For Reference

Not to be taken from this room

08/05

AMERICAN
DECADES
PRIMARY SOURCES

1920–1929

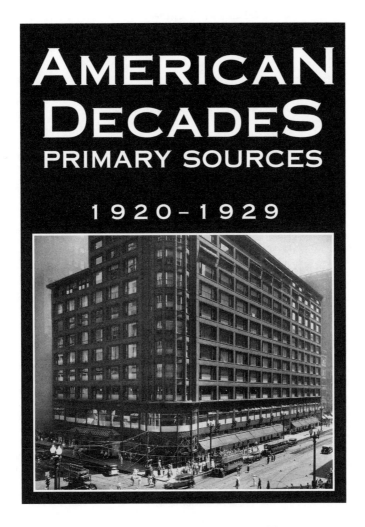

AMERICAN DECADES
PRIMARY SOURCES
1920–1929

CYNTHIA ROSE, PROJECT EDITOR

GALE®

THOMSON
™
GALE

Detroit • New York • San Diego • San Francisco • Cleveland • New Haven, Conn. • Waterville, Maine • London • Munich

THOMSON
GALE

American Decades Primary Sources, 1920–1929

Project Editor
Cynthia Rose

Editorial
Jason M. Everett, Rachel J. Kain, Pamela A. Dear, Andrew C. Claps, Thomas Carson, Kathleen Droste, Lynn U. Koch, Christy Justice, Michael D. Lesniak, Nancy Matuszak, John F. McCoy, Michael Reade, Rebecca Parks, Mark Mikula, Polly A. Rapp, Mark Springer

Data Capture
Civie A. Green, Beverly Jendrowski, Gwendolyn S. Tucker

Permissions
Margaret Abendroth, Margaret A. Chamberlain, Lori Hines, Jacqueline Key, Mari Masalin-Cooper, William Sampson, Shalice Shah-Caldwell, Kim Smilay, Sheila Spencer, Ann Taylor

Indexing Services
Lynne Maday, John Magee

Imaging and Multimedia
Randy Bassett, Dean Dauphinais, Leitha Etheridge-Sims, Mary K. Grimes, Lezlie Light, Daniel W. Newell, David G. Oblender, Christine O'Bryan, Kelly A. Quin, Luke A. Rademacher, Denay Wilding, Robyn V. Young

Product Design
Michelle DiMercurio

Composition and Electronic Prepress
Evi Seoud

Manufacturing
Rita Wimberley

For permission to use material from this product, submit your request via Web at http://gale-edit.com/permissions, or you may download our Permissions Request form and submit your request by fax or mail to:

Permissions Department
The Gale Group, Inc.
27500 Drake Rd.
Farmington Hills, MI 48331-3535
Permissions Hotline:
248-699-8006 or 800-877-4253, ext. 8006
Fax: 248-699-8074 or 800-762-4058

Cover photographs reproduced by permission of AP/Wide World Photos (Al Capone, left), Bettmann/Corbis (Schlesinger & Mayer/Carson, Pirie, Scott department store, designed by Louis Sullivan, background), The Library of Congress (Charles Lindbergh, right; floor of the New York Stock Exchange, center); Underwood & Underwood/Corbis (Flappers dancing the Charleston, spine).

Since this page cannot legibly accommodate all copyright notices, the acknowledgments constitute an extension of the copyright notice.

While every effort has been made to ensure the reliability of the information presented in this publication, The Gale Group, Inc. does not guarantee the accuracy of the data contained herein. The Gale Group, Inc. accepts no payment for listing; and inclusion in the publication of any organization, agency, institution, publication, service, or individual does not imply endorsement of the editors or publisher. Errors brought to the attention of the publisher and verified to the satisfaction of the publisher will be corrected in future editions.

LIBRARY OF CONGRESS CATALOGING-IN-PUBLICATION DATA

American decades primary sources / edited by Cynthia Rose.
    v. cm.
Includes bibliographical references and index.
Contents: [1] 1900-1909 — [2] 1910-1919 — [3] 1920-1929 — [4] 1930-1939 — [5] 1940-1949 — [6] 1950-1959 — [7] 1960-1969 — [8] 1970-1979 — [9] 1980-1989 — [10] 1990-1999.
    ISBN 0-7876-6587-8 (set : hardcover : alk. paper) — ISBN 0-7876-6588-6 (v. 1 : hardcover : alk. paper) — ISBN 0-7876-6589-4 (v. 2 : hardcover : alk. paper) — ISBN 0-7876-6590-8 (v. 3 : hardcover : alk. paper) — ISBN 0-7876-6591-6 (v. 4 : hardcover : alk. paper) — ISBN 0-7876-6592-4 (v. 5 : hardcover : alk. paper) — ISBN 0-7876-6593-2 (v. 6 : hardcover : alk. paper) — ISBN 0-7876-6594-0 (v. 7 : hardcover : alk. paper) — ISBN 0-7876-6595-9 (v. 8 : hardcover : alk. paper) — ISBN 0-7876-6596-7 (v. 9 : hardcover : alk. paper) — ISBN 0-7876-6597? (v. 10 : hardcover : alk. paper)
    1. United States—Civilization—20th century—Sources. I. Rose, Cynthia.
E169.1.A471977 2004
973.91—dc21

2002008155

3 1559 00174 8829

CONTENTS

Entries are arranged in chronological order by date of primary source. For entries with one primary source, the entry title is the primary source title. Entries with more than one primary source have an overall entry title, followed by the titles of the primary sources.

Business and the Economy

Education

Fashion and Design

Government and Politics

Law and Justice

Medicine and Health

Religion

ADVISORS AND CONTRIBUTORS

Advisors

CARL A. ANTONUCCI JR. has spent the past ten years as a reference librarian at various colleges and universities. Currently director of library services at Capital Community College, he holds two master's degrees and is a doctoral candidate at Providence College. He particularly enjoys researching Rhode Island political history during the 1960s and 1970s.

KATHY ARSENAULT is the dean of library at the University of South Florida, St. Petersburg's Poynter Library. She holds a master's degree in Library Science. She has written numerous book reviews for *Library Journal*, and has published articles in such publications as the *Journal of the Florida Medical Association* and *Collection Management*.

JAMES RETTIG holds two master's degrees. He has written numerous articles and has edited *Distinguished Classics of Reference Publishing* (1992). University librarian at the University of Richmond, he is the recipient of three American Library Association awards: the Isadore Gilbert Mudge Citation (1988), the G.K. Hall Award for Library Literature (1993), and the Louis Shores-Oryx Press Award (1995).

HILDA K. WEISBURG is the head library media specialist at Morristown High School Library and specializes in building school library media programs. She has several publications to her credit, including *The School Librarians Workshop, Puzzles, Patterns, and Problem Solving: Creative Connections to Critical Thinking*, and *Learning, Linking & Critical Thinking: Information Strategies for the K-12 Library Media Curriculum*.

Contributors

DENNIS A. CASTILLO received his doctorate in the History of Christianity from the University of Chicago. Currently an associate professor of Church History at Christ the King Seminary in East Aurora, New York, he is at work on his first book, *The Maltese Cross: A Military History of Malta*. A Detroit native, he now lives in Buffalo, New York.
Chapter: Religion.

PAUL G. CONNORS earned a doctorate in American History from Loyola University in Chicago. He has a strong interest in Great Lakes maritime history, and has contributed the article "Beaver Island Ice Walkers" to *Michigan History*. He has worked for the Michigan Legislative Service Bureau as a research analyst since 1996.
Essay: Using Primary Sources. *Chapter:* Government and Politics. *Chronologies:* Selected Events Outside the United States; Government and Politics, Sports chapters. *General Resources:* General, Government and Politics, Sports.

CHRISTOPHER CUMO is a staff writer for *The Adjunct Advocate Magazine*. Formerly an adjunct professor of

History at Walsh University, he has written two books, *A History of the Ohio Agricultural Experiment Station, 1882–1997,* and *Seeds of Change,* and has contributed to numerous scholarly journals. He also holds a doctorate in History from the University of Akron.

Chapter: Science and Technology. *Chapter Chronologies, General Resources:* Business and the Economy, Education, Medicine and Health, Science and Technology.

MICHAEL R. FEIN is an adjunct faculty member at Lesley University in Cambridge, Massachusetts. He is presently at work on a doctoral dissertation on twentieth century highway politics in New York. He has also contributed articles to *The Encyclopedia of New York State* and written book reviews for the *Business History Review.*

Chapter: Business and the Economy.

JENNIFER HELLER holds bachelor's degrees in Religious Studies and English Education, as well as a master's in Curriculum and Instruction, all from the University of Kansas. She has been an adjunct associate professor at Johnson County Community College in Kansas since 1998. She is currently at work on a dissertation on contemporary women's religious literature.

Chapter Chronology, General Resources: Religion.

DAVID M. HOLFORD has worked as an adjunct instructor at Ohio University, Park College, and Columbus State Community College; education curator for the Ohio Historical Society; and held editorial positions at Glencoe/McGraw Hill and Holt, Rinehard, and Winston. He also holds a doctorate History from Ohio State University. A freelance writer/editor since 1996, he has published *Herbert Hoover* (1999) and *Abraham Lincoln and the Emancipation Proclamation* (2002).

Chapter Chronologies, General Resources: Lifestyles and Social Trends, The Media.

JONATHAN KOLKEY is the author of *The New Right, 1960–1968,* and *Germany on the March: A Reinterpretation of War and Domestic Politics Over the Past Two Centuries.* He earned a Ph.D. in History from UCLA. Currently an instructor at West Los Angeles College, he is at work on *The Decision for War,* a comprehensive historical study of the politics and decision-making process behind war. Dr. Kolkey lives in Playa Del Rey, California.

Chapter: Lifestyles and Social Trends.

SCOTT A. MERRIMAN currently works as a part-time instructor at the University of Kentucky and is finishing his doctoral dissertation on Espionage and Sedition Acts in the Sixth Court of Appeals. He has contributed to *The History Highway* and *History.edu,* among others. Scott is a resident of Lexington, Kentucky.

Chapters: Law and Justice, Medicine and Health.

MURRY R. NELSON is the author of *Children and Social Studies—Creative Teaching in the Elementary Classroom, The Future of Social Studies,* and *The Originals: The New York Celtics Invent Modern Basketball.* His research interests include professional basketball history before 1950, curriculum history, and the history and foundations of social studies.

Chapter: Sports.

KRISTINA PETERSON earned her bachelor's degree in Psychology from Northland College. She also holds an M.A. in Education from the College of William and Mary, as well as a Ph.D. in History and Philosophy of Education from the University of Minnesota.

Chapter: Education.

DAN PROSTERMAN is an adjunct professor of history at St. Francis College, as well as an adjunct lecturer at Pace University. He holds an M.A. in History at New York University and is working on his doctoral dissertation on the subject of anti-Communism in New York City during the Great Depression and World War II.

Chapter: The Media.

LORNA BIDDLE RINEAR is the editor and coauthor of *The Complete Idiot's Guide to Women's History.* A Ph.D. candidate at Rutger's University, she holds a B.A. from Wellesley College and a master's degree from Boston College. She resides in Bellingham, Massachusetts.

Chapter Chronologies, General Resources: The Arts, Fashion and Design.

MARY HERTZ SCARBROUGH earned both her B.A. in English and German and her J.D. from the Univeristy of South Dakota. Prior to becoming a freelance writer in 1996, she worked as a law clerk in the Federal District Court for the District of South Dakota and as legal counsel for the Immigration and Naturalization Service. She lives in Storm Lake, Iowa, with her husband and three daughters.

Chapter Chronology, General Resources: Law and Justice.

ALICE WU holds a B.A. in English from Wellesley College, as well as an M.F.A. in Sculpture from Yale University. An artist and fashion designer, she lives in New York City.

Chapter: The Arts, Fashion and Design.

ACKNOWLEDGMENTS

Following is a list of the copyright holders who have granted us permission to reproduce material in this volume of American Decades Primary Sources. *Every effort has been made to trace copyright, but if omissions have been made, please let us know.*

Copyrighted material in *American Decades Primary Sources, 1920–1929,* was reproduced from the following periodicals: *Harpers Magazine,* v. 158, May 1929. —*The New York Times,* February 15, 1929. Copyright © 1929 by *The New York Times Co.* Reproduced by permission. —Nobel Lecture, May 23, 1924. © The Nobel Foundation 1923. Reproduced by permission. —Nobel Lecture, December 12, 1927. © The Nobel Foundation 1927. Reproduced by permission. —Smith, Bessie. From "Jail House Blues." Copyright © 1931 by Bessie Smith, renewed, 1974 by Frank Music Corp. All rights reserved. Reproduced by permission.

Copyrighted material in *American Decades Primary Sources, 1920–1929,* was reproduced from the following books: Bourke-White, Margaret. From "Skyscrapers and Advertising," in *Portrait of Myself.* Simon and Schuster, 1963. Copyright © 1963 by Margaret Bourke-White. All rights reserved. Reproduced by permission. —Brooks, Louise. From "Pabst and Lulu," in *Lulu in Hollywood.* Alfred A. Knopf, 1982. Copyright © 1974, 1982 by Louise Brooks. All rights reserved. Reproduced by permission of Alfred A. Knopf, a division of Random House, Inc. and Penguin Books Ltd. —Busch, Noel F. From "Time: The Weekly News-Magazine," in *Briton Hadden: A Biography of the Co-Founder of TIME.* Farrar, Straus and Company, 1949. Copyright © 1949 by Noel F. Busch. All rights reserved. Reproduced by permission of Farrar, Straus and Giroux, LLC. —Covello, Leonard. From *The Heart is the Teacher.* McGraw Hill, 1958. Copyright © 1958 by McGraw Hill. All rights reserved.

—Dawson, James P. From "Boxing," in *Sport's Golden Age: A Close-Up of the Fabulous Twenties.* Edited by Allison Danzig and Peter Brandwein. Harper & Brothers, 1948. Copyright 1948 by Harper & Brothers, renewed © 1976 by Allison Danzig. All rights reserved. Reproduced by permission of HarperCollins Publishers Inc. —Fosdick, Harry Emerson. From "The Fundamentalist Controversy," in *The Living of These Days: An Autobiography.* Harper & Row Publishers, 1956. Copyright © 1956 by Harper & Row Publishers, Incorporated, renewed 1984 by Dorothy Fosdick and Elinor F. Downs. All rights reserved. Reproduced by permission of HarperCollins Publishers Inc. —Marks, Robert W. From *The Dymaxion World of Buckminster Fuller.* Reinhold Publishing Corporation, 1960. Design and illustrations by R. Buckminster Fuller. Courtesy, The Estate of R. Buckminster Fuller. Reproduced by permission. —From "Al Smith's Presidential Campaign," in *Documents of American Catholic History.* The Bruce Publishing Company, 1962. Copyright © 1962 by John Tracy Ellis. All rights reserved. —From "Cecil Mack (1884–1944)," in *Reading Lyrics.* Edited by Robert Gottlieb and Robert Kimball. Pantheon Books, 2000. Copyright © 2000 by Robert Gottlieb and Robert Kimball. All rights reserved. Reproduced by permission of Pantheon Books, a division of Random House, Inc. —From "J. Edgar Hoover to Lewis J. Baley," in *The Marcus Garvey and Universal Negro Improvement Association Papers, Volume III, September 1920–August 1921.* Edited by Robert A. Hill, Emory J. Tolbert, Deborah Forczek. University of California Press,

About the Set

American Decades Primary Sources is a ten-volume collection of more than two thousand primary sources on twentieth-century American history and culture. Each volume comprises about two hundred primary sources in 160–170 entries. Primary sources are enhanced by informative context, with illustrative images and sidebars—many of which are primary sources in their own right—adding perspective and a deeper understanding of both the primary sources and the milieu from which they originated.

Designed for students and teachers at the high school and undergraduate levels, as well as researchers and history buffs, *American Decades Primary Sources* meets the growing demand for primary source material.

Conceived as both a stand-alone reference and a companion to the popular *American Decades* set, *American Decades Primary Sources* is organized in the same subject-specific chapters for compatibility and ease of use.

Primary Sources

To provide fresh insights into the key events and figures of the century, thirty historians and four advisors selected unique primary sources far beyond the typical speeches, government documents, and literary works. Screenplays, scrapbooks, sports box scores, patent applications, college course outlines, military codes of conduct, environmental sculptures, and CD liner notes are but a sampling of the more than seventy-five types of primary sources included.

Diversity is shown not only in the wide range of primary source types, but in the range of subjects and opinions, and the frequent combination of primary sources in entries. Multiple perspectives in religious, political, artistic, and scientific thought demonstrate the commitment of *American Decades Primary Sources* to diversity, in addition to the inclusion of considerable content displaying ethnic, racial, and gender diversity. *American Decades Primary Sources* presents a variety of perspectives on issues and events, encouraging the reader to consider subjects more fully and critically.

American Decades Primary Sources' innovative approach often presents related primary sources in an entry. The primary sources act as contextual material for each other—creating a unique opportunity to understand each and its place in history, as well as their relation to one another. These may be point-counterpoint arguments, a variety of diverse opinions, or direct responses to another primary source. One example is President Franklin Delano Roosevelt's letter to clergy at the height of the Great Depression, with responses by a diverse group of religious leaders from across the country.

Multiple primary sources created by particularly significant individuals—Dr. Martin Luther King, Jr., for example—reside in *American Decades Primary Sources*. Multiple primary sources on particularly significant subjects are often presented in more than one chapter of a volume, or in more than one decade, providing opportunities to see the significance and impact of an event or figure from many angles and historical perspectives. For example, seven primary sources on the controversial Scopes "monkey" trial are found in five chapters of the

1920s volume. Primary sources on evolutionary theory may be found in earlier and later volumes, allowing the reader to see and analyze the development of thought across time.

Entry Organization

Contextual material uses standardized rubrics that will soon become familiar to the reader, making the entries more accessible and allowing for easy comparison. Introduction and Significance essays—brief and focused—cover the historical background, contributing factors, importance, and impact of the primary source, encouraging the reader to think critically—not only about the primary source, but also about the way history is constructed. Key Facts and a Synopsis provide quick access and recognition of the primary sources, and the Further Resources are a stepping-stone to additional study.

Additional Features

Subject chronologies and thorough tables of contents (listing titles, authors, and dates) begin each chapter. The main table of contents assembles this information conveniently at the front of the book. An essay on using primary sources, a chronology of selected events outside the United States during the twentieth century, substantial general and subject resources, and primary source-type and general indexes enrich *American Decades Primary Sources*.

The ten volumes of *American Decades Primary Sources* provide a vast array of primary sources integrated with supporting content and user-friendly features.

This value-laden set gives the reader an unparalleled opportunity to travel into the past, to relive important events, to encounter key figures, and to gain a deep and full understanding of America in the twentieth century.

Acknowledgments

A number of people contributed to the successful completion of this project. The editor wishes to acknowledge them with thanks: Eugenia Bradley, Luann Brennan, Neva Carter, Katrina Coach, Pamela S. Dear, Nikita L. Greene, Madeline Harris, Alesia James, Cynthia Jones, Pamela M. Kalte, Arlene Ann Kevonian, Frances L. Monroe, Charles B. Montney, Katherine H. Nemeh, James E. Person, Tyra Y. Phillips, Elizabeth Pilette, Noah Schusterbauer, Andrew Specht, Susan Strickland, Karissa Walker, Tracey Watson, and Jennifer M. York.

Contact Us

The editors of *American Decades Primary Sources* welcome your comments, suggestions, and questions. Please direct all correspondence to:

Editor, *American Decades Primary Sources*
The Gale Group, Inc.
27500 Drake Road
Farmington Hills, MI 48331–3535
(800) 877–4253

For email inquiries, please visit the Gale website at www.gale.com, and click on the Contact Us tab.

ABOUT THE VOLUME

The "Roaring Twenties" was a roaring decade indeed. The passage of the Volstead Act prohibited the sale and consumption of alcohol and spawned a black market network of smuggling and speakeasies. Gangsters like Al Capone captured the public's imagination. Fashionable, fun-loving women wore short skirts and even shorter hair. They, and a growing number of the public, danced to jazz music, and the popular Cotton Club in Chicago was open to both African Americans and whites. Business was booming in many industries and, for the first time, people were buying on credit. Speculation in the stock market was at an all-time high as a "get rich quick" mentality took hold, but the artificially inflated bubble burst on October 24, 1929. The stock market crash closed out the 1920s with a bang. The following documents are just a sampling of the offerings available in this volume.

Highlights of Primary Sources, 1920–1929

- *New York Dada* first and only issue of Dadaist magazine by Man Ray

- Maidenform Brassiere Patent drawings and documentation, text facsimile

- Alfred E. Smith's speech on Religious Bigotry

- Reports and memos by J. Edgar Hoover, both as a special agent and Justice Department Attorney, on the activities of black nationalist Marcus Garvey

- "The Four Horsemen" of Notre Dame football: article by Grantland Rice and photograph of the players

- "Far From Well," book review by author and poet Dorothy Parker

- "Plan—Isometric and Elevation of a Minimum Dymaxion home and patent application by R. Buckminster Fuller

- *Handbook for Guardians of Camp Fire Girls,* 1924

- "Open Letter to the Pullman Company," by A. Philip Randolph, founder of the Brotherhood of Sleeping Car Porters

- Journal entry of May 5, 1926, by Robert Goddard documenting the launch of the first liquid-fuel rocket

- *Daily Worker* editorial cartoons covering the trial, sentencing, and execution of Sacco and Vanzetti

- Photograph of American Indian Chiefs Frank Seelatse and Jimmy Noah Saluskin

- *The Care and Feeding of Children,* a guidebook for new parents

Volume Structure and Content

Front matter

- Table of Contents—lists primary sources, authors, and dates of origin, by chapter and chronologically within chapters.

- About the Set, About the Volume, About the Entry essays—guide the reader through the set and promote ease of use.

- Highlights of Primary Sources—a quick look at a dozen or so primary sources gives the reader a feel for the decade and the volume's contents.

- How to Use Primary Sources—provides a crash course in reading and interpreting primary sources.

- Selected Events Outside the United States—lends additional context in which to place the decade's primary sources.

Chapters:

- The Arts
- Business and the Economy
- Education
- Fashion and Design
- Government and Politics
- Law and Justice
- Lifestyles and Social Trends
- The Media
- Medicine and Health
- Religion
- Science and Technology
- Sports

Chapter structure

- Chapter table of contents—lists primary sources, authors, and dates of origin chronologically, showing each source's place in the decade.

- Chapter chronology—highlights the decade's important events in the chapter's subject.

- Primary sources—displays sources surrounded by contextual material.

Back matter

- General Resources—promotes further inquiry with books, periodicals, websites, and audio and visual media, all organized into general and subject-specific sections.

- General Index—provides comprehensive access to primary sources, people, events, and subjects, and cross-referencing to enhance comparison and analysis.

- Primary Source Type Index—locates primary sources by category, giving readers an opportunity to easily analyze sources across genres.

ABOUT THE ENTRY

The primary source is the centerpiece and main focus of each entry in *American Decades Primary Sources*. In keeping with the philosophy that much of the benefit from using primary sources derives from the reader's own process of inquiry, the contextual material surrounding each entry provides access and ease of use, as well as giving the reader a springboard for delving into the primary source. Rubrics identify each section and enable the reader to navigate entries with ease.

Entry structure

- Key Facts—essential information pertaining to the primary source, including full title, author, source type, source citation, and notes about the author.

- Introduction—historical background and contributing factors for the primary source.

- Significance—importance and impact of the primary source, at the time and since.

- Primary Source—in text, text facsimile, or image format; full or excerpted.

- Synopsis—encapsulated introduction to the primary source.

- Further Resources—books, periodicals, websites, and audio and visual material.

Navigating an Entry

Entry elements are numbered and reproduced here, with an explanation of the data contained in these elements explained immediately thereafter according to the corresponding numeral.

Primary Source/Entry Title, Primary Source Type

•1• **"Ego"**
•2• Magazine article

•1• **PRIMARY SOURCE/ENTRY TITLE** The entry title is the primary source title for entries with one primary source. Entry titles appear as catchwords at the top outer margin of each page.

•2• **PRIMARY SOURCE TYPE** The type of primary source is listed just below the title. When assigning source types, great weight was given to how the author of the primary source categorized it. If a primary source comprised more than one type—for example, an article about art in the United States that included paintings, or a scientific essay that included graphs and photographs—each primary source type included in the entry appears below the title.

Composite Entry Title

•3• Debate Over *The Birth of a Nation*

•1• **"Capitalizing Race Hatred"**
•2• Editorial

•1• **"Reply to the *New York Globe*"**

•2• Letter

•3• **COMPOSITE ENTRY TITLE** An overarching entry title is used for entries with more than one primary source, with the primary source titles and types below.

Key Facts

•4• **By:** Norman Mailer

•5• **Date:** March 19, 1971

•6• **Source:** Mailer, Norman. "Ego." *Life* 70, March 19, 1971, 30, 32–36.

•7• **About the Author:** Norman Mailer (1923–) was born in Long Branch, New Jersey. After graduating from Harvard and military service in World War II (1939–1945), Mailer began writing, publishing his first book, the best-selling novel *The Naked and the Dead,* in 1948. Mailer has written over thirty books, including novels, plays, political commentary, and essay collections, as well as numerous magazine articles. He won the Pulitzer Prize in 1969 and 1979. ∎

•4• **AUTHOR OR ORIGINATOR** The name of the author or originator of the primary source begins the Key Facts section.

•5• **DATE OF ORIGIN** The date of origin of the primary source appears in this field, and may differ from the date of publication in the source citation below it; for example, speeches are often given before they are published.

•6• **SOURCE CITATION** The source citation is a full bibliographic citation, giving original publication data as well as reprint and/or online availability (usually both the deep-link and home-page URLs).

•7• **ABOUT THE AUTHOR** A brief bio of the author or originator of the primary source gives birth and death dates and a quick overview of the person's life. This rubric has been customized in some cases. If the primary source is the autobiography of an artist, the term "author" appears; however, if the primary source is a work of art, the term "artist" is used, showing the person's direct relationship to the primary source. Terms like "inventor" and "designer" are used similarly. For primary sources created by a group, "organization" may have been used instead of "author." If an author is anonymous or unknown, a brief "About the Publication" sketch may appear.

Introduction and Significance Essays

•8• **Introduction**

. . . As images from the Vietnam War (1964–1975) flashed onto television screens across the United States in the late 1960s, however, some reporters took a more active role in questioning the pronouncements of public officials. The broad cul-tural changes of the 1960s, including a sweeping suspicion of authority figures by younger people, also encouraged a more restive spirit in the reporting corps. By the end of the decade, the phrase "Gonzo Journalism" was coined to describe the new breed of reporter: young, rebellious, and unafraid to get personally involved in the story at hand. . . .

•8• **INTRODUCTION** The introduction is a brief essay on the contributing factors and historical context of the primary source. Intended to promote understanding and jump-start the reader's curiosity, this section may also describe an artist's approach, the nature of a scientific problem, or the struggles of a sports figure. If more than one primary source is included in the entry, the introduction and significance address each one, and often the relationship between them.

•9• **Significance**

Critics of the new style of journalism maintained that the emphasis on personalities and celebrity did not necessarily lead to better reporting. As political reporting seemed to focus more on personalities and images and less on substantive issues, some observers feared that the American public was ill-served by the new style of journalism. Others argued that the media had also encouraged political apathy among the public by superficial reporting. . . .

•9• **SIGNIFICANCE** The significance discusses the importance and impact of the primary source. This section may touch on how it was regarded at the time and since, its place in history, any awards given, related developments, and so on.

Primary Source Header, Synopsis, Primary Source

•10• **Primary Source**

The Boys on the Bus [excerpt]

•11• **SYNOPSIS:** A boisterous account of Senator George McGovern's ultimately unsuccessful 1972 presidential bid, Crouse's work popularized the term "pack journalism," describing the herd mentality that gripped reporters focusing endlessly on the same topic. In later years, political advisors would become more adept at "spinning" news stories to their candidates' advantage, but the essential dynamics of pack journalism remain in place.

•12• The feverish atmosphere was halfway between a high school bus trip to Washington and a gambler's jet junket to Las Vegas, where small-time Mafiosi were lured into betting away their restaurants. There was giddy camaraderie mixed with fear and low-grade hysteria. To file a story late, or to make one glaring factual error, was to chance losing everything—one's job, one's expense account, one's drinking buddies, one's mad-dash existence, and the methedrine buzz that comes from knowing stories that the public would not know for hours and secrets that the public would never know. Therefore reporters channeled their gambling instincts into late-night poker games and private bets on the outcome of the elections. When it came to writing a story, they were as cautious as diamond-cutters. . . .

•10• PRIMARY SOURCE HEADER The primary source header signals the beginning of the primary source, and "[excerpt]" is attached if the source does not appear in full.

•11• SYNOPSIS The synopsis gives a brief overview of the primary source.

•12• PRIMARY SOURCE The primary source may appear excerpted or in full, and may appear as text, text facsimile (photographic reproduction of the original text), image, or graphic display (such as a table, chart, or graph).

Text Primary Sources

The majority of primary sources are reproduced as plain text. The font and leading of the primary sources are distinct from that of the context—to provide a visual clue to the change, as well as to facilitate ease of reading. Often, the original formatting of the text was preserved in order to more accurately represent the original (screenplays, for example). In order to respect the integrity of the primary sources, content some readers may consider sensitive was retained where it was deemed to be integral to the source. Text facsimile formatting was used sparingly and where the original provided additional value (for example, Aaron Copland's typing and handwritten notes on "Notes for a Cowboy Ballet").

Narrative Break

•13•   I told him I'd rest and then fix him something to eat when he got home. I could hear someone enter his office then, and Medgar laughed at something that was said. "I've got to go, honey. See you tonight. I love you." "All right," I said. "Take care." Those were our last words to each other.

■ ■ ■

Medgar had told me that President Kennedy was speaking on civil rights that night, and I made a mental note of the time. We ate alone, the children and I. It had become a habit now to set only four places for supper. Medgar's chair stared at us, and the children, who had heard

about the President's address to the nation, planned to watch it with me. There was something on later that they all wanted to see, and they begged to be allowed to wait up for Medgar to return home. School was out, and I knew that Van would fall asleep anyway, so I agreed.

•13• NARRATIVE BREAK A narrative break appears where there is a significant amount of elided material, beyond what ellipses would indicate (for example, excerpts from a nonfiction work's introduction and second chapter, or sections of dialogue from two acts of a play).

Image Primary Sources

Primary source images (whether photographs, text facsimiles, or graphic displays) are bordered with a distinctive double rule. The Primary Source header and Synopsis appear under the image, with the image reduced in size to accommodate the synopsis. For multipart images, the synopsis appears only under the first part of the image; subsequent parts have brief captions.

•14• "Art: U.S. Scene": *The Tornado* by John Steuart Curry **(2 OF 4)**

•14• PRIMARY SOURCE IMAGE HEADER The primary source image header assists the reader in tracking the images in a series. Also, the primary source header listed here indicates a primary source with both text and image components. The text of the *Time* magazine article "Art: U.S. Scene," appears with four of the paintings from the article. Under each painting, the title of the article appears first, followed by a colon, then the title of the painting. The header for the text component has a similar structure, with the term "magazine article" after the colon. Inclusion of images or graphic elements from primary sources, and their designation in the entry as main primary sources, is discretionary.

Further Resources

•15• Further Resources

BOOKS
Dixon, Phil. *The Negro Baseball Leagues, 1867–1955: A Photographic History.* Mattituck, N.Y.: Amereon House, 1992.

PERIODICALS
"Steven Spielberg: The Director Says It's Good-Bye to Spaceships and Hello to Relationships." *American Film* 13, no. 8, June 1988, 12–16.

WEBSITES
Architecture and Interior Design for 20th Century America, 1935–1955. American Memory digital primary source collection, Library of Congress. Available online at http://memory.loc.gov/ammem/gschtml/gotthome

.html; website home page: http://memory.loc.gov
/ammem/ammemhome.html (accessed March 27, 2003).

AUDIO AND VISUAL MEDIA

E.T.: The Extra-Terrestrial. Original release, 1982, Universal. Directed by Steven Spielberg. Widescreen Collector's Edition DVD, 2002, Universal Studios.

•15• **FURTHER RESOURCES** A brief list of resources provides a stepping stone to further study. If it's known that a resource contains additional primary source material specifically related to the entry, a brief note in italics appears at the end of the citation. For websites, both the deep link and home page usually appear.

USING PRIMARY SOURCES

The philosopher R.G. Collingwood once said, "Every new generation must rewrite history in its own way." What Collingwood meant is that new events alter our perceptions of the past and necessitate that each generation interpret the past in a different light. For example, since September 11, 2001, and the "War on Terrorism," the collapse of the Soviet Union seemingly is no longer as historically important as the rise of Islamic fundamentalism, which was once only a minor concern. Seen from this viewpoint, history is not a rigid set of boring facts, but a fascinating, ever-changing field of study. Much of this fascination rests on the fact that historical interpretation is based on the reading of primary sources. To historians and students alike, primary sources are ambiguous objects because their underlying meanings are often not crystal clear. To learn a primary document's meaning(s), students must identify its main subject and recreate the historical context in which the document was created. In addition, students must compare the document with other primary sources from the same historical time and place. Further, students must cross-examine the primary source by asking of it a series of probing investigative questions.

To properly analyze a primary source, it is important that students become "active" rather than "casual" readers. As in reading a chemistry or algebra textbook, historical documents require students to analyze them carefully and extract specific information. In other words, history requires students to read "beyond the text" and focus on what the primary source tells us about the person or group and the era in which they lived. Unlike chemistry and algebra, however, historical primary sources have the additional benefit of being part of a larger, interesting story full of drama, suspense, and hidden agendas. In order to detect and identify key historical themes, students need to keep in mind a set of questions. For example, Who created the primary source? Why did the person create it? What is the subject? What problem is being addressed? Who was the intended audience? How was the primary source received and how was it used? What are the most important characteristics of this person or group for understanding the primary source? For example, what were the authors' biases? What was their social class? Their race? Their gender? Their occupation? Once these questions have been answered reasonably, the primary source can be used as a piece of historical evidence to interpret history.

In each *American Decades Primary Sources* volume, students will study examples of the following categories of primary sources:

- Firsthand accounts of historic events by witnesses and participants. This category includes diary entries, letters, newspaper articles, oral-history interviews, memoirs, and legal testimony.

- Documents representing the official views of the nation's leaders or of their political opponents. These include court decisions, policy statements, political speeches, party platforms, petitions, legislative debates, press releases, and federal and state laws.

- Government statistics and reports on such topics as birth, employment, marriage, death, and taxation.

- Advertisers' images and jingles. Although designed to persuade consumers to purchase commodities or to adopt specific attitudes, advertisements can also be valuable sources of information about popular beliefs and concerns.

- Works of art, including paintings, symphonies, play scripts, photographs, murals, novels, and poems.

- The products of mass culture: cartoons, comic books, movies, radio scripts, and popular songs.

- Material artifacts. These are everyday objects that survived from the period in question. Examples include household appliances and furnishings, recipes, and clothing.

- Secondary sources. In some cases, secondary sources may be treated as primary sources. For example, from 1836 to 1920, public schools across America purchased 122 million copies of a series of textbooks called the McGuffey Reader. Although current textbooks have more instructional value, the Reader is an invaluable primary source. It provides important insights into the unifying morals and cultural values that shaped the world-view of several generations of Americans, who differed in ethnicity, race, class, and religion.

Each of the above-mentioned categories of primary sources reveals different types of historical information. A politician's diary, memoirs, or collection of letters, for example, often provide students with the politicians' unguarded, private thoughts and emotions concerning daily life and public events. Though these documents may be a truer reflection of the person's character and aspirations, students must keep in mind that when people write about themselves, they tend to put themselves at the center of the historical event or cast themselves in the best possible light. On the other hand, the politician's public speeches may be more cautious, less controversial, and limited to advancing his or her political party's goals or platform.

Like personal diaries, advertisements reveal other types of historical information. What information does the WAVES poster on this page reveal?

John Phillip Faller, a prolific commercial artist known for his *Saturday Evening Post* covers, designed this recruitment poster in 1944. It was one of over three hundred posters he produced for the U.S. Navy while enrolled in that service during World War II. The purpose of the poster was to encourage women to enlist in the WAVES (Women Accepted for Volunteer Emergency Service), a women's auxiliary to the Navy established in

COURTESY OF THE NAVAL HISTORICAL FOUNDATION. REPRODUCED BY PERMISSION.

1942. It depicts a schoolgirl gazing admiringly at a photograph of a proud, happy WAVE (perhaps an older sister), thus portraying the military service as an appropriate and admirable aspiration for women during wartime. However, what type of military service? Does the poster encourage women to enlist in military combat like World War II male recruitment posters? Does it reflect gender bias? What does this poster reveal about how the military and society in general feel about women in the military? Does the poster reflect current military and societal attitudes toward women in the military? How many women joined the WAVES? What type of duties did they perform?

Like personal diaries, photographs reveal other types of historical information. What information does the next photograph reveal?

Today, we take electricity for granted. However, in 1935, although 90 percent of city dwellers in America had electricity, only 10 percent of rural Americans did. Private utility companies refused to string electric lines

to isolated farms, arguing that the endeavor was too expensive and that most farmers were too poor to afford it anyway. As part of the Second New Deal, President Franklin Delano Roosevelt issued an executive order creating the Rural Electrification Administration (REA). The REA lent money at low interest rates to utility companies to bring electricity to rural America. By 1950, 90 percent of rural America had electricity. This photograph depicts a 1930s tenant farmer's house in Greene County, Georgia. Specifically, it shows a brand-new electric meter on the wall. The picture presents a host of questions: What was rural life like without electricity? How did electricity impact the lives of rural Americans, particularly rural Georgians? How many rural Georgians did not have electricity in the 1930s? Did Georgia have more electricity-connected farms than other Southern states? What was the poverty rate in rural Georgia, particularly among rural African Americans? Did rural electricity help lift farmers out of poverty?

Like personal diaries, official documents reveal other types of historical information. What information does the next document, a memo, reveal?

From the perspective of the early twenty-first century, in a democratic society, integration of the armed services seems to have been inevitable. For much of American history, however, African Americans were prevented from joining the military, and when they did enlist they were segregated into black units. In 1940, of the nearly 170,000-man Navy, only 4,007, or 2.3 percent, were African American personnel. The vast majority of these men worked in the mess halls as stewards—or, as labeled by the black press, "seagoing bellhops." In this official document, the chairman of the General Board refers to compliance with a directive that would enlist African Americans into positions of "unlimited general service." Who issued the directive? What was the motivation behind the new directive? Who were the members of the General Board? How much authority did they wield? Why did the Navy restrict African Americans to the "messman branch"? Notice the use of the term "colored race." Why was this term used and what did it imply? What did the board conclude? When did the Navy become integrated? Who was primarily responsible for integrating the Navy?

CONFIDENTIAL

DOD Dir. 5200.10, June 29, 1960
NND by *RB* date Oct 5, 1961

DOWNGRADED AT 3 YEAR INTERVALS;
DECLASSIFIED AFTER 12 YEARS
DOD DIR 5200.10 NARS-NT

G.B. No. 421
(Serial No. 201)
SECRET
                                              Feb 3, 1942

From: Chairman General Board.
To: Secretary of the Navy.

Subject: Enlistment of men of colored race to other than
             Messman branch.

Ref: (a) SecNav let. (SC)P14-4/MM (03200A)/Gen of
             Jan 16, 1942.

        1.   The General Board, complying with the directive
contained in reference (a), has given careful attention to the
problem of enlisting in the Navy, men of the colored race
in other than the messman branch.

        2.   The General Board has endeavored to examine the
problem placed before it in a realistic manner.

A.   Should negroes be enlisted for **unlimited** general service?

                (a) Enlistment for general service implies that the
individual may be sent anywhere, - to any ship or station where
he is needed. Men on board ship live in particularly close
association; in their messes, one man sits beside another; their
hammocks or bunks are close together; in their common tasks they
work side by side; and in particular tasks such as those of a
gun's crew, they form a closely knit, highly coordinated team.
How many white men would choose, of their own accord, that their
closest associates in sleeping quarters, at mess, and in a gun's
crew should be of another race? How many would accept such
conditions, if required to do so, without resentment and just
as a matter of course? The General Board believes that the
answer is "Few, if any," and further believes that if the issue were
forced, there would be a lowering of contentment, teamwork
and discipline in the service.

                (b) One of the tennets of the recruiting service
is that each recruit for general service is potentially a leading
petty officer. It is true that some men never do become petty
officers, and that when recruiting white men, it is not possible
to establish which will be found worthy of and secure promotion
and which will not. If negroes are recruited for general service,
it can be said at once that few will obtain advancement to petty
officers. With every desire to be fair, officers and leading
petty officers in general will not recommend negroes for promotion
to positions of authority over white men.

DOWNGRADED AND
DECLASSIFIED   - 1 -   CONFIDENTIAL

The General Board is convinced that the enlistment of negroes for unlimited general service is unadvisable.

B.   Should negroes be enlisted in general service but detailed in special ratings or for special ships or units?

(a) The ratings now in use in the naval service cover every phase of naval activity, and no new ratings are deemed necessary merely to promote the enlistment of negroes.

(b) At first thought, it might appear that assignment of negroes to certain vessels, and in particular to small vessels of the patrol type, would be feasible. In this connection, the following table is of interest:

Type of Ship	Total Crew	Men in Pay Grades 1 to 4	Men in Pay Grades 5 to 7 (Non-rated)
Battleship	1892	666	1226
Light Cruiser (10,000 ton)	988	365	623
Destroyer (1630 ton)	206	109	97
Submarine	54	47	7
Patrol Boat (180 foot)	55	36	19
Patrol Boat (110 foot)	20	15	5

NOTE: Pay grades 1 to 4 include Chief Petty Officers and Petty Officers, 1st, 2nd and 3rd Class; also Firemen, 1st Class and a few other ratings requiring length of service and experience equal to that required for qualification of Petty Officers, 3rd class. Pay grades 5 to 7 include all other non-rated men and recruits.

There are no negro officers and so few negro petty officers in the Navy at present that any vessels to which negroes might be assigned must have white officers and white petty officers. Examination of the table shows the small number of men in other than petty officer ratings that might be assigned to patrol vessels and in- dicates to the General Board that such assignments would not be happy ones. The assignment of negroes to the larger ships, where well over one-half of the crews are non-rated men, with mixture of whites and negroes, would inevitably lead to discontent on the part of one or the other, resulting in clashes and lowering of the efficiency of the vessels and of the Navy.

- 2 -

The material collected in these volumes of *American Decades Primary Sources* are significant because they will introduce students to a wide variety of historical sources that were created by those who participated in or witnessed the historical event. These primary sources not only vividly describe historical events, but also reveal the subjective perceptions and biases of their authors. Students should read these documents "actively," and with the contextual assistance of the introductory material, history will become relevant and entertaining.

—Paul G. Connors

CHRONOLOGY OF SELECTED WORLD EVENTS OUTSIDE THE UNITED STATES, 1920-1929

1920

- Agatha Christie publishes *The Mysterious Affair at Styles,* introducing Hercule Poirot.

- On January 10, the Treaty of Versailles takes effect.

- On January 13, workers attack the Reichstag, the German parliament, during rioting in Berlin.

- In February, physicist William D. Harkins posits the existence of the neutron, a subatomic particle with neutral charge and mass equal to that of a proton.

- On March 7, Russia invades Poland, which, on April 20, counterattacks into Russia.

- On March 10, three hundred thousand workers in India go on strike against British rule.

- On March 11, the Syrian Congress declares Syrian independence and proclaims Prince Faisal king.

- On April 6, French troops occupy Darmstadt, Frankfurt, Hamburg, Hamau, and Dieburg in an attempt to force German troops to leave the Ruhr, Germany's industrial region.

- On April 7, Italy recognizes the state of Albania, which Italian troops occupy.

- From April 23 to April 25, the Allies grant Armenia independence under United States protection, and declare Syria a French mandate, Mesopotamia (Iraq) a British mandate, and Palestine a Jewish state under British protection.

- On May 16, Pope Benedict XV canonizes Joan of Arc.

- Russia invades Persia (Iran), which Britain occupies.

- On June 2, German physicist Max Planck delivers his Nobel lecture.

- On July 10, Peking comes under martial law after conflict between President Hsu Shihchang and the Chinese military.

- On July 12, Russia recognizes Lithuanian independence.

- On July 23, Britain names its East Africa protectorate the colony of Kenya.

- On July 24, the Treaty of Saint-Germain designates Austria's boundaries.

- On August 9, the Treaty of Trianon defines Hungary's boundaries.

- On August 10, the Treaty of Sèvres sets Turkey's boundaries.

- On August 14, the Summer Olympics begin in Antwerp, Belgium.

- On August 22, five hundred thousand Italian workers take over more than five hundred factories to protest economic and political difficulties.

- On September 25, twenty-five die in anti-Japanese protests in Gensan, Korea.

- On September 26, five thousand attacks on individuals and property cause more than one hundred deaths in Ireland.

- From November 18 to November 20, Germans plunder the Jewish Quarter in Prague.

- On November 26, Russia drives Turkish troops out of Armenia.

- On November 29, Russian leader Vladimir I. Lenin disavows all Soviet treaties, agreements, and debts.

- On December 12, German physicist Walter H. Nernst receives the Nobel Prize in chemistry for his discovery of the Third Law of Thermodynamics, which states that the entropy (amount of disorder) of a crystal is zero at absolute zero (-273 degrees Celsius).

- On December 16, an earthquake in northern China kills more than one hundred thousand people.

- On December 24, Russia conquers the country of Georgia, making it a Soviet republic.

1921

- Pablo Picasso paints *Three Musicians.*
- On February 9, the first Indian parliament under the Government of India Act of 1919 convenes in New Delhi.
- On February 21, Gen. Reza Khan launches a coup d'état against British rule in Persia (Iran) and establishes an independent government.
- On March 24, Greece invades Turkey to enforce the Treaty of Sèvres, establishing an Allies-supported government in Turkey.
- On March 31, Coal miners strike in Great Britain.
- On May 1, Arabs and Jews clash in Jaffa, Palestine, killing twenty-seven, all Jews.
- From May to July, German war criminals are tried at Leipzig, Germany.
- On July 21, Moroccan rebels, led by Abd-el-Krim, defeat a Spanish force, killing twelve thousand, and establish the Republic of the Riff.
- On July 27, Canadian Frederick Grant Banting discovers insulin, for which he shares the 1923 Nobel Prize in medicine.
- On July 29, Adolf Hitler is elected chairman and dictator of the Nazi Party in Munich, Germany.
- On August 23, Britain installs Emir Faisal as king of Iraq, formerly Mesopotamia.
- On September 12, Russia declares war on Bessarabia, a new Romanian province.
- On October 19, Portuguese troops assassinate premier António Granjó and several officials.
- On November 4, a fanatic assassinates Hara Takashi, the first commoner to become premier of Japan.
- On November 11, the Washington Armaments Conference convenes.
- On December 6, the British government signs a treaty with the Dail Eireann (Assembly of Ireland) to establish the Irish Free State.
- On December 8, the United States, Japan, England, and France sign the Four-Power Treaty for the arbitration and mediation of economic disputes.
- On December 10, French novelist Anatole France receives the Nobel Prize in literature.
- On December 16, Russian composer Sergey Prokofiev solos in the premiere of his *Piano Concerto No. 3* in Chicago, Illinois.

1922

- James Joyce publishes *Ulysses* in Paris.
- The silent movie classic of German expressionist horror, *Nosferatu,* directed by F.W. Murnau, is released.
- Centre Court at Wimbledon is built in London.

- On January 22, Pope Benedict XV dies at age sixty-five.
- On February 6, the College of the Cardinals elects Achille Cardinal Ratti, who takes the name Pius XI.
- On February 15, the International Court of Justice is established at The Hague, in the Netherlands.
- On February 18, Britain grants Egypt titular independence but maintains military bases throughout the country.
- On February 25, Henri-Désiré Landru, the modern Bluebeard, is guillotined in Versailles, France, for the murder of ten women and a young boy.
- On March 3, Italian Fascists seize the disputed port city of Fiume, which had been independent from both Italy and Yugoslavia.
- On March 15, four hundred followers of revolutionary Irish leader Eamon de Valera capture Limerick and evict conservative officials in the Free State government.
- On March 18, the British government sentences Indian nationalist leader Mohandas Gandhi to six years in prison for sedition.
- On April 3, Joseph Stalin becomes general secretary of the Central Committee of the Russian Communist Party.
- On April 16, Germany and Russia sign the Treaty of Rapallo to promote trade and military cooperation.
- On September 14, Great Britain sends a fleet of warships to the Dardanelles after Turkish troops rout the Greek army in Smyrna and destroy the city.
- On October 28, Benito Mussolini leads Italian Fascists in a march on Rome.
- On November 20, the Lausanne Conference convenes in Switzerland to rewrite the Treaty of Sèvres.
- On November 26, British archaeologists, many of them wealthy amateurs, begin to excavate the tomb of Pharoah Tutankhamen near Luxor, Egypt.
- On December 6, the Free State government replaces the provisional government in Ireland, establishing the Irish Free State.
- On December 11, Danish physicist Niels Bohr receives the Nobel Prize in physics for his work on the structure of the hydrogen atom.
- On December 12, British physicist Frederick Soddy delivers his Nobel lecture.
- On December 30, Russian leaders establish the Union of Soviet Socialist Republics (U.S.S.R.).

1923

- Kahlil Gibran publishes *The Prophet,* a meditative prose poem.
- German theologian Martin Buber publishes *Ich und Du (I and Thou),* in Vienna, Austria.
- On January 10, France sends one hundred thousand troops into the Ruhr to seize German assets as war reparations.
- On February 1, Yaqui Indian soldiers suppress a trolley car strike in Mexico City, killing fourteen and wounding thirty.

- On April 5, George Edward Stanhope Molyneux Herbert, Fifth Earl of Carnarvon, an amateur Egyptologist who is financing excavation of the tomb of Pharoah Tutankhamen, dies in Cairo following an insect bite. Sensationalists in the British press speculate that an Egyptian spell on the tomb had killed Stanhope.

- In April, a priest finds old manuscripts in a vault of a church in Sienna, Italy. Musicologists confirm them as compositions of the eighteenth century Venetian composer Antonio Vivaldi.

- On April 5, Soviet troops massacre 340 Ukrainian peasants for protesting the execution of Roman Catholic vicar general Constantine Butchkavitch six days earlier.

- On June 9, army officers overthrow Aleksandur Stamboliyski, premier of Bulgaria and leader of the Peasant Party.

- On July 11, Albert Einstein delivers his Nobel lecture.

- On August 27, the murder of an Italian delegation on the Greek-Albanian border precipitates an international crisis.

- On September 1, an earthquake, with more than three hundred shocks, destroys Tokyo and Yokohama, Japan, killing 143,000.

- On September 10, the League of Nations votes to admit the Irish Free State.

- On September 13, General Miguel Primo de Rivera seizes power in Spain with the approval of King Alfonso XIII.

- On September 28, the League of Nations admits Ethiopia despite British protests over Ethiopia's practice of slavery.

- On October 24, clashes between police and communist revolutionaries in Hamburg, Germany, kill 44 and wound 350.

- On October 28, Reza Khan, minister of war in Persia (Iran), declares himself prime minister.

- On October 29, three weeks after Turkish troops occupy Istanbul, the Grand Assembly in Turkey proclaims a republic and elects a new president, Mustafa Kemal, and a new premier, Ismet Pasha, ending six centuries of Ottoman rule.

- On November 8, the Nazis, led by Adolf Hitler, fail to overthrow the German government.

- On December 5, Mexican rebels revolt in Vera Cruz against the government of Álvaro Obregón.

- On December 6, an international fleet of warships begins assembling at Canton after Sun Yat-sen, leader of southern China, threatens to close the port.

- On December 15, Irish poet William Butler Yeats receives the Nobel Prize in literature.

- On December 24, Martial law is declared in Honduras, and opponents of President Rafael López Gutiérrez are imprisoned.

1924

- German novelist Thomas Mann publishes *Der Zauberberg* (*The Magic Mountain*), set in a Swiss tuberculosis sanitarium.

- On January 18, Joseph Stalin engineers a plot by the executive committee of the Communist International to exile Russian Communist leader Leon Trotsky, who retires to the Crimea.

- On January 21, Vladimir I. Lenin dies at age fifty-three, leaving Joseph Stalin to consolidate power in the Soviet Union.

- On January 22, the British Labour Party wins its first election, making Ramsay MacDonald the first Labour prime minister.

- On January 25, the first Winter Olympics open in Chamonix, France.

- On January 27, the Treaty of Rome between Italy and Yugoslavia determines that Italy will take the disputed port of Fiume but cede Porto Barros to Yugoslavia.

- On February 1, Britain becomes the first nation to extend diplomatic recognition to the Soviet Union.

- On February 12, British authorities open the sarcophagus of Pharoah Tutankhamen for the first time in four thousand years.

- On April 6, rigged elections give Mussolini's Fascist Party a huge majority in the Italian parliament.

- On April 13, Greek citizens vote to make their country a republic, effective May 1.

- On May 4, the eighth Summer Olympics open in Paris.

- On May 11, rioting between communists and monarchists in Halle, Germany, kills thirty.

- On June 10, fascists murder socialist Giacomo Matteotti, a critic of Mussolini.

- In August, British anatomist Raymond Dart discovers the ancient skull of a six-year-old child in South Africa and christens a new species, *Autralopithecus africanus*.

- On September 8, a military junta in Chile overthrows the liberal government of President Arturo Alessandri Palma.

- On September 10, the Soviet republic of Georgia revolts against the Soviet Union in a desire for independence.

- On October 13, Ibn Sa'ud, sultan of Nedj and leader of the Arabian Wahabis, captures Mecca, a sacred city for Muslims, to expand his dominion in the Arabian Peninsula.

- On November 19, the assassination of Sir Lee Stack, commander of the Anglo-Egyptian army and British governor general of the Sudan, leads Britain to reassert its authority in Egypt.

- On November 30, London sends photographs to New York City.

- On December 6, France begins arresting Russian Communists throughout the country.

1925

- Russian Dmitry Shostakovich composes his first symphony.

- Russian Sergey Eisenstein produces the movie *The Battleship Potemkin*.

- Franz Kafka's novel *Der Prozess* (The Trial) is published posthumously.

- On January 7, Germany elects a socialist, Paul Loebe, president of the Reichstag.

- On February 24, Kurdish rebels, under Sheik Said, revolt against the Turkish government.
- On April 15, Bolsheviks in Bulgaria, backed by Soviet agents, attempt to assassinate the Bulgarian czar, Boris III.
- From April 18 to April 19, military leaders attempt a coup against the democratic government of Portugal's Manuel Teixeira Gomes.
- On April 26, voters elect Field Marshal Paul von Hindenburg, at age seventy-eight, president of Germany in a run-off election.
- On May 15, the Italian parliament grants women limited voting rights.
- On June 10, the Presbyterian, Methodist, and Congregational Churches in Canada merge to form the United Church of Canada.
- On June 19, the French and Spanish armies, allied against the Riffs in Morocco, begin to blockade all shipments to Morocco in an attempt to prevent arms smuggling.
- On July 18, L'Exposition Internationale des Arts Décoratifs et Industriels Modernes (known as the Paris Exposition) opens and provides a venue and the name for art deco.
- On August 7, Druze rebels in Syria kill two hundred French soldiers and wound six hundred more in a revolt against the French.
- On August 21, Bulgarian and Greek troops skirmish near the tiny Turkish town of Demir Hissár, beginning a six-week border dispute between Bulgaria and Greece.
- In September, German physicist Wehrner Heisenberg announces the Uncertainty Principle.
- On September 15, Russian Bolsheviks revolt in Bessarabia, killing fifty Romanian troops, but the Romanian army crushes the revolt.
- On October 16, seven European nations negotiate at Locarno, Switzerland, a series of treaties that guarantee post World War I borders.
- In December, British dramatist George Bernard Shaw receives the Nobel Prize in literature.

1926

- Director Fritz Lang premieres the film *Metropolis,* a critique of power and technology.
- Ninette de Valois founds Britain's Academy of Choreographic Art, later the Royal Ballet.
- English writer A.A. Milne publishes *Winnie-the-Pooh,* the first in a series of children's books.
- On January 3, General Theodoros Pangalos leads a military coup in Greece and declares himself dictator.
- On March 8, the League of Nations calls a special session to admit Germany to membership but adjourns because of complications raised by Brazil and Spain over permanent seating on the council.
- On April 7, British woman, Violet Gibson, shoots Benito Mussolini, whose injuries are slight.

- On April 25, Reza Khan, prime minister of Persia (Iran), becomes shah, reigning as Reza Shah Pahlavi.
- On May 1, British coal miners go on strike.
- On May 2, Nicaraguan rebels, under Augusto César Sandino, launch a rebellion against the conservative government of Emiliano Chamorro Vargas.
- On May 12, a coup led by Marshal Józef Pilsudski overthrows the Polish government of Wincenty Witos.
- On May 28, Portuguese General Gomes da Costa deposes President Bernardino Machado.
- On July 14, President Mustafa Kemal Pasha of Turkey has fifteen members of the Young Turk Party executed for plotting against the government.
- On December 25, Yoshihito, emperor of Japan, dies at forty-seven. His son, Hirohito, will preside over a military expansion that leads Japan to attack the U.S. naval base at Pearl Harbor, Hawaii, on December 7, 1941.

1927

- On January 6, wireless communication connects London and New York City and is available to the public.
- On March 7, an earthquake in Osaka and Kobe, Japan, kills five thousand.
- On April 7, the British government in India convicts eighteen men of antigovernment activity and sentences three to death.
- On April 18, Nationalist Kuomintang leader Chiang Kai-shek splits with Chinese Communists and sets up a government at Nanjing.
- In May, German physicist Erwin Schroedinger announces that one can understand an atom as the interaction of waves.
- On May 4, the United States negotiates an end to the civil war in Nicaragua.
- On May 12, British agents seize documents intended to undermine the British government in a raid on the headquarters of the Soviet propaganda office in London.
- On May 15, excavation begins on the ancient Roman city of Herculaneum in southern Italy, which Mount Vesuvius had buried in an eruption in 79 C.E.
- On May 21, Charles Lindbergh arrives in Paris and is greeted by ecstatic crowds after a thirty-three-and-one-half-hour nonstop flight from New York City.
- On May 22, an earthquake in northern China kills more than two hundred thousand people.
- On June 1, prohibition ends in Ontario, Canada, after eighteen years.
- On July 15, socialists and monarchists clash in Vienna, Austria, killing eighty-nine and injuring more than six hundred.
- On August 29, Hindus and Moslems clash in India, killing three hundred and injuring almost three thousand.
- On October 2, France expels the Soviet ambassador for encouraging communists to rebel against the French government.

- On October 20, anthropologist Davidson Black discovers the first fragment of a skull of an early man.
- On November 12, Joseph Stalin expels Leon Trotsky and his followers from the Communist Party and banishes them to the Soviet provinces.
- On December 2, voters elect Olga Rudel-Zeunek the first female president of the Austrian senate.
- On December 10, French philosopher Henri Bergson receives the Nobel Prize in literature.
- On December 14, Britain grants Iraq a nominal independence but maintains military bases throughout the country.

1928

- Sergey Eisenstein premieres in the Soviet Union a film on the Russian Revolution, *October.*
- An early classic surrealist film, *Un Chien Andalou* (An Andalusian Dog), by Luis Buñuel, Salvador Dali, and others, premieres in France.
- French composer Maurice Ravel composes *Boléro,* among the most popular compositions of the twentieth century.
- D.H. Lawrence publishes *Lady Chatterley's Lover,* in Florence, Italy. Critics condemn its sexuality as obscene.
- On January 6, Pope Pius XI issues an encyclical condemning "Pan-Christian unity."
- On February 2, Transjordan signs a treaty with Britain creating an independent constitutional monarchy.
- On February 11, the second Winter Olympics opens in Saint Moritz, Switzerland.
- On March 2, Egypt rejects a treaty with Britain, limiting Egyptian sovereignty.
- On March 22, Spain revokes its September 1926 decision to resign from the League of Nations.
- On March 25, General Carmona is elected president of Portugal.
- On April 12, German financier Gunther von Huenefeld completes the first successful east to west transatlantic flight.
- On April 24, Chinese Nationalist forces led by Chiang Kai-shek capture Peking.
- On May 17, the ninth Summer Olympics open in Amsterdam, Holland.
- On June 7, the League of Nations cites Hungary for importing five freight cars of machine-gun parts from Italy in violation of the Treaty of Trianon.
- On June 18, Norwegian explorer Roald Amundsen disappears with his pilot and crew while attempting to rescue a stranded polar expedition.
- On July 2, Great Britain lowers the voting age for women from thirty to twenty-one, the voting age for British men.
- On July 10, Japan withdraws troops from Shandong, China.
- On July 19, King Faud of Egypt suspends the Egyptian parliament and assumes control under British authority.
- On August 27, twenty-three nations sign the Pact of Paris, which attempts to outlaw war.

- On August 27, Mustafa Kemal Pasha, president of Turkey, replaces the Arabic alphabet with the Roman alphabet.
- On September 12, Spain arrests more than two thousand protesters on the fifth anniversary of the dictatorship of Miguel Primo de Rivera.
- On October 7, Ras Tafari becomes king of Ethiopia, and on November 2, 1930, he is named king of kings with the title Haile Selassie I.
- On November 25, mountain tribes in Afghanistan revolt against King Amanollah to protest his reforms.
- On December 24, Hungarian police charge leaders of the Fascist Party with treason.

1929

- Erich Maria Remarque publishes *Im Westen Nichts Neues* (All Quiet on the Western Front), in Germany.
- British novelist Virginia Woolf publishes *A Room of One's Own,* in England.
- The French Army begins building the Maginot Line, a system of fortifications on the French-German border, to deter another German invasion of France.
- On January 5, Alexander I, king of the Serbs, Croats, and Slovenes since August 1921, proclaims himself dictator.
- On January 16, Joseph Stalin expels Leon Trotsky from European Russia and on January 23 arrests 150 of Trotsky's followers on charges of conspiracy.
- On February 11, Benito Mussolini and the Roman Catholic Church sign the Lateran treaties, creating Vatican City—a 108.7-acre section of Rome encompassing Saint Peter's Church and the Vatican—as a sovereign state ruled by the Pope.
- On May 1, communists riot in Berlin, killing twenty and injuring fifty.
- On May 20, Germany signs the Pact of Paris, outlawing war.
- On August 22, Arabs attack Jews in the British mandate of Palestine, killing hundreds.
- On October 20, the new state of Tadzhikistan joins the U.S.S.R.
- On November 17, the Soviet Politburo of the Central Committee of the Soviet Communist Party expels moderate leader Nikolay Bukharin from the U.S.S.R.
- On December 5, U.S. Marines quell a revolt against American control in Haiti.
- On December 10, German novelist Thomas Mann receives the Nobel Prize in literature.
- On December 12, French physicist Louis de Broglie receives the Nobel Prize in physics for his discovery that electrons have the properties of waves.
- On December 21, police arrest seventy in Mexico after discovery of a plot to assassinate public officials.

1

THE ARTS

ALICE WU

Entries are arranged in chronological order by date of primary source. For entries with one primary source, the entry title is the same as the primary source title. Entries with more than one primary source have an overall entry title, followed by the titles of the primary sources.

Edna St. Vincent Millay, *A Few Figs from Thistles;* Carl Sandburg, *Smoke and Steel;* E. A. Robinson, *Lancelot.*

POPULAR SONGS: Ted Lewis, "When My Baby Smiles at Me"; Paul Whiteman, "Whispering"; Al Jolson, "My Mammy" and "Avalon"; Bert Williams, "When the Moon Shines on the Moonshine"; Mamie Smith, "Crazy Blues"; Van & Schenck, "After You Get What You Want, You Don't Want It"; Ben Selvin, "Dardanella"; Nora Bayes, "Japanese Sandman"; Original Dixieland Jazz Band, "Margie"; Billy Murray, "I'll see You in C-U-B-A."

Important Events in The Arts, 1920–1929

1920

- *The Americanization of Edward Bok* by Edward W. Bok and *Main Street* by Sinclair Lewis are the year's sellers.
- Marcel Duchamp, Man Ray, and Katherine Dreier organize the New York Societé Anonyme for promoting modern art.
- The Pavley-Oukrainsky Ballet of the Chicago Civic Opera is the first American Ballet Company.
- Reginald de Koven's opera *Rip Van Winkle* is performed by the Chicago Opera Association.
- The Juilliard Foundation is established in New York to encourage music in the United States.
- Joseph Stella paints *Brooklyn Bridge.*
- Thomas Hart Benton paints *Portrait of Josie West.*
- Arturo Toscanini and the LaScala Orchestra give their first American performances.
- Jo Davidson sculpts *Gertrude Stein.*
- Lorado Taft sculpts *Fountain of Time.*
- On February 2, Eugene O'Neill's *Beyond the Horizon* opens at New York's Morosco Theater. It wins the 1920 Pulitzer Prize.
- On June 7, *George White's Scandals* opens with songs by George Gershwin.
- On November 1, Eugene O'Neill's *The Emperor Jones* opens.
- On December 21, Zona Gale's *Miss Lulu Bett* opens. It will win the 1921 Pulitzer Prize for drama.

MOVIES: *Dr. Jekyll and Mr. Hyde,* starring John Barrymore and Nita Naldi; *Way Down East,* starring Lillian Gish and Richard Barthelmess, directed by D. W. Griffith; *The Mark of Zorro,* starring Douglas Fairbanks; *Pollyanna,* starring Mary Pickford; *The Kid,* starring Charlie Chaplin.

FICTION: F. Scott Fitzgerald, *This Side of Paradise* and *Flappers and Philosophers;* Sinclair Lewis, *Main Street;* Sherwood Anderson, *Poor White;* Willa Cather, *Youth and the Bright Medusa;* Zane Grey, *The Man of the Forest;* Peter B. Kyne, *Kindred of the Dust;* Harold Bell Wright, *The Re-Creation of Brian Kent;* James Oliver Curwood, *The River's End;* Joseph C. Lincoln, *The Portygee.*

POETRY: T. S. Eliot, *Poems;* Ezra Pound, *Umbra* and *Hugh Selwyn Mauberley;* William Carlos Williams, *Kora in Hell;*

1921

- *The Brimming Cup* by Dorothy Canfield is the best seller of 1921.
- A collection of whimsical sketches titled *All Things Considered* by Robert Benchley, humorist, drama critic, and film actor is published.
- Charles Ives composes *Thirty-Four Songs for Voices and Piano.*
- Howard Hansen composes *Concerto for Organ, Strings, and Harp.*
- The Eastman School of Music opens in Rochester, New York.
- *The Cabinet of Doctor Caligari,* a German film emphasizing new art forms, is shown in the U.S.
- Stuart Davis paints *Bull Durham.*
- Isadora Duncan opens a dance school in Moscow.
- Charles Demuth paints *Roofs and Steeples.*
- Arthur G. Dove paints *Thunderstorm.*
- John Marin paints *Off Stonington.*
- Phillips Memorial Gallery opens in Washington, D.C.—the first American museum of modern art.
- On May 23, *Shuffle Along,* with music by Eubie Blake and Noble Sissle, opens; it is the first African American Broadway musical directed and written by African Americans.
- On June 1, Eugene O'Neill's *Gold* opens.
- On August 13, *Dulcy,* a play by Marc Connelly opens.
- On November 2, Eugene O'Neill's *Anna Christie* opens, and wins the 1922 Pulitzer Prize for drama.
- On November 10, Eugene O'Neill's *The Straw* opens.
- On December 30, Sergei Prokofiev's opera *The Love for Three Oranges* has its world premiere at the Chicago Civic Opera.

MOVIES: *The Four Horsemen of the Apocalypse,* starring Rudolph Valentino; *Tol'able David,* starring Richard Barthelmess; *The Three Musketeers,* starring Douglas Fairbanks; *Little Lord Fauntleroy,* starring Mary Pickford.

FICTION: John Dos Passos, *Three Soldiers;* Sherwood Anderson, *The Triumph of the Egg;* Ring W. Lardner, *The Big Town;* Donald Ogden Stewart, *A Parody Outline of History;* Booth Tarkington, *Alice Adams;* Dorothy Canfield, *The Brimming Cup;* Zane Grey, *The Mysterious Rider;* Edith Wharton, *The Age of Innocence.*

POETRY: Edna St. Vincent Millay, *Second April;* Marianne Moore, *Poems;* E. A. Robinson, *Collected Poems.*

POPULAR SONGS: Fanny Brice, "Second Hand Rose"; Van & Schenck, "Ain't We Got Fun?"; Lottie Gee, "I'm Just Wild About Harry"; Eddie Cantor, "Ma! (He's Making Eyes at Me)"; Charles Davis, "Shuffle Along"; Eubie Blake, "Bandana Days"; Al Jolson, "April Showers"; Isham Jones, "Wabash Blues"; John Steel, "Say It With Music"; Zez Confrey, "Kitten on the Keys."

1922

- George Antheil composes *Airplane Sonata* and *Death of the Machines*.
- Aaron Copland composes *Passacaglia for Piano*.
- George Bellows paints *The White House*.
- Maurice Prendergast paints *Acadia*.
- Howard Hansen composes *Symphony No.1*.
- On February 20, Marc Connelly's play *To the Ladies* opens.
- On March 9, Eugene O'Neill's *The Hairy Ape* opens.
- On May 23, *Abie's Irish Rose* by Anne Nichols opens; this comedy about a Catholic/Jewish marriage sets a record of 2,327 Broadway performances.
- On November 7, *Rain*, based on W. Somerset Maugham's "Miss Thompson," starring Jeanne Eagels, opens.
- On November 7, *The '49ers*, book by Marc Connelly, opens.
- On November 13, *Merton of the Movies*, a play by Marc Connelly, opens.

MOVIES: *The Prisoner of Zenda*, starring Ramon Novarro; *Orphans of the Storm*, starring Lillian and Dorothy Gish, directed by D. W. Griffith; *Blood and Sand*, starring Rudolph Valentino; *Foolish Wives*, directed by and starring Erich Von Stroheim; *Robin Hood*, starring Douglas Fairbanks; *Nanook of the North*, pioneer documentary directed by Robert Flaherty.

FICTION: Sinclair Lewis, *Babbitt*; James Joyce, *Ulysses*; E. E. Cummings, *The Enormous Room*; Willa Cather, *One of Ours*; Emerson Hough, *The Covered Wagon*; F. Scott Fitzgerald, *Tales of the Jazz Age*.

POETRY: T. S. Eliot, *The Waste Land*.

POPULAR SONGS: Al Jolson, "Toot Toot Tootsie"; Paul Whiteman, "Chicago"; Harry Creamer & Turner Layton, "Way Down Yonder in New Orleans"; Irene Bordoni, "Do It Again"; Sophie Tucker, "Lovin' Sam the Sheik of Alabam'"; Gallagher & Sheean, "Mr. Gallagher and Mr. Sheean"; The Georgians, "I Wish I Could Shimmy Like My Sister Kate"; Van & Schenck, "Carolina in the Morning."

1923

- *Etiquette* by Emily Post is the best seller of 1923.
- Edna St. Vincent Millay wins the Pulitzer Prize for poetry.
- Roger Sessions composes *The Black Maskers*.
- George Bellows paints *Between Rounds*.
- Charles Sheeler paints *Bucks County Barn*.
- Rockwell Kent paints *Shadows of Evening*.
- On February 10, *Icebound* by Owen Davis opens, winning 1923 Pulitzer Prize for drama.

- On February 16, Bessie Smith makes her first recordings ("Down Hearted Blues" and "Gulf Coast Blues").
- On March 19, *The Adding Machine* by Elmer Rice opens; it is an early expressionistic drama.
- From March 30 to March 31, the first dance marathon in the United States is held at Audubon Ballroom in New York City.
- On April 6, Louis Armstrong records his first solo on "Chimes Blues" with King Oliver's Creole Jazz Band.
- *Helen of Troy*, a musical, book by Marc Connelly, opens.
- On September 16, the Mikhail Mordkin ballet company, with Martha Graham, opens in the *Greenwich Village Follies* at the Sam S. Shubert Theater in New York City, running for 127 performances.
- On October 29, *Runnin' Wild* opens; the all-African American musical with songs by James P. Johnson and Cecil Mack introduces "Charleston."
- *The Deep Tangled Wildwood*, a play by Marc Connelly, opens.

MOVIES: *Safety Last*, starring Harold Lloyd; *The Ten Commandments*, starring Richard Dix and Rod LaRocque, directed by Cecil B. DeMille; *The Covered Wagon*, directed by James Cruze and starring Lois Wilson; *The Hunchback of Notre Dame*, starring Lon Chaney; *The Pilgrim*, starring Charlie Chaplin.

FICTION: Sherwood Anderson, *Horses and Men* and *Many Marriages*; Willa Cather, *A Lost Lady*; Ernest Hemingway, *3 Stories & 10 Poems*; Jean Toomer, *Cane*.

POETRY: E. E. Cummings, *Tulips and Chimneys*; Robert Frost, *New Hampshire*; Edna St. Vincent Millay, *The Ballad of the Harp-Weaver*; Kahlil Gibran, *The Prophet*; Wallace Stevens, *Harmonium*.

POPULAR SONGS: Billy Jones, "Yes, We Have No Bananas"; Jelly Roll Morton, "Mr. Jelly Lord"; Van & Schenck, "Who's Sorry Now?" and "That Old Gang of Mine"; Elisabeth Welch, "Charleston"; Wendell Hall, "It Ain't Gonna Rain No Mo'"; Jones & Hare, "Barney Google"; Sophie Tucker, "You've Got to See Mamma Ev'ry Night or You Can't See Mamma at All"; Bessie Smith, "Down Hearted Blues"; Paul Whiteman, "Linger Awhile" and "Three O'Clock in the Morning."

1924

- *So Big* by Edna Ferber is the best seller of 1924. She wins the 1924 Pulitzer Prize for literature.
- Aaron Copland composes *Symphony for Organ and Orchestra*.
- John Alden Carpenter composes *Skyscrapers*.
- George Bellows paints *Dempsey and Firpo*.
- Georgia O'Keeffe paints *Dark Abstraction*.
- Michel Fokine forms the American Ballet.
- Arthur G. Dove paints *Portrait of Ralph Dusenberry*.
- Serge Koussevitsky is appointed head of the Boston Symphony.
- George Antheil composes *Ballet Mécanique*.

- Ferde Grofé composes *Mississippi Suite.*
- Charles Ives composes *Three Pieces for Two Pianos.*
- Juilliard Graduate School is established with a $15 million endowment and Ernest Hutchinson as dean.
- Metro-Goldwyn-Mayer is formed with Louis B. Mayer president and Irving Thalberg second vice president and head of production.
- On February 5, *Hell-Bent fer Heaven* by Hatcher Hughes opens and wins the Pulitzer Prize.
- On February 12, *Beggar on Horseback* a play by Marc Connelly opens.
- On February 18, Bix Beiderbecke records "Fidgety Feet" and "Jazz Me Blues" with The Wolverines.
- On February 24, George Gershwin's *Rhapsody in Blue* is performed by Paul Whiteman's orchestra at New York's Aeolian Hall, bringing respectability to jazz.
- In March, Alfred Stieglitz presents art by Georgia O'Keefe at the Anderson Galleries.
- On May 15, Eugene O'Neill's *All God's Chillun Got Wings* opens—the play is controversial because its subject is miscegenation.
- On September 2, *Rose Marie* opens with songs by Rudolph Friml and Otto Harbach.
- On September 5, *What Price Glory?* the most popular U.S. war play of the 1920s, by Maxwell Anderson and Laurence Stallings opens, starring Louis Wolheim and William Boyd. Later, it becomes a movie.
- In November, Duke Ellington's Washingtonians make their first recordings ("Choo Choo" and "Rainy Nights").
- On November 3, Eugene O'Neill's *S. S. Glencairn* opens at the Provincetown Playhouse.
- On November 11, Eugene O'Neill's *Desire Under the Elms* opens at the Greenwich Village Theatre in New York City.
- On November 24, *They Knew What They Wanted* by Sidney Howard opens. It wins the 1925 Pulitzer Prize.
- On December 1, *Lady, Be Good!* opens with songs by George and Ira Gershwin at the Liberty Theater; it stars Fred and Adele Astaire.
- On December 2, *The Student Prince* opens with music by Sigmund Romberg.

MOVIES: *The Thief of Baghdad,* starring Douglas Fairbanks; *Monsieur Beaucaire,* starring Rudolph Valentino; *Greed,* starring ZaSu Pitts, directed by Erich Von Stroheim; *He Who Gets Slapped,* starring Lon Chaney; *Sherlock Holmes, Jr.,* starring Buster Keaton; *The Iron Horse,* starring George O'Brien, directed by John Ford; *Beau Brummel,* starring John Barrymore.

FICTION: James Gould Cozzens, *Confusion;* Ring W. Lardner, *How to Write Short Stories;* Edith Wharton, *Old New York;* Louis Bromfield, *The Green Bay Tree;* Edna Ferber, *So Big;* Ernest Hemingway, *in our time;* Herman Melville (posthumously), *Billy Budd;* Glenway Wescott, *The Apple of the Eye.*

POETRY: Robinson Jeffers, *Tamar;* Marianne Moore, *Observations;* Edgar Lee Masters, *The New Spoon River Anthology;* John Crowe Ransom, *Chills and Fever.*

POPULAR SONGS: Blossom Seeley, "Alabamy Bound"; Marion Harris, "It Had to Be You"; Winnie Lightner, "Somebody Loves Me"; Mary Ellis & Dennis King, "Indian Love Call"; Isham Jones, "I'll See You in My Dreams"; Al Jolson, "California, Here I Come" and "The One I Love"; Fred & Adele Astaire & Cliff Edwards, "Fascinating Rhythm"; Walter Catlett, "Oh Lady, Be Good"; Grace Moore & John Steel, "What'll I Do?"; Cliff Edwards, "Just Give Me a June Night, the Moonlight, and You."

1925

- *The Private Life of Helen of Troy* by John Erskine, *Gentlemen Prefer Blonds* by Anita Loos, *The Man Nobody Knows* by Bruce Barton are the year's best sellers.
- John Alden Carpenter composes *Jazz Orchestra Pieces.*
- Paul Whiteman's orchestra performs George Gershwin's *135th Street* at Carnegie Hall in New York.
- Alfred Stieglitz presents art by Arthur Dove, Marsden Hartley, John Marin, Charles Demuth, Paul Strand and Georgia O'Keefe at the Anderson Galleries.
- Alain Locke, a professor at Howard University, publishes *The New Negro,* an anthology of writings by various African American writers, making him a spokesperson for the African American community.
- Edward Hopper paints *House by the Railroad.*
- Man Ray paints *Sugar Loaves.*
- Paul Manship sculpts *Flight of Europa.*
- John D. Rockefeller funds The Cloisters, a museum dedicated to medieval art and architecture, built using architectural elements of several medieval cloisters from France on the banks of the Hudson River in New York City.
- The John Simon Guggenheim Memorial Foundation is founded to provide fellowships to artists and scholars in order that they may pursue research in any field of knowledge or creation in any of the arts.
- On March 23, a revival of *Beggars on Horseback* by Marc Connelly opens.
- On May 17, *Garrick Gaieties* opens with songs by Richard Rodgers and Lorenz Hart.
- From September 1 to October 31, the Denishawn dancers are the first American dance company to tour Asia.
- On September 21, *The Vagabond King* opens with music by Rudolph Friml.
- On September 22, *Sunny* opens with songs by Jerome Kern, Otto Harbach, and Oscar Hammerstein II; it stars Marilyn Miller, Clifton Webb, and Jack Donahue.
- On October 12, *Craig's Wife* by George Kelly opens. It wins the 1926 Pulitzer Prize.
- On November 12, Louis Armstrong makes his first recording ("Gut Bucket Blues") with the Hot Five.
- On December 3, George Gershwin's *Concerto in F for Piano and Orchestra* premieres at Carnegie Hall in New York City.
- On December 8, *The Coconuts* opens with songs by Irving Berlin; it stars the Marx Brothers.

MOVIES: *The Phantom of the Opera,* starring Lon Chaney; *Grass,* directed by Merian C. Cooper; *The Gold Rush,* starring Charlie Chaplin; *The Freshman,* starring Harold Lloyd; *The Merry Widow,* starring Mae Murray and John Gilbert, directed by Erich Von Stroheim; *The Big Parade,* starring John Gilbert; *Ben-Hur,* starring Ramon Novarro and Francis X. Bushman.

FICTION: F. Scott Fitzgerald, *The Great Gatsby;* Ernest Hemingway, *In Our Time;* Theodore Dreiser, *An American Tragedy;* Sinclair Lewis, *Arrowsmith;* John Dos Passos, *Manhattan Transfer;* Ellen Glasgow, *Barren Ground;* Anita Loos, *"Gentlemen Prefer Blondes";* John Erskine, *The Private Life of Helen of Troy;* Anzia Yezierska, *Bread Givers.*

POETRY: E. E. Cummings, *& and XLI Poems;* T. S. Eliot, *The Hollow Men;* Robinson Jeffers, *Roan Stallion, Tamar and Other Poems;* Ezra Pound, *A Draft of XVI Cantos;* Amy Lowell, *What's O'Clock;* Countee Cullen, *Color.*

POPULAR SONGS: Al Jolson, "Swanee" and "I'm Sitting on the Top of the World"; Louise Groody & Charles Winninger, "I Want to be Happy"; Louise Groody & John Barker, "Tea for Two"; Eddie Cantor, "If You Knew Susie Like I Know Susie"; Ben Bernie, "Sweet Georgia Brown"; Cliff Edwards, "Sleepy Time Gal"; Ethel Waters, "Dinah"; June Cochrane & Sterling Holloway, "Manhattan"; Fred Waring's Pennsylvanians, "Collegiate"; Vincent Lopez, "Always"; Gene Austin, "Yes Sir, That's My Baby" and "Five Foot Two, Eyes of Blue;—Has Anybody Seen My Girl?"

1926

• *Elmer Gantry* by Sinclair Lewis, *The Story of Philosophy* by Will Durant, and *Topper* by Thorne Smith are the year's best sellers.

• Walt Kuhn paints *Dressing Room.*

• Thomas Hart Benton paints *The Lord Is My Shepherd.*

• Paul Manship sculpts *Indian Hunter.*

• Bix Beiderbecke joins Frankie Trumbauer's band at the Arcadia Ballroom in Saint Louis.

• Margaret H'Doubler establishes the first dance department at the University of Wisconsin.

• On January 23, Eugene O'Neill's *The Great God Brown* opens at the Greenwich Village Theatre in New York City.

• On February 15, Marc Connelly's play *The Wisdom Tooth Brown* opens.

• On March 17, *The Girl Friend* opens with songs by Richard Rodgers and Lorenz Hart.

• On April 18, the first professional performance is given by Martha Graham & Trio at the 48th Street Theater in New York.

• On June 19, George Antheil's *Ballet Mécanique* is performed in Paris.

• On August 26, Warner Brothers' *Don Juan,* the first motion picture with sound, opens.

• On September 15, Jelly Roll Morton makes his first recordings ("Black Bottom Stomp," "Smokehouse Blues," and "The Chant") with The Red Hot Peppers.

• On November 8, *Oh, Kay!* opens with songs by George and Ira Gershwin; it stars Victor Moore and Gertrude Lawrence.

• On November 30, *The Desert Song* opens with songs by Sigmund Romberg, Otto Harbach, and Oscar Hammerstein II.

• On December 30, *In Abraham's Bosom* an all African American drama by Paul Green opens. It wins the 1927 Pulitzer Prize.

MOVIES: *Beau Geste,* starring Ronald Colman; *The Strong Man,* starring Harry Langdon; *The Sea Beast,* starring John Barrymore; *What Price Glory?,* starring Victor McLaglen and Edmund Lowe; *The Black Pirate,* starring Douglas Fairbanks (first Technicolor movie); *La Boheme,* starring Lillian Gish and John Gilbert; *The Son of the Sheik,* starring Rudolph Valentino; *The Torrent,* starring Greta Garbo.

FICTION: Ernest Hemingway, *The Sun Also Rises;* William Faulkner, *Soldiers' Pay;* Willa Cather, *My Mortal Enemy;* Edna Ferber, *Show Boat;* Ellen Glasgow, *The Romantic Comedians;* Ring W. Lardner, *The Love Nest;* Thornton Wilder, *The Cabala;* Thorne Smith, *Topper;* Earl Derr Biggers, *The Chinese Parrot;* F. Scott Fitzgerald, *All the Sad Young Men.*

POETRY: Hart Crane, *White Buildings;* Langston Hughes, *The Weary Blues;* Sara Teasdale, *Dark of the Moon.*

POPULAR SONGS: Ann Pennington, "Black Bottom"; Melody Sheiks, "The Blue Room" and "The Girl Friend"; McKinney's Cotton Pickers, "If I Could Be with You One Hour To-Night"; Georgie Price, "Bye Bye Blackbird"; Abe Lyman, "What Can I Say After I Say I'm Sorry?"; Al Jolson, "Breezin' Along With the Breeze"; Harry Richman, "The Birth of the Blues"; Eddie Cantor, "Baby Face"; Gertrude Lawrence, "Someone to Watch Over Me" and "Do-Do-Do"; Sophie Tucker, "When the Red, Red Robin Comes Bob, Bob, Bobbin' Along"; Louis Armstrong, "Heebie Jeebies"; Duke Ellington, "East St. Louis Toodle-oo."

1927

• *The Bridge of San Luis Rey* by Thornton Wilder is the best seller of 1927.

• Roy Harris composes *Concerto for Piano, Clarinet, and String Quartet.*

• Roger Sessions composes *Symphony in E Minor.*

• Aaron Copland composes *Concerto for Piano and Orchestra.*

• Edward Hopper paints *Manhattan Bridge.*

• Georgia O'Keeffe paints *Radiator Building.*

• Charles Demuth paints *My Egypt.*

• The Ford Motor Company hires Charles Sheeler to photograph its River Rouge plant.

• Ansel Adams takes photographs of Yosemite National Park; the results include a study titled "Monolith, the Face of Half Dome, Yosemite National Park."

• Mahonri Young sculpts *Right to the Jaw.*

• On January 26, *Saturday's Children* by Maxwell Anderson opens.

• On January 31, *The Road to Rome* by Robert E. Sherwood opens; it stars Jane Cowl.

- On February 17, Deems Taylor's opera *King's Henchmen,* libretto by poet Edna St. Vincent Millay, premieres at the Metropolitan Opera in New York City.
- On April 25, *Hit the Deck* opens with songs by Vincent Youmans and Lee Robin.
- On September 6, *Good News* opens with songs by Ray Henderson, B. G. DeSylva, and Lew Brown.
- On September 8, Bix Beiderbecke records "In a Mist."
- On September 13, *The Wild Man of Borneo,* a play by Marc Connelly opens.
- On November 3, *A Connecticut Yankee* opens with songs by Richard Rodgers and Lorenz Hart.
- On November 22, *Funny Face* opens with songs by George and Ira Gershwin; it stars Fred and Adele Astaire.
- On December 4, Duke Ellington's orchestra begins a long engagement at the Cotton Club in Harlem.
- On December 27, *Show Boat* opens with songs by Jerome Kern and Oscar Hammerstein II; it stars Helen Morgan, Charles Winninger, and Edna May Oliver.
- On December 27, *Paris Bound* by Philip Barry opens.

MOVIES: *The Jazz Singer,* starring Al Jolson; *The Scarlet Letter,* starring Lillian Gish; *It,* starring Clara Bow; *The General,* starring Buster Keaton; *Wings,* starring Buddy Rogers and Clara Bow; *Underworld,* directed by Joseph von Sternberg and starring George Bancroft, Evelyn Brent, and Clive Brook; *Flesh and the Devil,* starring John Gilbert and Greta Garbo; *Seventh Heaven,* starring Janet Gaynor and Charles Farrell; *Love,* starring John Gilbert and Greta Garbo; *The King of Kings,* directed by Cecil B. DeMille; *Student Prince,* directed by Ernst Lubitsch; *The Way of All Flesh,* starring Emil Jannings.

FICTION: Conrad Aiken, *Blue Voyage;* James Branch Cabell, *Something About Eve;* Willa Cather, *Death Comes to the Archbishop;* William Faulkner, *Mosquitoes;* Julia Peterkin, *Black April;* Upton Sinclair, *Oil!;* Edith Wharton, *Twilight Sleep;* S. S. Van Dine, *The Canary Murder Case;* Thornton Wilder, *The Bridge of San Luis Rey;* Sinclair Lewis, *Elmer Gantry.*

POETRY: Countee Cullen, *The Ballad of the Brown Girl: An Old Ballad Retold, Caroling Dusk,* and *Copper Sun;* Langston Hughes, *Fine Clothes to the Jew;* Don Marquis, *Archy and Mehitabel;* E. A. Robinson, *Tristram.*

POPULAR SONGS: Jules Bledsoe, "Ol' Man River"; Helen Morgan, "Bill"; and "Can't Help Lovin' Dat Man"; Norma Terris, Howard Marsh, Charles Winninger & Edna May Oliver, "Why Do I Love You?"; Fred Astaire, "'S Wonderful"; Fain & Dunn, "Let a Smile Be Your Umbrella"; Belle Baker, "Blue Skies"; William Gaxton & Constance Carpenter, "My Heart Stood Still" and "Thou Swell"; John Price Jones & Mary Lawler, "The Best Things in Life are Free"; Frank Fay, "Me and My Shadow"; Gene Austin, "My Blue Heaven"; Ruth Etting, "It All Depends on You"; Vernon Dalhart, "Lindbergh, Eagle of the U.S.A."

1928

- Virgil Thomson composes *Four Saints in Three Acts;* the libretto is by Gertrude Stein.

- John Alden Carpenter composes *String Quartet.*
- Arturo Toscanini becomes conductor of the New York Philharmonic.
- Walter Piston composes *Symphonic Piece.*
- Charles Demuth paints *I Saw the Figure 5 in Gold.*
- Charles Sheeler paints *River Rouge Industrial Plant.*
- John Steuart Curry paints *Baptism in Kansas.*
- John Sloan paints *Sixth Avenue Elevated at Third Street.*
- *Le Sacre du Printemps* is produced featuring dancer Martha Graham.
- The ballet *Apollo,* choreographed by George Ballanchine for the Ballets Russes, energizes classical ballet with a jolt of modernism.
- *The Oxford English Dictionary* is published.
- The Doris Humphrey-Charles Weidman dance company is formed in New York.
- Ansel Adams is hired as the official photographer of the Sierra Club, a conservationist organization.
- Alexander Calder creates a caricature in the form of a wire sculpture titled *The Hostess.*
- Louis Hart conducts the dance composition classes at the Neighborhood Playhouse in New York.
- On January 9, Eugene O'Neill's *Marco Millions* opens at the Guild Theatre in New York City.
- On January 10, *Rosalie* opens with songs by George and Ira Gershwin, P. G. Wodehouse, and Sigmund Romberg; it stars Marilyn Miller, Frank Morgan, and Jack Donahue.
- On January 30, Eugene O'Neill's *Strange Interlude* opens at the John Golden Theatre in New York City. It wins the Pulitzer Prize.
- On May 9, *Blackbirds of 1928* opens at the Liberty Theater with songs by Jimmy McHugh and Dorothy Fields; the all-African American cast stars Bill Robinson and Adelaide Hall.
- On May 15, Walt Disney releases to theaters the first Mickey Mouse cartoon *Plane Crazy* in which Mickey emulates his hero Charles Lindberg. In black and white, and without sound, it runs almost six minutes. In 1929, it is released again, this time with sound.
- On June 10, "Dance Derby of the Century" starts at Madison Square Garden in New York and runs for 481 hours.
- On July 28, Walt Disney releases the first Mickey Mouse cartoon with sound *Steamboat Willie,* running seven minutes.
- On August 14, *The Front Page* by Charles MacArthur and Ben Hecht opens; the newspaper melodrama stars Lee Tracy and Osgood Perkins.
- On September 19, *New Moon* opens with songs by Sigmund Romberg and Oscar Hammerstein II.
- On October 23, *Animal Crackers* opens with songs by Harry Ruby and Bert Kalamar; it stars the Marx Brothers.
- On November 26, *Holiday* by Philip Barry opens; it stars Hope Williams.

- On December 4, *Whoopee* with songs by Walter Donaldson and Gus Kahn opens; it stars Eddie Cantor and Ruth Etting.

- On December 13, George Gershwin's symphonic poem *An American in Paris* premieres at Carnegie Hall in New York City.

MOVIES: *The Wedding March,* starring Erich Von Stroheim and ZaSu Pitts, directed by Von Stroheim; *Lilac Time,* starring Colleen Moore and Gary Cooper; *The Circus,* starring Charlie Chaplin; *The Singing Fool,* starring Al Jolson; *Our Dancing Daughters,* starring Joan Crawford.

FICTION: Djuna Barnes, *Ryder;* Upton Sinclair, *Boston;* Glenway Wescott, *Goodbye, Wisconsin;* Edith Wharton, *The Children;* Earl Derr Biggers, *Behind That Curtain;* Viña Delmar, *Bad Girl.*

POETRY: Stephen Vincent Benét, *John Brown's Body;* Robert Frost, *West-Running Brook;* Robinson Jeffers, *Cawder;* Ezra Pound, *A Draft of Cantos XVII to XXVII;* Allen Tate, *Mr. Pope.*

POPULAR SONGS: Helen Kane, "I Wanna Be Loved By You"; Bix Beiderbecke with Paul Whiteman, "Thou Swell"; Gene Austin, "Ramona"; Evelyn Herbert, "Lover, Come Back to Me"; Ona Munson & Jack Whiting, "You're the Cream in My Coffee"; Ben Bernie, Peggy Chamberlin & June O'Dea, "Crazy Rhythm"; Ruth Etting, "Love Me or Leave Me"; Eddie Cantor, "Makin' Whoopee"; Rudy Vallee, "Sweet Lorraine"; Ruth Etting, "I'll Get By"; Jimmie Rodgers, "Blue Yodel."

1929

- *The Magnificent Obsession* by Lloyd C. Douglas and *Believe It or Not* by Robert L. Ripley are the best sellers of 1929.

- Samuel Barber composes *Serenade for String Quartet.*

- Walter Piston composes *Viola Concerto.*

- Roy Harris composes *American Portraits.*

- Edward Hopper paints *The Lighthouse at Two Lights.*

- Charles Sheeler paints *Upper Deck,* a portrait of the USS *Majestic,* achieving photographic quality with paint.

- Thomas Hart Benton paints *Georgia Cotton Pickers.*

- Arthur G. Dove paints *Foghorns.*

- Alexander Calder sculpts *Circus.*

- Saul Baizerman sculpts *Hod Carrier.*

- Isamu Noguchi sculpts *Martha Graham.*

- Fats Waller composes "Honeysuckle Rose," "Ain't Misbehavin'," and "Black and Blue."

- The Museum of Modern Art is founded in New York City.

- On January 10, Elmer Rice's *Street Scene* opens at the Playhouse Theater in New York City. It wins the Pulitzer Prize.

- On February 11, Eugene O'Neill's *Dynamo* opens at the Martin Beck Theater in New York City.

- On July 2, *Showgirl* opens with songs by George and Ira Gershwin; it stars Ruby Keeler and Jimmy Durante.

- On November 27, *Fifty Million Frenchmen* opens with songs by Cole Porter.

MOVIES: *The Taming of the Shrew,* starring Mary Pickford and Douglas Fairbanks; *The Love Parade,* starring Jeanette MacDonald and Maurice Chevalier, directed by Ernst Lubitsch; *Hallelujah,* directed by King Vidor; *The Broadway Melody,* starring Charles King and Bessie Love; *In Old Arizona,* starring Warner Baxter; *Coquette,* starring Mary Pickford.

FICTION: Ernest Hemingway, *A Farewell to Arms;* Thomas Wolfe, *Look Homeward, Angel;* William Faulkner, *Sartoris* and *The Sound and the Fury;* Sinclair Lewis, *Dodsworth;* Frederic Dannay and Manfred Lee (Ellery Queen), *The Roman Hat Mystery;* Ellen Glasgow, *They Stooped to Folly;* Dashiell Hammett, *The Dain Curse* and *Red Harvest;* Theodore Dreiser, *A Galley of Women;* Ring W. Lardner, *Round Up;* Claude McKay, *Banjo;* John Steinbeck, *Cup of Gold;* Edith Wharton, *Hudson River Bracketed;* Chic Sale, *The Specialist;* Oliver LaFarge, *Laughing Boy;* Lloyd C. Douglas, *The Magnificent Obsession;* S. S. Van Dine, *The Bishop Murder Case.*

POETRY: Robinson Jeffers, *Dear Judas;* Conrad Aiken, *Selected Poems;* Louise Bogan, *Dark Summer;* Countee Cullen, *The Black Christ;* E. A. Robinson, *Cavender's House.*

POPULAR SONGS: Nick Lucas, "Tiptoe Through the Tulips With Me"; Cliff Edwards, The Rounders & The Brox Sisters, "Singin' in the Rain"; Ethel Waters, "Am I Blue?"; Rudy Vallee, "I'm Just a Vagabond Lover"; Lillian Taiz & John Hundley, "With a Song in My Heart"; Louis Armstrong, "Ain't Misbehavin'"; William Gaxton & Genevieve Tobin, "You Do Something to Me"; Ruth Etting, "Button Up Your Overcoat"; Libby Holman, "Moanin' Low"; Helen Morgan, "Why Was I Born?"; Al Jolson, "Liza"; Charles King, "Broadway Melody."

"The New O'Neill Play"

Theater review

By: Alexander Woollcott

Date: November 7, 1920

Source: Woollcott, Alexander. "The New O'Neill Play." Review of *The Emperor Jones* by Eugene O'Neill. *The New York Times,* November 7, 1920. Available online at http://www.eoneill.com/artifacts/reviews/ej1_times.htm; website homepage: http://www.eoneill.com (accessed March 14, 2003).

About the Author: Eugene O'Neill (1888–1953) was born in a Broadway hotel room and died in a Boston hotel room. The son of a popular actor, O'Neill turned dramatic writing into a serious art form. He received four Pulitzer Prizes and a Nobel Prize for his contributions to American theater. O'Neill achieved recognition first for his experimental, expressionistic dramas, and later for his mature work in the realist style. ∎

Actor Charles Gilpin as Emperor Jones. Gilpin was the first black actor to play a lead role in a white stage production. **THE YALE COLLECTION OF AMERICAN LITERATURE, BEINECKE RARE BOOK AND MANUSCRIPT LIBRARY. REPRODUCED BY PERMISSION.**

Introduction

Eugene O'Neill despised the clichéd plots and exaggerated gestures of popular American drama at the beginning of the twentieth century. He preferred instead the realism of works by European playwrights such as Bernard Shaw, Henrik Ibsen, and August Strindberg. In keeping with his inclination toward realism, O'Neill was one of the first white playwrights to feature African American actors in lead roles. Until this time, theatrical productions featured African Americans primarily in song-and-dance routines; African American characters were played by white actors in blackface.

O'Neill's first drama featuring African American characters was the one-act play *Moon of the Caribees* (1918). This would be the playwright's last conventional production in terms of character portrayal. The following year, he debuted *The Dreamy Kid,* which starred African American actors in each of its four roles. In 1920, the Provincetown Players premiered O'Neill's *The Emperor Jones,* starring the popular Charles Gilpin in the lead role of Brutus Jones. Gilpin had already established himself as one of the most prominent African American actors of his time, and was considered the natural choice to play Brutus Jones.

The play depicts the tragedy of Brutus Jones, a former Pullman porter and escaped convict marooned on a Carib-

bean island. With the help of Cockney adventurer Henry Smithers, Jones convinces the island's natives that he is a magician. They crown him emperor, but he exploits his subjects, thereby turning them into his enemies. To escape an uprising, Jones flees into the jungle. There, specters of his victims taunt him; he encounters nightmare visions from the past. Ultimately, Jones is destroyed by the natives he had oppressed. O'Neill based his play on the real-life story of Vilbrun Guillame Sam, former president of Haiti. To ensure the realism of his production, the playwright traveled to Honduras in 1909 in order to experience first-hand life among the indigenous of the rainforest.

Significance

The Emperor Jones was an immediate success. Reviews of the play emphasized Gilpin's outstanding performance and consistently reminded readers that for the first time in theatrical history, a white production featured an African American actor in a black leading role.

The play was not without controversy, however. Although it was the first production of its kind to explore the issue of race, it did so in an overtly stereotypical manner. Brutus Jones was an ignorant, haughty anti-hero who eventually fell victim to his own fears and superstitions. Gilpin

A scene from the premiere of the Provincetown Players' groundbreaking production of Eugene O' Neill's *The Emperor Jones* on November 1, 1920. THE YALE COLLECTION OF AMERICAN LITERATURE, BEINECKE RARE BOOK AND MANUSCRIPT LIBRARY. REPRODUCED BY PERMISSION.

pointed this out in numerous interviews when he expressed satisfaction only in receiving recognition for his talent as an actor and not as a representative for his race. Eventually, the actor took it upon himself to change lines he felt were offensive to African Americans. Paul Robeson, who later played Brutus Jones in the film version of the play, expressed regret over his part in the production as well.

The film version of *The Emperor Jones* garnered favorable reviews from the African American press at first, but was eventually denounced by African American organizations such as the United Negro Improvement Association and the NAACP. Contemporary productions continue to explore the play and its complicated legacy through further experimentation, such as casting white actors as Brutus Jones and utilizing video and audio effects made available by the latest technologies.

Primary Source

"The New O'Neill Play"

> **SYNOPSIS:** Alexander Woollcott, a prominent writer and critic, reviewed the debut of *The Emperor Jones*. He and other critics unanimously praised Gilpin's portrayal of Brutus Jones as well as the unique staging of the play. Respected journalist Heywood Broun

said of Gilpin, "[He] gives the most thrilling performance we have seen anywhere this season."

The Provincetown Players began their new season in Macdougal Street last week with the impetus of a new play by the as yet unbridled Eugene O'Neill, an extraordinarily striking and dramatic study of panic fear which is called "The Emperor Jones." It reinforces the impression that for strength and originality he has no rival among the American writers for the stage.

Though this new play of his is so clumsily produced that its presentation consists largely of long, unventilated intermissions interspersed with fragmentary scenes, it weaves a most potent spell, thanks partly to the force and cunning of the author, thanks partly in the admirable playing of Charles S. Gilpin in a title role so predominant that the play is little more than a dramatic monologue. His is an uncommonly powerful and imaginative performance, in several respects unsurpassed this season in New York. Mr. Gilpin is a negro.

The Emperor Jones is a burly darky from the States who has broken jail there and escaped as a

Charles Gilpin

Charles Gilpin (1878–1930), actor and singer, was born in Richmond, Virginia, the youngest of fourteen children. Ending his formal education at the age of twelve, he then trained as a printer before running away to tour with vaudeville troupes. By 1916, he had helped organize the Lafayette Players, Harlem's first theater group. Gilpin earned his living as a printer, barber, and an elevator operator in between acting jobs. His 1919 Broadway debut was in John Drinkwater's *Abraham Lincoln,* in which he portrayed a former slave. The play was wildly successful and established Gilpin as a prominent performer. For his role as Brutus Jones in O'Neill's *The Emperor Jones,* Gilpin was honored by the Drama League as one of the ten persons contributing most to American theater in 1920; the NAACP awarded him its Springarn Medal, and *The New Republic* named him among the greatest artists of the American stage.

Gilpin's success was short-lived. In an effort to make his character less offensive to blacks, Gilpin began changing his lines without approval. In addition, he was losing his battle with alcohol. The combination caused him to be replaced by Paul Robeson, whose role as Brutus Jones propelled his career as it once did Gilpin's. Gilpin appeared in several other plays—none of them as successful as *The Emperor Jones*—until losing his voice in 1926. He died an impoverished elevator operator.

stowaway to what the program describes as "a West Indian island not yet self-determined by white marines." There, thanks a good deal to the American business philosophy he had picked up as a half-preoccupied porter listening wide-eyed in the smoking rooms of the Pullman cars back home, he is sufficiently bold, ingenious and unscrupulous to make himself ruler within two years. He has moved unharmed among his sullen subjects by virtue of a legend of his invention that only a silver bullet could harm [him]—this part of the play, at least, is not Mr. O'Neill's invention—but now, when he has squeezed from his domain just about all the wealth it will yield, he suspects it would be well for him to take flight. As the play begins, the measured sound of a beating tom-tom in the hills gives warning that the natives are in conclave there, using all manner of incantations to work up their courage to the point of rebellion.

The hour of Emperor Jones has come, and nightfall finds him already at the edge of the distant forest, through whose trackless waste he knows a way to safety and freedom. He has food hidden there and, anyway, his revolver carries five bullets for his enemies and one of silver for himself in case he is ever really cornered.

It is a bold, self-reliant adventurer who strikes out into the jungle at sunset. It is a confused, broken, naked, half-crazed creature who, at dawn, stumbles blindly back to his starting place, only to find the natives calmly waiting there to shoot him down with bullets they have been piously molding according to his own prescription.

The forest has broken him. Full of strange sounds and shadows, it conjures up visions of his own and his ancestral past. These haunt him, and i[n] each crises of fear he fires wildly into the darkness and goes crashing on through the underbrush, losing his way, wasting all of his defense, signaling his path, and waking a thousand sinister echoes to work still more upon his terrible fear.

It begins with the rattle of invisible dice in the darkness, and then, as in a little clearing, he suddenly sees the squatting darky he had slain back home in a gamblers' quarrel. He plunges on, but only to find himself once more strangely caught in the old chain gang, while the guard cracks that same whip whose stinging lash had goaded him to another murder. Then, as his fear quickens, the forest fills with old-fashioned people who stare at him and bid for him. They seem to be standing him on some sort of block. They examine his teeth, test his strength, flex his biceps. The scene yields only to the galley of a slave ship, and his own cries of terror take up the rhythmic lamentation of his people. Finally, it is a race memory of old Congo fears which drives him shrieking back through the forest to the very clearing whence he had started and where now his death so complacently awaits him.

From first to last, through all of the agonizing circle of his flight, he is followed by the dull beat, beat, beat, of the tom-tom, ever nearer, ever faster, till it seems to be playing an ominous accompaniment to his mounting panic. The heightening effect of this device is much as you might imagine.

The Provincetown Players have squanderously invested in cushions for their celebrated seats and a concrete dome to catch and dissolve their lights, so that even on their little stage they can now get such illusions of distance and the wide outdoors as few of their uptown rivals can achieve. But of immeasurably greater importance in their present enterprise, they have acquired an actor, one who has it in him to invoke the pity and the terror and inde-scribable foreboding which are part of the secret of "The Emperor Jones."

Further Resources

BOOKS

Anderson, Jervis. *This Was Harlem.* New York: Farrar Straus Giroux, 1982.

Beckerman, Bernard, and Howard Siegman, eds. *On Stage.* New York: Arno Press with Quadrangle/New York Times Book Co., 1973.

Bogard, Travis. *Contour in Time: The Plays of Eugene O'Neill.* New York: Oxford University Press, 1988.

Hatch, James Vernon. *Lost Plays of the Harlem Renaissance, 1920–1940.* Detroit: Wayne State University Press, 1996.

Hill, Errol, ed. *The Theater of Black Americans.* Vol. 2. Englewood Cliffs, N.J.: Prentice-Hall, 1980.

Kellner, Bruce. *The Harlem Renaissance.* New York: Methuen, 1984.

Klotman, Phyllis Rauch. *Frame by Frame.* Bloomington: Indiana University Press, 1979.

Patterson, Lindsay, ed. *Anthology of the American Negro in the Theatre; A Critical Approach.* 2nd ed. New York: Publishers Company, 1970.

Sampson, Henry T. *The Ghost Walks.* Metuchen, N.J.: Scarecrow Press, 1988.

PERIODICALS

Krasner, David, "Whose Role Is It Anyway?: Charles Gilpin and the Harlem Renaissance." *African American Review* 29, 1995, 483–496.

INTERVIEWS

"An Interview with Charles Gilpin." *The Best of the Brownies' Book.* Edited by Dianne Johnson-Feelings. New York: Oxford University Press, 1996.

New York Dada

Magazine cover; Magazine articles

By: Man Ray

Date: 1921

Source: Ray, Man, ed. *New York Dada.* April 1921. Beinecke Rare Book and Manuscript Library, Yale University.

About the Author: Emmanuel Rudnitsky (1890–1976) was born in Philadelphia and grew up in Brooklyn. At fifteen, the aspiring artist shortened his name to Man Ray. Never one to adhere to any particular artistic style or medium, Ray created a diverse body of work. In 1921, Ray moved to Paris, where he produced his most experimental art. He was the only American artist to figure prominently in both the Dada and Surrealist art movements. ∎

Introduction

In 1915, Ray met the French artist Marcel Duchamp, who was living in the United States at the time. The two became lifelong friends and together they formed the New York branch of the Dada movement.

Dada was invented in 1916 in Zurich, Switzerland. Writers and artists initiating the movement included Jean Arp, Hugo Ball, and Tristan Tzara. Dada was the radical rejection of traditional culture, and it attempted to do away with the artistic boundaries previously separating art, drama, and poetry. It was an attitude that could be applied to any artistic discipline, rather than to a particular form or style. Dada gave way to Surrealism by 1922, but has had a lasting influence throughout art. The Dadaists were considered extremely radical at the time. For instance, they used theories of chance, collage, audience confrontation, inventive typography, visual poetry, and abstraction in their art. The Dadaists were the first to present "found" objects as art; they called these combinations of everyday objects "readymades." Dada's innovations are now considered basic artistic concepts.

After World War I, the Zurich Dadaists moved to Paris, often presenting their artistic activities in the form of performances and publications.

Significance

Ray and Marcel Duchamp collaborated on many projects, including the publication of the only issue of *New York Dada* in 1921. *New York Dada* is a foldout magazine featuring works by and about well-known artists of the day. Duchamp's cover art for the magazine features a bottle of *Belle Haleine* perfume modified with a photograph of himself dressed up as alter ego Rose Sélavy.

Shortly after producing *New York Dada,* Ray followed Duchamp to move to Paris. "Dada cannot live in New York," Duchamp had said. In Paris, Ray made his first experimental films and produced his most famous photographic works. Ray invented "rayographs," cameraless prints created by placing objects directly onto photographic paper and exposing them to the light.

Ray was also a highly successful commercial photographer. He was lauded for his technical prowess and innovative portraiture. His images were prominently featured in *Vanity Fair,* and he was a principal photographer for *Harper's Bazaar,* a position that soon made his work instantly recognizable to the general public. His photo compositions were featured in numerous exhibitions as he reached the height of his fame in the mid-1930s.

Dadaism was a fringe movement whose leaders were icons of the Bohemian lifestyle of the day. As a movement whose mission was to buck the Establishment, its very popularity was something of a conundrum. Ray was

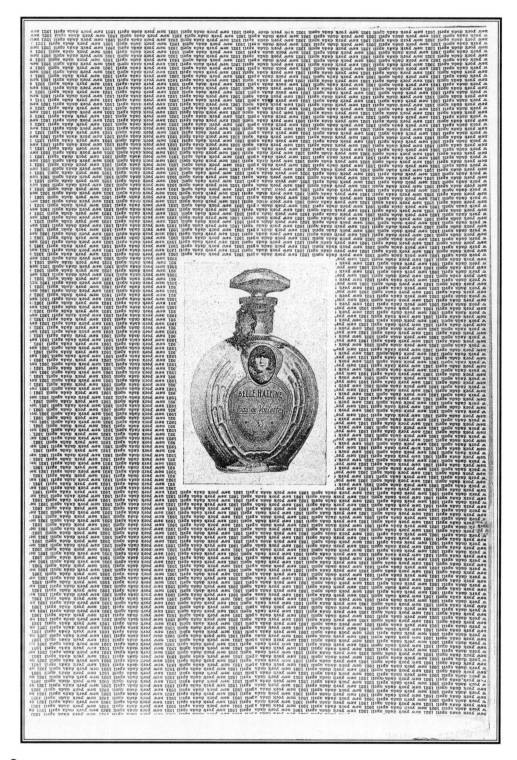

Primary Source

New York Dada, Cover (1 OF 5)

SYNOPSIS: Cover of the first and only issue of *New York Dada* magazine, created by Man Ray. The cover art is by Marcel Duchamp. Ray invited Dada godfather Tristan Tzara to write the introduction to the magazine. Its pages also include a cartoon by Rube Goldberg, satirical writings, and poetry by the eccentric Baroness Elsa von Freitag-Loringhoven. The graphic design of *New York Dada* was unusual for its time. The type runs in all directions, and the printed word is often used for visual effect, not just to convey the meaning of the word itself. © 2003 MAN RAY TRUST/ARTISTS RIGHTS SOCIETY (ARS) NY/ADAGP, PARIS. REPRODUCED BY PERMISSION.

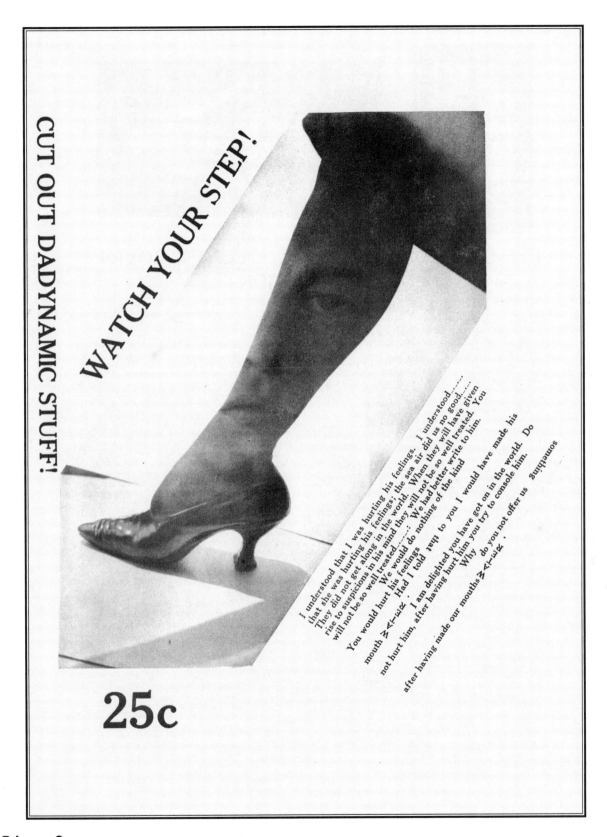

CUT OUT DADYNAMIC STUFF!

WATCH YOUR STEP!

25c

Primary Source

New York Dada, Page 1 (2 OF 5)

Page of *New York Dada* Magazine from 1921, priced at 25 cents. © 2003 MAN RAY TRUST/ARTISTS RIGHTS SOCIETY (ARS)

NY/ADAGP, PARIS. REPRODUCED BY PERMISSION.

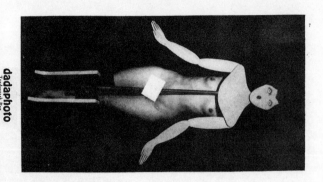

EYE-COVER   ART-COVER   CORSET-COVER

AUTHÓRIZATION

NEW YORK-DADA:

You ask for authorization to name your periodical Dada. But Dada belongs to everybody. I know excellent people who have the name Dada. Mr. Jean Dada; Mr. Gaston de Dada; Fr. Picabia's dog is called Zizi de Dada; in G. Ribemont-Dessaigne's play, the pope is likewise named Zizi de Dada. I could cite dozens of examples. Dada belongs to everybody. Like the idea of God or of the tooth-brush. There are people who are very dada, more dada; there are dadas everywere all over and in every individual. Like God and the tooth1brush (an excellent invention, by the way).

Dada is a new type; a mixture of man, naphthaline, sponge, animal made of ebonite and beefsteak, prepared with soap for cleansing the brain. Good teeth are the making of the stomach and beautiful teeth are the making of a charming smile. Halleluiah of ancient oil and injection of rubber.

There is nothing abnormal about my choice of Dada for the name of my review. In Switzerland I was in the company of friends and was hunting the dictionary for a word appropriate to the sonorities of all languages. Night was upon us when a green hand placed its ugliness on the page of Larousse—pointing very precisely to Dada—my choice was made. I lit a cigarette and drank a demitasse.

For Dada was to say nothing and to lead to no explanation of this offshoot of relationship which is not a dogma nor a school, but rather a constellation of individuals and of free facets.

Dada existed before us (the Holy Virgin) but one cannot deny its magical power to add to this already existing spirit and impulses of penetration and diversity that characterizes its present form.

There is nothing more incomprehensible than Dada.

Nothing more indefinable.

With the best will in the world I cannot tell you what I think of it.

The journalists who say that Dada is a pretext are right, but it is a pretext for something I do not know.

Dada has penetrated into every hamlet; Dada is the best paying concern of the day.

Therefore, Madam, be on your guard and realize that a really dada product is a different thing from a glossy label.

Dada abolishes "nuances." Nuances do not exist in words but only in some atrophied brains whose cells are too jammed. Dada is an anti "nuance" cream. The simple motions that serve as signs for deaf-mutes are quite adequate to express the four or five mysteries we have discovered within 7 or 8,000 years. Dada offers all kinds of advantages. Dada will soon be able to boast of having shown people that to say "right" instead of "left" is neither less nor too logical, that red and valise are the same thing; that 2765 = 34; that "fool" is a merit; that yes = no. Strong influences are making themselves felt in politics, in commerce, in language. The whole world and what's in it has slid to the left along with us. Dada has inserted its syringe into hot bread, to speak allegorically into language. Little by little (large by large) it destroys it. Everything collapses with logic. And we shall see certain liberties we constantly take in the sphere of sentiment, social life, morals, once more become normal standards. These liberties no longer will be looked upon as crime, but as itches.

I will close with a little international song: Order from the publishing house "La Sirene" 7 rue Pasquier, Paris, DADAGLOBE, the work of dadas from all over the world. Tell your bookseller that this book will soon be out of print. You will have many agreeable surprises.

Read Dadaglobe if you have troubles. Dadaglobe is in press. Here are some of its colloborators:

Paul Citroen (Amsterdam); Baader Daimonides; R. Hausmann; W. Heartfield; H. Hoech; R. Huelsenbeck; G. Grosz; Fried Hardy Worm (Berlin); Clement Pansaers (Bruxelles); Mac Robber (Calcutta); Jacques Edwards (Chili); Baargeld, Armada v. Dulgedalzen, Max Ernst, F. Haubrich (Cologne); K. Schwitters (Hannovre); J. K. Bonset (Leyde); Guillermo de Torre (Madrid); Gino Cantarelli; E. Bacchi, A. Fiozzi (Mantoue); Krusenitch (Moscou); A. Vagts (Munich); W. C. Arensberg, Gabrielle Buffet, Marcel Duchamp; Adon Lacroix; Baroness v. Loringhoven; Man Ray; Joseph Stella; E. Varese; A. Stieglitz; M. Hartley; C. Kahler (New York); Louis Aragon; C. Brancusi; André Breton; M. Buffet; S. Charchoune; J. Crotti; Suzanne Duchamp; Paul Eluard; Benjamin Peret; Francis Picabia; G. Ribemont-Dessaignes; J. Rigaut, Soubeyran; Ph. Soupault, Tristan Tzara (Paris); Melchior Vischer (Prague); J. Evola (Rome); Arp; S. Taeuber (Zurich).

The incalculable number of pages of reproductions and of text is a guaranty of the success of the book. Articles of luxury, of prime necessity, articles indispensable to hygiene and to the heart, toilet articles of an intimate nature.

Such, Madame, do we prepare for Dadaglobe; for you need look no further than to the use of articles prepared without Dada to account for the fact that the skin of your heart is chapped; that the so precious enamel of your intelligence is cracking; also for the presence of those tiny wrinkles still imperceptible but nevertheless disquieting.

All this and much else in Dadaglobe.   TRISTAN TZARA.

Primary Source

New York Dada, Page 2 (3 OF 5)

Page from *New York Dada* featuring "Authorization" and Dadaist images. © 2003 MAN RAY TRUST/ARTISTS RIGHTS SOCIETY (ARS) NY/ADAGP, PARIS. REPRODUCED BY PERMISSION.

R. Goldberg

I WILL NOW PROVE
THAT A BULLET DOESN'T
LOSE ANY OF ITS SPEED
WHEN IT GOES AROUND
CORNERS.

VENTILATION

On the question of proper ventilation opinions radically differ. It seems impossible to please all. It is our aim, however, to cater to the wishes of the majority. The conductor of this vehicle will gladly be governed accordingly. Your cooperation will be appreciated.

DADATAXI, Limited.

PUG DEBS MAKE SOCIETY BOW

Marsden Hartley May Make a Couple—
Coming Out Party Next Friday

A beautiful pair of rough-eared debutantes will lead the grand socking cotillion in Madison Square Garden when Mina Loy gives a coming-out party for her Queensberry proteges. Mina will introduce the Marsden Hartleys and the Joseph Stellas to society next week, and everybody who is who is who-er than ever that night.

Master Marsden will be attired in a neat but not gaudy set of tight-fitting gloves and will have a V-back in front and on both sides. —He will wear very short skirts gathered at the waist with a nickel's worth of live leather belting. His slippers will be heavily jewelled with brass eyelets, and a luxurious pair of dime laces will be woven in and out of the hooks. He may or may not wear socks. He has always been known as a daring dresser.

Attire of Debutantes.

Master Joseph will wear a flesh-colored complexion, with the exception of his full-dress tights. He has created a furore in society by appearing at informal morning battles with coattails on his tights. The usual procedure at matinee massacres is for the guest of honor to wear tuxedo trunks with Bull Durham trimmings. He will affect the six-ounce suede glove with hard bandages and a little concrete in 'em if possible. His tights will be silk and he wears them very short.

Before the pug-debs are introduced, Miss Loy will turn a gold spigot and flocks of butterflies will be released from their cages. They will be released through the magnificent Garden, which has been especially decorated with extra dust for the occasion. Each butterfly will flit around and then light on some particular head. If you get two oleofleas on your dome, try and keep it a secret.

Description of Ring

The ring will be from the Renaissance period with natural wood splinters. The gong will sound curfew chimes at the end of each round. It will be played by a specially imported pack of Swiss gong ringers. The ropes will be velvet and hung like portieres. Edgar Varese, the violinist, has donated a piece of concert resin to be used on the canvas flooring, which will be made in Persia. Incidentally, the tights worn by the fighters will be made by Tweeble-ham, of London, purveyor to the Queen by highest award.

Master Marsden will give his first dance to his brother pug-deb Joseph, which will probably fill Marsden's card for the evening. Visiting diplomats in the gallery de luxe will please refrain from asking for waltzes.

—With apologies to "Bugs" Baer.

YOURS WITH DEVOTION

trumpets and drums.

Dearest Saltimbanques_____
       beatrice_____muriel_____
  shaw___not garden___   mary___
      "when they go the other way"
      OTHER WAY___dearest___:
                REMEMBER_____
Mary so knowing_____emma_____emily_____
               beatrice_____muriel_____
  bandwaggon of heavenly saltimbanques_____
yes yes___girlies_____performance at eleven in the late afternoon_____
    wires all spread_____canvas_____stretched_____
special thunderstorm to be pulled___for YOU____for YOU____
and YOU_____and YOU_____and YOU_____
    saltimbanques come straight from HEAven_____
Toto_____ella_____and ethel_____
french nacre_____frigidity english_____
ALL_____ALL_____ALL_____ALL_____ALL_____
               hurdygurdy-merrygoround_____
Offset of delicious word DISGUST_____
    saltimbanques are from HEAven_____
eh bien TOTO____et toi___ELLA_____so murderously
aware-IMPECCABLE ELLA_____BERtie_____
             having given us
the difficulties of   to feel
    SNIPESHOOTING in the gutters of the
         STRAND_____
with a prince albert to cover those votive limbs
  hungrier for chops___than for the immoral
    NUdeness of the TRuth_____
shall we invite minnie_____that one who had the courage_____
              to run_____
the gamut_____from hedda to hannele_____
  never___glorious one___having to my knowledge
    taken advantage of any innocent word in our
        novel SPEECH_____

and lily?
      lena, naturellement_____
        most perfect legs since Pauline Hall
        so the old ducks say.
    shall we phone for Lily?_____
    saltimbanques are from HEAven_____
        c'est tout___ma chere_____

TOTO___pav_____
    WATTS___Pav____
give us these gentlemen pavs_____who turn PIROUETTES
  into handsprings____standing upon skates
          of wood_____and upon
          muscles of chalcedony_____

  saltimbanques are from HEAven_____
beatrice_____and muriel_____
    astarte of the SKATING rink____
      juno of the TIGHT wire_____
Puppets pull their own strings if having the
        intelligence___of bea_____
        and Muri_____
        they pull them well_____
          WELL_____I said_____
           W_E_L_L_____
saltimbanques are from HEAven_____
  Franklin and CHarles____muscles___muscles___muscles____
  George and dicky_____lines___lines___lines____

  saltimbanques are from HEAven_____

Experience__without____expurgation_____
  everyone's rabelaisian step-parent_____
  evryone damned by mrs. beterouge_____

I have a thousand mouchoirs____
          Phyllis and Phillippe_____
send us many another bandwaggon, GOD_____
  filled with saltimbanques like
    FRanklin and CHarles_____
      and TOTO_____and ETHEL_____and ELLA_____
You have heard what I said_____
    SALTIMBANQUES ARE STRAIGHT
          from heaven_____
    That's all, infinitely all_____
        That's all__
        ALL.
          ALL.
         ALL.

  Dance hellions, all of you_____
    for your very lives_____

Baroness Elsa von Freytag-Loringhoven

Primary Source

New York Dada, Page 4 (5 OF 5)

The collage style of this page from Man Ray's *New York Dada* magazine was typical of Dadaist art. © 2003 MAN RAY
TRUST/ARTISTS RIGHTS SOCIETY (ARS) NY/ADAGP, PARIS. REPRODUCED BY PERMISSION.

Ware, Katherine, and Emmanuelle de L'Ecotais. *Man Ray, 1890–1976.* Köln: Taschen, 2000.

Whitney Museum of Art. *Making of Mischief: Dada Invades New York.* New York: Harry Abrams, 1996.

PERIODICALS

Glueck, Grace. "They Were Two Wild Ones, Make No Mistake: Kiki of Montparnasse and Baroness Elsa von Freytag-Loringhoven." *The New York Times,* May 3, 2002.

WEBSITES

"Dada Online." Available online at http://www.peak.org /~dadaist/ (accessed July 7, 2002).

"International Dada Archive." The University of Iowa Libraries. Available online at http://www.lib.uiowa.edu/dada /index.html (accessed July 7, 2002).

"Man Ray Trust." Available online at http://www.manraytrust .com/ (accessed July 7, 2002).

Baroness Elsa von Freitag-Loringhoven and Kiki of Montparnasse

Elsa von Freitag-Loringhoven (1874–1927) was a New York-based artist and poet who created fanciful sculptures and outlandish costumes for herself. Her counterpart in Paris was Kiki of Montparnasse (1901–1953), a painter and café singer of bawdy ballads. The two women never met, but were both strong-willed, flamboyant characters, members of the Dada-Surrealist circle who captivated their audiences and were inspirations to key artistic figures, including Ernest Hemingway, Jean Cocteau, and Tsuguharu Foujita.

Elsa von Freitag-Loringhoven was born in Swinemünde, a small German seaport. At eighteen, she began to study art and made her way to New York and met Leopold, the Baron of Freitag-Loringhoven. They married in 1913, and when he died, Elsa simply kept using the name and title. She was a striking image, going about her daily business in her vermillion-dyed short hair and homemade hats trimmed with vegetables gilt in gold.

Ray met Kiki soon upon his arrival in Paris, where she was already something of a legend. Some called her "the queen of the artists' quarter Montparnasse." He was instantly interested in photographing her. They were lovers for eight years, and she appears in some of Ray's most famous images, such as *Noir et Blanche* (1926) and *Le Violon d'Ingres* (1924). *Le Violon d'Ingres* features Kiki's back imprinted with two "f"-shaped sound holes. The title is French for "hobby," and literally means "the violin of Ingres." This is an example of Ray's sense of humor. The famous eighteenth-century painter and draughtsman Jean Auguste Dominique Ingres was a second violin in the Capitol orchestra and thought himself a virtuoso, while his Parisian friends considered him musically challenged.

without question one of the most prominent Dadaists, and today he is considered a pioneer in photography not only as an art, but as a means of visual communication.

Further Resources

BOOKS

Martin, Julie, and Billy Klüve. *Kiki's Paris: Artists and Lovers 1900–1930.* New York: Henry N. Abrams, 1989.

Ray, Man. *Self Portrait.* New York: Little, Brown and Company, 1988.

Richter, Hans. *Dada Art and Anti-Art.* Trans. David Britt. New York: Oxford University Press/World of Art Series, 1965.

Documenting the Eskimos

My Eskimo Friends

Memoir

By: Robert Joseph Flaherty

Date: 1922

Source: Flaherty, Robert J. *My Eskimo Friends.* New York: Doubleday, Page & Co., 1924, 133–136.

Scene from *Nanook of the North*

Film still

By: Robert Joseph Flaherty

Date: 1922

Source: The Kobal Collection. Reproduced by permission.

About the Author: Robert Joseph Flaherty (1884–1951), was an explorer, prospector, mapmaker, and pioneering documentary filmmaker. His acclaimed *Nanook of the North* (1922) and subsequent film work earned him the title of "the father of the documentary." Born in Iron Mountain, Michigan, Flaherty grew up in isolated mining towns and camps, learning to hunt and track from Native American friends. He met his future wife, Frances Hubbard, while attending Michigan College of Mines. She became Flaherty's lifelong collaborator and promoter. ■

Introduction

Robert Flaherty earned his reputation and developed his outdoor expertise while working for various mining expeditions. In 1910 he was hired by Canadian railroad builder William Mackenzie to explore the Hudson Bay's east coast. This assignment introduced Flaherty to the region's Eskimos. In the next few years, Flaherty made two

"How I Filmed 'Nanook of the North'"

My equipment included seventy-five thousand feet of film, a Haulberg electric light plant and projector and two Akeley cameras and a printing machine so that I could make prints of film as it was exposed and project the pictures on the screen so that thereby the Eskimo would be able to see and understand wherever mistakes were made. . . .

When in December the snow lay heavy on the ground the Eskimo abandoned their topecks of sealskin and the village of snow igloos sprung up around my wintering post. They snow-walled my little hut up to the eves with thick blocks of snow. It was as thick walled as a fortress. My kitchen was their rendezvous—there was always a five-gallon pail of tea steeping on the stove and sea biscuit in the barrel. My little gramophone, too, was common property. Caruso, Farrar, Ricardo-Martin, McCormick served their turns with Harry Lauder, Al Jolson and Jazz King orchestras. Caruso in the Pagliacci prologue with its tragic ending was to them the most comic record of the lot. It sent them into peals of laughter and to rolling on the floor.

The difficulties of film development and printing during the winter were many. That convenience of civilization which I most missed was running water. For instance, in the film washing, three barrels of water for every hundred feet was required. The water hole, then eight feet of ice, had to be kept open all winter long and water clotted with particles of ice had to be taken, a barrel at a time, from a distance of more than a quarter of a mile away. When I mention that over fifty thousand feet of film was developed over the winter with no assistance save from my Eskimo and at the slow rate of eight hundred feet a day one can understand somewhat the amount of time and labor involved.

SOURCE: Flaherty, Robert J. "How I Filmed 'Nanook of the North.'" *World's Work,* October 1922, 632–640.

explorations of the island, traveling by foot, by sled, and by canoe. He mapped the region (one of the Belcher Islands is now named for him), took still photographs, and became friendly with the native Inuit.

For his next trip to the Hudson Bay, Mackenzie convinced Flaherty to bring along a movie camera. Flaherty then bought a Bell and Howell camera and took a three-week film class before his 1913 expedition. On this trip, he shot more than seventy thousand feet of film, about seventeen hours' worth of footage. He made one print of the footage when he returned to Toronto. A dropped cigarette ash destroyed the original nitrate negative of this film. Determined to make a new film, and with the encouragement of Frances, Flaherty used the surviving, unedited print of the first movie and compiled a book, *The Drawings of Ennoesweetok of the Sikosilingmiut Tribe of the Eskimo,* to secure financial backing for his project. John Revillon of Revillon Frères, a French furrier company, agreed to sponsor Flaherty.

In 1920, Flaherty returned to the Hudson Bay region for the exclusive purpose of making a film. This new film became the now-classic *Nanook of the North,* the story of the hunter Nanook, his wife Nyla, and their child, and their struggle to survive under harsh Arctic conditions. It was released in 1922 to commercial and critical success.

Significance

Nanook of the North became the greatest popular and critical success of any nonfiction film of its time. Flaherty's storytelling abilities and his camera artistry ensured the film's celebrated status. Although *Nanook* was not the first "documentary," or even the first film shot in an exotic location using native actors, it demonstrated to filmmakers and studio heads that nonfiction films could be low cost, as well as highly profitable. *Nanook* created a new excitement for the film industry and filmgoers alike. Audiences were keen for documentaries.

Flaherty's films were primarily created as dramas. Some rituals and events of *Nanook* were even staged. For the opening scene, Flaherty creates the illusion of six Inuits emerging from a single kayak. He and Inuit friends built a half-igloo for the interior scenes, as studio lighting was not available. Nanook's struggle with a seal was actually a tug-of-war with men hidden off-camera. While some of Flaherty's portrayals of the vanishing way of Inuit life were fictionalized, oftentimes the risk of physical danger to Nanook and the others was authentic. By the time of the film's commercial release, Allariallak, the Inuit who portrayed "Nanook the Bear," had died of starvation on a deer hunt.

Flaherty spent years filming the Eskimos of Canada, going through reels of film with no guarantee of financial gain. In the end, his talent for editing the footage into a beautiful, moving narrative made *Nanook of the North* enduringly appealing to the public. Flaherty secured more documentary projects and the opportunity to travel the world. However, the independent filmmaker found working under Hollywood studio conditions too restrictive. In his lifetime, he directed only seven features and two short films. These included *Moana* (1926), shot in Samoa and backed by Paramount; and film projects financed outside the industry such as his last work, *Louisiana Story* (1948), sponsored by Standard Oil, about oil workers and the bay-

A scene from the film *Nanook of the North,* directed by Robert Flaherty, 1924. THE KOBAL COLLECTION. REPRODUCED BY PERMISSION.

ous. The film won that year's Venice Film Festival's International Prize for its "lyrical beauty."

Primary Source

My Eskimo Friends [excerpt]

SYNOPSIS: *My Eskimo Friends* recalls Flaherty's experiences living among the Inuit and working on the project that would become the classic silent film *Nanook of the North.* This volume is a reworking of Flaherty's writings prior to the completion and release of *Nanook of the North.*

As luck would have it, the first film to be made was that of a walrus hunt. From Nanook I first heard of the "Walrus Island." On its south end, a surf-bound beach, there were in summer, he said, many walrus, judging from signs that had been seen by a winter sealing crowd of Eskimos who at one time had been caught there by a break-up of the ice. "The people do not go out to the island in summer," he continued, "for not only is it out of sight of land, but it is ringed with heavy surf—dangerous landing for kayaks. But for a long time I have had my eyes on your whaleboat," said he, "and I am sure, if the seas are smooth, it is big enough for crossing over, and just the thing for landing."

Through the busy weeks that followed, time and time again Nanook reminded me of the many, many moons it was since he had hunted walrus. One morning I woke up to see the profile of rising ground just beyond my window covered with topeks. Nanook popped his head in through the door. They were Eskimos from the north, he said, far away. "And among them," eagerly he continued, "is the very man who saw the walrus signs on Walrus Island."

Nanook was off, to return in a moment more leading the great man through the door. We talked iviuk through the hour. "Suppose we go," said I in conclusion, "do you know that you and your men may have to give up making a kill, if it interferes with my film? Will you remember it is the picture of you hunting the iviuk that I want, and not their meat?"

"Yes, yes, the aggie will come first," earnestly he assured me. "Not a man will stir, not a harpoon will be thrown until you give the sign. It is my word." We shook hands and agreed to start next day.

For three days we lay along the coast, before the big seas outside died down. The wind began blowing off the land. We broke out our leg-o'-mutton. Before the day was half done a film of gray far out in the west told us we were in sight of Walrus Island. By nightfall we closed in to the thundering shadow that was its shore.

For hours we lounged around the luxury of a drift-wood fire, soaking in its warmth and speculating on our chance for the morrow. When daylight came we made off to where the stranger had told us he had found the walrus signs. It was a crescent of beach pounded by the surf. While we looked around, one after another the heads of a school of walrus, their wicked tusks gleaming in the sun, shot up above the sea.

By night all my stock of film was exposed. The whaleboat was full of walrus meat and ivory. Nanook never had such walrus-hunting and never had I such filming, as that on Walrus Island.

Three days later the post bell clangs out the welcome news that the kablunak is about to show his iviuk aggie. Men, old men, women, old women, boys, girls, and small children file in to the factor's house. Soon there is not an inch of space to spare. The trader turns down the lamps. The projector light shoots over the shocks of heads upon the blanket which is the screen.

Then the picture. A figure appears. There is silence. They do not understand. "See, it is Nanook!" the trader cries. The Nanook in the flesh laughs his embarrassment. "Ah! ah! ah!" they all exclaim. Then silence. The figure moves. The silence deepens. They cannot understand. They turn their heads. They stare at the projector. They stare at its beam of magic light. They stare at Nanook, the most surprised of all, and again their heads turn toward the screen. They follow the figure which now snakes toward the background. There is something in the background. The something moves. It lifts its head.

"Iviuk! iviuk!" shakes the room. The figure stands up, harpoon poised in hand.

"Be sure of your harpoon! be sure of your harpoon!" the audience cries.

The figure strikes down; the walrus roll off into the sea. More figures rush in; they grab the harpoon line. For dear life they hold on.

"Hold him! hold him!" shout the men. "Hold him! hold him!" squeal the women. "Hold him! hold him!" pipe the children.

The walrus's mate dives in, and by locking tusks attempts rescue.

"Hold him!" gasps the crowd.

Nanook and his crew, although their arms seem to be breaking, hold on. But slowly and surely the threshing walrus drags the figures nearer sea.

"Hold him! hold him!" they despair. They are breathing hard. "Dig in! dig in! they rasp, as Nanook's feet slip another inch through the sand.

Deep silence. Suddenly the line sags, the crew, like a flash, draw in the slack, and inch by inch the walrus is pulled in to shore. Bedlam rocks the house.

The fame of the film spread far up and down the coast. Every strange Eskimo that came into the post Nanook brought before me and begged that he be shown the iviuk aggie.

Further Resources

BOOKS
Griffith, Richard. *The World of Robert Flaherty.* New York: Duell, Sloan and Pearce, 1953.

Ruby, Jay. *Robert J. Flaherty, a Biography.* Philadelphia: University of Pennsylvania Press, 1983.

WEBSITES
"Robert J. Flaherty—Web Resources for Scholars." Temple University. Available online at http://nimbus.ocis.temple.edu/~jruby/wava/Flaherty/; website home page: http://www.nimbus.ocis.temple.edu (accessed July 7, 2002).

Silver, Alain. "Robert Flaherty's *Nanook of the North.*" *Oneworld Magazine.* Available online at http://www.oneworldmagazine.org/seek/nanook/main.htm; website home page: http://www.oneworldmagazine.org (accessed July 7, 2002).

AUDIO AND VISUAL MEDIA
Flaherty, Robert. *Nanook of the North.* Videocassette, 1922.

Selections from *The Book of American Negro Poetry*

Preface to *The Book of American Negro Poetry*
Essay

By: James Weldon Johnson
Date: 1922
Source: Johnson, James Weldon. Preface to *The Book of American Negro Poetry*. New York: Harcourt, Brace & World, 1922. Reprint, New York: Harcourt, Brace & World, 1958.

"If We Must Die"
Poem

By: Claude McKay
Date: 1922
Source: McKay, Claude. "If We Must Die." In *The Book of American Negro Poetry,* James Weldon Johnson, ed. New York: Harcourt, Brace & World, Inc., 1922. Reprint, New York: Harcourt, Brace & World, Inc., 1958, 168–169.
About the Author: James Weldon Johnson (1871–1938) is considered the elder statesman of the Harlem Renaissance. In addition to his numerous literary contributions, he was an NAACP organizer and a U.S. consul to Venezuela. Johnson penned the famous "Lift Ev'ry Voice and Sing," the song known as the "Negro National Anthem." Claude McKay (1889–1948), born in Jamaica, came to the United States in 1912 to attend the Tuskegee Institute. His poetry recorded reactionary views on the injustices of African American life in America, and he wrote with an honesty and bluntness that was lacking in the work of his fellow poets. *Harlem Shadows* (1922), a volume of McKay's poetry, solidified his reputation as one of the great poets of the Harlem Renaissance. ∎

Introduction

At the beginning of the twentieth century, several middle-class New York African American families moved north to the newly built suburb of Harlem. This caused a "white flight," and real estate prices in the area dropped, attracting educated African Americans to the community, as well as laborers wanting to escape the blatant institutional racism and low wages of the South.

Patrons of the arts, including A'Lelia Walker and Carl van Vechten, helped an emerging African American arts scene flourish. By the twenties, Harlem was a center of cultural activity, and the era came to be known as the Harlem Renaissance. It encompassed literature, photography, painting, and music, and had a major effect on the nationwide mood of wanting to define a uniquely American culture. For the first time, African American artists began gaining

Author James Weldon Johnson, editor of *The Book of American Negro Poetry.* © CORBIS. REPRODUCED BY PERMISSION.

widespread attention for expressing their experiences of living as a African Americans in the United States.

In 1924, the publication of Jessie Redmon Fauset's (1882–1961) first novel, *There is Confusion,* was celebrated at a gala dinner also considered the Harlem Renaissance's "grand opening." Other Harlem Renaissance literary figures include Zora Neale Hurston, Nella Larsen, and Jean Toomer. Duke Ellington and Cab Calloway brought jazz to international prominence with their appearances at the legendary Harlem Cotton Club. Photographer James VanDerZee captured the spirit of the era with his portraits of the Harlem community. The Harlem Renaissance ended in the thirties with the Great Depression and the death of major arts patron A'Lelia Walker in 1934.

Significance

The Book of American Negro Poetry (1922) was the first anthology of African American poetry published in the United States. Selected and edited by James Weldon Johnson in the nascent years of the Harlem Renaissance, the anthology was a historic event. The forty poets collected here included not only the best of the Harlem Renaissance writers—W.E.B. Du Bois, Anne Spencer, Paul Laurence Dunbar, and Jessie Redmon Fauset—but their precursors as well, and emerging poets who rose to prominence later. Biographical entries accompanied the selections, giving readers additional interest in Johnson's project.

Johnson worked hard to encourage the ambitions of young African American writers, and was highly conscious of the biased viewpoints that the anthology might receive from white critics. Johnson's concerns regarding the latter may have made his discrediting of the literary convention of "Negro dialect" all the more emphatic. Johnson felt that "Negro dialect" could only convey pathos or humor. Later, literary giants such as Zora Neale Hurston would challenge this viewpoint, but Johnson felt it was his duty as a highly visible African American intellectual to present both the history of "Negro dialect" use in literature, as well as a critique of it.

A second edition of the highly popular anthology was released in 1933, with the addition of Arna Bontemps, Countee Cullen, Langston Hughes, and other young poets who were beginning to influence the literary scene. Many of the poets in both editions are still widely read and studied today, and Johnson's anthology invaluably presents their work in its original context, thus defining the burgeoning Harlem Renaissance.

Primary Source

Preface to *The Book of American Negro Poetry* [excerpt]

SYNOPSIS: In this excerpt from the Preface to the 1922 edition of *The Book of American Negro Poetry*, Johnson comments on the shift away from the "dialect" which had previously defined African American poetry for both African Amerian and white audiences. Modern African American poets began to challenge racial stereotypes in an effort to be recognized simply as poets. Claude McKay's "If We Must Die" represents this effort.

. . . It may be surprising to many to see how little of the poetry being written by Negro poets today is being written in Negro dialect. The newer Negro poets show a tendency to discard dialect; much of the subject-matter which went into the making of traditional dialect poetry, 'possums, watermelons, etc., they have discarded altogether, at least, as poetic material. This tendency will, no doubt, be regretted by the majority of white readers; and, indeed, it would be a distinct loss if the American Negro poets threw away this quaint and musical folk speech as a medium of expression. And yet, after all, these poets are working through a problem not realized by the reader, and, perhaps, by many of these poets themselves not realized consciously. They are trying to break away from, not

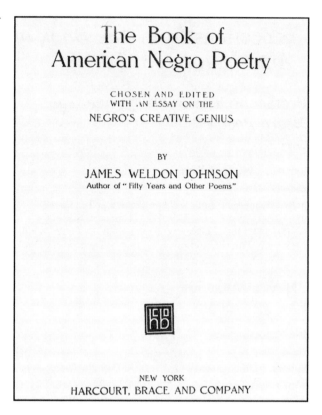

The Book of
American Negro Poetry

CHOSEN AND EDITED
WITH AN ESSAY ON THE
NEGRO'S CREATIVE GENIUS

BY

JAMES WELDON JOHNSON
Author of " Fifty Years and Other Poems"

NEW YORK
HARCOURT, BRACE AND COMPANY

Title page of *The Book of American Negro Poetry,* the first comprehensive collection of poetry by African Americans ever published. **COURTESY OF THE GRADUATE LIBRARY, UNIVERSITY OF MICHIGAN. REPRODUCED BY PERMISSION.**

Negro dialect itself, but the limitations on Negro dialect imposed by the fixing effects of long convention.

The Negro in the United States has achieved or been placed in a certain artistic niche. When he is thought of artistically, it is as a happy-go-lucky, singing, shuffling, banjo-picking being or as a more or less pathetic figure. The picture of him is in a log cabin amid fields of cotton or along the levees. Negro dialect is naturally and by long association the exact instrument for voicing this phase of Negro life; and by that very exactness it is an instrument with but two full stops, humor and pathos. So even when he confines himself to purely racial themes, the Aframerican poet realizes that there are phases of Negro life in the United States which cannot be treated in the dialect either adequately or artistically. Take, for example, the phases rising out of life in Harlem, that most wonderful Negro city in the world. I do not deny that a Negro in a log cabin is more picturesque than a Negro in a Harlem flat, but the Negro in the Harlem flat is here, and he is but part of a group growing everywhere

Poets Featured in the Second Edition of *The Book of American Negro Poetry*

Several authors were added to a second edition of the compilation in 1931, some of whom are featured here. Many of these poets went on to become some of the most famous writers of the Harlem Renaissance and African American literary history.

Gwendolyn Bennett (1902–1981)—poet, short-story writer, journalist, graphic artist, teacher, and arts activist—was one of the most versatile figures in the Harlem Renaissance. Bennett was a member of the Harlem Artists Guild (an African American graphic arts alliance), and she participated in the New York City Works Progress Administration Federal Arts Project (1935–1941). The twenties were her most productive period as a creative writer, when Johnson recognized Bennett as "a lyric poet of power."

Countee Cullen (1903–1946) was one of the most prolific poets of his generation. His best work explored themes pertinent to the lives of black Americans, but without emphasizing dialect or stereotypes. Cullen's lyrical style was inspired by English poet John Keats. Among his published volumes of poetry are *Color* (1925), *Copper Sun* (1927), and *The Black Christ* (1929). Cullen's only novel, *One Way to Heaven* (1931), described the joys and difficulties of living in Harlem.

Langston Hughes (1902–1967), known as the Poet Laureate of Harlem, made innovative use of jazz rhythms and the oral and improvisational traditions of black folk culture in his work. His first published poem, "The Negro Speaks of Rivers," appeared in the *Crisis* magazine in 1921 while Hughes was a student at Columbia University. Johnson selected Hughes for *The Book of Negro Poetry* well before Hughes began to rise to literary prominence in the late twenties.

Helene Johnson (1905–1995) received her first public recognition when James Weldon Johnson and Robert Frost selected three of her poems for prizes in a 1926 competition. She defied the conventions of women's literature by writing poems on erotic themes, as well as on the aesthetic, gender, and racial politics of the time. Johnson was adept at various verse forms, from the sonnet to the improvisational style of black vernacular.

in the country, a group whose ideals are becoming increasingly more vital than those of the traditionally artistic group, even if its members are less picturesque.

What the colored poet in the United States needs to do is something like what Synge did for the Irish; he needs to find a form that will express the racial spirit by symbols from within rather than by symbols from without, such as the mere mutilation of English spelling and pronunciation. He needs a form that is freer and larger than dialect, but which will still hold the racial flavor; a form expressing the imagery, the idioms, the peculiar turns of thought, and the distinctive humor and pathos, too, of the Negro, but which will also be capable of voicing the deepest and highest emotions and aspirations, and allow of the widest range of subjects and the widest scope of treatment. . . .

In stating the need for Aframerican poets in the United States to work out a new and distinctive form of expression I do not wish to be understood to hold any theory that they should limit themselves to Negro poetry, to racial themes; the sooner they are able to write *American* poetry spontaneously, the better. Nevertheless, I believe that the richest contribution the Negro poet can make to the American literature of the future will be the fusion into it of his own individual artistic gifts.

Primary Source

"If We Must Die"

SYNOPSIS: Claude McKay's poem is an example of the type of solid work coming out of the Harlem Renaissance. McKay challenged racial stereotypes and wanted to be seen simply as a poet.

If we must die—let it not be like hogs
Hunted and penned in an inglorious spot,
While round us bark the mad and hungry dogs,
Making their mock at our accursed lot.
If we must die—oh, let us nobly die,
So that our precious blood may not be shed
In vain; then even the monsters we defy
Shall be constrained to honor us though dead!
Oh, Kinsmen! We must meet the common foe;
Though far outnumbered, let us show us brave,
And for their thousand blows deal one deathblow!
What though before us lies the open grave?
Like men we'll face the murderous, cowardly pack,
Pressed to the wall, dying, but fighting back!

Further Resources

BOOKS

Bloom, Harold, ed. *Black American Poets and Dramatists of the Harlem Renaissance*. New York: Chelsea House Publishers, 1995.

Bontemps, Arna, ed. *The Harlem Renaissance Remembered*. New York: Dodd, Mead, 1984.

Fauset, Jessie Redmon. *There Is Confusion*. Boston: Northeastern University Press, 1989.

Lewis, David Levering, ed. *The Portable Harlem Renaissance Reader.* New York: Viking, 1994.

Mitchell, Verner D., ed. *This Waiting for Love: Helene Johnson, Poet of the Harlem Renaissance.* Amherst: University of Massachusetts Press, 2000.

Roses, Lorraine Elena, and Ruth Elizabeth Randolph, eds. *Harlem's Glory: Black Women Writing, 1900–1950.* Cambridge, Mass.: Harvard University Press, 1996.

Watson, Steve. *The Harlem Renaissance.* New York: Pantheon, 1995.

Wilson, Sondra Kathryn, ed. *The Crisis Reader: Stories, Poetry, and Essays from the N.A.A.C.P.'s Crisis Magazine.* New York: Modern Library, 1999.

Art of Alfred Stieglitz

"How I Came to Photograph Clouds"

Magazine article

By: Alfred Stieglitz

Date: September 19, 1923

Source: Stieglitz, Alfred. "How I Came to Photograph Clouds," *Amateur Photographer and Photography* 56, no. 1816, 1923, 255. Reprinted in *Stieglitz on Photography.* New York: Aperture, 2000, 235–238.

Photographs by Alfred Stieglitz

Photographs

By: Alfred Stieglitz

Date: 1922, 1929

Source: "Clouds, Music No. 1, Lake George," "Equivalent." 1922, 1929. George Eastman House.

About the Author: Alfred Stieglitz (1864–1946), born in Hoboken, New Jersey, was a highly influential photographer, writer, and art dealer. Stieglitz devoted his life to promoting photography as an art form. He was a major supporter of American modernist painting, exhibiting artists such as Arthur Dove and Charles Demuth. Stieglitz also organized the first exhibitions in America of work by European artists Pablo Picasso, Henri Matisse, Paul Cézanne, and others. He married the painter Georgia O'Keeffe in 1924. ∎

Introduction

When Stieglitz began exploring photography in the 1880s, the medium was primarily regarded as a mostly professional tool for descriptive and recording purposes. Camera equipment was complicated and unwieldy. During a stay in Germany, he felt encouraged to become an artist and immersed himself in mastering photography. Challenging the notion that photography could be done only in proper daylight, he discovered how to create perfect negatives even under low-light conditions. Stieglitz produced some of the first successful images of subjects difficult to photograph, such as rain, skies, and snow.

Stieglitz returned to New York and edited *American Amateur Photographer.* He founded his own publications such as *Camera Notes and Camera Work,* and organized Photo-Secession, a loose group of photographers. He was the foremost authority on photographic techniques, as well as a champion of modern art in other disciplines. Stieglitz exhibited American modernist artists in his various galleries, 291 (1905–1917), The Intimate Gallery (1925–1929), and An American Place (1929–1946). These exhibitions advanced the careers of important American artists such as Edward Steichen, John Marin, Georgia O'Keeffe, Marsden Hartley, Man Ray, and countless others.

Born in 1864 during the Civil War (1861–1865), Stieglitz witnessed some of the most profound changes America has ever experienced. He lived through two world wars, the Great Depression, and the nation's shift from agriculture to industrialization. As he predicted, photography would become a major force in the twentieth century, profoundly altering all aspects of culture and the arts.

Significance

Alfred Stieglitz was extremely influential in promoting the art value of photography and its expressive powers. He believed that making his own photographs could give him spiritual insight to his own life. To Stieglitz, form was far more important than the subject matter of the photograph. In his images he carefully composed shapes, lines, and tones to convey emotional and psychological meaning.

His first series of cloud photographs, published in 1922, was titled "Music: A Sequence of Ten Cloud Photographs." Stieglitz also called them "Clouds in Ten Movements," and "Music: A Series of Ten Pictures." He was searching for a title that would best describe how the images demonstrated what he called the "metaphorical power of the photograph." Continuing to explore cloud imagery and its relationship to emotions, he developed a second series of cloud photographs called "Equivalents" in 1925. With this series, Stieglitz felt he had finally achieved his intentions. The name "Equivalents" emphasized his belief that the images could depict emotional states. For instance, the dark skies, low-hanging black clouds, and barren landscape in some photographs evoke the tumult in Stieglitz's own familial life at the time.

Primary Source

Photographs by Alfred Stieglitz (1 OF 2)

SYNOPSIS: "Clouds, Music No. 1, Lake George" by Alfred Stieglitz, 1922. COURTESY GEORGE EASTMAN HOUSE. REPRODUCED BY PERMISSION.

At the time of the shooting of "Equivalents," Stieglitz was experiencing a number of life-altering revelations. His daughter was to be married, and she was pregnant with his first grandchild. His mother had just died, and he and wife Georgia O'Keeffe were contemplating having children of their own. His estate was falling apart, and life in general was in disarray. These events led him to photograph clouds for the next decade.

Stieglitz won numerous prizes in various photographic competitions. In 1923, he became the first photographer to be included in a major American museum collection when the Museum of Fine Arts acquired some of his photographs. In the following year, Stieglitz was the first photographer invited to send his work to the Metropolitan Museum of Art.

Primary Source

"How I Came to Photograph Clouds"

SYNOPSIS: Alfred Stieglitz photographed clouds from the hilltop near his family's home by Lake George in upstate New York. He presented the cloud series as small 8 x 10 or 4 x 5 contact prints glued to matte board. These photographs greatly influenced fellow photographers Edward Weston, Ansel Adams, and Minor White—all of whom also photographed clouds.

As for the cloud series perhaps it will interest you how that came about.

Last summer when manuscripts were sent in by the various contributors for the issue of the publi-

Primary Source

Photographs by Alfred Stieglitz (2 OF 2)

SYNOPSIS: "Equivalent" by Alfred Stieglitz, 1929. COURTESY GEORGE EASTMAN HOUSE. REPRODUCED BY PERMISSION.

cation, "M.S.S." devoted to photography, and its aesthetic significance, Waldo Frank—one of America's young literary lights, author of "Our America," etc.—wrote that he believed the secret power in my photography was due to the power of hypnotism I had over my sitters, etc.

I was amazed when I read the statement. I wondered what he had to say about the street scenes—the trees, interiors—and other subjects, the photographs of which he had admired so much: or whether he felt they too were due to my powers of hypnotism. Certainly a lax statement coming from one professing himself profound and fair thinking, and interested in enlightening. It happened that the same morning in which I read this contribution my brother-in-law (lawyer and musician) out of the clear sky announced to me that he couldn't understand how one as supposedly musical as I could have given up entirely playing the piano. I looked at him and smiled—and I thought: even he does not seem to understand. He plays the violin. The violin takes up no space: the piano does. The piano needs looking after by a professional, etc. I simply couldn't afford a piano, even when I was supposedly rich. It was not merely a question of money.

Thirty-five or more years ago I spent a few days in Mürren (Switzerland), and I was experimenting with ortho plates. Clouds and their relationship to the rest of the world, and clouds for themselves, interested me, and clouds which were most difficult to photograph—nearly impossible. Ever since then clouds have been in my mind most powerfully at times, and I always knew I'd follow up the experiment made over thirty-five years ago. I always watched clouds. Studied them. Had unusual opportunities up here on this hillside. What Frank had said annoyed me: what my brother-in-law said also annoyed me. I was in the midst of my summer's photographing, trying to add to my knowledge, to the work I had done. Always evolving—always going more and more deeply into life—into photography.

My mother was dying. Our estate was going to pieces. The old horse of thirty-seven was being kept alive by the seventy-year-old coachman. I, full of the feeling of to-day: all about me disintegration—slow but sure: dying chestnut trees—all the chestnuts in this country have been dying for years: the pines doomed too—diseased: I, poor, but at work: the world in a great mess: the human being a queer animal—not as dignified as our giant chestnut tree on the hill. So I made up my mind I'd answer Mr. Frank and my brother-in-law. I'd finally do something I had

in mind for years. I'd make a series of cloud pictures. I told Miss O'Keeffe of my ideas. I wanted to photograph clouds to find out what I had learned in forty years about photography. Through clouds to put down my philosophy of life—to show that my photographs were not due to subject matter—not to special trees, or faces, or interiors, to special privileges, clouds were there for everyone—no tax as yet on them—free.

So I began to work with the clouds—and it was great excitement—daily for weeks. Every time I developed I was so wrought up, always believing I had nearly gotten what I was after—but had failed. A most tantalising sequence of days and weeks. I knew exactly what I was after. I had told Miss O'Keeffe I wanted a series of photographs which when seen by Ernest Bloch (the great composer) he would exclaim: Music! music! Man, why that is music! How did you ever do that? And he would point to violins, and flutes, and oboes, and brass, full of enthusiasm, and would say he'd have to write a symphony called "Clouds." Not like Debussy's but *much, much more.*

And when finally I had my series of ten photographs printed, and Bloch saw them—what I said I wanted to happen happened *verbatim.*

Straight photographs, all gaslight paper, except one palladiotype. All in the power of every photographer of all time, and I satisfied [myself that] I had learned something during the 40 years. It's 40 years this year that I began in Berlin with Vogel.

Now if the cloud series are due to my power of hypnotism I plead "Guilty." Only some "Pictorial photographers" when they came to the exhibition seemed totally blind to the cloud pictures. My photographs look like photographs—and in their eyes they therefore can't be art. As if they had the slightest idea of art or photography—or any idea of life. My aim is increasingly to make my photographs look so much like photographs that unless one has *eyes* and *sees,* they won't be seen—and still everyone will never forget them having once looked at them. I wonder if that is clear.

Further Resources

BOOKS

Doty, Robert. *Photo-Secession: Stieglitz and the Fine-Art Movement in Photography.* New York: Dover, 1978.

Frank, Waldo, Lewis Mumford, Dorothy Norman, Paul Rosenfeld, and Harold Rugg, eds. *America and Alfred Stieglitz: A Collective Portrait.* 1934. Reprint, New York: Octagon Books, 1975.

Greenough, Sarah, and Juan Hamilton. *Alfred Stieglitz: Photographs & Writings.* Exh. cat., National Gallery of Art. 1983. Reprint, 1999.

Greenough, Sarah, et al. *Modern Art and America: Alfred Stieglitz and His New York Galleries.* Exh. cat., National Gallery of Art. Washington, 2001.

Homer, William Innes. *Alfred Stieglitz and the Photo-Secession.* Boston: Little Brown & Co., 1983.

Lowe, Sue Davidson. *Stieglitz: A Memoir/Biography.* New York: MFA Publications, 1983.

Norman, Dorothy. *Alfred Stieglitz: An American Seer.* New York: Aperture Foundation, 1990.

Peterson, Christian A. *Alfred Stieglitz's Camera Notes.* New York: W. W. Norton & Company, Inc., 1996.

Richter, Peter-Cornell. *Georgia O'Keeffe and Alfred Stieglitz.* New York: Prestel Publishing, 2000.

Stieglitz, Alfred. *Stieglitz on Photography: Selected Essays and Notes by Alfred Stieglitz.* Richard Whelan and Sarah Greenough, eds. New York: Aperture Foundation, 1999.

Whelan, Richard. *Alfred Stieglitz: A Biography.* Boston: Little, Brown, 1995.

Wood, John. *The Art of the Autochrome: The Birth of Color Photography.* Iowa City: University of Iowa Press, 1993.

Bessie Smith's Blues

"Jailhouse Blues;" "Young Woman's Blues;" "Backwater Blues"

Songs

By: Bessie Smith

Date: 1923–1927

Source: Smith, Bessie. "Jailhouse Blues" recorded September 21, 1923. Copyright 1931 (renewed), 1974 by Frank Music Corp. "Young Woman's Blues" recorded October 1926 on Columbia 14179-D. Empress Music, 1927. "Backwater Blues" recorded February 17, 1927, on Columbia 14195-D. Lyrics reproduced in Davis, Angela Y., *Blues Legacies and Black Feminism.* New York: Pantheon, 1998.

About the Musician: Known as the "Empress of the Blues," Bessie Smith (189?–1937) was born into poverty in Chattanooga, Tennessee. Orphaned at a young age and raised by siblings, Smith earned money as a street musician and started touring with a vaudeville show as a dancer in 1912. A protégé of legendary blueswoman "Ma" Rainey, she eventually became the most respected African American singer of her generation, influencing female vocalists from Billie Holiday to Janis Joplin. She was killed in an automobile accident outside Clarksdale, Mississippi. ■

Introduction

Standing six feet tall and weighing two hundred pounds, Bessie Smith was an imposing figure. She ap-peared on stage wearing lavish gowns, singing in a powerful yet seductive voice. Smith became popular with both African American and white audiences, but preferred to perform for mostly African American audiences on her tours throughout the United States. By the early 1920s, she was one of the most popular blues singers on the vaudeville circuit, but was consistently told by producers that her voice was "too rough" to merit a recording contract.

Finally, in 1923, Smith was signed by Columbia Records. Accompanied by pianist Clarence Williams, she recorded Alberta Hunter's "Down Hearted Blues" as well as Williams's song "Gulf Coast Blues." The record sold more than 750,000 copies, establishing Smith as a blues star. She followed up her initial success with a string of original compositions, many of which are regarded as blues standards of the highest order, including 1923's "Jailhouse Blues," 1926's "Young Woman's Blues," and 1927's "Backwater Blues."

Smith had an extraordinary ability to manipulate her pitch in the loudest portion of her range. In her live performances, she incorporated unusual phrasing, moaning, and growling, rather than relying on the lyrics to convey the emotion of her songs. Her naturally resonant voice easily projected across packed audiences in large venues, even without a microphone.

To emphasize her vocal prowess, most of Smith's early recordings featured just piano accompaniment. She also recorded with celebrated musicians, including Fletcher Henderson, James P. Johnson, Louis Armstrong, and Coleman Hawkins. Many critics consider her version of "St. Louis Blues" with Armstrong one of the finest recordings of the 1920s. Smith recorded over 160 songs for Columbia until the label dropped her in 1931, citing faltering record sales affected by the Depression, the advent of radio, and sound movies.

Significance

Unlike many artists of her era, Bessie Smith wrote much of her own material. Despite being musically illiterate, she had an uncanny knack for conveying the violence and chaos of her offstage existence. With her life marked by alcohol and drug abuse, bisexuality, and violent encounters with husband Jack Gee (and sometimes with his various girlfriends), Smith had a deep wellspring from which to draw her blues.

Her songs are simple but brilliant tales of spurned women, unfaithful men, and defiance in the face of a merciless, racist world. "Jailhouse Blues" is a perfect example of this defiance. Despite being imprisoned, the song's main character is anything but meek and contrite, threatening to retaliate against a male guard who is making sexual advances toward her.

Smith's lyrics rarely portray women as incapacitated by broken hearts or self-doubt. In fact, many of her songs reject the conventions of romance and marriage. "Young Woman's Blues" is such an example. Here, the protagonist is clearly not interested in marriage, and expresses no particular regret that her nameless man has left her, perhaps tired of her infidelities.

Not all of Smith's songs dealt with relationship issues. "Backwater Blues," for example, directly addresses social concerns. Written after Smith witnessed a flood destroy Southern homes, the song conveys the racism underlying the relief effort, as African American and white victims receive differential treatment. "Backwater Blues" sold tremendously well, a testament to Smith's ability to portray human pain while still retaining commercial appeal.

Primary Source

"Jailhouse Blues"

SYNOPSIS: Bessie Smith's song—"Jailhouse Blues" —is a blues classic, about defiance in the face of a merciless, racist world.

Lord this house is gonna get raided! Yes, sir!

Thirty days in jail with my back turned to the wall, to the wall
Thirty days in jail with my back turned to the wall.
Look here Mister Jailkeeper put another girl in my stall.

I don't mind bein' in jail but I got to stay there so long, so long.
I don't mind bein' in jail but I got to stay there so long, so long.
Well ev'ry friend I had has done shook hands and gone.

You better stop your man from ticklin' me under my chin, under my chin
You better stop your man from ticklin' under me under my chin
'Cause if he keeps on ticklin' I'm sure gonna take him on in.

Good mornin' blues, blues how do you do? How do you do?
Good mornin' blues, blues how do you do?
Well, I just come here to have a few words with you

Primary Source

"Young Woman's Blues"

SYNOPSIS: "Young Woman's Blues," another blues classic by Bessie Smith, rejects the conventions of romance and marriage for women.

Woke up this mornin' when chickens was crowin' for day
Felt on the right side of my pilla', my man had gone away

Influential blues singer and songwriter Bessie Smith was a well respected performer in her day. **THE BETTMANN ARCHIVE. REPRODUCED BY PERMISSION.**

By his pilla' he left a note readin' "I'm sorry, Jane, you got my goat.
No time to marry, no time to settle down"

I'm a young woman and ain't done runnin' 'round
I'm a young woman and ain't done runnin' 'round
Some people call me a hobo, some call me a bum

Nobody knows my name, nobody knows what I've done
I'm as good as any woman in your town
I ain't no high yeller, I'm a deep killer of brown
I ain't gonna marry, ain't gonna settle down
I'm gonna drink good moonshine and rub these browns down

See that long lonesome road
Lawd, you know it's gotta and I'm a good woman
 and I can get plenty men

Primary Source

"Backwater Blues"

> **SYNOPSIS:** "Backwater Blues"—this third song of Bessie Smith is also a blues classic which conveys the racism which underlies relief efforts for African American and white flood victims.

When it rains five days and the skies turn dark as
 night
When it rains five days and the skies turn dark as
 night
Then trouble's takin' place in the lowlands at night.

I woke up one mornin', can't even get out of my door
I woke up one mornin', can't even get out of my door
There was enough trouble to make a poor girl wonder
 where she wanna go.

Then they rowed a little boat about five miles 'cross
 the pond
Then they rowed a little boat about five miles 'cross
 the pond.
I packed all of my clothes, throwed 'em in and they
 rowed me along

When it thunders and lightnin', and the wind begins
 to blow
When it thunders and lightnin', and the wind begins
 to blow
There's thousands of people ain't got no place to go.

Then I went and stood up on some high old
 lonesome hill
Then I went and stood up on some high old
 lonesome hill
Then looked down on the house where I used to live

Backwater blues done caused me to pack my things
 and go
Backwater blues done caused me to pack my things
 and go
'Cause my house fell down and I can't live there no
 mo'

Mmmmmmmmm, I can't move no mo'
Mmmmmmmmm, I can't move no mo'
There ain't no place for a poor old girl to go

Further Resources

BOOKS

Bogle, Donald. *Brown Sugar: 80 Years of America's Black Female Superstars.* New York: Da Capo, 1990.

Eberhardt, Clifford. *Out of Chattanooga: The Bessie Smith Story.* Chattanooga, Tenn.: Ebco, 1993.

Feinstein, Elaine. *Bessie Smith: Empress of the Blues.* Middlesex, U.K.: Penguin, 1985.

Grimes, Sara. *BackWaterBlues: In Search of Bessie Smith.* Amherst, Mass.: Rose Island, 2001.

Jones, Hettie. *Big Star Fallin' Mama: Five Women in Black Music.* New York: Viking, 1995.

Moore, Carman. *Somebody's Angel Child: The Story of Bessie Smith.* New York: Thomas Y. Crowell, 1969.

AUDIO AND VISUAL MEDIA

Bessie Smith: American Blues Singers. Films for the Humanities. Videocassette, 1988.

Bessie Smith and Friends, 1929–1941. Videofidelity. Videocassette, 1986.

"From the Memoirs of a Private Detective"

Magazine article

By: Dashiell Hammett

Date: 1923

Source: Hammett, Dashiell. "From the Memoirs of a Private Detective." *The Smart Set,* March 1923. Reprinted in The Thrilling Detective Website. Available online at http://www .thrillingdetective.com/trivia/hammett2.htm; website home page: http://www.thrillingdetective.com/index.html (accessed August 14, 2002).

About the Author: Writer Dashiell Hammett (1894–1961) originated the "hardboiled" detective story genre. Born in Maryland, Hammett dropped out of school at thirteen to help support his family. He was a messenger boy, railroad clerk, and stevedore before starting detective work in 1915. Hammett's fiction drew on his investigative experiences. His most famous story, *The Maltese Falcon,* was a bestselling novel in 1930 and became a classic film featuring Humphrey Bogart in 1941. ∎

Introduction

Hammett worked as an operative at the famed Pinkerton Detective Agency, based in San Francisco, California. He was one of Pinkerton's top "shadows," an expert at tailing subjects. He left the agency to enlist in the army in World War I (1914–1918), and while on duty in the Motor Ambulance Corp, he contracted tuberculosis. Forced to give up detective work, Hammett began writing fictional stories about his Pinkerton experiences.

Hammett published his first short story in 1922 in the upscale society magazine, *The Smart Set.* However, his fiction explored the darker side of human nature—greed, revenge, corruption—and was much better suited to crime magazines of the time. The most popular of these, *Black Mask,* featured Hammett's short story "Arson Plus" in its October 1, 1923, issue. The story introduced an unnamed private eye known as The Continental Op. Under the pseudonym Peter Collinson, Hammett began regularly publishing The Op stories in *Black Mask* through the end of the 1920s.

Hammett's Op was the first believable detective hero in American fiction. He was a short, overweight detective with an unshakeable sense of justice. Like Hammett, The Op was employed by a San Francisco detective agency. He was gruff, tough, and dedicated to his job. The Op stories, numbering more than three dozen, were told in the first person in Hammett's characteristically terse style. Hammett's writing introduced a realism not found in earlier, highly intellectualized mystery novels, and was extremely successful with the public.

Hammett dropped The Op and introduced a new character, Sam Spade, in the September 1929 issue of *Black Mask.* This cover story, *The Maltese Falcon,* became Hammett's most famous work, and was published in four monthly installments. In 1930, the installments were collected and published as a novel, which became a bestseller and went through several reprints that same year.

Significance

Like The Op, Sam Spade was a private investigator, a taciturn loner with a dark view of society. He often worked outside of the law. Sam Spade and Miles Archer are partners in a San Francisco detective agency. Although Spade does not particularly like his partner, when he is found murdered, Spade must solve the case.

The Maltese Falcon remains one of the true classics of the "hard-boiled" genre. The novel epitomizes what became the "hard-boiled" story standard: character, inner conflict, and human behavior are emphasized as much as the complex crime plot. The story also provides insight on the political or moral climate of its era.

The Maltese Falcon was adapted for film three times. The third version, starring Humphrey Bogart, and written and directed by John Huston, was released by Warner Brothers in 1941. Bogart's performance is the definitive portrayal of the unorthodox detective. The film is a cinematic landmark, influencing countless suspense movies and television series. Its success spawned more short stories featuring Sam Spade, a comic book adaptation of *The Maltese Falcon* by Rodlow Williard in 1946, and a radio show called *The Adventures of Sam Spade.*

Dashiell Hammett was politically active in the defense of civil liberties. However, his leftist views attracted the attention of McCarthyites in the fifties, putting an end to his popularity. When he refused to name suspected communists, Hammett was convicted and sentenced to six months in prison in 1951. The radio producers promptly pretended Hammett didn't exist. Sam Spade continued to be profitable, but when the producers decided to develop a Spade television series, the task was given to other writers.

Hammett faded away from literary prominence and died in relative poverty in New York City. In addition to

Dashiell Hammett was a preeminent author of hard-boiled detective fiction. THE LIBRARY OF CONGRESS.

the more than ninety fictional works published in his lifetime—which included the popular series, "The Thin Man"—Hammett also wrote screenplays, book reviews, poetry, and nonfiction articles.

Primary Source

"From the Memoirs of a Private Detective"

SYNOPSIS: "From the Memoirs of a Private Detective" originally appeared in the March 1923 issue of *The Smart Set,* a high-society magazine. The magazine published Hammett's first stories at the beginning of his writing career, when he often published under the pseudonyms Peter Collinson, Dughall Hammett, and Jane Hammett. The article recounts some of Hammett's thoughts and adventures from his Pinkerton days.

1. Wishing to get some information from members of the WCTU in an Oregon city, I introduced myself as the secretary of the Butte City Purity League. One of them read me a long discourse on the erotic effects of cigarettes upon young girls. Subsequent experiments proved this tip worthless.

2. A man whom I was shadowing went out into the country for a walk one Sunday afternoon and lost

his bearings completely. I had to direct him back to the city.

3. House burglary is probably the poorest paid trade in the world. I have never known anyone to make a living at it. But for that matter few criminals of any class are self-supporting unless they toil at something legitimate between times. Most of them, however, live on their women.

4. I know an operative who, while looking for pickpockets at the Havre de Grace race track, had his wallet stolen. He later became an official in an Eastern detective agency.

5. Three times I have been mistaken for a Prohibition agent, but never had any trouble clearing myself.

6. Taking a prisoner from a ranch near Gilt Edge, Mont., to Lewistown one night, my machine broke down and we had to sit there until daylight. The prisoner, who stoutly affirmed his innocence, was clothed only in overalls and shirt. After shivering all night on the front seat his morale was low, and I had no difficulty in getting a complete confession from him while walking to the nearest ranch early the following morning.

7. Of all the men embezzling from their employers with whom I have had contact, I can't remember a dozen who smoked, drank, or had any of the vices in which bonding companies are so interested.

8. I was once falsely accused of perjury and had to perjure myself to escape arrest.

9. A detective official in San Francisco once substituted "truthful" for "voracious" in one of my reports on the grounds that the client might not understand the latter. A few days later in another report "simulate" became "quicken" for the same reason.

10. Of all the nationalities in hauled into the criminal courts, the Greek is the most difficult to convict. He simply denies everything, no matter how conclusive the proof may be; and nothing impresses a jury as a bare statement of fact, regardless of the fact's inherent improbability or obvious absurdity in the face of overwhelming contrary evidence.

11. I know a man who will forge the impressions of any set of fingers in the world for $50.

12. I have never known a man capable of turning out first-rate work in a trade, a profession or an art, who was a professional criminal.

13. I know a detective who once attempted to disguise himself thoroughly. The first policeman he met took him into custody.

14. I know a deputy sheriff in Montana who, approaching the cabin of a homesteader for whose arrest he had a warrant, was confronted by the homesteader with a rifle in his hands. The deputy sheriff drew his revolver and tried to shoot over the homesteader's head to frighten him. The range was long and a strong wind was blowing. The bullet knocked the rifle from the homesteader's hands. As time went by the deputy sheriff came to accept as the truth the reputation for expertness that this incident gave him, and he not only let his friends enter him in a shooting contest, but wagered everything he owned upon his skill. When the contest was held he missed the target completely with all six shots.

15. Once in Seattle the wife of a fugitive swindler offered to sell me a photograph of her husband for $15. I knew where I could get one free so I didn't buy it.

16. I was once engaged to discharge a woman's housekeeper.

17. The slang in use among criminals is for the most part a conscious, artificial growth, designed more to confuse outsiders than for any other purpose, but sometimes it is singularly expressive; for instance, two-time loser—one who has been convicted twice; and the older gone to read and write—found it advisable to go away for a while.

18. Pocket-picking is the easiest to master of all the criminal trades. Anyone who is not crippled can become adept in a day.

19. In 1917, in Washington DC, I met a young lady who did not remark that my work must be very interesting.

20. Even where the criminal makes no attempt to efface the prints of his fingers, but leaves them all over the scene of the crime, the chances are about one in ten of finding a print that is sufficiently clear to be of any value.

21. The chief of police of a Southern city once gave me a description of a man, complete even to the mole on his neck, but neglected to mention that he had only one arm.

22. I know a forger who left his wife because she learned to smoke cigarettes while he was serving a term in prison.

23. Second only to Doctor Jekyll and Mr. Hyde is Raffles in the affections of the daily press. The phrase "gentleman crook" is used on the slightest provocation. A composite portrait of the gentry upon whom the newspapers have bestowed this title

would show a laudanum-drinker, with a large rhine-stone-horseshow aglow in the soiled bosom of his shirt below a bow-tie, leering at his victim, and saying: "Now don't get scared, lady, I ain't gonna crack you on the bean. I ain't a rough-neck!"

24. The cleverest and most uniformly successful detective I have ever known is extremely myopic.

25. Going from the larger cities out into the remote, rural communities one finds a steadily decreasing percentage of crimes that have to do with money and a proportionate increase in the frequency of sex as a criminal motive.

26. While trying to peer into the upper story of a roadhouse in northern California one night—and the man I was looking for was in Seattle at the time—part of the porch crumbled under me and I fell, spraining an ankle. The proprietor of the roadhouse gave me water to bathe it in.

27. The chief difference between the exceptionally knotty problem facing the detective of fiction and that facing the real detective is that in the former there is usually a paucity of clues, and in the latter altogether too many.

28. I know a man who once stole a Ferris wheel.

29. That the lawbreaker is invariably sooner or later apprehended is probably the least challenged of extant myths. And yet the files of every detective bureau bulge with the records of unsolved mysteries and uncaught criminals.

Further Resources

BOOKS

Dooley, Dennis. *Dashiell Hammett.* New York: Frederick Ungar, 1984.

Johnson, Diane. *Dashiell Hammett: A Life.* New York: Random House, 1983.

Layman, Richard, and Julie Rivett. *Selected Letters of Dashiell Hammett.* New York: Counterpoint, 2001.

Margolies, Edward. *Which Way Did He Go? The Private Eye in Dashiell Hammett, Raymond Chandler, Chester Himes and Ross MacDonald.* New York: Holmes & Meier, 1982.

Mellen, Joan. *The Legendary Passion of Lillian Hellman and Dashiell Hammett.* New York: HarperCollins, 1996.

Muller, Marcia, and Bill Pronzini, eds. *Detective Duos.* New York: Oxford University Press, 1997.

Nolan, William F. *The Black Mask Boys: Masters in the Hard-Boiled School of Detective Fiction.* New York: Morrow, 1983.

Nolan, William F. *Dashiell Hammett: A Life on the Edge.* New York: Congdon and Weed, 1983.

Rhapsody in Blue
Musical composition

By: George Gershwin

Date: January 7, 1924

Source: Gershwin, George. *Rhapsody in Blue.* January 7, 1924. Piano and Orchestra: Arr. from Old Catalog. Reprinted in Jablonski, Edward, and Lawrence D. Stewart, *The Gershwin Years.* New York: Doubleday and Company, 1958, p. 82.

About the Author: George Gershwin (1898–1937) was born and raised in Brooklyn, New York. His first job in the music business was as sheet music promoter at Remick's, in the neighborhood known as Tin Pan Alley. He sat in a little booth at a piano so customers could listen to him play the latest tunes. In 1924, he began collaborating with his brother Ira. Together, they produced some of the most enduring songs in American history. George Gershwin died of a brain hemorrhage at the age of thirty-nine. ∎

Introduction

Gershwin composed the score for George White's *Scandals* of 1922, a musical revue rivaling Florence Ziegfield's Follies. In *Scandals,* Gershwin also presented his first "serious" work, a one-act opera titled *Blue Monday.* The piece, played by a full orchestra, infused jazz elements

George Gershwin poses next to a piano displaying the sheet music for his famous composition, *Rhapsody in Blue.* **GETTY IMAGES. REPRODUCED BY PERMISSION.**

Primary Source

Rhapsody in Blue

SYNOPSIS: The first page of the manuscript for *Rhapsody in Blue*. George Gershwin, as composer and pianist, premiered *Rhapsody in Blue* on January 12, 1924. Gershwin barely finished *Rhapsody* in time, since he had been concurrently working on a musical comedy. For *Rhapsody*, Gershwin even left the final piano part blank, intending to improvise during the performance itself. The opening bars of the piece feature the famous, soaring trill of a solo clarinet. FIRST PAGE OF SHEET MUSIC FOR "RHAPSODY IN BLUE, FOR JAZZ, BAND, AND PIANO," BY GEORGE GERSHWIN, JANUARY 7, 1924. © 1924, RENEWED WB MUSIC CORP. ALL RIGHTS RESERVED. USED BY PERMISSION OF WARNER BROS. PUBLICATIONS U.S. INC., MIAMI, FLORIDA 33014 into classical music, resulting in a sound previously un-heard-of. *Blue Monday* received scathing reviews and was withdrawn from *Scandals* after only one night's performance. However, Paul Whiteman, who led the *Scandals* orchestra, liked the piece so much he continued to perform it periodically under the name "135th Street." Whiteman supported Gershwin's experimental mixing of musical styles. Although *Blue Monday* was not a success, many of its themes anticipated Gershwin's masterpiece, the opera *Porgy and Bess* (1934). *Porgy and Bess* became the most famous and controversial opera of the twentieth century.

As in the other arts of the 1920s, music looked for its own, distinctly American, style. Gershwin grew up with ragtime and came of age as jazz developed into the first true American musical invention. Jazz was an early success with the public and began to be considered a legitimate form even by music critics, but was denounced by ministers as the root of the decade's evils. Gershwin responded to jazz by mixing it with traditional music and the other popular styles of the day—Broadway and opera. He created his own new style of composition, an American music not heard before. Gershwin's work marked the beginning of jazz mixed into classical, orchestrated music.

Eva Gauthier, a highly respected French singer who was on a performance tour in the United States, gave a concert at New York's Aeolian Hall. Gershwin appeared for the first time on stage performing his own compositions during that same recital on November 1, 1923. This brought his songs into a more serious context. The evening, entitled "A Recital of Ancient and Modern Music for Voice," received positive reviews.

Significance

With jazz becoming more lucrative, Paul Whiteman and other band leaders raced to capitalize on the emerging genre's rapidly growing popularity. Whiteman and Gershwin informally discussed presenting a "jazz concert" sometime in the indefinite future. When a rival conductor announced his own jazz concert date, Gershwin rushed to complete a "piano concerto" he was working on. Whiteman then persuaded Gershwin to develop the piece for his orchestra. Gershwin called this new jazz concerto *Rhapsody in Blue*.

Whiteman arranged a concert for February 12, 1924, at the Aeolian Concert Hall on 43rd Street. He titled the evening "An Experiment in Modern Music." Musical luminaries were chosen as the judges to determine an answer to the question, "What Is American Music?" Despite a snowstorm, crowds appeared for the evening's performance, and many were turned away because the hall was overcrowded. Prominent arts figures filled the audience, such as Carl Van Vechten and Fannie Hurst, and the panel

---

"Whiteman Judges Named: Committee Will Decide 'What Is American Music'"

Among the members of the committee of judges who will pass on "What Is American Music?" at the Paul Whiteman concert to be given at Aeolian Hall, Tuesday afternoon, February 12, will be Serge Rachmaninoff, Jascha Heifetz, Efrem Zimbalist, and Alma Gluck.

Leonard Leibling, editor of "The Musical Courier," will be chairman of the critics' committee, which is to be composed of the leading musical critics of the United States.

This question of "just what is American music?" has aroused a tremendous interest in music circles and Mr. Whiteman is receiving every phase of manuscript, from blues to symphonies.

George Gershwin is at work on a jazz concerto, Irving Berlin is writing a syncopated tone poem and Victor Herbert is working on an American suite.

SOURCE: "Whiteman Judges Named." *New York Tribune.* January 4, 1924. Reprinted in Jablonski, Edward, and Lawrence D. Stewart, *The Gershwin Years.* New York: Doubleday, 1958.

---

boasted Jascha Heifetz and Sergei Rachmaninoff among its judges. The program featured twenty-three works. *Rhapsody in Blue* was the second-to-last number, and it roused an audience that, by then, had largely fallen asleep. The performance received a standing ovation, and Gershwin's work was lauded as an American phenomenon.

George and his brother Ira enjoyed stellar careers as individuals in the music business. Following the success of *Rhapsody in Blue*'s premiere, George continued to compose orchestral works while beginning to work more closely with Ira. Later that year, on December 24, 1924, the Gershwin brothers debuted the musical comedy *Lady Be Good,* premiering at the Liberty Theater in Manhattan. This would be the official beginning of their long collaboration with one another. Other highly regarded orchestral works by George Gershwin are *Concerto in F* (1925), *Second Rhapsody* (1926), and *An American in Paris* (1928).

Further Resources

BOOKS

Capote, Truman. *The Muses Are Heard.* New York: Random House, 1956.

Jablonski, Edward. *Gershwin: A Biography.* New York: Da Capo Press, 1988.

Kresh, Paul M. *An American Rhapsody: The Story of George Gershwin.* New York: Lodestar Books/E.P. Dutton, 1988.

Schiff, David. *Gershwin, Rhapsody in Blue.* New York: Cambridge University Press, 1997.

Vernon, Roland. *Introducing Gershwin.* London: Belitha Press Ltd., 1996.

WEBSITES

James, Jeffrey. "What Gershwin Really Wrote: The Original Manuscript for the *Rhapsody in Blue.*" Available online at http://www.jamesarts.com/AZRHAPNOTE.htm (accessed January 21, 2003).

The Official George and Ira Gershwin Site. Available online at http://www.gershwin.com/ (accessed July 7, 2002).

Dempsey and Firpo
Painting

By: George Bellows

Date: 1924

Source: Bellows, George. *Dempsey and Firpo,* 1924. Available online at http://lcweb.loc.gov/exhibits/treasures/images/s206.1.jpg (accessed July 7, 2002).

About the Author: George Wesley Bellows (1882–1925) was born in Columbus, Ohio, and studied at Ohio State University. He enjoyed a career as a semiprofessional baseball player before moving to New York in 1904 to study art. Bellows achieved early fame with his bold paintings of prizefighters and scenes of everyday urban life. His work embodied a new and controversial form of social realism, later known as the Ashcan School of painting. ■

Introduction

Bellows studied painting with Philadelphia-born artist Robert Henri, leader of an artistic movement that became known as the Ashcan School. The movement rejected then-popular French Impressionism as well as American paintings of romanticized open prairies and Western landscapes. Instead, Ashcan artists sought to depict life in a rapidly changing America with a stark realism. Through their paintings, they addressed the social problems of urban life such as slum overcrowding and the ethnic ghettoes in New York City. The Ashcan School was named for these unrelentingly dark and dirty representations of city life.

Although Bellows was a generation younger than most of the Ashcan artists, he became one of the movement's most prominent figures. His images depicted the extremes of New York life, from construction workers, street children, and screaming crowds to mannered portraits of the elite. While often appearing grotesque, Bellows's characters seem alive, caught in dramatic moments. His paintings demonstrate an unusually bold use of color

George Bellows was involved in the Ashcan or Realist school of painting. © CORBIS. REPRODUCED BY PERMISSION.

for his time. The compositions are often extremely dense, creating movement and expressionistic effects.

From 1911 to 1917, Bellows also contributed illustrations to the radical journal *The Masses.* He was a member of the editorial board and participated in the circle of activists including left-wing artists such as John Sloan and Stuart Davis. Bellows, deeply influenced by the events of World War I (1914–1918), produced several antiwar drawings, including an incisive attack on Woodrow Wilson's Espionage Act, *Blessed Are the Peacemakers.*

Significance

Bellows first received widespread attention for his oil painting *Stag at Sharkey's* (1907), depicting a boxing match. At the time, prizefighting was illegal in New York, but underground athletic clubs such as Sharkey's—the equivalent of prohibition-era speakeasies—were extremely popular.

Bellows's paintings appealed to the general public at a time when it was unusual for fine artists to depict sports or everyday events, while fine art critics also praised his technique as a draftsman and handling of paint. *Dempsey and Firpo,* completed by Bellows as both an oil painting and as a lithographic print in 1924, is still

Primary Source

Dempsey and Firpo

SYNOPSIS: Bellows completed both a large oil painting (51 x 63 1/4 in.) and lithograph (18 x 22 1/4 in.) of *Dempsey and Firpo* in 1924. This image was one of his last paintings and is part of the permanent collection of the Whitney Museum of Modern Art, New York, New York. Bellows has included his self-portrait in the lower left corner of the print. © GEOFFREY CLEMENTS/CORBIS. REPRODUCED BY PERMISSION.

considered one of the most important American artworks depicting a sporting event.

On September 14, 1923, boxers Jack Dempsey and Luis Firpo fought at the Polo Grounds in New York. This legendary boxing match has often been referred to as "the most violent four minutes in boxing." Bellows captures the moment in the first round when Firpo sends Dempsey through the ropes and onto a press writer. Later in the same round, Dempsey returned to knock Firpo down seven times. In round two, Dempsey knocked out Firpo, thereby defending his heavyweight boxing title.

Bellows had begun experimenting in lithography in 1916, a medium once used solely for commercial print-

ing purposes but well-suited for displaying his mastery of draftsmanship and tonality. Bellows was an influential promoter of lithography as a distinct fine art medium. Lithographic prints are created by drawing directly onto a specially treated surface, undergoing a complicated printing process capable of producing a range of effects from the deepest blacks to subtle gradations of tone and lightness.

Bellows worked with the most highly respected commercial lithographers of his time, first with George C. Miller, and then with Bolton Brown. He produced nearly two hundred lithographs from 1916 to 1924, often reinterpreting his early paintings as large-scale lithographic prints, including *Stag at Sharkey's.* As a lithographic print, *Dempsey and Firpo* was easily circulated, and it quickly became an American classic. During World War II (1939–1945), the U.S. armed forces distributed a reproduction of the image to soldiers in camps and hospitals.

Further Resources

BOOKS

Atkinson, D. Scott. *An American Pulse: the Lithographs of George Wesley Bellows.* San Diego, Calif.: San Diego Museum of Art, 1999.

Doezema, Marianne. *George Bellows and Urban America.* New Haven, Conn.: Yale University Press, 1992.

Kahn, Robert. *A Flame of Pure Fire: Jack Dempsey and the Roaring '20s.* New York: Harcourt, 2000.

Perlman, Bernard B. *Painters of the Ashcan School: The Immortal Eight.* New York: Dover Publications, 1988.

Prather, Marla F. *History of Modern Art.* 4th ed. New York: Harry N. Abrams, Inc., 1998.

Zurier, Rebecca. *Metropolitan Lives: The Ashcan Artists and Their New York.* Washington, D.C.: National Museum of American Art, 1995.

Calder's Circus
Sculpture

By: Alexander Calder

Date: 1926–1931

Source: Calder, Alexander. *Calder's Circus.* 1926–31.

About the Author: Alexander Calder (1898–1976) was born into a family of artists. Though his degree was in engineering, his interests eventually turned to art, and Calder enrolled at the Art Students League in New York. In addition to the mobiles and large sculptures that made him famous, Calder's body of work included jewelry, wood carvings, bronze figurines, tapestries, and paintings. He received the United Nations Peace Medal in 1975. Today, his work is displayed in museums across the globe. ■

Introduction

Before Calder became famous for his sculptures, he was a young artist who liked to draw people and animals. In his mid-twenties, he supported his studies at the Art Students League by doing work as a commercial illustrator. Calder was hired to make drawings of the Ringling Brothers Barnum and Bailey Circus for *The National Police Gazette.* He also had a yearlong pass to the Bronx Zoo, and made hundreds of drawings which were published in his first book, *Animal Sketching,* in 1926.

Calder made his first sculptures at this time, using wire and string. These materials were ideal for translat-

ing the simple, one-line drawings of his early years. He would bend wire to create realistic figures and portraits, as if to make a three-dimensional line drawing.

Later in the year, after exhibiting his first show of oil paintings, Calder went to Paris. Shortly after his arrival, he began a miniature version of a circus made from wire, cork, wood scraps, fabrics, and other found materials. By 1927 Calder was regularly inviting artists to his studio in Montparnasse to watch him "perform" the circus. *Calder's Circus* featured tiny wire clowns, horses, and acrobats with articulated joints. Calder, like a ringmaster, would move the tiny players to make them dance, walk tightrope, and lift weights. Word of this fantastic work quickly spread throughout the Paris avant-garde.

Through 1930 Calder continued to perform, mend, and add to his *Circus.* In Paris, he made his living from these performances, pursued painting, and created new toys and small sculptures. The small sculptures made from wire and metal plates would in time become more sophisticated, developing into what is considered Calder's mature work: the colorful abstract mobiles and sculptures found in public spaces all over the world.

Significance

Calder's Circus marked the beginning of this artist's mobiles, the artistic creations for which he is most famous.

The Brass Family by Alexander Calder, 1927. © **GEOFFREY CLEMENTS/CORBIS. REPRODUCED BY PERMISSION.**

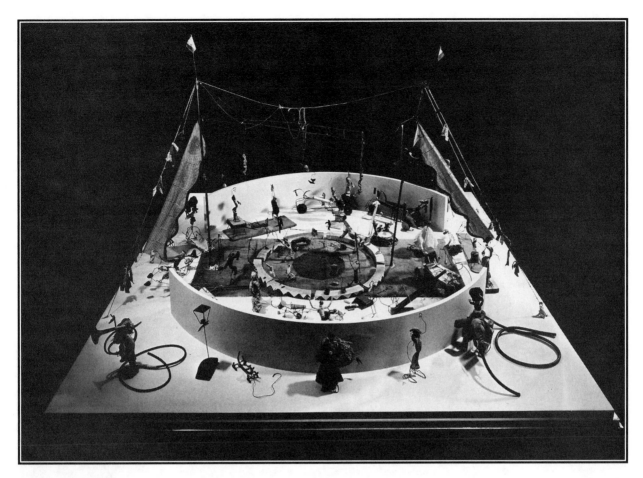

Primary Source

Calder's Circus

SYNOPSIS: *Calder's Circus* by Alexander Calder, 1926–1931. In the 1930s, Calder brought *Circus* to the United States and continued to delight audiences with his performances. Too delicate to be handled or transported, *Circus* is now permanently installed at the Whitney Museum of American Art in New York City. In 1961 filmmaker Carlos Vilardebo created *Calder's Circus,* a short film featuring Calder performing the circus in his studio for friends while his wife keeps up the gramophone in the background. PURCHASE, WITH FUNDS FROM A PUBLIC FUNDRAISING CAMPAIGN IN MAY 1982. ONE HALF THE FUNDS WERE CONTRIBUTED BY THE ROBERT WOOD JOHNSON, JR., CHARITABLE TRUST. ADDITIONAL MAJOR DONATIONS WERE GIVEN BY THE LAUDER FOUNDATION; THE ROBERT LEHMAN FOUNDATION, INC.; THE HOWARD AND JEAN LIPMAN FOUNDATION, INC.; AN ANONYMOUS DONOR; THE T.M. EVANS FOUNDATION, INC.; MACANDREWS & FORBES GROUP, INCORPORATED; THE DEWITT WALLACE FUND, INC.; MARTIN AND AGNETA GRUSS; ANNE PHILLIPS; MR. AND MRS. LAURANCE S. ROCKEFELLER; THE SIMON FOUNDATION, INC.; MARYLOU WHITNEY; BANKERS TRUST COMPANY; MR. AND MRS. KENNETH N. DAYTON; JOEL AND ANNE EHRENKANZ; IRVIN AND KENNETH FELD; FLORA WHITNEY MILLER. MORE THAN 500 INDIVIDUALS FROM 26 STATES AND ABROAD ALSO CONTRIBUTED TO THE CAMPAIGN.

Always interested in the way things move, some of his early sculptures were hand-cranked or motorized. However, Calder soon realized that the mechanized movements did not have the visual effect he desired in his work. He discovered that by hanging his sculptures, a slight breeze could create a fluid, natural movement. His friend, French artist Marcel Duchamp, first applied the term "mobile" (meaning "capable of moving") to Calder's hanging abstractions. Unknowingly, Calder had invented an art form.

Calder's admiration for the work of Surrealist painter Joan Miró and modernist painter Piet Mondrian also led to an important new direction in his work. Miró and Mondrian were not simply making abstract images; they made paintings of colors and shapes with no direct reference to the outside world. Calder's own sculpture gradually became less representational and more abstract.

Calder's sculptures were unlike any other; they were the first sculptures to incorporate movement. His works were modestly sized and not monumental, and consistently embodied a playfulness not found in "serious" art of the time. In addition to creating hundreds of small mobiles, Calder went on to create large, sedentary sculptures as well, called "stabiles." Using similar colorful abstract forms, he made giant metal structures that retained the whimsical quality characteristic of the smaller kinetic pieces. In 1943 the Museum of Modern Art in New York gave him a solo exhibition, which featured his mobiles and stabiles.

Further Resources

BOOKS

Kalman, Maira. *Roarr!: Calder's Circus.* New York: Doubleday & Company, Inc., 1993.

Krauss, Rosalind. *Passages in Modern Sculpture.* Cambridge, Mass.: MIT Press, 1988.

Lipman, Jean. *Calder's Universe.* West Sussex, England: Running Press Book Publishers, 1999.

Prather, Marla. *Alexander Calder 1898–1976.* New Haven, Conn.: Yale University Press, 1998.

WEBSITES

"Alexander Calder: The Breakthrough Years, 1925–1934." San Francisco Museum of Modern Art. Available online at http://www.sfmoma.org/espace/calder/calder_intro.html; website home page: http://www.sfmoma.org (accessed July 7, 2002).

Calder Foundation. Available online at http://www.calder.org/ (accessed July 7, 2002).

"Oral History Interview With Alexander Calder at Perls Gallery, October 26, 1971." Smithsonian Archives of American Art. Available online at http://artarchives.si.edu/oral-hist/calder71.htm; website home page: http://artarchives .si.edu (accessed July 7, 2002).

The General
Movie stills

By: Buster Keaton

Date: 1927

Source: Keaton, Buster. *The General.* 76 min. Hollywood, Calif.: United Artists, 1927. Videocassette.

About the Author: Joseph Frank Keaton VI (1895–1966), writer, director, and star of silent film comedies, was born

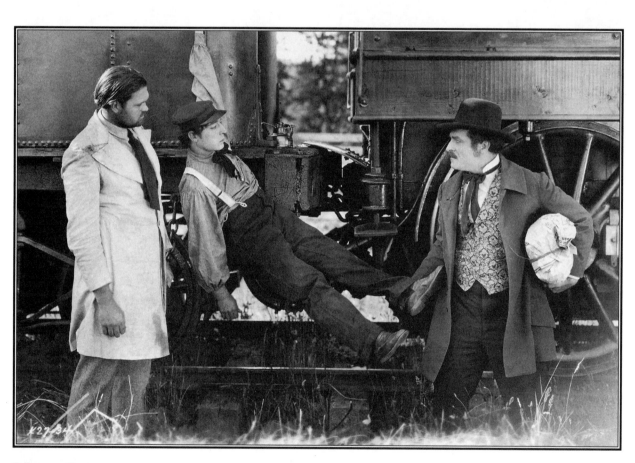

Primary Source

The General (1 OF 3)

SYNOPSIS: Buster Keaton as Johnnie Gray, holds on to a railroad car in a scene from *The General*. When Johnnie is rejected by the Confederate Army because they need him more as a civilian engineer than as a soldier, his sweetheart, Annabelle Lee, believes Johnnie is simply shirking his manly responsibility, and she leaves him. Fate intervenes when both train and sweetheart are kidnapped. Johnnie is unaware that Annabelle is part of the stolen booty. He is determined to rescue the train, and the great locomotive chase begins. © BETTMANN/CORBIS. REPRODUCED BY PERMISSION.

Primary Source

The General (2 OF 3)

This scene from *The General* depicts an element of dark comedy that audiences found disturbing compared to Buster Keaton's previous slapstick films. © BETTMANN/CORBIS. REPRODUCED BY PERMISSION.

into a family of vaudevillians. He was christened "Buster" after a family friend saw the six-month-old child tumble down a flight of stairs unharmed. "What a buster your kid took!" the friend exclaimed to Buster's parents. Young Buster performed in the family act "The Three Keatons" until 1917, when he quit to pursue his own career. By 1920 he had established the Buster Keaton Studio, where he became a master of the cinematic medium and its role in comedy. Keaton is remembered for his deadpan humor and inventive sight gags. ■

Introduction

Buster Keaton grew up being tossed around by his father in what was considered the roughest act in vaudeville. This early experience earned him the nickname, "The Human Mop," and sent his father before child-labor authorities more than once. Rumors persist to this day that the young Keaton was a victim of child abuse, but no court documents or reports from family or friends support this claim. In fact, Keaton used his childhood performances to perfect the incredible and sometimes dangerous stunts that would later earn him fame in Hollywood.

"The Three Keatons" disbanded in 1917 when Buster left the act to escape his father's drinking binges, which had worsened to the point where performing with him was unsafe. By that time, Keaton had decided to forge his own path, and he set out on making himself a silent film star. Early in his career, he met the legendary Fatty Arbuckle, and the two paired up to produce some of the most successful silent films ever made.

Much of Keaton's work was slapstick, but his humor also had a subtle, more subdued side, and a number of his films are considered satire, with undercurrents of black comedy and fantasy. Moviegoers loved Keaton for his endless stunts—all of which he performed himself. His list of

Primary Source

The General (3 OF 3)

Buster Keaton as Johnnie Gray, trying to rescue a stolen train in *The General*. © CORBIS. REPRODUCED BY PERMISSION.

injuries was long: a foot crushed in an elevator, a broken nose, a near drowning, and even a broken neck. The silent era was ideal for Keaton's talents; with no words to capture the audience, complete focus was on the actors.

The General, Keaton's favorite project and now considered his finest film, marked the beginning of the end of the silent era. Keaton wrote, starred, and directed the film. Set in the Civil War (1861–1865) era, *The General* was based on William Pittenger's *The Great Locomotive Chase,* a true story of Union Captain Anderson's seizure of a Confederate train near Atlanta, Georgia, and his attempt to ride it back into the Union.

Significance

The plot of *The General* predominantly consists of two train chases across the same territory. *The General* was a spectacular action film in its time, and also demonstrated that cinematography was an art in itself. Keaton's film is an artistic masterpiece, from his stoic performance to the ingenious sight gags and visual effects. The action involves water tanks, a large piece of timber, a rolling cannon on wheels, unattached railroad cars, collapsing bridges, the unpredictable forces of Nature, and of course the famous locomotive chases, some of the longest and most elaborate ever filmed in cinematic history.

The General was a box-office disappointment when it premiered in 1927. Its production costs—including a $42,000 train wreck, the most expensive single shot in film history at the time—made it unlikely that the film would recoup any of its investments, and the studio lost money. Expecting a slapstick comedy, film critics and audiences did not like the film either, complaining of

Keaton's strange brand of humor and his indelicate approach toward the still-sensitive topic of the Civil War. *The General* had few sustained laughs, and the jokes were often placed in scenes of carnage. *The General* was one of the last films over which Keaton had complete artistic control, and it was not widely appreciated until it was rediscovered decades later.

In 1928 Keaton closed his studio to join MGM. However, his career faltered, his marriage ended, and his struggles with alcoholism cost him many acting jobs. Keaton defected to Columbia Pictures, where he made short films. He despised the work and was reduced to ever smaller and smaller roles. When *The General* was shown at a film festival in 1945, filmgoers were finally ready to appreciate Buster's work. In 1959 he received a special Oscar "for his unique talents which brought immortal comedies to the screen." His career gradually rebounded, and today his silent films are regarded as comedic as well as cinematic masterpieces.

Further Resources

BOOKS

Bengston, John. *Silent Echoes: Discovering Early Hollywood Through the Films of Buster Keaton.* Santa Monica, Calif.: Santa Monica Press, 2000.

The Day Buster Smiled: The 1926 Filming of The General. *Cottage Grove, Ore.: Cottage Grove Historical Society, 1998.*

Higgins, Dick. *Buster Keaton Enters into Paradise.* Kingston, N.Y.: Left Hand Books, 1994.

Keaton, Buster, and Charles T. Samuels. *My Wonderful World of Slapstick.* New York: Da Capo Press, 1990.

Keaton, Eleanor, Kevin Brownlow and Jeffrey Vance. *Buster Keaton Remembered.* New York: H.N. Abrams, 1994.

Kerr, Walter. *The Silent Clowns.* New York: Da Capo, 1990, 1975.

Kline, Jim. *The Complete Films of Buster Keaton.* New York: Carol Pub. Group, 1993.

MacCann, Richard Dyer. *The Silent Comedians.* Metuchen, N.J.: Scarecrow Press; Iowa City, Iowa: Image & Idea, 1993.

Mitchell, Glenn. *A–Z of Silent Film Comedy: An Illustrated Companion.* London: B.T. Batsford, Ltd., 1999.

WEBSITES

The International Buster Keaton Society. Available online at http://www.busterkeaton.com (accessed January 25, 2003).

The Jazz Singer

Screenplay

By: Alfred A. Cohn

Date: 1927

Source: Cohn, Alfred A. "Shooting Script." *The Jazz Singer.* 1927. Reprinted on the Al Jolson Society Official Website.

Available online at http://www.jolson.org/works/film/js/jazzscript.html; website home page: http://www.jolson.org (accessed October 10, 2002).

About the Author: Alfred A. Cohn (1880–1951) was a prolific Hollywood screenwriter. His screenplay for Warner Brothers' *The Jazz Singer* (1927) was based on Samson Raphaelson's highly successful Broadway play, "The Day of Atonement." *The Jazz Singer* starred Al Jolson (1886–1950), already a singing sensation and often called the "World's Greatest Entertainer." Jolson, born Asa Yoelson, emigrated with his family from Lithuania and grew up in Washington D.C. He and his elder brother Hirsch (later Harry) performed in vaudeville as Harry & Al Jolson. When the brothers parted ways, Al joined a minstrel troupe, began to secure bit parts on Broadway, and eventually became his generation's most charismatic performer. ■

Introduction

Warner Brothers' *The Jazz Singer,* directed by Alan Crosland, is a cinematic landmark. It is considered Hollywood's first "talkie" film, even though it was not the first Vitaphone (sound-on-disk) film. *The Jazz Singer* was the first feature-length production in which spoken dialogue was synchronized with dramatic action. Until this time, films had previously required accompaniment by a piano or organ when shown in a theater, and title cards provided the characters' dialogue. In April 1923, inventor Lee de Forest introduced early sound-on-film movies using his Phonofilm process in a New York City theater. Phonofilm featured a superior sound quality to Tri-Ergon, the first sound-on-film technology, invented in Germany. No full-length film, however, had synchronized sound and action until *The Jazz Singer* began shooting in July 1927.

The hit Broadway show starred George Jessel, who had hoped to get the title role in the film version. Instead, Warner Brothers cast Al Jolson. The producers had not planned for dialogue; the film was to feature six songs and use title cards. However, caught up in the emotion of his rendition of "Dirty Hands, Dirty Face," Jolson ad-libbed what became the first spoken words in a feature-length film: "Wait a minute! Wait a minute! You ain't heard nothin' yet!"

The Jazz Singer is actually only a partial talkie. There are only a few scenes where dialogue is spoken synchronously with the acting; the film relies heavily on title cards, sound effects accompanying the action, and the musical themes given to each individual character in the film. However, the film is remarkable for its implementation of musical sequences. These scenes are sound-synchronized, featuring songs with voice and musical accompaniment. Al Jolson's extended sequence singing for and talking to his mother (portrayed by Eugenie Besserer) particularly touched filmgoers. However, the film then returns to title cards when Jakie has a dramatic confrontation with his father (Warren Olander).

A 1927 billboard advertisement for the Warner Bros. film, *The Jazz Singer,* declares it "a supreme triumph" because it was the first "talkie."
© BETTMANN/CORBIS. REPRODUCED BY PERMISSION.

Significance

When *The Jazz Singer* premiered on October 6, 1927, it was a revolutionary experience for filmgoers everywhere. The audiences were enthralled by Jolson's performance, and the success of the film gave Jolson a second career in the movies. *The Jazz Singer* earned more than three million dollars, making it one of the highest-grossing films of the 1920s, and it saved Warner Brothers from bankruptcy. Alfred A. Cohn was nominated for an Academy Award for Best Adapted Screenplay in 1927. Warner Brothers received an Academy Award Special Award for "the pioneer talking picture, which has revolutionized the industry." The studio produced the first full talkie (or all-dialogue) picture a year later, with *Lights of New York* (1928), a gangster film.

The film was also praised for its music. The score consists of traditional Jewish music (with a performance of "Kol Nidre" by famed cantor Rabbi Rosenblatt), classical music, and popular songs, including Irving Berlin's "Blue Skies," which marked the composer's early entry into Hollywood.

The Jazz Singer is loosely based on Al Jolson's own youth and rise to fame. The lead character is a teenage Jakie Rabinowitz, who breaks his family's five-genera-

tional tradition of cantors. To his rabbi father's dismay, young Jakie does not want to sing holy songs in the synagogue, preferring to belt out popular tunes in bars and nightclubs. He runs away, recreating himself as Jack Robin. The story follows Jakie's rise to fame as a hugely successful singer. Like Al Jolson, the fictional Jakie/Jack first achieves stardom with his blackface routine. The then-popular theatrical practice of blackface, or "blacking up" (white performers using skin-darkening makeup) has since become a complex issue, but it was a central part of Jolson's dramatic personality. Performers at the time often believed that audiences enjoyed blackface routines more than acts in which the white performers went onstage without such makeup.

Primary Source

The Jazz Singer [excerpt]

> **SYNOPSIS:** Jakie has returned home for a visit on the way to his star debut, only to discover that he must choose between his family and his ambition. He has an emotional reunion with his mother, while his father, who cannot believe his son is wasting his talent as a "jazz singer," refuses to speak to Jakie. This document has been slightly modified from its original format for clarity's sake.

FULL SHOT ROOM

Sara walks over to the piano as Jack sits down and starts to play a jazzy tune. He gets through several bars when the front door opens and the cantor appears. He hesitates at the unwonted sounds coming from his cherished piano.

CLOSE-UP CANTOR

His brows knit in a deep frown as he listens a moment. Then he takes a resolute step forward.

FULL SHOT ROOM FROM DOOR

As the cantor enters the room, he takes out his glasses and adjusts them. Sara sees him coming and she puts a hand on Jack's arm to stop him, telling him that his father has arrived. Jack swings around on the stool, gets up, and hurries over to greet his father. As Jack puts out his hand, the cantor makes no effort to take it. Sara hurries forward.

CLOSE SHOT THREE

Jack is saying, "Why, hello, Papa!" The cantor remains impassive as the frown deepens. Sara goes to him and, pointing to Jack, says eagerly to her husband:

> "Look, it's your son—he said 'Hello, Papa' to you."

Al Jolson as Jack Robin, sings for his mother Sara Rabinowitz, played by Eugenie Besserer, in one of the more famous sequences of *The Jazz Singer,* 1927. © UNDERWOOD & UNDERWOOD/CORBIS. REPRODUCED BY PERMISSION.

Jack nods in corroboration of this news. The cantor merely stiffens.

CLOSE-UP CANTOR

He glares at Jack as he demands:

"What you mean, coming in my house and playing on my piano your music from the streets—your jazz?"

CLOSE SHOT GROUP

Jack is abashed at this. He hesitates and Sara rushes in and takes the blame for Jack playing. She pleads with the old man to welcome Jack, but he remains adamant. He again points a condemning finger at Jack.

CLOSE-UP FATHER

He almost shouts at him:

"I taught you to sing to God—to be a cantor like your fathers. But you liked better to sing in beer halls than in the temple. You're the same now."

CLOSE SHOT GROUP

Sara takes the cantor's hand and pleads with him, saying that Jack doesn't deserve such treatment. Jack assumes also a pleading attitude. Sara tells the cantor to remember that it is his birthday. At this Jack goes to his bag.

CLOSE-UP JACK AT CHAIR

He is rummaging in the bag excitedly and fishes out a package. He looks up and says:

"Sure, Papa, I remembered it was your birthday. See, I brought you a present too."

He unwraps it, disclosing a prayer shawl.

CLOSE-UP CANTOR AND WIFE

Sara is talking to him excitedly, telling him how wonderful that Jakie should remember all these years, his papa's birthday. The cantor is beginning to weaken under this assault. Sara leaves him for Jack.

MED. SHOT ROOM

Sara goes over to Jack excitedly and takes the shawl from him. As she sees it, there is just a second's change when she sees with dismay that it is another prayer shawl. Her manner changes immediately to one of excited delight. As Jack looks appealingly at his father, Sara holds up the shawl for him.

CLOSE-UP SARA

As she holds up the shawl, stroking its soft folds affectionately, she says:

"See, Papa, just what you needed—a nice new prayer shawl."

She starts toward him.

MED. SHOT GROUP

Jack follows Sara to the side of the old man. He takes the shawl from her and addressing his father says, almost tearfully:

"Many happy returns of the day to our cantor. Ever hear that before when I was a little boy, Papa?"

CLOSE SHOT GROUP

As the cantor stands impassively, Sara takes his arm and says to him:

"Look, Papa, Jakie is making you a speech, like when he was a little boy on your birthday."

The cantor looks up as though from a reverie and, bowing in a dignified manner, says: "Thank you." He makes no effort to take the shawl, which Sara takes. She exclaims upon the fine weave and cloth, saying it is the best one the cantor has ever had, etc. Jack grows more embarrassed as the cantor shows no sign of relenting and shifts from one foot to another. He finally looks away from his father to his mother and, taking the cue from her, remarks:

"Sure, it's a good one—the best money could buy."

The old man shows interest at this. He repeats the boy's words. There is a question in his manner, or a conclusion, but seizing upon it as an opening, Jack eagerly declares:

"Sure, Papa, I'm making plenty jack. And I'm going to make more. Ain't many can put over a Mammy song like me."

He continues talking about his work. The old man's eyes assume a steely glitter. Jack continues talking glibly.

CLOSE-UP FATHER

He glares at Jack. Finally he holds up a hand for silence, then snaps out:

"So you sing your dirty songs in theaters now! First on the sidewalks, then beer halls and now theaters."

CLOSE-UP GROUP

Sara tries to stop the old man. Jack, surprised at this new attack, tries to defend himself. The old man doesn't want to listen. Finally Jack, aroused now to the fact that he must fight to get the respect of his father, demands that his father listen to him. He grasps his father's hand. The old man stares at him in surprise. He starts to protest and Jack silences him.

CLOSE-UP JACK

He leans forward as he says, earnestly:

"You taught me to sing—and you told me that music was the voice of God—and it is just as honorable to sing in the theater as in the synagogue."

CLOSE-UP FATHER AND SON

As Jack finishes [speaking], he endeavors to continue but the old man stops him. He points to the door. Jack, with a gesture of defeat, turns away from him, toward the chair upon which are his things.

Further Resources

BOOKS

Alexander, Michael. *Jazz Age Jews.* Princeton, N.J.: Princeton University Press, 2001.

Goldman, Herbert G. *Jolson: The Legend Comes to Life.* New York: Oxford University Press, 1988.

Heinze, Andrew R. *Adapting to Abundance: Jewish Immigrants, Mass Consumption, and the Search for American Identity.* New York: Columbia University Press, 1990.

Lhamon, W. T. *Raising Cain: Blackface Performance from Jim Crow to Hip Hop.* Cambridge, Mass.: Harvard University Press, 1998.

McClelland, Doug. *Blackface to Blacklist: Al Jolson, Larry Parks, and 'The Jolson Story'.* Metuchen, N.J.: Scarecrow Press, 1987.

Oberfirst, Robert. *Al Jolson: You Ain't Heard Nothin' Yet.* San Diego, Calif.: A.S. Barnes, 1980.

Sarris, Andrew. *You Ain't Heard Nothin' Yet: The American Talking Film.* New York: Oxford University Press, 1998.

Toll, Robert. *Blacking Up: The Minstrel Show in Nineteenth-Century America.* New York: Oxford University Press, 1974.

WEBSITES

Al Jolson: The World's Greatest Entertainer. Available online at http://www.jolson.org (accessed January 25, 2003).

"Blue Skies"

Musical composition

By: Irving Berlin

Date: 1927

Source: Berlin, Irving. "Blue Skies." New York: Irving Berlin, Inc., 1927.

About the Author: Born Israel Isidore Baline in Mohilev, Russia, Irving Berlin (1888–1989) moved to New York with his family in 1893. Israel changed his name to Irving Berlin and taught himself enough piano to begin writing songs. He sold his first song in 1907 and scored his first big hit with "Alexander's Ragtime Band" in 1911. Though he never learned to read music, he composed around fifteen hundred songs, among them such classics as "Blue Skies," "White Christmas," and "God Bless America." ∎

Introduction

Before the heyday of recorded music, the burgeoning music industry made its profits through the sale of sheet music, and the stars of the day were the songwriters, rather than performers. Berlin began his career as a songwriter for "Tin Pan Alley," the name given to the scores of sheet music publishers in New York during the late nineteenth and early twentieth centuries. Berlin enjoyed success from his first published song, "Marie From Sunny Italy," in 1907, and achieved international fame in 1911 with "Alexander's Ragtime Band." The czar's army band in Berlin's native Russia even recorded a version of the song.

Always eager to retain control of his work, Berlin founded his own publishing company in 1919, and even built his own theater—The Music Box—both of which survive today. During the twenties, Berlin's "Music Box Revues" became the most fashionable shows on Broadway. In 1927 Berlin wrote "Puttin' on the Ritz," a song emblematic of the Jazz Age, and notable also because its premiere marked the first performance of an interracial vocal ensemble.

Berlin's later success came from his songs for Broadway and for movies, and he would often rework songs from his stage revues for use in motion pictures. His favorite performers were Fred Astaire and Ethel Merman, because he felt they enunciated well and gave the lyrics as much importance as the melody. Merman sang the lead role in Berlin's *Annie Get Your Gun* on Broadway and popularized his song, "There's No Business Like Show Business." Astaire played in many of Berlin's musical revues and films. Berlin provided the score for three Fred Astaire and Ginger Rogers movies, including *Top Hat* (1933), featuring "Cheek to Cheek." Another Berlin classic, "White Christmas," first appeared as a movie song in 1942's *Holiday Inn.*

Irving Berlin sings at the dedication of City Hall in Los Angeles, 1928. © BETTMANN/CORBIS. REPRODUCED BY PERMISSION.

Primary Source

"Blue Skies," Cover (1 OF 5)

SYNOPSIS: The original cover of the sheet music for "Blue Skies" featured an illustration of Belle Baker tying strings around three embarrassed-looking men. Two of them bore a striking resemblance to the composer-lyricist duo Rodgers and Hart. The song returned to the number one spot on the bestseller charts as a Willie Nelson rendition—fifty-two years after its debut. COURTESY OF THE ESTATE OF IRVING BERLIN.

Primary Source

"Blue Skies," Inside Cover (2 OF 5)
Advertisement for another Irving Berlin composition, "Because I Love You," inside cover of "Blue Skies," 1927. "BECAUSE I LOVE YOU." WORDS AND MUSIC BY IRVING BERLIN. © COPYRIGHT 1926 BY IRVING BERLIN. COPYRIGHT RENEWED. INTERNATIONAL COPYRIGHT SECURED. ALL RIGHTS RESERVED.

Primary Source

"Blue Skies," Page 3 (3 OF 5)

Page three of "Blue Skies" by Irving Berlin, 1927. "BLUE SKIES." WORDS AND MUSIC BY IRVING BERLIN. © COPYRIGHT 1927 BY IRVING BERLIN. COPYRIGHT RENEWED. INTERNATIONAL COPYRIGHT SECURED. ALL RIGHTS RESERVED.

Primary Source

"Blue Skies," Page 5 (5 OF 5)

Page five of "Blue Skies" by Irving Berlin, 1927. "BLUE SKIES." WORDS AND MUSIC BY IRVING BERLIN. © COPYRIGHT 1927 BY IRVING BERLIN. COPYRIGHT RENEWED. INTERNATIONAL COPYRIGHT SECURED. ALL RIGHTS RESERVED.

Significance

Irving Berlin never learned to read music and could only play the piano using the black keys (F sharp minor). To compensate, he used a "transposing" piano. By pulling a simple lever, this instrument enabled Berlin to shift the key of a song, and he employed a transcriber to take down the song in musical notation while he sang or played it. Berlin was an unsophisticated musician compared with George Gershwin, Cole Porter, and other accomplished composers of his time, but the simplicity of his best songs captured the hearts of American music lovers.

In 1926 singer Belle Baker was to make her Broadway debut in the musical *Betsy*. The famous composing duo Rodgers and Hart wrote the score. On the eve of her debut, Baker was in despair. She felt that neither of the two solos she was to sing gave her a chance to show off her booming voice, so she called on her good friend, Berlin. It took him all night, but the result of his tireless effort was "Blue Skies." Baker loved it, and the tune was given to an arranger.

Neither Rodgers nor Hart had any idea what Baker had in mind. So on opening night, when she opened her mouth to sing the first line of "Blue Skies," no one was more shocked than they to hear what poured forth. Her interpretation of the song stopped the show cold, and audiences couldn't get enough. The audience demanded twenty-eight encores, twenty-seven of which she performed flawlessly. On the last one, she fumbled her lines. The spotlight trained on Berlin, who stood up in the front row and fed her the lyrics. *Betsy* closed after just thirty-nine performances, but the song became a hit that has been recorded by dozens of performers and is recognized even today.

Further Resources

BOOKS

Barrett, Mary Ellin. *Irving Berlin: A Daughter's Memoir*. New York: Alfred A. Knopf, 1994.

Bergreen, Laurence. *As Thousands Cheer: The Life of Irving Berlin*. New York: Viking, 1990.

Berlin, Irving. *The Complete Lyrics of Irving Berlin*. Robert Kimball and Linda Emmett, eds. New York: Knopf, 2000.

Furia, Philip. *Irving Berlin: A Life in Song*. New York: Schirmer Books, 1998.

Jablonski, Edward. *Irving Berlin: American Troubador*. New York: Alfred A. Knopf, 1999.

Whitcomb, Ian. *Irving Berlin & Ragtime America*. New York: Limelight Editions, 1988.

"Far from Well"

Book review

By: Dorothy Parker

Date: October 20, 1928

Source: Parker, Dorothy. *Constant Reader*. New York: Viking Press, 1970. (A reprint of *The New Yorker* review).

About the Author: Dorothy Parker (1893–1967) began her literary career writing reviews and fashion captions for magazines such as *Vogue* and *Vanity Fair*. She was once fired for writing a particularly sarcastic theater review. Parker was a core member of the legendary Algonquin Round Table, a group of literary types famous for their witty verbal exchanges. Parker also wrote short stories, poetry, and plays. She was a bitter, self-destructive character. Despite two (unsuccessful) suicide attempts, she outlived most of her hard-drinking peers. ∎

Introduction

In 1919, Dorothy Parker and other literary and theater types began to meet for informal lunches at the Algonquin Hotel in New York. The group became known as the Algonquin Round Table, famous for their rapid-fire exchange of clever insults and caustic wit. They made incisive observations on the society around them, skewering friends and foes alike. The Algonquins' core members included Franklin Pierce Adams, George S. Kaufman, Robert Benchley, comedian Harpo Marx, Alexander Woollcott (drama critic for *The New York Times*), and Harold Ross (the founder of *The New Yorker*). Parker was the only regular female member of the group. Actress Tallulah Bankhead and playwright Noel Coward made occasional appearances.

The Algonquins were extremely quick with words. They had very high standards, although they disdained formal academic-style criticism, adapting instead a casual but nevertheless tough attitude towards the work of their peers. Fueled by ambition, mutual ego-boosting, and liquor, they were very critical yet supportive of one another. By 1925, the Round Table was nationally famous. This private clique became the stuff of gossip columns for the public's amusement. At the time, New York City was the cultural center of the United States, and Americans were riveted by the Algonquins' biting commentary on society. Curious onlookers went to the hotel hoping for just a glimpse of the intellectual elite.

The Algonquins eventually scattered, and the famous luncheons faded from the public eye. Parker's own career flourished. In 1929, she won an O. Henry Prize for her short story "Big Blonde," the tale of a self-destructive flapper. Parker's plays were mostly unsuccessful, but her short, witty poems were highly regarded. She had no heirs and left everything to Dr. Martin Luther King, Jr., when she died in 1967. After his assassination the following

Author and columnist Dorothy Parker started her career as a drama critic. © BETTMANN/CORBIS. REPRODUCED BY PERMISSION.

year, Parker's literary rights were transferred to the NAACP. Her ashes are located at the NAACP headquarters in Baltimore, Maryland.

Significance

At a time when very few Americans graduated even from junior high school, the Algonquin Round Table represented the epitome of cultural sophistication. Its members were highly educated, with college diplomas and literary pedigrees spanning the most respected newspapers and magazines of the day. The Algonquins' commentaries filled newspaper gossip columns written by Adams, reaching every corner of the United States. The hotel's proprietor even encouraged the Algonquins by providing them with a large, round table. As a result of this active self-promoting, the Algonquins achieved a reputation of mythic proportions. The group embodied the spirit and abandon of the Roaring Twenties, and its members were uninhibited freethinkers who demonstrated that intellectual debate was alive in America. Their witticisms are often quoted.

The Round Table produced some fruitful artistic relationships. Playwright George Kaufman collaborated with Edna Ferber and Marc Connelly on *Dulcy* and *The Royal Family,* two of his best comedies. Harold Ross

hired Parker as a book reviewer and Robert Benchley as a drama critic for his new publication *The New Yorker.*

Several factors contributed to the demise of the Round Table. The mood during the Depression era was markedly more sober than the fun-loving 1920s, and some members moved to Hollywood to pursue their ambitions. Robert Sherwood and Robert Benchley, who had been living at the Algonquin Hotel, moved out and away from distraction in order to concentrate on their writing. Among the more serious issues discussed amidst the Algonquins was the nationally debated case of Sacco and Vanzetti. Their controversial execution in 1927 subdued even these rabble-rousers. Parker, who believed strongly in the pair's innocence, commented shortly afterwards, "I had heard someone say and so I said too, that ridicule is the most effective weapon. Well, now I know that there are things that never have been funny and never will be. And I know that ridicule may be a shield but it is not a weapon."

Primary Source

"Far from Well"

SYNOPSIS: Every week from October 1927 through May 1928, a book review column appeared in *The New Yorker* magazine. It was an open secret that its author, known only as the "Constant Reader," was really Dorothy Parker. The following review of *The House at Pooh Corner* is typical of Parker's vituperative style.

The more it
SNOWs-tiddely-pom,
The more it
GOES-tiddely-pom
The more it
GOES-tiddely-pom
On
Snowing.

And nobody
KNOWS-tiddely-pom,
How cold my
TOES-tiddely-pom
How cold my
TOES-tiddely-pom
Are
Growing.

The above lyric is culled from the fifth page of Mr. A. A. Milne's new book, *The House at Pooh Corner,* for, although the work is in prose, there are frequent droppings into more cadenced whimsy. This one is designated as a "Hum," that pops into the head of Winnie-the-Pooh as he is standing outside Piglet's house in the snow, jumping up and down to keep warm. It "seemed to him a Good Hum, such as is Hummed Hopefully to Others." In fact, so Good a Hum did it seem that he and Piglet started right out through the snow to Hum It Hopefully to Eeyore. Oh, darn—there I've gone and given away the plot. Oh, I could bite my tongue out.

As they are trotting along against the flakes, Piglet begins to weaken a bit.

"'Pooh,' he said at last and a little timidly, because he didn't want Pooh to think he was Giving In, 'I was just wondering. How would it be if we went home now and practised your song, and then sang it to Eeyore tomorrow—or—or the next day, when we happen to see him.'

"'That's a very good idea, Piglet,' said Pooh. 'We'll practise it now as we go along. But it's no good going home to practise it, because it's a special Outdoor Song which Has To Be Sung In The Snow.'

"'Are you sure?' asked Piglet anxiously.

"'Well, you'll see, Piglet, when you listen. Because this is how it begins. *The more it snows, tiddely-pom—*'

"'Tiddely what?' said Piglet." (He took, as you might say, the very words out of your correspondent's mouth.)

"'Pom,' said Pooh. 'I put that in to make it more hummy.'"

And it is that word "hummy," my darlings, that marks the first place in *The House at Pooh Corner* at which Tonstant Weader Fwowed up.

Further Resources

BOOKS

Crews, Frederick C. *The Pooh Perplex, A Freshman Casebook.* New York: Dutton, 1963.

Drennen, Robert E. *The Algonquin Wits.* Secaucus, N.J.: Citadel, 1968.

Gains, James R. *Wit's End: Days and Nights of the Algonquin Round Table.* New York: Harcourt Brace & Jovanovich, 1977.

Keats, John. *You Might As Well Live: The Life and Times of Dorothy Parker.* New York: Simon & Schuster, 1970.

Meade, Marion. *Dorothy Parker: What Fresh Hell is This?* New York: Villard Books, 1988.

Parker, Dorothy. *Not Much Fun: The Lost Poems of Dorothy Parker.* New York: Scribner, 1996.

———. *The Portable Dorothy Parker.* New York: Viking Press, 1985.

PERIODICALS

Kinney, Arthur F. "Dorothy Parker's Letters to Alexander Woollcott." *Massachusetts Review,* 30, 3, Fall 1989, 487–515.

AUDIO AND VISUAL MEDIA

Robert Benchley and the Knights of the Algonquin. Kino on Video. Directed by Robert Benchley. Videocassette, 1928–1941.

Steamboat Willie
Screenplay

By: Ub Iwerks and Walt Disney

Date: 1928

Source: *Steamboat Willie.* Directed by Walt Disney. Disney Studios, 1928. Script reprinted in Finch, Christopher, *The Art of Walt Disney: From Mickey Mouse to the Magic Kingdoms.* New York: H.N. Abrams, 1999, 22.

About the Artists: Ubbe Iwwerks (1901–1971) is widely credited with sketching the world-famous cartoon character Mickey Mouse. He simplified the spelling of his name to Ub Iwerks when he joined Walt Disney's California animation studio in 1924. Iwerks was a pioneering animator and won two Academy Awards for his technical achievements. His innovations enabled Disney Studios to become a leader in photographic and animation special effects. He also revolutionized the art of film restoration, pioneering the so-called wet gate system of eliminating scratches on old films by printing them under liquid.

Walter Elias Disney (1901–1966) is an iconic figure in American entertainment, responsible for creating some of the world's most beloved cartoon characters. On the strength of such classic children's films as *Snow White and the Seven Dwarfs* (1937), *Pinocchio* (1940), *Fantasia* (1940), and *Peter Pan* (1953), Disney built his fledgling Disney Studios into a global empire worth billions of dollars. He was also responsible for building two of the world's most recognizable tourist attractions: Disneyland Park in California and Walt Disney World Resort in Florida. ■

Introduction

Ub Iwerks and Walt Disney first met in 1920 at the Pesmen-Rubin Commercial Art Studio in Kansas City, Missouri, where they created artwork for local newspaper advertisements. Later that year, the two formed their own company, Iwerks-Disney Commercial Artists. When Disney opened his own company, Laugh-O-gram Films, in 1922, he asked Iwerks to be his head animator.

The 1920s was an extremely prolific time for the Iwerks-Disney team. Laugh-O-gram Films produced six cartoon shorts, which were shown before feature-film presentations. Disney wrote the stories and directed, and Iwerks created the artwork. At the time, animation was steadily gaining in popularity, and Laugh-O-gram Films quickly established itself as a player in the new art form, particularly with its innovative *Alice Comedies* series, which combined cartoon characters with live-action film.

Scene # 27.

C.U. Mickey drumming on bucket and utensils.....Goose in crate showing at left of scene....Little Kitten walks across scene ' MEOW'ING ' as it walks across.....Mickey sees it and puts his foot on its head and pulls its tail in time to music.... and cat lets out yells in time to last half of Verse.....He sees goose, lets cat go and picks up goose.... puts its body under his arm and pumps it in and out as he head and neck back and forth like TROMBONE— in time to verse......
SOUND EFFECTS....Squeaky cat sounds, ...WA - WA- WA- effect with sliding trombone as he plays on GOOSE....

Scene # 29.

Medium shot of little girl turning goats tail like crank....and music of ' Turkey in the Straw ' comes out his mouth like hand organ....

As she cranks che does crazy clog dance........

Scene # 30.

C.U. of Mickey drumming on bucket Old cows head sticking in left side of scene....she is chewing in time to music.....she reaches over and licks Mickeys face with her long tongue....then smiles (shows teeth) Mickey sees teeth....opens her mouth wide and hammers on her teeth like playing Xylophone....plays in time to music....runs up and down scale, etc.
Just as he is about to finish two large feet(the Captains) walk into right side of scene and stop....Mickey finishes piece with 'Ta-da-de-da-da-... on cows horns....pulls out her tongue and strums 'Dum - Dum...' on it...and turns around to girl with smile....He sees feet...looks upslowly...when he sees its Captain he acts surprised...

65

Primary Source

Steamboat Willie

SYNOPSIS: The early Mickey was a mischievous character. In this excerpt from the continuity script for *Steamboat Willie,* he drives Pete's river steamer. Pete yells at Mickey for horsing around, and Mickey picks up Minnie's cow and puts it on the boat. Minnie runs on the boat to retrieve her cow, and after a goat eats some sheet music, Mickey and Minnie begin playing the folk tune "Turkey in the Straw," using animals as instruments. EVEREST HOUSE PUBLISHERS, 1982. © 1982 DISNEY ENTERPRISES, INC. REPRODUCED BY PERMISSION.

However, the company was forced to file for bankruptcy after its distributor defaulted on payments. Disney then moved his operation to Los Angeles, where he founded The Walt Disney Company. In 1927, Iwerks and Disney created a new character, Oswald the Lucky Rabbit, who was featured in a series even more successful than *Alice.*

Mickey Mouse was conceived in March 1928, when Disney lost the Oswald character to his New York-based financial backer and distributor, Charles Mintz. Disney and his wife, Lillian, had traveled to New York to ask Mintz for more money to improve the quality of the Oswald series. Mintz refused, taking the character away from Disney and giving it to another animation studio. Disney then spent the train ride back to Los Angeles developing a new character, a little mouse in red velvet pants. Originally, Disney wanted to name him "Mortimer," but Lillian thought it was too pretentious and suggested "Mickey" instead. Mickey looked very much like Oswald, but with short, round ears.

Upon his return, Disney and Iwerks began working on the first Mickey Mouse cartoon. Completed in May 1928 and consisting of seven minutes of animation and thousands of drawings, *Plane Crazy* was singlehandedly animated by Iwerks. Athough no distributor wanted to buy the film, Disney Studios began production on another silent Mickey cartoon, *The Gallopin' Gaucho.* Then the enormous success of Warner Bros.' *The Jazz Singer,* starring Al Jolson, inspired Disney to create the first synchronous sound cartoon. Disney and Iwerks began work on another Mickey short, *Steamboat Willie,* based on Buster Keaton's 1928 silent film *Steamboat Bill, Jr.*

Significance

Steamboat Willie was the first cartoon designed for, and synchronized with, a soundtrack. The short made its screen debut at New York's Colony Theater on November 18, 1928, which is now considered Mickey Mouse's official "birthday." It was booked for a two-week run, appearing before the crime drama *Gang War.* By the end of its run, *Steamboat Willie* had made an enormous impact, astonishing audiences and leaving them wondering how "make-believe" cartoon characters could possibly talk, play instruments, and move to a musical beat.

The success of *Steamboat Willie* made Mickey Mouse into Disney Studios' first major star. Disney even added soundtracks to the first two Mickey cartoons in order to offer exhibitors a package of three shorts. Mickey Mouse quickly became an international personality and the foundation of Disney's commercial and creative enterprises. His popularity enabled Disney to create more animated shorts. A second cartoon series, *Silly Symphonies,* also largely animated by Iwerks, was a success when it debuted in 1929.

Later that same year, Iwerks was approached with the chance to run his own animation studio. Intrigued by the opportunity, he parted ways with Disney. However, his animation studio foundered after a few years, and after a ten-year period working with Columbia and Warner, Iwerks returned to work at Disney Studios. This time, he primarily worked as an inventor and researcher rather than an animator. He created the sophisticated camera tricks in *The Parent Trap* (1961) and made further advancements in combining live-action and animation in *Mary Poppins* (1964). He also worked outside of Disney, winning an Academy Award for his special-effects work on Alfred Hitchcock's *The Birds* (1963).

Further Resources

BOOKS

Canemaker, John. *Walt Disney's Nine Old Men.* New York: Disney Editions, 2001.

Iwerks, Leslie, and John D. Kenworthy. *The Hand Behind the Mouse.* New York: Disney Editions, 2001.

Maltin, Leonard. *Of Mice and Magic: A History of American Animated Cartoons.* New York: New American Library, 1987.

Merritt, Russell, and J.B. Kaufman. *Walt in Wonderland: The Silent Films of Walt Disney.* Baltimore, Md.: Johns Hopkins University Press, 2001.

Mosley, Leonard. *Disney's World.* Chelsea, Mich.: Scarborough House, 1990.

Thomas, Frank, and Ollie Johnston. *Disney Animation: The Illusion of Life.* New York: Abbeville, 1984.

Watts, Steven. *The Magic Kingdom: Walt Disney and the American Way of Life.* New York: Houghton Mifflin, 1997.

PERIODICALS

Tannenbaum, Barbara. "The Obscure History of Mickey Mouse." *Los Angeles Times Magazine,* May 12, 2002, 20–21.

WEBSITES

"The Encyclopedia of Disney Animated Shorts." Teemings. Available online at http://www.teemings.com/shorts/disney /index.html; website home page: http://www.teemings.com (accessed March 7, 2003).

FilmSound.org. Available online at http://www.filmsound.org (accessed January 26, 2003).

Lulu in Hollywood
Memoir

By: Louise Brooks

Date: 1982

Source: Brooks, Louise, *Lulu in Hollywood.* 1982. Reprint, Minneapolis: University of Minnesota, 2000, 104–106.

Actress Louise Brooks in the film *Pandora's Box.* Although best known for this role, Brooks appeared in 24 films from 1925 to 1938. **THE KOBAL COLLECTION. REPRODUCED BY PERMISSION.**

About the Author: Louise Brooks (1906–1985) was born in Cherryvale, Kansas. Brooks aspired to be a dancer but became a silent film star instead. *Pandora's Box* (1928), directed by G.W. Pabst, remains her most famous work. Her short, dark hair became synonymous with the flapper look. Brooks retired from acting in 1938. She appeared in only twenty-five films during her career and lived in seclusion until her death in Rochester, New York. ∎

Introduction

Louise Brooks's father was a lawyer. Her mother, Myra Brooks, was more interested in playing the piano and reading books than attending to maternal duties. Nevertheless, Mrs. Brooks instilled in her daughter a love of the arts and literature, and took her to the Denishawn dance concert that inspired Louise to become a performer. Mrs. Brooks also cut off little Louise's braids, creating what would become her signature hairstyle, then called a "Buster Brown." As a film star Louise Brooks was often known as "The Girl in the Black Helmet."

Brooks first arrived in New York at age fifteen to study dance at the Denishawn School, the leading modern dance troupe at the time. Martha Graham was already a part of Denishawn. The two admired each other and became friends; Louise Brooks later remarked that she had learned to act from watching Martha Graham dance.

After completing several tours with Denishawn during the 1922–1923 season, Brooks appeared as a chorus girl in George White's "Scandals" in 1924. The following year, she sailed with a friend to Europe, and gained employment as a dancer at London's *Cafe de Paris.* Audiences loved her, and she was the first to dance the Charleston in London. Upon her return to the United States, Brooks was hired as a showgirl in the 1925 Ziegfield Follies. She left the Follies to sign a contract with Paramount and appeared in the films *The Street of Forgotten Women* (1925), *The American Venus* (1925), and *Love 'Em and Leave 'Em* (1926). These early works were well-received but unremarkable. Brooks also appeared in *It's the Old Army Game* (1926) with W.C. Fields, whom she had befriended earlier when they both had acts in the Follies.

Significance

Brooks retired from film by the end of the 1930s. After living in upstate New York in seclusion, far from Hollywood and the very public life which characterized her youth, Brooks published her memoirs as *Lulu in Hollywood* in 1982, a collection of essays about her years in the limelight. Her autobiography traces her dreams and foibles along the way to becoming the icon of an era, including valuable vignettes about notable performers, writers, and directors of her time. For instance, she gives an insider's portrait of W.C. Fields, detailing her preference for his stage rather than film perfomances.

Brooks describes her sexual awakening in those early years in New York as she learned to style herself, in fact, into the era's most prominent female sex symbol. While rich "gentlemen" could provide struggling young actresses and dancers with much-needed social mobility, jewels, and fine gowns, Brooks would rather retain her independence. Even if other young stars could exploit these sexual liaisons, Brooks suggests some ambivalence towards her own behavior, although she makes no reference to any specific instances of the extent to which she played the game herself. Her essays also reveal little of her own romantic affairs. The performances she was most famous for may ultimately be the only insight to her allure. Brooks's role in *Pandora's Box* became an artistic opportunity to reflect upon her attitudes toward sexuality and stardom.

Ultimately, her "artistic differences" would turn her into a Hollywood pariah. Brooks left Hollywood the very day the studio completed shooting the silent version of *The Canary Murder Case* (1929). The film was to be turned into a talkie. Brooks refused to do the sound takes and returned to Germany to work with Pabst on another film, *Diary of a Lost Girl* (1929). Afterwards, she worked on a few more films in the United States, but Hollywood was no longer interested in her. As a star of silent films,

Director G.W. Pabst, at work on a movie set in the 1920s. **THE KOBAL COLLECTION. REPRODUCED BY PERMISSION.**

Brooks had little opportunity to actually voice her artistic opinions. Leaving Hollywood, Brooks devoted herself to painting, writing, and studying film, making extensive use of the film archive at the George Eastman House in her town of Rochester, New York.

Primary Source

Lulu in Hollywood [excerpt]

SYNOPSIS: Louise Brooks had demonstrated her fierce independence from her days as a young dancer from Kansas. Although eager to shed her "provincialism" and become more sophisticated, she wanted to create her image only on her own terms. This independent spirit made her an icon of the Jazz Age but also compromised her film career.

It had pleased me on the day I finished the silent version of *The Canary Murder Case* for Paramount to leave Hollywood for Berlin to work for Pabst. When I got back to New York after finishing *Pandora's Box,* Paramount's New York office called to order me to get on the train at once for Hollywood. They were making *The Canary Murder Case* into a talkie and needed me for retakes. When I said I wouldn't go, they sent a man round with a contract. When I still said I wouldn't go, they offered me any amount of money I might ask, to save the great expense of reshooting and dubbing in another voice. In the end, after they were finally convinced that nothing would induce me to do the retakes, I signed a release (gratis) for all my pictures, and they dubbed in Margaret Livingston's voice in *The Canary Murder Case.* But the whole thing—the money that Paramount was forced to "spend," the affront to the studio—made them so angry that they sent out a story, widely publicized and believed, that they had let me go because I was no good in talkies.

In Hollywood, I was a pretty flibbertigibbet whose charm for the executive department decreased with every increase in her fan mail. In Berlin, I stepped onto the station platform to meet Pabst and became an actress. I would be treated by him with a kind of decency and respect unknown to me in Hollywood. It was just as if Pabst had sat in on my whole life and career and knew exactly where I needed assurance and protection. And, just as his understanding of me reached back to his knowledge of a past we did not have to speak about, so it was with the present. For although we were together constantly—on the set, at lunch, often for dinner and the theatre—he seldom spoke to me. Yet he would appear at the dressmaker's at the moment I was about to go into the classic act of ripping off an offensive wedding dress; he would banish a call boy who roared at me through the dressing-room door; he would refuse after the first day's rushes, which secretly upset me, to let me see the rushes ever again. All that I thought and all his reactions seemed to pass between us in a kind of wordless communication. To other people surrounding him, he would talk endlessly in that watchful way of his, smiling, intense; speaking quietly, with his wonderful, hissing precision. But to me he might speak never a word all morning, and then at lunch turn suddenly and say, "Loueess, tomorrow morning you must be ready to do a big fight scene with Kortner," or "This afternoon, in the first scene, you are going to cry." That was how he directed me. With an intelligent actor, he would sit in exhaustive explanation; with an old ham, he would speak the language of the theatre. But in my case, by some magic, he would saturate me with one clear emotion and turn me loose. And it was the same with the plot. Pabst never strained my mind with anything not pertinent to the immediate action. But if I made that picture with only the dimmest notion of what it was about, on my second picture with Pabst, *Diary of a Lost Girl,* I had no idea at all of its plot or meaning till I saw it twenty-seven years later, at Eastman House.

And it was during the making of *Diary of a Lost Girl*—on the last day of shooting, to be exact—that Pabst moved into my future. We were sitting gloomily at a table in the garden of a little café, watching the workmen while they dug the grave for a burial scene, when he decided to let me have it. Several weeks before, in Paris, he had met some friends of mine—rich Americans with whom I spent every hour away from work. And he was angry: first, because he thought they prevented me from staying in Germany, learning the language, and becoming a serious actress, as he wanted; and second, because he looked upon them as spoiled children who would amuse themselves with me for a time and then discard me like an old toy. "Your life is exactly Lulu's," he said, "and you will end the same way."

At that time, knowing so little of what he meant by "Lulu," I just sat sullenly glaring at him, trying not to listen. Fifteen years later, in Hollywood, with all his predictions closing in on me, I heard his words again—hissing back to me. And, listening this time, I packed my trunks and went home to Kansas. But the strangest thing of all in my relationship with Mr. Pabst was the revelation tucked away in a footnote written by Richard Griffith in his book *The Film*

Since Then. He identified me as "Louise Brooks, whom Pabst brought to Germany from Hollywood to play in *Pandora's Box,* whose whole life and career were altered thereby." When I read that, thirty years after I refused to go back to Hollywood to do those retakes on *The Canary Murder Case,* I finally understood why.

Further Resources

BOOKS

Bjork, Angela, and Daniela Turudich. *Vintage Face: Period Looks from the 20s, 30s, 40s, and 50s.* Long Beach, Calif.: Streamline Press, 2001.

Brooks, Louise. *The Fundamentals of Good Ballroom Dancing.* Wichita, Kans.: 1940.

Churchill, Allen. *The Theatrical Twenties.* New York: McGraw-Hill, 1975.

Dijkstra, Bram. *Evil Sisters: The Threat of Female Sexuality in Twentieth-Century Culture.* New York: Henry Holt, 1997.

Higashi, Sumiko. *Virgins, Vamps and Flappers.* St. Albans, Vt.: Eden Press Women's Publications, 1978.

McDowall, Roddy. *Double Exposure.* New York: Delacorte Press, 1966.

Normant, Serge, Ranee Palone Flynn, and Bridget Foley. *Femme Fatale: Famous Beauties Then and Now.* New York: Viking Studio, 2001.

Pabst, G.W. *Pandora's Box (Lulu).* New York: Simon & Schuster, 1971.

Paris, Barry. *Louise Brooks.* New York: Alfred A. Knopf, 1989.

Sherman, Jane. *Denishawn: The Enduring Influence.* Boston: Twayne Publishers, 1983.

WEBSITES

"Louise Brooks: Life & Times." *The Louise Brooks Society.* Available online at http://www.pandorasbox.com/louisebrooks /lifeandtimes.html (accessed July 7, 2002).

Blood Memory

Memoir

By: Martha Graham

Date: 1991

Source: *Blood Memory.* New York: Doubleday, 1991.

About the Author: Martha Graham (1894–1991)—dancer, choreographer, teacher—was born in Allegheny, Pennsylvania, in 1894 and later moved with her family to California. She began her training relatively late; it was after seeing a performance by modern dance pioneer Ruth St. Denis in 1912 that Graham aspired to become a dancer herself. She established the Martha Graham Contemporary Dance School in New York in 1927. Graham retired from dancing in 1969 but kept choreographing. She died at the age of ninety-six. ■

Introduction

Martha Graham's father was a psychiatrist. She always remembered how he had talked to her about how the body's movements indicate inner emotions. In 1916, Graham enrolled in Ruth St. Denis's school, the Denishawn School of Dancing. Denishawn was famous for its highly theatrical productions, lavish costumes, and new forms of movement. At the time, Graham was not considered beautiful: Denishawn's ideal dancer was blonde and blue-eyed. Graham's severe features and dark hair created a striking contrast to her classmates. She quickly distinguished herself with her expressive talents and individuality—as well as what she called her "black Irish temper"—but was rarely chosen to perform in the school's concerts, more often relegated to designing and sewing costumes. However, her dancing had caught the attention of one of her instructors, Ted Shawn—St. Denis's husband—and he finally put Graham in a performance when "Miss Ruth" was sick and unable to dance. From then on, Graham refused to be shut away in the costume shop, declaring that she could be a dancer or a costume designer, but not both. Graham was selected to go on performance tours with Denishawn within the following year.

After leaving Denishawn, she moved to New York City and danced in the Greenwich Village Follies from 1923 to 1925. She sent her earnings to family in California. Unscrupulous dealings by a formerly entrusted family caretaker had devastated the family's resources and left them destitute after the death of Graham's father.

Graham was rebellious, and although she made a good living from her showstopping solo performances at the Follies, she did not feel that the popular revue suited her artistic aspirations. Feeling restless and ambitious, she left to form her own company in 1926 and that same year presented her first professional performance at the 48th Street Theater in New York City.

Significance

After the success of the 1926 concert, Graham went on to develop a reputation for both her performances and her teaching. At a time when the public still clung to nineteenth-century ballet traditions, her work was often criticized and lampooned by other performers, from Fanny Brice (Graham's dance "Revolt" was reinvented as "Rewolt") to Danny Kaye (he created a mock dance troupe called "The Graham Crackers"), but never ignored. Graham herself was far from humorless, however, and in *Blood Memory* she acknowledges and even applauds Fanny Brice's comedic Graham imitations. Graham also enjoyed a stint as mystery celebrity radio announcer "Miss Hush," so named for her husky voice.

Dancer and choreographer Martha Graham as she appeared in her first concert, "A Study in Lacquer," April 18, 1926. COURTESY GEORGE EASTMAN HOUSE. REPRODUCED BY PERMISSION.

Graham had often struggled to make ends meet. But with the help of friends and benefactors, and through sheer determination, she kept her dance company touring the world and her school full of students. She taught well into her later years, working with students of all levels as well as with performers such as Gregory Peck, Madonna, Kathleen Turner, Liza Minnelli, and Woody Allen. Graham crossed paths with many famous artists including Man Ray, Alfred Stieglitz, and Alexander Calder. Isamu Noguchi designed many of Graham's costumes and stage sets. Imogen Cunningham created dramatic photographic figure studies of her. *Appalachian Spring,* with its score by Aaron Copland, was created by the exchange of innumerable letters between Graham and the American composer, while they lived on opposite coasts.

In 1932, Graham received her first Guggenheim Fellowship and used the award to travel to Mexico. She received a second Guggenheim in 1950. Her works often addressed the social issues of her time, from the Great Depression to World War II (1939–1945). She was awarded the Presidential Medal of Freedom in 1976.

Primary Source

Blood Memory [excerpt]

> **SYNOPSIS:** Martha Graham died shortly after the publication of her autobiography, *Blood Memory*. The following passage recounts her determination to present her own unique work and presents the circumstances of her inaugural public performance.

At this time, I could not afford to buy books but would always go to the Gotham Book Mart on West Forty-seventh Street, which was owned by Frances Steloff. She had been a little Jewish immigrant girl from Russia, who was so poor in Saratoga Springs she sold flowers to make money. She just loved books and had this great respect for knowledge. She used to give me books to take home because I couldn't afford them. She had a blond cat that wandered everyplace, all over the tables and the piles of books.

Frances was very generous with the writers and other artists of the time. No one had much money then. I remember once when Edmund Wilson came into the shop. He said, "Frances, I need to cash a check."

Frances said, "Now Edmund, don't bother me, I'm busy. Just go to the cash register and take what you need and leave a little piece of paper saying how much it is."

I was so impressed by this I almost fainted dead away. He went to the cash register, took what he needed, and left.

During one particularly hectic Christmas I assisted Frances in the store. A sailor came in and I helped him find a book he was searching for. When Frances put me on the cash register I did something wrong to ruin the roll of tape that wound around it. The customers began to line up at the front desk until Frances came to my rescue. I would also help her wrap books, because at this time they were not put in bags but were wrapped with paper and twine.

Frances believed in me and without ever having seen me dance signed a loan for one thousand dollars for my first concert. I was a nobody, but I was given one chance to prove myself. I wanted to gamble on being judged on Broadway, and not perform in my studio just for friends. I went to Mr. Green, of the *Greenwich Village Follies,* and asked if I could have his theater for one night, just to show what I could do. He said, "Yes, you can. If you fail, you will go back into the *Follies* for one year." We could use his theatre on a Sunday, but the show had to be billed as a sacred concert because of the blue laws forbidding dance performances.

That first concert was held at the 48th Street Theatre on April 18, 1926. I danced solos to the music of Schumann, Debussy, Ravel, and others. Louis Horst was my accompanist. With my trio of girls from Rochester, we danced "Chorale" to the music of Cesar Franck and "Clair de lune" to the music of Claude Debussy. I did many dances, and everything I did was influenced by Denishawn. There was an audience. They came because I was such a curiosity—a woman who could do her own work. Although there was a snowstorm that night, at the second intermission Mr. Green came backstage and said, "You made it." I didn't have to return. My path was clear.

■ ■ ■

One woman, a friend of Miss Ruth's who had seen me dance at Denishawn, came backstage after my first solo performance. She was dressed as a woman of the late nineteenth century. She wore a many-layered, cluttered dress, a fur hat with feathers on it, great beads and all. She said, "Martha, this is simply dreadful. How long do you expect to keep this up?"

I said, "As long as I've got an audience."

That's been my criterion. Sometimes the audiences have been very small, but they have sustained me. The response of Miss Ruth's friend was typical. To many people, I was a heretic. A heretic is a woman who is put upon in all she does, a woman who is frightened. Everyplace she goes she goes against the heavy beat and footsteps of those she opposes. Maybe she is a heretic in a religious way, maybe in a social way. I felt at the time that I was a heretic. I was outside the realm of women. I did not dance the way that people danced. I had what I called a contraction and a release. I used the floor. I used the flexed foot. I showed effort. My foot was bare. In many ways I showed onstage what most people came to the theatre to avoid.

Three years later I created a dance called *Heretic.* I decided that morning that the costumes were wrong. I went down to the Lower East Side, to Delancey Street to my favorite fabric shop, and bought wool jersey for eighteen cents a yard. I went back to the studio, we made our costumes, and by evening we were ready. Onstage I danced the woman in white, while the others in my company were dressed in black. They became a wall of defiance that I could not break. The music, an old Breton song, would stop, and the women in black formed another group. I was the heretic desperately trying to force myself free of the darkness of my oppressors.

I had made up my mind that I was going to rely on the audience, on the people who bought tickets, not just on those whom I had invited and who wanted me to succeed. Some people did not. They thought I was extremely ugly and that I did some dreadful things.

I remember years later my mother said to me, "Martha, I don't see why you have to present such dreadful women on the stage. You're really rather sweet when you're at home."

I'd rather an audience like me than dislike me, but I'd rather they disliked me than be apathetic, because that is the kiss of death. I know because I have had both. . . .

Further Resources

BOOKS

Bird, Dorothy, and Joyce Greenberg. *Bird's Eye View: Dancing With Martha Graham and on Broadway.* Pittsburgh: University of Pittsburgh Press, 1997.

de Mille, Agnes. *Martha: The Life and Work of Martha Graham.* New York: Vintage Books, 1992.

Freedman, Russell. *Martha Graham: A Dancer's Life.* New York: Clarion Books, 1998.

Graham, Martha. *The Notebooks of Martha Graham.* New York: Harcourt Brace Jovanovich, 1973.

Mazo, Joseph H. *Prime Movers: The Makers of Modern Dance in America.* New York: Morrow, 1977.

Pratt, Paula Bryan. *The Importance of Martha Graham.* San Diego, Calif.: Lucent Books, 1995.

2

BUSINESS AND THE ECONOMY

MICHAEL R. FEIN

Entries are arranged in chronological order by date of primary source. For entries with one primary source, the entry title is the same as the primary source title. Entries with more than one primary source have an overall entry title, followed by the titles of the primary sources.

Important Events in Business and the Economy, 1920–1929

1920

- Agricultural economists expect U.S. food prices to fall 72 percent. European farmers resume production after World War I, leaving U.S. farmers little opportunity to export surplus to Europe.

- In January, 10 percent of U.S. women worked outside the home.

- From January to May, the Federal Reserve Board raised interest rates from 4 to 7 percent to contract the money supply and thus counteract the threat of inflation.

- On January 2, U.S. Attorney General A. Mitchell Palmer accuses the Industrial Workers of the World (IWW) of plotting to strike the railroads.

- On January 5, the Radio Corporation of America is founded with $20 million capital.

- On January 16, Prohibition begins; America goes dry.

- On February 28, Congress passes the Esch-Cummins Act, restoring railroads to private ownership and establishing the Railroad Labor Board.

- On June 2, Congress passes the Merchant Marine Act to stimulate U.S. shipping.

- On July 1, U.S. workers strike as railroads cut wages 10 to 20 percent and as the Railway Labor Board approves cuts of 12 percent.

- On September 8, U.S. transcontinental airmail service begins with a flight from New York to San Francisco.

- On November 2, radio station KDKA begins regular broadcasting from Pittsburgh, Pennsylvania.

- On December 10, Pitney-Bowes introduces the postage meter.

- On December 19, the U.S. Supreme Court in *Traux* v. *Carrigan* declares the Arizona picketing law unconstitutional.

- On December 28, Amalgamated Clothing Workers begins a six-month strike against clothing "sweatshops."

1921

- The Ford Motor Company announces a schedule to produce one million vehicles each year.

- The Women's Bureau, a division of the Labor Department, reports that eight million females are in the labor force, 80 percent of them in clerical work.

- GM's market share rises to 12 percent under the leadership of Alfred P. Sloan.

- Food surplus erodes prices to 85 percent of the levels of 1919; cotton falls to eleven cents per pound, down from forty-two cents.

- On January 1, Ford Motor Company controlled 55 percent of the U.S. auto market.

- On January 3, the U.S. Supreme Court rules that trade unions are subject to antitrust prosecution under the Sherman Anti-Trust Act, despite the fact that the Clayton Act had exempted unions.

- On March 10, the first White Castle hamburger outlet opens in Wichita, Kansas.

- On April 14, Congress tries to relieve farm distress by enacting a tariff on imported food in hopes of protecting U.S. farmers from foreign competition.

- On May 10, Ford Motor Company announces assets of more than $345 million.

- On June 25, Samuel Gompers is elected head of the American Federation of Labor for the fortieth time.

- In July, William Crapo Durant, formerly of General Motors, founds Durant Motors to produce the Durant 4, selling at $850.

- On September 26, Secretary of Commerce Herbert Hoover announces a plan to ease unemployment from the 1920–1921 recession.

- In November, Congress cut taxes on the wealthiest Americans from 65 to 50 percent of their income.

- In December, U.S. Treasury bonds paid 4.8 percent interest. By April 1922 interest would drop to 3.2 percent.

- On December 31, the Census Bureau estimates that the United States has 387,000 miles of surfaced roads, up from 190,476 in 1909.

1922

- Wills Sainte Claire announces the development of a new automobile to compete in the Stutz-Duesenberg market.

- Durant Motors introduces its Stor, priced at $348 to compete with the Model T. Ford cuts its Model T prices to retaliate.

- In February, Standard Oil announces an eight-hour day for oil-field workers.

- In February, six hundred thousand coal miners begin a four-month strike to protest pay cuts.

- On February 2, the Amoskeag Textile Mill in Manchester, New Hampshire, announces a wage cut of 20 percent and an increase in hours from forty-eight to fifty-two per week.

- On February 9, Congress creates a War Foreign Debt Commission to negotiate the terms under which Britain and France will repay U.S. loans.

- On July 1, the U.S. Railroad Labor Board announces a 13 percent wage cut for four hundred thousand workers.

In July, four hundred thousand railroad workers throughout the U.S. went on strike to protest wage cuts.

- On September 1, U.S. Attorney General Harry Daugherty ordered the four hundred thousand railroad strikers back to work or face arrest for defying his order.

- On September 18, railway shopmen abandon their two-month strike.

- On September 19, Congress passes the Fordney-McCumber Tariff Act, raising tariffs to the levels of the 1909 Payne-Aldrich Act to protect U.S. businesses from foreign imports.

- In October, Ford Motor Company acquires the Lincoln Company for $12 million.

1923

- GM puts its Chevrolet Division under the direction of William S. Knudsen, formerly of Ford, in an effort to make Chevrolet more competitive with Ford.

- Cotton prices drop to eleven cents per pound on U.S. markets.

- The U.S. Department of Commerce projects that over the next six years corporate profits will increase by 62 percent, dividends by 65 percent, and wages by 11 percent.

- PanAmerican Airways announces that it will buy nine navy flying boats to use in the New York City air-taxi service it is founding.

- Hudson Motors introduces a closed sedan selling for little more than its open model.

- On March 4, Congress enacts the Agricultural Credits Act, to loan farmers money.

- On May 4, the U.S. Supreme Court invalidates minimum-wage laws in *Adkins* v. *Children's Hospital.*

- From June to September, wholesale prices fall 5 percent, evidence that consumers are not spending money.

- On August 2, U.S. Steel reduces its standard twelve-hour workday to eight hours; the eight-hour day will allow the corporation to hire seven thousand additional workers.

- In October, Zenith Radio is founded in Chicago.

- In November, Congress cuts taxes on the wealthiest Americans from 50 to 40 percent.

- In December, the Federal Reserve Board buys $510 million in U.S. Treasury bonds, in hopes of raising interest on bonds and thereby making them attractive to investors.

- In December, union membership is 3.6 million, down from more than 5 million three years earlier.

1924

- Investors trade 2.2 million shares of stocks and bonds, the highest number to that date.

- The Central Railroad of New Jersey unveils the first U.S. diesel-electric locomotive.

- GM's Oakland becomes the first U.S. auto to be painted with Du Pont Duco paint, which cuts days off the time required to paint cars.

- Continental Baking Company is founded in Chicago, consolidating more than one hundred bakeries to become the largest baking chain in the United States.

- Southern Railway introduces the Crescent Limited that will run between New York and New Orleans; it has both a five-dollar premium fare and a regular fare.

- Union Carbide and Carbon Company introduces Prestone, an auto antifreeze that costs five dollars per gallon.

- On January 1, A&P operates 11,913 stores.

- On January 1, Ford has ten thousand U.S. dealerships.

- On January 1, 2.5 million Americans own a radio compared to 2,000 in 1920.

- On February 14, Thomas J. Watson changes the name of his company to International Business Machines (IBM).

- From April to July, the Mayflower (Washington, D.C.), the Parker House (Boston), the Palmer House (Chicago), the Peabody (Memphis), the Boca Raton (Palm Beach), The Breakers (Palm Beach), and the Miami Biltmore (Coral Gables) open as luxury hotels.

- On April 1, Dillon, Read and Company acquires Dodge Motor Company for $146 million, the largest automobile-industry transaction to date.

- In June, the new Chrysler Corporation announces it will sell a new car for fifteen hundred dollars.

1925

- As cities and suburbs grow upward and outward, Americans spend more than $6 billion on building and construction.

- To fulfill a contract for transporting airmail from San Francisco to Chicago, William Boeing produces the 40A, the first plane capable of flying over the Sierra Nevada and Rocky Mountains with twelve hundred pounds of mail.

- On January 17, President Calvin Coolidge says, in an address to the Society of American Newspaper Editors, "The business of America is business."

- On February 2, the Kelly Air Mail Act authorizes the U.S. Postal Department to contract for airmail carriage; rates are high enough to attract air carriers.

- In March, Walter P. Chrysler produces the first Chrysler automobile.

- On December 2, Gimbel Brothers acquires Philadelphia's Kaufmann & Bauer store.

- On December 8, President Calvin Coolidge tells Congress that he opposes cancellation of British and French war debts.

1926

- The Santa Fe *Super Chief* begins service from Chicago to Los Angeles in fifty-eight hours.

- J. C. Penney Company opens its five hundredth store; it will soon reach 1,495 outlets.

- An automobile census shows that 72 percent of autos are closed models; in 1916 only 2 percent had been.

- Sears, Roebuck distributes fifteen million catalogues and twenty-three million special announcements per year.

- On February 26, President Coolidge signs legislation reducing federal income and inheritance taxes, a policy that benefits the wealthy who stand to inherit fortunes rather than the poor who inherit nothing.

- In April, Greyhound Corporation begins service with GM as its major stockholder.

- On May 5, the United States and France agree on a schedule of debt repayment to the U.S. Treasury.

- On May 20, Western Air Express begins service; it will later become Trans-World Airlines (TWA).

- In June, Ford Motor Company takes over production of the Lincoln, adding a high-priced car to the Ford line.

- On July 6, a survey shows that one of six Americans owns an automobile.

- On September 19, a hurricane strikes Florida, damaging thousands of homes. Newspaper reports of the damage frighten away investors, and the speculative bubble in Florida real estate bursts.

- In November, Congress cuts taxes on the wealthiest Americans from 40 to 20 percent. Since November 1921 the wealthiest Americans have seen their taxes decline more than threefold, from 65 to 20 percent.

- In December, U.S. auto production reaches four million per year, up nearly eightfold from 1919.

1927

- The Franklin automobile, which has an air-cooled engine, is introduced.

- The New York Central Railroad refurbishes the *Twentieth Century Limited* with a new Hudson locomotive; archrival Pennsylvania Railroad upgrades its *Broadway Limited.*

- In February, Boston's Statler Hotel opens with 1,150 rooms.

- On February 1, the Royal Hawaiian Hotel opens in Honolulu.

- In April, Washington's Hay-Adams Hotel opens on Lafayette Square.

- On April 7, television is introduced in a U.S. demonstration, but investors are wary.

- In May, David Sarnoff's RCA splits into two networks (the Red and the Blue) to bring about more efficient management.

- In May, Chrysler introduces the Plymouth and will soon introduce the DeSoto, a midpriced car.

- On May 25, President Calvin Coolidge signs a law to regulate radio broadcasting.

- On September 5, Ford Motor Company announces that some employees will work a forty-hour week at the same pay they received for longer hours.

- In October, New Jersey's Newark Airport opens to relieve traffic to and from New York.

- On October 19, Juan Trippe of Pan American Airways announces airmail service to and from Cuba.

- In November, Ford unveils the Model A, announced on May 25, 1927, to worldwide publicity.

- In December, GM announces a $2.60-per-share dividend totaling $65 million, the largest dividend in American history.

1928

- NBC broadcasts the Will Rogers program nationwide to an audience of millions.

- A. P. Giannini founds the TransAmerica Corporation.

- New York Central Railroad earns $10 million as business travel soars.

- Stearns-Knight introduces an automobile to compete at the high-price level.

- David Gerber introduces improved baby foods to be sold through grocery stores.

- Ford brings out its popular wood-sided station wagon.

- Walter P. Chrysler announces plans for a seventy-seven-floor office building in Manhattan.

- Marmon, a producer of expensive cars, introduces the Roosevelt to compete in the medium-price market.

- Gruman Aircraft opens a plant on Long Island, New York.

- On January 7, President Calvin Coolidge assures Americans that the economy is robust. Investors respond by buying stocks, spurring a Wall Street boom.

- In May, *Time* magazine inaugurates an aeronautics department to cover the airline industry.

- On May 27, Congress passes the Jones-White Act, subsidizing U.S. shipping in hopes of encouraging U.S. exports.

- In June, Stutz, which had produced the legendary Bear Cat, declares bankruptcy.

- On July 30, George Eastman of Kodak introduces color motion pictures.

- In August, President Calvin Coolidge vetoes a farm subsidy plan, calling it a "price fixing scheme."

- In September, Republican presidential candidate Herbert Hoover declares that the end of poverty is in sight.

- In November, Chrysler acquires Dodge Brothers and becomes one of the "big three," alongside Ford and General Motors.

- In November, Macy's department store, hoping to entice Christmas shoppers, announces it has increased its sales staff to 12,500 and enlarged its floor space to 1.5 million square feet.

1929

- Press reports estimate Henry Ford's income at $14 million.

- GM completes a Detroit office building that dominates the city and a New York office estimated to cost $60 million.

- Commercial airlines fly thirty million miles and carry 180,000 passengers.

- Electric refrigerator sales reach eight hundred thousand, up from seventy-five thousand in 1925.

- Curtiss-Wright is created by the merger of two pioneer aircraft builders.

- On January 1, the U.S. auto industry accounts for 13 percent of the value of all manufactured goods.

- On January 1, seventy-one percent of U.S. families have incomes below twenty-five hundred dollars; the average weekly wage is twenty-eight dollars.

- On January 12, James J. Hill, president of the Great Northern Railroad, dedicates the new eight-mile-long Cascade Tunnel.

- On February 23, the Brotherhood of Sleeping Car Porters, headed by A. Philip Randolph, becomes the first African American union to affiliate with the American Federation of Labor.

- On March 17, GM announces plans to acquire the German auto firm Opel.

- On July 7, Transcontinental Air Transport announces a plan to offer coast-to-coast service using air carriers over flatlands and rail carriers in the mountains.

- In August, farm laborers earn $2.30 a day, the same as their pay, adjusted for inflation, in 1914.

- On September 11, the Fokker F32, the world's longest passenger plane, is unveiled.

- From October to December, unemployment rose from five hundred thousand to more than 4 million.

- On October 24, Black Thursday, the New York Stock Exchange lost more than $20 million, its worst single-day losses to date.

- From October 24 to November 30 the New York Stock Exchange lost some $26 billion.

- On October 29, Black Tuesday, the New York Stock Exchange loses $14 million.

- On December 31, President Herbert Hoover declares that the economy is sound.

mary source collection, Library of Congress. Available online at http://memory.loc.gov/ammem/award97/codhtml /hawphome.html; website home page: http://memory.loc.gov (accessed February 14, 2003).

About the Photographer: Harry Mellon Rhoads (1880 or 1881–1975) was born in Unionville, Pennsylvania, and attended school in Denver, Colorado. He remained there, working as a newspaper photographer for the *Denver Republican* and the *Rocky Mountain News.* Rhoads's thousands of photographs leave a record both of his times (he retired in 1969), and of his often humorous perspective on them.

Women in the Office

"Heap of Papers" and "Three Women at Desk"

Photographs

By: Harry Mellon Rhoads
Date: ca. 1920–1930
Source: Rhoads, Harry Mellon. "Three Women at Desk" and "Heap of Papers." ca. 1920–1930. *History of the American West, 1860–1920: Photographs from the Collection of the Denver Public Library.* American Memory digital pri-

"Washington School for Secretaries"

Photograph

By: Theodor Horydczak
Date: ca. 1920–1950
Source: Horydczak, Theodor. "Washington School for Secretaries." ca. 1920. *Washington as It Was: Photographs of Theodor Horydczak.* American Memory digital primary source collection, Library of Congress. Available online at http://memory.loc.gov/ammem/thchtml/thhome.html; website home page: http://memory.loc.gov/ (accessed February 14, 2003).

Primary Source

"Heap of Papers"
SYNOPSIS: Harry Rhoads's flip image of a woman buried beneath a heap of papers, high heels kicked in the air, perpetuates the demeaning stereotype of the "sexy secretary" common in the 1920s. DENVER PUBLIC LIBRARY, WESTERN HISTORY COLLECTION, HARRY M. RHOADS, RH-1429. REPRODUCED BY PERMISSION.

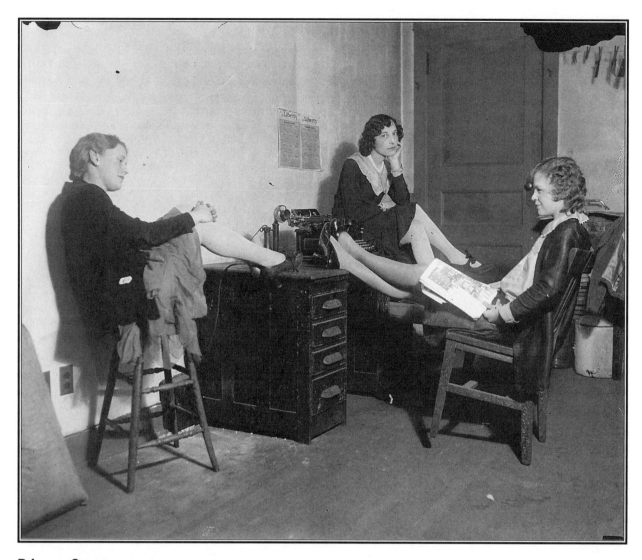

Primary Source

"Three Women at Desk"

SYNOPSIS: Harry Rhoads's photo of women at a desk captures them among new workplace technologies such as the telephone and typewriter. DENVER PUBLIC LIBRARY, WESTERN HISTORY COLLECTION, HARRY M. RHOADS, RH-1828. REPRODUCED BY PERMISSION.

About the Photographer: Though the details of the life of Theodor Horydczak (c. 1890–1971) are in doubt, he is believed to have been born in Eastern Europe and to have served as a photographer in the U.S. Army Signal Corps during World War I. From 1921 until 1959 he captured scenes from daily life out of his studio in Washington, D.C.

"The Girl on the Job"

Newspaper article

By: Jessie Roberts

Date: 1922

Source: Roberts, Jessie. "The Girl on the Job: Clerical Work." *The Union* 17, no. 44, 1922, 2. Reproduced in "The African-American Experience in Ohio, 1850–1920." Ohio

Historical Society. Available online at http://dbs.ohiohistory.org/africanam/det.cfm?ID=1751; website home page http://www.ohiohistory.org/index.html (accessed February 14, 2003).

About the Author: Jessie Roberts wrote for the Cincinnati, Ohio-based *Union,* an African-American newspaper owned and edited by Wendell Phillips Dabney. Renowned for its journalistic integrity, the *Union* reached both black and white readers. ■

Introduction

In the half century prior to 1930, the gender composition of the American office workforce shifted dramatically. Whereas in the nineteenth-century clerical work had been an almost exclusively male profession, by the end of the 1920s most office workers were women. Women dominated the fields of typing and stenography;

Primary Source

"Washington School for Secretaries"

SYNOPSIS: Theodor Horydczak's photo depicts the new ranks of women typists being readied for the corporate world at a Washington secretarial school. THEODOR HORYDCZAK COLLECTION (LIBRARY OF CONGRESS).

by 1930 they accounted for half of the nation's book-keepers, accountants, and cashiers.

The most significant factor accounting for these new opportunities for women was the rapid expansion of big business—and its corporate hierarchies—during this period. As firms organized on regional and national scales, they relied on legions of clerical workers in their effort to function in ever larger markets. Since women were traditionally paid between forty and sixty percent of men's salaries, they provided a cheap labor pool from which to draw. Women's dominance in clerical work was also pegged to the popularization of the typewriter. Since this technology was a new one, it had never been "man's work," and was thus unconstrained by the older, gendered workplace traditions.

Scientific management methods permeated American business thought during the early twentieth century, and it was not long before proponents of rational organization sought to apply it to the office. As had been the case in industrial work, as offices expanded, they established extensive hierarchies that positioned de-skilled clerical workers at the bottom and well-paid managers at the top. But unlike factory work, office work was rapidly

dividing along gender lines. Whereas nineteenth-century male clerks had considered themselves "apprentice capitalists," the ladder of advancement had been cut off for the female office workers of the early twentieth century.

Significance

By the 1920s, much of American business had been reorganized in such a way that allowed women into the workplace in great numbers. As Jessie Roberts's article 1922 article in *The Union* mentions, more and more women were working in clerical positions in banks and railroad offices. But despite the male bank official's comment in the article regarding the future possibility of women bank presidents, women office workers were generally seen as working-class operatives rather than potential managers. Theodor Horydczak's photograph of a secretatarial school class documents how women came to dominate the clerical world.

Drawing on widely held assumptions about gender roles, women were incorporated into "rational" work hierarchies that re-created the domestic patriarchal order inside the office space. Even in this era of the "New Woman," the managerial class justified the degradation of women's clerical work in countless ways. Women, it was asserted, were temperamental, and they worked for "pin money" or took jobs only as a way station on the road to marriage. As Harry Rhoads's photos of attractive, high-heeled secretaries suggest, the gender hierarchies of workplace power were also reinforced by the sexualization of women in the office.

Under these assumptions, literate men were pulled into management, while high-school-educated women entered the firm at the lower ranks. Once this gender divide had been established, traditional gender roles, which subordinated women in domestic life, could be exploited to ease labor-management relations.

Women might rise within the firm hierarchy to supervise a typing pool or serve as a private secretary. But these advanced positions only stabilized the larger business structure—since women were unlikely to aspire to management, they served as a buffer between managers and workers, taking orders while presenting no threat to ambitious male managers.

Primary Source

"The Girl on the Job"

> **SYNOPSIS:** In Jessie Roberts's 1922 article, she optimistically describes the new work opportunities available to women.

Clerical Work

During the war women went into railroad work in large numbers, and took over jobs that were unsuited to them, because the need was there to be filled. Since peace has come they have left these positions. But many women are still working for the railroads in clerical positions and they are liked for the work. The salaries are good, and the treatment of the women is said to be excellent. Where these are required the railroads have provided rest and lunch rooms, and there are matrons whose business it is to see that the women are comfortably situated and cared for.

In the banks, too, women are going more and more into clerical work. They are working as cashiers and assistant cashiers, and in the branches for women customers they hold jobs as paying tellers and adjustors. The work is agreeable to women who have a sound training in book-keeping, the associations are pleasant, and there will be more opportunities for advancement as the strangeness of having women work in banks wears off. In many banks with a large woman clientele a woman is employed to advise these clients in regard to investments. This is a position of trust and importance.

One high official of a large bank that employs many women in various positions said that he found them efficient, trustworthy and capable.

"I don't know whether we shall ever have many women as presidents of banks, but I don't see why we shouldn't," he remarked. "After all, it's up to the women."

Further Resources

BOOKS

Chafe, William H. *The American Woman: Her Changing Social, Economic, and Political Roles, 1920–1970.* New York: Oxford University Press, 1972.

Davies, Margery W. *Woman's Place is at the Typewriter: Office Work and Office Workers, 1870–1930.* Philadelphia: Temple University Press, 1982.

PERIODICALS

Rotella, Elyce J. "The Transformation of the American Office: Changes in Employment and Technology." *Journal of Economic History* 41, March 1981, 51–57.

WEBSITES

"Who Won the Debate over the Equal Rights Amendment in the 1920s?" Women and Social Movements in the United States. Available online at http://womhist.binghamton.edu /era/intro.htm; website home page http://womhist.binghamton.edu/index.html (accessed February 25, 2003).

"The Negro Working Woman"
Essay

By: Mary Louise Williams

Date: 1923

Source: Williams, Mary Louise. "The Negro Working Woman: What She Faces in Making a Living." *The Messenger,* 5, July 1923, 763. Reprinted in Foner, Philip S., and Ronald L. Lewis. *Black Workers: A Documentary History from Colonial Times to the Present.* Philadelphia: Temple University Press, 1989, 389–391.

About the Author: Little is known about Mary Louise Williams except what she reveals about herself in the excerpt below. An educated, light-skinned, African American woman, she was probably born in upstate New York in the late 1890s. Williams traveled throughout the urban North, writing about her experiences with work and racism. *The Messenger,* the journal in which Williams's essay appeared, was founded by the socialist and African American labor activist A. Philip Randolph. Published in Harlem from 1917 to 1928, and directed at a African American audience, it had a radical, socialist bent. ∎

Introduction

Literacy rates rose steadily in the early twentieth century as access to public schools increased. Women tended to get more schooling than men, who were often pulled into the workforce at an earlier age. But as a whole, the chances that a young person would attend high school increased from one in ten in 1900 to one in two in 1930. Race had little effect on literacy rates in the urban North; by 1930, African American women were as literate as their white counterparts.

Better education helped many white women find better-paying jobs, and, indeed, white women entered factory, clerical, and sales work in record numbers during the 1920s. But racism kept educated African American women from enjoying the benefits of their education to the same degree. They found that despite their personal qualifications, they were shuttled into menial tasks, primarily domestic service, where the white mistress-African American servant roles resonant of American slavery could be re-created.

When African American women did manage to gain access to more remunerative work, they still faced discriminatory hurdles. In industrial work, segregation kept African American women from gaining union membership and thus denied them the benefits for which white unions fought: higher wages, better working conditions, and seniority privileges. In clerical work, which for whites had been thoroughly feminized by the 1920s, racial prejudices ensured that African American men outnumbered African American women four to one. In retail work, African American women were restricted from coming into contact with white customers, and thus relegated to behind-the-scenes work. Montgomery Ward, a mail-order house, employed the largest number of African American women clerks in the 1920s precisely because these women would not directly encounter white consumers. And in sales and other service industries, African American and white employees were segregated within the workplace, often eating in separate (and unequal) facilities.

Significance

As Mary Louise Williams's essay reveals, in the 1920s, educational training mattered less to prospective employers than the shade of one's skin. As a light-skinned African American, Williams secured a position in a department store. The "question of color" never arose, but she was summarily dismissed when a coworker met her mother (who had darker skin than her daughter) and called attention to her racial identity. Later, when applying for a position in another store, she found that the only job for which an educated African American woman could apply was as a bootblack. The manager sought a high-school graduate not because of her skills, but to ensure that she was not an "objectionable Negro." Ultimately he refused to offer Williams the menial job because she looked too white.

Williams seemed to defy racial categorization, making it especially difficult for her to find work in a society that operated under strict racial coding. She found little comfort in her ability to "pass" for white; for her, sidestepping racial prejudice meant stepping outside the currents of African American women's history. She also was ambivalent about the potential for racial uplift. The large African American community in Cleveland, where she lived for several years, supported a wide range of African American-operated businesses. And advocacy organizations, like the National Association for the Advancement of Colored People and the Phillis Wheatley Home (misspelled as "Phyllis Wheaty" in Williams's essay) for working girls, provided important job-placement services. But this was not enough. Broad-based racial discrimination continued to set tight limits on the opportunities for African American women to enjoy the benefits of their education.

Primary Source

"The Negro Working Woman"

> **SYNOPSIS:** In this essay, Mary Louise Williams describes her experience in the world of work. After being fired from a New York department store when it was discovered that she was African American, Williams began a work odyssey which took her first to the factory (where segregated unions kept her from advancement) and then to Cleveland, Ohio. World War I offered her the chance to take on work befitting her education, but she lost that job to the returning veteran. In the end, Williams returned to New York where she worked as a door-to-door magazine saleswoman. While this work allowed her to leave behind the institutional segregation of her earlier jobs, she faced racial prejudice on a much more intimate level, having doors slammed in her face one day, being mistaken for a prostitute the next.

My working career started a few years back in a small city in New York State, with a high school education. After graduation, being filled with the enthusiasm of youth, I naturally turned my thoughts to "something different."

I applied to several offices for employment, seeking even as inferior a position as addressing envelopes. At every place I met with disappointment. None felt they could use colored help in that capacity.

By this time I felt somewhat like a peacock who had looked at his feet. Now, I worked around at odd jobs and housework until one day I received a surprise.

Through the kind intercession of the Vice-President of a manufactory I was given an opportunity in its perfume department. I was to act as forelady and stock clerk. I made good. The management, being so well pleased, doubled my salary after a year's service. No question of color ever arose. In the course of a few more months I was walking home

Students of the National Training School for Women and Girls in Washington, DC, pose for a group photo. Vocational education, such as clerical and domestic training was emphasized, though many classical education subjects were also taught. THE LIBRARY OF CONGRESS.

with a co-worker and met my mother. Naturally I was proud of her and wanted my friends to meet her. At the corner, as had been our habit, we separated. Next morning I was summoned to the office. You can imagine my surprise upon finding my services were no longer needed. Mr. Vice-President softened it as best he could: "There is no fault with your work, but the girls will not work with a Negro. We would gladly keep you if we could, but it is better to lose one girl than to lose twenty."

On another occasion I answered an advertisement in the paper worded thus: "Wanted: a young colored girl, high school graduate preferred. Apply Dey's Department Store." I dressed with care expecting to find at least a saleslady's opening. Just picture for yourself my chagrin upon learning they desired a bootblack in the ladies' rest room! The reason they wanted an educated girl was to keep their wealthy customers from coming in contact with objectionable Negroes. I had no chance to refuse the job because Mr. T. said I looked too much like a Caucasian and he could not use me. He finally hired a high school graduate who had trained two years for a teacher. Is it not a pity that a colored girl must be educated to qualify as a bootblack?

Finding no real openings for me in the clerical line, I turned my attention to shop work. I did this for three reasons. First, it gave me more time for myself than housework. Second, I received a more liberal reward per hour for my services. Third, it placed me on a more equal basis with the other workers although I needed no education other than to read and write. At this work I made just enough money to make both ends meet and sometimes I had to stretch pretty hard to do so, especially when we had a holiday. Naturally I received a little less pay than the white workers. The difference in pay was due possibly to the open shop. In this city there is no colored garment workers' union and the white unions do take the Negro in. In the shops the Negro has no chance of advancement.

I heard so much about Cleveland. I went there and found conditions more favorable, due probably to the fact that the Negro himself was more enterprising. Here I found a Negro Vaudeville employing all Negro help. There were also colored doctors, lawyers, clubs, hotels, rooming houses, ice cream parlors, drug stores, and restaurants. These were all using colored help. The Phyllis Wheatly Home and the National Association for the Advancement of Colored People took an active part in placing girls in suitable positions. Still there were many girls uncared for.

I happened to be one of these and took a job to wash glasses and silver in a white hotel. I found hotel conditions here very much as they were at home. Though we ate the same food as the whites, we ate at the dishwashers' table, men and women eating together. Here I worked nine hours a day for forty dollars a month. Out of this paid carfare twice a day, for one meal a day, four dollars a week for a room, and one dollar for laundry. This left me very little for the pleasures of life. I was about discouraged when the assistant steward was taken up in the draft. After this the head steward had quite a job to keep this place filled. So I braved the lion in his den and the result was I became the assistant. It was really a man's job. I had to take care of the storeroom and coolers also to keep track of the cost of keeping up the various parts of the hotel. I probably would be there yet only peace was declared and with it came the return of the former assistant steward. This position afforded me so many luxuries of life that it showed me what a joy work would be to the Negro woman if given a position and salary instead of a job and wages.

Being a little homesick I returned. Somehow I expected to see conditions changed. With the exception of a few elevator operators, girls to dust china and furniture, two or three girls to rearrange stock behind white salesladies, and a few more women working in shops, I found no change. Oh, yes, I found three women working as salesladies, but as these were "passing" they mean less than nothing in the history of the Negro Woman.

Not being able to find anything that pleased me I turned my attention to canvassing. Even now I feel a loathing for this work. If I called at the front door I was directed to the rear. In many instances the door was shut in my face before I could make my errand known. Others treated me well, but that expression of incredulity upon seeing a Negro agent spoke louder than words. Some business men would give me an audience, sometimes with an order. Others received me with so much attention I felt they thought my magazines were only a camouflage.

And since there is a general tendency to expand the field of her operations, manual and mental, let us say with Longfellow:

Out of the shadow of night
The world moves into light,
It is daybreak everywhere!

Further Resources

BOOKS

Jones, Jacqueline. *Labor of Love, Labor of Sorrow: Black Women, Work, and the Family from Slavery to Present.* New York: Basic Books, 1985.

Perry, Charles R. *The Negro in the Department Store Industry.* Philadelphia: University of Pennsylvania Press, 1971.

PERIODICALS

Clark-Lewis, Elizabeth. "'This Work Had an End': African-American Domestic Workers in Washington, D.C., 1910–1940." Reprinted in Kish Sklar, Kathryn, and Dublin, Thomas, eds. *Women and Power in American History: A Reader, Vol. II From 1870.* Englewood Cliffs, N.J.: Prentice Hall, 1991.

AUDIO AND VISUAL MEDIA

Freedom Bags. PBS. Produced by Elizabeth Clark-Lewis and Stanley Nelson. Videocassette, 1980.

Twelfth Annual Report of the Secretary of Commerce, 1924

Report

By: Herbert Hoover

Date: 1924

Source: Hoover, Herbert. *Twelfth Annual Report of the Secretary of Commerce, 1924.* Washington, D.C.: U.S. Government Printing Office, 1924, 10–16, 18–19, 22–24. Excerpted in Shannon, David A. "The Government Administrator as Efficiency Expert," in *Progressivism and Postwar Disillusionment: 1898–1928.* New York: McGraw Hill, 1966, 320–29.

About the Author: Herbert Hoover (1874–1964) was born in West Branch, Iowa. An engineer and successful businessman, he entered public life as a relief administrator during World War I. Rejecting Democratic and Republican entreaties to run for president in 1920, he served instead as Secretary of Commerce under Presidents Warren Harding and Calvin Coolidge (1921–1928). When Coolidge chose not to run for reelection, this time Hoover accepted the Republican nomination and became America's thirty-first president (1929–1933). Hoover's presidency was overshadowed by the Great Depression, and he is largely remembered for his failure to cope with that national crisis. The philanthropic work and advanced economic ideas that propelled him to the nation's highest office are often overlooked. ∎

Introduction

Herbert Hoover agreed to accept the position of Secretary of the Commerce Department on the condition that he have a hand in all the administration's economic policies. President Harding assented, and Hoover immediately set about reorganizing a department that had once been of little consequence. Persuading Congress to provide him with a vastly increased budget, Hoover restructured the Commerce Department, hiring thousands of new employees to help set national economic policy in a wide variety of sectors: trade, industry, agriculture, transportation, and communication.

But Hoover was not interested in establishing "Big Government." Rather, he hoped to use the Commerce Department's resources in a cooperative effort to bring order to the American economy. Hoover relied heavily on national trade associations to govern themselves, providing public support for the elimination of waste, inefficiency, and destructive competition. The public-private partnership that Hoover envisioned—what has been termed an "associative state"—presented a middle way between raw capitalist individualism and state-sponsored socialism.

To bring about this new economic order, Hoover's wide-ranging Commerce Department developed initiatives on a variety of issues. The department tackled unemployment and the recurring problems of the business cycle in a highly publicized conference in 1921. Hoover used this model repeatedly during his tenure as secretary, organizing hundreds more publicity campaigns to bring about socially efficient management in chronically disorganized fields (such as mining and housing construction) and emerging new ones (including electricity, radio, and aviation). By 1924, when Hoover issued this annual report, the Commerce Department had become one of the most active government agencies in the nation.

Significance

Through his work at the Commerce Department, Hoover achieved a near-iconic position in the business world. In an era still fascinated by Frederick Taylor's principles of scientific management, which sought greater efficiency through the rationalization of industry, Hoover's engineering approach to national economic reorganization drew wide praise. The 1920s promised a "New Era" in business-government relations, promoting economic development, limiting wasteful competition, and soothing labor relations through cooperative rather than authoritarian means. Hoover's 1924 Commerce Department report, which details government efforts to resolve unemployment crises, inefficient modes of production, and poorly networked infrastructure, reflects his intense faith in his ability to transform all aspects of American economic life.

Despite general satisfaction with the Commerce Department's new role in the economy, the ideal of the associative state was difficult to achieve. For instance, in the area of unemployment, strong anti-statist political traditions hindered real reform. Congress was reluctant to support the department's recommended program of public works designed to offset dips in the business cycle.

State and city governments proved equally averse to initiating broad programmatic change.

Members of the business community, too, were often wary about entering into cooperative arrangements that might run counter to their personal self-interest. Industrial managers were especially hesitant about enacting new labor standards. Hoover had argued that shorter workdays and higher pay would reduce overproduction and increase consumption, creating a more efficient, more profitable economy. But his reliance on cooperative alliances with industrial organizations tended to sap the strength of labor unions and limit gains by workers during the 1920s. With the onset of the Great Depression in 1929, these cooperative arrangements collapsed, leaving the federal government ill-equipped to manage a national economic crisis.

Primary Source

Twelfth Annual Report of the Secretary of Commerce, 1924 [excerpt]

SYNOPSIS: In this report, Herbert Hoover outlines the myriad ways in which his department sought to reduce waste and inefficiency in the American economy. Citing the department's work in reducing unemployment, coordinating electric power and lighting systems, and bringing standardization to production, Hoover explains how government agencies, in cooperation with private trade associations, can fine-tune the economy sector by sector.

Outside of the very large functions of the department in the promotion of foreign trade, in aid to navigation, in provision of systematic economic information, and in cooperation with commerce and industry to advance productivity, a definite constructive national program has been developed for the elimination of waste in our economic system. The need is plain. The American standard of living is the product of high wages to producers and low prices to consumers. The road to national progress lies in increasing real wages through proportionately lower prices. The one and only way is to improve methods and processes and to eliminate waste. Just as 20 years ago we undertook nation-wide conservation of natural resources, so now we must undertake nation-wide elimination of waste. Regulation and laws are of but minor effect on these fundamental things. But by well-directed economic forces, by cooperation in the community we can not only maintain American standards of living—we can raise them.

We have the highest ingenuity and efficiency in the operation of our industry and commerce of any nation in the world. Yet our economic machine is far from perfect. Wastes are legion. There are wastes which arise from wide-spread unemployment during depressions, and from speculation and overproduction in booms; wastes attributable to labor turnover and the stress of labor conflicts; wastes due to intermittent and seasonal production, as in the coal and construction industries; vast wastes from strictures in commerce due to inadequate transportation, such as the lack of sufficient terminals; wastes caused by excessive variations in products; wastes in materials arising from lack of efficient processes; wastes by fire; and wastes in human life. . . .

Unemployment and the Business Cycle

The greatest waste is periodic slackening of production and resultant unemployment. At the beginning of this administration there were 4,500,000 unemployed. To meet this situation, and acting under the direction of President Harding, I called in September, 1921, the First National Conference on Unemployment. This conference had as its primary purpose the promotion of temporary relief measures, but had in view a broader consideration of the whole problem of business slumps. The relief measures adopted by the conference proved so successful that we overcame unemployment in much less time than in any other depression in our history. While formulating emergency measures, however, the responsible business men, labor leaders, and economists of the conference agreed fully with the proposal that exhaustive investigations should be made of the whole problem, with a view to the abiding minimization of this waste.

In pursuance of this objective I appointed a committee on business cycles and unemployment, which brought in its report in April, 1923. The committee found that slumps in business are due fundamentally to the economic collapse from the wastes, extravagance, speculation, inflation, overexpansion, and relaxation of effort by labor developed during booms. . . .

■ ■ ■

Interconnection of Electric Power and Lighting Systems

In October, 1923, with the approval of the President, I called a conference of the representatives of the State utility commissions of the 11 States from Maine to Maryland to consider what cooperative steps the Federal and State authorities could properly take to promote interconnection of power systems in those States. At this conference I outlined the problem in the following terms:

This conference is not conceived as more Government in business. The public authorities are already deeply in the power business through many forms of regulation and a very large measure of control of power sources. The thought here is that coordination between public authorities and industries may secure further consummation of a great advance in the development of a great service to the public.

The reason and need for this discussion are simply that engineering science has brought us to the threshold of a new era in the development of electric power. This era promises great reductions in power cost and wide expansion of its use. Fundamentally, this new stage in progress is due to the perfection of high voltage, longer transmission, and more perfect mechanical development in generation of power. We can now undertake the cheaper sources of power from water sources further afield, such as the St. Lawrence, and cheaper generation from coal through larger and more favorably placed coal generation plants. We can secure great economies in distribution through the interconnection of load between systems, for thus we secure a reduction of the amount of reserve equipment, a better average load factor through pooling the effect of day and seasonal variations, together with wider diversification of use by increased industrial consumption. We can assure more security in the power supply from the effect of coal strikes and from transportation interruptions.

All this means the liquidity of power over whole groups of States. At once power distribution spreads across State lines and into diverse legal jurisdictions. We are, therefore, confronted not only with problems of the coordination in the industries of their engineering, financial, and ownership problems, but also with new legal problems in State rights and Federal relations to power distribution. . . .

The savings in these 11 States resulting from a coordinated and fully developed electrical power system, would, by the time it could be erected, amount to a conservation of about 50,000,000 tons of coal per annum; an annual saving could be made of over $500,000,000 per annum at an additional capital outlay of about $1,250,000,000. In this area we are to-day producing something like 9,000,000 horsepower by direct steam and individual plant generation, a substantial part of which could be transferred to central generation with great economy. . . .

The indirect results both human and material are even more important than these figures I have given would imply. They take no account of vast losses to industry and commerce by the actual interruption and threatened interruption of fuel supplies to our several hundred thousand independent power units; no account of the relief to shippers from our already over-burdened transportation and terminal facilities; no account of the increased production of our factories from cheaper power; no account of the larger extension of power into farm and home; no account of the reduction of physical labor and increase of comfort. . . .

■ ■ ■

This conference recommended the formation of the Northeastern Superpower Committee under my chairmanship. The members of the committee have been designated by the governors of the various States representing their utilities commissions, together with representatives of the War Department, the Federal Power Commission, the United States Geological Survey, and the Department of Commerce. An engineering subcommittee, comprised of engineers of the various State utilities commissions and Federal engineers, brought in its report on April 14, 1924. This report deals comprehensively with the problems above outlined and with the major technical steps necessary to bring about the technical development required. Already a number of these steps have been undertaken by the various power systems throughout this area.

Studies as to the legal problems involved in interconnection over State lines, having in mind the involved and varying forms of regulation in different States, are being made by a legal subcommittee with a view to determining some basis of uniformity in such regulation.

It would be desirable to cover other areas of the country in the same fashion. . . .

Simplified Practice

A large field in the elimination of waste lies in the direction of simplified nomenclature, grades, and variations in dimensions of industrial products. The Division of Simplified Practice established early in 1921, serves as a centralizing agency in bringing together producers, distributors, and consumers, when so requested by any of these groups, for the purpose of assisting these interests in their mutual efforts to eliminate waste in production and distribution. Here the particular waste attacked was that caused by unnecessary diversification of practice or character resulting in the accumulation of excessive and consequently expensive, stocks of seldom-used varieties. Soon after the division was established the national brick manufacturers brought to its attention the need for simplifying the number of sizes of paving bricks. It developed that no less than 66 sizes were actually being manufactured and sold. This department promptly called a conference of all interested parties, with the result that varieties of paving brick were reduced by mutual consent from 66 to 11. Since then there has been a further reduction to 5 varieties. . . .

Two national conferences of lumber manufacturers, dealers, consumers, and architects have been held and successfully established standard nomenclature, grades, and sizes for softwood lumber calling for a 60 per cent elimination of the present variety in yard lumber. Similar effort is under way in hardwood. The application of simplified practice to automotive parts, gas water heaters, steam boiler parts and fittings, hacksaw blades, pocket knives, shotgun shells, drills, and nearly a hundred other commodities, is being developed by those engaged in their manufacture, sale, and use, with the cooperation of the department.

The department has received the widest approval from the leaders in the industries affected that the simplified practice work is steadily decreasing the volume of retail stocks, production costs, and selling expenses, at the same time strengthening employment by allowing manufacture of standard articles for stock. Estimated annual savings by the industries as a result of this method of national waste elimination range from half a million dollars in one commodity field to a quarter of a billion dollars in another. These savings eventually find their way back to the consumer either in lower prices or better quality or both. All such efforts definitely advance competition. . . .

Trade Associations

One of the most important agencies through which the elimination of waste may be promoted is the trade association. It is true that a small minority of these associations have been in the past used as cloaks for restraint of trade by such activities as open-price associations and other attempts to control distribution or prices. It is equally true that the vast majority of trade associations have no such purpose and do no such things. The dividing line, however, between what activities are in the public

Herbert Hoover was secretary of commerce before he resigned to run for president in 1928. **THE LIBRARY OF CONGRESS.**

and types, eliminating excess varieties, and establishing grades and qualities, thus reducing the amount of stocks thrust upon the retailer and at the same time enabling factories to operate more regularly to stocks of standard requirements.

Elimination of misdirected credit and aid in the collection of accounts.

Provision for the settlement of trade disputes by arbitration.

Stamping out of unfair practices and misrepresentation in business or as to goods.

Promotion of the welfare of employees, by the improvement of working conditions, sanitation, safety appliances, accident prevention, housing conditions, and matters of like character.

Economy in insurance by handling that of all members, including fire, industrial, indemnity, or group insurance.

Economies in transportation through common agencies for settlement of rate matters, classification, car supply, auditing transportation bills, and the study of competitive transportation agencies.

Elimination of waste in processes by the establishment of laboratories for technical and scientific research.

Further Resources

BOOKS

Barber, William. *From New Era to New Deal: Herbert Hoover, the Economists, and American Economic Policy, 1921–1933.* Cambridge, Mass.: Cambridge University Press, 1985.

Hawley, Ellis, ed. *Herbert Hoover as Secretary of Commerce, 1921–1928.* Iowa City, Iowa: University of Iowa Press, 1981.

Wilson, Joan Hoff. *Herbert Hoover: Forgotten Progressive.* Boston: Little, Brown, 1975.

PERIODICALS

Galambos, Louis. "The Emerging Organizational Synthesis in Modern American History." *Business History Review* 44, Autumn 1970, 279–290.

Hawley, Ellis. "Herbert Hoover, the Commerce Secretariat, and the Vision of an Associative State." *Journal of American History,* 61, June 1974, 116–140.

WEBSITES

Herbert Hoover Presidential Library and Museum. Available online at http://www.hoover.archives.gov/index.html (accessed February 23, 2003).

interest and what are not in the public interest is not to-day clearly defined either by the law or by court decision. In consequence of recent decisions of the courts many associations are fearful of proceeding with work of vital public importance, and we are losing the value of much admirable activity. At the same time we are keeping alive the possibility of wrongful acts. It is imperative that some definition should be made by which an assurance of legality in proper conduct can be had, and by which illegality or improper conduct may be more vigorously attacked.

In the elimination of waste, trade associations have been among the most constructive agencies of the country, and will be far more so if the solution can be found to the above question. Their waste elimination activities extend in many directions, of which the following are but a part:

Collection and distribution of statistics as to actual production, capacity production, stocks on hand, shipments, orders on hand, cancellations, number of employees, and such other data as will enable the industry and its consumers intelligently to judge future demands and supply.

Elimination of waste and reductions in cost of production and distribution by standardizing sizes

The Real Estate Boom

Speech before the Birmingham, Michigan, Real Estate Board

Speech

By: James Couzens

Date: October 7, 1925

Source: Couzens, James. Speech before the Birmingham, Michigan, Real Estate Board, October 7, 1925. "James Couzens Papers." *Prosperity and Thrift: The Coolidge Era and the Consumer Economy, 1921–1929.* American Memory digital primary source collection, Library of Congress. Available online at http://memory.loc.gov/ammem/coolhtml /coolhome.html; website home page: http://memory.loc.gov (accessed May 14, 2003).

About the Author: James Couzens (1872–1936) moved to Detroit, Michigan, from his Chatham, Ontario, birthplace in 1890. Couzens spent his early career working closely with Henry Ford during the extraordinary growth and development of the Ford Motor Company. Couzens parted ways with Ford in 1919, when he successfully ran for mayor of Detroit. He remained in public life until his death, serving fourteen years as a U.S. Senator.

"Florida Frenzy"

Magazine article

By: Gertrude Mathews Shelby

Date: 1926

Source: Shelby, Gertrude Mathews. "Florida Frenzy." *Harper's Monthly,* January 1926, 177. Reprinted in Mowry, George, ed., *The Twenties: Fords, Flappers, and Fanatics.* Englewood Cliffs, N.J.: Prentice-Hall, Inc., 1963, 33–38.

About the Author: Gertrude Mathews Shelby (1881–1937), writer, anthropologist, and geographer, traveled extensively in the course of her research of African and African diasporic culture. As her article on American's frenzied migration to Florida reveals, she occasionally turned her anthropologist's eye on her own culture. ■

Introduction

Suburban construction increased dramatically in the 1920s. The cessation of wartime material restrictions, rising economic prosperity, and the drift of urban and rural residents into new suburban communities prompted real estate booms across the country. Manhattan, Detroit, Cleveland, and Los Angeles residents spilled into the growing suburban domains of Queens, Grosse Pointe, Shaker Heights, and Beverly Hills.

By far the most frenzied new construction took place on the Florida peninsula. It was once considered little more than muggy swampland, but in the early twentieth century, developers reenvisioned the area as a vacation paradise. Railroads and highways opened up Florida's coastline, bringing not only the wealthy, but also middle-class tourists. Hoping to turn the Florida coast into an American Riviera, private developers planned resort communities such as Boca Raton, Palm Beach, and Tampa Bay. By the end of the 1920s, the population of Miami, one of the most popular new locations, had grown by 400 percent.

Historians account for southern Florida's tremendous growth in numerous ways. A strong military presence during World War I prompted early development. Illegal liquor traffic (from the nearby Bahamas) during Prohibition helped bring new money into the state, as did the emerging tourist trade. And pro-business state legislation, including the prohibition of state income and inheritance taxes, helped draw permanent residents of great wealth (for example, Alfred duPont) to the Sunshine State.

Significance

Rapid suburbanization offered plenty of opportunity for unscrupulous business dealings, as brokers and investors speculated on rising land values. But pleas from public officials, such as Senator James Couzens of Michigan, asking local real estate agents to adhere to strict standards of business ethics, largely fell on deaf ears.

The rush of new capital resources into Florida fueled an era of easy credit during the early 1920s, credit which further facilitated land development and land speculation. Florida was being developed so quickly that many found real estate investment extremely profitable. Waterfront property values soared, and modest ventures soon produced enormous returns. Vacationers cashed in on the booming economy, as did many Northerners who purchased land without ever having seen it. The contagious excitement of the boom atmosphere was captured in Gertrude Mathews Shelby's article "Florida Frenzy," published in the January 1926 issue of *Harper's Monthly.*

The boom peaked in 1925. Real estate costs had soared far beyond any real relation to value; they reflected only an inflated sense of what someone else might pay. But land sales remained profitable only as long as there were interested customers, and the buying frenzy could not be sustained interminably. Real estate empires, built up in an era of easy finance and limited public oversight, collapsed by 1926. New Florida towns, which had built sewers, paved roads, and installed lights in preparation for newcomers, now found that they had overbuilt. The new residents (and their tax contributions) never materialized. When the Hurricane of 1926 devastated the Florida coastline, much of it was never reconstructed and the Florida Land Boom was over.

The boom and bust in Florida construction and development, with its get-rich-quick schemes, its loosely regulated transactions, and its vacillating fortunes, can serve as a microcosm of the national economy in the 1920s and 1930s. Economic prosperity and easy credit helped fuel rapid development, but it was development based on overvalued resources in an underregulated market. When the speculative frenzy was spent, the subsequent crash was severe. In the midst of the Great Depression, these parallels were seen more clearly, perhaps as a warning sign that had been missed.

Primary Source

Speech before the Birmingham, Michigan, Real Estate Board [excerpt]

SYNOPSIS: In a speech before Michigan real estate agents, Michigan Senator James Couzens implores the profession to stand up to its code, selling land based on actual rather than inflated values.

I come here tonight with mixed emotions and opinions as to the real-estate business and those engaged in it. What I have to say will, of course, not be agreed to by all, or perhaps none, but what I voice will at least be my own observations. . . .

The real estate business should not be called a "game." I remember in the early days of the motor car business, our dealers and salesmen used to refer to the automobile business as the "automobile game" and to this I took violent objection. I contended that the automobile business was not a gambling business: it was not a game of chance. The real estate men must, I think, take this position. It is usually speculation and gambling that makes business a game. It doesn't take a great deal of brains, it seems to me, to be a speculator, but it does take it, I think, to be a steady, reliable business man. No body hurts your business as much as those connected with the business, who take advantage of a customer's ignorance.

President Coolidge said at your national gathering last year in Washington, "You are the sellers of America." Don't oversell it. You are the progressives of the community, the merchants of optimism and confidence and to maintain that you must have a code of ethics. You have a code: I hope you will adhere to it. In the preamble to your code, adopted at your Washington meeting in 1924, is the following: "Underlying all is the land. Upon its wide utilization and widely allocated ownership depend the survival and growth of free institutions and of our civilization."

The realtor is the instrumentality handling land resources of the nation. The real estate man's first duty is to know the facts and be sure to tell them to his client. You are the middleman who must render service to both sides.

Some philosopher has said, "A deal in which one side gets the best of it is not good business—the ideal basis is to trade something you need less for something you need more, and do it on an equitable basis. The realtors' idealism should be taken seriously. There have been too many frauds in the past. Get the public to understand that we are passing the stage of business for business sake; that we recognize a social duty as well as to make money. Make it so that an agent, or a speculator is not a realtor. Every customer should be a part of your business and you should realize that you have no business without the customer, that he is first, last and all the time, that your merchandise, your premises, your ability is valueless without the customer. A business trade is not legitimate unless morally good. High pressure salesmanship doesn't mean exaggeration. A man can be square and win. Some men, however, seem to gain without being square, but who knows what is in their conscience. Every man isn't happy just because he has money, every man isn't contented because he is rich. I am satisfied that many men who have money wish they had gotten it otherwise. The doubtful part, however, is that he has become softened physically and weakened mentally with the physical comforts that money can buy to such an extent that he has lost his stamina and ability to say "No" to a crooked deal.

Your National Association of Realestate Boards adopted an article in June 1924, as follows:

It is the duty of every realtor to protect the public against fraud, misrepresentation or unethical practices in connection with real estate transactions.

Are you individually living up to it?

Primary Source

"Florida Frenzy" [excerpt]

SYNOPSIS: In "Florida Frenzy," Gertrude Mathews Shelby describes her experience in Florida land speculation. At times Shelby adopts a critical distance, but she is soon tempted to join the buying mania.

The smell of money in Florida, which attracts men as the smell of blood attracts a wild animal, became ripe and strong last spring. The whole United

States began to catch whiffs of it. Pungent tales of immense quick wealth carried far.

"Let's drive down this summer when it's quiet," said canny people to one another in whispers, "and pick up some land cheap."

Concealing their destination from neighbors who might think them crazy, they climbed into the flivver, or big car, or truck, and stole rapidly down to Florida.

Once there, they found themselves in the midst of the mightiest and swiftest popular migration of history—a migration like the possessive pilgrimage of army ants or the seasonal flight of myriads of blackbirds. From everywhere came the land-seekers, the profit-seekers. Automobiles moved along the eighteen-foot-wide Dixie Highway, the main artery of East Coast traffic, in a dense, struggling stream. Immense busses bearing subdivision names rumbled down loaded with "prospects" from Mobile, Atlanta, Columbia, or from northern steamers discharging at Jacksonville. A broken-down truck one day stopped a friend of mine in a line. The license plates were from eighteen different states, from Massachusetts to Oregon. Most of the cars brimmed over with mother, father, grandmother, several children, and the dog, enticed by three years of insidious publicity about the miracles of Florida land values.

The first stories of the realty magicians had been disseminated through small city and country newspapers, particularly in the Middle West. Systematic propaganda stressed the undeniable fact that Florida was an unappreciated playground. Yet that was far less effective advertising than the beautiful, costly free balls given by one subdivision in certain cities. Those who attended shortly afterwards received a new invitation, to go without charge and view lots priced from one thousand dollars up.

Lured by the free trip, many went. Those who bought at the current prices and promptly resold made money. Other subdivisions met the competition, offsetting the overhead by arbitrary periodic raises in all lot prices. Whole states got the Florida habit. The big migration began.

Millions—variously estimated from three to ten—visited Florida last year, investing three hundred million dollars, and bank deposits swelled till they neared the half-billion mark in July.

The newcomers found themselves in a land where farming was practically at a standstill. Fresh vegetables were almost unobtainable; everybody uses canned goods. All food brought top New York prices. Railroads and steamships were inadequate to carry enough food, supplies, and passengers. For more than thirty days at midsummer an embargo was effective against building materials because a food famine (not the first) threatened. In September the prohibition extended to household goods, bottled drinks, and—chewing gum! . . .

Joining the great migration this summer, I went inclined to scoff. Were the others also confident that they possessed average good sense and were not likely to be fooled much?

Probably. I was lost. I gambled. I won. I remained to turn land salesman. Not only with no superiority, but with defiant shame rather than triumph, I confess—not brag—that on a piker's purchase I made in a month about $13,000. Not much, perhaps, but a lot to a little buyer on a little bet.

In June an old and trusted friend turned loose upon our family a colony of Florida boom bacilli. It was a year since I had heard from this particular friend. He was down and out, owing to domestic tragedy topped by financial reverses. Suddenly he bobbed up again rehabilitated, with $100,000 to his credit made in Florida since November, 1924. His associate made more than $600,000 in six months. . . .

We sailed from Philadelphia. On the boat I was amazed to find myself already a "prospect." Brokers on shipboard enviously assumed that our friend, like the usual land-octopus, had encircled wealthy prey in New York. A protectively inclined Philadelphian warned me in private, "Don't be drawn in. I wish I'd never seen Florida. It's a magnificent state. Money is to be made still. But speculation is hog-wild. People do things they'd never be guilty of at home. I've done them myself. I'm sewed up now in a company whose president, I've discovered, is a crook who failed at everything but bootlegging. If you enjoy a good night's sleep now, stay out." His protectorship was rather unflattering. Feeling superior, I thanked him. But when I landed at Miami I saw the significance of his warning. The whizzing pace of the people in tropical heat (for it *is* hot in Florida in summer—dripping hot) showed their frantic excitement. There was a sparkle in every eye, honest or dishonest. At the hotel, humming night as well as day with unwonted activity, a man in the next room took advantage of the after-midnight rates joyfully to long-distance New York.

"Momma! Momma! Is that you, Momma? This is Moe! I bought ten t'ousand acres today. Yes, ten t'ousand. Vat? Vat you say? Vy—Momma! How should I tell you where that land iss? I don't know myself!"

When, in those first days as a prospect, I was rushed by motor car and boat all over the Gold Coast, that millionaire-jeweled strip seventy-two miles long and two to seven miles wide from Miami and Palm Beach, between the Everglades and the Ocean, I was confronted everywhere by evidences of boom hysteria. On a street corner a woman selected a choice lot from a beautiful plat shown her by a complete stranger and paid him fifteen hundred dollars in crumpled carefully hoarded bills. He gave her a receipt, but vanished. There was no land. . . .

On one of the innumerable Florida busses, bumbling overbearingly down the blisteringly hot Dixie Highway toward Miami, my neighbor was a young woman of most refined appearance, an exceedingly pretty brunette in white crêpe de chine gown and hat. Only her handkerchief-edge hinted at mourning. As usual, the bus joggled loose all reserves.

"Florida? Wonderful! Came with a special party two weeks ago. Bought the third day. Invested everything. They guarantee I'll double by February. Madly absorbing place! My husband died three weeks ago. I nursed him over a year with cancer. Yet *I've actually forgotten I ever had a husband. And I loved him, too, at that!*" Values and customs are temporarily topsy-turvy in Florida.

What happens to Florida "sourdoughs" on arrival? Few come fortified with even the names of reliable firms. Notorious as well as honest promoters lie in wait for the gambling horde. Like wolves, they stir up the sheep, stampede them, allow them no time for recovery. They must decide instantaneously.

Again and again I declared that I had no intention to buy, but nobody let me forget for an instant I was a prospect. As upon others, the power of suggestion doubtless worked on me. It is subtly flattering to be the implied possessor of wealth. The kingdoms of the world appeared to be displayed for my choice. To help me choose, I like everyone else, was accosted repeatedly on Miami streets, offered free dinners and bus trips, besides a deal of entertainment, conscious and unconscious, by high-pressure salesmen. . . .

On account of an inherited notion of conduct towards those with whom one breaks bread, I refused all such bait. On my independent investigations salesmen found me unusually inquisitive. One, trying to sell me a $3500 lot, reproved me. "Those things don't matter. All Florida is good. What you are really buying is the bottom of the climate. Or the Gulf Stream. All you've got to do is to *get the rich consciousness.* There's the dotted line—you'll make a fortune."

Authentic quick-wealth tales, including innumerable lot transactions, multiplied astoundingly. They were not cases of twenty-five-dollar land proved worth one hundred dollars, but of prices which had pyramided high into the thousands. When I saw the sort of people who were making actual money my hesitation appeared ridiculous. I resolved to invest. I tried to assume an attitude of faith. I said aloud, indiscreetly, "Resisting enthusiasm and using intelligence—"

I was interrupted scornfully. "That's just it. The people who have made real fortunes check their brains before leaving home. Buy anywhere. You can't lose."

Those last three sentences, boom-slogans, were mainly true in 1924. But I for one refused to credit them in 1925. Clinging to such wits and caution as remained to me, that first week I studied the land itself from Miami to Fort Lauderdale, to Palm Beach, to Jupiter and Fort Pierce. Like everyone else I yearned to own a bit of the ocean rim. But shore acreage was held mainly in parcels priced at a million or worse. Beach lots for the little piker in good subdivisions cost now from $7000 to $75,000, according to location. Even on good terms that sort of thing was not for me. Biting off too much leads to acute financial indigestion. Perhaps I could find a doll-ranch—the traditional five acres with orange trees.

I searched. Some orchards still stand. Many have been mowed down by subdivisioners with an eye to front-foot prices. The fields, the wilderness, are side-walked and handsomely lampposted. The main ocean boulevard of the little city in which we were staying at the moment has not yet a sidewalk, yet checkerboards of cement, often approached through a showy archway, mark the strangely empty site of many a soldout backwoods subdivision. The raw land is being laid out as if for an exposition. Surveyors' theodolites are seen everywhere. Roadmaking is a great industry. The available supply of wood is used up for lot-stakes.

Yet, houses, usually of hollow tile, pop out like the measles—they weren't there yesterday. Florida's table, I concluded, was being spread as rapidly as possible for an immense population, invited to occupy not only what it is believed will be a continuous pleasure city seventy-two miles long between Palm Beach and Miami, but the entire

Brick roads curve around Spring Bayou in Tarpon Springs, Florida. The city attracted diverse groups of settlers in the late 1800s and early-1900s, including wealthy northerners seeking warm winter homes, and Greek immigrants, who established a thriving sponge-diving industry. **THE LIBRARY OF CONGRESS.**

state, with twenty-two million acres capable of development.

Searching continually for some deal to fit my modest purse, I found that the only ranch tracts priced within my reach were six or seven miles back in the Everglades. No Everglades for me, I decided, until reclamation is completed.

I then was offered by a reputable firm a great bargain in a city lot for $1000, an unusually low price. Well-located $3000 fifty-foot lots are rather scarce. This bonanza turned out to be a hole, a rockpit—and I reflected on the credulous millions who buy lots from plats without ever visiting the land!

But to set against this experience I had one of exactly the opposite sort which left me with a sharp sense of personal loss. An unimportant-looking lot several blocks from the center of Fort Lauderdale (whose population is fifteen thousand) on Las Olas Boulevard had been offered me about a week before at $60,000. I didn't consider it. It now resold for $75,000.

"It doesn't matter what the price is, if your location is where the buying is lively," I was told. "You get in and get out on the binder, or earnest money. If you had paid down $2500 you would have had thirty days after the abstract was satisfactorily completed and the title was approved before the first payment was due. You turn around quickly and sell your purchase-contract for a lump sum, or advance the price per acre as much as the market dictates. Arrange terms so that your resale will bring in sufficient cash to meet the first payment, to pay the usual commission, and if possible to double your outlay, or better. In addition you will have paper profits which figure perhaps several hundred per cent—even a thousand—on the amount you put into the pot. The next man assumes your obligation. You ride on his money. He passes the buck to somebody else if he can."

"But what happens if I can't resell?"

"You're out of luck unless you are prepared to dig up the required amount for the first payment. You don't get your binder back. But it's not so hazardous as it sounds, with the market in this condition."

Imagine how I felt two weeks later still when the same lot resold for $95,000. By risking $2500 with faith I could have made $35,000 clear, enough to live on some years. Terror of an insecure old age suddenly assumed exaggerated proportions. Right then and there I succumbed to the boom bacillus. I would gamble outright. The illusion of investment vanished. . . .

Further Resources

BOOKS

Allen, Frederick Lewis. "Home Sweet Florida." In *Only Yesterday: An Informal History of the 1920s.* New York: Harper and Row, 1931.

Frazer, William, and John J. Guthrie, Jr. *The Florida Land Boom: Speculation, Money, and the Banks.* Westport, Conn.: Quorum Books, 1995.

Vickers, Raymond B. *Panic in Paradise: Florida's Banking Crash of 1926.* Tuscaloosa, Ala.: University of Alabama Press, 1994.

WEBSITES

"Exploring Florida: Florida's Land Boom." Florida Center for Instructional Technology. Available online at http://fcit .coedu.usf.edu/florida/lessons/ld_boom/ld_boom1.htm; website home page http://fcit.coedu.usf.edu/florida/default.htm (accessed February 20, 2003).

Installment Buying

"How to Budget, How to Pay, The Budget Credit Book Shows the Way"

Pamphlet

By: John Wanamaker Department Store, New York

Date: December 1925

Source: "How to Budget, How to Pay, The Budget Credit Book Shows the Way." New York: John Wanamaker, 1925, 2, 6–7, 12–13. Reproduced in "Calvin Coolidge Papers. Credit-Installment Plan Buying 1926–29." *Prosperity and Thrift: The Coolidge Era and the Consumer Economy, 1921–1929.* American Memory digital primary source collection, Library of Congress. Available online at http://memory.loc.gov/ammem/coolhtml/coolhome.html; website home page: http://memory.loc.gov (accessed May 12, 2003).

About the Organization: John Wanamaker opened his first store in Philadelphia in 1876; it is considered the first retail department store in the United States. In 1896 he opened a store in New York City, and about a dozen other Wanamaker stores were opened in the Northeast during the early twentieth century. Along with retail magnates Marshall Field and Edward Filene, Wanamaker set the standard for large-scale urban sales, modern marketing, and consumer credit programs. Wanamaker department stores remained in operation until 1995.

Letter to Calvin Coolidge

Letter

By: George Talbot

Date: January 14, 1926

Source: Talbot, George. Letter to Calvin Coolidge, January 14, 1926. Reproduced in "Calvin Coolidge Papers. Credit-Installment Plan Buying 1926–29." *Prosperity and Thrift: The Coolidge Era and the Consumer Economy, 1921–1929.* American Memory digital primary source collection, Library of Congress. Available online at http://memory.loc.gov/ammem/coolhtml/coolhome.html; website home page: http://memory.loc.gov (accessed May 12, 2003).

About the Author: George Talbot, a Boston clothier, was one of many independent businessmen who criticized President Calvin Coolidge in response to a press report indicating his support for installment buying plans. ∎

Introduction

By 1900, department stores had largely replaced the smaller dry-goods retailers that had prospered in the nineteenth century. These new mass retailers offered a wide selection of consumer goods. And like big business (which relied on economies of mass production), department stores used their capacity for mass distribution to lower costs and eliminate smaller competitors. During the early twentieth century, department stores such as Mar-

shall Field's in Chicago, Macy's in New York, Filene's in Boston, and Wanamaker in Philadelphia, consolidated their control over retail selling. In the process, they built ever larger palaces of consumption and helped shape the consumer revolution of the 1920s.

Shifting ideas about debt and credit practices were integral to the success of department stores. Though the notion of thrift held significant cultural resonance in the nineteenth century, credit had always played a role in consumer interactions. Nineteenth-century Americans borrowed and lent, relying on a network of friends and relations, pawnbrokers, loan sharks, mortgage agents, and retailers. These lending practices were private, informal, and varied in respectability.

Of America's myriad financial practices, installment buying, so critical to the credit revolution of the 1920s, underwent the most marked transformation. Once considered little more than a con game designed to fool prospective customers into overpaying for goods, it soon found middle-class respectability under a new name: the finance plan. It took time for the stigma of installment purchases to disappear, but soon American consumers were financing the purchase of expensive durable goods (from farm implements and sewing machines to automobiles and furniture) through regularly scheduled payments. Department stores, which once prided themselves on trading only for cash (they argued that a no-credit policy helped to keep prices low), soon were selling most of their big-ticket items on credit.

Significance

The 1920s have been described as the "prosperity decade." As never before, Americans were moving into homes and filling them with furniture and appliances. Department stores promoted ever-shifting fashions, fueling sales of everything from European designer clothing to the latest face creams and perfumes. Credit accounts allowed customers immediate access to goods and helped bring these items within reach of those with modest budgets. Through pamphlets like "How to Budget, How to Pay, The Budget Credit Book Shows the Way" and broadcasts on store-owned radio stations, Wanamaker, like other department stores, actively promoted installment buying, which dramatically boosted sales.

This new consumer culture was built upon the designs of mass retailers and implemented through their extension of credit to consumers. Since installment buying was integral to this transformation, it often served as the scapegoat for those who were unhappy with the consumer revolution. Small business owners, who were unable to manage extensive credit programs, were the loudest critics. In January 1926, newspaper columnists reported that President Calvin Coolidge had endorsed buying on

A BUDGET ACCOUNT at Wanamakers

is a *thrift* account because it teaches, not only how to spend wisely, but how to save. It is limited to the purchase of home merchandise because the building of a home (within the house or apartment) is an investment that will bear much interest in joy and comfort with the passing years.

A Budget Account is a savings plan which permits the satisfaction of possession first and accepts payment in convenient sums—as the money is saved.

Budgeting is the control of investment. It prevents over-spending and puts more "sense" in the buying dollar. A Budget Account is a Savings account turned around. Instead of depositing in small sums to get your principal, you get the principal at the start and follow with small deposits.

PAGE
2

Primary Source

"How to Budget, How to Pay, The Budget Credit Book Shows the Way: A Budget Account at Wanamakers"

SYNOPSIS: This 1925 pamphlet, distributed by the John Wanamaker department store in New York, promoted installment buying. The first excerpt is from the pamphlet's introductory essay, which asserts that a "budget account" is a "thrift account" that helps consumers manage their purchases and "spend wisely." The second excerpt is taken from an address by the "Director of Wanamaker Budget Service," which was broadcast by the department store's own radio station and then reproduced in the pamphlet. THE LIBRARY OF CONGRESS.

Telephone Congress 2360
Post Office Box 5309

Established 1844
Incorporated 1887

Talbot Company

Manufactures and sells at wholesale and retail

Men's Clothing

"BOSTON MADE"
(Trade Mark)

395-403 Washington Street
Boston 5, Massachusetts

January 14, 1926

Calvin Coolidge, President,
Washington, D. C.

My dear President Coolidge:-

I have noticed in the papers lately items
which say that you endorse the installment plan
of buying articles.

Like all paper items, of course this is
open to great doubt in my mind, but I enclose
one clipping, taken from the Boston Herald on
this date, and I cannot believe that this is true.

To illustrate, a short time ago a man
was riding in the state of Maine. Seated in the
next seat were two ladies, who were going to some
convention -

No.1 said to No.2: "Have you an automobile yet?"
No.2 replies: "No, I talked it over with John and
he felt that we could not afford one."
NO.1: "Mrs Budge, who lives in your town has one,
and they are not as well off as you are."
The reply was:- "Yes, I know they have one. Their
second installment came due and they had no means
to pay it."
"What did they do, lose their car?"
"No, they got the money and paid the installment."
"How did they get the money?"
"They sold their cook stove."
"How could they get along without a cook stove?"
"They didn't. They bought another on the installment plan."

This is a true story.

Admiring as I do what you have done for
thrift and living within means, by example and
principle which I admire, imagine the condition
of this family and also of all families who purchase on the installment plan.

First, it destroys all feeling, second,
they mortgage their future, third, it induces
them to buy luxuries which are not proper for

Primary Source

George Talbot to Calvin Coolidge, January 14, 1926, Page 1 (1 OF 2)

SYNOPSIS: George Talbot, a Boston clothier, wrote this letter in response to a press report indicating President Coolidge's support for installment buying plans. In it, Talbot attacks installment buying as mortgaging the future. THE LIBRARY OF CONGRESS.

[5582]

Telephone Congress 2360
Post Office Box 5309

Established 1844
Incorporated 1887

Talbot Company

Manufactures and sells at wholesale and retail

Men's Clothing

"BOSTON MADE"

(Trade Mark)

395-403 Washington Street

Boston 5, Massachusetts

-2-

Calvin Coolidge, President

them to have, and if continued, will ruin practically every one who indulges in buying things that are not necessary, by mortgaging their entire future.

Apologizing for addressing you on this matter, but with the feeling that it is a most vital proposition, I am,

Yours most sincerely,

GNT/B

George N Talbot

Nothing laid by for the rainy day which comes to all —

Primary Source

George Talbot to Calvin Coolidge, January 14, 1926, Page 2 (2 OF 2)
Page 2 of the George Talbot Letter to Calvin Coolidge. THE LIBRARY OF CONGRESS.

installment plans at a press conference. His remark generated an outpouring of responses, many from independent businessmen. Among them was a letter to the president from a Boston clothier named George Talbot. Talbot and others argued that purchases made on credit enticed consumers to live beyond their means, forgoing necessities for newly available luxury items.

But others defended the institution, seeing in it an advance over pay-as-you-go methods. Still others thought that by enlarging the power of the consumer, credit purchases increased consumer demands and opened the market for producers and manufacturers. One historian has argued that the 1920s credit revolution should not be seen as reckless hedonism; rather, installment buying practices—with their regularly slated payments—represent nothing so much as the emergence of "regulated abundance."

Primary Source

"How to Budget, How to Pay, The Budget Credit Book Shows the Way" [excerpt]

The Effect of Budgeting on the American Home

Address given over the Radio, Station WEAF, December, 1925

The question has been asked, "What effect has a Budget on the American home?"

We might ask just as reasonably "What effect has a Budget on our Government at Washington?"

From the experience of several years as a Budget specialist, I can truthfully answer that there seems almost no part of family life that a Budget will not affect for the better. No two cases are alike, but they all have this in common: That we can get more out of life by using our brains than by living in a haphazard way and simply hoping for the best.

A great deal has been said in the past of how to make money. Stories of success are built around making money or saving money, but we are just waking up to the fact that there is a great field that has not been studied—the spending of money, that is, the wise spending of money.

This touches the American home more closely than anything else, for it is the home that spends the money. The head of the house earns money, but all his efforts are wasted if the housewife cannot spend it wisely. Therefore she must look to her laurels.

But how is the housewife to learn? Schools will take up the subject before long, but in the mean-

time we must learn to work with the tools we have at hand, and make our own methods.

The only way to begin is to begin—and, like charity, we must begin at home. The problem brought to a budget specialist every day is this, "My income is $1,000 or $5,000 or $100,000, but I don't have enough to go around. What shall I do?"

The answer is "Nobody ever has enough." Fast as the income may grow, demands of the family will grow faster, unless regulated. You might as well face that fact—first as last. It will never be any different. But we shall see what we can do to make your money go further and we are sure this can be done by making out a plan, a careful plan to cover as much ground as possible. That is all there really is to a budget. . . .

How often we hear the expression, "All the other women have fur coats." Or "All the other girls are having motor cars." And the hard-working head of the house makes one more painful effort to get the things which he cannot afford so that the family shall be happy.

Seeing women as I do, I am sure that the majority would not want luxuries at such a price. What other women have is not the question. The question is—"Do fur coats and motor cars fit the family income?" No one knows unless you have a budget. So get out the budget quickly. If luxuries fit in—you can have them with a light heart. If not, it is well to get the agony over. It saves a lot of wear and tear!

It is the place of the women in the home to do the most for the family budget. The man has business to keep him thinking. But don't leave him out. The Budget will never be a success unless the family works as one.

A tragic young woman came to me one day and said—"My husband and I are at the parting of the ways. Unless something is done we must separate. I don't know what to do."

I answered—"That seems too bad. What can we do for you?" She replied—"He says I am extravagant. Perhaps I am. I always have bills. My parents are dead. I was brought up care free. I don't know anything about managing. I don't know anything about money."

The sympathy she aroused took the very practical form of making out a budget our cure-all. We went into the matter thoroughly. The poor child was indeed ignorant. She had been trying to pay a lot of bills every month, far in excess of her allowance.

We made a plan. I told her to take the figures back and show them to her husband. He would see at once that she could not pay $150 worth of bills with $100 and keep out of debt. It seems that he was a very busy man, and had gotten the idea that she was frivolous.

He was older than she. He had not entered into her problems. After another visit she went away with a workable budget. Three months later she came back so joyous and oh so pretty. It was a happy story she told.

Her husband was so proud of her trying to learn that he increased her allowance generously. Better still—he began to rely on her judgment. She had earned his respect. She never had an unpaid bill. She had already saved a considerable sum.

Who shall say that a budget is dry figures—when it unites a family? In this case—it turned a sad woman into a beauty, which certainly ought to appeal to every woman.

Further Resources

BOOKS

Calder, Lendol. *Financing the American Dream: A Cultural History of Consumer Credit.* Princeton, N.J.: Princeton University Press, 1999.

Leach, William. *Land of Desire: Merchants, Power, and the Rise of a New American Culture.* New York: Vintage Books, 1993.

Olney, Martha L. *Buy Now, Pay Later: Advertising, Credit, and Consumer Durables in the 1920s.* Chapel Hill, N.C.: University of North Carolina Press, 1991.

WEBSITES

Murphy, Sharon. "The Advertising of Installment Plans." *Essays in History.* Corcoran Department of History, University of Virginia. Available online at http://etext.lib.virginia .edu/journals/EH/Murphy.html; website home page http:// etext.virginia.edu/journals/EH/ (accessed February 25, 2003).

Regulating Radio

Speech on Radio Regulation Given to the U.S. House of Representatives

Speech

By: Luther A. Johnson
Date: March 13, 1926
Source: Johnson, Luther A. Speech on radio regulation given to the U.S. House of Representatives, March 13, 1926. *Congressional Record* 67, 5558, March 13, 1926.

About the Author: Luther Alexander Johnson (1875–1965) was born and raised in Navarro County, Texas. Johnson practiced law, working first as a district attorney, then in private practice. Active in Democratic politics, he represented his north-central Texas community in the U.S. Congress from 1923 until 1946.

Letter to Congress Regarding Pending Radio Regulation

Letter

By: National Radio Coordinating Committee
Date: December 2, 1926
Source: National Radio Coordinating Committee. Letter to Congress regarding pending radio regulation, December 2, 1926. Reproduced in "Calvin Coolidge Papers. Radio— General 1923–29." *Prosperity and Thrift: The Coolidge Era and the Consumer Economy, 1921–1929.* American Memory digital primary source collection, Library of Congress. Available online at http://memory.loc.gov/ammem/coolhtml/cool home.html; website home page: http://memory.loc.gov (accessed May 12, 2003).

About the Organization: The National Radio Coordinating Committee, an umbrella organization representing radio broadcasters, manufacturers, amateur groups, and listeners' associations, worked closely with public officials in the 1920s as Congress and the Commerce Department debated radio regulation. ■

Introduction

Radio emerged in the first decades of the twentieth century as an advanced form of wireless telegraph, first transmitting Morse code messages, and—after further innovations in transmitters and receivers—music and speech. In radio's early years, its primary service was in ship-to-ship and ship-to-shore communications. The armed forces, especially the Navy, adapted the new technology to military uses during World War I.

Radio expanded dramatically in the early 1920s. Within two years of the first major broadcast—the 1920 presidential election returns by Pittsburgh's KDKA station—three million Americans owned radios. The number of broadcasting stations shot up from thirty in 1922 to 556 in 1923 to 734 in 1927. Soon the airwaves were crowded with amateurs and stations operated by universities, municipalities, religious organizations, labor unions, and trade associations. Chain broadcasting appeared in 1926, when a network of radio stations organized under the National Broadcasting Company.

Broadcasting revolutionized the radio industry during the 1920s. Yet it still operated under the supervision of the Commerce Department, which had been authorized by Congress to regulate radio in order to control its early maritime uses. As the number of broadcasters increased during the early 1920s, with only 189 available broadcast frequencies, many feared that chaos would rule the air. Secretary of Commerce Herbert Hoover sought to manage this situation by limiting the number of new broadcasting licenses and by creating complex time-sharing arrangements among competing stations. But it was not clear that the old radio law gave Hoover the power to act unilaterally. Plagued with continuing interference, members of both the radio industry and the listening public called upon Congress to better regulate this new technology.

Hoover called four radio conferences in the early 1920s in an effort to have the industry regulate itself. But by 1926, after several court cases severely limited Hoover's regulatory authority, Congress moved to enact stronger radio legislation.

Significance

In his speech before Congress on March 13, 1926, Representative Luther A. Johnson voiced his support for radio regulation. Contrasting radio's limited spectrum to the limitless potential of newspapers, Johnson argued that radio must be regulated in order to preserve free speech.

As its December 1926 letter to Congress demonstrates, the National Radio Coordinating Committee (NRCC) also supported stronger regulation. The NRCC letter urged immediate Congressional action, in part to secure the position of existing broadcasters against new competition.

Wary that radio—a medium with immense social and political significance—might drift into a market-regulated, property rights system, Congress established the Federal Radio Commission (FRC) in 1927. First Amendment restrictions meant the FRC could not directly regulate content, but it was empowered to grant broadcast licenses according to "public interest, convenience, and necessity."

The passage of the Federal Radio Act of 1927, which was recodified in the Federal Communications Act of 1934, accomplished Congress's top two priorities: it resolved the problem of broadcast interference and maintained public control over the airwaves. These were issues of no small importance, safeguarding against mass-media monopolies and establishing doctrines such as the equal-time rule, which ensured politicians of differing viewpoints access to the air. But the act had other consequences: it checked the rapid growth of radio broadcasting and favored incumbent, networked broadcasters at the expense of smaller, marginal stations. In so doing, Congress ensured that radio would not be monopolized, but neither would it be the source of diverse and competing voices it once was.

Primary Source

Speech on Radio Regulation Given to the U.S. House of Representatives [excerpt]

SYNOPSIS: In this excerpt, Representative Luther A. Johnson makes a claim for the significance of radio as a social and political medium. Government must prevent monopoly ownership of radio stations, he argues, in order to preserve "freedom of the air."

There is no agency so fraught with possibilities for service of good or evil to the American people as the radio. As a means of entertainment, education, information, and communication it has limitless possibilities. The power of the press will not be comparable to that of broadcasting stations when the industry is fully developed. If the development continues as rapidly in the future as in the past, it will only be a few years before these broadcasting stations, if operated by chain stations, will simultaneously reach an audience of over half of our entire citizenship, and bring messages to the fireside of nearly every home in America. They can mold and crystallize sentiment as no agency in the past has been able to do. If the strong arm of the law does not prevent monopoly ownership and make discrimination by such stations illegal, American thought and American politics will be largely at the mercy of those who operate these stations. For publicity is the most powerful weapon that can be wielded in a Republic, and when such a weapon is placed in the hands of one, or a single selfish group is permitted to either tacitly or otherwise acquire ownership and dominate these broadcasting stations throughout the country, then woe be to those who dare to differ with them. It will be impossible to compete with them in reaching the ears of the American public.

Subsidy of radio broadcasting would be far more effective and dangerous than subsidy of the press. For if every newspaper in the United States could be purchased by some trust or combination, independent and competing newspapers could be established. But if the broadcasting stations, which are necessarily limited in number, can be acquired, or even a majority of the high-powered stations owned and controlled by a trust, then the public will be helpless to establish others, unless the Government protects them in this right. Freedom of the air will be impossible if the Government either licenses or permits monopoly ownership of radio sending stations.

Announcing the
National Broadcasting Company, Inc.

National radio broadcasting with better programs permanently assured by this important action of the *Radio Corporation of America* in the interest of the listening public

THE RADIO CORPORATION OF AMERICA is the largest distributor of radio receiving sets in the world. It handles the entire output in this field of the Westinghouse and General Electric factories.

It does not say this boastfully. It does not say it with apology. It says it for the purpose of making clear the fact that it is more largely interested, more selfishly interested, if you please, in the best possible broadcasting in the United States than anyone else.

Radio for 26,000,000 Homes

The market for receiving sets in the future will be determined largely by the quantity and quality of the programs broadcast.

We say quantity because they must be diversified enough so that some of them will appeal to all possible listeners.

We say quality because each program must be the best of its kind. If that ideal were to be reached, no home in the United States could afford to be without a radio receiving set.

Today the best available statistics indicate that 5,000,000 homes are equipped, and 21,000,000 homes remain to be supplied.

Radio receiving sets of the best reproductive quality should be made available for all, and we hope to make them cheap enough so that all may buy.

The day has gone by when the radio receiving set is a plaything. It must now be an instrument of service.

WEAF Purchased for $1,000,000

The Radio Corporation of America, therefore, is interested, just as the public is, in having the most adequate programs broadcast. It is interested, as the public is, in having them comprehensive and free from discrimination.

Any use of radio transmission which causes the public to feel that the quality of the programs is not the highest, that the use of radio is not the broadest and best use in the public interest, that it is used for political advantage or selfish power, will be detrimental to the public interest in radio, and therefore to the Radio Corporation of America.

To insure, therefore, the development of this great service, the Radio Corporation of America has purchased for one million dollars station WEAF from the American Telephone and Telegraph Company, that company having decided to retire from the broadcasting business.

The Radio Corporation of America will assume active control of that station on November 15.

National Broadcasting Company Organized

The Radio Corporation of America has decided to incorporate that station, which has achieved such a deservedly high reputation for the quality and character of its programs, under the name of the National Broadcasting Company, Inc.

The Purpose of the New Company

The purpose of that company will be to provide the best program available for broadcasting in the United States.

The National Broadcasting Company will not only broadcast these programs through station WEAF, but it will make them available to other broadcasting stations throughout the country so far as it may be practicable to do so, and they may desire to take them.

It is hoped that arrangements may be made so that every event of national importance may be broadcast widely throughout the United States.

No Monopoly of the Air

The Radio Corporation of America is not in any sense seeking a monopoly of the air. That would be a liability rather than an asset. It is seeking, however, to provide machinery which will insure a national distribution of national programs, and a wider distribution of programs of the highest quality.

If others will engage in this business the Radio Corporation of America will welcome their action, whether it be cooperative or competitive.

If other radio manufacturing companies, competitors of the Radio Corporation of America, wish to use the facilities of the National Broadcasting Company for the purpose of making known to the public their receiving sets, they may do so on the same terms as accorded to other clients.

The necessity of providing adequate broadcasting is apparent. The problem of finding the best means of doing it is yet experimental. The Radio Corporation of America is making this experiment in the interest of the art and the furtherance of the industry.

A Public Advisory Council

In order that the National Broadcasting Company may be advised as to the best type of program, that discrimination may be avoided, that the public may be assured that the broadcasting is being done in the fairest and best way, always allowing for human frailties and human performance, it has created an Advisory Council, composed of twelve members, to be chosen as representative of various shades of public opinion, which will from time to time give it the benefit of their judgment and suggestion. The members of this Council will be announced as soon as their acceptance shall have been obtained.

M. H. Aylesworth to be President

The President of the new National Broadcasting Company will be M. H. Aylesworth, for many years Managing Director of the National Electric Light Association. He will perform the executive and administrative duties of the corporation.

Mr. Aylesworth, while not hitherto identified with the radio industry or broadcasting, has had public experience as Chairman of the Colorado Public Utilities Commission, and, through his work with the association which represents the electrical industry, has a broad understanding of the technical problems which measure the pace of broadcasting.

One of his major responsibilities will be to see that the operations of the National Broadcasting Company reflect enlightened public opinion, which expresses itself so promptly the morning after any error of taste or judgment or departure from fair play.

We have no hesitation in recommending the National Broadcasting Company to the people of the United States.

It will need the help of all listeners. It will make mistakes. If the public will make known its views to the officials of the company from time to time, we are confident that the new broadcasting company will be an instrument of great public service.

RADIO CORPORATION OF AMERICA

OWEN D. YOUNG, *Chairman of the Board*   JAMES G. HARBORD, *President*

The National Broadcasting Company (NBC) was one of the first broadcasting networks when it was formed in 1926, and had 48 affiliate stations. THE LIBRARY OF CONGRESS.

Primary Source

Letter to Congress Regarding Pending Radio Regulation [excerpt]

SYNOPSIS: In this excerpt, the National Radio Coordinating Committee (NRCC) states its support of the pending radio regulation, asking Congress to "prevent confusion in the air."

Dear Senator:

The Coordinating Committee of the radio industry, representing all branches of that industry, the organized transmitting amateurs, some 16,000 in number; through one of the signers hereof, many organized Broadcast Listeners' Leagues of the United States and, through our many contacts, the great unorganized radio listening public, takes this opportunity to present to the members of the Conference Committee of the Senate and the House the views of the radio industry and the public as a whole on the legislation which is pending in conference.

These views are the result of a very careful study of the problems not only confronting the industry, but confronting you as the men who are immediately responsible for the legislation. We submit these views with the knowledge that they express the attitude of the radio industry and the radio public on the vital matters which are before you, and in the hope that they may be of material assistance to you in your consideration of legislation.

If this Committee, which is truly and wholly representative of radio in America, can be of assistance to the members of the Conference Committee of the Senate and the House, we are at your service.

Emergency Control

It is the opinion of the Coordinating Committee that it is highly essential to secure legislation controlling radio during this session of Congress. To this end it appears that two distinct steps are necessary.

1. The enactment of an emergency control measure, which will prevent the further complication of an already complicated situation by prohibiting the issuance of any more licenses for the operation of radio broadcasting stations after December 6, 1926.

2. The bringing out of conference of a comprehensive and adequate general law governing the whole radio industry.

The emergency control measure is necessary, in our opinion, because broadcasting stations are now increasing at such a rate—to be specific, one a day—as to cause not only confusion on the air but the possibility of even greater confusion. It is estimated reliably that there are now more than twenty million citizens of the United States who are enthusiastic listeners to radio programs; that more than five million citizens of the United States are the owners of radio receiving sets; that the investment of these citizens as individuals in radio is upwards of $1,800,000,000, to say nothing of the investment which broadcasting companies and commercial operators have in the industry.

Unless immediate steps are taken by Congress to prevent confusion in the air, this great radio listening public, together with its large investment in radio, is likely to suffer a tremendous injury.

Equally important is the threatened interruption of the flow of information regarding agricultural and market reports, upon which our farmers have come to depend, through the medium of the radio.

Rights

In our consideration of the Bills in your Committee, we find a specific statement and several references to a principle of "vested property rights."

We have arrived at the conclusion that a distinction must be made as between vested rights as against the United States and such other rights included in this term as persons, firms, companies or corporations may have against each other.

It is the opinion of the Coordinating Committee that it is fair, just and reasonable, and in confirmation of the interpretation of the common law, that there be provided in any radio law a recognition of rights as between individual broadcasters as distinguished from the vested rights of the United States which will be in effect at the time and in the form prescribed in the legislation following your conference report.

We believe that the theory of the right of priority of operation, should be thoroughly defined. In effect this seems that the allocation and use of wave lengths shall be determined on the basis of these factors:

1. The length of time during which stations, existing at the time this Act becomes law, have operated.

2. The character of service rendered by them.

3. The requirements of their zones and communities for radio service.

The above principles should be so written into the law that there will be no limitation of the effect thereof.

This Committee has examined with great care both the Senate and House Bills where reference is made to vested rights either directly or by implication, and as a result have decided for themselves upon a policy which is believed to meet with the objects and desires of the paragraphs mentioned, and yet provides a recognition of rights between individual broadcasters based upon the common law.

To state it briefly, the doctrine which we have developed may be said to be as follows. A broadcaster has no vested rights as against the United States Government; but he has certain clearly defined rights as against other broadcasters.

It is only fair and just, in our opinion, that recognition be given to those broadcasters who have invested substantial sums of money in broadcasting plant and equipment, and who have served the public properly. It would be unfair, in our opinion, to consider a late comer in the business of broadcasting—especially those who might be licensed subsequent to the time of the passage of this proposed legislation—to have equal rights or to be placed upon the same basis as a broadcaster who has served the public well and has a substantial investment.

Therefore, we believe the proposed law should specifically provide in a lawful manner for a recognition of this doctrine wherever it may appear.

Further Resources

BOOKS

Barnouw, Eric. *A Tower in Babel: A History of Broadcasting in the United States to 1933.* New York: Oxford, 1966.

Bensman, Marvin. *Beginning of Broadcast Regulation in the Twentieth Century.* Jefferson, N.C.: McFarland and Co., 2000.

Rosen, Philip T. *The Modern Stentors: Radio Broadcasters and the Federal Government, 1920–1934.* Westport, Conn.: Greenwood Press, 1980.

PERIODICALS

Aitken, Hugh G.J. "Allocating the Spectrum: The Origins of Radio Regulation." *Technology and Culture* 35, 1994, 686–716.

Coase, Ronald H. "The Federal Communications Commission." *Journal of Law and Economics* 2, 1959, 1–40.

Hazlett, Thomas W. "The Rationality of U.S. Regulation of the Broadcast Spectrum." *Journal of Law and Economics* 33, 1990, 133–175.

"The Shop Chairmen, the Rank and File and the 'Prosanis' Label"

Newspaper article

By: *Justice*

Date: April 2, 1926

Source: "The Shop Chairmen, the Rank and File and the 'Prosanis' Label." *Justice* 8, no. 14, April 2, 1926, 5. Reproduced in "*Justice: Official Organ of the International Ladies' Garment Workers' Union*: Selected Issue from 1926." *Prosperity and Thrift: The Coolidge Era and the Consumer Economy, 1921–1929.* American Memory digital primary source collection, Library of Congress. Available online at http://memory.loc.gov/ammem/coolhtml/coolhome.html; website homepage: http://memory.loc.gov (accessed May 12, 2003).

About the Publication: The International Ladies' Garment Workers' Union (ILGWU) was founded in 1900 as a federation of local cloak-makers' unions. At first it attracted little membership, but following the "Uprising of the Twenty Thousand," an industry-wide garment workers' strike in 1909, tens of thousands of workers swelled its ranks. The widely circulated union newspaper, *Justice,* published articles relating to socialism, ILGWU activities, and other labor news. In 1995, ILGWU became part of UNITE (Union of Needletrades, Industrial and Textile Employees). ∎

Introduction

As early as 1900, upper- and middle-class consumers' groups such as the National Consumers' League endeavored to improve working conditions in the garment industry by educating consumers about the origins of their purchases. Their chief weapon in this publicity campaign was the union label—a tag sewn into clothes indicating that the manufacturer had complied with local labor standards. The union label crusade was, however, tremendously difficult to implement effectively. Its success depended on unions' ability to agree on standards, companies' readiness to accept them, retailers' willingness to stock union-label goods, and consumers' eagerness to purchase them. And of course, there were plenty of nonunionized garment workers who were not helped by the union label movement.

Under these conditions, the union label faired poorly at first, and its use was limited to a handful of key urban centers with a strong union presence, among them New York City and Boston. The situation improved after strikes in the needle trades produced a new labor "protocol" in 1910. Among other things, the agreement established the Joint Board of Sanitary Control, an organization composed of representatives from the ILGWU and other garment unions, the clothing industry, and the public. The Sanitary Board was authorized to inspect factories and to ensure that their management was upholding agreed-upon labor standards, including working hours, safety and sanitary conditions, and the prohibition of child labor. If the manufacturers were in compliance, then the "white label" on their products would serve as a seal of approval.

Despite the Sanitary Board's fight for the union label, it remained a localized, voluntary movement, dependent on union support and appeals to wealthy women who wanted to use their power as consumers to reform working conditions. In 1924, Governor Al Smith of New York proposed that all of New York's unionized cloak industry be required to use the Sanitary Board's label. To this end the board, in conjunction with the ILGWU, began a new label campaign in 1925, on the fifteenth anniversary of the labor protocol of 1910. The new label would be called "Prosanis," a term derived from the Latin words for "for health."

Significance

The 1920s turned out to be a poor time to spearhead a new union label campaign. Bitter divides between communist, socialist, and anarchist factions consumed much of the union's energy. Under the presidency of Morris Sigman (1923–1928) the ILGWU grew increasingly embattled as its leaders struggled to avoid a communist takeover. Members of the union's leftist locals were suspended; they later reorganized in protest to the ILGWU leadership. Their Joint Action Committee, a coalition of communist labor leaders, charged Sigman with violating union democracy and began to draw support from the dispossessed locals. Over the next several years, the union struggled to maintain a sense of unity while communist and noncommunist factions vied for control.

Internecine warfare drew the union's attention away from Governor Smith's labor commission and its proposal to require union labels throughout the garment industry. At the same time, the Joint Board of Sanitary Control was having trouble gaining support among retailers in ensuring that they stock only union-label merchandise. Large Manhattan department stores such as Macy's, Altman's, and Lord and Taylor, often relied on their own reputations to vouchsafe the quality of their goods and were thus reluctant to place any label inside their garments other than their own. Educating customers to look for the label—when factories neglected to use it and stores were reluctant to stock union-label goods— was thus a slow and uneven process. Despite the growth of consumer power during the prosperous 1920s, it remained exceedingly difficult to channel that power toward better working conditions.

Written by an inspector from the Joint Board of Sanitary Control's label division, this article in the April 2,

Justice was the official newsletter of the ILGWU and presented articles on national and international labor news as well as information on ILGWU activities. **THE LIBRARY OF CONGRESS.**

1926, issue of the ILGWU's newspaper *Justice* is a first-hand account of the workings of garment factories of the time. It provides an explanation of why the Prosanis label met with little success: Factory operators were often unwilling to spend the extra money for union labels. Shoppers were frequently indifferent to the origin of their purchases. And even union members, already overtaxed in the workplace and distracted by internal union divisions, failed to stand firmly behind the union label.

Primary Source

"The Shop Chairmen, the Rank and File and the 'Prosanis' Label" [excerpt]

SYNOPSIS: In this article from the ILGWU's newspaper *Justice,* an inspector from the Joint Board of Sanitary Control's label division explains the difficulties faced by supporters of the union label and sweatshop reform.

Impressions of An Inspector

Dr. Henry Moskowitz, Director of the Label Division of the Joint Board of Sanitary Control, asked me, as an inspector in his Division, to write a short article on my impressions as to the attitude of the

The Consumer Revolution

[Arthur W. Calhoun, an instructor at the Brockwood Labor College, describes in the April 2, 1926 issue of *Justice* how the extension of credit to laborers has made them consumers as well, providing access to more luxury goods and, by virtue of the economic expansion their consumption engendered, greater employment opportunities. But, he prophetically argues, unchecked industrial growth will eventually result in overproduction and economic collapse. Workers, customers, managers, and producers all struggled to renegotiate their roles during the consumer revolution of the 1920s.]

The workers have learned a lesson from the boss; they have learned how to spend money before they get it. The boss has known that for a long time, and he is now practicing it so well that nearly all business is done on credit. If the business man were forced to pay cash, the whole of industry would be prostrated.

But the wise men tell us that it's one thing to go into debt for machinery and equipment that will yield a product for sale and another thing to go into debt for a radio outfit or a player piano, which will give a good time maybe but will not turn out anything to sell and pay the debt. Very likely there's something in that contrast.

Is there as much in it, do you suppose, as the wise men say? Everybody knows that the American workers have during the past year bought millions of dollars worth of goods on credit. Suppose they had not done it! Suppose they had harkened to the advice "Pay as you go!" What then? Evidently the goods would have stayed in the stores and killed the market for new production. In other words, buying on credit has kept trade going and has made it possible to keep up production to a point far above what it would have been if there had been no credit.

The tale does not stop there. Because people bought on credit and thus made a market that otherwise would not have existed, there was work for many who would otherwise have been idle and thus the pay envelopes were fattened with real dollars that would otherwise never have left the coffers of the financiers who keep the boss going. Thus power on the market; it represents so many dollars itself, and their expenditure puts dollars into pay envelopes that would otherwise have been flat. There's almost magic in it.

One thing's sure, the instalment plan has helped to keep the wheels turning; but how long can such a game keep up? No one has ever yet invented a perpetual motion machine. What will happen when everybody is in debt to the limit of his credit?

But where is the limit? If there had been no credit buying, business would have been dull, industry would have been sluggish, and the total wages of the workers would have been low. Consequently, their credit would have been poor and small. But someone released a flow of credit and it swelled the streams of trade and industry, so that wages totalled more and the workers automatically had better credit and could buy still more on the instalment plan. Within limits, credit buying evidently can expand itself to great dimensions.

Now if credit were only well enough managed to provide a continual flow of purchasing power sufficient to keep all the wheels of industry turning full time, then the actual earning power of the workers would be at a maximum.

SOURCE: Calhoun, Arthur W. "The Workers Have Learned a Lesson." *Justice* 8, no. 14, April 2, 1926, 5, 7. Reproduced in "*Justice: Official Organ of the International Ladies' Garment Workers' Union*: Selected Issue from 1926." *Prosperity and Thrift: The Coolidge Era and the Consumer Economy, 1921–1929.* American Memory digital primary source collection, Library of Congress. Available online at http://memory.loc.gov/ammem /coolhtml/coolhome.html; website homepage: http://memory.loc.gov (accessed May 12, 2003).

chairmen and the operators in the factories in the cloak and dress industries towards the "Prosanis" Label. It is not easy to do this in a short article. As an inspector in the Label Division for the past fifteen months, I have made so many observations that I could fill a number of articles without difficulty. It will require more than one to record all my impressions.

Most of the chairmen, not speaking of the operators, do not understand why and for what purpose the Union has introduced the label. And, not knowing the purpose, they do not carefully see that each garment going out of their union shops carries a "Prosanis" label. . . .

My general impression is that the label is not used even fifty per cent in the cloak industry; in the dress industry it is still worse. I find in most cases that the fault lies with the chairmen. Of course, the operators themselves are far from being entirely innocent in the matter. In those shops where the chairman himself is responsible for the general union conditions, he also gives his attention to the label. He will not work without labels. As soon as the supply of labels is exhausted, no work is permitted to continue until a new supply is purchased. In very few cases do the members of the firm act against the wish of the chairman for more labels. The price of the label is so nominal that it does not pay for the firm to put itself in wrong with the workers as well as with the Union.

In other factories, the chairmen have instructed the pressers not to press any garments that do not carry the "Prosanis" label. As soon as the presser receives a garment without it, he is asked to give it back to the operator.

I am sorry to say that there are only a few shops where the two examples cited above exist. In most of the factories, as mentioned before this desirable condition is not found. Usually the chairmen are negligent and indifferent. They do not care whether the manufacturers for whom they work buy labels or not. They care even less whether the labels are actually being used. In fact, they themselves, look upon the label as rather a nuisance. Of course, the firms use such negligent chairmen for their own purposes. They do not then bother to buy labels and all garments are shipped without having them sewn on. These firms naturally regard the label as a case of easy arithmetic. Each label costs one-half cent. They only figure on the number of half-cents they save themselves. They do not see further than their noses, and they do not take into consideration that the saving of a penny now may in the end cost them a hundred times as much.

The label does not only safeguard the interests of the union workers: it also safeguards the interests of the union contractors. However, this is not all. The label is the only means by which the union firm and workers can defend themselves against the unscrupulous competition of the open sweatshop. Even the strongest union and the most devoted trade unions have no other means of recognizing a union-made garment from those made in a non-union shop. . . .

What motives have the shop chairmen for not using the label? They do not pay for the labels, but they can control the sending of bundle goods to non-union shops. Why don't they do it? Why are they so negligent? Why do they take such a small interest in the label?

I have spoken to hundreds of chairmen about this. When I tell them the purpose of the label, they are astounded as if confronted with a new truth. They had never previously been told why and for what purpose the label has been introduced and of what use it is to the industry. The Union has not educated them as to the usefulness of the label. In this respect, the chairmen and the operators are not guilty. It is the fault of the Union which has forgotten to educate their members as to the use and purpose of the "Prosanis" label.

Another observation made must also be mentioned here. At the time of the inner struggle in the Union, the "Prosanis" label suffered. At that time,

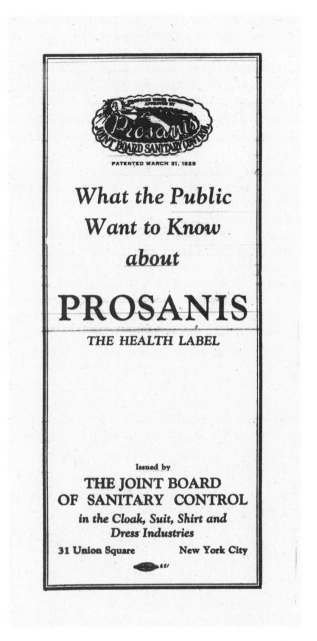

The Prosanis label on an item of clothing indicated to consumers that it was manufactured under working conditions approved by the union. **THE LIBRARY OF CONGRESS.**

most of the factories stopped using the labels and some are not using it yet. The chairmen and operators will not again use the label until informed by the Union to do so. Another excuse, and a legitimate one, is that the business agents, when they inspect the factories, do not even mention the label, and do not inspect the garments to see whether they carry it. Naturally, from the attitude of the business agents, the workers and chairmen conclude that the Union is indifferent to the label.

The Union can do much to better conditions. The business agents should be asked to look for the label upon the inspection of a factory; and to speak to the shop chairman regarding it. At all general, section and shop meetings, attention should be given to the label and its purposes and use explained.

And, another thing: if a manufacturer or a worker disregards any one of the rules in the agreement between the manufacturer and the Union, he is brought before the Grievance Committee and is punished in accordance with his ofense. Now, one of the rules in the agreement is that each and every garment must carry a "Prosanis" label. This rule is broken day in and day out and the breaker of this rule is never called to account for it. The manufacturer and the workers know that they can get away with it, and therefore nothing is done with regard to the label. Why is this? Is the label of such insignificance in the eyes of the Union leaders that it does not pay for them to take action against this.

Besides the manufacturers who have purchased labels, but have not used them one hundred per cent, there are many who have never purchased at all. This fact impresses those who have bought. What does the Union do in order to compel these firms to purchase in accordance with the agreement?

Further Resources

BOOKS

Stein, Leon. *Out of the Sweatshop: The Struggle for Industrial Democracy.* New York: Quadrangle, 1977.

Tyler, Gus. *Look for the Union Label: A History of the International Ladies' Garment Workers' Union.* Armonk, N.Y.: M.E. Sharpe, 1995.

WEBSITES

"Histories of UNITE! and Its Predecessor Unions: A Selective Scholarly Bibliography." The Kheel Center for Labor-Management Documentation and Archives, Cornell University. Available online at http://www.ilr.cornell.edu/library/kheelcenter/guides/unite; website home page http://campusgw.library.cornell.edu/ (accessed February 25, 2003).

"Look for the Union Label." Unite! History. Available online at http://www.uniteunion.org/research/song.html; website home page http://www.uniteunion.org/whatisunite/whatis.html (accessed February 21, 2003).

National Consumers League Papers: "Prosanis" Label. *Prosperity and Thrift: The Coolidge Era and the Consumer Economy, 1921–1929.* American Memory digital primary source collection, Library of Congress. Available online at http://memory.loc.gov/ammem/coolhtml/coolhome.html; website home page: http://memory.loc.gov (accessed May 14, 2003).

"No Backward Step in Federal Aid For Road Building Can Be Taken"

Magazine article

By: Simeon D. Fess

Date: 1926

Source: Fess, Simeon D. "No Backward Step in Federal Aid for Road Building Can Be Taken." *American Motorist* 18, no. 2, February 1926, 12, 38, 40. Reproduced in "*American Motorist:* Selected Issues from 1926." *Prosperity and Thrift: The Coolidge Era and the Consumer Economy, 1921–1929.* American Memory digital primary source collection, Library of Congress. Available online at http://memory.loc.gov/ammem/coolhtml/coolhome.html; website homepage: http://memory.loc.gov (accessed May 14, 2003).

About the Author: Simeon Davison Fess (1861–1936) was born in Ohio. Fess attended Ohio Northern University and the University of Chicago, where he studied law and American history. In 1907, Fess assumed the presidency of Antioch College, an office he held for a decade. During that time he entered Ohio state politics, later serving as a U.S. congressman (1913–1923) and a U.S. senator (1924–1935). A staunch Republican and a renowned orator, Fess delivered the keynote address at the party's 1928 convention. Fess lost his reelection bid in 1935, and died the following year. ∎

Introduction

Before 1900, most public roads were cared for by local governments. These country roads were often in rough condition, and private transportation systems—railroads, steamboats, and canals—handled most long-distance traffic. Between the 1880s and the 1910s, however, "good roads" advocates lobbied for the improvement of the nation's highways. They met with some success: a handful of states assumed responsibility for hard-surfacing highways within their borders. Efforts to create a national highway commission did not fare as well. Instead, Congress enacted the 1916 Federal Aid Road Act, a compromise measure that offered federal assistance but kept road-building authority in the hands of state governments.

The 1916 federal act promised to support state road-building programs on a matching basis, provided that states meet certain requirements, such as the establishment of a state highway department under the control of engineers. Highway engineers were charged with depoliticizing state highway construction and providing rational, apolitical expertise. But even with the highway program under the control of engineers, questions remained as to which roads would be improved: national touring routes, intercity highways, or rural, farm-to-market roads. The 1916 act was silent on this issue, but a revised 1921 act declared that federal aid would be directed toward a national system. In 1925, a plan was adopted for coordinating and numbering routes in the U.S. highway system.

In this excerpt from the February 1926 issue of *American Motorist,* a publication of the American Automobile Association, Republican Senator Simeon D. Fess of Ohio defends the federal aid highway program.

Significance

The 1920s represented the golden age of highway building. World War I and the brief economic recession that followed it limited the impact of the 1916 act. But between 1921 and 1936, the states built more than 420,000 miles of improved highways. In 1929, automobile registrations reached 26.5 million; by that year every state had adopted the gasoline tax, which was soon the major source of revenue for highway construction.

The willingness with which Americans accepted the gasoline tax and the strong support they gave highway construction programs reveals how quickly the nation sur rendered to the pleasures of automobility. The middle-class family car became commonplace in the 1920s, as did a host of new industries designed to accommodate motorists: drive-in movies, fast-food chains, motorist campgrounds, and motels. Proponents of highway development like Senator Fess accurately assessed Americans' growing commitment to a car culture, and drew on this new enthusiasm in support of maintaining federal aid for highway development.

The extensive public resources devoted to road building were consistent with the tenets of an associationalist state—a style of governance in which public agencies cooperate with private industries in order to promote economic growth. By supporting highway construction, the state and federal governments fostered increased automobile use, which in turn encouraged the growth of auto manufacturers, allied materials producers (like oil, steel, and rubber), and tourist industries.

But the federal aid highway program of the 1920s was also indicative of an increasingly dynamic federalism. Whereas public roads had once been the product of local administration, by the 1920s, highway development was directed by officials at the local, state, and federal levels of government. As the nation initiated a public works project that continues to this day, it drew on the rich tradition of federalism to tackle a project that was national in scope, yet state and local in implementation.

Primary Source

"No Backward Step in Federal Aid For Road Building Can Be Taken"

SYNOPSIS: In this February 1926 article, Senator Simeon Fess reminds readers that Americans spent more than $8 billion a year on the purchase and upkeep of automobiles. In light of this, he maintains that the $481 million appropriated by Congress in the first decade of federal road aid was not excessive.

"Federal Funds for Road Building are a Fitting Appropriation to a Public Necessity Indisputably National in Character," Declares Senator Fess

Federal Aid for highways is now in its tenth year. The projected system is two-thirds completed, and the plans for the improvement of the remaining one-third are moving along in accord with a well-thought-out program of ordered economy. This has been accomplished without extravagance. It is believed that our interstate roads are at the moment lagging behind the gigantic requirements of highway transportation.

To date, the United States Treasury has actually paid out approximately $481,000,000 as the Government's share of Federal Aid highway expenditures, while Congress has authorized up to July, 1927, the expenditure of $690,000,000 on the Federal Aid system. A very considerable amount, you will say. But the total paid out to date is about one-half of the sum we spend in one year on the Army and the Navy, and the total authorization up to 1927 is far short of the sum of $940,000,000 that one class of road users, namely, the owners of motor vehicles, has paid into the Treasury since 1918.

Government Committed to Federal Aid

Propaganda hostile to Federal Aid is active, but I am convinced that it will not succeed. The scrapping of the Federal Aid policy at this stage of progress is out of the question. It is a policy to which the Government is committed, not only because of Federal Aid to the States under the Act of 1921, but also because Congress and the country are convinced that in cooperating in the work of national road building, the Government is following the constitutional obligations, namely, that it shall assume responsibility for national defense, for post offices and post roads, for the development of commerce between the States, all in the interest of and for the promotion of the national welfare. Measured in terms of results secured and advantages accruing from Government participation in road building, few Federal functions are giving the people more for the funds expended, and no Federal function that I know of partakes of a more truly national character.

Before proceeding further, let us examine briefly some of the objections raised by the critics of Federal Aid. Their arguments are specious and they will not stand the acid test of facts or of sound logic. For example, we are told that this is a sectional matter, that the eastern States are paying for road building in the western States. But what are the facts? An analysis of the figures of Federal expenditures for the last fiscal year shows that the New England, Middle Atlantic and East North Central States which contain only 13.7 per cent of the land area of the country, received 28.2 per cent of the Federal Aid. It shows that the Mountain and Pacific Coast States, which constitute 39.6 per cent of the total land area of the country received only 18.8 per cent of Federal Aid.

The expenditures for last year clearly demonstrate that every State and every section of the country takes advantage of every cent available from Federal sources under the law, and that there is nowhere a demand for a let-down in Government aid and participation.

It would be difficult to conceive of a more fallacious argument than that put forward by those who contend that the necessity for Federal participation in highway construction lies in the far West or in the Middle West and South. The necessity is in no wise sectional but is in all respects national. It is even more essential that the populous sections of the East should have an adequate system of highways.

There is a totally erroneous impression that the roads in the East have generally been built. It is true that road improvement was begun in that section at an early date, but every mile of the original construction is being rebuilt to meet present-day traffic requirements and the Federal funds are as eagerly used in this section as in any other. The Eastern States are benefiting to a marked degree by this Federal service for the very reason that their population is dense and that the number of interstate roads is great.

The West in Need of Roads

Federal participation in the sparsely settled States of the West is not different in principle, although the need is more acute by reason of long stretches of sparsely settled areas in which the Federal Government still holds a large percentage of the land. High mountain passes and desert stretches must be crossed with adequate highways before we shall have that tie between the different sections of the country that will lead to a greater unity of purpose and broader understanding which are in themselves worthy objectives of the Federal Aid highway system.

That the Western States are alive to their responsibility in the matter of road building and are not leaving the job to the Federal Government or to the Eastern States is proven by the heavy per capita expenditures which they annually apply to highways, for such expenditures are not equaled in any other section of the country. There is no one effort for unifying the whole country into one people like road building, which connects all the people into one family.

There is another false premise underlying the arguments against Federal Aid. They imply constantly that these highways benefit this or that section. They overlook the fact that in these days, travel on the main highways is not limited to the borders of any county or any State. In some States there are important highways today on which it is known that more than half the traffic originates in other States. There are many counties traversed by main roads on which not more than ten per cent of the traffic originates within the county. The through highways in which the Government is interested are essentially intercity roads. Yet these roads pass through counties in which there are no cities. If the residents of such counties are to be called upon to pay for the improvement of these roads we could certainly not expect them to pay for a type of improvement that is more expensive than their own local traffic needs will justify. Here is where Government, State and local cooperation plays a vital part, and is sound economically as well as governmentally.

Does Not Destroy State Initiative

We are often told that Government participation in road building tends to destroy State and local initiative. This statement is not supported by the facts. It may be said in answer that of the one billion dollars expended on all types of highways in the United States last year, the Federal Government supplied approximately ten per cent while ninety per cent of the funds were supplied by States and counties. Considering the vital interest of the Government itself, this was certainly not a disproportionate or an exorbitant amount, and might raise the question of fulfilment of Federal duty.

It is worthy of notice in this connection that of the designated Federal Aid highway system, the States have completed or have under construction 65,000 miles without a cent of aid from the Federal Government, as compared with the 57,560 miles which have been completed or undertaken with aid

A gas station and automotive product billboards line North Broad Street in Philadelphia in 1922. Roadway construction and the automotive industry expanded greatly during the 1920s. **HARTMAN CENTER FOR SALES, ADVERTISING, AND MARKETING HISTORY, DUKE UNIVERSITY RARE BOOK, MANUSCRIPT, AND SPECIAL COLLECTIONS LIBRARY.**

from the Government. This does not look as if the States were laying down on the job.

Equally untenable is the charge that the providing of funds from the United States Treasury has encouraged extravagance. . . .

Imagine what would happen if the States and the counties were spending a billion dollars a year with a view only to the requirements of States and local units and without any consideration for the requirements of interstate transportation. We might have roads, but we never would have a national system of highways. Federal Aid has enabled us to escape such a contingency.

At the present rate of construction, and if nothing happens to retard progress, we will, within five more years, have a continuous interstate highway system connecting every city of five thousand population or larger, and every section of it improved to take care of the requirements of present dense traffic. Therefore, I say again, that funds from the Federal Treasury to be diverted to the improvement of interstate roads are in no sense a discrimination against wealthy States, are in no wise a charitable

contribution from the rich to the poor, but rather a fitting appropriation to a public necessity indisputably national in character. On the other hand, I agree fully with President Coolidge that Federal funds should be used for interstate highways only, but this principle has been observed since the launching of the Federal Aid program.

The problem of highway construction and operation is so gigantic that I sometimes doubt if the public at large appreciate its magnitude. Statements as to expenditures for highways confront us much more frequently than statements as to the cost of vehicular operation over the highways.

Occasionally one hears the complaint that the billion dollars, one-tenth from the Federal Government, three-tenths from the States and six-tenths from local sources, annually expended for highway construction and maintenance in the United States is excessive. How many of those who give voice to this complaint, I wonder, realize that the American people pay each year more than $8,000,000,000 for the purchase, upkeep and operation of motor vehicles; or that the annual sales of new cars and trucks amount to more than double the billion dollars expenditure for roads; or that if all the new cars and trucks sold each year were parked in a single line on the new roads built in the same year, the intervals between them would be less than five feet each? Yet these are the simple facts.

The entire cost of highway construction and upkeep is only about ten per cent of the whole bill for highway transportation. That ten per cent cannot be escaped, because if the highways are not improved and maintained, the addition to the operating bill, already ninety per cent of the total, will more than offset whatever is denied the roads. In the end, if such a policy of denial were persisted in, our $15,000,000,000 investment in highway rolling stock would become practically useless because of highway deterioration.

The Government is not spending too much for highways. Apart from every other consideration, the users of the highway receive a splendid dividend in cheaper transportation. The difference between the cost of operation over improved and unimproved highways would pay for the cost of improvement in a comparatively few number of years. From this standpoint, no Federal expenditure is paying a higher dividend to our people than the annual appropriation for highways. To scrap this Federal policy would be nothing short of disaster. Public sentiment would not stand for it and national self-interest commits the Government to the fulfillment of the present program. Not until this program is completed can we have assurance that we have a true national highway system.

Further Resources

BOOKS

Fein, Michael R. "Public Works: New York Road Building and the American State, 1880–1956." Ph.D. diss., Brandeis University, 2003.

Flink, James J. *The Automobile Age.* Cambridge, Mass.: MIT Press, 1988.

Goddard, Stephen B. *Getting There: The Epic Struggle Between Road and Rail in the American Century.* New York: Basic Books, 1994.

Seely, Bruce. *Building the American Highway System: Engineers as Policy Makers.* Philadelphia: Temple University Press, 1987.

PERIODICALS

Paxson, Frederic L. "The American Highway Movement, 1916–1935." *American Historical Review* 101, January 1946, 236–253.

Seely, Bruce. "Railroads, Good Roads, and Motor Vehicles: Managing Technological Change." *Railroad History Bulletin,* 155, Autumn 1986, 35–63.

WEBSITES

"Highway History." The U.S. Department of Transportation, Federal Highway Administration. Available online at http://www.fhwa.dot.gov/infrastructure/history.htm; website home page http://www.fhwa.dot.gov/index.html (accessed February 21, 2003).

Calvin Coolidge and Nicaragua

"Message to Congress on Nicaragua"
Message

By: Calvin Coolidge

Date: January 10, 1927

Source: Coolidge, Calvin. "Message to Congress on Nicaragua, January 10, 1927." *Congressional Record,* 69th Congress, 2nd session, 1927, vol. 68, 1324–1326. Reprinted in Romero, Francine Sanders, ed. *Presidents from Theodore Roosevelt through Coolidge: Debating the Issues in Pro and Con Primary Documents.* Westport, Conn.: Greenwood Press, 2000, 215–217.

About the Author: Calvin Coolidge (1872–1933), the nation's thirtieth president, spent most of his life in politics. A conservative Republican, he rose through the ranks from Northampton, Massachusetts, city councilor to Massachusetts governor in the span of two decades. As governor, Coolidge gained national recognition when he intervened in a Boston police strike in 1919. The following year he was nominated by his party to run as vice president on Warren Harding's ticket. When Harding died in 1923, Coolidge became president. Easily reelected in 1924, Coolidge presided over an era of economic prosperity assisted by pro-business policies.

"Coolidge Crossing the Gulf"
Political cartoon

By: Art Young

Date: February 1927

Source: Young, Art. "Coolidge Crossing the Gulf." *New Masses,* February, 1927. Reproduced in "Prosperity and Thrift: The Coolidge Era and the Consumer Economy, 1921–1929." *Prosperity and Thrift: The Coolidge Era and the Consumer Economy, 1921–1929.* American Memory digital primary source collection, Library of Congress. Available online at http://memory.loc.gov/ammem/coolhtml/coolhome.html; website home page: http://memory.loc.gov (accessed May 12, 2003).

About the Author: Art Young (1866–1943) was an illustrator whose work appeared in a variety of publications, including the *Chicago Daily News,* the *Evening Journal,* and a socialist magazine called *The Masses.* His political cartoons could be interpreted in many ways, as he strove to expose with his drawings the hypocrisy behind official images. The

U.S. government, in 1917, claimed that cartoons by Young and his compatriots at *The Masses* violated the Espionage Act. The magazine was forced to close, while a jury trial for the accused failed to bring a conviction. ∎

Introduction

As American economic power increased during the last quarter of the nineteenth century, so too did its economic interest in Latin America. In an effort to consolidate its hemispheric supremacy, the United States supported independence movements in Central American and Caribbean nations, replacing European colonial regimes with ones more friendly to America and to American investment. The opening of the canal route through Panama, the construction of railroads, and the establishment of American companies (including fruit and coffee plantations) all contributed to the growing American presence in Latin America.

When European trading patterns were disrupted during World War I, American investors turned even greater attention southward. European investment dwindled during the hostilities, as American entrepreneurs opened up new operations in Latin America. The pro-business sentiment of the time—which many felt contributed to American domestic prosperity—was visible in foreign affairs as well. Through the easing of antitrust and banking regulations, the U.S. government encouraged the expansion of American economic activity in Latin America in an effort to make America the banking center for the entire hemisphere.

By the 1920s, Americans administered Nicaragua's customs, banking, and railroad systems. The loans necessary to develop the country's infrastructure had been negotiated by the U.S. State Department. This steady flow of money, directed by American political and corporate elites, was integral to the maintenance of the Conservative administration in Nicaragua, presided over by Adolfo Díaz—the Nicaraguan president who had been supported by American military interventions during the Taft administration.

As a further means of preserving domestic tranquility, U.S. Marines remained posted in the country until Nicaraguan Liberals and Conservatives called a truce in 1925. But the compromise government collapsed within weeks. Revolutions and counterrevolutions rocked Nicaragua for two years. When Díaz was nominated as a compromise leader in 1927, President Calvin Coolidge and Secretary of State Frank Kellogg deployed 2,000 Marines to support his administration and to put down the nationalist revolution led by Augusto Sandino. A few days later, on January 10, 1927, Coolidge sent a written statement to Congress, explaining the reasons for the American military intervention.

Significance

Nicaragua, like other Latin American nations, was often depicted in the popular press as a scruffy, delinquent child, in need of Uncle Sam's supervision. The Coolidge administration capitalized on this stereotype and used it both to justify American involvement in the affairs of other nations and to downplay the significance of its military actions. Thus America became a policeman, Sandino a bandit. Fears that Mexican Bolsheviks supported Díaz's political opponents tapped into American anticommunist sentiment and provided one more reason to suppress the Nicaragua revolution.

For others though, the Nicaraguan military intervention reflected nothing more than strict economic interest. Liberal magazines such as the *Nation* and radical presses like the socialist *New Masses* criticized the United States for what they saw as blatant international bullying. From their perspective, U.S. Marines were sent in to meddle with another country's political process in order to ensure friendly leadership, protect American citizens' existing investments, and guard American access to Nicaraguan resources (including a possible new canal route). Opponents of the invasion thought that in light of America's own revolutionary origins, it was especially hypocritical to refuse to recognize an administration that had gained control through violent means.

In his January 10, 1927, message, Coolidge reminded Congress that Nicaragua and other Latin American countries had signed a treaty (at America's behest) stating that governments that attain power through violent revolution should not be recognized. But his main concern, Coolidge wrote, remained the safety of Americans, their property, and their investments. Protecting these, Coolidge maintained, required the use of armed force to bring about political stability.

Primary Source

"Message to Congress on Nicaragua" [excerpt]

> **SYNOPSIS:** In this excerpt, President Coolidge defends the deployment of American armed forces in Nicaragua. The United States, he says, has "a moral obligation" to help "prevent revolution and disorder" in Central America.

While conditions in Nicaragua and the action of this government pertaining thereto have in general been made public, I think the time has arrived for me officially to inform the Congress more in detail of the events leading up to the present disturbances and conditions which seriously threaten American lives and property, endanger the stability of all Central America, and put in jeopardy the rights granted

Secretary of State Frank Kellogg (right) stands with chairman of the Senate Foreign Relations Committee William Borah in 1927. Kellogg justified U.S. involvement in Nicaragua to the committee, stating that communist activity was on the rise in Mexico and Central America, thus posing a threat to the United States. **THE LIBRARY OF CONGRESS.**

by Nicaragua to the United States for the construction of a canal.

It is well known that in 1912 the United States intervened in Nicaragua with a large force and put down a revolution, and that from that time to 1925 a legation guard of American Marines was, with the consent of the Nicaragua government, kept in Managua to protect American lives and property. In 1923 representatives of the five Central American countries, namely, Costa Rica, Guatemala, Honduras, Nicaragua, and Salvador, at the invitation of the United States, met in Washington and entered into a series of treaties.

These treaties dealt with limitation of armament, a Central American tribunal for arbitration, and the general subject of peace and amity. . . .

The United States was not a party to this treaty, but it was made in Washington under the auspices of the secretary of state, and this government has felt a moral obligation to apply its principles in order to encourage the Central American states in their efforts to prevent revolution and disorder. The treaty, it may be noted in passing, was signed on behalf of Nicaragua by Emiliano Chamorro himself, who afterwards assumed the presidency in violation thereof and thereby contributed to the creation of the present difficulty.

■ ■ ■

Immediately following the inauguration of President Díaz, and frequently since that date, he has appealed to the United States for support, has informed this government of the aid which Mexico

Primary Source

"Coolidge Crossing the Gulf"

SYNOPSIS: In this political cartoon, which appeared in the February, 1927, issue of the socialist journal *New Masses,* President Calvin Coolidge and Secretary of State Frank Kellogg, along with other "interests," are depicted in a re-creation of the painting *Washington Crossing the Delaware.* Noted political cartoonist Art Young (1866–1943) offers a twofold radical critique of American involvement in Nicaragua. He condemns Coolidge for acting on behalf of monied interests, but he also suggests that America has adopted a double standard regarding political revolution. Recalling America's own revolutionary campaign under George Washington, the artist implies that the United States has forsaken that tradition for economic imperialism. THE LIBRARY OF CONGRESS.

is giving to the revolutionists, and has stated that he is unable solely because of the aid given by Mexico to the revolutionists to protect the lives and property of American citizens and other foreigners.

■ ■ ■

For many years numerous Americans have been living in Nicaragua, developing its industries and carrying on business. At the present time there are large investments in lumbering, mining, coffee growing, banana culture, shipping, and also in general mercantile and other collateral business. All these people and these industries have been encouraged by the Nicaraguan government. That government has at all times owed them protection, but the United States has occasionally been obliged to send naval forces for their proper protection. In the present crisis such forces are requested by the Nicaraguan government, which protests to the United States its

inability to protect these interests and states that any measures which the United States deems appropriate for their protection will be satisfactory to the Nicaraguan government.

In addition to these industries now in existence, the government of Nicaragua . . . granted in perpetuity to the United States the exclusive proprietary rights necessary and convenient for the construction, operation, and maintenance of an oceanic canal. . . .

There is no question that if the revolution continues, American investments and business interests in Nicaragua will be very seriously affected, if not destroyed. . . .

. . . The proprietary rights of the United States in the Nicaraguan canal route, with the necessary implications growing out of it affecting the Panama Canal, together with the obligations flowing from the investments of all classes of our citizens in

Nicaragua, place us in a position of peculiar responsibility. I am sure it is not the desire of the United States to intervene in the internal affairs of Nicaragua or of any other Central American republic. Nevertheless, it must be said that we have a very definite and special interest in the maintenance of order and good government in Nicaragua at the present time, and that the stability, prosperity, and independence of all Central American countries can never be a matter of indifference to us.

The United States cannot, therefore, fail to view with deep concern any serious threat to stability and constitutional government in Nicaragua tending toward anarchy and jeopardizing American interests, especially if such state of affairs is contributed to or brought about by outside influences or by any foreign power. It has always been and remains the policy of the United States in such circumstances to take the steps that may be necessary for the preservation and protection of the lives, the property, and the interest of its citizens and of this government itself. In this respect I propose to follow the path of my predecessors.

Consequently, I have deemed it my duty to use the powers committed to me to ensure the adequate protection of all American interests in Nicaragua, whether they be endangered by internal strife or by outside interference in the affairs of that republic.

Further Resources

BOOKS

Krenn, Michael L. *U.S. Policy Toward Economic Nationalism in Latin America, 1917–1929.* Wilmington, Del.: Scholarly Resources, 1990.

Musicant, Ivan. *The Banana Wars: A History of United States Military Intervention in Latin America from the Spanish-American War to the Invasion of Panama.* New York: Macmillan Publishing Co., 1990.

Sharbach, Sarah E. *Stereotypes of Latin America, Press Images and U.S. Foreign Policy, 1920–1930.* New York: Garland Publishing, 1993.

PERIODICALS

Salisbury, Richard V. "Mexico, the United States, and the 1926–1927 Nicaraguan Crisis." *Hispanic American Historical Review* 66, May 1986, 319–39.

WEBSITES

"Frank Billings Kellogg." Nobel e-Museum. Available online at http://www.nobel.se/peace/laureates/1929/kellogg-bio.html; website home page http://www.nobel.se/index.html (accessed February 24, 2003).

"Open Letter to the Pullman Company"

Letter

By: A. Philip Randolph

Date: June 4, 1927

Source: Randolph, A. Philip. "Open Letter to the Pullman Company, June 4, 1927." *The Messenger* 9, July 1927, 237–41. Reprinted in Foner, Philip S., and Ronald L. Lewis. *Black Workers: A Documentary History from Colonial Times to the Present.* Philadelphia: Temple University Press, 1989, 392–403. Original letter in the Lowell M. Greenlaw Papers, Chicago Historical Society.

About the Author: Asa Philip Randolph (1889–1979) was born in Crescent City, Florida, and educated at the Cookman Institute, Florida's first high school for African Americans. He moved to New York City in 1911, where he enrolled at City College and became active in socialist politics. Randolph co-founded the radical magazine, *The Messenger* in 1917. In 1925, Randolph helped to organize the Brotherhood of Sleeping Car Porters, the first predominantly African American union. A prominent spokesman for the rights of African American workers, he subsequently organized campaigns against discrimination in federal defense jobs and in the U.S. military in the 1940s. Randolph continued to fight for racial and economic justice in the 1950s and 1960s and was hailed as an elder statesman in the civil rights movement. ∎

Introduction

George Pullman founded the Pullman Palace Car Company in 1867 in an effort to realize his vision of comfortable, long-distance rail travel. His Pullman sleeper cars offered a wide variety of amenities: from sleeping berths and baggage handling to drink service and shoe shines. These services were provided by porters, who were all African American men, many recently freed from slavery.

The Pullman Company quickly became the nation's largest employer of African American labor. The company sought African American porters exclusively for several reasons. They could be paid low wages, they offered white passengers a form of status achieved by having an African American servant, and they offered a level of privacy based on the social distance demanded by existing codes of racial etiquette. The company recruited widely in the South, where traditions of service were believed to be stronger.

Pullman porters gained in status within the African American community in the early twentieth century. Having traded in the laborer's denims or the clothes of the field hand for the porter's uniform, the highly mobile, better-paid porters were associated with a northern, urbane cosmopolitanism. But the work was demeaning. The African American porters had to work round the clock, sleeping in the men's lounge on four-hour shifts. And the porters' heavy dependence on tips meant adhering to strict racially defined behavior and deference.

Entrenched economic racism kept porters' wages low and working conditions substandard into the 1920s. Efforts by porters to organize themselves had failed several times in the first two decades of the century. A nascent advocacy organization, the Pullman Porters and Maids Protective Association, was quickly dismantled after the Pullman Corporation established its own company union, the Employee Representation Plan (ERP). Even after an ERP wage conference in 1924, wages still remained well below those necessary to maintain a minimum standard of living.

The Brotherhood of Sleeping Car Porters (BSCP) was founded in 1925 by a small cell of porters in New York City. They called upon A. Philip Randolph, a socialist editor and orator, to help lead the fledgling union. Randolph had an uphill battle. Many porters were reluctant to join the union out of a sense of gratitude toward what was perceived as corporate benevolence. Others feared company reprisals. For this reason, the BSCP met in secret and kept its membership lists clandestine.

During the union's early years, Randolph faced persistent attacks from the company, but also from the African American community, who wondered if an African American union was in the porters' or the community's best interest. Some of this criticism was legitimate; some reflected blatant efforts by the Pullman Company to buy off African American leadership. And though Randolph was an anticommunist, his socialist politics left him—and the union—open to charges of radicalism. In such a contested situation, it remained difficult for Randolph to draw the porters away from their alliance with white capitalists and toward African American union leadership. This effort was further hampered by white trade unionists, who resisted union integration.

Significance

Randolph published his open letter to the Pullman Company in *The Messenger* on June 4, 1927. The letter was designed to attract publicity for the porters' cause, but also to defuse the burgeoning hostility directed at it. The company did not respond to the letter, but internal memoranda suggest that it was read and discussed. The Pullman Company defended its racially defined wage scale, arguing that while porters were paid less than white workers, they were better paid than other African American workers. When the company refused to bargain with the BSCP, Randolph threatened a strike in 1928. But strong resistance from the company and poor relations with other railway unions undercut the strike, and it did not come to pass. The Brotherhood struggled for several more years until the more favorable political climate of the New Deal brought about union recognition by the company and a charter from the American Federation of Labor's white leadership.

Primary Source

"Open Letter to the Pullman Company" [excerpt]

> **SYNOPSIS:** In this public letter, A. Philip Randolph describes the origins and purposes of the Brotherhood of Sleeping Car Porters and argues that the company has treated the porters unfairly based on their race.

Mr. E. F. Cary, President,
The Pullman Company,
Pullman Building,
Chicago, Ill.

Dear Sir:

I am addressing you this letter in order to acquaint you, first hand, with every phase of the development of the Movement to organize the Pullman porters in order that your attitude toward this Movement may rest upon a basis of understanding.

First, why did the Pullman porters organize? I think it is a sound business policy that you frankly face the question and honestly seek an answer. Doubtless, you can recall several previous efforts on the part of the porters to organize, especially during the war. Each time the main question at issue was wages and working conditions. Evidently, the porters felt then that organization would enable them to improve their condition. Then the United States Government, through the Railroad Administration Department, of which Messrs. McAdoo and Hines were Director Generals, encouraged the organization of railroad employees. With a view of adjusting disputes between carriers and employees with facility and dispatch, the Government set up the Board of Wages and Working Conditions. This Board was replaced by the United States Railroad Labor Board, which was set up under the Transportation Act upon the restoration of railroads to private hands, in 1920.

During this time you organized the Employment Representation Plan for the Pullman porters. It functioned for about six years unchallenged. On August 25, 1925, the Brotherhood of Sleeping Car Porters was born. It was the outgrowth of long deep-seated grievances which had been partly expressed and partly unexpressed, grievances because of poor working conditions which the Employee Representation Plan failed to remedy. These are not imagined but very real grievances which cannot and ought not to be summarily ignored, either by the Company or the porters. Despite several wage conferences under the Plan, five years after its inauguration, porters received a wage of only $67.50 a month, thereby being compelled to rely, for a living, on tips, which a scientific survey by the New York Labor Bureau revealed averaged only $58.15 a month, out of which an average occupational expense of $33.82 must come. This brought an income of only $1,154.16 a year, whereas, the United States Bureau of Labor Statistics has set $2,040.75 as the minimum yearly wage upon which an American family can live in health and decency. Coupled with this, the systematic oppression of some of your local officials, the inability of porters to get a fair hearing on charges made against them under your Plan, the failure of porters to get an adequate redress for their grievances, the obvious Company control of the Plan, made organization among the porters, as among your conductors, necessary and inevitable. I am sure I need not tell you that porters would not always be content to work the long hours of 350 or more a month under that 11,000 mileage basis without compensation for overtime.

May I say that the Employee Representation Plan, the Pullman Porters Benefit Association, Field Days, Quartets, Bands, Stock Distribution Plans, Free Insurance, Courtesy and Honor Rolls do not constitute a fundamental, fair or permanent solution of the problem of unrest which the above-named conditions are bound to foster, engender and inculcate. Such, then, is the basic reason for the beginning of the Brotherhood.

Who Began it?

In order that your mind might be disabused of any misrepresentation about the origin of the Brotherhood, permit me to assure you, backed up by our records, that the Pullman porters in your employ, began the Movement to organize the porters and maids. In the home of Mr. W. H. Des Verney, a porter, thirty-seven years in your service, the first meeting was called. At that meeting, Mr. Roy Lancaster, seventeen years a porter and A. L. Totten, nine years a porter, both of whom served as officials of the Employee Representation Plan and the Pullman Porters Benefit Association, were present. I was the only person invited there who had never served the Company. But I am certain that you will admit that porters have as much right to secure a person who was never a porter to represent their organization as the stockholders of the Pullman Company have to employ an attorney or statistician, not a stockholder, to represent them.

Who Compose it?

And the Brotherhood is composed of Pullman porters. Nor are they all young men. The survey by the Labor Bureau of New York showed that the average service-ages of the members of the Brotherhood are a fraction over nine years. It may be interesting for you to know that all of the organizing committees, which are the local executive and administrative machinery of the Brotherhood, are composed of the oldest and most responsible men in your service, service-ages ranging from ten to forty years.

Who Control the Brotherhood?

The control of the Brotherhood is in the hands of the porters who finance it by their monthly dues, and assessments when essential. Contrary to unfounded charges, none of the leaders of the Union are either Atheists or Communists. Its leaders do not oppose the United States Government or advocate irreligion. The Brotherhood is perfectly willing to permit the Pullman Company or any body of disinterested, responsible citizens, to institute an investigation to establish the truth or falsity of our claim.

Purpose of Brotherhood

The organization is seeking lawfully to secure better wages, improved working conditions for the porters and maids through the approved and accepted method of collective bargaining. This principle is recognized in both state and federal statutes. The new Railway Labor Act, which you supported, as a member of the Association of Railway Executives, provides under the head of General Duties, in Section 2 that "All disputes between a carrier and its employees shall be considered, and, if possible, decided with all expedition in conference between representatives designated and authorized so to confer respectively, by the carriers and by the employees thereof interested in the dispute. Third, Representatives, for the purposes of this Act, shall be designated by the respective parties in such manner as may be provided in their corporate organization or unincorporated association, or by other means of collective action, without interference, influence or coercion exercised by either party over the self-organization or designation of representatives by the other."

The right of self-organization on the part of the employees of carriers is clearly and cogently set forth in the aforementioned Act which of course, I am sure you do not deny, since you were a party to its formulation and enactment.

The fact that you recognize the right of your employees to organize and bargain collectively with you is shown by your jointly setting up of an Adjustment

Board with the Pullman conductors under the Act. Thus, I am confident that you would not consciously and deliberately seek to deny the porters a right which you recognize and accord the conductors.

But the purpose of the Brotherhood is not only to secure more wages and better working conditions, it is as sincerely concerned and interested in a high standard of service as you are, for we realize that as the company grows and develops into a bigger, better and more prosperous enterprise, the possibilities of improvement for the porters and maids increase, also. . . .

The Brotherhood is much more prepared, spiritually and intellectually, to secure this creative, constructive response and discipline than you can through your Employee Representation Plan, because the former, the Brotherhood, emanates from within, as an expression of the spirit and life and hopes and faith of the porters in themselves, whereas, the latter, the Plan, is imposed upon them from without—which social psychology will show— can hardly make for a higher morale that will reflect itself in a finer quality of service. . . .

Progress of Company

The material progress of the Pullman service industry has been marvelous, unprecedented. The entire American public has been the beneficiary of the constructive resourcefulness and ingenuity of its management in mechanical elaboration and perfection of physical equipment.

From the wooden, kerosene-lamp miniature sleeper, has developed the magnificent, richly decorated and furnished standard sixteen section sleeper, and your very recent addition, the fourteen-room car, which probably represents the last word in luxury and comfort, in transit, on rails. . . .

Progress of Porters and Maids

I need not tell you that, in the nature of things, it would be impossible for the porters and maids to be a part of this phenomenal progress, playing a considerable and basic part in giving its existence, without being profoundly influenced intellectually and spiritually. In very truth, the porter of fifty years ago, with the wicker-lamp, wooden car mind, could no more properly handle the deluxe standard sleeping, parlor, buffet, room, observation, steel cars of today than could the wooden, wicker-lamp cars of yesterday meet the rigid and exacting industrial and social requirements of modern travel. The former only re-

quired a porter with a primitive, rural mind; the latter, a porter with an alert, urbanized mind. I think you will agree that the vast progress of the Company would not have been possible with the porter with the slow-moving rural mind. A person needs much more urbanization to be able efficiently to handle the highly elaborated mechanism of the Pullman car. And along with the transformation of the rural mind of the porter into an urban mind, goes a progressive change in worth, service technique and competency and productivity. But accompanying this urbanization and improvement in the productive ability of the porter, go the needs, desires, interests, hopes and demands of an urban citizen.

The history of all social psychology shows that the latter inevitably follows the former. The wage increases you have granted are based upon the assumption that a porter of today, with an urban mind, is worth more to the Company than a porter of yesterday, with a rural mind. . . .

Attitude of Company to Conductors

. . . I am sure you would not join hands in the adoption of a course of action which you thought was harmful to the Company and conductors. Thus, I think you will agree that the porters and the public are justified in assuming by your recognition of the conductors' union that you don't consider the principle of self-organization, self-designation of representatives for collective bargaining, as inimical to the welfare and interests of the Company, the conductors or the porters and maids.

Therefore, I assume that the question of organization will not be an issue if it can be demonstrated that the porters and maids want it, which, of course, is a logical position. If the porters didn't want organization, the Brotherhood could not well claim that they did, since such a claim is subject to verification by a disinterested Government body, the United States Mediation Board.

No legitimate objection can be raised against the organization of porters on the grounds that it will destroy discipline, for, in the first place a bonafide functioning organization of porters and maids has never existed; hence no grounds of fact exist upon which to base such an assumption. Moreover, it is perfectly unfair to predicate attributes and behavior of a group of men and women under conditions they have never experienced. Instead of organization subverting discipline, it will greatly improve it, since the very organization of porters presupposes, implies and indicates their susceptibility

A Pullman porter shines the shoes of sleeping passengers. **ARCHIVE PHOTOS. REPRODUCED BY PERMISSION.**

to discipline, for discipline is nothing more than the implicit acceptance of, and obedience to, definite rules of behavior, which is the recognized condition of organization.

But if organization is believed by you to be injurious to the discipline of the porters, why do you maintain the Employees Representation Plan for them? It is my understanding that you allege the Plan to be an organization; hence, rendering another form of organization superfluous and unnecessary. . . .

Train Crews and the Brotherhood

If associated effort as between the various sections of labor personnel in a given industry makes for increased production, so will associated effort between two industrial groups, say, the train crews and the Pullman crews, make for a larger total efficiency on a given train, as well as a larger specific efficiency of each individual industrial group. Concretely, the Pullman service will surely be the beneficiary of the cooperation between the train crews and the Pullman crews. This is obvious because the work relates at certain points. But such cooperation would hardly be possible if the train crews feel that

a large section of the Pullman crews are scabs, their enemies. Scabs are despised by all union men which emotionally prevents willing and helpful cooperation. This accounts for the support which the Brotherhood receives from the standard railroad unions. It is, therefore, palpably to the interest of the Company to have the porters and maids organized into bonafide union which other railroad unions will respect and recognize. . . .

Attitude of Negro Public

You have only to canvass Negro public opinion to find a virtual unanimity of interest in the success of the Brotherhood. It is viewed as the most significant economic movement of racial progress instituted in the last half century. The most outstanding Negro organizations and leaders such as the National Association for the Advancement of Colored People, the leaders of the National Urban League, the National Federation of Colored Women's Clubs, the Shriners, The Elks, The Interdenominational Ministerial Alliance of New York, the members of which are preaching Brotherhood sermons, the International Negro Ministerial Alliance of America, the Negro Race Congress, headed by Dr. Jernigan of Washington, and practically the entire Negro press, stand behind the Brotherhood.

The White Public

Of the attitude of the white public, doubtless you are to some extent aware, for you surely know of the public prominence of a large number of the men and women who compose our Committee of One Hundred. It certainly speaks definitely for the responsibility of our movement. None of the persons, who are members of the Committee, can be accused of readily affixing their names to anything in which they have no confidence. Especially, would they be hesitant about venturing into the Brotherhood, implicit with big and far-reaching principles, unless they were committed to its program.

Permit me herewith to reassure you that the Brotherhood stands ready to submit to, and abide by, the Watson-Parker Bill, which has established the procedure of mediation or arbitration of disputes between self-organized employees and carriers. We feel that the dispute between the membership of the Brotherhood which embraces the majority of your employees of this class of service, and the Pullman Company can be amicably adjudged through mediation or arbitration as provided in the law.

If you feel that the Brotherhood has no case, I am sure you would not be opposed to having this fact established through fair and impartial arbitration as provided by the Act, since you could sustain no loss, but only secure a reaffirmation of your contention. If the Brotherhood has a case, I think you will also agree that it would be industrially inexpedient to deny same, since it could only tend to give force to a continuing vexatious condition of discontent among the porters and maids, which will render an eventual definite handling of the situation through mediation, arbitration or direct conference, advisable and imperative. . . .

Respectfully yours,
A. Philip Randolph,
General Organizer, Brotherhood of Sleeping Car Porters.

Further Resources

BOOKS

Harris, William H. *Keeping the Faith: A. Philip Randolph, Milton P. Webster, and the Brotherhood of Sleeping Car Porters, 1925–37.* Urbana: University of Illinois Press, 1977.

Santino, Jack. *Miles of Smiles, Years of Struggle: Stories of Black Pullman Porters.* Urbana, Ill.: University of Illinois Press, 1989.

PERIODICALS

Harris, William H. "A. Philip Randolph as a Charismatic Leader." *Journal of Negro History* 64, Autumn 1979, 301–315.

Hutchinson, George. "Mediating 'Race' and the 'Nation': The Cultural Politics of *The Messenger*." *African-American Review* 28, Winter 1994, 531–548.

WEBSIZES

"A. Philip Randolph: For Jobs and Freedom." PBS Online. Available online at http://www.pbs.org/weta/apr/aprprogram .html; website home page http://www.pbs.org/ (accessed February 20, 2003).

AUDIO AND VISUAL MEDIA

A. Philip Randolph: For Jobs and Freedom. PBS. Produced and directed by Dante J. James. Videocassette, 1998.

"The Present Status and Future Prospects of Chains of Department Stores"

Speech

By: Edward A. Filene

Date: 1927

Source: Filene, Edward A. "The Present Status and Future Prospects of Chains of Department Stores: An Address Delivered before the American Economic Association, Washington, D.C., December 27, 1927." Transcript reproduced in *Prosperity and Thrift: The Coolidge Era and the Consumer Economy, 1921–1929.* American Memory digital primary source collection, Library of Congress. Available online at http://memory .loc.gov/ammem/coolhtml/coolhome.html; website home page: http://memory.loc.gov (accessed May 12, 2003).

About the Author: Edward Albert Filene (1860–1937) was born in Salem, Massachusetts. Along with his brother Lincoln, Edward established Filene's department store in downtown Boston. This pioneering business blended mass distribution, scientific management, and novel forms of sales (including the "bargain basement") to become one of the nation's most thriving retail establishments. Following the success of his department store, Edward Filene helped found the United States Chamber of Commerce. He also chaired the War Shipping Committee during World War I, was active in civic reform movements, and wrote widely about economic and political issues. ∎

Introduction

Chain stores—that is, individually managed retail businesses owned by a single company—emerged in the late nineteenth century. The first chain was founded in 1859 by the Great Atlantic & Pacific Tea Company; it's now the A&P grocery-store chain. But chain stores did not spring into full bloom until the early twentieth century. James Cash Penney, a pioneer in chain-store retailing, opened his first store in Kemmerer, Wyoming, in 1902. After joining with Earl Sams in 1907, Penney expanded the chain in the 1910s and 1920s. There were 312 J.C. Penney stores in 1920, earning $42.8 million; by the end of the decade there were 1,395 stores, earning $209.7 million.

Cash-and-carry chain stores quickly outpaced even the largest of the old department stores like Filene's and Macy's, which had higher costs imposed by extra services such as deliveries and credit. Moreover, they simply could not compete with the economies of scale that benefited multiple-store chains. By the early 1920s, chain grocery stores had horned in on local merchants; by the end of the decade, chains of variety stores (e.g., Woolworth's), drugstores (Walgreen's), and shoe stores (Kinney's) threatened established independent retailers. Even Sears, Roebuck, and Company, the pathbreaking mail-order house, opened retail outlets in conjunction with its existing distribution centers in order to boost sales during the postwar recession.

Significance

The chain stores offered a new means of cutting distribution costs and lowering prices for the consumer. Independent stores had always bought from wholesalers, who in turn had purchased goods in large quantities from producers. Each took its share, and the price of goods rose accordingly. Chain stores, which had the capacity to purchase goods in larger quantities than independent merchants (and even large department stores), upset this established order by acting as both wholesaler purchasers and retailer sellers. Size had other benefits: since advertising costs could be distributed widely among all the stores, chain stores could afford to run national advertising campaigns and inundate consumers with their appeals.

Chain-store sales skyrocketed in the 1920s as the number of stores increased. Even though independent stores far outnumbered chain stores, the chains' sales volume grew out of proportion to their numbers. Not surprisingly, this generated great concern. Leading department-store owners, including Edward Filene, recognized the threat the chain stores posed to established retailers—advantages of scale not so different from the ones they had employed against dry-goods houses in the late nineteenth century. But whereas Filene advocated adopting the chain stores' methods, others resisted the trend. Communities staged boycotts, citizens campaigned to keep local money in local stores, and independent merchants' associations lobbied for protective legislation. By the late 1920s, states had considered dozens of acts (some of doubtful constitutionality) designed to curtail chain-store expansion or to prohibitively tax them.

The growth of chain stores had been so explosive during the 1920s that many feared they would entirely smother independent retailers. But firms could not continue to open new stores forever. By the 1930s, the trend shifted away from more openings and toward the enlargement of existing stores. This trend was heightened by the increase in restrictive legislation and the collapse of the stock market, which dried up the capital necessary to support expansion. Nonetheless, chain stores continued to play a large role in the American economy, from the supermarkets of the 1950s to the big-box retailers of today.

Primary Source

"The Present Status and Future Prospects of Chain Stores in America" [excerpt]

> **SYNOPSIS:** In this speech, Edward A. Filene, department store magnate, explains how chain stores profited by removing obstacles from the stream of distribution. In order for independent department stores to survive, Filene argues, they themselves must merge into chains—"chains within chains"— in order to remain competitive.

Chains of department stores will, before very long, dominate the retail field.

We are right now in the midst of epoch making changes in methods of distribution. Mass production has made mass distribution necessary.

Although production costs are constantly decreasing, due to mass production methods, the spread between the production cost and what the consumer pays is on the average greater today than when I entered the retail business some forty years ago. Certain types of retailing are in effect dams in the stream of distribution—a stream which should be broad, deep and swift flowing.

Chain stores have shown how to remove many of the obstructions in the distribution stream. It is true that as yet department stores have not been hard pressed. But unless they organize so as to conform to the new trend in distribution methods, chain stores will so organize that they will combine the advantages of the department stores with the manifest advantages which the chains already have.

In one way or another great chains of department stores are certain to develop. One way is for the existing department stores to form themselves into chains. Each department of each store will then become a unit of a chain of similar departments. There will be chains within chains.

If department stores fail to do this, then the existing chains in different lines will get together. They will occupy buildings of the department store type, and organize to function successfully in competition with the most successful department stores. . . .

How Chain Stores Have Grown

First: In 1925 the S. S. Kresge Company operated 304 five and ten cent stores and did a total business of $105,965,610. As of July 8, 1927 it operated 400 stores. For the first eleven months of 1927 its sales have been $110,722,047. In November its sales were $12,010,892.

Second: To show that this success is not an isolated case, consider the fact that had an investor bought $1,000 worth of the capital stock of each of 10 chain store systems as recently as 1912, the market value of his $10,000 investment would today be more than $300,000.

Third: That this growth is still going on is shown by figures for the first 11 months of 1927. Twenty-two chain store systems did an aggregate business in that period of $848,035,385—an increase of 15.8% over the sales for the same period of 1926.

There are more than fifty fields in which important chains are spreading with amazing rapidity.

I foretold the success of the chain stores because I saw that they were fundamentally more in accord with basic economic law than were most of the other stores of that period. I was aware of the weaknesses of the then current methods of retailing. Painstaking study had convinced me that mass distribution, which would make mass production possible, was the way out. The chains supplied a means for securing mass distribution.

Some of the weaknesses of distribution had already been overcome by the great department store. Among other advantages it had buying power and skilled management far beyond that of the small store. But even so, it was far from a perfect tool of distribution, and for that reason the chain store came and succeeded.

According to figures gathered by the Chamber of Commerce of the United States, the sales of chain stores have doubled in the past eight years, while in the same time the sales of department stores have increased only 31%. Such a difference is practical proof that chains are more nearly in accordance with fundamental economic law, and that they conform to the best current business trends.

The Advantages of Department Stores Over Chains

The outstanding advantages which the department store has over the chain specialty store are:

1. Better local generalship with the consequent ability to get direct and swift action.
2. Many departments, including "service" departments, under the same roof. This makes shopping easier, more comfortable, and much more attractive.
3. Closer contact between the management and community served. The department store is a "good citizen," active in the community of which it is a part.
4. Departments which are unprofitable during certain seasons can be "carried" by the more profitable departments.

The Advantages of Chains Over Department Stores

Among others, the chains have the following important advantages over department stores:

1. Greater purchasing power and, through centralized buying, a lower buying expense.
2. A greater degree of specialization.
3. Greater ability to work out "best" methods which are then standardized.

Why the Chain Has Greater Buying Power than a Department Store

It sometimes comes as a surprise to learn that the purchasing power of even a large department store is exceeded by that of an average size chain, but it is true.

That is one of the reasons for the great prosperity of the chains. No department store can buy in such quantities as the large chain. Macy's, one of the best stores in the world, cannot sell as many ten cent hammers as Woolworth; therefore Woolworth can buy that kind of hammer cheaper than Macy. No department store can sell as much canned goods as the A. & P., nor so much dress goods as the J. C. Penney chain.

Why Great Buying Power is an Advantage

The buying power of the department store is sufficient to enable it to deal directly with manufacturers, eliminating wholesalers and jobbers, thus saving the middlemen's profit and expense. But it cannot buy sufficiently large quantities to make the most efficient mass production possible.

It used to be thought that large buying power was valuable solely as a club with which to hammer down prices—often to the point where the manufacturer lost money. Before the methods of mass production were understood that was usually the aim. But now mass production methods enable manufacturers to make larger profits, although selling at a low price, than they could make at a much higher price for a smaller order.

The chain store's ability to place large orders for a single kind of goods enables the manufacturer to achieve great economies. He must, perforce, pass much of this saving on to the chain store, which in turn passes on all or most of the saving to the consumer. Inevitably this stimulates sales. It is that, largely, which accounts for the fact that the sales of the chains are growing far faster than the sales of individual department stores.

The Present Status of Department Store Chains

One of the first chains of department stores was the J. C. Penney Company which started 25 years ago with one store. From the beginning it grew steadily and rapidly. Yet since 1914—during the last half of its existence—the number of stores has increased 1452% and the average sales per store have increased 183%. It now operates, according to the latest available statistics, 885 stores. . . .

Suits are sold at Dayton's department store in Minneapolis, 1929. The early-twentieth century saw the growth of department stores that sold ready-to-wear clothing. © MINNESOTA HISTORICAL SOCIETY/CORBIS. REPRODUCED BY PERMISSION.

Chains of large department stores such as I foresee will not have the fault of dissimilarity. The stores will be very similar. These chains will combine the advantages of department stores and of the existing chain stores—and properly organized, they will be able to eliminate most of the weaknesses of both types.

What Department Store Chains Will Be Like

The future chains of department stores will have six outstanding characteristics as to organization, namely:

1. They will cater to customers of all degrees of buying power and all tastes.

2. They will concentrate on three full line price levels.

3. Departments will be highly specialized.

4. Buying will to a large degree be centralized.

5. A delicate balance between centralization and decentralization will be maintained.

6. Policies will be based on *facts*—not on opinions. . . .

How Large Will the Department Store Chains Be?

These many advantages that I have touched on make it certain in my opinion that in the near future we shall see chains of department stores which even in these days of Gargantuan businesses can be called "gigantic."

Further Resources

BOOKS

Johnson, Gerald W. *Liberal's Progress: Edward A. Filene: Shopkeeper to Social Statesman.* New York: Coward-McCann, 1948.

Lebhar, Godfrey M. *Chain Stores in America, 1859–1950.* New York: Chain Store Publishing Corporation, 1952.

Tedlow, Richard. "Nineteenth-Century Retailing and the Rise of the Department Store." *The Coming of Managerial Cap-*

italism: A Casebook in the History of American Economic Institutions. Homewood, Ill: Irwin, 310–326.

Walsh, William I. The Rise & Decline of the Great Atlantic & Pacific Tea Company. Secaucus, N.J: Lyle Stuart Inc., 1986.

WEBSITES

"History and Guiding Philosophy." JCPenney. Available online at http://www.jcpenney.net/company/history/history.htm; website home page: http://www.jcpenney.net (accessed February 25, 2003).

Federal Farm Policy

"McNary-Haugen Veto Message, May 23, 1928"

Message

By: Calvin Coolidge

Date: May 23, 1928

Source: Coolidge, Calvin. "McNary-Haugen Veto Message, May 23, 1928." Congressional Record, 70th Congress, First session, 1928, vol. 69, 9524–9526. Reprinted in Romero, Francine Sanders, ed. Presidents from Theodore Roosevelt through Coolidge: Debating the Issues in Pro and Con Primary Documents. Westport, Conn.: Greenwood Press, 2000, 221–223.

About the Author: Born in Vermont to a farming family, Calvin Coolidge (1872–1933) nonetheless spent most of his life in politics. A conservative Republican, he rose through the ranks from city councilor to Massachusetts governor in the span of two decades. Coolidge gained national recognition during his intervention in a Boston police strike in 1919. The following year he was nominated by his party to run as vice president on Warren Harding's ticket. When Harding died in 1923, Coolidge became the nation's thirtieth president. Easily reelected in 1924, Coolidge presided over an era of economic prosperity assisted by pro-business policies.

"Reflections on Farm Relief, December 1928"

Journal article

By: Rexford G. Tugwell

Date: 1929

Source: Tugwell, Rexford G. "Reflections on Farm Relief, December 1928." Political Science Quarterly 43, 1929, 481–97. Reprinted in Romero, Francine Sanders, ed. Presidents from Theodore Roosevelt through Coolidge: Debating the Issues in Pro and Con Primary Documents. Westport, Conn.: Greenwood Press, 2000, 224–225.

About the Author: Rexford Guy Tugwell (1891–1979) was born in upstate New York. After receiving his doctorate from the Wharton School of Finance and Commerce, he taught

economics at several institutions, serving on the faculty of Columbia University during the 1920s. President Franklin D. Roosevelt pulled Tugwell into his "Brain Trust" in 1933. An advocate of national economic planning, he worked on relief measures in the Agriculture Department and the Resettlement Administration until his resignation in 1937. Tugwell served in a variety of other governmental and corporate roles until 1946, when he returned full time to teaching, research, and writing. ∎

Introduction

The 1920s were a prosperous times for many Americans, but the farming community did not share in the nation's abundance. American farmers had enjoyed a golden age of agriculture in the years before and during World War I (1914–1918), when prices were high and markets ample. But by the 1920s, they faced the problem of chronic overproduction. Farmers had consistently relied on European markets to soak up surplus production, but after the war, new competitors in Europe, Africa, and Asia cut deeply into American foreign trade. American domestic consumption also declined during these years as immigration restrictions and tendencies toward smaller families slowed population increase. These trends were compounded by higher agricultural productivity due to the increased use of tractors and the consolidation of smaller farms—which further enlarged the nation's agricultural surplus.

As a result, farm prices dropped precipitously during the economic depression of 1920–1921, and farm relief became an increasingly significant political issue over the course of the decade. Even though urban dwellers outnumbered rural folk by 1920, farmers carried more political heft than their numbers would indicate. Farmers were a key constituent of the dominant Republican party, and they drew on a longstanding tradition of American agrarianism. Their pleas for assistance were difficult to ignore, and by 1924 Secretary of Commerce Herbert Hoover organized an agricultural conference to establish farm policy for the Coolidge administration. A longtime proponent of associative governance, Hoover supported loans to farming cooperatives and encouraged agricultural diversification. But this thinking ignored the fact that voluntary farming programs had typically been dismal failures, incapable of overcoming economic individualism.

George N. Peek, an official at Moline Plow Company, made his living selling agricultural implements to farmers. Since Peek could not sell to farmers without cash, he took it on himself to devise a plan that would offer them a decent return on their labor. Peek envisioned a system in which farm prices would be pegged to pre-war levels, and then kept in "parity" by adjusting farm prices to the general price index. In order to support these inflated prices, Peek proposed that a government corporation purchase surplus produce and sell it at lower world prices in foreign markets. The loss could then be charged to farmers in the form of an equalizing fee, but farmers would still receive higher returns than if they had sold all of their produce at world prices.

Peek won converts in Secretary of Agriculture Henry A. Wallace and in Congress, where Oregon Senator Charles McNary and Iowa Representative Gilbert Haugen introduced a bill that followed Peek's plan. Peek was evangelical in his campaign for the bill, and he soon rallied American farmers to his cause. Drawing on a general sense of agrarian discontent with a government that appeared to be in the service of industrialists, agriculturalists were ripe to support any plan that might improve their relative economic position. Progressive economists such as Rexford Tugwell also endorsed the plan, which offered an escape from chronic agricultural depression.

Despite the growth of a farming bloc in support of McNary-Haugenism, its proponents had great difficulty securing its passage. Businessmen decried it as inimical to the American spirit of free enterprise, and laborers worried about the effect on their grocery bills. When cotton prices plummeted in 1925, bringing Southern cotton growers into the McNary-Haugen fold, internal divisions within the agricultural community led to further disagreements, this time about the details of the price support program and its administration.

Under these conditions, the bill failed in 1924, and again, in a modified version, in 1925. New bills were introduced in 1927 and 1928, but they were vetoed by President Calvin Coolidge in increasingly caustic language that reflected the growing conservatism of the time.

Significance

The broad array of opposition (which Coolidge helped cultivate) made the veto politically palatable. Moreover, Coolidge had deep reservations about the logic of the system. He agreed with economists who argued that inflated prices would likely prompt farmers to rotate marginal acreage into production and further increase surpluses. He believed that agricultural diversity would make the program an administrative impossibility. And he thought that artificially high farm prices would increase the cost of living while subsidizing foreign consumers who could purchase produce below cost.

The Hoover administration eventually passed the Agricultural Marketing Act in 1929. It provided government money to support prices and encourage farming cooperatives, but carried no provision for exporting surpluses overseas. When the Great Depression drove farm prices down even further, this program lost hundreds of millions of dollars. Not until economist Rexford Tugwell

and Secretary Wallace drafted the Agricultural Adjustment Act of 1933, which paid farmers to reduce their acreage, did farm policy begin to directly address the problem of overproduction.

Primary Source

"McNary-Haugen Veto Message, May 23, 1928" [excerpt]

> **SYNOPSIS:** In this excerpt, President Calvin Coolidge explains why the McNary-Haugen measure fails to address the problem of overproduction and serves only to increase government bureaucracy.

The recurring problem of surpluses in farm products has long been a subject of deep concern to the entire nation, and any economically sound, workable solution of it would command not only the approval but the profound gratitude of our people. The present measure, however, falls far short of that most desirable objective; indeed, although it purports to provide farm relief by lessening the cares of our greatest industry, it not only fails to accomplish that purpose but actually heaps even higher its burdens of political control, of distribution costs, and of foreign competition.

It embodies a formidable array of perils for agriculture which are all the more menacing because of their being obscured in a maze of ponderously futile bureaucratic paraphernalia. . . .

A detailed analysis of all of the objections to the measure would involve a document of truly formidable proportions. However, its major weaknesses and perils may be summarized under six headings:

1. *Price fixing.* This measure is as cruelly deceptive in its disguise as governmental price-fixing legislation and involves quite as unmistakably the impossible scheme of attempted governmental control of buying and selling of agricultural products through political agencies as any of the other so-called surplus control bills. In fact, in certain respects, it is much broader and more flagrant in its scope.

■ ■ ■

These provisions would disappoint the farmer by naïvely implying that the law of supply and demand can thus be legislatively distorted in his favor. Economic history is filled with the evidences of the ghastly futility of such attempts. Fiat prices match the folly of fiat money. . . .

2. *The equalization fee,* which is the kernel of this legislation, is a sales tax upon the entire community. It is in no sense a mere contribution to be made by the producers themselves, as has been represented by supporters of the measure. It can be assessed upon the commodities in transit to the consumer and its burdens can often unmistakably be passed on to him.

■ ■ ■

Incidentally, this taxation or fee would not be for purposes of revenue in the accepted sense but would simply yield a subsidy for the special benefit of particular groups of processors and exporters. It would be a consumption or sales tax on the vital necessities of life, regulated not by the ability of the people to pay but only by the requirements and export losses of various trading intermediaries. It would be difficult indeed to conceive of a more flagrant case of the employment of all of the coercive powers of the government for the profit of a small number of specially privileged groups. . . .

3. *Widespread bureaucracy.* A bureaucratic tyranny of unprecedented proportions would be let down upon the backs of the farm industry and its distributors throughout the nation in connection with the enforcement of this measure. Thousands of contracts involving scores of different grades, quantities, and varieties of products would have to be signed by the board with the 4,400 millers, the 1,200 meat-packing plants, the 3,000 or more cotton and woolen mills, and the 2,700 canners. If this bill had been in operation in 1925, it would have involved collections upon an aggregate of over 16 billion units of wheat, corn, and cotton.

■ ■ ■

4. *Encouragement to profiteering and wasteful distribution by middlemen.* As was pointed out in the veto last year, it seems almost incredible that the farmers of this country are being offered this scheme of legislative relief in which the only persons who are guaranteed to benefit are the exporters, packers, millers, canners, spinners, and other processors. Their profits are definitely assured. They have, in other words, no particular incentive toward careful operation, since each of them holding a contract, no matter how unscrupulous, wasteful, or inefficient his operations may have been, would be fully reimbursed for all of his losses.

■ ■ ■

5. *Stimulation of overproduction.* The bill runs counter to an economic law as well settled as the

Senator Charles McNary (left) and Representative Gilbert Haugen shake hands after President Hoover signed a modified version of the McNary-Haugen Bill, shortly after succeeding Coolidge in the oval office. **THE LIBRARY OF CONGRESS.**

law of gravitation. Increased prices decrease consumption; they also increase production. These two conditions are the very ones that spell disaster to the whole program. . . .

6. *Aid to our foreign agricultural competitors.* This measure continues, as did its predecessor, to give substantial aid to the foreign competitors of American agriculture and industry. It continues the amazing proposal to supply foreign workers with cheaper food than those of the United States, and this at the expense of the American farm industry, thereby encouraging both the foreign peasant, whose produce is not burdened with the costs of any equalization fees, and also affording through reduced food prices the means of cutting the wage rates paid by foreign manufacturers. . . .

This is indeed an extraordinary process of economic reasoning, if such it could be called. Certainly it is a flagrant case of direct, insidious attack upon our whole agricultural and industrial strength.

By the inevitable stimulation of production the bill can only mean an increase of exportable surplus to be dumped in the world market. This in turn will bring about a constantly decreasing world price, which will soon reach so low a figure that a whole-sale curtailment of production in this country with its attendant demoralization and heavy losses would be certain. Where is the advantage of dragging our farmers into such folly?

Furthermore, as the board undertakes to dump the steadily mounting surplus into foreign countries at the low-cost figures, it will come into direct conflict with the dumping and similar trade laws of many foreign lands which are interested in the maintenance of their own agricultural industries. We might, therefore, expect immediately a series of drastic, retaliatory discriminations on the part of these consumer countries. This will drive our surplus into narrower market channels and force even further price reductions, with consequent increases in the burdens of the equalization tax.

Primary Source

"Reflections on Farm Relief, December 1928" [excerpt]

SYNOPSIS: In this excerpt from an article in the *Political Science Quarterly,* economist Rexford Guy Tugwell reviews the problems of American farming and praises the McNary-Haugen bill as a fine piece of social legislation.

Eight years of gradually liquidating depression have incalculably injured the nation's agricultural plant. Fertility has been depleted, equipment has run down, man-power has deteriorated. Not only farmers themselves, but all thoughtful social observers are seriously concerned that some ingenuity and some public action should be enlisted and at once. At best farming suffers needless handicaps. Back to 1913 is not good enough. For, strictly speaking, what happened between 1920 and 1928 is nothing new in our history. Indeed a more or less organized agrarian revolt is nothing new. If we were to look backward we should see that each of those phenomena we call the business cycle and which, in Europe, they call the economic rhythm, has had similar consequences for rural folks. . . .

. . . The disadvantage of farmers is measured roughly by the fact that they lose more in depression than they gain in prosperity, and that this continues to be true, with a periodical exploitation of those engaged in this activity for the benefit of those engaged in other pursuits.

■■■

The McNary-Haugen idea was that this price disparity, recurrently so disastrous, might be traced to the economic rule that small surpluses have disproportionate effects on prices and that this situation might be relieved by the segregation of this small percentage which has such great consequences. It might then be disposed of safely in either of two ways: storage or export. Coöperative storage, assisted by government financing, might enable farmers to wait for favorable markets. At least marketing could be spread throughout the year. Dumping abroad, with proper management of import duties, could be done at any price, provided the elimination of the surplus was complete; for then domestic prices could be kept at a level which would yield a profit on the whole of any crop. This device, it was argued, would at least admit farmers to the American protective system on an equality with other industries.

■■■

All this was objected to by Mr. Coolidge as unconstitutional and as administratively impossible. There is doubt as to constitutionality, but it is only doubt; and that decision belongs to the courts. As to the complexity of administration, this is a charge which might be brought against almost any governmental device. Simplicity is desirable, but lack of it ought not to prevent the adoption of a desirable policy. Besides, the scheme, if complex, was necessarily so. It may be better to do something difficult than to do nothing at all. His real objection was a stubborn determination to do nothing. New England minds revolt against any economic proposal which is more socially oriented than Vermont shopkeeping. But the veto stood.

The scheme seemed workable enough, and administratively possible, provided only that foreign governments made no retaliatory moves to protect their own farmers, and that the surpluses in question did not grow so big, with profit insurance, as to prove unwieldy. But obviously it applied mostly to exportable (or easily stored) products; and, quite as obviously it depended upon a huge coöperative organization among farmers of which only the barest beginnings were to be discerned.

■■■

Mr. Coolidge inherited the puzzle of farmers penalized for productivity. But puzzles do not worry him. Besides he held it certain that prosperity would recur in his time to justify inaction. The obstinate persistence of the farm leaders in pointing out the remarkable duration of the depression and the certainty of its recurrence has annoyed him, but not unbearably. His last McNary-Haugen veto lacked something of aplomb; it was even sharp. But it may be doubted whether it satisfied everyone that the economics of New England shop-keeping is adequate to the solution of the difficulty.

■ ■ ■

. . . Indeed the more I study the Bill of 1928 the deeper my admiration becomes. As a piece of social legislation it surpasses anything an American Congress ever framed. The remaining troublesome consideration is its dependence on a non-existent coöperative structure. Perhaps, however, ways around this difficulty may be found.

Further Resources

BOOKS

Ferrell, Robert H. *The Presidency of Calvin Coolidge.* Lawrence, Kans.: University of Kansas Press, 1998.

Fite, Gilbert C. *George N. Peek and the Fight for Farm Parity.* Norman, Okla.: University of Oklahoma Press, 1954.

Kirschner, Don S. *City and Country: Rural Responses to Urbanization in the 1920s.* Westport, Conn.: Greenwood Press, 1970.

Saloutos, Theodore, and John D. Hicks. *Agricultural Discontent in the Middle West: 1900–1939.* Madison: University of Wisconsin Press, 1951.

Sternsher, Bernard. *Rexford Tugwell and the New Deal.* New Brunswick, N.J.: Rutgers University Press, 1964.

PERIODICALS

Hoffman, Elizabeth, and Gary D. Libecap. "Institutional Choice and the Development of U.S. Agricultural Policies in the 1920s." *Journal of Economic History* 51, June 1991, 397–411.

WEBSITES

"Calvin Coolidge Papers. McNary-Haugen Bill, 1923–28." In *Prosperity and Thrift: The Coolidge Era and the Consumer Economy, 1921–1929.* American Memory digital primary source collection, Library of Congress. Available online at http://memory.loc.gov/ammem/coolhtml/coolhome.html; website home page: http://memory.loc.gov (accessed May 12, 2003).

"Hamlin Memorandum and Diary Extracts, Showing Federal Reserve Board Response to 1927 Recession and Stock Market: July 1, 1927–January 4, 1929"

Diary

By: Charles Sumner Hamlin

Date: 1928–1929

Source: Hamlin, Charles S. "Hamlin Memorandum and Diary Extracts, Showing Federal Reserve Board Response to 1927 Recession and Stock Market: July 1, 1927–January 4, 1929." Charles Hamlin Papers, 877–879, 880, 881–883, 888–890, 896–900, 920–921, 932. Reproduced in *Prosperity and Thrift: The Coolidge Era and the Consumer Economy, 1921–1929.* American Memory digital primary source collection, Library of Congress. Available online at http://memory.loc.gov/ammem/coolhtml/coolhome.html; website home page: http://memory.loc.gov (accessed May 12, 2003).

About the Author: Charles Sumner Hamlin (1861–1938) was born in Boston, Massachusetts, and earned undergraduate, master's and law degrees at Harvard University. He practiced law in Boston and was active in Democratic politics; he ran for state senate twice and Massachusetts secretary of state and governor, each time unsuccessfully. He was assistant secretary of the treasury from 1893 to 1897, and again from 1913 to 1914. Hamlin served on the Federal Reserve Board for over two decades, first as chairman from 1914 to 1916, then on the Board of Governors until 1936, and finally as special counsel until his death in 1938. ■

Introduction

Chartered in 1913, the Federal Reserve System created a centralized banking agency controlled by a Board of Governors and twelve regional federal reserve banks. The Federal Reserve Board, in conjunction with these regional banks, was charged with the creation of a more stable, flexible, and responsive monetary system. Financial panic in 1907 had led Congress to investigate the possibility of central banking. The Federal Reserve System, which emerged six years later, had the advantages of a national regulatory agency, but allowed for regional differentiation and therefore alleviated the American public's discomfort with the idea of a concentrated banking power.

As a bankers' bank, or a "lender of last resort," the Federal Reserve banks shaped monetary policy by setting reserve requirements, establishing discount rates, and influencing the cost of credit through the purchase or sale of government securities. Each of these techniques served to tighten or loosen available credit in the economy. But in the 1920s, when the Fed (as the Reserve System is sometimes called) was relatively new and still controversial, it was reluctant to overly manipulate the market. Indeed, some of the regional reserve banks were so strong that the Fed had difficulty dictating monetary policy.

A longtime member of the board, Charles Sumner Hamlin kept extensive diaries that chronicled the work of the Federal Reserve Board.

Significance

The Fed struggled to set effective monetary policy during the 1920s, a time of general economic prosperity. The rise in U.S. gold holdings and the Fed's low discount rate combined to lower the cost of credit. This in turn fueled stock market speculation. Brokers' loans (money loaned to purchase stocks) increased by more than 400 percent between 1921 and 1928. The Fed's Board of Governors recognized that excessive speculation could have dire consequences and sought to reduce the volume of credit by raising the discount rate and by selling off hundreds of millions of dollars in U.S. government securities.

This was not enough to stem the speculative tide, however, and the Fed soon realized that it could do little more than call upon member banks to exercise restraint in making speculative loans. When the New York Stock Exchange crashed in the fall of 1929, the Fed was widely criticized: first for having done too little to slow the economy in advance of the crash, and later for not doing enough to ease the Great Depression that followed.

Clearly the Fed had not developed a monetary policy during the 1920s strong enough to ward off economic collapse; but neither had it been granted the authority at its inception to do much more than monitor bank reserves and ensure an elastic currency. Closely managing economic expansion—and operating as an active player in the marketplace—was simply outside of its original mandate. Charles Sumner Hamlin's personal diary, which carefully documented the Fed's early history, offers a unique insider's perspective on the board and on the events leading up to the crash of 1929. These excerpts describe how board members, including Hamlin himself, understood the turbulent economic times in which they lived, and how they sought to bring order to the economy as market speculation became ever more frenzied.

Primary Source

"Hamlin Memorandum and Diary Extracts, Showing Federal Reserve Board Response to 1927

Recession and Stock Market: July 1, 1927–January 4, 1929" [excerpt]

SYNOPSIS: These excerpts were culled by Charles Sumner Hamlin, inveterate diarist and longtime Federal Reserve Board member, as part of his effort to write a history of the Federal Reserve Board. In the diary entries, Hamlin refers to himself as C. S. H. Others mentioned in the entries are Treasury Secretary Andrew Mellon, and Senate Banking Committee Chairman Carter Glass. The "governors" are governors of the Federal Reserve Board. The other men mentioned are bankers at Federal Reserve banks in different cities. The excerpts show that the Federal Reserve Board was concerned about stock market speculation but uncertain if they should attempt to control it, and if so, how.

January 6, 1928, Friday

Governor [Roy A.] Young comes up to our room—he has taken a room at the Lee House temporarily. He said the President in the morning had given out a statement as to the stock speculation situation in New York, stating that he had inquired at the Treasury and was satisfied there was nothing alarming in the situation; that Secretary Mellon told him he could not remember any talk with the President on this matter. Governor Young fears that when this is published tomorrow it will cause another value of speculation. . . .

January 10, 1928, Tuesday

Governor Young told C.S.H. a reporter told him there was a rumor that the New York Stock Exchange would shortly issue a warning against brokers loans and stock exchange speculation.

This will be a blow at Coolidge. C.S.H. cannot understand how Coolidge could have made such an extraordinary statement. He must have been deceived by stock manipulators. Governor Young also said he thought the New York directors wanted to put up rates and that Hoxton was there saying Richmond wanted to put up rates and that he should advise Richmond to wait until after Open Market Committee.

The consensus of opinion of Board seemed to be that we should first sell securities and we voted to authorize committee to sell from 50 to 75 millions, as Case, for Committee requested.

I fear that nothing short of a rate increase will cope with the situation caused by Coolidge's statement to Press.

January 11, 1928, Wednesday

McGarrah, Woolley and Raeburn of the Federal Reserve Bank of the New York before Board. We discussed rate situation. McGarrah felt time was near to increase rates although he agreed that first we might sell some more securities.

Wooley said there were faint signs of improvement in business from the present recession and that he feared a general increase might retard or kill this growth.

Raeburn believed rates should be increased and that it would not hurt business.

All agreed however that securities should be sold first.

Raeburn said that Coolidge's statement would not deceive professional operators in stocks but that it would encourage small investors to hold or increase these investments; that the statement was most unfortunate.

Governor Young said securities should be sold first; that a change in discount rates does not change the quantity of credit, while a sale of securities does and that this was the better course. Present: Secretary Mellon, Governor Young, C.S.H., [Governor Edward H.] Cunningham and [Governor Edmund] Platt. Board took up recommendations of Committee. . . .

March 7, 1928, Wednesday

Governor Young, Platt, C.S.H. and Cunningham went before Banking and Currency Committee on the LaFollette resolution on brokers loans. Professor Sprauge of Harvard also was there. C.S.H. got Board's consent to ask Sprague to come down yesterday as he wished to consult him, as did possibly some other Board members, before we testified. C.S.H. told Senator Glass Sprague was to be here and suggested to him to get the Committee to ask Sprague to appear, not as representing Board but as an independent witness—which Senator Glass did.

Sprague testified first and made a very good impression. The Governor Young testified in general as follows:

1. Cannot tell whether brokers loans are unduly excessive or not.

2. They seem to be well collateralled and safe from banking standpoint.

3. They are not depriving commerce or agriculture of a dollar of credit.

4. As a fact the bank loans are less today than in 1922.

Charles S. Hamlin served on the Federal Reserve Board for over two decades. **THE LIBRARY OF CONGRESS.**

5. The increase is practically all in money lent on call by those other than banks, e.g. corporations, etc.

6. Of the bank loans the New York banks have decreased and out of town banks decreased.

7. Today practically no banks which are constantly in debt for rediscounts have large loans on call. The few which are gradually reducing their call loans.

8. If banks loan on call to any increasing extent and are perpetual reductions the Federal Reserve Board would admonish them as it has in the past (1925) and will in the future.

9. Federal Reserve rediscounts are in general not being used to obtain call loan funds.

10. No new legislation is considered necessary as the Federal Reserve Banks can cope with the situation under present law.

11. If speculative loans increased so as to react on general business or to encourage business speculation the Federal Reserve Banks can put up rates and sell securities in open market.

Governor Young did not say that the recent rate increase and sales of securities were for purpose of reducing brokers loans, but put it largely on ground of gold movements. . . .

C.S.H. was called to testify. He said Governor Young had covered the case completely and his testimony would be largely cumulative so he had nothing to add but would be glad to answer any questions. The hour was late, the Committee was tired, and no questions were put to C.S.H.

Cunningham then read a statement to the Committee. He did not seek to justify brokers loans in any way but agreed they were not now depriving any farmer or business man of credit.

C.S.H. would approve an increase of rates and selling securities to control stock market speculation only when such speculation was interfering with agriculture or commercial credit or exciting similar speculation in business even then C.S.H. would regret necessity of putting up rates for the farmer and business man generally because of stock gambling on Wall Street or speculation on commodities among some business men. This would be so especially at a time when crops were moving. . . .

April 16, 1928, Monday

Received letter from Governor [W.P.G.] Harding. Directors oppose putting up rates on collateral notes. Executive committee willing to put up discount rate to 4-1/2%. Asks Board to let him know today what action Board would take if rate increased. Says no particular need of increase so far as Boston district is concerned but Reserve ratio is low enough to justify increase.

If executive committee votes to increase will not be because of any specific local condition but merely expression of willingless to help out general situation.

C.S.H. at once talked with Platt. Platt called up New York—Case said was selling considerable amount of securities, hoped Boston would increase. Platt saw Mellon. Mellon did not object to increase. Said would not cause any disasterous break in market but might slow it up.

In P.M. Miller came in—Governor Harding had just talked with him. Said discounts had greatly increased and proceeds were being used in stock market and he thought rate should be raised (not consistent with his letter to me).

Miller at first thought we ought to act at once and have meeting and tell Harding so. Later he veered around and felt we ought to ask Governor Harding at least to wait until directors meeting Thursday—that putting up rates would chill business, etc.

Finally we agreed to ask Governor Harding not to act through executive committee tomorrow but to wait at least until Board meeting Thursday.

April 17, 1928, Tuesday

Board received application from Boston for increase in all rates from 4 to 4-1/2%. No quorum present. Only Platt, Miller, James and C.S.H. Curtiss called up C.S.H. and said the directors were unanimous; that their decision was based entirely on local conditions; that their earning assets had increased 40 millions since Saturday; that their reserve percent was 56; that they feared further trouble and hoped Board would decide Case at once. All this C.S.H. reported to Board. C.S.H. read Governor Harding's personal letter to him dated Saturday, April 14 and said conditions had changed and matter had become a purely local one. He said that to refuse the application on ground that New York should take care of it by further sales of Government securities would be equivalent to saying that New York was the Central Bank of United States.

Miller, who on Monday told Platt and C.S.H. we should promptly approve, now turned a somersault and said that to approve it would be to announce formally that Board would try to control speculation on stock exchange through discount rates.

C.S.H. replied that Governor Harding and Curtiss said the proceeds of the discounts were being used for speculative loans; that theoretically, the Federal Reserve Bank could decline to rediscount under such conditions; that this, of course, was impracticable as all the banks were involved and it would be equivalent to splitting up the Federal Reserve Bank; that if the Bank could refuse altogether it could put up rates to discourage such transaction. Miller said if the Bank should refuse to rediscount it would be a great stroke. James agreed with Miller. C.S.H. said the Federal Reserve Bank of Boston could not sell securities as could New York and that rate increase was its only practicable remedy; that it would be monstrous to say to Boston—New York cannot or does not sell enough securities, therefore, Boston must suffer in silence.

James said he thought the pressure at New York was producing results and was forcing borrowers to borrow at Boston. C.S.H. said if this was so it would be absurd to refuse to allow Boston to protect itself by rate increase. James did not answer this.

Secretary Mellon was tied up with Farm Loan Board and could not come in to make a quorum, therefore, we adjourned until tomorrow.

April 18, 1928, Wednesday

Board met. Present Secretary Mellon, Miller, Platt, James, and C.S.H. C.S.H. moved to approve Boston rate.

Discussed from 10 to 12, Miller talking almost incessantly against it. Tried to have matter go over until Friday for full Board meeting or until Monday. Miller said he was satisfied New York was putting pressure on market which might settle question before Friday if Boston would wait. Said he could never vote to control stock speculation by increasing discount rates etc., etc. C.S.H. reminded him that in fall of 1925 he earnestly favored advance in New York rate to control speculative activity; that New York Bank said it had it in hand through direct pressure that Cunningham moved to put in an increase (from 3-1/2 to 4%) in New York over the heads of the New York directors and though defeated by Board, Miller voted for it with Cunningham.

C.S.H. said Miller's arguments would have some force if we were a central bank at Washington and Boston a branch, but that Boston is an indispensable bank and unanimously asked for increase because of increasing rediscounts and falling reserves, its present reserve—about 57%—being the lowest of any Reserve Bank; that he, C.S.H., would not hesitate to vote to increase rates where a speculative movement was interfering or threatening to interfere with business, commerce and agriculture; that he felt this condition was at hand.

Finally Board adjourned until 2:30.

At 2:30 reconvened. Same members present. Miller said he had just been talking with Case in New York; that Case was discouraged and said the situation was getting out of hand; that money was coming into New York for speculative purposes and that he could identify 50 millions as coming from Boston.

Secretary Mellon who had patiently listened to Miller all the morning, answering all his argument, said he did not feel Board could overrule the Boston directors who expressly based their decision on the local situation, and he called for a vote.

Miller said he felt impelled to change his morning vote (a tie, C.S.H. and Platt Yes. Miller and James, No. Secretary Mellon for present, not voting) and vote Aye.

The vote was taken and stood. Aye—Secretary Mellon, Platt, C.S.H. and Miller. No—James. . . .

September 28, 1928, Friday

Meeting of Federal Advisory Council. Discussed the rate question. Governor Young said the Board might possibly soon have before it two requests: to increase rates at Chicago from 5 to 5 1/3; to reduce rates at Cleveland from 5 to 4 1/2%; that the Board would satisfying itself to grant both. The Council seemed generally to oppose both, taking ground that to lower Cleveland rate to 4 1/2 would be construed as a change of policy of the System which would start up stock exchange speculation.

Mr. Goebel of Kansas City said that if total conditions warranted a lower rate at Cleveland it should be put in.

The consensus of opinion was that the 5% rate was not injuring business. Mr. Alexander said that the fact that business men had to pay at least 6% was depressing.

He agreed with Governor Young that the discount rate at the present time was a national question but said he believed all rates should go down to 4 1/2%; that this would stimulate business. He said the general feeling was that the Federal Reserve System was trying to control stock exchange speculative rates and that in his judgement speculation could not be controlled by discount rates. He favored a 4 1/2% rate to show the country that the System was not trying to regulate the stock exchange. He said he did not agree with those who claimed that lowering rates from 4 to 3 1/2% in August 1927, was a mistaken policy but that we might have gone back to the 4% rate a little sooner than we did.

He said he was extremely puzzled at the speculation in New York and felt we could not control it. He said liquidation or a break was certain to come but he could not say when nor understand why it had not come before this; that even if a 4-1/2% rate might further encourage speculation it would in the long run correct itself; that many of the booming stocks were not so overvalued as the country seemed to think.

He was asked what would happen if the corporations, etc. suddenly withdrew, say, 500 millions of the money now on call. He said there would have to be a liquidation and that the banks would not take over these loans. Governor Young said in such case we might have a panic. Later, Alexander qualified this statement and said the banks would help as far as able and the system also must do its part. . . .

December 31, 1928, Monday

Miller put in a resolution to effect that the present spread between Federal Reserve and stock market call loan and other speculative loans tends to tempt member banks into pushing Federal Reserve credit into stock exchange market, and asking the banks what they are going to do to correct this in 1929.

Governor Young vigorously objected saying that resolution meant that banks having call loans should be refused rediscounts. On vote:

Aye—Miller; C.S.H.; James; Cunningham; and Platt.

No—Governor Young. Not voting, Comptroller.

C.S.H. said he voted Aye on the interpretation that resolution was not intended to mean that the Board believed that speculative loans were necessarily illegal; nor that a bank should be refused rediscounts to make good reserves when the deficiency was in part due to speculative, loans, but that it merely pointed out a danger and asked banks how they proposed to meet it in 1929. . . .

Further Resources

BOOKS

Livingston, James. *Origin of the Federal Reserve System.* Ithaca, N.Y.: Cornell University Press, 1986.

Moore, Carl H. *The Federal Reserve System: A History of the First 75 Years.* Jefferson, N.C.: McFarland & Co. Publishers, 1990.

West, Robert Craig. *Banking Reform and the Federal Reserve, 1863–1923.* Ithaca, N.Y.: Cornell University Press, 1977.

PERIODICALS

Field, Alexander J. "A New Interpretation of the Onset of the Great Depression." *Journal of Economic History* 44, June 1984, 489–498.

WEBSITES

Federal Reserve Education. Available online at http://www .federalreserveeducation.org (accessed February 24, 2003).

"A New Era . . . an Economic Revolution of the Profoundest Character"

Magazine article

By: John Moody

Date: 1928

Source: Moody, John. "A New Era . . . an Economic Revolution of the Profoundest Character." *The Atlantic Monthly* 142, August 1928, 255–262. Reprinted in Shannon, David A., ed. *Progressivism and Postwar Disillusionment: 1898–1928.* New York: McGraw-Hill, 1966, 312–319.

About the Author: John Moody (1868–1958) was a financial analyst, a prolific author, and the president of Moody's Investors Services. Beginning in 1900, his company published *Moody's Manual,* an index that eventually profiled and rated thousands of corporations. By the 1920s, Moody's writings were part of the canon of American economic thought, and his opinion of Wall Street was widely respected. ∎

Introduction

There was ample justification to think that the American economy had entered a new era by the late 1920s. Industrial productivity soared during the decade, fueled by electrification, technological innovations, and streamlined systems of production and distribution. New consumer goods, from antifreeze fluids to wristwatches, flooded the market. New materials discovered as the result of wartime research—including plastics, rayon, and cellophane—revolutionized manufacturing. The growth and consolidation of businesses (among them chain stores, banks, and light and power companies) promised lower prices through economies of scale. Nowhere was the confidence in American economic growth more clear than in the frenzied building that dominated the decade. Homes and highways were constructed at record rates. Cities boasted new skylines with ever taller skyscrapers. Resort communities like those on the Florida peninsula mushroomed.

The year 1928 was a golden year for business. National economic prosperity seemed to offer all things to all people: large profits for employers, new homes and products for consumers, better wages and working conditions for laborers. That year, in his state of the union address, Calvin Coolidge proclaimed that no president had ever before presided over such prosperity. That year was also the beginning of the Great Bull Market. From the spring of 1928, stock prices rose steadily, drawing in new investors willing to join in a speculative market that seemed to have no losers. The impact of these changes was not lost on financial analyst John Moody, who described the American economic transformation of the 1920s in an article that appeared in the August 1928 issue of *Atlantic Monthly*. With the causes of previous depressions largely eliminated, Moody thought that the economic future appeared promising.

Significance

Unlike previous bursts of economic expansion, the 1920s offered financial analysts like Moody plenty of reasons to believe that this boom would not end in the inevitable bust. The United States was now a leader in the world economy, becoming a creditor nation and rising in relative commercial strength since World War I

(1914–18). And new domestic regulations—especially the Federal Reserve System—promised a greater degree of control over the market. Under these conditions, it appeared to the chorus of bull market boosters that America had opened the way to unrelenting economic growth.

By 1929 the stock market provided the economy's major thrust. As more and more money was poured into stocks, the monetary supply contracted, causing interest rates to rise. Other market indicators—such as declining housing construction—suggested that a downturn was in the offing. But the stock market was followed with avid and unswerving interest, as more and more Americans invested and its value continued to soar.

This broad cultural enthusiasm for the market was remarkable. Before the war, progressive reformers had attacked business interests as narrow, selfish profit mongers. Reformers promoted social welfare legislation that reined in free enterprise and offered greater protection to workers. But a decade of prosperity had put the perpetuation of business stability above these concerns on the national agenda. Not until the economy tumbled in late 1929 would the reformers' voices, once stifled by the rising tide of business conservatism and economic prosperity, ring loudly again.

Primary Source

"A New Era . . . an Economic Revolution of the Profoundest Character" [excerpt]

> **SYNOPSIS:** In this excerpt from an article in the August 1928 issue of *Atlantic Monthly,* noted financial analyst John Moody exudes an optimism in the United States' economic future that was typical of the period. Moody asserts that all of the factors behind previous depressions, among which he includes attempts to regulate business, have been eliminated. Thus he claims that unprecedented gains in prosperity during the 1920s will continue indefinitely. This confidence proved to be ill-founded—the stock market crash of 1929 occurred little more than a year later, triggering the Great Depression.

The trend of American security prices since 1922 presents a remarkable picture. Never before in the history of Wall Street has such a record been displayed. Before the Great War, so-called 'bull markets' sometimes ran two or three years without serious interruption. But now we have witnessed a bull market which had its inception nearly six years ago. And this market, instead of culminating in reaction, depression, or panic, as, according to all orthodox rules of the past, it should long ago have done, has this year been making such spectacular records for

itself that the entire financial world has been amazed.

Nearly all of the accredited seers and economic experts have been at a loss to explain it. . . . The Wall Street stock market, which, according to all rules of the old logic, should have 'petered out' two years ago and was then believed to be overdue for a wide-open crash, has this year displayed new and mysterious force. And even though the country has been going through a moderate business depression,—though credit conditions are beginning to display considerable strain, interest rates have long been rising, and brokers' loans have been soaring,—still the great bull market has gone on. . . .

As a concrete illustration of what has happened in the Wall Street markets since 1923, certain exhibits of the price changes in standard, representative investment stocks and bonds have recently been compiled by the writer. In the field of railroad stocks, taking twenty-six representative dividend-paying issues, there has been an average advance in prices of about 100 per cent from the levels of 1923. . . . In the public-utility field, an investor who had diversified a similar sum in twenty-seven representative stocks would recently have had a profit of over 200 per cent. . . . In the industrial list, an investment in thirty representative issues (the sum being equally divided between all) recently showed a profit of over 230 per cent. . . .

. . . [T]his continuous upward tendency in security prices since 1923 has not been confined to stocks alone. Investors in the highest-grade seasoned railroad bonds have reaped profits of 20 per cent or more during the period; purchasers of standard foreign dollar bonds in 1923 now find themselves with profits of from 20 per cent to 30 per cent on their original investments. In this general connection, the writer recently compiled a diversified list of American railroad bonds, foreign dollar bonds, railroad, public utility, and industrial stocks, and bank and trust-company stocks. Assuming that an investor had spread the specific sum of $100,000 in this list, in approximately equal amounts, he would now find himself with a capital value of nearly $400,000.

There has been strong emphasis laid for many months on what are called the dangers of the speculative situation and high market values by practically every public commentator. Dangers are present, it is true, and the thoughtless and venturesome speculator in these days runs great risk of having his fingers burned. But the average financial commentator or critic is too prone to hark back to the experiences of the years before the war and draw parallels with years like 1893, 1903, and 1907; years in which great bull movements culminated and were followed by depressions or panics. There is a similar tendency to ring the changes constantly on what happened immediately at the end of the wild post-war inflation period of 1919 and early 1920. It is confidently asserted that what happened in those years will presently happen again. And yet, notwithstanding the wide and persistent preaching of this orthodox doctrine, we have this year witnessed powerful financial interests and numerous shrewd, 'long-pull' investors purchasing vast blocks of high-priced standard shares and putting these shares in their strong boxes.

What is the correct explanation of it all? . . . A careful examination of all the facts seems to indicate that there are some fundamental factors of moment behind this extraordinary Wall Street situation; and it is the purpose of this article to attempt to bring some of these fundamental things to light.

II

It will be agreed by all thoughtful persons that to interpret the present intelligently one must first turn to a study of the past. But in turning to the past one should first give due weight to the fact that causes which greatly affected events in past years may no longer exist; that laws, customs, methods, perspectives, as well as the position and resources of the nation, may have materially changed. Let us examine for a moment the panic and depression periods of 1893, 1903, and 1907.

These years were all preceded by bull markets which, superficially at least, bore many of the earmarks of the present bull market. . . . But the panics or depressions that followed closely on the heels of the booms of 1892, 1902, and 1906 were primarily caused, in all three cases, by certain outstanding factors which no longer exist in this country. . . .

Consequently, in comparing the pre-war past with the post-war present, we must first give due weight to the fact that the fundamental causes of the disasters mentioned have now been eliminated. Looking backward, as we now can, it is readily enough demonstrated that in the period of twenty years or more preceding the Great War there never was a time in which one could fairly count on a long period of sustained prosperity in this country. Banking conditions were always unsound; a large part of

the period was checkered with radical antitrust legislation; socialistic ideas were rampant in all directions; the financing of this initial era of big business was in large part crude, unscientific, and ill considered. It was the period of the 'trust-buster,' the muckraker, and the 'undesirable citizen,' and, in its later years, the shadows of the Great War were dropping down over the world.

The saner method for attempting an analysis of the present is to seek for the background of the years which have gone by since the close of the war; especially those years which have intervened since the deflation collapse of 1920 and 1921. The background of these half-dozen years far more completely explains the present and indicates the probable future than any research, however exhaustive, into the generation which preceded the Great War. . . .

. . . [C]ertain other fundamental facts should be brought to the front. The most important is that the position of the United States in relation to the rest of the world had completely changed. We had become a mighty creditor nation, whereas in the decades before the war we were still a borrowing nation. The sudden and dramatic events of the war period had increased the wealth and resources of this country to an extent which perhaps would not otherwise have been equaled within a generation or more; and, because of the exhaustion of Europe, the relative position of the United States had been made even stronger. An immense increase in our plant and producing capacity had also taken place as a result of abnormal war activities after 1914 and all through the war years. Thus, at the signing of the peace, this country was completely equipped for a vast new expansion in its wealth-producing activities.

Another vital fact which had gone far to stabilize fundamental financial and business conditions in America was the founding of the Federal Reserve Banking System. . . . By the opening of 1923, the Federal Reserve Law had demonstrated its thorough practicality and value, and thus had secured the general confidence of the business interests of the country. The old breeder of financial panics, the National Banking Law, which had been a menace to American progress for two decades, had now been replaced by a modern, scientific reserve system which embodied an elastic currency and an orderly control of the money market. . . .

After the war had closed and the wild speculative period of profiteering had collapsed, a declining tendency immediately set in in commodity prices. Margins of profit narrowed or entirely disappeared,

In this illustration, passengers of a transatlantic liner travel in great luxury. The 1920s were a period of prosperity for many. © HISTORICAL PICTURE ARCHIVE/CORBIS. REPRODUCED BY PERMISSION.

and thus the old temptation for expanding inventories or buying goods or raw materials in anticipation of sharply rising prices was completely eliminated. A very direct and increasing impetus was thus given to the modern American effort toward the more scientific development of mass production and distribution, the speeding up of production, and the cutting out of waste and excess motion in all industrial activities. . . .

Coincident with the growing efficiency in manufacturing and business methods, there was fully under way by 1923 a rapid development of new mechanical inventions in almost every business line. Old methods were being eliminated and new labor and time-saving devices installed as never before. Profits were being sought more and more through the elimination and cutting down of unnecessary costs rather than in mere attempts to increase volume and profit through possible advancing prices.

This tendency was further accelerated by the continuous trend toward consolidation of small units into large; by the larger development of the chain-store and direct-delivery systems, with the resulting elimination of the middle man.

This general evolution in production and distribution was of course immensely stimulated by the perfecting of methods, going on all over the country, for the larger mobilization of investment capital; the gathering together, for the uses of industry and for direct investment in the big business and corporate enterprises of the times, of the surplus savings of the people. We were rapidly becoming a nation of investors—investors in our own industries from one end of the country to the other.

With the gradual disappearance of the war and post-war problems and the final adjustment of relations with our former Allies, and with the adjustment of our people to the habit of accepting the higher level of prices and cost of living as 'normal,' a new stabilization of political and labor interests took form. No longer were the people agitated by the pre-war political issues of tariff, antimonopoly, and 'trust-busting'; labor was no longer aggressively urging socialistic legislation; issues which had split the Republican Party in 1912, such as the recall of judges, initiative and referendum, direct election of senators, and woman suffrage, were either settled or forgotten; the League of Nations issue and the 'Wilson policies' had been pushed aside by the return of the Republicans to power in 1920. Labor was being quite uniformly employed on the new and higher wage scales and was beginning to share more and more in the profits of industry, while the general public were feeling the influences of growing stability and prosperity. As increasing numbers became investors in the rising corporate activities of the continent, the sentiment pervaded more and more widely that business enterprise and wealth production thrive best under political noninterference, though with proper and necessary regulation. This changing attitude of the people was well reflected in the national election of 1924, when the strongest argument which returned President Coolidge to office was the maintenance of business stability. . . .

No one can examine the panorama of business and finance in America during the past half-dozen years without realizing that we are living in a new era; that we have been going through an economic revolution of the profoundest character. America's world of to-day is not the world of twenty years ago.

In fact, a new age is taking form throughout the entire civilized world; civilization is taking on new aspects. We are only now beginning to realize, perhaps, that this modern, mechanistic civilization in which we live is now in the process of perfecting itself. Political problems nowadays are looming less large in the minds of men than are economic factors. The public more and more are thinking in terms of industry, wealth production, efficiency of method, income, and profits. What this portends for the longer future, no one can say; but it is a fact of great significance, nevertheless.

III

. . . [T]here seem to be many reasons for believing that the coming period may prove quite as stable and constructive in this country as have the five past years, if not more so. And, though the prices of investment securities of standard quality look high to us to-day, they easily may, by 1933, be quoted in many cases at far higher values. . . .

There is every indication that the steady growth in the wealth and savings of the American people which has been going on without material interruption for years, and is still persisting, will continue through many years to come, thus adding steadily to and maintaining a relative plethora of available capital and credit; a plethora which has by no means been offset thus far by the immense outpour of new securities or the heavy borrowings of foreign peoples. Capital, credit, and confidence are practically interchangeable terms in our modern, mechanistic civilization. In the last analysis, their plenitude depends on faith; that is, faith in the future. . . .

Not the least important fact of this new age in which we live is the profound change which has taken place within recent years in the public attitude toward corporate enterprise. To-day it is estimated that more than 15,000,000 Americans own stocks and bonds and governmental obligations, and the number is still growing by leaps and bounds. When it is realized that twenty years ago not more than 500,000 security investors existed in the United States, the significance of this fact will be recognized. . . .

It is not for a moment intended to imply that in this new era the old-fashioned principles of causes and effect have lost their meaning. There is still as much truth as ever in the axiom that what is pushed up in speculative Wall Street is certain sooner or later to be pushed down. We have had demonstration enough, during the past five years, as values have been rising, that rash stock-market speculation is as dangerous as ever. The impressive thing, however, has been the gradual, though fluctuating, upward trend from year to year and the relative maintenance of values at the higher levels, regardless of business reactions, of temporary recessions in profits, money-market fluctuations, or such seemingly abnormal things as the heavy outflow of gold to Europe. . . .

The mistake that many, no doubt, make is to assume that times have not fundamentally changed. They have changed. We are living in a new era, and Wall Street, in its present condition and activity, broadly stated, is simply reflecting this new era. It will continue to reflect it as the years go by, and if, as has been assumed, the present national and world trends continue without material change through the next decade, it is obvious enough that security values during future years will rise to higher levels.

But it should finally be emphasized that, though we are in the midst of a new and remarkable era, we have not reached the millennium. We should not assume that business reactions, periods of recession, and unsettlement, are to be abolished, or that Wall Street will enjoy an uninterrupted bull market indefinitely. Plenty of shocks will come in the months and years ahead to the speculator and gambler, and perhaps there will be more than one massacre of the innocents in Wall Street during the coming year or two. This seems likely enough, if only because of the vast increase in our 'lamb' population.

Further Resources

BOOKS

Leuchtenburg, William F. *The Perils of Prosperity, 1914–1932.* Chicago: University of Chicago Press, 1958, 1993.

Moody, John. *The Long Road Home.* New York: Macmillan, 1933.

———. *Fast By the Road.* New York: Macmillan, 1942.

WEBSITES

Herbert Hoover Presidential Library and Museum. Available online at http://hoover.archives.gov/exhibits/ (accessed February 25, 2003).

"Brokers and Suckers"

Magazine article

By: Robert Ryan

Date: 1928

Source: Ryan, Robert. "Brokers and Suckers." *The Nation,* August 15, 1928, 154. Reprinted in Mowry, George, ed. *The Twenties: Fords, Flappers, and Fanatics.* Englewood Cliffs, N.J.: Prentice-Hall, Inc., 1963, 38–42.

About the Author: Little is known about the details of Robert Ryan's life. He published the piece (excerpted below) in *The Nation* following a two-month stint in a busy Wall Street brokerage firm during the summer of 1928. Founded in 1865 *The Nation* is the United States' oldest weekly magazine. Established in the liberal-reform tradition, the journal is still well-known for publishing intelligent political and social commentary. ∎

Introduction

So much of the New Era economy of the 1920s was built on salesmanship—of cars, consumer goods, and real estate. Investments were no different. New ranks of slick bankers and brokers aggressively marketed bonds to new investors in the early 1920s. As the stock market improved, the promise of spectacular profits drew increasing numbers of people to invest in riskier equities. One estimate claims the number of people owning stocks rose from half a million to fifteen million in the two decades before 1928, in part due to the shady dealings Robert

Ryan described in his expose of Wall Street firms, published in a 1928 issue of *The Nation.*

New means were developed to facilitate the entrance of this throng of new investors into the market. One was the investment trust: a forerunner to modern mutual funds, the investment companies allowed small investors to diversify their holdings by buying into the trust and combining their assets with others in an actively managed account. Another technique was buying "on margin." This meant financing the purchase of a large volume of stock using a mix of cash and brokers' loans. The cash was the "margin" and could be anywhere from ten to seventy percent of the cost of the total transaction. If the stock's value fell below the amount necessary to cover the loan, the buyer had to put up more money, or risk losing his entire investment. It was a fantastic system when the market was on the rise, allowing investors to reap large profits on small investments.

The aggressive marketing of brokers and the new methods of investment allowed individuals to control vast pools of common stocks and to ride the waves of the market in previously unavailable ways. As New Era financiers, economists, and analysts debated how long the bull market could last, they grew ever more worried about the effect of the flood of speculators and amateur traders on the financial climate. Was all this activity inflating stock value? Was the market being manipulated to capitalize on short-term volatility at the expense of long-term growth?

Significance

By the summer of 1929, many financial observers thought that the market was overheated. Concerned that market speculation was driving the price of stocks too high, the Federal Reserve Board sought to discourage market speculation. But few could foresee the crash that was to come. Prices tumbled during the last week of October amid frantic trading. Driven in part by margin buying, a system that could not withstand dramatic downturns, the slide continued into mid-November. Private bankers tried in vain to stem the rapid sell-off, but they could do little to restore the lack of confidence in the market's profitability.

At the time, blame for the crash and the following depression was laid on the "speculative orgy" of trading that had characterized the previous eighteen months. But scholars now tend to doubt these conclusions. Advances in productivity underlay the rise in stock prices in most sectors, and the Great Depression, notable for its length and severity, lingered and deepened for reasons which were not directly linked to the market collapse.

Other factors combined to turn what might have been a brief recession into a global economic depression. The maintenance of an inflexible gold standard, the raising of barriers to foreign trade, and the liquidation of international investments have all been offered as reasons for the Great Depression. Leading industrial nations—Britain, France, Germany, Austria, and the United States—all suffered from a contraction of investment, excess production, under-consumption, and a decline in foreign trade. To be sure, the panic on Wall Street spread from investors to bank depositors, and the failure of banks led to the shriveling of credit, which had underpinned 1920s prosperity. But the Great Depression was more deeply rooted in the inherent instability of the world economy.

If the stock market crash of 1929 did not directly *cause* the Great Depression, it still remains significant as a cultural touchstone. The market's dizzying heights had been central to New Era psychology; its collapse now signified that era's failures. The economic advances of the 1920s, once unassailable, were now reinterpreted as the product of giddy excess. The democratization of the stock market, once enthusiastically trumpeted, despite the warnings by writers like Ryan, now appeared as so many lambs being led to the slaughter.

Primary Source

"Brokers and Suckers" [excerpt]

> **SYNOPSIS:** In this excerpt from his article in the August 15, 1928 issue of *The Nation*, Robert Ryan recounts his experience in a Wall Street brokerage firm. Ryan reveals how even in what was considered a respectable investment house, sales practices routinely discriminated against and took advantage of small investors.

During the spring months of this year the customers' rooms of Wall Street's brokerage houses were overflowing with a new type of speculator. In these broad rooms you could see feverish young men and heated elders, eyes intent upon the ticker tape. The ranks of the inexperienced—the "suckers"— were swelled by numbers of men who had been attracted by newspaper stories of the big, easy profits to be made in a tremendous bull market, of millions captured overnight by the Fisher Brothers, Arthur Cutten, and Durant. At first these newcomers risked a few hundred dollars with some broker they knew, discovered that it was easy to make money this way, and finally made their headquarters in the broker's large customer's room, bringing with them their entire checking and savings accounts.

These amateurs were not schooled in markets that had seen stringent, panicky drops in prices. They came in on a rising tide. They speculated on tips, on

hunches, on "follow-the-leader" principles. When a stock rose sharply they all jumped for it—and frequently were left holding the bag of higher prices. They would sell or buy on the slightest notice, usually obeying implicitly the advice of their broker.

Out of this combustible desire to trade in and out of the market, abuses have arisen. Some brokers, none too scrupulous, have taken advantage of the helplessness of the small customer. The broker can make more commissions by rapid trading than by holding stocks for real appreciation in value, and he knows that this particular type of customer is here today and gone tomorrow. He must make commissions while the money shines.

Sometime ago I spent about two months in a busy broker's office. I had been offered a position as customer's man (to get new accounts and keep them posted on the market's doings). As I wanted to see whether I would like this work, I asked for a two months' period in which to learn the business. The broker with whom I became associated is considered reliable and honest, and the offer was supposedly an attractive one. I sat in the private office of the president and was thus able to follow quite minutely the methods by which he conducted his business. Years of experience with ordinary business had given me no hint of the practices I saw occur as everyday procedure—in the main practices highly prejudicial to the average customer's interest. So astonished was I that I questioned several other Wall Street brokers, only to find that the practices I saw were common enough on the Street, indulged in more or less generally by large and small firms. . . .

I shall list here a few of the incidents I witnessed while in the office. On Thursday the partner of Mr. X, whose name I shall conceal, had bought some shares of Arabian bank stock at $440 a share. This stock was not listed on the Stock Exchange but was dealt in by over-the-counter houses (houses which deal in unlisted securities). These firms make their own prices, determined solely by the demand for the stock. There is usually a marked difference in quotations by these houses, and the practice is to call several of them before buying in order to get the best price. On Friday morning a customer of Mr. X telephoned an order to sell 50 shares of Arabian bank stock. Mr. X obtained his permission to sell "at the best price." He called to his partner, "Want any more of that Arabian bank stock?"

"At what price?" answered Mr. Y. "I paid $440 a share yesterday."

"You can have this for less," said Mr. X. "I've got a market order. The market is 415 bid, 445 offered. Want it at 415?"

"Sure," said Mr. Y. And the customer was informed that it was too bad he got such a low price—but after all, "we sold it at the market."

The dishonesty of this transaction lies in the fact that if several firms had been called and the stock offered for sale, a better price could have been obtained, for this was an active stock in good demand with a wide difference between the bid-and-ask prices.

Incident No. 2: This firm was "bullish" on a certain stock—they believed its price would go higher. Suddenly a panic developed in the stock and it began to decline at a rapid rate. The large and small customers who owned the stock all began selling at once. When the selling confirmations came in, Mr. X announced that no selling prices could be given out until all the orders were checked. In the next half hour Mr. X and his partners selected those sales which had brought the best prices, allotted these best prices to their larger customers, and allowed the small fry to get what was left. This is obviously unfair discrimination. A record is kept by the order clerk of the sequence in which the selling orders are placed. Consequently, the prices of the sales should have been allotted in that order. "Of course," Mr. X remarked, "we make most money from our large customers, and we must keep them satisfied."

Incident No. 3: The broker charges a standard—and substantial—commission on the orders he executes, yet it is common practice among all firms to borrow money at, let us say, 5 per cent and charge 6 per cent to their customers who buy on margin. The Stock Exchange has ruled that brokers may charge their customers the exact amount of interest, or more than the exact amount, that they themselves have to pay when they borrow the money in the open market or from banks; but in no case may brokers charge the customers *less* than the brokers pay in borrowing the money. This rule has been promulgated in order that brokers may not offer the extra inducement of a reduced interest rate to large speculators in order to acquire them as customers. This rule does away with a great deal of cut-throat competition; but in practice the large customer is actually charged the same amount of interest as the broker pays or very little more, while the small customer pays an average of ¾ of one per cent additional on all money which he uses when buying on margin. This ¾ of one per cent, various brokers have

"I'm in the Market For You"

Recorded just months after the crash, this song written by George Olsen and performed by Fred Mac-Murray hopes for romantic dividends where financial ones failed.

I'll have to see my broker
Find out what he can do.
'Cause I'm in the market for you.

There won't be any joker,
With margin I'm all through.
'Cause I want you outright it's true.

You're going up, up, up in my estimation.
I want a thousand shares of your caresses too.

We'll count the hugs and kisses,
When dividends are due,
'Cause I'm in the market for you.

SOURCE: Olsen, George. "I'm in the Market for You." Recorded February 9, 1930, on the Victor recording label. Lyrics and .wav file reproduced at "The Crash of 1929," The Jazz Age Page. Available at online at http://www.btinternet.com/~dreklind/thecrash.htm; website home page http://www.btinternet.com/~dreklind/Jazzhome.htm (accessed February 25, 2003).

told me, is intended to cover the entire overhead cost of their business. This means that the commissions which are paid for buying or selling the stock are net income to the brokerage house. It is easy to understand why brokerage houses insist that they are justified in charging this so-called "service fee" for negotiating a loan for a client.

Incident No. 4: Mr. X stepped into the customers' room and announced with a great show of sagacity that "Pomegranate A" was a purchase at current prices, and that he advised immediate purchase. His advice was quickly followed; there was general buying by the customers who thought they saw an opportunity to make some quick money. A few minutes later Mr. X notified one of his large customers that he had sold 1,500 shares of "Pomegranate A" at excellent prices, and received the client's congratulations for a good "execution." Those customers in the big room who bought on Mr. X's advice paid 6 per cent or more on their money, and watched the stock drop in value. The story behind this transaction was enlightening. Mr. X's large customer had heard from a director of "Pomegranate A" that the quarterly dividend would not be paid and that this fact would be announced in a few days. Knowing that the stock would drop in price after such an announcement, Mr. X's customer gave

High and Low Prices of Leading Stocks, 1929

	High price Sept. 3, 1929	Low price Nov. 13, 1929
American Can	$181^7/_8$	86
American Telephone & Telegraph	304	$197^1/_4$
Anaconda Copper	$131^1/_2$	70
General Electric	$396^1/_4$	$168^1/_8$
General Motors	$72^3/_4$	36
Montgomery Ward	$137^7/_8$	$49^1/_4$
New York Central	$256^3/_8$	160
Radio	101	28
Union Carbide & Carbon	$137^7/_8$	59
United States Steel	$261^3/_4$	150
Westinghouse E & M	$289^7/_8$	$102^5/_8$
Woolworth	$100^3/_8$	$52^1/_4$
Electric Bond & Share	$186^3/_4$	$50^1/_4$

SOURCE: Allen, Frederick Lewis. *Only Yesterday: An Informal History of the Nineteen-Twenties.* New York and London: Harper & Brothers Publishers, 1931, p. 337.

immediate orders to sell at the current prices. Mr. X knew that "Pomegranate A" was a volatile stock and that if he dumped 1,500 shares on the market it would break the price of the stock. So, by getting his small customers to buy these shares, he placed a cushion under the stock to absorb the 1,500 shares he was selling. He sold at no sacrifice and induced his smaller customers to buy stock which he knew would decline in value.

Incident No. 5: A "pool" is made to maintain current prices in a certain stock or push those prices higher. Mr. X was in a pool to raise the price on "New York Rug." This pool had made a substantial profit by the time its price had been shoved up to $212 a share. Thereupon the members of the pool decided to liquidate their holdings and take their profits. Mr. X knew that this stock was not worth $212 a share and that when the pool had distributed its holdings the stock would drop in value. Mr. X had put a large number of his customers into this stock at high prices. When any of them called to inquire about it he answered cheerfully, "It's good for $250 a share. Yes, I'm holding mine." So his customers held on.

When Mr. X and his friends had finished taking their profits by selling the stock and the news had come out on the floor that the pool had disbanded there was a great deal of "short selling." (If you believe a stock is selling at a price above its real value, you sell it and buy it back at a lower price—if you are lucky.) These "short sales" forced the stock down, and it was only then that Mr. X telephoned

his customers that he understood the stock was a sale at once, and watched his customers receive much lower prices.

Incident No. 6: Mr. X advised all his customers to buy "Rotton Apples Common." Since Mr. X's firm helped to finance the stock issue their interest in selling this stock could hardly be wholly disinterested.

It would be simple to multiply these incidents and cite other practices, but what I suggested in the first part of this article has, I believe, been amply shown: in every case under my observation the broker felt that he must give the advantage, even though it were a dishonest advantage, to his large customer, for the large customer is his bread and butter and his profits. The small investor or speculator remains completely unaware of these practices. In a rising market such methods may be employed without losing the customer's business, for a speculator will overlook small irregularities as long as he continues to make money; while in a declining market the broker gets away with an equal amount of dishonesty, the customer blames the results on market drops. If a customer loses all his money, or so dislikes the actions of Mr. X's firm that he withdraws his business, Mr. X is completely unconcerned. As he remarked to me: "Suckers are born every minute; the glamor of easy money gets them all. One goes, two come in. Win or lose, we get our commissions." It is an easy-going philosophy which has been so completely proved true by many Wall Street brokers that they have no reason to revise it.

How such practices can be stopped I do not know; nor do I imagine that it is within the power of the Stock Exchange authorities to prevent them. I do believe that one step ahead would be to forbid all brokerage houses or their employees to transact business for themselves, to compel them to act solely as customers' agents. Surely this would make them a trifle more disinterested in the advice they give their clients.

In the meantime Mr. X's firm is making money hand over fist. In another month they will move to quarters three times their present space.

Further Resources

BOOKS

Bierman, Harold J., Jr. *The Causes of the 1929 Stock Market Crash: A Speculative Orgy of a New Era?* Westport, Conn.: Greenwood Press, 1998.

Galbraith, John Kenneth. *The Great Crash.* Boston: Houghton Mifflin, 1955.

A New York man tries to sell his roadster after the stock market crash. While the market had fluctuated in the preceding months, many investors did not at all foresee loss to that extent. © UPI/CORBIS-BETTMANN. REPRODUCED BY PERMISSION.

James, Harold. *The End of Globalization: Lessons from the Great Depression.* Cambridge: Harvard University Press, 2001.

Klein, Maury. *Rainbow's End: The Crash of 1929.* New York: Oxford University Press, 2001.

WEBSITES

"The 1929 Stock Market Crash." University of Melbourne. Available online at http://www.arts.unimelb.edu.au/amu/ucr /student/1997/Yee/1929.htm (accessed February 25, 2003).

"Stock Market Crash." Timeline from *The First Measured Century.* PBS Online. Available online at http://www.pbs.org /fmc/timeline/estockmktcrash.htm; website home page: http:// www.pbs.org/ (accessed February 25, 2003).

The Southern Urban Negro as Consumer

Report, Advertisements

By: Paul Kenneth Edwards

Date: 1932

Source: Edwards, Paul Kenneth. *The Southern Urban Negro as Consumer,* 1932. Reprint, College Park, Md.: McGrath

Publishing Company, 1969, 246–51. Reproduced in *Prosperity and Thrift: The Coolidge Era and the Consumer Economy, 1921–1929.* American Memory digital primary source collection, Library of Congress. Available online at http://memory .loc.gov/ammem/coolhtml/coolhome.html; website home page: http://memory.loc.gov (accessed May 14, 2003).

About the Author: Throughout his career, Paul Kenneth Edwards (1898–1959) devoted his scholarly energies to understanding the mind of the black consumer. He received his doctorate in economics from Harvard University, taught at Ursinus College and the University of Virginia, and worked at Harvard's Bureau of Business Research and the Department of Agriculture before arriving at Fisk University. There he conducted his pioneering study of the consumption patterns of urban African Americans during the 1920s. When Fisk created the Institute of Race Relations in 1944, Edwards joined that prestigious group of African American scholars, which also included Charles Johnson, E. Franklin Frazier, Horace Mann Bond, and Bertram Doyle. ∎

Introduction

The 1920s were a time of creative outpouring for African Americans. Writers sought to better understand the African American's "two-ness" in W. E. B. DuBois's phrase: the dilemma of racial distinctiveness and intimate connectedness to America. Political groups, such as the National Association for the Advancement of Colored People, organized to advocate racial justice. And scholars like Paul Kenneth Edwards and others at African American academic institutions produced voluminous scholarship during this period in an effort to explain the social and economic conditions of African Americans.

This torrent of artistic, political, and academic work reflected a spirit of cultural revolution: the artistic and intellectual fervor centered in New York was termed the Harlem Renaissance; the broad movement of racial uplift was referred to as the era of the "New Negro." This new expressiveness also reflected the growing strength and activism of a black middle and upper class. These men and women staffed the organizations and served on the faculty of institutions dedicated to African American advancement. And in this age of mass consumption, they became a significant presence in the market as well.

Significance

Edwards's study of southern black consumers reveals the extensive and varied use of the African American image in mass advertising. With the rise of national advertising in the post-slavery era, many corporations chose to incorporate plantation images into their ad campaigns. Drawing on popular minstrel show imagery and depictions of Southern blacks as docile and happy servants, figures such as Aunt Jemima and Uncle Tom were used to sell pancake batter mixes and hot cereals to white folks.

Other corporations avoided these most stereotypical presentations of African Americans. For instance, record companies recognized a growing market for black music and selected images that, though often exoticizing or romanticizing African Americans, avoided the most alienating depictions redolent of slavery. And black entrepreneurs, including cosmetics tycoon Madam C.J. Walker, employed realistic representations of African Americans in their ads. In both instances, black- and white-owned corporations acknowledged the growing importance of African Americans' buying power.

Ads like those for Madam Walker's beauty products dignified rather than degraded black women. But they also played into white standards of beauty. Ads for African American skin-care products might have avoided racist caricatures, but the "skin whiteners" being sold promoted a definition of beauty that excluded dark skin. As African American men and women struggled during the 1920s to redefine themselves in contrast to older stereotypes, they found that the world of mass advertising offered conflicting and often offensive images.

Primary Source

The Southern Urban Negro as Consumer [excerpt]

SYNOPSIS: This excerpt is from Paul Kenneth Edwards's socioeconomic study of black consumers in the urban South. In this section on race, advertising, and mass marketing, he describes African Americans' reactions to the depiction of black people in nationally distributed advertisements for products such as Cream of Wheat cereal and Madam C. J. Walker's beauty products.

Types of Negro Character Illustrations Most Pleasing and Most Displeasing to Negroes

Because of the significant influence in advertising copy of elements having to do with the Negro race—in particular, the Negro character illustration—either toward developing a favorable reaction to the brand of product advertised, or toward building up a barrier of hostility to it, it was believed worth while to find out, on the one hand, the types of Negro character illustrations most pleasing to Negroes, and, on the other hand, the types most displeasing to them. In an effort to do this, fifteen advertisements were selected containing illustrations of about every type of Negro character used in advertising copy today. The same groups of housewives and family heads used in the preceding tests were then asked to pick from this collection those advertisements in which the Negro character illustration pleased them very much and those in which the Negro character was exceedingly displeasing.

Three advertisements used by the Cream of Wheat Company in 1914 were among the fifteen selected for this study. The illustrations of these advertisements proved to be highly displeasing to more of the 240 individuals interviewed than any of the others. One of them is reproduced on page 247. An understanding of what there is about this illustration which gained the ill will of so many Negroes can best be obtained by reading the selected criticisms which follow:

1. White boy is driving colored man.
2. Don't like idea of white boy driving old Negro.
3. Degrades Negroes in appearance and dress.
4. Pictures wrong side of Negro.
5. White boy driving Negro and calling him "Uncle."
6. Don't like colored man pulling white child.
7. Makes colored people look foolish.
8. White boy using colored man for horse.
9. White boy driving colored man—Negro servant.
10. Don't like colored man being horse for white boy.
11. Not true to life.

SELLING APPEALS FOR THE NEGRO   247

"GIDDAP, UNCLE!"

Painted by Edw. V. Brewer for Cream of Wheat Co.   Copyright 1914 by Cream of Wheat Co.

Figure 20.—Cream of Wheat Advertisement in Which the Negro Character Illustration Proved to Be Exceedingly Displeasing to a Majority of the Negroes of All Occupation Classes Interviewed. (Published through the Courtesy of the Cream of Wheat Corporation.)

Primary Source

Advertisements: Cream of Wheat Advertisement from *The Southern Urban Negro as Consumer* (1 OF 3)

SYNOPSIS: These three images accompanied the text of Paul Kenneth Edwards's socioeconomic study of African American consumers in the urban South. The Uncle Tom caricature often took the form of a childlike black male servant, who despite being constantly demeaned and harassed, remained cheerfully submissive. It was a common image in household product advertising in the early century. THE LIBRARY OF CONGRESS.

Figure 22.—Advertisement of a Product of the Madame C. J. Walker Company in Which the Negro Character Illustration Proved to Be Particularly Pleasing to a Majority of the Negroes of All Occupation Classes Interviewed.

Primary Source

Advertisements: Madam C. J. Walker Face Powder Advertisement from *The Southern Urban Negro as Consumer* (2 OF 3)

The Madam C.J. Walker Manufacturing Company factory employed around 3,000 black men and women in its manufacture of cosmetic products. Madam Walker founded her business around 1905. THE LIBRARY OF CONGRESS.

Three MINUTES A DAY

... with this beauty aid works miracles to any complexion

Alluring Beauty

can be yours by using Dr. Fred Palmer's Skin Whitener Preparations just "three minutes" a day This complete and easy-to-use home beauty treatment is a quick and sure way to remove ugly blackheads, pimples and blotches

and to bring out all of your fascinating loveliness, by reviving that dull, lifeless, sallow skin and giving it a smooth, light and captivating appearance

Dr. Fred Palmer's Skin Whitener Ointment clears and lightens the darkest skin giving it a feminine exquisiteness that gets more charming every day. The dainty Skin Whitener Soap cleanses the skin. smoothes away the roughness and gets rid of that "shiny" appearance The Face Powder in addition to keeping the skin soft. smooth and velvety also clings to the skin and lasts so long that constant powdering is unnecessary one application frequently lasting all day , , and the famous Hair Dresser is a toilet necessity that no woman now-a-days can very well be without, it keeps your hair soft and glossy and in place hours and hours after one application

Any of the above Dr Fred Palmer's Skin Whitener Preparations can be purchased at any drug store for 25c each, or sent postpaid upon receipt of price—four for $1 00 A generous trial sample of the Skin Whitener Soap and Face Powder sent for 4c in stamps

DR FRED PALMER'S LABORATORIES
Dept 9   ATLANTA GEORGIA

DR. FRED PALMER'S SKIN WHITENER Preparations

"keeps your complexion youthful"

Figure 23.—Advertisement of a Product of Dr. Fred Palmer's Laboratories in Which the Negro Character Illustration Proved to Be Particularly Pleasing to a Majority of the Negroes of All Occupation Classes Interviewed.

Primary Source

Advertisements: Dr. Fred Palmer's Skin Whitener Tone and Bleach Cream Advertisement from *The Southern Urban Negro as Consumer* (3 OF 3)

The Dr. Fred Palmer brand today manufactures a similar product called Skin Whitener Tone and Bleach Cream. THE LIBRARY OF CONGRESS.

12. Dislike idea of white boy making fool out of Negro.

13. Boy should not be striking Negro.

14. Makes light of Negro. General appearance disgusts me.

15. Dislike white boy striking Negro man.

16. This is burlesquing the Negro.

17. Dislike making monkey of colored folks.

18. Dislike white boy having Negro hitched up as servant.

19. Dislike "take-off" of Negro.

20. Makes fun of the Negro.

21. Takes off Negro and does not represent usual type.

22. Ignorance is exaggerated.

23. Don't like idea of colored man making fool of himself over white child.

24. Dislike advertising to public at expense of Negro.

25. Picture exaggerated.

26. Portrays old "Uncle Tom" type of Negro.

27. Portrays obsolete and objectionable type.

28. Portrays colored people burlesqued.

29. Disgusting. Shows old-time Negro instead of modern.

30. This is true, but should not be pictured publicly.

Two advertisements are reproduced on pages 252–53 which contain illustrations of Negro characters pleasing to a large majority of the individuals interviewed. One of these advertisements concerns the products of the Madame Walker Company, a large Negro manufacturing enterprise, and was clipped from a Negro magazine. The other is for a bleaching cream and was found in a Negro weekly newspaper. The comment made by the majority who found the illustrations of these two advertisements particularly pleasing was that here were illustrations which pictured the Negro as he really is, not caricatured, degraded, or made fun of; that here the Negro was dignified and made to look as he is striving to look, and not as he looked in ante-bellum days; that here was the new Negro.

Further Resources

BOOKS

Bundles, A'Lelia. *On Her Own Ground: The Life and Times of Madam C.J. Walker.* New York: Scribners, 2001.

Kern-Foxworth, Marilyn. *Aunt Jemima, Uncle Ben, and Rastus: Blacks in Advertising, Yesterday, Today, and Tomorrow.* Westport, Conn.: Greenwood Press, 1994.

Manring, M. M. *Slave in a Box: The Strange Career of Aunt Jemima.* Charlottesville, Va.: University Press of Virginia, 1998.

PERIODICALS

Cohen, Lizabeth. "Encountering Mass Culture at the Grass Roots: The Experience of Chicago Workers in the 1920s." *American Quarterly* 41, March 1989, 6–33.

WEBSITES

Madam C. J. Walker, 1867–1919, Entrepreneur, Philanthropist, Social Activist. Available online at http://www.madam-cjwalker.com/ (accessed February 19, 2003).

3

EDUCATION

KRISTINA PETERSON

Entries are arranged in chronological order by date of primary source. For entries with one primary source, the entry title is the same as the primary source title. Entries with more than one primary source have an overall entry title, followed by the titles of the primary sources.

Important Events in Education, 1920–1929

1920

- The U.S. Census reports 21,578,000 students in public schools. College enrollment is 597,000 students, while U.S. population exceeds 100 million.
- The Lusk Laws require New York teachers to take loyalty oaths.
- Junior colleges open in Arizona and Iowa.
- Ellwood P. Cubberley of Stanford University publishes *The History of Education.*
- In February, psychologist John B. Watson resigns his professorship at Johns Hopkins University in Baltimore, Maryland, after rumors surface that he had dated a former student following a divorce from his first wife.
- In May, Arthur Holly Compton becomes Wayman Crow Professor of Physics at Washington University in Saint Louis, Missouri, and one of the most highly paid professors in the U.S.
- In September, Clark University in Worcester, Massachusetts, opens the first graduate school of geography.
- In September, educators Ernest Jackman and Helen Parkhurst in Dalton, Massachusetts, first use the Dalton Plan of instruction.
- In November, Susan Miller Dorsey becomes the first female superintendent of the Los Angeles schools.
- From December 4 to December 10, teachers and administrators celebrate the first American Education Week.

1921

- About two hundred institutions of higher education award master's degrees, and nearly fifty offer doctorates.
- Junior colleges open in Texas.
- On January 18, the New York State school commissioner makes public-school teachers subject to dismissal for membership in the Communist Party.
- In May, former Democratic presidential candidate William Jennings Bryan launches a campaign against the teaching of evolution in U.S. public schools.
- On June 4, Robert Andrews Millikan becomes director of the Norman Bridge Laboratory of Physics at the California Institute of Technology in Pasadena, California. Millikan's eminence brings immediate status to the laboratory.

- In August, astronomer Harlow Shapley becomes director of the Harvard College Observatory.
- In the fall, the fifth annual report of the Federal Board for Vocational Education declares that between July 1, 1920, and June 30, 1921, the board cooperated with the states in the vocational training of 305,224 students in 3,859 schools. The most popular areas were home economics, trade and industry, and agriculture.

1922

- John Franklin Bobbitt publishes *Curriculum-making in Los Angeles.*
- George S. Counts publishes *The Selective Character of American Secondary Education.*
- John Dewey's *Human Nature and Conduct* draws national attention.

1923

- On March 6, the U.S. Supreme Court, in *Meyer v. Nebraska,* forbids schools from banning foreign-language instruction when the intent is to shield students from the language and customs of countries whose political and economic systems differ from those of the U.S.
- In the winter, the New York state legislature repeals the Lusk Laws, which had required New York teachers to profess their loyalty to the U.S.
- On October 16, the New York State Court of Appeals upholds a law requiring mandatory educational and literacy tests for new voters.

1924

- William McAndrew becomes superintendent of the Chicago School System.
- On May 21, the General Assembly of the Presbyterian Church at San Antonio, Texas, opposes the teaching of the theory of evolution in Texas schools.
- On October 4, tobacco millionaire James B. Duke gives $47 million to Trinity College in North Carolina. In 1925 the Board of Trustees renames the college Duke University.

1925

- In January, physicist and Nobel laureate Albert Abraham Michelson becomes the first Distinguished Service Professor at the University of Chicago.
- On January 11, the Tennessee state legislature forbids the teaching of "any theory that denies the story of the Divine creation of man as taught in the Bible and to teach instead that man has descended from a lower order of animals."
- On May 13, the Florida House of Representatives passes a bill requiring daily Bible readings in all public schools. Civil libertarians condemn the law as a violation of the Establishment Clause of the First Amendment.
- On June 1, the U.S. Supreme Court, in *Pierce v. Society of Sisters,* strikes down an Oregon law requiring all children to attend public schools. The Court rules that student attendance

at a private school satisfies Oregon's compulsory attendance law.

- On July 13, John T. Scopes goes on trial in Dayton, Tennessee, for teaching evolution in violation of the January 11 state law forbidding the teaching of evolution in Tennessee public schools.

- On October 16, Texas governor Miriam Ferguson issues an executive order forbidding public-school teachers from using textbooks that discuss evolution. The Texas State Text Book Board, acting on Ferguson's executive order, bans the use of such textbooks from its public schools.

1926

- Carter Godwin Woodson wins the NAACP Spingarn Medal for his promotion of the study of African American history.

- A New York state court hears a challenge to the White Plains, New York, school board requirement that its public schools teach religion one hour per week.

- On February 9, the Board of Education prohibits the teaching of the theory of evolution in Atlanta, Georgia, public schools.

- On July 28, the Virginia Supreme Court, in *Flory v. Smith,* affirms that the Virginia state legislature has the authority to enact any law governing public education, provided its laws do not contradict federal law or the U.S. Constitution.

1927

- William McAndrew is fired as superintendent of the Chicago School System.

- Samuel Morison publishes *The Oxford History of the United States.*

- New York University establishes seven summer schools in European universities; these schools will grant college credit for courses taught by American professors.

1928

- George S. Counts publishes *School and Society in Chicago.*

- In May, embryologist Thomas Hunt Morgan accepts an invitation from the California Institute of Technology to organize and staff its Division of Biology.

- In October, Vernon Louis Parrington's *Main Currents in American Thought* wins the Pulitzer Prize for history.

1929

- The Carnegie Foundation for the Advancement of Teaching reports that intercollegiate athletics is a "Roman Circus."

- Public-school enrollment is 25,678,000, and enrollment in colleges and universities is more than 1,000,000. The U.S. population is 121,770,000.

- In January, the historically African American Spelman College, Morehouse College, and Atlanta University agree to share facilities, faculty, and students, welding the three into a center for the education of African Americans.

- On June 30, Susan Miller Dorsey retires as superintendent of the Los Angeles schools.

"Memoranda Accompanying the Vetoes of the Lusk Laws"

Memo

By: Alfred E. Smith

Date: 1920

Source: Moskowitz, Henry, ed. *Progressive Democracy: Addresses and State Papers of Alfred E. Smith*. New York: Harcourt, Brace, 1928, 275–276.

About the Author: Alfred E. Smith (1873–1944) was born on the Lower East Side of New York, the child of second-generation immigrants. With only an eighth-grade education, Smith went on to become a New York State assemblyman, governor of New York for four terms, and, in 1928, the Democratic presidential candidate. As New York governor (1919–1921 and 1923–1929), he worked to pass legislation to improve social welfare and preserve the rights of individuals. ■

Introduction

The "Lusk Laws" were passed during the "Red Scare" following World War I (1914–1918), a period marked by a distrust and fear of radicals and foreigners, especially those individuals thought to represent the socialist ideals that had recently spread throughout Europe following the Bolshevik Revolution in Russia. Economic woes, waves of immigrants entering the country, and labor struggles all fed the growing paranoia.

It was in this context that the New York legislature formed, in 1919, the Joint Legislative Committee to Investigate Seditious Activities, headed by Senator Clayton Lusk. This group, known as the Lusk Committee, conducted an investigation of a large number of organizations and individuals suspected of advocating the overthrow of the U.S. government. Tactics used included raiding the headquarters of suspect organizations, seizing documents, infiltrating groups, and investigating individuals found on membership lists. Thousands of people were arrested. The committee produced an enormous report entitled "Revolutionary Radicalism: Its History, Purpose and Tactics."

In the report, the Lusk Committee stressed that education is the key to forming citizens loyal to American

"The Need of Loyalty Oaths for Teachers"

Of the three so-called Lusk bills in the Legislature against the Socialists, the Teacher's Loyalty bill has been passed by both houses. It requires public school teachers to obtain from the Board of Regents a certificate of loyalty to the State and Federal Constitutions and the laws and institutions of the United States. Such certification is sorely needed. There has been only too much evidence of the success of the Socialists in imparting their fatal doctrines to young and ductile minds. It is incredible that the State should allow schools or teachers whose teaching is for the express purpose of destroying the State. The danger is not that any loyal teacher will be disqualified, but that disloyal teachers will profess loyalty.

SOURCE: *The New York Times*, April 22, 1920.

institutions and values. Teachers, the report states, because they are in a position to directly influence students, must "possess character above reproach and should be loyal to the institutions and laws of the government they represent." Regarding the public school teacher, the report asserts that "If he does not approve of the present social system or the structure of our government he is at liberty to entertain those ideas, but must surrender his public office."

Based on the report and recommendations of the committee, the New York legislature passed the Lusk Bills, two of which concerned education. The first of these required all public school teachers to sign an oath of loyalty "to the institutions of the United States and of the State of New York and the laws thereof." The second bill required certain private schools to show that their activities were not "detrimental to the public interest" in order to obtain a license to operate.

Significance

The Lusk Bills were passed at a time when many individual rights and liberties were sacrificed to the goal of protecting Americans and American institutions from foreign and subversive forces. Calls for loyalty oaths were not the only way schools and teachers were affected by this social climate. A 1923 Nebraska law, for example, banned the teaching of foreign languages, and a 1922 Oregon law required all students to attend public schools only. These laws aimed to increase the uniformity of the American population and reduce the influence of radicals and subversives.

By vetoing the Lusk Bills, Governor Smith took a stand for the academic freedom of teachers and their right to freedom of speech and thought. Smith stated that such laws, far from protecting democracy, are themselves destructive of "the foundations of democratic education." Although Smith vetoed the Lusk Laws, his successor, Governor Nathan Miller, signed them into law. Smith ran for office again with the promise to repeal the Lusk Laws as part of his campaign. He was reelected in 1923 and repealed the laws.

The roller-coaster-like history of the Lusk Laws illustrates the intensity of the debate over the protection of the American way of life on the one hand, and the individual freedoms that are part of that life on the other. Schools and teachers are often impacted by this recurring battle. Decisions regarding the way that young minds are shaped in society are seen by many groups as key to the question: Should students be educated for loyalty to existing systems or for critical inquiry?

Primary Source

"Memoranda Accompanying the Vetoes of the Lusk Laws" [excerpt]

SYNOPSIS: In the following memorandum, Governor Alfred E. Smith describes his reasoning behind his veto of the Lusk Bill that required each teacher to obtain a certificate from the Commissioner of Education indicating that he or she is morally upright and loyal to the United States and New York State governments. Smith defends teachers' freedom of speech and thought.

Albany, May 18, 1920.

Memorandum filed with Senate Bill, Int. No. 1121, Printed No. 1275, Assembly Reprint No. 2165, entitled:

An act to amend the education law, in relation to the qualifications of teachers, and making an appropriation for expenses.

NOT APPROVED.

This bill provides that every public-school teacher in the State shall obtain a certificate from the Commissioner of Education to the effect that he or she is of good moral character, and has shown satisfactorily that he or she will support the State and Federal Constitutions and is loyal "to the institutions and laws thereof." The certificate may be revoked without hearing on the ground that the commissioner may find that the teacher is not "loyal to the institutions of the United States and of the State of New York and the laws thereof." The test established is not what the teacher teaches, but what the teacher believes, and the effect of the bill would be to make

New York Governor Alfred Smith was a vocal opponent of the movement to have teachers take a loyalty oath, calling it unjust and discriminatory. **THE LIBRARY OF CONGRESS.**

the Commissioner of Education the sole and arbitrary dictator of the personnel of the teaching force of the State in its public schools.

This bill must be judged by what can be done under its provisions. It permits one man to place upon any teacher the stigma of disloyalty and this even without hearing or trial. No man is so omniscient or wise as to have entrusted to him such arbitrary and complete power not only to condemn any individual teacher, but to decree what belief or opinion is opposed to the institutions of the country.

No teacher could continue to teach if he or she entertained any objection, however conscientious, to any existing institution. If this law had been in force prior to the abolition of slavery, opposition to that institution which was protected by the Constitution and its laws would have been just cause for the disqualification of a teacher. There is required of the teacher not only loyalty to the Constitution and the laws of the State but also loyalty to what is described as the institutions of the United States and of the State of New York.

Opposition to any presently established institution, no matter how intelligent, conscientious, or disinterested this opposition might be, would be sufficient to disqualify the teacher. Every teacher would be at the mercy of his colleagues, his pupils, and their parents, and any word or act of the teacher might be held by the commissioner to indicate an attitude hostile to some of "the institutions of the United States" or of the State.

The bill unjustly discriminates against teachers as a class. It deprives teachers of their right to freedom of thought; it limits the teaching staff of the public schools to those only who lack the courage or the mind to exercise their legal right to just criticism of existing institutions. The bill confers upon the Commissioner of Education a power of interference with the freedom of opinion which strikes at the foundations of democratic education.

The bill is, therefore, disapproved.

(Signed) Alfred E. Smith

Further Resources

BOOKS

Eldot, Paula. *Governor Alfred E. Smith: The Politician as Reformer.* New York: Garland, 1983.

Finan, Christopher M. *Alfred E. Smith: The Happy Warrior.* New York: Hill and Wang, 2002.

Kovel, Joel. *Red Hunting in the Promised Land: Anticommunism and the Making of America.* New York: Basic Books, 1994.

WEBSITES

"Alfred E. Smith, U.S. Politician." History Channel: Speeches. Available online at http://www.historychannel.com/speeches/archive/speech_278.html; website home page: http://www.historychannel.com/ (accessed March 12, 2003).

Education on the Dalton Plan

Nonfiction work

By: Helen Parkhurst

Date: 1922

Source: Parkhurst, Helen. *Education on the Dalton Plan.* New York: Dutton, 1922, 18–24, 27–30.

About the Author: Helen Parkhurst (1887–1973) began her career in education as a teacher in a one-room school. She studied in Italy under Maria Montessori and served as Montessori's representative in the United States. Based on her experiences in Montessori's school, Parkhurst developed a "laboratory plan" that she implemented in Dalton, Massachusetts. She lectured extensively abroad and produced several radio programs about education. Parkhurst is recognized as a leader in the progressive education movement. ∎

Introduction

Helen Parkhurst and the Dalton Plan were part of the progressive education movement that began in the 1870s and continued through the 1950s. The movement emphasized social reform through education, the use of psychology and scientific study in education, education for the "whole child," a more practical and relevant curriculum, freedom and self-expression for students, a curriculum derived from students' interests, school as socialization, and teaching how to think rather than what to think.

The progressive education movement had it origins in the attempts of the education system to cope with the problems of urbanization, immigration, and industrialization. In addition to these factors, child labor and compulsory school laws put additional pressures on the education system. Schools were faced with ever-larger numbers of students from a variety of ethnic backgrounds and social classes in the context of a rapidly changing world of new technologies and social patterns. The traditional educational methods of regimentation and memorization would no longer be sufficient. Many new types of curriculum and methods were based on the progressive movement.

In developing the Dalton Plan, Parkhurst was influenced by a number of writers, including John Dewey and Maria Montessori. The plan emphasizes freedom, cooperation, responsibility, individual differences, and school as a social community with interdependent members.

Under the Dalton Plan, the curriculum is divided into monthly "jobs" for each subject. Students sign individual contracts indicating acceptance of the work to be done. Students are also given an overview of the year's work so that they can envision the smaller tasks as part of a coherent whole. They are free to approach the tasks in their own way and to organize their time as they see fit. A room or "laboratory" is assigned to each subject, with students moving freely from one room to another, working individually or in groups as appropriate. A student must finish one job before moving on to another and must make similar progress in all subjects.

After working out many details of what she originally called the "laboratory plan," Parkhurst first put it into practice at a school for "crippled boys." The plan was then adopted by the high school in Dalton, Massachusetts, from which the new name was derived. The word "laboratory," Parkhurst feared, might be misunderstood. In 1919 she founded the Children's University School, later called the Dalton School, in New York City.

Significance

The progressive education movement meant different things to different people. The many facets of the movement allowed an individual interpretation to emphasize some aspects while downplaying others. In addition, the focus of the movement as a whole changed over time. The Dalton plan represents one important educational approach that grew out of the postwar version of progressive education. Prior to World War I (1914–1918), the movement emphasized social reform through education. Progressives worked to make schools for the urban poor more humane and relevant to students' lives. After the war, individual development and freedom for the child took center stage.

While the Dalton Plan is sometimes viewed as an implementation of the ideas of philosopher John Dewey, Parkhurst's plan deviates from Dewey's ideas in at least one important way. Dewey believed that the curriculum, at least during the early years of education, should proceed from the student's interests. The Dalton Plan, on the other hand, uses lessons that are prepared by the teacher and arranged in a set sequence. While the student does not choose what to study, he or she does have the freedom to decide how and when to approach the work. The Dalton plan does closely match Dewey's view of the school as a social community where students work together and teachers serve as resources for students rather than taskmasters. And unlike many others at the time who attempted to apply Dewey's ideas to the classroom by simply letting children do whatever they pleased, Parkhurst understood that, for Dewey, "freedom is not license."

Interest in Helen Parkhurst's ideas and the Dalton Plan continues in the United States, Europe, Japan, and elsewhere. The Dalton School, a private school using Parkhurst's approach, remains in operation in New York City.

Primary Source

Education on the Dalton Plan [excerpt]

SYNOPSIS: In the following excerpts from the chapter entitled "The Plan in Principle," Helen Parkhurst outlines the educational philosophy behind the development of the Dalton Plan. She emphasizes the importance of freedom and responsibility for students within the context of a school that is an interdependent social community. The outcome, she asserts, will be more efficient learning, and students who will be responsible and productive members of a democratic society.

Broadly speaking the old type of school may be said to stand for *culture,* while the modern type of school stands for *experience.* The Dalton Laboratory Plan is primarily a way whereby both these aims can be reconciled and achieved.

The acquisition of culture is a form of experience, and as such is an element in the business of living with which school ought to be as intimately concerned as is adult existence. But it will never become so until the school as a whole is reorganized so that it can function like a community—a community whose essential condition is freedom for the individual to develop himself.

The ideal freedom is not license, still less indiscipline. It is, in fact, the very reverse of both. The child who "does as he likes" is not a free child. He is, on the contrary, apt to become the slave of bad habits, selfish and quite unfit for community life. Under these circumstances he needs some means of liberating his energy before he can grow into a harmonious, responsible being, able and willing to lend himself consciously to co-operation with his fellows for their common benefit. The Dalton Laboratory Plan provides that means by diverting his energy to the pursuit and organization of his own studies in his own way. It gives him that mental and moral liberty which we recognize as so necessary on the physical plane in order to insure his bodily well-being. Antisocial qualities and activities are, after all, merely misdirected energy.

Freedom is therefore, the first principle of the Dalton Laboratory Plan. From the academic, or cultured, point of view, the pupil must be made free to continue his work upon any subject in which he is absorbed without interruption, because when interested he is mentally keener, more alert, and more capable of mastering any difficulty that may arise in the course of his study. Under the new method there are no bells to tear him away at an appointed hour and chain him pedagogically to another subject and another teacher. Thus treated, the energy of the pupil automatically runs to waste. Such arbitrary transfers are indeed as uneconomic as if we were to turn an electric stove on and off at stated intervals for no reason. Unless a pupil is permitted to absorb knowledge at his own rate of speed he will never learn anything thoroughly. Freedom is taking his own time. To take someone else's time is slavery.

The second principle of the Dalton Laboratory Plan is co-operation or, as I prefer to call it, the interaction of group life. There is a passage in Dr. John Dewey's *Democracy and Education* which admirably defines this idea. "The object of a democratic education," he writes, "is not merely to make an individual an intelligent participator in the life of his immediate group, but to bring the various groups into such constant interaction that no individual, no economic group, could presume to live independently of others."

Under the old educational system a pupil can and often does live outside his group, touching it only when he passes in company with his fellows over the common mental highway called the curriculum. This easily ends in his becoming antisocial, and if so he carries this handicap with him when he leaves school for the wider domain of life. Such a pupil may even be "an intelligent participator" in the life of his form or class, just as a teacher may be. But a democratic institution demands more than this. Real social living is more than contact; it is co-operation and interaction. A school cannot reflect the social experience which is the fruit of community life unless all its parts, or groups, develop those intimate relations one with the other and that interdependence which, outside school, binds men and nations together.

Conditions are created by the Dalton Laboratory Plan in which the pupil, in order to enjoy them, involuntarily functions as a member of a social community. He is accepted or rejected by this community according as his functioning, or conduct is social or the reverse. The law operates in school just as it does in the world of men and women. To be effective this law must not be imposed, but unwritten, an emanation as it were of the atmosphere breathed by the community. The value of community life lies in the service it renders in making each free individual composing it perpetually conscious that he, as a member, is a co-worker responsible to, and for, the whole.

This constitutes a problem in school procedure. It should be so organized that neither pupil nor teacher can isolate themselves, nor escape their due share in the activities and in the difficulties of others. We all know the teachers who hang up their personality each morning as they hang up their coats. Outside school these people have human interests and human charm which they do not dare to exhibit when with their pupils lest they should in so doing seem to abrogate their authority. The Dalton Laboratory Plan has no use for the parade of such fictitious authority, which is restrictive, not educative. Instead of promoting order it provokes indiscipline. It is fatal to the idea of a school as a vital social unit.

Equally, from the pupil's point of view, is the child when submitted to the action of arbitrary authority and to immutable rules and regulations, in-

capable of developing a social consciousness which is the prelude to that social experience so indispensable as a preparation for manhood and womanhood. Academically considered, the old system is just as fatal as it is from the social point of view. A child never voluntarily undertakes anything that he does not understand. The choice of his games or pursuits is determined by a clear estimate of his capabilities to excel in them. Having the responsibility of his choice his mind acts like a powerful microscope, taking in and weighing every aspect of the problem he must master in order to ensure success. Given the same free conditions his mind would act on the problems of study in exactly the same way. Under the Dalton Laboratory Plan we place the work problem squarely before him, indicating the standard which has to be attained. After that he is allowed to tackle it as he thinks fit in his own way and at his own speed. Responsibility for the result will develop not only his latent intellectual powers, but also his judgment and character.

But in order that he may accomplish this educative process—in order that he may be led to educate himself—we must give him an opportunity to survey the whole of the task we set. To win the race he must first get a clear view of the goal. It would be well to lay a whole twelvemonth's work before the pupil at the beginning of the school year. This will give him a perspective of the plan of his education. He will thus be able to judge of the steps he must take each month and each week so that he may cover the whole road, instead of going blindly forward with no idea either of the road or the goal. How so handicapped can a child be expected to be interested in the race even to desire to win it? How can a teacher hope to turn out a well-equipped human being unless he takes the trouble to study the psychology of the child? Both for master and for pupil a perception of their job is essential. Education is, after all, a co-operative task. Their success or failure in it is interlocked.

Children learn, if we would only believe it, just as men and women learn, by adjusting means to ends. What does a pupil do when given, as he is given by the Dalton Laboratory Plan, responsibility for the performance of such and such work? Instinctively he seeks the best way of achieving it. Then having decided, he proceeds to act upon that decision. Supposing his plan does not seem to fit his purpose, he discards it and tries another. Later on he may find it profitable to consult his fellow students engaged in a similar task. Discussion helps to clarify his ideas and also his plan of procedure.

When he comes to the end the finished achievement takes on all the splendour of success. It embodies all he has thought and felt and lived during the time it has taken to complete. This is real experience. It is culture acquired through individual development and through collective co-operation. It is no longer school—it is life.

Not only will this method of education stimulate the deepest interest and the highest powers in a student, but it will teach him how to proportion effort to attainment. In his book upon the principles of war General Foch says: "Economy of forces consists in throwing all the forces at one's disposition at a given time upon one point." So the child's attack upon his problem of work should be facilitated by allowing him to concentrate all his forces upon the subject that claims his interest at one particular moment. He will in this case not only do more work, but better work too. The Dalton Laboratory Plan permits pupils to budget their time and to spend it according to their need. . . .

I have carefully guarded against the temptation to make my plan a stereotyped cast-iron thing ready to fit any school anywhere. So long as the principle that animates it is preserved, it can be modified in practice in accordance with the circumstances of the school and the judgment of the staff. For this reason I refrain from dogmatizing on what subjects should be included in the curriculum, or by what standards the achievement of pupils should be measured. Above all, I do not want to canalize the life-blood of citizenship. On this point I can say that the curriculum of any school should vary according to the needs of the pupils, and even in schools where it is designed to serve a definite academic purpose, this aspect should not be lost sight of as it often is. Until the educational world wakes to the fact that curriculum is not the chief problem of society, we shall, I fear, continue to handicap our youth by viewing it through the wrong end of the telescope.

To-day we think too much of curricula and too little about the boys and girls. The Dalton Plan is not a panacea for academic ailments. It is a plan through which the teacher can get at the problem of child psychology and the pupil at the problem of learning. It diagnoses school situations in terms of boys and girls. Subject difficulties concern students, not teachers. The curriculum is but our technique, a means to an end. The instrument to be played upon is the boy or girl.

Under the conditions that exist in the average school the energies of these boys and girls cannot flow freely. The top-heavy organization has been built up for the instructor, and with it teachers are expected to solve their problems. But I contend that the real problem of education is not a teacher's but a pupil's problem. All the difficulties that harass the teacher are created by the unsolved difficulties of the pupils. When the latter disappear the former will vanish also, but not before the school organization and its attendant machinery has been re-made for the pupil, who is rendered inefficient and irritable by being compelled to use a mechanism that is not his own.

The first thing, therefore, is to remove all impediments that prevent the pupil from getting at his problem. Only he knows what his real difficulties are, and unless he becomes skilled in dispersing them he will become skilled in concealing them. Hitherto our educational system has been content to tap the surface water of his energy. Now we must try to reach and release the deep well of his natural powers. In doing so we shall assist and encourage the expression of his life-force and harness it to the work of education. This is not to be achieved by doing the pupil's work for him, but by making it possible for him to do his own work. Harmony between teacher and pupil is essential if we would avoid those emotional conflicts which are the most distracting among the ills the old type of school is heir to.

Experience of the Dalton Laboratory Plan shows, moreover, that it is beneficial to the pupils morally as well as mentally. Where it is put into operation conflicts cease, disorder disappears. The resistance generated in the child by the old inelastic machinery to the process of learning is transformed into acquiescence, and then into interest and industry as soon as he is released to carry out the educational programme in his own way. Freedom and responsibility together perform the miracle.

Briefly summarized, the aim of the Dalton Plan is a synthetic aim. It suggests a simple and economic way by means of which the school as a whole can function as a community. The conditions under which the pupils live and work are the chief factors of their environment, and a favourable environment is one which provides opportunities for spiritual as well as mental growth. It is the social experience accompanying the tasks, not the tasks themselves, which stimulates and furthers both these kinds of growth. Thus the Dalton Plan lays emphasis upon the importance of the child's living while he does his work, and the manner in which he acts as a member of society, rather than upon the subjects of this curriculum. It is the sum total of these twin experiences which determines his character and his knowledge.

Further Resources

BOOKS

Cremin, Lawrence Arthur. *The Transformation of the School: Progressivism in American Education, 1876–1957.* New York: Knopf, 1961.

Dewey, Evelyn. *The Dalton Laboratory Plan.* New York: Dutton, 1922.

Lynch, Albert John. *The Rise And Progress of the Dalton Plan: Reflections and Opinions After More Than Three Years' Working of the Plan.* London: G. Philip & Son, 1926.

Parkhurst, Helen. *Exploring the Child's World.* New York: Appleton-Century-Crofts, 1951.

———. *Growing Pains.* Garden City, N.Y.: Doubleday, 1962.

WEBSITES

"The Dalton School." Available online at http://www.dalton .org/ (accessed March 6, 2003).

"Dalton International." Available online at http://www .daltoninternational.org/ (accessed March 6, 2003).

"Educational Determinism; Or Democracy and the I.Q."

Journal article

By: William C. Bagley

Date: 1922

Source: Bagley, William C. "Educational Determinism; Or Democracy and the I.Q." *School and Society* 15, no. 380, April 8, 1922, 373–384.

About the Author: William Chandler Bagley (1874–1946) received a Ph.D. in psychology from Cornell University in 1900. He served as professor of education at the University of Illinois and Teachers College, Columbia. Bagley stressed improved teacher education and professionalism and emphasized the social aims of education versus the focus on individualism common in his time. He was a leader in the essentialism movement that advocated a curriculum leading to a common cultural foundation for all students. ■

Introduction

The publication of Charles Darwin's *On the Origin of Species* in 1859 laid the foundation for a shift in thinking about the study of human behavior, which previously had been the domain of religion and philosophy. The theory of evolution led many to begin to think about humans as part of the natural world and therefore legitimate subjects of scientific inquiry. During the 1890s, William James and others pioneered the "New Psychology" based on "objective" methods, including psychological mea-

surement. In 1905, Alfred Binet in France began to experiment with intelligence testing and developed the concept of an intelligence scale based on "mental ages."

Lewis Terman produced a revision of Binet's test, the widely used *Stanford-Binet,* and popularized the concept of the intelligence quotient, or IQ, a measure of mental age in comparison to chronological age. Terman's views on intelligence and IQ represented the extreme of determinism. He believed that intelligence was largely hereditary and unchanging and that intelligence tests could accurately measure this ability and predict future occupational and educational outcomes. Terman advocated the use of IQ tests to identify and segregate the "feeble minded" who "clog the educational machinery." The environment was a minimal factor: schools could do little to change a person's intellectual ability. Terman viewed intelligence tests as a means to reform—tests could eliminate guesswork in classifying individual students and thereby reduce waste in schools. Many students, in Terman's view, could not benefit from much academic training and would be better off in vocational classes.

The use of intelligence tests spread rapidly through the schools in the 1920s, accompanied by an increase in differentiation, or grouping students by ability. While ability grouping already existed, the use of intelligence tests to classify students was new. Schools, inundated by increasing enrollments and a more diverse student population, found in intelligence tests a supposedly "scientific" way to group students for increased efficiency.

Significance

William C. Bagley was a principal participant in a major controversy of the 1920s resulting from the use of intelligence tests in schools. Many, including Bagley, were critical of deterministic views such as Terman's and the use of IQ scores to permanently track students toward a particular educational and occupational destiny. Critics charged that psychologists could not agree on a definition of intelligence, much less accurately measure it. Many pointed to environment as a major factor—tests, they claimed, measured how much a student had learned, not innate ability. In addition, the differences in scores between racial and ethnic groups, which Terman attributed to the innate inferiority of certain groups, led critics to disparage the tests as culturally biased. In 1922, Walter Lippmann, in a series of articles in the *New Republic,* introduced these criticisms to the public, sparking a great deal of debate.

In the arena of professional psychologists and educators, Bagley's essay, "Educational Determinism; Or Democracy and the I.Q.," initiated an intellectual sparring match between himself and Terman. Bagley did not oppose the use of intelligence tests in general but rather what he saw as their misuse to classify students and label some as "uneducable." Terman charged Bagley with being unscientific and dismissed the idea that those with low ability can improve through education. The Terman-Bagley debate was a major feature of the professional controversy over intelligence testing during the 1920s.

Intelligence tests, and their critics, are a feature of schooling in the early twenty-first century. Increasingly since the 1960s and 1970s, charges have been made that IQ tests are biased toward the white and middle class and measure achievement within a particular cultural framework rather than innate ability. Howard Gardner introduced the concept of multiple intelligences in the 1980s, challenging the notion of intelligence as a single type of ability. Yet, intelligence tests continue to be used as a means to classify students, especially for special education services, and the practice of "tracking" students also continues.

Primary Source

"Educational Determinism; Or Democracy and the I.Q." [excerpt]

SYNOPSIS: In this essay, Bagley argues against the use of tests to classify students, since, he believed, intellectual ability is not inborn and unchanging but rather influenced by environment. Therefore, schools can and should help students overcome deficiencies in their backgrounds. Schools in a democracy should be "levelers," giving every student, regardless of social class, an even start in life.

Educator and author William C. Bagley. He was a proponent of the essentialist school curriculum, which emphasized core, rather than vocational, subjects in education. **THE LIBRARY OF CONGRESS.**

As used in this discussion, educational determinism means the attitude of mind consequent upon the conviction or the assumption that the influence of education is very narrowly circumscribed by traits or capacities which, for each individual, are both innate and in themselves practically unmodified by experience or training. This attitude is no new thing; within the past ten years, however, it has been given an emphatic sanction and a very widely extended currency by the development of mental measurements, and particularly by the hypothesis of "general intelligence" which has been brought into high relief by the measurement investigations. It is the purpose of the present paper to show that the sanction which mental measurements apparently give to educational determinism is based, not upon the facts that measurements reveal, but upon the hypotheses and assumptions that the development of the measures has involved: that these hypotheses and assumptions, while doubtless justified for certain purposes, are at basis questionable in the last degree; and that the present tendency to extend

them *ad libitum* beyond a very restricted field is fraught with educational and social dangers of so serious and far-reaching a character as to cause the gravest concern. I shall also attempt to show that, even if the assumptions are granted, many of the fatalistic inferences drawn from the data in hand are not justified. . . .

In the first place, in order to prove that I am not attacking a man of straw, I shall present documentary evidence showing the extent to which some of the alleged facts and interpretations in the field of intelligence testing have been generalized in fatalistic conclusions. I may take as an example the apparent support that these alleged facts and interpretations give to those who oppose the expenditure of public funds necessary to provide on a universal scale education of the type that will be needed if the ideals of democracy are to be realized. I quote from an editorial in a recent issue of the *Highway,* an English educational journal:

> Last month we drew attention to the significance of Lord Inchcape's observation that there are "limitations of the economic usefulness of education." The *Pall Mall Gazette* has

now gone one better. It has made the discovery (on the authority of Dr. R. R. Rusk, lecturer on education to St. Andrew's University), that 70 per cent of the children of this country "will never develop any more intelligence than that which should be possessed at the age of fourteen, and, consequently, further education is wasted on them." Of the remaining thirty "only four will be found fit to take an Honours degree at the university."

This "discovery," the result, we are told, of psychological tests made on children in America, Germany and Scotland (but not apparently in England) has suggested to the *Pall Mall's* correspondent a method whereby "education will be improved and, at the same time, expenditure decreased." In future a series of tests applied to each child between the ages of three and twelve will enable the authorities to know exactly which of them is fit for further continued education; so that "a great economy would be effected through the removal from school of a large number of dull and useless children," and "better provision would be made to develop the brain of the supernormal child."

. . . Let me now, with due humility, examine the basic assumption that underlies the whole theory of mental measurements. Native mentality or native intelligence, the determinist himself will admit, is not directly measured by the tests. What is measured? Let me again quote Mr. Colvin:

> "We never measure inborn intelligence; we always measure acquired intelligence, but we infer from differences in acquired intelligence, differences in native endowment when we compare individuals in a group who have had common experiences and note the differences in the attainment of these individuals."

(Yearbook, p. 19; italics in original.)

This, then, is the assumption back of the I. Q. which is playing so important a part now in our educational programs and which threatens to overturn the entire theory and practice of democratic education. The validity of mental measurements and of every inference that is drawn from the alleged facts that the measurements have disclosed is based upon the assumption that *with respect to the materials of the tests* the environment, the experience, the education, the stimulation, and the inspiration of those compared have been identical. . . . But the contributions of experience have become so numerous and influential and these vary so widely even among individuals of fairly homogeneous groups that it is the height of absurdity to contend that it is a native and unmodified factor that is being measured. Yet this contention is made the basis of sweeping

conclusions regarding what education can or cannot do. If the determinist claims scientific validity for these extensions of his theory I say without fear of contradiction that no theory in the whole history of science has been based on a group of assumptions so questionable. . . .

I wish to dwell a little on this cool proposal to separate the sheep from the goats at the close of the sixth school year. With the constancy of the persistence of the I. Q. still in doubt the edict has gone forth that, "for all practical purposes," it is safe to predict a child's future at the age of twelve. It is "safe," in other words, to stamp the twelve-year-old child with the brand of permanent inferiority. It is "safe" to neglect the broader education of mediocre and dull children, to let them be satisfied with a narrow specific training that will fit them only for routine work, and to reserve the higher privileges for the "gifted" children. With his instruments of selection admittedly faulty, with his measures that measure something that no one has yet been able to define, the determinist proposes this policy and seeks to justify his proposal on the high grounds of social welfare and especially of social progress. . . .

I come now to the most fundamental tendency of the theories which the determinist has constructed, again not on the basis of his facts, but upon the basis of his assumptions. I refer to the inevitable application of his inferences, with all the their questionable logic, to the theory of democracy and to the ideals of democratic education. . . .

"Equity" of opportunity, then, is the only real democracy, according to the determinist. Give every child opportunity, he says, opportunity to develop precisely as his original nature dictates, this one into an artisan, that one into an artist; this one into a machine operative, that one into a "captain of industry"; this one into a clerk; that one into a "merchant prince"; this one into a teacher, that one into an "educator." The determinist is very skeptical about the possibility of teaching some lessons; but he apparently has no doubt that one lesson can be effectively and universally taught. Every man, he nonchalantly assumes, can be taught to know his own place, appreciate his own limitations, and mind his own business. . . .

Let us come to the real issue, namely, the need of democracy for a high level of trained and informed intelligence as a basis for collective judgement and collective action. We can not dodge this issue by saying that those who can not readily "take" this kind of education may take some other kind that is far better for them individually. This may be true, but let us not deceive ourselves by calling it democratic. It is not democracy as a theory but as a stupendous fact that education must consider. *The development of democracy has been unquestionably toward the education of the common man to a position of supreme collective control.* Within a century in our own country, the franchise has been made universal. Our government is a representative government in form; in fact, it is coming every day closer to a type of direct government controlled by the great masses of the people. It is this variety of democracy that has lately spread through the world. It is this variety of democracy that was imperiled in 1914 and saved in 1918. *It can not now be a question of going back to an early form of social control.* It is now, as it has never been before, a "race between education and annihilation." If education is to save civilization it must lift the common man to new levels—*and not so much to new levels of industrial efficiency as to new levels of thinking and feeling.*

What has the determinist to propose in place of this program? He would apply his intelligence tests to discover the future leaders. Having thus selected them in advance he would give them every advantage and stimulus to turn their native abilities to the benefit of society.

I shall not dwell upon perfectly obvious obstacles in the way of this solution. It would be easy to show that an intellectual aristocracy is just as reprehensible as an aristocracy based upon family or upon wealth and perhaps even more likely to arouse the resentment of the "common man." Nor shall I worry much over the contention that the future "leaders" whom the determinist would select now and train for their future responsibilities should have such training in order to sensitize them to the responsibilities that they must assume. With no fear of contradiction, I can affirm that the safest guarantee of sincere and responsible leadership lies in a level of informed intelligence among the rank and file that will enable the common man to choose his leaders wisely, scrutinize their programs with sagacity and, in the pungent slang of the day, tell them "where to get off" when they go wrong.

There is, however, a factor connected with this matter of "leadership" that merits the most serious attention. The qualities that make for democratic leadership, far from being exclusively intellectual qualities, are not even predominantly so. They are rather "human" qualities, such as sympathy, tact, humor, and sociability, and "moral" qualities, such as integrity, industry, persistence, courage, and loyalty. Men and women of average or below-average mentality may possess these qualities in such abundance that they become leaders inevitably. It is of the greatest importance that these men and women be prepared through education for the responsibilities that will devolve upon them. . . .

The great mistake of the determinist has been to confine his thinking to organic evolution; he thinks only of the forces and factors that governed progress from the dawn of life to the dawn of mind. He forgets that, with the dawn of mind, new forces were let loose which transformed the entire character and course of progress. He forgets that, with the dawn of language, still other forces were let loose—for from that time on the common man was able to share the thoughts and feelings of the most gifted of his immediate fellows. He forgets how this great force of common experience was immeasurably broadened and strengthened by the art of writing and the art of printing which made it possible for the common man not only to enter into the experience of his immediate fellows, but almost literally to stand upon the shoulders of all the tall and sun-crowned men who had gone before. He forgets that the development of the universal school is the latest act in this great drama of social evolution. It is doubtless true that the school cannot increase the sum total of mentality, but it can and does increase the sum total of trained and informed intelligence. There are, indeed, good reasons for believing that the *average* level of native mentality has not been raised significantly throughout the entire course of recorded history—but something has assuredly been happening during these six or seven thousand years.

Personally I have still to be convinced that this progress of social evolution will disappoint the world in its rich promise to bring humankind into a real brotherhood. What education has already done is only a feeble portent of what education can and will do as its forces become better organized and more keenly alive to their tremendous possibilities and their tremendous responsibilities.

Further Resources
BOOKS
Bagley, William Chandler. *Determinism in Education.* Baltimore: Warwick & York, 1925.

Chapman, Paul Davis. *Schools as Sorters: Lewis M. Terman, Applied Psychology, and the Intelligence Testing Movement, 1890–1930.* New York: New York University Press, 1988.

Gardner, Howard. *Frames of Mind: The Theory of Multiple Intelligences.* New York: Basic Books, 1983.

Gould, Stephen Jay. *The Mismeasure of Man.* New York: Norton, 1996.

Herrnstein, Richard J., and Murray, Charles. *The Bell Curve: Intelligence and Class Structure in American Life.* New York: Free Press, 1994.

Sokal, Michael M. *Psychological Testing and American Society, 1890–1930.* New Brunswick, N.J.: Rutgers University Press, 1987.

PERIODICALS

Lippmann, Walter. "The Mental Age of Americans." *New Republic* 32, no. 412, October 25, 1922, 213–215.

———. "The Mystery of the 'A' Men." *New Republic* 32, no. 413, November 1, 1922, 246–248.

———. "The Reliability of Intelligence Tests." *New Republic* 32, no. 414, November 8, 1922, 275–277.

———. "The Abuse of the Tests." *New Republic* 32, no. 415, November 15, 1922, 297–298.

———. "Tests of Hereditary Intelligence." *New Republic* 32, no. 416, November 22, 1922, 328–330.

———. "A Future for the Tests." *New Republic* 33, no. 417, November 29, 1922, 9–11.

WEBSITES

"History of Influences in the Development of Intelligence Theory and Testing." Indiana University. Available online at http://www.indiana.edu/~intell/index2.html; website home page: http://www.indiana.edu/ (accessed March 13, 2003).

Meyer v. Nebraska

Supreme Court decision

By: James Clark McReynolds

Date: June 4, 1923

Source: *Meyer v. Nebraska.* 262 U.S. 390 (1923).

About the Author: Justice James Clark McReynolds (1862–1946) was born in Elkton, Kentucky. He studied law at the University of Virginia, earning a degree in 1884, and served as a professor of law at Vanderbilt University. In 1903 President Theodore Roosevelt (served 1901–1909) appointed McReynolds Assistant Attorney General for the Antitrust Division in the Department of Justice. He later became Attorney General, and was appointed by President Woodrow Wilson (served 1913–1921) to the Supreme Court in 1914. He served as a Supreme Court justice for twenty-six years until his retirement in 1941. ■

Introduction

In 1920, a Nebraska private school teacher was convicted of teaching a ten-year-old child a Bible story in the German language. This act was in violation of a state law, passed in 1919, that prohibited the teaching of modern foreign languages in any school to any child who had not passed the eighth grade. The teacher, Robert Meyer,

appealed the decision to the Nebraska Supreme Court and the conviction was upheld. Meyer again appealed to the U.S. Supreme Court, which determined the Nebraska law to be unconstitutional and overturned his conviction. Two justices, Oliver Wendell Holmes and George Sutherland, dissented.

The Nebraska law was passed in the period after World War I (1914–1918), which was characterized by widespread suspicion and fear of foreigners, Jews, Catholics, Communists, and Socialists. The Nebraska Supreme Court, in its decision upholding the conviction of Meyer, argued that children of foreigners who grow up speaking the language of their native country created a situation that "was found to be inimical to our own safety" because such children would naturally develop "ideas and sentiments foreign to the best interests of this country." The German language was especially fear-inducing since Germany had been an enemy in the recent war.

The decision of the U.S. Supreme Court in this case was based on its judgment that the Nebraska law violated the Fourteenth Amendment by infringing on the liberty of both teachers and students. The Fourteenth Amendment states that it is not permissible to "deprive any person of life, liberty, or property without due process of law." In this instance, the Court determined that the liberty of modern language teachers to engage in a "useful and honorable" profession and the liberty of parents to hire such teachers for this purpose were violated.

While the Court recognized that states do have the power to regulate education, it pointed out that they may not unreasonably infringe on the liberties of others as happened in this case. The decision indicated that while the State of Nebraska was justified in wanting to improve and unify its citizens, it may not accomplish this goal by unconstitutional means.

Significance

Meyer v. Nebraska is an important decision that helped to clarify the boundary between the rights of the state to compel children to attend school and to regulate the curriculum of both public and private schools, and the rights of parents to make reasonable choices in terms of the education of their children. The Court maintains that the Nebraska law was not a reasonable use of the state's power because there was no evidence to suggest that a child having knowledge of German or any other modern language constituted a real threat to the state or its citizens. Parents, on the other hand, have the right to allow their children to learn a foreign language. Foreign language instruction has an accepted place in the school curriculum and, the Court points out, early childhood is the time when foreign languages are most easily learned.

The *Meyer* decision became an important precedent for later cases. *Meyer v. Nebraska* was cited in the decision in the landmark 1925 U.S. Supreme Court case *Pierce v. Society of Sisters,* in which the Court declared an Oregon law compelling children to attend only public schools unconstitutional. Both the Nebraska and the Oregon law were found to infringe on parents' liberty to make choices for their children's education, and consequently were in violation of the Fourteenth Amendment. The decision in *Meyer* was one of the first in which the Court included in Fourteenth Amendment liberties rights not mentioned specifically in the Constitution. In the opinion of the Court, these rights include "without doubt . . . the right of the individual to contract, to engage in any of the common occupations of life, to acquire useful knowledge, to marry, establish a home and bring up children. . . ."

Primary Source

Meyer v. Nebraska [excerpt]

SYNOPSIS: The following excerpt from the text of the Supreme Court's decision in *Meyer v. Nebraska* includes a summary of the facts of the case, the text of the Nebraska law in question, and the main points of the Court's reasoning behind the decision. Justice McReynolds, who delivered the opinion of the Court, includes a lengthy excerpt from the Nebraska Supreme Court's decision upholding Meyer's conviction. The case was argued on February 23, 1923, and was decided on June 4, 1923.

Mr. Justice McReynolds delivered the opinion of the Court.

Plaintiff in error was tried and convicted in the district court for Hamilton county, Nebraska, under an information which charged that on May 25, 1920, while an instructor in Zion Parochial School he unlawfully taught the subject of reading in the German language to Raymond Parpart, a child of 10 years, who had not attained and successfully passed the eighth grade. The information is based upon "An act relating to the teaching of foreign languages in the state of Nebraska," approved April 9, 1919, which follows [Laws 1919, c.249.]:

Section 1. No person, individually or as a teacher, shall, in any private, denominational, parochial or public school, teach any subject to any person in any language than the English language.

Sec. 2. Languages, other than the English language, may be taught as languages only after a pupil shall have attained and successfully passed the eighth grade as evidenced by a certificate of graduation issued by the county superintendent of the county in which the child resides.

Sec. 3. Any person who violates any of the provisions of this act shall be deemed guilty of a misdemeanor and upon conviction, shall be subject to a fine of not less than twenty-five dollars ($25), nor more than one hundred dollars ($100) or be confined in the county jail for any period not exceeding thirty days for each offense.

Sec. 4. Whereas, an emergency exists, this act shall be in force from and after its passage and approval.

The Supreme Court of the State affirmed the judgment of conviction. 107 Neb. 657. It declared the offense charged and established was "the direct and intentional teaching of the German language as a distinct subject to a child who had not passed the eighth grade," in the parochial school maintained by Zion Evangelical Lutheran Congregation, a collection of Biblical stories being used therefor. And it held that the statute forbidding this did not conflict with the Fourteenth Amendment, but was a valid exercise of the police power. The following excerpts from the opinion sufficiently indicate the reasons advanced to support the conclusion.

The salutary purpose of the statute is clear. The legislature had seen the baneful effects of permitting foreigners, who had taken residence in this country, to rear and educate their children in the language of their native land. The result of that condition was found to be inimical to our own safety. To allow the children of foreigners, who had emigrated here, to be taught from early childhood the language of the country of their parents was to rear them with that language as their mother tongue. It was to educate them so that they must always think in that language, and, as a consequence, naturally inculcate in them the ideas and sentiments foreign to the best interests of this country. The statute, therefore, was intended not only to require that the education of all children be conducted in the English language, but that, until they had grown into that language and until it had become a part of them, they should not in the schools be taught any other language. The obvious purpose of this statute was that the English language should be and become the mother tongue of all children reared in this state. The enactment of such a statute comes reasonably within the police power of the state. *Pohl v. State,* 132 N. E. (Ohio) 20; *State v. Bartels,* 181 N. W. (Ia.) 508.

It is suggested that the law is an unwarranted restriction, in that it applies to all citizens of the state and arbitrarily interferes with the rights of citizens who are not of foreign ancestry, and prevents them, without reason, from having their children taught foreign languages in school. That argument is not well taken, for it assumes that every citizen finds himself restrained by the statute. The hours which a child is able to devote to study in the confinement of school are limited. It must have ample time for exercise or play. Its daily capacity for learning is comparatively small. A selection of subjects for its education, therefore, from among the many that might be taught, is obviously necessary. The legislature no doubt had in mind the practical operation of the law. The law affects few citizens, except those of foreign lineage. Other citizens, in their selection of studies, except perhaps in rare instances, have never deemed it of importance to teach their children foreign languages before such children have reached the eighth grade. In the legislative mind, the salutary effect of the statute no doubt outweighed the restriction upon the citizens generally, which, it appears, was a restriction of no real consequence.

The problem for our determination is whether the statute as construed and applied unreasonably infringes the liberty guaranteed to the plaintiff in error by the Fourteenth Amendment. "No state shall . . . deprive any person of life, liberty, or property without due process of law."

While this Court has not attempted to define with exactness the liberty thus guaranteed, the term has received much consideration and some of the included things have been definitely stated. Without doubt, it denotes not merely freedom from bodily restraint but also the right of the individual to contract, to engage in any of the common occupations of life, to acquire useful knowledge, to marry, establish a home and bring up children, to worship God according to the dictates of his own conscience, and generally to enjoy those privileges long recognized at common law as essential to the orderly pursuit of happiness by free men. . . . The established doctrine is that this liberty may not be interfered with, under the guise of protecting the public interest, by legislative action which is arbitrary or without reasonable relation to some purpose within the competency of the State to effect. Determination by the legislature of what constitutes proper exercise of police power is not final or conclusive but is subject to supervision by the courts. *Lawton v. Steele,* 152 U. S. 133, 137.

The American people have always regarded education and acquisition of knowledge as matters of supreme importance which should be diligently promoted. The Ordinance of 1787 declares, "Religion, morality, and knowledge being necessary to good government and the happiness of mankind, schools and the means of education shall forever be encouraged." Corresponding to the right of control, it is the natural duty of the parent to give his children education suitable to their station in life; and nearly all the States, including Nebraska, enforce this obligation by compulsory laws.

Practically, education of the young is only possible in schools conducted by especially qualified persons who devote themselves thereto. The calling always has been regarded as useful and honorable, essential, indeed, to the public welfare. Mere knowledge of the German language cannot reasonably be regarded as harmful. Heretofore it has been commonly looked upon as helpful and desirable. Plaintiff in error taught this language in school as part of his occupation. His right thus to teach and the right of parents to engage him so to instruct their children, we think, are within the liberty of the Amendment.

The challenged statute forbids the teaching in school of any subject except in English; also the teaching of any other language until the pupil has attained and successfully passed the eighth grade, which is not usually accomplished before the age of twelve. The Supreme Court of the State has held that "the so-called ancient or dead languages" are not "within the spirit or the purpose of the act." *Nebraska District of Evangelical Lutheran Synod v. McKelvie,* 187 N. W. 927. Latin, Greek, Hebrew are not proscribed; but German, French, Spanish, Italian, and every other alien speech are within the ban. Evidently the legislature has attempted materially to interfere with the calling of modern language teachers, with the opportunities of pupils to acquire knowledge, and with the power of parents to control the education of their own.

It is said the purpose of the legislation was to promote civic development by inhibiting training and education of the immature in foreign tongues and ideals before they could learn English and acquire American ideals, and "that the English language should be and become the mother tongue of all children reared in this State." It is also affirmed that the foreign born population is very large, that certain communities commonly use foreign words, follow foreign leaders, move in a foreign atmosphere, and that the children are thereby hindered from becoming citizens of the most useful type and the public safety is imperiled.

That the State may do much, go very far, indeed, in order to improve the quality of its citizens, physically, mentally and morally, is clear; but the individual has certain fundamental rights which must be respected. The protection of the Constitution extends to all, to those who speak other languages as well as to those born with English on the tongue. Perhaps it would be highly advantageous if all had ready understanding of our ordinary speech, but this cannot be coerced by methods which conflict with the Constitution—a desirable end cannot be promoted by prohibited means.

For the welfare of his Ideal Commonwealth, Plato suggested a law which should provide: "That the wives of our guardians are to be common, and their children are to be common, and no parent is to know his own child, nor any child his parent. . . . The proper officers will take the offspring of the good parents to the pen or fold, and there they will deposit them with certain nurses who dwell in a separate quarter; but the offspring of the inferior, or of the better when they chance to be deformed, will be put away in some mysterious, unknown place, as they should be." In order to submerge the individual and develop ideal citizens, Sparta assembled the males at seven into barracks and intrusted their subsequent education and training to official guardians. Although such measures have been deliberately approved by men of great genius, their ideas touching the relation between individual and State were wholly different from those upon which our institutions rest; and it hardly will be affirmed that any legislature could impose such restrictions upon the people of a State without doing violence to both letter and spirit of the Constitution.

The desire of the legislature to foster a homogeneous people with American ideals prepared readily to understand current discussions of civic matters is easy to appreciate. Unfortunate experiences during the late war and aversion toward every characteristic of truculent adversaries were certainly enough to quicken that aspiration. But the means adopted, we think, exceed the limitations upon the power of the State and conflict with rights assured to plaintiff in error. The interference is plain enough and no adequate reason therefor in time of peace and domestic tranquility has been shown.

The power of the State to compel attendance at some school and to make reasonable regulations for all schools, including a requirement that they shall give instructions in English, is not questioned. Nor has challenge been made of the State's power to prescribe a curriculum for institutions which it supports. Those matters are not within the present controversy. Our concern is with the prohibition approved by the Supreme Court. *Adams v. Tanner, supra,* p. 594, pointed out that mere abuse incident to an occupation ordinarily useful is not enough to justify its abolition, although regulation may be entirely proper. No emergency has arisen which renders knowledge by a child of some language other than English so clearly harmful as to justify its inhibition with the consequent infringement of rights long freely enjoyed. We are constrained to conclude that the statute as applied is arbitrary and without reasonable relation to any end within the competency of the State.

As the statute undertakes to interfere only with teaching which involves a modern language, leaving complete freedom as to other matters, there seems no adequate foundation for the suggestion that the purpose was to protect the child's health by limiting his mental activities. It is well known that proficiency in a foreign language seldom comes to one not instructed at an early age, and experience shows that this is not injurious to the health, morals or understanding of the ordinary child.

The judgment of the court below must be reversed and the cause remanded for further proceedings not inconsistent with this opinion.

Reversed.

Further Resources

BOOKS

Alexander, Kern, and M. David Alexander. *American Public School Law,* 5th ed. Belmont, Calif.: West/Thomson Learning, 2001.

Spurlock, Clark. *Education and the Supreme Court.* Urbana: University of Illinois Press, 1955.

Taylor, Bonnie B. *Education and the Law: A Dictionary.* Santa Barbara, Calif.: ABC-CLIO, 1996.

PERIODICALS

Ross, William G. "The Contemporary Significance of *Meyer v. Nebraska* and *Pierce v. Society of Sisters.*" *Akron Law Review* 34, 2000, 177–207.

WEBSITES

"Legal Information Institute." Cornell Law School. Available online at http://www.law.cornell.edu/ (accessed March 10, 2003).

"The Supreme Court Historical Society." Available online at http://www.supremecourthistory.org/index.html; website home page: http://www.supremecourthistory.org (accessed March 10, 2003).

"Children of Loneliness"

Short story

By: Anzia Yezierska

Date: 1923

Source: Yezierska, Anzia. "Children of Loneliness." Reprinted in *How I Found America: Collected Stories of Anzia Yezierska.* New York: Persea Books, 224–228.

About the Author: Anzia Yezierska (18??–1970) was a Polish-Jewish immigrant who came to the United States when she was about ten years old. She graduated from Columbia University in 1904 and during the 1920s was a successful and acclaimed author writing mainly of the immigrant experience in America. One of her books, *Hungry Hearts,* was made into a silent film in 1922. Although she was largely ignored by publishers after the 1920s, academic interest in her life and work, especially among feminist scholars, has increased in recent years. ■

Introduction

Anzia Yezierska wrote about the lives of immigrants in America. Her work grew out of her own experiences and those of people she knew. Yezierska's Polish-Jewish family came to America about 1890 when she was nine or ten years old (accurate birth records do not exist). Immigration officers, unable to spell or pronounce the Polish names, changed the family's last name to Mayer and each member received an American name—Anzia became "Hattie." The family settled in a tenement and Yezierska began school while her older sisters went to work as seamstresses in sweatshops. She helped support her family by making paper bags and selling them to street merchants; later she was employed as a servant and a factory worker.

Chafing against what she felt were the unreasonable restrictions of her traditional family, Yezierska defied the wishes of her father, an orthodox rabbi, and prepared for college by attending night school after work. She saved enough money to go to normal school for a year and then received a scholarship to attend Columbia University to become a cooking teacher.

At Columbia, Yezierska felt constrained by the curriculum required for her course of study. She yearned to take literature classes but her schedule enabled her to attend only a few. The professors and students, she felt, looked down on her. She had been sent by philanthropists to be a cooking teacher—an appropriate goal, they thought, for a poor immigrant. However, she changed her name back to Anzia Yezierska and began to write.

Although she was college educated, she "wrote in the guise of an untutored immigrant" according to a biography written by her daughter, Louise. Readers found her work "exotic" and were charmed by the rags-to-riches story of this literary "sweatshop Cinderella."

As Yezierska attained higher levels of education and became increasingly Americanized, she grew critical of her parents, brothers, and sisters. She detested her parents' Old World ways, was appalled at her sisters' domesticity and obedience to their husbands, and resented her brothers' attempts to curtail her freedom. She eventually alienated herself from most of her family. Yet she never felt at home within the culture of educated, Anglo-Saxon Americans. Yezierska wavered throughout her life, alternately returning to, and escaping from, the ghetto.

Significance

Much of Yezierska's work is autobiographical or semiautobiographical. She drew on the events of her own life, especially her striving for education and freedom from Old World ways. The theme of the Americanized child caught between cultures was a frequent one in her writing.

While intensely personal, Yezierska's work also reflects the experiences and feelings of many foreign-born children educated in America. The goal of public schools during this time period was to mold the children of immigrants to fit American standards, often with the blessing of parents. Teachers and parents alike wanted academic and economic success for their children. But this success came with a price—parents and children were divided by a wide cultural chasm. Mothers and fathers who had worked and sacrificed to send their children to school now found themselves the target of criticism and scorn. Children, accustomed to new ways of living and thinking, were repelled by their parents' "backward ways."

Many mainstream Americans of the time became acquainted with the immigrant experience through Yezierska's work and knowledge of her life. The picture was a romantic one and fit into most Americans' conceptions of the United States as a beacon of opportunity for the foreign born: the poor immigrant arrives in America, works hard, and, through opportunities such as the public schools, finds success and happiness. However, readers also learned that the picture was not entirely positive. Americanization, education, and success in the new country were often accompanied by feelings of rootlessness, alienation, and loneliness.

Primary Source

"Children of Loneliness" [excerpt]

SYNOPSIS: In this excerpt from one of Yezierska's short stories, Rachel's experiences parallel those of the author. Rachel has graduated from college and now is critical of her parents: "two lumps of ignorance and superstition." Her parents are bewil-

Immigrant children eat their first Christmas dinner in the United States in 1920. © BETTMANN/CORBIS. REPRODUCED BY PERMISSION.

dered and wounded by her response to them and their culture. In shame and anger, Rachel flees her parents' tenement, blaming them for her predicament and vowing to live her life as she pleases.

"Oh, Mother, can't you use a fork?" exclaimed Rachel as Mrs. Ravinsky took the shell of the baked potato in her fingers and raised it to her watering mouth.

"Here, *Teacherin* mine, you want me to learn in my old age how to put the bite in my mouth?" The mother dropped the potato back into her plate, too wounded to eat. Wiping her hands on her blue-checked apron, she turned her glance to her husband, at the opposite side of the table.

"Yankev," she said bitterly, "stick your bone on a fork. Our *teacherin* said she dassn't touch no eatings with the hands."

"All my teachers died already in the old country," retorted the old man. "I ain't going to learn nothing new no more from my American daughter." He continued to suck the marrow out of the bone with that noisy relish that was so exasperating to Rachel.

"It's no use," stormed the girl, jumping up from the table in disgust; "I'll never be able to stand it here with you people."

"'You people?' What do you mean by 'you people?'" shouted the old man, lashed into fury by his daughter's words. "You think you got a different skin from us because you went to college?"

"It drives me wild to hear you crunching bones like savages. If you people won't change, I shall have to move and live by myself."

Yankev Ravinsky threw the half-gnawed bone upon the table with such vehemence that a plate broke into fragments.

"You witch you!" he cried in a hoarse voice tense with rage. "Move by yourself! We lived without you while you was away in college, and we can get on without you further. God ain't going to turn his nose on us because we ain't got table manners from America. A hell she made from this house since she got home."

"*Shah!* Yankev *leben,*" pleaded the mother, "the neighbors are opening the windows to listen to our hollering. Let us have a little quiet for a while till the eating is over."

But the accumulated hurts and insults that the old man had borne in the one week since his daughter's return from college had reached the breaking-point. His face was convulsed, his eyes flashed, and his lips were flecked with froth as he burst out into a volley of scorn:

"You think you can put our necks in a chain and learn us new tricks? You think you can make us over for Americans? We got through till fifty years of our lives eating in our own way—"

"Wo is me, Yankev *leben*!" entreated his wife. "Why can't we choke ourselves with our troubles? Why must the whole world know how we are tearing ourselves by the heads? In all Essex Street, in all New York, there ain't such fights like by us."

Her pleadings were in vain. There was no stopping Yankev Ravinsky once his wrath was roused. His daughter's insistence upon the use of a knife and a fork spelled apostasy, Anti-Semitism, and the aping of the Gentiles.

Like a prophet of old condemning unrighteousness, he ran the gamut of denunciation, rising to heights of fury that were sublime and godlike, and sinking from sheer exhaustion to abusive bitterness.

"*Pfui* on all your American colleges! *Pfui* on the morals of America! No respect for old age. No fear of God. Stepping with your feet on all the laws of the holy Torah. A fire should burn out the whole new generation. They should sink into the earth, like Korah."

"Look at him cursing and burning! Just because I insist on their changing their terrible table manners. One would think I was killing them."

"Do you got to use a gun to kill?" cried the old man, little red threads darting out of the whites of his eyes.

"Who is doing the killing? Aren't you choking the life out of me? Aren't you dragging me by the hair to the darkness of past ages every minute of the day? I'd die of shame if one of my college friends should open the door while you people are eating."

"You—you—"

The old man was on the point of striking his daughter when his wife seized the hand he raised.

"*Mincha*! Yankev, you forgot *Mincha*!"

This reminder was a flash of inspiration on Mrs. Ravinsky's part, the only thing that could have ended the quarreling instantly. *Mincha* was the prayer just before sunset of the orthodox Jews. This religious rite was so automatic with the old man that at his wife's mention of *Mincha* everything was immediately shut out, and Yankev Ravinsky rushed to a corner of the room to pray.

"*Ashrai Yoishwai Waisahuh!*"

"Happy are they who dwell in Thy house. Ever shall I praise Thee. *Selah*! Great is the Lord, and exceedingly to be praised, and His greatness is unsearchable. On the majesty and glory of Thy splendor, and on Thy marvelous deeds, will I mediate."

The shelter from the storms of life that the artist finds in his art, Yankev Ravinsky found in his prescribed communion with God. All the despair caused by his daughter's apostasy, the insults and disappointments he suffered, were in his sobbing voice. But as he entered into the spirit of his prayer, he felt the man of flesh drop away in the outflow of God around him. His voice mellowed, the rigid wrinkles of his face softened, the hard glitter of anger and comdemnation in his eyes was transmuted into the light of love as he went on:

"The Lord is gracious and merciful; slow to anger and of great loving-kindness. To all that call upon Him in truth He will hear their cry and save them."

Oblivious to the passing and repassing of his wife as she warmed anew the unfinished dinner, he continued:

"Put not your trust in princes, in the son of man in whom there is no help." Here Reb Ravinsky paused long enough to make a silent confession for the sin of having placed his hope on his daughter instead of on God. His whole body bowed with the sense of guilt. Then in a moment his humility was transfigured into exaltation. Sorrow for sin dissolved in joy as he became more deeply aware of God's unfailing protection.

"Happy is he who hath the God of Jacob for his help, whose hope is in the Lord his God. He healeth the broken in heart, and bindeth up their wounds."

A healing balm filled his soul as he returned to the table, where the steaming hot food awaited him. Rachel sat near the window pretending to read a book. Her mother did not urge her to join them at the table, fearing another outbreak, and the meal continued in silence.

The girl's thoughts surged hotly as she glanced from her father to her mother. A chasm of four centuries could not have separated her more completely from them than her four years at Cornell.

"To think that I was born one of these creatures! It's an insult to my soul. What kinship have I with these two lumps of ignorance and superstition? They're ugly and gross and stupid. I'm all sensitive nerves. They want to wallow in dirt."

She closed her eyes to shut out the sight of her parents as they silently ate together, unmindful of the dirt and confusion.

"How is it possible that I lived with them and like them only four years ago? What is it in me that so quickly gets accustomed to the best? Beauty and cleanliness are as natural to me as if I'd been born on Fifth Avenue instead of the dirt of Essex Street."

A vision of Frank Baker passed before her. Her last long talk with him out under the trees in college still lingered in her heart. She felt that she had only to be with him again to carry forward the beautiful friendship that had sprung up between them. He had promised to come shortly to New York. How could she possibly introduce such a born and bred American to her low, ignorant, dirty parents?

"I might as well tear the thought of Frank Baker out of my heart," she told herself. "If he just once sees the pigsty of a home I come from, if he just sees the table manners of my father and mother, he'll fly through the ceiling."

Timidly, Mrs. Ravinsky turned to her daughter.

"Ain't you going to give a taste to the eating?"

No answer.

"I fried the *lotkes* special' for you—"

"I can't stand your fried, greasy stuff."

"Ain't even my cooking good no more either?" Her gnarled, hard-worked hands clutched at her breast. "God from the world, for what do I need yet any more my life? Nothing I do for my child is no use no more."

Her head sank; her whole body seemed to shrivel and grow old with the sense of her own futility.

"How I was hurrying to run by the butcher before everybody else, so as to pick out the grandest, fattest piece of brust!" she wailed, tears streaming down her face. "And I put my hand away from my heart and put a whole fresh egg into the lotkes, and I stuffed the stove full of coal like a millionaire so as to get the *lotkes* fried so nice and brown, and now you give a kick on everything I done—"

"Fool woman," shouted her husband, "stop laying yourself on the ground for your daughter to step on you! What more can you expect from a child raised up in America? What more can you expect but that she should spit in your face and make dirt from you?" His eyes, hot and dry under their lids, flashed from his wife to his daughter. "The old Jewish eating is poison to her; she must have *trefa* ham—only forbidden food."

Bitter laughter shook him.

"Woman, how you patted yourself with pride before all the neighbors, boasting of our great American daughter coming home from college! This is our daughter, our pride, our hope, our pillow for our old age that we were dreaming about! This is our American *teacherin*! A Jew-hater, an Anti-Semite we brought into the world, a betrayer of our race who hates her own father and mother like a Russian Czar once hated a Jew. She makes herself so refined, she can't stand it when we use the knife or fork the wrong way; but her heart is of a brutal Cossack, and she spills her own father's and mother's blood like water."

Every word he uttered seared Rachel's soul like burning acid. She felt herself becoming a witch, a she-devil, under the spell of his accusations.

"You want me to love you yet?" She turned upon her father like an avenging fury. "If there's any evil hatred in my soul, you have roused it with your cursed preaching."

"*Oi-i-i!* Highest One! pity Yourself on us!" Mrs. Ravinsky wrung her hands. "Rachel, Yankev, let there be an end to this knife-stabbing! Gottuniu! my flesh is torn to pieces!"

Unheeding her mother's pleading, Rachel rushed to the closet where she kept her things.

"I was a crazy idiot to think that I could live with you people under one roof." She flung on her hat and coat and bolted for the door.

Mrs. Ravinsky seized Rachel's arm in a passionate entreaty.

"My child, my heart, my life, what do you mean? Where are you going?"

"I mean to get out of this hell of a home this very minute," she said, tearing loose from her mother's clutching hands.

"Wo is me! My child! We'll be to shame and to laughter by the whole world. What will people say?"

"Let them say! My life is my own; I'll live as I please." She slammed the door in her mother's face.

"They want me to love them yet," ran the mad thoughts in Rachel's brain as she hurried through the streets, not knowing where she was going, not caring. "Vampires, bloodsuckers fastened on my flesh! Black shadow blighting every ray of light that ever came my way! Other parents scheme and plan and wear themselves out to give their child a chance, but they put dead stones in front of every chance I made for myself."

With the cruelty of youth to everything not youth, Rachel reasoned:

"They have no rights, no claims over me like other parents who do things for their children. It was my own brains, my own courage, my own iron will that forced my way out of the sweatshop to my present position in the public schools. I owe them nothing, nothing, nothing."

Further Resources

BOOKS

Henriksen, Louise Levitas. *Anzia Yezierska: A Writer's Life.* New Brunswick: Rutgers University Press, 1988.

Schoen, Carol B. *Anzia Yezierska.* Boston: Twayne, 1982.

Yezierska, Anzia. *Hungry Hearts.* New York: Houghton Mifflin, 1920.

———. *Salome of the Tenements.* New York: Boni and Liveright, 1923.

———. *Bread Givers: A Novel.* Garden City, N.Y.: Doubleday, Page, 1925.

———. *Red Ribbon on a White Horse.* New York: Scribner, 1950.

PERIODICALS

Laufer, Pearl D. "Between Two Worlds: The Fiction of Anzia Yezierska." *DAI* 42, no. 11, May 1982, 4827A.

Levinson, Melanie. "'To Make Myself for a Person': 'Passing' Narratives and the Divided Self in the Work of Anzia Yezierska." *Studies in American Jewish Literature* 13, 1994, 2–9.

VIDEOCASSETTES

Hungry Hearts. Directed by E. Mason Hopper. National Center for Jewish Film. Videocassette, 1993.

"A Statement of the Principles of Progressive Education"

Journal article

By: The Progressive Education Association
Date: April 1924
Source: "A Statement of the Principles of Progressive Education." *Progressive Education* 1, no. 1, April 1924, p. 2.

Reprinted in *Readings in American Educational History.* Edgar W. Knight and Clifton L. Hall, eds. New York: Appleton-Century Crofts, 1951, 528–529.

About the Author: Eugene Randolph Smith (1876–?), one of the founding members of the Progressive Education Association, graduated from Syracuse University, where he taught mathematics. He also taught in public schools and in Brooklyn Polytechnic High School. In 1912, he was asked to organize the Park School in Baltimore. Subsequently, Smith was appointed headmaster of the Beaver Country Day School in Chestnut Hill, Massachusetts. ■

Introduction

The progressive education movement, begun during the late nineteenth century, was a response to a number of changes impacting American schools. An increasing population, new child labor and compulsory school laws, and waves of non-English-speaking immigrants put pressures on schools, especially in urban areas. It became increasingly clear that the old classical curriculum would no longer be adequate. Progressive educators introduced a number of reforms intended to improve the lives of poor and immigrant students attending urban public schools. The emphasis was on practical and humanizing measures such as free lunch programs, health and hygiene classes, and vocational training.

By contrast, the variety of progressive education dominant after World War I (1914–1918) was focused on "child-centered" education: creativity, individual expression, and freedom for the child. This new strain of progressive education was largely confined to private schools for the privileged. Common to both eras was a willingness to experiment, a concern for the "whole child," and a rejection of traditional methods and curriculum.

It was in the context of 1920s postwar progressivism that the Progressive Education Association (PEA) was founded in 1919. While many saw the progressive movement as having its origin in the PEA, clearly the movement had been under way for some time. That the PEA was allied with the newer trends in progressive education is evident from its "Statement of Principles of Progressive Education," adopted by the organization in 1920. Much emphasis is placed on individual freedom and self-expression while none of the prewar social reform is evident.

The "seven principles" appeared in the association's journal, *Progressive Education,* from 1924 until 1929, after which they were withdrawn. The 1930s and the start of the Great Depression led some progressive educators to emphasize the schools as agents of social reform rather than only for individual development. Also, the PEA had become a large, successful organization attracting a more diverse membership. While the original principles no longer represented the views of the membership, subsequent statements of educational philosophy were either never formally adopted or received without enthusiasm by members. The organization began to diminish in importance by the early 1940s, and by 1955 was officially disbanded. Several factors played a role, one of which was that progressive education was under attack as the cause of schools perceived to be overly concerned with social development to the neglect of intellectual development.

Significance

The PEA and the larger progressive education movement became synonymous in the public mind. The PEA gave the movement a tangible form for the education profession and the public and embodied many of the same ideals and beliefs—not surprising, as most of the main leaders of the movement became involved, in one way or another, with the organization.

Consequently, many accepted the seven principles as the tenets of the movement as a whole. While the seven principles were, at best, only a partial statement of the ideals of the larger movement, the more complete and detailed philosophical statements such as John Dewey's *Democracy and Education* are long, difficult, and ponderous—few teachers or parents read them.

While the PEA was dismantled and the term "progressive education" became a pejorative (negative) one, some of the reforms sought by both the movement and the association have become the prevailing approach and are accepted as commonsense educational practice. Applications of the seven principles are readily observable in the schools of the early twenty-first century: It is the rare teacher or school that relies exclusively on memorization and recitation, ignoring the issue of student interest and motivation. Opportunities for self-expression are commonplace. Few would argue against the need for attention to student health and physical development and do away with physical and health education, playgrounds, and clean, well-ventilated buildings. Strengthening the school-home connection is a major issue. Though derogatory opinions depicting progressive schools as "free-for-alls" continue to linger, ultimately the movement and the Progressive Education Association had an enormous impact on the educational thinking and practice of Americans.

Primary Source

"A Statement of the Principles of Progressive Education"

> **SYNOPSIS:** The following statement was adopted by the PEA in 1920 and featured on the inside cover of its journal from 1924 to 1929. It was written by a committee headed by Eugene Randolph Smith. Its

emphasis reflects the variety of progressive education dominant in the 1920s: "child-centered" education featuring individual expression, the development of the "whole child," and student motivation.

I. Freedom to Develop Naturally

The conduct of the pupil should be governed by himself according to the social needs of his community, rather than by arbitrary laws. Full opportunity for initiative and self-expression should be provided, together with an environment rich in interesting material that is available for the free use of every pupil.

II. Interest, the Motive of All Work

Interest should be satisfied and developed through: (1) Direct and indirect contact with the world and its activities, and use of the experience thus gained. (2) Application of knowledge gained, and correlation between different subjects. (3) The consciousness of achievement.

III. The Teacher a Guide, Not a Task-Master

It is essential that teachers should believe in the aims and general principles of Progressive Education and that they should have latitude for the development of initiative and originality.

Progressive teachers will encourage the use of all the senses, training the pupils in both observation and judgment; and instead of hearing recitations only, will spend most of the time teaching how to use various sources of information, including life activities as well as books; how to reason about the information thus acquired; and how to express forcefully and logically the conclusions reached.

Ideal teaching conditions demand that classes be small, especially in the elementary school years.

IV. Scientific Study of Pupil Development

School records should not be confined to the marks given by teachers to show the advancement of the pupils in their study of subjects, but should also include both objective and subjective reports on those physical, mental, moral and social characteristics which affect both school and adult life, and which can be influenced by the school and the home. Such records should be used as a guide for the treatment of each pupil, and should also serve to focus the attention of the teacher on the all-important work of development rather than on simply teaching subject matter.

V. Greater Attention to All that Affects the Child's Physical Development

One of the first considerations of Progressive Education is the health of the pupils. Much more room in which to move about, better light and air, clean and well ventilated buildings, easier access to the out-of-doors and greater use of it, are all necessary. There should be frequent use of adequate playgrounds. The teachers should observe closely the physical conditions of each pupil and, in co-operation with the home, make abounding health the first objective of childhood.

VI. Co-operation Between School and Home to Meet the Needs of Child Life

The school should provide, with the home, as much as is possible of all that the natural interests and activities of the child demand, especially during the elementary school years. These conditions can come about only through intelligent co-operation between parents and teachers.

VII. The Progressive School a Leader in Educational Movements

The Progressive School should be a leader in educational movements. It should be a laboratory where new ideas, if worthy, meet encouragement; where tradition alone does not rule, but the best of the past is leavened with the discoveries of today, and the result is freely added to the sum of educational knowledge.

Further Resources

BOOKS

Cremin, Lawrence A. *The Transformation of the School: Progressivism in American Education, 1876–1957.* New York: Knopf, 1961.

Dewey, John. *Dewey on Education: Selections.* Martin S. Dworkin, ed. New York: Teachers College Press, 1959.

Graham, Patricia Albjerg. *Progressive Education: From Arcady to Academe: A History of the Progressive Education Association, 1919–1955.* New York: Teachers College Press, 1967.

WEBSITES

Schugurensky, Daniel, and Natalie Aguirre. "1919: The Progressive Education Association is Founded." Available online at http://fcis.oise.utoronto.ca/~daniel_schugurensky/assignment1/1919pea.html; website home page: http://fcis.oise.utoronto.ca/ (accessed March 11, 2003).

Scopes v. Tennessee
Court case

By: Grafton Green

Date: January 17, 1927

Source: *Scopes v. Tennessee,* 154 Tenn. 105 (1927). Reprinted in *The South Western Reporter* vol. 289. St. Paul, Minn.: West Publishing, 1927.

About the Author: Grafton Green (1872–1947) graduated from Cumberland University and was admitted to the Tennessee Bar Association in 1893. He practiced general law in Nashville until becoming a justice of the Tennessee Supreme Court in 1910. Green served as chief justice from 1923 to 1947, the longest tenure of any judge on the Tennessee Supreme Court. ∎

Introduction

In 1925, the Tennessee legislature passed the Butler Act, making it illegal, in any school supported by public funds, "to teach any theory that denies the story of the Divine creation of man as taught in the Bible and to teach instead that man has descended from a lower order of animals." The American Civil Liberties Union (ACLU) advertised for teachers willing to challenge the law and offered to provide for the cost of legal defense.

In Dayton, Tennessee, a town experiencing difficult economic times, several town leaders looking for a way to attract attention and dollars to Dayton developed a plan to put a teacher on trial for violation of the recently passed law. They asked John Scopes, a high school physics and math teacher and football coach, to volunteer. He had been substituting temporarily for the regular biology teacher and indicated that he had probably taught evolution, since it was included in the text for the class. He agreed to be the defendant and the group had him arrested.

At the trial, the defense was headed by Clarence Darrow, a lawyer famous for defending labor leaders. The prosecution was led by William Jennings Bryan, a strongly religious politician who opposed evolutionary theory. Darrow argued that banning the teaching of evolution in public schools was unconstitutional because it advanced a particular religious viewpoint. Bryan's main argument was that taxpayers fund the public schools and, therefore, have a right to determine the nature of the curriculum.

The jury found Scopes guilty and the judge fined him $100. The ACLU paid the fine, and in 1926 appealed the case to the Tennessee Supreme Court. The court overturned the conviction on a technical point: By Tennessee state law, any fine greater than $50 must be imposed by the jury rather than the judge. In their decision, the justices of the state supreme court made it clear that they did not believe that the law banning the teaching of evolution was unconstitutional.

Significance

The trial attracted a great deal of media attention, drawing large numbers of people to Dayton. People all over the country and in Europe followed in the newspapers the progress of what came to be known as "The Monkey Trial," in reference to the evolutionary theory that humans descended from apes. A play, *Inherit the Wind,* two movie versions of the same name, and a handful of songs were inspired by the events in Dayton.

One of the most influential trials in American history, the Scopes trial and the mythology surrounding it continue to play a part in the way many Americans view the relationship between religion and science in the schools and the larger society.

The Tennessee legislature repealed the Butler Act in 1967. In 1968, the Supreme Court, in *Epperson v. Arkansas,* found unconstitutional a similar law in Arkansas. While no state currently has a law banning the teaching of evolution in public schools, the controversy continues in the early twenty-first century as religious fundamentalists fight to include biblical creationism in the classroom alongside evolutionary theory.

John Scopes was arrested and tried for teaching Charles Darwin's theory of evolution to high school students. **AP/WIDE WORLD PHOTOS. REPRODUCED BY PERMISSION.**

Primary Source

Scopes v. Tennessee [excerpt]

SYNOPSIS: In these excerpts from the decision of the Tennessee Supreme Court in *Scopes v. Tennessee,* the court concludes that the Butler Act is not unconstitutional on several grounds: The law did not violate Scopes' Fourteenth Amendment liberties because the state has a right to set limits on how state employees perform their duties. Scopes was free to teach the theory of evolution outside of school. The law does not constitute a preference to a particular religion since a belief in creation is not linked to any one religion. In addition, the court noted, the law does not require the teaching of creation, but only forbids the teaching of any contradictory theory, specifically evolution. However, the court reversed Scopes' conviction on a technicality. The case was decided January 17, 1927.

[Chief Justice Grafton Green delivered the opinion of the Court]

Scopes was convicted of a violation of chapter 27 of the Acts of 1925, for that he did teach in the public schools of Rhea county a certain theory that denied the story of the divine creation of man, as taught in the Bible, and did teach instead thereof that man had descended from a lower order of ani-

mals. After a verdict of guilty by the jury, the trial judge imposed a fine of $100, and Scopes brought the case to this court by an appeal in the nature of a writ of error. . . .

Chapter 27 of the Acts of 1925, known as the Tennessee Anti-Evolution Act is set out in the margin.

While the act was not drafted with as much care as could have been desired, nevertheless there seems to be no great difficulty in determining its meaning. It is entitled:

> An act prohibiting the teaching of the evolution theory in all the Universities, normals and all other public schools in Tennessee, which are supported in whole or in part by the public school funds of the state, and to provide penalties for the violations thereof.

Evolution, like prohibition, is a broad term. In recent bickering, however, evolution has been understood to mean the theory which holds that man has developed from some pre-existing lower type. . . .

Thus defining evolution, this act's title clearly indicates the purpose of the Statute to be the prohibition of teaching in the schools of the state that

Tennessee Anti-Evolution Act

[The following is a footnote from the opening paragraphs of the *Scopes v. State of Tennessee* Supreme Court decision. It is from Chapter 27 of the Acts of 1925, also known as the Tennessee Anti-Evolution Act.]

An act prohibiting the teaching of the evolution theory in all the Universities, normals and other public schools of Tennessee, which are supported in whole or in part by the public school funds of the state, and to provide penalties for the violations thereof

Section 1. Be it enacted by the General Assembly of the state of Tennessee, that it shall be unlawful for any teacher in any of the Universities, normals and all other public schools of the state which are supported in whole or in part by the public school funds of the state, to teach any theory that denies the story of the divine creation of man as taught in the Bible and to teach instead that man has descended from a lower order of animals.

Sec. 2. Be it further enacted, that any teacher found guilty of the violation of this act, shall be guilty of a misdemeanor and upon conviction shall be fined not less than one hundred ($100.00) dollars nor more than five hundred ($500.00) dollars for each offense.

Sec. 3. Be it further enacted, that this act take effect from and after its passage, the public welfare requiring it.

SOURCE: *Scopes v. State of Tennessee,* 154 Tenn. 105 (1927). Reprinted in *The South Western Reporter* vol. 289. St. Paul, Mn.: West Publishing, 1927.

---

man has developed or descended from some lower type or order of animals.

When the draftsman came to express this purpose in the body of the act, he first forbade the teaching of "any theory that denies the story of the divine creation of man, as taught in the Bible"—his conception evidently being that to forbid the denial of the Bible story would ban the teaching of evolution. To make the purpose more explicit, he added that it should be unlawful to teach "that man had descended from a lower order of animals." . . .

[1] It is contended that the statute violates section 8 of article 1 of the Tennessee Constitution, and section 1 of the Fourteenth Amendment of the Constitution of the United States—the law of the land clause of the state Constitution, and the due process of law clause of the federal Constitution, which are practically equivalent in meaning.

We think there is little merit in this contention. The plaintiff in error was a teacher in the public schools of Rhea county. He was an employee of the state of Tennessee or of a municipal agency of the state. He was under contract with the state to work in an institution of the state. He had no right or privilege to serve the state except upon such terms as the state prescribed. His liberty, his privilege, his immunity to teach and proclaim the theory of evolution, elsewhere than in the service of the state, was in no wise touched by this law.

The statute before us is not an exercise of the police power of the state undertaking to regulate the conduct and contracts of individuals in their dealings with each other. On the other hand, it is an act of the state as a corporation, a proprietor, an employer. It is a declaration of a master as to the character of work the master's servant shall, or rather shall not, perform. In dealing with its own employees engaged upon its own work, the state is not hampered by the limitations of section 8 of article 1 of the Tennessee Constitution, nor of the Fourteenth Amendment to the Constitution of the United States. . . .

Since the state may prescribe the character and the hours of labor of the employees on its works, just as freely may it say what kind of work shall be performed in its service, what shall be taught in its schools, so far at least as section 8 of article 1 of the Tennessee Constitution, and the Fourteenth Amendment to the Constitution of the United States, are concerned.

But it is urged that chapter 27 of the Acts of 1925 conflicts with section 12 of article 11, the educational clause, and section 3 of article 1, the religious clause, of the Tennessee Constitution. It is to be doubted if the plaintiff in error, before us only as the state's employee, is sufficiently protected by these constitutional provisions to justify him in raising such questions. Nevertheless, as the state appears to concede that these objections are properly here made, the court will consider them.

[2] The relevant portion of section 12 of article 11 of the Constitution is in these words:

***It shall be the duty of the General Assembly in all future periods of this government, to cherish literature and science.

The argument is that the theory of the descent of man from a lower order of animals is now established by the preponderance of scientific thought and that the prohibition of the teaching of such theory is a violation of the legislative duty to cherish science.

While this clause of the Constitution has been mentioned in several of our cases, these references have been casual, and no act of the Legislature has ever been held inoperative by reason of such provision. In one of the opinions in *Green v. Allen,* 5 Humph. (24 Tenn.) 170, the provision was said to be directory. Although this court is loath to say that any language of the Constitution is merely directory (*State v. Burrow,* 119 Tenn. 376, 104 S. W. 526, 14 Ann Cas. 809; *Webb v. Carter,* 129 Tenn. 182, 165 S. W. 426), we are driven to the conclusion that this particular admonition must be so treated. It is too vague to be enforced by any court. To cherish science means to nourish, to encourage, to foster science.

In no case can the court directly compel the Legislature to perform its duty. In a plain case the court can prevent the Legislature from transgressing its duty under the Constitution by declaring ineffective such a legislative act. The case, however, must be plain, and the legislative act is always given the benefit of any doubt.

If a bequest were made to a private trustee with the avails of which he should cherish science, and there was nothing more, such a bequest would be void for uncertainty. *Green v. Allen,* 5 Humph. (24 Tenn.) 170, *Ewell v. Sneed,* 136 Tenn. 602, 191 S. W. 131, 5 A. L. R. 303, and the cases cited. It could not be enforced as a charitable use in the absence of prerogative power in this respect which the courts of Tennessee do not possess. A bequest in such terms would be so indefinite that our courts could not direct a proper application of the trust fund nor prevent its misapplication. The object of such a trust could not be ascertained.

If the courts of Tennessee are without power to direct the administration of such a trust by an individual, how can they supervise the administration of such a trust by the Legislature? It is a matter of far more delicacy to undertake the restriction of a coordinate branch of government to the terms of a trust imposed by the Constitution than to confine an individual trustee to the terms of the instrument under which he functions. If language be so indefinite as to preclude judicial restraint of an individual, such language could not possibly excuse judicial restraint of the General Assembly.

If the Legislature thinks that, by reason of popular prejudice, the cause of education and the study of science generally will be promoted by forbidding the teaching of evolution in the schools of the state, we can conceive of no ground to justify the court's interference. The courts cannot sit in judgment on such acts of the Legislature or its agents and determine whether or not the omission or addition of a particular course of study tends "to cherish science."

[3] The last serious criticism made of the act is that it contravenes the provision of section 3 of article 1 of the Constitution, "that no preference shall ever be given, by law, to any religious establishment or mode of worship."

The language quoted is a part of our Bill of Rights, was contained in our first Constitution of the state adopted in 1796, and has been brought down into the present Constitution.

At the time of the adoption of our first Constitution, this government had recently been established and the recollection of previous conditions was fresh. England and Scotland maintained state churches as did some of the Colonies, and it was intended by this clause of the Constitution to prevent any such undertaking in Tennessee.

We are not able to see how the prohibition of teaching the theory that man has descended from a lower order of animals gives preference to any religious establishment or mode of worship. So far as we know, there is no religious establishment or organized body that has in its creed or confession of faith any article denying or affirming such a theory. So far as we know, the denial or affirmation of such a theory does not enter into any recognized mode of worship. Since this cause has been pending in this court, we have been favored, in addition to briefs of counsel and various amici curiae, with a multitude of resolutions, addresses, and communications from scientific bodies, religious factions, and individuals giving us the benefit of their views upon the theory of evolution. Examination of these contributions indicates that Protestants, Catholics, and Jews are divided among themselves in their beliefs, and that there is no unanimity among the members of any religious establishment as to this subject. Belief or unbelief in the theory of evolution is no more a characteristic of any religious establishment or mode of worship than is belief or unbelief in the wisdom of the prohibition laws. It would appear that members of the same churches quite generally disagree as to these things.

Furthermore, chapter 277 of the Acts of 1925 *requires* the teaching of nothing. It only *forbids* the teaching of evolution of man from a lower order of animals. Chapter 102 of the Acts of 1915 requires that ten verses from the Bible be read each day at the opening of every public school, without comment, and provided the teacher does not read the same verses more than twice during any session. It is also provided in this Act that pupils may be excused from the Bible readings upon the written request of their parents.

As the law thus stands, while the theory of evolution of man may not be taught in the schools of the state, nothing contrary to that theory is required to be taught. It could scarcely be said that the statutory scriptural reading just mentioned would amount to teaching of a contrary theory.

Our school authorities are therefore quite free to determine how they shall act in this state of the law. Those in charge of the educational affairs of the state are men and women of discernment and culture. If they believe that the teaching of the science of biology had been so hampered by chapter 27 of the Acts of 1925 as to render such an effort no longer desirable, this course of study may be entirely omitted from the curriculum of our schools. If this be regarded as a misfortune, it must be charged to the Legislature. It should be repeated that the act of 1925 deals with nothing but the evolution of man from a lower order of animals.

It is not necessary now to determine the exact scope of the religious preference clause of the Constitution and other language of that section. The situation does not call for such an attempt. Section 3 of article 1 is binding alike on the Legislature and the school authorities. So far we are clear that the Legislature has not crossed these constitutional limitations. If hereafter the school authorities should go beyond such limits, a case can then be brought to the courts.

Much has been said in argument about the motives of the Legislature in passing this Act. But the validity of a statute must be determined by its natural and legal effect, rather than proclaimed motives. *Lochner v. New York,* 198 U. S. 45, 25 S. Ct. 539, 49 L. Ed. 937, 3 Ann Cas. 1133; *Grainger v. Douglas Park Jockey Club* (C. C. A.) 148 F. 513, 8 Ann. Cas. 997; R. C. L. III, 81.

Some other questions are made, but in our opinion they do not merit discussion, and the assignments of error raising such questions are overruled.

[4] This record disclosed that the jury found the defendant below guilty, but did not assess the fine. The trial judge himself undertook to impose the minimum fine of $100 authorized by the statute. This was error. Under section 14 of article 6 of the Constitution of Tennessee, a fine in excess of $50 must be assessed by a jury. The statute before us does not permit the imposition of a smaller fine than $100.

Since a jury alone can impose the penalty this act requires, and as a matter of course no different penalty can be inflicted, the trial judge exceeded his jurisdiction in levying this fine, and we are without power to correct his error. The judgment must accordingly be reversed. *Upchurch v. State,* 153 Tenn. 198, 281 S. W. 462.

The Court is informed that the plaintiff in error is no longer in the service of the state. We see nothing to be gained by prolonging the life of this bizarre case. On the contrary, we think the peace and dignity of the state, which all criminal prosecutions are brought to redress, will be the better conserved by the entry of a nolle prosequi herein. Such a course is suggested to the Attorney General.

Further Resources

BOOKS

Alexander, Kern, and M. David Alexander. *American Public School Law,* 5th ed. Belmont, Calif.: West/Thomson Learning, 2001.

Conkin, Paul Keith. *When All the Gods Trembled: Darwinism, Scopes, and American Intellectuals.* Lanham, Md.: Rowman and Littlefield, 1998.

Larson, Edward J. *Summer for the Gods: The Scopes Trial and America's Continuing Debate over Science and Religion.* New York: Basic Books, 1997.

Lawrence, Jerome, and Robert E. Lee. *Inherit the Wind.* New York: Random House, 1955.

Taylor, Bonnie B. *Education and the Law: A Dictionary.* Santa Barbara, Calif.: ABC-CLIO, 1996.

Tompkins, Jerry R., ed. *D-Days at Dayton: Reflections on the Scopes Trial.* Baton Rouge: Louisiana State University Press, 1965.

WEBSITES

"American Experience: Monkey Trial." PBS. Available online at http://www.pbs.org/wgbh/amex/monkeytrial/; website home page: http://www.pbs.org/ (accessed March 11, 2003).

"The Scopes Trial." The Ohio State University Department of History. Available online at http://www.history.ohio-state.edu/projects/clash/Scopes/scopes-page1.htm; website home page: http://www.history.ohio-state.edu/ (accessed March 11, 2003).

"Scopes Trial Home Page." University of Missouri–Kansas City School of Law. Available online at http://www.law.umkc.edu/faculty/projects/ftrials/scopes/scopes.htm; website home page: http://www.law.umkc.edu/ (accessed March 11, 2003).

AUDIO AND VISUAL MEDIA

Inherit the Wind. Directed by Stanley Kramer. 1960. MGM/UA Home Video.

Monkey Trial. American Experience Series. Directed by Christine Lesiak. PBS Home Video. Videocassette, 2002.

"The Teacher Goes Job-Hunting"

Magazine article

By: Thomas Minehan

Date: June 1, 1927

Source: Minehan, Thomas. "The Teacher Goes Job-Hunting." *The Nation* 124, no. 3230, June 1, 1927, 605–606.

About the Author: Thomas Minehan (dates unknown), a sociologist and high school teacher, received a master's degree from the University of Minnesota in 1933. During the Great Depression, he lived as a hobo in order to study the lives of the transient homeless. Struck by the number of children he encountered, he wrote *Boy and Girl Tramps of America,* which was the inspiration for a PBS documentary, *Riding the Rails: Teenagers on the Move During the Depression.* ∎

Introduction

Historically, teaching in schools has been regarded by the America public as a low-status job requiring few qualifications and offering little pay. Initially, most teachers were men who were considered unfit for any other profession or who taught temporarily as they prepared for higher-level careers. By 1870, the majority of schoolteachers were women. While public opinion held that women were inferior teachers and unable to handle discipline problems, the argument that women could be hired at one-third to one-half the salary of men was persuasive to many. By the turn of the twentieth century, teaching was commonly regarded as a women's profession and, therefore, not deserving of high pay or respect. Since female teachers were commonly forbidden to marry or risked losing their jobs, teaching came to be viewed as the domain of "unmarriageable" women or men unsuccessful at finding anything better in terms of employment.

In addition to, and in spite of, the lack of respect or monetary reward, teachers had to cope with an unusual set of expectations outside of school. Teachers were required to take on extra responsibilities, such as Sunday school and charity work. Because, it was argued, teachers should be role models for their students, they were under close observation by community members. Social activities were often banned. Teachers also found their personal religious and political beliefs under scrutiny.

In the 1920s, teachers in search of a position had to go to lengthy efforts to achieve a job that was often a politically made decision by those doing the hiring. THE LIBRARY OF CONGRESS.

During the period of intense paranoia and xenophobia following World War I (1914–1918), teachers were often required to sign loyalty oaths to keep their jobs, and Roman Catholics and Jews faced discrimination in hiring. In addition, teachers were often at the mercy of the social mores and values of individual communities. For example, one town required membership in the Ku Klux Klan as a condition of employment and another prohibited it.

The early twentieth century saw an enormous increase in the expectations for teachers. No longer would it be sufficient for teachers to impart the basics to children through recitation and the threat of the rod. Teachers of this period found that they needed to be familiar with new and complex methods, expanded curricula, and child psychology. Despite these developments, teachers continued to lag far behind other professionals in status, pay, and autonomy.

Significance

"The Teacher Goes Job-Hunting" documents experiences common to many teachers during the 1920s. The article is an example of efforts by reformers of the time to draw public attention to the plight of teachers and other problems within the educational system. Greater awareness of the conditions faced by teachers facilitated progress toward reform.

Efforts toward the professionalization of teaching begun before and during the 1920s include the formation of professional organizations such as the National Education Association (NEA) and unions such as the American Federation of Teachers (AFT). Professional organizations enabled teachers to work as a group toward other reforms such as tenure, freedom of political association, and higher pay.

Progressive educators such as John Dewey contributed to the professionalization of teaching through the development of university departments of education and a broader, more liberal arts–oriented curriculum for teacher training programs. Increasingly, states required teachers to have higher levels of education and to earn certificates.

While many of these developments occurred before the 1920s, Minehan's article clearly showed that many teachers continued to wait for reform. Even in the early 2000s, teachers struggle with issues of lower status and pay compared to other professions.

Primary Source

"The Teacher Goes Job-Hunting"

SYNOPSIS: In this article, the author draws attention to the plight of schoolteachers in the 1920s: they were underpaid, undervalued, and deprived of normal adult freedoms. Teachers were subjected to a lengthy and invasive application process that resulted in being selected on the basis of religion, race, and politics rather than relevant qualifications.

[*This is the second section of Mr. Minehan's articles on teachers as job-hunters. The first appeared in last week's* Nation.]

Devious as are the means through which a teacher gets a job, the method of application is more devious still. To anybody who has ever sought employment in the ordinary channels of business, the amount of correspondence carried on over even a sixty-dollar-a-month job is amazing.

In order to register in any agency a teacher has to furnish a complete record of his education and experience, a recent photograph, and from three to five references to verify all of his statements. The agency will then send him notice of some vacancy. The teacher writes a letter of application, giving full information in regard to his qualifications—education, experience, degrees, certificates held, and references. In addition, he incloses a photograph of himself and copies of three or four testimonials. At the same time, the agency sends the school authorities a complete record of the candidate together with copies of the references which it has received. If the school authorities are going to consider the applicant they will answer his letter by sending a blank calling for information in regard to education, experience, degrees, certificates held, and references. The teacher has already supplied all this information, the agency has answered similar inquiries, and it has supported all these statements with copies of confidential references which it has received, yet the teacher, if he wants to be considered, must supply all the information once more. This is a good time, if the teacher has two or three more testimonials, to send them, and the experienced job-hunter invariably does. Meanwhile, the school authorities write to the teacher's references. In order to play safe the teacher will, if he is wise, have some friends in the educational and business world write letters to the school authorities urging his appointment. After a few days, the school board receives answers from the references. These together with the testimonials and letters of recommendation are examined. All are satisfactory, but there is unfortunately something lacking. The teacher has not presented prima facie evidence that he is a believer—a true Christian, and an active Sunday school worker. Nor has he presented a medical certificate. More correspondence and a letter from a minister and a doctor is forwarded to the school authorities. At last all of the facts are in. After receiving similar information from fifteen or twenty candidates, the school board meets one night and on the basis of race, political, or religious prejudice appoints the applicant whom they or the agency had decided on in the first place.

Why then did they bother about applications, references, and testimonials from a dozen individuals? Simply to convince the man who is footing the bill that he is getting his money's worth. The more work the school board can make, the more generous the secretarial and office allowance the taxpayers can be induced to provide, the more plums there will be to distribute among followers. I know of a superintendent who was able to get an assistant and a stenographer simply by showing the county board an enormous stack of letters and references on his desk, which he assured them had to be answered. Next year the assistant looked after all routine work, the stenographer answered all mail, and the superintendent spent most of his time tabulating the results of a questionnaire which he had the stenographer copy into a doctor's thesis for him, and as a result of this work he got a raise in salary and a new job.

The correspondence carried on between the applying teacher and the school board is often curious. The school authorities in almost all cases want to know about the applicant's most personal habits. Does he smoke cigarettes? Is she fond of dancing? Will she teach Sunday school and take part in B. Y. P. U. work? Will he make a good basso in the local choir? Will she fall in love with any of the town swains? Will he cast immodest glances at the knees of his flapper pupils? Will the teacher be able to put on a weekly program that will permit every pupil to appear at advantage before the fond mammas? These and a hundred other questions must be answered before the school authorities will appoint the teacher. The strongest recommendation a teacher can have for most jobs in Dixie is to be a Baptist. The strongest recommendation a teacher can have for most jobs in Minnesota is to be a Scandinavian. Many teachers are selected because they happen to be of the same nationality or religious faith as the superintendent. I have known brilliant young teachers who found it absolutely impossible to get jobs simply because they were Jews. I have known of Catholics who have been removed in order to have teachers of other religious faiths appointed. Any teacher suspected of being a radical is never retained longer than it takes the board to meet, and in some States backwoods communities do not care to consider a graduate from any of the liberal universities.

Sometimes the school authorities require other qualifications than those of a religious, moral, or academic nature. I recall a letter I received from a principal in Alabama advising me of my appointment as an instructor in his school. The letter closed with this paragraph:

> But let me tell you right now that you would not be a success at this school if you are not a fighter. If you would hesitate to toss an unruly boy out of the window or cowhide him into submission this is no place for you. That was the trouble with the last man I had. He could not fight and was always calling on me to do his fighting for him. I want a man who can do his own fighting and is ready to fight at the drop of the hat.

After drawing some unpleasant comparisons between one hundred and fifty dollars a month and the earnings of a "fighter," I declined his generous offer and I suggested that in the future when he had need of teachers he communicate with Tex Rickard.

A school in Missouri wanted me to sign a resignation with a contract. The resignation was to be effective together with the forfeiture of all salary that might be due me if I should smoke a cigarette, pipe, or cigar at any time, in any place during the period my contract was to run. I did not sign. A girl of my acquaintance went out to Montana a few years ago after signing a similar contract except that the prohibition was against dancing on school nights. After the first of the year there was no money in the county treasury. She was paid in driblets until the end of May. When she applied for the remainder of her wages, she was presented with evidence showing she had been at a dance one night in March and consequently no further money was owed her.

The end is not yet. A woman received a contract from a small village along the seacoast of North Carolina. It contained the usual stipulations in regard to certification, boarding at the dormitory, sacrificing pay while unable to work, and in addition the following clauses:

> I promise to take a vital interest in all phases of Sunday-school work, donating of my time, service, and money without stint for the uplift and benefit of the community.
>
> I promise to abstain from all dancing, immodest dressing, and any other conduct unbecoming a teacher and a lady.
>
> I promise not to go out with any young men except in so far as it may be necessary to stimulate Sunday-school work.
>
> I promise not to fall in love, to become engaged, or secretly married.
>
> I promise to remain in the dormitory or on the school grounds when not actively engaged in school or church work elsewhere.
>
> I promise not to encourage or tolerate the least familiarity on the part of any of my boy pupils.
>
> I promise to sleep at least eight hours a night, to eat carefully, and to take every precaution to keep in the best of health and spirits in order that I may be better able to render efficient service to my pupils.
>
> I promise to remember that I owe a duty to the townspeople who are paying me my wages, that I owe respect to the school board and the superintendent that hired me, and that I shall consider myself at all times the willing servant of the school board and the townspeople and that I shall cooperate with them to the limit of my ability in any movement aimed at the betterment of the town, the pupils, or the schools.

This, remember, for a job paying eighty-five dollars a month for seven and half months in a little town of three or four hundred persons, located in the mosquito and fever district of North Carolina, where half the inhabitants can not read or write.

This is the most restrictive contract I have ever seen, but anyone who is familiar with the conditions of restraint under which the average teacher works and with the attitude of the community toward the teacher cannot help admiring its frankness. There are hundreds of places where every provision mentioned in that contract is enforced. A teacher may not be required in writing to teach Sunday school, but the teacher who fails to do so will not be re-elected. A teacher may not have to promise not to fall in love but if she does she had better marry as soon as possible, for in nine cases out of ten she will find herself out of a job the next year. A teacher may not have to sign a pledge to sleep at least eight hours a night, but the teacher who wants his job will not keep a light going long after curfew.

Everywhere it is the same. The mails, the fire department, the police department, almost any other division of public service is relatively immune from prying supervision. Not so the schools. There is no reform too ridiculous to find favor and support in the schools. Twenty years ago the prohibitionists began to make it impossible for any man who did not abhor the word rum to get or hold a job in our public-school system. Today the anti-tobacco leagues are making it increasingly difficult for any man who smokes to get work outside the large cities. In fully half the school districts of the country the churchmen completely dominate the teachers. Some States will not grant a teacher a certificate no matter what his academic qualifications, unless he presents an affidavit from some minister showing that he is a good church member.

There are, of course, other reasons besides moral ones for the continual shifting of teachers. Teachers become tired of towns and want to change. Towns become tired of teachers and want new blood. There is more bossing and bickering among school-teachers than among any other class of workers. The principal and supervisor are always interfering with the teacher, the superintendent and school board interfering with the principal and supervisor, and the parent-teachers' associations with all of them. The boarding-houses take advantage of the teacher because, in most cases, the teacher has no other place to go. The administrative officers are much more tyrannical than in any other occupation. They know that the teacher will not quit in the middle of the term; to do so means not merely quitting

a job but quitting the profession entirely. The teacher who does not work to get a good recommendation from his present employer has small chance of a new job in the fall. The teacher keeps his grievances to himself, knowing that in a few months' time he can leave town and need never come back. He eats the humble pie that is placed before him, smiles, and placates the powers that be. Next spring he will go job-hunting and next fall, if his references are first-class, he will have a new job.

Further Resources

BOOKS

Altenbaugh, Richard J., ed. *The Teacher's Voice: A Social History of Teaching in Twentieth Century America.* Washington, D.C.: Falmer Press, 1992.

Butts, R. Freeman, and Lawrence A. Cremin. *A History of Education in American Culture.* New York: Holt, 1953.

Hofstadter, Richard. *Anti-Intellectualism in American Life.* New York: Knopf, 1963.

Gong Lum v. Rice

Supreme Court decision

By: William Howard Taft

Date: 1927

Source: *Gong Lum v. Rice.* 275 U.S. 78 (1927).

About the Author: William Howard Taft (1857–1930) served as Chief Justice of the Supreme Court from 1921 to 1930. He graduated from Cincinnati Law School and earned a bachelor's degree from Yale University. Prior to being nominated to the Supreme Court, he served as Solicitor General, civilian governor of the Philippines, Secretary of War, joint chairman of the War Labor Board, and president of the United States (served 1909–1913). No one else has ever held the offices of both a chief justice and president. ■

Introduction

In 1924, a Mississippi child, Martha Lum, began attending Rosedale Consolidated High School, a school reserved for whites, at the start of the academic year. At lunchtime on her first day, she was told she would not be allowed to return to school on the grounds that, as a child of Chinese descent, she was considered to be "colored" and might only attend a public or private school accepting colored children.

Her father, Gong Lum, sued the trustees of the school and the Mississippi State Superintendent of Education (Rice) for Martha to be allowed to attend Rosedale Consolidated. He argued that he was a taxpayer who helped to support the schools, that Martha was not "colored" but rather pure Chinese, and that she was not afforded equal

African American children in a segregated school similar to the one Martha Lum was asked to attend. **THE LIBRARY OF CONGRESS.**

protection under the law since there are no schools in the district or country for Chinese children. The lawyer for the Lum family asserted that the intent of segregation was to protect the white race from the supposed evils of race mixing and that the state may not expose members of other races to the same risk by failing to provide separate schools for each race.

The trustees of the high school argued that Martha Lum had access to a public education of equal quality at the local school for colored students and that the district is not required to provide schools for each race. "Colored," they argued, is defined by the State of Mississippi as "not white."

A Mississippi trial court ruled in favor of Gong Lum, but Rice appealed to the Supreme Court of Mississippi, which reversed the lower court ruling. Gong Lum then appealed to the U.S. Supreme Court, which ruled in favor of the school district on the grounds that a school was available to Martha Lum that served "brown, yellow or black" students and that, therefore, she was afforded equal protection of the laws.

Significance

Gong Lum v. Rice affirmed previous rulings by the Court involving segregation. In delivering the opinion of the Court, Chief Justice Taft made reference to these earlier cases to justify the decision against Gong Lum.

In *Plessy v. Ferguson* (1896), the Court ruled that states could maintain a system of "separate but equal" in the provision of accommodations on passenger trains because the application of the "equal protection" clause of the Fourteenth Amendment was subject to a recognition of "established usages, customs, and traditions of the people." And the Court ruled in a 1899 case, *Cumming v. County Board of Education,* that it would not interfere with how a state chose to conduct their schools unless there was a "clear and unmistakable disregard of rights secured by the supreme law of the land" and school segregation could not be considered a violation of any constitutional rights.

Gong Lum v. Rice demonstrated the Court's continued willingness to uphold the "separate but equal" doctrine as well as to turn a blind eye to the obvious fact that "colored" schools were clearly inferior by any measure to those designated for whites. In the *Gong Lum* decision, the Court extended the doctrine in *Plessy* to include Asians and other nonwhites.

It would not be until *Brown v. Board of Education* in 1954 that the Court would determine school segregation to be inherently unconstitutional.

Primary Source

Gong Lum v. Rice [excerpt]

SYNOPSIS: In the following excerpt from the decision of the Supreme Court in *Gong Lum v. Rice,* Chief Justice Taft sets forth the main points of the Court's reasoning behind its decision in this case. As support for the Supreme Court's decision, he quotes the decision of the Mississippi State Supreme Court in favor of Rice. According to Taft, this case did not present a "new question" and therefore did not require a detailed argument to support the decision. Rather, Taft cites past decisions of the Court in favor of allowing states to determine their own laws regarding segregation without federal interference. The case was argued on October 12, 1927, and was decided on November 21, 1927.

Mr. Chief Justice Taft delivered the opinion of the Court.

This was a petition for Mandamus filed in the state Circuit Court of Mississippi for the First Judicial District of Bolivar County.

Gong Lum is a resident of Mississippi, resides in the Rosedale Consolidated High School District, and is the father of Martha Lum. He is engaged in the mercantile business. Neither he nor she was connected with the consular service or any other service of the government of China, or any government, at the time of her birth. She was nine years old when the petition was filed, having been born January 21, 1915, and she sued by her next friend, Chew How, who is a native born citizen of the United States and the State of Mississippi. The petition alleged that she was of good moral character and between the ages of five and twenty-one years, and that, as she was such a citizen and an educable child, it became her father's duty under the law to send her to school; that she desired to attend the Rosedale Consolidated High School; that at the opening of the school she appeared as a pupil, but at the noon recess she was notified by the superintendent that she would not be allowed to return to the school; that an order had been issued by the Board of Trustees, who are made defendants, excluding her from attending the school solely on the ground that she was of Chinese descent and not a member of the white or Caucasian race, and that their order had been made in pursuance to instructions from the State Superintendent of Education of Mississippi, who is also made a defendant.

The petitioners further show that there is no school maintained in the District for the education of children of Chinese descent, and none established in Bolivar County where she could attend. . . .

The petition alleged that . . . the legislature has provided for the establishment and for the payment of the expenses of the Rosedale Consolidated High School, and that the plaintiff, Gong Lum, the petitioner's father, is a taxpayer and helps to support and maintain the school; that Martha Lum is an educable child, is entitled to attend the school as a pupil, and that this is the only school conducted in the district available for her as a pupil; that the right to attend it is a valuable right; that she is not a member of the colored race nor is she of mixed blood, but that she is pure Chinese; that she is by the action of the board of trustees and the State Superintendent discriminated against directly and denied her right to be a member of the Rosedale School; that the school authorities have no discretion under the law as to her admission as a pupil in the school, but that they continue without authority of law to deny her the right to attend it as a pupil. For these reasons the writ of mandamus is prayed for against the defendants commanding them and each of them to desist from discriminating against her on account of her race or ancestry and to give her the same rights and privileges that other educable children between the ages of five and twenty-one are granted in the Rosedale Consolidated High School.

The petition was demurred to by the defendants on the ground, among others, that the bill showed on its face that plaintiff is a member of the Mongolian or yellow race, and therefore not entitled to attend the schools provided by law in the State of Mississippi for children of the white or Caucasian race.

The trial court overruled the demurrer and ordered that a writ of mandamus issue to the defendants as prayed in the petition.

The defendants then appealed to the Supreme Court of Mississippi, which heard the case. *Rice v. Gong Lum,* 139 Miss. 760. In its opinion, it directed its attention to the proper construction of § 207 of the State Constitution of 1890, which provides:

Separate schools shall be maintained for children of the white and colored races.

The Court held that this provision of the Constitution divided the educable children into those of the pure white or Caucasian race, on the one hand, and the brown, yellow, and black races, on the other, and therefore that Martha Lum of the Mongolian or yellow race could not insist on being classed with the whites under this constitutional division. The Court said:

The legislature is not compelled to provide separate schools for each of the colored races, and, unless and until it does provide such schools and provide for segregation of the other races, such races are entitled to have the benefit of the colored public schools. Under our statutes a colored public school exists in every county and in some convenient district in which every colored child is entitled to obtain an education. These schools are within the reach of all the children of the state, and the plaintiff does not show by her petition that she applied for admission to such schools. On the contrary the petitioner takes the position that because there are no separate public schools for Mongolians that she is entitled to enter the white public schools in preference to the colored public schools. A consolidated school in this state is simply a common school conducted as other common schools are conducted; the only distinction being that two or more school districts have been consolidated into one school. Such consolidation is entirely discretionary with the county school board having reference to the condition existing in the particular territory. Where a school district has an unusual amount of territory, with an unusual valuation of property therein, it may levy additional taxes. But the other common schools under similar statutes have the same power.

If the plaintiff desires, she may attend the colored public schools of her district, or, if she does not so desire, she may go to a private school. The compulsory school law of this state does not require the attendance at a public school, and a parent under the decisions of the Supreme Court of the United States has a right to educate his child in a private school if he so desires. But plaintiff is not entitled to attend a white public school.

As we have seen, the plaintiffs aver that the Rosedale Consolidated High School is the only school conducted in that district available for Martha Lum as a pupil. They also aver that there is no school maintained in the district of Bolivar county for the education of Chinese children and none in the county. How are these averments to be reconciled with the statement of the State Supreme Court that colored schools are maintained in every county by virtue of the Constitution? This seems to be explained, in the language of the State Supreme Court, as follows:

By statute it is provided that all the territory of each county of the state shall be divided into school districts separately for the white and colored races; that is to say, the whole territory is to be divided into white school districts, and then a new division of the county for colored school districts. In other words, the statutory scheme is to make the districts outside of the separate school districts, districts for the particular race, white or colored, so that the territorial limits of the school districts need not be the same, but the territory embraced in a school district for the colored race may not be the same territory embraced in the school district for the white race, and *vice versa,* which system of creating the common school districts for the two races, white and colored, do not require schools for each race as such to be maintained in each district, but each child, no matter from what territory, is assigned to some school district, the school buildings being separately located and separately controlled, but each having the same curriculum, and each having the same number of months of school term, if the attendance is maintained for the said statutory period, which school district of the common or public schools has certain privileges, among which is to maintain a public school by local taxation for a longer period of time than the said term of four months under named conditions which apply alike to the common schools for the white and colored races.

We must assume then that there are school districts for colored children in Bolivar county, but that no colored school is within the limits of the Rosedale Consolidated High School District. This is not inconsistent with there being, at a place outside of that district and in a different district, a colored school which the plaintiff Martha Lum, may conveniently attend. If so, she is not denied, under the existing school system, the right to attend and enjoy the privileges of a common school education in a colored school. If it were otherwise, the petition should have contained an allegation showing it. Had the petition alleged specifically that there was no colored school in Martha Lum's neighborhood to which she could conveniently go, a different question would have been presented, and this, without regard to the State Supreme Court's construction of the State Constitution as limiting the white schools provided for the education of children of the white or Caucasian race. But we do not find the petition to present such a situation.

The case then reduces itself to the question whether a state can be said to afford to a child of Chinese ancestry born in this country, and a citizen of the United States, equal protection of the laws by giving her the opportunity for a common school education in a school which receives only colored children of the brown, yellow or black races.

The right and power of the state to regulate the method of providing for the education of its youth at public expense is clear. In *Cumming v. Richmond County Board of Education,* 175 U. S. 528, 545, persons of color sued the Board of Education to enjoin it from maintaining a high school for white children without providing a similar school for colored children which had existed and had been discontinued. Mr. Justice Harlan, in delivering the opinion of the Court, said:

> Under the circumstances disclosed, we cannot say that this action of the state court was, within the meaning of the Fourteenth Amendment, a denial by the State to the plaintiffs and to those associated with them of the equal protection of the laws, or of any privileges belonging to them as citizens of the United States. We may add that while all admit that the benefits and burdens of public taxation must be shared by citizens without discrimination against any class on account of their race, the education of the people in schools maintained by state taxation is a matter belonging to the respective States, and any interference on the part of Federal authority with the management of such schools can not be justified except in the case of a clear and unmistakable disregard of rights secured by the supreme law of the land.

The question here is whether a Chinese citizen of the United States is denied equal protection of the laws when he is classed among the colored races and furnished facilities for education equal to that offered to all, whether white, brown, yellow or black. Were this a new question, it would call for very full argument and consideration, but we think that it is the same question which has been many times decided to be within the constitutional power of the state legislature to settle without intervention of the federal courts under the Federal Constitution. . . .

In *Plessy v. Ferguson,* 163 U. S. 537, 544, 545, in upholding the validity under the Fourteenth Amendment of a statute of Louisiana requiring the separation of the white and colored races in railway coaches, a more difficult question than this, this Court, speaking of permitted race separation, said:

> The most common instance of this is connected with the establishment of separate schools for white and colored children, which has been held to be a valid exercise of the legislative power even by courts of States where the political rights of the colored race have been longest and most earnestly enforced.

The case of *Roberts v. City of Boston, supra,* in which Chief Justice Shaw of the Supreme Judicial Court of Massachusetts, announced the opinion of that court upholding the separation of colored and white schools under a state constitutional injunction of equal protection, the same as the Fourteenth Amendment, was then referred to, and this Court continued:

> "Similar laws have been enacted by Congress under its general power of legislation over the District of Columbia, Rev. Stat. D. C. §§ 281, 282, 283, 310, 319, as well as by the legislatures of many of the States, and have been generally, if not uniformly, sustained by the Courts," citing many of the cases above named.

Most of the cases cited arose, it is true, over the establishment of separate schools as between white pupils and black pupils, but we can not think that the question is any different or that any different result can be reached, assuming the cases above cited to be rightly decided, where the issue is as between white pupils and the pupils of the yellow races. The decision is within the discretion of the state in regulating its public schools and does not conflict with the Fourteenth Amendment. The judgment of the Supreme Court of Mississippi is

> *Affirmed.*

Further Resources

BOOKS

Alexander, Kern, and M. David Alexander. *American Public School Law,* 5th ed. Belmont, Calif.: West/Thomson Learning, 2001.

Spurlock, Clark. *Education and the Supreme Court.* Urbana, Ill.: University of Illinois Press, 1955.

WEBSITES

"Legal Information Institute." Cornell Law School. Available online at http://www.law.cornell.edu/ (accessed March 10, 2003).

"The Supreme Court Historical Society." supremecourthistory .org. Available online at http://www.supremecourthistory .org/index.html; website home page: http://www .supremecourthistory.org (accessed March 10, 2003).

"Progressive Education and the Science of Education"

Speech

By: John Dewey

Date: 1928

Source: Dewey, John. "Progressive Education and the Science of Education." *Progressive Education* 5, 1928, 197–204. Reprinted in *Dewey on Education: Selections with an Introduction and Notes.* Martin S. Dworkin, ed. New York: Teachers College Press, 1959, 113–126.

About the Author: John Dewey (1859–1952), had a long and prolific career that deeply impacted the intellectual life of the nation and the world. While his work spanned the fields of psychology, politics, and social issues, he is probably best known as a philosopher of education. In 1894, he was appointed head of the department of philosophy, psychology and pedagogy at the University of Chicago. In 1904, he left Chicago to join the faculty at Columbia. He remained at Columbia until his retirement in 1939. Dewey continued to write and speak until the end of his long life in 1952. ■

John Dewey has been closely associated with the progressive education movement. **THE LIBRARY OF CONGRESS.**

Introduction

Dewey believed that education should, at least for young children, begin with the interests and motivations that the child brings to school. He referred to these interests as "dawning capacities," emphasizing that they are not ends in themselves but rather indications of what the child is capable of and about to be capable of. The purpose of education is growth, but not in just any direction. The teacher, because of his or her greater experience and wisdom, guides the child to the next step. For Dewey, the primary way that teachers should do this is by selecting environmental influences that best influence the proper growth of the child. One of these environmental influences is the organizing of the school as a real social community in which the child learns values and discipline by being an active participant. Rather than forcing students to learn abstract symbols (such as language and numbers) out of the context in which they might have meaning, students learn by experience and by doing, starting with projects they are intrinsically motivated to do. In the process, a student learns abstract symbols when they become needed as tools to accomplish his or her own goals. Dewey viewed education as a means to social progress and reform. Because the world is always changing, children can be best prepared to be effective and responsible citizens by being taught how to think, not what to think. Education should be focused on the practical and useful.

John Dewey has been closely associated with the progressive education movement that began in the 1870s and continued through the 1950s. The movement promoted education as a means to social reform and advo-

cated a psychological and scientific approach to schooling. For Progressives, education should emphasize the whole child through a more practical and relevant curriculum, increased freedom and self-expression for students, an attention to students' interests, and viewing schooling as the process of socialization.

While the progressive education movement arose out of the interaction of many social forces, some have credited (or blamed!) Dewey for the movement as a whole and for the various educational innovations that have been associated with it. And many within the movement identified Dewey as their leader and guide. A multitude of new schools, programs, approaches, methods, curricula, and materials appeared under the banner of "progressive education" and were introduced as practical applications of Dewey's philosophy. Yet Dewey himself often disagreed with these approaches and methods. Misinterpretations of his work spawned educational programs that bore little resemblance to his original ideas.

One explanation for the gap between Dewey's philosophy and its application in the progressive movement is Dewey's difficult and often ambiguous writing. This lack of clarity sometimes enables readers to see what they want to see in his work. Dewey was, and remains, much discussed but little read. Oversimplifications abound. His leadership role in the progressive education movement has been compared to that of a reverently misinterpreted prophet, rather than of a carefully obeyed commander.

Significance

"Progressive Education and the Science of Education" is an important example of Dewey's attempts to correct misconceptions of his work and to guide the progressive education movement in more fruitful directions.

It is significant that Dewey had refused to associate himself with the Progressive Education Association from its founding in 1919. In 1928, however, he accepted an honorary presidency of the organization and delivered this address in which he offers criticisms of the progressive education movement and clarifies misunderstandings regarding his philosophy.

Dewey carried on this struggle with his "disciples" in the progressive education movement for the duration of his career. Where Dewey wrote of freedom in education there were, inevitably, some who would interpret this to mean "letting the child do whatever he or she wants." When he discussed the concept of experimental schools, some assumed this meant having no plan or direction. Even in the early twenty-first century, the phrase "progressive education" can evoke such caricatures in the minds of proponents and detractors alike.

Primary Source

"Progressive Education and the Science of Education" [excerpt]

SYNOPSIS: In these excerpts from an address to members of the Progressive Education Association, Dewey urges progressive educators to turn away from a "negative" phase in the movement where the goal is simply not to do what had been done in traditional schooling. Instead, educators should turn their attention to a systematic and intelligent process of developing organized subject matter and studying "the conditions favorable to learning." In this way, progressive educators would make a genuine contribution to the science of education.

What is Progressive Education? What is the meaning of experiment in education, of an experimental school? What can such schools as are represented here do for other schools, in which the great, indefinitely the greater, number of children receive their instruction and discipline? What can rightfully be expected from the work of these progressive schools in the way of a contribution to intelligent and stable educational practice; especially what can be expected in the way of a contribution to educational theory? Are there common elements, intellectual and moral, in the various undertakings here represented? Or is each school going its own way, having for its foundation the desires and preferences of the particular person who happens to be in charge? Is experimentation a process of trying anything at least once, of putting into immediate effect any "happy thought" that comes to mind, or does it rest upon principles which are adopted at least as a working hypothesis? Are actual results consistently observed and used to check an underlying hypothesis so that the latter develops intellectually? Can we be content if from the various progressive schools there emanate suggestions which radiate to other schools to enliven and vitalize their work; or should we demand that out of the cooperative undertakings of the various schools a coherent body of educational principles shall gradually emerge as a distinctive contribution to the theory of education? . . .

Let us then reduce our questions to a single one and ask, What is the distinctive relation of progressive education to the science of education, understanding by science a body of verified facts and tested principles which may give intellectual guidance to the practical operating of schools? . . .

As the working operations of schools differ, so must the intellectual theories devised from those operations. Since the practice of progressive education differs from that of the traditional schools, it would be absurd to suppose that the intellectual formulation and organization which fits one type will hold for the other. . . .

While what has been said may have a tendency to relieve educators in progressive schools from undue anxiety about the criticism that they are unscientific—a criticism levelled from the point of view of theory appropriate to schools of quite a different purpose and procedure—it is not intended to exempt them from responsibility for contributions of an organized, systematic, intellectual quality. The contrary is the case. All new and reforming movements pass through a stage in which what is most evident is a negative phase, one of protest, of deviation, and innovation. It would be surprising indeed if this were not true of the progressive educational movement. For instance, the formality and fixity of traditional schools seemed oppressive, restrictive. Hence in a school which departs from these ideals and methods, freedom is at first most naturally conceived as removal of artificial and benumbing restrictions. Removal, abolition are, however, negative things, so in time it comes to be seen that such freedom is no end in itself, nothing to be satisfied with and to stay by, but marks at most an opportunity to do something of a positive and constructive sort.

Now I wonder whether this earlier and more negative phase of progressive education has not upon the whole run its course, and whether the time has not arrived in which these schools are undertaking a more constructively organized function. One thing is sure: in the degree in which they enter upon organized constructive work, they are bound to make definite contributions to building up the theoretical or intellectual side of education. Whether this be called science or philosophy of education, I for one, care little; but if they do not *intellectually* organize their own work, while they may do much in making the lives of the children committed to them more joyous and more vital, they contribute only incidental scraps to the science of education.

The word organization has been freely used. This word suggests the nature of the problem. Organization and administration are words associated together in the traditional scheme, hence organization conveys the idea of something external and set. But reaction from this sort of organization only creates a demand for another sort. Any genuine intellectual organization is flexible and moving, but it does not lack its own internal principles of order and continuity. An experimental school is under the temptation to improvise its subject-matter. It must take advantage of unexpected events and turn to account unexpected questions and interests. Yet if it permits improvisation to dictate its course, the result is a jerky, discontinuous movement which works against the possibility of making any important contribution to educational subject-matter. Incidents are momentary, but the use made of them should not be momentary or short-lived. They are to be brought within the scope of a developing whole of content and purpose, which is a whole because it has continuity and consecutiveness in its parts. There is no single subject-matter which all schools must adopt, but in every school there should be some significant subject-matters undergoing growth and formulation. . . .

An exaggerated illustration, amounting to a caricature, may perhaps make the point clearer. Suppose there is a school in which pupils are surrounded with a wealth of material objects, apparatus, and tools of all sorts. Suppose they are simply asked what they would like to do and then told in effect to "go to it," the teacher keeping hands—and mind, too—off. *What* are they going to do? What assurance is there that what they do is anything more than the expression, and exhaustion, of a momentary impulse in interest? The supposition does not, you may say, correspond to any fact. But what are the implications of the opposite principle? Where can we stop as we get away from the principle contained in the illustration? Of necessity—and this is as true of the traditional school as of a progressive—the start, the first move, the initial impulse in action, must proceed from the pupil. You can lead a horse to water but you can't make him drink. But whence comes his idea of *what* to do? That must come from what he has already heard or seen; or from what he sees some other child doing. It comes as a suggestion from beyond himself, from the environment, he being not an originator of the idea and purpose but a vehicle through which his surroundings past and present suggest something to him. That such suggestions are likely to be chance ideas, soon exhausted, is highly probable. I think observation will show that when a child enters upon a really fruitful and consecutively developing activity, it is because, and in as far as, he has previously engaged in some complex and gradually unfolding activity which has left him a question he wishes to prove further or with the idea of some piece of work still to be accomplished to bring his occupation to completion. Otherwise he is at the mercy of chance suggestion, and chance suggestions are not likely to lead to anything significant or fruitful.

While in outward form, these remarks are given to show that the teacher, as the member of the group having the riper and fuller experience and the greater insight into the possibilities of continuous development found in any suggested project, has not only the right but the duty to suggest lines of activity, and to show that there need not be any fear of adult imposition provided the teacher knows children as well as subjects, their import is not exhausted in bringing out this fact. Their basic purport is to show that progressive schools by virtue of being progressive, and not in spite of that fact, are under the necessity of finding projects which involve an orderly development and inter-connection of subject-matter, since otherwise there can be no sufficiently complex and long-span undertaking. The opportunity and the need impose a responsibility. Progressive teachers may and can work out and present to other teachers for trial and criticism definite and organized bodies of knowledge, together with a listing of sources from which additional information of the same sort can be secured. If it is asked how the presentation of such bodies of knowledge would differ from the standardized texts of traditional schools, the answer is easy. In the first place, the material would be associated with and derived from occupational activities or prolonged courses of action undertaken by the pupils themselves. In the second place, the material presented would not be something to be literally followed by other teachers and students, but would be indications of the intellectual possibilities of this and that course of activity—statements on the basis of carefully directed and observed experience of the questions that have arisen in connection with them and of the kind of information found useful in answering them, and of where that knowledge can be had. No second experience would exactly duplicate the course of the first; but the presentation of material of this kind would liberate and direct the activities of any teacher in dealing with the distinctive emergencies and needs that would arise in re-undertaking the same general type of project. Further material thus developed would be added, and a large and yet free body of related subject-matter would gradually be built up.

As I have touched in a cursory manner upon the surface of a number of topics, it may be well in closing to summarize. In substance, the previous discussion has tried to elicit at least two contributions which progressive schools may make to that type of a science of education which corresponds to their own type of procedure. One is the development of organized subject-matter just spoken of. The other is a study of the conditions favorable to learning. As I have already said there are certain traits characteristic of progressive schools which are not ends in themselves but which are opportunities to be used. These reduce themselves to opportunities for *learning,* for gaining knowledge, mastering definite modes of skill or techniques, and acquiring socially desirable attitudes and habits—the three chief aspects of learning, I should suppose. Now of necessity the contribution from the side of traditional schools to this general topic is concerned chiefly with methods of teaching, or, if it passes beyond that point, to the methods of study adopted by students. But from the standpoint of progressive education, the question of method takes on a new and still largely untouched form. It is no longer a question of how the teacher is to instruct or how the pupil is to study. The problem is to find what conditions must be fulfilled in order that study and learning will naturally and necessarily take place, what conditions must be present so that pupils will make the responses which cannot help having learning as their consequence. The pupil's mind is no longer to be on study or learning. It is given to doing the things that the situation calls for, while learn-ing is the result. The method of the teacher, on the other hand, becomes a matter of finding the conditions which call out self-educative activity, or learning, and of cooperating with the activities of the pupils so that they have learning as their consequence.

A series of constantly multiplying careful reports on conditions which experience has shown in actual cases to be favorable and unfavorable to learning would revolutionize the whole subject of method. The problem is complex and difficult. Learning involves, as just said, at least three factors: knowledge, skill, and character. Each of these must be studied. It requires judgment and art to select from the total circumstances of a case just what elements are the causal conditions of learning, which are influential, and which secondary or irrelevant. It requires candor and sincerity to keep track of failures as well as successes and to estimate the relative degree of success obtained. It requires trained and acute observation to note the indications of progress in learning, and even more to detect their causes—a much more highly skilled kind of observation that is needed to note the results of mechanically applied tests. Yet the progress of a science of education depends upon the systematic accumulation of just this sort of material. Solution of the problem of discovering the cause of learning is an endless process. But no advance will be made in the solution till a start is made, and the freer and more experimental character of progressive schools places the responsibility for making the start squarely upon them.

I hardly need remind you that I have definitely limited the field of discussion to one point: the relation of progressive education to the development of a science of education. As I began with questions, I end with one: Is not the time here when the progressive movement is sufficiently established so that it may now consider the intellectual contribution which it may make to the art of education, to the art which is the most difficult and the most important of all human arts?

Further Resources
BOOKS

Cremin, Lawrence A. *The Transformation of the School: Progressivism in American Education, 1876–1957.* New York: Knopf, 1961.

Dewey, John. *Experience and Education.* New York: Macmillan, 1938.

Dewey, John, and Evelyn Dewey. *Schools of To-morrow.* New York: Dutton, 1915.

Dykhuizen, George. *The Life and Mind of John Dewey.* Carbondale: Southern Illinois University Press, 1973.

WEBSITES

"The Center for Dewey Studies." Southern Illinois University. Available online at http://www.siu.edu/~deweyctr/; website home page: http://www.siu.edu/ (accessed March 11, 2003).

"The John Dewey Society for the Study of Education and Culture." Available online at http://cuip.uchicago.edu/jds/; website home page: http://cuip.net/cuip/ (accessed March 11, 2003).

VIDEOCASSETTES

John Dewey: His Life and Work. Directed by Frances W. Davidson. Davidson Films. Videocassette, 2001.

School and Society in Chicago

Nonfiction work

By: George S. Counts

Date: 1928

Source: Counts, George S. *School and Society in Chicago.* New York: Harcourt, Brace, 1928, 3–12.

About the Author: George S. Counts (1889–1974) earned a B.A. from Baker University and a Ph.D. from the University of Chicago. He taught at several universities before joining the faculty at Teachers College, Columbia University in 1927, where he remained until 1955. Counts was concerned with American democracy and education in the context of social and technological change. He was also a noted scholar in comparative education. ■

Introduction

The progressive education movement was characterized by a diversity of aims and viewpoints and evolved over the course of its existence from the late nineteenth century through the 1950s. Prior to World War I (1914–1918), progressives focused on social reform within schools in urban areas, developing programs to meet the needs of the lower class, immigrant students who flooded the city schools. By contrast, postwar progressivism during the prosperous and free-wheeling 1920s emphasized creative self-expression in child-centered schools serving the children of the middle and upper-middle class. As the Great Depression deepened during the 1930s, individual expression seemed less relevant and many progressives began to take a closer look at the role of the schools in the larger society.

Fundamental shifts in American society prompted progressives to advocate for changes in education. Waves of immigration, child labor laws, and compulsory school laws resulted in larger and more diverse student bodies. Now that almost all children from the various social classes and cultural groups were attending schools, the old classical curriculum for the college-bound no longer

seemed appropriate.

In addition, America was becoming a largely urban society. Historically, the U.S. had been a nation of farmers; by the 1920s, more people were living in urban areas and encountering some of the problems and issues of industrial capitalism. Progressive educators were asking: What type of education will children need to function successfully in this new context? How will schools need to change?

For some progressives, the focus on the school within the context of society was the key to answering these questions. Educational institutions do not exist in a vacuum. A variety of forces act upon the schools in a complex industrial society and these need to be studied. This group of progressives also viewed schools as instruments of social change.

Significance

George S. Counts was a major voice for the branch of progressive thought emphasizing the schools' responsiveness to the larger society and its role in social change. He studied the influence of industrial capitalism on the schools of Chicago and concluded that efforts toward curriculum reform and innovative new methods, however sound these may be, were futile until the distribution of power and control in the schools was reorganized to reflect the realities of the new social context.

Schools, Counts argued, were organized to suit the small-town context in which they were formed. He emphasized the complexity of the circumstances in which modern urban public schools operated. A diverse array of organizations, demographic groups, and other special interests pressured the schools from all sides, lured by the huge budgets and potential propaganda opportunities of the public schools. Every group wanted to put in its two cents and secure its piece of the pie.

Counts studied the schools in Chicago as representative of the situation in other large urban centers. Looking beyond the bizarre events and "flapdoodle" surrounding the ouster of a school superintendent, Counts determined that the problem was not the influence of the various societal groups on the schools, but the lack of a "stable, enduring, and balanced connection" between the schools and the society in which they are embedded. Schools, Counts contended, could not be above politics. The solution would not be to insulate schools from the interest groups, but to make schools more responsive to them. Rather than a school board made up of the upper-class appointees of the mayor, the board members needed to reflect the various groups. Instead of "under the table" approaches, the very real differences in opinion could be "brought out into the clear sunlight of discussion." In addition, education policy decisions should be placed in the hands of a well-trained and organized teaching force.

Published in the late 1920s, *School and Society in Chicago* anticipated the shift the progressive education movement would take in the 1930s toward an emphasis on schools embedded within a social context.

Primary Source

School and Society in Chicago [excerpt]

SYNOPSIS: In this excerpt from *School and Society in Chicago*, George S. Counts outlines the events surrounding the dismissal of Chicago superintendent of schools William McAndrew. While the bizarre nature of some of aspects of the Chicago affair are unique, Counts makes the case that the underlying causes are common to all urban schools systems at the time.

The Triumph of the Politicians

A reader of the New York *Times* on the morning of August 30, 1927, might have found on the twenty-fifth page of that issue the following special despatch:

> Chicago, August 29.—William McAndrew, Superintendent of Schools, was suspended this afternoon at a special meeting of the Board of Education by a vote of six to five on charges of insubordination. Hearing on the charges was set for September 29.

This despatch marked the culmination of a long series of events in the political and educational history of Chicago. By action of the board of education the superintendent was removed from office six months before the expiration of his contract, and the effort of William Hale Thompson to redeem an election pledge, made during the mayoralty campaign in the spring, thus entered expeditiously upon its final stages. During the campaign the latter had said that, if elected mayor, he would drive Mr. McAndrew from Chicago and purge the public school system of anti-American propaganda. After his election in April by a plurality of 85,000, in a total vote of approximately 1,000,000, he left no stone unturned to achieve this end. Consequently, on the twenty-ninth of August the superintendent was suspended from office, and four weeks later he was placed on trial before the board of education. The immediate charge on which he was arraigned was that of insubordination; the more remote charge was that of being a "stool pigeon of the King of England"; while the true reasons for the action were probably of an altogether different order.

From the moment the first gun was fired in this fight on the part of the mayor to oust the superin-

tendent, a colorful spectacle was unfolded on the shores of Lake Michigan. Charges and counter-charges, often personal in nature, were made by both sides; and the case attracted much attention and was given wide publicity. From the Atlantic to the Pacific and from the Great Lakes to the Gulf the daily press, with an ever-watchful eye for the sensational, reported the dramatic and striking incidents of the trial. The more substantial publications of the week and the month ran many articles which were designed to acquaint the thinking public with the underlying forces at work in the situation. Reports of the case were even carried to other lands, there to add strength to the widespread dogma that America is peopled by semi-civilized tribes. The English press in particular, and naturally because of the anti-British attack of the mayor, watched and reported the barbarous assault on the public schools of Chicago. As a consequence the American citizen who passes beyond the borders of his own country is almost certain to be asked embarrassing questions regarding the state of education and culture in the United States.

The reports which emanated from Chicago during the heat of the battle might well cause the most stable mind, unfamiliar with American politics, to doubt its own sanity. When one hears that William McAndrew, a man with a record of forty years of distinguished service in the schools of his country, takes orders from the King of England; when one hears that all but one of the eight histories used in the schools of Chicago contain "false and insidious teachings of alienism"; when one hears that with unimportant exceptions American historians are either directly or indirectly in the pay of foreign governments; when one hears that the University of Chicago is not an institution genuinely dedicated to the advancement of learning but rather a cleverly disguised agency of anti-American propaganda; when one hears that the public libraries of the city of Chicago have fallen into the hands of enemies of the nation and are covertly instilling treasonable sentiments into the minds of their patrons; when one hears that under the preceding mayor, a man of Irish descent and Catholic persuasion, the entire city administration had become the tool of scheming British statesmen—in a word, when one hears charge upon charge, each rivaling its fellow in stupidity, and when one learns that not only did these utterances not spell political disaster for the man who made them, but rather that they were one of the means whereby he elevated himself to office, one naturally begins to doubt that *Alice in Wonderland* was a fiction of the mind and not an authentic account of actual happenings somewhere on the planet.

What is the meaning of this drama which is being enacted in the second city of the nation? Here is something which, though familiar to every student of politics and to every practical school administrator, is not covered in the textbooks on school administration. Is it comedy, or is it tragedy? And is one supposed to laugh or to weep? To the cynic who views the entire human spectacle with amused detachment, it is comedy—and a very proper occasion for laughter; but to the citizen who feels himself identified in some measure with the fortunes of the republic, it is tragedy—and the only fitting response is tears. Moreover, in proportion as the social background of case is examined, the less of comedy does it seem to contain. He who surveys the Chicago situation can only wonder whether man has not created a social mechanism so complex and intricate as to defy his understanding.

In order to orient the reader with regard to this attack upon the superintendent in the name of patriotism, the historical background should be briefly sketched. From 1915 to 1923 William Hale Thompson served two successive terms as mayor of Chicago. The second of his two administrations was marked by a political invasion of the schools of the most shameless order. Mr. Charles E. Chadsey, an able superintendent, was illegally removed from office before he had scarcely entered upon his duties; the board of education was packed with henchmen of the city hall and the political machine; and the public school treasury was raided again and again by grafters and embezzlers. Revolting against this gross mismanagement of the public interest, the people of Chicago in the spring of 1923 elected to the mayor's office a man pledged to keep his hands off the board of education. In the early weeks of the following year Mr. William McAndrew was appointed superintendent of the Chicago schools. He proceeded to administer the system of education with vigor, to claim all the prerogatives of office to which he was entitled under law, and to launch a bold and comprehensive program of educational reform. Among other things he abolished the teachers' councils, advocated the junior high school, supported the platoon system, introduced a testing program, altered the administrative and supervisory organization, and unflinchingly opposed political interference in the conduct of the schools. So bitter was the opposition aroused by these reforms that the personality of the superintendent was made a vital issue in the mayoralty fight in 1927. Mr. Thomp-

son, sensing the possibilities in the situation, attacked Mr. McAndrew on the grounds of Americanism, promised to remove him from office if elected, and thus attracted to his camp the discontented elements of the city.

What the "trial" of the superintendent which followed the election of Mr. Thompson actually means to the schools and children of Chicago has been set forth by the Public School Emergency Committee. This committee, headed by some of Chicago's ablest and most disinterested citizens, issued the following statement in January, 1928:

> The curtain is about to rise on the last scene of the mock trial of Superintendent McAndrew. After dragging out the proceedings until his term is over, the Superintendent will be dismissed. What makes this affair a farce is:
>
> 1. The fact that the majority of the Board of Education were pledged to dismiss McAndrew before they were appointed. They could not be honest with the power that appointed them and honest with the Superintendent at the same time. Who can be fairly tried by a jury pledged to return a verdict against him? This is not legal justice but political lynch law.
>
> 2. The trial was conducted by the man who made the charges, as prosecutor, judge, and part of the jury.
>
> 3. The *technical* charge against the Superintendent was that of insubordination, but during the proceedings every kind of testimony was admitted from any one who cared to come before the Board with any kind of complaint or grievance.
>
> 4. The president of the Board, prosecutor and judge and jury, himself voted for the introduction of the textbooks charged against the Superintendent. When he votes against McAndrew, he votes against himself.
>
> 5. Loose-mouthed talkers never before heard of in the world of patriotic endeavor were brought in from coast to coast, but not the slightest effort was made to find out the facts from those qualified to speak of the Superintendent's standing as a civic leader and teacher of youth.
>
> 6. The hearings were deliberately delayed from week to week in order that McAndrew might not have an opportunity to bring his case into court and obtain substantial justice there. The purpose was to defeat the ends of justice and substitute the plans of politicians.
>
> The sorry proceedings now coming to a close in the dismissal of a competent official by a packed board constitute the saddest page in the history of the Chicago schools and in fact of all American education. Never in so

unblushing and brutal a fashion has the spoils system dared to lay its hands upon our public schools. Never have there been proceedings so hypocritical and insincere. Never has patriotism been so brazenly invoked to cover up the designs of a plundering crew of political pirates.

The real purpose of this farce is to cover up plans to make the schools of Chicago a part of a political machine and to distract attention from what is really going on behind the scenes, at this very time. When they say patriotism they mean plunder. When they say America First they mean Chicago last. Behind the picture of Washington lurk the conspirators who seek to make the school funds, the school lands, school contracts, school textbooks of this city serve the purpose of political scoundrels; in short, to make the public schools a private asset.

When the president of the Board, already pledged, and five other members of the Board, already pledged, and the attorney of the Board, already pledged, finally summon courage to vote on the charges they agreed upon months ago, they will lynch the Superintendent; and will set up a hilarious cry of triumph. But the public will know that this has been a roaring farce; that every elementary principle of justice has been violated; that the most shameless unfair methods have been employed. All over America school teachers will know that a great crime has been committed against the educational profession; and citizens everywhere will know that dirty politics is behind the mask of patriotism. Within a few months the fathers and mothers of Chicago will know that the little school children of Chicago have been betrayed into the clutches of political wolves.

Fundamental Americanism is supposed to guarantee a speedy trial on clear charges by a free and impartial court. In the McAndrew case the School Board, in the name of Americanism, exhibits a puppet "judge," presiding over a packed "court" whose decision has been announced in advance denying to the accused elementary rights that are the common heritage of all American citizens. A crew of political buccaneers, lost to all sense of sportsmanship and fair play, has made a bonfire of the bill of rights while hoisting aloft the picture of George Washington to detract attention from the blow directed at the vitals of real Americanism.

If there is even a modicum of truth in this statement, the condition of the Chicago schools today is indeed tragic and the welfare of Chicago children is being sacrificed to the ambitions of politicians. But however deplorable this might be, if it presented no general aspects, it would scarcely warrant detailed study, unless perhaps the object of such study were the preservation of some rare form of human behavior for a sociological museum. As a matter of fact the Chicago situation exhibits only too many features which are familiar to the eye of the student of politics. It merits the most attentive consideration of all persons interested in the future of public education, because nothing less than the future of public education is at stake. The picture presented by Chicago today is not unique in the history of that city, it is not peculiar to the southwestern shores of Lake Michigan, and it is far more complicated in its pattern than is apparent to the casual observer. The present assault on the Chicago schools casts a shadow of uncertainty over the American faith in the public school and raises a doubt regarding the efficacy of those social arrangements through which public education is controlled in a democratic society of the American type.

For more than a generation the Chicago system of public education has been the victim of political manipulation. Only rarely within the memory of the oldest inhabitant have the schools of this city experienced tranquility. In 1922 the practices of the board of education were made the object of a grand-jury investigation, and members of the board were indicted and given prison sentences. In 1919 the superintendent of schools was locked out of his office by order of the police department, and certain members of the board were convicted of conspiracy in the circuit court. In 1917 and 1918 two separate boards of education existed and struggled for supremacy until one of them was declared illegal by the supreme court of the state of Illinois. In 1913, in order to secure a board which would do his bidding, the mayor removed four recalcitrant members from office. A protracted battle in the courts followed, and the members were reinstated. In 1907, for similar reasons and with similar results, seven members of the board were removed from office by action of the mayor. So the history of the schools might be traced from decade to decade far back into the past. Always the same sordid story of political interference with the management of the schools and the general subordination of the fortunes of public education to the passions and selfish interests of organized minorities would be revealed. There is ample precedent for much that has occurred during the past year in Chicago.

Moreover, Chicago is after all an American city and is not essentially different from the other great industrial and commercial centers of the nation. In practically no large city of the country will the history of the control of education bear careful scrutiny. The most that may be said is that some cities have better records than others, and that in a particular city the record is not equally unsavory all of the time. Whether one goes to Boston, New York, Philadelphia, Baltimore, Pittsburgh, Cleveland, Chicago, St. Louis, New Orleans, Seattle, or San Francisco, the situation will be found much the same.

Further Resources

BOOKS

Counts, George S. *The Social Composition of Boards of Education: A Study in the Social Control of Public Education.* Chicago: University of Chicago, 1927.

———. *Secondary Education and Industrialism.* Cambridge, Mass.: Harvard University Press, 1929.

Cremin, Lawrence A. *The Transformation of the School: Progressivism in American Education, 1876–1957.* New York: Knopf, 1961.

Graham, Patricia Albjerg. *Progressive Education: From Arcady to Academe; A History of the Progressive Education Association, 1919–1955.* New York: Teachers College Press, 1967.

Gutek, Gerald, L. *George S. Counts and American Civilization: The Educator as Social Theorist.* Macon, Ga.: Mercer University Press, 1984.

"Some 'Defects and Excesses of Present-Day Athletic Contests,' 1929"

Report

By: Henry S. Pritchett

Date: 1929

Source: Pritchett, Henry S. "Some 'Defects and Excesses of Present-Day Athletic Contests,' 1929." In *American College Athletics,* Bulletin Number Twenty-Three. Howard J. Savage, ed. New York: Carnegie Foundation for the Advancement of Teaching, 1929. Preface, xiv–xvii. Reprinted in *Readings in American Educational History.* Edgar W. Knight and Clifton L. Hall, eds. New York: Appleton-Century Crofts, 1951, 598–601.

About the Author: Henry S. Pritchett (1857–1939) received a bachelor's degree in 1875 from the Collegiate Institute at Glasgow, Missouri. In 1895, he earned a doctorate in astronomy from the University of Munich. Pritchett was a professor of astronomy at Washington University, superintendent of the United States Coast and Geodetic Survey, and president of the Massachusetts Institute of Technology (M.I.T.). He was president of the Carnegie Foundation for the Advancement of Teaching from 1905 to 1930. ■

Introduction

College sports have been characterized by commercialism from their very beginnings. The 1852 rowing contest between Harvard and Yale was arranged by a railroad superintendent who, wanting to draw well-to-do passengers to the occasion, promised athletes "unlimited alcohol" and "lavish prizes." The 1860s and 1870s saw the founding and growth of intercollegiate sports associations in rowing, baseball, track and field, and football. Football soon dominated college sports and became big business by the end of the 1880s. Some $25,000 in gate receipts were sold for each Yale-Princeton game, and Yale had a $100,000 football slush fund.

It is not surprising that with such high stakes, problems began to surface. Colleges paid nonstudents to play, enrolled players as "students" long enough to play a game or two, and offered a variety of perks such as jobs and free meals to lure players. Injuries and deaths were common due to inadequate protective equipment and the dangerous "flying wedge" formation—330 college football players were killed in games from 1890 to 1905. President Theodore Roosevelt (served 1901–1909) threatened to halt college football unless reforms were made. As a result, the Intercollegiate Athletic Association of the United States (IAAUS) was founded in 1905. Five years later, the IAAUS changed its name to the National Collegiate Athletic Association (NCAA). Improvements were made in player safety and standardization of play, but cheating in the form of illegal recruiting and subsidizing of players actually increased.

Meanwhile, some college presidents and professors became concerned about the growing emphasis on athletics over academics. In 1931, the president of the University of Chicago, Robert Hutchins, wrote:

> College is not a great athletic association and social club in which provision is made, merely incidentally, for intellectual activity on the part of the physically and socially unfit. College is an association of scholars in which provision is made for the development of traits and powers which must be cultivated, in addition to those which are purely intellectual, if one is to become a well-balanced and useful member of any community.

However, faculty groups attempting to rein in the excesses and abuses of college sports were often at odds with alumni groups.

Significance

American College Athletics was the first comprehensive study of college sports, covering administration, coaching, subsidizing and recruiting, financial aspects, the role of the press, and effects on athletes. The report identified the main problem in college sports as "commercialism, and

The development of competitive sports in colleges had, by the 1920s, impacted sports in secondary schools. **THE LIBRARY OF CONGRESS.**

a negligent attitude toward the educational opportunity for which the college exists." The main purpose of college sports was found to be "financial and commercial" rather than educational. Most institutions—more than three-fourths of the colleges studied—were not operating under the principles of amateurism.

The study was front-page news when it was released in October 1929. Extensive media coverage of responses to the report continued over the next year. College administrators typically denied its validity in general or its applicability to their own institution. However, Howard Savage, the author, was able to refute the charges of critics, and in 1930 the NCAA endorsed the report.

Despite this success in bringing abuses in college athletics to the attention of colleges and the general public, there is little evidence that it prompted either long-term or short-term reform. The next two decades saw significant growth in commercialized college athletics and the cheating that accompanied such growth. *New York Herald Tribune* sports editor Stanley Woodward, writing in November 1946, decried the "chicanery" and "double-dealing" of 1940s college football and noted that "should the Carnegie Foundation launch an investigation of college football right now, the mild breaches of etiquette uncovered [in the 1920s] would assume a remote innocence which would only cause snickers among the post-war pirates of 1946."

In the early twenty-first century, scandals continue to surface. Newspapers report evidence of illegal recruiting, special "rinky dink" classes for athletes, and "tutors" who write papers for football players. The role of athletics within the college or university is still unclear—are sports part of the educational program or a business?

Primary Source

"Some 'Defects and Excesses of Present-Day Athletic Contests,' 1929" [excerpt]

SYNOPSIS: In the preface to *American College Athletics,* Henry S. Pritchett, president of the Carnegie Foundation, summarizes the problems found in college sports, including the negative effects on the student-athlete, recruiting and subsidizing, the role of the press, commercialism, and the role of alumni.

The preceding pages have dealt with a complicated situation of which organized athletics are but one factor. It remains to summarize the particular defects and excesses of present-day athletic contests as set forth in detail in the chapters of this report. The game of football looms large in any account of the growth of professionalism in college games. This does not mean that other sports are untouched by the influences that have converted football into a professional vocation.

The unfavorable results upon students through the athletic development may be briefly stated in the following terms:

1. The extreme development of competitive games in the colleges has reacted upon the secondary schools. The college athlete begins his athletic career before he gets to college.

2. Once in college the student who goes in for competitive sports, and in particular for football, finds himself under a pressure, hard to resist to give his whole time and thought to his athletic career. No college boy training for a major team can have much time for thought or study.

3. The college athlete, often a boy from a modest home, finds himself suddenly a most important man in the college life. He begins to live on a scale never before imagined. A special table is provided. Sport clothes and expensive trips are furnished him out of the athletic chest. He jumps at one bound to a plane of living of which he never before knew, all at the expense of some fund of which he knows lit-

tle. When he drops back to a scale of living such as his own means can afford, the result is sometimes disastrous.

4. He works (for it is work, not play) under paid professional coaches whose business it is to develop the boy to be an effective unit in a team. The coach of to-day is no doubt a more cultivated man than the coach of twenty years ago. But any father who has listened to the professional coaching a college team will have some misgivings as to the cultural value of the process.

5. Inter-college athletics are highly competitive. Every college or university longs for a winning team in its group. The coach is on the alert to bring the most promising athletes in the secondary schools to his college team. A system of recruiting and subsidizing has grown up, under which boys are offered pecuniary and other inducements to enter a particular college. The system is demoralizing and corrupt, alike for the boy who takes the money and for the agent who arranges it, and for the whole group of college and secondary school boys who know about it.

6. Much discussion has been had as to the part the college graduate should have in the government of his college. In the matter of competitive athletics the college alumnus has, in the main, played a sorry role. It is one thing for an "old grad" to go back and coach the boys of his college as at Oxford or Cambridge, where there are no professional coaches and no gate receipts. It is quite another thing for an American college graduate to pay money to high school boys, either directly or indirectly, in order to enlist their services for a college team. The process is not only unsportsmanlike, it is immoral to the last degree. The great body of college graduates are wholly innocent in this matter. Most college men wish their college to win. Those who seek to compass that end by recruiting and subsidizing constitute a small, but active, minority, working oftentimes without the knowledge of the college authorities. This constitutes the most disgraceful phase of recent inter-college athletics.

7. The relation of organized sports to the health of college students is not a simple question. The information to deal with it completely is not yet at hand. A chapter of the report is devoted to this subject. In general it may be said that the relation of college organized sports to the health of the individual student is one dependent on the good sense exhibited by the college boy in participating in such sports, and to the quality of the advice he receives from the college medical officer.

8. For many games the strict organization and the tendency to commercialize the sport has taken the joy out of the game. In football, for example, great numbers of boys do not play football, as in English schools and colleges, for the fun of it. A few play intensely. The great body of students are on-lookers.

9. Finally, it is to be said that the blaze of publicity in which the college athlete lives is a demoralizing influence for the boy himself and no less so for his college.

It goes without saying that fifty thousand people (not an unusual attendance) could not be gathered to witness a football game, through the mere pull of college loyalty or interest in the sport. The bulk of the spectators do not understand the game. They are drawn to this spectacle through wide spread and continuous publicity. The relation of the press to the inter-college sports is described in detail in a chapter devoted to that subject. It is sufficient here to add a brief statement.

The American daily, or weekly, paper lives on its advertising, not on the subscriptions paid by its readers. The news policy of the paper is determined by this fundamental fact. It desires to print the things that will be eagerly read by the great body of every-day men and women who shop in the stores. The working woman likes to read of the fine clothes of the society belle, her husband delights in the startling accounts of fights or the details of the professional baseball games. The paper, being human, supplies the kind of news the advertisers like. It prints much for those of wider interests, but it follows the desires of its great advertising constituency all the time.

This has led to a form of personal news-telling unknown in any other country. In no other nation of the world will a college boy find his photograph in the metropolitan paper because he plays on a college team. All this is part of the newspaper effort to reach the advertiser. The situation is regrettable alike for journalism and for the public good. But it exists.

Into this game of publicity the university of the present day enters eagerly. It desires for itself the publicity that the newspapers can supply. It wants students, it wants popularity, but above all it wants money and always more money.

The athlete is the most available publicity material the college has. A great scientific discovery will make good press material for a few days, but nothing to compare to that of the performance of a first-class athlete. Thousands are interested in the athlete all the time, while the scientist is at best only a passing show.

And so it happens that the athlete lives in the white light of publicity and his photograph adorns the front pages of metropolitan (which means New York, Boston, Chicago, San Francisco, Los Angeles, New Orleans, and a hundred other) dailies. It must be an unusual boy who can keep his perspective under such circumstances. Why should the college boy be subjected to this régime merely to enable some thousands of attractive young reporters to make a living?

Further Resources

BOOKS

Dealy, Francis X., Jr. *Win at Any Cost: The Sell Out of College Athletics.* New York: Carol Publishing Group, 1990.

Smith, Ronald A. *Sports and Freedom: The Rise of Big-Time College Athletics.* New York; Oxford University Press, 1988.

Thelin, John R. *Games Colleges Play: Scandal and Reform in Intercollegiate Athletics.* Baltimore, Md.: Johns Hopkins University Press, 1994.

Zimbalist, Andrew. *Unpaid Professionals: Commercialism and Conflict in Big-Time College Sports.* Princeton, N.J.: Princeton University Press, 1999.

WEBSITES

"NCAA Online." Available online at http://www.ncaa.org/ (accessed March 5, 2003).

AUDIO AND VISUAL MEDIA

Horse Feathers. Directed by Norman McLeod. 1932. MCA Home Video.

Saturday's Heroes. Directed by Edward Killy. RKO Radio Pictures. Motion picture, 1937.

Hero for a Day. Directed by Harold Young. Universal Pictures. Motion picture, 1939.

The Heart Is the Teacher
Memoir

By: Leonard Covello

Date: 1958

Source: Covello, Leonard, with Guido D'Agostino. *The Heart Is the Teacher.* New York: McGraw-Hill, 1958. Excerpted in *The Work of Teachers in America: A Social History Through Stories.* Rosetta Marantz Cohen and Samuel Scheer, eds. Mahwah, N.J.: Erlbaum, 1997, 216–221.

About the Author: Leonard Covello (1887–1982) came to America with his family from Italy at the age of eight. He was a teacher, advocate for the Italian American community,

and proponent of the inclusion of Italian in the curriculum alongside other modern languages. He received a bachelor's degree from Columbia University and later earned a Ph.D. from New York University. As a high school teacher and principal, Covello was actively involved in the lives of his students and their families and communities. ■

Introduction

Prior to the 1880s, most immigrants who came to the United States were from Northern Europe—mainly England, Ireland, Germany, and Scandinavia. After this date, increasing numbers of new arrivals were from Southern and Eastern Europe. By 1900, these groups made up the majority of the foreign-born entering the country. This latter group, originating mainly from Italy, Austria-Hungary, and Russia, differed from the first wave of immigrants in that they were more likely to be Roman Catholic and illiterate in their own language. While the Northern European immigrants headed for farms in the interior of the country, those from Southern and Eastern Europe tended to form insulated communities, or ghettoes, within the urban areas of the Northeast. Because these tightly knit communities enabled immigrants to retain their own languages and customs, they did not assimilate into American society as quickly as had previous immigrants.

These trends in immigration coincided with, and possibly contributed to, a post–World War I (1914–1918) period of heightened nationalism, patriotism, and nativism accompanied by a climate promoting fear of anything foreign or unfamiliar. Many native-born Northern European Protestants were apprehensive about the large numbers of Catholics entering the country. Others felt that the values, beliefs, and lifestyles of the latest newcomers were too different from American culture. In 1922, a member of the Daughters of the American Revolution asked, "What can you expect of the Americanism of the man whose breath always reeks of garlic?" It seemed to many as if the American way of life was in jeopardy.

It was in this context that American schools faced the challenge of educating the vast numbers of new immigrant children. Charged by the public with the task of assimilating these students, educators responded in different ways. For most, the answer was to eradicate all vestiges of the old culture and replace it with American values, beliefs, customs, and language. These educators encouraged students to speak English only, and lamented the presence of foreign languages spoken by students' families at home. They argued that students needed to learn to read, speak, and write English in order to be successful in their new culture; allowing students to continue to speak their native language would slow or permanently damage this process. In addition, "English-only" policies were motivated by a concern for the country as a whole—

large numbers of non-English speaking people threatened the unity of the nation.

Significance

Leonard Covello's work to include the Italian language as a curricular option for the children of Italian immigrants represents a significant minority viewpoint within the context of the time. While bilingual education was viewed by many as slowing the Americanization process and furthering the segregation of ethnic groups, the proponents of cultural pluralism advocated including students' language of origin in the curriculum. Covello's approach, while not widely adopted at the time, was an important alternative that encouraged students to retain connections with their culture of origin while at the same time learning to make their way successfully in their new country. Covello modeled this approach in his own life. Highly successful within the context of American education, he also maintained life-long ties to Italian culture.

In the early twenty-first century, as immigration again reaches high levels, the same issues confront Americans. Covello's approach prefigured what has become referred to as "multiculturalism" or "education for diversity." Though it is far more popular than in the 1920s, there remain important objections to multiculturalism, including bilingual education, in the schools: Are students slower to learn English if they are instructed even part of the school day in their first language? Does encouraging students to retain significant aspects of their original culture exacerbate existing racial and ethnic tensions? If the United States is more of a "salad bowl" than a "melting pot," what effect does this have on its citizens' sense of being a unified country?

Primary Source

The Heart Is the Teacher

> **SYNOPSIS:** In this excerpt from his memoir, Leonard Covello describes his efforts to make Italian part of the high school curriculum on an equal footing with other modern languages. He views his advocacy for bilingual education as an important part of his overall concern for the student within the context of his family, culture, and community.

In September, 1920, I again stepped into a classroom and looked into the faces of about twenty-five boys who formed my first class in Italian at De Witt Clinton, perhaps the only Italian class in any public school in the country at that time. Our efforts and struggles prior to the war had succeeded, and there was a deep satisfaction in this achievement. Surely the language and culture of Italy held a place beside that of France, Germany, or Spain. Surely the

student from the lower or upper East Side had a right to that spiritual lift that comes from knowing that the achievements of one's people have been recognized.

For this basic belief those of us who espoused this simple cause were often criticized by fellow teachers and by the general public. They argued that we were keeping the boys "foreigners." The boys were in America now and should use English exclusively. I was myself accused of "segregating" my students, and more than once by Italian-Americans themselves. The war had strengthened the idea of conformity. Americanization meant the casting off of everything that was "alien," especially the language and culture of national origin. Yet the amazing paradox lay in the fact that it was perfectly all right for the Italo-American boy to study Latin or French, German or Spanish.

Fortunately, at De Witt Clinton, we had the approval of Dr. Francis H. Paul, the principal, who was sympathetic with our point of view. It was he who had made the *Circolo* possible in the first place and who had later approved the introduction of the teaching of Italian.

Dr. Paul called me into his office one day not long after my return and spoke about the problem of the rapidly increasing number of students of Italian origin now coming to Clinton from all over the city. "These boys are not easy to handle," he said, sitting on the edge of his desk. "To put it bluntly, it will be your job to look after these boys. I will see to it that your schedule is changed so that you will have time to take care of them. In short, Leonard, from now on I want you to be the father-confessor of these East Side boys."

In an out-of-the-way corner of the De Witt Clinton building, I found a small room that was being used as a stock room. Together with some of my students I spent several Saturdays cleaning and painting and putting it in shape for an office. The room had a very narrow window and just enough space for a desk, a few file cabinets, some chairs, and a mimeographing machine. It wasn't much of an office, but it was good enough for a beginning. It was good enough for the first office of the first Italian Department in the public schools of New York City.

In this two-by-four office I held conferences, handled disciplinary problems, interviewed parents, and planned our work. For the very first time in my experience as a teacher I began to have a feeling of inner satisfaction which rose from the knowledge that here was a job that I really wanted to do. All my thoughts about a professorship or becoming a medical school doctor faded, never to be revived. No longer was I merely teaching a language or a subject. Here I was grappling with *all* the problems affecting the boys coming to me for help.

Often I would be working in my office, late in the afternoon, and a knock would come on the door, hesitant, reluctant, and I would know at once that it was another of my boys coming to me for help or advice. When the knock came during school hours I could almost be sure it had to do with a school problem. But when it sounded out of the stillness of the deserted corridors, I could be equally sure that the problem was a personal one.

At this moment I can still see Joe D'Angelo sitting in my chair near my desk. He was a tall boy, weighing about one hundred and eighty pounds, dressed in a new suit and carrying a derby. To make it easier for him to talk I kept my eyes on the narrow knot of his tie while he fumbled to explain why he had come. He was going to a party. His companions were waiting for him outside the school. "I had to see you first, Mr. Covello. I gotta get this thing off my chest. It's the old man. He keeps hittin' me all the time. No matter what I say or do he's gotta start cloutin' me. He's a big guy and he works on the docks, and it hurts, and I can't stand it no more."

"If he really hurts you . . . ," I started to say.

Joe D'Angelo shook his head. "That's not it." He held out a bony fist across the desk for my observation. "What he don't know is I've been fighting around the Jersey clubs a lot under the name of Kid Angel. I'm pretty good. That's what he don't know. If I hit him I could put him in the hospital. That's what I'm scared of. It's gonna happen and it would kill my mother."

After a silence I said, "How is it you never told them at home about the boxing?"

"Because ever since I was a little kid my mother has been telling everybody that I was going to be a lawyer."

"While you want to be a fighter?"

"No. I want to be a lawyer. But I make a couple of bucks in these club matches. I get a kick out of it, and I don't have to work in a store or a factory after school. Only thing is, I could never make them believe it."

I sent Joe off to his party and told him to spend the night with his uncle who lived in the Bronx.

Then I took the subway downtown to the "Little Italy" of Greenwich Village. The D'Angelo family lived in one of those red brick tenements on Mac-Dougal Street. As I entered the downstairs hall and caught the odor of garlic and tomato sauce, I felt right at home. Pappa D'Angelo himself, clad in his undershirt, answered the door. He was short, with heavy shoulders and a gray moustache, and an iron-gray stubble of hair covered his head and became a mattress of gray on his chest. He looked at me, wiped his mouth with a bright, checkered napkin, and was about to slam the door in my face. When he caught the name De Witt Clinton, his manner changed.

"*Perdona!* Scuse me, please. I think you was selling piano or something." He gently took hold of my arm and ushered me inside, directly into the kitchen. "Ninitta," he said to the middle-aged woman seated at the table. "Get up. Get one more plate. Is the teacher from the school where Joe go. Clintona." Suddenly he stopped dead. "Is Joe?" he shouted. "What he do? He do something bad? That why you here? I kill him! I break all the bones in his head!"

The mother started to cover her face with her hands in anticipation of some terrible calamity. I took hold of the father's arm and, wagging my free hand in a characteristic Italian gesture, at the same time speaking in the Neapolitan dialect, said, "Who said anything about Joe being a bad boy? Joe is a good boy. He is a very good student."

When both father and mother got over the staggering fact that I could not only speak Italian but could even speak the dialect, they made me sit down and eat a dish of sausage and peppers. "It is an honor. You will do us a great honor, Signor Maestro," Pappa D'Angelo insisted, in the most flowery language at his command. "Also a glass of wine. A gentle glass of wine made with my own hands. So he is a good student, Giuseppe? And good he should be." He extended a massive paw. "With this instrument I have taught him right from wrong. Respect for his elders. For those who instruct him in the school. In the old tradition. In this way he will become educated and become a lawyer and not work on the docks like his father."

"Exactly," I agreed, rolling a mouthful of wine over my tongue. "It is just that I have come to see you about. Giuseppe is getting too big. You have to handle him differently, now."

"I have been telling him this again and again," the mother broke in.

"Quiet," Pappa D'Angelo said. "Where is the harm in a father correcting his son? This is something new. Something American. I have heard of it but I do not understand. Only this very evening I had to give Giuseppe a lesson in economy. A derby! Imagine, a boy buying and wearing a derby. To go to work in a factory!"

"With me," I said, "it was shiny shoes with buttons. Besides it was his own money—money he earned with his own hands."

"Which changes nothing at all."

"But which makes for impatience and loss of temper. He is getting too old for you to knock him around. He is afraid that one day he is going to forget himself and hurt you. That is what he is afraid of."

It was a joke. Pappa D'Angelo started to laugh. He downed a full glass of wine and heaved his powerful chest. "Ha, ha. Now he thinks he can lick his pappa." He slammed his fist down on the table. "Wait he come home, I show him. I show him who the boss in this house, lilla snotnose!" All of a sudden he was so mad at his son again that he could only talk the language of the docks.

"Wait a minute," I said. "Calm down. Do you know what kind of work your son does when he is not at school? Do you know how he makes the money that he gives you here at home and that paid for the derby?"

I told them as simply as I could that their son was not working in a factory but was making money as a prize fighter.

The father did not get it right away. "A fighter," he asked, "with the hands?"

"With the hands. A boxer. I have been told that even though he is very young, he is good. He would have a future as a fighter. But Joe does not want to be a fighter. He fights so that he can earn money to be a lawyer. But he is afraid when you beat him that someday he is going to forget you are his father."

"*Madonna!*" the mother breathed.

Pappa D'Angelo rocked his head. After a while, as if this were not enough, he scratched it furiously. He looked at me sheepishly. He started to smile. The smile broadened into a grin.

"That lilla sonamangonia!" he said.

That was my encounter with the D'Angelo family. There were so many others in those days that sometimes it seems as if I spent almost as much time in the homes of my students as I did at the

school. There was Nick Barone, who didn't show up in class for a couple of days. He worked on an ice wagon after school, and one of the big ice blocks toppled over and smashed his hand, landing him in the hospital. Nick had spoken to me about his parents. They could speak no English at all and both mother and father worked at home doing stitching and needle piece work for the garment industry— the common exploitation of the time. They had little or no contact at all with the outside world.

The Barone family lived in the Italian section around 28th Street and Second Avenue. I went there after school and found the small tenement flat in a state of turmoil—crowded with neighbors, and the mother and father carrying on so that I thought for sure Nick had passed away. When I was finally able to make them understand who I was, both parents grabbed my hands, imploring me to save Nick before it was too late.

"He will die there," the father lamented. "Everyone knows what goes on in a hospital—the last stage before the grave. A soul could die in a torment of thirst and no one would lift a finger to bring you a glass of water."

"Old superstitions about hospitals," I sought to explain; "stories from the old country when distances were great and knowledge of medicine limited and the patient almost always died before reaching the hospital. It is different now."

"But we could take such wonderful care of him at home here," the mother entreated. "I could cook him a chicken, make him broth and pastina and food to get well. The good Lord knows what they will feed him there, if anything."

After I had managed to calm them somewhat, I had both the mother and father put on their best clothes and I took them to the hospital, where up until now they had not dared to go. We found Nick sitting up in bed, joking with a nurse and having a gay time with his companions in the ward. When one of the interns even spoke to them in Italian, their attitude changed to one of great wonderment.

On the way home from the hospital the father turned to me with an expression of guilt and deep embarrassment. "You must forgive us. There are many things here we know nothing about. It is hard to change old ideas and the way we think even though we see the changes every day in our children."

He shook his head. "If only everybody in the world could speak the same tongue, then perhaps things would not be quite so hard to understand."

And the more I came into contact with the family life of my boys, the more I became aware of the vital importance of language in the double orientation—to family and to community—of the immigrant child.

Though Italian was now being taught as a first language in De Witt Clinton, it was not being taught as a first language in other high schools. A student could study Italian only after he had had a year of Latin, French, or Spanish. We determined to do what was necessary—have the Board of Education of New York City pass a by-law placing Italian on an equal footing with the other languages.

The campaign to accomplish this involved civic leaders, interested citizens, and members of the Italian Teachers Association, particularly Professor Mario E. Cosenza of City College, who was president of this association for many years.

We invited parents to entertainments at which our students put on plays in Italian, we publicized the campaign in the Italian newspapers, and we had conferences at the Board of Education. The most effective part of the campaign was the home visits that we made—speaking to the individual parents about signing petitions to introduce Italian in a particular school.

How many homes I entered at this period where I had to guide a trembling hand in the signing of an "X"! How many cups of coffee I drank, jet black with just a speck of sugar, while explaining our purpose. The parents were usually astonished that they should be consulted in the matter of what was to be taught to their children. They couldn't believe the schools were really interested in their opinion.

"Signor Maestro, we are people who never had any education. In Italy we worked in the fields from when the sun came up in the morning until it went down at night. In America we work, but we hope that with our children it will be different. That is why we came to America. But do not ask us to decide things we know nothing about."

Our visits usually turned into a lesson in democracy, trying to make the immigrant understand his rights and privileges. "Would you prefer your son to study Italian, or some other foreign language?"

"What a question! Naturally, we prefer him to study our own language. But *real* Italian. Italian as you speak it, Signor Maestro—the Italian of our great men, of Garibaldi."

In May, 1922, through our work and the help of Salvatore Cotillo, New York State Senator elected by the East Harlem community, the Board of Education placed Italian on an equal footing with other languages in the schools of New York City.

I had longed for the day when I would have just one class in Italian to teach. Never did I imagine that in the space of a few years there would be hundreds of boys studying Italian at Clinton—and that there would be five teachers in the Italian Department.

Further Resources

BOOKS

Castellanos, Diego, with Pamela Leggio. *The Best of Two Worlds: Bilingual-Bicultural Education in the U.S.* Trenton, N.J.: New Jersey State Department of Education, 1983.

Crawford, James. *Bilingual Education: History, Politics, Theory, and Practice.* Trenton, N.J.: Crane, 1989.

Cremin, Lawrence A. *The Transformation of the School: Progressivism in American Education, 1876–1957.* New York: Knopf, 1961.

Glazer, Nathan, and Daniel Patrick Moynihan. *Beyond the Melting Pot: The Negroes, Puerto Ricans, Jews, Italians, and Irish of New York City.* Cambridge, Mass.: M.I.T. Press, 1970.

Lintelman, Joy K. *The Go-Betweens: The Lives of Immigrant Children.* Minneapolis: University Art Museum, University of Minnesota, 1986.

Peebles, Robert Whitney. *Leonard Covello: A Study of an Immigrant's Contribution to New York City.* New York: Arno Press, 1968.

Perrone, Vito. *Teacher With a Heart: Reflections on Leonard Covello and Community.* New York: Teachers College Press, 1998.

PERIODICALS

Covello, Leonard. "Interview with Leonard Covello." *Urban Review* 3, January 1969.

WEBSITES

"Immigration History Research Center." University of Minnesota. Available online at http://www1.umn.edu/ihrc/; website home page: http://www1.umn.edu/ (accessed March 12, 2003).

4

FASHION AND DESIGN

ALICE WU

Entries are arranged in chronological order by date of primary source. For entries with one primary source, the entry title is the same as the primary source title. Entries with more than one primary source have an overall entry title, followed by the titles of the primary sources.

Important Events in Fashion and Design, 1920–1929

1920

- Women's hems range from ankle length to calf length.

- A new three-button sports coat in cartridge cloth—the fabric used to hold powder charges during World War I—becomes a predecessor of the light-weight men's summer suit.

- Architect Addison Mizner constructs Palm Beach, Florida, Spanish-style mansions with exotic names (Villa de Sarmiento, El Mirasol) for such millionaires as A. J. Drexel Biddle, George and Isabel Dodge, and Harold S. Vanderbilt.

- John Manning Van Heusen introduces a semi-stiff three-ply detached collar.

- In New York City Raymond H. Dietrich and Thomas L. Hibbard found LeBaron Carrossiers, an "automotive architecture" firm.

- Men's suits with two pairs of pants become popular.

- On February 16, James H. Sherburne, chairman of a Massachusetts state commission, reports that working-class purchases of silk stockings and other "long-desired luxuries" have contributed to a 92 percent boost in the cost of living in the state since 1914.

- In September, Henry M. Leland introduces the Model L Lincoln, which he envisions as a "permanent car," so well made that it will never wear out or fail.

1921

- Jantzen presents a clinging knit one-piece bathing suit in men's and women's styles. Advertized as "the suit that changed bathing to swimming," it features a scoop-necked, sleeveless tunic attached to trunks and is decorated with stripes at the chest, hips, and thighs.

- High-buttoned shoes for men are replaced by oxfords, low-cut shoes that tie.

- Men's wristwatches become popular.

- Belted Norfolk jackets worn with either flannel slacks or knickers are popular sportswear for younger men.

- Among dress accessories for men are spats and canes.

- The Duesenberg Automobile and Motor Company introduces the Model A Duesenberg, the first U.S. straight-eight and first U.S. automobile with overhead camshaft and hydraulic brakes.

- On March 4, Warren G. Harding arrives at his inauguration in a Packard Twin-Six; he is the first president-elect to ride in an automobile to inaugural ceremonies.

- In May, construction begins on Chicago's Wrigley Building, which has a thirty-two-story tower and 442,000 square feet of office space; completed in 1924, its architects are Graham, Anderson, Probst, and White.

1922

- Architectural delineator Hugh Ferriss executes and publishes his influential drawings of the four stages of skyscraper construction.

- The Ford Motor Company buys the Lincoln Motor Company from Henry M. Leland, who had also founded Cadillac in 1903; Edsel Ford, Henry Ford's son, plans to develop the Lincoln as Ford's luxury car.

- German architect Ludwig Mies van der Rohe introduces "ribbon windows"—glass evenly divided by concrete slabs—in plans for an office building; Mies van der Rohe later will use this style of window in many of his European and American buildings.

- Dr. Lulu Hunt Peters's *Diet and Health with Key to the Calories* (1918) appears on the best-seller lists, where it will remain through 1926; for two years—1924 and 1925—it heads the nonfiction list.

- The Prince of Wales wears a Fair Isles sweater with knickers while playing golf at St. Andrews, Scotland, and starts a rage in America and Europe for these brightly colored, patterned wool sweaters.

- The women's "slouch" suit, with jacket bloused over a hip-level belt, becomes popular.

- On May 5, Coco Chanel introduces Chanel No. 5, which will become the world's best-known perfume.

- On May 30, the Lincoln Memorial, styled as a Greek Doric temple, is dedicated; the building has been designed by architect Henry Bacon, and the statue of the seated Lincoln has been sculpted by Daniel Chester French.

- In July, *Fruit, Garden and Home* is first published as a monthly magazine by Edwin Thomas Meredith in Des Moines, Iowa. In August 1924, it is renamed *Better Homes & Gardens,* and by 1928 it becomes the first magazine to achieve one million in circulation without featuring fiction or fashions.

- On December 23, a Gothic-style plan by John Mead Howells and Raymond M. Hood is announced as the winner of the international competition for the design of Col. Robert R. McCormick's Chicago Tribune Tower; the second-place design is by Finland's Eliel Saarinen. Response to the Saarinen's losing design causes him to emigrate to the U.S., where his entry influences the design of the Empire State Building, the Chysler Building, the Daily News Building, and Rockefeller Center.

- Charles F. Kettering develops fast-drying Duco lacquer, which brings color to mass-produced cars.

- The "cake-eater's suit" is adopted by many noncollegiate young men.

- Ida Cohen Rosenthal founds the Maiden Form Brassiere Company, later renamed Maidenform.

- The "shingle" cut—an extremely short hairstyle with a single curl pulled forward from each ear onto each cheek—is increasingly seen in Europe and the United States.

- Felt cloche hats that are pulled down low on the forehead and feature small, slightly upturned brims in front and back are gaining popularity in Paris and America. The cloche is the perfect hat for the shingle cut.

- Artificial silk (rayon) stockings, often seamless and flesh-colored, are being worn with shorter skirts.

- The excavation of King Tutankhamen's tomb, which began in late 1922, produces a rage for "Egyptian" accessories.

- The upscale Bergdorf Goodman women's fashion store opens a ready-to-wear department at its original Fifth Avenue location.

- On February 22, the first successful U.S. chinchilla farm—which has seven males and four females—is established in Los Angeles.

- In June, Packard introduces its popular Single-Eight motor car.

1924

- Architect Louis H. Sullivan publishes his influential book *The Autobiography of an Idea.*

- Lewis Mumford publishes his architectural study *Sticks and Stones: A Study of American Architecture and Civilization.*

- Henry Wright and Clarence S. Stein begin constructing the first of their planned communities, Sunnyside Gardens (completed in 1928) in Queens, New York; in 1928, they start work on a second "garden community," Radburn, New Jersey.

- Women adopt dramatic accessories, including long strings of pearls draped over the shoulders and bracelets circling the biceps.

- Heavy makeup and plucked, redrawn eyebrows are popular with women.

- Raymond Hood's black-and-gold American Radiator Building is completed in New York City.

- Loew's State Theater, one of Thomas W. Lamb's most famous "hard-top" movie palaces, opens in Saint Louis.

- Men adopt blue blazers and round-toed oxfords.

- Double-breasted suits worn with vests and bow ties remain popular with men.

- Macy's, one of the country's best-known retailers of men's and women's ready-to-wear fashions, completes an addition to its 34th Street building. Further additions in 1928 and 1931 take up all but two small corners of the city block between Broadway and Seventh Avenue, making Macy's the world's largest department store under one roof. The store boasts two million square feet of floor space.

- Elsa Maxwell is hired as a press agent for couturier Jean Patou.

- On August 29, Edward, Prince of Wales, arrives in New York; he charms the country and continues to exert a strong influence on men's fashion in Europe and America.

- In September, Gimbel Brothers opens an upscale clothing store, Saks & Company, later to be called Saks Fifth Avenue.

- Addison Mizner begins construction of Boca Raton, but his plans for the city are abandoned when the Florida real-estate market collapses in spring 1926.

- In fall, Jean Patou imports six American girls to help model fashions in his Paris couture house.

1925

- Chanel introduces her short, open, collarless cardigan jacket as part of her Chanel suit.

- Skirts rise to knee length.

- Oxford bags—voluminous pants—are adopted by American college men.

- Antoine de Paris opens a hair salon at Saks Fifth Avenue.

- Tans for women become popular, as do skin lotions and moisturizers.

- Inlaid and embossed linoleums are introduced.

- In Chicago, the Tribune Tower, designed by John Mead Howells and Raymond Hood, is completed; it is one of the most eclectic skyscrapers ever built. The 1922 competition for its design stipulated only that the building be the "world's most beautiful office building."

- For the first time, more American men wear attached-collar shirts than wear detached-collar ones.

- Raymond H. Dietrich leaves LeBaron, Inc., and founds Dietrich, Inc., an automobile-custom-design firm in Detroit.

- Four-piece knickerbocker suits—knickers, jacket, vest, and traditional trousers—are widely sold.

- On July 18, the Exposition Internationale des Arts Décoratifs et Industriels Modernes opens in Paris.

1926

- The cocktail dress becomes popular as speakeasy attire for women.

- French tennis player René Lacoste introduces the knit, short-sleeved Lacoste tennis or polo shirt with a crocodile emblem on the chest.

- New York's monumental Standard Oil Building, designed by Carrère and Hastings, is completed.

- Construction begins on William Van Alen's Chrysler Building (completed in 1930); this graceful New York City skyscraper becomes an embodiment of both Art Deco style and 1920s American exuberance.

- Chanel introduces the "little black dress," which *Vogue* labels "a Ford," a serviceable, enduring success.

- On February 19, the ballet *Skyscrapers,* scored by John Alden and commissioned by Sergei Diaghilev, premieres at the Metropolitan Opera House. The ballet uses jazz idiom to celebrate the most significant development in metropolitan architecture during the 1920s.

1927

- The Avalon, the greatest of John Eberson's "atmospheric" movie palaces, opens in Chicago.

- *Toward a New Architecture,* an English translation of Le Corbusier's *Vers une architecture* (1923), is published in New York.

- Elsa Schiaparelli makes her fashion debut with her trompe l'oeil (optical illusion) sweater.

- General Motors adds an Art and Colour Section, which is headed by the young automotive designer Harley J. Earl; it is the first styling department established by an American automobile company.

- Grauman's Chinese Theater (architects Meyer, designer Raymond Kennedy), one of the legendary American movie palaces, opens in Hollywood.

- On March 11, the Roxy Theater, the "Cathedral of the Motion Picture," opens at Seventh Avenue and 50th Street in New York City with the premiere of Gloria Swanson's *The Love of Sunya.* The creation of Samuel L. Rothafel (Roxy), it is the most lavish of American movie palaces.

- On May 25, Henry Ford announces that the Model A Ford will be produced and the Model T discontinued. Ford assembly lines begin manufacturing the new automobiles in October, and the first Model A display cars appear in November.

1928

- Architect R. Buckminster Fuller introduces his prefabricated Dymaxion House, a hexagonal module suspended from a central utility mast with outer walls of glass.

- The Packard, the most popular of the American luxury cars, achieves sales of fifty thousand.

- Fashion designer Hattie Carnegie opens a dress shop on East 49th Street in New York City.

- Hollywood costume designer Adrian introduces the slouch hat, which will supplant the cloche, in the Greta Garbo movie *A Woman of Affairs.*

- The trench coat and the similar French aviator coat replace the long yellow slicker as favorite rain wear on Ivy League campuses.

- The Model A Ford is offered in a wood-sided station-wagon version, the first large-scale production of this type of automobile body.

- The Model BB Splendid Stutz is introduced.

- The Designers' Gallery Show, which tours ten major American cities, displays modernistic designs.

- On January 1, the Milam Building, the first air-conditioned office building in the United States, opens in San Antonio, Texas.

- On December 1, the Model J Duesenberg, one of America's most spectacular automobiles, is introduced at the New York Automobile Salon.

1929

- Built-in furniture becomes popular.

- German architect Mies van der Rohe premieres the Barcelona chair at the Barcelona Fair. This chair features curved steel legs and back supports topped by leather-covered foam-rubber cushions.

- *Middletown: A Study in American Culture,* by Robert S. Lynd and Helen Merrell Lynd, is published. Among the subjects it treats are the tastes in homes, clothing, and automobiles of the citizens of Middletown (actually Muncie, Indiana).

- Construction begins on Shreve, Lamb, and Harmon's Empire State Building in New York City; the tallest building in the world, it is completed in 1931.

- Ground is broken for Raymond Hood's modernist McGraw-Hill Building, which is finished in 1932.

- Howe and Lescaze's Philadelphia Savings Fund Society Building (completed in 1932) is under construction; it is an early expression of International Style in America.

- During this year, American women purchase an average of one pound of powder and eight rouge compacts apiece.

- Hugh Ferriss's visionary *The Metropolis of Tomorrow* is published.

- The United States has 377 skyscrapers that are more than twenty stories high; 188 of them are in New York City.

- In February, the Metropolitan Museum of Art opens its Contemporary American Decorative Arts Show, displaying modernist rooms by five major American designers.

- Jean Patou's spring show restores the natural waistline and bustline to women's dresses.

- In his fall show, Patou drops skirt lengths. His 1929 shows are credited with killing the "garçonne"—or "little boy"—look and with ushering in the dominant style in women's fashion during the 1930s.

Young Men's Fashions of the 1920s

"Shorts: A Coming Fashion"

Magazine article

By: *The Boys' Outfitter*

Date: April 1920

Source: Lovat. "Shorts: A Coming Fashion." *The Boys' Outfitter,* April 1920. Available online at http://histclo.hispeed .com/chron/c19201.html; website home page: http://histclo .hispeed.com (accessed September 27, 2002).

"My First Long Pants"

Memoir

By: Julius Raskin

Date: 1998

Source: Raskin, Julius. "My First Long Pants." 1998. Available online at http://histclo.hispeed.com/style/pants/long/long1.html; website home page: http://histclo.hispeed.com (accessed January 13, 2003).

About the Authors: *The Boys' Outfitter* was a trade magazine published from 1919 until 1932, when it was absorbed by another publication, *Boy's Buyer. The Boys' Outfitter* included illustrated advertisements showing the latest boys' fashions, including what boys in England and France were wearing and what trends were likely to develop in the upcoming season.

Julius Raskin (1906–1996) was born in New York. He attended college at City College of New York, where he was a star basketball player. ■

Introduction

In the 1920s, menswear was more casual than it had been in previous decades. Clothing was made from natural, easy-care fibers such as cotton and wool. Simpler clothing styles for both adults and children resulted from changes in the household routine. Before the 1920s, well-off families hired servants to assist with the chore of laundering. In the 1920s, more women entered the workforce, and immigration restrictions decreased the availability of servants. Modern, labor-saving conveniences such as electricity and running water came to most homes, and washing machines were available, making clothes that were easy to care for more appealing to the American consumer.

Although they did not undergo changes as radical as the fashions for women and girls during the decade, men's fashions of the 1920s were youth-inspired. College students became particularly influential in male fashions, since American prosperity in the 1920s resulted in a huge increase in the numbers of young men continuing their education beyond the high-school years.

Ivy League men attended "tea dances" at New York City hotels, socializing with female students, debutantes, and young actresses. Cake was often the refreshment of choice at these parties. The silhouette popularized by these young men—a narrow-shouldered suit jacket with wide-legged trousers—came to be called the "cake-eater's suit." Eventually a more extreme version of the suit, with a slope-shouldered jacket and trousers that flared like bell bottoms, was adopted by "noncollegiate types," turning the cake-eater's suit into a symbol of the "lower classes."

English styles remained the standard for the neatly dressed young man of status. By 1925, the collegiates had moved on to another extreme style, the "Oxford Bags," or "baggies." English students had adopted the style to subvert university dress codes, which forbade short pants. Oxford Bags were cropped, cuffed trousers as wide as 25 inches around the legs; they hung four inches below the knees and were worn with a short jacket. Trenchcoats were popular at this time; college men particularly favored Burberry trenchcoats, a belted, gabardine affair worn by the British officers of World War I. Edward, Prince of Wales, was also viewed as a model for young Americans. He became a style icon for his charming manner and casual but elegant dress.

Sports figures such as Bobby Jones (golf), Johnny Weissmuller (swimming), and the ubiquitous college athlete also set fashion standards for young men in the 1920s. America's admiration for its cultural heroes also was reflected in fashions of the time. Charles Lindbergh's 1927 nonstop Atlantic flight set a trend for leather driving jackets and coats.

Fashions for younger boys also changed in the 1920s. Men's fashion had long been distinct from the clothing for young boys. Now, boys' clothes became less girlish. The Little Lord Fauntleroy look of the late nineteenth century, consisting of velveteen breeches and shirts with lacy collars, was replaced by more casual knicker suits for young American boys through the teen years. Their fashions began to look more like miniature versions of adult clothing, although long pants continued to be considered men's attire.

Significance

"Shorts: A Coming Fashion" and "My First Long Pants" offer insights into the attitudes that people had towards the clothing worn for boys and young men of the 1920s.

"Shorts: A Coming Fashion" is interesting not only because it claims to predict a trend but because it also notes how the boys of the era were styling themselves. Fashion is made not only by the design of the garment, but also by how the wearer chooses to express himself—for example, by pulling his knickers below the knees. The manufacturer is likely to show how the garment is worn "properly," while the customer, the young man, is the one who actually will set the trend by the expressive manner in which he wears his clothing.

"My First Long Pants" reflects the symbolic value that long pants had in the 1920s. For the young men of the time, the change from shorts to long pants was a rite of passage, a visible sign of their transition into young adulthood.

Primary Source

"Shorts: A Coming Fashion" [excerpt]

SYNOPSIS: As the decade progressed, high-school-aged boys moved away from the knickers associated with younger boys and began wearing mostly longer, knee-length shorts before heading off to college and changing their style once more. The following article from *The Boys' Outfitter,* a menswear journal, promotes the wearing of short pants for ease of movement.

I venture to prophesy that during Nineteen Twenty we shall witness the successful introduction of short pants, otherwise known as "shorts" in boys' school and play suits. Prominent students of boys' fashions agree with my prediction. The subject is so interesting that I am giving these two pages to it alone.

Well do I remember the "shorts" of my boyhood days; tight-fitting things that bound the muscles of my thighs so that after riding a bicycle, say to Brighton Beach, I would look upon them and marvel that they did not burst apart.

But the "shorts" that have been known hereabouts in recent years are those which the Boy Scouts have as a part of their regulation outfit. They are almost as loose as running pants, but of course in khaki, and they are used for the big outdoors, being too loose and light in weight to look well for any dignified occasion.

Illustration of man in four-button Norfolk suit, popular among young men at Princeton University, December 6, 1922. **CHICAGO APPAREL GAZETTE.**

Advertisement for Carleton Clothing Co. featuring illustration of a young man in a three-button suit wearing a hat and carrying a schoolbook. April 11, 1928. CHICAGO APPAREL GAZETTE.

The "shorts" that I believe will soon appear on the market are . . . a cross between the snug-fitting pants of unhappy memory and the modern khakis of sport. The length of them is to a point just above the bend of the knee. And that, apart from the boy's fondness for easy garments, which are best adapted for romping, is one reason for heralding them as a coming fashion. The boy of today wants to wear leggings and to have his knees bare during the warmer months.

This desire has been apparent in recent summers, when many boys have worn knickers fastened above the knee and leggings, though the two clearly do not go well together. Knees bend easier when there's nothing on them, you know, and that's what boys' knees are doing most of the time during waking hours. . . .

One particular reason why I am glad to see this new mode in the making is that the way the older boys wear their knickers nowadays is getting on my nerves. It seems that in the peculiar code of their clan, "only kids wear their knickers fastened below the knees." The older boys pull them down below the knees, making an unsightly effect for which they were never intended. The new "shorts" will remove this practice for all time—I hope.

Primary Source

"My First Long Pants"

SYNOPSIS: In this personal essay, Julius "Tubby" Raskin (1906–1996), a native New Yorker, recalled the first summer that he dressed like a man, and the new activities for which he wore his new "uniform."

History records the introduction of bobbed hair in 1921 as a milestone in women's liberation. But the archives neglect an emancipation epic of equal moment that year: my discard of knee pants, long underwear, suspenders, and high button shoes, for the long pants and accessories to which becoming 16 years old now enfranchised me. In those times, only on that 16th birthday did the magical moment arrive when boys dared dress like men.

Like my other clothes, my first long-pants suit was a hand-me-down from my brother. The pants were too long, the waist too wide, the jacket too small, the sleeves too short. I never raised or bent my arms to lift the trouser cuffs off the ground. But I wore that suit as proudly as if it had been tailored just for me in the most fashionable Fifth Avenue store.

Come of age, I savored a liberal sampling of life's heady pleasures. I saw Babe Ruth hit a home run at the Polo Grounds. I sat on the open upper deck of the Fifth Avenue bus, from Washington

Advertisement for "Gleneagles" new fall line of clothing for men and boys. Popular styles of the day included knickers and long pants with wide legs. July 10, 1929. **CHICAGO APPAREL GAZETTE.**

Square to Fort George, riding the length of Fifth Avenue and Riverside Drive, all New York at my feet.

I made a weekly pilgrimage to Coney Island: daredevil rides at Luna Park; at Steeplechase, the crazy mirrors and mad clowns, the hidden air jets ballooning the skirts of flustered but flattered females; Felt man's [sic] hot dogs; the carousel; corn on the cob, jelly apples; games of skill and chance.

I fancied myself a man-about-town, as my now sophisticated taste in entertainment turned from movies and vaudeville to the Broadway theater. I discovered Leblang's discount ticket agency, below

Gray's drug store, near Times Square; a real bargain basement, where seats to Broadway shows sold at half price. Then came the mad dash to the theater, imagining myself an All-American halfback, as I ran broken-field style through the streets. Every such night on Times Square was another New Year's Eve: the crush of pleasure-bound crowds, spectacular electric signs, the traffic and noises.

My first Leblang purchase was "Rain," starring Jeanne Eagels. A dramatization of the Somerset Maugham story of a South Seas prostitute, it was the sex-shocker of the times, and denounced as pornography by moralists. Its frank sex treatment alerted me to gaps in my education which I thereupon firmly resolved to eradicate by dint of conscientious field research.

I patronized the local poolroom, our neighborhood cultural center operated by the wrestling Zbysko brothers, out of which Mom dragged me regularly. Wladek and Stanislaus faced their most fearsome ring rivals with less trepidation than they did Mom's wrathful scorn, delivered in pungent Polish. I smoked and drank beer in the alley of our tenement house.

A reckless adventurer, I survived spine-tingling rides in my uncle's new Reo car: over the Harlem Bridge, onto the practically private Boston Post Road, past the Bronx fields and farms, out into the open country to the uncharted reaches of the Connecticut wilderness.

Irresolute signs of maturity began to assert themselves. I nursed with tender solicitude the vagrant facial hairs which sprouted weed-like in forlorn loneliness. My voice fluttered unpredictably between basso and soprano. The geometry of girls mesmerized me. My despisement of the boys who talked to them, pariahs until now, began to yield to grudging envy.

Girls had always been as repugnant as relatives. Although still scornful of the illogic of their ways, I no longer crossed to the other side or pretended not to see them when they came down the street. Their presence had acquired a bewildering power to dry my throat, muddle my speech, quicken my pulse, shorten my breath, and befuddle my brain.

Sunday afternoon parties with the girls replaced the sacred traditional game of box-ball with the boys. Ostensibly, we socialized: We gave imitations of our favorite movie and vaudeville performers; we danced in the delicious semi-embrace of the long-ago style to music which pleasured the ear with melodies one could remember, sing, and whistle—another world from the frenetic gyrations of the tribal calisthenics called social dancing today, and the deafening yawp of rock-and-roll called music.

But the real agenda of those Sunday seances were the kissing games: spin-the-bottle and post office. I kissed the girls and—rapture sublime—was kissed back sweet times beyond counting. I applied the lessons learned from Rudolph Valentino on the screen instead of my until-then heart throb: Tom Mix and his Wonder Horse Tony.

That first long-pants suit marked the end of one life and the beginning of another. My suits since then have cost much more, and have been more fashionable. But no other rivals the special place of that first one.

Further Resources

BOOKS
Blum, Stella, ed. *Everyday Fashions of the Twenties.* New York: Dover Publications, 1981.

Burns, Leslie Davis, and Nancy C. Bryant. *The Business of Fashion.* New York: Fairchild Publications, 1997.

Chenoune, Farid. *A History of Men's Fashion.* Translated from French by Deke Dusinberre. Paris: Flammarion, 1993.

Esquire's Encyclopedia of 20th-Century Men's Fashion. New York: McGraw Hill, 1973.

Horsham, Michael. *'20s & '30s Style.* London: Quintet Publishing, 1989.

Peacock, John. *Men's Fashion: The Complete Sourcebook.* New York: Thames & Hudson, 1996.

PERIODICALS
La Ferla, Ruth. "Boys to Men: Fashion Pack Turns Younger." *The New York Times,* July 14, 2002.

The Arrow Collar Man

Arrow Collars and Shirts Advertisement

Poster

By: J.C. Leyendecker
Date: 1920s
Source: Leyendecker, J.C. Arrow Collars and Shirts Advertisement. Created for Cluett, Peabody, & Co, Inc. Library of Congress, Prints and Photographs Division. Available online at http://lcweb2.loc.gov/pp/mdbquery.html (accessed May 11, 2003).

Primary Source

Arrow Collars and Shirts Advertisement

SYNOPSIS: The Arrow Collar Man was one of the first sex symbols created to sell a product. J.C. Leyendecker succeeded in devising sensual images of the male face and form in a manner that appealed to women and men, both straight and gay, without alienating any segment of his intended audience. THE LIBRARY OF CONGRESS.

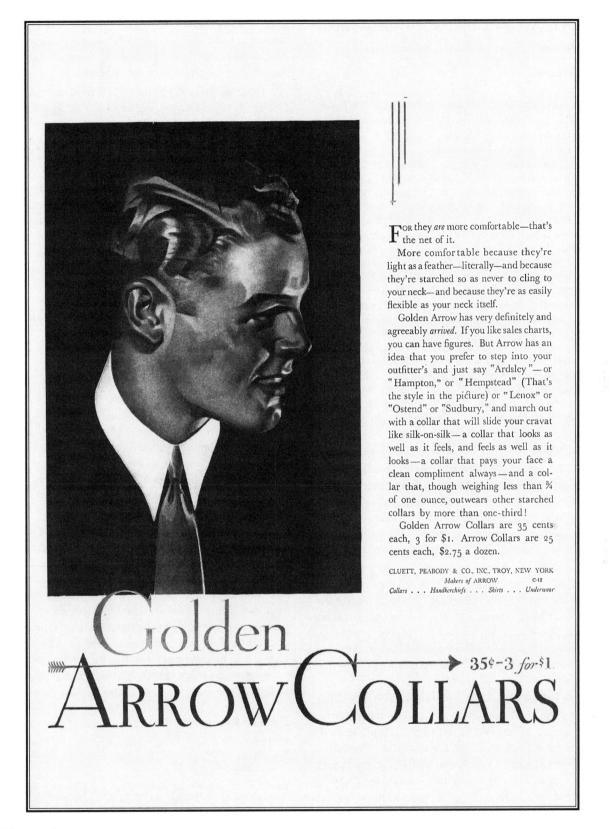

FOR they *are* more comfortable—that's the net of it.

More comfortable because they're light as a feather—literally—and because they're starched so as never to cling to your neck—and because they're as easily flexible as your neck itself.

Golden Arrow has very definitely and agreeably *arrived*. If you like sales charts, you can have figures. But Arrow has an idea that you prefer to step into your outfitter's and just say "Ardsley"—or "Hampton," or "Hempstead" (That's the style in the picture) or "Lenox" or "Ostend" or "Sudbury," and march out with a collar that will slide your cravat like silk-on-silk—a collar that looks as well as it feels, and feels as well as it looks—a collar that pays your face a clean compliment always—and a collar that, though weighing less than ¾ of one ounce, outwears other starched collars by more than one-third!

Golden Arrow Collars are 35 cents each, 3 for $1. Arrow Collars are 25 cents each, $2.75 a dozen.

CLUETT, PEABODY & CO., INC., TROY, NEW YORK
Makers of ARROW   C-12
Collars . . . Handkerchiefs . . . Shirts . . . Underwear

Golden
ARROW COLLARS

35¢-3 *for* $1

Primary Source

Golden Arrow Collars Advertisement

Golden Arrow Collars was a line of softer collars marketed to younger men who thought stiff, starched collars were out of style. THE ADVERTISING ARCHIVE LTD. REPRODUCED BY PERMISSION.

Golden Arrow Collars Advertisement

Advertisement

By: J.C. Leyendecker

Date: 1922

Source: Leyendecker, J.C. Golden Arrow Collars Advertisement. The Advertising Archive. The Kobal Collection.

About the Artist: Joseph Christian Leyendecker (1874–1951), artist and commercial illustrator, was born in Germany, and immigrated with his family to America in 1882. Upon completion of his formal schooling in 1889, Leyendecker apprenticed himself to Chicago publishers J. Manz & Co., where he was soon promoted to staff illustrator. His work received widespread attention when he won a cover illustration contest for the popular *Century Magazine* in 1898. Soon after, he was selling his illustrations to publications such as *Colliers* magazine. In 1900, Leyendecker moved to New York to be closer to the center of the publishing industry. In 1905, he began working for Cluett, Peabody Inc., the Troy, New York–based manufacturer of Arrow collars and shirts; he would lead the company's advertising efforts for nearly twenty-five years. Leyendecker also devised major advertising campaigns for the House of Kuppenheimer, another menswear designer, and for Ivory Soap and Kellogg's. His work also appeared in books and magazines—he illustrated more than 320 covers for *The Saturday Evening Post*. For nearly forty years, the *Post*'s New Year's covers featured the image of "Baby New Year," a Leyendecker creation. ■

Introduction

At the turn of the twentieth century, retailers began selling men's dress shirts separately from the collars. Detachable collars provided an economical means of adding variety to a man's wardrobe. The acquisition of detachable collars was regarded as a status symbol—it was said that a true gentleman had to have at least six.

Cluett, Peabody commissioned Leyendecker to devise an advertising campaign to help sell their detachable collars for men's shirts. Leyendecker's creation, the Arrow Collar Man, became one of the most successful advertising icons in American history, helping to make the company into the best-selling collar brand in America. His advertisements pushed annual company sales to over $32 million.

After World War I, however, men wanted a softer, more relaxed look, and high, stiff collars started to fall out of favor. By the end of the 1920s, Cluett, Peabody decided to sell whole shirts. The company adopted the advertising slogan, "Only Arrow Shirts have the famous Arrow Collar." The success of the shirts led the company to expand into other areas of menswear, including undergarments, knit shirts, and trousers.

Significance

The Arrow Collar Man became a cultural icon. Smartly dressed, dignified, and handsome, he symbolized taste, manners, and quality, and represented the ideal American male. The advertisements were paintings of actual models, and Cluett, Peabody received mountains of fan letters each time a new face debuted.

Leyendecker's first Arrow Collar Man model was Charles Beach. The two developed a relationship that lasted over forty years, until Leyendecker's death. Beach is variously described as Leyendecker's model, gardener, and secretary, although many scholars also believe that he was Leyendecker's lover and companion. In a repressive era when homosexuality was unspoken and gay culture was only in its nascent stages, J.C. Leyendecker kept an extremely low profile even as the images he created appeared everywhere. Very little documentation of his personal life remains. An intensely private person, he ordered all of his drawings and personal papers destroyed after his death. Leyendecker's paintings were designed to be mechanically reproduced, and so the originals were often discarded. As a result, Leyendecker's works became now popular collectibles.

The Arrow Collar Man represented an advertising innovation, the first use of sexually suggestive imagery to sell sundry items. Hollywood film stars Frederic March and John Barrymore, as well as now-forgotten actors such as Reed Howes, Brian Donlevy, Jack Mulhall, and Neil Hamilton, were all Arrow Collar men before they achieved their screen-idol status. Movies were just becoming more accessible to the mass market, and to the public, the new screen idols were simply extensions of the popular images of male sexuality readily available to the adoring public through the print media.

Leyendecker's career and the popularity of the Arrow Collar Man both reached their pinnacles in the 1920s. The Arrow Collar Man was such an advertising success that the 1923 musical play, *Helen of Troy, New York,* featured him as its main subject. Written by George S. Kaufman and Marc Connolly, two of Broadway's most prominent playwrights at the time, the play satirizes the emergence of the new corporate culture pervading American life. The advertisement for the show featured a young woman gazing longingly at a picture of the Arrow Collar Man.

Further Resources

BOOKS

Pitz, Henry C. *200 Years of American Illustration.* New York: Random House, 1977.

Reed, Walt, and Roger Reed. *The Illustrator in America: 1880–1980.* New York: Madison Square Press, 1984.

Schau, Michael. *J. C. Leyendecker.* New York: Watson-Guptill Publications, 1974.

PERIODICALS

Kriss, Gary. "The Father of the New Year's Baby." *New York Times,* December 27, 1998.

Martin, Richard. "American Chronicle: J.C. Leyendecker's Icons of Time." *Journal of American Culture,* Spring 1996, 57–85.

Martin, Richard. "J.C. Leyendecker and the Homoerotic Invention of Men's Fashion Icons, 1910–1930." *Prospects: An Annual Journal of American Cultural Studies* 21, 1996, 453–470.

Pettinga, Steve. "In Celebration of Cherubs: J.C. Leyendecker's *Saturday Evening Post* Covers." *The Saturday Evening Post* 267, Jan.–Feb. 1995, 56–61.

WEBSITES

"J.C. Leyendecker: A Retrospective." *The Norman Rockwell Museum.* Available online at http:www.tfaoi.com/newsmu /nmus21b.htm; website home page: http://www.nrm.org (accessed January 13, 2003).

AUDIO AND VISUAL MEDIA

J.C. Leyendecker: The Great American Illustrator. Kultur Home Video, 2002, VHS.

Egyptian Influence on Fashion

"They Watch Egypt for Fashion News"

Newspaper article

By: *The New York Times*

Date: February 18, 1923

Source: "They Watch Egypt for Fashion News." *The New York Times,* February 18, 1923, 3.

"Egypt Dominates Fashion Show Here"; Shoecraft Advertisement

Newspaper article, advertisement

By: *The New York Times*

Date: February 25, 1923

Source: "Egypt Dominates Fashion Show Here," Shoecraft Advertisement. *The New York Times,* February 25, 1923, 12, 15.

Notes About the Publication: Founded in 1850 as the *Daily Times, The New York Times* was originally a relatively obscure local paper. By the early twentieth century, however, it had grown into a widely known, widely read news source. Its banner, "All the News That's Fit to Print," is recognized across the United States and throughout the world. ∎

Introduction

The Egyptian craze that swept 1920s fashion was fueled by newspaper coverage of the latest treasures unearthed from King Tut's tomb. American designers in particular were quick to incorporate Egyptian motifs; within months, they created entire collections based on the Egyptian look.

The Tut influence was seen throughout the design world. In fashion it affected everything from textile prints to dress silhouettes. Shoe designers were inspired by the variety of materials used in the fragments of the ancient Egyptian sandals, and soon (as the *Times* predicted) sandals became a trend. Jewelry made with lapis lazuli, turquoise, and carnelian became popular, too. Furniture designers adapted Egyptian scarab, sphinx, falcon, and floral imagery to embellish sleek, streamlined furniture. Graphic artists imitated the Egyptian tomb paintings' use of bold outlines and repetitions of simple geometric patterns, as demonstrated by the design of many newspaper advertisements of the time.

Significance

The Tut craze marked the first time designers responded so unanimously to a contemporary world event. American designers were particularly keen on exploiting the fad for all things Egyptian as another "weapon" against the dominance of Parisian fashion. In numerous newspaper interviews, American garment and textile industry spokespersons proudly declared that Paris was too slow to catch on to the public's desire for the Egyptian look.

The exaggeratedly elongated limbs of the Egyptian tomb paintings appealed to the fashionable public, which then favored the slim and boyish look of the flapper. Dresses of this era streamlined the female silhouette, using fewer lines and solid forms to de-emphasize the body's natural curves. The Egyptian look was in tune with this trend, and many of the Tut-inspired designs consisted of sleeveless barrel-shaped dresses that simply slipped over the head, usually made in flowing materials. TJ Mitchell and Co., a silk manufacturing company, even trademarked the name "Luxor Silk" and promoted its use for manufacturing underclothes.

By looking to the ancients, designers of the day were inspired to create a modern, minimalist look for the design-conscious consumer. Even as the public's interest in the tomb discoveries waned within the following seasons, the Egyptian influence left its indelible imprint on the look of clothing, jewelry, furniture, and graphic design of the 1920s.

Primary Source

"They Watch Egypt for Fashion News" [excerpt]

SYNOPSIS: Newspaper coverage of the discovery of the tomb of Tutankhamen sparked worldwide interest in all things Egyptian. In addition to the latest news on the archeological excavation, *The New York Times* was soon running reports about Egyptian influences on American fashion. This one was published on February 18, 1923.

Nobody is watching the revelations from the tomb of Tut-ankh-Ahmen with greater interest than the designers and costumers, according to J.M. Gidding of J.M. Gidding & Co., who said yesterday that every great Egyptian collection in the world was crowded with style designers, jewelers, cabinetmakers, workers in ceramics, and even architects. The modern coiffure creator, beauty specialist and cosmetic manufacturer are said to be equally interested.

One of the greatest revolutions in dress was predicted by Mr. Gidding, who said that designers all over the world were under high pressure to produce vivid and colorful embroiders in the Egyptian fashion.

Pierre C. Cartier said that the discoveries in the tomb would bring in some sweeping changes in fashions in jewelry to meet the demands of the public for things Egyptian.

The milliner and hairdresser are probably confronted by the greatest problem. Tut-ankh-Ahmen's headdress was a thing of monumental proportions, ornamental in front with a gold inlaid cobra about to strike. Fantastic and elaborate wings were much worn by the great ladies of ancient Egypt. The modern method of marcelling, curling and frizzing hair are simple things beside the ancient Egyptian treatment of it. Some of the coiffures displayed on the Nile a few thousand years ago must have required weeks of work. A few look as if each individual hair had been strung with beads. Other styles indicate that each individual hair was separately treated. Bobbed hair and bobbed wigs reigned for some seasons. . . .

"These discoveries will undoubtedly have a revolutionary effect on dress and many other things," said Mr. Gidding. "This is being assisted by a reaction from the dress prevailing for so many years during and after the war. There has never been a time when the designer has had to keep so carefully in touch with news. It is necessary to keep posted constantly by cable. Every museum and library of Egyptology in Europe and this country is haunted by designers and style-makers.

"The influence of high color combinations and peculiar Egyptian figures will be felt everywhere. The wide publicity is causing a great demand for these things, and people generally are delighted with the change to brighter colors and to embroidery and patterns based on the Egyptian. It is hard to tell how far this will go, but, besides taking colors and designs from Egypt, we may find it necessary to adopt new kinds of costumes from the Egyptian. There is already a tendency in the direction of various loose-fitting things."

Primary Source

"Egypt Dominates Fashion Show Here: Designs Copied from Luxor Pictures Decorate Many Suit Models" [excerpt]

SYNOPSIS: On February 25, 1923, *The New York Times* featured yet another article on the Egyptian trend in fashion. This report focused on a trade association's fashion show.

Only American designs were shown last night at the Fashion Review of the United Cloak and Suit Designers' Association of America at the Hotel Savoy. The Egyptian influence was more pronounced than ever, and among the models were copies of the designs and inscriptions on the pictures recently received from Luxor and these were cleverly worked into wraps and gowns.

The wrap which won the competition prize in the association was of black velvet and had a hathor, or sacred cow, copied from the picture published in *The New York Times* recently, on the yoke at the front.

The pattern was carried out with beads, as was the design of a scarab which reached to the bottom of the wrap at the back. The bright colors which seemed to be subdued by age are said to be exact reproductions of those found in the museum. Satin of a new Egyptian clay shade lined the wrap.

In an address which preceded the show Alexandre M. Grean, honorary President of the organization, said that America now was in a better mood to produce styles than Europe and predicted that the Egyptian models would prolong the vogue for bobbed hair and short skirts.

"American fashions are now a success," said Mr. Grean. "This country leads the world in fashion shows and there is hardly a city of any importance that has not a fashion show at least twice a year. The supply in this country is now so satisfying that I am afraid the buyers who went to Paris this season for new models are coming home rather disappointed. Paris has not taken up the Egyptian trend

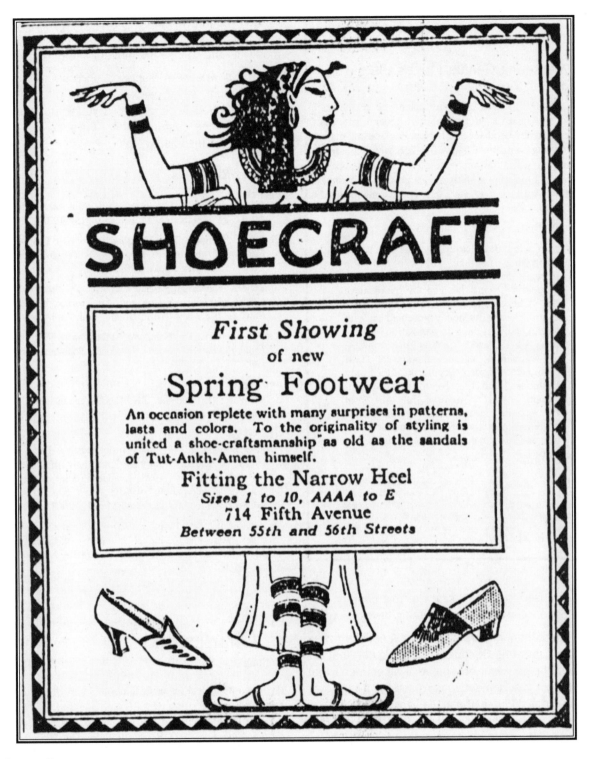

Primary Source

Shoecraft Advertisement

SYNOPSIS: This advertisement that appeared in the February 25, 1923, issue of *The New York Times* reveals that Tut-inspired attire was in New York stores less than four months after the discovery of Tutankhamen's tomb. The Shoecraft store ad reflects an Egyptian-inspired spring line of footwear. COPYRIGHT © 1923 BY THE NEW YORK TIMES CO. REPRODUCED BY PERMISSION.

A Marketing Genius Makes the Most of the King Tut Trend

In 1923, Edward Bernays, an image consulting pioneer, devised a surefire publicity generator for his client Cheney Brothers, an old New England silk manufacturing company. Cheney Brothers would award a young American woman designer a scholarship to take a trip to Egypt to study the excavations and come back to America to create some silk designs inspired by what she saw:

As Bernays wrote in a report:

In a few days Hazel Slaughter, a charming young American girl who had won prizes at the textile exhibition and at the Art Student's League, became the recipient of the Cheney Brothers Tut-ankin-Amen award. Horace B. Cheney presented her with a scholarship at the Silk Exposition on February 12, 1923 and *The New York Times,* in a two-column headline announced, "Girl Designer Awarded Scholarship to Study Fashions From the Tomb of Tut-ankin-Amen." . . . Overnight a little girl from Brooklyn became the heroine of a glamorous adventure that focused much publicity on her and on Cheney Brothers' pioneering spirit in silk design.

SOURCE: Bernays, Edward L. "Typescript on Art in the Fashion Industry, 1923–1927: Cheney Brothers." *Prosperity and Thrift: The Coolidge Era and the Consumer Economy, 1921–1929.* American Memory digital primary source collection, Library of Congress. Available online at http://memory.loc.gov/ammem/coolhtml/coolhome.html; website home page: http://memory.loc.gov (accessed May 12, 2003).

by products of some of our great textile houses. However, it is a dangerous theme. Do not exaggerate it, modify it, and choose the most beautiful parts only."

The gowns were displayed on a small stage in the ballroom, which was decorated with Egyptian draperies. Nadine Egronaya, a young Russian girl, dressed in the costume of an Egyptian slave, announced the models.

Further Resources

BOOKS

Corson, Richard, *Fashions in Makeup, from Ancient to Modern Times.* London: Owen, Peter Limited, 1972.

Cosgrave, Bronwyn. *The Complete History of Costume and Fashion: From Ancient Egypt to the Present Day.* New York: Checkmark Books, 2001.

Holkeboer, Katherine Strand. *Patterns for Theatrical Costumes: Garments, Trims, and Accessories from Ancient Egypt to 1915.* New York: Drama Book Publishers, 1992.

Reeves, Nicholas. *The Complete Tutankhamun: The King, the Tomb, the Royal Treasure.* New York: Thames and Hudson, 1995.

PERIODICALS

Cohen, R.H. "Tut and the '20s: The 'Egyptian look.'" *Art in America* 67, 1979, 97.

WEBSITES

Orzada, Belinda T. "Egyptian Influences on Dress in the 1920s." Twentieth Century Design: Ethnic Influences, University of Delaware, 1998. Available online at http://udel.edu/~orzada/egypt.htm; website home page: http://udel.edu/~orzada/toc.htm (accessed May 12, 2003).

Yeager, J. "History of Fashion: 1920–1930." American Vintage Blues. Available online at http://www.vintageblues.com/history2.htm (accessed January 15, 2003).

as vigorously as the designers of this country, and this vogue will overshadow anything else this year.

"The continual propaganda for American styles has done its work. Of course I do not mean that designers should never go abroad. I recommend that they go, for it is an education to see the things over there, but I do urge these designers not to copy those things blindly just because they can be called 'imported.' America is in a better mood to produce styles today than Europe. Over there they are war mad, while we are occupying ourselves with fashions, a much pleasanter and healthier amusement. America has produced recently distinct types of young girls' clothes that are most interesting.

"Egyptians had more than one silhouette. The Egyptian trend in clothes was on before the discovery of the tomb of Tut-ankh-Ahmen, as you will find

"Charleston"

Song

By: Cecil Mack and James P. Johnson

Date: 1923

Source: Mack, Cecil, and James P. Johnson. "Charleston." Warner Bros., Inc., 1923. Reprinted in Gottlieb, Robert, and Robert Kimball, eds. *Reading Lyrics.* New York: Pantheon Books, 2000.

About the Artists: Cecil Mack (1883–1944), born Richard C. McPherson in Norfolk, Virginia, wrote lyrics to many popular songs from the turn of the twentieth century through the 1920s, the height of his career. Though he lacked formal training in music or theater—he attended Lincoln University in Pennsylvania and the University of Pennsylvania Medical School for one semester—he was extremely successful in show business. Mack published his first lyrics in 1901, and

Joan Crawford, who was a Charleston dance champion before she became a film star, dances the Charleston in *Our Dancing Daughters,* 1928. HULTON/ARCHIVE. REPRODUCED BY PERMISSION.

early in 1905 he organized the Gotham Music Publishing Company, which published songs primarily composed by African Americans, including Mack's own work. Later that year, Gotham Music merged with the Attucks Music Publishing Company to form the Gotham-Attucks Music Publishing Company. Under Mack's leadership, Gotham-Attucks became a highly influential company, helping to open doors for African Americans in the music business. Mack was also was an early member of the American Society of Composers, Authors and Publishers.

James P. Johnson (1891–1955) was a pianist, a highly prolific and versatile composer, and a major influence in the development of jazz. He began performing publicly at seventeen, sometimes recording under the name Jimmy Johnson. Johnson originated a piano-playing style known as "stride" that was a link between ragtime and jazz. His instrumental compositions were extremely popular between 1910 and 1920. He was a music teacher to Fats Waller, performed with Bessie Smith and Fletcher Henderson, among many others, and was a major influence on Duke Ellington. ∎

Introduction

James P. Johnson often played piano at dances in Harlem for African American longshoremen and seamen recently moved from southern ports. He was particularly inspired by the Gullahs. The Gullahs are an ethnic group descended from freed slaves who settled in the coastal regions of the Carolinas and Georgia and who maintained some of their West African language and culture. Their dance styles inspired Johnson's playing style, which came to be known as "stride." Johnson originally composed the tune "Charleston" in 1913 and played it at the Harlem dances. The steps were already known among African American dancers at the time, but most Americans were not aware of the Charleston song or dance for another decade.

After the success of their 1921 show *Shuffle Along* (the first all-African American Broadway show), the vaudeville team Flournoy E. Miller and Aubrey Lyles invited Johnson and lyricist Cecil Mack to provide the songs for their next show, *Runnin' Wild.* One of these songs, "Charleston," featured the dance that became an emblem of the 1920s. Done in 4/4 time, it was essentially a kickstep combined with flailing arms: step back with the right foot, kick back with the left, step forward with the left, kick back with the right; arms bent, swing elbows. *Runnin' Wild,* which opened in 1923, was highly profitable in New York and went on tour throughout the United States. Since dancing was the premier form of entertainment and recreational activity of the era, the popularity of the musical, especially on the road, helped the Charleston craze spread like wildfire.

Significance

Individually, both Cecil Mack and James Johnson were important figures on the music scene, so it is not surprising that their collaboration met with success. "Charleston" became Mack's and Johnson's greatest composition, garnering profits and creating a legendary dance trend.

The popularity of *Shuffle Along, Runnin' Wild,* and other such shows helped break down barriers that had prevented African American-produced entertainment from prospering. African American dancers had been doing the Charleston in private social clubs for years, but it took a lavish Broadway production to introduce the dance to scores of white audiences across America.

Soon everyone wanted to dance the Charleston. The dance was considered outrageous and scandalous, yet it was eagerly adopted by those who wanted to be daring and challenge social norms. Some white employers went so far as to require that potential hires for domestic help be able to teach them how to do the steps. The Charleston became indelibly associated with the "flappers," fashionable young ladies who were so-named for the way that their arms flapped wildly as they did the dance. A number of movie stars launched their show-business careers by winning Charleston dance contests, including Joan Crawford and Ginger Rogers, who became Fred Astaire's long-time movie dance partner.

Primary Source

"Charleston"

SYNOPSIS: The Charleston was originally considered an "exhibition" dance, strictly for professionals. But it became wildly popular nonetheless. Though the craze faded out by 1926, the Charleston is still the dance most emblematic of the 1920s. While "Charleston" remains one of the most well-known tunes of the era, Cecil Mack's original lyrics are seldom heard.

Carolina, Carolina,
At last they've got you on the map.
With a new tune,
A funny blue tune,
With a peculiar snap!
You may not be able to buck or wing,
Fox-trot, two-step, or even sing,
If you ain't got religion in your feet
You can do this prance and do it neat.

Charleston!
Charleston!
Made in Carolina.
Some dance,
Some prance,
I'll say.
There's nothing finer than the Charleston,
Charleston.
Lord, how you can shuffle.
Ev'ry step you do
Leads to something new,
Man, I'm telling you
It's a lapazoo.
Buck dance
Wing dance
Will be a back number,
But the Charleston,
The new Charleston,
That dance is surely a comer.
Sometime
You'll dance it one time,
The dance called the Charleston,
Made in South Caroline.

Further Resources

BOOKS

Brown, Scott E. *James P. Johnson: A Case of Mistaken Identity.* Metuchen, N.J.: Scarecrow Press and the Institute of Jazz Studies, Rutgers University, 1986.

Driver, Ian. *A Century of Dance.* London: Hamlyn, 2000.

Kallen, Stuart A. *The Roaring Twenties.* San Diego: Greenhaven Press, 2002.

The Making of a Mosaic: An Introduction to the Music and Dance of the Americas. New York: National Dance Institute, 1992.

Villacorta, Aurora S. *Charleston, Anyone?* Danville, Ill.: Interstate Printers & Publishers, 1978.

Walker, Bemis. *How to Charleston Correctly.* Minneapolis: Great Northern Publishing Co., 1926.

The 1926 edition of *Life* magazine features an illustration of a man and woman doing the Charleston. © **CORBIS. REPRODUCED BY PERMISSION.**

PERIODICALS

"Headlines: Charleston Forever." *Time* 29, June 1959, 54.

Parish, Paul. "A Revival in Full Swing." *Dance Magazine,* September 1999.

Thompson, Robert Farris. "An Aesthetic of the Cool: West African Dance." *African Forum* 2, 1966, 85–102.

"The 25 Most Important Events in Black Music History." *Ebony,* June 2000.

AUDIO AND VISUAL MEDIA

Dancetime! 500 Years of Social Dance, Volume II. Dancetime Publications. Directed by Carol Teten. Videocassette, 1998.

The Roaring Twenties. Schlessinger Video Productions. Videocassette, 1996.

World of Swing #6—From Partner Charleston to Lindy Charleston. World of Swing Series. Directed by Bärbl Kaufer and Marcus Koch. Videocassette, 2000.

Red Diving Girl

Advertisements

By: Jantzen, Inc.
Date: 1924, 1928

Primary Source

Red Diving Girl (1 OF 2)

SYNOPSIS: With a popular advertising logo, innovative swimsuit designs, and marketing efforts that promoted swimming as an athletic activity, the Jantzen company spearheaded the development of swimwear as a new segment of the fashion industry. THE ADVERTISING ARCHIVE LTD. REPRODUCED BY PERMISSION.

Source: Jantzen. "The Nation's Swimming Suit" and "Blonde or Brunette" advertisements. 1924; 1928.

About the Organization: Jantzen, Inc., is one of the oldest swimsuit makers in the United States. Incorporated in 1910 in Portland, Oregon, it began as the Portland Knitting Company, manufacturing sweaters. By the 1920s, the company had renamed itself Jantzen, Inc., and was focused on manufacturing swimwear. ∎

Introduction

In 1913, Portland Knitting received an order for a custom pair of wool trunks for a rower to wear while working out in the Pacific Northwest's chilly waters. The company's two owners, John Zehntbauer and Carl Jantzen, devised a knitted garment, ribbed like a sweater cuff. The rower was extremely pleased, and Zehntbauer and Jantzen decided to produce swimsuits of the same material. These suits featured a "rib stitch" consisting of elasticized material that retained its shape whether wet or dry. The one-piece design for both men and women sold well, even though it weighed two pounds when dry and nine pounds when wet.

During the 1920s, swimsuit styles underwent additional transformations. The once-favored sailor costumes with short skirts were giving way to new skirtless suits that covered less and less of the body. The decade's most popular style, for both men and women, was the maillot,

a two-piece consisting of a vest-shaped top extending to the upper thigh, and shorts. A more conservative one-piece version was essentially the top and shorts of the maillot assembled from a single piece of fabric. By the end of the decade, armholes were cut deeper and the shorts became shorter for comfort and ease of movement. However, men's topless suits were not commonly worn in the United States until 1935.

In 1921, Jantzen introduced a new advertising image, a female diver in a red swimsuit. The company featured the *Red Diving Girl* in its catalogue and erected billboards with the image along highways in San Francisco and Los Angeles. The original *Red Diving Girl* wore a striped pom-pom hat, a swimsuit with striped legs, and long socks. In 1928, artist Frank Clark created an updated version of the Red Diving Girl logo—no pom-pom, no stripes, and no socks.

In 1923, Jantzen introduced a comparatively lightweight swimsuit made from 100 percent virgin wool, and advertised it as "the suit that changed bathing to swimming." This slogan was at times used in ads featuring the *Red Diving Girl.*

Significance

Jantzen's innovations both in swimwear design and in its promotional methods created a new segment of the

Primary Source

Red Diving Girl **(2 OF 2)**
A Jantzen swimsuit advertisement from a 1928 edition of the *The Saturday Evening Post*. THE ADVERTISING ARCHIVE LTD. REPRODUCED BY PERMISSION.

fashion industry—and increased the popularity of swimming as a leisure activity.

The *Red Diving Girl* was an extremely popular and successful advertising image. When it became a fad to paste cutouts of the girl on the windshields of automobiles, Jantzen responded by creating stickers. This was one of the greatest retail-marketing devices of the century. The company distributed 10 million of the decals in the 1920s. A number of states refused to grant driver's licenses to those who displayed such a risque image on their automobiles, a rule that was impossible to enforce. In 1924, Massachusetts even banned the Jantzen Girl stickers from auto windshields, but being "banned in Boston," of course, meant even more publicity for the company.

Jantzen also fueled demand for its new swimwear products by offering free swimming lessons in cities across the country. At the time, swimming was growing in popularity as a recreational activity; "for health and beauty" was the motto. Johnny Weissmuller, a 1924 Olympic swimming champion (who went on to portray Tarzan in Hollywood films), appeared in a publicity photograph wearing his Jantzen suit. In Hawaii, Duke Kahanamoku, another Olympian, also made public appearances in a Jantzen. These were early examples of celebrity endorsements.

Fashion took on a greater influence in the sales of swimwear in the 1920s. Jantzen and other swimwear manufacturers began to consider the latest fads in the fashion world and quickly adapted these trends into swimwear designs. While swimwear silhouettes were still fairly limited, Jantzen provided the consumer with a variety of colors from which to choose. Previously, most suits were black or striped navy and white. Janzten offered a far greater range of colors and color combinations and used the phrase "Color Harmony" to suggest that there was a Jantzen swimsuit in a color flattering to every swimmer.

Swimsuit sales during the 1920s grew in the United States, Europe, and Asia, and the Red Diving Girl became a familiar symbol around the world.

Further Resources

BOOKS

Lencek, Lena, and Gideon Bosker. *Making Waves.* San Francisco: Chronicle Books, 1988.

Martin, Richard, and Harold Koda. *SPLASH! A History of Swimwear.* New York: Rizzoli International, 1990.

Probert, Christina. *Swimwear in Vogue Since 1910.* New York: Abbeville Press, 1981.

WEBSITES

Hsueh, Roselyn and Christina Lau, "Evolution of Swimwear." *Women's Swimwear.* Available online at http://www.ocf .berkeley.edu/~roseying/ids110/1FRAME.HTM (accessed January 13, 2003).

"Jantzen Knitting Mills Collection, 1925–1977." The Archives Center of the Smithsonian National Museum of American History. Available online at http://americanhistory.si.edu /archives/d9233.htm; website home page: http://american-history.si.edu/archives/b-1.htm (accessed January 13, 2003).

The Autobiography of an Idea
Memoir

By: Louis Sullivan

Date: 1924

Source: Sullivan, Louis H. *The Autobiography of an Idea.* New York: Press of the American Institute of Architects, 1924; reprint, New York: Dover Publications, 1956, 311–314

About the Author: Louis H. Sullivan (1856–1924) was considered the "Dean of American Architects." Born in Boston, he studied architecture at Massachusetts Institute of Technology and at the École des Beaux Arts in Paris. He received his early training as a draftsman in the studios of Frank Furness and William LeBaron Jenney in Chicago. In 1883, at the age of twenty-five, Sullivan established an architectural firm with Dankmar Adler, a German engineer. Adler & Sullivan designed more than 180 buildings. Sullivan was a mentor for Frank Lloyd Wright, who joined the firm of Adler & Sullivan in 1887. Sullivan was an important member of the Chicago School, a group of architects and critics with strong views about the negative effects of modernization on American architecture. The group was highly influential throughout the decades following the Chicago Fire of 1871, which had created a great demand and need for new buildings. ∎

Introduction

In the late nineteenth century, architects and city planners realized that vertical expansion was the only solution to the growing problem of land shortage, and so the great skyscraper race began. At the time, large buildings were structures of masonry held up by supporting walls. In 1882, the "Montauk Block" (since demolished) was built in Chicago; designed by the firm of Burnham

Architect Louis Henry Sullivan designed a number of buildings in the Chicago area, noted for their modern and naturalistic aesthetic.
SULLIVAN, LOUIS HENRY, PHOTOGRAPH.

and Root it reached the previously unprecedented height of nine stories. But wall-bearing masonry construction was an inefficient means of making commercial structures, and it soon gave way to the use of a lightweight steel framework, like a skeleton that could be covered with a much thinner layer of stone. In 1885, William LeBaron Jenney designed the first building in which the exterior walls were entirely supported on a steel frame, the Home Insurance Company Building in Chicago.

Louis Sullivan felt that these architectural innovations required a new attitude about the design of these new structures. Although he coined the famous dictum "form follows function," and believed that an object's structure should reflect the purpose for which it was created, Sullivan did not feel that design should not be limited by utilitarianism. To Sullivan, "function" referred to more than simply the practical and structural considerations of architectural design. He insisted that architecture had a civic responsibility and a spiritual function that encompassed society's values, aspirations, and spiritual needs. Therefore, the design and ornamentation of a building should be more than simply a means of making the object look better—they should reflect human beings' connections to nature and democratic ideals.

Sullivan created buildings that were simple geometric forms embellished with elaborate, organically inspired designs. For a time, other architects followed his approach. But the Columbian Exposition that took place in Chicago in 1893 had a classical architectural theme, and Renaissance classicism became fashionable in American architecture again.

Sullivan's practice began to decline, particularly after Adler retired in 1895. By 1918, Sullivan was deeply impoverished and was forced to give up the office in his own Auditorium Building. He subsisted on commission fees from the various small bank projects, published articles, and received financial help from charitable friends. He promoted his architectural philosophy, which came be called "organic architecture," in *The Autobiography of an Idea* and *A System of Architectural Ornament,* published shortly before his death in 1924.

Significance

Louis Sullivan was the first architect to truly weld the aesthetic and industrial innovations involved in the creation of the skyscraper into a unified whole. Sullivan showed how the simplicity and strength of the steel frame could also serve as a major decorative element of the building design. Many other architects followed Sullivan's example of combining new building techniques with classical and medieval architectural forms. This blend of steel construction and stylistic revival produced some of the greatest skyscrapers of the early twentieth century, such as Cass Gilbert's Woolworth Building (1911–1913) in New York City and Raymond Hood and John Mead Howells' Tribune Tower (1922–1925) in Chicago.

By the 1920s, Sullivan's accomplishments had been obscured by the newest architectural fashions, such as those forged by his former protégé Frank Lloyd Wright. But Sullivan's ability to combine materials paved the way for modern architecture, even if his flowery style became unfashionable in favor of the sleek, minimalist styles that would come to define architecture in the first half of the twentieth century.

Primary Source

Autobiography of an Idea [excerpt]

SYNOPSIS: In his book, Louis Sullivan promoted his architectural philosophy, which was based on the premise that building designs should be used to uplift the spirituality of the individual, not to demonstrate social status or wealth. In the following selection, Sullivan recounts the early days of the skyscraper.

Detail of the cast-iron entrance to Carson, Pirie, Scott & Co. building, designed by Louis Sullivan. **THE LIBRARY OF CONGRESS.**

. . . It became evident that the very tall masonry office building was in its nature economically unfit as ground values steadily rose. Not only did its thick walls entail loss of space and therefore revenue, but its unavoidably small window openings could not furnish the proper and desirable ratio of glass area to rentable floor area.

Thus arose a crisis, a seeming *impasse.* What was to do? Architects made attempts at solutions by carrying the outer spans of floor loads on cast columns next to the masonry piers, but this method was of small avail, and of limited application as to height. The attempts, moreover, did not rest on any basic principle, therefore the squabblings as to priority are so much piffle. The problem of the tall office building had not been solved, because the solution had not been sought within the problem itself—within its inherent nature. And it may be here remarked that after years of observation, that the truth most difficult to grasp, especially by the intellectuals, is this truth: That every problem of whatsoever name or nature, contains and suggests its own solution; and, the solution reached, it is invariably found to be simple in nature, basic, and clearly allied to common sense. . . .

Schlesinger & Mayer/Carson, Pirie, Scott department store, designed by Louis Sullivan in 1889, Chicago, Illinois. © BETTMANN/CORBIS. REPRODUCED BY PERMISSION.

So in this instance, the Chicago activity in erecting high buildings finally attracted the attention of the local sales managers of Eastern rolling mills; and their engineers were set at work. The mills for some time past had been rolling those structural shapes that had long been in use in bridge work. Their own ground work thus was prepared. It was a matter of vision in salesmanship based upon engineering imagination and technique. Thus the idea of a steel frame which should carry all the load was tentatively presented to Chicago architects.

The passion to *sell* is the impelling power in American life. Manufacturing is subsidiary and adventitious. But selling must be based on a semblance of service—the satisfaction of a need. The need was there, the capacity to satisfy was there, but contact was not there. Then came the flash of imagination which saw the single thing. The trick was turned; and there swiftly came into being something new under the sun. For the true steel-frame structure stands unique in the flowing of man and his works; a brilliant material example of man's capacity to satisfy his needs through the exercise of his natural powers. . . .

The architects of Chicago welcomed the steel frame and did something with it. The architects of the East were appalled by it and could make no contribution to it. In fact, the tall office buildings fronting the narrow streets and lanes of lower New York were provincialisms, gross departures from the law of common sense. For the tall office building loses its validity when the surroundings are uncongenial to its nature; and when such buildings are crowded together upon narrow streets or lanes they become mutually destructive. The social significance of the tall building is in finality its most important phase. In and by itself, considered *solus* so to speak, the lofty steel frame makes a powerful appeal to the architectural imagination where there is any. Where imagination is absent and its place usurped by timid pedantry the case is hopeless. The appeal and the inspiration lie, of course, in the element of loftiness, in the suggestion of slenderness and aspiration, the soaring quality as of a thing rising from the earth as a unitary utterance, Dionysian in beauty. The failure to perceive this simple truth has resulted in a throng of monstrosities, snobbish and maudlin or brashly insolent and thick lipped in speech; in either case a defamation and denial of man's finest powers.

In Chicago the tall office building would seem to have arisen spontaneously in response to favoring physical conditions, and the economic pressure as then sanctified, combined with the daring of promoters.

The construction and mechanical equipment soon developed into engineering triumphs. Architects, with a considerable measure of success, undertook to give a commensurate external treatment. The art of design in Chicago had begun to take on a recognizable character of its own. The future looked bright.

Further Resources

BOOKS

Condit, Carl W. *The Chicago School of Architecture*. Chicago: University of Chicago Press, 1964.

Frampton, Kenneth. *Modern Architecture 1851–1945*. New York: Rizzoli, 1983.

Morrison, Hugh. *Louis Sullivan: Prophet of Modern Architecture*. New York: The Museum of Modern Art and W.W. Norton, 1935.

Roth, Leland M. *A Concise History of American Architecture*. New York: Harper and Row, 1979.

Sullivan, Louis H. *A System of Architectural Ornament*. New York: Rizzoli, 1990.

Szarkowski, John. *The Idea of Louis Sullivan*. Boston: Bulfinch Press, 2000.

Twombly, Robert, and Narciso G. Menocal. *Louis Sullivan: The Poetry of Architecture.* New York: W.W. Norton, 2000.

Van Zanten, David. *Sullivan's City.* New York: W.W. Norton, 2000.

Wit, Wim de, ed. *Louis Sullivan: The Function of Ornament.* New York: W.W. Norton, 1986.

PERIODICALS

Lewis, Michael J. "Louis Sullivan After Functionalism." *The New Criterion,* 20, no. 1, September 2001.

WEBSITES

Howe, Jeffrey. "Louis Sullivan." A Digital Archive of American Architecture. Available online at http://www.bc.edu/bc _org/avp/cas/fnart/fa267/sullivan.html; website home page: http://www.bc.edu/bc_org/avp/cas/fnart/default.html (accessed January 14, 2003).

"Louis H. Sullivan." The Great Buildings Collection. Available online at http://www.greatbuildings.com/architects/Louis _H._Sullivan.html; website home page: http://www.great buildings.com (accessed January 14, 2003).

Miller, C. "Lieber-Meister—Louis Sullivan, The Architect and his Work." Broadacre All-Wright Site. Available online at http://www.geocities.com/SoHo/1469/sullivan.html; website home page: http://www.geocities.com/SoHo/1469/flw.html (accessed January 14, 2003).

AUDIO AND VISUAL MEDIA

Louis Sullivan: The Function of Ornament. Chicago Historical Society. Directed by Drew Browning. Videocassette, 1986.

"Here We Are Again! Confidential Tips on What to See at the Show"

Magazine article

By: George W. Sutton, Jr.

Date: January 1926

Source: Sutton, George W., Jr. "Here We Are Again! Confidential Tips on What to See at the Show." *American Motorist,* January 1926, 14, 46. *Prosperity and Thrift: The Coolidge Era and the Consumer Economy, 1921–1929.* American Memory digital primary source collection, Library of Congress. Available online at http://memory.loc.gov/ammem /coolhtml/coolhome.html; website home page: http://memory .loc.gov (accessed May 3, 2003).

About the Publication: A booming car market in the 1920s spawned numerous motoring-enthusiast magazines. Mass production brought down automobile prices—while a luxury car cost thousands, a Ford Model T could be bought for under $400 in 1925. An automobile culture was emerging, and membership in the American Automobile Association, an organization for drivers established in 1902, grew exponentially. AAA's magazine, *American Motorist,* contained practical advice on road travel and good driving skills, along with articles chronicling the growth of the automobile industry. ∎

Introduction

Fashion had been associated with driving since its earliest days, when only the wealthy could afford automobiles. The first cars were open-air, covered only with a simple bonnet, so that passengers were often exposed to the elements. Protective gear included long coats to shield clothes from the dust raised while driving on dirt roads; large hats, veils, and scarves; and goggles to block out small pebbles and other debris. However, the cars themselves offered little opportunity for making a fashion statement. The models varied very little in appearance and were available only in black.

In the early 1920s, General Motors, under the leadership of company president Alfred Sloan, began to devote more attention to automotive styling. Sloan created price and style categories and introduced new models annually. Technical advances of the decade included four-wheel brakes, automatic engine temperature control, shock absorbers, automatic choking, and adjustable front seats. As car technology improved, the rides along bumpy roads became more comfortable. Costs fell as manufacturing volume increased, and driving a car became more affordable.

Automobile enthusiasts' interest in appearances was finally satisfied by the car companies' newfound ability to provide choices in colors and styling. In 1923, GM engineer Charles Kettering invented Duco, an exterior body paint made from nitrocellulose lacquer. Before Duco, it took three weeks for the paint on a car to dry. Duco reduced drying time to 13.5 hours, freeing up valuable factory resources.

In 1924, "True Blue" was introduced as the first new car color, revolutionizing car fashions. A Duco finish became a status symbol because it was initially available exclusively on luxury Oakland automobiles; it was eventually offered on lower-end models as well. In 1927, GM instituted the Art & Color Section, a division of the company devoted to automotive styling. Harley Earl, who developed the streamlined 1927 Cadillac LaSalle, was hired as the industry's first designer. Since cars were motion machines, Earl said, their styling ought to suggest their speed and power.

Significance

The modern age of advertising had begun, and the automobile industry was positioned at forefront of the consumer revolution. Rising standards of living convinced buyers to equate use of new products with the middle-class American Dream. In the 1920s, American consumers were no longer satisfied with utility alone in their clothing, home décor, furniture—or automobiles. Car design had previously been dictated by function, but advancements enabled manufacturers to turn automobiles

February, 1926   AMERICAN MOTORIST   35

THIS IS A STUDEBAKER YEAR

Coral Gables Country Club, Miami, Florida

The Studebaker Standard Six Sport-Roadster $1295 *f.o.b. factory*

A CAR that calls to the open spaces! A car with the "up-and-away" spirit! Trim as a greyhound, fleet as the wind!

According to the rating of the Society of Automotive Engineers, the Studebaker Standard Six Sport-Roadster is the most powerful roadster of its size and weight in the world. Nineteen roadsters with less rated horsepower sell at prices $80 to $1505 above that of this Standard Six.

In appearance, this roadster has few equals at any price. The long, low body is richly finished in two-tone lacquer—rear deck and wheels in deep blue, the rest of the body in a slightly lighter shade. The collapsible top with boot is blue-gray. Windshield wings and nickel-plated radiator add smartness.

Ample room for three passengers. Leather upholstery of an attractive blue. The seatback is ad-

justable. Comfort is further insured by full-size balloon tires and long flexible springs. There is a compartment for golf sticks or packages behind the seat and liberal room for luggage under the rear deck.

Equipment is unusually complete, including front bumper and rear bumperettes; spare tire, tube and cover; automatic windshield cleaner; rear-view mirror; sun visor; 8-day clock; gasoline gauge; automatic spark control; lighting control on steering wheel; oil and gas filters; air cleaner; coincidental lock to ignition and steering gear.

Like every Studebaker, the Standard Six Sport-Roadster is Unit-Built, on the One-Profit basis. This enables Studebaker to offer you a car with scores of thousands of miles of excess transportation—a car of much finer quality, at an exceptionally low price.

THE STUDEBAKER CORPORATION OF AMERICA, SOUTH BEND, INDIANA

This advertisement for a Studebaker Roadster promotes the car as a friend to leisure. **THE LIBRARY OF CONGRESS.**

from mere engineering feats into works of art—or at least fine design.

The evolving image of the car and driving were reflected in publications such as *Your Car: A Magazine of Romance, Fact and Fiction.* Its 1925 issues featured short stories about cars and articles about the joys of road travel. Pictorials such as "Spring Styles for Women Motorists," associating fashion with female drivers, and "Stars and their Cars," photographs of celebrities with their vehicles, further inspired consumer fantasies. Car shows, in which automobile manufacturers displayed their newest makes and models, added to the public's growing interest in cars as status symbols and fashion statements.

Primary Source

"Here We Are Again! Confidential Tips on What to See at the Show" [excerpt]

SYNOPSIS: In the 1920s, automobile manufacturers appealed to the consumer with new options in styling and colors. No longer built only for utility, cars could be accessorized with the latest gadgets and trims. *American Motorist* featured this humorous article previewing the cars and accessories to be featured at the 1926 New York Automobile Show.

The time of year has arrived when all eyes are turned toward the automobile shows and the new models for next year. Thousands of eager motorists cannot tear themselves away from their radio sets long enough to give the shows a bit of personal attention, so, for these busy souls, it will be my pleasure to set forth, in the following paragraphs, a short and pithy interpretation of the 1926 motoring developments and a more or less accurate description of the many new motoring gems the manufacturers are offering for our delectation or something like that. Very well, let us proceed onward.

The Trend of Design

As revealed at the show which has come back to New York from Nova Scotia, in other words back to the Grand Central Palace from the Bronx, nothing could equal the energy with which the car makers are aiming their cars at definite classes of people. For instance:

Sport Cars for the Youthful

People who are not far from their childhood, either first or second, are being much intrigued by the new sport roadsters which are appearing in such splendiferous numbers in the various booths. The color schemes of some of them are most interesting in appearance, appetizing, one might say, like Irish stews with their delicately colored carrots, beets and onions. These cars have compartments for golf clubs lined with fleece so the bottles won't break. One sensational model has on its dashboard, instead of the old-fashioned whip socket, a little spigot releasing, at the touch of a dainty feminine hand, the desired amount of charged water. Yes, the sport cars are sportier than ever.

There will be several sedans in the show—four hundred of them to be exact. Strange as it may seem, many of the younger set are adopting sedans and coupes for sport purposes. The reason of this is that they have invented a new game. A group of them get together and buy cars having the largest possible blind spots in the driving compartments. They then go out on a crowded road at night and the game is to see who will stay alive the longest. Of course points are given by the referee—or referee-ess—for any pedestrians or other vermin demolished in the course of the contest.

It is a thrilling sport, but a few of the manufacturers at the show will show that they refuse to enter into the spirit of the thing and are making their front corner pillars out of little narrow metal strips, so there is no excuse for getting "deceased" through this cause or of hitting human, animal or vegetable matter on the road. Blame Jordan, the New-Day Jewett, Stutz, Pierce-Arrow and some of the other progressive ones for spoiling this lively sport.

Last year there was a cry "Any car without four-wheel brakes is obsolete." This didn't turn out to be quite true, but let's, in the name of safety and common sense, invent a new one and hope it will be true before another twelve months have dripped by, to the effect that "Any car with blind spots is obsolete."

Cars for Old People

There ain't no such animal as an old person any more. Even the seventy-year-old ossified dowager who, until now, has rolled up Fifth Avenue in a Brewster brougham, surveying the world and its sweetie with jaundiced eyes and a sour stomach, has had her car painted white, green and purple, dyed and shingled her hair, had her face lifted a few times and is taking Charleston lessons from some sofa chamelion. Therefore, there is no longer any need for cars designed for old people, except occasionally for those wonderful Cunningham sport hearses when some great-grandmother believes too implicitly what her bootlegger tells her about the age and quality of his "pre-war" stuff. It's a fast age, lads, a fast age. Naturally there will be no old people's cars at the show.

Accessories and Features

The show will be a riot of accessories. The makers of cars, parts and fittings have done wonders in supplying us with windshield wings, air filters, ventilators, vanity bags and a host of other useful and practical thingamajigs to make our motoring better and wiser. This year they've added a lot of long-needed novelties.

The Studebakers at the show will be equipped with a hot-air filter to be used on the person who insists on talking to the driver and says, "Oh, John, look at that lovely slaughter house," or "See the pink cow," when John is busy trying to keep the car from going over a precipice.

One of the new Buick models has a calendar on the dashboard so the driver can tell how many months it has been since he filled the grease cups. Another interesting device, revealed for the first time in the accessory section, is a fully equipped diving suit for the use of owners in swimming out after div-

The Ford Coupe was marketed as a safe, practical car, reliable even in the snow. **THE LIBRARY OF CONGRESS.**

ing under their cars to empty the oil out of the crankcase.

An intriguing gadget newly offered is a tooled leather bag containing a dainty stick of dynamite to employ in opening the greasing plug on the differential.

And so it goes, improvements everywhere, on every one of the new cars, to improve our motoring in a thousand different ways. Why the makers of one car have even supplied a substantial tent in which the family may rest while father is trying to find out why the car won't run or to live in while father is trying to find hotel accommodations in Florida.

There will be a lot of propaganda going around the show advocating birth control for Fords. They're turning them out nine thousand a day now. It doesn't seem respectable.

Yes, there has been great progress in the motor world during the past year. The national campaign for safety has been a howling success. Instead of killing 19,875 people in 1924, the fatalities for 1925 were only 19,877. The campaign for the elimination of railroad grade crossings has also been successful beyond the wildest dreams because a

Auto Trends in the Twenties

As portrayed at the New York Show, the aggregate American automobile for 1926 will have a smaller engine, the roof line or top of the body will be lower and the wheelbase shorter, although bodies will be more comfortable than ever before. Colors will range throughout almost the entire spectrum and will be presented in unusual combinations which are most attractive. The best evidence of the latter tendency are the new Fords which have been available for some time. Even these depart from Henry Ford's one-time statement that his customers could have any color they chose providing it was black.

SOURCE: Carver, Walter. "What the Show Will Show: Smaller Engines, Lower-Built Bodies and Many Bright-Colored Cars Mark the Trend in Design of the 1926 Car." *American Motorist,* January 1926, 10. *Prosperity and Thrift: The Coolidge Era and the Consumer Economy, 1921–1929.* American Memory digital primary source collection, Library of Congress. Available online at http://memory.loc.gov/ammem /coolhtml/coolhome.html; website home page: http://memory.loc.gov (accessed May 3, 2003).

large branch of the Boston and Maine railroad was abandoned; thus eliminating three grade crossings.

Traffic, especially in big cities, has been vastly improved. Instead of taking forty minutes as formerly to drive from Forty-seventh Street, New York, to the Grand Central Station at Forty-second Street, it now takes only a little over an hour.

And they're going to build 5,000,000 of them next year!

Further Resources

BOOKS

Adler, Dennis. *Packard.* New York: Motorbooks, 1998.

Adler, Dennis, and Pat Teberg. *The Art of the Automobile: The 100 Greatest Cars.* New York: HarperInformation, 2000.

Cleveland, Reginald McIntosh, and S.T. Williamson. *The Road Is Yours: The Story of the Automobile and the Men Behind It.* New York: Greystone Press, 1951.

Curcio, Vincent. *Chrysler: The Life and Times of an Automotive Genius.* New York: Oxford University Press, 2000.

Madsen, Axel. *The Deal Maker: How William C. Durant Made General Motors.* New York: John Wiley & Sons, 1999.

Sloan, Alfred Pritchard. *My Years with General Motors.* New York: Doubleday, 1990.

WEBSITES

"Harley Earl 1893–1969." Idaho Corvette Page. Available online at http://www.idavette.net/HistFact/earl.htm; website home page: http://www.idavette.net (accessed January 14, 2003).

Koma, Victor. "Why the "Y-Job?: Harley Earl and the Buick Dream Car." PreWarBuick.com. Available online at http://www.prewarbuick.com/id377.htm; website home page http://www.prewarbuick.com (accessed January 14, 2003).

Teresko, John. "GM Rediscovers Styling." *Industry Week,* December 18, 2001. Available online at http://www.industry week.com/Columns/asp/columns.asp?ColumnID=843; website home page: http://www.industryweek.com (accessed January 14, 2003).

"What Price Beauty? Practical Budgets for Furnishings"

Magazine article

By: Mrs. Charles Bradley Sanders

Date: January 1926

Source: Sanders, Mrs. Charles Bradley. "What Price Beauty? Practical Budgets for Furnishings." *The Delineator* 82, no. 2, January 1926, 20, 55–57. *Prosperity and Thrift: The Coolidge Era and the Consumer Economy, 1921–1929.* American Memory digital primary source collection, Library of Congress. Available online at http://memory.loc.gov /ammem/coolhtml/coolhome.html; website home page: http://memory.loc.gov (accessed January 8, 2003).

About the Publication: *The Delineator,* a monthly publication of Butterick Publishing Company (purveyor of dress patterns, often adapted from European fashions), was founded in 1872. Originally intended to market Butterick patterns, it quickly became a women's general-interest magazine. It specialized in fashion editorials, often with sketches of the latest Paris fashions and patterns based on these designer looks so that readers could sew the latest styles at home. The magazine also included articles about the latest trends in homemaking. ∎

Introduction

While the 1920s in Europe saw the genesis of the sleek, simplistic lines of Art Deco and the mechanistic steel, glass, and leather furniture of the Bauhaus, these styles appealed to only a small minority of American homemakers at the time. Most Americans in the 1920s preferred to decorate their homes with understated pieces in combination with the latest modern conveniences. These innovations—the telephone, radio, and phonograph—were often hidden in traditionally designed cabinetry. Mass production of furniture and home accessories had reached a peak, allowing homemakers on tight budgets to purchase inexpensive furniture in period styles from Colonial to Louis XIV. Much furniture and interior decoration retained vestiges of the Victorian style

Page 20   THE DELINEATOR, January, 1926

What price Beauty?

Practical budgets for furnishings

By MRS. CHARLES BRADLEY SANDERS

The individuality of the family is largely expressed by the home in which it lives.

To determine how much shall be spent for this home and its furnishings requires thoughtful planning. The amount once determined, no matter how small, should not be spent without careful study and a firm resolution to challenge every purchase for permanent satisfaction.

Our DELINEATOR bride and groom, George and Mary, take up their furniture budget problem in this article. Mrs. Charles Bradley Sanders, the author, is Director of THE DELINEATOR'S House Decoration and Home Building Department and has helped thousands of readers in their efforts to make a more beautiful home environment. Her budget plans reflect her wide experience and knowledge of values.

Martha Van Rensselaer

Home-making Department

Edited by MARTHA VAN RENSSELAER,
Director of the New York State College of Home Economics, Cornell University~

reading matter, automobile and personal expenses for all of these; consequently, you must be willing to cut a little on theaters or sports togs to make the home you so love contain touches of loveliness. Never cut from savings, not even for the price of beauty; that is the Golden Rule of budgeting.

Real beauty does not mean a display of elaborate objects, but rather a combination of articles of good line, form and color, placed in appropriate settings and in attractive groups.

The object of this article is primarily to assist those attempting to live on a budget to make their houses, or apartments, as charming as their means will permit; also to give them a complete and helpful list of the articles necessary to furnish properly and attractively such homes, and to estimate the cost of complete furnishing of certain homes, namely: Homes No. 1, No. 2 and No. 3,

YOUR FURNITURE UPKEEP

Your home is never finished. A rug wears, a table needs refinishing, new curtains are necessary—all these must be allowed for in the yearly budget. We have a leaflet that will outline your furniture needs for ten years. It shows what must be spent on each of the houses in this article for new furnishings, renovation and cleaning. It also suggests ways of avoiding wear and tear on furniture and house.

A two-cent stamp to cover postage will bring you this and our leaflet on the KITCHEN BUDGET. Space in this article is too limited to give kitchen furnishings in detail; therefore we have prepared a special leaflet on the subject. This shows how attractive and efficient kitchens may be furnished on three different incomes and gives the cost of equipment.

Address the Home-Making Department of THE DELINEATOR, Butterick Building, New York.

SMALL PIECES OF GOOD
DESIGN MAY BE USED
FOR THE ODD CORNERS

CAREFUL PLANNING WILL RESULT IN
ROOMS OF A DEFINITE CHARM

INCREASING INCOMES ALLOW LATITUDE
IN THE CHOICE OF ACCESSORIES

A LOW CONSOLE MAY
CONCEAL A TALKING
MACHINE OR RADIO

A LIVING-ROOM RESTFUL AND DISTINCTIVE IN ITS APPOINTMENTS

WHAT price are you willing to pay for a beautiful home—not just a furnished house or apartment, but for a place which contains charm and expresses your artistic individuality with objects of interest and beauty? The price is usually that of denial. In fact, the whole purpose of a budget is to place before yourself your economic life, and to make cold-blooded decisions as to what you are willing to have and what to do without.

Most budgets, no matter how large the income, allow not more than five per cent. of the total for furnishing, and when classified on the budget sheet. it usually comes under the general heading of "advancement." "Advancement" as a heading is suggested as a point of departure in compiling a budget and includes, usually, besides furnishings, entertainment, travel,

furnished to fit three grades of income— $1,800, $3,000 and $5,000.

FUNDAMENTALS OF GOOD DECORATION

The room which often receives the greatest attention when the new home is being furnished is the living-room, since comfortable living and charm of arrangement are more generally appreciated there. The furnishings, then, should be selected for quality, comfort and informal good style, which may be interpreted through inexpensive as well as expensive articles and fabrics. Before choosing, consider all periods, colors and styles; decide which most pleases your fancy, and concentrate on that particular period and its variations. The quintness of Early American, the regalness of the Georgian, the daintiness and beauty of the French, and the sturdiness of the Spanish, Italian and Early English periods have their particular appeal to the individual, and

Continued on page 55

Primary Source

What Price Beauty? Practical Budgets for Furnishings, Page 1 (1 OF 4)

SYNOPSIS: Home magazines of the 1920s frequently published articles demonstrating how to decorate a home on a modest budget. This article from *The Delineator* suggested how to properly decorate a home at four budget levels, with a detailed list of what furniture and decorations for the household to purchase. The homemaker was, of course, encouraged to make the curtains and slipcovers in order to further cut costs. THE LIBRARY OF CONGRESS.

WHAT PRICE BEAUTY?

Continued from page 20

no budget is so small that one or two good foundation pieces of any of these periods can not be indulged in and added to occasionally.

Each period, too, has its appropriate background, and consideration must be expended on whether it will be soft-colored paint, wallpaper or wall fabric which will complete the setting and give individuality to what would otherwise be a commonplace assortment of furniture. All furniture and accessories, whether in suites or single pieces, should be chosen for correct design and grace of line. Proper scale is difficult for amateurs to grasp in the flush of buying and developing a home, but to develop ultimately a successful room, one must bear in mind the size of the room to be furnished and, if possible, have the articles sent home on approval before definitely purchasing them. Then, if they do not conform with the size and proportion of the room, they can easily be exchanged. A good rule to follow in selecting furniture and hangings is to avoid that which strikes you as eccentric or elaborate in a shop. A bizarre piece of furnishing will show up doubly prominent in a home. In furnishing rooms that are low and long, you will notice at once that they should not contain high, narrow pieces of furniture; neither should high, small rooms be furnished with short, broad pieces.

No house or apartment can be considered properly furnished unless it first meets the needs of the occupants. Comfortable chairs, beds, sofas, good tables and rugs are the most important articles, and should be the best the family can afford. The amount of furnishings required for a room necessarily depends upon the size of the room, the requirements of the family and the amount of money available for furniture. Hominess and beauty are consistent with simplicity and economy; thus the following simple lists of furnishings are offered as a guide to those whose enthusiasm for a home may bring about expenditures on inappropriate objects.

WE WILL now suppose that George and Mary—our budget bride and groom—were able during their engagement to save $600 and received approximately $150 worth of wedding gifts, or the equivalent in credits at shops, thus making $750 in all on which to embark on a career of home-making. Mary, of course, will be counted on to make all her curtains, bedspreads, etc., and paint her own furniture. Their yearly income, as we have stated in a previous budget article, is $1,800 a year. A total of $480 of that, or $40 per month, is set aside for shelter. In some localities very small houses, more generally only three or four rooms at the most, may be leased for that sum. Again, we will suppose that they have leased a combination living-room and dining-room, a bedroom, kitchen and bath, and the problem of furnishing so often confronts them. In some places a combination kitchen and dining-room is easier to obtain than a living-room-dining-room combination, so we have listed the furnishings for such a room, and the list may be substituted when necessary.

HOME NO. 1—INCOME, $1,800

Allowance for furnishings, $750, or its equivalent in credits, gifts or furniture on hand.

The prices indicated are only approximate, as they vary in different shops and localities.

COMBINATION LIVING AND DINING-ROOM

Rug. Linen or wool fiber	$ 25.00
Table. Drop - leaf, gate - legged, or square or round soft-wood kitchen type, or table and bench combined, unpainted	20.00
Chairs. Four, to m a t c h wood in table, with plain wood, cane or reed seats; or soft-wood kitchen type of chairs, painted to match table; the latter chairs may have small pads of cretonne or rep fastened by tapes, at $3.75 each . .	15.00
Serving - Table or Small Sideboard. In any of the hard wood or painted soft woods, or an individual piece such as a low-boy, chest of drawers or console with drawers for linen, silver, etc. .	55.00

6   16

Sofa, Day-Bed or Combination of Both. Covered with denim, rep or poplin	$ 30.00
Armchair. Wicker, n a t u r a l or painted; cushions of rep or cretonne like draperies or sofa cover	12.00
Armchair. S m a l l overstuffed, in striped or figured denim or damask, or slat-back, rush seat . . .	45.00
Desk. Small flat-top, or combination desk and bookcase	25.00
Desk-Chair. Use straight diningchair	12.00
Book-Shelves. Under windows, or in corner, or built around and over radiator as a disguise for material only	15.00
Table. Small end-table or soft-wood stool, painted, for smoking appointments	3.75
Lamp. One wrought-iron or wood floor-lamp, with paper or muslin shade	12.50
Waste-Paper Basket. Dark wicker or metal	1.50
Curtains	14.00
Decorative Accessories and Utensils. One or two pictures, or any interesting strip of brocade, embroidery or shawl, but not both. One or two bright, colorful pottery vases or bowls. Flat and hollow silverware, kitchen utensils, table linens and china	130.00
TOTAL FOR ABOVE ROOM . . .	**$415.75**

COMBINATION KITCHEN AND DINING-ROOM
(Alternative)

One Table. Small, round pine table, painted any soft, neutral shade	$ 20.00
Four Chairs. Pine, painted to match the table	15.00
Sideboard. Welsh dresser, table or chest of drawers	55.00
One Hanging Dish-Rack or small serving-table for linen, silver, etc.	15.00
Decorative Accessories and Utensils. Brass or pottery candlesticks, bowl for fruit, chintz or cretonne window-shades; hanging, metal flower-basket with English ivy. Kitchen utensils, silver and china and table linens	125.00
TOTAL FOR ABOVE ROOM . . .	**$230.00**

This last figure does not include kitchen cabinet, refrigerator, range or floor covering.

BEDROOM

Three Small Rugs. Rag, braided or strips of carpet	$ 20.00
Bed. Double, or two single beds, painted light or in dark colors, in wood or metal. Bedspread of seersucker, crape or cretonne . .	80.00
Bed Linens, Blankets, Quilt	30.00
Two Chests of Drawers. Painted to match beds	60.00
Two Mirrors. Painted frames to match chest of drawers, or antique gilt	16.00
One Armchair and Cushions. Wicker, natural or painted	8.50
One Straight Chair. Rush bottom, painted to match chest of drawers	3.75
One Small Bed Table. Next to bed for lamp, books, etc.	6.00
One Chest. At end of bed for linens, clothes, etc.	18.00
Curtains	6.00
Accessories. Toilet articles and small lamp	25.00
TOTAL FOR ABOVE ROOM . . .	**$273.25**

KITCHEN

Table	$ 10.00
Curtains	2.00
Stool and Utensils	23.00
TOTAL	**$ 35.00**

The above total does not include kitchen cabinet, refrigerator, range or floor covering.

BATHROOM

Linens	$ 12.00
Fixtures	8.00
Mirror	4.00
Curtains	2.00
TOTAL	**$ 26.00**

TOTAL EXPENDED ON HOME No. 1 $750.00

HOME NO. 2—FIVE ROOMS

Yearly income, $3,000. Allowance for furnishings, $1,700, or its equivalent in credits, gifts or furniture on hand.

HALL

Floor Coverings. Over hard wood, p a i n t e d, or linoleum-covered floors. One or two rugs—wool braided, Wilton, Brussels, Axminster, or linen or wool fiber rugs	$ 10.00
Table. Console type with drawers, drop-leaf, or small table with a drawer, in any of the hard woods or painted soft woods . . .	12.00
Mirror or Picture. Over table; antique gilt, hard wood or painted frame	12.00
Chair. One straight, hard wood or painted chair, upholstered, rush or wood slats	8.00
TOTAL	**$ 42.00**

LIVING-ROOM

Floor Coverings. Rugs and carpets should be preferably the Wiltons, chenilles or Axminsters. Linen fiber, wool fiber, wool braided or hooked rugs. It is a matter of choice whether one large or several small rugs be used	$ 75.00
Table. In any of the hard woods or painted soft woods; square or oblong, depending on the shape of the room, such as an oblong library table, refectory, a square drop-leaf, gate-legged or plain wood table, painted	40.00
Sofa. Small or overstuffed, wicker or hard wood, with cushions . .	139.00
Armchair. Either entirely overstuffed, upholstered seat and back only, or upholstered seat and wooden back, such as plain, overstuffed velours chair or wing chair	45.00
Armchair. In any of the hard woods; type such as a Windsors or ladderback, with wood or rush seats . .	13.00
Wicker Armchair. Natural color or painted, with or without cushions	12.00
Desk. In any of the hard woods; type, small Colonial secretary with bookcase above, or small flat-top desk	40.00
Desk-Chair. Straight chair with wood or rush seat, to correspond in wood and style with desk . .	10.00
End-Table or Sewing-Table or Stand. In any of the hard woods or painted; low, round or square . .	14.00
Bookcase or Book-Shelves. Bookcase with or without doors; straightline type, or built-in book-shelves, painted or stained to match woodwork	30.00
Two Lamps. Tall wooden or metal reading-lamp with silk or paper shade	20.00
Clock. Simple design in wood, metal or leather	15.00
Waste-Paper Basket. Metal, wicker, wood or fiber	3.00
Decorative Accessories. P o t t e r y, brass or copper vases; bowls, candlesticks, sofa cushions, tablerunners or mats in duvetyn, velours, old brocade, heavy silks, or to correspond with materials used in overdraperies	30.00
Desk Appointments. Brass, bronze, leather or wood. Book-ends in wood or metal; ash-trays of enamel, glass, brass, or other metal, or wood; library shears and smoking appointments	8.00

Continued on page 56

Primary Source

"What Price Beauty? Practical Budgets for Furnishings," Page 2 (2 OF 4)

List of prices of interior design elements from article, "What Price Beauty?" from the January 1926 issue of *The Delineator*.

THE LIBRARY OF CONGRESS.

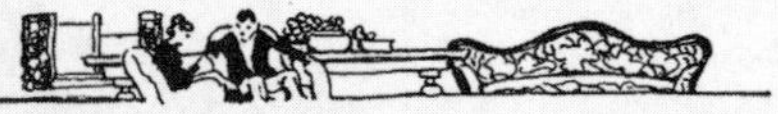

WHAT PRICE BEAUTY?

Concluded from page 55

Pictures. In antique gilt or natural wood frames; subjects in oil, water-colors, engravings, etchings or colored prints of interest to family and friends 25.00
Talking-Machine. In console cabinet or smaller case in any of the hard woods, chosen to correspond with the other furniture in the room 45.00
Curtains 20.00

Total for above room . . . $584.00

Dining-Room

Floor Coverings. Rugs such as Wiltons, velvets, chenilles, Axminsters, linen fiber, grass fiber or wool braided rugs are appropriate for the small dining-room . . $ 50.00
Table. In any of the hard woods or painted soft woods. It may be a round or square extension table or of drop-leaf or gate-leg type . 59.50
Chairs. Six, to match the dining-table in wood and design 36.00
Sideboard. To match the dining-table in wood and design. Or it may be an interesting chest of drawers, low-boy or large console 67.50
Mirror. Long, oblong or upright, in gold-leaf, silver-leaf, antique gilt, wood or painted frame 15.50
Pictures. One or two. These may be in gold-leaf, antique gilt, natural wood or painted frame . . . 16.00
China 50.00
Silver 100.00
Linens 20.00
Curtains 10.00

Total for above room . . . $424.50

Adults' Bedroom

Floor Coverings. Rugs such as velvets, Brussels, Wiltons, braided rag rugs, linen rugs or straw matting by the yard . . . . $ 30.00
Beds. Twin beds or double bed, in any of the hard woods, natural-wood finish or painted, or metal beds painted; woven-wire springs; mattress of good composition filler; two pillows, blankets, comforter. Bedspread preferably of washable material 150.00
Dresser. Or a broad chest of drawers, with or without attached mirror, similar to bed in style and finish. Metal furniture in excellent design is now made to match beds 50.00
Chiffonier, Chifforobe or High-Boy. Similar to dresser in finish and style, or it may be an individual chest of drawers 40.00
Small Table or Night-Stand. For bedside use; same wood and style as other bedroom furniture; or an individual piece, antique or modern, of period design 10.00
Lamp. Wood, pottery or metal base, with paper or light-colored silk shade 6.00
Armchair. Of wicker, or low, overstuffed, upholstered in light-colored silk or cotton material . . . 8.00
Straight Chair. This should be similar to other bedroom furniture . 8.00
Mirror. Mirror, with antique gilt, painted or wood frame, should be hung over chests of drawers or low-boys 15.00
Pictures. One or two, with natural-wood or painted frames; subjects may be of the more intimate type, such as family photographs or subjects of particular interest and association to the occupants of the room 10.00
Decorative Accessories for Ladies. Toilet articles in ivory or wood. Fresh cotton in small container or bag for guest. Lamp of wood, metal or pottery on bedside table, with shade of paper or chintz.
Hangers, shoe-trees and shoe-brushes in closet. 25.00
Decorative Accessories for Gentlemen. Toilet articles in ivory or wood. Clothes, hat and shoe-brushes available. Plenty of coat and trousers hangers; shoe-trees and shoe-cloths available in closet . . 15.00
Curtains 8.00

Total for above room . . . $375.00

Children's Room

Floor Coverings. Rugs or linoleum. Wilton, Brussels, hooked or braided rugs, or strips of coco-matting . . . . $ 20.00
Beds. Single beds, wood or metal. If the room is shared by two boys, use two single beds, in dark wood or metal, preferably of the day-bed type in dark wood, dull finish or painted finish. If the room is occupied by two girls, have light-colored wood or painted beds . . 70.00
One Mirror. Wood frame, hung low 8.00
Table. A low one to match dresser, or painted to match chairs . . . 12.00
Pictures. One or two dark-wood frames; subjects, those of interest to boys (or girls) 6.00
Curtains. Denims, reps and heavy sunfasts make appropriate curtains, bedspreads and bureau-scarfs for boys; cotton crapes, cretonnes and swisses for girls . . 10.00

Total for above room . . . $126.00

Linens and Blankets for all beds . . $ 78.00

Kitchen

Table . . . . $ 10.00
Stool 4.00
Utensils and Kitchen Linens . . . 40.00

Total for above room . . . $ 54.00

The above total does not include kitchen cabinet, range, refrigerator or floor covering.

Bathroom

Fixtures . . . . $ 10.00
Curtains 2.00
Hamper 3.50

Total for above room . . . $ 15.50

Total expended on Home No. 2 $1,699.00

HOME NO. 3—SEVEN ROOMS

Salary $5,000 per year. Allowance for furnishings, $2,800, or its equivalent in credits or furniture on hand.

Hall

Floor Coverings. Rugs, long runners, square or oblong, depending on the shape of the hall, of Wilton, Brussels, Axminster, wool-braided or any short-nap carpet, preferably in small design . . . . . . $ 25.00
Table. Small or medium size, in any of the hard woods or painted soft woods; drop-leaf, square, oblong or console shape 20.00
Chairs. Two straight chairs, with or without rush, cane or upholstered seats, in any of the hard woods, or dark-painted furniture 15.00
Accessories. Card-tray of wood, silver or brass, and a stone or pottery vase for flowers or branches are all that will be needed 5.00

Total for above room . . . $ 65.00

Living-Room

Floor Coverings. Carpets, rugs or linoleum . . . . $ 85.00
Table. In any of the hard woods or painted soft woods; square or oblong, depending on the shape of the room, such as an oblong library table, refectory, a square, drop-leaf, gate-leg or plain wood table, painted 45.00
Sofa. Either entirely overstuffed, or with wood frame, upholstered . . 200.00
Armchair. Either entirely overstuffed, upholstered seat and back only, or upholstered seat and wooden back, such as plain overstuffed velours chair, wing chair, Chippendale or French tapestry and needlework 60.00
Armchair. In any of the hard woods; type such as Windsor or ladder-back, with wood or rush seat . . 25.00
Desk. In any of the hard woods; type, block front or flat-top desk 65.00
Desk-Chair. Straight chair with upholstered, wood or rush seat, to correspond in wood and style with desk 15.00
End-Tables or Stools. In any of the hard woods or painted soft woods; low, round, square, oblong or kidney-shaped 24.00
Bookcase or Book-Shelves. Bookcase with or without doors; straight-line type or built-in book-shelves, painted or stained to match woodwork 50.00
Armchair. Partly upholstered . . . 35.00
Lamps. Tall, wooden or metal reading-lamp, with silk or paper shade; a table-lamp of wood, metal or pottery base, with silk, chintz, muslin or paper shade . . 40.00
Waste-Paper Basket. Wicker, wood or fiber 5.00
Decorative Accessories. Small foot-stool, pottery, brass or copper vases, bowls, candlesticks, sofa-cushions, table-runners or mats in duvetyn, velours, old brocade, heavy silks, or to correspond with materials used in overdraperies 30.00
Curtains 45.00
Pictures. Antique gilt or natural-wood frames; subjects in oils, water-colors, engravings, etchings or colored prints of interest to the family and friends 30.00
**Fireplace* (if any). Solid brass or steel andirons, fire-screen, stand containing pinchers, poker and hearth-brush, a wood-box or wood-basket 30.00
Radio. On small stand or table, with stool or chair to match . . 75.00

Total for above room . . . $859.00

Dining-Room

Floor Coverings. Carpets, rugs or linoleum . . . . $ 75.00
Table. In any of the hard woods or painted soft woods. Round or square extension, drop-leaf, gate-leg or refectory, in a reproduction of any of the straight or curved line periods 75.00
Chairs. Six, to match in wood and design the dining-table, or of some similar wood, or a dark painted finish of a period or style similar to that of the table . . . 72.00
Sideboard. To match the table in wood and design. Or it may be an interesting old chest of drawers, spinet, low-boy, or large console with drawers 130.00
**Serving-Table.* To match the sideboard in wood and design. Or it may be a small low-boy, a console with folding top, a gate-leg table or a small chest of drawers . . . 35.00
**Pictures.* Few are necessary in a dining-room. These may be in gold-leaf, antique gilt, natural-wood or painted frames 10.00
Curtains 20.00
China and Silver 200.00
Table Linens 40.00

Total for above room . . . $657.00

Adults' Bedroom

Floor Coverings. Linoleum or straw matting; rugs, such as velvets, Brussels, Wiltons, braided, rag rugs, linen rugs or straw matting by the yard . . . . $ 40.00
Beds. Twin beds 160.00
Dresser. Or a broad chest of drawers, with or without attached mirror, similar to beds in style and finish; or it may be an individual piece, antique or modern, of period design 60.00
Chiffonier, Chifforobe or High-Boy. Similar to dresser in finish and style; or it may be an individual piece, antique or modern, of period design 45.00
Dressing-Table, Toilet-Table or Low-Boy. Similar to chiffonier in style and finish; or it may be an individual piece, antique or modern, of period design. A flounced dressing-table is appropriate, with French or Early-American period furniture, or in country houses where no period is suggested, but is a dust collector and is not recommended for general use . . . 25.00
Dressing-Chair, Bench or Stool. For convenience at dressing-table. Same wood and style as dressing-table 10.00
Small Table or Night-Stand. For bedside use. Should be of same wood and style as other bedroom furniture, or an individual piece, antique or modern, of period design 10.00
Straight Chair. Hard wood 8.50
Lamp. Wood, pottery or metal base, with paper or light-colored silk shade 12.00
Mirrors. If dresser, chiffonier and dressing-table have no mirrors attached, mirrors with antique gilt, gold-leaf, painted or wood frames should be hung over chests of drawers or low-boys 15.00
Pictures. Subjects may be of the more intimate type, such as family photographs or subjects of particular interest and association to the occupants of the room 10.00
Decorative Accessories for Ladies. Toilet articles in silver, ivory, tortoise-shell or wood 25.00
Decorative Accessories for Gentlemen. Toilet articles in silver, ivory, tortoise-shell or wood. Clothes-, hat- and shoe-brushes available. Plenty of coat and trousers hangers, and shoe-trees and shoe-cloths available in closet 15.00

Total for above room . . . $435.50

Guest-Room*

Floor Coverings. Rugs, linoleum or straw matting. Hooked, braided or linen fiber rugs. . . . . . . $ 40.00
Beds. Twin beds in any of the hard woods, natural finish or painted 100.00
Dresser or Chest of Drawers. Similar to bed in finish and style, or an individual antique or modern piece, or a painted chest. 40.00
Flounce Dressing-Table. A flounce dressing-table may be made over a wooden frame or kitchen table at slight expense 15.00
Mirror. If the dresser and dressing-table have no mirrors, two antique gilt, gold-leaf or painted frames will be necessary, hung against the wall over the dresser and dressing-table 15.00
Armchair or Slipper-Chair. Low wicker, painted wood or overstuffed, upholstered in flowered or dainty material 15.00
Chair. One straight chair, either natural wood or painted, for use at desk 7.00
Desk. Natural wood, flat-top or spinet type 20.00
Table. Small bedside table to match the other furniture, with a small drawer 10.00
Lamp. Wood, pottery or metal base in some dainty, unusual design or color 10.00
Pictures. Not more than two. The subjects should interest the guests 10.00
Appointments and Decorative Accessories. Note-paper, blotters, post-cards, stamps, pen and ink on desk. Hand-mirror, brush and comb, shoe-horn, button-hook, box of assorted dress and hair pins; dress-hangers, shoe-cloth, shoe pockets or rack in the closet. Small carafe pitcher or thermos bottle and glass for water; small bag or basket with threads, needles, etc. Vase or bowl in pottery or glass for flowers. A few current magazines and small books. Special rack in bathroom for guest-towels and soap if there is no guest-bath 15.00
Curtains 8.00

Total for above room . . . $305.00

*Many houses can not afford a guest-room. The list of appointments and decorative accessories given above will prove useful when one of the family rooms is made over to accommodate a guest.

*Accessory rather than necessary.

Primary Source

What Price Beauty? Practical Budgets for Furnishings, Page 3 (3 OF 4)

List of prices of interior design elements from article, "What Price Beauty?," from the January 1926 issue of *The Delineator,* continued. THE LIBRARY OF CONGRESS.

THE DELINEATOR, January, 1926

CHILDREN'S ROOM

Floor Coverings. Rugs, linoleum or
coco-matting. Brussels, velvet,
braided or rag rugs, or strips of
coco-matting . . . . $ 15.00

Bed. Single bed, wood or metal . . 40.00

*Dresser, High - Boy or Chest of
Drawers* 40.00

Mirror. If the dresser has no mirror
attached, a plain square or oblong
mirror of natural wood or antique
gilt 12.00

Chair. One straight wooden chair to
match dresser 3.75

Table. A low one 12.00

Lamp. For table, or on a bracket,
with glass or stout paper shade 8.00

Bookcase or Book-Shelves. For books,
trophies, etc., of simple lines to
match other furniture, or shelves
finished to match woodwork . . 8.00

Pictures. One or two in dark-wood
frames; subjects should be those
of interest to children 6.00

Curtains. Sunfasts make appropriate curtains, bedspreads and
bureau-scarfs 8.00

TOTAL FOR ABOVE ROOM . . . $152.75

Linens together with Blankets for all
the beds $200.00

KITCHEN

Electrical Equipment . . . . . . $ 12.00

Table 15.00

Curtains 3.00

Kitchen Linen and Utensils . . . 50.00

TOTAL FOR THIS ROOM . . . $ 80.00

The above total, as in the preceding budgets for Homes No. 1 and No. 2, does not
include kitchen cabinet, refrigerator, range or
floor covering.

BATHROOM

Fixtures . . . . $ 8.00

Stool 5.00

Bathroom Linens 30.00

TOTAL FOR ABOVE ROOM . . . $ 43.00

TOTAL COST OF FURNISHING HOME
No. 3 . . . . $2,797.25

*If you wish further help in any of your
problems of house decoration write to Mrs.
Charles Bradley Sanders.*

THE HOME GYMNASIUM

Concluded from page 21

pocketbook permit. When not in use they
can be unhooked from the ceiling and therefore take up very little room.

Indian clubs and dumb-bells—These are
bought in pairs, are cheap, and are desirable
if you have space enough to use them.

Talking-machine—An inexpensive talking-
machine is a good investment. Figure marching and wand drills are much more enjoyable
when done to music, and a book of directions
and a few records will make it possible to add
folk-dancing to your programs.

With this equipment or even with a bare
floor many enjoyable as well as profitable
programs can be arranged. All that is necessary is the initiative; that I am counting on
you to provide. If your club can meet twice
each week and will really get into the spirit
of the games, the members will have more fun
than they could have in almost any other
way, and will assure themselves of good
health and poise and confidence.

In our article next month we will describe
in detail the exercises and games that can be
enjoyed in such a home gymnasium.

AFTER ONE HUNDRED AND FIFTY YEARS

Concluded from page 8

In all plays there are three things to be
considered: scene-setting, costuming, lighting.
The scene of Independence Hall, with its
main desk and rounds of benches, can be
easily copied from pictures in American
school histories or from reproductions of
Colonel John Trumbull's famous painting.
Note that the costumes are all in sober
colors—grays, browns and black.

The scene outside Independence Hall is
more difficult.

When a school has a good stage equipment,
there may be a backdrop of sky (such as in
the Central High School at Cleveland)
against which Independence Hall stands in
silhouette, while the sides of the stage are
masked with real or scenic trees. When a
backdrop is not feasible, and a narrow forest-
age must be used with curtains for background, the scene must be *suggested*.

If a longer program than these Independence Hall scenes is desired, lighter themes
may precede this mighty theme, and since
Washington was the popular hero of the
Revolution, these one-act plays might center
around him.

For a light and delicate comedy, there is a
one-act play entitled "Washington's First
Defeat," by Charles Nirdlinger. It has been
very widely used by high schools and little
theaters. In it one sees the youthful Washington as the wooer of Lucy Grimes, who
failed to smile on his courtship.

But if another type of scene is desired—one
that catches the poetry, the fragrance, the
glamour of that vanished Colonial period—
then the wedding scene of Martha Custis and
George Washington from "Washington," by
Percy MacKaye, is one that lends itself to
festival feeling. The scene is out-of-doors,
just after the wedding ceremony has been
performed. There are the negro songs of
the rejoicing plantation hands in Virginia,
with melodies both gay and plaintive; then
comes the entrance of the brilliant bevy of
wedding guests—many with names familiar
to history. A wandering ballad singer adds
a quaint touch to the gathering, which ends
with a Virginia reel, led by George and
Martha Washington.

FOR a grade school there is a one-act
Colonial play that belongs to the years
just after the revolution, when the Declaration had become a fact. This is "Little Lady
Dresden: An Incident of Mount Vernon"
from "Short Plays from American History
and Literature," by Olive M. Price. The
scene is in the west parlor at Mount Vernon
and the characters include *George* and *Martha Washington, Lafayette, Nellie Custis,* and
Betty Warwick—The Little Lady Dresden of
the play, as well as some other children and
a negro servant.

For rural grade schools an episode of Washington's boyhood which is exceedingly easy

to stage because of its backwoods costumes
is "George Washington's Fortune" from
"Patriotic Plays and Pageants," by C. D.
Mackay. There is a legend that as a boy
Washington had his fortune told by a Gipsy,
and her predictions came true. This little
play portrays that early incident.

For clubs and churches an extremely colorful and practical *indoor* pageant "For Home
and Country" has been designed by Annie
Russell Marble and published in pamphlet
form. It can be given by a cast numbering
seventy-five to one hundred men, women
and children. All it requires in the way of
stage setting is an average auditorium platform, hung with curtains. This play briefly
outlines the chief epochs in American history, and is strikingly original in that it depends on group effects with no star parts.

If you live in a small place, instead of the
usual perspiring Fourth of July parade of
shirt sleeves, straw hats, firemen, and local
ads, why not have a parade suggesting
epochs of American history? Such a parade
can (with competent committees) be homemade. Have half a dozen or more flat trucks,
with marchers in between. America or
Uncle Sam leads the parade. Next come
Indians and a wigwam truck with pine trees
and canoe (camp-fire girls, local Red Men or
Daughters of Pocahontas). Next a Pilgrim
group, marchers, or a spinning-wheel float.
Next a wilderness float and a group of young
eighteenth-century surveyors round a camp-
fire, this group led by young George Washington in surveyor's costume. Boy scouts
could do this. Next come the minute men,
with a flag: "Don't tread *on* me." Next a
marching replica of "Spirit of '76" group.
Float, Liberty Enthroned. (Also, if given
in an New England village, as many "antiques and horribles" as possible, in order to
keep up this ancient Fourth of July tradition. They add color and humor.) Then
have a space. Then a replica of the Liberty
Bell swung from a cross tree and carried by
two Quakers. Space. A float of Betsy Ross
and the first flag, walking with her dozens of
girls in Colonial dress, carrying flowers.
Then a blue and lavender group; pink and
pale-green group; yellow and violet group.
Next the Spirit of 1926, with a placard carried stating this fact. This group can be arranged like that of '76, and consist of an air-
pilot, Red Cross ambulance man, and boy
scout.

THE first ceremonial to be acted on public
steps against a Greek pillared background was that devised by Hazel MacKaye
for the Treasury steps at Washington, D. C.;
and after that, at Winchester, a small town
in Massachusetts, she proved that a Colonial
pillared background can also be most effective. Thus a city or a smaller town, possessed of a town hall or house with Colonial

pillars and with or without a flight of steps,
can essay this exceedingly interesting outdoor experiment with its players costumed in
rainbow hues, or trailing clouds of glory of
purple, crimson, and gold. The steps can
be used for the tableaux and speaking,
and the space below the steps for symbolic
dances.

On the week of July Fourth, when a number of villages may wish to join in a special
celebration other than a parade or fire-works,
there is the novel idea of equipping a large
motor truck as a stage, and sending it from
village to village. Denizens of the shore-line
villages of the Eastern states from Maine to
Rhode Island look forward eagerly each year
to the Jitney Players an organization of
young people who travel about the country
with a truck, whereon they give one-act
plays. Such a traveling stage could be readily duplicated for community use.

FOR a Fourth of July evening celebration
on the village green, have a huge replica
of the Declaration fastened to a pole. Have
a town crier (in Colonial costume) go to and
fro, ringing his bell and crying: "Hear ye!
Hear ye! The Declaration is signed." Have
the green or common hung with red, white
and blue Japanese lanterns. Have the town
band. Have Uncle Sam in costume, assisted
by the Thirteen Original States. Make people welcome, and then have a series of events
to which you will find reference in this final
paragraph. For if you want to know how to
evolve Colonial costumes and make effective
scenery for a mere song; where to obtain suggestions for a park and playground festival,
as well as for children's tableaux; where to
find a suitable program for Fourth of July
night in the village green; where to get the
inexpensive books mentioned in this article,
besides others that are helpful, then S.S.S.
instead of S.O.S. In other words, Send for
the Service Sheet! It is yours for the asking, and contains all sorts of information on
producing pageants which THE DELINEATOR
wants you to have but which could not be
crowded into the space of one article.

THEIR JUBILEE

*This year, of all years, is one that some
groups can make particularly their own. If
you join a patriotic society you will be able to
take part in the colorful celebrations of an unusually interesting period.*

*You may be eligible to some of these clubs.
Our booklet PATRIOTIC ORGANIZA-
TIONS FOR WOMEN gives you the membership requirements and headquarters of the important societies. It is the most complete
directory yet published. The book costs twenty-
five cents and will be sent promptly if you
write the Entertainment Department of THE
DELINEATOR, Butterick Building, New York.*

Primary Source

"What Price Beauty? Practical Budgets for Furnishings," Page 4 (4 OF 4)

Last page of "What Price Beauty?" article from *The Delineator*, January 1926. THE LIBRARY OF CONGRESS.

popular since the end of the nineteenth century. Even lamps and chandeliers resembled old-fashioned candles, disguising any appearance of modern electrical fixtures.

Rising wages and general economic optimism, along with an increase in mechanization, gave rise to the notion of "leisure." Americans began to spend more time improving their home lives. Magazines introduced readers to the latest appliances and trends in home decorating and offered advice on improving homemaking skills. Articles on gardening, selecting appliances for the home, and purchasing and arranging furnishings filled the pages of these publications, along with recipes and feature stories on family issues.

Significance

In the 1920s, home magazines such as *The Delineator, Good Housekeeping, House Beautiful, Arts & Decoration,* and *Better Homes and Gardens* (founded in 1922 as *Fruit, Garden and Home* but renamed two years later) enjoyed a growing readership. This type of publication had been in existence since the late nineteenth century, but by the 1920s their appeal was increasing among members of the expanding American middle class. Readers of these magazines, whether they lived in cities, towns, or suburbs, aspired to a better quality of home life.

Magazine articles offered readers solutions to their everyday home-related problems, both practical and aesthetic. An article in the January 1926 issue of *The Delineator,* for example, asked "Has it Beauty?" It suggested that, with the increasing attention given to the design of utilitarian objects, consumers should look for beauty in material things as they would look for beauty in other life experiences. Readers were even encouraged to build their own homes—in the 1920s, *Better Homes and Gardens* offered house plans for two dollars a set. Among the most popular regular features in these magazines were "Homes of Famous Americans" and "The Delightful Vogue of House Naming," both of which appeared in early issues of *Better Homes and Gardens. Good Housekeeping* also featured fiction and poetry.

Although *The Delineator* ceased publication, several home magazines of the 1920s were still published eighty years later and home and decorating ("shelter") magazines remained popular. Many offered features and articles that were remarkably similar to those found in their predecessors.

Further Resources

BOOKS

Bayer, Patricia. *Art Deco Interiors: Decoration and Design Classics of the 1920s and 1930s.* New York: Thames and Hudson, 1998.

Foy, Jessica H., and Thomas J. Schlereth, eds. *American Home Life, 1880–1930: A Social History of Spaces and Services.* Knoxville: University of Tennessee Press, 1992.

Grier, Katherine C. *Culture & Comfort: Parlor Making and Middle-Class Identity, 1850–1930.* Washington: Smithsonian Institution Press, 1997.

Reiff, Daniel Drake. *Houses from Books: Treatises, Pattern Books, and Catalogs in American Architecture, 1738–1950.* University Park, Pa.: Pennsylvania State University Press, 2000.

Stilgoe, John R. *Borderland: Origins of the American Suburb, 1820–1939.* New Haven, Conn.: Yale University Press, 1988.

WEBSITES

"Butterick: Our History." Available online at http://www.butterick.com/bhc/pages/articles/histpgs/about.html; website home page: http://www.butterick.com (accessed January 15, 2003).

The Delineator, November 1920. Reproduced at OnlineCostumeball.com. Available online at http://www.onlinecostumeball.com/Delineator/Nov_1920/Paris/Trends.htm; website home page: www.costumegallery.com (accessed January 15, 2003).

Reuss, Carol. "Chesla C. Sherlock as First Editor of *Better Homes and Gardens.*" University of Iowa Special Collections. Available online at http://www.lib.uiowa.edu/spec-coll/Bai/reuss.htm; website home page:http://www.lib.uiowa.edu/spec-coll/ (accessed January 8, 2003).

Wagner, Christopher. "United States Fashion Publications and Children's Fashions: *The Delineator.*" Historical Boys' Clothing. Available online at http://histclo.hispeed.com/photo/mag/us/mus-del.html; website home page: http://histclo.hispeed.com (accessed January 15, 2003).

Maidenform Brassiere Patent

Patent application

By: William and Ida Rosenthal

Date: October 12, 1926

Source: Rosenthal, William. *United States Patent 1,648,464.* Granted November 8, 1927. United States Patent and Trademark Office. Available online at http://www.uspto.gov (accessed October 28, 2002).

About the Inventors: Ida Cohen Rosenthal (1886–1973) was born near Minsk, Russia, and emigrated to the United States in 1905. She was a dressmaker at Enid Frocks in New York City, the company that would become Maidenform, Inc. Ida's husband, William Rosenthal (18??–1958), also a Russian emigrant, oversaw the designing and tailoring at Enid Frocks. He was also an amateur sculptor. The success of their intimate apparel company enabled the Rosenthals to become major philanthropists in their later years. ∎

Patented Nov. 8, 1927.

1,648,464

UNITED STATES PATENT OFFICE.

WILLIAM ROSENTHAL, OF NEW YORK, N. Y., ASSIGNOR TO ENID MANUFACTURING COMPANY, OF NEW YORK, N. Y., A CORPORATION OF NEW YORK.

BRASSIÈRE.

Application filed October 12, 1926. Serial No. 141,086.

This invention relates broadly to a new brassière construction.

One of the objects of this invention is the provision of a brassière which is adapted to support the bust in a natural position, contrary to the old idea of brassières made to flatten down the bust.

A further object of this invention is the provision of a brassière formed with pockets attached to the back bands without shirring.

A further object of this invention is the provision of a novel brassière construction which includes an elastic insert serving two purposes, first, the joining of the two pockets together so as to make it mold between the breasts and mark the division, and second to lessen the strain of the brassière, which is tight fitted.

A still further object of this invention is the construction of a brassière having pockets therein, constructed of irregular shaped pieces to provide an arrangement without shirring.

A still further object of this invention is the arrangement of seams placed in such a position as to eliminate any strain or pressure on the breast, and a still further purpose is to have the elastic insert covered with silk or net shirring for beautifying purposes, which is very essential in women's wearing apparel.

A further object of this invention is the provision of a brassière formed with pockets attached to a band extended below and inside above the lower parts of the pockets to prevent the bust from slipping out.

These and many other objects are secured by the brassière construction disclosed herein.

This invention resides substantially in the combination, construction, arrangement and relative location of parts, all as will appear more fully hereinafter.

Referring to the drawings, in which the same reference numerals will be used throughout the several views to indicate the same or similar parts,

Figure 1 represents a perspective view of a brassière employing the novel principles of my construction.

Figure 2 represents a cross-sectional view taken on the line 2—2 of Figure 1, looking in the direction of the arrows.

Figure 3 represents a cross-sectional view taken on the line 3—3 of Figure 5 looking in the direction of the arrows.

Figure 4 represents an enlarged cross-sectional view taken on the same line as Figure 3.

Figure 5 is an enlarged detailed side elevational view of the elastic insert.

Figures 6 and 9 represent a portion of the elements which form the back band.

Figures 7 and 10 represent a portion of the piece which forms the upper portion of the pockets and Figures 8 and 11 represent the portion which forms the bottom portion of the pockets.

Figure 12 shows a rear elevational view of a modified form with a band forming with the pockets a receptacle for the breasts.

Figure 13 is an enlarged front elevational view of one of the pockets.

Figure 14 is a vertical cross-sectional view taken on line 14—14 of Fig. 12, looking in the direction of the arrows.

It has been found in actual experience with former constructions of brassières that there is a tendency for the brassière to cause irritation of the wearer's skin due to certain features of construction.

For instance, it has been found that the seams used in uniting the several elements of the brassière, being raised, cause this trouble, as well as the shirring used in joining the several parts together. Especially is this true of the shirring formed where the pockets are united to the elastic insert. The improved construction disclosed herein eliminates these difficulties.

Referring to the drawings, I have shown at 1, the two pieces 1, which form together the back band for supporting the pocket section on the body of the wearer. The pocket comprises the two pieces 2 and 3. The shape of the pieces 1, 2 and 3 are clearly shown in Figures 6 to 11. The two pieces 2 are provided with a V-shaped notch indicated by the reference numeral A and the two edges of the notch are drawn together and united to form the substantially vertical seam shown in Figure 1, and form the upper portion of the pockets. Since the drawing together of these edges will cause the element 2 to bulge and become convex, it is evident that this construction is readily adapted to form a pocket. The lace or net lining 4 is shown, which in the completed article will form a

Primary Source

Maidenform Brassiere Patent, Page 1 (1 OF 5)

SYNOPSIS: William and Ida Rosenthal, designers of the first Maidenform bra, were granted a patent for a brassiere designed to "support the bust in a natural position" in 1927. The Rosenthals went on to apply for more patents as their company continued to make improvements to their design, which eventually led to modern bra styles. U.S. GOVERNMENT PATENT OFFICE.

2 **1,648,464**

complete cover for the inside of the brassière. An elastic insert 6 is shown secured to the inner ends of the pockets and pieces of tape 7 are used to cover these seams as is clearly
5 shown in Figure 3. A net covering 5 is also provided for the elastic insert 6. The back band pieces 1 are attached to the pockets by means of seams and tape covering 7'; and this connection, as well as the connection of
10 the pockets to the elastic insert is formed without any shirring. The free ends of the back band are covered with the tape pieces 8 and applied with the usual hook and eye construction 9. Suitable straps 10 are provided
15 to support the brassière on the shoulders of the wearer. As is shown in Figure 2, the edges of the pieces 3 and 4 are bent back on themselves as shown at 11 and 12 and joined together to form a strong resistant bound
20 edge. As is clearly shown in Figure 1, the portion 3 fits into the flat V-shaped portion formed by the elements 2, when they are shaped as above described, and is joined to these edges to form the seams 13. It is at
25 once evident that by this construction a neat pocket arrangement is formed.

It may be pointed out then that by this construction a brassière is formed with relatively few seams which are all covered by a
30 lace or net lining and pieces of tape, so that the seams are not allowed direct contact with the skin. It will be evident that by this construction the resulting product is neat, and comprises relatively few parts. I consider
35 the particular pattern shapes devised by me to form the pocket construction one of the essential features of this invention, since I provide a method of constructing pockets and attaching them to the back band piece
40 of the elastic insert without shirring. The lace covering can be omitted if desired.

In the form of brassière shown in Figures 12, 13 and 14, the back pieces 1 and the fastening means 8 are used. An elastic insert 30
45 is also shown in the back bands. The pockets formed of the pieces 2 and 3 are shown

attached to the upper portions of the back band, which are wide in this construction, and are joined by the elastic insert 6 at 40. A band comprising the parts 31, 32 and 33
50 is united together and to the back bands by taped seams 34. The bottom edges of the pockets are united with the composite band by the seams 35, and a lace band 41 decorates and strengthens the upper free edge. All the
55 edges are strengthened by being bent back on themselves at 35, and tacked down. A receptacle for the breasts is formed between the pocket forming portions and the portions of the composite band between the seams 34
60 and 35. Shoulder straps 36 are provided with a series of button holes 37, adapted to form with the buttons 38 adjustable supports for the brassière.

I am, of course, aware that many changes
65 in the detail of construction and relative arrangement of parts will readily suggest themselves to those skilled in the art, and I do not, therefore, desire to be limited to the exact details disclosed by the way of illus-
70 tration, but rather to the spirit and scope of my invention as I define it in the appended claim.

What I seek to secure by United States Letters Patent is:
75

In a brassière construction as described the combination of two sets of two irregular shaped members secured together along three seams emanating from a single point to form breast receiving pockets, having an elastic
80 connection between them, a back band secured to each pocket and having means on the free ends of said back bands for detachably securing the brassière around the body of the wearer, and a flexible and distortable
85 lining for the brassière for protecting the wearer's body from said seams.

In testimony whereof I have hereunto set my hand on this 6th day of October, A. D., 1926.

WILLIAM ROSENTHAL.

Primary Source

Maidenform Brassiere Patent, Page 2 (2 OF 5)
Second page of textual portion of Maidenform bra patent. 1927. U.S. GOVERNMENT PATENT OFFICE.

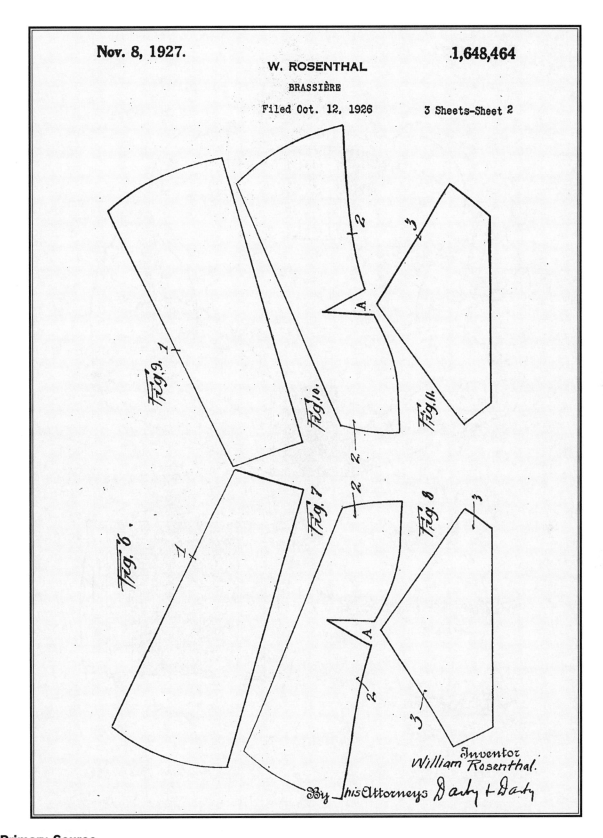

Nov. 8, 1927.

W. ROSENTHAL

BRASSIÈRE

Filed Oct. 12, 1926

3 Sheets-Sheet 2

1,648,464

Inventor
William Rosenthal.

By his Attorneys Darby + Darby

Primary Source

Maidenform Brassiere Patent, Page 3 (3 OF 5)
Patent application drawing showing pattern for pieces of main body of first Maidenform bra. 1927. U.S. GOVERNMENT PATENT OFFICE.

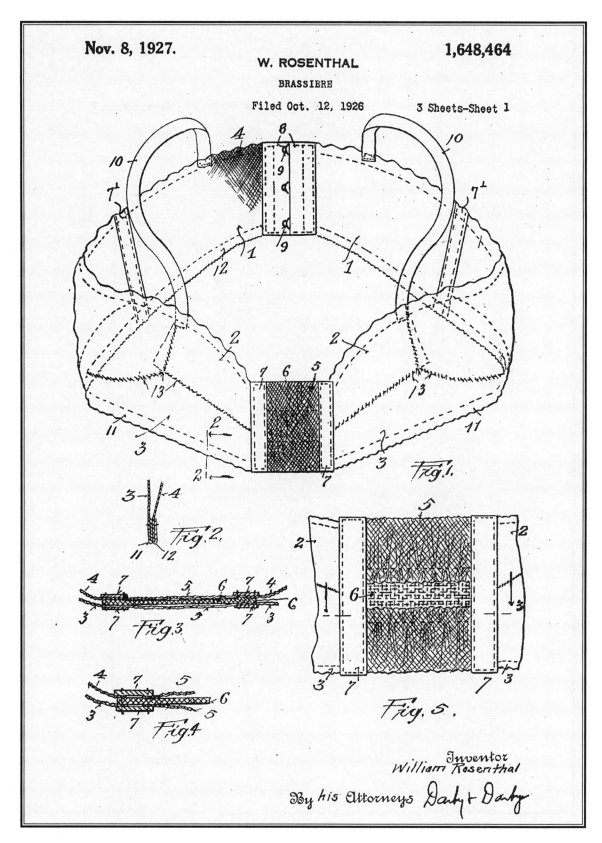

Nov. 8, 1927.

W. ROSENTHAL

BRASSIERE

Filed Oct. 12, 1926

1,648,464

3 Sheets—Sheet 1

Fig. 1.

Fig. 2.

Fig. 3.

Fig. 4.

Fig. 5.

Inventor
William Rosenthal

By his Attorneys Darby & Darby

Primary Source

Maidenform Brassiere Patent, Page 4 (4 OF 5)
Patent application drawing illustrating stitching and fasteners of Maidenform's first bra. 1927. U.S. GOVERNMENT PATENT OFFICE.

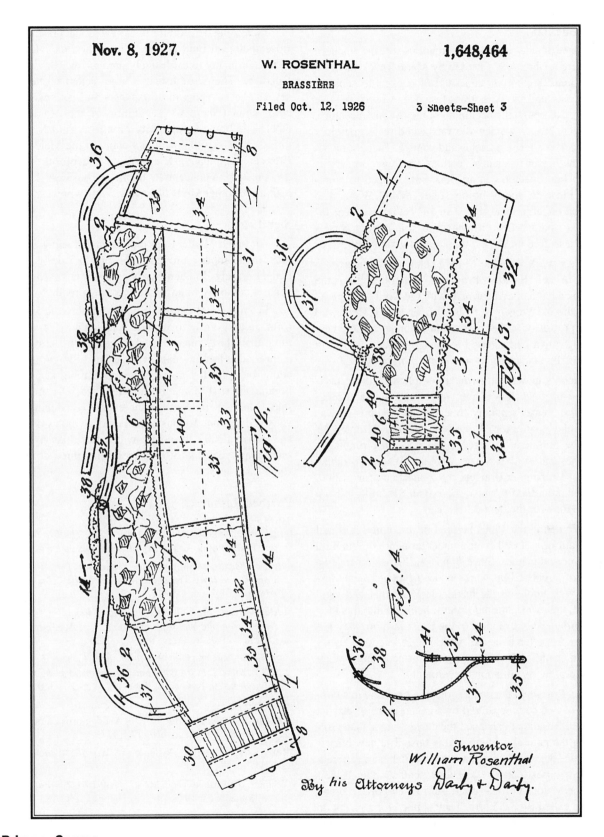

Nov. 8, 1927.   1,648,464

W. ROSENTHAL

BRASSIÈRE

Filed Oct. 12, 1926   3 Sheets-Sheet 3

Fig. 12.

Fig. 13.

Fig. 14.

Inventor
William Rosenthal
By his Attorneys Darby & Darby.

Primary Source

Maidenform Brassiere Patent, Page 5 (5 of 5)
Patent application drawing showing lace embellishment to be included on Maidenform's bras. 1927. U.S. GOVERNMENT PATENT OFFICE.

Introduction

One of the earliest incarnations of the modern brassiere, or bra, was patented by Marie Tucek in 1893. Her "breast supporter" consisted of pockets to separate the breasts, and shoulder straps fastened by hook-and-eye closures. Through the beginning of the twentieth century, however, proper women were expected to wear tightly laced corsets over camisoles and panties. Then women's fashions began to change, calling for looser undergarments. Improvements in artificial silks helped to popularize the new, looser-fitting styles. World War I also affected undergarment styles; in 1917, the U.S. War Industries Board called on women to stop buying corsets in order to free up 28,000 tons of metal annually.

New York socialite Mary Phelps Jacob received a patent for her "Backless Brassiere" in 1914. She was the first to patent an undergarment with the word "brassiere" (from the old French word for "upper arm"). Dismayed at the protrusion of her corset boning under a sheer new evening gown, she devised an undergarment consisting of two silk handkerchiefs and some pink ribbon.

Jacob's new undergarment complemented the fashions of the time. It was lightweight and soft, and separated the breasts naturally (but without support—it was rather like a halter top). Friends and family clamored for the new brassiere, but Jacobs did not enjoy running a business and sold her patent to the Warner Brothers Corset Company in Bridgeport, Connecticut, for $1,500. Warner proceeded to make more than $15 million from the patent over the next thirty years.

Women in the 1920s favored flesh-colored bras and cami-knickers, an all-in-one undergarment combining a camisole and panties. Since flapper fashions demanded a boyish flat chest, bras were bandeau-type garments fastened with hooks in the back. Ida Rosenthal and Enid Bissett, the owner of Enid Frocks, believed that this look was unflattering. Contrary to the latest fashion, they felt dresses fit better over the natural bust line, and that a woman spending money on a custom-made dress ought to have properly fitting undergarments.

Ida Rosenthal devised a prototype brassiere that consisted of two cups separated by a center piece of elastic. William Rosenthal enhanced the design into a shape following the natural contours of the bust. The new bra offered the breasts support and was available in different size categories (cup sizes). The Rosenthals named their creation Maiden Form, in contrast to a then-popular brand of bras called Boyish Form. They applied for a patent on the design in 1926 and were granted one the following year. Originally the bra was built into each dress made by Enid Frocks. But the Maiden Form was such a success that Enid Frocks began offering a separate bonus undergarment with each dress sold.

Increasing demand for their new product inspired the Rosenthals and Enid Bissett to form the Enid Manufacturing Company to exclusively produce the Maidenform Brassiere. They established a large factory in New Jersey. Advertisements in newspapers and national magazines helped increase recognition of the Maidenform label. The brand's popularity prompted Enid Manufacturing Company to change its name to the Maidenform Brassiere Company. Eventually Maidenform stopped dressmaking to concentrate on the bra business, later expanding to other kinds of lingerie and swimwear.

Significance

Although Maidenform did not manufacture the first bras, the company produced the first bra design to be bought widely. Maidenform was also the first intimate apparel company to advertise this new product.

From a small company of ten employees, Maidenform quickly grew to include a national sales team of more than thirty men to market the new bras, available in three sizes for the small, average, and full figure. "Variation" bras, for the average figure, retailing at $1 each, became the first Maidenform style to reach $1 million in sales. Maidenform continued to expand, producing innovative advertising for buses, billboards, window displays, and radio. In 2003, the company had more than five thousand employees and offered more than three dozen bra styles each season.

Further Resources

BOOKS

Farrell-Beck, Jane, and Colleen Gau. *Uplift: The Bra in America.* Philadelphia: University of Pennsylvania Press, 2002.

Fontanel, Béatrice. *Support and Seduction: The History of Corsets and Bras.* Translated by Willard Wood. New York: Abrams, 1997.

Steele, Valerie. *Fashion and Eroticism: Ideals of Feminine Beauty from the Victorian Era to the Jazz Age.* New York: Oxford University Press, 1985.

Vare, Ethlie Ann, and Greg Ptacek. *Patently Female: From AZT to TV Dinners: Stories of Women Inventors and Their Breakthrough Ideas.* New York: John Wiley & Sons, 2002.

PERIODICALS

"Dreams for Sale: How the One for Maidenform Came True." *Advertising Age,* September 12, 1977.

"The Mother Figure of Maidenform." *Working Woman,* April 1987.

"Women Who Made Their Mark." *New York Journal-American,* January 13, 1959.

WEBSITES

Maidenform Collection, 1922–1997. Smithsonian National Museum of History Archives. Available online at http:// americanhistory.si.edu/archives/d7585.htm; website home page: http://americanhistory.si.edu/archives (accessed January 15, 2003).

"Maidenform Timeline." Maidenform company website. Available online at http://www.maidenform.com/cgi-bin /maidenform/maidenform/timeline/timeline.jsp; website home page http:www.maidenform.com (accessed January 6, 2003).

Textile Designs of the 1920s

Americana Print: Pegs

Textile design

By: Charles Buckels Falls

Date: 1927

Source: Falls, Charles B. *Americana Print: Pegs.* 1927. Manufactured by Stehli Silks Corp., New York. In the collection of the Metropolitan Museum of Art, New York.

Rhapsody

Textile design

By: John Held Jr.

Date: 1927

Source: Held, John Jr. *Rhapsody.* 1927. Manufactured by Stehli Silks Corp., New York. In the collection of the Allentown Art Museum, Allentown, Pa.

Mothballs and Sugar

Textile design

By: Edward Steichen

Date: ca. 1927

Source: Steichen, Edward. *Mothballs and Sugar.* ca. 1927. Manufactured by Stehli Silks Corp., New York. In the collection of the Whitney Museum of American Art, New York.

Thrill

Textile design

By: Dwight Taylor

Date: 1927

Source: Taylor, Dwight. *Thrill.* 1927. Manufactured by Stehli Silks Corp., New York. In the collection of the Allentown Art Museum, Allentown, Pa.

About the Designers: Some of the best-known artists and designers of the 1920s created textile patterns. Stehli Silks, one of the leading silk manufacturers of the decade, emerged as the textile industry's top innovator of the time. The following artists and designers were among those commissioned by the company to produce textile designs.

Charles Buckels Falls (1874–1960) was a popular graphic artist and muralist. His *ABC Book of 1923* was one of the first modern American picture books, and he illustrated many other children's books as well. He also created posters and prints for the Marines and provided many cover illustrations

Art and Advertising

In 1923, Cheney Brothers, an old New England silk firm that was seeking to update its stodgy image, engaged the services of Edward L. Bernays. Born in Vienna and raised in the United States, Bernays (1891–1995) is considered the founder of the field of public relations. He devised elaborate advertising campaigns for corporate clients such as Procter & Gamble, Cartier, Best Foods, and Knox Gelatin, and also worked on behalf of many nonprofit organizations. In 1924, he was even hired to improve Calvin Coolidge's image before the presidential election. Bernays helped modernize the Cheney Brothers' image by commissioning artist Georgia O'Keeffe to create paintings for display in shop windows with Cheney silks. The accompanying ad copy read, "The newest fall colors are certain subtle shadings of red, brown, blue, green and gray, specific shades new to fashion. So exquisite are these hues that a modern artist symbolizes their charm in a series of paintings." Painter Marc Chagall, not yet famous at the time, also produced a colorful floral design for a similar Cheney project.

SOURCE: Bernays, Edward L. "Typescript on Art in the Fashion Industry, 1923–1927: Cheney Brothers." *Prosperity and Thrift: The Coolidge Era and the Consumer Economy, 1921-1929.* American Memory digital primary source collection, Library of Congress. Available online at http://memory.loc.gov/ammem/coolhtml/coolhome.html; website home page: http://memory.loc.gov (accessed May 12, 2003).

for pulp magazines of the time, including *The Shadow, Weird Tales,* and *Thrills of the Jungle.*

John Held Jr. (1889–1958) was one of the most prolific commercial illustrators of the 1920s. Held's images appeared in some of the era's most popular magazines, including *Vanity Fair, Harper's Bazaar,* and *Redbook.* His humorous drawings featured exaggerated, lanky figures in playful poses and vivid colors that reflected the spirit of the Jazz Age.

Edward Steichen (1879–1973) was born in Luxembourg and began exhibiting his paintings at the age of sixteen. He later moved to the United States and embarked on a career in photography. In collaboration with the noted photographer and gallery owner Alfred Stieglitz, he played an instrumental role in introducing modern art to Americans. He also promoted American artists throughout Europe. In the 1920s, Steichen was famous for his fashion and celebrity photography. He directed the Department of Photography at the Museum of Modern Art in New York from 1947 to 1962. ■

Introduction

After World War I, Americans felt a growing desire to break free of European influences in fashion, art, literature, music, and drama. In the field of industrial design,

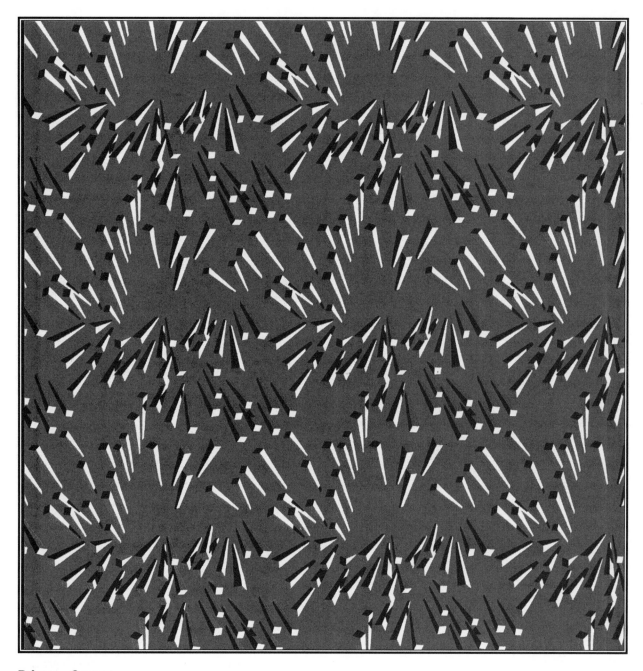

Primary Source

Americana Print: Pegs

SYNOPSIS: Charles B. Falls, an illustrator and graphic artist, created a playful design for Stehli. The "pegs," scattered on an ocean of bright color, give the illusion of actually being stuck into the surface of the fabric. Using a simple graphic device, Falls created a complex image that could appear both three-dimensional and yet abstract at the same time. THE METROPOLITAN MUSEUM OF ART, GIFT OF STEHLI SILKS CORPORATION, 1927. (27.243.2) PHOTOGRAPH © 2000 THE METROPOLITAN MUSEUM OF ART.

this resulted in an effort to create a modern style that was uniquely American. Until this time, American designers either took their influences from the latest European trends, including Art Deco, or regurgitated colonial-era designs that had been popular in the United States since the nation's Centennial Exposition in 1876. But reports from the 1925 Paris Exposition of Decorative Arts and Modern Industry, an influential exhibition devoted to demonstrating the importance of art in industrial production, convinced American designers that even as the country entered the Machine Age, its machine-made products could be pleasingly and thoughtfully designed.

Primary Source

Rhapsody

SYNOPSIS: Many of the new Stehli Silks designs incorporated images from popular culture. John Held Jr.'s *Rhapsody* depicts musicians performing George Gershwin's recently debuted jazz concerto. ALLENTOWN ART MUSEUM, GIFT OF KATE FOWLER MERLE-SMITH, 1978. (1978.26.524.1-3)

The resulting "Art in Industry" movement sought to promote awareness of industrial design, primarily through widespread newspaper campaigning. Manufacturing spokespersons declared that even everyday objects such as kitchen gadgets and furniture ought to incorporate some creativity in their design.

Significance

The "Art in Industry" movement particularly affected American textile manufacturing. Heightened publicity and public awareness spurred competition between various design houses and textile producers in the States. Advancements in silk production techniques and the invention of acetate and rayon also created a demand for new fabric colors and patterns that would appeal to the American public. Consumers, long accustomed to imitating the latest styles from Paris, now demanded American designs in American fabrics, as long as these colors and patterns were not drab.

In response, the textiles industry took an innovative approach to the design of new fabrics, hiring some of the best-known artists and designers of the decade to create textile patterns. Stehli Silks Corporation, along with Cheney Brothers, and H.R. Mallinson & Co., Inc., were the leaders of the 1920s and 1930s in the creation of innovative printed silks; all three manufacturers commissioned outside artistic talent. Inspired by popular imagery and social trends, the designers created bold, repetitive patterns of simple geometric forms, evoking the idea of the Machine Age. The wildly patterned, colorful prints

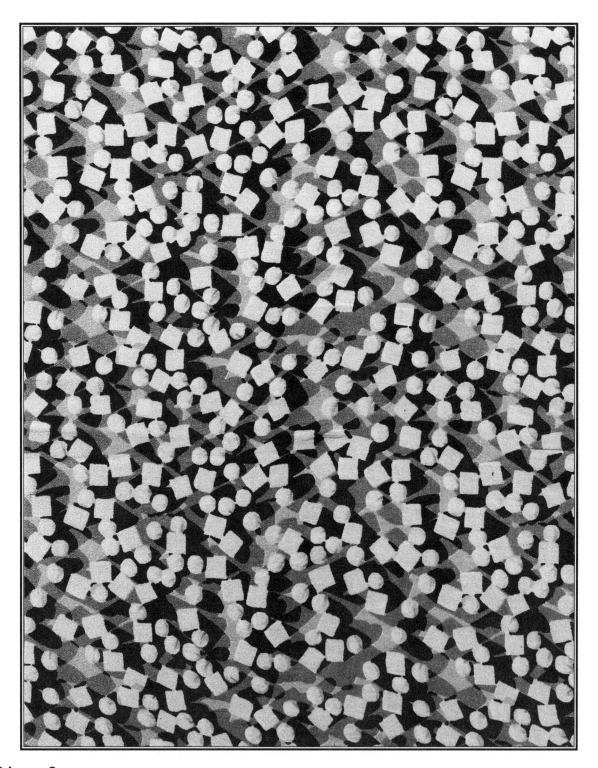

Primary Source

Mothballs and Sugar

SYNOPSIS: Edward Steichen's fabric designs for the Stehli Silks Corporation were derived from his abstract photographs of small, common items. An aerial reconnaissance photographer during World War I, Steichen photographed close-ups of clustered objects (matches and matchboxes, tacks, buttons with thread) from above. The shadows cast by the objects became part of the composition. THE NEWARK MUSEUM/ART RESOURCE, NY. REPRODUCED BY PERMISSION.

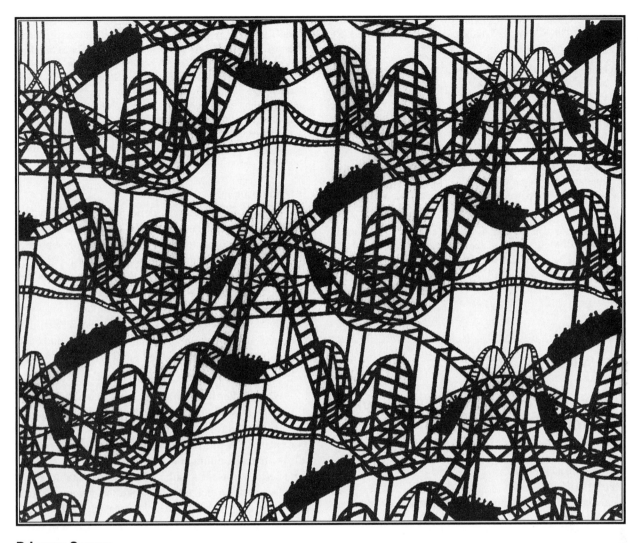

Primary Source

Thrill

SYNOPSIS: Inspired by Coney Island's then-newest attraction, the Cyclone roller coaster, Dwight Taylor's 1927 design *Thrill* perfectly captures the sinuous, topsy-turvy rush of the Roaring Twenties. ALLENTOWN ART MUSEUM, GIFT OF KATE FOWLER MERLE-SMITH, 1978. (1978.26.27)

captured the spirit of the Roaring Twenties—and were still appealing at the end of the century. Some of the textile patterns were reissued and continue to be available some eighty years later.

Competing textile companies began producing fabrics imprinted with motifs such as submarines, radios, teepees, and American icons such as Washington's home at Mount Vernon and the Grand Canyon. Style leaders cheered this Americanism. Even popular culture was translated into fabric. Ralph Barton easily reinvented his illustrations for the quintessential flapper novel, *Gentlemen Prefer Blondes* (1926), by Anita Loos, into fabric prints. Other imaginative designs of the 1920s featured Cheerios and the "It" girl, silent-film star Clara Bow. In

1927, artist Dwight Taylor designed a silk called *Thrill*. Imprinted with roller coasters, it was designed as an homage to Coney Island's Cyclone ride, which opened earlier that year. The development of a modern American design style was well under way.

Further Resources

BOOKS

Armitage, Shelley. *John Held Jr.: Illustrator of the Jazz Age.* New York: Syracuse University Press, 1989.

Bernays, Edward L. *Biography of an Idea.* New York: Simon & Schuster, 1965.

Boardman, Michelle. *All That Jazz: Printed Fashion Silks of the '20s and '30s.* Allentown, Pa.: Allentown Art Museum, 1998.

Haskell, Barbara. *The American Century: Art & Culture, 1900–1950.* New York: Whitney Museum of American Art, 1999.

Jackson, Lesley. *Twentieth-Century Pattern Design: Textile and Wallpaper Pioneers.* New York: Princeton Architectural Press, 2002.

Skinner, Tina. *Art Deco Textile Designs.* Atglen, Pa.: Schiffer Publishing Co., 1999.

WEBSITES

Horsley, Carter B. "Edward Steichen." *The City Review.* Available online at http://www.thecityreview.com/steichen.html; website home page: http://www.thecityreview.com/home.html (accessed January 14, 2003).

"John Held, Jr. and the Jazz Age: A Life in Art." The Norman Rockwell Museum. Available online at http://www.nrm.org/exhibits/held/bio.html; website home page: http://www.nrm.org (accessed January 14, 2003).

Dymaxion House

"Plan—Isometric and Elevation of a Minimum Dymaxion Home"

Architectural design

By: R. Buckminster Fuller

Date: 1927

Source: Fuller, R. Buckminster. "Plan—Isometric and Elevation of a Minimum Dymaxion Home." In Marks, Robert W. *The Dymaxion World of Buckminster Fuller.* New York: Reinhold Publishing, 1960, 82.

"4D House (1928)"

Personal journal

By: R. Buckminster Fuller

Date: 1928

Source: Fuller, R. Buckminster. "4D House (1928)." In the archives of the Buckminster Fuller Institute. Available online at http://www.bfi.org/4d_house_1928.htm; website home page: http://www.bfi.org (accessed July 31, 2002).

About the Designer: Richard Buckminster Fuller (1895–1983) was an inventor, mathematician, educator, philosopher, and poet. Born in Milton, Massachusetts, he attended Harvard and the U.S. Naval Academy, and served in the U.S. Navy. In the early 1920s, Fuller's four-year-old daughter died, and his company, which made the first modular housing units, folded. He contemplated suicide, but emerged from his crisis determined to do something "on behalf of all humanity." Particularly concerned with providing housing for all, Fuller began to develop designs for cheap, mass-produced shelter. Although he had no formal degrees in engineering or architecture, his investigations eventually led to his most famous invention, the geodesic dome—the world's lightest, strongest, and most cost-effective structure, patented in 1947. He became a research professor at Southern Illinois University in 1959 and in 1962 became the Norton professor of poetry at Harvard. In the 1960s and 1970s, he lectured and wrote frequently on his theories about socially and environmentally conscious design, promoting the idea that technology and planning could alleviate global problems facing humanity. Fuller was awarded twenty-five U.S. patents, received forty-seven honorary doctorates, and published twenty-eight books. ■

Introduction

In 1927, Fuller set to work designing a prefabricated housing unit, which he called "4D." The house consisted of walls and multiple levels of steel alloy cable-supported floor decks suspended around a central mast. The mast included vents to cool, clean, or heat the air and ensured that the house would be dust-free. The windowless walls consisted of transparent vacuum pane glass with a special shuttering system. 4D, if mass-produced, would be relatively affordable (costing as much as a car), and could be easily shipped and installed anywhere in the United States.

When Fuller filed his patent application in 1928, the 4D house was not ready for industrial production. The structure called for technology that was not yet available. For example, it was designed to be made with aluminum alloys, but aluminum was not used in buildings at the time because it was too soft and not heat-treatable. Fuller was certain these technologies would be developed soon, and he was right. Only five years later, the first heat-treated aluminum alloys came on the market, a development that launched the airplane industry.

Fuller's 4D house was featured in the art news section of the *Chicago Evening Post* in December 1928. Marshall Field's department store in Chicago felt that the 4D house would be a perfect complement to its new line of modern furniture and arranged to have a model displayed in the store. Advertising specialist Waldo Warren was assigned to work with Fuller on a new name for his "house of the future." The name "Dymaxion" is a fusion of the syllables from a few of Fuller's favorite words: "DYnamism," "MAXimum," and "tensION." In 1929, Marshall Field copyrighted the word "Dymaxion" in Fuller's name. Fuller began using "Dymaxion" as a brand name, and in 1932, he founded the Dymaxion Corporation to produce his innovative designs.

Fuller created a modified version of his design for the Marshall Field's display. This second model was a single-level, round, metallic house. Its spaceship-like appearance gave it a fantastic, futuristic quality, and it quickly became the better-known version of Fuller's design.

PLAN - ISOMETRIC - AND - ELEVATION OF A MINIMUM DYMAXION HOME

Primary Source

"Plan—Isometric and Elevation of a Minimum Dymaxion Home"

SYNOPSIS: Buckminster Fuller's Dymaxion House was inexpensive to produce, required little maintenance, an easily adaptable floor plan, and was strong enough to withstand earthquakes and storms. It even had such futuristic conveniences as storage areas and shelving units that would fold away at the wave of the hand. Only two prototypes were ever produced.

Buckminster Fuller poses near a model of his 4D, or "Dymaxion," House, 1929. © BETTMANN/CORBIS. REPRODUCED BY PERMISSION.

Significance

Dymaxion House, designed for maximum efficiency with minimal materials, was a product of Buckminster Fuller's environmentalist and conservationist philosophy—a philosophy that was unusual for his time. He embraced the age of mass production, believing that a conscientious application of technology could provide social benefits for humanity and maintain the earth's resources.

While Fuller had created a stir with the unveiling of 4D, he felt the design could be improved upon. Dymaxion House was one of the first steps toward the development of the geodesic dome, the invention for which Fuller is best known and one of the strongest structures ever designed.

Dymaxion Houses were never produced as Fuller envisioned. He built only two prototypes of the house, in 1946; both were purchased by Kansas investor William Graham. Graham's family lived in a hybridized version of the Dymaxion House, also called the Dymaxion

Dwelling Machine (or simply "Wichita House") well into the 1970s. In 1991, the Henry Ford Museum in Dearborn, Michigan, acquired the surviving prototype. The Dymaxion House was installed in the museum and opened to the public in 2001.

Although some of his ideas were considered offbeat and controversial, Fuller was ahead of his time in many respects. Considered a founder of the environmental design movement, he stressed technological efficiency ("getting more with less"), and coined the term "Spaceship Earth." Karen Goodman, who produced and directed a documentary file on Fuller, points out, "Fuller urged everyone to think globally and act ecologically long before most people had even heard those words."

Primary Source

"4D House (1928)"

SYNOPSIS: In this excerpt from his journal, Buckminster Fuller describes how the failure of his company, which made modular housing units, led to the development of his first home design, dubbed "4D." He also explains why the innovative design was never actually patented.

When, after getting up 240 Stockade System houses in the Eastern half of the United States, I discovered that I could not make money by introducing so new a process into the building world, I became interested in how we might use aircraft technologies to produce dwelling machines for humanity. I was convinced by my experience in the building world that its activities were thousands of years behind the development of environment controlling for the sea and the sky. The 4D House was a consequence of my attempt to bring that advanced technology to bear on human environment controlling. I was producing tensionally cohered structures, and the 4D House was the result. My patent attorney felt that it would be much more convincing to the patent examiners if the same principles were employed but resulted in a rectilinear structure of conventional appearance. While the patent application embodied all the principles of the 4D House, it looked like a conventional house.

I knew very little about the world of patenting. In the case of my first two patents, the joint one with my father-in-law and mine for the manufacturing process, all the work was done by my patent attorney, who did not consult with me after the first disclosure. It is the formal procedure of attorneys dealing with the U.S. patent office to file applications for patents that first make a philosophical disclosure of the state of the art in which the invention is operative, then carefully describe the invention with accompanying drawings, then list a series of claims of what the inventor feels is the most economical statement of that which he feels is his unique invention. Then after the list of claims is filed, the patent office examiner sends back what is called the first rejection, rejecting a number of the claims but allowing one or two. The attorney and the inventor have the opportunity to make two more resubmissions of the stated claims, hoping to restate them acceptably to the examiners. The examiner indicates which of the claims might be restated in a final submission. In all, there are four such exchanges between the claiming inventor and the patent examiner. The patent attorney I had for the 4D House changed partnership and moved out of town. He did not tell me that the first rejection by the patent office was anything but a rejection. I did not know that subsequent resubmission of the

patent was possible; I just assumed it was a final rejection and let it go. I knew I had a filing in the patent office of the invention and that it would serve as a first disclosure of my discovery from a scientific viewpoint.

Further Resources

BOOKS

Baldwin, J. *BuckyWorks: Buckminster Fuller's Ideas for Today.* New York: John Wiley & Sons, 1996.

Fuller, Buckminster. *Operating Manual for Spaceship Earth.* Carbondale: Southern Illinois University Press, 1969.

Krausse, Joachim, and Claude Lichenstein, eds. *Your Private Sky: R. Buckminster Fuller, The Art of Design Science.* Zurich: Lars Muller Publications, 1999.

Pawley, Martin, *Buckminster Fuller.* London: Taplinger Publishing Company, 1990.

PERIODICALS

Fuller, Buckminster. "Tree-Like Style of Dwelling Is Planned." *Chicago Evening Post Magazine of the Art World,* December 18, 1928, 5.

WEBSITES

Baldwin, J. "Dymaxion Houses." Thirteen Online. Available online at http://www.thirteen.org/bucky/house.html; website home page: http://www.thirteen.org (accessed January 10, 2003).

The Buckminster Fuller Institute. Available online at http://www.bfi.org (accessed January 10, 2003).

"Buckminster Fuller's Dymaxion House." In the collection of The Henry Ford Museum, Dearborn, Michigan. Available online at http://www.hfmgv.org/dymaxion/; website home page: http://www.hfmgv.org (accessed January 10, 2003).

AUDIO AND VISUAL MEDIA

Buckminster Fuller: Thinking Out Loud. PBS American Masters Series documentary. Directed by Karen Goodman and Kirk Simon. Videocassette, 1997.

The Schiaparelli Sweater

Clothing style

By: Elsa Schiaparelli

Date: 1927

Source: The Schiaparelli Sweater. In Schiaparelli, Elsa. *Shocking Life.* New York: E.P. Dutton, 1954, 33.

About the Designer: Elsa Schiaparelli (1896–1973) was born in Rome as a French citizen of Italian, Scottish, and Egyptian descent. Convent-educated, she studied languages and philosophy; a volume of her poetry was published when she was a teenager. In 1919, Schiaparelli moved to New York City with her husband, who subsequently abandoned her while she was pregnant. Schiaparelli had to reinvent herself in order to survive and raise her daughter. From forsaken

Primary Source

The Schiaparelli Sweater

SYNOPSIS: Elsa Schiaparelli's trompe l'oeil butterfly-bow sweater is a good example of the designer's innovative style, reflecting her humor and the influence of the art movements of the day. It is also an example of the more feminine fashions that followed on the heels of the slim flapper silhouette. FROM AN ILLUSTRATION IN *SHOCKING LIFE*, BY ELSA SCHIAPARELLI. J. M. DENT & SONS (ORION), E. P. DUTTON & COMPANY, 1954. COPYRIGHT 1954 ELSA SCHIAPARELLI. REPRODUCED BY PERMISSION OF DUTTON, A DIVISION OF PENGUIN GROUP (USA) INC.

wife and penniless foreigner, she became "Schiap," a noted fashion designer. From 1920 to 1921, Schiaparelli remained in the United States translating film scripts for Hollywood and working as a freelance writer. She became part of a circle of artists that included Edward Steichen, Paul Poiret, Man Ray, and Marcel Duchamp. She eventually worked with a friend, selling Paris-designed clothes in New York. In 1922, she returned to Paris and began designing and making her own clothes. Schiaparelli set up her first boutique in Paris in 1928 and was soon a successful designer. She opened another design studio in 1949 in New York City. Schiaparelli contin-

ued to write fashion articles even as she became a famous fashion designer. She also gave her designs witty names, often beginning with the letter "s." Her autobiography, *Shocking Life,* was published in 1954. ■

Introduction

In Paris in 1927, Elsa Schiaparelli spied a woman wearing a new kind of knit sweater. It was elastic and seemed to hold its shape. She struck up a conversation with the woman, who referred her to the Armenian

Fashion designer Elsa Schiaparelli. AP/WIDE WORLD PHOTOS.
REPRODUCED BY PERMISSION.

Dueling Designers

Elsa Schiaparelli openly acknowledged her rivalry with Gabrielle (Coco) Chanel. Chanel referred to Schiaparelli as "that Italian who's making clothes." Schiaparelli called Chanel "that dreary little bourgeoise . . . [who] specializes in cemeteries." At a costume ball in 1939, Chanel came dressed as herself and Schiaparelli came dressed as a Surrealist oak tree. Chanel dared Schiaparelli to dance with her, and then proceeded to purposely steer the tree into some lit candles. Of course the costume caught fire, and the other guests were finally able to put out the fire by spraying Schiaparelli with soda siphons.

SOURCE: White, Palmer. *Elsa Schiaparelli: Empress of Paris Fashion.* New York: Rizzoli, 1995.

woman who knit the tightly woven sweater, using a unique stitch. Schiaparelli asked the Armenian woman to knit a sweater that she had designed. It employed the artistic technique known as "trompe l'oeil" (French for "deceive the eye"), which involves creating the illusion of a three-dimensional object. Schiaparelli's trompe l'oeil sweater was solid color with what appeared to be a large floppy bow tied at the neck. But the bow was not real; the image of a bow was simply woven into the sweater in a contrasting color.

Schiaparelli wore her new design to a fashionable luncheon, and an excited buyer from Lord and Taylor of Fifth Avenue immediately placed an order for forty trompe l'oeil sweaters. They became enormously popular and were featured in the latest fashion magazines with rave reviews. Other fashion designers began to produce hand-knit sweaters with designs on them, but they were always most closely and originally associated with "The House of Schiaparelli."

Significance

Elsa Schiaparelli first achieved widespread recognition and commercial success with her now-legendary trompe l'oeil sweater. The sweater was the first example of her signature use of surrealistic imagery in her fashions. The Dadaist and surrealist art movements were in their early stages at the time, and Schiaparelli went on to collaborate with many artists, including Jean Cocteau, Man Ray, Cecil Beaton, and Salvador Dali.

Schiaparelli arrived on the fashion radar just as the flapper look was beginning to go out of style. Fashion was returning to a more feminine silhouette. Schiaparelli's use of the bias cut gave her clothes a drape emphasizing the female figure. The boldness of her patterning as well as these sharp silhouettes made for very striking photographic images, and Schiaparelli's designs frequently appeared in fashion magazines. The sense of humor in Schiaparelli's designs also greatly appealed to the public. She created accessories such as fish buttons and newspaper-printed scarves. Schiaparelli invented and named colors such as "ice blue" and "shocking pink." She created perfumes in unusual packaging with intriguing names, including *Sleeping, Snuff, So Sweet,* and *Shocking You.*

Further Resources

BOOKS

Latour, Anny. *Kings of Fashion*. London: Weidenfeld and Nicolson, 1958, 195–197.

Martin, Richard. *Fashion and Surrealism*. New York: Rizzoli, 1987.

Penn, Irving, and Diana Vreeland. *Inventive Paris Clothes, 1909–1939*. London: Thames and Hudson, 1977.

Schiaparelli, Elsa. *Shocking Life*. New York: Dutton, 1954.

PERIODICALS

Presley, Ann Beth. "Fifty Years of Change: Societal Attitudes and Women's Fashions, 1900–1950." *The Historian,* Winter 1998.

Glueck, Grace. "When the Blithe Led the Blithe: High '30s Style." *New York Times,* November 8, 2002, 35.

WEBSITES

"Elsa Schiaparelli." ArtandCulture.com. Available online at http://www.artandculture.com/cgi-bin/WebObjects/ACLive .woa/wa/artist?id=1314; website home page: http://www .artandculture.com (accessed January 16, 2003).

The Metropolis of Tomorrow

Essay, Architectural designs

By: Hugh Ferriss

Date: 1929

Source: Ferriss, Hugh. *The Metropolis of Tomorrow.* New York: Ives Washburn, 1929, 15–17, 59, 65, 69, 87.

About the Author: Hugh Ferriss (1889–1962) was America's foremost "delineator"—architectural renderer—in the 1920s and throughout the next three decades. Ferriss received an architecture degree from Washington University in St. Louis in 1911, then worked for two years as a draftsman for Cass Gilbert, architect of the Woolworth Building in New York City. In 1915, he started a career as an independent delineator. By 1921, Ferriss was already well known and highly sought after. He documented existing architecture and was commissioned by more than a hundred architectural firms to create presentation drawings for proposed building projects. He also produced design sketches for city planners, trade journals, newspapers and magazines, and advertisements. Ferriss's futuristic cityscapes were displayed in department store windows and architecture shows. His work greatly influenced the film, painting, and architecture of his time. ■

Introduction

In 1922, Ferriss collaborated with skyscraper architect and city planner Harvey Wiley Corbett to publish a series of drawings entitled "The Four Stages of Skyscraper Construction," which was received with much excitement by the design community. The drawings illustrated the ziggurat form that became popular with skyscraper architects. In 1916, New York passed laws (since revised) demanding that skyscrapers be built with setbacks in order to maintain light and air circulation at street level. Ferriss and Corbett responded to this mandate by layering smaller blocks on top of larger ones, at aesthetically pleasing proportions. This radical new silhouette dominated the urban architecture of the 1920s.

Later, Corbett commissioned Ferriss to illustrate a solution to the growing problem of traffic congestion in the city. Surpassing the inventiveness of the ziggurat idea, Ferriss and Corbett imagined a fantastic urban utopia with separate levels for pedestrian and automobile traffic. The two visionaries proposed a truly vertical Manhattan in which this double-decked system of roads and overhead walkways would ease the inconvenience and dangers of city life.

In addition to his commercial assignments, Ferriss provided his own response to rapid urban development with his classic collection of drawings and essays, *The Metropolis of Tomorrow,* first published in 1929. The book reproduces more than sixty of Ferriss's architectural renderings. The drawings are grouped in three sections, each accompanied by Ferriss's own commentary. "Cities of Today" includes drawings of what he believed were the best examples of contemporary urban architecture, including Chicago's Tribune Tower, New York's Chrysler Building, and Detroit's Penobscot Building. The section titled "Projected Trends" has some drawings focusing on the benefits of setback buildings, and others illustrating possible catastrophic results from a lack of proper urban planning. In the book's final section, "An Imaginary Metropolis," Ferriss proposes an ideal city, consisting of three separate zones for business, science, and art, all grouped around a large park.

Significance

Metropolis of Tomorrow is considered a classic by architects and artists. Its moody, futuristic charcoal drawings are among the twentieth century's most iconic imaginings of urban architecture. The book has been reprinted several times, and Ferriss's drawings have been featured in major retrospective exhibitions.

But the book was more than a showcase for Ferriss's art. He used it to voice his concerns about the costs of urban development to both builders and to people. Even in this early stage of urban development, Ferriss sensed that there was little consideration for the individual. Architects and designers are often criticized for a lack of social concern, favoring design flair over function and humanity, and Ferriss may have been one of the earliest figures to remind the design community that the very purpose of design is to improve the lives of individuals.

While his ideas for future cities were never seriously considered by urban planners, Ferriss's visionary draw-

Primary Source

The Metropolis of Tomorrow: Architectural design (1 OF 4)
SYNOPSIS: *The Lure of the City,* from *The Metropolis of Tomorrow* by Hugh Ferriss, 1929. REPRINTED FROM HUGH FERRISS, *THE METROPOLIS OF TOMORROW.* NEW YORK: IVES WASHBURN, 1929.

ings reached a large audience and created a greater public awareness of the possibilities and pitfalls that the future held for the American metropolis.

Primary Source

The Metropolis of Tomorrow: Essay [excerpt]

    SYNOPSIS: In his classic 1929 book, Hugh Ferriss both depicts and describes his vision of the city of the future. In this selection from the "Cities of Today" section of his classic book, Hugh Ferriss writes as if from high atop a skyscraper in Manhattan, comparing the vantage point to a box seat at the theater. Likewise, he says, the monumental structures of the city are merely stage sets for the human drama going on below. As more and more skyscrapers were being built, Ferriss maintained that architects should keep people and their needs in mind.

A first impression of the contemporary city—let us say, the view of New York from the work-room in which most of these drawings were made . . . is not unlike the sketch on the opposite page. This, indeed, is to the author the familiar morning scene. But there are occasional mornings when, with an early fog not yet dispersed, one finds oneself, on stepping onto the parapet, the spectator of an even more nebulous panorama. . . . To an imaginative spectator, it might seem that he is perched in some elevated stage box to witness some gigantic spectacle, some cyclopean drama of forms; and that the curtain has not yet risen.

There is a moment of curiosity, even for those who have seen the play before, since in all probability they are about to view some newly arisen steel skeleton, some tower or even some street which was not in yesterday's performance . . . in due succession the other architectural principals lift their pinnacles into vision: the Brooklyn skyscraper group, the Municipal building, the Woolworth. . . . As mysteriously as though being created, a Metropolis ap-

Primary Source

The Metropolis of Tomorrow: Architectural design **(2 OF 4)**

SYNOPSIS: *Overhead Traffic-Ways,* from *The Metropolis of Tomorrow* by Hugh Ferriss, 1929. REPRINTED FROM HUGH FERRISS, *THE METROPOLIS OF TOMORROW.* NEW YORK: IVES WASHBURN, 1929.

Primary Source

The Metropolis of Tomorrow: Architectural design (3 OF 4)
SYNOPSIS: *Churches Aloft,* from *The Metropolis of Tomorrow* by Hugh Ferriss, 1929. REPRINTED FROM HUGH FERRISS, *THE ME-TROPOLIS OF TOMORROW.* NEW YORK: IVES WASHBURN, 1929.

Primary Source

The Metropolis of Tomorrow: Architectural design (4 OF 4)

SYNOPSIS: *Verticals on Wide Avenues,* from *The Metropolis of Tomorrow* by Hugh Ferriss, 1929. REPRINTED FROM HUGH FER-
RISS, *THE METROPOLIS OF TOMORROW.* NEW YORK: IVES WASHBURN, 1929.

pears. Obviously, we can now conclude, it is to be a city of closely juxtaposed verticals. And indeed, it is not until considerably later, when the mists have been completely dispersed that there is revealed far below—through bridge and river and avenue—the presence of any horizontal base whatever for these cloud-capped towers.

One further discovery remains to be made: on a close scrutiny of the streets, certain minute, moving objects can be unmistakably distinguished. The city apparently contains, away down there—human beings!

The discovery gives one pause. Between the colossal inanimate forms and those mote-like creatures darting in and out among their foundations, there is such a contrast, such discrepancy in scale, that certain questions force their attention on the mind.

What is the relation between these two? Are those tiny specks the actual intelligences of the situation, and this towered mass something which, as it were, those ants have marvelously excreted?

Or are these masses of steel and glass the embodiment of some blind and mechanical force that has imposed itself, as though from without, on a helpless humanity?

At first glance, one might well imagine the latter. Nevertheless, there is but one view which can be taken; there is but one fact that can—in these pages, at least—serve as our criterion. The drama which, from this balcony, we have been witnessing is, first and foremost, a human drama. Those vast architectural forms are only a stage set. It is those specks of figures down there below who are, in reality, the principals of the play.

But what influences have these actors and this stage reciprocally upon on another? How perfectly or imperfectly have the actors expressed themselves in their constructions—how well have the architects designed the set? And how great is the influence which the architectural background exercises over the actors—and is it a beneficient one?

. . . Is the set well designed? Indeed, it is not designed at all! It is true that in individual fragments of the set here and there—in individual buildings—we see the conscious hand of the architect. But in speaking, as we are, of the city as a whole, it is impossible to say that it did more than come to be built; we must admit that, as a whole, it is not work of conscious design.

And nevertheless it is a faithful expression! Architecture never lies. Architecture invariably expresses its Age correctly. Admire or condemn as you may, yonder skyscrapers faithfully express both the characteristic structural skill and the characteristic urge—for money; yonder tiers of apartments represent the last word in scientific ingenuity and the last word but one in desire for physical comfort.

As regards the effect which the "set" is having upon the actors: it is unquestionably enormous . . . the character of the architectural forms and spaces which all people habitually encounter are powerful agencies in determining the nature of their thoughts, their emotions and their actions, however unconscious of this they may be . . . everybody is influenced by the house he inhabits, be it harmonious or mean, by the streets in which he walks and by the buildings among which he finds himself.

Are not the inhabitants of most of our American cities continually glancing at the rising masses of office or apartment buildings whose thin coating of architectural confectionery disguises, but does not alter, the fact that they were fashioned to meet not so much the human needs of the occupants as the financial appetites of the property owners? Do we not traverse, in our daily walks, districts which are stupid and miscellaneous rather than logical or serene—and move, day long, through an absence of viewpoint, vista, axis, relation, or plan? Such an environment silently but relentlessly impresses its qualities upon the human psyche.

The contemplation of the actual Metropolis as a whole cannot but lead us at last to the realization of a human population unconsciously reacting to forms which came into existence without conscious design.

A hope, however, may begin to define itself in our minds. May there not yet arise, perhaps in another generation, architects who, appreciating the influence unconsciously received, will learn consciously to direct it?

But we may postpone more general conclusions until we have examined, at closer view, the existing facts. Let us go down into the streets. . . .

Further Resources

BOOKS

Ferriss, Hugh. *Power in Buildings: An Artist's View of Contemporary Architecture.* Santa Monica, Calif.: Hennessey & Ingalls, 1998.

Leich, Jean Ferriss, *Architectural Visions: The Drawings of Hugh Ferriss.* New York: Whitney Library of Design, 1980.

PERIODICALS

Little, Richard. "Review: Metropolis of Tomorrow." *Journal of Urban Technology* 7, issue 1, April 2000, 103–104.

WEBSITES

Axelrod, Jeremiah Borenstein. "'Los Angeles is not the city it could have been': Cultural Representation, Traffic, and Urban Modernity in Jazz Age America." The 3 Cities Project Electronic Book. Available online at http://www.nottingham .ac.uk/3cities/axelrod.htm#1039; website home page: http:// www.nottingham.ac.uk/3cities/index.php (accessed January 9, 2003).

Middleton, David. "Drawing Towards Metropolis." *January Magazine,* October 1998. Available online at http://www .januarymagazine.com/artcult/metro.html; website home page http://www.januarymagazine.com.

Men at Work

Nonfiction work, Photographs

By: Lewis W. Hine

Date: 1932

Source: Hine, Lewis W. "The Spirit of Industry." Introduction to *Men At Work: Photographic Studies of Modern Men and Machines.* New York: Dover, 1977.

About the Author: Lewis Wickes Hine (1874–1940) was born in Oshkosh, Wisconsin. While teaching at the Ethical Culture School in New York City, he began using the camera as an educational tool and to record school activities. Hine developed an interest in social photography while documenting immigrants arriving at Ellis Island, and took on freelance assignments for the National Child Labor Committee. His images of child laborers throughout the United States helped bring about legislative reforms. Hine also produced influential photo essays on the activities of the American Red Cross in World War I, on New York tenements, and on miners and factory workers. ∎

Introduction

Planning for the Empire State Building began in 1928. The architecture firm of Shreve, Lamb, & Harmon Associates was retained to design the commercial office tower. Construction began in January 1930, and the building was completed in just sixteen months. At 102 stories, or 1,252 feet high, the Empire became the tallest skyscraper in the world, surpassing the Chrysler Building. The Empire remained the tallest skyscraper until 1975, when the twin towers of the World Trade Center were completed.

Designed in the late 1920s, the Empire State Building reflects the late Art Deco style, which was very popular at the time. But it was designed with flamboyance not common to the architecture of its era. A steel frame with stone cladding, the building features setbacks at the lower levels (mandated by a 1916 New York law) that permitted the upper floors to shoot up as a straight tower. The Empire State Building is one of the very few skyscrapers with four facades instead of a single one facing

Primary Source

Men at Work: Photographs (1 OF 4)

SYNOPSIS: "A Worker Hanging on Two Steel Beams," by Lewis Hine, 1930. NEW YORK PUBLIC LIBRARY. REPRODUCED BY PERMISSION.

the avenue. At the top of its 102 stories are an observation platform and a pylon, crowned with a television transmission antenna. Shreve, Lamb, & Harmon ensured the building's investors would maximize their returns by completing the project quickly and by filling the building with tenants as soon as possible. The Empire State Building was celebrated by the public as an architectural feat and a commercial success, and it continues to be a landmark attraction, "The Eighth Wonder of the World."

Lewis Hine was already a well-known photographer when he was hired to photograph the construction of the Empire State Building. In the 1920s, he achieved recognition for his ongoing series of "Work Portraits." The Empire State Building construction photographs are less spontaneous than Hine's earlier works; the hazardous working conditions necessitated careful planning and composition of these images. He photographed riveters, bricklayers, welders, and ironworkers in precarious positions high above the city as they secured the framework of the building. Hine even arranged to be swung out in a specially designed "basket" past the building site, 1,000 feet in the air, in order to capture the best vantage points.

Primary Source

Men at Work: Photographs (2 OF 4)

SYNOPSIS: "Icarus Atop Empire State," by Lewis Hine, 1930. NEW YORK PUBLIC LIBRARY. REPRODUCED BY PERMISSION.

In 1932, Hine published *Men at Work,* a book featuring these photographs as well as selected images from previous industrial photo-essays.

Significance

Throughout the 1920s, Lewis Hine often documented the negative aspects of labor and industrialization, such as the dangerous working conditions in factories. In contrast, his series of Empire State Building construction photographs celebrated the post–World War I American labor force. Hine portrayed the Empire's construction workers as a proud and dignified team, and he presented the erection of the Empire as a monument to progress.

Hine's style of documentary photography set the standard for delivering social messages through the medium. His interests as a photographer lay in capturing how mechanical advancements could lift the burden of hard labor from the worker. A sociologist and humanist, Hine consistently chose the worker as his main subject, and many of his images became iconic representations of labor.

Since there is little documentation of what the construction workers actually thought of the project, Hine's portraits of men working on the Empire State Building also provide a rare glimpse into the experience of building what was then the world's tallest building.

Primary Source

Men at Work: Nonfiction work [excerpt]

> **SYNOPSIS:** In his introduction to *Men at Work,* an essay titled "The Spirit of Industry," Hine praises

Primary Source

Men at Work: Photographs **(3 OF 4)**
SYNOPSIS: "View of the building rising to about sixteen stories" by Lewis Hine, 1930. NEW YORK PUBLIC LIBRARY. REPRODUCED BY PERMISSION.

the bravery and skill of the workers he photographed. This time using words rather than pictures, he reasserted his belief in the primary importance of human beings in an age of machines and soaring skyscapers.

This is a book of Men at Work; men of courage, skill, daring and imagination. Cities do not build themselves, machines cannot make machines, unless back of them all are the brains and toil of men. We call this the Machine Age. But the more machines we use the more do we need real men to make and direct them.

I have toiled in many industries and associated with thousands of workers. I have brought some of them here to meet you. Some of them are heroes; all of them persons it is a privilege to know. I will take you into the heart of modern industry where machines and skyscrapers are being made, where the character of the men is being put into the motors, the airplanes, the dynamos upon which the life and happiness of millions of us depend.

Then the more you see of modern machines, the more may you, too, respect the men who make them and manipulate them.

Further Resources

BOOKS

Gutman, Judith Mara. *Lewis W. Hine and the American Social Conscience.* New York: Walker, 1967.

Hine, Lewis Wickes. *The Empire State Building.* New York: Prestel Press, 1998.

Primary Source

Men at Work: Photographs (4 of 4)
SYNOPSIS: "View of Empire State Building," by Lewis Hine, 1930. COURTESY GEORGE EASTMAN HOUSE. REPRODUCED BY PERMISSION.

Kaplan, Daile, ed. *Photo Story: Selected Letters and Photographs of Lewis W. Hine.* Washington, D.C.: Smithsonian Institution Press, 1992.

Pacelle, Mitchell. *Empire: A Tale of Obsession, Betrayal, and the Battle for an American Icon.* New York: John Wiley & Sons, 2001.

Rosenblum, Walter, Naomi Rosenblum, and Alan Trachtenberg. *America & Lewis Hine: Photographs 1904–1940.* New York: Aperture, 1977.

Smith, G.E. Kidder. *Looking at Architecture.* New York: Harry N. Abrams, 1990.

Steinorth, Karl, ed. *Lewis Hine: Passionate Journey Photographs, 1905–1937.* Zurich: Edition Stemmle, 1997.

Willis, Carol, ed. *Building the Empire State.* New York: W.W. Norton & Company, 1998.

PERIODICALS

Millstein, Barbara Head. "Lewis Wickes Hine: The Final Years." *Magazine Antiques,* November 1, 1998.

Wright, Leigh Martinez. "Spiders in the Sky." *Smithsonian* 32, issue 10, January 2002, 17–18.

WEBSITES

The Empire State Building Official Internet Site. Available online at http://www.esbnyc.com (accessed January 7, 2003).

"Lewis Wickes Hine: The Construction of the Empire State Building, 1930–1931." The Miriam & Ira Wallach Division of Art, Prints and Photographs: Photography Collection, New York Public Library. Available online at http://www.nypl.org/research/chss/spe/art/photo/hinex/empire/empire.html; website home page: www.nypl.org (accessed January 7, 2003).

AUDIO AND VISUAL MEDIA

Modern Marvels: Empire State Building. Modern Marvels. Videocassette, 1994.

Portrait of Myself
Autobiography

By: Margaret Bourke-White

Date: 1963

Source: Bourke-White, Margaret. *Portrait of Myself.* New York: Simon & Schuster, 1963, 76–80.

About the Author: Margaret Bourke-White (1904–1971) was born in the Bronx in New York City and raised in rural New Jersey. Although she received her undergraduate degree in herpetology (the study of reptiles), she had a long-standing interest in photography and became a commercial photographer upon completing college. She quickly established herself as a top industrial photographer, beginning with her first assignments for Otis Steel Company in Cleveland, Ohio, in 1927. Her work then garnered the attention of magazine publishers, and she was hired as the first photographer for *Fortune* magazine when it debuted in 1929. She moved to New York, where she created magazine photo-essays and took on advertising assignments as well. Her work appeared on the first cover of *Life* magazine in 1935. Bourke-White became a leader in the new field of photojournalism, documenting the suffering during the Depression and serving as a war correspondent in combat zones during World War II. After retiring from photography, she wrote six books on her international travels. ∎

Introduction

In 1928, Margaret Bourke-White was hired to photograph the Chrysler factory in Detroit, and was subsequently sent to New York to document the construction of the Chrysler Building. To substantiate their claim that the new building was the tallest in the world, Chrysler executives wanted to prove that the towering spire was an essential structural element and not merely ornamental.

Designed by architect William van Alen (1883–1954), the building was originally commissioned by building contractor William H. Reynolds, who then sold it to automotive magnate Walter P. Chrysler. Chrysler wanted to own "a bold structure, declaring the glories of the modern age."

The Chrysler Building has a steel framework. It is one of the earliest examples of the use of stainless steel over a large exposed building surface. As required by New York zoning laws set in 1916—mandating that tall buildings provide for light and air circulation at the ground level—the design of the Chrysler utilizes setbacks. Each setback boasts a unique decorative treatment of the masonry walls. Other ornamental designs include monumentally scaled basket-weave designs, gargoyles, brilliant radiator caps, and a band of abstract automobile shapes.

Construction of the Chrysler Building began in 1928. When it was completed in 1930, it stood seventy-seven stories and 1,046 feet high, surpassing the 927-foot Bank of Manhattan. However, the Chrysler triumph was short-lived. The Empire State Building, at a height of 1,250 feet, was completed the following year.

Significance

Even though the Chrysler Building lost its hold on the title of the world's tallest building, the skyscraper remains the finest example of Art Deco architecture in America.

Margaret Bourke-White's memoir is a firsthand look at the construction of this famous building. It also offers insights into a time when captains of industry were vying for the prestige of creating the tallest buildings in the world. The public took an active interest in what Bourke-White calls "this battle of the skyscapers," and as she points out, the buildings' owners took full advantage of the publicity value of the construction projects. Bourke-White's assignment to photograph the construction of the Chrysler Building was just one example of this.

The Chrysler Building was often described as a "celebration of financial excess." Murals adorn the walls and ceiling of the lobby, lined with pink African marble and chrome steel. It once housed an elite club on its 66th, 67th and 68th floors. The Cloud Club, as it was known then, was rumored to be a speakeasy for Manhattan's rich and famous during the Prohibition years. Mr. Chrysler had an apartment on the upper floors, and Bourke-White set up her photographic studio in the building as well. Through her amusing description of her studio and her

work life in the Chrysler Building, the photographer offers readers a glimpse inside the glamorous skyscraper, which still retains a hold on the public imagination.

Primary Source

Portrait of Myself [excerpt]

SYNOPSIS: In a chapter of her autobiography titled "Skyscapers and Advertising," Margaret Bourke-White recounts photographing the construction of the Chrysler Building and her experiences in her photography studio on the building's 61st floor.

. . . I am grateful to [history] for getting me in the right place at the right time to photograph a most curious event—a heaven-climbing contest which could take place only in America—indeed, only in Manhattan, where a tight little island must pile itself layer on layer upward if it was to grow at all.

In this battle of the skyscrapers, the chief contenders were the 927-foot Bank of Manhattan and the unfinished Chrysler Building, slated to rise to more than 1,000 feet, and I was brought in as a sort of war correspondent on the Chrysler side. The scene of battle was that relatively narrow band of atmosphere ranging from 800–1,200 feet above the sidewalks of New York. Who can doubt that this was a forerunner of the contest for outer space which would follow after a quarter of a century? Then, as now, a principal target was prestige. A skyscraper was a tall and strong feather in the cap of that ultra-rare individual who could afford to build one.

For forty years the championship was held at 792 feet by a tower ornamented in the Gothic style and erected literally on dimes and nickels: the Woolworth Tower. Certainly Mr. Walter Percy Chrysler was aware of the stupendous advertising value generated when the world's highest building bears the name of your product. And this was where I came in.

A dastardly rumor had been circulated, undoubtedly by some busy banker, that the Chrysler Building would not actually surpass the Bank of Manhattan, despite the Chrysler claim of total supremacy at 1,046 feet. The insinuation was that the Chryslers were merely pasting on an ornamental steel tower to gain the few feet needed to make the world's record. I had been photographing the mile-long Chrysler factory in Detroit and was given the job in New York of taking progress pictures of each stage of construction to show that the tower was an integral part of the building. The Chryslers need not have gone to such lengths to prove their supremacy, be-

"Margaret Bourke-White on the Chrysler Building." New York, 1931. © THE ESTATE OF MARGARET BOURKE-WHITE. REPRODUCED BY
PERMISSION.

cause in one short year it did not matter anyway. All the man-made structures of this planet would be topped by a spire rising to the magnificent height of 1,250 feet, freezing the world's altitude record to date, and built by a man named Smith.

Fortune ran one or two of the Chrysler Building pictures. I don't know whether the photographs proved anything except that a photographer has to work in all kinds of weather. I had to take pictures during the midwinter of 1929–30, 800 feet above the street, working on a tower that swayed 8 feet in the wind, often in subfreezing temperatures, but all this did not bother me too much. . . .

Heights held no terrors for me. I was lucky in having a God-given sense of balance and also a great deal of practice in my childhood. My sister Ruth and I had a pact to walk the entire distance to school and back on the thin edges of fences. It was a point of honor to dismount only for crossroads and brooks. Here on the heights of the Chrysler tower, I had additional instruction from the welders and riveters who gave me a valuable rule which I have often remembered and acted upon: when you are working at 800 feet above the ground, make believe that you are 8 feet up and relax, take it easy. The problems are really exactly the same.

On the sixty-first floor, the workmen started building some curious structures which overhung 42nd Street and Lexington Avenue below. When I learned these were to be gargoyles a la Notre Dame, but made of stainless steel as more suitable for the twentieth century, I decided that here would be my new studio. There was no place in the world that I would accept as a substitute. I was ready to close my studio in Cleveland in order to be nearer *Fortune,* but it was the gargoyles which gave me the final spurt into New York.

It was surprisingly difficult to get my studio space. The Chrysler people seemed to think that since I was female, young, and not too plain, I would surely get married before much time went by. That would put a stop to all this photography business, and then who would pay the rent? *Fortune* helped me to get the studio space. This did not mean any concession on the part of my august landlords, in the size of the rent, which was as high per square foot as any in the city. It was just that the privilege of paying rent became mine.

My first step was to apply for the job as Chrysler Building janitor. This was not because I wanted to run up and down its seventy-seven stories with a floor mop. I wanted to live in my studio, and there was a New York City law which stipulated that no one could live in an office building except the janitor. I was turned down for the position of janitor. Some other more fortunate tenant, perhaps one of the Chryslers themselves, had beaten me to it. I loved my studio so that I hated to go home at night. Frequently I worked the whole night through until dawn came and the mist rolled back revealing the great city below. I would brush my teeth, run out for a hot breakfast and come back to work. I hoped this was legal.

It turned out that I had not one but a pair of gargoyles resplendent in stainless steel and pointing to the southeast. This was certainly the world's highest studio, and I think it was the world's most beautiful studio, too. It was furnished and decorated in the most modern simplicity by John Vassos, who is a man of considerable designing talent and also a dear friend. Vassos has a strong feeling for unadorned materials. I had a clear glass desk, a tropical fish tank which was built into a wall, and natural wood and aluminum were used everywhere.

I loved the view so much that I often crawled out on the gargoyles, which projected over the street 800 feet below, to take pictures of the changing moods of the city. I had a large terrace where I gave parties and a small terrace where I kept two pet alligators which a friend had sent me from Florida. The alligators, plus a few turtles, reminded me pleasantly of the herpetology days of my childhood. At feeding time, I tossed the alligators big slabs of raw beef which they playfully tore from each other. They grew very fast and ate a great deal, even bolting down several of my turtles, shell and all. I thought they would find this meal quite indigestible, but they calmly slept it off. It astonished me to find the law of the jungle operating in a penthouse at the top of a skyscraper.

Further Resources
BOOKS

Callahan, Sean. *The Photographs of Margaret Bourke-White.* Greenwich, Conn.: New York Graphic Society, 1972.

Curtis, William J.R. *Modern Architecture Since 1900.* Upper Saddle River, N.J.: Prentice Hall, 1996.

Goldberg, Vicki. *Margaret Bourke-White, a Biography.* Reading, Mass.: Addison-Wesley, 1987.

Gossel, Peter, and Gabriele Leuthauser. *Architecture in the Twentieth Century.* New York: Taschen, 2001.

Keller, Emily. *Margaret Bourke-White: A Photographer's Life.* Minneapolis: Lerner, 1996.

Shivers, Natalie. *Chrysler Building.* Princeton, N.J.: Princeton Architectural Press, 1999.

PERIODICALS

Ellis, William S. "Skyscrapers." *National Geographic,* February 1989, 140A–73.

Pierpont, Claudia Roth. "The Silver Spire: Dreaming up the Chrysler Building." *The New Yorker,* November 18, 2002, 74–81.

WEBSITES

Chrysler Building. Available online at http://www.chrysler building.org (accessed January 6, 2003).

"Chrysler Building." Great Buildings Online. Available online at http://www.greatbuildings.com/buildings/Chrysler_Building .html; website home page: http://www.greatbuildings.com (accessed January 6, 2003).

Horsley, Carter B. "The Chrysler Building." *The City Review.* Available online at http://www.thecityreview.com/chryslerb .html; website home page: http://www.thecityreview.com (accessed January 16, 2003).

Zacharek, Stephanie. "The Chrysler Building." Salon.com, February 25, 2002. Available online at http://archive.salon.com /ent/masterpiece/2002/02/25/chrysler/; website home page: http://www.salon.com (accessed January 16, 2003).

AUDIO AND VISUAL MEDIA

Building Big: Skyscrapers. PBS. Videocassette, 2000.

Matthews, Kevin. *The Great Buildings Collection.* Artifice. CD-ROM, 2001.

5

GOVERNMENT AND POLITICS

PAUL G. CONNORS

Entries are arranged in chronological order by date of primary source. For entries with one primary source, the entry title is the same as the primary source title. Entries with more than one primary source have an overall entry title, followed by the titles of the primary sources.

Important Events in Government and Politics, 1920–1929

1920

- The 1920 census reports that 105,710,620 people live in the United States and that for the first time urban residents outnumber rural residents. The center of population is 8.3 miles southeast of Spencer, Indiana.

- On January 16, the Eighteenth Amendment to the Constitution, which prohibits the manufacture, sale, and transportation of alcoholic beverages, goes into effect.

- On March 19, the United States Senate rejects the Treaty of Versailles.

- From May 8 to May 14, the Socialist Nationalist Convention meeting in New York City again nominates Eugene V. Debs for President and Seymour Stedman for Vice-President. Since 1918, Debs has been serving a ten-year prison sentence for violating the Espionage Act.

- From June 8 to June 12, the National Republican Convention meeting in Chicago nominates Senator Warren G. Harding from Ohio for President on the tenth ballot. Governor Calvin Coolidge of Massachusetts is nominated for Vice-President.

- From June 28 to July 5, the National Democratic Convention meeting in San Francisco nominates Governor James M. Cox of Ohio for President and former Secretary of the Navy Franklin Delano Roosevelt for Vice-President.

- On November 2, with his campaign slogan "back to normalcy," Warren G. Harding receives 404 electoral votes and 60 percent of the popular vote to become the President of the United States.

1921

- On March 4, Warren G. Harding is inaugurated as twenty-ninth President of the United States.

- On May 19, Congress enacts the First Immigration Quota Act, restricting immigration to the United States from any European country to 3 percent of the individuals of that nationality in the United States at the time of the 1910 census. The act also creates an annual ceiling of 355,000 immigrants.

- On June 20, Alice Robertson of Oklahoma is the first woman to preside over the United States House of Representatives, remaining at the podium for thirty minutes.

- On June 30, former President William Howard Taft is appointed and confirmed Chief Justice of the United States Supreme Court.

- On August 25, because the United States fails to ratify the Versailles Treaty, the United States and Germany sign a peace treaty in Berlin to officially recognize the end of World War I.

- On November 2, Congress votes to designate November 11—Armistice Day—a national holiday.

- On December 23, President Harding pardons Eugene V. Debs, who was convicted under the Espionage Act.

1922

- On February 6, the Washington Conference on arms reduction ends with agreements on three important treaties—the Four-Power Treaty, the Five-Power Treaty, and the Nine-Power Treaty.

- On April 7, Secretary of the Interior Albert B. Fall leases Naval Reserve No. 3 (Teapot Dome) to Harry F. Sinclair without competitive bidding. In turn, Sinclair sells the reserve to the Mammoth Oil Company for $160 million of stock.

- On May 15, the United States Supreme Court declares the federal child labor law unconstitutional.

- On June 14, in a silent march in Washington, D.C., African Americans from every state demonstrate their support for the Dyer Anti-Lynching Bill.

- On September 19, President Harding vetoes the Veteran's Bonus Bill.

- On October 3, Rebecca Felton, age eighty-seven, of Georgia becomes the first female United States Senator. Her term, to which the governor of Georgia appointed her following the death of Senator Thomas Watson, lasts only one day.

1923

- On March 4, Congress passes the Agricultural Credits Act, making low-interest loans available to farmers.

- On April 9, the United States Supreme Court rules the minimum-wage law for women and children in Washington, D.C., is unconstitutional in *Adkins* v. *Children's Hospital.*

- On August 2, after a week of illness, President Harding dies of what at the time is thought to be food poisoning (Japanese crabs). Some press reports accuse the First Lady of killing him to gain his lucrative estate.

- On August 3, Calvin Coolidge is sworn in as the thirtieth President of the United States by his father at Plymouth, Vermont.

- On September 15, Oklahoma Governor J. C. Walton places his state under martial law to counteract Ku Klux Klan racial violence.

- On November 19, the Oklahoma Legislature impeaches and removes Governor Walton from office.

1924

- On March 1, the United States Senate passes a resolution calling for an investigation of United States Attorney General Harry M. Daugherty in the ever-widening Teapot Dome scandal.

- On April 15, the United States Senate votes unanimously to bar all Japanese immigrants from the United States, except for ministers, educators, and their families.

- On May 19, Congress overrides President Coolidge's veto of the Veterans' Bonus Bill, which allocates $2 billion for veterans of the Great War.

- On May 26, Congress passes the National Origins Act, lowering the European immigration quota to 150,000 per year and making the 1890 census the basis for determining each nation's share of that quota.

- On June 2, President Coolidge signs into law the Indian Citizenship Act.

- On June 2, President Coolidge signs into law the Revenue Act of 1924. This act reduces the income tax rate by 25 percent and eliminates excises taxes, in part, on candy, yachts, motor boats, and telephone and telegraph messages.

- From June 10 to June 12, the Republican National Convention meeting in Cleveland, Ohio nominates Calvin Coolidge for President and Charles Gates Dawes of Illinois for Vice-President. For the first time, convention proceedings are broadcast live by radio throughout the country.

- On June 19, the National Convention of the Farmer Labor Party meeting at St. Paul, Minnesota nominates Duncan MacDonald of Illinois for President and William Bouck of Washington for Vice-President.

- From June 24 to July 10, the National Convention of the Democratic Party meeting in New York City nominates John W. Davis of West Virginia for President and William Jennings Bryan's brother Charles W. Bryan of Nebraska for Vice-President.

- On June 30, a federal grand jury indicts Albert B. Hall and Harry F. Sinclair for bribery and conspiracy to defraud the United States government in the Teapot Dome scandal.

- On July 4, the Conference for Progressive Political Action meeting at Cleveland, Ohio nominates Senator Robert M. La Follette of Wisconsin for President and Senator Burton K. Wheeler of Montana for Vice-President.

- On July 11, the Workers' Party (Communist) nominates William Z. Foster for President and Benjamin Gitlow for Vice-President.

- On November 4, Calvin Coolidge is elected President of the United States with 382 electoral votes and 54 percent of the popular vote. Republicans regain control of Congress. Nellie G. Ross is elected Governor of Wyoming and Miriam Ferguson is elected Governor of Texas.

- On December 13, Samuel Gompers, the longtime President of the American Federation of Labor, dies at the age of seventy-four.

1925

- On February 16, Frank B. Kellogg is appointed Secretary of State.

- On March 4, Calvin Coolidge is sworn in as President and begins his first full term.

- On April 3, indictments against Albert B. Fall and Harry F. Sinclair in the Teapot Dome scandal are overturned on a technicality in federal court. The federal government appeals the decision.

- On May 5, John Scopes, a biology teacher in Dayton, Tennessee, is arrested for violating the state law prohibiting the teaching of evolution.

- On May 27, the federal government drops its bribery charge against Albert B. Hall and Harry F. Sinclair. However, the two men are reindicted on the charge of criminal conspiracy to defraud the government.

- On July 21, Scopes is found guilty of violating the state law prohibiting the teaching of evolution and is fined one hundred dollars. Five days later, William Jennings Bryan, who assisted the prosecution, dies at the age of sixty-five.

1926

- On March 3, the United States Senate ratifies a treaty with Mexico to prevent smuggling of narcotics, liquor, and aliens across the border.

- On April 7, the United States Attorney General informs the United States Senate Prohibition Committee that since the passage of the Volstead Act the bootleg trade is estimated at $3.6 billion.

- On October 25, the United States Supreme Court upholds the president's exclusive power to remove executive officers from their appointed positions.

- On December 16, Albert B. Fall is acquitted of the charge of conspiring to defraud the government in the Elk Hills Naval Oil Reserve.

1927

- On January 15, the Tennessee Supreme Court upholds the state's anti-evolution law, but dismisses the case against John Scopes and voids the one hundred dollar fine.

- On March 7, the United States Supreme Court rules that a Texas law excluding African Americans from voting in the Democratic primary is unconstitutional. Justice Oliver Wendell Holmes Jr. maintains that the law is a direct infringement of the Fourteenth Amendment.

- On April 6, President Coolidge vetoes an act of the Philippine Legislature that would have allowed the Filipinos to vote on independence from the United States.

- On August 23, Sacco and Vanzetti are executed in prison in Massachusetts. Celestino Madeiros, who had confessed to the 1920 murders and had claimed that Sacco and Vanzetti were innocent, was also executed.

- On October 10, the United States Supreme Court invalidates the leases of the Teapot Dome government oil reserves in Wyoming made by former Secretary of the Interior Albert B. Fall in 1922.

1928

- On February 21, District of Columbia Court finds Harry Sinclair guilty of contempt for hiring private detectives to follow and spy on jury members in the Teapot Dome scandal. Sinclair is sentenced to six months imprisonment.

1928

- On April 13, the National Socialist Party Convention meeting in New York City nominates Norman Thomas for President and James H. Maurer for Vice-President.

- On April 21, Harry Sinclair, in his second trial, is acquitted by the District of Columbia Court jury of conspiracy with Albert B. Fall to defraud the federal government in the Teapot Dome scandal.

- On May 27, the First National Convention of Workers Party (Communist) meeting in New York nominates William Z. Foster for President and Benjamin Gitlow for Vice-President.

- From June 12 to June 15, the Republican National Convention meeting Kansas City nominates Herbert Hoover for President and Charles Curtis for Vice-President.

- From June 26 to June 29, the Democratic National Convention meeting in Houston nominates Alfred E. Smith of New York for President and Joseph T. Robinson of Arkansas for Vice-President.

- On July 11, the Farm Labor Party nominates George W. Norris for President and W. J. Vereen for Vice-President.

- On July 12, the National Prohibition Convention meeting in Chicago nominates William F. Varney for President and James A. Edgerton for Vice-President.

- On August 27, the United States signs the utopian Kellogg-Briand Pact that renounces war as "an instrument of national policy."

- On November 6, Republican candidates Herbert Hoover and Charles Curtis capture the White House in an election land-slide, carrying forty states, 444 electoral votes, and 58 percent of the popular vote.

- On November 27, "to keep the crooks out" of government work, the U.S. Civil Service Commission announces plans to install fingerprinting systems in 250 cities.

1929

- On January 1, Franklin D. Roosevelt is sworn in as New York's new Governor, succeeding Alfred Smith, who lost his bid to become the first Irish-Catholic President of the United States.

- On January 15, the United States Senate ratifies the Kellogg-Briand Pact on a vote of 85-1.

- On March 4, Herbert Hoover is inaugurated as the thirty-first President of the United States.

- On June 18, Congress passes a reapportionment bill, which gives the President the authority to reapportion Congress after each decennial census if Congress fails to act. President Hoover believes that the legislation is necessary because Congress has refused to reapportion congressional districts on the basis of the 1920 census.

- On October 25, Albert B. Fall is found guilty of accepting a bribe as Secretary of the Interior in the Teapot Dome scandal. He is sentenced to one year imprisonment and fined one hundred thousand dollars.

- On October 29, on what comes to be known as "Black Tuesday," the Dow Jones Industrial Average on Wall Street plummets 30.57 points and $30 billion disappears.

- On December 22, the Fascist League of America headquartered in New York City is disbanded.

"Return to Normalcy"
Speech

By: Warren G. Harding

Date: May 14, 1920

Source: Harding, Warren G. "Warren G. Harding Calls for a "Return to Normalcy," Boston, Mass., May 14, 1920. Available online at http://www.pbs.org/greatspeeches/timeline /w_harding_s.html; website home page: http://www.pbs.org (accessed January 28, 2003).

About the Author: Historians consider Warren Harding (1865–1923), the twenty-ninth president of the United States, as among the nation's worst presidents, largely because his administration was the most corrupt in American history. Born near Marion, Ohio, he began his career as a newspaper publisher. He was elected to the Ohio Senate, served as the state's lieutenant governor, and ran unsuccessfully for Ohio governor. He was elected to the U.S. Senate in 1914 and served as president from 1921 until he died in office. ■

President Warren G. Harding called on the nation to "return to normalcy" in a 1920 speech. Harding throws out the first ball at a baseball game, arguably illustrating the return from matters of war to "normal" American pastimes. **AP/WIDE WORLD PHOTOS. REPRODUCED BY PERMISSION.**

Introduction

In 1919, Harry M. Daugherty, who headed the Ohio Republican Party and would later serve as Harding's attorney general, began circulating Harding's name as candidate for the presidency. The nomination was up for grabs because none of the major candidates had widespread support. In 1920, at the Republican convention, delegates cast nine ballots and were unable to choose a consensus candidate. At midnight, party leaders met behind closed doors and decided to back Harding, who was popular because he had taken few controversial stands over the years and therefore had made no lasting political enemies. Massachusetts governor Calvin Coolidge joined Harding on the Republican ticket. The Democrats, after forty-four ballots, nominated another Ohioan, three-term progressive governor James M. Cox, as their presidential nominee and Franklin D. Roosevelt of New York as his running mate. The Democratic nominees reflected the party's determination to continue Woodrow Wilson's progressive agenda, which he called New Freedom.

Wilsonian progressivism, which had begun under President Theodore Roosevelt, harnessed the power of government to advance the cause of social justice by regulating big business. To protect the weaker members of society, the Wilson administration broke up some large businesses, established fair rules for doing business, and provided a graduated tax on personal incomes. However, Wilson's policies alienated many Americans who believed that the power of government had grown too broad. Americans also tired of Wilson's World War I crusade to promote worldwide democracy, along with his call for self-sacrifice at home and abroad. Disillusioned also with the violent labor strikes of 1919, and the poisonous atmosphere of the Red Scare (the fear of communists), America longed for peace, security, and prosperity.

Significance

In the election of 1920, Harding reassured the American people that he would not embark on any new crusades or demand self-sacrifice to save Europe. As a result, he won in a landslide, giving him the largest margin of victory any presidential candidate ever received—60.4 percent of the popular vote and 404 electoral votes. In addition, Republican majorities took control of both houses of Congress. However, fewer than 50 percent of the eligible voters went to the polls.

Uninterested electors, primarily newly enfranchised working-class women, apparently did not care who was president. Though scandal and inattention to the problems of the day marred his presidency, his victory is seen as a bridge between Wilsonian idealism and the laissez-faire business culture of the Coolidge and Hoover years.

Primary Source

"Return to Normalcy" [excerpt]

SYNOPSIS: On May 14, 1920, in Boston, Massachusetts, Warren Harding recited the famous line, "America's present need is not heroics, but healing; not nostrums, but normalcy, not revolution, but restoration." This speech not only cautioned America not to return to Theodore Roosevelt's activism and Woodrow Wilson's idealism but also coined the word *normalcy* as a substitute for *normality*.

There isn't anything the matter with world civilization, except that humanity is viewing it through a vision impaired in a cataclysmal war. Poise has been disturbed, and nerves have been racked, and fever has rendered men irrational; sometimes there have been draughts upon the dangerous cup of barbarity, and men have wandered far from safe paths, but the human procession still marches in the right direction.

America's present need is not heroics, but healing; not nostrums, but normalcy; not revolution, but restoration; not agitation, but adjustment; not surgery, but serenity; not the dramatic, but the dispassionate; not experiment, but equipoise; not submergence in internationality, but sustainment in triumphant nationality.

It is one thing to battle successfully against world domination by military autocracy, because the infinite God never intended such a program, but it is quite another thing to revise human nature and suspend the fundamental laws of life and all of life's acquirements. . . .

This republic has its ample tasks. If we put an end to false economics which lure humanity to utter chaos, ours will be the commanding example of world leadership today. If we can prove a representative popular government under which a citizenship seeks what it may do for the government rather than what the government may do for individuals, we shall do more to make democracy safe for the world than all armed conflict ever recorded.

The world needs to be reminded that all human ills are not curable by legislation, and that quantity of statutory enactment and excess of government offer no substitute for quality of citizenship.

The problems of maintained civilization are not to be solved by a transfer of responsibility from citizenship to government, and no eminent page in history was ever drafted by the standards of mediocrity. More, no government is worthy of the name which is directed by influence on the one hand, or moved by intimidation on the other. . . .

My best judgment of America's needs is to steady down, to get squarely on our feet, to make sure of the right path. Let's get out of the fevered delirium of war, with the hallucination that all the money in the world is to be made in the madness of war and the wildness of its aftermath. Let us stop to consider that tranquillity at home is more precious than peace abroad, and that both our good fortune and our eminence are dependent on the normal forward stride of all the American people. . . .

Further Resources

BOOKS

Britton, Nan. *The President's Daughter.* New York: Elizabeth Ann Guild, 1927.

Murray, Robert K. *The Politics of Normalcy: Governmental Theory and Practice in the Harding-Coolidge Era.* New York: Norton, 1973.

Russell, Francis. *The Shadow of Blooming Grove: Warren G. Harding in His Times.* New York: McGraw-Hill, 1968.

PERIODICALS

Anthony, Carl Sferrazza. "The Duchess: First Lady Florence Harding and the Tragedy of Being Ahead of Her Time." *Social Science Journal* 37 no. 4, 2000, 503–515.

Kauffman, Bill. "A President, His Paperboy & the Socialist." *American Enterprise* 13, January/February 2002, 52.

WEBSITES

Library of Congress. "American Leaders Speak: Recordings from World War I and the 1920 Election." Available online at http://memory.loc.gov/ammem/nfhtml/nfhome.html; website home page: http://www.loc.gov/ (accessed January 28, 2003).

"Warren Harding: The Return to Normalcy President." *The American President.* Available online at http://www.americanpresident.org/KoTrain/Courses/WH/WH_In_Brief.htm; website home page: http://www.americanpresident.org/the_series.htm (accessed January 28, 2003).

Nineteenth Amendment

Constitutional amendment

By: U.S. Congress
Date: 1920

Source: Nineteenth Amendment to the U.S. Constitution. 1920. National Archives and Records Administration. Available online at http://www.archives.gov/exhibit_hall/charters _of_freedom/constitution/19th_amendment.html; website home page: http://www.archives.gov (accessed May 15, 2003). ∎

Introduction

At the time of its founding, the United States did not explicitly prohibit women from voting in public elections. It was only when women agitated for suffrage that state legislatures clarified their constitutions to deny them the vote. From 1776 to 1784, women lost the right to vote in New York, Massachusetts, and New Hampshire. Fourteen years later, New Jersey, which granted the vote to all inhabitants "worth" fifty pounds, revoked women's right to vote, a right that the state had recognized since the crafting of its constitution in 1776. In addition to not being able to vote, unmarried women, either by law or local custom, were prohibited from jury service, public speaking, holding public office, attending college, or earning a living outside the positions of teacher, seamstress, servant, or mill worker. A married woman not only had to live within the same restrictions as unmarried women but could not enter into legal contracts, sue in court, divorce, gain child custody, or own personal property. In 1848, at the Seneca Falls Convention in New York, Elizabeth Cady Stanton and Lucretia Mott, along with other reformers both men and women, drew up the "Declarations of Sentiments." The declarations called for equal opportunities for women and gave voice to the first formal demand for women's right to vote. In 1866, U.S. Representative James Brooks of New York introduced the first woman suffrage amendment. The measure, which would have amended the Fourteenth Amendment, failed. In 1878, Senator A.A. Sargent of California introduced a similar amendment that was not acted upon until 1887, when the Senate defeated it

Significance

Most eastern states were firmly opposed to women's suffrage, in contrast to states in the West. In 1890, Wyoming became the first state since New Jersey to grant women full enfranchisement in its constitution. It was soon followed by Colorado (1893), Utah (1896), and Idaho (1896). Although women's suffrage had been granted in only nine states, there were considerable grounds for optimism that a constitutional amendment could be passed. By 1910, almost eight million women had entered the workforce, which had been dominated by men. Also, the Progressive movement controlled both the Democratic and Republican parties. These middle-class reformers realized that giving women the right to vote would improve their chances of passing other progressive reforms such as pure food and drug laws, conserva-

tion, abolition of child labor, and direct election of U.S. senators. Further, women played invaluable roles in World War I. As nurses, factory workers, and patriotic volunteers, they proved to male critics that they could shoulder important civic responsibilities. In 1918 President Woodrow Wilson, who had opposed a federal women's suffrage amendment, gave it his unqualified endorsement. According to the president, "It seems to me that every consideration of justice and of public advantage calls for the immediate adoption of that amendment and its submission forthwith to the legislatures of the several states."

In 1920, the United States joined New Zealand (1893), Australia (1902), Russia (1917), and Canada, Germany, and England (1919) in granting women the right to vote after three-quarters of the states voted to ratify the Nineteenth Amendment. Immediately, 26 million women were finally given a say in the government of their country. The landmark fulfilled nearly a century and a half of struggle to achieve full political rights for women. Nevertheless, this important milestone was just another step in a continuing battle for complete equality between the sexes.

Primary Source

Nineteenth Amendment

SYNOPSIS: In 1918, the House of Representatives passed the suffrage amendment 257 to 136, but it was defeated in the Senate. In May 1919, the House again passed the measure, 304 to 89, and in June the Senate passed it on a 56 to 25 vote. By the next year, the Nineteenth Amendment officially granted women the right to vote.

Sixty-Sixth Congress of the United States of America;

At the First Session,

Begun and held at the City of Washington on Monday, the nineteenth day of May, one thousand nine hundred and nineteen.

Joint Resolution

Proposing an amendment to the Constitution extending the right of suffrage to women.

Resolved by the Senate and House of Representatives of the United States of America in Congress assembled (two-thirds of each House concurring therein), That the following article is proposed as an amendment to the Constitution, which shall be valid to all intents and purposes as part of the Constitution when ratified by the legislatures of three-fourths of the several States.

The Nineteenth Amendment, also known as the Equal Rights Amendment, recognized the legitimacy of the women's suffrage movement by granting women the right to vote. **AP/WIDE WORLD PHOTOS. REPRODUCED BY PERMISSION.**

"Article——.

"The right of citizens of the United States to vote shall not be denied or abridged by the United States or by any State on account of sex.

"Congress shall have power to enforce this article by appropriate legislation."

Speaker of the House of Representatives.
Vice President of the United States and President of the Senate.

Further Resources

BOOKS

DuBois, Ellen. *Feminism and Suffrage: The Emergence of an Independent Women's Movement in America, 1848–1869.* Ithaca, N.Y.: Cornell University Press, 1978.

Flexner, Eleanor. *Century of Struggle: The Woman's Rights Movement in the United States.* Cambridge, Mass.: Belknap Press, 1975.

Griffith, Elisabeth. *In Her Own Right: The Life of Elizabeth Cady Stanton.* New York: Oxford Press, 1984.

PERIODICALS

Burkhalter, Nancy. "Women's Magazines and the Suffrage Movement: Did They Help or Hinder the Cause?" *Journal of American Culture* 19 (Summer 1996), 13–24.

Moore, Sarah J. "Making a Spectacle of Suffrage: The National Woman Suffrage Pageant, 1913." *Journal of American Culture* 20 (Spring 1917), 89–103.

WEBSITES

Halsall, Paul, ed. "Internet Sourcebooks History Project: Internet Modern History Sourcebook: Passage of the 19th Amendment 1919–1920: Articles from *The New York Times*." Available online at http://www.fordham.edu/halsall /mod/1920womensvote.html; website home page: http://www .fordham.edu/halsall/mod/modsbook.html (accessed January 28, 2003).

Library of Congress. "Votes for Women: Selections from the National American Woman Suffrage Association Collection, 1848–1921." Available online at http://lcweb2.loc.gov /ammem/naw/; website home page: http://www.loc.gov/ (accessed January 28, 2003).

Anti-Lynching Publicity Program
Meeting minutes

By: National Association for the Advancement of Colored People

Date: June 1922

Source: NAACP Anti-Lynching Papers, Anti-Lynching Publicity Program. Available online at http://www.fcii.arizona

.edu/hist396a/amungarro/executive_committee_of_the_anti.htm (accessed January 28, 2003).

About the Organization: On President Abraham Lincoln's birthdate in 1909, Ida Wells and W.E.B. DuBois helped organized the National Association for the Advancement of Colored People (NAACP) in response to the lynchings of African Americans. In 1919, the organization published *Thirty Years of Lynching in the United States: 1889–1919* to call attention to the issue. In 1922, it supported federal legislation prohibiting lynchings. ■

Introduction

The term *lynch* originated during the American Revolution. Amid the fighting and subsequent breakdown in civil authority, Colonel Charles Lynch, a prosperous Virginian plantation owner, established a "court" in his front yard and punished pro-British colonials, usually by beating them. As the American people migrated westward across the Allegheny Mountains in the postwar years, lynching was associated with vigilantism, in which citizens, assuming the role of judge, jury, and executioner, swiftly disciplined gamblers, cattle rustlers, horse thieves, and other outlaws.

With the end of Reconstruction in 1877 and the subsequent passage of discriminatory Jim Crow laws, southern and border states ended black participation in the region's political, legal, and economic affairs. To preserve white supremacy, lynchings became almost common occurrences, particularly in small rural towns. Between 1892, when reliable statistics were first collected, and 1951, a conservative estimate of the total number of lynchings is 4,730, of whom 3,437 were black. Ninety percent of all such lynchings occurred in the Deep South. Two-thirds of the remaining 10 percent occurred in the six border states. Mississippi recorded the most lynchings of African Americans with 539, followed by Georgia with 453, Texas with 411, Louisiana with 279, and Alabama with 251. These brutal acts continued into the twentieth century. In 1919, 79 blacks were lynched, 10 while still wearing their World War I uniforms. Between 1918 and 1927, 416 blacks were lynched, 42 of whom were burned alive.

To a large degree, lynchings were less a manner of punishment than an act of intimidation and terror. Southern whites justified lynchings as a necessary measure to protect white women from black rapists. From 1892 to 1951, however, only 25 percent of black lynching victims were even charged with, let alone convicted of, either rape or attempted rape. Undoubtedly, many of the accused were lynched for committing minor offenses or no offenses at all. Moreover, lynchings were not secretive acts of cruelty. To the contrary, by the 1890s, lynchings had evolved into public recreational events. Across the South and border states, small-town newspapers alerted their readers of upcoming lynchings. To increase

Two black men were pulled from the county jail and lynched from a tree before a crowd of onlookers. GETTY IMAGES. REPRODUCED BY PERMISSION.

attendance, railroads sold excursion tickets to would-be visitors. On lynch day, white families and their children assembled to watch the gruesome spectacle. Typically, blacks were first burned, maimed, and dismembered, and then faced the hangman's noose. Afterward, souvenir seekers often sliced off the victims' fingers, toes, ears, and genitalia.

Significance

From the 1890s to the 1930s, sixteen southern and border states enacted laws outlawing lynchings, but state and local governments rarely indicted or sentenced lynchers, often because officials were personally sympathetic to the perpetrators. In 1922, the NAACP encouraged Representative Leonidas Dyer, a Missouri Republican, to sponsor antilynching legislation. Dyer had been deeply affected by recent riots in East St. Louis, Illinois, where policeman shot blacks and mobs burned homes occupied by African Americans and threw black children into the fires. The measure passed the House but failed in the Senate. The bill was reintroduced in 1927 and 1940, but each time the Senate failed to pass it. Southern lawmakers argued that the bill was unconstitutional, for it infringed upon states' rights. Even though it did not pass, the Dyer bill was important because it repeatedly called attention to the

Men and women march in a 1922 protest against the lynching of blacks and in support of federal intervention to stop the practice.
© BETTMANN/CORBIS. REPRODUCED BY PERMISSION.

problem. Moreover, after it was first introduced in 1922, the number of lynchings began to decline. Between 1922 and 1940, the number of annual lynchings in the United States dropped more than 90 percent, from 57 to 5.

Primary Source

Anti-Lynching Publicity Program

SYNOPSIS: In June 1922, the NAACP launched a sophisticated publicity campaign designed to ensure that the country was informed of the evil of lynchings. The NAACP sought to raise $1 million ($9.5 million in 2001 dollars) to pressure Congress and state legislatures to pass antilynching legislation and to inform the general public through newspaper advertisements. The following are minutes from the meeting of the Executive Committee of the NAACP's Anti-Lynching Crusaders.

The Executive Committee of the Anti-Lynching Crusaders held their Third meeting in New York with 5 states represented. The chairman, Mrs. M. B. Talbert, reported that the movement was splendidly started with over 700 key women in 25 states hard at work. Ultimate success seemed assured.

The Committee made the following statement in answer to many inquiries:

A. The movement owes its origin to Mrs. Helen Curtis who was inspired by a public statement of Congressman L. C. Dyer, made at the Annual Conference of the N.A.A.C.P. at Newark, June 1922, in which he said: "If 1,000,000 people were united in the demand from the Senate that the Dyer Bill be passed, there would be no question of its passage." A small committee does not believe in duplicating organizations.

B. The committee does not believe in duplicating organizations. We have enough and more organizations already for all the work there is to do. What we need is concentrated effort for specific objects. The committee, therefore, is organized to raise money for one object and then to disband January 1, 1923.

C. The one object of the Anti-Lynching Crusaders is to stop lynching and mob violence. There is no division of opinion on the imperative need of this among decent people, black and white.

D. The one clear and practical program so far outlined for the accomplishment of this end is that of the N.A.A.C.P. are honestly administered and publicity accounted for.

E. The Anti-Lynching Crusaders have, therefore, determined to raise $1,000,000 dollars or as much thereof as is possible by January 1st and to turn this sum over to the Anti-Lynching Fund of the N.A.A.C.P. in trust to be used to pass and enforce the Dyer Anti-Lynching and to put down mob violence.

F. Some have doubted if such a sum is necessary. It is; and we have asked the executive office of the N.A.A.C.P. to outline roughly how it could be effectively and economically expended. The statement follows: An Anti-Lynching program demands: 1. Publicity 2. Pressure upon Congress 3. Pressure upon state legislatures 4. Investigation 5. Legal processes.

   1. Publicity: The Negro has never given his cause proper publicity. We propose, if we can obtain the funds, a campaign of newspaper publicity patterned after the Red Cross and Child Welfare campaigns. A campaign where full page statements of the facts concerning lynching shall appear in every influential daily paper throughout the United States, and that this shall be repeated two, three or more times until not a single person who reads the daily papers shall be ignorant of the fact that we are the only country that burns human beings at the stake, that 3,436 people have been lynched, from 1888 to January 1, 1922 and that rape is not the primary cause of lynching. Such a campaign could be started for $10,000 and would, to be complete, cost $1,000,000.

   2. Pressure upon Congress: The country must be aroused by letters, telegrams and articles to pour in upon the Senate a stream of requests for immediate action. Such a campaign throughout the United States cannot be completely inaugurated for less than $25,000.

   3. Pressure upon State Legislatures: Our efforts to strengthen state laws must not for a moment lag. Three or four states have adequate anti-lynching laws. Campaigns must be inaugurated to secure the passage of such laws in other states. This should cost from $10,000 to $100,000. Moreover, if the Dyer Bill fails of passage before March, the present bill must be reintroduced in the next Congress. If the Dyer Anti-Lynching Bill is passed, the campaign against lynching, mob violence and legal defense has just begun and we must immediately be ready for two things:

   4. Investigation of every case of lynching and mob violence which occurs. These investigations must be far more th[o]rough than in the past for on them we must be able to build court cases with facts and witnesses. This will mean the use of detective agencies, local investigators, documentary research, etc. It is safe to say that in the next few years from $50,000 to $250,000 could be wisely and economically spent on such investigations.

   5. Legal processes: Finally, there are the actual law cases. The Federal Government will probably attend to the actual prosecutions but we must stand ready to help in the preparation of the cases, the gathering of witnesses, and the stimulation of

Anti-Lynching Prayer

This prayer was part of the campaign of the Anti-lynching crusaders. The prayer was to be prayed at noon during the months of October, November, and December. The Anti-Lynching Crusaders' statement calls upon women to integrate this prayer into their lives. Integrating the anti-lynching movement along with religion appealed to both black and white Christian women.

For Deliverance of the Colored People

Our Father who art in Heaven. Hallowed be thy Name.

Hear now, we beseech Thee, the prayer and petition of ten million American citizens of African descent, who this day approach Thy presence with one heart and voice. We thank Thee that Thou art no respecter of races, nations or persons; but all who love and serve find equal favor with Thee.

Thou didst stoop to the lowly estate of our fathers and mothers in the darker days of their enslavement, and didst hear their cry for deliverance rising up from the low ground of sorrows. May our faith in Thy power of deliverance be as simple and sincere and as soul-deep as theirs. Amidst the distractions and allurements of this worldly day, may we preserve the patrimony of the faith of our fathers.

We do not palliate misdeeds, nor would we shield the wrongdoer from the just penalty of crime. Let those who sin under the law perish by the law. But we pray Thee that accusation, suspicion and allegement of crime may not suffice for proof when one of our number is the victim. Let not the sins of the wicked be visited upon the heads of the guiltless.

We are slain all the day long in the land of our nativity, which is the land of our loyalty and of our love.

The vials of race vengeance are wreaked upon our defenceless heads. The inhuman thirst for human blood takes little heed of innocence or guilt. Any convenient victim identified with our race suffices to slake the accursed thirst. We are beaten with many stripes. Our bodies are bruised, burned and tortured and torn asunder for the ghoulish mirth of the blood lusty multitude. Whenever such atrocity is perpetrated upon any one of our number, because of his race, it is done unto us all. Vengeance and wrath are not invoked for the fit atonement of committed crime, nor yet for the just punishment of evildoers; but the sinister aim is to depress our spirit, enslave our souls and to give our name an evil repute in the eyes of the world.

Put it into the hearts of the people and the ruler of our own land that the true grandeur of this nation will not consist in political dominion or the mightiness of power or the magnitude of material things, but in justice, love and mercy.

We pray Thee to enlighten the understanding and nerve the hearts of our law-makers with the political wisdom and the moral courage to pass the Dyer Anti-Lynching Bill, now hanging in the balance of doubt and uncertainty.

Have mercy upon any of our legislators who may be so embittered with the gall of race hatred and fettered by the bonds of political iniquity as to advocate or apologize for lynching, rapine and murder.

Hear our prayer, relieve our distress, preserve our nation and save the world.

We ask it all for Jesus' sake. Amen.

SOURCE: "Prayer for Deliverance of the Colored People." NAACP Papers, Part 7: The Anti-Lynching Campaign, 1912–1955, Series B: Anti-Lynching Legislative and Publicity Files, 1916–1955. Library of Congress. Available online at http://womhist.binghamton.edu/lynch/doc13.htm; website home page: http://womhist.binghamton.edu (accessed May 5, 2003).

the interest of public minds. From $100,000 to $250,000 is a small estimate of the cost of preparing such cases. This means that not less than $100,000 ought to be available this moment for the anti-lynching campaign and that it will take at least $1,000,000 to stop lynching and mob violence in United States and provide legal defense. These figures may seem large. They are not large. The difficulty with us is that our ideas of the cost of emancipation have always been too small.

G. The Executive Committee of the Anti-Lynching Crusaders accepts this program and will seek earnestly to raise the necessary funds. In the raising of these funds, no salaries are being paid, and no commissions of any sort. The work of the Crusaders, both officers and others, is entirely voluntary and uncompensated in any way. Only actual expenses are being met and these are being met by funds raised outside of money contributed to the anti-lynching fund is to be held in trust by the Guaranty Trust Company of New York City to be turned over as directed.

Mrs. Grace Nail Johnson
Mrs. Alice Dunbar Nelson
Mrs. Lillian Alexander
Publicity Committee

Mrs. Mary B. Talbert
National Director

Further Resources

BOOKS

Cook, Fred J. *The Ku Klux Klan, America's Recurring Nightmare.* New York: J. Messner, 1980.

White, Walter. *Rope and Faggot.* New York: Arno, 1969.

Zangrando, Robert L. *The NAACP Crusade Against Lynching, 1909–1950.* Philadelphia: Temple University Press, 1980.

PERIODICALS

Blee, Kathleen M. "Women in the 1920s' Ku Klux Klan Movement." *Feminist Studies* 17, Spring 1991, 57–77.

Coben, Stanley. "Ordinary White Protestants: The KKK in the 1920s." *Journal of Social History* 28, Fall 1994, 155–165.

WEBSITES

Ferris State University. "Jim Crow Museum of Racist Memorabilia." Available online at http://www.ferris.edu/news /jimcrow/ (accessed January 28, 2003).

Temple University Center for African American History and Culture. "NAACP Anti-Lynching Campaign and Anti-Lynching Investigative Papers, 1912–1955." Available online at http://www.temple.edu/CAAHC/new_page_16.htm; website home page: http://www.temple.edu/CAAHC/ (accessed January 28, 2002).

The Pivot of Civilization

Nonfiction work

By: Margaret Sanger

Date: 1922

Source: Sanger, Margaret. *The Pivot of Civilization.* Elmsford, N.Y.: Maxwell Reprint Co., 1969. Available online at http://www.pro-life.net/sanger/pivot_05.htm (accessed January 29, 2003).

About the Author: Born in Cornell, New York, to Irish American parents, Margaret Sanger (1879–1966) was the leading American proponent of birth control until her death. The death of her mother at age fifty after bearing eleven children had a profound impact on Sanger, who believed that women had a right to control their sexual and reproductive lives. In 1921, she established the American Birth Control League, which became Planned Parenthood in 1942. ■

Introduction

In 1883, British scientist Francis Galton coined the term *eugenics,* from the Greek word for "good in birth." The term was first used to refer to the "science" of good breeding. In 1910, with the financial assistance of the Andrew Carnegie Institution, the Eugenics Record Office (ERO), a genetic research center, was established at Cold Harbor, New York. The ERO adapted the plant genetic experiments of Gregor Mendel into a social theory that sought to explain and predict complex traits and behaviors. ERO scientists visited insane asylums, prisons, and orphanages and compiled data by interviewing subjects,

Margaret Sanger, author of *The Pivot of Civilization,* alleged that organized charity was a symbol of "a malignant social disease" and that society should be acting to alleviate the problem rather than aid it. **THE LIBRARY OF CONGRESS.**

taking medical histories, and amassing family histories. In addition, ERO administered culturally biased IQ tests, which they incorrectly surmised were accurate measures of intelligence. From this "scientific evidence," eugenicists argued that Russians, Italians, and Jews, along with other immigrants from southern and eastern Europe, were "idiots" and "feebleminded." In turn, those Americans who traced their ancestry back to northern and western Europe were hardworking, frugal, and highly intelligent. This information was widely published and presented at professional seminars. To its upper- and middle-class believers, these studies seemed an objective, mathematical approach to solving the myriad social problems stemming from immigration. Further, these studies confirmed their convictions that the moral value of human beings was relative, or, in other words, that some people were better than others.

In the early decades of the twentieth century, eugenics was not a fringe movement. In 1906, J.H. Kellogg, the breakfast cereal tycoon, founded the Race Betterment Foundation in Battle Creek, Michigan, which hosted a number of eugenics conferences. After 1914, eugenics was taught at Harvard, Columbia, and Brown Universities. Eugenics was also popular among middle-class progressive reformers. After World War I, local eugenics societies were organized across the United States. In 1923, the American Eugenics Society (AES) was founded, and it quickly expanded into twenty-nine chapters nationwide. This group, fearing that the birthrate of the "idiot" lower classes was outpacing the birthrate of their own "intelligent" class, focused on three ways of improving humanity by breeding out the undesirable traits of those deemed less worthy. First, the group successfully advocated that the nation enact selective immigration restrictions, for in 1924, the Federal Immigration Act set up strict quotas limiting the number of immigrants from countries having "inferior stock." Second, eugenicists encouraged Americans from northern and western Europe not to marry outside their "race." Last, they denied the "unfit" the right to reproduce by involuntarily sterilizing alcoholics, paupers, criminals, sexual deviants, and others who had undesirable physical and personal traits. In 1907, Indiana was the first state to mandate compulsory sterilization of "degenerates." By 1914, eleven other states enacted similar laws. Eugenicists insisted that sterilization saved society, through state-funded welfare and private charities, millions of dollars. By 1941, 40,000 Americans had been involuntarily sterilized. Mandated sterilization soon spread to Switzerland, Scandinavia, and Nazi Germany, where American eugenics beliefs, combined with social Darwinism and anti-Semitism, produced the Holocaust.

Significance

The eugenics movement continues to thrive in twenty-first century America. Though scientists are not racist or anti-Semitic, they are concerned with directing the future of humanity's evolution. Through cloning and other advances in genetic medicine, scientists hope someday to preserve and perpetuate the "finest" genes of our species. Critics of genetic medicine fear that in the future, wealthy prospective parents will be able to select the physical, cognitive, and behavioral traits they desire for their children. However, after a few centuries of tinkering with the natural order, they believe that humanity will split into two separate groups, a homogeneous superrace and a diverse "natural" underclass.

Primary Source

The Pivot of Civilization [excerpt]

SYNOPSIS: In the mid-twentieth century, Margaret Sanger was one of the most influential women in America. Much of her notoriety came from this classic 1922 book. In this excerpt from Chapter 5, "The Cruelty of Charity," Sanger professes a eugenic philosophy and seeks to end federal and private funding that provided free medical and nursing facilities to immigrant mothers.

Fostering the good-for-nothing at the expense of the good is an extreme cruelty. It is a deliberate storing up of miseries for future generations. There is no greater curse to posterity than that of bequeathing them an increasing population of imbeciles.

Herbert Spencer

The last century has witnessed the rise and development of philanthropy and organized charity. Coincident with the all-conquering power of machinery and capitalistic control, with the unprecedented growth of great cities and industrial centers, and the creation of great proletarian populations, modern civilization has been confronted, to a degree hitherto unknown in human history, with the complex problem of sustaining human life in surroundings and under conditions flagrantly dysgenic.

The program, as I believe all competent authorities in contemporary philanthropy and organized charity would agree, has been altered in aim and purpose. It was first the outgrowth of humanitarian and altruistic idealism, perhaps not devoid of a strain of sentimentalism, of an idealism that was aroused by a desperate picture of human misery intensified by the industrial revolution. It has developed in later years into a program not so much aiming to succor the unfortunate victims of circumstances, as to effect what we may term social sanitation. Primarily, it is a program of self-protection. Contemporary philanthropy, I believe, recognizes that extreme poverty and overcrowded slums are veritable breeding-grounds of epidemics, disease, delinquency and dependency. Its aim, therefore, is to prevent the individual family from sinking to that abject condition in which it will become a much heavier burden upon society.

There is no need here to criticize the obvious limitations of organized charities in meeting the desperate problem of destitution. We are all familiar with these criticisms: the common indictment of "inefficiency" so often brought against public and privately endowed agencies. The charges include the high cost of administration; the pauperization of deserving poor, and the encouragement and fostering of the "undeserving"; the progressive destruction of self-respect and self-reliance by the paternalistic interference of social agencies; the impossibility of keeping pace with the ever-increasing multiplication of factors and influences responsible for the perpetuation of human misery; the misdirection and misappropriation of endowments; the absence of interorganization and coordination of the various agencies of church, state, and privately endowed institutions; the "crimes of charity" that are occasionally exposed in newspaper scandals. These and similar strictures we may ignore as irrelevant to our present purpose, as inevitable but not incurable faults that have been and are being eliminated in the slow but certain growth of a beneficent power in modern civilization. In reply to such criticisms, the protagonist of modern philanthropy might justly point to the honest and sincere workers and disinterested scientists it has mobilized, to the self-sacrificing and hard-working executives who have awakened public attention to the evils of poverty and the menace to the race engendered by misery and filth.

Even if we accept organized charity at its own valuation, and grant that it does the best it can, it is exposed to a more profound criticism. It reveals a fundamental and irremediable defect. Its very success, its very efficiency, its very necessity to the social order, are themselves the most unanswerable indictment. Organized charity itself is the symptom of a malignant social disease.

Those vast, complex, interrelated organizations aiming to control and to diminish the spread of misery and destitution and all the menacing evils that spring out of this sinisterly fertile soil, are the surest sign that our civilization has bred, is breeding and is perpetuating constantly increasing numbers of defectives, delinquents and dependents. My criticism, therefore, is not directed at the "failure" of philanthropy, but rather at its success.

These dangers inherent in the very idea of humanitarianism and altruism, dangers which have to-day produced their full harvest of human waste, of inequality and inefficiency, were fully recognized in the last century at the moment when such ideas were first put into practice. Readers of Huxley's attack on the Salvation Army will recall his penetrating and stimulating condemnation of the debauch of sentimentalism which expressed itself in so uncontrolled a fashion in the Victorian era. One of the most penetrating of American thinkers, Henry James, Sr., sixty or seventy years ago wrote: "I have been so long accustomed to see the most arrant deviltry transact itself in the name of benevolence, that the moment I hear a profession of good will from almost any quarter, I instinctively look around for a constable or place my hand within reach of a bell-rope. My ideal of human intercourse would be a state of things in which no man will ever stand in need of any other man's help, but will derive all his satisfaction from the great social tides which own no individual names. I am sure no man can be put in a position of de-

pendence upon another, without the other's very soon becoming—if he accepts the duties of the relation—utterly degraded out of his just human proportions. No man can play the Deity to his fellow man with impunity—I mean, spiritual impunity, of course. For see: if I am at all satisfied with that relation, if it contents me to be in a position of generosity towards others, I must be remarkably indifferent at bottom to the gross social inequality which permits that position, and, instead of resenting the enforced humiliation of my fellow man to myself in the interests of humanity, I acquiesce in it for the sake of the profit it yields to my own self-complacency. I do hope the reign of benevolence is over; until that event occurs, I am sure the reign of God will be impossible."

To-day, we may measure the evil effects of "benevolence" of this type, not merely upon those who have indulged in it, but upon the community at large. These effects have been reduced to statistics and we cannot, if we would, escape their significance. Look, for instance (since they are close at hand, and fairly representative of conditions elsewhere) at the total annual expenditures of public and private "charities and corrections" for the State of New York. For the year ending June 30, 1919, the expenditures of public institutions and agencies amounted to $33,936,205.88. The expenditures of privately supported and endowed institutions for the same year, amount to $58,100,530.98. This makes a total, for public and private charities and corrections of $92,036,736.86. A conservative estimate of the increase for the year (1920–1921) brings this figure approximately to one-hundred and twenty-five millions. These figures take on an eloquent significance if we compare them to the comparatively small amounts spent upon education, conservation of health and other constructive efforts. Thus, while the City of New York spent $7.35 per capita on public education in the year 1918, it spent on public charities no less than $2.66. Add to this last figure an even larger amount dispensed by private agencies, and we may derive some definite sense of the heavy burden of dependency, pauperism and delinquency upon the normal and healthy sections of the community.

Statistics now available also inform us that more than a million dollars are spent annually to support the public and private institutions in the state of New York for the segregation of the feeble-minded and the epileptic. A million and a half is spent for the up-keep of state prisons, those homes of the "defective delinquent." Insanity, which, we should remember, is to a great extent hereditary, annually drains from the state treasury no less than $11,985,695.55, and from private sources and endowments another twenty millions. When we learn further that the total number of inmates in public and private institutions in the State of New York—in alms-houses, reformatories, schools for the blind, deaf and mute, in insane asylums, in homes for the feeble-minded and epileptic—amounts practically to less than sixty-five thousand, an insignificant number compared to the total population, our eyes should be opened to the terrific cost to the community of this dead weight of human waste.

The United States Public Health Survey of the State of Oregon, recently published, shows that even a young community, rich in natural resources, and unusually progressive in legislative measures, is no less subject to this burden. Out of a total population of 783,000 it is estimated that more than 75,000 men, women and children are dependents, feeble-minded, or delinquents. Thus about 10 per cent. of the population is a constant drain on the finances, health, and future of that community. These figures represent a more definite and precise survey than the rough one indicated by the statistics of charities and correction for the State of New York. The figures yielded by this Oregon survey are also considerably lower than the average shown by the draft examination, a fact which indicates that they are not higher than might be obtained from other States.

Organized charity is thus confronted with the problem of feeble-mindedness and mental defect. But just as the State has so far neglected the problem of mental defect until this takes the form of criminal delinquency, so the tendency of our philanthropic and charitable agencies has been to pay no attention to the problem until it has expressed itself in terms of pauperism and delinquency. Such "benevolence" is not merely ineffectual; it is positively injurious to the community and the future of the race.

But there is a special type of philanthropy or benevolence, now widely advertised and advocated, both as a federal program and as worthy of private endowment, which strikes me as being more insidiously injurious than any other. This concerns itself directly with the function of maternity, and aims to supply GRATIS medical and nursing facilities to slum mothers. Such women are to be visited by nurses and to receive instruction in the "hygiene of pregnancy"; to be guided in making arrangements for confinements; to be invited to come to the doctor's clinics for examination and supervision. They are, we are informed, to "receive adequate care during pregnancy, at confinement, and for one month afterward." Thus are mothers and babies to be saved. "Childbearing is to be made safe." The work of the maternity centers in the various American cities in which they have already been established and in which they are supported by private contributions and endowment, it is hardly necessary to point out, is carried on among the poor and more docile sections of the city, among mothers least able, through poverty and ignorance, to afford the care and attention necessary for successful maternity. Now, as the findings of Tredgold and Karl Pearson and the British Eugenists so conclusively show, and as the infant mortality reports so thoroughly substantiate, a high rate of fecundity is always associated with the direst poverty, irresponsibility, mental defect, feeble-mindedness, and other transmissible taints. The effect of maternity endowments and maternity centers supported by private philanthropy would have, perhaps already have had, exactly the most dysgenic tendency. The new government program would facilitate the function of maternity among the very classes in which the absolute necessity is to discourage it.

Such "benevolence" is not merely superficial and near-sighted. It conceals a stupid cruelty, because it is not courageous enough to face unpleasant facts. Aside from the question of the unfitness of many women to become mothers, aside from the very definite deterioration in the human stock that such programs would inevitably hasten, we may question its value even to the normal though unfortunate mother. For it is never the intention of such philanthropy to give the poor over-burdened and often undernourished mother of the slum the opportunity to make the choice herself, to decide whether she wishes time after to time to bring children into the world. It merely says "Increase and multiply: We are prepared to help you do this." Whereas the great majority of mothers realize the grave responsibility they face in keeping alive and rearing the children they have already brought into the world, the maternity center would teach them how to have more. The poor woman is taught how to have her seventh child, when what she wants to know is how to avoid bringing into the world her eighth.

Such philanthropy, as Dean Inge has so unanswerably pointed out, is kind only to be cruel, and unwittingly promotes precisely the results most deprecated. It encourages the healthier and more normal sections of the world to shoulder the burden of unthinking and indiscriminate fecundity of others; which brings with it, as I think the reader must agree, a dead weight of human waste. Instead of decreasing and aiming to eliminate the stocks that are most detrimental to the future of the race and the world, it tends to render them to a menacing degree dominant.

Further Resources

BOOKS

Gordon, Linda. *Woman's Body, Woman's Right: A Social History of Birth Control in America.* New York: Grossman, 1976.

Pickens, D. *Eugenics and the Progressives.* Nashville, Tenn.: Vanderbilt University Press, 1968.

Sanger, Margaret. *Margaret Sanger: An Autobiography.* 1938. Reprint, New York: Cooper Square Press, 1999.

PERIODICALS

Sanger, Margaret. "Leaders and Revolutionaries of the 20th Century." *Time,* April 13, 1998, 93–94.

Vecoli, Rudolph. "Sterilization: A Progressive Measure?" *Wisconsin Magazine of History* 43, 1960, 190–202.

WEBSITES

New York University Department of History. "The Margaret Sanger Papers Project." Available online at http://www.nyu.edu/projects/sanger/ (accessed January 28, 2003).

"Canal-Boat Children"

Journal article

By: Children's Bureau, U.S. Department of Labor (Ethel M. Springer)

Date: February 1923

Source: Springer, Ethel M. "Canal-Boat Children," *Monthly Labor Review* 16, no. 2, February 1923. Available online at http://www.history.rochester.edu/canal/bib/springer/ (accessed January 28, 2003).

About the Organization: In 1906, Senator Albert Beveridge of Indiana sponsored a bill to "prevent the employment of children in factories and mines." Though the measure was defeated, reformers pressured Congress to create the federal Children's Bureau in the Department of Labor in 1912. The bureau was charged with investigating and reporting "upon all matters pertaining to the welfare of children and child life among all classes of our people." ∎

Introduction

In colonial America, child labor was not a subject of controversy. Children were an integral part of the agricultural economy. Not only did children labor on the homestead, they also were hired out to other farmers by their parents. It was not unusual for boys to begin their apprenticeship in a designated trade by the time they were ten years of age. Benjamin Franklin, for example, was apprenticed to work as a printer's assistance for his older brother at the age of twelve. In the early nineteenth century, child apprenticeships declined, but with the onset of the Industrial Revolution in the United States and the influx of Irish in the 1840s and southern and eastern Europeans after 1880, minors often found factory employment. Children were ideal factory workers because they were paid a fraction of an adult's wages, were easily managed, and were very difficult for labor unions to organize. By 1900, 18 percent of children between the ages of ten and fifteen were gainfully employed. Moreover, 25 percent of workers in southern cotton mills were below the age of fifteen, some as young a six or seven. Although many child workers labored in horrendous conditions, their incomes were vital for families who lived in dire poverty.

Attempts to prohibit child labor began prior to the Civil War. By 1863, seven states had passed laws limiting the hours of child workers to forty-eight per week, but often the laws were not strictly enforced. The use of child labor continued to rise throughout the late nineteenth century. In 1900, the national census revealed that 1,750,178 children between the ages of ten and fifteen were employed, an increase of more than one million since 1870. At the turn of the century, outraged middle-class progressives mounted a vigorous campaign to stamp out child labor. Armed with an array of statistics documenting the widespread use of child labor and poignant photographs dramatizing the poor working conditions of child laborers, the reformers lobbied states to end the practice. By 1914, reformers had persuaded nearly every state legislature to ban the employment in factories of young children, generally defined as under the age of fourteen, and to limit hours of work for older minors. However, child labor persisted as too many businessmen reaped excessive profits, too many politicians and judges were reluctant to regulate or intervene in the practice, and too many parents depended upon their children's labor for survival. As a result, it became clear that the states could not effectively curb child labor and progressives lobbied Congress, seeking federal legislation that would end child labor once and for all.

Significance

In 1916, the Children's Bureau undertook and published a series of studies of the conditions under which children worked in specific industries and occupations. The bureau chronicled boy mine workers in Pennsylvania, ten-year-olds working nearly all night making artificial flowers in grimy urban tenements, and barefoot children slaving in the hot southern sun picking onions,

Children Boating on Chesapeake and Ohio Canal, 1920

Classified by Age and Number of Seasons Worked

| Age | Number who had done boat work each specified number of seasons | | | | | | | | | | Not reported | Total | Number who had done no boatwork | Total |
	1	2	3	4	5	6	7	8	9	10 or more				
5 years or under	3	...	...	...	...	...	...	...	...	...	...	3	38	41
6 years	3	1	...	...	...	...	...	...	...	...	...	4	3	7
7 years	2	2	1	...	...	...	...	...	...	...	1	6	1	7
8 years	1	2	...	1	...	...	...	...	...	...	...	4	1	5
9 years	3	...	3	...	1	...	...	...	...	...	1	8	2	10
10 years	1	1	1	2	1	1	...	...	...	...	...	7	...	7
11 years	2	3	1	1	...	2	...	...	...	...	1	10	1	11
12 years	...	3	2	...	1	1	1	...	...	...	1	9	1	10
13 years	...	2	2	...	2	1	...	1	...	...	1	9	...	9
14 years	1	5	1	3	2	1	...	1	...	...	1	15	1	16
15 years	2	...	2	1	1	...	...	1	...	2	...	9	...	9
16 years	...	1	1	...	1	1	...	1	1	...	1	7	...	7
17 years	...	...	...	...	...	1	...	1	...	1	...	3	...	3
Total	18	20	14	8	9	8	1	5	1	3	7	94	48	142

SOURCE: Springer, Ethel M. "Canal Boat Children," *Monthly Labor Review*, vol. 16, no. 2, February 1923, p. 5.

cotton, and beets. That year, the Keating-Owen Child Labor Act was implemented, which barred interstate commerce in goods manufactured by the labor of children under the age of sixteen. Congress authorized the Children's Bureau to administer the new law, but the U.S. Supreme Court, in *Hammer v. Dagenhart* (1918), ruled the law unconstitutional. The court held that although children needed protection, the federal law intruded upon the ability of the states to regulate their own child labor laws. The Children's Bureau continued to investigate child labor violations, and in 1938 much of the exploitation was prohibited under the Fair Labor Standards Act.

Primary Source

"Canal-Boat Children" [excerpt]

SYNOPSIS: In 1921, the Children's Bureau received information of children living on canal boats on the Chesapeake and Ohio Canal, which extends 185 miles from Washington, D.C., to Cumberland, Maryland. The bureau investigated and found that although the number of children were few, the "living and working conditions presented unusually serious problems." The following article, written by Ethel M. Springer, sheds light on one facet of the child labor and welfare problem.

The Chesapeake and Ohio Canal extends from Washington, DC, to Cumberland, Md., along the eastern bank of the Potomac River, a distance of 185 miles, with an ascent of 609 feet which is overcome by means of 75 locks. The canal varies in width at the surface from 55 to 65 feet and at the bottom from 30 to 42 feet and has a depth of 6 feet throughout. The open season lasts approximately nine months, from early March till December. During the winter months it is customary to drain the canal to prevent damage which might be caused by freezing.

The principal cargo has always been bituminous coal mined in the mountains about Cumberland, which is transported to Georgetown. Boatmen said that they averaged two round trips a month, the distance from Cumberland to Georgetown being covered from six to eight days, and the return trip in from four to six days. Practically all the traffic at the time of the study was conducted by one company which owned the boats and employed captains to operate them. The policy of this company was to give preference to married men on the ground that a married man is steadier in his job than a single man, and that the presence of his wife and children on a boat raises the moral tone. For the year 1920, the company reported that all but 7 of the 66 captains oil its pay roll were married men.

Of the 59 captains who were married, 41 were found who had their children with them during the season studied. The number of children found accompanying their families was 135 (70 boys and 65 girls); of these, 48 were under 7 years of age. In addition to these children there were found on canal boats 7 boys who wore employed as deck hands by captains to whom they were not related. One of these boys was 11 years of age, four were 14, one was 15, and one 16 years of age. It is known that not all the families were located and interviewed and it is probable that the number of independent child workers found is still less indicative of the actual number on the canal boats, inasmuch as they were even more difficult to locate than families.

The operation of canal boats is an occupation handed down from father to son. Said one mother: "The children are brought up on the boat and don't know nothin' else, and that is the only reason they take up 'boating.' Boys work for their fathers until they are big enough to get a boat of their own, and it's always easy to get a boat." Several men complained that they knew "nothing else" and realized that their children would have the same disadvantage. Most of the fathers had begun boating before they were 13 years of age; but since the majority had begun by helping their own fathers they did not become "captains" at an especially early age, many of them not until they were 25 years or over. Four men, however, had become captains before they were 16. The mother of one of these had died when he was 12 years of age, leaving $2,100 in cash to each of 14 children. The boy boated for one season with an older brother, receiving as compensation for the season's work, an overcoat, a "made" (as distinguished from homemade) suit of clothes, and $7.50. When he was 14 he bought his own boat and team of mules and became an independent captain. During the first season he saved $700 and "lived like a lord." He began with practically no education, and though he had been a captain for 54 years he had never learned to read and write. Several of his sons became boatmen and at the time of the study a 16-year-old grandson was boating with him.

All the captains included in the study were native white. Seven were illiterate. Their wives also were all native white. Five of them were illiterate. One captain, who had begun boating with his father when he was 5 years of age, said that altogether he had gone to school only 29 months. By the time he reached the fourth grade the children of his own age had long since completed the grammar grades and he was ashamed to go into classes with younger boys and girls. He seemed to regret his own lack of education and said that when his little girl was old enough to go to school he should stop boating.

Operation of Boats

The operation of the old-fashioned canal boat used on the Chesapeake and Ohio Canal consists

The Federal Children's Bureau found in 1921 that living and working conditions for children presented "serious problems" on canal boats on the Ohio and Chesapeake Canal. © HULTON-DEUTSCH COLLECTION/CORBIS. REPRODUCED BY PERMISSION.

in driving the mules and in steering the boat. The mules are harnessed tandem to two long ropes or "lines" attached to the bow of the boat. From two to five mules are used by "spells," two or three mules being stabled in the fore cabin at rest while the others draw. The boathands take turns at driving, either walking beside the mules or riding the leader. Although the captains usually do some of the driving, especially if the boat travels at night, they consider it a child's job during the day. In dry weather the towpath, which is level except at the approaches to the locks, is well beaten down and easy to walk on, but in summer the work is wearisome and hot. In wet weather the path is muddy and slippery, and consequently shoes and clothing get very hard wear. One captain considered himself the best father on the canal because he provided his boys with rubber boots.

Steering the boat is accomplished by means of the "stick" located on the quarter-deck at the stern of the boat. This controls the rudder or "paddle," and may be guided by the pilot standing or sitting against it. As there is practically no current to change the direction of the boat, the operation is very simple and the mother of the family often steers while doing household tasks that permit. A young child can steer a light boat, as the stick moves easily, but to steer loaded boats requires strength. The only complications in steering occur at the locks or when other canal boats are passed.

Locks are 15 feet wide and approximately 100 feet long. The usual method of opening and shut-

Efforts to reform child labor succeeded in effecting some change, but it remained a profitable business practice in the 1920s.
HULTON/ARCHIVE. REPRODUCED BY PERMISSION.

ting them is by pushing heavy beams which extend from the swinging gates on each side. At the time of the study the lock tenders were mostly old men who were assisted by the women and children of their families; the boat workers, however, frequently helped to operate the locks as it is sometimes necessary for several persons to brace themselves against the beams of the gates. . . . Boats approach the locks so slowly that the steersman has ample time to fit the boat into the lock. Careful calculation, however, is required as the locks are only one foot wider than the boats. . . . A severe jolt against the wall of the lock has been known to sink a boat. When the boat is in the lock, the boatmen untie the mules and make the boat fast by wrapping ropes around heavy posts which are driven deep into the ground near the lock wall. After a lock is filled or emptied the boatmen pull in their ropes and steer the boat through. If another boat is waiting to enter a lock as one leaves it, great care must be exercised by the steersmen of both boats.

Hours of Boat Work

Hours of travel on the canal were practically continuous. Fifteen hours a day was the minimum re-

ported by any of the boat families; 18 was the number of hours most frequently reported; and several families stated they worked longer. One family had operated its boat without taking any intervals for rest. "It never rains, snows, or blows for a boatman, and a boatman never has no Sundays," explained one father. "We don't know it's Sunday," said another, "till we see some folks along the way, dressed up and a-goin' to Sunday school." One captain and his wife who reported working 15 hours a day employed no crew but depended on the assistance of two children, a girl 14 years of age and a boy of 5. The girl did almost all the driving, usually riding muleback, and the parents steered. The little boy helped with the driving, but did not drive for more than a mile or two at a time. The boat was kept moving until the girl could drive no longer, then the boat was tied up for the night. "We'd boat longer hours if the driver felt like it," said the father. . . .

Boat Work Done by Children

Only the limitations of their physical strength prevented children from performing all operations connected with canal boats. Consequently when they reported that they had done boat work it meant that they had assisted in all parts of the work. The older children, of course, bore heavier burdens than the younger.

. . . [Ninety-four] children, or all except 7 of those over 6 years of age, were found assisting in the work. Twenty-one of the children of the children had begun to help when they were not more than 6 years of age, and 8 of these had begun when not more than 5. The following stories illustrate the life of the boat children.

One of the boating households consisted of four persons—the captain and his assistant "deck hand," the captain's wife, and their 11-year-old daughter. The child had been driving, steering, and doing housework for "several years," but she did not like boating and got very lonely. Her father said that she could do anything the "hand" could do, but he felt it necessary to hire a man because, as he put it, "you have to rest once in a while." "The women and children are as good as the men," he said. "If it weren't for the children the canal wouldn't run a day." The girl's school attendance for the year 1920–21 had been 89 days out of 177, or 50 percent of the school term.

An 11-year-old boy who had been helping his father since he was 6 years old had become his father's "right-hand man." This boy was one of a family of seven children, two older than he, one a girl of 7, and three others under 6 years of age. "A boat is a poor place for little children," said the father, "for all they can do is to go in and out of the cabin." The four older children were accustomed to helping with the boat work, but the father depended especially on the 11-year-old boy. He could do any sort of work and often drove for long hours, and even well into the night. His school attendance in 1920–21 was only 93 days out of a possible 178. The father himself commented on this poor record and said that while he regretted it he was obliged to "boat" his children as he could not afford with his large family to hire extra help.

One 17-year-old girl boasted that she had been working on canal boats for 12 seasons. The mother of this girl had had 17 children, 8 of whom were living. Of the 9 children who had died, 8 had died in infancy. The 2 oldest living children had married and left home. The remaining 6 children, including the 17-year-old girl, 2 boys who were 15 and 12 years of age, respectively, and 3 girls, aged 11, 6, and 2 traveled with their parents on the canal. All except the youngest were regular boat hands, having begun to work when 6 years of age. The mother stated that for many years it had not been necessary for them to employ a crew as they had plenty of their "own hands." During the season selected for study their boat had traveled 19 hours a day 7 days a week. While the 6-year-old girl was allowed to go to bed at 8 and presumably had lighter duties than the others, the 4 older children worked on shifts all day long, snatching a nap now and then. They went to bed at 10 p. m. and had to be up and ready to start· again at 3 a. m. The oldest girl had stopped school on completing the fourth grade. The 4 other children who had been in school during 1920–21 had records which showed attendance varying from 29 percent to 73 percent of the term. The 15-year-old boy, with an attendance record of 29.6 percent, had just completed the fourth grade and was not planning to return to school in the fall.

Further Resources

BOOKS

Abbott, Grace. *The Child and the State.* Chicago: University of Chicago Press, 1938.

Trattner, Walter. *Crusade for the Children: A History of the National Child Labor Committee and Child Labor Reform in American.* Chicago: Quadrangle Books, 1970.

Wickes, Lewis. *Lewis Hine and the Crusade Against Child Labor.* New York: Clarion, 1994.

PERIODICALS
Baldwin, Peter C. "Nocturnal Habits and Dark Wisdom: The American Response to Children in the Streets at Nights." *Journal of Social History* 35, Spring 2002, 593–611.

Carp, Wayne, E. "The Rise and Fall of the U.S. Children's Bureau." *Reviews in American History* 25 no. 4, 1997, 606–611.

WEBSITES
The History Place. "Child Labor in America 1908–1912: Photographs by Lewis W. Hines." Available online at http://www.historyplace.com/unitedstates/childlabor/ (accessed January 28, 2003).

Ohio State University History Department. "Child Labor and Child Labor Reform in American History." Available online at http://www.history.ohio-state.edu/projects/childlabor/; website home page: http://www.history.ohio-state.edu/default.htm (accessed January 28, 2003).

"The Negro's Greatest Enemy"
Magazine article

By: Marcus Garvey

Date: September 1923

Source: Garvey, Marcus. "The Negro's Greatest Enemy." *Current History* 18 (September 1923). Available online http://www.isop.ucla.edu/mgpp/sample01.htm (accessed January 28, 2003).

About the Author: In 1916, Marcus Garvey (1887–1940) emigrated from his native Jamaica to New York City. A committed black nationalist, he created the Universal Negro Improvement Association (UNIA), which promoted a self-help philosophy and promised racial grandeur in the "Empire of Africa." A controversial figure, Garvey successfully tapped into growing African American aspirations for justice, wealth, and a sense of communal identity. He ran afoul of the federal government and was deported to Jamaica in 1927. ■

Introduction

Between 1910 and 1930, close to one million rural southern african americans, or 13 percent of the region's African American population, joined the "Great Migration" to northern cities. In some cases, entire church congregations and nearly entire communities fled the South to start anew in New York City, Philadelphia, and Chicago. African Americans left their southern homes not only to escape disenfranchisement, segregation, and violence but to seek personal freedom and economic opportunity. Life in the urban industrial North was far different from that in the rural South. The majority of men in this migration, who had previously worked as sharecroppers and tenant farmers, found jobs in steel mills, shipyards, munitions plants, and railroad yards. Further, they were

Marcus Garvey founded the Universal Negro Improvement Association (UNIA). THE BETTMANN ARCHIVE. REPRODUCED BY PERMISSION.

segregated and concentrated into poverty-stricken, crime-ridden ghettos. For example, Harlem, a white middle-class residential section of New York City as late as 1910, had 50,000 African Americans in 1914, 73,000 in 1920, and 165,000 in 1930. However, some aspects of city life were similar to country living. Working-class whites, fearful of losing their jobs and status, lashed out against the newly arriving African Americans. In 1918, race riots raged in two dozen northern cities.

The northern urban experience and the tragic shortcomings of American democracy altered African American attitudes toward their racial identity. Thousands of African Americans found inspiration in the racial separatism and African nationalism of Marcus Garvey. When he arrived in New York in 1916 at the invitation of Booker T. Washington, the charismatic Garvey sought to create a "New Negro" by instilling a sense of racial pride in mostly lower-middle-class blacks. Dressed in elaborate braided uniforms and plumed hats, Garvey urged African Americans to take greater pride in their culture and achievements. He taught them that both God and Christ were African American. In addition, he began an international African American movement to reclaim their ancestral homeland from European imperialism. Coining the slogan "Back to Africa," he taught his fol-

lowers that "the black man must work out his salvation in his motherland."

In 1917, he launched the UNIA, whose goal was to help African Americans gain economic and political independence entirely outside of white society. In two years, the UNIA had established 1,100 chapters in forty countries. With tens of thousands of supporters, the UNIA was the largest secular organization in African American history. With African American investments, he established a newspaper and founded stores, restaurants, and other African American businesses, including a company that manufactured African American dolls. His biggest entrepreneurial project was the Black Star Line, a steamship company that was to be owned and operated by African Americans.

Significance

Despite immense talent, Garvey failed to realize his dream. His brand of African American separatism ran counter to the integrationist policy of W.E.B. Du Bois and the National Association for the Advancement of Colored People (NAACP), which sought to bring whites and African Americans together to fight discrimination. Further, Garvey was a poor businessman, and the Black Star Line financially collapsed. Afterwards, the FBI arrested him for using the mails to defraud shareholders, and he was sentenced to five years in jail, though President Calvin Coolidge commuted the sentence and he was deported to Jamaica. With his movement crumbling in America, Garvey moved to London and become somewhat of a recluse. Garvey is an important figure because he demonstrated that organized urban African Americans were a potentially powerful force in the struggle for African American freedom. His memory inspired Malcolm X, whose parents belonged to the UNIA, and other African American nationalists in the 1960s.

Primary Source

"The Negro's Greatest Enemy" [excerpt]

> **SYNOPSIS:** In September 1923, Garvey, while imprisoned for mail fraud in New York City, wrote his most detailed autobiographical account. He wrote that in every country he had ever visited blacks were treated as second-class citizens. Inspired to create a black nation in Africa, Garvey realizes that the biggest obstacle to his dream was not whites, but blacks.

I was born in the Island of Jamaica, British West Indies, on Aug. 17, 1887. My parents were black negroes. My father was a man of brilliant intellect and dashing courage. He was unafraid of consequences. He took human chances in the course of life, as most bold men do, and he failed at the

Nurses participate in a 1922 parade through Harlem in New York City to support the annual world convention of the Universal Negro Improvement Association. © UNDERWOOD & UNDERWOOD/CORBIS. REPRODUCED BY PERMISSION.

close of his career. He once had a fortune; he died poor. My mother was a sober and conscientious Christian, too soft and good for the time in which she lived. She was the direct opposite of my father. He was severe, firm, determined, bold and strong, refusing to yield even to superior forces if he believed he was right. My mother, on the other hand, was always willing to return a smile for a blow, and ever ready to bestow charity upon her enemy. Of this strange combination I was born thirty-six years ago, and ushered into a world of sin, the flesh an[d] the devil.

I grew up with other black and white boys. I was never whipped by any, but made them all respect the strength of my arms. I got my education from many sources—through private tutors, two public schools, two grammar or high schools and two colleges. My teachers were men and women of varied experiences and abilities; four of them were eminent preachers. They studied me and I studied them. With some I became friendly in after years, others and I drifted apart, because as a boy they wanted to whip me, and I simply refused to be whipped. I was not made to be whipped. It annoys me to be defeated;

hence to me, to be once defeated is to find cause for an everlasting struggle to reach the top.

I became a printer's apprentice at an early age, while still attending school. My apprentice master was a highly educated and alert man. In the affairs of business and the world he had no peer. He taught me many things before I reached twelve, and at fourteen I had enough intelligence and experience to manage men. I was strong and manly, and I made them respect me. I developed a strong and forceful character, and have maintained it still.

To me, at home in my early days, there was no difference between white and black. One of my father's properties, the place where I lived most of the time, was adjoining that of a white man. He had three girls and two boys; the Wesleyan minister, another white man whose church my parents attended, also had property adjoining ours. He had three girls and one boy. All of us were playmates. We romped and were happy children playmates together. The little white girl whom I liked most knew no better than I did myself. We were two innocent fools who never dreamed of a race feeling and problem. As a child, I went to school with white boys and girls, like all other negroes. We were not called negroes then. I never heard the term negro used once until I was about fourteen.

At fourteen my little white playmate and I parted. Her parents thought the time had come to separate us and draw the color line. They sent her and another sister to Edinburgh, Scotland, and told her that she was never to write or try to get in touch with me, for I was a "nigger." It was then that I found for the first time that there was some difference in humanity, and that there were different races, each having its own separate and distinct social life. I did not care about the separation after I was told about it, because I never thought all during our childhood association that the girl and the rest of the children of her race were better than I was; in fact, they used to look up to me. So I simply had no regrets. I only thought them "fresh."

After my first lesson in race distinction, I never thought of playing with white girls any more, even if they might be next door neighbors. At home my sister's company was good enough for me, and at school I made friends with the colored girls next to me. White boys and I used to frolic together. We played cricket and baseball, ran races and rode bicycles together, took each other to the river and to the sea beach to learn to swim, and made boyish efforts while out in deep water to drown each other,

making a sprint for shore crying out "shark, shark, shark." In all our experiences, however, only one black boy was drowned. He went under on a Friday afternoon after school hours, and his parents found him afloat half eaten by sharks on the following Sunday afternoon. Since then we boys never went back to sea.

"You Are Black"

At maturity the black and white boys separated, and took different courses in life. I grew up then to see the difference between the races more and more. My schoolmates as young men did not know or remember me any more. Then I realized that I had to make a fight for a place in the world, that it was not so easy to pass on to office and position: Personally, however, I had not much difficulty in finding and holding a place for myself, for I was aggressive. At eighteen I had an excellent position as manager of a large printing establishment having under my control several men old enough to be my grandfathers. But I got mixed up with public life. I started to take an interest in the politics of my country, and then I saw the injustice done to my race because it was black, and I became dissatisfied on that account. I went traveling to South and Central America and parts of the West Indies to find out if it was so elsewhere, and I found the same situation. I set sail for Europe to find out if it was different there, and again I found the same stumbling-block—"You are black." I read of the conditions in America. I read "Up From Slavery," by Booker T. Washington, and then my doom—if I may so call it—of being a race leader dawned upon me in London after I had traveled through almost half of Europe.

I asked, "Where is the black man's Government?" "Where is his King and his kingdom?" "Where is his President, his country, and his ambassador, his army, his navy, his men of big affairs?" I could not find them, and then I declared, "I will help to make them."

Becoming naturally restless for the opportunity of doing something [for] the advancement of my race, I was determined that the black man would not continue to be kicked about by all the other races and nations of the world, as I saw it in the West Indies, South and Central America and Europe, and as I read of it in America. My young and ambitious mind led me into flights of great imagination. I saw before me then, even as I do now, a new world of black men, not peons, serfs, dogs and slaves, but a nation of sturdy men making their impress upon civilization and causing a new light to dawn upon the human race. I could not remain in London any more. My brain was afire. There was a world of thought to conquer. I had to start ere it became too late and the work be not done. Immediately I boarded a ship at Southampton for Jamaica, where I arrived on July 15, 1914. The Universal Negro Improvement Association and African Communities (Imperial) League was founded and organized five days after my arrival, with the program of uniting all the negro peoples of the world into one great body to establish a country and Government absolutely their own.

Where did the name of the organization come from? It was while speaking to a West Indian negro who was a passenger with me from Southampton, who was returning home to the West Indies from Basutoland with his Basuto wife, that I further learned of the horrors of native life in Africa. He related to me in conversation such horrible and pitiable tales that my heart bled within me. Retiring from the conversation to my cabin, all day and the following night I pondered over the subject matter of that conversation, and at midnight, lying flat on my back, the vision and thought came to me that I should name the organization the Universal Negro Improvement Association and African Communities (Imperial) League. Such a name I thought would embrace the purpose of all black humanity. Thus to the world a name was born, a movement created, and a man became known.

I really never knew there was so much color prejudice in Jamaica, my own native home, until I started the work of the Universal Negro Improvement Association. We started immediately before the war. I had just returned from a successful trip to Europe, which was an exceptional achievement for a black man. The daily papers wrote me up with big headlines and told of my movement. But nobody wanted to be a negro. "Garvey is crazy; he has lost his head," "Is that the use he is going to make of his experience and intelligence?"—such were the criticisms passed upon me. Men and women as black as I, and even more so, had believed themselves white under the West Indian order of societal. I was simply an impossible man to use openly the term "negro;" yet every one beneath his breath was calling the black man a negro.

I had to decide whether to please my friends and be one of the "black-whites" of Jamaica, and be reasonably prosperous, or come out openly and defend and help improve and protect the integrity of the black millions and suffer. I decided to do the latter, hence my offence against "colored-black-white" society in the colonies and America. I was openly hated and persecuted by some of these colored men of the island who did not want to be classified as negroes, but as white. They hated me worse than poison. They opposed me at every step, but I had a large number of white friends, who encouraged and helped me. Notable among them were the then Governor of the Colony, the Colonial Secretary and several other prominent men. But they were afraid of offending the "colored gentry" that were passing for white. Hence my fight had to be made alone. I spent hundreds of pounds (sterling) helping the organization to gain a footing. I also gave up all my time to the promulgation of its ideals. I became a marked man, but I was determined that the work should be done.

Further Resources

BOOKS

Cronon, E. David. *Black Moses: The Story of Marcus Garvey.* Madison, Wis.: University of Wisconsin Press, 1986.

DeCaro, Louis A. *Malcolm and the Cross: The Nation of Islam, Malcolm X and Christianity.* New York: New York University Press, 1998.

Stein, Judith. *The World of Marcus Garvey: Race and Class in Modern Society.* Baton Rouge, La.: Louisiana State University, 1985.

PERIODICALS

Henderson, Errol A. "Black Nationalism and Rap Music." *Journal of Black Studies* 26, January 1996, 308–339.

Tolbert, Emory J. "Federal Surveillance of Marcus Garvey and the U.N.I.A." *Journal of Ethnic Studies* 14, Winter 1987, 25–46.

WEBSITES

James S. Coleman African Studies Center, University of California at Los Angeles. "The Marcus Garvey and Universal Negro Improvement Association Papers Project." Available online at http://www.isop.ucla.edu/mgpp/default.htm; website home page: http://www.isop.ucla.edu/jscasc/ (accessed January 28, 2003).

The Universal Negro Improvement Association and the African Communities League home page. Available online at http://www.unia-acl.org/ (accessed January 28, 2003).

Nativism versus Immigration

"Guarding the Gates Against Undesirables"

Magazine article

By: Ku Klux Klan

Date: April 1924

Source: "Guarding the Gates Against Undesirables." *Current Opinion,* April 1924, 400–401.

About the Organization: The Ku Klux Klan was organized in 1866, in Pulaski, Tennessee, located near the Alabama border. The Klan's mysterious name derives from the Greek word *kuklos,* meaning circle, the oldest symbol of unity.

Speech by Robert H. Clancy

Speech

By: Robert H. Clancy

Date: 1924

Source: Clancy, Robert H. Speech. *Congressional Record,* 68th Congress, 1st Session, Washington, D.C.: Government Printing Office, 1924, vol. 65, 5929–5932.

About the Author: Robert H. Clancy (1882–1962) was a four-term Republican congressman from Detroit, Michigan. In the 1920s, Clancy represented a large constituency of first-generation Polish, Italian, and Jewish voters. As an Irish American whose immigrant forebears experienced discrimination, Clancy fought to protect his supporters from native hostility. ∎

Introduction

Klan intimidation and violence originated in the resentment and hatred harbored against former slaves, who achieved freedom and political power after the Civil War (1861–1865). Originally, the Klan was a six-member social club of predominately Scottish American veterans of the Confederate army. Soon, the group included members from surrounding towns and evolved into the most notorious paramilitary terrorist organization in American history. Claiming to be ghosts of Confederate soldiers, the Klan dressed in long, flowing white robes, high conical cardboard hats, and masks that made the wearers seem abnormally tall. Determined to drive blacks and sympathetic whites out of politics and restore white supremacy, the Klan roamed the countryside at night, dragging blacks from their homes, whipping and shooting them, then destroying their property. Between 1868 and 1870, the Klan was instrumental in removing Republican state governments from the Democratic strongholds of North Carolina, Tennessee, and Georgia. With the end of Reconstruction and the restoration of white supremacy, the organization nearly disappeared by the mid-1870s.

The Immigration Act of 1924 set stricter regulations on immigrants hoping to enter the United States to start a new life. **LIBRARY OF CONGRESS/CORBIS. REPRODUCED BY PERMISSION.**

In 1915, the preacher William J. Simmons, who held a Thanksgiving Day cross-burning ceremony atop Stone Mountain, Georgia, revived the Klan. Simmons was influenced by the film *The Birth of a Nation,* directed by D.W. Griffith. The epic movie, the first full-length film, depicted the Klan as heroes, uniting postwar North and South and suppressing villainous blacks who controlled the South. The movie was a box office smash, earning more money than any other film until *Snow White and the Seven Dwarfs* in 1937. More importantly, it was a tremendous recruiting and propaganda tool. Following its release, the Klan became a national organization. Unlike the 1870s version that was rooted in the South and the border states, the "new" Klan of the 1920s, with a membership that totaled over three million, had spread to Maine, Indiana, Oklahoma, Kansas, Oregon, and California.

The twentieth-century Klan targeted newly arriving Catholics and Jews, as well as African Americans. This hatred stemmed from the fact that Klan membership, Protestants whose ancestors had emigrated generations before from northern and western Europe, were hostile to unrestricted immigration. They believed that Italians and Russian Jews, along with other immigrants, were genetically inferior and through inbreeding threatened to mongrelize the American population. By halting unrestricted immigration, which the federal government did in 1924, the Klan hoped to preserve a mythical America of hardworking, churchgoing, small-town citizens, all white, Anglo-Saxon, and Protestant.

Significance

Contrary to its present-day image of a racist fringe group, the Klan of the 1920s was an integral aspect of mainstream America. In 1924, the society nearly tore apart the Democratic Party when convention delegates voted down a resolution condemning the Klan before nominating the anti-Klan candidate John W. Davis for president on the 103rd ballot. A year later, 40,000 hooded Klansmen marched down Pennsylvania Avenue past the White House. The society, whose sympathizers included President Woodrow Wilson, wielded significant power within the House of Representatives, where an estimated seventy-five members openly identified with the Klan, and the Senate, which consistently opposed antilynching legislation. The success of the new Klan was short-lived. In 1924, David C. Stephenson, the powerful Grand Dragon of the Indiana Klan, was convicted of kidnapping and raping his secretary, who later committed suicide. The demoralized rank-and-file deserted the organization, and by the end of World War II (1939–1945) it had largely disbanded.

Primary Source

"Guarding the Gates Against Undesirables" [excerpt]

> **SYNOPSIS:** In April 1924, Congress debated the Johnson-Reed Act, which shaped immigration policy by limiting entrants from southern and eastern Europe. The Klan supported the act because it believed that immigrants from Poland, Italy, and Russia could not assimilate into the dominant culture to become "good" Americans.

The struggle continues over the Johnson bill to restrict immigration to two per cent. of each national group domiciled here in 1890. The opposition comes mainly from certain groups of Southern and Eastern Europeans, and individuals representing them. Specifically the opposition comes from Congressmen representing districts in which compact blocks of Italians, Poles, Russians, Greeks and Slavs now reside.

Against these unassimilated and unassimilable peoples the proposed measure would discriminate. They all represent the newer immigration. Before 1890 the United States received mainly folk from northern and western Europe. Since 1890 the majority have come from southern and eastern Europe. By basing the quotas upon the 1890 census Italian immigration would be cut down from over forty thousand to under four thousand, the Russians from over twenty thousand to under two thousand, and the Poles from about twenty thousand to five thousand, admissible in one year. The new bill would not greatly reduce the number who would come in from the United Kingdom, Sweden, Norway, Denmark, France and Germany. These groups have made no protest against a measure which aims to cut the immigration total approximately in half, from about three hundred and sixty thousand to about one hundred and eighty thousand persons. . . .

There is no blinking the fact that certain races do not fuse with us, and have no intention of trying to become Americans. The Poles, for example, are determined to remain Polish. No doubt this is good Polish patriotism, but it is very poor Americanism. The Polish Diet, as the Indianapolis *News* points out, has adopted a resolution asking the government to request the Holy See to use its influence with the Catholic hierarchy in the United States to permit the continued use of the Polish language in Polish Catholic churches and parochial schools. A dispatch from Warsaw declares that the resolution is part of an effort to stop "the systematic Americanization of the Poles"! Nevertheless, as the *News* declares, if we are to permit any Poles to come here in the future, "the systematic Americanization" of them must continue.

Primary Source

Speech by Robert H. Clancy

> **SYNOPSIS:** Robert Clancy opposed the Johnson-Reed Act as "un-American" because it discriminated against the foreign born.

Since the foundations of the American commonwealth were laid in colonial times over 300 years ago, vigorous complaint and more or less bitter persecution have been aimed at newcomers to our shores. Also the congressional reports of about 1840 are full of abuse of English, Scotch, Welsh immigrants as paupers, criminals, and so forth.

Old citizens in Detroit of Irish and German descent have told me of the fierce tirades and propaganda directed against the great waves of Irish and Germans who came over from 1840 on for a few decades to escape civil, racial, and religious persecution in their native lands.

The "Know-Nothings," lineal ancestors of the Ku-Klux Klan, bitterly denounced the Irish and Germans as mongrels, scum, foreigners, and a menace to our institutions, much as other great branches of the Caucasian race of glorious history and antecedents are berated to-day. All are riff-raff, unassimilables, "foreign devils," swine not fit to associate with the great chosen people—a form of national pride and hallucination as old as the division of races and nations.

But to-day it is the Italians, Spanish, Poles, Jews, Greeks, Russians, Balkanians, and so forth, who are the racial lepers. And it is eminently fitting and proper that so many Members of this House with names as Irish as Paddy's pig, are taking the floor these days to attack once more as their kind has attacked for seven bloody centuries the fearful fallacy of chosen peoples and inferior peoples. The fearful fallacy is that one is made to rule and the other to be abominated. . . .

In this bill we find racial discrimination at its worst—a deliberate attempt to go back 84 years in our census taken every 10 years so that a blow may be aimed at peoples of eastern and southern Europe, particularly at our recent allies in the Great War—Poland and Italy.

Jews In Detroit Are Good Citizens

Of course the Jews too are aimed at, not directly, because they have no country in Europe they can call their own, but they are set down among the inferior peoples. Much of the animus against Poland and Russia, old and new, with the countries that have arisen from the ruins of the dead Czar's European dominions, is directed against the Jew.

We have many American citizens of Jewish descent in Detroit, tens of thousands of them—active in every profession and every walk of life. They are particularly active in charities and merchandising. One of our greatest judges, if not the greatest, is a Jew. Surely no fair-minded person with a knowledge of the facts can say the Jews of Detroit are a menace to the city's or the country's well-being. . . .

Italian Citizens Are Not Inferior

Forty or fifty thousand Italian-Americans live in my district in Detroit. They are found in all walks and classes of life—common hard labor, the trades, business, law, medicine, dentistry, art, literature, banking, and so forth.

They rapidly become Americanized, build homes, and make themselves into good citizens. They brought hardihood, physique, hope, and good humor with them from their outdoor life in Sunny Italy, and they bear up under the terrific strain of life and work in busy Detroit.

One finds them by thousands digging streets, sewers, and building foundations, and in the automobile and iron and steel fabric factories of various sorts. They do the hard work that the native-born American dislikes. Rapidly they rise in life and join the so-called middle and upper classes. . . .

The Italian-Americans of Detroit played a glorious part in the Great War. They showed themselves as patriotic as the native born in offering the supreme sacrifice.

In all, I am informed, over 300,000 Italian-speaking soldiers enlisted in the American Army, almost 10 percent of our total fighting force. Italians formed about 4 percent of the population of the United States and they formed 10 percent of the American military force. Their casualties were 12 percent. . . .

Detroit Satisfied With The Poles

I wish to take the liberty of informing the House that from my personal knowledge and observation of tens of thousands of Polish-Americans living in my district in Detroit that their Americanism and patriotism are unassailable from any fair or just standpoint.

The Polish-Americans are as industrious and as frugal and as loyal to our institutions as any class of people who have come to the shores of this country in the past 300 years. They are essentially home builders, and they have come to this country to stay. They learn the English language as quickly as possible, and take pride in the rapidity with which they become assimilated and adopt our institutions.

Figures available to all show that in Detroit in the World War the proportion of American volunteers of Polish blood was greater than the proportion of American volunteers of Polish blood was greater than the proportion of Americans of any other racial descent. . . . Polish-Americans do not merit slander nor defamation. If not granted charitable or sympathetic judgment, they are at least entitled to justice and to the high place they have won in American and European history and citizenship.

The forces behind the Johnson bill and some of its champions in Congress charge that opposition to the racial discrimination feature of the 1800 quota basis arises from "foreign blocs." They would give the impression that 100 per cent Americans are for it and that the sympathies of its opponents are of the "foreign-bloc" variety, and bear stigma of being "hyphenates." I meet that challenge willingly. I feel my Americanism will stand any test.

Every American Had Foreign Ancestors

The foreign born of my district writhe under the charge of being called "hyphenates." The people of my own family were all hyphenates—English-Americans, German-Americans, Irish-Americans. They began to come in the first ship or so after the *Mayflower*. But they did not come too early to miss the charge of anti-Americanism. Roger Williams was driven out of the Puritan colony of Salem to die in the wilderness because he objected "violently" to blue laws and the burning or hanging of rheumatic old women on witchcraft charges. He would not "assimilate" and was "a grave menace to American institutions and democratic government."

My family put 11 men and boys into the Revolutionary War, and I am sure they and their women and children did not suffer so bitterly and sacrifice until it hurt to establish the autocracy of bigotry and intolerance which exists in many quarters to-day in this country. Some of these men and boys shed their blood and left their bodies to rot on American battle fields. To me real Americanism and the American flag are the product of the blood of men and of the tears of women and children of a different type than the rampant "Americanizers" of to-day.

My mother's father fought in the Civil War, leaving his six small children in Detroit when he marched away to the southern battle fields to fight against racial distinctions and protect his country.

My mother's little brother, about 14 years old, and the eldest child, fired by the traditions of his family, plodded off to the battle fields to do his bit. He aspired to be a drummer boy and inspire the men in battle, but he was found too small to carry a drum and was put at the ignominious task of driving army mules, hauling cannons and wagons.

I learned more of the spirit of American history at my mother's knee than I ever learned in my four years of high school study of American history and in my five and a half years of study at the great University of Michigan.

All that study convinces me that the racial discriminations of this bill are un-American. . . .

It must never be forgotten also that the Johnson bill, although it claims to favor the northern and western European peoples only, does so on a basis

of comparison with the southern and western European peoples. The Johnson bill cuts down materially the number of immigrants allowed to come from northern and western Europe, the so-called Nordic peoples. . . .

Then I would be true to the principles for which my forefathers fought and true to the real spirit of the magnificent United States of to-day. I can not stultify myself by voting for the present bill and overwhelm my country with racial hatreds and racial lines and antagonisms drawn even tighter than they are to-day. [Applause.]

Further Resources

BOOKS

Chalmers, David. *Hooded Americanism: The First Century of the Ku Klux Klan 1865–1965.* Garden City, N.Y.: Doubleday, 1987.

Trelease, Allen W. *White Terror: The Ku Klux Klan Conspiracy and Southern Reconstruction.* New York: Harper & Row, 1971.

Wyn, Craig Wade. *The Fiery Cross: The Ku Klux Klan in America.* New York: Simon and Schuster, 1987.

PERIODICALS

Coben, Stanley. "Ordinary White Protestants: The KKK in the 1920s." *Journal of Social History* 28, Fall 1994, 155–65.

Dessommes, Nancy Bishop. "Hollywood in Hoods: The Portrayal of the Ku Klux Klan in Popular Film." *Journal of Popular Culture* 32, no. 4, 1999, 13–23.

WEBSITES

Dirks, Tim. "The Birth of a Nation (1915)." *Greatest Films.* Available online at http://www.filmsite.org/birt.html; website home page: http://www.filmsite.org/index.html (accessed January 28, 2003).

Ohio State University Department of History. "Immigration Restriction" and "Ku Klux Klan." *Clash of Cultures in the 1910s and 1920s.* Available online at http://www.history.ohio-state.edu/projects/clash/Imm_KKK/antiimmigrationKKK-index.htm; website home page: http://www.history.ohio-state.edu/projects/clash/default.htm (accessed January 28, 2003).

Taxation: The People's Business
Nonfiction work

By: Andrew W. Mellon

Date: 1924

Source: Mellon, Andrew W. *Taxation: The People's Business.* New York: Macmillan, 1924, 9–14.

About the Author: Andrew W. Mellon (1855–1937) was the son of a successful banker. In 1874, he joined his father's banking firm and eight years later became its owner. Mellon exhibited a remarkable ability for investing in promising businesses and was a major shareowner of some of the nation's leading aluminum, coal, and oil businesses. He was also a philanthropist, donating his world-renowned art collection and $10 million to the National Gallery of Art in Washington, D.C. ■

Introduction

A fiscally conservative Republican, Andrew W. Mellon was the third richest man in the United States, worth an estimated $700 million, or $5.9 billion in 2001 dollars. Despite—or perhaps because of—his great wealth, Mellon left the private sector to devote his career to public service. In 1921, at the age of sixty-six, he joined the cabinet of President Warren G. Harding as treasury secretary. His accomplishments in this capacity earned him reappointments by Presidents Calvin Coolidge and Herbert Hoover. In part, he accepted the government position out of patriotism, for the nation faced dire post-World War I economic problems. Among the most pressing was the inefficient manner in which the government managed its fiscal resources. For example, Congress never enacted a balanced budget. Instead, it haphazardly appropriated money to each department, trusting that at the end of the year income and expenditures would balance—which they often did not. Such practices, in combination with borrowing to finance American participation in World War I, caused the national debt to balloon to $26 billion by 1921.

Under Mellon's leadership, Congress passed the Budget and Accounting Act of 1921, which created a director of the budget to oversee the executive budget process and prepare a unified budget. By the end of his third year as secretary, the annual budget was reduced to $3.5 billion and the national debt was reduced by $3 billion. Moreover, under Mellon's leadership the government produced annual revenue surpluses. Because of these surpluses, Mellon sought to overhaul the entire federal tax system. In 1917, under the War Revenue Act, the U.S. scrapped the 13 percent flat tax in favor of a graduated tax. This tax fell disproportionately on the rich as the maximum individual rate rose to 67 percent. Throughout the war years, the graduated tax raised huge sums of revenue needed to defeat Germany and the Central Powers. After the war, however, the tax hampered economic expansion. The rich, in order to avoid excessive tax rates, withdrew their money from the private sector and invested it in tax-exempt government bonds. In response, Mellon proposed the "Mellon Plan," which became the basis for the Revenue Acts of 1924 and 1926. The plan reduced the maximum individual tax rate from 67 percent to 25 percent. The acts also exempted most families by providing a $2,500 exemption, plus $400 for each dependent. Mellon also persuaded Congress to reduce inheritance and excise taxes, which had been imposed during World War I. In 1928, Congress continued to cut taxes by eliminating most excise taxes and lowering corporate tax rates. Consequently, by the end of the decade the largest two hundred corporations increased their assets from $43 billion to $81 billion.

Significance

Admirers saw Mellon as the greatest secretary of the treasury since Alexander Hamilton. By 1926, a person earning $1 million annually paid less than a third of the income tax that he had paid in 1920. Moreover, the national debt was reduced from $26 billion in 1921 to $16 billion in 1930. Freed from oppressive taxation, the rich pulled their capital from tax-exempt bonds and invested in the private sector, which created jobs for the working class. Today, this form of economics is called "trickle down" or "supply-side" economics, which was popular during the presidency of Ronald Reagan. However, critics of the Mellon Plan argue that the freeing up of private capital fueled the wild speculation that led to the stock market crash of 1929 and the Great Depression.

Primary Source

Taxation: The People's Business [excerpt]

SYNOPSIS: In this 1924 book, Mellon argued that tax policy should not be a partisan, political issue. To do so breeds class resentment that serves only to divide America. Instead, sound tax policy must be based strictly on a nonpartisan, economic basis and benefit the poor as much as the rich. The following excerpt is from Chapter 1, "Fundamental Principles."

The problem of the Government is to fix rates which will bring in a maximum amount of revenue to the Treasury and at the same time bear not too heavily on the taxpayer or on business enterprises. A sound tax policy must take into consideration three factors. It must produce sufficient revenue for the Government; it must lessen, so far as possible, the burden of taxation on those least able to bear it; and it must also remove those influences which might retard the continued steady development of business and industry on which, in the last analysis, so much of our prosperity depends. Furthermore, a permanent tax system should be designed not merely for one or two years nor for the effect it may have on any given class of taxpayers, but should be worked out with regard to conditions over a long period and with a view to its ultimate effect on the prosperity of the country as a whole.

Calvin Coolidge signed the income tax bill, also called the Mellon tax bill, into law on February 26, 1926. © CORBIS. REPRODUCED BY
PERMISSION.

These are the principles on which the Treasury's tax policy is based, and any revision of taxes which ignores these fundamental principles will prove merely a make-shift and must eventually be replaced by a system based on economic, rather than political, considerations.

There is no reason why the question of taxation should not be approached from a non-partisan and business viewpoint. In recent years, in any discussion of tax revision, the question which has caused most controversy is the proposed reduction of the surtaxes. Yet recommendations for such reductions have not been confined to either Republican or Democratic administrations. My own recommendations on this subject were in line with similar ones made by Secretaries Houston and Glass, both of whom served under a Democratic President. Tax revision should never be made the football either of partisan or class politics but should be worked out by those who have made a careful study of the subject in its larger aspects and are prepared to recommend the course which, in the end, will prove for the country's best interest.

I have never viewed taxation as a means of rewarding one class of taxpayers or punishing another.

If such a point of view ever controls our public policy, the traditions of freedom, justice and equality of opportunity, which are the distinguishing characteristics of our American civilization, will have disappeared and in their place we shall have class legislation with all its attendant evils. The man who seeks to perpetuate prejudice and class hatred is doing America an ill service. In attempting to promote or to defeat legislation by arraying one class of taxpayers against another, he shows a complete misconception of those principles of equality on which the country was founded. Any man of energy and initiative in this country can get what he wants out of life. But when that initiative is crippled by legislation or by a tax system which denies him the right to receive a reasonable share of his earnings, then he will no longer exert himself and the country will be deprived of the energy on which its continued greatness depends.

This condition has already begun to make itself felt as a result of the present unsound basis of taxation. The existing tax system is an inheritance from the war. During that time the highest taxes ever levied by any country were borne uncomplainingly by the American people for the purpose of defraying the unusual and ever-increasing expenses incident to the successful conduct of a great war. Normal tax rates were increased, and a system of surtaxes was evolved in order to make the man of large income pay more proportionately than the smaller taxpayer. If he had twice as much income, he paid not twice, but three or four times as much tax. For a short time the surtaxes yielded a large revenue. But since the close of the war people have come to look upon them as a business expense and have treated them accordingly by avoiding payment as much as possible. The history of taxation shows that taxes which are inherently excessive are not paid. The high rates inevitably put pressure upon the taxpayer to withdraw his capital from productive business and invest it in tax-exempt securities or to find other lawful methods of avoiding the realization of taxable income. The result is that the sources of taxation are drying up; wealth is failing to carry its share of the tax burden; and capital is being diverted into channels which yield neither revenue to the Government nor profit to the people.

Before the period of the war, taxes as high as those now in effect would have been thought fantastic and impossible of payment. As a result of the patriotic desire of the people to contribute to the limit to the successful prosecution of the war, high taxes were assessed and ungrudgingly paid. Upon the conclusion of peace and the gradual removal of war-time conditions of business, the opportunity is presented to Congress to make the tax structure of the United States conform more closely to normal conditions and to remove the inequalities in that structure which directly injure our prosperity and cause strains upon our economic fabric. There is no question of the fact that if the country is to go forward in the future as it has in the past, we must make sure that all retarding influences are removed.

Further Resources

BOOKS

Finley, David E. *A Standard of Excellence: Andrew W. Mellon Founds the National Gallery of Art at Washington.* Washington, D.C.: Smithsonian Institution Press, 1973.

Hersh, Burton. *The Mellon Family: A Fortune in History.* New York: Morrow, 1978.

O'Connor, Harvey. *Mellon's Millions, the Biography of a Fortune; The Life and Times of Andrew W. Mellon.* New York: John Day, 1933.

PERIODICALS

Higgs, Robert. "Regime Uncertainty: Why the Great Depression Lasted So Long and Why Prosperity Resumed After the War." *The Independent Review* 1, Spring 1997, 560–573.

Reed, Lawrence W. *Great Myths of the Great Depression.* January 1, 1998. Mackinac Center for Public Policy. Available online at: http://www.mackinac.org/4014 (accessed January 28, 2003).

WEBSITES

National Gallery of Art. "From the Tour: Founding Benefactors of the National Gallery of Art." Available online at http://www.nga.gov/collection/gallery/ggfound/ggfound-987 .0.html; website home page: http://www.nga.gov/home.htm (accessed January 28, 2003).

Tennessee Laws Regarding the Teaching of Evolution

"Chapter No. 27, House Bill No. 185"; "Chapter No. 237, House Bill No. 48"

Laws

By: Tennessee House of Representatives

Date: March 13, 1925, and March 13, 1967

Source: Chapter No. 27, House Bill No. 185. Public Acts of the State of Tennessee Passed by the Sixty-Fourth General Assembly, 1925.; Chapter No. 237, House Bill No. 48. Public Acts of the State of Tennessee Passed by the Eighty-Fifth General Assembly, 1967.; Available online at http://www.law .umkc.edu/faculty/projects/ftrials/scopes/tennstat.htm; website home page: http://www.law.umkc.edu/ (accessed January 28, 2003).

About the Author: In 1925, state representative John Butler sponsored Tennessee's anti-evolution act. Four years earlier, Butler had listened to a Baptist preacher warn the congregation that Darwinism was being taught in all public schools. Butler, who had three boys in school, was outraged that state public schools were undermining his efforts to raise his children as Christians by teaching evolution. Promising to change the law if elected into office, Butler was overwhelming endorsed by district voters. Twenty-five years later the Tennessee House repealed the 1925 law. ∎

Introduction

In many ways, the culture of the 1920s was defined by radio, movies, advertising, and mass-circulation magazines, all promoting a secular culture that celebrated consumerism, social mobility, leisure time, and sexuality. This "modern" culture clashed with "traditional" culture, which honored the values enshrined in Protestant fundamentalism: family, home, frugality, hard work, and belief in a literal interpretation of the Bible. Modern Americans, who dismissed traditionalists as "hayseed fanatics," championed evolution, which held that mankind evolved from primates.

John Scopes (seated second from left) and others gather around the table where their discussion of the theory of evolution began and ultimately led to Scopes' prosecution in a Tennessee court. © UNDERWOOD & UNDERWOOD/CORBIS. REPRODUCED BY PERMISSION.

In the 1920s, three-time Democratic presidential candidate and U.S. Secretary of State William Jennings Bryan launched a crusade to forbid schoolteachers in state high schools from teaching any theory that denied the biblical account of divine creation. Bryan was concerned not only about the corrupting influences of modern culture but also that Darwin's theories were being used by believers in the popular eugenics movement to justify the sterilization of the "feebleminded." By 1925, Tennessee and several other southern and border states passed laws imposing this fundamentalist view on public education. When the American Civil Liberties Union announced that it would finance a test case challenging the law's con-

stitutionality, John Scopes, a young biology instructor from Dayton, Tennessee, agreed to teach the theory that man had descended from other primates. The so-called Monkey Trial, which sought to decide Scopes's innocence or guilt and the constitutionality of the state statue, was overshadowed by the clash between traditional and modern values.

In July 1925, over five thousand spectators converged on Dayton, a town of 1,800 people nestled in the Cumberland Mountains. This trial soon took on a carnival atmosphere that included vendors selling Bibles, toy monkeys, hot dogs, and lemonade. Those who could not attend the trial in person could listen to it on the radio, for it was the first jury trial brought to the public by live radio broadcasts. At the trial, defense lawyer Clarence Darrow, an avowed agnostic, defended Scopes. The World Christian Fundamentalism Association hired Bryan, one of the greatest orators in American history, to assist the prosecution. Darrow's sole witness was Bryan, who agreed to provide expert testimony on the Bible.

From the perspective of the press, Darrow's cross-examination of Bryan was flawless, as the lawyer used the power of scientific reason to trump religious faith. Bryan, who believed in a literal interpretation the scriptures, testified that the world was created in six days; that Jonah had been swallowed by a whale; that Eve literally had been made from Adam's rib; and that in 2348 B.C., the world had been flooded, nearly destroying all living things except for the animals in Noah's ark. From the perspective of the twelve jurors, however, eleven of whom attended church on a regular basis, Bryan had truthfully spoken the word of God. To the surprise of none, the jury declared Scopes guilty and the judge fined him $100.

Significance

A year after the trial, the Tennessee Supreme Court, in *Scopes v. State,* overturned the decision on a technicality. Instead of sending the suit back to Dayton for retrial, the court dismissed the matter, concluding, "Nothing is to be gained by prolonging the life of this bizarre case." The Scopes trial was a victory for the forces of evolution. In 1925, fifteen states had anti-evolution legislation pending in their state legislatures, but only Mississippi and Arkansas enacted them. Moreover, evolution continued to be taught in Tennessee. The constitutional issues in Scopes went unaddressed until 1968, when the U.S. Supreme Court, in *Epperson v. Arkansas,* overturned a similar Arkansas law.

Primary Source

"Chapter No. 27, House Bill No. 185"

SYNOPSIS: On March 21, 1925, Tennessee governor Austin Peay signed H.B. No. 185 into law. The act prohibited all state public schools from teaching evolution. Schoolteachers who violated the law were guilty of a misdemeanor and fined between $100 to $500, a significant portion of the teacher's salary in the early twentieth century.

Public Acts of the State of Tennessee Passed by the Sixty-Fourth General Assembly, 1925

Chapter No. 27
House Bill No. 185
(By Mr. Butler)

An Act prohibiting the teaching of the Evolution Theory in all the Universities, Normals and all other public schools of Tennessee, which are supported in whole or in part by the public school funds of the State, and to provide penalties for the violations thereof.

Section 1. *Be it enacted by the General Assembly of the State of Tennessee,* That it shall be unlawful for any teacher in any of the Universities, Normals and all other public schools of the State which are supported in whole or in part by the public school funds of the State, to teach any theory that denies the story of the Divine Creation of man as taught in the Bible, and to teach instead that man has descended from a lower order of animals.

Section 2. *Be it further enacted,* That any teacher found guilty of the violation of this Act, Shall be guilty of a misdemeanor and upon conviction, shall be fined not less than One Hundred $ (100.00) Dollars nor more than Five Hundred ($ 500.00) Dollars for each offense.

Section 3. *Be it further enacted,* That this Act take effect from and after its passage, the public welfare requiring it.

Passed March 13, 1925

W. F. Barry,
Speaker of the House of Representatives
L. D. Hill,
Speaker of the Senate

Approved March 21, 1925.

Austin Peay,
Governor.

Primary Source

"Chapter No. 237, House Bill No. 48"

SYNOPSIS: In 1967, this Act was passed to repeal Tennessee's law forbidding the teaching of evolution in the schools.

Public Acts of the State of Tennessee Passed by the Eighty-Fifth General Assembly, 1967

Chapter No. 237
House Bill No. 48
(By Smith, Galbreath, Bradley)

Substituted for: Senate Bill No. 46
(By Elam)

An Act to repeal Section 498 - 1922, Tennessee Code Annotated, prohibiting the teaching of evolution.

Be it enacted by the General Assembly of the State of Tennessee:

Section 1. Section 49 - 1922, Tennessee Code Annotated, is repealed.

Section 2. This Act shall take effect September 1, 1967.

Passed: May 13, 1967

James H. Cummings,
Speaker of the House of Representatives

Frank C. Gorrell,
Speaker of the Senate

Approved: May 17, 1967.

Buford Ellington,
Governor.

Further Resources

BOOKS

Blake. Arthur. *The Scopes Trial; Defending the Right to Teach.* Brookfield, Conn.: Millbrook Press, 1994.

Driemen, John Evans. *Clarence Darrow.* New York: Chelsea House, 1992.

Ipsen, D.C. *Eye of the Whirlwind: The Story of John Scopes.* Reading, Mass.: Addison-Wesley, 1973.

PERIODICALS

Lisby, Gregory C., and Linda L. Harris. "Georgia Reporters at the Scopes Trial: A Comparison of Newspaper Coverage." *Georgia Historical Quarterly* 75, 1991, 784–803.

Ragsdale, W.B. "Three Weeks in Dayton."*American Heritage* 26, 1975, 38–41, 99–103.

WEBSITES

CourtTV Online. "The Scopes Monkey Trial." Available online at http://www.courttv.com/greatesttrials/scopes/ (accessed January 28, 2003).

Linder, Douglas. "Famous Trials in American History: Tennessee vs. John Scopes: 'The Monkey Trial.'" Available online at http://www.law.umkc.edu/faculty/projects/ftrials/scopes/scopes.htm; website home page: http://www.law.umkc.edu/faculty/projects/ftrials/ftrials.htm (accessed January 28, 2003).

Letter from Nicola Sacco to His Son, Dante

Letter

By: Nicola Sacco

Date: August 18, 1927

Source: Sacco, Nicola. "The Letters of Sacco and Vanzetti." Available online at Court TV Online. *The Greatest Trials of All Time.*

http://www.courttv.com/greatesttrials/sacco.vanzetti/sacco_letter.html; website home page: http://www.courttv.com/ (accessed January 28, 2003).

About the Author: Nicola Sacco (1891–1927) emigrated from southern Italy to Massachusetts in 1908. In 1912, he married an Italian woman, Rosina, and a year later their son, Dante, was born. Politically, Sacco was an active member of a radical Italian anarchist group that aligned itself with violent labor unionists and antiwar propagandists. In 1920, amid the hysteria of the "Red Scare," Sacco and Bartolomeo Vanzetti were found guilty of first-degree murder and sent to the electric chair. ∎

Introduction

Following World War I, the U.S. economy boomed as consumers spent wartime savings for automobiles, homes, and other goods that had been in short supply during the war. This pent-up demand for consumer goods resulted in temporary shortages, which accelerated the rate of inflation. Inflation, in turn, sparked labor unrest and violence as unions struck for increased wages. In 1919, four million workers, or 20 percent of the labor force, went on strike at one time or another. Many Americans associated the strikers with lower-class, unskilled immigrant Italians. Between 1884 and 1920, approximately seven million Italians arrived in New York City before migrating to other parts of the country like Boston. In addition, many Americans associated the strikers with political radicals—communists, socialists, and anarchists, 90 percent of whom were foreign born. Hatred of foreign radicals approached hysteria in April 1919 when anarchists plotted to send thirty dynamite bombs to U.S. Attorney General A. Mitchell Palmer, capitalists J.P. Morgan and John D. Rockefeller, and U.S. Supreme Court Justice Oliver Wendell Holmes Jr. Although the plot was foiled, an Italian anarchist later blew himself up on the stairs of Palmer's Washington home. Palmer also suspected that Russian communists sought to overthrow the American government on November 7, 1919, the second anniversary of the Russian Revolution. These real and imagined acts of domestic terrorism caused many Americans to demand that radicals be ruthlessly suppressed. As a result, 10,000 suspected "Reds" and "Anarchists" were arrested in what became known as the Palmer Raids.

On the afternoon of April 15, 1920, in Braintree, Massachusetts, a paymaster and his bodyguard were transporting the Slater & Morill Shoe Company's payroll of $15,776. The men were approached by two thieves, who fired six shots and murdered the two employees before eluding capture in a stolen Buick. Three weeks later, Nicola Sacco and Bartolomeo Vanzetti, who were not original suspects in the robbery, were arrested in a police sting operation. In Sacco's pocket, the authorities discovered a Colt automatic handgun and a

Nicola Sacco poses with his wife and son in a 1927 photo that was submitted as evidence, along with other material, in an attempt to get a trial review of his case. © BETTMANN/CORBIS. REPRODUCED BY PERMISSION.

handbill for an upcoming anarchist meeting. During the six-week trial, Sacco testified that on the day of the murders, he was at the Italian consulate in nearby Boston inquiring about a passport. Recently, he had received word that his mother, whom he had not seen in twelve years, had died in Italy. Sacco also testified that after leaving the consulate, he ate at Boni's Restaurant, and several witnesses confirmed his story. The prosecution presented ballistics evidence that one of the six bullet shells found at the murder scene had been fired from a Colt and was consistent with being fired from Sacco's pistol. In July 1921, Sacco and Vanzetti were found guilty of murder in the first degree. After numerous appeals, the two were executed by electric chair in August 1927 at Charlestown State Prison in Massachusetts.

Significance

To many Americans, the Red Scare and fear of foreign radicalism were the central issues on trial in the Sacco and Vanzetti case and played a paramount role in their convictions and sentencing. Consequently, the men became international symbols for the oppressed immigrant and martyrs for a generation of 1920s radicals. Although early opinion was almost unanimous that they

were innocent of murder and had been unjustly executed, new evidence has emerged to challenge conventional thought. Modern ballistics studies of Sacco's gun indicate that he may indeed have been guilty, though not Vanzetti. However, no single account or any ballistics test has been able to put all doubts about innocence or guilt completely to rest.

Primary Source

Letter from Nicola Sacco to His Son, Dante

> **SYNOPSIS:** Sacco was more than a mere symbol to radical elements. He was a man who had been denied, rightly or wrongly, the opportunity to watch his two young children grow up. Nine days before his execution, Sacco composed a touching letter to his son Dante, named after the early Renaissance Italian poet.

My Dear Son and Companion:

Since the day I saw you last I had always the idea to write you this letter, but the length of my hunger strike and the thought I might not be able to explain myself, made me put if off all this time.

The other day, I ended my hunger strike and just as soon as I did that I thought of you to write to you, but I find that I did not have enough strength and I cannot finish it at one time. However, I want to get it down in any way before they take us again to the death-house, because it is my conviction that just as soon as the court refused a new trial to us they will take us there. And between Friday and Monday, if nothing happens, they will electrocute us right after midnight, on August 22nd. Therefore, here I am, right with you with love and with open heart as ever I was yesterday.

I never thought that our inseparable life could be separated, but the thought of seven dolorous years makes it seem it did come, but then it has not changed really the unrest and the heartbeat of affection. That has remained as it was. More. I say that our ineffable affection reciprocal, is today more than any other time, of course. That is not only a great deal but it is grand because you can see the real brotherly love, not only in joy but also and more in the struggle of suffering. Remember this, Dante. We have demonstrated this, and modesty apart, we are proud of it.

Much we have suffered during this long Calvary. We protest today as we protested yesterday. We protest always for our freedom.

If I stopped hunger strike the other day, it was because there was no more sign of life in me. Be-

Nicola Sacco (right) walks handcuffed to Bartolomeo Vanzetti, with whom he was prosecuted for radical activity. **ARCHIVE PHOTOS, INC. REPRODUCED BY PERMISSION.**

cause I protested with my hunger strike yesterday as today I protest for life and not for death.

I sacrificed because I wanted to come back to the embrace of your dear little sister Ines and your mother and all the beloved friends and comrades of life and not death. So Son, today life begins to revive slow and calm, but yet without horizon and always with sadness and visions of death.

Well, my dear boy, after your mother had talked to me so much and I had dreamed of you day and night, how joyful it was to see you at last. To have talked with you like we used to in the days—in those days. Much I told you on that visit and more I wanted to say, but I saw that you will remain the same affectionate boy, faithful to your mother who loves you so much, and I did not want to hurt your sensibilities any longer, because I am sure that you will continue to be the same boy and remember what I have told you. I knew that and what here I am going to tell you will touch your sensibilities, but don't cry Dante, because many tears have been wasted, as your mother's have been wasted for seven years, and never did any good. So, Son, instead of crying, be strong, so as to be able to comfort your mother, and when you want to distract your mother from the

discouraging sourness, I will tell you what I used to do. To take her for a long walk in the quiet country, gathering wild flowers here and there, resting under the shade of trees, between the harmony of the vivid stream and the gentle tranquility of the mother-nature, and I am sure that she will enjoy this very much, as you surely would be happy for it. But remember always, Dante, in the play of happiness, don't you use all for yourself only, but down yourself just one step, at your side and help the weak ones that cry for help, help the prosecuted and the victim, because that [they] are your better friends; they are the comrades that fight and fall as your father and Bartolo fought and fell yesterday for the conquest of the joy of freedom for all and the poor workers. In this struggle of life you will find more love and you will be loved.

I am sure that from what your mother told me about what you said during these last terrible days when I was lying in the iniquitous death-house—that description gave me happiness because it showed you will be the beloved boy I had always dreamed.

Therefore whatever should happen tomorrow, nobody knows, but if they should kill us, you must not forget to look at your friends and comrades with the

Your Father and Companion

smiling gaze of gratitude as you look at your beloved ones, because they love you as they love everyone of the fallen persecuted comrades. I tell you, your father that is all the life to you, your father that loved you and saw them, and knows their noble faith (that is mine) their supreme sacrifice that they are still doing for our freedom, for I have fought with them, and they are the ones that still hold the last of our hope that today they can still save us from electro-cution, it is the struggle and fight between the rich and the poor for safety and freedom, Son, which you will understand in the future of your years to come, of this unrest and struggle of life's death.

Much I thought of you when I was lying in the death-house—the singing, the kind tender voices of the children from the playground, where there was all the life and the joy of liberty-just one step from the wall which contains the buried agony of three buried souls. It would remind me so often of you and your sister Ines, and I wish I could see you every moment. But I feel better that you did not come to the death-house so that you could not see the hor-rible picture of three lying in agony waiting to be elec-trocuted, because I do not know what effect it would have on your young age. But then, in another way if you were not so sensitive it would be very useful to your tomorrow when you could use this horrible mem-ory to hold up to the world the shame of the coun-try in this cruel persecution and unjust death. Yes, Dante, they can crucify our bodies today as they are doing, but they cannot destroy our ideas, that will remain for the youth of the future to come.

Dante, when I said three human lives buried, I meant to say that with us there is another young man by the name of Celestino Maderios that is to be electrocuted at the same time with us. He has been twice before in that horrible death-house, that should be destroyed with the hammers of real progress—that horrible house that will shame for-ever the future of the citizens of Massachusetts. They should destroy that house and put up a factory or school, to teach many of the hundreds of the poor orphan boys of the world.

Dante, I say once more to love and be nearest to your mother and the beloved ones in these sad days, and I am sure that with your brave heart and kind goodness they will feel less discomfort. And you will also not forget to love me a little for I do—O, Sonny!, thinking so much and so often of you.

Best fraternal greetings to all the beloved ones, love and kisses to your little Ines and mother. Most hearty affectionate embrace.

P.S. Bartolo send you the most affectionate greetings. I hope that your mother will help you to understand this letter because I could have written much better and more simple, if I was feeling good. But I am so weak.

Further Resources

BOOKS

D'Attilio, Robert, Jane Manthorn et al. *Sacco Vanzetti: Devel-opments and Reconsiderations, 1979.* Boston: Boston Pub-lic Library, 1979.

Dickinson, Alice. *The Sacco-Vanzetti Case, 1920–27: Com-monwealth of Massachusetts vs. Nicola Sacco and Bar-tolomeo Vanzetti.* New York: F. Watts, 1972.

Joughin, Louis, and Edmund M. Morgan. *The Legacy of Sacco and Vanzetti.* Princeton, N.J.: Princeton University Press. 1978.

PERIODICALS

Frankfurter, Felix. "The Case of Sacco and Vanzetti." *Atlantic Monthly,* March 1927. Available online at http://www.theatlantic.com/unbound/flashbks/oj/frankff.htm (accessed January 28, 2003).

Porter, Katherine Ann. "The Never-ending Wrong." *Atlantic Monthly,* June 1977. Available online at http://www.theatlantic.com/unbound/flashbks/oj/porterf.htm (accessed January 28, 2003).

WEBSITES

Linder, Douglas. "Famous American Trials: The Trial of Sacco and Vanzetti, 1921." Available online at http://www.law.umkc.edu/faculty/projects/ftrials/SaccoV/SaccoV.htm; website home page: http://www.law.umkc.edu/faculty/projects/ftrials/ftrials.htm (accessed January 28, 2003).

"Native American Chiefs Frank Seelatse and Jimmy Noah Saluskin of the Yakima Tribe"

Photograph

By: National Photo Company Collection

Date: 1927

Source: National Photo Company Collection. "Native Ameri-can chiefs Frank Seelatse and Chief Jimmy Noah Saluskin of the Yakima tribe." LC-USZ62-92917 DLC. Library of Con-gress American Memory Collection. Available online at http://memory.loc.gov/ (accessed January 28, 2003).

About the Subjects: Native American Chiefs Frank Seelatse and Jimmy Noah Saluskin were members of the Yakima tribe from eastern Washington State. The tribe called themselves *Waptailmim,* meaning "people-of-the-narrows," because their

294 ■ GOVERNMENT AND POLITICS

AMERICAN DECADES PRIMARY SOURCES, 1920-1929

Primary Source

"Native American Chiefs Frank Seelatse and Jimmy Noah Saluskin of the Yakima Tribe"
SYNOPSIS: In 1927, Yakima chiefs Frank Seelatse and Jimmy Noah Saluskin posed in full native dress in front of the U.S. Capitol building in Washington, D.C. The photo was taken three years after the signing of the General Citizen Act granting Native Americans full citizenship rights. Prior to the act, many Native Americans were denied the right to vote, sue in court, enter into legal contracts, or hold state and federal elective office. THE LIBRARY OF CONGRESS.

village was located near Union Gap along the Yakima River. In 1804, the Yakima encountered Meriwether Lewis and William Clark, whose report on the abundant wildlife and rich soil attracted white settlement. By 1875, the Yakima's traditional culture had been critically undermined. ■

Introduction

The U.S. Constitution contains little mention of Native Americans. The Constitution gives Congress the powers to make war and peace, enter into treaties, and regulate commerce with the tribes in the same manner in which it interacts with foreign countries. In theory, Congress treated the tribes as independent, sovereign nations. In reality, however, the tribes were treated as subservient, and to a significant degree they were dependent upon government. Moreover, Native Americans were not citizens and therefore did not have the same civil liberties and constitutional rights as white Americans.

The question of whether Native Americans should have been considered American citizens was part of the debate surrounding adoption of the Fourteenth Amendment to the Constitution in 1868. The amendment granted citizenship status to all newly freed slaves who were born or naturalized in America. To some members of Congress, the amendment was broad enough to include Native Americans. In 1870, a Senate committee examined this issue and later reported that Native Americans had not become citizens because, as members of independent tribes, they were not subject to the jurisdiction of the United States. The committee's decision was widely accepted. It was not clear, however, whether the Fourteenth Amendment applied to those who voluntarily severed their tribal ties and assimilated into white society. The issue was resolved in 1884 when the U.S. Supreme Court, in *Elk v. Wilkins,* ruled that Native Americans who voluntarily withdrew from their tribe and became participating members in white society were not citizens. To become a naturalized citizen required a specific congressional act.

Many Americans believed that Native Americans deserved to be citizens. However, the question was when to bestow citizenship upon them. Should Congress pass an act giving all Native Americans immediate citizenship, or should citizenship be seen as an award granted only to those who were willing to assimilate into white society? In 1887, Congress passed the Dawes Severalty Act, which linked Native American citizenship to taking land in severalty. Henry L. Dawes, the sponsor of the act, believed that it was impossible to civilize Native Americans without turning them into farmers. Under the act, reservations with good agricultural and grazing land that had been held in common by all tribal members were divided up and allotted to individual members. The act sought to protect their allotments from

corrupt whites by holding them in trust for twenty-five years. At the end of the trust period, during which it was assumed that the Native Americans would have been assimilated, Native Americans would receive title to the land and become citizens subject to state and territorial laws. This law disappointed reformers who believed that they should be granted immediate citizenship. Moreover, reformers were disturbed because the law did not apply to those still residing on reservations whose lands were not allotted.

Significance

In November 1919, the definitions underlying Native American citizenship were broadened to include World War I veterans who received an honorable discharge. As a result, a majority of Native Americans had now attained citizenship. But because Native Americans served so valiantly in the Great War, pressure built to grant all Native Americans citizenship. In 1924, Homer P. Snyder of New York sponsored the General Citizenship Act, which bestowed citizenship on all Native Americans born in the United States. Because the right to vote was governed by state law, however, some states barred Native Americans from voting. In 1962, Arizona became the last state to enfranchise Native Americans.

Further Resources

BOOKS

Berkhofer, Robert F., Jr. *The White Man's Indian: Images of the American Indian from Columbus to the Present.* New York: Random House, 1978.

Prucha, Francis, Paul. *The Great Father: The United States Government and the American Indians.* Vol. 2. Lincoln, Neb.: University of Nebraska Press, 1984.

Utley, Robert M. *The Indian Frontier of the American West, 1846–1890.* Albuquerque, N.M.: University of New Mexico Press, 1984.

PERIODICALS

Barsh, Russel L. "American Indians in the Great War." *Ethnohistory* 38, Summer 1991, 294.

Tate, Michael L. "From Scout to Doughboy: The National Debate Over Integrating American Indians into the Military, 1891–1918." *Western Historical Quarterly* 17, no. 4, October 1986, 434–435.

WEBSITES

Clarke Historical Library, Central Michigan University. "Indian Treaties: Their Ongoing Importance to Michigan Residents: Federal Education Policy & Off-Reservation Schools 1870–1933." Available online at http://www.lib.cmich.edu /clarke/indian/treatyeducation.htm (accessed January 28, 2003).

Library of Congress. "American Memory: Today in History." Available online at http://memory.loc.gov/ammem/today/jun02 .html; website home page:http://www.memory.loc.gov/ (accessed January 28, 2003).

The Problem of Indian Administration

Report

By: Lewis Meriam

Date: February 21, 1928

Source: Meriam, Lewis. *The Problem of Indian Administration.* Report of a Survey made at the request of the Honorable Hubert Work, Secretary of the Interior, submitted to him on February 21, 1928. Institute for Government Research Studies in Administration. Baltimore, Md.: Johns Hopkins Press, 1928. Available online at http://www.alaskool.org /native_ed/research_reports/IndianAdmin/Indian_Admin _Problms.html; website home page: http://www.alaskool.org/ (accessed January 29, 2003).

About the Author: In 1906, Lewis Meriam graduated from Harvard with a law degree and a master's degree in government and economic studies. In 1916, he joined the staff of the newly organized Institute of Government Relations (IGR). The IGR was founded by a select group of progressive social scientists and Republican businessmen who sought to bring nonpartisan budgetary efficiency to the executive appropriation process. In 1926, the IGR became the Brookings Institution, a nonpartisan, independent research organization. ■

Introduction

For nearly four centuries, Native Americans have been subjected to numerous methods designed to assimilate them into "civilized" Euro-American society. The most effective means has been formal education. The earliest attempt to educate Native Americans began in Jamestown. In 1616, John Rolfe and his wife Pocahontas sailed to England and successfully lobbied the King of England to contribute substantial revenue to establish an Indian college. In 1622, Henrico College was set to open, but the endeavor failed following the Indian slaughter of 347 colonists. As a result, colonists were more concerned with warring with the tribes than with educating them.

In the early decades of the nineteenth century, the U.S. government accepted partial responsibility for Native American education, funding missionaries who established reservation schools aimed at "Christianizing the heathen savages" so that they could be rapidly absorbed into white civilization. After the Civil War, the government assumed more direct responsibility for Native American education by establishing off-reservation boarding schools, reservation-based day schools, and industrial schools. In 1889, the course of Indian education was dramatically altered with the appointment of Thomas Jefferson Morgan as commissioner of the Bureau of Indian Affairs. Morgan announced that the federal government would be solely responsible for Native American education, as it would no longer delegate such responsibilities to religious groups. In addition, he sought dramatic increases in federal funding to increase the number of Indian schools. From 1889 to the end of the century, the number of Indian schools increased from 239, with 11,552 students, to 307 schools with 21,568 students. Over this period, federal appropriations increased from $1.3 million to $3 million.

The government's expanded involvement in Native American education paradoxically resulted in greater health risks for its beneficiaries. As more and more children crowded into government schools, the incidence of contagious diseases skyrocketed, causing increased rates in morbidity. In 1912, President William Howard Taft sent a special message to Congress on Indian health. The president revealed that in many parts of Indian country, the death rate was 35 per 1,000, compared to 15 per 1,000 for the United States as a whole. In response, Congress urged the U.S. Public Health Service to conduct a wide-ranging study. Out of an estimated 322,715 Native Americans, the agency examined an 40,000. The study revealed that Indian schools were generally overcrowded, unsanitary, and served poor food. As a result, the study concluded, nearly 30 percent of Native American children living at boarding schools had contracted the eye disease trachoma, which had quickly spread to the reservations when the students returned home to visit. In addition, the study found that tuberculosis was rampant.

Significance

In response to President Taft's concerns, Congress over the next several years increased annual appropriations to combat disease and alleviate poor living conditions among Native Americans. However, the public health of Native Americans failed to improve. In the 1920s, reformer John Collier, president of the American Indian Defense Association, along with John D. Rockefeller lamented the state of Indian health. They charged the government with inefficiency and corruption and demanded that an independent entity investigate the agency. In 1926, the Brookings Institution launched a comprehensive survey of Indian public health. Its findings and recommendations were widely distributed. Embarrassed into action by public outrage over the poor treatment of Native American children, the Hoover administration almost doubled spending on Indian schools between 1928 and 1933.

Primary Source

The Problem of Indian Administration [excerpt]

SYNOPSIS: In 1926, social scientist Lewis Meriam and his research team spent seven months investigating the conditions of Native Americans. They visited ninety-five reservations, agencies, hospitals, and schools, as well as many off-reservation Indian communities. Meriam argued that insufficient funds resulted in poor health, particularly among children. The following excerpt is from Chapter 1 of his report.

General Summary of Findings and Recommendations

The Conditions Among the Indians

An overwhelming majority of the Indians are poor, even extremely poor, and they are not adjusted to the economic and social system of the dominant white civilization.

The poverty of the Indians and their lack of adjustment to the dominant economic and social systems produce the vicious circle ordinarily found among any people under such circumstances. Because of interrelationships, causes cannot be differentiated from effects. The only course is to state briefly the conditions found that are part of this vicious circle of poverty and maladjustment.

Health

The health of the Indians as compared with that of the general population is bad. Although accurate mortality and morbidity statistics are commonly lacking, the existing evidence warrants the statement that both the general death rate and the infant mortality rate are high. Tuberculosis is extremely prevalent. Trachoma, a communicable disease which produces blindness, is a major problem because of its great prevalence and the danger of its spreading among both the Indians and the whites.

Living Conditions

The prevailing living conditions among the great majority of the Indians are conducive to the development and spread of disease. With comparatively few exceptions, the diet of the Indians is bad. It is generally insufficient in quantity, lacking in variety, and poorly prepared. The two great preventive elements in diet, milk, and fruits and green vegetables, are notably absent. Most tribes use fruits and vegetables in season, but even then the supply is ordinarily insufficient. The use of milk is rare, and it is generally not available even for infants. Babies, when weaned, are ordinarily put on substantially the same diet as older children and adults, a diet consisting mainly of meats and starches.

The housing conditions are likewise conducive to bad health. Both in the primitive dwellings and in the majority of more or less permanent homes which in some cases have replaced them, there is great overcrowding, so that all members of the family are exposed to any disease that develops, and it is virtually impossible in any way even partially to isolate a person suffering from a communicable disease. In certain jurisdictions, notably the Osage and the Kiowa, the government has stimulated the building of modern homes, bungalows, or even more pretentious dwellings, but most of the permanent houses that have replaced primitive dwellings are small shacks with few rooms and with inadequate provision for ventilation. Education in housekeeping and sanitation has not proceeded far enough so that the Indians living in these more or less permanent shacks practice ventilation and domestic cleanliness. From the standpoint of health, it is probably true that the temporary, primitive dwellings that were not fairly air-tight and were frequently abandoned were more sanitary than the permanent homes that have replaced them. The furnishing of the primitive dwellings and of the shacks is limited. Although many of them still have very primitive arrangements for cooking and heating, the use of modern cook stoves and utensils is far more general than the use of beds, and the use of beds in turn is far more common than the use of any kind of easily washable bed covering.

Sanitary facilities are generally lacking. Except among the relatively few well-to-do Indians, the houses seldom have a private water supply or any toilet facilities whatever. Even privies are exceptional. Water is ordinarily carried considerable distances from natural springs or streams, or occasionally from wells. In many sections the supply is inadequate, although in some jurisdictions, notably in the desert country of the Southwest, the government has materially improved the situation, an activity that is appreciated by the Indians.

Economic Conditions

The income of the typical Indian family is low and the earned income extremely low. From the standpoint of the white man, the typical Indian is not industrious, nor is he an effective worker when he does work. Much of his activity is expended in lines which produce a relatively small return either in goods or money. He generally ekes out an existence through unearned income from leases of his land, the sale of land, per capita payments from tribal funds, or in exceptional cases through rations given him by the government. The number of Indians who are supporting themselves through their own efforts, according to what a white man would regard as the minimum standard of health and decency, is extremely small. What little they secure from their own efforts or from other sources is rarely effectively used.

The main occupations of the men are some outdoor work, mostly of an agricultural nature, but the number of real farmers is comparatively small. A considerable proportion engage more or less casually in unskilled labor. By many Indians several different kinds of activity are followed spasmodically: a little agriculture, a little fishing, hunting, trapping, wood cutting, or gathering of native products, occasional labor and hauling, and a great deal of just idling. Very seldom do the Indians work about their homes as the typical white man does. Although the permanent structures in which they live after giving up primitive dwellings are simple and such as they might easily build and develop for themselves, little evidence of such activity was seen. Even where more advanced Indians occupied structures similar to those occupied by neighboring whites, it was almost always possible to tell the Indian homes from the white by the fact that the white man did much more than the Indian in keeping his house in condition.

In justice to the Indians, it should be said that many of them are living on lands from which a trained and experienced white man could scarcely wrest a reasonable living. In some instances the land originally set apart for the Indians was of little value for agricultural operations other than grazing. In other instances part of the land was excellent but the Indians did not appreciate its value. Often when individual allotments were made, they chose for themselves the poorer parts, because those parts were near a domestic water supply or a source of firewood, or because they furnished some native product important to the Indians in their primitive life. Frequently the better sections of the land originally set apart for the Indians have fallen into the hands of the whites, and the Indians have retreated to the poorer lands remote from markets.

In many places crops can be raised only by the practice of irrigation. Many Indians in the Southwest are successful in a small way with their own primitive systems of irrigation. When modern, highly developed irrigation systems have been supplied by governmental activities, the Indians have rarely been ready to make effective use of the land and water. If the modern irrigation enterprise has been successful from an economic standpoint, the tendency has been for whites to gain possession of the land either by purchase or by leases. If the enterprise has not been economically a success, the Indians generally retain possession of the land, but they do not

The Meriam report, completed by Lewis Meriam and a team of researchers, criticized the government for not providing sufficient funding, which resulted in poor health for Native Americans both on and off reservations. **DENVER PUBLIC LIBRARY, WESTERN HISTORY COLLECTION, H.S. POLEY, P-310. REPRODUCED BY PERMISSION.**

know how to use it effectively and get much less out of it than a white man would.

The remoteness of their homes often prevents them from easily securing opportunities for wage earning, nor do they have many contacts with persons dwelling in urban communities where they might find employment. Even the boys and girls graduating from government schools have comparatively little vocational guidance or aid in finding profitable employment.

When all these factors are taken into consideration, it is not surprising to find low incomes: low standards of living, and poor health. . . .

The Work of the Government in Behalf of the Indians

The work of the government directed toward the education and advancement of the Indian himself, as distinguished from the control and conservation of his property, is largely ineffective. The chief explanation of the deficiency in this work lies in the fact that the government has not appropriated

Native Americans have, over history, been subjected to numerous methods designed to assimilate them into "civilized" Euro-American society, including style of dress and education. As Indian children crowded into government schools, incidences of contagious diseases skyrocketed, leading the government to evaluate Indian health. **THE LIBRARY OF CONGRESS.**

enough funds to permit the Indian Service to employ an adequate personnel properly qualified for the task before it.

Absence of Well-Considered, Broad Educational Program

The outstanding evidence of the lack of an adequate, well-trained personnel is the absence of any well considered, broad educational program for the Service as a whole. Here the word education is used in its widest sense and includes not only school training for children but also activities for the training of adults to aid them in adjusting themselves to the dominant social and economic life which confronts them. It embraces education in economic production and in living standards necessary for the maintenance of health and decency.

Work for the Promotion of Health

The inadequacy of appropriations has prevented the development of an adequate system of public health administration and medical relief work for the Indians. The number of doctors, nurses, and dentists is insufficient. Because of small appropriations the salaries for the personnel in health work are ma-

terially below those paid by the government in its other activities concerned with public health and medical relief, specifically the Public Health Service, the Army, the Navy, and the Veterans' Bureau, as well as below those paid by private organizations for similar services. Since its salaries are sub-standard, the Indian Service has not been able to set reasonably high entrance qualifications and to adhere to them. In the case of doctors, the standards set for entrance have been too low. In the case of public health nurses the standards have been reasonable, but it has not been possible to secure at the salary offered a sufficient number of applicants, so that many people have to be employed temporarily who do not possess the required qualifications. Often untrained, inexperienced field matrons are attempting to perform duties which would be fairly difficult for a well-trained, experienced public health nurse. For general nursing positions, it has often been necessary to substitute for properly trained nurses, practical nurses, some of whom possess few qualifications for the work.

The hospitals, sanatoria, and sanatorium schools maintained by the Service, despite a few exceptions, must be generally characterized as lacking in personnel, equipment, management, and design. The statement is sometimes made that, since the Indians live according to a low scale, it is not necessary for the government to furnish hospital facilities for them which are comparable with those supplied for poor white people in a progressive community. The survey staff regards this basis of judging facilities as unsound. The question is whether the hospitals and sanatoria are efficient institutions for the care and treatment of patients, and this question must generally be answered in the negative.

Although the present administration has made a praiseworthy forward step in the reorganization of the Indian medical service and has secured from the Public Health Service a well-qualified director for the chief position, it is hampered at every turn by the limitations of its present staff and equipment and by lack of funds for development. Under the present administration, too, a real beginning has been made in public health nursing. Despite these recent promising developments, it is still true that the Indian Service is markedly deficient in the field of public health and preventive medicine. The preventive work in combating the two important diseases of tuberculosis and trachoma can only be characterized as weak. The same word must be applied to the efforts toward preventing infant mortality and the diseases of children. Here and there some effective work is done in maternity cases, just about enough to demonstrate that competent, tactful physicians can induce a very considerable number of Indian women to have professional care in childbirth and to advance beyond the crude, unsanitary, and at times, even brutal primitive practices.

Another striking need is for the development of the public health clinic, an agency extremely effective in locating cases of tuberculosis and other communicable diseases in their incipiency and thus permitting of the early treatment of the sufferer when there is still chance to help him, and also making it possible to exercise some control over contagion. The number of public health clinics in the Indian Service is small, and the two or three deserving the name are of recent origin and are not adequately equipped.

Vital statistics have been called the handmaid of preventive medicine. They are indispensable for the efficient planning, development, and operation of a sound program for conservation of public health. The Indian Service has not yet been successful in overcoming the great difficulties inherent in securing vital statistics for the Indians and, moreover, its

physicians in general have tended to neglect the important work of keeping case histories and other records basic to a public health program. The result is that the directing personnel of the Indian Service and the Department of the Interior, the Bureau of the Budget, and Congress and its committees lack the information essential for planning, development, and control. Under such circumstances it is inevitable that some of the money actually appropriated and expended will be wasted, if it is not almost equally inevitable that appropriations will not be proportional to needs.

Because of these numerous defects in the medical service, it is not surprising to find that serious errors have been made in the treatment of Indians suffering from trachoma. Practically entirely ignoring the view held by many students of the disease that a close relationship exists between trachoma and dietary deficiencies, the Service for some years pinned its faith on a serious, radical operation for cure without carefully watching results and checking the degree of success achieved. The Service has now recognized the marked limitations of this radical procedure and has stopped its wholesale use. Serious errors of this nature are likely to occur in a service which is so seriously understaffed that following up cases and checking results are neglected. This serious operation was unquestionably performed on many Indians who did not need it, and, because of the difficulties in diagnosis of trachoma, upon some Indians who did not even have the disease.

Formal Education of Indian Children

For several years the general policy of the Indian Service has been directed away from the boarding school for Indian children and toward the public schools and Indian day schools. More Indian children are now in public schools maintained by the state or local governments than in special Indian schools maintained by the nation. It is, however, still the fact that the boarding school, either reservation or non-reservation, is the dominant characteristic of the school system maintained by the national government for its Indian wards.

The survey staff finds itself obliged to say frankly and unequivocally that the provisions for the care of the Indian children in boarding schools are grossly inadequate.

The outstanding deficiency is in the diet furnished the Indian children, many of whom are below normal health. The diet is deficient in quantity, quality, and variety. The effort has been made to feed the children on a per capita of eleven cents a day, plus what can be produced on the school farm, including the dairy. At a few, very few, schools, the farm and the dairy are sufficiently productive to be a highly important factor in raising the standard of the diet, but even at the best schools these sources do not fully meet the requirements for the health and development of the children. At the worst schools, the situation is serious in the extreme. The major diseases of the Indians are tuberculosis and trachoma. Tuberculosis unquestionably can best be combated by a preventive, curative diet and proper living conditions, and a considerable amount of evidence suggests that the same may prove true of trachoma. The great protective foods are milk and fruit and vegetables, particularly fresh green vegetables. The diet of the Indian children in boarding schools is generally notably lacking in these preventive foods. Although the Indian Service has established a quart of milk a day per pupil as the standard, it has been able to achieve this standard in very few schools. At the special school for children suffering from trachoma, now in operation at Fort Defiance, Arizona, milk is not part of the normal diet. The little produced is mainly consumed in the hospital where children acutely ill are sent. It may be seriously questioned whether the Indian Service could do very much better than it does without more adequate appropriations.

Next to dietary deficiencies comes overcrowding in dormitories. The boarding schools are crowded materially beyond their capacities. A device frequently resorted to in an effort to increase dormitory capacity without great expense is the addition of large sleeping porches. They are in themselves reasonably satisfactory, but they shut off light and air from the inside rooms, which are still filled with beds beyond their capacity. The toilet facilities have in many cases not been increased proportionately to the increase in pupils, and they are fairly frequently not properly maintained or conveniently located. The supply of soap and towels has been inadequate.

The medical service rendered the boarding school children is not up to a reasonable standard. Physical examinations are often superficial and enough provision is not made for the correction of remediable defects.

Further Resources
BOOKS
Brown, Dee. *Bury My Heart at Wounded Knee: An Indian History of the American West.* New York: Henry Holt, 1970.

Hoxie, Frederick E. *Talking Back to Civilization: Indian Voices from the Progressive Era.* Boston: Bedford, 2001.

Iverson, Peter. *"We Are Still Here": American Indians in the Twentieth Century.* Wheeling, Ill.: Harlan Davidson, 1998.

PERIODICALS
Bovey, Seth. "Dances with Stereotypes: Western Films and the Myth of the Noble Red Man." *South Dakota Review* 31 no. 1, 1993, 115–122.

Critchlow, Donald T. "Lewis Meriam, Expertise, and Indian Reform." *The Historian* 23, 1981, 325–344.

WEBSITES
Clarke Historical Library, Central Michigan University. "Indian Treaties: Their Ongoing Importance to Michigan Residents: Federal Education Policy & Off-Reservation Schools 1870–1933." Available online at http://www.lib.cmich.edu /clarke/indian/treatyeducation.htm (accessed January 28, 2003).

Public Broadcasting Service. "Documents on the Sand Creek Massacre." New Perspectives on the West. Available online at http://www.pbs.org/weta/thewest/resources/archives/four /sandcrk.htm; website home page: http://www.pbs.org (accessed January 29, 2003).

Behind the Scenes in Candy Factories
Report

By: Consumers' League of New York

Date: March 1928

Source: Consumers' League of New York. *Behind the Scenes in Candy Factories.* New York: Consumers' League of New York, 1928. Reprinted in the Library of Congress American Memory Collection. Available online at http:// memory.loc.gov (accessed January 29, 2003).

About the Author: Frances Perkins (1882–1965), who wrote this report for the Consumers' League of New York, was influenced by the investigative muckraking journalists Lincoln Steffens, Jacob Riis, and Upton Sinclair, along with her involvement in Jane Addams's Hull House. In 1910, she headed the National Consumers' League and successfully fought to shorten the work week for women to fifty-four hours. In 1933, President Franklin D. Roosevelt appointed her to head the Department of Labor—the first woman in American history to hold a cabinet position. ■

Introduction

The National Consumers' League (NCL) was probably the most effective middle-class voluntary women's reform organization in American history. In 1899, Florence Kelley was appointed secretary of the New York Consumers' League and helped establish sixty-four local consumers' leagues throughout the country under the umbrella of the national organization. Before arriving in New York, Kelley had been a leader in Chicago's anti-sweatshop movement and was the chief inspector for the Illinois Bureau of Statistics and Labor. She was coauthor of the report "The Sweating System of Chicago," which documented that six-and-half-day workweeks and starvation wage levels were commonplace among women and children. In 1893, Illinois passed an anti-sweatshop act that provided for an eight-hour day for women. In 1895, the state supreme court declared the act unconstitutional.

The NCL's constitution stated that it was "concerned that goods be produced and distributed at reasonable prices and in adequate quantity, but under fair, safe, and healthy working conditions that foster quality products for consumers and a decent standard of living for workers." To fulfill these goals, the league campaigned for minimum wage and eight-hour workday laws. It lobbied state lawmakers and pressured department stores and garment makers to reform their practices through the "White Label" campaign. To educate the general public, the league published in local newspapers a list of retail establishments that met basic working standards. These labels were important because a large segment of the public were immigrants and did not speak English. The labels informed them which products were manufactured in compliance with state factory laws and were not made by workers under the age of sixteen. Consumers were urged to boycott manufacturers who did not met NCL approval.

In 1908, the NCL embarked upon a campaign to uphold the Oregon ten-hour workday law. In 1903, Oregon had enacted a law limiting workdays for women employed in factories and laundries to ten hours. Afterwards, laundry owner Curt Muller of Portland ordered Mrs. Elmer Gotcher to work more hours than the law allowed. After the state supreme court upheld the statute's constitutionality, the U.S. Supreme Court agreed to hear the case, *Muller v. Oregon*, in 1908. The NCL hired future Supreme Court Justice Louis D. Brandeis to defend the law. With the assistance of Florence Kelley, Brandeis used an innovative strategy of citing sociological data and evidence demonstrating the connection between women's poor health and long work hours. The Court upheld the law.

Significance

The NCL had an enormous impact on women's labor issues. By 1914, the league had signed formal White Label agreements with sixty-eight garment manufacturers. Four years later, that successful campaign could be ended because many states had enacted and enforced laws that were consistent with league requirements. Moreover, the NCL's sociological evidence in the *Muller* case was used by other states to uphold laws protecting women

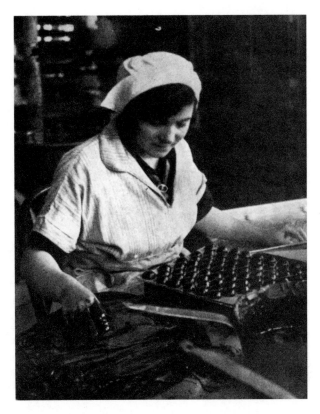

The National Consumer's League of New York found in 1928 that women candy-makers earned the lowest wage. **THE LIBRARY OF CONGRESS.**

workers. Currently, the NCL is the oldest national consumer organization in the United States.

Primary Source

Behind the Scenes in Candy Factories [excerpt]

> **SYNOPSIS:** In 1928, the Consumers' League of New York investigated twenty-five candy factories, ranging from the "little loft factory in the dirty side street turning out the cheapest grade of lollipop" to the large, modern factory in New York City. Of the five major industries in the state that employed women, the candy industry paid the lowest wages. In particular, the report documents the unsanitary conditions in the factories.

A Week in a Candy Factory

Long before eight the line of job-hunters began gathering at *****'s in answer to the advertisement for both experienced and inexperienced candy workers. The middle-aged women were the first to arrive and the most determined. There were no benches or chairs, so we stood about, first on one foot, then on the other, or tried to edge around near the wall so we could lean against it. Within half an hour there were sixty or seventy women crowded

The NCL's main goal was with the production and distribution of goods "at reasonable prices and in adequate quantity, but under fair, safe and healthy working conditions that foster quality products for consumers and a decent standard of living for workers." To fulfill these concerns, the league campaigned for minimum wage and eight-hour workday laws. **THE CENTER FOR AMERICAN HISTORY AND GENERAL LIBRARIES, UNIVERSITY OF TEXAS AT AUSTIN. REPRODUCED BY PERMISSION.**

into the tiny hall. Latecomers, those arriving after 8:30, were not able to get inside. Most of the girls were young, in their early teens, it seemed, but the few older ones were around fifty. Italian girls predominated with a scattering of Polish and Irish. Two girls were Porto Rican and spoke no word of English. One of them was strikingly beautiful. Among the older women was one I had met the week before looking for another job. She was in her fifties and unmarried and she told me she was being turned down everywhere because of her age. She was a pale, frail little thing. Later when she got turned down again, and I left her at the door, she was headed toward the ***** Biscuit Co. on the trail of a rumor picked up in the lobby.

At 9:30, we were sent upstairs by the watchman and here the personnel manager interviewed us singly. The older women were turned aside with the assurance, "I am sure you wouldn't want this kind of work. We need strong, young girls to run back and forth." After they had left fifteen of us were hired for all kinds of work. We had to fill out application blanks, quite a job for the slower girls, and those that finished first were hired.

A team of five of us was put to work in the "Art Department" under a hard-boiled Irish forelady. I soon found she was hated by both porters and girls and reviling her was their chief pastime.

The girl in charge of our table was a thin little Italian with paper-white face and large eyes. She hated her job and was continually wishing she was married. She had been here two years, had started at $14 a week and had never been increased. The only promotion, she said, was to be put on piece work. A woman wrapper at a near-by table was working on piece. Her hands flew so fast one could scarcely see them. Her face was strained and tense, her eyes never left her boxes and paper. I asked how much she could average. "About $18 a week at this season," she replied without looking up. But she didn't do piece work all the time, the little Italian said. She was getting "too many shakes," in her wrapping.

The smallest girl on the new team, though not the youngest, was 19. She had been married a year but had left her husband and was now living at home. She would tell us long, sad tales of her married life.

About 11 o'clock I went to the dressing room to wash my hands. The place was fairly clean, although the odor was bad and on the walls were signs informing the girls that they must wash their hands after using the toilets. I looked about for soap and towels. The little liquid soap bowls were all empty and there were no towels in sight. "How do you wipe your hands?" I asked. "On toilet paper, or on your shimmy, if you like," answered one girl. The other girls in the place walked out without the formality of washing.

Our department was called the Ice Box. The temperature was a little above 50° and although most of the girls wore sweaters, they shivered at their work. The girls who tied and wrapped were permitted to sit on iron stools. But the cold from the floor crept up the metal and helped in the chilling process. Many of the girls had very bad colds. Two young Jewish girls who worked with us got disgusted at the cold and bored with the monotony of the work. We were tying a piece of tin-foiled candy to the leg of a chocolate turkey with a piece of yellow ribbon. After one of the forelady's harangues they decided to quit at once and went to tell her so. An argument followed in which the forelady's voice rose loud and shrill. "Go to hell, you old cat," shouted one of the girls and the two departed.

The three of us who were left at the table were much impressed by this show of independence. Jessie, the little Italian, told infamous stories about the forelady but when she appeared we all bent over our work and did not reply to her abuse.

At the 45-minute lunch period the girls retired to the cloak room on the same floor with the lunches they had brought from home. A stock room girl made coffee and sold it at three cents a cup. A few of us who had not brought lunch this first day slipped across the street to a lunch counter where we could get a bowl of soup or a sandwich for ten cents. The place was full of workmen and the air thick with frying grease but it was the only restaurant in the neighborhood. "Some of the factories have swell lunch rooms and serve you tea or coffee and sugar free," one youngster informed me. "But even at that, this is the best place I've worked in. Not so much overtime and they don't speed you so. I worked at ***** a year for $12 a week—a rotten dump, too. Here they start you at $14. I suppose they keep you there forever, too."

Further Resources

BOOKS

Jensen, Joan M., and Sue Davidson, eds. *A Needle, a Bobbin, a Strike: Women Needleworkers in America.* Philadelphia: Temple University Press, 1984.

Lehrer, Susan. *Origins of Protective Labor Legislation for Women, 1905–1925.* Albany, N.Y.: State University of New York Press, 1987.

Sklar, Kathryn Kish, ed. *The Autobiography of Florence Kelley: Notes of Sixty Years.* Chicago: Charles Kerr, 1986.

PERIODICALS

Sklar, Kathryn Kish. "Hull House as a Community of Women Reformers in the 1890's." *Signs: Journal of Women in Culture and Society* 10, Summer 1985, 657–677.

Wandersee, Winifred, D. "I'd Rather Pass a Law than Organize a Union": Frances Perkins and the Reformist Approach to Organized Labor." *Labor History* 34, no. 1, Winter 1993, 5.

WEBSITES

Crozier, William, et al. "On the Lower East Side: Observations of Life in Lower Manhattan at the Turn of the Century." *Lower Manhattan Project.* Available online at http://tenant.net/Community/LES/contents.html (accessed January 29, 2003).

Sklar, Kathryn Kish, and Jamie Tyler. "How Did Florence Kelley's Campaign against Sweatshops in Chicago in the 1890s Contribute to State Formation?" *Women in Social Movements in the United States, 1775–2000.* Available online at http://womhist.binghamton.edu/factory/intro.htm; website home page: http://www.womhist.binghamton.edu/index.html (accessed January 29, 2003).

Leases Upon Naval Oil Reserves and Activities of the Continental Trading Co. (LTD.) of Canada

Report

By: U.S. Senate Committee on Public Lands and Surveys

Date: May 28, 1928

Source: U.S. Senate Committee on Public Lands and Surveys. *Leases Upon Naval Oil Reserves and Activities of the Continental Trading Co. (Ltd.) of Canada.* 70th Cong., 1st sess., May 28, 1928. S. Supplemental Report No. 70–1326, Pt. 2, at 3. Available online at http://www.brook.edu/dybdocroot/gs/ic/teapotdome/teapotdome.htm; website home page: http://www.brook.edu (accessed January 29, 2003).

About the Author: In April 1922, Wyoming senator John Kendrick introduced a Senate resolution that launched one of the most important Senate investigations in U.S. history. Earlier, *The Wall Street Journal* had reported a secret deal in which Albert B. Fall, secretary of the interior, had leased Wyoming's Teapot Dome oil reserve to a petroleum company. Six years later, the committee released its scathing report on the incident. ∎

Introduction

In the presidential election of 1920, Republican Warren G. Harding emerged the winner. The Republican

Party had been confident because it correctly assessed that the county was weary of the progressivism of Presidents Theodore Roosevelt and Woodrow Wilson. Harding was personally honest, but his administration was the most corrupt in American history, as the president doled out executive offices to swindlers, gamblers, and heavy drinkers collectively known as the "Ohio Gang." The administration's worst offender was Secretary of the Interior Albert B. Fall, who was implicated in the notorious Teapot Dome scandal.

In 1920, the U.S. Navy assumed responsibility for three petroleum-rich parcels of land located in Elk Hills and Buena Vista, California, and Salt Creek, Wyoming. The topography of the Wyoming parcel was shaped like a teapot, giving the scandal its name. These natural resources were essential to national security and were to remain in reserve for use by the Navy in case of war. Private interests and some politicians were opposed to leaving the reserves untapped, claiming that American oil companies were capable of meeting the Navy's fuel needs. As a U.S. senator, Fall was a longtime foe of such conservation programs. In 1921, as secretary of the interior, he persuaded the Navy that his department was better suited to manage the reserves. Once the properties were under his jurisdiction, Fall leased Teapot Dome to the Mammoth Oil Company, a subsidiary of Standard Oil. In return, he received $300,000 in cash and negotiable securities. It was estimated at the time that the naval reserves were worth $500,000,000.

In the spring of 1923, the press and congressional leaders learned about the brewing Teapot Dome scandal. Distressed by the swirling allegations, President Harding left Washington, D.C., for a tour of the West, but he could not escape the damning news. The mounting stress took its toll on Harding, who was afflicted with high blood pressure and an enlarged heart. While he was returning from Alaska, it was reported that he contracted food poisoning from contaminated Japanese crabs, but it is more likely that he suffered a massive heart attack. He died in San Francisco in August. Rumors soon swirled around the death of the president. A tabloid book published in 1930 claimed that the president's wife poisoned him to prevent him from being implicated in the corruption. Incidentally, Mrs. Harding received most of her husband's estate, valued at $850,000.

Significance

In October 1923, two months after Harding's death, the Senate Public Lands Committee launched an investigation and discovered that Fall had illegally leased government-owned naval reserves. No one was convicted of conspiring to defraud the government, but Fall was fined $100,000 and sentenced to one year imprisonment for accepting a bribe—the first former cabinet officer to go to prison. In 1927, the U.S. Supreme Court, in *Mammoth Oil Company v. United States,* revoked the leases, and the two reserves were returned to the government. The Teapot Dome incident, with its partisan conflict over the Senate's investigatory role in the scandal, was the 1920s equivalent to Watergate, which led to President Richard M. Nixon's resignation in 1974. At issue in 1924 was whether the executive branch, which included the Justice Department and the office of the attorney general, could impartially investigate other members of the presidential administration. Congressional skepticism forced President Calvin Coolidge to nominate two special counsels to investigate the matter. Therefore, the Teapot Dome scandal set precedent for the appointment of special counsel outside of the Justice Department to investigate possible wrongdoing in the executive branch.

Primary Source

Leases upon Naval Oil Reserves and Activities of the Continental Trading Co. (LTD.) of Canada

> **SYNOPSIS:** On May 28, 1928, the Senate Committee on Public Lands and Surveys submitted its preliminary report on the Teapot Dome Scandal. After six years of investigation, this damning report "uncovered the slimiest of slimy trails beaten by privilege." Among the worst offenses was the ability of the wealthy to finesse the legal system to bring about their acquittals.

Conceived in darkness and selfishness and dedicated to the proposition that the cause of privilege and the privileged must be served!

That, in a few words, is the sum and substance of the real story of the looting of the naval oil reserves and the formation and operations of the Continental Trading Co. of Canada, which the Committee on Public Lands and Surveys has had under investigation by virtue of Senate Resolution 101 of the Seventieth Congress, and Senate Resolutions 282 and 294 of the Sixty-seventh Congress.

In preparing this report in response to the aforementioned resolutions, the desires and requirements of the Senate with relation to a report have been construed to include:

1. The committee findings with relation to protection, or lack of protection, accorded the rights and equities of the Government of the United States in, and the preservation of, its natural resources as embodied in its naval oil reserves.

2. The committee findings with relation to its inquiry into the affairs of the Continental Trading

The Senate Committee investigating the Teapot Dome/Elk Hills oil leases hears testimony in 1924. © BETTMANN/CORBIS. REPRODUCED BY
PERMISSION.

Co. of Canada; the purpose of its organization, the source of its profit, the uses to which this profit was put or the uses for which it was probably intended; its connection, if any, with the leasing of the naval oil reserves; and its influence upon the political and economic life of the Nation.

3. In view of developments which have been the outgrowth of the investigation, it is felt that there should be incorporated in this report a citation of such benefits as have come out of the investigation thus far.

4. It is further felt that any final report should include a review of the contention of those men and institutions which have been thrown on the defensive as a result of the disclosures made by the investigation; that such a review should be offered for the purpose of showing how unreasonable their contention often has been, and how evasive, misleading, and false these men and institutions have in many cases been while presuming to throw light upon the matter under inquiry and while under oath to tell the truth, the whole truth, and nothing but the truth.

5. Finally, in its report the committee is expected to at least suggest such recommendations for legislation as many be considered necessary to further safeguard the naval oil reserves or other necessary security.

This Report Not Final

This report should under no circumstances be considered necessarily a final report.

The committee is still without knowledge of the uses to which about a third of the profits of the Continental Trading Co. were put. Representation is made that the one-fourth share which went to James O'Neil was finally given by O'Neil to the oil company of which he was the head official at the time he received the said profits. The bonds which were thus paid over to the oil company were not the Continental Trading Co. bonds, however. It may be that O'Neil still possessed the original bonds received as profit from the Continental Trading Co., but there has as yet developed no opportunity to ascertain this.

In addition to this quarter share of said profits, there is unaccounted for a portion of those bonds received by Harry F. Sinclair. Since the investigation has disclosed that approximately a half of his share

Investigation into the Teapot Dome scandal revealed that the U.S. Secretary of the Interior, Albert B. Fall, transferred government oil resources to Edward Doheny and Harry Sinclair without competitive bidding. The Supreme Court later restored the oil fields to the U.S. government. © BETTMANN/CORBIS. REPRODUCED BY PERMISSION.

entered channels which have been considered of a corrupt nature, it seems essential that every possible means ought to be exhausted to learn of the uses to which that portion unaccounted for was put.

Not all avenues of information with relation to the questions under investigation can be considered exhausted before the testimony of H.S. Osler, one H.M. Blackmer, and one James E. O'Neil has been made available. These three men were principals in the entire question under investigation, but they have all absented themselves from the continent during the time their testimony has been sought. The first has found trips abroad convenient upon occasions when it was indicated that the investigation would seek his personal testimony. The other two have been fugitives from justice since the inauguration of this inquiry in 1923.

Persistence and patience have been the first essential in winning virtually every bit of material information which has been secured by the committee. There ought not be haste and impatience now in bringing the inquiry to a quick close.

What Investigation Discloses

The investigation thus far discloses that the leasing of the naval oil reserves constitutes criminal conspiracy against the rights, interests, and properties of the United States unparalleled in the history of this or any other civilized nation.

Never has the world known a case involving a degree of fraud, quite evident bribery, thievery, conspiracy, and corruption to compare with what has come to be known as the Teapot Dome-Elk Hills-Continental Trading Co. case. The leases in the case are estimated to be worth not less than $500,000,000, and were consummated, to use the language of the Supreme Court of the United States, "by conspiracy, corruption, and fraud."

The investigation has uncovered the slimiest of slimy trails beaten by privilege. The investigation has shown, let us hope, privilege at its worst. The trail is one of dishonesty, greed, violation of law, secrecy, concealment, evasion, falsehood, and cunning. It is a trail of betrayals by trusted and presumably honorable men—betrayals of a government, of certain business interests and the people who trusted and honored them; it is a trail showing a flagrant degree of the exercise of political power and influence, and the power and influence of great wealth upon individuals and political parties; it is the trail of despoilers and schemers, far more dangerous to the well-being of our Nation and our democracy than all those who have been deported from our shores in all time as undesirable citizens. And in the end the story is one of the crushing of brilliant careers when finally the light was played upon those who schemed those unhealthy schemes born in darkness.

Slow to unfold itself, and slow in being unraveled, the tale of those who engineered, aided, and abetted in the naval oil-reserve leases and the affairs of the Continental Trading Co. goes beyond the most fertile imagination. The enormity of the offenses involved in these transactions is increased by the fact that these great oil reserves, created by the acts of Presidents Taft, Roosevelt, and Wilson, were essential to the national defense and were intended to be held inviolate until they were actually needed for the use of the Navy by reason of the depletion of other oil reserves or for some other great national emergency.

In addition to the startling story which the investigation itself has unfolded there are results, the direct outgrowth of facts uncovered by it, to further startle and stagger any mind which has followed the case. Among such results are the various court actions which the investigation has made inescapable, and the results of these actions.

The acquittal verdicts which followed the Fall-Doheny and the Fall-Sinclair trials have been considered most deplorable failures of justice on every side, excepting only the side of privilege. These failures have been of such nature as to prove the need for such changes in court procedure as will make advantage no more easily available to the criminal of great means than to the offender who comes out of the most lowly classes. Great means in these particular cases have won delays and purchased talent which have served to divert the mind from and cloud the real offenses and criminal acts attendant thereon. Justice has been proven, not a thing to be applied to and enjoyed by all alike, but, instead a commodity to be brought and otherwise influenced by wealth, and able lawyers in the Congress and out would contribute mightily to the cause of our democracy if they would devote themselves to such legislation as would make justice reach out to one and all alike.

The delays which have been attendant upon the trial of cases growing out of the naval oil leases is not to the credit of the order that prevails now with respect to the dispensation of justice. Because of these permissible delays we become the laughing stock of the world. Then there are the ins and outs and technicalities which do no permit, when expensive legal talent is on guard and objects the offering of all evidence bearing upon the case at trial.

The complaints offered by the jurors, who voted an acquittal in one of the cases growing out of the leasing of the naval oil reserves, to the effect that one learned more about the case from the newspapers he read after being relieved from duty on the jury which voted the acquittal then he had learned during the entire course of the trial, which ran over many days, is a case in point when it is agreed on every hand that the newspapers made no false presentations in its representations. Greed will be served through means, corrupt if need be, so long as there remains the chance to play with and break-down the true purpose of law. Conspiracies can be anticipated so long as conspirators are shown to have a chance for trial before juries which can be denied knowledge of all conditions and facts attendant upon that act of conspiracy.

Further Resources

BOOKS

Diner, Hasia. "Teapot Dome, 1924." In Arthur M. Schlesinger Jr., and Roger Bruns, eds., *Congress Investigates: A Docu-*

mented History, 1972–1974. New York: Chelsea House, 1975.

Fall, Albert. *The Memoirs of Albert B. Fall.* David Stratton, ed. El Paso, Tex.: Texas Western, 1966.

Noggle, Burl. *Teapot Dome: Oil and Politics in the 1920s.* New York: Norton, 1965.

PERIODICALS

Stratton, David. "Two Western Senators and Teapot Dome: Thomas J. Walsh and Albert B. Fall." *Pacific Northwest Quarterly* 65, April 1974, 57–65.

Weinberg, Myra Engers. "For GOP, Roaring '20s Ended with a Whimper." *Congressional Quarterly Weekly Report* 55, August 16, 1997, 1970.

WEBSITES

Bennett, Leslie. "One Lesson From History: Appointment of Special Counsel and the Investigation of the Teapot Dome Scandal." American Enterprise Institute and the Brookings Institution Project on the Independent Counsel Statute. Available online at http://www.brook.edu/gs/research/projects /ic/teapotdome/teapotdome.htm; website home page: http:// www.brook.edu/dybdocroot/default.htm (accessed January 29, 2003).

"Revisiting Watergate." *The Washington Post.* Available online at http://www.washingtonpost.com/wp-srv/national/longterm /watergate/front.htm; website home page: http://www .washingtonpost.com (accessed January 29, 2003).

Kellogg-Briand Pact

Treaty

By: Frank Kellogg and Aristide Briand

Date: August 27, 1928

Source: Kellogg-Briand Pact, 1928. *United States Statues at Large,* vol. 46, part 2, p. 2343. Reprinted in the Avalon Project at Yale Law School. "The Kellogg-Briand Pact and Associated Documents." Available online at http://www.yale.edu/lawweb/avalon/kbpact/kbpact.htm (accessed January 28, 2003).

About the Author: Frank Kellogg (1856–1937) was one of the premier attorneys in the United States. As a "trustbuster," he won antitrust suits against the General Paper Company, Union Pacific Railroad, and the Standard Oil Company. In 1925, he became the U.S. secretary of state, and in 1929 he won the Nobel Peace Prize. Aristide Briand (1862–1932) served in the French government for over thirty years, dating from his election to the Chamber of Deputies in 1902. He served as premier and at the time of the pact was minister for foreign affairs. In 1926, he won the Nobel Peace Prize. ∎

Introduction

By the conclusion of World War I (1914–1918), over 116,000 Americans had lost their lives, and another 234,000 were wounded. As a result, the vast majority of Americans wanted to withdraw from international affairs

Calvin Coolidge looks on as Frank Kellogg, the U.S. Secretary of State, signs the Kellogg-Briand Pact in 1929 © BETTMANN/CORBIS.
REPRODUCED BY PERMISSION.

because isolation was seen as the best opportunity for lasting peace. In 1920, the U.S. Senate, which had serious concerns about America's possible loss of sovereignty, voted not to participate in either the League of Nations or the World Court. In 1921, though, Congress reduced the size of the country's armed forces from a high of 4,355,000 mobilized during the war to 250,000. President Coolidge summed up the view of many Americans when he said, "The people have had all the war, all the taxation, and all the military service that they want."

In 1923, Edward W. Bok, former editor of the *Ladies' Home Journal,* the best-selling magazine at the time, held a contest calling for a proposal for preserving international peace. The winner would win the American Peace Prize and $100,000 in cash. Bok was swamped with thousands of suggestions. Even Franklin Roosevelt, the future president, crafted a plan while recuperating from polio. The vast majority of entries were from idealists who believed that merely revealing and criticizing the moral shortcomings of war could attain peace. Such thinking culminated in the signing of the Kellogg-Briand Pact in 1928.

On April 6, 1927, Aristide Briand, the French foreign minister, published an open letter to the American public proposing a bilateral treaty of perpetual friendship that would "outlaw" war forever between the longtime allies.

Briand wanted the formal agreement in part because he feared a possible attack by a resurgent Germany. Secretary of State Frank B. Kellogg feared that such an alliance would involve the United States in the type of foreign entanglement that the nation had avoided since George Washington's administration. Ultimately, such a treaty could drag the United States into another European war. However, William Jennings Bryan and other prominent isolationists found the offer fascinating and urged Kellogg to negotiate such a treaty. Later that year, Kellogg countered with a broader multilateral treaty proposal to include all nations, but with the provision that "every nation is free at all times . . . to defend its territory from attack and it alone is competent to decide when circumstances require war in self-defense." Briand, like his American counterpart and the American diplomatic corps, realized that such a proposal was pointless but could not resist public pressure to negotiate the treaty. Thus, the Kellogg-Briand Pact, renouncing war as a method of foreign policy, was drafted and ratified by the United States and several other nations, including Australia, Canada, Czechoslovakia, Great Britain, Germany, India, and Italy.

Significance

In January 1929, the Senate ratified the Kellogg-Briand Pact by a vote of 85 to 1. The vote, like the treaty itself, was empty of meaning. The effectiveness of the treaty was hampered by its structural weaknesses. For example, what should be the course of action after diplomacy failed to provide for a peaceful solution? Why should a nation comply with its moralistic vision if the treaty provided no verifiable system of monitoring its "former" enemies or provided substantial penalties for violations? The level of seriousness that the signatories attached to the treaty soon became clear. After ratification, the Senate moved to its next order of business, appropriating $274 million for navy rearmament. In 1931, Japan invaded Manchuria, Italy attacked Ethiopia four years later, and Germany occupied Austria in 1938. Fourteen years after its signing, all the signatories were belligerents in World War II.

Primary Source

Kellogg-Briand Pact

SYNOPSIS: On August 27, 1928, in Paris, diplomats from fifteen nations, including the United States, France, Great Britain, Japan, and Italy, signed the Kellogg-Briand Pact. The signatories pledged to renounce "war as an instrument of national policy." They also promised that if their country resorted to war, they "should be denied the benefits furnished by this Treaty," though it was uncertain what these benefits were. Eventually, sixty-two nations ratified the pact, including the United States on January 17, 1929.

By the President of the United States of America

A Proclamation

WHEREAS a Treaty between the President of the United States Of America, the President of the German Reich, His Majesty the King of the Belgians, the President of the French Republic, His Majesty the King of Great Britain, Ireland and the British Dominions beyond the Seas, Emperor of India, His Majesty the King of Italy, His Majesty the Emperor of Japan, the President of the Republic of Poland, and the President of the Czechoslovak Republic, providing for the renunciation of war as an instrument of national policy, was concluded and signed by their respective Plenipotontiaries at Paris on the twenty-seventh day of August, one thousand nine hundred and twenty-eight, the original of which Treaty, being in the English and the French languages, is word for word as follows:

THE PRESIDENT OF THE GERMAN REICH, THE PRESIDENT OF THE UNITED STATES OF AMERICA, HIS MAJESTY THE KING OF THE BELGIANS, THE PRESIDENT OF THE FRENCH REPUBLIC, HIS MAJESTY THE KING OF GREAT BRITAIN IRELAND AND

THE BRITISH DOMINIONS BEYOND THE SEAS, EMPEROR OF INDIA, HIS MAJESTY THE KING OF ITALY, HIS MAJESTY THE EMPEROR OF JAPAN, THE PRESIDENT OF THE REPUBLIC OF POLAND THE PRESIDENT OF THE CZECHOSLOVAK REPUBLIC,

Deeply sensible of their solemn duty to promote the welfare of mankind;

Persuaded that the time has, come when a frank renunciation of war as an instrument of national policy should be made to the end that the peaceful and friendly relations now existing between their peoples may be perpetuated;

Convinced that all changes in their relations with one another should be sought only by pacific means and be the result of a peaceful and orderly process, and that any signatory Power which shall hereafter seek to promote its national interests by resort to war a should be denied the benefits furnished by this Treaty;

Hopeful that, encouraged by their example, all the other nations of the world will join in this humane endeavor and by adhering to the present Treaty as soon as it comes into force bring their peoples within the scope of its beneficent provisions, thus uniting the civilized nations of the world in a common renunciation of war as an instrument of their national policy;

Have decided to conclude a Treaty and for that purpose have appointed as their respective Plenipotentiaries:

THE PRESIDENT OF THE GERMAN REICH:

Dr Gustav STRESEMANN, Minister of Foreign Affairs;

THE PRESIDENT OF THE UNITED STATES OF AMERICA:

The Honorable Frank B. KELLOGG, Secretary of State;

HIS MAJESTY THE KING OF THE BELGIANS:

Mr Paul HYMANS, Minister for Foreign Affairs, Minister of State;

THE PRESIDENT OF THE FRENCH REPUBLIC:

Mr. Aristide BRIAND Minister for Foreign Affairs;

HIS MAJESTY THE KING OF GREAT BRITAIN, IRELAND AND THE BRITISH DOMINIONS BEYOND THE SEAS, EMPEROR OF INDIA:

For GREAT BRITAIN and NORTHERN IRELAND and all parts of the British Empire which are not separate Members of the League of Nations:

The Right Honourable Lord CUSHENDUN, Chancellor of the Duchy of Lancaster, Acting-Secretary of State for Foreign Affairs;

For the DOMINION OF CANADA:

The Right Honourable William Lyon MACKENZIE KING, Prime Minister and Minister for External Affairs;

For the COMMONWEALTH of AUSTRALIA:

The Honourable Alexander John McLACHLAN, Member of the Executive Federal Council;

For the DOMINION OF NEW ZEALAND:

The Honourable Sir Christopher James PARR High Commissioner for New Zealand in Great Britain;

For the UNION OF SOUTH AFRICA:

The Honourable Jacobus Stephanus SMIT, High Commissioner for the Union of South Africa in Great Britain;

For the IRISH FREE STATE:

Mr. William Thomas COSGRAVE, President of the Executive Council;

For INDIA:

The Right Honourable Lord CUSHENDUN, Chancellor of the Duchy of Lancaster, Acting Secretary of State for Foreign Affairs;

HIS MAJESTY THE KING OF ITALY:

Count Gaetano MANZONI, his Ambassador Extraordinary and Plenipotentiary at Paris.

HIS MAJESTY THE EMPEROR OF JAPAN:

Count UCHIDA, Privy Councillor;

THE PRESIDENT OF THE REPUBLIC OF POLAND:

Mr. A. ZALESKI, Minister for Foreign Affairs;

THE PRESIDENT OF THE CZECHOSLOVAK REPUBLIC:

Dr Eduard BENES, Minister for Foreign Affairs;

who, having communicated to one another their full powers found in good and due form have agreed upon the following articles:

Article I

The High Contracting Parties solemnly declare in the names of their respective peoples that they condemn recourse to war for the solution of international controversies, and renounce it, as an instrument of national policy in their relations with one another.

Article II

The High Contracting Parties agree that the settlement or solution of all disputes or conflicts of whatever nature or of whatever origin they may be, which may arise among them, shall never be sought except by pacific means.

Article III

The present Treaty shall be ratified by the High Contracting Parties named in the Preamble in accordance with their respective constitutional requirements, and shall take effect as between them as soon as all their several instruments of ratification shall have been deposited at Washington.

This Treaty shall, when it has come into effect as prescribed in the preceding paragraph, remain open as long as may be necessary for adherence by all the other Powers of the world. Every instrument evidencing the adherence of a Power shall be deposited at Washington and the Treaty shall immediately upon such deposit become effective as; between the Power thus adhering and the other Powers parties hereto.

It shall be the duty of the Government of the United States to furnish each Government named in the Preamble and every Government subsequently adhering to this Treaty with a certified copy of the Treaty and of every instrument of ratification or adherence. It shall also be the duty of the Government of the United States telegraphically to notify such Governments immediately upon the deposit with it of each instrument of ratification or adherence.

IN FAITH WHEREOF the respective Plenipotentiaries have signed this Treaty in the French and English languages both texts having equal force, and hereunto affix their seals.

DONE at Paris, the twenty seventh day of August in the year one thousand nine hundred and twenty-eight.

[Seal] GUSTAV STRESEMANN

[Seal] FRANK B KELLOGG

[Seal] PAUL HYMANS

[Seal] ARI BRIAND

[Seal] CUSHENDUN

[Seal] W. L. MACKENZIE KING

[Seal] A J MCLACHLAN

[Seal] C. J. PARR

[Seal] J S. SMIT

[Seal] LIAM T.MACCOSGAIR

[Seal] CUSHENDUN

[Seal] G. MANZONI

[Seal] UCHIDA

[Seal] AUGUST ZALESKI

[Seal] DR EDWARD BENES

Certified to be a true copy of the signed original deposited with the Government of the United States of America.

FRANK B. KELLOGG

Secretary of State of the United States of America

AND WHEREAS it is stipulated in the said Treaty that it shall take effect as between the High Contracting Parties as soon as all the several instruments of ratification shall have been deposited at Washington;

AND WHEREAS the said Treaty has been duly ratified on the parts of all the High Contracting Parties and their several instruments of ratification have been deposited with the Government of the United States of America, the last on July 24, 1929;

NOW THEREFORE, be it known that I, Herbert Hoover, President of the United States of America, have caused the said Treaty to be made public, to the end that the same and every article and clause thereof may be observed and fulfilled with good faith by the United States and the citizens thereof.

IN TESTIMONY WHEREOF, I have hereunto set my hand and caused the seal of the United States to be affixed.

DONE at the city of Washington this twenty-fourth day of July in the year of our Lord one thousand nine hundred and twenty-nine, and of the Independence of the United States of America the one hundred and fifty-fourth

HERBERT HOOVER

By the President:

HENRY L STIMSON

Secretary of State

Further Resources

BOOKS

Bryn-Jones, David. *Frank B. Kellogg: A Biography.* New York: Putnam, 1937.

Ellis, L. Ethan. *Frank B. Kellogg and American Foreign Relations, 1925–1929.* New Brunswick, N.J.: Rutgers University Press, 1961.

Ferrell, Robert H. *Peace in Their Time: The Origins of the Kellogg-Briand Pact.* New Haven, Conn.: Yale University Press, 1952.

PERIODICALS

Kellogg, Frank B., "The War Prevention Policy of the United States." *American Journal of International Law* 22, 1928, 253–261.

Mead, Walter Russell. "The American Foreign Policy Legacy." *Foreign Affairs* 81, January/February 2002, 163–176.

WEBSITES

Halsall, Paul, ed. "Internet Modern History Sourcebook: Imperialism." *Internet History Sourcebooks Project, Fordham University.* Available online at http://www.fordham.edu/halsall/mod/modsbook34.html; website home page: http://www.fordham.edu/halsall/index.html (accessed January 28, 2003).

Zwick, Jim. "Anti-Imperialism in the United States, 1898–1935." Available online at http://www.library.csi.cuny.edu/dept/history/lavender/ai.html (accessed January 28, 2003).

"Rugged Individualism"
Speech

By: Herbert Hoover

Date: October 22, 1928

Source: Hoover, Herbert. "Rugged Individualism" Presidential Campaign Speech, New York, N.Y., October 22, 1928. Available online at The History Net: http://history1900s.about.com/ (accessed January 29, 2003).

About the Author: Herbert Clark Hoover (1874–1964) was the first American president born west of the Mississippi River. In 1883, he was orphaned when his mother died of pneumonia. In 1895, he graduated with a geology degree from Stanford University in California. By the age of forty, the skilled mineral engineer owned Burma silver mines and was a self-made multimillionaire. Hoover became president at the onset of the Great Depression. ■

Introduction

During World War I, Herbert Hoover earned a reputation as a great humanitarian. When war erupted in August 1914, the U.S. Embassy in London, where Hoover had been residing, requested that he organize a committee to evacuate 120,000 stranded Americans in Europe. The committee made available $1 million in loans, along with providing food and lodging in England and then passage to America. Hoover also organized the Committee for the Relief of Belgium. The Germans had occupied the small nation and refused to divert food away from their army to Belgian civilians. Without any government assistance, Hoover raised $1 billion to buy food and medicine, enough to supply 10 million people every day of the war.

Presidential candidate Herbert Hoover speaks at Madison Square Garden in New York City on October 22, 1928. **AP/WIDE WORLD PHOTOS. REPRODUCED BY PERMISSION.**

President Woodrow Wilson subsequently asked Hoover to head the U.S. Food Administration, which oversaw the rationing of food and household material for the war effort. After the war, Wilson appointed him to administer the European Relief and Rehabilitation Administration, which distributed thirty-four million tons of American food and clothing to twenty war-ravaged nations.

In 1920, President Warren G. Harding appointed Hoover secretary of commerce, a position he retained under President Calvin Coolidge. In 1928, Hoover announced his intention to run for the presidency. He united

a Republican Party deeply split into progressive and conservative wings. That year, the Democratic Party nominated Alfred E. Smith, the four-time governor of New York and son of Irish-Catholic immigrants. On paper, the two men were complete opposites. Smith was the first Catholic to run for the presidency and encountered opposition and hostility from Protestant leaders, who warned that a Catholic president would turn the reins of government over to the pope. In addition, Smith embodied working-class urban values. Born in the slums of New York City's Lower East Side, he was closely associated with the corrupt machine politics of Tammany Hall. He also supported the manufacture and distribution of alcoholic beverages. In contrast, Hoover was a Protestant (Quaker) from rural Middle America who supported Prohibition, which was very popular in the South and the West.

In November 1928, Hoover won in a landslide, carrying 58 percent of the popular vote and 444 electoral votes. He carried forty states, including Smith's own New York. Smith carried the big cities of New York, Boston, Cleveland, St. Louis, and San Francisco, but only 41 percent of the popular vote and 87 electoral votes.

Significance

In the election, Hoover was the beneficiary of Coolidge's prosperity. After World War I and the postwar depression of 1921 and 1922, the United States had become the world's leading economic power. During the Roaring '20s, national industrial production rose by an incredible 40 percent. A construction boom created new suburbs circling American cities and urban skyscrapers that illustrated American strength and ingenuity. However, this wealth was based on a shaky foundation as farmers suffered from low prices and debt. Certain industries, particularly textiles and coal mining, experienced high unemployment. Further, the real wages of industrial workers failed to keep pace with productivity and corporate profits. This created underconsumption, since many consumers could not afford the goods they produced.

Primary Source

"Rugged Individualism" [excerpt]

SYNOPSIS: On October 22, 1928, Herbert Hoover closed his presidential campaign with his "Rugged Individualism" speech. The speech exemplified American conservative philosophy, which stressed that the recent prosperity was due to "rugged individualism," limited government, and private enterprise. In contrast, Hoover criticized the "socialistic" Democrats for wanting to increase the power of government to solve societal ills.

By adherence to the principles of decentralized self-government, ordered liberty, equal opportunity, and freedom to the individual, our American experiment in human welfare has yielded a degree of well-being unparalleled in all the world. It has come nearer to the abolition of poverty, to the abolition of fear of want, than humanity has ever reached before. Progress of the past seven years is the proof of it. This alone furnishes the answer to our opponents, who ask us to introduce destructive elements into the system by which this has been accomplished.

We were challenged with a choice between the American system of rugged individualism and a European philosophy of state socialism.

Let us see what this system has done for us in our recent years of difficult and trying reconstruction and then solemnly ask ourselves if we now wish to abandon it.

As a nation we came out of the War with great losses. We made no profits from it. The apparent increases in wages were at that time fictitious. We were poorer as a nation when we emerged from the War. Yet during these last eight years we have recovered from these losses and increased our national income by over one-third, even if we discount the inflation of the dollar. That there has been a wide diffusion of our gain in wealth and income is marked by a hundred proofs. I know of no better test of the improved conditions of the average family than the combined increase in assets of life and industrial insurance, building and loan associations, and savings deposits. These are the savings banks of the average man. These agencies alone have, in seven years, increased by nearly one-hundred percent, to the gigantic sum of over fifty billions of dollars, or nearly one-sixth of our whole national wealth. We have increased in home ownership, we have expanded the investments of the average man.

In addition to these evidences of larger savings, our people are steadily increasing their spending for higher standards of living. Today there are almost nine automobiles for each ten families, where seven and one-half years ago, only enough automobiles were running to average less than four for each ten families. The slogan of progress is changing from the full dinner pail to the full garage. Our people have more to eat, better things to wear, and better homes. We have even gained in elbow room, for the increase of residential floor space is over twenty-five percent with less than ten percent increase in our number of people. Wages have increased, the cost of living has decreased. The job of every man and woman has been made more secure. We have in this short period decreased the fear of poverty, the fear of unemployment, the fear of old age; and these are fears that are the greatest calamities of human kind.

All this progress means far more than greater creature comforts. It finds a thousand interpretations into a greater and fuller life. A score of new helps save the drudgery of the home. In seven years, we have added seventy per cent to the electric power at the elbows of our workers and further promoted them from carriers of burdens to directors of machines. We have steadily reduced the sweat in human labor. Our hours of labor are lessened; our leisure has increased. We have expanded our parks and playgrounds. We have nearly doubled our attendance at games. We pour into outdoor recreation in every direction. The visitors at our national parks have trebled, and we have so increased the number of sportsmen fishing in our streams and lakes that the longer time between bites is becoming a political issue. In these seven and one-half years, the radio has brought music and laughter, education and political discussion to almost every fireside.

Springing from our prosperity with its greater freedom, its vast endowment of scientific research, and the greater resources with which to care for public health, we have, according to our insurance actuaries, during this short period since the War, lengthened the average span of life by nearly eight years. We have reduced infant mortality, we have vastly decreased the days of illness and suffering in the life of every man and woman. We have improved the facilities for the care of the crippled and helpless and deranged.

From our increasing resources, we have expanded our educational system in eight years from an outlay of twelve hundred-millions to twenty-seven hundred-millions of dollars. The education of our youth has become almost our largest and certainly our most important activity. From our greater income, and thus our ability to free youth from toil, we have increased the attendance in our grade schools by fourteen percent, in our high schools by eighty percent, and in our institutions of higher learning by ninety-five percent. Today we have more youth in these institutions of higher learning twice over than all the rest of the world put together. We have made notable progress in literature, in art, and in public taste.

We have made progress in the leadership of every branch of American life. Never in our history was the leadership in our economic life more distinguished in its abilities than today, and it has grown greatly in its consciousness of public responsibility. Leadership in our professions and in moral and spiritual affairs of our country was never of a higher order. And our magnificent educational system is bringing forward a host of recruits for the succession to this leadership.

I do not need to recite more figures and more evidence. I cannot believe that the American people wish to abandon, or in any way to weaken, the principles of economic freedom and self-government which have been maintained by the Republican Party, and which have produced results so amazing and so stimulating to the spiritual as well as to the material advance of the nation.

Further Resources

BOOKS

Bernstein, Irving. *The Lean Years: A History of the American Worker, 1920–1933.* Boston: Houghton Mifflin, 1960.

Burner, David. *Herbert Hoover: A Public Life.* New York: Knopf, 1979.

Smith, Richard Norton. *An Uncommon Man: The Triumph of Herbert Hoover.* New York: Simon and Schuster, 1984.

PERIODICALS

Bergman, Gregory. "The 1920s and the 1980s—A Comparison." *Monthly Review,* October 1986, 112–137.

Hirshbein, Laura Davidow. "The Flapper and the Fogy: Representations of Gender and Age in the 1920s." *Journal of Family History* 26, January 2001, 112–137.

WEBSITES

Internet Public Library. "Herbert Clark Hoover." Available online at http://www.ipl.org/div/potus/hchoover.html; website home page: http://www.ipl.org (accessed January 29, 2003).

"Herbert Hoover: The Engineer President." The American President. Available online at http://www.americanpresident.org /KoTrain/Courses/HH/HH_In_Brief.htm; website home page: http://www.americanpresident.org (accessed January 29, 2003).

6

LAW AND JUSTICE

SCOTT A. MERRIMAN

Entries are arranged in chronological order by date of primary source. For entries with one primary source, the entry title is the same as the primary source title. Entries with more than one primary source have an overall entry title, followed by the titles of the primary sources.

Important Events in Law and Justice, 1920–1929

1920

• On January 2, federal agents begin nationwide raids on suspected political radicals. More than four thousand people are detained in thirty-three cities.

• On January 5, the U.S. Supreme Court upholds the constitutionality of the Volstead Act, the legislative measure passed to implement the Eighteenth Amendment, which prohibited the manufacture, sale, or transport of alcoholic beverages in the United States.

• On January 16, Prohibition officially begins.

• On April 19, the U.S. Supreme Court rules that to implement an international treaty, Congress may enact legislation that otherwise might be construed as a violation of an individual state's sovereignty.

• On May 5, Nicola Sacco and Bartolomeo Vanzetti, known anarchists, are arrested for the murder of two men during a payroll robbery in South Braintree, Massachusetts, some weeks earlier.

• On May 15, Chicago gangster "Big Jim" Colosimo, who has been shot to death, is given the first "gangland funeral." It is attended by movie and opera stars, judges, and Johnny Torrio, who is suspected of having arranged the hit.

• On June 7, the U.S. Supreme Court rules that the Eighteenth Amendment is constitutional. This ruling abrogates all existing state laws that permit the sale of light wines and beer. The justices also declare that Congress has the authority to define what constitutes an intoxicating liquor.

• On August 26, by proclamation President Woodrow Wilson declares the ratification of the Nineteenth Amendment, which prohibits the denial of suffrage based solely on gender.

1921

• On January 3, the U.S. Supreme Court rules that a secondary labor boycott initiated during a strike constitutes an illegal restraint of trade, and that such boycotts can be prohibited by federal-court injunctions.

• On May 19, Chief Justice Edward D. White dies.

• On July 11, former president William Howard Taft realizes a lifelong dream when he is sworn in as chief justice. He is the only former president ever to serve on the high court.

• On August 2, a Chicago jury hands down its verdicts in the "Black Sox" scandal and acquits former Chicago White Sox team players and others of conspiring to defraud the public.

• On September 10, Sacco and Vanzetti are convicted on all charges, including murder.

• On December 19, the U.S. Supreme Court voids an Arizona law forbidding employers to seek court injunctions to bar picketing by striking workers.

• On December 23, President Warren G. Harding pardons Eugene V. Debs, Congressman Victor Berger of Wisconsin, and all others convicted under the Sedition Act of 1918 and other measures designed to curb dissent during World War I.

1922

• On March 27, the U.S. Supreme Court declares it lawful for a state judge to issue an order that directs federal authorities to remand a federal prisoner to state custody for prosecution. Such transfers must have the prior consent of the U.S. Department of Justice.

• On April 22, a New York State court judge rules that Dr. William J. Johnston, a physician, has violated a state obscenity law by printing and distributing a booklet titled *Love In Marriage*. Johnston is fined $250.

• On May 15, the U.S. Supreme Court voids a federal law that places a flat tax on the net profits of a business that employs child labor to produce goods sold through interstate commerce. The court rules that the law is a violation of the sovereign powers reserved to the various states in the Tenth Amendment.

• On September 18, John H. Clark, associate justice, resigns from the Supreme Court in order to promote U.S. participation in the League of Nations.

• On October 2, George Sutherland joins the Supreme Court as an associate justice.

• On November 13, William R. Day, associate justice, retires.

• On December 1, the U.S. Supreme Court rules that federal and state authorities both may prosecute a person caught in a specific instance of bootlegging, stating that such joint prosecutions do not violate the Double-Jeopardy Clause of the Fifth Amendment.

• On December 31, Mahlon Pitney retires from the Supreme Court.

1923

• On January 2, Pierce Butler is sworn in as a justice of the U.S. Supreme Court.

• On February 19, Edward T. Sanford is sworn in as an associate justice to the Supreme Court.

• On April 9, the U.S. Supreme Court rules that a law setting a minimum wage for female workers in the District of Columbia is unconstitutional.

• On June 4, in *Meyer* v. *Nebraska* the U.S. Supreme Court strikes down a Nebraska criminal statute that bars the teaching of all foreign languages to grammar-school pupils.

• On June 8, the Supreme Court affirms that a New York law on sedition is constitutional.

• On September 15, Governor J. C. Walton of Oklahoma declares martial law because of widespread violence caused by the Ku Klux Klan. Over the next three weeks several thousand Klansmen are detained by state military forces.

1924

• On February 8, the first execution by gas takes place in Carson City, Nevada.

• On March 28, President Coolidge dismisses Attorney General Harry Daugherty for his involvement in various scandals during the Harding administration. Daugherty is succeeded by Harlan Fiske Stone, the dean of Columbia University Law School.

• On May 21, fourteen-year-old Bobby Franks is murdered by Nathan Leopold Jr. and Richard Loeb, students at the University of Chicago.

• On June 2, Leopold and Loeb are arrested in Chicago. The wealthy Leopold and Loeb families retain famous trial lawyer Clarence Darrow, who mounts an insanity defense.

• On August 2, George Shiras Jr. retired associate justice of the Supreme Court, dies. Shiras served on the high court from 1892 to 1903.

• On September 10, Leopold and Loeb are found guilty of murder but are sentenced by "reason of insanity" to life imprisonment rather than death.

• On December 9, President Coolidge nominates Attorney General Stone to fill a vacancy on the Supreme Court.

• On December 9, Mahlon Pitney dies. Pitney was appointed to the Supreme Court by President Taft in 1912 and served until 1922.

• On December 19, Stone persuades Coolidge to appoint Acting Director J. Edgar Hoover as the permanent head of the Federal Bureau of Investigation (FBI).

1925

• On January 5, Associate Justice Joseph McKenna retires from the Supreme Court.

• On January 28, Stone is questioned by the full Senate Judiciary Committee, becoming the first Supreme Court nominee to undergo scrutiny by the committee.

• On February 2, the Senate confirms Stone's appointment to the U.S. Supreme Court by a vote of 71-6.

• On February 4, Charles R. Forbes, head of the Veterans' Bureau under President Harding, is sentenced to two years in prison for fraud, conspiracy, and bribery.

• On March 13, a law prohibiting the teaching of evolution takes effect in Tennessee.

• In March, after escaping an attempt on his life, Chicago gang boss Johnny Torrio hands over his crime empire to Al Capone and retires to Italy with between $10 million and $30 million.

• On March 2, in *Ex parte Grossman,* the U.S. Supreme Court rules that President Calvin Coolidge's pardon of a man convicted of criminal contempt of court was within the powers granted to the president by the constitution.

• On March 2, Harlan Fiske Stone is sworn in as an associate justice on the Supreme Court.

• On March 3, the U.S. Supreme Court upholds the right of federal prohibition agents to confiscate all alcoholic beverages that are found during routine searches of automobiles. The court rules that such searches are not violations of the Fourth Amendment.

• On May 5, John T. Scopes, a high-school science teacher, is arrested in Dayton, Tennessee, for violating a state law that bars the teaching of evolution in public schools.

• On May 6, the U.S. Treasury Department uses U.S. Coast Guard vessels to wage an all-out campaign against rumrunners who have been increasing the scope of their activities along the Atlantic Seaboard.

• On June 1, in *Pierce* v. *Society of Sisters,* the U.S. Supreme Court invalidates an Oregon law that makes it compulsory for all children between the ages of eight and sixteen to attend public school.

• On June 8, in *Gitlow* v. *New York,* the U.S. Supreme Court finds no violation of the First Amendment as it upholds a New York law that punishes the advocacy of overthrowing the government.

• On June 28, at a conference in Chicago, a coalition of radical political groups creates the International Labor Defense Fund (ILDF) to help various "political prisoners" procure legal assistance against criminal prosecution.

• On July 10, in Dayton, Tennessee, the Scopes "Monkey" Trial begins. Clarence Darrow leads the defense; William Jennings Bryan assists the prosecution.

• On July 21, John T. Scopes is convicted in a Tennessee state court of violating Tennessee law by teaching evolution. His conviction is later overturned.

• On September 9, a white mob in Detroit, Michigan, attacks the home of Dr. Ossian Sweet, an African American physician who has recently moved into an all-white neighborhood. After firing on the crowd in self-defense and killing one attacker, Sweet and eleven associates are arrested for murder.

• On November 21, David C. Stephenson, grand dragon of the Ku Klux Klan in Indiana, is found guilty of second-degree murder.

1926

• On February 12, after two inconclusive trials, prosecutors drop murder charges against all defendants in the Sweet case except one, Ossian Sweet's brother Henry.

• On February 19, the U.S. Supreme Court rules that a defendant's right to a fair trial, as guaranteed by the Sixth Amendment, would be denied if a "mob atmosphere" dominates trial proceedings.

• On May 14, with Clarence Darrow as his defense attorney, Henry Sweet is declared innocent by an all-white jury.

• On May 24, the U.S. Supreme Court declares the constitutionality of restrictive property covenants, discriminatory pacts designed to prevent members of various minorities from residing within a community. The court rules that such covenants violate neither the Fourteenth nor the Fifteenth Amendment.

- On May 24, Joseph McKenna, who retired from the Supreme Court in 1925, dies.

1927

-

- On February 28, the U.S. Supreme Court declares that all oil contracts and leases granted to oil magnate Edward L. Doheny by former secretary of the interior Albert B. Fall are illegal, fraudulent, and corrupt.

- On March 7, the U.S. Supreme Court orders the state of Texas to pay an indemnity of five thousand dollars to L. A. Nixon, an African American who had been denied the right to vote in the Texas Democratic primary election of 1924.

- On June 10, the three-member Lowell Commission, appointed by Governor Alvan T. Fuller of Massachusetts, declares Sacco and Vanzetti guilty as charged.

- On August 23, after the U.S. Supreme Court refuses to grant a final reprieve, Sacco and Vanzetti are executed at the Charlestown State Penitentiary in Massachusetts.

- On November 21, the U.S. Supreme Court upholds the right of the state of Mississippi to place all nonwhite pupils in segregated public schools.

1928

- On February 9, the U.S. Supreme Court strikes down a New Jersey law that has created a commission to regulate the business practices of employment agencies operating in that state.

- On June 4, in *Olmstead* v. *U.S.,* the U.S. Supreme Court upholds the right of federal agents to wiretap private telephones without first obtaining judicial approval. The case was overturned in 1967 in *Katz* v. *U.S.*.

1929

- On February 14, gunmen working for Al Capone, the leading racketeer in Chicago, execute seven members of a rival gang. This crime becomes known as the Saint Valentine's Day Massacre.

- On April 9, the Canadian government protests the sinking of *I'm Alone,* a vessel of Canadian registry, some two hundred miles off the Florida coast by a U.S. Coast Guard cutter whose crew had suspected that the ship was being used by rumrunners.

- On May 7, the U.S. Supreme Court sustains the right of the federal government to deny citizenship to any immigrant who directly declares an unwillingness to fulfill military service, whatever the circumstance.

Gitlow v. New York

Supreme Court decision

By: Edward Sanford and Oliver Wendell Holmes Jr.

Date: June 8, 1920

Source: *Gitlow v. People of State of New York* 268 U.S. 652 (1925). Available online at http://caselaw.lp.findlaw.com /scripts/getcase.pl?court=US&vol;=268&invol;=652; website home page: http://caselaw.lp.findlaw.com (accessed February 7, 2003).

About the Authors: Edward Sanford (1865–1930) was appointed to the court in 1923 by President Harding (served 1921–1923). One of his most well-known decisions held that, in addition to the federal government, states must uphold some provisions of the Bill of Rights.

Oliver Wendell Holmes Jr. (1841–1935) served in the Union army in the Civil War. In 1902, President Theodore Roosevelt (served 1901–1909) appointed him associate justice to the United States Supreme Court. He did not resign until 1932. ∎

Introduction

Free speech was not a topic discussed often in Supreme Court decisions in the nineteenth century. *Schenck v. U.S.* represented the first time in the twentieth century that free speech came across the docket. That case upheld the *Espionage Act* and suggested that speech could be repressed when it presented a "clear and present danger" to the United States. The Supreme Court continued in this vein, as all six cases involving the Espionage and Sedition Acts upheld the *Schenck* precedent. However, in *Abrams v. U.S.,* a second strand of free speech thought appeared in the Court. Abrams had been convicted for disseminating leaflets opposing the United States intervention in the Russian Revolution. In his dissent in that case, Justice Holmes suggested that *Schenck* had been correctly decided, but that Abrams did not present a clear and present danger. Holmes argued that in general, "the ultimate good is better reached by free trade in ideas." Thus, Holmes suggested that free speech needed to be protected.

All six of the Espionage and Sedition Act cases brought before the Court involved federal law. The law in *Gitlow,* though, was a state law preventing criminal anarchy, which brought up the question of which free speech guarantees the states had to respect. The First Amendment only restricted Congress, and the question arose as to what controls are placed on state laws. *Barron v. Baltimore* (1833) had held that the Bill of Rights did not apply to the states. The Fourteenth Amendment applied due process guarantees against the states, but the definition of due process remained in question. The Supreme Court in 1884 held that due process did not include requirements of a grand jury indictment or the privilege against self-incrimination, but they had not dealt with the issue of free speech. In *Gitlow,* they addressed that issue for the first time when they examined the conviction of a Communist Party leader.

Significance

Though the Court upheld Gitlow's conviction, it significantly expanded the definition of "due process" to include freedom of speech and the press inside its protection. This, in turn, increased the amount of speech state laws had to permit. The court next revisited the issue in *Whitney v. California,* upholding a state law prohibiting syndicalism (supporting the overthrow of the government), and upholding the conviction of Anna Whitney for her membership in the Communist Labor Party of America. In the 1931 case of *Stromberg v. California,* the Supreme Court specifically incorporated the First Amendment into the Fourteenth Amendment, striking down a state law which prohibited the displaying of a red flag as an element of anarchism. The law was struck down because it was so broadly worded as to allow the state to imprison those who were protesting peacefully and civilly and thus well within their First Amendment rights. In that same year, the Supreme Court struck down a Minnesota law that broadly banned "malicious, scandalous, or defamatory" newspapers as also being so broad as to violate the First Amendment. The Supreme Court also began, in the famous Scottsboro Boys cases, to expand the due process clause to include some guarantees of a fair trial, which began to weaken the court's 1884 decision. It was not until the Warren Court, however, that the due process clause was broadened to near the width it had at the end of the twentieth century, prohibiting the use of evidence seized illegally, establishing the right to counsel, and forcing states to read prisoners their rights. By 1969, only seven of the twenty-six provisions of the Bill of Rights had not been incorporated against the states. Thus, *Gitlow* was the first step toward a nationalization of the Bill of Rights.

Primary Source

Gitlow v. New York [excerpt]

SYNOPSIS: Justice Sanford first states that Gitlow's pamphlet is not abstract and therefore not immune

Benjamin Gitlow's conviction noted that freedom of speech and freedom of the press were protected against intrusion by the state.
© BETTMANN/CORBIS. REPRODUCED BY PERMISSION.

from prosecution. He establishes the state's right to limit freedom of speech when it is abused. Then he upholds Gitlow's conviction under the law. Holmes' dissent states that Gitlow's pamphlet had no hope of inciting any revolution. The case was argued on November 23, 1923, and decided on June 8, 1925.

Mr. Justice Sanford delivered the opinion of the Court. . . .

The precise question presented, and the only question which we can consider under this writ of error, then is, whether the statute, as construed and applied in this case, by the State courts, deprived the defendant of his liberty of expression in violation of the due process clause of the Fourteenth Amendment.

The statute does not penalize the utterance or publication of abstract "doctrine" or academic discussion having no quality of incitement to any concrete action. It is not aimed against mere historical or philosophical essays. It does not restrain the advocacy of changes in the form of government by constitutional and lawful means. What it prohibits

is language advocating, advising or teaching the overthrow of organized government by unlawful means. . . .

The Manifesto, plainly, is neither the statement of abstract doctrine nor, as suggested by counsel, mere prediction that industrial disturbances and revolutionary mass strikes will result spontaneously in an inevitable process of evolution in the economic system. It advocates and urges in fervent language mass action which shall progressively foment industrial disturbances and through political mass strikes and revolutionary mass action overthrow and destroy organized parliamentary government. It concludes with a call to action in these words:

> The proletariat revolution and the Communist reconstruction of society—the struggle for these—is now indispensable. . . . The Communist International calls the proletariat of the world to the final struggle!

This is not the expression of philosophical abstraction, the mere prediction of future events; it is the language of direct incitement. . . .

For present purposes we may and do assume that freedom of speech and of the press—which are protected by the First Amendment from abridgment by Congress—are among the fundamental personal rights and "liberties" protected by the due process clause of the Fourteenth Amendment from impairment by the States. . ..

It is a fundamental principle, long established, that the freedom of speech and of the press which is secured by the Constitution, does not confer an absolute right to speak or publish, without responsibility, whatever one may choose, or an unrestricted and unbridled license that gives immunity for every possible use of language and prevents the punishment of those who abuse this freedom. . . .

That a State in the exercise of its police power may punish those who abuse this freedom by utterances inimical to the public welfare, tending to corrupt public morals, incite to crime, or disturb the public peace, is not open to question. . . .

By enacting the present statute the State has determined, through its legislative body, that utterances advocating the overthrow of organized government by force, violence and unlawful means, are so inimical to the general welfare and involve such danger of substantive evil that they may be penalized in the exercise of its police power. That determination must be given great weight. Every presumption is to be indulged in favor of the validity of the statute. . . . That utterances inciting to the overthrow of organized government by unlawful means, present a sufficient danger of substantive evil to bring their punishment within the range of legislative discretion, is clear. Such utterances, by their very nature, involve danger to the public peace and to the security of the State. They threaten breaches of the peace and ultimate revolution. And the immediate danger is none the less real and substantial, because the effect of a given utterance cannot be accurately foreseen. The State cannot reasonably be required to measure the danger from every such utterance in the nice balance of a jeweler's scale. A single revolutionary spark may kindle a fire that, smouldering for a time, may burst into a sweeping and destructive conflagration. . . .

We cannot hold that the present statute is an arbitrary or unreasonable exercise of the police power of the State unwarrantably infringing the freedom of speech or press; and we must and do sustain its constitutionality. . . .

the judgment of the Court of Appeals is

Affirmed.

Mr. Justice Holmes (dissenting).

. . . If what I think the correct test is applied it is manifest that there was no present danger of an attempt to overthrow the government by force on the part of the admittedly small minority who shared the defendant's views. It is said that this manifesto was more than a theory, that it was an incitement. Every idea is an incitement. It offers itself for belief and if believed it is acted on unless some other belief outweighs it or some failure of energy stifles the movement at its birth. The only difference between the expression of an opinion and an incitement in the narrower sense is the speaker's enthusiasm for the result. Eloquence may set fire to reason. But whatever may be thought of the redundant discourse before us it had no chance of starting a present conflagration. . . .

If the publication of this document had been laid as an attempt to induce an uprising against government at once and not at some indefinite time in the future it would have presented a different question. The object would have been one with which the law might deal, subject to the doubt whether there was any danger that the publication could produce any result, or in other words, whether it was not futile and too remote from possible consequences. But the indictment alleges the publication and nothing more.

Further Resources

BOOKS

Eastlan, Terry. *Freedom of Expression in the Supreme Court: The Defining Cases.* Washington, D.C.: Rowman & Littlefield, 2000.

Gitlow, Benjamin. *Gitlow v. New York.* Wilmington, Del.: Michael Glazier, 1978.

Gitlow, Benjamin, and Clarence Darrow and Bartow S. Weeks. *The "Red Ruby" Address to the Jury.* New York: Labor Party, United States of America, 1920.

Gitlow, Benjamin, and Walter Nelles. *Supreme Court of the United States, October Term, 1922, Benjamin Gitlow, Petitioner-In-Error, Against People of the State of New York, Defendant-In-Error: Brief for Petitioner In Support of Application to the Full Court for Writ of Error.* New York: Hecla Press, 1922.

Worton, Stanley N. *Freedom of Speech and Press.* Rochelle Park, N.J.: Hayden Book Co., 1975.

The Black Sox Scandal

"The Black Sox Trial: Trial Summations"

Court case

By: Lawyers for prosecution and defense

Date: July 29, 1921

Source: "The Black Sox Trial: Trial Summations (Excerpts)." University of Missouri-Kansas City School of Law's Famous American Trials: The Black Sox Trial: 1921. Available online at http://www.law.umkc.edu/faculty/projects /ftrials/blacksox/trialsummations.html; website home page: http://www.law.umkc.edu (accessed February 11, 2003).

Statement of Commissioner Landis

Statement

By: Kenesaw Mountain Landis

Date: August 4, 1921

Source: Landis, Kenesaw Mountain. "Statement of Commissioner Landis: August 4, 1921." University of Missouri–Kansas City School of Law's Famous American Trials: The Black Sox Trial: 1921. Available online at http://www.law .umkc.edu/faculty/projects/ftrials/blacksox/commissionerdec .html; website home page: http://www.law.umkc.edu (accessed February 11, 2003).

About the Author: Kenesaw Mountain Landis (1866–1944) served as baseball commissioner from 1920 until his death in 1944, the longest term ever served. Prior to that, he was a federal district court judge who presided over the trials of Victor Berger under the Espionage Act, among many others. He is most famous for banning eight men from baseball in the Black Sox Scandal. ■

Joseph "Shoeless Joe" Jackson, a member of the Chicago White Sox baseball team, was a key player in the "Black Sox Scandal." **AP/WIDE WORLD PHOTOS. REPRODUCED BY PERMISSION.**

Introduction

Baseball had achieved nationwide popularity by 1869. In that year, the first professional baseball team, the Cincinnati Red Stockings, formed and went on a nationwide barnstorming tour. The Red Stockings were undefeated in that sixty-nine-game campaign. Teams formed in other cities, and in 1876, the National League was founded. The American League formed a bit later in 1901, and in 1903, the first World Series was played between the Boston Red Sox (of the American League) and the Pittsburgh Pirates (of the American League). The game had great appeal to working-class people, especially men, and was played before large crowds.

Baseball was not without its difficulties, however. Players complained about their salaries and sometimes staged holdouts in attempts to get more money. "Barnstorming" tours, where league teams would travel and play against various local teams, took place during the off season. Franchises moved and there were unruly fans

and players. A third league—the Federal League—was formed for a time, but it was defeated by the American and National Leagues. During World War I (1914–1918), in the 1918 season, the game came under attack, with many players having to get defense jobs or go into the military.

With World War I in the past, the 1919 season found the game back in full swing. Attendance was up, evidence that the American people were ready to get things back to normal. The Chicago White Sox won the American League and the Cincinnati Reds surprisingly won the National League. The Chicago White Sox were favored in the Series, which had been increased from seven games to nine, but the Reds won the series in eight. The news that several White Sox players had apparently accepted bribes to throw the series did not come out until September of the following year, when a Chicago grand jury indicted a number of ballplayers for fixing the Series, and those players were banned for the season.

Significance

In response to this scandal, the major leagues hired their first commissioner, Kenesaw Mountain Landis, who was paid the astronomical sum of $42,500 a year. He was also given dictatorial powers. The players were eventually acquitted by a jury, but Commissioner Landis refused to allow any of the players to return, banning all eight for life. Thus the men escaped jail time but still were unable to play the game of their dreams. Commissioner Landis ruled with an iron hand for the rest of his tenure, acting in the way he thought was best for the game, even while continuing to support baseball's policy of segregation. He was commissioner for twenty-five years. Commissioners since Landis have also suspended or banned players in smaller numbers. The most recent well-known player is Pete Rose, who was suspended by A. Bartlett Giamatti after an investigator's findings that Rose gambled on baseball. Soon after Rose was suspended, Giamatti died of a heart attack. It is unclear whether Giamatti intended for Rose to be suspended for life, but succeeding commissioners (when baseball has had a commissioner) have not acted to lift the ban.

For both Rose and those banned in the Black Sox scandal, the suspension from baseball has had other consequences—the Hall of Fame has refused the admission of those players. Rose, with his record 4,256 hits, and "Shoeless Joe" Jackson, whose .356 lifetime batting average ranks third only to that of Ty Cobb and Roger Hornsby, clearly would deserve consideration if they were not ineligible for consideration. Despite fan-based signature drives, no commissioner has ever reconsidered any suspensions.

This Chicago White Sox team was involved in the "Black Sox Scandal" of 1919, and although exonerated, eight players were banned from playing baseball. **NATIONAL BASEBALL LIBRARY & ARCHIVE, COOPERSTOWN, NY.**

Primary Source

"The Black Sox Trial: Trial Summations [excerpt]"

SYNOPSIS: The prosecution proclaims the ballplayers guilty by their own admission and says these men have "swindled America." The prosecution continues by defending the owners, pointing out that the players were not cheated as they might claim to be. The defense opens by pointing out that the elements of conspiracy had never been proven. The defense concludes by arguing that these men have been framed.

Summation for the Prosecution by Assistant State's Attorney, Edward Prindeville (July 29, 1921):

What more convincing proof do you want than the statement by the ballplayers? Joe Jackson, Eddie Cicotte, and Williams sold out the American public for a paltry $20,000. They collected the money, but they could not keep quiet. Their consciences would not let them rest. When the scandal broke, they sought out the State's Attorney's office and made their confessions voluntarily. Cicotte told his story to Chief Justice MacDonald. Then he told it to the Grand Jury. He was followed to the Grand Jury room by Jackson and Williams. On evidence which they gave the jurors, Bill Burns, the State's star witness, was indicted. They have called Burns a squealer, but I tell you that he owes his connection in the case to what these defendant ballplayers have confessed. . . .

This is an unusual case as it deals with a class of men who are involved in the great national game which all red-blooded men follow. This game, gentlemen, has been the subject of a crime. The public, the club owners, even the small boys on the sandlots have been swindled. That is why these defendants are charged with conspiracy.

This conspiracy started when Eddie Cicotte told Burns in New York that if the White Sox won the pennant there was something on and he would let him in on it. All the way through you will find that Cicotte's statements are corroborated by Burns and vice versa.

Cicotte was advised of his rights, yet he told his story. He told of the ten thousand dollars he got under his pillow. He told of meeting his pals and talking over the conspiracy details. He told of watching while his companions filed one by one from the meeting place so as not to raise suspicions of the honest players. Then what did this idol of the diamond do? He went home and took the ten thousand dollars from under his pillow. Of course he was uneasy!

Then, the gamblers met again on the morning before the World Series began. The gamblers accepted the players' terms. It was agreed that Cicotte should lose the first game. Of course he lost. With ten thousand dollars in his pocket, how could you expect him to keep his balance and win. The weight would bear him down!

Gentlemen, you will find that Burns was also corroborated in his testimony by Joe Jackson and Williams. Jackson tells you he got the five thousand dollars after the fourth game—

[O'Brien, interrupting: "I suppose that sharpened his batting average!"]

He certainly was batting 1000% when he got the $5,000! Swede Pisberg then tells you he had a cold. The only trouble with him was that he had an overdose of conspiracy in his hide. You recall the defendants said they could not win for Kerr because he was a busher. Abe Attell told them to win and they won! There is no pitcher on God's green earth who could have won that ball game if the defendants had not backed him up!

I say, gentlemen, that the evidence shows that a swindle and a con game has been worked on the American people. The crime in this case warrants the most severe punishment of the law. This country is for sending criminals to the penitentiary whether they are idols of the baseball diamond or gangsters guilty of robbery with a gun. Unless the jury, by convicting the ballplayers in this trial, does its part to stamp out gambling that is corrupting baseball, I predict restrictive legislation for baseball such as has been enacted for boxing and horseracing.

The State is asking in this case for a verdict of guilty with five years in the penitentiary and a fine of $2,000 for each defendant.

Summation for the Prosecution by Assistant State's Attorney George Gorman:

The attorneys for the defense will ask for mercy. They point out that Lefty Williams got only five hundred dollars a month for his services. They charge that Charles Comiskey, the grand old man of baseball, is persecuting the players because he has tried to clean out rottenness in the national game. Gentlemen, Charles Comiskey wants to keep the game clean for the American public and I will tell you now that if the owners don't get busy when rottenness crops up, baseball won't last long.

Comiskey gave these men a job. And here we find the defendants deliberately conspiring to injure and destroy his business. They have hit at Billy Maharg, the man who corroborated him. They tell you, at least three of their clients, Eddie Cicotte, Lefty Williams, and Joe Jackson have condemned themselves so badly that I don't see how you can acquit them. In his confession, Eddie Cicotte tells how the games were fixed. Then we have the spectacle of the public going to the game believing it was on the square. Thousands of men throughout the chilly hours of the night, crouched in line waiting for the opening for the first World Series game. All morning they waited, eating a sandwich, perhaps never daring to leave their places for a moment. There they waited to see the great Cicotte pitch a ball game. Gentlemen, they went to see a ball game. But all they saw was a con game!

August 1, 1921: Summation for the Defense by Attorney Ben Short (for the players):

The State failed to establish criminal conspiracy. There may have been an agreement entered by the defendants to take the gambler's money, but it has not been shown the players had any intention of defrauding the public or of bringing the game into ill repute. They believed any arrangement they may have made was a secret one and would, therefore, reflect no discredit on the national pastime or injure the business of their employer as it would never be detected! . . .

Summation for the Defense by A. Morgan Frumberg (for the gamblers):

Arnold Rothstein came here to Chicago during the Grand Jury investigation and immediately went to Alfred Austrian, the White Sox attorney. What bowing and scraping must have taken place when 'Arnold the Just,' the millionaire gambler, entered the sanctum of "Alfred the Great." By his own testimony, Mr.

Austrian admits conducting the financier to the Grand Jury and bringing him back unindicted! . . .

Why was [Rothstein] not indicted? Why were Brown, Sullivan, Attell, and Chase allowed to escape? Why were these underpaid ballplayers, these penny-ante gamblers from Des Moines and St. Louis, who may have bet a few nickels on the World Series, brought here to be the goats in this case? Ask the powers in baseball. Ask Ban Johnson who pulled the strings in this case. Ask him who saved Arnold Rothstein!

Summation for the Defense by Michael Ahearn:

Ban Johnson was the directing genius of the prosecution. His hand runs like a scarlet thread through the whole prosecution. Johnson is boss. The czar of Russia never had more power over his subjects than Johnson has over the American League. He controlled the case. His money hired Burns and Maharg to dig up evidence. He sent Maharg on a wild-goose chase to Mexico to find Burns. The State's attorneys have no more control over the prosecution than a bat boy has over the direction of play in a World Series game.

Maharg came to court as an auto worker, but he flashed enough diamonds on his fingers to buy a flock of autos. And Burns has been proved a liar in a score of instances. He said he talked to Gandil in Chicago after the second game. He lied. He said he talked to the ballplayers on the morning before the opening game. He lied. He makes me think of a drink of moonshine: It looks good, but when you drink it gives you a stomachache!

Primary Source

Statement of Commissioner Landis

> **SYNOPSIS:** All of the players involved in the scandal are banned from baseball forever by Commissioner Landis.

Regardless of the verdict of juries, no player who throws a ball game, no player that undertakes or promises to throw a ball game, no player that sits in conference with a bunch of crooked players and gamblers where the ways and means of throwing a game are discussed and does not promptly tell his club about it, will ever play professional baseball.

Further Resources

BOOKS

Asinof, Eliot. *Eight Men Out.* New York: Holt, 1987.

Cottrell, Robert C. *Blackball, the Black Sox, and the Babe: Baseball's Crucial 1920 Season.* Jefferson, N.C.: McFarland, 2002.

Fleitz, David L. *Shoeless: The Life and Times of Joe Jackson.* Jefferson, N.C.: McFarland & Co., 2001.

Gropman, Donald. *Say It Ain't So, Joe!: The True Story of Shoeless Joe.* New York: Carol Pub. Group, 1992.

Pietrusza, David. *Judge and Jury: The Life and Times of Judge Kenesaw Mountain Landis.* South Bend, Ind.: Diamond Communications, 1998.

AUDIO AND VISUAL MEDIA

Field of Dreams. Universal City, Calif.: Universal Home Video. Videocassette, 1998.

Eugene Debs' Release

"Debs Is Released, Prisoners Joining Crowd in Ovation"; "The Release of Debs"

Newspaper article, Editorial

By: *The New York Times*
Date: December 26, 1921
Source: "Debs Is Released, Prisoners Joining Crowd in Ovation." *The New York Times,* December 26, 1921, 1, 6. "The Release of Debs." *The New York Times,* December 26, 1921, 12.
About the Publication: Founded in 1850 as the *New-York Daily Times, The New York Times* was originally a relatively obscure local paper. However, by the early twentieth century, it had grown into a widely read news source. Its banner reading "All the News That's Fit to Print" is recognized throughout the world. ∎

Introduction

Five-time Socialist presidential candidate Eugene Debs was a leading labor advocate in America. He rose to national prominence in the early 1890s as president of the American Railway Union. The union participated in the Chicago Pullman Strike in 1894. The government, at the behest of the Pullman Company, went to court and obtained an injunction against Debs and the other union leaders, which was upheld at the Supreme Court level in *In re Debs* (1895). Debs remained active in Socialist politics, and received nine hundred thousand votes for president, or 6 percent, in 1912. With the start of World War I, many Socialists took a strong antiwar stance, and Debs attracted significant federal attention. In Canton, Ohio, on June 16, 1918, Debs gave an impassioned speech in which he praised three Ohio socialists who had been imprisoned nearby for opposing the draft. Debs also praised Kate Richards O'Hare, who had been jailed under the Espionage and Sedition Acts.

Debs was arrested for this speech and put on trial in September 1918 under the Espionage and Sedition Acts. Debs' main defense, other than contesting the claims of some prosecution witnesses, was to attempt to sway the jury by another impassioned speech. In it, Debs stated, "I have been accused of obstructing the war. I admit it. Gentleman, I abhor war." Eugene Debs appealed his conviction all the way to the Supreme Court, where it was upheld in March 1919. After that, Debs was imprisoned, first in West Virginia and then in Atlanta, where he remained until pardoned.

Eugene Debs' conviction served as a rallying point for many radicals. People wrote letters, mailed postcards, and sent telegrams in protest. Debs was nominated to be the Socialist Party's candidate for President in 1920, and from jail he attracted 919,000 votes, or 3.4 percent. Clearly, Debs was not going to fade into the background. Many pushed President Wilson to pardon Debs, and he flatly refused. Harding, though, was more open to the issue. He considered the opinions of his attorney general and cabinet and pardoned Debs.

Significance

Warren Harding's pardon of Debs was a blessing to Debs himself. It allowed him to return home to his family and enjoy a late Christmas dinner with his wife. Harding's pardon also, in many ways, allowed the nation to close the book on World War I. By the time of Debs' pardon, most Espionage Act prisoners had either been pardoned or their sentences had expired. Some refused to apply for pardons, but in December 1923, the Department of Justice decided to unconditionally pardon the remainder of the prisoners. By June 1924, all of the Espionage and Sedition Acts defendants had been released from prison. In pardoning Debs, Harding also demonstrated his tolerance for differing views, a quality Wilson lacked. Not everyone agreed with Harding, however, as the *New York Times* editorial shows here, and many conservative groups condemned the pardon. Many of these same groups found the original sentence far too lenient, with some even preferring firing squads for dissidents.

Harding's view was more popular in World War II than was Wilson's, as no prosecutions under the Espionage and Sedition Acts were undertaken. However, tolerance for a variety of viewpoints did not control racial prejudices. Minorities of German and Italian heritage were generally left alone. Exceptions to this were that German and Italian Americans who were not citizens were generally kept under curfew for a short amount of time. Japanese Americans, though, were discriminated against very heavily, with 110,000—two-thirds of whom were American citizens—relocated to internment camps.

Primary Source

"Debs Is Released, Prisoners Joining Crowd in Ovation"

> **SYNOPSIS:** This article chronicles Debs' behavior at his release as well as that of the crowd surrounding him. It also notes the numerous false sightings journalists had to endure while waiting for Debs to emerge.

"Debs Is Released, Prisoners Joining Crowd In Ovation"

Atlanta, Dec. 25.—Beaming his pleasure at release, with the ovation of the crowd outside and the shouts of approbation of a thousand prisoners in his ears, Eugene V. Debs, Socialist leader and several times a candidate for President, walked out of the United States penitentiary here at 11:30 o'clock this morning into the Christmas sunlight, free again after serving two and a half years of a ten-year sentence for violation of the Espionage law. His liberation was an act of executive clemency on the part of President Harding, who commuted his sentence, effective Christmas Day.

At 12:30 o'clock, the prisoner, his brother, Theodore Debs, and a party of others, including Miss Lucy Robbins of the American Federation of Labor and Miss Celia Rotter of the Debs Freedom Conference, who had awaited his release, boarded a train for Washington "to confer with Attorney General Daugherty, which was a condition of my release," Debs said.

"Then I am going to my dear little wife in Terre Haute as fast as the train will take me," he said.

Waves Hat to Prisoners

When the iron doors swung closed behind the Socialist chief and he walked down the steps and toward the outer gates between Warden J. E. Dyche and Deputy Warden L. J. Fletcher, a roar of cheers swept out from the prisoners. Debs raised his hat in one hand and his cane in the other and waved back at them. He continued to wave while they continued to cheer him until he reached the gates, where a battery of movie cameras was in action.

Debs smiled and chatted and acted like a schoolboy going home on vacation. At the prison gates he gripped hands fervently and kissed the women and men alike who had gathered to welcome him to liberty.

Debs was apparently in the best of health. He had jocularly remarked a few minutes before, when somebody told him he looked well kept, that "the

Warden didn't want my appearance to be a reflection on his institution."

At the gates Debs willingly posed for the cameramen. They also had been cranking away furiously as his friends rushed to meet him and received warm handclasps and joyful kisses from their leader. Mrs. H. I. Flanagan, her husband and two children, who live near the prison, were among the first to reach him. He kissed them and then kissed them again at the request of the movie men while cameras clicked.

Extra Fare to Russian Relief

Debs then entered an automobile with the Warden and was driven to the terminal station. There Debs declared the party would ride in a day coach to Washington and the Pullman fare would be devoted to the Russian Relief Fund.

At dawn this morning newspaper men and photographers renewed a vigil started two days ago, when Debs' release was expected hourly. Until the last the prison officials had maintained strict secrecy as to the hour of his release and this led to two amusing incidents, as others emerging from the prison were mistaken for Debs.

As the morning wore on it was whispered in the waiting group that Debs had secretly been taken out by a rear exit and was even then speeding home. His attorney, Sam Castleton, and newspaper men refused to credit this story. Suddenly the doors were swung open, a group descended to a waiting car and sped out of the grounds. A roar of cheering went up from the inmates.

"That's Debs," somebody shouted. Castleton, who had been waiting with others in his own car, threw in the clutch and gave chase. He finally caught the warden's flying automobile only to find that it was another released prisoner going away.

By the time this excitement subsided the doors opened to permit the departure of another group, who started toward the gate on foot.

"You can't fool me," yelled one of the watchers. "I've seen him a hundred times. That's Debs in front." Movie machines played on the party and the newspaper men rushed to the gate.

"No, I'm not Debs," explained the man in front when he met the crowd. "My name is W. M. Jones of 311 Pulliam Street. I have been accused of looking like Lincoln, but nobody ever told me before that I resembled Debs. I am a teacher in Sunday school at the First Christian Church. These gentlemen with me are members of various denominations of the

Well-known socialist Eugene Debs shown here in his prison garb shortly before his release from prison. © BETTMANN/CORBIS. REPRODUCED BY PERMISSION.

city, and we were holding religious services in the prison."

Debs Makes No Statement

A few minutes preceding the release of Debs, orders were issued by Warden Dyche permitting newspaper men to enter the prison and meet him, but he stated that they would not be allowed to get interviews.

Warden Dyche first conducted newspaper men through the big dining room of the institution, beautifully decorated in Christmas green and red, and the kitchen, where savory odors told of the Christmas dinner in the ovens. A painted Santa Claus and team of reindeers, nearly life-size, hung on the wall of the dining room. The warden said this was the work of a prisoner. Other Christmas works of art adorning the walls, he said, were done by inmates.

Debs, when seen by the newpaper men said he had no statement to make at the present time, either regarding his future or any further move for the release of all the so called "political" prisoners, though he expressed sympathy with the movement.

Later, at the terminal before boarding a train for Washington, he remarked that "I left 2,200 men back there in prison and they all should be given their liberty."

Just before leaving Atlanta, Debs told newspaper men that he had intended visiting the grave of Mrs. Mary L. McClendon, one of Georgia's most famous women and a leader in W. C. T. U. and equal suffrage movements. While he was in prison, he said, Mrs. McClendon had sent him a bouquet of roses, and he had intended to place a wreath of flowers on her grave. This he would be unable to do, he said, on account of the fact that he had to go to Washington to see Attorney General Daugherty, rather than to Terre Haute, as first planned.

Debs had been confined in the penitentiary here since June 13, 1919. He was convicted in the Federal Court at Cleveland, Ohio, Sept. 8, 1918, on a charge of violating the Espionage act. He was sentenced to serve a term of ten years and was first sent to the Federal prison at Moundville, W. Va., and later transferred to Atlanta.

Washington, Dec. 25.—Attorney General Daugherty said tonight he expected Eugene V. Debs, who was released from the Atlanta Penitentiary today, to call at the Department of Justice to discuss the commutation of his sentence by President Harding.

When Debs was in Washington recently it was decided, Mr. Daugherty said, that in the event Debs was released or his sentence commuted, it might be well for him to come to Washington for a final conference. There was no reason, however, the Attorney General added, that Debs should be formally obliged to come here, as was indicated by the released Socialist leader when he stepped from the prison in Atlanta.

Primary Source

"The Release of Debs"

SYNOPSIS: Published the day of his release, this editorial attacks Debs on all fronts. His supporters are criticized as shallow and unpatriotic.

Mr. Harding and his advisers haven't been able to find, at least they don't give, even a colorable reason for releasing Eugene V. Debs. He was convicted on evidence he admitted to be truthful, as he did the perfect fairness of all his trial for violating the Espionage Act by attempting to incite insubordination, disloyalty and mutiny in the army and navy, by obstructing and attempting to obstruct recruiting and enlistment, and by language meant to incite resistance to the United States and to aid its enemies in the war. He did all in his power to injure his country and to further the victory of its armed foes.

If he had been a mere ordinary murderer, the radicals and the swarm of sentimentalists wouldn't have lifted a finger for him. His crime was far more dangerous. He sought to murder the State. At once the loose lips of the sentimental squad overflowed with words. The Rev. Cream Cheeses, the weekly organs of nursery revolution, the miscellaneous small fry of weak heads and leaky lachrymal ducts, and the whole Socialist Party worked their hardest to deliver from the jail that he was sanctifying this martyr of "free speech." Mr. Wilson was obdurate. Mr. Harding is made of gentler stuff. Unrepentant, triumphant, Debs emerges, bright with his prison halo, to continue his beneficent labors as "a flaming revolutionist" and "a Bolshevik."

To him, in spite of his unrepented guilt, attaches the respect due to a brave and constant man. Why should justice be weak and this great criminal strong? The apologia from the White House is curious. Though admittedly guilty,

> he was by no means, however, as rabid and outspoken in his expressions as many others, and but for the prominence and far-reaching effect of his words very probably might not have received the sentence he did.

Debs' speech at the Ohio Socialist State Convention, June 16, 1918, was sufficiently rabid and outspoken, wasn't it? His position made him the most conspicuous and dangerous violator of the law. If he hadn't deserved the ten years' sentence, he wouldn't have got it—that is what the naïve passage quoted amounts to. With holy simplicity the apologia continues:

> He is an old man, not strong physically. He is a sum of much personal charm and impressive personality, which qualifications make him a dangerous man calculated to mislead the unthinking and affording excuse for those with criminal intent.

Debs is 66. Apparently only robust criminals should be imprisoned. The country has reason to be a little suspicious of ailing prisoners. Their health is sometimes miraculously restored when they get out. This man is dangerous. Therefore release him. This tiger is a man-killer. Let him loose. Singular apologia!

At last a few drops of milk are squeezed from the cocoanut:

> Under all circumstances it was believed that the ends of justice would be sufficiently met and it would be a gracious act to release this prisoner.

The ends of justice are met by defeating them. After two years and eight months of imprisonment in a jail where he seems to be regarded as a saint, prophet and prize exhibition, Debs comes out to begin again. His release is notice to all persons that the United States will not seriously punish the most perilous assailants of its safety and life. At the worst, they will only have to be immured for a little while. Then, if their friends make hubbub enough, a gracious act of mercy will open the doors of the prison.

Egg-nog was a more harmless form of "Dickens Christmas Book spirit" than this gift of freedom to noxious criminals. The majority of the American people will not approve this commutation. A shallow, howling, whining minority has had its way. Another case of Burke's grasshoppers and the cattle under the oak.

Further Resources

BOOKS

Ginger, Ray. *The Bending Cross: A Biography of Eugene Victor Debs.* New Brunswick, N.J.: Rutgers University Press, 1949.

Salvatore, Nick. *Eugene V. Debs: Citizen and Socialist.* Urbana, Ill.: University of Illinois Press, 1982.

Schneirov, Richard, Shelton Stromquist, and Nick Salvatore, eds. *The Pullman Strike and the Crisis of the 1890s: Essays on Labor and Politics.* Chicago: University of Illinois Press, 1999.

Young, Marguerite. *Harp Song for a Radical: the Life and Times of Eugene Victor Debs.* New York: Knopf, 1999.

PERIODICALS

Zinn, Howard. "Eugene V. Debs and the Idea of Socialism." *The Progressive* 63, 1, January 1, 1999, 16.

WEBSITES

Official Site of the Eugene V. Debs Foundation. Available online at http://www.eugenevdebs.com/pages/found.htm; website home page: http://www.eugenevdebs.com (accessed February 7, 2003).

Rare Books and Special Collections Quick Links: Databases and Lists. "Debs Collection." Indiana State University. Available online at http://odin.indstate.edu/level1.dir/cml/rbsc/rare2.html#Debs; website home page: http://odin.indstate.edu (accessed February 7, 2003).

Vetrovec, David. "Debs Collection: Index to Newspaper Clippings and Selected Articles." Indiana State University. Available online at http://odin.indstate.edu/level1.dir/cml/rbsc/debs/filmindx.html; website home page: http://www.odin.indstate.edu (accessed February 7, 2003).

Zwick, Jim, ed. "Political Cartoons and Cartoonists: Envy-A. Mitchell Palmer and Eugene Debs." *Detroit News,* rpt. *Current Opinion* 69 (July 1920). Available online at http://www.boondocksnet.com/gallery/cartoons/reds/reds200700a.html; website home page: http://www.boondocksnet.com (accessed February 7, 2003).

Bailey v. Drexel Furniture Company

Supreme Court decision

By: William Howard Taft

Date: May 15, 1922

Source: *Bailey v. Drexel Furniture Company* 259 U.S. 20 (1922). Cornell University Law School's Legal Information Institute. Available online at http://www2.law.cornell.edu/cgibin/foliocgi.exe/historic/query=%5Bgroup+f_children!3A%5D/doc/%7Bt13348%7D/hit_headings/words=4/pageitems=%7Bbody%7D; website home page: http://www.law.cornell.edu/ (accessed February 7, 2003).

About the Author: William Howard Taft (1857–1930) was a federal appellate judge, a governor of the Philippines, and secretary of war under President Theodore Roosevelt before winning the presidential election himself in 1908. He deeply loved judging and aspired to be chief justice of the U.S. Supreme Court. He achieved this goal in 1921 when he was selected to replace Edward White in that position. ∎

Introduction

Child labor has long been an item of concern in American history. Educators wished to end it in order to keep children in school, and reformers saw the long work hours and terrible conditions as being harmful to American youth. Around 1900, approximately 1.7 million children worked. Ten percent of girls aged ten to fifteen and 20 percent of all boys held jobs. Very young boys were "breaker boys" who separated coal from the slate, and their gloveless fingers bled as they worked. Many states did act to end abuses. By 1900, thirty-eight states had passed some sort of child labor law. However, these laws had many loopholes, and agriculture was frequently exempted.

The laws also allowed for long work days—up to ten hours—and allowed children to begin working at the age of ten. Many reformers saw the federal government as the ultimate solution. In 1916, Congress passed the *Keating-Owen Act,* which banned the shipment of goods produced using child labor in interstate commerce. Congress based the act on other acts banning the shipment of dangerous goods in interstate commerce. This law was tested in the Supreme Court in *Hammer v. Dagenhart* (1918). In this case, Roland Dagenhart, father of seven-year-old Reuben and fourteen-year-old John, both of whom worked at a cotton mill, challenged the bill, which prohibited Reuben from working and limited John to working eight hours per day. The Supreme Court said a ban on a dangerous item, such as adulterated food, was legal, but the products of child labor were not dangerous in and of themselves and so could not be banned. The Supreme Court examined congressional intent for the law, stating that this was a regulation of production, not interstate

A child labor law imposing a 10 percent tax on the net profits of any firm that employed child labor was overturned in the *Bailey v. Drexel Furniture Company* case. **THE LIBRARY OF CONGRESS.**

commerce, and so should not be allowed. The Court also held that the law invaded powers reserved to the state under the Tenth Amendment. Congress then passed another child labor law imposing a 10 percent tax on the net profits of any firm which employed child labor. It is this law that was tested in *Bailey.*

Significance

The Supreme Court held this law to be an abuse of the federal taxing power and an invasion of the powers of the states. The states, under the Tenth Amendment, are generally held to have those powers not held by federal government or the people, and Chief Justice Taft invoked that amendment to strike down this law. Taft also stated, correctly, that this tax was a penalty rather than a revenue enhancement, but Taft ignored the fact that punitive taxes had been upheld before. Thus, the efforts of those who wanted to ban child labor were stopped. During the conservative 1920s, efforts to ban child labor generally were unsuccessful. With the New Deal, however, these efforts began again. Congress banned child labor in the Fair Labor Standards Act (1938) by prohibiting the shipment in interstate commerce of any good produced at a factory where child labor had been used in the past thirty days. While this act went further than the one struck down in

Hammer, it was deemed constitutional by the Supreme Court in 1941. Controls on child labor have also been generally adopted by most states. However, the precedent set in Bailey represented a sizable hindrance to reformers for the rest of the 1920s and well into the 1930s.

Primary Source

Bailey v. Drexel Furniture Company [excerpt]

SYNOPSIS: Taft first states that the law in question required employers to follow a specific course of action or be subject to a penalty. Therefore, he says, the law is intended as a prohibition rather than a revenue enhancement. Moreover, he states that the Tenth Amendment gives states, rather than the federal government, power to make laws regulating child labor. Therefore, he rules the Child Labor Tax Law invalid. The case was argued on March 8, 1922, and was decided on May 15, 1922.

Mr. Chief Justice Taft delivered the opinion of the Court.

. . . The law is attacked on the ground that it is a regulation of the employment of child labor in the States—exclusively state function under the Federal Constitution and within the reservations of the Tenth

Amendment. It is defended on the ground that it is a mere excise tax levied by the Congress of the United States under its broad power of taxation conferred by §8, Article I, of the Federal Constitution. We must construe the law and interpret the intent and meaning of Congress from the language of the act. The words are to be given their ordinary meaning unless the context shows that they are differently used. Does this law impose a tax with only that incidental restraint and regulation which a tax must inevitably involve? Or does it regulate by the use of the so-called tax as a penalty? If a tax, it is clearly an excise. If it were an excise on a commodity or other thing of value we might not be permitted under previous decisions of this court to infer solely from its heavy burden that the act intends a prohibition instead of a tax. But this act is more. It provides a heavy exaction for a departure from a detailed and specified course of conduct in business. That course of business is that employers shall employ in mines and quarries, children of an age greater than sixteen years; in mills and factories, children of an age greater than fourteen years, and shall prevent children of less than sixteen years in mills and factories from working more than eight hours a day or six days in the week. If an employer departs from this prescribed course of business, he is to pay to the Government one-tenth of his entire net income in the business for a full year. The amount is not to be proportioned in any degree to the extent or frequency of the departures, but is to be paid by the employed in full measure whether he employs five hundred children for a year, or employs only one for a day. Moreover, if he does not know the child is within the named age limit, he is not to pay; that is to say, it is only where he knowingly departs from the prescribed course that payment is to be exacted. Scienter is associated with penalties not with taxes. The employer's factory is to be subject to inspection at any time not only by the taxing officers of the Treasury, the Department normally charged with the collection of taxes, but also by the Secretary of Labor and his subordinates whose normal function is the advancement and protection of the welfare of the workers. In the light of these features of the act, a court must be blind not to see that the so-called tax is imposed to stop employment of children within the age limits prescribed. Its prohibitory and regulatory effect and purpose are palpable. All others can see and understand this. How can we properly shut our minds to it?

It is the high duty and function of this court in cases regularly brought to its bar to decline to rec-

These children holding signs saying "We Want to Go to School" demonstrated the need to enact effective child labor laws. **THE LIBRARY OF CONGRESS.**

ognize or enforce seeming laws of Congress, dealing with subjects not entrusted to Congress but left or committed by the supreme law of the land to control of the States. We can not avoid the duty even though it require us to refuse to give effect to legislation designed to promote the highest good. The good sought in unconstitutional legislation is an insidious feature because it leads citizens and legislators of good purpose to promote it without thought of the serious breach it will make in the ark of our covenant or the harm which will come from breaking down recognized standards. In the maintenance of local self government, on the one hand, and the national power, on the other, our country has been able to endure and prosper for near a century and a half.

Out of a proper respect for the acts of a coordinate branch of the Government, this court has gone far to sustain taxing acts as such, even though there has been ground for suspecting from the weight of the tax it was intended to destroy its subject. But, in the act before us, the presumption of validity cannot prevail, because the proof of the contrary is found on the very face of its provisions. Grant the validity of this law, and all that Congress would need to do, hereafter, in seeking to take over to its control any one of the great number of subjects of public interest, jurisdiction of which the States have never parted with, and which are reserved to them by the Tenth Amendment, would be to enact a detailed measure of complete regulation of the subject and enforce it by a so-called tax upon departures from it. To give such magic to the word "tax" would be to break down all constitutional limitation of the powers of Congress and completely wipe out the sovereignty of the States.

The difference between a tax and a penalty is sometimes difficult to define and yet the consequences of the distinction in the required method of their collection often are important. Where the sovereign enacting the law has power to impose both tax and a penalty the difference between revenue production and mere regulation may be immaterial, but not so when one sovereign can impose a tax only, and the power of regulation rests in another. Taxes are occasionally imposed in the discretion of the legislature on proper subjects with the primary motive of obtaining revenue from them and with the incidental motive of discouraging them by making their continuance onerous. They do not lose their character as taxes because of the incidental motive. But there comes a time in the extension of the penalizing features of the so-called tax when it loses its character as such and becomes a mere penalty with the characteristics of regulation and punishment. Such is the case in the law before us. Although Congress does not invalidate the contract of employment or expressly declare that the employment within the mentioned ages is illegal, it does exhibit its intent practically to achieve the latter result by adopting the criteria of wrongdoing and imposing its principal consequence on those who transgress its standard. The case before us cannot be distinguished from that of *Hammer v. Dagenhart* . . .

In the case at the bar, Congress in the name of a tax which on the face of the act is a penalty seeks to do the same thing, and the effort must be equally futile.

The analogy of the Dagenhart Case is clear. The congressional power over interstate commerce is, within its proper scope, just as complete and unlimited as the congressional power to tax, and the legislative motive in its exercise is just as free from judicial suspicion and inquiry. Yet when Congress threatened to stop interstate commerce in ordinary and necessary commodities, unobjectionable

as subjects of transportation, and to deny the same to the people of a State in order to coerce them into compliance with Congress's regulation of State concerns, the court said this was not in fact regulation of interstate commerce, but rather that of State concerns and was valid. So here the so-called tax is a penalty to coerce people of a State to act as Congress wishes them to act in respect of a matter completely the business of the State government under the Federal Constitution . . .

For the reasons given, we must hold the Child Labor Tax Law invalid and the judgment of the District Court is

Affirmed.

Mr. Justice Clarke dissents.

Further Resources

BOOKS

Burton, David Henry. *Taft, Holmes, and the 1920s Court: An Appraisal.* Madison, N.J.: Fairleigh Dickinson University Press, 1998.

Forastieri, Valenti. *Children at Work: Health and Safety Risks.* Geneva: International Labour Office, 1997.

Hobbs, Sandy, Jim McKechnie, and Michael Lavalette. *Child Labor: A World History Companion.* Santa Barbara, Calif.: ABC-CLIO, 1999.

New York Labor Legacy Project. *From Forge to Fast Food: a History of Child Labor in New York State.* Troy, N.Y.: Council for Citizenship Education, Russell Sage College, 1995.

Trattner, Walter I. *Crusade for the Children: A History of the National Child Labor Committee and Child Labor Reform in America.* Chicago: Quadrangle Books, 1970.

PERIODICALS

Galloway, Russell W. "The Taft Court (1921–29)." *Santa Clara Law Review* 25, 1, Winter 1985, 1–64.

The New York Times. "Child Labor 1915–1919." Sanford, N.C.: Microfilming Corp. of America, 1981.

"Criminal Justice in Cleveland"

Study

By: Felix Frankfurter and Roscoe Pound

Date: 1922

Source: Frankfurter, Felix, and Roscoe Pound. "Criminal Justice In Cleveland." Excerpt reprinted in Hall, Kermit L., William M. Wiecek, and Paul Finkelman. *American Legal History: Cases and Materials,* 2nd ed. New York: Oxford University Press, 1996, 443–445.

About the Authors: Felix Frankfurter (1882–1965), before his Supreme Court appointment in 1939, was a Harvard law professor who advised President Franklin Roosevelt (served 1933–1945). His strong nationalism appears in many of the opinions he wrote while on the bench.

Roscoe Pound (1870–1964) was a professor at Harvard from 1910 to 1936 and dean of their Law School from 1916 to 1936. He was a progressive in the 1910s and 1920s. ∎

Introduction

The annals of early America are rife with accounts of crimes and punishments. Crime was a local concern in the early years of the United States, and punishment was more on people's minds than was prevention. With the rise of progressivism, a political movement active in the early 1900s, this attitude changed. This change took place not just in America, however. The writings of Emile Durkheim in France sought to explain what he saw as the runaway crime rate, and he put the blame on the rapid urbanization of the population. The whole science of sociology had, as one of its main goals, the understanding of society. Progressives were particularly interested in removing political corruption and bossism (a political system in which the control centered around one powerful figure), which they saw as hampering government and police work. However, some of what the progressives saw as corruption was actually political bosses providing benefits to their constituents before the existence of welfare and government programs. Progressives wanted to improve society through a variety of mechanisms and hence were quite interested in preventing crime. One of the main aims of progressivism was to fully understand society and its flaws, and progressives believed that when a society was fully understood, its problems could be solved. Going hand-in-hand with this understanding was a belief in college-trained experts, who progressives thought were best able to comprehend and understand the issues. This desire for understanding is what led to a study of crime in Cleveland.

Significance

This study clashes with the attitude of those who argue that the present crime rate is the highest rate ever, and that things were good in the past and are bad now. Crime has been a societal concern for decades. Modern citizens complain that criminals "get away with murder" and are not punished for their sins, but the fact that their complaints echo those from some eighty years earlier demonstrates the enduring nature of this concern. This study also demonstrates that progressives relied on progressive solutions. The study calls for understanding the causes of crime and for relying on experts, and, as noted before, this dependence on experts is a hallmark of the progressive era. A third point to note is how the study identifies "un-Americanism" as the cause of this crime, vilifying immigrants as the source of crime, even though no statistics are presented for this racist attitude. This echoes the comments of some later

Women employees training to defend Cleveland Trust Company's main vault in the 1920s. HULTON/ARCHIVE. REPRODUCED BY PERMISSION.

twentieth-century writers like conservative columnist Pat Buchanan. It is interesting to note that the authors use statistics to bolster their case when they want to but make sweeping conclusions without statistical support ("lack of homogeneity" causing crime) when that is desirous. Another note of interest is how the progressives, despite their desire to understand crime, do not consider the environment in which criminals were raised when searching for motivation or reasons for turning to lives of crime. Such questions would not be raised until several decades after this report was written. Nor do these progressives analyze why the number of crimes dropped between 1917 and 1921, even though the study does note the improvement. The study identifies the police force as something that needs to be changed—in a progressive way—with the use of experts and an increased use of "technique." Besides demonstrating that societies and groups view crime through the lens of their own perspectives, the progressives' study of crime in Cleveland illuminates the fact that crime is by no means a new concern.

Primary Source

"Criminal Justice in Cleveland" [excerpt]

SYNOPSIS: The Cleveland study was the first of its kind in two respects. First, its intent was to be an

Roscoe Pound was one of the legal scholars hired to write about the criminal justice system in Cleveland, illuminating the Progressive belief in the causes of crime. **THE LIBRARY OF CONGRESS.**

objective scientific study of the administration of justice, whereas previous studies were largely partisan efforts. It also studied an entire local justice system rather than isolating specific aspects for investigation. This study was the model for many commissions and studies that followed.

A cursory examination of the problem of crime in Cleveland produces some startling facts. For the year 1920 Cleveland, with approximately 800,000 population, had six times as many murders as London, with 8,000,000 population. For every robbery or assault with intent to rob committed during this same period in London there were 17 such crimes committed in Cleveland. Cleveland had as many murders during the first three months of the present year as London had during all of 1920. . . . There are more robberies and assaults to rob in Cleveland every year than in all England, Scotland, and Wales put together. In 1919 there were 2,327 automobiles stolen in Cleveland; in London there were 290; in Liverpool, 10.

Comparisons of this kind between Cleveland, on the one hand, and European cities, on the other, could be almost indefinitely extended. . . . And yet, compared with other American cities, Cleveland's

record does not show to any special disadvantage. For the first quarter of 1921 there were four more murders committed in Detroit than in Cleveland, and nearly twice as many automobiles stolen in Detroit. During the first three months of 1921 St. Louis had 481 robberies, while Cleveland had 272; for the same period complaints of burglary and house-breaking in St. Louis numbered 1,106, as compared to 565 such complaints in Cleveland. For this same period the number of murders in Buffalo, a much smaller city, equaled those in Cleveland, and burglaries, housebreakings, and larcenies were almost as numerous. In 1919 Chicago, more than three times the size of Cleveland, had 293 murders and manslaughters, compared with Cleveland's 55, so that the ratio was easily two to one in Cleveland's favor; the 1920 statistics of the two cities show an even better proportion for Cleveland.

On the other side of the scale, for the first three months of the present year Cleveland had more than twice the number of robberies and assaults to rob that Detroit had, and a similar large proportion of burglaries and housebreakings. During this period there were 296 automobiles stolen in St. Louis, as against 446 in Cleveland. Cleveland is approximately three times larger than Toledo, and yet in 1920 Cleveland had 87 murders, while Toledo had only 11.

Another basis of comparison is between the crime statistics of Cleveland in 1921 and Cleveland in former years. For the first six months of 1921, the period in which this survey was carried on, the number of murders committed in Cleveland was 15. For the same period in 1920 the number of murders was 30. . . . The following figures show the average number of complaints for the first quarter of each of the four years from 1917 to 1920 inclusive, classified according to four outstanding crimes:

Robbery and assault to rob 283

Burglary and larceny 418

Murder 17

Automobiles driven away 361

The following figures give the number of complaints of the same crimes for the first quarter of 1921:

Robbery and assault to rob 272

Burglary and larceny 265

Murder 6

Automobiles driven away 446

Obviously, there has been some improvement within the last four years.

All in all, crime conditions are no more vicious in Cleveland than they are in other American cities. . . . In this respect, therefore, Cleveland's problem is the problem of America, for the same causes that are maintaining the high crime rate of Chicago, St. Louis, New York, Detroit, and San Francisco are operating here.

What are these causes? Here we can only hint at some of the deeper social and economic causes. The lack of homogeneity in our population and its increasing instability, the absence of settled habits and traditions of order, the breakdown of the administration of criminal law in the United States, and the many avenues by which offenders can escape punishment, our easy habit of passing laws which do not represent community standards or desires, our lack of cohesive industrial organization, our distrust of experts in the management of governmental enterprises—all these are undoubtedly contributing factors.

But there is another factor, still more potent: police machinery in the United States has not kept pace with modern demands. It has developed no effective technique to master the burden which modern social and industrial conditions impose. Clinging to old traditions, bound by old practices which business and industry long ago discarded, employing a personnel poorly adapted to its purposes, it grinds away on its perfunctory task without self-criticism, without imagination, and with little initiative.

Further Resources

BOOKS

Barton, Josef J. *Peasants and Strangers: Italians, Rumanians, and Slovaks in an American City, 1890–1950.* Cambridge, Mass.: Harvard University Press, 1975.

Campbell, Thomas F., and Edward M. Miggins, eds. *The Birth of Modern Cleveland, 1865–1930.* Cleveland: Western Reserve Historical Society, 1988.

Hartsfield, Larry K. *The American Response to Professional Crime, 1870–1917.* Westport, Conn.: Greenwood Press, 1985.

Parrish, Michael E. *Felix Frankfurter and His Times.* New York: Free Press, 1982.

Porter, Philip Wiley. *Cleveland: Confused City on a Seesaw.* Columbus: Ohio State University Press, 1976.

Potter, Claire Bond. *War on Crime: Bandits, G-men, and the Politics of Mass Culture.* New Brunswick, N.J.: Rutgers University Press, 1998.

Two Perspectives on the Scopes Trial

Tennessee v. John T. Scopes

Testimony

By: Clarence Darrow, William Jennings Bryan

Date: July 9, 1925

Source: Darrow, Clarence, William Jennings Bryan. *The State of Tennessee v. John T. Scopes 1925.* Reprinted in Marcus, Robert, and Anthony Marcus, ed. *On Trial Vol. 2, American History Through Court Proceedings and Hearings.* St. James, N.Y.: Brandywine Press, 1998, 107–108, 111–115, 117–118.

About the Authors: Clarence Darrow (1857–1938), as a trial defense lawyer, was famous for winning high-profile cases with a combination of intellect and eloquence. He was among the first to save a client from execution by using an insanity plea.

William Jennings Bryan (1860–1925) was the unsuccessful Democratic nominee for president in 1896, 1900, and 1908. A famously effective speaker, he was a leading figure in the Populist and Progressive reform movements. He served as secretary of state from 1913–1915. In his last decade, Bryan was best known for his support of conservative Christian causes.

"'The Monkey Trial': A Reporter's Account"

Editorial

By: H.L. Mencken

Date: 1925

Source: Mencken, H.L. "The Monkey Trial: A Reporter's Account." Available online at http://www.law.umkc.edu /faculty/projects/ftrials/scopes/menk.htm; website home page: http://www.law.umkc.edu (accessed February 10, 2003).

About the Authors: Reporter H.L. Mencken (1880–1956) wrote for the *Baltimore Sun* throughout the 1920s and 1930s. His popularity waned during the Depression, but he enjoyed renewed success with the personal narratives written before his death. ■

Introduction

Charles Darwin published *On the Origin of Species by Means of Natural Selection* in 1859. His basic idea was that all plants and animals had evolved over a long period of time from earlier and simpler forms of life, a process known as organic evolution. It was not until 1871, with *The Descent of Man,* that he argued man was a "co-descendant" with other mammals from a common ancestor. Though Catholicism was somewhat tolerant of the idea, most Protestant faiths disagreed fervently with it. Protestant fundamentalist sects argued for an outright ban on Darwin and a suppression of his book, as they argued for a literal interpretation of the Bible. The Protestant rejection of Darwin was especially strong in the American South. Many liberal protestants had accepted, somewhat, the ideas of Darwin, but fundamentalists had not. Fundamentalism was strongest in the small towns and countryside of the South, and these areas rejected modernization and Darwinism hand in hand. In 1925, Tennessee passed the Butler Act, making illegal the teaching, in a public school, of "any theory that denies the story of the Divine Creation of man as taught in the Bible, and to teach instead that man has descended from a lower order of animals." Several people in Dayton, Tennessee, wanted to generate publicity for the town to encourage visitors, as the economy had been suffering. They recruited John T. Scopes, a math teacher at the high school, to challenge the law. The case gained national attention, and people flocked to Dayton. William Jennings Bryan, a believer in the literal meaning of the Bible, joined the prosecution team, while Clarence Darrow, the period's most famous criminal defense lawyer, volunteered for the defense. H.L. Mencken, a famous journalist, went to Dayton and recorded his acerbic commentary. Darrow wanted to prove the "truth" of Darwinism by calling upon scientists to testify, but the court ruled this issue irrelevant, as the violation of the law was the only pertinent issue. Darrow then decided to call Bryan as an expert on the Bible, and Bryan accepted the challenge. Part of the bargain was that Bryan was going to have a chance to cross-examine Darrow on scientific issues after Darrow was done examining Bryan on the Bible. The judge did not allow the jury to witness the exchange.

Significance

What began as a quiet, normal exchange between lawyer and witness ended up as a feud. Darrow relentlessly hounded Bryan and got him to admit what he wanted: The Bible should not always be interpreted literally. The judge—a believer in Creationism—cut Bryan's testimony short and demanded it be stricken from the record, and he hurried the case to the jury. Bryan never had the chance to cross-examine Darrow. Scopes was convicted and fined one hundred dollars, which he never had to pay. Scopes's fine was overturned by a higher court on the technical grounds that a jury could not impose a fine of over fifty dollars. This case accomplished the goal of those who put Scopes "up to it," as it brought many people to Dayton and generated revenue and attention for the town. Technically, the law was upheld, but the trial brought ridicule to the fundamentalists and basically halted the anti-Darwinian forces. No additional states passed anti-Darwin laws in the 1920s. Many southern states, and some northern

ones, however, adopted informal policies against evolution, buying textbooks which slighted evolution and hiring teachers who ignored that subject. State curriculum committees followed this trend, choosing the term "change over time" instead of "evolution" and neglecting the topic on their state exams. This trend persisted throughout the century.

Bryan collapsed soon after this trial and died five days later. Darrow went on successfully to argue other famous cases, including the Scottsboro Boys case.

Primary Source

Tennessee v. John T. Scopes [excerpt]

SYNOPSIS: John T. Scopes was the only defendant Clarence Darrow ever represented free of charge. Approaching the age of seventy when he set foot in Dayton, Darrow had an intolerance of intolerance that only intensified with age. William Jennings Bryan was no match for Darrow's scrutiny; many people consider Bryan's testimony as the weapon that destroyed him both as a legend and a man.

The Court: Mr. Bryan, you are not objecting to going on the stand?

Mr. Bryan: Not at all.

The Court: Do you want Mr. Bryan sworn?

Mr. Darrow: No.

Mr. Bryan: I can make affirmation; I can say, "So help me God, I will tell the truth."

Mr. Darrow: No, I take it you will tell the truth, Mr. Bryan.

Q: You have given considerable study to the Bible, haven't you, Mr. Bryan?

A: Yes, sir, I have tried to.

Q: But you have written and published articles almost weekly, and sometimes have made interpretations of various things.

A: I would not say interpretations, Mr. Darrow, but comments on the lesson.

Q: If you comment to any extent, these comments have been interpretations?

A: I presume that any discussion might be to some extent interpretations, but they have not been primarily intended as interpretations.

Q: Then you have made a general study of it?

A: Yes, I have; I have studied the Bible for about fifty years, or some time more than that, but, of course, I have studied it more as I have become older than when I was but a boy.

Q: Do you claim that everything in the Bible should be literally interpreted?

A: I believe everything in the Bible should be accepted as it is given there; some of the Bible is given illustratively. For instance: "Ye are the salt of the earth." I would not insist that man was actually salt, or that he had flesh of salt, but it is used in the sense of salt as saving God's people.

Q: But when you read that Jonah swallowed the whale—or that the whale swallowed Jonah—excuse me please—how do you literally interpret that?

A: When I read that a big fish swallowed Jonah—it does not say whale.

Q: Doesn't it? Are you sure?

A: That is my recollection of it. A big fish, and I believe it; and I believe in a God who can make a whale and can make a man and make both do what He pleases.

Q: Mr. Bryan, doesn't the New Testament say whale?

A: I am not sure. My impression is that it says fish; but it does not make so much difference; I merely called your attention to where it says fish—it does not say whale.

Q: But in the New Testament it says whale, doesn't it?

A: That may be true; I cannot remember in my own mind what I read about it.

Q: Now, you say, the big fish swallowed Jonah, and he there remained how long? Three days? And then he spewed him upon the land. You believe that the big fish was made to swallow Jonah?

A: I am not prepared to say that; the Bible merely says it was done.

Q: You don't know whether it was the ordinary run of fish, or made for that purpose?

A: You may guess; you evolutionists guess.

Q: But when we do guess, we have a sense to guess right.

A: But do not do it often.

Q: You are not prepared to say whether that fish was made especially to swallow a man or not?

A: The Bible doesn't say, so I am not prepared to say.

Q: You don't know whether that was fixed up specially for the purpose?

A: No, the Bible doesn't say.

Q: But you do believe He made them—that He made such a fish and that it was big enough to swallow Jonah?

A: Yes, sir. Let me add: one miracle is just as easy to believe as another.

Q: It is for me.

A: It is for me.

Q: Just as hard?

A: It is hard to believe for you, but easy for me. A miracle is a thing performed beyond what man can perform. When you get beyond what man can do, you get within the realm of miracles; and it is just as easy to believe the miracle of Jonah as any other miracle in the Bible.

Q: Perfectly easy to believe that Jonah swallowed the whale?

A: If the Bible said so; the Bible doesn't make as extreme statements as evolutionists do.

Mr. Darrow: That may be a question, Mr. Bryan, about some of those you have known.

A: The only thing is, you have a definition of fact that includes imagination.

Q: And you have a definition that excludes everything but imagination.

Gen. Stewart [a colleague of Bryan]: I object to that as argumentative.

The Witness: You—

Mr. Darrow: The witness must not argue with me, either.

Q: Do you consider the story of Jonah and the whale a miracle?

A: I think it is. . . .

Q: You believe that all the living things that were not contained in Noah's ark were destroyed.

A: I think the fish may have lived.

Q: Outside of the fish?

A: I cannot say.

Q: You cannot say?

A: No, I accept that just as it is; I have no proof to the contrary.

Q: I am asking you whether you believe?

A: I do.

Q: That all living things outside of the fish were destroyed?

A: What I say about the fish is merely a matter of humor.

Q: I understand.

The Witness: Due to the fact a man wrote up here the other day to ask whether all the fish were destroyed, and the gentleman who received the letter told him the fish may have lived.

Q: I am referring to the fish, too.

A: I accept that as the Bible gives it and I have never found any reason for denying, disputing, or rejecting it.

Q: Let us make it definite, 2,348 years?

A: I didn't say that. That is the time given there [indicating the King James edition of the Bible] but I don't pretend to say that is exact.

Q: You never figured it out, these generations, yourself?

A: No, sir; not myself.

Q: But the Bible you have offered in evidence says, 2,340 something, so that 4,200 years ago there was not a living thing on the earth, excepting the people on the ark and the animals on the ark and the fishes?

A: There have been living things before that.

Q: I mean at that time.

A: After that.

Q: Don't you know there are any number of civilizations that are traced back to more than 5,000 years?

A: I know we have people who trace things back according to the number of ciphers they have. But I am not satisfied they are accurate.

Q: You are not satisfied there is any civilization that can be traced back 5,000 years?

A: I would not want to say there is because I have no evidence of it.

Q: Would you say there is not?

A: Well, so far as I know, but when the scientists differ from 24,000,000 to 306,000,000 in their opinion as to how long ago life came here. I want them to be nearer, to come nearer together, before they demand of me to give up my belief in the Bible.

Q: Do you say that you do not believe that there were any civilizations on this earth that reach back beyond 5,000 years?

A: I am not satisfied by any evidence that I have seen.

Q: I didn't ask you what you are satisfied with. I asked you if you believe it?

The Witness: Will you let me answer it?

The Court: Go right on.

The Witness: I am satisfied by no evidence that I have found that would justify me in accepting the opinions of these men against what I believe to be the inspired Word of God.

Q: And you believe every nation, every organization of men, every animal, in the world outside of the fishes—

The Witness: The fish, I want you to understand, is merely a matter of humor. . . .

Q: You believe that every civilization on the earth and every living thing, except possibly the fishes, that came out of the ark were wiped out by the flood?

A: At that time.

Q: At that time. And then whatever human beings, including all the tribes, that inhabited the world, and have inhabited the world, and who run their pedigree straight back, and all the animals, have come onto the earth since the flood?

A: Yes.

Q: Within 4,200 years. Do you know a scientific man on the face of the earth that believes any such thing?

A: I cannot say, but I know some scientific men who dispute entirely the antiquity of man as testified to by other scientific men.

Q: Oh, that does not answer the question. Do you know of a single scientific man on the face of the earth that believes any such thing as you stated, about the antiquity of man?

A: I don't think I have ever asked one the direct question.

Q: Quite important, isn't it?

A: If I had nothing else to do except speculate on what our remote ancestors were and what our remote descendants have been, but I have been more interested in Christians going on right now to make it much more important than speculation on either the past or the future.

Q: You have never had any interest in the age of the various races and people and civilization and animals that exist upon the earth today, is that right?

A: I have never felt a great deal of interest in the effort that has been made to dispute the Bible by the speculations of men, or the investigations of men.

Q: Are you the only human being on earth who knows what the Bible means?

Gen. Stewart: I object.

The Court: Sustained.

Mr. Darrow: You do know that there are thousands of people who profess to be Christians who believe the earth is much more ancient and that the human race is much more ancient?

A: I think there may be.

Q: And you never have investigated to find out how long man has been on the earth?

A: I have never found it necessary—

Q: For any reason, whatever it is?

A: To examine every speculation; but if I had done it I never would have done anything else.

Q: I ask for a direct answer.

A: I do not expect to find out all those things, and I do not expect to find out about races.

Q: I didn't ask you that. Now, I ask you if you know if it was interesting enough or important enough for you to try to find out about how old these ancient civilizations were?

A: No; I have not made a study of it.

Q: Don't you know that the ancient civilizations of China are 6,000 or 7,000 years old, at the very least?

A: No; but they would not run back beyond the creation, according to the Bible, 6,000 years.

Q: You don't know how old they are, is that right?

A: I don't know how old they are, but probably you do. I think you would give preference to anybody who opposed the Bible, and I give the preference to the Bible.

Q: I see. Well, you are welcome to your opinion. Have you any idea how old the Egyptian civilization is?

A: No.

Q: Do you know of any record in the world, outside of the story of the Bible, which conforms to any statement that it is 4,200 years ago or thereabouts that all life was wiped off the face of the earth?

A: I think they have found records.

Q: Do you know of any?

A: Records reciting the flood but I am not an authority on the subject of any records, that describe that a flood existed 4,200 years ago, or about that time, which wiped all life off the earth.

A: The recollection of what I have read on that subject is not distinct enough to say whether the records attempted to fix a time, but I have seen in the discoveries of archaeologists where they have found records that described the flood.

Q: Mr. Bryan, don't you know that there are many old religions that describe the flood?

A: No, I don't know.

Q: You know there are others besides the Jewish?

A: I don't know whether these are the record of any other religion or refer to this flood.

Q: Don't you ever examine religion so far to know that?

A: Outside of the Bible?

Q: Yes.

A: No; I have not examined to know that, generally.

Q: You have never examined any other religions?

A: Yes, sir.

Q: have you ever read anything about the origins of religions?

A: Not a great deal.

Q: You have never examined any other religions?

A: Yes, sir.

Q: And you don't know whether any other religion ever gave a similar account of the destruction of the earth by the flood?

A: The Christian religion has satisfied me, and I have never felt it necessary to look up some competing religions. . . .

Q: Would you say that the earth was only 4,000 years old?

A: Oh, no; I think it is much older than that.

Q: How much?

A: I couldn't say.

Q: Do you say whether the Bible itself says it is older than that?

A: I don't think the Bible says itself whether it is older or not.

Q: Do you think the earth was made in six days?

A: Not six days of twenty-four hours?

Q: Doesn't it say so?

A: No, sir. . . .

Mr. Bryan: [Darrow's] purpose is to cast ridicule on everybody who believes in the Bible, and I am perfectly willing that the world shall know that these gentlemen have no other purpose than ridiculing every Christian who believes in the Bible.

Mr. Darrow: We have the purpose of preventing bigots and ignoramuses from controlling the education of the United States and you know it, and that is all.

Mr. Bryan: I am glad to bring out the statement. I want the world to know that this evidence is not for the view Mr. Darrow and his associates have filed affidavits here stating, the purpose of which, as I understand it, is to show that the Bible story is not true.

Mr. Malone: Mr. Bryan seems anxious to get some evidence in the record that would tend to show that those affidavits are not true.

Mr. Bryan: I am not trying to get anything into the record. I am simply trying to protect the Word of God against the greatest atheist or agnostic in the United States. I want the papers to know I am not afraid to get on the stand in front of him and let him do his worst. . . .

Mr. Darrow: I wish I could get a picture of these clackers. . . .

Q: Do you believe the story of the temptation of Eve by the serpent?

A: I do.

Q: . . . thenceforth and forever should suffer the pains of childbirth in the reproduction of the earth?

A: I believe what it says, and I believe the fact as fully—

Q: That is what it says, doesn't it?

A: Yes.

Q: And for that reason, every woman born of woman, who has to carry on the race, the reason they have childbirth pains is because Eve tempted Adam in the Garden of Eden?

A: I will believe just what the Bible says. I ask to put that in the language of the Bible, for I prefer that to your language. Read the Bible and I will answer.

Q: All right, I will do that.

[*Darrow reads from Genesis 3:15–16.*]

A: I accept it as it is.

Q: And you believe that came about because Eve tempted Adam to eat the fruit?

A: Just as it says.

Q: And you believe that is the reason that God made the serpent to go on his belly after he tempted Eve?

A: I believe the Bible as it is, and I do not permit you to put your language in the place of the language of the Almighty. You read that Bible and ask me questions, and I will answer them. I will not answer your questions in your language.

Q: I will read it to you from the Bible: "And the Lord God said unto the serpent, Because thou hast done this, thou art cursed above all cattle, and above every beast of the field; upon thy belly shalt thou go and dust shalt thou eat all the days of thy life." Do you think that is why the serpent is compelled to crawl upon its belly?

A: I believe that.

Q: Have you any idea how the snake went before that time?

A: No, sir.

Q: Do you know whether he walked on his tail or not?

A: No, sir. I have no way to know.

Q: Now, you refer to the cloud that was put in the heaven after the flood, the rainbow. Do you believe in that?

A: Read it.

Q: All right, I will read it for you.

Mr. Bryan: Your Honor, I think I can shorten this testimony. The only purpose Mr. Darrow has is to slur at the Bible, but I will answer his question. I will answer it all at once, and I have no objection in the world, I want the world to know that this man, who does not believe in a God, is trying to use a court in Tennessee—

Mr. Darrow: I object to that.

Mr. Bryan: [continuing] to slur at it and while it will require time I am

Mr. Darrow: I object to your statement. I am examining you on your fool ideas that no intelligent Christian on earth believes.

The Court: Court is adjourned.

Primary Source

"'The Monkey Trial': A Reporter's Account"

SYNOPSIS: H.L. Mencken was known for his sarcastic wit, and many people found his commentaries offensive. In writing about the Scopes Trial, he suggested that not only were the southern townspeople descended from monkeys, but that they were actual monkeys themselves.

July 9

On the eve of the great contest Dayton is full of sickening surges and tremors of doubt. Five or six weeks ago, when the infidel Scopes was first laid by the heels, there was no uncertainty in all this smiling valley. The town boomers leaped to the assault as one man. Here was an unexampled, almost a miraculous chance to get Dayton upon the front pages, to make it talked about, to put it upon the map. But how now?

Today, with the curtain barely rung up and the worst buffooneries to come, it is obvious to even town boomers that getting upon the map, like patriotism, is not enough. The getting there must be managed discreetly, adroitly, with careful regard to psychological niceties. The boomers of Dayton, alas, had no skill at such things, and the experts they called in were all quacks. The result now turns the communal liver to water. Two months ago the town was obscure and happy. Today it is a universal joke.

I have been attending the permanent town meeting that goes on in Robinson's drug store, trying to find out what the town optimists have saved from the wreck. All I can find is a sort of mystical confidence that God will somehow come to the rescue to reward His old and faithful partisans as they deserve—that good will flow eventually out of what now seems to be heavily evil. More specifically, it is believed that settlers will be attracted to the town as to some refuge from the atheism of the great urban Sodoms and Gomorrah.

But will these refugees bring any money with them? Will they buy lots and build houses? Will they light the fires of the cold and silent blast furnace down the railroad tracks? On these points, I regret to report, optimism has to call in theology to aid it. Prayer can accomplish a lot. It can cure diabetes, find lost pocketbooks and retain husbands from beating their wives. But is prayer made any more officious by giving a circus first? Coming to this thought, Dayton begins to sweat.

H.L. Mencken wrote an account of the Scopes "Monkey Trial" in which he implies that humans not only share a common ancestor with primates but are themselves monkeys. © BETTMANN/CORBIS. REPRODUCED BY PERMISSION.

The town, I confess, greatly surprised me. I expected to find a squalid Southern village, with darkies snoozing on the horse blocks, pigs rooting under the houses and the inhabitants full of hookworm and malaria. What I found was a country town of charm and even beauty . . .

July 10 (the first day)

The town boomers have banqueted Darrow as well as Bryan, but there is no mistaking which of the two has the crowd, which means the venire of tried and true men. Bryan has been oozing around the country since his first day here, addressing this organization and that, presenting the indubitable Word of God in his caressing, ingratiating way, and so making unanimity doubly unanimous. From the defense yesterday came hints that he was making hay before the sun had legally begun to shine—even that it was a sort of contempt of court. But no Daytonian believes anything of the sort. What Bryan says doesn't seem to these congenial Baptists and Methodists to be argument; it seems to be a mere graceful statement to the obvious . . .

Victory or Defeat?

While some viewed the conviction of Scopes in 1925 as a sign of worse things to come for those who accepted evolution, in reality it was the last act in the decades-long struggle that had been taking place within Protestantism between modernists and Fundamentalists. Liberal theologians had been trying to demonstrate an affinity between religion and progress. To do this, religion in general and the Bible in particular needed to be subjected to the same critical standards as any other field of study. Such an analysis and questioning of traditional beliefs and texts was regarded as impious by religious conservatives. The most aggressive of these, the Fundamentalists, were in particular threatened by the teaching of evolution, which was believed to discredit the Bible's teachings on the creation of the world.

This struggle within Protestantism was already unfortunate when it was a matter of questioning the orthodoxy of professors and pastors. When this controversy was displayed before the world during the *Scopes* trial, the real loser was religion itself, whether it was of the liberal or conservative variety. The noted American religious historian Robert Handy stated, "The prestige of Protestantism was further lessened by the bitter controversy between fundamentalists and modernists. . . . A law prohibiting the teaching of evolution was upheld, but the fundamentalist movement was discredited and soon receded. Neither side really won. . . . With its bitter polemics and personal attacks, the struggle further harmed organized religion in a time of disillusionment and spiritual hunger."

July 11

The selection of a jury to try Scopes, which went on all yesterday afternoon in the atmosphere of a blast furnace, showed to what extreme lengths the salvation of the local primates has been pushed. It was obvious after a few rounds that the jury would be unanimously hot for Genesis. The most that Mr. Darrow could hope for was to sneak in a few bold enough to declare publicly that they would have to hear the evidence against Scopes before condemning him. The slightest sign of anything further brought forth a peremptory challenge from the State. Once a man was challenged without examination for simply admitting that he did not belong formally to any church. Another time a panel man who confessed that he was prejudiced against evolution got a hearty round of applause from the crowd . . .

In brief this is a strictly Christian community, and such is its notion of fairness, justice and due process of law. Try to picture a town made up wholly of Dr. Crabbes and Dr. Kellys, and you will have a reasonably accurate image of it. Its people are simply unable to imagine a man who rejects the literal authority of the Bible. The most they can conjure up, straining until they are red in the face, is a man who is in error about the meaning of this or that text. Thus one accused of heresy among them is like one accused of boiling his grandmother to make soap in Maryland . . .

July 13 (the second day)

It would be hard to imagine a more moral town than Dayton. If it has any bootleggers, no visitor has heard of them. Ten minutes after I arrived a leading citizen offered me a drink made up half of white mule and half of coca cola, but he seems to have been simply indulging himself in a naughty gesture. No fancy woman has been seen in the town since the end of the McKinley administration. There is no gambling. There is no place to dance. The relatively wicked, when they would indulge themselves, go to Robinson's drug store and debate theology . . .

July 14 (the third day)

The net effect of Clarence Darrow's great speech yesterday seems to be preciously the same as if he had bawled it up a rainspout in the interior of Afghanistan. That is, locally, upon the process against the infidel Scopes, upon the so-called minds of these fundamentalists of upland Tennessee. You have but a dim notice of it who have only read it. It was not designed for reading, but for hearing. The clangtint of it was as important as the logic. It rose like a wind and ended like a flourish of bugles. The very judge on the bench, toward the end of it, began to look uneasy. But the morons in the audience, when it was over, simply hissed it.

During the whole time of its delivery the old mountebank, Bryan, sat tight-lipped and unmoved. There is, of course, no reason why it should have shaken him. He has these hillbillies locked up in his pen and he knows it. His brand is on them. He is at home among them. Since his earliest days, indeed, his chief strength has been among the folk of remote hills and forlorn and lonely farms. Now with his political aspirations all gone to pot, he turns to them for religious consolations. They understand his peculiar imbecilities. His nonsense is their ideal of sense. When he deluges them with his theologic

John Scopes stood before the judges as he was convicted of teaching evolution in school and fined $100. This conviction was later overturned.
© BETTMANN/CORBIS. REPRODUCED BY PERMISSION.

bilge they rejoice like pilgrims disporting in the river Jordan . . .

July 15 (the fourth day)

A preacher of any sect that admit the literal authenticity of Genesis is free to gather a crowd at any time and talk all he wants. More, he may engage in a disputation with any expert. I have heard at least a hundred such discussions, and some of them have been very acrimonious. But the instant a speaker utters a word against divine revelation he begins to disturb the peace and is liable to immediate arrest and confinement in the calaboose beside the railroad tracks . . .

July 16 (the fifth day)

In view of the fact that everyone here looks for the jury to bring in a verdict of guilty, it might be ex-

pected that the prosecution would show a considerable amiability and allow the defense a rather free play. Instead, it is contesting every point very vigorously and taking every advantage of its greatly superior familiarity with local procedure. There is, in fact, a considerable heat in the trial. Bryan and the local lawyers for the State sit glaring at the defense all day and even the Attorney-General, A. T. Stewart, who is supposed to have secret doubts about fundamentalism, has shown such pugnacity that it has already brought him to forced apologies.

The high point of yesterday's proceedings was reached with the appearance of Dr. Maynard M. Metcalf of the Johns Hopkins. The doctor is a somewhat chubby man of bland mien, and during the first part of his testimony, with the jury present, the prosecution apparently viewed his with great equanimity. But the instant he was asked a question bearing directly upon the case at bar there was a flurry in the Bryan pen and Stewart was on his feet with protests. Another question followed, with more and hotter protests. The judge then excluded the jury and the show began.

What ensued was, on the surface, a harmless enough dialogue between Dr. Metcalf and Darrow, but underneath there was tense drama. At the first question Bryan came out from behind the State's table and planted himself directly in front of Dr. Metcalf, and not ten feet away. The two McKenzies followed, with young Sue Hicks at their heels.

Then began one of the clearest, most succinct and withal most eloquent presentations of the case for the evolutionists that I have ever heard. The doctor was never at a loss for a word, and his ideas flowed freely and smoothly. Darrow steered him magnificently. A word or two and he was howling down the wind. Another and he hauled up to discharge a broadside. There was no cocksureness in him. Instead he was rather cautious and deprecatory and sometimes he halted and confessed his ignorance. But what he got over before he finished was a superb counterblast to the fundamentalist buncombe. The jury, at least, in theory heard nothing of it, but it went whooping into the radio and it went banging into the face of Bryan . . .

This old buzzard, having failed to raise the mob against its rulers, now prepares to raise it against its teachers. He can never be the peasants' President, but there is still a chance to be the peasants' Pope. He leads a new crusade, his bald head glistening, his face streaming with sweat, his chest heaving beneath his rumpled alpaca coat. One somehow pities him, despite his so palpable imbecilities. It is a tragedy, indeed, to begin life as a hero and to end it as a buffoon. But let no one, laughing at him, underestimate the magic that lies in his black, malignant eye, his frayed but still eloquent voice. He can shake and inflame these poor ignoramuses as no other man among us can shake and inflame them, and he is desperately eager to order the charge.

In Tennessee he is drilling his army. The big battles, he believes, will be fought elsewhere.

July 17 (the sixth day)

Malone was in good voice. It was a great day for Ireland. And for the defense. For Malone not only out-yelled Bryan, he also plainly out-generaled and out-argued him. His speech, indeed, was one of the best presentations of the case against the fundamentalist rubbish that I have ever heard.

It was simple in structure, it was clear in reasoning, and at its high points it was overwhelmingly eloquent. It was not long, but it covered the whole ground and it let off many a gaudy skyrocket, and so it conquered even the fundamentalist. At its end they gave it a tremendous cheer—a cheer at least four times as hearty as that given to Bryan. For these rustics delight in speechifying, and know when it is good. The devil's logic cannot fetch them, but they are not above taking a voluptuous pleasure in his lascivious phrases . . .

July 18

All that remains of the great cause of the State of Tennessee against the infidel Scopes is the formal business of bumping off the defendant. There may be some legal jousting on Monday and some gaudy oratory on Tuesday, but the main battle is over, with Genesis completely triumphant. Judge Raulston finished the benign business yesterday morning by leaping with soft judicial hosannas into the arms of the prosecution. The sole commentary of the sardonic Darrow consisted of bringing down a metaphorical custard pie upon the occiput of the learned jurist.

"I hope," said the latter nervously, "that counsel intends no reflection upon this court."

Darrow hunched his shoulders and looked out of the window dreamily.

"Your honor," he said, "is, of course, entitled to hope." . . .

The Scopes trial, from the start, has been carried on in a manner exactly fitted to the anti-evolution law and the simian imbecility under it. There hasn't been the slightest pretense to decorum. The rustic judge, a candidate for re-election, has postured the yokels like a clown in a ten-cent side show, and almost every word he has uttered has been an undisguised appeal to their prejudices and superstitions. The chief prosecuting attorney, beginning like a competent lawyer and a man of self-respect, ended like a convert at a Billy Sunday revival. It fell to him, finally, to make a clear and astounding statement of theory of justice prevailing under fundamentalism. What he said, in brief, was that a man accused of infidelity had no rights whatever under Tennessee law . . .

Darrow has lost this case. It was lost long before he came to Dayton. But it seems to me that he has nevertheless performed a great public service by fighting it to a finish and in a perfectly serious way. Let no one mistake it for comedy, farcical though it may be in all its details. It serves notice on the country that Neanderthal man is organizing in these forlorn backwaters of the land, led by a fanatic, rid of sense and devoid of conscience. Tennessee, challenging him too timorously and too late, now sees its courts converted into camp meetings and its Bill of Rights made a mock of by its sworn officers of the law. There are other States that had better look to their arsenals before the Hun is at their gates.

Further Resources

BOOKS

Caudill, Edward, Edward J. Larson and Jesse Fox Mayshark. *The Scopes Trial: a Photographic History.* Knoxville: University of Tennessee Press, 2000.

Godfrey, Laurie R. *Scientists Confront Creationism.* New York: W.W. Norton, 1983.

Larson, Edward J. *Summer for the Gods: The Scopes Trial and America's Continuing Debate Over Science and Religion.* New York: BasicBooks, 1997.

Numbers, Ronald L. *The Creationists.* New York: A.A. Knopf, 1992.

Scopes, John Thomas, and James Presley. *Center of the Storm; Memoirs of John T. Scopes.* New York: Holt, Rinehart and Winston, 1967.

PERIODICALS

Moore, Randy. "The Lingering Impact of the Scopes Trial on High School Biology Textbooks." *BioScience,* 51, 2001, 790–796.

Downfall of "Grand Dragon" David C. Stephenson

"Indiana Assembly Linked to 'Dragon'"

Newspaper article

By: Associated Press
Date: November 10, 1925
Source: "Indiana Assembly Linked to 'Dragon.'" *The New York Times,* November 10, 1925, 6.

"Finds Ex-Klan Head Murdered Woman"

Newspaper article

By: Associated Press
Date: November 15, 1925
Source: "Finds Ex-Klan Head Murdered Woman." *The New York Times,* November 15, 1925, 1, 23.

"Stephenson Receives Sentence for Life"

Newspaper article

By: Associated Press
Date: November 17, 1925
Source: "Stephenson Receives Sentence for Life." *The New York Times,* November 17, 1925, 10.

About the Organization: The Associated Press was formed in 1848 to allow competing newspapers to pool some of their news-gathering resources. The organization relied heavily on telegraph communications in its early years. As time passed, newspapers developed the technology to receive their news via telephone and their pictures via Wirephoto. The AP first allowed its news to be broadcast on the radio in 1920. Technological advances changed its method of transmitting news throughout the twentieth century, and by the turn of the century digital speed enhanced its communications. ■

Introduction

After the Civil War (1861–1865), vigilante justice increased rapidly in the United States, especially in the South. The Ku Klux Klan was formed in the 1860s in the South to force the former slaves to submit to their former masters. By the end of Reconstruction, the KKK had largely been silenced, but white supremacy in the South had also been assured.

The beginning of the twentieth century brought U.S. involvement in World War I (1914–1918), and many pacifists disagreed with this. Vigilantes tried to force everyone to support the war and did cause many to mute their protests. Thus was the vigilante tradition revived, and it was still strong in the 1920s. During World War I, the KKK was reborn as well. The book *The Clansman* and the film based on it—*Birth of a Nation*—glorified the role of the Klan during Reconstruction, and these were two of the factors responsible for the resurgence of the Klan.

The Klan in the 1920s, though, were not just racists but "equal opportunity bigots," hating anyone that was not White Anglo-Saxon Protestant (WASP). The group had more than five million members. Its goals included enforcing traditional morality, restricting immigration, promoting "traditional" values, protesting modernity, and preventing promiscuity. The KKK had members throughout America, not just the South, with the largest Klan group in Indiana.

The "Grand Dragon," or leader of the Klan in Indiana, was a man named David C. Stephenson. Stephenson gained political power and legitimacy and turned the Klan into a powerful force in the state. All of this came to an end when he was charged with murder. He and his henchmen abducted state house secretary Madge Oberholtzer and forcibly held her prisoner for several days. Although the legal documents refer to the abuse she suffered as "mistreatment," she was actually raped and beaten repeatedly. She attempted suicide with poison, but did not succeed, and she died nearly a month later from her infected wounds, after informing the authorities of her abduction and imprisonment, leading to Stephenson's arrest and trial for murder.

Significance

The immediate result of Stephenson's conviction was a long jail sentence. After not being pardoned by the Governor of Indiana, who was a political ally, Stephenson handed over Klan documents to the government, which revealed great corruption in the organization. Having lost its legitimacy and regarded as immoral and corrupt, the Klan was finished as a political force.

The Klan then disappeared from the forefront of American life, dropping to less than thirty thousand official members, but it did not disappear altogether. After the trial, the Klan and similar groups ruled much of Southern life, preventing African Americans from asserting themselves. Attempts by the NAACP and others to organize in the South frequently brought lynchings and arson, even though the Klan remained publicly quiet. Many rural areas were also controlled by the Klan.

The Klan next reappeared in the 1950s, when white supremacy was finally challenged in the South. The vigilante violence became front-page news again, and White Citizens' Councils formed to publicly denounce the Supreme Court and liberalism. Some of the more well-known vigilante incidents include the bombing of a church in Birmingham, which killed four young girls, and the murder of Medgar Evers. Official forces also participated in violence, as it was the police who killed three civil rights workers in Mississippi in 1965.

The federal government mobilized against Klan violence by the late 1960s. With the removal of J. Edgar Hoover from the FBI, the FBI also became interested in protecting civil rights. Individuals sued and won large damage awards against the Klan, which also weakened it. Thus, by the start of the 1980s, the Klan had been largely marginalized. However, the proliferation of hate group sites on the Internet at the turn of the century demonstrate that the Klan, and other groups like it, had by no means been eradicated.

Primary Source

"Indiana Assembly Linked to 'Dragon'"

> **SYNOPSIS:** This article chronicles the trial of KKK Grand Dragon and accused murderer D.C. Stephen-

son, demonstrating how strong the KKK was in Indiana by linking the Grand Dragon with members of the Indiana Assembly.

Indiana Assembly Linked to 'Dragon'
Murder Trial Witnesses Tell How Legislators Consulted Accused Klan Chief.

Primary Tactics Revealed
Railroad Men Say They Saw No Signs of Miss Oberholtzer's Being Forced into Train.

NOBLESVILLE, Ind., Nov. 9 *(AP)*.—An insight into D. C. Stephenson's activities during the last primary campaign and at the 1925 session of the Indiana Legislature was given here today at the murder trial of the former Ku Klux Klan leader.

Continuing its assault on the dying declaration in which Madge Oberholtzer charged her abduction and the attack upon her to Stephenson, Earl Klenck and Earl Gentry, the defense sought to refute the girl's contention that she was forced through the Union Station at Indianapolis and on to a Pullman car. The testimony of three station employes was offered.

Nine other witnesses occupied the stand during the day, most of them to corroborate earlier defense testimony that Miss Oberholtzer was a frequent visitor prior to the time of her alleged abduction at the Indianapolis office where D.C. Stephenson presided over the Ku Klux Klan of Indiana as its Grand Dragon. It was from their testimony that the political angle developed.

Foster Straider, Stephenson's office secretary; Robert James, former clerk in Stephenson's office; Miss Maxine Elliott, a stenographer for the chief defendant; Raymond Donahue, a former Klan organizer, and Ralph Rigdon, a Klan member and a friend of Stephenson, all told of seeing the girl at Stephenson's office in January and February.

Political Chiefs Called on Dragon

The State obtained from all of them on cross-examination, names of other Indianans who were frequent visitors at the Dragon's office—among them men and women who were political leaders and members of the 1925 Indiana Legislature.

The State developed that Straider served Stephenson when the latter was in charge of the Ku Klux Klan at Columbus, Ohio, and that he came to Indianapolis soon after his chief in 1923.

Donahue, an Indianapolis real estate salesman, said he rented offices for Stephenson. On

D.C. Stephenson, former Grand Dragon of the Klu Klux Klan (fourth from the left), is shown on the steps of the courthouse where he was on trial for murder. © BETTMANN/CORBIS. REPRODUCED BY PERMISSION.

cross-examination he said he was under contract to Stephenson when engaged in Ku Klux Klan work as an organizer.

During the last session of the Legislature the witness said he had seen Senator Delbert Blackburn of Vanderburg County; Ralph Rigdon, who testified earlier in the day; Robert Duncan of Indianapolis, Chairman of the Public Morals Committee in the Indiana House of Representatives; and several women in Stephenson's office. Madge Oberholtzer was a frequent visitor, he insisted.

Donahue said he had lived in Washington, D. C., Ohio and Minnesota. He was a Ku Klux Klan organizer in the District of Columbia and two States, he testified.

Tells of Victory in Primary

Rigdon said he had worked with Stephenson during the Indiana primary campaign in 1924. He said

most of the men Stephenson supported were elected.

On cross-examination Rigdon testified that many members of the 1925 Indiana General Assembly had visited Stephenson's Indianapolis office during the session. He said he was a daily visitor at the Legislature; but that he was not interested in any particular legislation.

The first witness on the point of Miss Oberholtzer's passage through the Union Station, David Giblin, gatekeeper at the turnstile leading to the Monon tracks, declared that on the night of March 15, the date on which the State alleges the girl was put forcibly on a Pullman car of a Monon train bound for Hammond, Ind., he heard no outcry and that everybody passed through the gates without aid and one at a time.

Two more employes, Jess J. Kemper, night station master, and Wilbur C. Schwier, engineer for the

Indianapolis Union Railway, brought maps and plans of the terminal to the witness stand and described the methods of reaching out-going trains from the street. A train could be reached, they said, without going through the gates, but such methods were forbidden or involved extensive difficulties.

Primary Source

"Finds Ex-Klan Head Murdered Woman"

> **SYNOPSIS:** This article reports on the Oberholtzer murder case, detailing everything from Stephenson's political power to the crime itself and finally, the sentence meted out.

Finds Ex-Klan Head Murdered Woman

Indiana Jury Convicts Stephenson in Second Degree—Penalty is 20 Years.

Acquits Other Defendants

Former Grand Dragon and State Political Power Described as "Monster" by Prosecutor.

Noblesville, Ind., Nov. 14 *(AP)*.—Imprisonment for twenty years in the State Prison is the price which a jury determined today. D.C. Stephenson, former Grand Dragon of the Indiana Ku Klux Klan, shall pay for causing the death of Madge Oberholtzer.

A panel composed of ten farmers, one business man and a truck driver reached a verdict of guilty in less than six hours. Earl Klenck and Earl Gentry, body guards of Stephenson and charged jointly with the abduction and attack on the woman last March, were acquitted. Miss Oberholtzer took poison in a Hammond (Ind.) hotel after mistreatment at the hands of Stephenson, she averred, and died at her Indianapolis home twenty-nine days later.

Murder in the second degree was the finding of the jury. It calls automatically for twenty years' servitude.

Notice of Appeal Is Given

Stephenson took the verdict without flinching. A short laugh and a shake of the head were his only apparent reactions.

"Surrender?" he said as he lay on his bunk a few minutes later in the cell that has been his home for several months. "I am just beginning to fight. The last chapter has not been written." Floyd Christian of defense counsel notified Judge Sparks that a motion of appeal would be filed. Stephenson will be removed to the State prison pending appeal.

State legislators and other politicians flocked to his office in Indianapolis, when he was Grand Dragon of the Klan, it was shown by testimony at his trial. He was in constant communication, the State charged, with a large group of State Senators and Representatives sitting in the Legislature last January and February.

"I am the law in Indiana," was the statement attributed to Stephenson by the State—a statement ascribed to him by Madge Oberholtzer in her dying declaration, which played so big a part in his conviction and a statement which the prosecution repeated again and again as it pleaded with the jury to sentence him to death.

Klenck and Gentry followed their leader back to his cell, scorning the knowledge that they were free. He finally prevailed on them to leave him.

Stephenson Called "a Monster"

Excoriated yesterday in the State's closing arguments, the three defendants were assailed with new fury today by Ralph Kane, who spoke for the prosecution for more than two hours, and closed sixteen hours of argument. He called Stephenson a "hideous monster" and a "serpent who should be put away for the protection of the daughters of the future."

The three defendants sat unmoved during the verbal lashing.

"These men are criminals," declared the prosecutor. "By their acts, they drove that girl to the position that she believed life held nothing for her but shame, and she took poison. They are as guilty of murder as though they had stabbed her in the heart. Now is the time to act to protect the daughters of the future."

Reads Woman's Dying Statement

The prosecutor then read from her dying statement a description of the mistreatment the woman said she had received at the hands of Stephenson and his co-defendants. This mistreatment, the State contended, caused infected wounds which caused her death, the poison she took with suicidal intent not having a fatal effect.

"Shamed and humiliated, she felt she had nothing to live for," Mr. Kane continued. "These men murdered her. I want to demonstrate to Stephenson, to Klenck, To Gentry, to Inman and all the rest that in Indiana, the law is supreme. Put them away so others will be safe from them."

In charging the jury, the court said: "A person cannot be held criminally responsible for a homicide unless his act is said to be the cause of death. But a person may . . . be guilty of the crime of murder as an indirect result of his unlawful acts. In such cases, it must appear, however, that the act of the deceased which destroyed his or her life falls under the influence of fear: (1) As such a step as a reasonable man or woman might take; (2) that the apprehension was of immediate violence or injury; (3) that the apprehension of violence must have been well grounded; (4) the act of the deceased must have been the natural and probable consequence of the unlawful conduct of other person.

"One who inflicts injuries on another is deemed . . . guilty of homicide if the injury contributes mediately or immediately to death. The fact that other causes contributed to the death does not relieve the actor of responsibilities."

Stephenson Once Political Power

D.C. Stephenson and his co-defendants were indicted on a charge of first degree murder by an Indiana Grand Jury on April 18 last, following an extensive inquiry into the death of Miss Oberholtzer. The murder charge was filed on the allegation that the three men failed to provide medical aid for Miss Oberholtzer after she had taken poison at a Hammond, Ind., hotel, where it was alleged she was forcibly held by abduction by Stephenson and his companions and that the actual cause of her death was infection, due to wounds inflicted by Stephenson.

The case caused intense interest throughout Indiana because it involved the Klan and the political power of the organization.

Four years ago Stephenson was virtually unknown in Indiana. Then he rapidly forged ahead by organizing the Ku Klux Klan throughout the State. When the Klan first entered the State he was a small-town politician in Evansville, but through his efforts, the hooded order gained in strength, particularly in the southwestern part of the State, and he was elected Grand Dragon of the Indiana branch. With the backing of 400,000 Klansmen, he entered State politics and organized a powerful machine. Even though he afterward came to loggerheads with the national leaders of the Klan and was ousted from the order he managed to retain his political power.

At the time of his arrest he was generally looked on as the ultimate logical candidate for a seat in the United States Senate. During the Gubernatorial campaign of 1924, he was active in the support of Governor Jackson, who was generally regarded as having been elected by the Klan supporters.

Stephenson first met Miss Oberholtzer when both were lobbying for favorable action on legislation before the General Assembly.

According to the story told to her parents and to Dr. John E. Kingsbury before her death, Miss Oberholtzer was lured to Stephenson's house on the night of March 15, forced to take a drink, kidnapped, and then taken on a train to Hammond. She was assaulted, she said, at a hotel in Hammond by Stephenson and the following day she obtained some poison and drank it. Stephenson and the others then took her back to Indianapolis by automobile, she said, refusing to get medical attention for her. She was kept a prisoner until the morning of March 17, when she was taken to her home. She died a month later.

A change of venue was obtained by counsel for Stephenson and he was placed on trial on Oct. 12. Thirteen days were taken up in obtaining a jury and then a vain but strenuous fight was waged by his attorneys against the admission in evidence of the girl's dying statement. The defense contended that the woman committed suicide and that she accompanied Stephenson and his companions as a free agent.

Primary Source

"Stephenson Receives Sentence for Life"

> **SYNOPSIS:** This is the announcement of the prison sentence for KKK Grand Dragon D.C. Stephenson.

Ex-Klan Leader in Dramatic Speech Denies Having Slain Miss Oberholtzer

NOBLESVILLE, Ind., Nov. 16 *(AP).*—Smiling and debonair, trying his best to radiate confidence, D.C. Stephenson, former Grand Dragon of the Indiana Ku Klux Klan, today heard Judge Will M. Sparks sentence him to life imprisonment, for the murder of Madge Oberholtzer.

Further Resources

BOOKS

Blee, Kathleen M. *Women of the Klan: Racism and Gender in the 1920s.* Berkeley: University of California Press, 1991.

Lutholtz, M. William. *Grand Dragon: D.C. Stephenson and the Ku Klux Klan in Indiana.* West Lafayette, Ind.: Purdue University Press, 1991.

MacLean, Nancy. *Behind the Mask of Chivalry: The Making of the Second Ku Klux Klan.* New York: Oxford University Press, 1994.

Moore, Leonard Joseph. *Citizen Klansmen: The Ku Klux Klan in Indiana, 1921–1928.* Chapel Hill: University of North Carolina Press, 1991.

Tucker, Richard K. *The Dragon and the Cross: The Rise and Fall of the Ku Klux Klan in Middle America.* Hamden, Conn.: Archon Books, 1991.

Corrigan v. Buckley

Supreme Court decision

By: Edward Sanford

Date: May 24, 1926

Source: Sanford, Edward. *Corrigan v. Buckley* 271 U.S. 323. (1926). Available online at http://caselaw.lp.findlaw.com /scripts/getcase.pl?court=US&vol=271&invol=323; website home page: http://caselaw.lp.findlaw.com (accessed February 11, 2003)

About the Author: Conservative Justice Edward Sanford (1865–1930) was appointed to the Supreme Court in 1923 by President Warren Harding (served 1921–1923) after serving as a federal trial judge in Tennessee. He allied himself with Chief Justice William Howard Taft and, along with some of the other justices, spent his Sunday afternoons at the Chief Justice's home. One of his most well-known decisions held that states, in addition to the federal government, must uphold some provisions of the Bill of Rights. ∎

Introduction

One device adopted by segregationists in the 1910s was the restrictive zoning ordinance. Aimed to keep African Americans out of white areas, such ordinances effectively denied African Americans their civil rights. They became the subject of a federal lawsuit in *Buchanan v. Warley.* Marking one of the first National Association for the Advancement of Colored People (NAACP) appearances before the Supreme Court, the case was a civil rights victory, resulting in restrictive zoning laws being declared unconstitutional. However, the Supreme Court ruling only affected the segregationists' lawmaking abilities. After the *Buchanan* decision, individuals began placing racially restrictive covenants in their private land contracts and deeds. These effectively prohibited the sale of land to African Americans and prevented African Americans from occupying some properties. Housing organizations also formed to discourage the sale of property to African Americans, and in Chicago, during the Red Summer of 1919, several homes were bombed to frighten African Americans into leaving white neighborhoods.

The question then became whether restrictive covenants were legal, and the controlling factor in any court decision would be whether or not there was enough "state action" in the covenants. The Supreme Court had, as early as 1883, in the Civil Rights cases, limited the Fourteenth Amendment and the Civil Rights Act of 1875 by declaring that mere private discrimination did not constitute state action, even in public accommodations.

Significance

The segregationists won this case, and restrictive covenants were declared legal. The Supreme Court closed its eyes to the fact that these covenants were enforced in state courts, which by its very nature involved state action. It would not be until 1947 that the Supreme Court would change its attitude. In *Shelley v. Kraemer* in that year, the Court held, by a 6-0 vote, that restrictive covenants were not enforceable. Even at that time, the Supreme Court did not prevent these codes from being put into housing contracts but prevented state and federal courts from enforcing them. In *Shelley,* the Court took notice that contract provisions cannot be enforced without court action. This makes the courts a partner to any contract, showing the inanity of the *Corrigan* Court's ruling that restrictive covenants were merely private. Even *Shelley* was not a total victory, though, as two very important federal agencies—the Federal Housing Authority and the Veterans Administration—still discriminated by not giving loans to African Americans who wanted to move into white areas. This prevented many African Americans from participating in the great suburbanization of the 1950s. African Americans were not able to build on the victory of *Shelley v. Kraemer* until the Civil Rights Act of 1968 *(Fair Housing Act).* This act forbade racial discrimination in loans from banks, in renting, and in home selling, and it empowered the federal government to act to remedy discrimination. There still are discrimination problems today in housing, but *Shelley* was an important victory—*Corrigan* delayed that victory for twenty-two years.

Primary Source

Corrigan v. Buckley

> **SYNOPSIS:** Sanford summarizes the covenant, initially signed by Corrigan, which essentially prevented the sale of certain land to African Americans for twenty-one years. As that time has not yet passed, other signers of the covenant now wish to forbid Corrigan from selling her land to an African American. He then dismisses the case because, he states, the Fifth and Fourteenth amendments do not apply to the behavior of individuals, and restrictive covenants represent only the actions of individuals. The case was argued on January 8, 1926, and was decided on May 24, 1926.

White tenants protested African Americans moving into their neighborhood in the 1920s and in later decades. © CORBIS. REPRODUCED BY PERMISSION.

Mr. Justice Sanford delivered the opinion of the Court.

This is a suit in equity brought by John J. Buckley in the Supreme Court of the District of Columbia against Irene H. Corrigan and Helen Curtis, to enjoin the conveyance of certain real estate from one to the other of the defendants.

The case made by the bill is this: The parties are citizens of the United States, residing in the District. The plaintiff and the defendant Corrigan are white persons, and the defendant Curtis is a person of the negro race. In 1921, thirty white persons, including the plaintiff and the defendant Corrigan, owning twenty-five parcels of land, improved by dwelling houses, situated on Street, between 18th and New Hampshire avenue, in the City of Washington, executed an indenture, duly recorded, in which they recited that for their mutual benefit and the best interests of the neighborhood comprising these properties, they mutually covenanted and agreed that no part of these properties should ever be used or occupied by, or sold, leased or given to, any person of the negro race or blood; and that this covenant should run with the land and bind their respective heirs and assigns for twenty-one years from and after its date.

In 1922, the defendants entered into a contract by which the defendant Corrigan, although knowing the defendant Curtis to be a person of the negro race, agreed to [271 U.S. 323, 328] sell her a certain lot, with dwelling house, included within the terms of the indenture, and the defendant Curtis, although knowing of the existence and terms of the indenture, agreed to purchase it. The defendant Curtis demanded that this contract of sale be carried out, and, despite the protest of other parties to the indenture, the defendant Corrigan had stated that she would convey the lot to the defendant Curtis.

The bill alleged that this would cause irreparable injury to the plaintiff and the other parties to the indenture, and that the plaintiff, having no adequate remedy at law, was entitled to have the covenant of the defendant Corrigan specifically enforced in equity by an injunction preventing the defendants from carrying the contract of sale into effect; and prayed, in substance, that the defendant Corrigan be enjoined during twenty-one years from the date of the indenture, from conveying the lot to the defendant

Curtis, and that the defendant Curtis be enjoined from taking title to the lot during such period, and from using or occupying it.

The defendant Corrigan moved to dismiss the bill on the grounds that the "indenture or covenant made the basis of said bill" is (1) "void in that the same is contrary to and in violation of the Constitution of the United States," and (2) "is void in that the same is contrary to public policy." And the defendant Curtis moved to dismiss the bill on the ground that it appears therein that the indenture or covenant "is void, in that it attempts to deprive the defendant, the said Helen Curtis, and others of property, without due process of law; abridges the privilege and immunities of citizens of the United States, including the defendant Helen Curtis, and other persons within this jurisdiction (and denies them) the equal protection of the law, and therefore, is forbidden by the Constitution of the United States, and especially by the Fifth, Thirteenth, and Fourteenth [271 U.S. 323, 329] Amendments thereof, and the Laws enacted is aid and under the sanction of the said Thirteenth and Fourteenth Amendments."

Both of these motions to dismiss were overruled, with leave to answer. 52 Wash. Law Rep. 402. And the defendants having elected to stand on their motions, a final decree was entered enjoining them as prayed in the bill. This was affirmed, on appeal, by the Court of Appeals of the District. 55 App. D. C. 30, 299 F. 899. The defendants then prayed an appeal to this Court on the ground that such review was authorized under the provisions of section 250 of the Judicial Code (Comp. St. 1227)—as it then stood, before the amendment made by the Jurisdictional Act of 1925—in that the case was one "involving the construction or application of the Constitution of the United States" (paragraph 3), and "in which the construction of" certain laws of the United States, namely, sections 1977, 1978, 1979 of the Revised Statutes (Comp. St. 3925, 3931, 3932) were "drawn in question" by them (paragraph 6). This appeal was allowed, in June, 1924.

The mere assertion that the case is one involving the construction or application of the Constitution, and in which the construction of federal laws is drawn in question, does not, however, authorize this Court to entertain the appeal; and it is our duty to decline jurisdiction if the record does not present such a constitutional or statutory question substantial in character and properly raised below. *Sugarman v. United States,* 249 U.S. 182, 184, 39 S. Ct.

191; *Zucht v. King,* 260 U.S. 174, 176, 43 S. Ct. 24. And under well settled rules, jurisdiction is wanting if such questions are so unsubstantial as to be plainly without color of merit and frivolous. *Wilson v. North Carolina,* 169 U.S. 586, 595, 18 S. Ct. 435; *Delmar Jockey Club v. Missouri,* 210 U.S. 324, 335,28 S. Ct. 732; *Binderup v. Pathe Exchange,* 263 U.S. 291, 305, 44 S. Ct. 96; *Moore v. New York Cotton Exchange,* 270 U.S. 593, 46 S. Ct. 367, No. 200, decided April 12, 1926.

Under the pleadings in the present case the only constitutional question involved was that arising under the [271 U.S. 323, 330] assertions in the motions to dismiss that the indenture or covenant which is the basis of the bill, is "void" in that it is contrary to and forbidden by the Fifth, Thirteenth and Fourteenth Amendments. This contention is entirely lacking in substance or color of merit. The Fifth Amendment "is a limitation only upon the powers of the General Government," *Talton v. Mayes,* 163 U.S. 376, 382,16 S. Ct. 986, 988 (41 L. Ed. 196), and is not directed against the action of individuals. The Thirteenth Amendment denouncing slavery and involuntary servitude, that is, a condition of enforced compulsory service of one to another does not in other matters protect the individual rights of persons of the negro race. *Hodges v. United States,* 203 U.S. 1, 16, 18 S., 27 S. Ct. 6. And the prohibitions of the Fourteenth Amendment "have reference to State action exclusively, and not to any action of private individuals." *Virginia v. Rives,* 100 U.S. 313, 318; *United States v. Harris,* 106 U.S. 629, 639, 1 S. Ct. 601. "It is State action of a particular character that is prohibited. Individual invasion of individual rights is not the subject-matter of the Amendment." Civil Rights Cases, 109 U.S. 3, 11, 3 S. Ct. 18, 21 (27 L. Ed. 835). It is obvious that none of these amendments prohibited private individuals from entering into contracts respecting the control and disposition of their own property; and there is no color whatever for the contention that they rendered the indenture void. And plainly, the claim urged in this Court that they were to be looked to, in connection with the provisions of the Revised Statutes and the decisions of the courts, in determining the contention, earnestly pressed, that the indenture is void as being "against public policy," does not involve a constitutional question within the meaning of the Code provision.

The claim that the defendants drew in question the "construction" of sections 1977, 1978 and 1979 of the Revised Statutes, is equally unsubstantial. The only question raised as to these statutes under the pleadings was the [271 U.S. 323, 331] assertion in the motion interposed by the defendant Curtis, that the indenture is void in that it is forbidden by the laws enacted in aid and under the sanction of the Thirteenth and Fourteenth Amendments. Assuming that this contention drew in question the "construction" of these statutes, as distinguished from their "application," it is obvious, upon their face, that while they provide, inter alia, that all persons and citizens shall have equal right with white citizens to make contracts and acquire property, they, like the Constitutional Amendment under whose sanction they were enacted, do not in any manner prohibit or invalidate contracts entered into by private individuals in respect to the control and disposition of their own property. There is no color for the contention that they rendered the indenture void; nor was it claimed in this Court that they had, in and of themselves, any such effect.

We therefore conclude that neither the constitutional nor statutory questions relied on as grounds for the appeal to this Court have any substantial quality or color of merit, or afford any jurisdictional basis for the appeal.

And while it was further urged in this Court that the decrees of the courts below in themselves deprived the defendants of their liberty and property without due process of law, in violation of the Fifth and Fourteenth Amendments, this contention likewise cannot serve as a jurisdictional basis for the appeal. Assuming that such a contention, if of a substantial character, might have constituted ground for an appeal under paragraph 3 of the Code provision, it was not raised by the petition for the appeal or by any assignment of error, either in the Court of Appeals or in this Court; and it likewise is lacking is substance. The defendants were given a full hearing in both courts; they were not denied any constitutional or statutory right; and there is no semblance of ground for any contention that the decrees were so plainly arbitrary [271 U.S. 323, 332] and contrary to law as to be acts of mere spoliation. See *Delmar Jockey Club v. Missouri,* supra, 335 (28 S. Ct. 732). Mere error of a court, if any there be, in a judgment entered after a full hearing, does not constitute a denial of due process of law. *Central Land Co. v. Laidley,* 159 U.S. 103, 112, 16 S. Ct. 80; *Jones v. Buffalo Creek Coal Co.,* 245 U.S. 328, 329, 38 S. Ct. 121.

It results that, in the absence of any substantial constitutional or statutory question giving us jurisdiction of this appeal under the provisions of section 250 of the Judicial Code, we cannot determine upon the merits the contentions earnestly pressed by the defendants in this court that the indenture is not only void because contrary to public policy, but is also of such a discriminatory character that a court of equity will not lend its aid by enforcing the specific performance of the covenant. These are questions involving a consideration of rules not expressed in any constitutional or statutory provision, but claimed to be a part of the common or general law in force in the District of Columbia; and, plainly, they may not be reviewed under this appeal unless jurisdiction of the case is otherwise acquired.

Hence, without a consideration of these questions, the appeal must be, and is dismissed for want of jurisdiction.

Further Resources

BOOKS

Avins, Alfred. *Open Occupancy vs. Forced Housing Under the Fourteenth Amendment: A Symposium on Anti-Discrimination Legislation, Freedom of Choice, and Property Rights in Housing.* New York: Bookmailer, 1963.

Miller, Loren. *The Petitioners: The Story of the Supreme Court of the United States and the Negro.* New York: Pantheon Books, 1966.

Vose, Clement E. *Caucasians Only: The Supreme Court, the NAACP, and the Restrictive Covenant Cases.* Berkeley: University of California Press, 1959.

WEBSITES

Orfield, Gary. "Housing Segregation: Causes, Effects, Possible Cures: Address Before the National Press Club." Available online at http://www.civilrightsproject.harvard.edu/research /metro/call_housinggary.php; website home page: http: //www.law.harvard.edu (accessed February 11, 2003).

Smith, J. Clay. "James Adali Cobb: Lawyer, Law Teacher, Judge, and Generous Man." Available online at http://www .law.howard.edu/alumni/legalgiants/huslgiantmar2k2.htm; website home page: http://www.law.howard.edu (accessed: February 11, 2003).

Nixon v. Herndon

Supreme Court decision

By: Oliver Wendell Holmes Jr.

Date: March 7, 1927

Source: Homes, Oliver Wendell, Jr. *Nixon v. Herndon* 273 U.S. 536 (1927). Available online at http://caselaw.lp.findlaw .com/scripts/getcase.pl?court=US&vol=273&invol=536; website home page: http://caselaw.lp.findlaw.com (accessed February 11, 2003).

About the Author: Oliver Wendell Holmes Jr. (1835–1941) served in the Union army in the Civil War (1861–1865) from 1861 to 1864. He joined the Massachusetts Supreme Court as an associate justice in 1883. In 1899, he became chief justice of that organization, and, in 1902, President Theodore Roosevelt (served 1901–1909) appointed him associate justice to the U.S. Supreme Court, at the age of sixty-one. He served for thirty years and resigned in 1932. ■

Introduction

After the Civil War, Congress passed three Reconstruction amendments—the Thirteenth, which ended slavery; the Fourteenth, which granted equal protection of the laws, due process, and priviliges and immunities to the ex-slaves; and the Fifteenth, which provided that "the right of citizens of the United States to vote shall not be denied or abridged by the United States or by any state on the basis of race, color or previous condition of servitude." That last amendment would seem to confer the vote to all male citizens. However, the Supreme Court, in *United States v. Reese* (1876), held that the Fifteenth Amendment did "not confer the right of suffrage upon anyone." Congress was limited in its power to enforce this amendment, and it was mostly left up to the states. During the 1880s and 1890s, the appeal of the Populist Party threatened the power structure in the South, and rich whites took action to prevent blacks from voting with such measures as the literacy test and poll taxes. These methods were upheld by the Supreme Court in *Williams v. Mississippi* (1898). Poor whites, who were often loyal Democrats, though, were disenfranchised by these methods, and so southern legislators created the "grandfather clause." This allowed the descendants of those who had voted before 1866 to vote without restriction, which of course excluded nearly all blacks, who in turn had to maneuver through the poll taxes and the literacy tests. The grandfather clause was struck down by the Supreme Court in *United States v. Guinn* (1915).

However, in 1923, Texas banned African Americans from voting in the Democratic Party primary, even while allowing registered blacks to vote in the general election. This restriction was important, as Democratic candidates almost universally won elections across the south between 1870 and 1960. This was the issue brought before the Supreme Court in *Nixon v. Herndon*.

Significance

The Supreme Court ruled that Texas's white primary was unconstitutional. However, the Court's ruling here did not end the question of the Democratic primary. The question came directly in front of the Supreme Court again in *Nixon v. Condon* (1932). The state of Texas allowed each political party to decide who was eligible to vote in its primaries. Essentially, this meant that the state allowed

the Democratic Party to perpetuate the white primary, in spite of the Court's ruling, and in such a way as to appear to be doing something different. The Supreme Court ruled the same way in *Condon* as it did in *Herndon:* unconstitutional. The Democrats were not finished blocking black voters, though, as they (theoretically independently and without enabling legislation from the state) called a state convention, which passed a resolution limiting participation in the primaries to white voters. The Supreme Court in 1935 allowed this, since it did not involve, in the eyes of the court, "state action." State action is vital, as both the Fifteenth and Fourteenth Amendments ban only state discrimination, not all discrimination. The issue did not return to the Supreme Court until 1944 in *Smith v. Allwright,* in which the Supreme Court finally banned the white primary. This ruling did not end discrimination in the South, however. The poll tax had to be outlawed through a constitutional amendment, and no court decision could change the views of southern registrars who were firmly opposed to any blacks voting. It finally took federal legislation in the 1965 Voting Rights Act to give most African Americans in the South a chance to vote. When this occurred, the southern Democratic Party became much more liberal, and in response many conservative southern whites fled the Democratic Party for the Republican. *Allwright* thus eventually led to a change in the nation and in politics, but the road to that change began with *Nixon v. Herndon.*

Primary Source

Nixon v. Herndon [excerpt]

SYNOPSIS: Justice Holmes first summarizes the complaint: the plaintiff has experienced discrimination because he has been prevented from voting in the Texas Democratic primaries. Then, he upholds this complaint because the plaintiff's Fourteenth Amendment rights have been infringed upon. The case was argued on January 4, 1927, and was decided on March 7, 1927.

Mr. Justice Holmes delivered the opinion of the Court.

This is an action against the Judges of Elections for refusing to permit the plaintiff to vote at a primary election in Texas. It lays the damages at five thousand dollars. The petition alleges that the plaintiff is a negro, a citizen of the United States and of Texas and a resident of El Paso, and in every way qualified to vote, as set forth in detail, except that the statute to be mentioned interferes with his right; that on July 26, 1924, a primary election was held at El Paso for the nomination of candidates for a senator and representatives in Congress and State and other offices, upon the Democratic ticket; that [273 U.S. 536, 540] the plaintiff, being a member of the Democratic party, sought to vote but was denied the right by defendants; that the denial was based upon a statute of Texas enacted in May, 1923 (Acts 38th Leg. 2d Called Sess. (1923) c. 32, 1 (Vernon's Ann. Civ. St. 1925, art. 3107)), and designated article 3093a, by the words of which "in no event shall a negro be eligible to participate in a Democratic party primary election held in the State of Texas," etc., and that this statute is contrary to the Fourteenth and Fifteenth Amendments to the Constitution of the United States. The defendants moved to dismiss upon the ground that the subject-matter of the suit was political and not within the jurisdiction of the Court and that no violation of the Amendments was shown. The suit was dismissed and a writ of error was taken directly to this Court. Here no argument was made on behalf of the defendants but a brief was allowed to be filed by the Attorney General of the State.

The objection that the subject-matter of the suit is political is little more than a play upon words. Of course the petition concerns political action but it alleges and seeks to recover for private damage. That private damage may be caused by such political action and may be recovered for in suit at law hardly has been doubted for over two hundred years, since *Ashby v. White,* 2 Ld. Raym. 938, 3 Ld. Raym. 320, and has been recognized by this Court. *Wiley v. Sinkler,* 179 U.S. 58, 64, 65 S., 21 S. Ct. 17; *Giles v. Harris,* 189 U.S. 475, 485, 23 S. Ct. 639. See also Judicial Code, 24(11), (12), (14); Act of March 3, 1911, c. 231; 36 Stat. 1087, 1092 (Comp. St. 991). If the defendants' conduct was a wrong to the plaintiff the same reasons that allow a recovery for denying the plaintiff a vote at a final election allow it for denying a vote at the primary election that may determine the final result.

The important question is whether the statute can be sustained. But although we state it as a question the answer does not seem to us open to a doubt. We find it unnecessary to consider the Fifteenth Amendment, because [273 U.S. 536, 541] it seems to us hard to imagine a more direct and obvious infringement of the Fourteenth. That Amendment, while it applies to all, was passed, as we know, with a special intent to protect the blacks from discrimination against them. *Slaughter House Cases,* 16 Wall. 36; *Strauder v. West Virginia,* 100 U.S. 303. That Amendment "not only gave citizenship and the privileges of citizenship to persons of color, but it denied to any State the power to with-

hold from them the equal protection of the laws. . . . What is this but declaring that the law in the States shall be the same for the black as for the white; that all persons, whether colored or white, shall stand equal before the laws of the States, and, in regard to the colored race, for whose protection the amendment was primarily designed, that no discrimination shall be made against them by law because of their color?" Quoted from the last case in *Buchanan v. Warley,* 245 U.S. 60, 77, 38 S. Ct. 16, 19 (62 L. Ed. 149, L. R. A. 1918C, 210, Ann. Cas. 1918A, 1201). See *Yick Wo v. Hopkins,* 118 U.S. 356, 374, 6 S. Ct. 1064. The statute of Texas in the teeth of the prohibitions referred to assumes to forbid negroes to take part in a primary election the importance of which we have indicated, discriminating against them by the distinction of color alone. States may do a good deal of classifying that it is difficult to believe rational, but there are limits, and it is too clear for extended argument that color cannot be made the basis of a statutory classification affecting the right set up in this case.

Judgment reversed.

Further Resources

BOOKS

Bryson, Conrey. *Dr. Lawrence A. Nixon and the White Primary.* El Paso: Texas Western Press, 1974.

In the Supreme Court of the United States. Reply Brief for Plaintiff-in-Error. 926:117 (October, 1926 term). New York: Hecla Press, 1977.

Marshall, Louis, Moorfield Storey, Arthur B. Spingarn, et al. *In the Supreme Court of the United States, October Term, 1926 No. 117. L.A. Nixon, Plaintiff-in-Error, Against C.C. Herndon and Charles Porras, Defendants-in-Error. In error to the District Court of the United States for the Western District of Texas. Reply Brief For Plaintiff-in-Error.* New York: Hecla Press, 1926.

NAACP legal file. Cases supported—*Nixon v. Herndon,* 1924-1929. Frederick, Md.: University Publications of America, 1986.

Scriabine, Christine Brendel, Rebecca Spears Schwartz, Rue Anne Wood, and Thomas Nast. *Black Voting Rights: The Fight for Equality.* Amawalk, N.Y.: Golden Owl, 1993.

Buck v. Bell

Supreme Court decision

By: Oliver Wendell Holmes Jr.

Date: May 2, 1927

Source: Holmes, Oliver Wendell, Jr. *Buck v. Bell.* 274 U.S.

200 (1927). Available at http://caselaw.lp.findlaw.com/scripts /getcase.pl?navby=search&court=US&case=/us/274/200.html; website home page: http://caselaw.lp.findlaw.com (accessed February 11, 2003).

About the Author: Oliver Wendell Holmes Jr. (1835–1941) served in the Union army in the Civil War (1861–1865) from 1861 to 1864. He joined the Massachusetts Supreme Court as an associate justice in 1883. In 1899, he became chief justice of that organization, and, in 1902, President Theodore Roosevelt (served 1901–1909) appointed him associate justice to the U.S. Supreme Court. He served for thirty years and resigned in 1932. ∎

Introduction

Science greatly advanced during the nineteenth century, both in terms of reputation and knowledge, especially in the field of genetics. Some people came to believe that everything was controlled by genes. Progressivists combined this belief with their desire for improvement to argue for sterilization of certain people. This program came to be called eugenics, which held that certain people were inherently destined to inferiority and superiority, and that the "better" genetic characteristics should be encouraged. If one believes this, and if one has the progressive desire to improve society, it is only a short step toward the other half of the "genetic equation"—that the "worse" genetic characteristics should be discouraged, perhaps by sterilization. A 1924 law in Virginia allowed exactly this to happen, but it was by no means the first law of its kind. Indiana was the first, in 1907, and twelve states had adopted such laws by 1912. By 1924, three thousand people had been involuntarily sterilized, with most being in California. Virginia claimed that "heredity plays an important part in the transmission of insanity, idiocy, imbecility, epilepsy, and crime."

Carrie Buck was the first person chosen to be sterilized in Virginia. She had a child at seventeen, and her mother was already institutionalized in a mental asylum. Virginia officials claimed that Carrie and her mother shared the genetic trait of sexual promiscuity. One national expert, without physically examining her, provided written testimony supporting the sterilization and describing Carrie as "feeble minded." Carrie's child, Vivian, was examined at seven months old, and one nurse testified that Vivian had a "look" that was "not quite normal." All three Bucks were tested and found to be below average. Thus, an order for sterilization was given, and this became a test case for the law.

Significance

The Supreme Court upheld this law, and Justice Holmes calculated: "It is better for all the world, if instead of waiting to execute degenerate offspring for crime or to let them starve for their imbecility, society can prevent those who are manifestly unfit from continuing their kind. . . . Three generations of imbeciles are enough." However, there were not truly three generations of imbeciles. Carrie had not been sexually promiscuous, but rather, she was a victim of rape. Carrie also lived out her life without being considered retarded by those who knew her. Her daughter, Vivian, was on the honor roll in first grade; by the age of eight, she was dead, most likely due to any one of the preventable diseases common among the poverty-stricken.

At the trial, one doctor's opinion of the Buck family was: "these people belong to the shiftless, ignorant, and worthless class of antisocial whites of the South." Carrie's sister, Doris, was sterilized as well. Surgeons lied and told Doris that the operation was for a burst appendix and a rupture. Later, when she and her husband had difficulty trying to conceive children, they consulted numerous hospitals. No one noticed she had had a tubal ligation. She finally found out in 1979. Upon hearing the news, Doris said that she "broke down and cried. My husband and me wanted children desperately. We were crazy about them. I never knew what they'd done to me."

Some eighty-three hundred Virginians were sterilized under this statute, which was in effect until 1972. Across the country, sixty thousand people were involuntarily sterilized, with thirty-three states having sterilization statutes. The same law Virginia used as a model was also used in Nazi Germany, where more than 350,000 people were sterilized. The use of sterilization has been narrowed, but *Buck v. Bell* has never been overturned.

Primary Source

Buck v. Bell [excerpt]

SYNOPSIS: Justice Holmes first notes the law being challenged and then describes Carrie Buck. Holmes returns to the law, describing its purposes, and the safeguards in place to prevent abuse of the patient's rights. The opinion then notes that all must sacrifice sometimes for the good of the state, and that "three generations of imbeciles are enough," which justified the sterilization. The case was argued on April 22, 1927, and was decided on May 2, 1927.

Mr. Justice Holmes delivered the opinion of the Court.

This is a writ of error to review a judgment of the Supreme Court of Appeals of the State of Virginia, affirming a judgment of the Circuit Court of Amherst County, by which the defendant in error, the superintendent of the State Colony for Epileptics and Feeble Minded, was ordered to perform the operation of salpingectomy upon Carrie Buck, the plaintiff in error, for the purpose of making her sterile. The case comes here upon the contention that the statute authorizing the judgment is void under the Fourteenth Amendment as denying to the plaintiff in error due process of law and the equal protection of the laws.

Carrie Buck is a feeble-minded white woman who was committed to the State Colony above mentioned in due form. She is the daughter of a feeble-minded mother in the same institution, and the mother of an illegitimate feeble-minded child. She was eighteen years old at the time of the trial of her case in the Circuit Court in the latter part of 1924. An Act of Virginia approved March 20, 1924 (Laws 1924, c. 394) recites that the health of the patient and the welfare of society may be promoted in certain cases by the sterilization of mental defectives, under careful safeguard, etc.; that the sterilization may be effected in males by vasectomy and in females by salpingectomy, without serious pain or substantial danger to life; that the Commonwealth is supporting in various institutions many defective persons who if now discharged would become a menace but if incapable of procreating might be discharged with safety and become self supporting with benefit to themselves and to society; and that experience has shown that heredity plays an important part in the transmission of insanity, imbecility, etc. The statute then enacts that whenever the superintendent of certain institutions including the above named State Colony shall be of opinion that it is for the best interest of the patients and of society that an inmate under his care should be sexually sterilized, he may have the operation performed upon any patient afflicted with hereditary forms of insanity, imbecility, etc., on complying with the very careful provisions by which the act protects the patients from possible abuse.

The superintendent first presents a petition to the special board of directors of his hospital or colony, stating the facts and the grounds for his opinion, verified by affidavit. Notice of the petition and of the time and place of the hearing in the institution is to be served upon the inmate, and also upon his guardian, and if there is no guardian the superintendent is to apply to the Circuit Court of the County to appoint one. If the inmate is a minor notice also is to be given to his parents, if any, with a copy of the petition. The board is to see to it that the inmate may attend the hearings if desired by him or his guardian. The evidence is all to be reduced to writing, and after the board has made its order for or against the operation, the superinten-

Carrie Buck, by order of the state of Virginia, was sterilized without her consent because she and her mother were said to have shared the genetic trait of sexual promiscuity. **COURTESY MRS. A. T. NEWBERRY, BLAND, VIRGINIA.**

dent, or the inmate, or his guardian, may appeal to the Circuit Court of the County. The Circuit Court may consider the record of the board and the evidence before it and such other admissible evidence as may be offered, and may affirm, revise, or reverse the order of the board and enter such order as it deems just. Finally any party may apply to the Supreme Court of Appeals, which, if it grants the appeal, is to hear the case upon the record of the trial in the Circuit Court and may enter such order as it thinks the Circuit Court should have entered. There can be no doubt that so far as procedure is concerned the rights of the patient are most carefully considered, and as every step in this case was taken in scrupulous compliance with the statute and after months of observation, there is no doubt that in that respect the plaintiff in error has had due process at law.

The attack is not upon the procedure but upon the substantive law. It seems to be contended that in no circumstances could such an order be justified. It certainly is contended that the order cannot be justified upon the existing grounds. The judgment finds the facts that have been recited and that

Carrie Buck "is the probable potential parent of socially inadequate offspring, likewise afflicted, that she may be sexually sterilized without detriment to her general health and that her welfare and that of society will be promoted by her sterilization," and thereupon makes the order. In view of the general declarations of the Legislature and the specific findings of the Court obviously we cannot say as matter of law that the grounds do not exist, and if they exist they justify the result. We have seen more than once that the public welfare may call upon the best citizens for their lives. It would be strange if it could not call upon those who already sap the strength of the State for these lesser sacrifices, often not felt to be such by those concerned, in order to prevent our being swamped with incompetence. It is better for all the world, if instead of waiting to execute degenerate offspring for crime, or to let them starve for their imbecility, society can prevent those who are manifestly unfit from continuing their kind. The principle that sustains compulsory vaccination is broad enough to cover cutting the Fallopian tubes. . . . Three generations of imbeciles are enough. But, it is said, however it might be if this reasoning were applied generally, it fails when it is confined to the small number who are in the institutions named and is not applied to the multitude outside. It is the usual last resort of constitutional arguments to point out shortcomings of this sort. But the answer is that the law does all that is needed when it does all that it can, indicates a policy, applies it to all within the lines, and seeks to bring within the lines all similarly situated so far and so fast as its means allow. Of course so far as the operations enable those who otherwise must be kept confined to be returned to the world, and thus open the asylum to others, the equality aimed at will be more nearly reached.

Judgment affirmed.

Mr. Justice Butler dissents.

Further Resources

BOOKS

Carson, Elof Axel. *The Unfit: A History of a Bad Idea.* Cold Spring Harbor, N.Y.: Cold Spring Harbor Laboratory Press, 2001.

Gould, Stephen Jay. *The Mismeasure of Man.* New York: Norton, 1996.

Kevles, Daniel J. *In the Name of Eugenics: Genetics and the Uses of Human Heredity.* New York: Knopf, 1985.

Kuhl, Stefan. *The Nazi Connection: Eugenics, American Racism, and German National Socialism.* Oxford: Oxford University Press, 2002.

Larson, Edward J. *Sex, Race, and Science: Eugenics in the Deep South.* Baltimore, Md.: Johns Hopkins University Press, 1996.

Novick, Sheldon M. *Honorable Justice: The Life of Oliver Wendell Holmes.* Boston: Little, Brown, 1989.

WEBSITES

Miklos, David."None Without Hope: Buck vs. Bell at 75." Gene Almanac. Available online at http://www.dnalc.org/resources /buckvbell.html; website home page: http://www.dnalc.org (accessed, February 11, 2003).

Whitney v. California

Supreme Court decision

By: Louis D. Brandeis

Date: May 16, 1927

Source: Brandeis, Louis D. *Whitney v. People of State of California.* 274 U.S. 357 (1927). Available at http://caselaw.lp.findlaw.com/scripts/getcase.pl?court=US& vol;=274&invol;=357; website home page: http://caselaw.lp .findlaw.com (accessed February 11, 2003).

About the Author: Louis D. Brandeis (1856–1941), the first Jewish member of the Supreme Court, was raised in Louisville, Kentucky. He graduated from Harvard with one of the highest grade point averages in the history of the school. Nominated to the Supreme Court by President Woodrow Wilson (served 1913–1921) in 1916, he is famous for being one of the Court's most brilliant jurists and for his thorough examinations of cases. ∎

Introduction

Freedom of speech, enshrined in the Bill of Rights, was added to the U.S. Constitution in 1791, just two years after its original ratification. The meaning of freedom of speech was not tested greatly during the eighteenth century, though, as the only major violation came in the Alien and Sedition Acts, by which the Federalists criminalized opposition to their party. These acts were repealed (or had already expired) when Thomas Jefferson came into office, and the fines assessed against anti-Federalists were refunded. Free speech also did not originally apply against the states, as decided in *Barron v. Baltimore.* Free speech was somewhat restricted in the Civil War (1861–1865), as Lincoln's opponents were sometimes jailed. The Supreme Court, however, never ruled on that question. The first real opportunity for the Supreme Court to draw the parameters of the First Amendment was during World War I (1914–1918), when it upheld all six cases that came before it under the Espionage and Sedition Acts. The Court, in the words of Oliver Wendell Holmes, held that speech could be restricted when it created a "clear and present danger."

Some cracks in the court's unanimity came in the last three Espionage Act cases, where Holmes and Brandeis generally dissented, suggesting that the acts criminalized did not create such a danger.

In *Gilbert v. Minnesota,* the Court upheld a conviction under a state law prohibiting interference with the draft. Brandeis dissented, suggesting implicitly that the law violated the Fourteenth Amendment, meaning that the states could not violate the freedom of speech. The Court took another step in that direction in 1925, when, in *Gitlow v. New York,* it held that freedom of speech and freedom of the press were protected against intrusion by the state. The next time the Supreme Court had an opportunity to rule on the First Amendment in the context of a state law was the *Whitney* case. Anita Whitney was the niece of Supreme Court Justice Stephen J. Field and a member of the Communist Labor Party of America. Her membership in the party earned her conviction under California's *Criminal Syndicalism Act.*

Significance

Whitney failed to raise the issue of freedom of speech at trial, and for this reason the Supreme Court chose not to raise the issue. At the time, and still for the most part throughout the rest of the century, appellate courts would generally not rule on issues that were not introduced at trial. Holmes and Brandeis concurred in the result, meaning that they agreed that Whitney had been properly convicted under the arguments advanced at the trial. Holmes and Brandeis, however, presented a ringing defense of freedom of speech, and the need for that freedom in their concurrence. They left little doubt that there would be a high barrier to state infringement of freedom of speech on the next occasion that the issue came before the Supreme Court and had been raised in the trial court. In 1931, in the case of *Stromberg v. California,* the Supreme Court struck down a California law prohibiting the display of a red flag as a symbol of anarchism. The same year, the Court struck down a Minnesota law that allowed the suppression of any defamatory, scandalous, or malicious newspaper reporting because that law violated freedom of the press. The Supreme Court continued to expand free speech and in *Brandenburg v. Ohio* (1969), the Court allowed speech to be restricted only "where such advocacy [of illegal activities] is directed to inciting or producing imminent lawless action." In *Brandenburg,* the court directly reversed *Whitney.* The *Brandenburg* standard remained in use into the twenty-first century.

Primary Source

Whitney v. California [excerpt]

SYNOPSIS: The majority opinion, not included here, sustained the conviction. Brandeis concurred, argu-

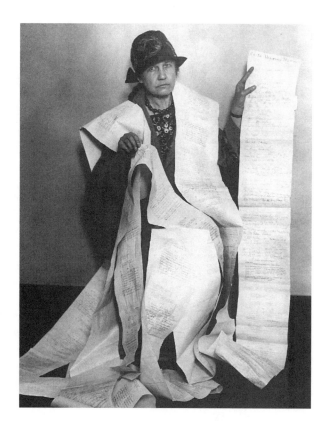

Alice Mosgrove holds a petition on behalf of Anita Whitney signed by her followers. © BETTMANN/CORBIS. REPRODUCED BY PERMISSION.

ing that the Fourteenth Amendment protects free speech through the First Amendment. He went on to say that speech can only be restricted when a "clear and present danger" exists and concludes "there must be the probability of serious injury to the state" for the state to be allowed to restrict free speech. The case was argued March 18, 1926, and was decided on May 16, 1927.

Mr. Justice Brandeis (concurring.)

. . . Despite arguments to the contrary which had seemed to me persuasive, it is settled that the due process clause of the Fourteenth Amendment applies to matters of substantive law as well as to matters of procedure. Thus all fundamental rights comprised within the term liberty are protected by the federal Constitution from invasion by the states. The right of free speech, the right to teach and the right of assembly are, of course, fundamental rights. . . . These may not be denied or abridged. But, although the rights of free speech and assembly are fundamental, they are not in their nature absolute. Their exercise is subject to restriction, if the particular restriction proposed is required in order to protect the state from destruction or from serious injury,

Anita Whitney, a member in the Communist Labor Party of America, was convicted under California's Criminal Syndicalism Act.
© BETTMANN/CORBIS. REPRODUCED BY PERMISSION.

political, economic or moral. That the necessity which is essential to a valid restriction does not exist unless speech would produce, or is intended to produce, a clear and imminent danger of some substantive evil which the state constitutionally may seek to prevent has been settled. . . . It is said to be the function of the Legislature to determine whether at a particular time and under the particular circumstances the formation of, or assembly with, a society organized to advocate criminal syndicalism constitutes a clear and present danger of substantive evil; and that by enacting the law here in question the Legislature of California determined that question in the affirmative. . . . Legislature must obviously decide, in the first instance, whether a danger exists which calls for a particular protective measure. But where a statute is valid only in case certain conditions exist, the enactment of the statute cannot alone establish the facts which are essential to its validity. Prohibitory legislation has repeatedly been held invalid, because unnecessary, where the denial of liberty involved was that of engaging in a particular business. The powers of the courts to strike down an offending law are no less when the interests involved are not property rights, but the fundamental personal rights of free speech and assembly.

This court has not yet fixed the standard by which to determine when a danger shall be deemed clear; how remote the danger may be and yet be deemed present; and what degree of evil shall be deemed sufficiently substantial to justify resort to abridgment of free speech and assembly as the means of protection. To reach sound conclusions on these matters, we must bear in mind why a state is, ordinarily, denied the power to prohibit dissemination of social, economic and political doctrine which a vast majority of its citizens believes to be false and fraught with evil consequence. Those who won our independence believed that the final end of the state was to make men free to develop their faculties, and that in its government the deliberative forces should prevail over the arbitrary. They valued liberty both as an end and as a means. They believed liberty to the secret of happiness and courage to be the secret of liberty. They believed that freedom to think as you will and to speak as you think are means indispensable to the discovery and spread of political truth; that without free speech and assembly discussion would be futile; that with them, discussion affords ordinarily adequate protection against the dissemination of noxious doctrine; that the greatest menace to freedom is an inert people; that public discussion is a political duty; and that this should be a fundamental principle of the American government. They recognized the risks to which all human institutions are subject. But they knew that order cannot be secured merely through fear of punishment for its infraction; that it is hazardous to discourage thought, hope and imagination; that fear breeds repression; that repression breeds hate; that hate menaces stable government; that the path of safety lies in the opportunity to discuss freely supposed grievances and proposed remedies; and that the fitting remedy for evil counsels is good ones. Believing in the power of reason as applied through public discussion, they eschewed silence coerced by law—the argument of force in its worst form. Recognizing the occasional tyrannies of governing majorities, they amended the Constitution so that free speech and assembly should be guaranteed.

Fear of serious injury cannot alone justify suppression of free speech and assembly. Men feared witches and burnt women. It is the function of speech to free men from the bondage of irrational fears. To justify suppression of free speech there must be reasonable ground to fear that serious evil will result if free speech is practiced. There must be reasonable ground to believe that the danger apprehended is imminent. There must be reasonable ground to believe that the evil to be prevented is a serious one. Every denunciation of existing law tends in some measure to increase the probability that there will be violation of it. Condonation of a breach enhances the probability. Expressions of approval add to the probability. Propagation of the criminal state of mind by teaching syndicalism increases it. Advocacy of lawbreaking heightens it still further. But even advocacy of violation, however reprehensible morally, is not a justification for denying free speech where the advocacy falls short of incitement and there is nothing to indicate that the advocacy would be immediately acted on. The wide difference between advocacy and incitement, between preparation and attempt, between assembling and conspiracy, must be borne in mind. In order to support a finding of clear and present danger it must be shown either that immediate serious violence was to be expected or was advocated, or that the past conduct furnished reason to believe that such advocacy was then contemplated. Those who won our independence by revolution were not cowards. They did not fear political change. They did not exalt order at the cost of liberty. To courageous, selfreliant men, with confidence in the power of free and fearless reasoning applied through the processes of popular government, no danger flowing from speech can be deemed clear and present, unless the incidence of the evil apprehended is so imminent that it may befall before there is opportunity for full discussion. If there be time to expose through discussion the falsehood and fallacies, to avert the evil by the processes of education, the remedy to be applied is more speech, not enforced silence. Only an emergency can justify repression. Such must be the rule if authority is to be reconciled with freedom. Such, in my opinion, is the command of the Constitution. It is therefore always open to Americans to challenge a law abridging free speech and assembly by showing that there was no emergency justifying it.

Moreover, even imminent danger cannot justify resort to prohibition of these functions essential to effective democracy, unless the evil apprehended is relatively serious. Prohibition of free speech and assembly is a measure so stringent that it would be inappropriate as the means for averting a relatively trivial harm to society. A police measure may be unconstitutional merely because the remedy, although effective as means of protection, is unduly harsh or oppressive. Thus, a state might, in the exercise of its police power, make any trespass upon the land of another a crime, regardless of the results or of the intent or purpose of the trespasser. It might, also, punish an attempt, a conspiracy, or an incitement to commit the trespass. But it is hardly conceivable that this court would hold constitutional a statute which punished as a felony the mere voluntary assembly with a society formed to teach that pedestrians had the moral right to cross uninclosed, unposted, waste lands and to advocate their doing so, even if there was imminent danger that advocacy would lead to a trespass. The fact that speech is likely to result in some violence or in destruction of property is not enough to justify its suppression. There must be the probability of serious injury to the State. Among free men, the deterrents ordinarily to be applied to prevent crime are education and punishment for violations of the law, not abridgment of the rights of free speech and assembly.

Further Resources

BOOKS

Eastland, Terry. *Freedom of Expression in the Supreme Court: The Defining Cases.* Lanham, Md., Washington, D.C.: Rowman & Littlefield, 2000.

Huemann, Milton, Thomas W. Church, and David P. Redlawsk. *Hate Speech on Campus: Cases, Case Studies, and Commentary.* Boston: Northeastern University Press, 1997.

The Pardon of Charlotte Anita Whitney. Sacramento: California State Printing Office, 1927.

Richmond, Al. *Native Daughter: The Story of Anita Whitney.* San Francisco: Anita Whitney 75th Anniversary Committee, 1942.

Whitney, Charlotte Anita. *Whitney v. California.* Wilmington, Del.: Michael Glazier, 1978.

WEBSITES

"Whitney v. California." Civnet.org. Available online at http://www.civnet.org/resources/teach/basic/part7/44.htm; website home page: http://www.civnet.org (accessed February 11, 2003).

Olmstead v. U.S.

Supreme Court decision

By: Louis D. Brandeis

Date: June 4, 1928

Source: Brandeis, Louis D. *Olmstead v. U.S.* 277 U.S. 438 (1928). Landmark Supreme Court Rulings, 1857–2002. Available online at http://faculty.uml.edu/sgallagher/olmstead.htm; website home page: http://faculty.uml.edu/ (accessed February 11, 2003).

About the Author: Louis D. Brandeis (1856–1941), the first Jewish member of the Supreme Court, was raised in Louisville, Kentucky. He graduated from Harvard with one of the highest grade point averages in the history of the school. Nominated for the Supreme Court in 1916 by President Woodrow Wilson (served 1913–1921), Brandeis is famous for being one of the Court's most brilliant jurists and for his thorough examinations of cases. ■

Introduction

The Fourth Amendment protects a person from being searched without probable cause and protects a person's home from being searched without a search warrant. These rights were outlined in the Bill of Rights, defining those protections in eighteenth-century terms. The federal government was prohibited from using evidence illegally seized after the *Weeks* case of 1914. The question arises, though, of how these amendments should be construed when they come to situations that were not current when the Bill of Rights was written. If the amendments are limited to only those situations present in the eighteenth century, then the government could effectively force an individual to incriminate himself, even while not violating the letter of the Constitution. On the other hand, if the amendment is stretched too far, then the intent of the framers, assuming that can be determined, may be disregarded.

The United States had adopted Prohibition, in the Eighteenth Amendment, following World War I (1914–1918). Throughout the nineteenth century, there was a continuing push for temperance—people limiting their consumption of alcohol—and prohibition—a complete ban on alcohol. Some progressives were in favor of prohibition, as they saw alcohol ruining lives and believed society would be better off without it. Factory owners also saw prohibition as a way to increase productivity.

Mr. Olmstead was a prominent illegal liquor distributor in the state of Washington. He employed about fifty people and sold millions of dollars of liquor. In order to prosecute him, federal officials tapped his phones without a warrant, never actually going onto his property to tap those phones. The question here was whether the Fourth Amendment prohibited this action.

Significance

The Supreme Court, in the majority opinion not included here, held that the Fourth Amendment only protects one's house or other physical items, and since there was no trespass into Olmstead's house to install the tap, then no violation occurred. Brandeis, in the opinion reprinted here, argues that the meaning of the Fourth Amendment needs to evolve with the modernization of crime-fighting technology. Brandeis also invokes the Fifth Amendment, saying that when privacy is violated and that evidence is used in court, then that amendment is violated. Brandeis also argues that if law enforcement commits a crime while gathering evidence, the evidence is not usable. That would have barred the prosecution, as it was illegal in Washington state to tap phones. Taft however, thought that federal agents could still legally use the taps. Brandeis also argues that the Constitution protects both criminals and everyone else, and he further argues that government must respect the rules of law, just as everyone else does. Both of these were revolutionary ideas. The *Communications Act of 1934* addressed wiretapping by prohibiting it except with the consent of one of the parties. The Court significantly expanded the idea of privacy in *Griswold v. Connecticut,* overruling a law banning the use of contraceptives. In 1967, the Court returned to the issue of wiretapping, overruling a conviction based on the recording of a phone call made from a public phone booth. This decision, *Katz v. U.S.* overturned Olmstead. The next year, Congress passed the Crime Control Act, prohibiting employers from wiretapping employees and limiting the government's power to wiretap phones. That same year, Congress acted to ban the use of electronic surveillance and wiretaps without a warrant. Brandeis wanted the Constitution to be modernized in the area of privacy, and his ideas have formed the foundation for all civil-libertarian cases involving privacy.

Primary Source

Olmstead v. U.S. [excerpt]

SYNOPSIS: Brandeis's basic argument in this case is that the right to be left alone is the most essential right of free people. He has been called visionary for his claim that the Constitution needs to evolve along with the ever-changing landscape of criminal investigative technology, and his dissent is one of the most oft-quoted in legal history. The case was argued on February 20–21, 1928, and decided on June 4, 1928.

Mr. Justice Brandeis (dissenting)

The government makes no attempt to defend the methods employed by its officers. Indeed, it concedes that, if wire tapping can be deemed a search and seizure within the Fourth Amendment, such wire tapping as was practiced in the case at bar was an unreasonable search and seizure, and that the evidence thus obtained was inadmissible. But it relies on the language of the amendment, and it claims that the protection given thereby cannot properly be held to include a telephone conversation. . . .

When the Fourth and Fifth Amendments were adopted, 'the form that evil had theretofore taken' had been necessarily simple. Force and violence were then the only means known to man by which a government could directly effect self-incrimination. It could compel the individual to testify—a compulsion effected, if need be, by torture. It could secure possession of his papers and other articles incident to his private life—a seizure effected, if need be, by breaking and entry. Protection against such invasion of 'the sanctities of a man's home and the privacies of life' was provided in the Fourth and Fifth Amendments by specific language. Boyd v. United States. But 'time works changes, brings into existence new conditions and purposes.' Subtler and more far-reaching means of invading privacy have become available to the government. Discovery and invention have made it possible for the government, by means far more effective than stretching upon the rack, to obtain disclosure in court of what is whispered in the closet. Moreover, 'in the application of a Constitution, our contemplation cannot be only of what has been, but of what may be.' The progress of science in furnishing the government with means of espionage is not likely to stop with wire tapping. Ways may some day be developed by

which the government, without removing papers from secret drawers, can reproduce them in court, and by which it will be enabled to expose to a jury the most intimate occurrences of the home. Advances in the psychic and related sciences may bring means of exploring unexpressed beliefs, thoughts and emotions. 'That places the liberty of every man in the hands of every petty officer' was said by James Otis of much lesser intrusions than these. To Lord Camden a far slighter intrusion seemed 'subversive of all the comforts of society.' Can it be that the Constitution affords no protection against such invasions of individual security? . . .

Decisions of this court applying the principle of the Boyd Case have settled these things. Unjustified search and seizure violates the Fourth Amendment, whatever the character of the paper; whether the paper when taken by the federal officers was in the home, in an office, or elsewhere; whether the taking was effected by force, by fraud, or in the orderly process of a court's procedure. From these decisions, it follows necessarily that the amendment is violated by the officer's reading the paper without a physical seizure, without his even touching it, and that use, in any criminal proceeding, of the contents of the paper so examined—as where they are testified to by a federal officer who thus saw the document . . . —any such use constitutes a violation of the Fifth Amendment.

. . . The makers of our Constitution undertook to secure conditions favorable to the pursuit of happiness. They recognized the significance of man's spiritual nature, of his feelings and of his intellect. They knew that only a part of the pain, pleasure and satisfactions of life are to be found in material things. They sought to protect Americans in their beliefs, their thoughts, their emotions and their sensations. They conferred, as against the government, the right to be let alone—the most comprehensive of rights and the right most valued by civilized men. To protect that right, every unjustifiable intrusion by the government upon the privacy of the individual, whatever the means employed, must be deemed a violation of the Fourth Amendment. And the use, as evidence in a criminal proceeding, of facts ascertained by such intrusion must be deemed a violation of the Fifth.

Applying to the Fourth and Fifth Amendments the established rule of construction, the defendants' objections to the evidence obtained by wire tapping must, in my opinion, be sustained. It is, of course, immaterial where the physical connection with the telephone wires leading into the defendants' premises was made. And it is also immaterial that the intrusion was in aid of law enforcement. Experience should teach us to be most on our guard to protect liberty when the government's purposes are beneficent. Men born to freedom are naturally alert to repel invasion of their liberty by evil-minded rulers. The greatest dangers to liberty lurk in insidious encroachment by men of zeal, well-meaning but without understanding.

Independently of the constitutional question, I am of opinion that the judgment should be reversed. By the laws of Washington, wire tapping is a crime. Pierce's Code 1921, 8976 (18). To prove its case, the government was obliged to lay bare the crimes committed by its officers on its behalf. A federal court should not permit such a prosecution to continue. . . .

When these unlawful acts were committed they were crimes only of the officers individually. The government was innocent, . . . for no federal official is authorized to commit a crime on its behalf. When the government, having full knowledge, sought, through the Department of Justice, to avail itself of the fruits of these acts in order to accomplish its own ends, it assumed moral responsibility for the officers' crimes. . . . [A]nd if this court should permit the government, by means of its officers' crimes, to effect its purpose of punishing the defendants, there would seem to be present all the elements of a ratification. If so, the government itself would become a lawbreaker.

. . . The governing principle has long been settled. It is that a court will not redress a wrong when he who invokes its aid has unclean hands. The maxim of unclean hands comes from courts of equity. But the principle prevails also in courts of law. Its common application is in civil actions between private parties. Where the government is the actor, the reasons for applying it are even more persuasive. Where the remedies invoked are those of the criminal law, the reasons are compelling.

The door of a court is not barred because the plaintiff has committed a crime. The confirmed criminal is as much entitled to redress as his most virtuous fellow citizen; no record of crime, however long, makes one an outlaw. The court's aid is denied only when he who seeks it has violated the law in connection with the very transaction as to which he seeks legal redress. Then aid is denied despite the defendant's wrong. It is denied in order to maintain respect for law; in order to promote confidence in the administration of justice; in order to preserve the judicial process from contamination. The rule is one, not of action, but of inaction. . . . A defense may be waived. It is waived when not pleaded. But the objection that the plaintiff comes with unclean hands will be taken by the court itself. It will be taken despite the wish to the contrary of all the parties to the litigation. The court protects itself.

Decency, security, and liberty alike demand that government officials shall be subjected to the same rules of conduct that are commands to the citizen. In a government of laws, existence of the government will be imperiled if it fails to observe the law scrupulously. Our government is the potent, the omnipresent teacher. For good or for ill, it teaches the whole people by its example. Crime is contagious. If the government becomes a lawbreaker, it breeds contempt for law; it invites every man to become a law unto himself; it invites anarchy. To declare that in the administration of the criminal law the end justifies the means—to declare that the government may commit crimes in order to secure the conviction of a private criminal—would bring terrible retribution. Against that pernicious doctrine this court should resolutely set its face.

Further Resources

BOOKS

Frankfurter, Felix. ed. *Mr. Justice Brandeis.* New York: Da Capo Press, 1972.

Gross, David C. *A Justice for All the People: Louis D. Brandeis.* New York: Lodestar Books, 1987.

National Lawyers Guild. *Electronic Surveillance Project, Raising and Litigating Electronic Surveillance Claims in Criminal Cases.*

McLean, Deckle. *Privacy and Its Invasion.* Westport, Conn.: Praeger, 1995.

Urofsky, Melvin I. *Louis D. Brandeis and the Progressive Tradition.* Boston: Little, Brown, 1981.

Ware, Willis H. *Information Technology, Crime and the Law.* Santa Monica, Calif.: Rand, 1982.

"7 Chicago Gangsters Slain By Firing Squad of Rivals, Some in Police Uniforms"

Newspaper article

By: *The New York Times*
Date: February 15, 1929

Source: "7 Chicago Gangsters Slain By Firing Squad of Rivals, Some in Police Uniforms." *New York Times,* February 15, 1929, 1–2.

About the Organization: Founded in 1850 as the *New York Daily Times, The New York Times* was originally a relatively obscure local paper. However, by the early part of the twentieth century, it had grown into a widely read news source. Its banner reading "All the News That's Fit to Print" is recognized throughout the world. ■

Introduction

Congress passed the Eighteenth Amendment in 1919, banning the production of alcohol in the United States. Prohibition had been high on the wish list of moral reformers throughout the nineteenth century, as the reformers believed it would protect families and improve people; industrialists thought it would increase productivity to have sober workers. Prohibition was widely (and wildly) unsuccessful, though, and organized crime grew up to provide illegal alcohol. One problem with Prohibition was the fact that the federal government hired only fifteen hundred agents to enforce the law, and the Volsted Act, which enforced the Eighteenth Amendment, was constantly underfunded. Local law enforcement generally did not help the federal government.

Chicago was one of the main hubs of the illegal alcohol trade, with Al Capone as one of Chicago's most vibrant figures. Capone was born in New York City in 1899 and moved to Chicago in 1919. There he quickly established himself as a savvy businessman, and within a few years he controlled the city's speakeasies, brothels, race tracks, bookie joints, and gambling houses. He rose to prominence by eliminating "Big Jim" Colissimo, the crime boss of Chicago. As a reward, Chicago's gangs allowed him to manage the alcohol trade in Chicago. Wishing to be rid of "Bugs" Moran, a rival crime boss, Capone hired "Machine Gun" McGurn to carry out the hit. The subsequent murders came to be known as the St. Valentine's Day Massacre.

Significance

Ironically, the victims of the massacre did not include "Bugs." The intended target had seen the fake police car pulling up and left. The only person to survive the execution long enough to speak to authorities was Frank Gusenberg, who refused to name the killers. The police had little evidence, and both Capone and McGurn had alibis. The Valentine's Day Massacre, though, was the beginning of the end for Capone. President Herbert Hoover (served 1929–1933) persuaded the IRS and the Bureau of Prohibition to break up Capone's crime ring. The Bureau of Prohibition's task force, led by Elliot Ness, recruited a team of "Untouchables" to go after him. Ness did manage to make a dent in Capone's liquor trade, but the gangster was never tried on the Prohibition violations.

Capone took a proactive approach toward his pursuers, opening a soup kitchen in the midst of the Great Depression to garner public support and killing off his enemies as well as a reporter who was going to betray him. Capone, though, had not paid taxes on any of his illegal earnings, and the government found a ledger of his illegal activities. Capone originally agreed to a light sentence for his crimes. The government agreed to this as well, fearing that he would either bribe the jurors or kill the government witnesses. Judge James Wilkerson nixed the plea agreement, and a trial was scheduled. As predicted, Capone planned to bribe the jury. Wilkerson outwitted Capone, however, by switching his jury panel with that of another judge. For this reason, Capone was convicted on some of the counts. Wilkerson then sentenced Capone to eleven years in prison. Though Capone was first sentenced to Atlanta, he was transferred to Alcatraz Island in San Francisco Bay. While in prison, Capone began to suffer from the syphilis he had contracted as a youth. Soon after leaving prison, he required medical treatment. His health slowly declined, and he died in 1947.

The activities of Capone and the other bootleggers, and the efforts of the federal government to stop them, continued to captivate the nation's attention, as they spurred movies such as *Scarface,* named for Capone's nickname, and *The Untouchables,* which is loosely based on the records of the federal task force sent to shut down Capone.

Primary Source

"7 Chicago Gangsters Slain by Firing Squad of Rivals, Some in Police Uniforms"

SYNOPSIS: Capone's henchmen dressed in police uniforms the morning of the massacre. Moran's men thought they were victims of a raid, so they lined up against a wall with their hands in the air. Capone's gang fired more than 150 bullets into the seven men, killing six of them.

Chicago gangland leaders observed Valentine's Day with machine guns and a stream of bullets and as a result seven members of the George (Bugs) Moran–Dion O'Banion, North Side gang are dead in the most cold-blooded gang massacre in the history of this city's underworld.

The seven gang warriors were trapped in a beer-distributors' rendezvous at 2122 North Clark Street, lined up against the wall by four men, two of whom were in police uniforms, and executed with the precision of a firing squad.

The killings have stunned citizens of Chicago as well as the Police Department, and while tonight there was no solution, the one outstanding cause was illicit liquor traffic.

The dead as identified by the police, were:

Clark, James, alias Frank Meyer and Albert Kashellek, convicted robber and burglar; brother-in-law of George Moran, the gang leader.

Gusenberg, Frank, who died after the others were killed, but refused to talk.

Gusenberg, Peter, brother of Frank, a notorious gunman for the O'Banion-Weiss-Drucci-Moran faction.

May, John, auto mechanic, thought to be a safeblower before joining Moran gang.

Schwimmer, Dr. Reinhart H., a resident of Hotel Parkway, an optometrist, with offices in the Capitol Building, known as a companion of gangsters, but lacking a criminal record.

Snyder, John, alias Arthur Hayes, Adam Hoyer, Adam Hyers; convicted robber and confidence man.

Weinshank, Albert, henchman of Moran and strongarm agent of Chicago cleaning and dyeing industry.

The dead, the greatest in point of numbers since Chicago gang killings began in 1924 with the assassination of Dion O'Banion, were the remnants of the "mob" organized by O'Banion, later captained by Hymie Weiss and Peter Gusenberg and recently commanded by George (Bugs) Moran.

Capone's Name Is Mentioned

One name loomed in the police investigation under way this afternoon and tonight. It was that of Alphonse (Scarface) Capone, gang leader extraordinary.

Six of the slain gangsters died in their tracks on the floor of the North Clark Street garage, a block from Lincoln Park and its fine residential neighborhood. A seventh, with twenty or more bullets in his body, died within an hour.

The police found more than 100 empty machine gun shells strewing the floor of the execution room, and there was a report that Moran had been taken out alive by the marauders.

Police Commissioner William F. Russell and his First Deputy Commissioner, John Stege, were bewildered tonight over the fact that the ambush was arranged by two men in police uniforms, wearing police badges, and the fact that the other killers arrived at the scene in an automobile resembling a detective bureau squad car.

Police Declare "War to the Finish"

Tonight an underworld round-up unparalleled in the annals of the Police Department is under way.

"It's a war to the finish," Commissioner Russell said. "I've never known of a challenge like this—the killers posing as policemen—but now the challenge has been made, it's accepted. We're going to make this the knell of gangdom in Chicago."

Reconstructing the massacre as it occurred, police and prosecuting officials were of the opinion that the men were victims of their own cupidity as well as the wrath of their enemies, for they had been stood up against the brick wall of the garage, their backs, rather than their faces, toward the executioners.

Victims Invaded at Breakfast

This morning about 10 o'clock seven men were sitting about the garage, two in the front, five others behind a wooden partition in the garage proper, according to the investigators' theory.

Four of the men were gathered about an electric stove on which bubbled a pot of coffee. A box of crackers and a half-dozen cups completed the breakfast layout. The men munched away, in between telephone calls.

The fifth man, John May, the mechanic, is believed to have been puttering about the trucks, one of which was loaded with a new wooden beer vat.

There was a noise outside that rose above the clatter of Clark Street traffic, sounding like a police gong. The front door of the garage opened.

In marched two men wearing the uniforms of policemen, their stars gleaming against the blue of the cloth. Two men in civilian attire followed them. All were armed, the first two with sub-machine guns, the last two with sawed off shotguns.

Swift Execution Accomplished

The two men in the front office threw up their hands, apparently believing a regular police raid was in progress, and marched to the rear. There was a scramble among the men about the improvised breakfast tables as they saw the police uniforms.

One of the men in police uniform probably gave the order to line up, face to the wall, and, sighting

This gangland-style slaughter in Chicago on February 14, 1929, became known as the "St. Valentine's Day Massacre." **AP/WIDE WORLD PHOTOS, REPRODUCED BY PERMISSION.**

May, made him join the others. As the seven stood staring at the whitewashed wall, they were swiftly deprived of their weapons.

Then, it is believed, came the order to "give it to them" and the roar of the shotguns mingled with the rat-a-tat of the machine gun, a clatter like that of a gigantic typewriter.

Evidently May, incredulous that he, an ordinary mechanic, should be included, made a mad leap only to drop within six inches of a man wielding a shotgun.

The machine-gunners probably sprayed the heap of dead on the floor and then the four executioners marched out.

A tailor glanced up from his pressing iron next door, and a woman living near by ran to the street. They saw what appeared to be two men under arrest, their hands in the air, followed by two policemen.

The four climbed into what looked like a police squad car, a fifth man sitting at the wheel, the motor humming. The car roared south in Clark Street, sweeping around the wrong side of a street car, and was lost in the traffic.

When police arrived upon the scene they found six of the men dead. The seventh, Frank Gusenberg, was crawling on the floor toward Police Lieutenant Tom Loftus. Gusenberg died within an hour at the Alexandrian Hospital.

The majority of the victims were dangerous men, with reputations equal to the worst, Deputy Commissioner Stege said.

"Where is 'Bugs' Moran?" Stege asked when his officers discovered the automobile which Moran was supposed to own.

Then came the story that perhaps he was one of the men who walked out of the garage, hands high above his head, followed by the pseudo policemen.

Squads were dispatched to seek Moran. Others were sent after information concerning "Scarface Al" Capone's whereabouts. The latter group came back with word that Capone was at his Winter home in Miami, Fla.

The police recalled that the Aiello brothers' gang of North Side Sicilians had a year or so ago affiliated themselves with the Moran gang, and that the Aiellos and the Caponites were deadly enemies. But no Aiellos were found.

Coroner Herman N. Bundesen reached the garage within a half hour after the fusillade. The bodies were photographed and searched.

Cash and Diamond Rings on Bodies

Lieutenants John L. Sullivan and Otto Erianson of the Homicide Bureau checked the identifications and kept records of search results.

Peter Gusenberg had a large diamond ring and $447 in cash.

Albert Weinshank proved to be the cousin of a former State representative of the same family name. Weinshank, who recently took an "executive position" with the Central Cleaners and Dyers Company, had only $18 in cash, but he had a fine diamond ring and a bankbook showing an account in the name of A. H. Shanks.

Then a body was identified as that of John Snyder, alias Adam Meyers, alias Adam Hyers, alias Hayes. It was said that Snyder was owner of the Fairview Kennels, a dog track rivaling Capone's Hawthorne course. Chief Egan was told that Snyder was the "brains" of the Moran "mob." Snyder had $1,399.

The body of May, the overall-clad mechanic, had only a few dollars in the pockets. He was the father of seven children. A machine gun bullet had penetrated two medals of St. Christopher.

The fifth of the five bodies in the row, flat on their backs with their heads to the south, was recorded as that of Reinhardt H. Schwimmer, an optometrist. Despite his having no police record, it is said that he recently boasted that he was in the alcohol business and could have any one "taken for a ride."

Closer to the door, face down, with his head to the east, lay John Clark, brother-in-law of Moran, and rated as a killer with many notches in his guns. His clothes contained $681.

Woman's Story Aids Police

"Bullet marks on the wall," Captain Thomas Condon observed and it was seen that few of the pellets missed their marks, for there were only seven or eight places where the detectives were sure bullets had struck.

Each of the victims had six to ten bullets shot through him. A high-powered electric bulb overhead flooded the execution chamber with a glare of white light. Chained in a corner was a huge police dog, which strained on its fastenings and snarled at the detectives.

The police expressed amazement that the seven gangsters had been induced to face the wall and certain death without a struggle and without resistance.

"That bunch always went well armed," a police captain said.

An explanation was seen in the story of Mrs. Alphonsine Morin, who lives just across the street from the garage. She told of seeing men she thought were policemen coming out after hearing the shooting.

"Two men in uniforms had rifles or shotguns as they came out the door," she said, "and there were two or three men walking ahead of them with their hands up in the air. It looked as though the police were making an arrest and they all got into an automobile and drove away."

"Quite simple," Chief Egan commented. "They would never have got that gang to line up unless they came in police uniforms."

Typical of his life, Frank Gusenberg refused during his last hour to tell the police anything. He was conscious, but he kept defying the police who sought names from him.

Assistant State's Attorney David Stansbury was put in charge of the investigation tonight by State's Attorney John A. Swanson. The police, prosecutor and the Federal authorities were all working together to get trace of the slayers.

Theories about who plotted and carried out the execution were numerous.

"Hi-jackers, no doubt," Chief of Detectives John Egan termed the dead men. Other theories were:

That the victims had been "hoisting" trucks of booze, Canadian beer, alcohol and fine liquors en route from Detroit, and the "Purple Gang" of Detroit had sallied out for vengeance.

That they were involved in the bitter competition of rival organizations of cleaning and dyeing establishments, the Moran gang protecting the North Side concerns and the Capone outfit the Becker system.

That it was a sequel to the sentencing of Alderman Titus Haffa yesterday to two years in Leavenworth Prison for violating the prohibition law. Haffa's ward adjoins the domain which Moran had ruled.

Other detectives said the killing was the work of the Capone "mob."

"It is the answer of the Sicilians for the killing of Tony Lombardo, and it is a logical sequel to the series of murders starting five years ago with the mowing down on O'Banion," one declared.

North Side Gang "Dynasty" Falls

Gang warfare in Chicago began with the slaying of Dion O'Banion in November, 1924. In the fifty months since then, thirty-eight murders, most of them attributed to the enmity between the North Side band founded by O'Banion and the West Side syndicate established by John Torrio and turned over to Al Capone, have been recorded.

Today's massacre marked the end of the proud North Side dynasty which began with O'Banion. O'Banion yielded to Hymie Weiss who was replaced by "Schemer" Drucci, who was succeeded by "Bugs" Moran. And Moran tonight was missing while seven of his chief aids lay dead.

Back to the assassination of Jim Colosimo, a vice lord in 1920 when prohibition was new and profitable violations were beginning to be realized, the police traced the series of slayings which reached a climax today. But it was not until O'Banion's murder that lines were sharply drawn between the gangs.

Al Capone was suspected of masterminding the "St. Valentine's Day Massacre" in order to eliminate rival gang members. AP/WIDE WORLD PHOTOS. REPRODUCED BY PERMISSION.

On Nov. 10, 1924, three men stepped into O'Banion's floral shop across from the Holy Name Cathedral. He stepped forward with his famous sunny smile, his hand extended in greeting. Three revolvers cracked and he sank dead among his flowers. It was a declaration of war by the West Side against the North Side.

Further Resources

BOOKS

Kobler, John. *Capone: The Life and World of Al Capone.* New York: Putnam, 1971.

Murray, Jesse George. *The Legacy of Al Capone: Portraits and Annals of Chicago's Public Enemies.* New York: Putnam, 1975.

Schoenberg, Robert J. *Mr. Capone.* New York: William Morrow, 1992.

Tucker, Kenneth. *Eliot Ness and The Untouchables: The Historical Reality and the Film and Television Depictions.* Jefferson, N.C.: McFarland, 2000.

AUDIO AND VISUAL MEDIA

Mamet, David. *The Untouchables.* Produced by Art Linson, directed by Brian De Palma. Hollywood, Calif.: Paramount, 2000.

7

LIFESTYLES AND SOCIAL TRENDS

JONATHAN MARTIN KOLKEY

Entries are arranged in chronological order by date of primary source. For entries with one primary source, the entry title is the same as the primary source title. Entries with more than one primary source have an overall entry title, followed by the titles of the primary sources.

Important Events in Lifestyles and Social Trends, 1920–1929

1920

- The U.S. Census reports that the population of the United States is 105,710,620. For the first time in census history, the U.S. population is less than 50 percent rural; and the population earning their living through farming is less than 30 percent.

- In this year 80 percent of all women in their thirties are married.

- Women make up 23.6 percent of the American workforce, and 8.3 million women work outside their homes.

- Thirteen percent of Americans are first-generation immigrants.

- The median size of the American family is 4.3 people, a drop from 4.7 in 1900. Average life expectancy is 54 years, up from 49 years in 1900.

- Birth control advocate Margaret Sanger campaigns for birth control as a means to women's personal and economic freedom.

- Prohibition results in increases in sales of coffee, tea, soft drinks, and ice cream sodas.

- Silk stockings are out and rayon hose from the DuPont Fibersilk Company are in. Frigidaire refrigerators are replacing the old icebox. Pogo sticks are introduced. New brand name products include La Choy Chinese food, Campfire marshmallows, and Baby Ruth candy bars—named for the daughter of former president Grover Cleveland.

- A vacuum cleaner costs forty dollars on the installment plan—two dollars down and four dollars monthly.

- Templar, Stanley Steamer, Stephens, Salient, Overland, Stutz, Hupmobile, Maxwell, Pierce-Arrow, Milburn Electric, Liberty, Peerless, Ford, Chevrolet, Hudson, Packard, and Cadillac are some of the cars on the U.S. market.

- On January 16, the Volstead National Prohibition Act goes into effect, providing enforcement for the Eighteenth Amendment. In Norfolk, Virginia, ten thousand supporters join evangelist Billy Sunday in celebrating the event. But almost immediately, portable stills are offered in hardware stores for six dollars, and speakeasies begin to appear.

- On June 5, the Women's Bureau, a new federal agency to promote the welfare of women workers, is approved by Congress.

- From August 1 to August 2, the national convention of the Universal Negro Improvement Association, founded by Marcus Garvey, meets in New York City. Twenty-five thousand African Americans hear Garvey speak at a rally in Madison Square Garden.

- On August 26, the Nineteenth Amendment takes effect, granting women the right to vote.

1921

- The American Medical Association (AMA) endorses alcohol by prescription: a maximum of 2.5 gallons of beer per year can be prescribed for a range of complaints.

- Freudian psychology has become a fad. Partygoers corner psychologist guests at social gatherings and ask for psychoanalysis. For those who cannot afford treatment at clinics in Europe, popular books like *Sex Problems Solved* or *Ten Thousand Dreams Interpreted* offer self-help at home.

- The Education Act regulates working conditions for children under fourteen.

- Forty-three billion cigarettes are consumed annually, in spite of antismoking laws in fourteen states. College girls often are expelled if caught smoking. Iowa legalizes the sale of cigarettes to adults.

- On January 16, after one year of Prohibition, bootleggers thrive, and many people make bathtub gin and home brew.

- On May 19, the Emergency Quota Act restricts immigration to 358,000 people per year, a drastic decrease from the more than one million immigrants who entered annually in the years before World War I. In addition, nearly half of the entrance visas are limited to British immigrants. The 1917 ban on Asian workers is continued.

- In August, the reemergence of the Ku Klux Klan brings lawlessness, whippings, brandings, tarrings, and destruction of property to African Americans and Catholics in the South.

- In September, Dallas businessman J.G. Kirby opens the Pig Stand. The roadside establishment serves barbecued pork sandwiches to motorists in their cars.

- On September 8, the first Miss America pageant is won by Margaret Gorman of Washington, D.C.

- On November 2, Margaret Sanger founds the American Birth Control League in New York, combining the National Birth Control League (established by Sanger in 1914) with the Voluntary Parenthood League (begun by Mary Dennett in 1919). In 1923, Sanger establishes the Birth Control Clinical Research Bureau in New York City.

1922

- Sociologist Katherine Bement Davis's survey of marital happiness among one thousand middle-class women reports that 116 respond as "happy."

- A study by the Bureau of Social Hygiene Committee of one thousand married women reports that 75 percent approve of birth control.

- Emily Post's *Etiquette in Society, in Business, in Politics, and at Home* is published and becomes a runaway best-seller.

- Advertising educates people about their appearance. Americans have learned about body odor, halitosis, and stained teeth. For example, they now know that Palmolive soap will give them a "school girl complexion" and that smoking Lucky Strikes protects the throat against excessive coughing.

- Radio is a national obsession. Many stay up late listening to concerts, sermons, anti-Communist Red Scare news, and sports. A hundred thousand radios are manufactured this year and sales reach $60 million.

- Thirty-five percent of households now have a telephone. The cost of a call from New York to San Francisco has fallen to $13.50. In 1915 it was $20.70.

- Mah-Jongg, an ancient Chinese game, is introduced in the United States; it quickly becomes a fad.

- The Harlem Renaissance, a flourishing of African American art and literature, begins in New York City.

- In May, the trade journal *American Hairdresser* reports that short, bobbed hair has become popular among certain stylish young women. *Vanity Fair* calls such women "flappers."

- On May 6, government officials announce that more than 50 African Americans have been lynched this year. Although a federal anti-lynching bill passes the House of Representatives during the year, it is killed in the Senate. African American leader Mary B. Talbot organizes the Anti-Lynching Crusade.

- In Fall, the U.S. Post Office in New York destroys hundreds of copies of James Joyce's *Ulysses,* a book that has been banned in the United States.

- On September 12, Episcopal bishops vote to omit the word *obey* from the marriage ceremony.

- On September 22, Congress passes the Cable Act, which grants independent citizenship to married women. Women who marry aliens no longer have to give up their citizenship.

1923

- Emile Coué, promoter of auto-suggestion, makes his first tour of the United States. He returns for his second tour in 1924.

- The newest movie star is Rin Tin Tin. The handsome dog is reported to have been found in a trench during World War I. His film success makes German Shepherds a popular household breed.

- On April 1, Alma Cummings becomes the first American marathon dance champion at the Audubon Ballroom in New York City. Within a month her record is broken by a group of eight young people. The record rises to 90 hours and 10 minutes. Another 1920s fad is launched.

- On October 24, African American migration to the North is estimated by the Department of Labor to be 500,000 within the past year.

- On October 29, the African American musical revue *Runnin' Wild* premieres on Broadway and introduces the Charleston, an exuberant, jazzy dance.

- On November 6, Jacob Schick patents the first electric razor.

- On November 15, Governor J.C. Walton calls out the National Guard and places Oklahoma under martial law. He blames the Ku Klux Klan for a rising tide of unrest and hatred in the state toward African Americans, Native Americans, Jews and immigrants. The Klan's growth has been strong in both Oklahoma and Texas in recent years. Pro-Klan state legislators call for a special session of the legislature to remove the governor from office.

- In December, the first Equal Rights Amendment is proposed in Congress.

1924

- The League of Women Voters establishes the Committee on Negro Problems.

- The most popular places to hide illegal liquor are heels of shoes, flasks form-fitted to women's thighs, folds of coats, and perfume bottles.

- Some 2.5 million radios are now in American homes. There were just two thousand in 1920.

- Clarence Birdseye introduces a process for freezing fish so that they can go immediately from freezer to oven, without thawing first. Other consumer developments of the year include the spin dryer, spiral-bound notebook, and permanent wave.

- The use of commercial laundries has increased 57 percent since 1914.

- Alvin "Shipwreck" Kelley begins his career as a flagpole sitter in front of a Hollywood theater and starts a fad in the United States.

- In April, a craze begins when new publishers Richard Simon and Max L. Schuster publish the first book of crossword puzzles.

- In May, actor Paul Robeson, who plays an African American man married to a white woman in Eugene O'Neill's *All God's Chillun Got Wings,* is threatened by the Ku Klux Klan. Police officers guard the Provincetown Playhouse.

- On May 26, Congress restricts immigration even more than it did in 1921. The Johnson-Reed Act cuts the 1921 quota in half, to just 164,000 European immigrants per year. In addition, all immigration from Asia is banned. The Ku Klux Klan is among the legislation's most vocal supporters. However, Japan's ambassador to the United States shows his nation's discontent by threatening to resign.

- On November 4, Miriam "Ma" Ferguson in Texas and Nellie Taylor Ross in Wyoming become the first women elected governor of a state.

1925

- The Model T Ford reaches its lowest price of $260. It had sold for $950 in 1909. Rental cars also are popular. Yellow Drive-It-Yourself Systems charges 12 cents per mile for a Ford and 22 cents for a six-cylinder car.

- Cosmetics is a $141 million industry.

- Prosperity increases, and 40 percent of the population earns at least $2,000 per year. The mass market for cars, radios, refrigerators, and vacuum cleaners increases.

- Public adulation of sports figures—such as baseball's Babe Ruth, boxing's Gene Tunney and Jack Dempsey, golf's Bobby Jones, and swimming's Johnny Weismuller—is at an all-time high.

- Earl Wise's potato chips prove so successful that he moves his business from his garage to a plant in Berwick, Pennsylvania.

- Bootleg-liquor prices regularly appear in the "Talk of the Town" section of a magazine new this year, *The New Yorker.*

- Surviving an attempt on his life, Chicago crime boss John Torrio turns his entire organization over to his former bodyguard Al Capone and retires to Italy.

- On May 13, the Florida legislature passes a law that requires daily Bible readings in the state's public schools.

- From July 10-21, the trial of high school teacher John Scopes takes place in Dayton, Tennessee. Scopes is accused of breaking the state's new law (passed March 21) against the teaching of evolution. Clarence Darrow, the nation's leading lawyer, defends him. Former secretary of state and three-time presidential candidate William Jennings Bryan heads the prosecution. Widely covered in newspapers and by radio, the "Monkey Trial" attracts national attention. Scopes is convicted and fined $100.

- On August 8, some 40,000 members of the Ku Klux Klan rally in Washington, D.C. The white-robed Klansmen march down Pennsylvania Avenue in a demonstration of the organization's renewed strength in America. Current membership is estimated at more than four million.

- In August, a land boom in Florida reaches its height. The state's population has exploded to more than a million since the end of World War I, as both tourists and migrants seek out the state's inviting warmth and sun.

- On October 16, the Texas State Text Book Board bans the discussion of evolution in school books in the state.

- On November 24, the Grand Dragon of the Indiana Ku Klux Klan is convicted of assault, kidnapping, and rape in the abduction and brutal beating of a young Indianapolis woman. The incident marks the beginning of a change in the public's perception of the Klan.

1926

- Two thousand people die from poisoned liquor during the year, as the illegal liquor trade brings in $3.5 billion.

- Movies become a favorite entertainment; more than 14,500 movie houses show four hundred films a year. The personality cult that has affected sports figures is beginning to spread to movie stars as well. Rudolph Valentino, Charlie Chaplin, and Greta Garbo cannot appear in public without being swamped by fans.

- Twelve percent of high school graduates go to college, of which there are more than twelve hundred to choose from.

- Scotch tape, zippers, safety glass, the pop-up electric toaster, and flavored yogurt are among the new products available this year.

- On March 7, the first transatlantic radiotelephone conversation—between New York and London—occurs.

- In August, thousands of mourners line Hollywood streets for Valentino's funeral. Reports of the handsome thirty-one-year-old film star's unexpected death on August 23 caused mass hysteria among women across America.

- In October, Henry Ford introduces a shorter, forty-hour workweek to combat overproduction in the auto industry. Industrial leaders are shocked, but the American Federation of Labor commends Ford's action.

- In November, the Supreme Court upholds a law limiting medical prescriptions of whiskey to one pint every ten days.

1927

- The American Birth Control League has fifty-five clinics in twelve states and thirty-seven thousand dues-paying members.

- Film producers add some sound to silent films and call them "part talkies."

- A survey reports a "loosening of manners and morals." Mrs. Bertrand Russell defends free love, and Judge Lindsey advocates "companionate [trial] marriage."

- Al Capone's gang nets $100 million in the bootleg trade; *rackets* is a new word.

- On April 19, actress Mae West is given a ten-day sentence and fined $500 in a New York court. West was arrested in April 1926, when public pressure forced police to close her play *Sex.* The star was busted for moving her navel—"up and down and from right to left" according to an undercover cop in the audience—while doing a belly dance on stage.

- On May 21, aviator Charles Lindbergh lands in Paris after completing the first solo flight across the Atlantic. The flight, which began in New York, took more than thirty-three hours. On his return to America, Lindbergh is honored in a parade down Broadway that features 1,800 tons of ticker tape, and in a 48-city national tour. A new dance, the Lindy Hop, is named for the aviator.

- On August 22, Poet Edna St. Vincent Millay is arrested outside the Boston courthouse during a deathwatch for Nicola Sacco and Bartolomeo Vanzetti. Others protesting the execution of the anarchists convicted of murder include three-fourths of the students enrolled at Harvard Law School, Harvard law professor Felix Frankfurter, writer Dorothy Parker, physicist Albert Einstein, social worker Jane Addams, and writer H.G. Wells. In spite of this protest, Sacco and Vanzetti are executed on August 23.

- On December 1, Henry Ford unveils his new Model A automobile. After producing 15 million of his "tin lizzies," Ford is trying to keep up with competitors like Chevrolet. His new car features shock absorbers, a speedometer, and more graceful lines than the Model T it is replacing.

1928

- A study shows that there are 116 divorces for every 1,000 marriages.

- Women's congressional representation reaches a high point of 7 elected congresswomen. Other women elected to office include 119 state representatives, 12 state senators, and 2 state treasurers.

- The federal government and the Coast Guard arrest seventy-five thousand people this year for Prohibition violations.

- Marathons continue to be a fad. In the ultimate dance marathon, ninety-one couples remain after competing for three weeks for a five thousand dollar prize. After 482 hours of dancing, the contest is suspended. The winner of the Noun and Verb Rodeo, a talk marathon, lasts 81 hours and 45 minutes.

- Real wages (adjusted for inflation) are up 33 percent from 1914.

- Drivers in the United States operate 78 percent of the world's motor vehicles—21,630,000 cars and 3,120,000 trucks.

- Brokers' loans to stock-market margin investors reach a record $4 billion.

1929

- The United States averages one car for every 1.3 families; 23.1 million automobiles are in use in the nation.

- Radio sales reach $852 million.

- There are 20,500 movie theaters in the United States. Almost half of them have sound.

- At least thirty-two thousand speakeasies thrive in New York City.

- The American Home Economics Association observes: "Homemaking still ranks first as the occupation employing the largest number of persons, expending the longest hours of labor."

- A study of 169,255 working women indicates that more than 46 percent are or have been married.

- Lynchings are on the decline; ten are reported this year.

- The United States has 70,950 stockbrokers, up from 26,609 in 1920.

- Roughly 4.5 million people put money in speculative "investment trusts."

- Seventy percent of Americans have incomes of less than three thousand dollars per year.

- Private citizens in the United States have $6 billion tied up in installment buying.

- On May 12, the first Academy Awards are presented by the Academy of Motion Picture Arts and Sciences.

- In September, Pickwick Stages, a Los Angeles company manufactures the first busses equipped with sleeping facilities for long distance travel.

- On September 3, the bull market peaks.

- On October 29, Black Tuesday: the stock market crashes. New York City mayor Jimmy Walker urges movie houses to show cheerful pictures in the wake of the crash.

- On November 13, the stock market hits bottom. Within weeks unemployment rises from seven hundred thousand to 3.1 million.

J. Edgar Hoover Monitors Marcus Garvey

Memo to Special Agent Ridgely

Memo

By: J. Edgar Hoover

Date: October 11, 1919

Source: Hoover, J. Edgar. Memo to Special Agent Ridgely. October 11, 1919. Reprinted in Hill, Robert A., ed. *The Marcus Garvey and Universal Negro Improvement Association Papers,* vol. II. Berkeley, Calif.: University of California Press, 1983, 72.

"Report by Special Agent P-138"

Report

By: J. Edgar Hoover

Date: August 6, 1920

Source: Hoover, J. Edgar. "Report by Special Agent P-138." August 6, 1920. Reprinted in Hill, Robert A., ed. *The Marcus Garvey and Universal Negro Improvement Association Papers,* vol. II. Berkeley, Calif.: University of California Press, 1983, 546–547.

Memo to Lewis J. Baley

Memo

By: J. Edgar Hoover

Date: February 11, 1921

Source: Hoover, J. Edgar. Memo to Lewis J. Baley, February 11, 1921. Reprinted in Hill, Robert A., ed. *The Marcus Garvey and Universal Negro Improvement Association Papers,* vol. III. Berkeley, Calif.: University of California Press, 1983, 177.

About the Author: J. Edgar Hoover (1895–1972), also known by the Bureau as Special Agent P138, headed the FBI from 1924 until his death in 1972. A fierce anti-Communist, Hoover saw himself as a bulwark against the spread of political radicalism (especially among disaffected minority groups) in the United States. ∎

Marcus Garvey (center), founder of the Universal Negro Improvement Association and African Communities League, was considered by those in government, including FBI Director J. Edgar Hoover, to be a radical and an agitator. © BETTMANN/CORBIS. REPRODUCED BY PERMISSION.

Introduction

America has doubtless never witnessed anyone like the legendary J. Edgar Hoover—a Washington, D.C., insider whose career spanned over fifty years and who in time became the veritable symbol of the nation's commitment to effective, impartial law enforcement. Along the way, Hoover's reputation reached near mythic proportions, indeed eventually rising to the status of a modern-day Wyatt Earp.

Hoover tended to personalize his job—first at the Justice Department's obscure Bureau of Investigation when, while serving under Wilson administration attorney general A. Mitchell Palmer, he supervised the federal government's crackdown on suspected radicals during the so-called 'Red Scare' of 1918–20. Second, after 1924 Hoover served as permanent director of the now-renamed Federal Bureau of Investigation (FBI)—a position he held until his death in 1972. Accordingly, various notorious felons with colorful names—John Dillinger, Machine Gun Kelly, Pretty Boy Floyd, Bonnie and Clyde, and Baby Face Nelson—were branded by Hoover as "public enemies" and then relentlessly pursued by Hoover's FBI in the same spirit that old frontier sheriffs chased down outlaws.

To Hoover, this pursuit was a game—a sort of one-on-one, man-to-man confrontation between the FBI director and his prey. Naturally, the American public often responded enthusiastically to Hoover's conspicuous display of bureaucratic bravado.

Significance

One of Hoover's lifelong obsessions was the potential threat of African American political and social unrest. At the beginning of his long career, Hoover made certain to keep close watch on Marcus Garvey, the Jamaican-born man who became America's first popular black nationalist leader. Having founded the Universal Negro Improvement Association in 1914, Garvey boldly challenged white America's most deeply held assumptions regarding race. Hoover came to view Garvey as a dangerous agitator—indeed, a likely subversive—and instructed his agents to monitor Garvey's activities. Meanwhile, as a resident alien, Garvey was vulnerable, for if convicted of any felony, he was subject to immediate deportation.

Clearly, Hoover paid close attention to his surveillance of Garvey and his movement. In the end, Hoover "got his man." Based on questionable evidence, Garvey was convicted in 1923 of mail fraud in connection with his ill-fated efforts to launch a steamship company—the Black Star Line. After his appeal failed, Garvey entered federal prison in 1925 to serve a five-year term. He was pardoned by President Calvin Coolidge, but then summarily deported in December 1927.

Four decades later, Hoover's FBI (again on direct orders from the director) pursued similar successful tactics to "neutralize" another generation of suspected African American "agitators," in particular, the radical Black Panthers.

Primary Source

Memo to Special Agent Ridgely

SYNOPSIS: In this letter, then Justice Department attorney J. Edgar Hoover expresses his concern regarding Marcus Garvey and his movement.

Washington, D.C., October 11, 1919

Memorandum for Mr. Ridgely.

I am transmitting herewith a communication which has come to my attention from the Panama Canal, Washington office, relative to the activities of MARCUS GARVEY. Garvey is a West-Indian negro and in addition to his activities in endeavoring to establish the Black Star Line Steamship Corporation he has also been particularly active among the radical elements in New York City in agitating the negro movement. Unfortunately, however, he has not as yet violated any federal law whereby he could be proceeded against on the grounds of being an undesirable alien, from the point of view of deportation. It occurs to me, however, from the attached clipping that there might be some proceeding against him for fraud in connection with his Black Star Line propaganda and for this reason I am transmitting the communication to you for your appropriate attention.

The following is a brief statement of Marcus Garvey and his activities:

Subject a native of the West Indies and one of the most prominent negro agitators in New York;

He is a founder of the Universal Negro Improvement Association and African Communities League;

He is the promulgator of the Black Star Line and is the managing editor of the Negro World;

He is an exceptionally fine orator, creating much excitement among the negroes through his steamship proposition;

In his paper the "Negro World" the Soviet Russian Rule is upheld and there is open advocation of Bolshevism. Respectfully,

J. E. Hoover

Primary Source

"Report by Special Agent P-138"

SYNOPSIS: Now a special agent with the Bureau of Investigation (renamed the Federal Bureau of Investigation in 1924), J. Edgar Hoover reports on his surveillance of Marcus Garvey's Universal Negro Improvement Association.

New York City 8/6/20

In Re: Negro Activities (Marcus Garvey)

Today [*4 August*] I visited Garvey's afternoon and evening sessions of the Convention now being held in Liberty Hall, which were well attended. The afternoon session was given over to hearing the reports of delegates. Two delegates of note spoke. One was from Hayti and the other from San Domingo. They expressed themselves as in hearty accord with the movement and think Garvey will be the Saviour of their country. They further pledged moral and financial support to carrying on and spreading of Garvey's anti-white propaganda. On the whole all the delegates['] reports played to the tune of "Down with the White Man."

So as to learn all that is possible regarding any Japanese activity among the Garvey followers, I succeeded today in getting in touch with Garvey's associate Editor of the "Negro World" who works in the office and very near to Garvey. This fellow's name is Hudson Price. During a lengthy conversation with him on the street this eve, commenting on the Madison Square Meeting, Sunday and Monday parades, etc., by a series of "drawing out" questions I learned from Price that there were two Japanese whom were very much in sympathy with Garvey's movement and he said that means a great deal to them as the Japs were smart people.

Price had a long talk with one of them especially who visited him at the office, told him to put a Japanese paper on the mailing list which he claims to represent in Tokio, Japan. But Price told me that this said Jap is a "big man" and was only using that as a farce. Price said that the name of this Jap was Kataran or Ketarama. He also stated that six weeks ago Katarama visited the office, 56 W. 135th St. Black Star Line Office, and handed him, Price, a news item which appeared in the Negro World. Of course, I expressed my sympathy with entire movement and affairs and asked Price to secure that particular [issue] of the paper for me which he promised to do.

Tonight Garvey spoke on the race question at length. He worked his followers up to a height of frenzied enthusiasm when he told them that for years the white man told them that everything which is black was bad or evil and everything which was white is good. That God was white. The devil was black, but now the negro must turn it the other way about that God is black and the Devil was white. The Negroes will therefore in future worship a Black God and not a White One.

I simply cite the foregoing to give an idea of the plans and method which Garvey used in playing on the crude minds and undeveloped faculties of his followers. Another favorite story of his is that it was the White man who killed Jesus and it was the Black man who helped Jesus to bear the cross up the hill of Calvary, hence God will always help the black man now. The foregoing Biblical story naturally touches the Religious Chord of his hearers.

The con[s]ensus of opinion which one can draw from the reports of the various delegates is that the greatest opposition which they encounter in their respective territory is from the Preachers and all the intelligent Negro Business and Professional men whose attitude is either right out hostility or a Hands Off policy. So far as I can see the movement has ceased to be simply a nationalist movement but among the followers it is like a religion. The majority of them are hard working poor men and women who absolutely refuse to think and reason for themselves. Of course men such as Rev. Easton and Brooks, Ferris, etc., are simply paid employees who must talk as Garvey wants them to or else lose their jobs.

After mixing in among the officers and followers of this movement I spoke with Garvey himself. Two days ago I met him in the street, shook his hands and congratulated him on the wonderful hit he made at Madison Square Garden. I am fully convinced that Garvey's teaching is without doubt a purely anti-white campaign and the Negro World is the instrument employed to spread the propaganda. That the various branches of the movement are only nucleus for further spreading of same. That he gives the leaders of these different branches high titles so as to let them feel important and carry on the work. That he is flirting with the leaders of the Irish, Egyptian, Indian and Japanese only so far as to further his aims. That Garvey is becoming bolder everyday, having been fed along with the hand clapping and cheers of his worshippers. That his followers are under the impression owing to Garvey's statement from the platform, that he has defied state and Government, outwitted the State District Attorney[,] hence he is looked upon as a black Moses. That the convention and movement is only stirring up race hatred and widening the gap between the Races which the other intelligent leaders took years to build up.

Primary Source

Memo to Lewis J. Baley

SYNOPSIS: In this memo, J. Edgar Hoover expresses his belief that Marcus Garvey was inciting "negro disturbances" in the United States, possibly under orders from a foreign government. He recommends that Garvey be allowed to leave the United States and then denied re-entry into the country.

Washington, D.C. February 11, 1921

Memorandum for Mr. Baley.

It is my desire to call your attention to the departure from this country, of MARCUS GARVEY, the well known negro agitator, publisher of the "Negro World" and president of the Universal Negro Improvement Association.

The activities of Garvey have been covered for some time in the past, in a confidential manner, and it has now come to our attention that he is contemplating leaving this country February [7th?] aboard the Black Line steamer "Ka[n]a[w]ha." Garvey who is a British subject, also contemplates securing a seaman's passport, in order that same will warrant his return to this country. I understand that his trip will take him to the West Indies.

For your further information on this subject, I desire to advise you that I have been under the impression for some time, although with a limited amount of proof, that Garvey's movement in this country, is subsidized to some extent by the British Government, further, that he through his emissaries, has been responsible to a considerable extent, for the negro disturbances.

In view of the above it is my desire, should Garvey leave this country, that he be denied entry in the future, and it is suggested that some such arrangement be made with the State Department in this matter.

Will you kindly advise this office as to the final disposition of this matter.

Respectfully,
J. E. Hoover

Further Resources

BOOKS

Cronon, Edmund D. *Black Moses: The Story of Marcus Garvey and the Universal Negro Improvement Association.* Madison, Wis.: University of Wisconsin Press, 1969.

Gentry, Curt. *J. Edgar Hoover: The Man and the Secrets.* New York: Plume, 1991.

Vincent, Theodore G. *Black Power and the Garvey Movement.* Berkeley, Calif.: Ramparts Press, 1971.

"'These Wild Young People': By One Of Them"

Magazine article

By: John F. Carter Jr.

Date: September 1920

Source: Carter, John F., Jr. "'These Wild Young People': By One Of Them." *The Atlantic Monthly,* September 1920, 301.

About the Author: A contributor to *The Atlantic Monthly,* author John F. Carter Jr., reflected the angst of American youth in the immediate post-World War I period. ∎

Introduction

In the eyes of some historians, the U.S. government oversold American participation in the First World War as a crusade to remake the world in the image of a democratic America. For instance, the Committee on Public Information, a Wilson administration agency led by one-time Progressive journalist George Creel, set the stage for later disillusionment by characterizing the struggle as "a Crusade not merely to rewin the tomb of Christ, but to bring back to earth the rule of right, the peace, goodwill to men and gentleness he taught." In his book *Reform and Reaction in Twentieth-Century American Politics,* historian John J. Broesamle notes: "Good Lord! Of course disillusionment and cynicism set in afterward. The goals and ideals had run not only beyond immediate reality, but beyond any possibility of reality."

Very soon after the guns had fallen silent, it became readily apparent that the First World War had not produced a more peaceful world; the bloody conflict was not destined to be the last war that the human race would ever fight—the "war to end all wars." On the home front, political repression, inflation, as well as social and racial conflict infected the land. Also, the wartime climate had allowed the adherents of national Prohibition to succeed in getting the Eighteenth Amendment passed. Finally, the devastating influenza epidemic of 1918–1919 claimed half a million American lives.

Significance

Hence, despite tremendous prosperity, the 1920s seemed anticlimactic, especially after the fervent moral atmosphere of the 1910s. Indeed, the 1920s was for some a time of profound disillusion. Many citizens lost faith in collective enterprises and instead resigned themselves to personal lives dedicated to the pursuit of material wealth and private pleasures.

The period immediately preceding American entry into the First World War has been superbly chronicled by historian Henry F. May in *The End of American Innocence: A Study of the First Years of Our Own Time, 1912–1917.* According to May, this era had featured an almost naïve social and cultural rebellion—but with a generally positive thrust. Unfortunately, in the postwar period this rebellion turned sour. American youth who had earlier embraced the future with optimism now, overwhelmed with despair, overwhelmingly viewed the future as relentlessly bleak. They blamed their elders for passing along to them what they deemed to be a totally dysfunctional world.

Luckily removed from the actual physical horrors of war, the American youth's rebellion assumed the form of a culture of hedonism. In contrast, European youth, recently dispatched by the millions to their death by their

Post-World War I youth were criticized by the previous generation for being too lacking in manners, too frank in speech, and too reckless, among other things. © BETTMANN/CORBIS. REPRODUCED BY PERMISSION.

governments in the recently concluded war, quickly lapsed into ultraradical political activity: anarchism, nihilism, communism, and fascism.

Primary Source

"'These Wild Young People': By One of Them"
[excerpt]

> **SYNOPSIS:** America entered World War I with such lofty goals and aspirations that a letdown was inevitable, especially soon after the conflict ended, when it had become painfully apparent that the war, despite the promises, had failed to usher in a new and better world. The widespread postwar sense of disillusionment, which particularly manifested itself among the young, was captured in the following article in *The Atlantic Monthly.*

For some months past the pages of our more conservative magazines have been crowded with pessimistic descriptions of the younger generation, as seen by their elders and, no doubt, their betters. Hardly a week goes by that I do not read some indignant treatise depicting our extravagance, the corruption of our manners, the futility of our existence, poured out in stiff, scared, shocked sentences before a sympathetic and horrified audience of fathers, mothers, and maiden aunts—but particularly maiden aunts.

In the May issue of the *Atlantic Monthly* appeared an article entitled "Polite Society," by a certain Mr. Grundy, the husband of a very old friend of my family. In kindly manner he

Mentioned our virtues, it is true,
But dwelt upon our vices, too.

"Chivalry and Modesty are dead. Modesty died first," quoth he, but expressed the pious hope that all might yet be well if the oldsters would but be content to "wait and see." His article is one of the best-tempered and most gentlemanly of this long series of Jeremiads against "these wild young people." It is significant that it should be anonymous. In reading it, I could not help but be drawn to Mr. Grundy personally, but was forced to the conclusion that he, like everyone else who is writing about my generation, has very little idea of what he is talking about. . . .

I would like to say a few things about my generation.

In the first place, I would like to observe that the older generation had certainly pretty well ruined this world before passing it on to us. They give us this Thing, knocked to pieces, leaky, red-hot, threatening to blow up; and then they are surprised that we don't accept it with the same attitude of pretty, decorous enthusiasm with which they received it, 'way back in the eighteen-nineties, nicely painted, smoothly running, practically fool-proof. "So simple that a child can run it!" But the child couldn't steer it. . . .

But still, everything, masked by ingrained hypocrisy and prudishness, seemed simple, beautiful, inevitable.

Now my generation is disillusionized, and, I think, to a certain extent, brutalized, by the cataclysm which *their* complacent folly engendered. The acceleration of life for us has been so great that into the last few years have been crowded the experiences and the ideas of a normal lifetime. We have in our unregenerate youth learned the practicality and the cynicism that is safe only in unregenerate old age. We have been forced to become realists overnight, instead of idealists, as was our birthright. We have seen man at his lowest, woman at her lightest, in the terrible moral chaos of Europe. We have been forced to question, and in many cases to discard, the religion of our fathers. We have seen hideous peculation, greed, anger, hatred, malice, and all uncharitableness, unmasked and rampant and unashamed. We have been forced to live in an atmosphere of "to-morrow we die," and so, naturally, we drank and were merry. We have seen the rottenness and shortcomings of all governments, even the best and most stable. We have seen entire social systems overthrown, and our own called in question. In short, we have seen the inherent beastliness of the human race revealed in an infernal apocalypse. . . .

But, in justice to my generation, I think that I must admit that most of us have realized that, whether or no it be worth while, we must all play the game, as long as we are in it. And I think that much of the hectic quality of our life is due to that fact and to that alone. We are faced with staggering problems and are forced to solve them, while the previous incumbents are permitted a graceful and untroubled death. All my friends are working and working hard. Most of the girls I know are working. In one way or another, often unconsciously, the great burden put upon us is being borne, and borne gallantly, by that immodest, unchivalrous set of ne'er-do-wells, so delightfully portrayed by Mr. Grundy and the amazing young Fitzgerald. A keen interest in po-

litical and social problems, and a determination to face the facts of life, ugly or beautiful, characterizes us, as it certainly did not characterize our fathers. We won't shut our eyes to the truths we have learned. We have faced so many unpleasant things already,—and faced them pretty well,—that it is natural that we should keep it up.

Now I think that this is the aspect of our generation that annoys the uncritical and deceives the unsuspecting oldsters who are now met in judgment upon us: our devastating and brutal frankness. And this is the quality in which we really differ from our predecessors. We are frank with each other, frank, or pretty nearly so, with our elders, frank in the way we feel toward life and this badly damaged world. . . .

The trouble with them is that they can't seem to realize that we are busy, that what pleasure we snatch must be incidental and feverishly hurried. We have to make the most of our time. We actually haven't got so much time for the noble procrastinations of modesty or for the elaborate rigmarole of chivalry, and little patience for the lovely formulas of an ineffective faith. Let them die for a while! They did not seem to serve the world too well in its black hour. If they are inherently good they will come back, vital and untarnished. But just now we have a lot of work, "old time is still a-flying," and we must gather rose-buds while we may.

Oh! I know that we are a pretty bad lot, but has not that been true of every preceding generation? At least we have the courage to act accordingly. Our music is distinctly barbaric, our girls are distinctly *not* a mixture of arbutus and barbed-wire. We drink when we can and what we can, we gamble, we are extravagant—but we work, and that's about all that we can be expected to do; for, after all, we have just discovered that we are all still very near to the Stone Age. The Grundys shake their heads. They'll *make* us be good. Prohibition is put through to stop our drinking, and hasn't stopped it. Bryan has plans to curtail our philanderings, and he won't do any good. A Draconian code is being hastily formulated at Washington and elsewhere, to prevent us from, by any chance, making any alteration in this present divinely constituted arrangement of things. . . .

We're men and women, long before our time, in the flower of our full-blooded youth. We have brought back into civil life some of the recklessness and ability that we were taught by war. We are also quite fatalistic in our outlook on the tepid perils of tame living. All may yet crash to the ground for aught that we can do about it. Terrible mistakes will be made, but *we* shall at least make them intelligently and insist, if we are to receive the strictures of the future, on doing pretty much as we choose now.

Oh! I suppose that it's too bad that we aren't humble, starry-eyed, shy, respectful innocents, standing reverently at their side for instructions, playing pretty little games, in which they no longer believe, except for us. But we aren't, and the best thing the oldsters can do about it is to go into their respective backyards and dig for worms, great big pink ones—for the Grundy tribe are now just about as important as they are, and they will doubtless make company more congenial and docile than "these wild young people," the men and women of my generation.

Further Resources

BOOKS

Cowley, Malcolm. *Exile's Return: A Literary Odyssey of the 1920s.* New York: Viking, 1969.

Fass, Paula S. *The Damned and the Beautiful: American Youth in the 1920's.* New York: Oxford University Press, 1977.

Statement of Mr. William Joseph Simmons

Testimony

By: William Joseph Simmons

Date: 1921

Source: Simmons, William Joseph. Statement of Mr. William Joseph Simmons, of Atlanta, Ga. *The Ku-Klux Klan: Hearings Before the Committee on Rules: House of Representatives,* 67th Cong., 1st sess. Washington, D.C.: United States Government Printing Office, 1921, 67–73.

About the Author: William Joseph Simmons (1880–1945) served in the Spanish-American War (1898). Although he never reached officer rank, he nonetheless adopted the title "Colonel," which he routinely employed throughout the remainder of his life. In 1915, galvanized by the favorable portrayal of the Ku Klux Klan in D.W. Griffith's epic silent motion picture *Birth of a Nation,* Simmons decided to form a new KKK—an organization that by 1921 had become the largest private paramilitary force in American history. ∎

Introduction

Born in the aftermath of Southern defeat, military occupation, and slave emancipation, the original Ku Klux Klan symbolized active resistance to Northern rule in a period of Southern white humiliation. Formed initially as a social club in 1865 in Tennessee shortly after the Civil

War's end, the Klan engaged in some highly publicized acts of intimidation and outright terror against both the Union soldiers patrolling the South to ensure law and order and against newly freed African Americans seeking to exercise their recently granted civil and political rights.

The Klan quickly drew the attention of the federal government. Congressional hearings on the organization in 1871 led to the passage of anti-Klan legislation and induced then-president Ulysses S. Grant (served 1869–1877) to dispatch additional troops to the region to combat the menace. These actions eventually stamped out the original Klan. Meanwhile, the gradual end of Northern-imposed Reconstruction and the eventual withdrawal of Northern occupation troops, coupled with the return of "white" home rule, effectively eliminated the perceived need for such an organization. By century's end, the original Southern KKK had become a distant echo of an era that most white Southerners would evidently have preferred to forget.

By 1915, however, the tense social, political, and cultural climate in America was doubtless ripe for the reappearance of such an organization. Not surprisingly, in that same year, the second KKK was born. With prewar anxiety running high in the nation, some other direct-action group might well have formed. But the reconstructed KKK enjoyed a measure of nostalgic legitimacy. The breakthrough silent film, director D.W. Griffith's *Birth of a Nation,* which opened in 1915, galvanized audiences (both North and South) with stunning scenes of the post-emancipation Klan members heroically rescuing vulnerable white women from the clutches of black "predators."

Significance

To a great degree, the revival of the Klan in 1915 reflected the "nationalizing" of America's heretofore largely Southern race problem, for the fifty-year post-emancipation period (1865–1915) had seen the African American population outside the South swell significantly. In addition, the burgeoning cities of the midwestern industrial states of Illinois, Indiana, and Ohio had meanwhile received a large influx of poor Southern whites—themselves seeking higher paying factory jobs and who brought northward with them their traditional Southern prejudices against African Americans.

After attending the spectacular premier of *Birth of a Nation* in Atlanta, Georgia, in 1915, self-styled "Colonel" William Joseph Simmons, a Spanish-American War veteran, decided to start a Klan movement—initially, it appears, as a mail-order business. But the movement swiftly spread across the nation, often serving as a sort of white Anglo-Saxon Protestant inquisition. The revived Klan of 1915 attacked not just African Americans but a host of other convenient targets that included Roman Catholics, Jews, recent immigrants, and social enemies such as prostitutes, pornographers, and saloon keepers.

Members of the Ku Klux Klan march down Washington, D.C.'s Pennsylvania Avenue in 1925. **NATIONAL ARCHIVE AND RECORDS ADMINISTRATION.**

In the early twenty-first century, observers remained divided over the essential nature of this reborn Klan, an organization that contained an estimated 4.5 million members at its peak of popularity in 1924. On the one hand, so large an organization as the Klan must surely have contained many normally law-abiding citizens, who probably joined in the same spirit that other Americans during this booster-driven era joined various lodges as well as business and professional organizations. Finally, in an ironic twist, although they were usually safe in oftentimes sympathetic rural and small-town America, Klansmen often found themselves harassed in large cities,

especially where Irish Catholics comprised a significant portion of the local police force. Complaints by Klan members of police brutality occasionally surfaced.

In the spirit of its investigation of 1871, the United States House of Representatives held hearings in October 1921 to assess the threat of what had clearly become the largest private paramilitary organization in the nation's history. During these proceedings, Simmons proved to be an intriguing witness. As expected, he defended the Klan from the usual charges of financial chicanery, intimidation of opponents, and outright violence. Any illegal activities Simmons not surprisingly attributed to opportunists.

Primary Source

Statement of Mr. William Joseph Simmons, of
Atlanta, Ga.

SYNOPSIS: "Colonel" William Joseph Simmons,
founder of the reborn Ku Klux Klan, appeared in
Washington to defend his controversial organization
before a House of Representatives committee. Despite the intense questioning, Simmons emerged
from the hearings as a strong, even eloquent, advocate for the Klan. His performance gave a further
boost to the KKK, which was already well on its way
to becoming the most significant private parami-li-
tary organization in American history.

My name is William Joseph Simmons, residing
in Atlanta, Ga. They call me "Colonel," largely out of
respect. Every lawyer in Georgia is called "Colonel,"
so they thought that I was as good as a lawyer, so
they call me that. However, since that matter has
been called into question. I am a veteran of the
Spanish-American War. I am a past commander of
my Spanish-American war veterans' post. I am a past
national aid-de-camp of the Spanish-American War
Veterans' Association and also a past provisional
division commander. I was at one time the senior
colonel in command of five regiments and colonel
of my own regiment of the uniform rank of the Wood-
men of the World, and I was known as "Colonel." I
have used that title on certain literature of the klan
for the reason that there are three other "W.J. Sim-
monses" in Atlanta, and for some time our mail got
confused. It is merely a designation. They accord it
to me as an honor and I appreciated it, but at no
time and in no place have I arrogated to myself the
fact that I was a colonel of the Army. I served there,
but I was under a colonel and I found out how the
colonels do. . . .

Twenty years ago I received the inspiration to
establish a fraternal, patriotic, secret order for the
purpose of memorializing the great heroes of our national history, inculcating and teaching practical fra-
ternity among men, to teach and encourage a
fervent, practical patriotism toward our country, and
to destroy from the hearts of men the Mason and
Dixon line and build thereupon a great American solidarity and a distinctive national conscience which
our country sorely stands in need of.

At that time I was a mere young man and knew
that my youth and immature thought would not permit me to successfully launch the movement, so I
kept my own counsel all through 15 subsequent
years, working, thinking, and preparing my head and
heart for the task of creating this institution for the

interest of our common country and for the promotion of real brotherhood among men. To this work
and to this end I dedicated my life and all my energies, after being thoroughly convinced that there was
a place for such a fraternal order and that the order
could and would fill that place.

It was in the month of October, 1915, that I decided to launch the movement. . . .

Through the dark hours of struggle and bitter
sacrifice incident to the launching of this movement,
for over nine long months I had an average of one
meal a day. I have fought a good fight. I have truly
kept the faith, and God permitting me, Mr. Chairman, I shall finish my course, with love toward all,
with malice toward none. I shall pursue the right as
God shall give me a vision of the right.

If the Knights of the Ku-Klux Klan has been a
lawless organization, as has been charged, it would
not have shown the remarkable growth it has, for in
the klan is as fine a body of representative citizens
as there is in the United States. In each community
where there is a klan will be found members from
the lending citizens, men who stand at the forefront
in their cities. These men would not stand for lawlessness.

It has been charged that the klan is a gigantic
swindle, run solely to enrich a few of the inside ring.
I, as the executive head of the klan, have received
during the past six years altogether approximately
$12,000, an average of $2,000 per year. I can not
be in any wise accurate in these figures, because I
have not run it up, but I may state just here that for
two or three years I received not a penny, only what
I could get out and do myself. I have also a home,
purchased by klan members, but not by the klan,
but by voluntary subscriptions of 25 cents and 50
cents and a dollar. This home is not completely paid
for, and I knew nothing of this until it was given to
me as a complete surprise as a birthday remembrance on the 6th day of last May by members of
the klan from every section of the country.

And I may add just here, from what has been
presented for my information regarding the home in
which I now reside, that property is in the hands of
a board of trustees who are looking after it; and they
told me, "When we get the home paid for then the
deed will be made to you; but we do not want you
to bother with that until it is all paid for." A board
of trustees is handling that home.

The secretary, treasurer, and other officials of
the klan receive salaries lower than they would re-

ceive from business institutions for their ability and for the work that each of them does. I introduce here, marked "Exhibit B," the pay roll and salaries paid and the expenses of the klan.

If the klan was seeking to enrich a few insiders the money would go into our pockets. Instead, we are spending the surplus money of the klan in the education of young men and women who are the very foundation of the Nation. . . .

The charge has been made that the klan takes the law into its own hands; that it terrorizes private citizens in many communities by lawless acts against person and property. These charges are untrue. I state, Mr. Chairman, that klans can not take action on anything outside of their lodge rooms or ceremonial duties unless they have an order, so to speak, written and signed by myself. That is a law in the klan to keep anyone within our membership from doing things—in other words, holding them in control—that contravene the law. Before God and this honorable committee, I have never authorized nor signed any kind of instructions that could in any way be construed as a violation of the law or to be carried out in violation of the law of my country.

There have been only a few instances where lawless acts have been alleged against individual members of the klan. You will notice I say "alleged," and there is a possibility that if individual members of the klan have committed acts of lawlessness that those same men were members of other fraternal orders, and should the other fraternal orders be condemned? No. In these instances the charter in that community was revoked or suspended, although the acts of the individual members were not the acts of the klan as a body and were condemned by all those disbanded klan members. The charter was revoked or suspended, as we have no room in our organization for those who take the law into their own hands, because to do so violates a most solemn oath. Individual members of other organizations have committed and been charged with outrages and crimes, but that does not condemn the whole order, as an order, of lawlessness. . . .

The klan does not countenance nor will it tolerate any lawless acts by its members. Instead we teach respect for the law, love of country, and a closer fellowship of service. I here introduce, marked Exhibit G, and will read later, the ritual, oath, and other secret books and works of the klan. In the oath attention is called to the section where all klan members swear to uphold and respect the law of

the United States, the State, county, and city where the members live. No man who would break his solemn oath by taking the law into his own hands is worthy of membership in any organization or worthy to be a citizen of our glorious country.

The charge has also been made that the klan as an organization gives an opportunity for evil-minded persons to threaten others, to satisfy their private grudges, and to commit outrages, using the klan as a cloak. This charge is absurd on its face when an examination of the records for the past 10 years will show that there were as many of these so-called outrages committed before the klan was organized as since its organization. . . .

I noticed some time ago that the klan was charged with outrages, or, rather, an outrage against a Negro in Arkansas, and I state to you as an honorable man that that particular outrage occurred in Arkansas 18 months before we had one member in Arkansas.

It has been charged that this organization incites to riot. Can that charge be substantiated? No; because no man can place his finger on any spot on the map of the United States in which a klan has been organized and well established where there has ever been a riot, racial or otherwise, and in every town where riots have occurred there is no klan there or was not there at the time of the riots.

The charge has also been made that the klan is organized for the purpose of assisting the enforcement of the law. Nothing to substantiate this charge has been produced, and there is no room in the United States for any organization organized for any such purpose. The law is supreme, and if we were organized for any such absurd purpose the klan would not have lived a year and could not have grown as it has.

The charge is made that we are organized to preach and teach religious intolerance, and especially that we are anti-Roman Catholic, anti-Jew, and anti-Negro. The conduct of the klan proves this absolutely untrue. Many alleged outrages have been attributed to the klan, but none of these were against Roman Catholics, Jews, and Negroes per se, and none were committed by the klan. It is indeed strange that if we organized to persecute the Roman Catholics, Jews, and Negroes that nothing has been done against them. In the United States the question is not and should never be whether a citizen is a Protestant, a Roman Catholic, a Jew, or a Negro, but whether he is a loyal American.

Since the fight against the klan we have been offered and urged to use, by those who are anti-Roman Catholic and not members of the klan, possibly the greatest existing mass of data and material against the Roman Catholics and Knights of Columbus. In this material, so we are told, there are affidavits and other personal testimony attributing to the Roman Catholics and Knights of Columbus in American more outrages and crimes than the klan has ever been charged with. Included in these charges against the Roman Catholics and Knights of Columbus are murder, whipping, tar and feathers, and crimes of all natures.

If the klan was anti-Roman Catholic we would have certainly used the material offered us, but the offer was received, although those making it are anxious that this evidence be presented to Congress. If the klan is to secure members on an anti-Roman Catholic, anti-Jew, and anti-Negro appeal, we do not want such members, and have never secured them in this way. Discussions involving any man's religious beliefs are never allowed in a meeting of the klan. If it ever occurs and the fact is made known to the proper officials of the klan, those who indulge in it, even the presiding officers who permit it, are rigidly penalized.

Further Resources

BOOKS

Horowitz, David A., ed. *Inside the Klavern: The Secret History of a Ku Klux Klan of the 1920s.* Carbondale Ill.: Southern Illinois University Press, 1999.

MacLean, Nancy. *Behind the Mask of Chivalry: The Making of the Second Ku Klux Klan.* New York: Oxford University Press, 1994.

Tucker, Richard K. *The Dragon and the Cross: The Rise and Fall of the Ku Klux Klan in Middle America.* Hamden, Conn.: Archon Books, 1991.

"Flapper Americana Novissima"

Magazine article

By: G. Stanley Hall

Date: June 1922

Source: Hall, G. Stanley. "Flapper Americana Novissima." *The Atlantic Monthly,* June 1922, 771, 773–774, 775, 776.

About the Author: Grenville Stanley Hall (1844–1924) was a longtime psychological and social observer who specialized in the field of adolescent development. ∎

Introduction

The term *flapper* appears to have made its American debut in the February 1915 issue of the New York–based satire/arts review, *The Smart Set: A Magazine of Cleverness.* In an article in the review, author Henry L. Mencken introduced the word, which seems to have already been in use over in Britain to describe a certain type of young woman. In the United States, up until that time, the French word *ingénue* was invariably employed.

According to Mencken, the flapper was a young, modern, sophisticated woman/child. Mencken lovingly described "this American Flapper. Her skirts have just reached her very trim and pretty ankles; her hair, newly coiled upon her skull, has just exposed the ravishing whiteness of her neck. A charming creature! . . . She is an enchantment through the plate glass of a limousine. Youth is hers, and hope, and romance, and—."

Significance

Meanwhile, from its more-or-less innocent origins, the term *flapper* had evolved by the early 1920s to the point where the word and the image that it evoked helped define the entire decade in much the same fashion that Rosie the Riveter helps define the American woman of the 1940s or the Happy Housewife of early black-and-white television situation comedies helps define the 1950s.

By the early 1920s, not only had the term *flapper* itself evolved but the entire constellation of ideas and images surrounding the word had likewise changed. The June 1922 edition of *The Atlantic Monthly* referred to the "Flapper Americana Novissima"—the last being an Italian word that signifies the latest model or the most recent trend. This phrase underscored the actual evolution of the ideal young American woman circa 1922.

According to this article, the American flapper was above all else fun in ways quite unlike her rather sedate Victorian-era grandmother. Not only did this "Flapper American Novissima" love to play—indeed often in competition with men—but she thoroughly enjoyed her leisure time. In fact, historians have chronicled changing attitudes toward work—indeed changing attitudes towards the entire meaning of life—that seem to have taken place by the 1920s. Gone were the days when, for instance, work was revered as a "calling" and an overall seriousness pervaded one's life. Instead, life was now to be enjoyed. And the material abundance so characteristic of modern America helped create a climate where, for many citizens—both men and women—partaking in the consumer culture had become the central purpose of one's existence. In essence, "Flapper American Novissima" had become the new norm.

During the 1920s flappers were girls known for their love of dance and jazz music and an appreciation for life's enjoyments. © UNDERWOOD & UNDERWOOD/CORBIS. REPRODUCED BY PERMISSION.

Primary Source

"Flapper Americana Novissima" [excerpt]

SYNOPSIS: Veteran psychologist and child-development expert G. Stanley Hall places the brief history of the young American flapper in perspective. Stanley contrasts the term circa its introduction to America in 1915 with the evolution of the term by the early 1920s.

When, years ago, I first heard the picturesque word 'Flapper' applied to a girl, I thought of a loose sail flapping in whatever wind may blow, and liable to upset the craft it is meant to impel. There was also in my mind the flitting and yet cruder mental imagery of a wash, just hung out to dry in the light and breeze, before it is starched and ironed for use. I was a little ashamed of this when the dictionary set me right by defining the word as a fledgling, yet in the nest, and vainly attempting to fly while its wings have only pinfeathers; and I recognized that thus the genius of 'slanguage' had made the squab the symbol of budding girlhood. This, too, had the advantage of a moral, implying what would happen if the young bird really ventured to trust itself to its pinions prematurely. . . .

We must, then, admit at the outset that the world has not yet found the right designation for this unique product of civilization, the girl in the early teens, who is just now undergoing such a marvelous development. But why bother about names? . . .

Let us start at random, with dancing, on which the flapper dotes as probably never before, in all the history of the terpsichorean art, made up of crazes as it has been, has anyone begun to do.

A good dance is as near heaven as the flapper can get and live. She dances at noon and at recess in the school gymnasium; and, if not in the school, at the restaurants between courses, or in the recreation and rest-rooms in factories and stores. She knows all the latest variations of the perennial fox-trot, the ungainly contortions of the camel walk; yields with abandon to the fascination of the tango; and if the floor is crowded, there is always room for the languorous and infantile toddle; and the cheek-to-cheek close formation—which one writer ascribes to the high cost of rent nowadays, which necessitates the maximum of motion in the minimum of space—has a lure of its own, for partners must sometimes cling together in order to move at all. Verticality of motion and, at least, the vibrations of the 'shimmy,' are always possible.

High-school girls told my informant that they 'park' their corsets when they go to dances, because they have been taught by their instructors in hygiene and physiology that to wear them is unfavorable to deep breathing, and that this is as necessary for freedom of motion as the gymnastic costume or the bath-suit at the seaside; and also that, to get the best out of the exercises of the ballroom, they must not be too much or too heavily clad to be able to keep cool. To her intimates she may confess that she dispenses with corsets (a growing fashion which manufacturers of these articles already regard with alarm) lest she be dubbed 'ironsides,' or left a wall-flower. Alas for the popularity of teachers who would limit any of these innovations, however much they may be supported by anxious and bewildered mothers, who know only the old-fashioned steps! Despite the decline of the ballet, theatrical managers who advertise for corps of stage-dancers report that they are overwhelmed by crowds of applicants.

The flapper, too, has developed very decided musical tastes. If she more rarely 'takes lessons' of any kind, she has many choice disks for the phonograph, and has a humming acquaintance with the most popular ditties; and if she rarely indulges in the cake-walk, she has a keen sense of ragtime and 'syncopation to the thirty-second note,' and her nerves are uniquely toned to jazz, with its shocks, discords, blariness, siren effects, animal and all other noises, and its heterogeneous tempos, in which every possible liberty is taken with rhythm.

Those who sell candies, ices, sodas, or 'sweetened wind,' are unanimous that flappers are their best customers. It somehow seems as if they could almost live on sweets; and their mothers complain that it interferes with the normality of their appetites, digestion, and nutrition generally. A girl may have acidulous tastes and love even pickles; but this is only a counterfoil. She discriminates flavors as acutely as do wine-tasters. She not only no longer chews gum, as she used to do, but eschews chewers of it, and even 'cuts' them—for on just this point I have cases. But she may munch sweetmeats at theatre, school, or even on the street. Thus the late sugar shortage was hardest on her; and how she throve so well with so short a ration of it in 'the good old times' is a puzzling mystery.

If she loves sweetmeats for their own sake, why this new love of perfumery so characteristic of her age? Is her own olfactory sense suddenly much more acute, or is she now like the flowers attracting insects—but human ones? Is there a correspondingly augmented acuity in this sense in the young man? Possibly, in thus making herself fragrant she is not thinking of him at all. If she is, and he has no *flair* for it, she has made a monumental mistake. This most interesting and very important problem must be left to future investigation. At any rate, all those who sell perfumery, who were interviewed, agreed that here, too, young girls are the best customers. . . .

At least half the movie films seem almost to have been made for the flapper; and her tastes and style, if not her very code of honor, are fashioned on them. Librarians report that she reads much less since the movies came. No home or other authority can keep her away; the only amelioration is to have reels more befitting her stage of life. . . .

But I am forgetting the curriculum. In college, some subjects attract girls, and others boys, each sex sometimes monopolizing certain courses. But in high school, wherever the elective system permits choice, most girls are usually found in classes where there are most boys. Girls, too, seem fonder of cultural subjects, and less, or at least later, addicted to those that are immediately vocational. They do far better in their studies with teachers whom they like; and I have heard of an attractive unmarried male teacher who was accused by his colleagues of marking the girls in his classes too high, but whose principal had the sagacity to see that the girls did far better work for him than for any other teacher and to realize the reason why.

In the secondary school the girl finds herself the intellectual equal of her male classmate, and far more mature at the same age in all social insights. Hence coeducation at this stage has brought her some slight disillusionment. Her boy classmates are not her ideal of the other sex, and so real lasting attachments, dating from this period, are rare. Perhaps associations and surroundings here bring also some disenchantment with her home environment, and even with her parents. But docile as she is, her heart of hearts is not in her textbooks or recitations, but always in life and persons; and she learns and adjusts herself to both with a facility and rapidity that are amazing. It is things outside her studies which seem to her, if indeed they are not in fact, far more important for her life. . . .

Never since civilization began has the girl in the early teens seemed so self-sufficient and sure of herself, or made such a break with the rigid traditions of propriety and convention which have hedged her in. From this, too, it follows that the tension which always exists between mothers and daughters has greatly increased, and there now sometimes seems to be almost a chasm between successive generations. If a note of loudness in dress or boisterousness in manner has crept in, and if she seems to know, or pretends to know, all that she needs, to become captain of her own soul, these are really only the gestures of shaking off old fetters. Perhaps her soul has long been ripening for such a revolt, and anxious to dissipate the mystery which seemed to others to envelop it. Let us hope that she is really more innocent and healthier in mind and body because she now knows and does earlier so much that was once admissible only later, if at all.

Further Resources
BOOKS

Kitch, Carolyn L. *The Girl on the Magazine Cover: The Origins of Visual Stereotypes in American Mass Media.* Chapel Hill, N.C.: University of North Carolina Press, 2001.

Latham, Angela J. *Posing a Threat: Flappers, Chorus Girls, and Other Brazen Performers of the American 1920s.* Hanover, N.H.: University Press of New England, 2000.

Prohibition's Supporters and Detractors

Address to Congress

Speech

By: Warren G. Harding

Date: December 8, 1922

Source: Harding, Warren G. Address to Congress. December 8, 1922. *Congressional Record: House of Representatives,* 67th Cong., 4th sess., vol. 64, part 1 (Washington, D.C.: United States Government Printing Office, 1922), 212.

About the Author: Ohio-born Warren G. Harding (1865–1923) served as president of the United States from 1921 to 1923. Elected by an overwhelming margin in 1920 over Democrat James Cox, the Republican Harding died in 1923 before he could finish serving out his first term.

"Jurors Go on Trial, Drank Up Evidence"

Newspaper article

By: *The New York Times*

Date: January 7, 1928

Source: "Jurors Go on Trial, Drank Up Evidence." *The New York Times,* January 7, 1928. ∎

Men and women increasingly sought out speakeasies during the 1920s to get around the government's prohibition of liquor sales and consumption. © BETTMANN/CORBIS. REPRODUCED BY PERMISSION.

Introduction

Many of the staunchest advocates of Prohibition had never been completely satisfied with the Eighteenth Amendment to the U.S. Constitution passed by Congress in December 1917 and finally ratified by the requisite number of states in January 1919. The Eighteenth Amendment mandating national Prohibition outlawed the manufacture, sale, and transportation of alcoholic beverages—clearly an attack on the business end of the liquor industry, which, curiously enough, mirrored the overall anticorporate thrust of the Progressive era. In the case of alcohol, critics blasted the liquor industry for allegedly making money by poisoning the public in much the same fashion that reformers decried filthy meat-packing plants that sold tainted food to consumers.

Nevertheless, the Eighteenth Amendment was never intended to impact the individual drinker, since the measure never actually outlawed either the purchase or the consumption of alcohol, in contrast to today's laws against both the sellers and buyers of illegal drugs.

Significance

The Eighteenth Amendment represented a well-crafted political compromise that appears, in the final analysis, to have satisfied no one. By neglecting to punish drinkers, a drastic step that few legislators favored, the measure could never have really worked. True Prohibition enforcement was doubtless doomed from the start. The somewhat lackadaisical opponents of Prohibition, many of whom had carelessly let the Eighteenth Amendment clear Congress in 1917 secure in their belief that the amendment would never be ratified, made sure that implementation of the new law would soon be nullified. Indeed the Volstead Act of October 1919, the measure designed to create the actual federal government machinery to enforce national Prohibition, was watered down to the point of ineffectiveness. For correctly gauging the temper of postwar public opinion, many politicians, recognizing that Prohibition had originally been enacted largely as a wartime measure, understood that many Americans did not want this policy actually implemented now that more normal peacetime conditions had returned.

Immediately after the official start of Prohibition in January 1920, problems of day-to-day enforcement surfaced with alarming regularity. In fact, President Warren G. Harding, a staunch public advocate of Prohibition (although a social drinker in private), noted these difficulties in his December 1922 address to Congress.

Enforcing Prohibition, law enforcement officers searched out illegal liquor stores while many in the population at large sought out speakeasies at which to whet their thirst for alcohol. © BETTMANN/CORBIS. REPRODUCED BY PERMISSION.

Primary Source

Address to Congress

SYNOPSIS: President Warren G. Harding, while acknowledging some of the practical problems associated with Prohibition, nonetheless reaffirms his strong support for the measure.

There is a demand for every living being in the United States to respect and abide by the laws of the Republic. [Applause.] Let men who are rending the moral fiber of the Republic through easy contempt for the prohibition law, because they think it restricts their personal liberty, remember that they set the example and breed a contempt for law which will ultimately destroy the Republic. [Applause.]

Constitutional prohibition has been adopted by the Nation. It is the supreme law of the land. In plain speaking, there are conditions relating to its enforcement which savor of nationwide scandal. It is the most demoralizing factor in our public life.

Most of our people assumed that the adoption of the eighteenth amendment meant the elimination of the question from our politics. On the contrary, it has been so intensified as an issue that many voters are disposed to make all political decisions with reference to this single question. It is distracting the public mind and prejudicing the judgment of the electorate.

The day is unlikely to come when the eighteenth amendment will be repealed. The fact may as well be recognized and our course adapted accordingly. If the statutory provisions for its enforcement are contrary to deliberate public opinion, which I do not believe, the rigorous and literal enforcement will concentrate public attention on any requisite modification. [Applause.] Such a course conforms with the law and saves the humiliation of the Government and the humiliation of our people before the world, and challenges the destructive forces engaged in widespread violation, official corruption, and individual demoralization.

The eighteenth amendment involves the concurrent authority of State and Federal Governments for the enforcement of the policy it defines. A certain lack of definiteness, through division of responsibility, is thus introduced. In order to bring about a full understanding of duties and responsibilities as thus distributed, I purpose to invite the governors of the States and Territories, at an early opportunity, to a conference with the Federal Executive authority. Out of the full and free considerations which will thus be possible, it is confidently believed, will emerge a more adequate comprehension of the whole problem and definite policies of National and State cooperation in administering the laws.

Primary Source

"Jurors Go On Trial, Drank Up Evidence"

SYNOPSIS: In this *New York Times* newspaper account of a bootlegger's trial in San Francisco, the jury not only acquitted the defendant but during deliberations actually drank the evidence.

In the same court where they heard testimony last Friday afternoon that acquitted a liquor defendant eight jurors went on trial today before Municipal Judge Ambrose to show cause why they should not be suspended from further jury service for drinking the evidence in the case.

The ninth member of the jury, A. A. Huelester, collapased soon after the Magistrate had assailed the jurors vigorously for a "breach of conduct." Mr. Huelesteer was removed to his home on orders of a county jail physician who examined him.

Though earlier in the day the Judge had discharged nine members of the jury when they refused to take the stand and deny consuming virtually all of the evidence against George Beven, hotel clerk. He finally appointed attorneys to represent them.

Sworn to tell the truth, the eight jurors took the stand and gave their stories as to what happened in the jury room during the three hours it took to determine the case of Beven, who was acquitted of violation of the State Prohibition act.

Judge Ambrose heard the charges of drinking the evidence in silence. The jurors all admitted drinking the pint of liquor which was the prosecution's chief exhibit against Beven. All denied it was consumed without an honorable motive. They stated it was sampled to determine whether it was of alcoholic content and actually constituted a violation of the liquor law.

The magistrate considered the pleadings of the two lawyers appointed by him to get at the facts of the case. He agreed to go over the circumstances again in his mind and decide Monday at 9:30 A.M. whether to reinstate the nine accused jurors.

The talesmen whose judicial status is to be determined are all Los Angeles residents and include five women.

Further Resources

BOOKS

Hallwas, John E. *The Bootlegger: A Story of Small-Town America.* Urbana, Ill.: University of Illinois Press, 1969.

Murray, Robert K. *The Harding Era: Warren G. Harding and His Administration.* Minneapolis, Minn.: University of Minnesota Press, 1969.

Sinclair, Andrew. *Prohibition: The Era of Excess.* Boston: Little, Brown, 1962.

Babbitt

Novel

By: Sinclair Lewis

Date: 1922

Source: Lewis, Sinclair. *Babbitt.* New York: Grosset & Dunlap, 1922, 1–10, 12–13.

About the Author: Sinclair Lewis (1885–1951) was one of modern America's most popular and well-respected novelists. His work combines strong characterization with biting social commentary. Along with *Babbitt,* some of Lewis's best-known novels include *Dodsworth, Main Street,* and *Elmer Gantry.* ∎

Introduction

Sinclair Lewis's masterpiece, the novel *Babbitt,* features a devastating portrait of the quintessential smug, complacent 1920s "Booster," George Babbitt, a man who buys into the empty materialism of post–World War I America. An unabashed cheerleader for his country, his social class, and his nation's prevailing business ethos, Babbitt fits perfectly the description of the ever-faithful bourgeois, for he is a conformist to the very depths of his soul. The character Babbitt has come to epitomize the dominant mind-set of the 1920s and symbolizes, perhaps as much as does the flapper or bootleg gin, the entire decade. The very word *Babbitt* has come to represent a type.

Significance

Despite the author's literary artistry, there is something slightly askew with Babbitt. For despite his avowed Republican "boosterism," he seems slightly out of place. For some readers, he seems too urban. He resides in the mythical Zenith, a good-sized generic American city, but a smaller town would seem a more appropriate setting for his kind. Moreover, he seems too enlightened, too aware of his predicament and the middle-class trap that he finds himself ensnared in unwittingly. He doesn't quite buy into the materialistic consumer myths of modern America and its work ethos. He recognizes a spiritual vacuum at the core of both himself and his America that denies human needs. He's tortured by self-doubts. In short, he's far too aware of being George Babbitt.

As a matter of fact, the novel tells us more about intellectuals like Sinclair Lewis and their perceptions of the 1920s. For the empty materialism that so disturbed them hardly appear, in hindsight, to have bothered the Babbitts at the time. The intellectual cannot fathom a world where such people are truly satisfied. This reflects an old theme in literature—that the bourgeoisie is not as smug as it might appear.

Primary Source

Babbitt [excerpt]

SYNOPSIS: In his masterpiece *Babbitt,* novelist Sinclair Lewis provides an unforgettable portrait of an America "booster" who, through his social conformity, adherence to Republicanism, and worship of materialism, reflects the prevailing ethos of the post–World War I United States.

I

The towers of Zenith aspired above the morning mist; austere towers of steel and cement and limestone, sturdy as cliffs and delicate as silver rods. They were neither citadels nor churches, but frankly and beautifully office-buildings.

The mist took pity on the fretted structures of earlier generations: the Post Office with its shingle-tortured mansard, the red brick minarets of hulking old houses, factories with stingy and sooted windows, wooden tenements colored like mud. The city was full of such grotesqueries, but the clean towers were thrusting them from the business center, and on the farther hills were shining new houses, homes—they seemed—for laughter and tranquillity.

Over a concrete bridge fled a limousine of long sleek hood and noiseless engine. These people in evening clothes were returning from an all-night rehearsal of a Little Theater play, an artistic adventure considerably illuminated by champagne. Below the bridge curved a railroad, a maze of green and crimson lights. The New York Flyer boomed past, and twenty lines of polished steel leaped into the glare.

In one of the skyscrapers the wires of the Associated Press were closing down. The telegraph operators wearily raised their celluloid eye-shades after a night of talking with Paris and Peking. Through the building crawled the scrubwomen, yawning, their old shoes slapping. The dawn mist spun away. Cues of men with lunch-boxes clumped toward the immensity of new factories, sheets of glass and hollow tile,

Author Sinclair Lewis satirized boosterism in his novels. **AP/WIDE WORLD PHOTOS. REPRODUCED BY PERMISSION.**

glittering shops where five thousand men worked beneath one roof, pouring out the honest wares that would be sold up the Euphrates and across the veldt. The whistles rolled out in greeting a chorus cheerful as the April dawn; the song of labor in a city built—it seemed—for giants.

II

There was nothing of the giant in the aspect of the man who was beginning to awaken on the sleeping-porch of a Dutch Colonial house in that residential district of Zenith known as Floral Heights.

His name was George F. Babbitt. He was forty-six years old now, in April, 1920, and he made nothing in particular, neither butter nor shoes nor poetry, but he was nimble in the calling of selling houses for more than people could afford to pay.

His large head was pink, his brown hair thin and dry. His face was babyish in slumber, despite his wrinkles and the red spectacle-dents on the slopes of his nose. He was not fat but he was exceedingly well fed; his cheeks were pads, and the unroughened hand which lay helpless upon the khaki-colored blanket was slightly puffy. He seemed prosperous, extremely married and unromantic; and altogether unromantic appeared this sleeping-porch, which looked on one sizable elm, two respectable grass-plots, a cement driveway, and a corrugated iron garage. Yet Babbitt was again dreaming of the fairy child, a dream more romantic than scarlet pagodas by a silver sea.

For years the fairy child had come to him. Where others saw but Georgie Babbitt, she discerned gallant youth. She waited for him, in the darkness beyond mysterious groves. When at last he could slip away from the crowded house he darted to her. His wife, his clamoring friends, sought to follow, but he escaped, the girl fleet beside him, and they crouched together on a shadowy hillside. She was so slim, so white, so eager! She cried that he was gay and valiant, that she would wait for him, that they would sail—

Rumble and bang of the milk-truck.

Babbitt moaned, turned over, struggled back toward his dream. He could see only her face now, beyond misty waters. The furnace-man slammed the basement door. A dog barked in the next yard. As Babbitt sank blissfully into a dim warm tide, the paper-carrier went by whistling, and the rolled-up *Advocate* thumped the front door. Babbitt roused, his stomach constricted with alarm. As he relaxed, he was pierced by the familiar and irritating rattle of some one cranking a Ford: snap-ah-ah, snap-ah-ah, snap-ah-ah. Himself a pious motorist, Babbitt cranked with the unseen driver, with him waited through taut hours for the roar of the starting engine, with him agonized as the roar ceased and again began the infernal patient snap-ah-ah—a round, flat sound, a shivering cold-morning sound, a sound infuriating and inescapable. Not till the rising voice of the motor told him that the Ford was moving was he released from the panting tension. He glanced once at his favorite tree, elm twigs against the gold patina of sky, and fumbled for sleep as for a drug. He who had been a boy very credulous of life was no longer greatly interested in the possible and improbable adventures of each new day.

He escaped from reality till the alarm-clock rang, at seven-twenty.

III

It was the best of nationally advertised and quantitatively produced alarm-clocks, with all modern attachments, including cathedral chime, intermittent alarm, and a phosphorescent dial. Babbitt was proud of being awakened by such a rich device.

Socially it was almost as creditable as buying expensive cord tires.

He sulkily admitted now that there was no more escape, but he lay and detested the grind of the real-estate business, and disliked his family, and disliked himself for disliking them. The evening before, he had played poker at Vergil Gunch's till midnight, and after such holidays he was irritable before breakfast. It may have been the tremendous home-brewed beer of the prohibition-era and the cigars to which that beer enticed him; it may have been resentment of return from this fine, bold man-world to a restricted region of wives and stenographers, and of suggestions not to smoke so much.

From the bedroom beside the sleeping-porch, his wife's detestably cheerful "Time to get up, Georgie boy," and the itchy sound, the brisk and scratchy sound, of combing hairs out of a stiff brush.

He grunted; he dragged his thick legs, in faded baby-blue pajamas, from under the khaki blanket; he sat on the edge of the cot, running his fingers through his wild hair, while his plump feet mechanically felt for his slippers. He looked regretfully at the blanket—forever a suggestion to him of freedom and heroism. He had bought it for a camping trip which had never come off. It symbolized gorgeous loafing, gorgeous cursing, virile flannel shirts.

He creaked to his feet, groaning at the waves of pain which passed behind his eyeballs. Though he waited for their scorching recurrence, he looked blurrily out at the yard. It delighted him, as always; it was the neat yard of a successful business man of Zenith, that is, it was perfection, and made him also perfect. He regarded the corrugated iron garage. For the three-hundred-and-sixty-fifth time in a year he reflected, "No class to that tin shack. Have to build me a frame garage. But by golly it's the only thing on the place that isn't up-to-date!" While he stared he thought of a community garage for his acreage development, Glen Oriole. He stopped puffing and jiggling. His arms were akimbo. His petulant, sleep-swollen face was set in harder lines. He suddenly seemed capable, an official, a man to contrive, to direct, to get things done.

On the vigor of his idea he was carried down the hard, clean, unused-looking hall into the bathroom.

Though the house was not large it had, like all houses on Floral Heights, an altogether royal bathroom of porcelain and glazed tile and metal sleek as silver. The towel-rack was a rod of clear glass set in nickel. The tub was long enough for a Prussian

Guard, and above the set bowl was a sensational exhibit of tooth-brush holder, shaving-brush holder, soap-dish, sponge-dish, and medicine-cabinet, so glittering and so ingenious that they resembled an electrical instrument-board. But the Babbitt whose god was Modern Appliances was not pleased. The air of the bathroom was thick with the smell of a heathen toothpaste. "Verona been at it again! 'Stead of sticking to Lilidol, like I've re-peat-ed-ly asked her, she's gone and gotten some confounded stinkum stuff that makes you sick!"

The bath-mat was wrinkled and the floor was wet. (His daughter Verona eccentrically took baths in the morning, now and then.) He slipped on the mat, and slid against the tub. He said "Damn!" Furiously he snatched up his tube of shaving-cream, furiously he lathered, with a belligerent slapping of the unctuous brush, furiously he raked his plump cheeks with a safety-razor. It pulled. The blade was dull. He said, "Damn—oh—oh—damn it!"

He hunted through the medicine-cabinet for a packet of new razor-blades (reflecting, as invariably, "Be cheaper to buy one of these dinguses and strop your own blades,") and when he discovered the packet, behind the round box of bicarbonate of soda, he thought ill of his wife for putting it there and very well of himself for not saying "Damn." But he did say it, immediately afterward, when with wet and soap-slippery fingers he tried to remove the horrible little envelope and crisp clinging oiled paper from the new blade.

Then there was the problem, oft-pondered, never solved, of what to do with the old blade, which might imperil the fingers of his young. As usual, he tossed it on top of the medicine-cabinet, with a mental note that some day he must remove the fifty or sixty other blades that were also temporarily piled up there. He finished his shaving in a growing testiness increased by his spinning headache and by the emptiness in his stomach. When he was done, his round face smooth and streamy and his eyes stinging from soapy water, he reached for a towel. The family towels were wet, wet and clammy and vile, all of them wet, he found, as he blindly snatched them—his own face-towel, his wife's, Verona's, Ted's, Tinka's, and the lone bath-towel with the huge welt of initial. Then George F. Babbitt did a dismaying thing. He wiped his face on the guest-towel! It was a pansy-embroidered trifle which always hung there to indicate that the Babbitts were in the best Floral Heights society. No one had ever used it. No guest had ever dared to. Guests secretively took a corner of the nearest regular towel.

He was raging, "By golly, here they go and use up all the towels, every doggone one of 'em, and they use 'em and get 'em all wet and sopping, and never put out a dry one for me—of course, I'm the goat!—and then I want one and—I'm the only person in the doggone house that's got the slightest doggone bit of consideration for other people and thoughtfulness and consider there may be others that may want to use the doggone bathroom after me and consider—"

He was pitching the chill abominations into the bath-tub, pleased by the vindictiveness of that desolate flapping sound; and in the midst his wife serenely trotted in, observed serenely, "Why Georgie dear, what are you doing? Are you going to wash out the towels? Why, you needn't wash out the towels. Oh, Georgie, you didn't go and use the guest-towel, did you?"

It is not recorded that he was able to answer.

For the first time in weeks he was sufficiently roused by his wife to look at her.

IV

Myra Babbitt—Mrs. George F. Babbitt—was definitely mature. She had creases from the corners of her mouth to the bottom of her chin, and her plump neck bagged. But the thing that marked her as having passed the line was that she no longer had reticences before her husband, and no longer worried about not having reticences. She was in a petticoat now, and corsets which bulged, and unaware of being seen in bulgy corsets. She had become so dully habituated to married life that in her full matronliness she was as sexless as an anemic nun. She was a good woman, a kind woman, a diligent woman, but no one, save perhaps Tinka her ten-year-old, was at all interested in her or entirely aware that she was alive.

After a rather thorough discussion of all the domestic and social aspects of towels she apologized to Babbitt for his having an alcoholic headache; and he recovered enough to endure the search for a B.V.D. undershirt which had, he pointed out, malevolently been concealed among his clean pajamas.

He was fairly amiable in the conference on the brown suit.

"What do you think, Myra?" He pawed at the clothes hunched on a chair in their bedroom, while she moved about mysteriously adjusting and patting her petticoat and, to his jaundiced eye, never seeming to get on with her dressing. "How about it? Shall I wear the brown suit another day?"

"Well, it looks awfully nice on you."

"I know, but gosh, it needs pressing."

"That's so. Perhaps it does."

"It certainly could stand being pressed, all right."

"Yes, perhaps it wouldn't hurt it to be pressed."

"But gee, the coat doesn't need pressing. No sense in having the whole darn suit pressed, when the coat doesn't need it."

"That's so."

"But the pants certainly need it, all right. Look at them—look at those wrinkles—the pants certainly do need pressing."

"That's so. Oh, Georgie, why couldn't you wear the brown coat with the blue trousers we were wondering what we'd do with them?"

"Good Lord! Did you ever in all my life know me to wear the coat of one suit and the pants of another? What do you think I am? A busted bookkeeper?"

"Well, why don't you put on the dark gray suit to-day, and stop in at the tailor and leave the brown trousers?"

"Well, they certainly need—Now where the devil is that gray suit? Oh, yes, here we are."

He was able to get through the other crises of dressing with comparative resoluteness and calm.

His first adornment was the sleeveless dimity B.V.D. undershirt, in which he resembled a small boy humorlessly wearing a cheesecloth tabard at a civic pageant. He never put on B.V.D.'s without thanking the God of Progress that he didn't wear tight, long, old-fashioned undergarments, like his father-in-law and partner, Henry Thompson. His second embellishment was combing and slicking back his hair. It gave him a tremendous forehead, arching up two inches beyond the former hair-line. But most wonder-working of all was the donning of his spectacles.

There is character in spectacles—the pretentious tortoise-shell, the meek pince-nez of the school teacher, the twisted silver-framed glasses of the old villager. Babbitt's spectacles had huge, circular, frameless lenses of the very best glass; the earpieces were thin bars of gold. In them he was the modern business man; one who gave orders to clerks and drove a car and played occasional golf and was scholarly in regard to Salesmanship. His head suddenly appeared not babyish but weighty, and you noted his heavy, blunt nose, his straight mouth and thick, long upper lip, his chin overfleshy but strong; with respect you beheld him put on the rest of his uniform as a Solid Citizen.

The gray suit was well cut, well made, and completely undistinguished. It was a standard suit. White piping on the V of the vest added a flavor of law and learning. His shoes were black laced boots, good boots, honest boots, standard boots, extraordinarily uninteresting boots. The only frivolity was in his purple knitted scarf. With considerable comment on the matter to Mrs. Babbitt (who, acrobatically fastening the back of her blouse to her skirt with a safety-pin, did not hear a word he said), he chose between the purple scarf and a tapestry effect with stringless brown harps among blown palms, and into it he thrust a snake-head pin with opal eyes.

A sensational event was changing from the brown suit to the gray the contents of his pockets. He was earnest about these objects. They were of eternal importance, like baseball or the Republican Party. They included a fountain pen and a silver pencil (always lacking a supply of new leads) which belonged in the righthand upper vest pocket. Without them he would have felt naked. On his watch-chain were a gold penknife, silver cigar-cutter, seven keys (the use of two of which he had forgotten), and incidentally a good watch. Depending from the chain was a large, yellowish elk's-tooth—proclamation of his membership in the Benevolent and Protective Order of Elks. Most significant of all was his loose-leaf pocket note-book, that modern and efficient note-book which contained the addresses of people whom he had forgotten, prudent memoranda of postal money-orders which had reached their destinations months ago, stamps which had lost their mucilage, clippings of verses by T. Cholmondeley Frink and of the newspaper editorials from which Babbitt got his opinions and his polysyllables, notes to be sure and do things which he did not intend to do, and one curious inscription—D.S.S. D.M.Y.P.D.F.

But he had no cigarette-case. No one had ever happened to give him one, so he hadn't the habit, and people who carried cigarette-cases he regarded as effeminate.

Last, he stuck in his lapel the Booster's Club button. With the conciseness of great art the button displayed two words: "Boosters—Pep!" It made Babbitt feel loyal and important. It associated him with Good Fellows, with men who were nice and human, and important in business circles. It was his V.C., his Legion of Honor ribbon, his Phi Beta Kappa key. . . .

V

Before he followed his wife, Babbitt stood at the westernmost window of their room. This residential settlement Floral Heights, was on a rise; and though the center of the city was three miles away—Zenith had between three and four hundred thousand inhabitants now—he could see the top of the Second National Tower, an Indiana limestone building of thirty-five stories.

Its shining walls rose against April sky to a simple cornice like a streak of white fire. Integrity was in the tower, and decision. It bore its strength lightly as a tall soldier. As Babbitt stared, the nervousness was soothed from his face, his slack chin lifted in reverence. All he articulated was "That's one lovely sight!" but he was inspired by the rhythm of the city; his love of it renewed. He beheld the tower as a temple-spire of the religion of business, a faith passionate, exalted, surpassing common men; and as he clumped down to breakfast he whistled the ballad "Oh, by gee, by gosh, by jingo" as though it were a hymn melancholy and noble.

Further Resources

BOOKS

Hutchisson, James M. *The Rise of Sinclair Lewis, 1920–1930.* University Park, Pa.: Pennsylvania State University Press, 1996.

Lingeman, Richard R. *Sinclair Lewis: Rebel from Main Street.* New York: Random House, 2002.

Mary Ware Dennett and Birth Control

Letter to the Members of the Senate and House of Representatives; Letter to the Members of the Senate Judiciary Committee

Letters

By: Mary Ware Dennett

Date: February 1923

Source: Dennett, Mary Ware. Mary Ware Dennett to the members of the Senate and House of Representatives, February 1923; Mary Ware Dennett to the members of the Senate Judiciary Committee, February 1923. In *Birth Control Laws: Shall We Keep Them Change Them or Abolish Them.* New York: Grafton Press, 1926, 110, 116–117.

About the Author: Mary Ware Dennett (1872–1947) was a pioneering advocate of birth control, family planning, and sex

education. A tireless crusader for her beliefs, she helped found the National Birth Control League, served as director of the Voluntary Parenthood League, and wrote the famous book *The Sex Side of Life.* ■

Introduction

Anthony Comstock left a curious legacy. The one-time leader of the New York Society for the Prevention of Vice and longtime official "censor" of the U.S. Post Office, this mid-nineteenth century moral crusader almost single-handedly induced Congress in 1873 to enact the country's first nationwide antiobscenity laws—in this case, authorizing postal authorities to deny use of the mails to publishers peddling what many (including Comstock) would deem objectionable materials.

By the early 1920s, the "Comstock Law" was clashing with the new birth control/family planning movement, which had come into being just before American entry into World War I (1914–1918). Groups such as Margaret Sanger's American Birth Control League (a forerunner of today's Planned Parenthood) and others had sought to amend the narrowly drawn Comstock statute to allow legitimate organizations to disseminate medical and health-related materials through the U.S. mail.

Significance

However, Sanger and others came up against the Comstock prohibition still in force, which, when interpreted literally, could be employed by government authorities to suppress the distribution of any sexually oriented materials. Accordingly, the 1920s witnessed a hotly contested battle to amend the Comstock statute so as to permit the dissemination of legitimate birth control and family planning information. This issue pitted newly liberated women, their male allies, and the medical community against churches and assorted self-styled moral defenders of their communities, many of whom were the strongest proponents of the recently enacted Prohibition law.

Meanwhile, America's politicians found themselves unwittingly caught between two forces. Many lawmakers, while personally sympathetic to amending the strict Comstock statute, feared the wrath of public opinion and so refused to support reform. Many political leaders maintained the same stance toward Prohibition; while they privately acknowledged its various shortcomings, they nonetheless refused to endorse repeal publicly.

Hence, despite compelling arguments, the reformers failed in their efforts during 1922–1923 to overturn the Comstock law. Meanwhile, despite the reluctance of

A growing number of people, including prominent physicians, began to support birth control measures during the 1920s. Margaret Sanger (seated, left) was head of a birth control clinical bureau charged in 1929 with violating the law. AP/WIDE WORLD PHOTOS. REPRODUCED BY PERMISSION.

the legislature to liberalize the laws, subsequent U.S. Supreme Court decisions did. The Comstock era finally ended with the Court's landmark 1965 ruling in *Griswold v. Connecticut* that struck down a state law that banned dissemination of information about contraceptive devices.

Primary Source

Letter to the Members of the Senate and House of Representatives

SYNOPSIS: Pioneering birth-control and family-planning advocate Mary Ware Dennett, the one-time director of the Voluntary Parenthood League, wrote letters to and vigorously lobbied the members of Congress in 1922–1923 to repeal the "Comstock statutes" to permit legitimate scientific and medical information to be delivered by the U.S. Post Office.

Gentlemen:

Just fifty years ago this month, Anthony Comstock showed to your predecessors specimens of the revolting, smutty literature which was then being circulated by conscienceless publishers among the young people of this country.

The Bill he proposed for the suppression of this traffic got almost instant support, as the abuse was flagrant and the proposed remedy a natural one. But by an obvious blunder the Bill was drawn to include all knowledge of contraception, when the aim of the Bill was only the suppression of this knowledge in connection with sex-perversions—a blunder which has meant injustice, hardship and insult to millions of parents ever since.

Now Congress is asked to correct that blunder, and just as Comstock showed your predecessors samples of the disgraceful traffic of the seventies, so we present to you herewith samples of the letters which the League constantly receives in great quantity from suffering parents whose lives are being made miserable by the error that was unwittingly made fifty years ago.

Just as Congress responded to the need presented to them in 1873, we ask you to respond to the need now presented to you in 1923, and to correct the blunder with as much speed as that in which it was originally made.

Yours very truly,
Voluntary Parenthood League.

Primary Source

Letter to the Members of the Senate Judiciary Committee

> Despite Dennett's many forceful letters to lawmakers, reprinted in her book *Birth Control Laws: Shall We Keep Them Change Them or Abolish Them,* Congress turned a deaf ear on her calls for birth control reform.

To the Members of the Senate Judiciary Committee:

In again urging you to report out the Cummins Bill (S4314) next Monday (February 26th), on behalf of my league, I beg you to think of the request in the most simple and human way possible.

The Bill is *simple* because it merely rectifies a blunder made by Congress 50 years ago. It was contraceptive knowledge in connection with sexual depravity that the original statute aimed to suppress, not the knowledge for normal use. The proof of this statement has previously been submitted to you.

The logic of the measure is also *simple,* for the application of this knowledge in controlling conception is not a crime, therefore it is absurd to maintain a law which deems it a crime to learn what that knowledge is.

I beg you to be *human* about it. Act on this measure as if the need for knowledge were your own, instead of that of millions of poor people. Suppose you were a young man on a small wage, with a frail wife and more children already than your pay could support, would you be patient on hearing that your Senators were "too busy" to spend the five minutes it would take to send this Bill on its way to passage? Suppose you had any one of the many good reasons that millions of parents have for needing desperately to get this knowledge in decent, scientific, reliable form, instead of from heresay and in abominable underground ways, wouldn't you put that need first? Would you stop to debate about the French birth-rate, or any other irrelevant question?

Without speaking personally of individual Senators, it is entirely justifiable to assume what Senators *really* think about this question, for the average birth-rate in their families and their children's families has proven it long ago. Can you then be any longer callous to the needs of millions of your poorer fellow citizens who, unlike you, are struggling with poverty and the whole train of worries induced by poverty?

And most of all, can you not break through the *fear,* which has held many of you back from acting promptly; fear not of public opinion but of each other, the flippant, facetious comment that comes easily to the lips of many men, even good and fine men—in their instinctive effort to cover the embarrassment they feel because this question touches upon sex? Many members have admitted that they were inhibited by this fear. But can you not forget it, through sympathy for the suffering of others? Isn't it more precious to you to be just and generous to your fellow citizens than to further indulge this fear, which in the last analysis could never be a source of real pride to you as a servant of the public?

Gratitude and respect await your favorable action.

> Yours very truly,
> Director of the V. P. L.

Further Resources

BOOKS

Chen, Constance M. *"The Sex Side of Life": Mary Ware Dennett's Pioneering Battle for Birth Control and Sex Education.* New York: New Press, 1996.

Gordon, Linda. *Woman's Body, Woman's Right: Birth Control in America.* New York: Penguin Books, 1990.

McCann, Carole R. *Birth Control Politics in the United States.* Ithaca, N.Y.: Cornell University Press, 1994.

"Rise and Present Peril of Mah Jong: The Chinese Game Has Escaped from Society's Chaperonage and Is on Its Own"

Magazine article

By: Helen Bullitt Lowry

Date: August 10, 1924

Source: Lowry, Helen Bullitt. "Rise and Present Peril of Mah Jong: The Chinese Game Has Escaped from Society's Chaperonage and Is on Its Own." *The New York Times Magazine,* August 10, 1924, 4.

About the Author: Helen Bullitt Lowry wrote feature articles on such topics as fashion and Atlantic City beauty pageants for the *The New York Times Magazine.* ∎

Introduction

Twentieth-century Americans enjoyed a love affair with board games: Monopoly in the 1930s, Scrabble in the 1950s, Risk in the 1960s, and backgammon and Trivial Pursuit in the 1980s. Meanwhile, the old standby, chess, was rediscovered during the early 1970s under the influence of chess champion Bobby Fischer.

However, this love affair appears to have started sometime in 1922 with the importation from Asia into America of the Chinese game Mah Jong—a sort of gin rummy played with elegantly carved rectangular pieces of tile. The rapid spread of this pastime constituted a triumph for the art of modern mass merchandising. As with most fads, the market quickly became saturated as various entrepreneurs sough to capitalize on the craze. At some point, the fad peaks and then recedes, never again to enjoy the initial level of popularity. At the conclusion of this cycle, most casual players have drifted away, leaving the field to hard-core enthusiasts. Such was the rise and fall of the 1920s Mah Jong mania.

Significance

The Mah Jong mania represents a significant milestone in the evolution of American popular culture, for Mah Jong was possibly the first major Asian fad to seize the imagination of the American people. Indeed, to a considerable degree, the introduction of Mah Jong coupled with the sudden popularity of Chinese food in the larger, more cosmopolitan cities constituted the moment in time when, for large numbers of Americans, the "mysterious Orient" had become decidedly less so. For an often virulently anti-Asian citizenry that still supported strict immigration laws, including a virtual ban on all Asian immigration, the "discovery" of Chinese culture through games and food represented a breakthrough of sorts that served as a portent for the future.

In retrospect, perhaps the time was ripe for this "discovery" of Chinese culture. The United States had become directly entangled in Asian affairs following the acquisition of the Philippines in 1898—the result of the Spanish-American War (1898). In the two decades following the American intervention in Beijing to suppress the nationalist Boxer Rebellion of 1900, the United States came face-to-face with the Chinese people. In fact, the 1911 Chinese Republican Revolution enjoyed broad support in America. Indeed some top Chinese leaders had strong personal ties to the United States.

Finally, it was of supreme significance that the first Asian fad to sweep America was Chinese Mah Jong, for the American public became acquainted with Chinese culture in a positive, nonthreatening fashion. Major American cities already sported a variety of Chinese restaurants by the 1920s, while Japan's sushi remained largely unknown to the American public until perhaps the 1970s. Therefore, during the 1930s, as political and military tensions escalated in Asia between China and Japan

before World War II (1939–1945), the American people reflexively supported the better-known Chinese side against the lesser-known Japanese—primarily, it appears, for sentimental reasons, which included the perceived friendship between the American and Chinese peoples.

Primary Source

"Rise and Present Peril of Mah Jong: The Chinese Game Has Escaped from Society's Chaperonage and Is on Its Own" [excerpt]

SYNOPSIS: Of all the various boardgame fads that have swept the United States during the twentieth-century, the introduction of the Chinese pastime Mah Jong, described in the following excerpts, doubtless had the most profound political impact. For the American public, exposed to Chinese culture before Japanese, tended to support China in its war with Japan during the 1930s.

Rumor has been about that the vogue for Mah Jong is on the wane. Rumor has even had it that Mah Jong is about to return to China, whence it hailed from, to take up its venerable life again far east of Suez. Rumor has indicated that the life of our missionaries in the "foreign field" is at last to be allowed to return to normalcy—without the embarrassment of their having to explain away the passion for China's own private gambling game in Christian Endeavored America. . . .

The wave of the Mah Jong craze has admittedly passed its crest. Yet there are more people playing Mah Jong today than there were a year ago, when the rage was hottest. The old bridge habitués and the cold-blooded society bridge gamblers have definitely returned to the ways of their fathers. This particularly applies to the Eastern seaboard, where the craze has had a year of it to run its course. But meanwhile an entirely new world of players has been called into being—made up of the sociable folk who are interested primarily in the "party" instead of in the scientific play or in the gaming—the brand of chatty beings who have been out of their element ever since the Right and Left Bower were ostracized from good society.

This year those who do not want to play Mah Jong no longer have to play to keep up Mah Jong appearances. It is no longer the "thing to do." Instead, it is now the thing one does, if one wants to do it. Mah Jong has passed out of its incense-burning period—its In-Chinese-Costume charity bazaar epoch. One no longer feels deliciously Oriental when uttering Chows and Pungs. Instead, the time has come when the game has got to make good as a way to spend the evening. It has definitely passed beyond its bijou period.

Witness the 10-cent decks of Mah Jong to be had at Woolworth's. So are $4.98 near-ivory sets prevalent at department stores. Two-dollar-and-a-half sets are syndicated in chain drug stores. There, alone, is indication enough that the purely fashionable period of Mah Jong has passed. Therein lies its present strength. Therein, too, lies the peril, which the commercial interests behind the game have brought upon it.

Those shadowy commercial interests behind the game and the social fortunes of the game itself are, in truth, inextricably interwoven—nor can one understand the dramatic story of its brilliant social fortune and of its present social hazards without realizing also the tale of its commercial backing.

Into the East the story carries us. Standard Oil business took J. P. Babcock into China and the region about Shanghai, where Mah Jong is the indigenous game alike of mandarins and coolies.

Babcock's first move—at least this is the way Oriental gossips tell the story—was to introduce the native game into the American Club at Shanghai, thereby cannily creating a demand in the smart American colony frequented by our naval officers. Having created the demand, he thriftily set about the business of supplying it. This next step necessitated the diplomatic achievement of getting Chinese sets translated into English. And it was only after vast Confucian difficulties that he prevailed upon the native workmen to engrave S, N, E, and W upon their native winds and Occidental numerals upon the dots, bams and cracks. Next he invented the name of Mah Jong and the handy titles of Chow, Pung and Woo. Then he got his invention patented. . . .

By reason of the American naval officers Mah Jong made the necessary jump across the Pacific and established itself in the smartest society of San Francisco. True, the Chinese version of Mah Jong had been played for a generation in the smart kitchens of the town, where many a month's wages had changed hands over the tiles. That was a mere detail. Smart San Francisco had not discovered Mah Jong. The $100 and $200 English-speaking sets on the market were just the commercial impetus needed. From the Golden Gate Mah Jong jumped the continent at one leap and established itself on the Eastern seaboard.

The Chinese game Mah Jong became a popular one with the American public during the 1920s. © KEREN SU/CORBIS. REPRODUCED BY PERMISSION.

From this point on—sinister isn't exactly the right word, "synthetic," that's it—influences behind the game begin to be realized. Society editors of the metropolitan sheets say that social pressure began to be felt from a dozen sources. The type of persons who have the reputation of commercializing their social position to mitigate the high cost of living were very much on the job.

So, too, were the serious "authorities" on auction bridge on the job. They straightway set themselves the task of becoming authorities on Mah Jong, and then issued their own "authoritative" textbooks on the subject. Also other persons who had never been authorities to any game suddenly announced themselves the final arbiters on Mah Jong—and likewise issued $2 books on its technique. . . .

All this while the actual industrial forces were gathering. Two hundred importing firms were developing their Mah Jong branches—many of them fly-by-night concerns, hastily capitalized for the purpose. In round numbers $1,500,000 worth of sets were imported in 1923. But that wasn't all. Four factories, three of them in New England and one in New

York, poured out ivory tiles. Across the water Germany and Austria chimed into the international anthem, until today the best cheap sets are coming from those two countries.

All in all, the capital invested in this fad runs high into the millions. If not a Senatorial lobby—at any rate a well-organized social lobby—was inevitable. Where the vogue for auction bridge had been the product of slow, unstimulated evolution, the craze for Mah Jong has certainly occurred more in accordance with Mr. Bryan's ideas on biology. . . .

We now come to the part played by the other 200 importers. They entered the field with a patented name already in existence. But the ancient game itself and its jewel-like tiles could no more be copyrighted than could a deck of cards. Mah Duke, Mah Cheuk, Mah Chang, Pung Chow were launched, also half a dozen cases of litigation. Each of these importers, too, was employing his own Chinese authorities And interpreters, who threw together quite a different set of simplified Oriental rulings. All of these commercial complications added to the chaos already in existence by reason of the hordes of self-made authorities.

So it has come about that society today is split into a dozen warring camps. The society folk of Washington can't play without warfare with the society folk of Baltimore. Nay more, each city is divided up into a dozen quarreling cliques that find that they cannot play with each other in peace, because this clique plays by Babcock and that clique by Foster. If there is one stranger in the crowd, the rules of warfare have to be discussed beforehand as meticulously as rulings of The Hague Tribunal were supposed to be discussed. . . .

Mah Jong is now paying the price for that insolent compromise with the traditions of the centuries. The very persons who took it up so excitedly just a year ago, are now quite frankly tired of its easy thrills. The people who were bridge habitués again.

There is that third great danger as well that menaces the game. I mean the actual democratizing of it. Mah Jong is no longer the exclusive plaything of the rich, as it was when a set called for the expenditure of $100. In the Summer and Fall of 1923 a gigantic commercial drive was launched by the manufacturers and importers of medium-priced sets.

From east to west and from north to south the democratic drive took its department store way. Itinerant demonstrators "played" Milwaukee and Kansas City, St. Paul and Des Moines and Chat-

tanooga. In plate-glass show windows of department stores they set up their stage business. Two little Chinese maids in native costume could there be seen playing with a $25 set against a background of lacquer—the all-too-familiar Hollywood version of the East and its sins and its mysteries. While, inside the store, a Mah Jong instructor, also in costume, gave gratuitous instruction to all who came inquiring—whether they purchased a set or whether they didn't.

So Mah Jong came into the possession of the great common people, of whom the Lord in His infinite wisdom (or carelessness) made so many. Today the majority of sets that are being sold are of the $5 and $10 variety. Mah Jong can no longer depend for its popularity on any artificial social prestige. Of no avail now organized efforts to restore that artificial prestige. For better or for worse, the game is irretrievably committed to the ways of democracy.

Further Resources

BOOKS

Shiu, Priscilla. *The Mystic Mah-Jongg Game.* New York: Exposition Press, 1973.

Whitney, Eleanor Noss. *A Mah Jong Handbook; How to Play, Score, and Win the Modern Game.* Rutland, Vt.: C.E. Tuttle, 1964.

Advertising Response: A Research Into Influences That Increase Sales

Nonfiction work

By: Howard McCormick Donovan

Date: 1924

Source: Donovan, H.M. *Advertising Response: A Research into Influences That Increase Sales.* Philadelphia: J.B. Lippincott, 1924, 19, 21–23, 24.

About the Author: Howard McCormick Donovan (1883–?) was a well-known advertising and marketing expert. ∎

Introduction

The 1920s witnessed the practical application of insights gleaned from both experimental psychology as well as from survey research methods to the age-old art of selling, which traditionally had been approached more or less intuitively. The 1920s saw the advent of modern

Advertising methods became increasingly targeted at the youth market during the 1920s. **THE LIBRARY OF CONGRESS.**

mass-marketing techniques designed to induce consumers to buy products and services. Also, the decade saw the rise of slick advertising and public relations firms dispensing advice to corporate clients from their office's on New York City's Madison Avenue.

In this atmosphere, an appreciation of the various "niche" markets appeared for the first time. First, a distinctive women's market materialized. Later in the 1920s, a distinctive "youth" market surfaced. This splintering of the consumer world would continue to be refined over the course of the twentieth century.

Significance

It remains an open question why it took so long to identify and cultivate such a youth market. In hindsight, a key finding culled from modern market research concerned the fact that many consumers who were introduced to brand names at an early age wound up retaining an affinity for such brands throughout their lifetime—an insight that should have long been self-evident. "Hook 'em while they're young" has today become standard mantra in the advertising world.

Although previous advertising campaigns had often emphasized the youthful aspects of various products and services, the 1920s saw a reversal—where youth actually appeared to set the pace. A clear message emerged that the pursuit of "fun" had now become a lifelong endeavor—a change reflecting the fact that long-standing attitudes toward the primacy of work had eroded. The 1920s may well have been the moment in time, some observers suggest, when the older work ethic began to be eclipsed by a new ethic of recreation and leisure that redefined the central purpose in the lives of millions of Americans.

Primary Source

The Advertising Response: A Research Into Influences That Increase Sales [excerpt]

SYNOPSIS: The American advertising and marketing industry seems to have discovered the so-called "youth market" during the 1920s, a distinctive niche with enormous economic potential. The subdivision of the larger market into numerous readily identifiable submarkets constitutes an important step in the evolution of modern American consumer culture. In this excerpt, Donovan discusses "The Age Factor," the title of Chapter 3 of *The Advertising Response.*

The Age Factor

Until recently practically nothing definite has been known concerning just what part youth played in the buying of goods. . . .

For many years manufacturers have known that it was good psychology to have a youthful appeal in the advertising of certain lines. Yet because the subject had been investigated only superficially, a full understanding of the influence of advertising on youth was impossible.

It was recognized that a youthful appeal in the advertising of men's and women's wear played on a human weakness. This appeal was certain to get a response both "from the young and those who wish to appear young." There was no question in the minds of advertisers that youth exerted considerable influence on the purchase of many articles other than those intended primarily for them, such as phonographs, and good use was made of this knowledge in the advertising. . . .

Let us consider a few of the many aspects of advertising and selling which are involved by the proposition of the appeal to youth. In the first place, psychologists agree that it is the associations gained in the formative period of youth that are stamped most indelibly upon the mind. These bear a dominant influence on the mental reactions of the individual for many years to come. Also, young people are responsive to almost anything new that strikes their fancy. Advertising which appeals especially to them not only produces sales most quickly, but, if it is continuous and adequate, forms a bond which is not easily broken.

What has been fixed in the students' minds at eighteen and nineteen will not desert them. They have been more or less permanently influenced in favor of certain brands because advertising during the most impressionable period of their lives has worn grooves in their brain structure that cannot easily be removed.

Briefly, the manufacturer who has appealed to young people in his advertising and succeeded in winning their favor to his brand, has successfully placed his competitors' lines at a disadvantage. This cannot be overcome without very great effort in sales work and a largely increased advertising expenditure.

It has been commonly noticed by retailers that at the beginning of a period of depression the older customers tighten up almost immediately and sales to them fall off. The younger people with their characteristic optimism keep right on with their purchases until they are actually forced by lack of cash to reduce their expenditures. When times improve, sales to the young get in full swing long before their elders will respond to any kind of advertising except reduction sales.

The reason for youthful appeal in advertising is only half told by emphasizing its indelible effect on the young. Their responsiveness to its message is greatest during the years from 17 to 30, which age group is largest in numbers as well as strongest in actual buying interest. Of equal importance is the dominant influence which youth exerts on sales to the older groups.

There is no question that modern youth sets the fashion in almost everything, and the extent to which maturity follows this lead is amazing. Today, fashions are actually being set by young people of high school age, and the range of their influence runs all the way from the purchase of automobiles to canned pineapple. Not a book, a magazine, or a play can meet even with ordinary success unless it appeals to youth. . . .

Youth is demanding a greater share of attention than ever before. It is imperative that manufacturers be awakened to a fuller realization of the power which youth exerts on the welfare of their businesses. Advertisers should take better advantage of the opportunities offered thereby.

Further Resources
BOOKS
Gilbert, Eugene. *Advertising and Marketing to Young People.* Pleasantville, N.Y.: Printers' Ink Books, 1957.

Mayer, Martin. *Madison Avenue, USA.* New York: Harper & Row, 1958.

Norris, James D. *Advertising and the Transformation of American Society, 1865–1920.* New York: Greenwood, 1990.

Handbook for Guardians of Camp Fire Girls
Handbook

By: Camp Fire Girls, Inc.

Date: 1924

Source: *Handbook for Guardians of Camp Fire Girls.* New York: Camp Fire Girls, Inc, 1924, 167–171, 173.

About the Author: Camp Fire Girls, Inc., was founded in 1910 by Dr. Luther Gulick and his wife, Charlotte. Initially their organization was known as "Camp Fire USA." ∎

Introduction
Tensions abound in American society between the ethos of individualism and the social pressure that demands conformity. The twentieth century American experience bounced between one extreme and the other. The relatively free-spirited 1910s and 1960s stand in marked contrast to the conformist 1950s and 1980s. Meanwhile, the decade of the 1920s, perhaps more so than any other period in recent American history, epitomizes an era when society exerted tremendous pressure to follow the crowd in order to gain acceptance.

The third decade of the century witnessed the "coming of age" of both advertising and public relations, which sought to use many of the theoretical insights gleaned from modern social science disciplines such as psychology, sociology, and anthropology. Since, in the 1920s, the overriding concern with many Americans was to be "popular," advertisers helped create anxieties that, not surprisingly, their own products and services magically alleviated. More scientifically, professional child-rearing manuals of the period repeatedly stressed the overarching importance of youngsters "fitting in" to the requirements of the group.

Significance

But what happens to those boys and girls who, for whatever reason, never quite "fit in" comfortably? What would ultimately become of them? The problem of how to engender sufficient conformity from children led to advice such as that found in the 1920s editions of the Camp Fire Girls Handbook.

That the Camp Fire Girls should seriously address this issue in its manual should come as no surprise. For the Camp Fire Girls, an organization akin to the Girl Scouts and Boy Scouts that burgeoned in the United States during the years just before American entry into World War I (1914–1918), was widely viewed as a wholesome antidote to many of the influences of modern life that adults feared. Accordingly, the Camp Fire Girls stressed group activity, along with social conformity and enjoyment of "good clean fun."

By making certain that all girls (including the "misfits") ultimately "fit in," the Camp Fire Girls pursued its avowed goal of turning raw young ladies into successful polished women.

Primary Source

Handbook for Guardians of Camp Fire Girls
[excerpt]

> **SYNOPSIS:** The Camp Fire Girls, like the Boy and Girl Scouts, was a youth organization that sprang up prior to American entry into World War I in large measure to provide a "wholesome" environment for kids who might otherwise be exposed to the allegedly "unwholesome" environment of that era. Once launched, these groups later comfortably reflected the dominant social ethos of the 1920s—conformity. The following excerpts, from Chapter 14, "The Unusual Girl and the Group," contain advice to Camp Fire Girl leaders on how to deal with members who don't "fit in."

The Unusual Girl and the Group

For the time, trouble, patience, and thought that you put into making your Camp Fire a success you ask no reward except that success for which you have striven. But is there any reward unasked for and unexpected which thrills you with more happiness than the knowledge that some one girl in your group has found herself through Camp Fire? Perhaps she comes to you and tells you in stumbling phrases, which your sympathetic understanding must fill out and interpret, what Camp Fire has done for her. Perhaps some of the other girls confide in you how much they like and respect a certain girl who they had thought at first would never make a companionable member of your Camp Fire. Perhaps no one says

anything to you but you cannot help feeling and knowing that the misfit about whom you had serious and secret misgivings is a misfit no longer but has found her way into the hearts and affections of the rest of your girls. . . .

Face the Problem

Tact is most important in dealing with the girl who for some reason does not seem to fit into your group—tact, and sympathy, and understanding, with common sense and the courage to act decisively if need be. Never, if you can help it, let the matter drift to the point where the girl has achieved a recognized unpopularity, for then it is most difficult to wipe out the unpleasant impression she has made on the other girls, and harder still to restore the girl's own self-confidence.

Each individual case must be dealt with in its own way and there lies a heavy responsibility for Guardians to shoulder. Psychologists have been working for some time on the personality difficulties of the problem child. It is too bad that so much of their work has been with the abnormal and delinquent children, probably because their needs are the most pressing and because they offer the most material for study. What we need for our guidance is the study of the somewhat unusual girl whose difficulties make her a problem although she is by no means abnormal or what we think of as a delinquent. However, there are certain basic things to consider if we would help a girl who for some reason is "different" to find her place in a Camp Fire Group. . . .

Look for Causes

In an article on the "Problem Child," by Phillis Blanchard and Richard H. Payne of the Child Guidance Clinic, they say of a child that "there are definite causes that produce his difficulties, that these causes are to be found in his physical, mental, or social life, and that, having been found, they can in many instances be removed or ameliorated." They also say, "Our conception of personality is not that it is a static, unchanging condition. We realize that physical ills, environmental influences and many other interlocking factors underlie the outward manifestations of personality. Therefore by medical and social treatment, and by enlisting the child's own cooperation in the correction of her difficulties, we may hope to produce marked changes in personality and bring it back to a normal state." It is, therefore, the duty of the Guardian to inform herself about her girls, especially the one or two who do not seem to be in accord with the rest of her group, in order ! that she may be able to help them make the necessary readjustment. . . .

What Can You Say?

It is seldom a wise thing to talk to the girl directly; it will tend to make her even more self conscious and perhaps so resentful as to undo any intended good. It is also a rather dangerous thing to talk the matter over specifically with the other girls, though this is sometimes necessary and the only solution to the problem. If you find that most of your girls are pointedly ignoring this one girl, or making fun of her, or antagonizing her, put a stop to it at once by a tactful talk with one or two of the leading spirits or with all of the girls. The way you do this will mean its success or failure. It is far better to present the matter to the girls as their duty to Camp Fire, rather than as a kindness to the individual girl. A Guardian might say to her girls, something like this:

> You are, perhaps, unconsciously, leaving Dorothy out of your games, your plans, and your conversation. She is naturally shy and reserved and the more you do this the more she will crawl into her own shell. We want a Camp Fire that works together as a whole, so we want Dorothy to be one with us. Let's try to make her realize she has her place. Don't let her feel your effort, but include her in everything you do, and make a point of talking to her about the things that interest her most. Soon I am sure she will forget to be shy and our Camp Fire will be the unit we want it to be. . . .

A Few General Suggestions

Do not try to force the shy girl. Let her take a small and inconspicuous part in the group activities at first, but gradually arouse her interest and stimulate her confidence in herself so that through working with the group she comes in time to lose some of her shyness and is no longer afraid to venture by herself.

Give the aggressive girl a job that will keep her busy, not necessarily one of leadership. If possible, make her feel that she is working for the good of the group and not for her own self exaltation. Competitions and games between groups are an excellent means of teaching an egotistic girl her place as one small unit in a group activity.

Do not over-stimulate the active girl. Help her to appreciate the excellence of achievement as opposed to the amount accomplished.

Attempts to include all children in a group to limit ostracism and maintain group cohesion were made by various organizations, including the Camp Fire Girls. **THE LIBRARY OF CONGRESS.**

Through the winning of Honors and through competition arouse the lethargic girl to participate in the group activities.

Make a selfish girl responsible for the happiness of someone younger or weaker than herself.

These are the merest generalizations. In the end you will have to work out your own problems in your own way, but do not be frightened or discouraged if fate brings to your group what seems to be a hopeless misfit. Very great will be your spiritual reward if through your tact and understanding you bring out the latent beauty in her girl-nature and make her an asset to your Camp Fire.

Further Resources
BOOKS
Ferris, Helen Josephine. *Girls' Clubs: The Organizational Management, A Manual for Leaders.* New York: Dutton, 1926.

Pendry, Elizabeth Ruth. *Organizations for Youth: Leisure Time and Character Building Procedures.* New York: McGraw-Hill, 1935.

"Into the Land of Talk"

Magazine article

By: Lydia Lion Roberts

Date: March 1926

Source: Roberts, Lydia Lion. "Into the Land of Talk." *American Cookery,* March 1926, 584–586.

About the Author: Lydia Lyon Roberts was a contributor to *American Cookery,* formerly known as *The Boston Cooking-School Magazine.* ∎

Introduction

Everyday gossip can provide a unique window into the prevailing mind-set of an era, especially the thoughts and aspirations of ordinary people. Unlike politics, or even some aspects of popular culture, gossip reflects the mundane, day-to-day concerns of average citizens. We can decipher a great deal about a society by examining exactly what men and women chat about during their idle time.

It remains remarkably difficult to analyze such gossip because much of it is unrecorded. We have tantalizing glimpses of marketplace chitchat handed down from ancient times in the classics. The characters in William Shakespeare's plays make frequent reference to the gossip of the street. But for the most part, gossip has inherent ethereal quality to it. Hence, it is hard to capture, let alone analyze.

Significance

Nonetheless, if various reports are to be believed, the content of American thought seems to have shifted significantly by the 1920s, a reflection, no doubt, of deeper economic and social changes transforming the lives of ordinary people. For openers, peoples' geographical horizons expanded dramatically with the widespread introduction of the automobile and the construction by the 1920s of a nationwide network of highways. This geographic mobility made it easier to get around and to bridge the large gaps between city and countryside. Then too, by the 1920s, the home telephone had become an ever-present feature of daily life. In addition, the advent of commercial radio along with the burgeoning popularity of the motion pictures increased people's perceptions of the larger universe outside their own communities.

Meanwhile, the partial liberation of women (including the right to vote granted in 1920), enhanced employment opportunities outside the home, and an upsurge in female college student enrollment served to transport women out of their normal domestic routine by opening up new possibilities. In many ways, women began to emulate men. The 1920s saw the advent of many woman's clubs and professional organizations, although they were on a smaller scale than what was to come later in the century.

Primary Source

"Into the Land of Talk" [excerpt]

> **SYNOPSIS:** The quality of mundane, day-to-day gossip appears to have changed in America by the 1920s—doubtless a reflection of certain social and economic transformations (urbanization, the automobile, motion pictures, radio, and the partial liberation of women) that had impacted the nation by the third decade of the twentieth century. The following article describes this new type of chitchat.

What do people talk about on the trains, in the clubs, at meetings and in the homes? Do men gossip more than women? Is there a difference in the subjects chosen to talk about between the younger and the older generation? Is the talk of the men more broad-minded than that of the women who are at home? Does the business woman have a wider range of talkitis than her home sisters? All these questions seethe in one's mind as one goes about, smiling and alert, but holding the thought of listening, listening, listening.

People talk about babies, movies, clothes, homes, religion, automobiles, books, women's latest fads and club work. They talk about other things, but these subjects seem to predominate as one listens in cloak rooms, living rooms, offices, street corners, repair stations and concerts.

Gossip seems to be fairly evenly divided between men and women, the male sex being perhaps a bit more alert and active on this score than the weaker sex. One has heard so much about women's gossip that it is rather a surprising adventure to find the mighty male just about as guilty. This listening game does broaden one's observations. There is a decided difference in the matter of gossip between the older generations, the women of sixty and more, and the younger. One hears much less gossip among the younger people. The older people seem to deal more with personal things, with more detail and smaller matters, especially those whose minds got their growth before the days of the automobile, radio and telephone. The gossip is not necessarily unkind, but it is trivial. The most interesting adventure in the talk of the older ones is to listen when they talk of old times. It is like reading an old story book, and is valuable in the light it sheds on other ways and customs. Whenever one is with older people it is decidedly worth while to draw them out on this subject.

Members of the Chicago Woman's Club meet outside of a building in Chicago, Illinois in 1928. **CHICAGO HISTORICAL SOCIETY. REPRODUCED BY PERMISSION.**

The work of the women's clubs certainly has made a decided change in the trend of women's talk. The noted speakers, the latest books, the customs of the different clubs, the work done by various organizations, the musical part of the programs, and international affairs, all form a prominent part of a clubwoman's talk. The women's clubs are doing for the home woman what business has done for the men—enlarging her viewpoint, giving her a better sense of proportion and showing her the many adventures of life all over the world. The business woman used to complain that the home woman could talk about nothing but beans and babies, but now the two types of women seem to meet on a mutual and pleasant ground. Women's clubs are bringing all types of women into closer relations, breaking barriers, and elevating the everlasting talk of the world.

Mention the word "baby" in any circle, start to tell a story of some proud parents' precocious youngster, and all talk of work, clubs or world affairs is immediately off the board and every one's attention centered on really important things. The magic word brings smiles in cars, shops, homes and streets. Men, women and children meet here on a common platform, the men being more guilty of boasting than the women. Two men will talk incessantly on a train trip about the merits of their offspring, just as much as the mothers. After listening to talk about babies the world seems a mellow, kind-hearted affair underneath its hard crust, and the air a bit brighter and cleaner.

Powder, rouge, short skirts and smoking get their share of the conversations, and the criticism, the blame, the arguments are directed, not at the so-called "flapper," but at her mother; the mother who follows the latest fad, the woman of apparent intelligence and charm who persists in adopting habits which are not up to the real ideal of the wholesome, modern woman. The talk about the "flapper mother" is serious, scornful, and thought-provoking.

Blessed be the automobile and the radio which have taken the women into the outside world and brought the world into the home. Men and women meet here on mutual interests and enthusiasms. It is lively, clean, interesting talk, with many flashes of humor, exciting experiences and wholesome rivalry. "What did you get last night?" "This set is better; I'll be over and show you how to fix yours." These two blessings have also brought their problems which are being earnestly discussed. What about the high-school boy with the automobile, the money spent on radio and cars, the late rides, the "radio widow," and the new trio—the boy, the girl, and the automobile?

We are being told there are no homes any more, and yet the talk about the home goes on, day after day. The planning of its affairs, the delight in new, efficient machinery for the home work, the never-failing interest in home decoration, the man whistling at his bench in the cellar, the woman humming over a new color scheme, the meeting and exchanging of ideas seem to show no slackening interest in the home. Women crowd the lectures on home products, on correct ways of doing everything in the home, and men still proudly talk in cars and offices of their prowess with tools, or the ways they are going to fix over the house. Even house-cleaning comes in for its share of attention, along with the radio.

Movies, books, travel and the theater are usually mentioned where any group of people of either sex assemble. There is a brisk interchange of comparisons, outspoken approval or otherwise, lively arguments over what to read and what not to read and why, over what to see and what son or daughter has already seen and read. Talk about travel always brings out personal experiences and often forms a slight bond between people who have been over the same route or visited the same places, and always there occurs that magic word "abroad." So many have already been that the others want to go, too, and there is hopeful talk of the cheaper rates, "so that perhaps we can go in a year or two."

The newspaper headlines and its line of talk is apt to depress one, but a month of listening, flitting here and there among the different groups of people, is quite otherwise. The talk of the world today is encouraging. It is brisk, frank and friendly. It is like the effect of a clean, clear east wind, stirring up the languorous summer day. People talk quickly, hopefully, with a looking-forward attitude to doing and being *more* in later years, rather than the old looking forward to "settling down" and growing stale. The old, good subjects of home and babies are still current talk, but it is mixed in with Europe and the new car, and Cadman on the radio, "that wonderful speaker at the club," and "the next thing this town needs." The talk of today centers on subjects on which both men and women, and home women and business women, city and country women may meet. It is talk which draws people together in mutual interests, ambitions, problems and plans.

Further Resources

BOOKS

Fitzgerald, F. Scott. *The Great Gatsby.* New York: Scribner's, 1925.

Walls, Jeannette. *Dish: The Inside Story of the World of Gossip.* New York: Spike, 2000.

"Fools and Their Money"

Magazine article

By: Keyes Winter

Date: August 1927

Source: Winter, Keyes. "Fools and Their Money." *Harpers Magazine,* August 1927, 361–362.

About the Author: Republican Keyes Winter served as assistant attorney general of New York State. ∎

Introduction

History is replete with examples of speculative booms that trapped the unwary: the seventeenth-century Dutch Tulip Craze, the eighteenth-century English South Sea Bubble, or the various modern-day Ponzi schemes that cheat investors out of their money. In these schemes, unsophisticated investors fall prey to inflated expectations while the "insiders" and the "smart money" have long since recognized the inevitable and have cashed out. In recent times, the "go-go" stock-market of the 1960s along with the gold and silver speculations of the late 1970s confirm showman P.T. Barnum's adage that there's a "sucker born every minute."

The most famous speculative bubble in American history was the stock-market mania of the 1920s. The proliferation of get-rich-quick schemes help define the Roaring Twenties as much as do flappers, Al Capone, and bootleg gin. Not only were stock prices wildly over-

American money practices were oftentimes incautious, with many purchases made on credit accounts and investments in questionable deals. These practices contributed to the stock market collapse of 1929 and the economic depression of the 1930s. **THE LIBRARY OF CONGRESS.**

inflated, but so too were Florida real estate (much of it swampland) and Texas oil wells.

Significance

At the height of the speculative mania in 1928, even normally subdued political and business leaders could be found adding their voices to the chorus cheering on the stock market to record new heights. Near the end of the boom, President Calvin Coolidge (served 1923–1929), himself the epitome of personal financial rectitude, went so far as to pronounce stocks a good bargain even at astronomical prices.

Meanwhile, an occasional voice did raise questions about the speculative bubble. Consumed with greed, many normally staid people lost all sense of reason and ignored the nostrum that whatever goes up must surely come down. One unambiguous warning came from Keyes Winter, the assistant attorney general of New York State. In pre–Great Depression America, the stock market was largely unregulated at the national level. Meanwhile, New York State, home to the largest stock exchange, provided the only semblance of supervision—although it proved to be vastly inadequate.

Primary Source

"Fools and Their Money" [excerpt]

SYNOPSIS: One of the few sober voices to surface during the late-1920s stock-market mania belonged to New York State assistant attorney general Keyes Winter, who clearly warned unwary investors against excessive speculation in a memorable *Harpers Magazine* article in August 1927. Winters' "Fools and Their Money" contained wise words of caution that most investors, swept away by the trading frenzy, refused to heed, to their ultimate regret.

It is a curious and ironic psychological fact that Americans, shrewd as in many ways they show themselves, should be almost universally the victims of some type of financial fraud. The national susceptibility to the swindler is historic, limited to no class or locality. Generations of otherwise hardheaded citizens of these United States have followed the mirage of preposterous profits until its inevitable fading left the deluded in the desert of reality, stripped of their savings of years. Nor has to-day's generation appeared to learn wisdom from the bitter experiences of predecessors. Our fathers and grandfathers hopefully purchased green goods and gold bricks. We, in the same spirit of get-rich-quick optimism, have bought German marks and stock in fly-by-night companies. The form of the dollar-alluring swindle changes, but its spirit remains the same.

Even some of the old forms are still practiced successfully. Crooks continue to offer to college boys and to more sophisticated persons so-called "wonderful bargains" in goods "smuggled off a ship." On a crowded subway platform in New York the other day a man approached a certain keen-eyed citizen with the old story of the valuable watch which he wanted to sell in a hurry.

"Do I look like that kind of a fool?" indignantly demanded this particular New Yorker. With him the game did not work, but it would not have been tried if it were not still working with others. And while for decades the investor in bogus mining shares has been a butt for ridicule in fiction and on the stage, it is a fact that worthless mines are just now the bait most popular with the ever-gullible American public. . . .

If safety is the first, the final, the everpresent thought of the average small investor in other parts of the world, taking a chance—the reverse of the safety principle—makes many an American play into the hands of the confidence man, the seller of worthless investments, the market rigger, all of whom promise miraculous gains. The guiding principles of such an ingenuous American's investing philosophy appear to include the gambling impulse, the desire to get something for nothing, the yearning, above all, to get rich quick without work.

This passion for riches seems to paralyze common caution and to destroy common sense. With ridiculous alacrity the sucker swallows the thinnest and most preposterous story told by the "con man." The latter need achieve no mastery of detail, no smooth chain of logic, no careful realism.

Whether the victim has inherited a little money, whether he—or she—has worked hard for years and saved a little—almost always the temptation to turn it into promised wealth proves irresistible. Most Americans are not content with what they have. They look about them and see the heads of big corporations enjoying millions and—so the envious observers mistakenly assume—doing little or no work for those millions. All the small fry long to be as well off; they worship the moneyed man. The cult of noble families, the aristocracy of landed estates, such powerful factors in the civilization of older communities have no place in our society. What kindles the imagination and emulation of Americans is the figure of the millionaire. He, to paraphrase the Persian poet, is the door to which they find no key—until they think they have found a key of gold in some swindler's offer of incredible returns for capital invested.

Often, too, this swindler reaches his victims by means of the little knowledge that is so dangerous. More than the citizens of most countries, Americans are a newspaper-reading public. They acquire at least a headline acquaintance with new discoveries, inventions, enterprises. Upon this popular stock of information, which may be sensational and garbled to the point of misinformation, the investment crook deliberately trades. I venture to say that the presses are even now printing millions of stock certificates in corporations holding holes in the ground near Weepah, the scene of a much-advertised recent gold strike. Tens of thousands of shares have been sold in worthless or even nonexistent motion picture and radio companies. Fake "bargains" in Florida real estate were among the financial best sellers a year ago.

Wistful aspirants for unearned increment often point out to one another that a fortune might have been amassed by any person lucky enough to have bought a few shares of telephone stock, or of Ford motor stock, when the telephone and the Ford car were new and unknown. What these dreamers do not realize is that the public never is given the chance to invest in such genuine bonanzas. When the promoters of an enterprise are really convinced that it will make them rich they do not want to sell stock in it to anybody and everybody. They want to keep that stock snugly in their own hands. The commonest assurance offered by the salesman of bogus stock that "you will double your money" is a plain indication that something is wrong. What man or organization with anything as good as this is passing it around!

To get rich quick, because being rich is the most desirable state; to take a gambler's chance on any scheme promising fortune without toil, especially if one has "seen something about it in the papers"—that is, perhaps, the synthesis of the American philosophy which, according to Mr. Andrew Mellon, Secretary of the Treasury, parts fools from no less than one billion seven hundred million dollars every year in the United States. Of this sum which he estimates is obtained by financial shysters at least half, in my opinion, is collected in New York—but *from* America. Because Wall Street is the hub of the country's legitimate financial operations, the Get-Rich-Quick Wallingfords prefer Wall Street as an impressive business address, but their operations radiate to every corner of the land.

Further Resources

BOOKS

Cohen, Bernice. *The Edge of Chaos: Financial Booms, Bubbles, Crashes, and Chaos.* Chichester, N.Y.: Wiley, 1997.

Galbraith, John Kenneth. *The Great Crash, 1929.* Boston: Houghton Mifflin, 1955.

Sobel, Robert. *The Money Manias: The Era of Great Speculation in America, 1770–1970.* New York: Weybright and Talley, 1974.

Discontinuing the Model T Ford

"Strut, Miss Lizzie!"

Editorial

By: *The Nation*
Date: December 14, 1927
Source: "Strut, Miss Lizzie!" *The Nation,* December 14, 1927, 672.

"The King Is Dead"

Magazine article

By: Margaret Marshall
Date: December 14, 1927
Source: Marshall, Margaret. "The King Is Dead." *The Nation,* December 14, 1927, 678.
About the Publication: *The Nation,* founded in 1865, has consistently been a voice for leftist viewpoints on politics, social issues, lifestyle trends, and the like. Margaret Marshall wrote for *The Nation.* ■

Introduction

It was remarked that you could purchase a Ford Model T in any color so long as it was basic black. In a nutshell, this statement captured automaker Henry Ford's lifelong commitment to producing and marketing a no-frills automobile, a "people's car," that would be affordable to countless millions of Americans. First sold in 1913, the legendary Model T achieved Ford's goal. The car was priced around $900 the year of introduction, but as a result of Ford's innovative assembly-line fabrication system, the price eventually came down to $260. Motoring had truly become accessible to the masses and hence an integral part of the American scene.

For many Americans, the Model T would become the first car that they ever owned. Of course, the car had its peculiarities. "Miss Lizzie," as she was affectionately called, was often hard to start. But although often cantankerous, Miss Lizzie was like a family member.

Elsewhere, Ford's rival, General Motors, a conglomerate cobbled together in 1908 by William C. Durant, gradually took aim at a more upscale automotive market. Unlike Fords, General Motors cars featured fashionable styling complete with fancy gadgets. The contest between General Motors and Ford became more pronounced by the 1920s as the decade's widespread prosperity allowed many Americans the luxury of spending more money to purchase higher quality automobiles.

Significance

At first, faced with the General Motors challenge, Henry Ford refused to budge. But eventually the need to face reality became clear. Consumer tastes had changed, and the shifting whims of contemporary fashion now necessitated improvements.

Thus, in 1927, the last Model T rolled off the assembly lines, and Ford factories were shut down for retooling in order to make way for the advent of the new Model A. Nevertheless, despite the change, General Motors continued to gain market share at Ford's expense. In truth, Henry Ford's no-frills ethic circa 1913 had become counterproductive. Many Americans now viewed own-

The Ford Model A was issued as an improvement on the popular Model T. © CORBIS. REPRODUCED BY PERMISSION.

ing stylish cars almost as part of their birthright. In the end, the advent of World War II (1914–1918), which led to government contracts for the production of military vehicles, may well have saved Henry Ford's company from extinction.

Primary Source

"Strut, Miss Lizzie!"

SYNOPSIS: The Model T, affectionately dubbed "Miss Lizzie" or "Tin Lizzy," was the ultimate no-frills car, and, as such, proved to be the victim of changing consumer tastes.

The international event of the moment is not, we regret to say, the Russian proposal to disarm instead of talking about it. Editorial writers may be stirred about such matters; diplomats may consider them solemnly or otherwise over their cigars. But the people—the people in Oshkosh and Hoboken, in Sauk Center, in San Francisco and New York, the people in China and Japan and London and Paris are agog over the new Ford car!

Never was publicity story so adroitly managed. A dozen times during the past few months alleged

details about the new car slipped out and were duly featured on the front pages of the newspapers. Each time solemn denials came from Edsel Ford, from the Ford plant in Detroit, from the great man himself. Yet the stories persisted: the car was to have a standard gear-shift and fourwheel brakes; it was to look just like the old one, only funnier; it was to be equipped with every sort of modern trick and contrivance; it was to double its price. It was rumored that behind a ten-foot fence in Detroit managers of the Ford plant were tearing around at sixty-five miles an hour; a fortnight ago pirated pictures of the new car were printed in the New York papers, pictures obtained by stealth by the enterprising editor of the *Weekly Argus* of Bridgeton, Michigan. And Edsel merely shook his head or his finger and refused to be quoted.

Yet it is doubtful if any amount of publicity, managed by ever so masterful a hand, could have produced the enormous interest that the plain people feel in the new car. Fifteen million of them have bought Fords. They have driven the old bus downhill past Packards and uphill behind everything else; they have driven in rain and snow and over the thawing roads of March; they have mended a door with a piece of string, they have cursed at side-curtains that

The Model T was discontinued by Ford Motor Company in the 1920s. AP/WIDE WORLD PHOTOS. REPRODUCED BY PERMISSION.

never came near to fitting, they have thrust a nail in to hold something that an honest bolt would have held better; they have loaded the old Ford high with farm produce, mattresses, baby carriages, 300-pound hogs, and with whatever handicap they have managed to get from where they started to where they wanted to go. It has been pointed out that men called the Ford car "she." Only when a tool with which man is served comes very near his heart does he deal with it so familiarly. The sailing ship, proud under its white can! vas, was "she," the old horse plodding through mud or sun; "she's a nice blade," says the woodsman of his favorite ax; and a pet cat or dog, whatever its sex, may be "she."

Out of this affection born of common use it is not strange that all America should be breathless to hear the real details at last, or that 375,000 advance orders for the new car should have been placed. But when we read in the China *Weekly Review* (Shanghai) that the new Ford will not be ready in October as previously announced or when we hear that buses are running up to London to places where the cars are on exhibition (admission 1/6) we realize that the whole world is cocking a respectful ear in the direction of Miss Lizzie Ford, U. S. A. And for all our rough familiarity with Lizzie, for all the jokes

that have been cracked at her expense, and all the abuse she has suffered from the owners of "real cars," there is something colossal in the spectacle of a little man in Detroit, Michigan, who out of his own head, whatever else may be lacking in that same head, drew an idea which has won the hearts of millions. Henry Ford did not invent the automobile; but he made it a success as no other man in the world has done. Incidentally he has made money by the hundred million; but only incidentally. The money can mean little to him—there is too much of it and his ideas of how to spend it are too elementary. But he has his fun all the same. And because of it, we have ours.

During the last quarter of a century machines have been carried to the farthest village in the country. Telephones, the telegraph, mechanical devices for the home and the barn. Yet what man thinks tenderly of his cream separator? And who looks on a telephone except with impatience and contumely? Henry Ford went with the machine wave that washed from one end of the country to the other and spread across two oceans, east and west. He alone won the hearts of his customers; and his product, even radically altered, is welcomed eagerly and affectionately—even though it means standing in a long line in the pouring rain to get the first sight of it, as last week it did—instead of with the suspicion and distrust that greets most new-fangled mechanical devices.

Primary Source

"The King is Dead"

> **SYNOPSIS:** This selection take a nostalgic look at the Model T Ford—the original "people's car"—which went out of production in 1927 in order to make way for the advent of the Ford Model A.

I entered the Empire Room at the Waldorf-Astoria to attend the private showing of the new Ford. Near the center of the room a group of people circled, looking down at something—like mourners viewing a corpse. Somewhere an orchestra was playing bad, sad music. Or perhaps it was the velvet hangings and the cut-glass chandeliers and the noiseless young men in tuxedos and stiff white fronts who hovered about and murmured softly in one's ear: "It has a miniature Lincoln transmission"; "They're going to make 12,000 a day"; "100,000 orders already from Greater New York"; "No parts of the old Ford are interchangeable with the new."

Then I noticed that the spectators were all dressed up in fur-trimmed evening wraps and raccoon coats and high-heeled pumps—so I knew it wasn't a funeral. The circling crowd was looking down at the new chassis from Detroit, so I looked too. I passed on to the new sedan, and the new coupe, and the new sport model, all arrayed in the refined new colors—gun metal, blue, dawn gray, Niagara blue, Arabian sand. Standard gear-shift, four-wheel brakes, foot throttle, gasoline gauge on the dash, speedometer—only a vestige of the old crank that required profane strength to spin—merely a hole, covered by a round shiny plate.

"Now we'll see how I look in a Ford," said a stringy dowager in evening dress.

At one end of the room the anatomy of Model A was laid out on a blue velvet tripod trimmed with gold braid. It was all very refined and quiet and a bit plushy.

Model T was one of the unpleasant facts of life. The family bought and confronted me with it one spring when I came home from school to spend the summer on the ranch. My brother, in overalls, backed it out of the shed and paraded in it up and down in front of the ranch-house. For a background there were the log barns and a wheat-field and then gray sagebrush in the distance, sweltering dry in the sun. The sound of hens cackling and a dog's bark and that funny Ford horn are bound together in my memory.

I hated Model T. I said I wouldn't ride in the ugly thing, sitting high and tinny on its four wheels. But I was young then. Soon I found—like several million others—that it "would go anywhere." It would, and did. It chased antelopes in African deserts—and farmers herded cows with it. Ditches, ruts, mountain roads, mudholes, high centers did not matter. "It took you anywhere and brought you back." And for a while that was enough for most people—so most people bought a Ford. Then they wanted to be "smart." They were not so much interested in going anywhere as they were in being seen going somewhere. Model T was sturdy, strong, brave. But it certainly was not smart.

Mr. Ford was wise. He knew Model T was done for. He had a problem, but it was rather simple. He merely made a car to order—price and all—to suit the predominant desires of present-day America.

Model A is here, irrevocably. "No parts of the new Ford are interchangeable with the old."

Of course not.

The king is dead.

Further Resources

BOOKS

Clymer, Floyd. *Henry's Wonderful Model T, 1908–1927.* New York: McGraw-Hill, 1955.

Collins, Peter, and David Horowitz. *The Fords: An American Epic.* New York: Summit Books, 1987.

Lacey, Robert. *Ford, the Man and the Machine.* Boston: Little, Brown, 1986.

This Smoking World

Nonfiction work

By: Albert Edward Hamilton

Date: 1927

Source: Hamilton, A.E. *This Smoking World.* New York: Century, 1927, 174–177, 182, 183–187.

About the Author: A.E. (Albert Edward) Hamilton (1887–?) was a widely recognized authority on tobacco. ∎

Introduction

Americans have always attached a great deal of cultural significance to smoking. During the 1920s, the cigarette became a conspicuous sign that, by emulating men who enjoyed the freedom to light up in public, newly liberated women had themselves finally "arrived." In addition, the triumph of the cigarette over its rivals—the cigar and the pipe—amply demonstrated the enormous power of the modern mass media to shape consumer tastes.

During the nineteenth century, the cigar and to a lesser extent the pipe had dominated Americans' smoking habits. The cigar, consisting of various layers of tobacco leaves, and the pipe were considered to be the only authentic smokes—the only ones acceptable for "respectable" people. In contrast, the cigar's cheap imitation, the lowly cigarette, containing lesser-quality ground tobacco wrapped in paper, was reserved for the "lower sorts," who evidently could not afford the genuine article.

Significance

By the 1920s, the once-despised cigarette had become increasingly popular. The popularity of cigarettes coincided with the rise in smoking among women. The burgeoning motion-picture industry deliberately provided a huge boost to the cigarette, for in an early version of a tactic that would one day be known in the industry as "product placement," Hollywood worked hard to portray the cigarette as a symbol of elegance and sophistication, in much the same fashion that the cigarette emerged as the symbol of rugged masculinity in the 1940s or adolescent rebellion in the 1950s.

The campaign against smoking during the early twentieth century paralleled the movement to outlaw the consumption of alcoholic beverages. The numerous problems associated with attempts to enforce Prohibition, however, induced politicians to shy away from any similar frontal assault on tobacco use. Indeed after the disastrous Prohibition experiment (1920–1933), the country was apparently in no mood for another such crusade.

By the end of the century, legislative successes chalked up by a new antismoking movement could be attributed largely to the fact that the smoking issue was presented as a personal and public health concern—not, as the earlier prohibitionists had often emphasized, a primarily moral one.

Primary Source

This Smoking World [excerpt]

SYNOPSIS: The impact of mass media on consumer tastes can be amply demonstrated by the triumph of the cigarette, which by the 1920s had easily become the dominant form of tobacco use in the United States. As A.E. Hamilton observes in "Our Ladies' Nicotine," Chapter 12 of his book, the cigarette's popularity was largely the result of clever marketing campaigns—especially those aimed at newly liberated women consumers.

Our Ladies' Nicotine

Her puffs of smoky violet
Twined in fantastic silhouette;
She blushed, laughed, coughed a little, yet
She smoked her brother's cigarette.

The question, Shall women smoke? has already been answered. They do. The number who are smoking is growing like the proverbial snowball. English and American women are the last to fall in line with their sisters of this smoking world. The immense increase in consumption of cigarettes in America has caused dismay to the fumiphobes, whose backfire of eloquent prophecy has been of little avail. Church, print, and even radio have been called upon to halt a growing custom which threatens national decadence and racial degeneration. From a metropolitan broadcasting station a mellow feminine voice cried out, not long ago, to tens of thousands of her fellow-kind:

> Tobacco is an octopus, spreading over the entire surface of the nation, sucking the life force, the moral zeal, and the capacity for spirtual development of the people, and giving them in return, what? Unspeakable suffering, both mental and physical, poisoned systems and drugged mentality, and enslaving them to the traders in tobacco. It is our God-inspired protest, yours and mine, that is going to exterminate both tobacco poison and the mentality that produces this plague of poisoned drugs in the United States.

Under a gay painting of two men and a woman, the men smoking cigarettes, the woman looking as though she wanted to, one reads the legend:

> You can light them all day and far into the night with never a loss of smoothness, mildness, and incomparable fragrance. First thing in the morning. Late at night. Before or after breakfast, lunch, or dinner. Light them as liberally as you choose, one after the other, as often as you desire the cheering comfort of a cigarette.

Such advertisements do not lie. They are quite true to fact—for the cigarettist. Their subtle danger lies in the suggestion of harmlessness. One infers immunity from throat troubles in smoothness, safety from poison in mildness, only wholesome content in the incomparable aroma. When from three to ten million dollars a year are spent for such educational propaganda, it becomes a significant problem in national health. Little wonder that there are those who would campaign to prohibit advertisements of tobacco as an unmixed blessing to mankind. But when agitators come back at the advertisers with such equally spectacular half-truths as the following, the

Cigarette smoking became increasingly fashionable during the 1920s. Though its unhealthy aspects were recognized, many men and women still engaged in the practice. **THE LIBRARY OF CONGRESS.**

case is made double perplexing. Says a prominent sanitarian:

> Should smoking become prevalent among girls and young women as it is at present among boys and young men, America would be doomed. There would be bred an inferior and degenerate race, and ultimate extermination would result. Our prisons, our reform schools and asylums would be filled to overflowing, for the cigarette is undoubtedly the maker of criminals. It is the breeder of nervous disorders and insanities.

If such an announcement could be run alongside every cigarette advertisement before the public, it would probably increase the consumption of tobacco materially. Every reasonable man or woman endowed with eyes and common sense would immediately react against such absurdly unfounded statements, and many would buy a pack of coffin nails at the next cigar stand by way of protest. . . .

Increasingly women smoke. No longer do they buy cigarettes in candy bags from the confectionery corner of a cigar stand, or wait about tobacco shops as though to use a telephone until no one is looking before making the desired purchase. . . .

For a time, smoking by American women will be largely governed by fashion. She who does not smoke may find herself in the same class with those who wear cotton stockings or fail to powder their noses. The custom, being set in "society," is imitated in widening circles, like those of a pebble dropped in a quiet pool. But, unlike the hang of a gown or the color of the stocking, the use of tobacco will not be so easily influenced by the dictates of style. Smoking is a subtler matter of physiology than dress and, as a mild drug habit, will not so easily be set aside as last year's hat or shoe. . . .

As to why women have taken up the practice of smoking, opinion is diverse, of course. Some lay the cause to the war, when women smoked to keep dough-boys company. Others attribute it to the inferred slump of moral standards following the war. One theory has it that knitting, crocheting, tatting, and their like having gone the way of spinning and weaving, women's hands are again idle and have welcomed the cigarette as a relief for nervous tension in their fingers. Or perhaps women, in their new emancipation of the vote and the hair-cut, are merely imitating men. The stage and the movie have made smoking women popular. The business woman has come, and the stress and strain of her day's work calls for a sedative for artificial rest. The journalist or author, active in imaginative creation, calls upon smoke for inspiration like the famous literary lights of recent history. These . . . are held up as partly accounting for woman's swing into the line of smokers.

Whatever the individual reasons may be, there is a larger social factor which relates to womankind. Smoke has so woven itself into the structure of society that even in many homes of those who never use tobacco the ash tray, ash-tray stand, humidor, tobacco jar, cigar box, and an assortment of cigarettes will be found as symbols of modern hospitality. The fashion of the day has introduced these things into the home. Etiquette demands the ritualistic "Have a cigar" on the part of a host, and this seems slowly giving way to "Have a cigarette." Few stop to analyze the reason why, and the automatism takes its place with shaking hands, tipping the hat, or commenting upon the weather. Smoking has become a pleasure that is taken for granted. The burden of proving that it is not a joy but a delusion, and of substituting for it something just as acceptable, has been placed squarely on the shoulders of those who, for one reason or another, remain opposed to the custom. . . .

Hand-bags, combination cigarette and vanity cases, elaborate cigarette holders, pipes at thirty dollars apiece, crystal ash trays, ivory cigarette boxes, assorted tobacconic dinner favors, and a variety of expensive knickknacks tempt the neophyte to begin the art of smoking.

Further Resources

BOOKS

Gately, Ian. *Tobacco: The Story of How Tobacco Seduced the World.* New York: Grove, 2001.

Goodman, Jordan. *Tobacco in History: The Cultures of Dependence.* New York: Routledge, 1993.

Men of Destiny

Nonfiction work

By: Walter Lippmann

Date: 1927

Source: Lippmann, Walter. *Men of Destiny.* New York: Macmillan, 1927, 35–36, 38–41.

About the Author: Walter Lippmann (1889–1974) was twentieth century America's premier syndicated columnist and political analyst. So great was Lippmann's impact that

Al Smith, right, governor of New York, reads a telegram sent from the Democratic Convention in Houston, Texas. Smith was the first Catholic to be a serious contender for the presidency of the United States and began a trend of greater acceptance of Catholics in prominent political posts. © **UNDERWOOD & UNDERWOOD/CORBIS. REPRODUCED BY PERMISSION.**

historian Ronald Steel saw fit to title his award-winning biography *Walter Lippmann and the American Century.* ∎

Introduction

"Demography is destiny." Perhaps nowhere is this saying so true as with politics, for long-term population trends involving birth rates and immigration have an impact on the political scene. Although founded largely by Protestants from northern and western Europe, since its inception the American colonies and later the new United States exhibited a rich ethnic diversity. The heavy Irish and German Catholic immigration of the period 1840–1860 created for the first time an American "Catholic" problem—an issue exploited by groups such as the virulently anti-Catholic "Know-Nothing Party."

A subsequent wave of Catholics (and Jews), this time largely from southern and eastern Europe, arrived during the period 1880–1921. In similar fashion, these newcomers engendered hostility from many native-born Protestants. The 1890s saw the formation of both the American Protective League as well as the Immigration Restriction League.

This second Catholic wave, which settled in America's largest urban centers, "came of age" politically in the 1920s. Guided by already established third- and fourth-generation Irish and German politicians, these non-Protestants began to flex their electoral muscle. Meanwhile, by the 1920s, the long-term migration pattern of countryside to city served to shift political power away from farms and small towns toward the urban areas generally.

Significance

New Yorker Al Smith, the descendant of the Irish wave of the 1840s and championed by the mass voting power of the later immigrant vote, emerged as America's first national Catholic political leader. First elected in 1918 as the Democratic governor of the nation's then most populous state, Smith was defeated for reelection in the 1920 Republican "earthquake" that sent Warren G. Harding (served 1921–1923) to the White House. But Smith soon rebounded to recapture the New York statehouse in 1922 and retain it in 1924 and again in 1926. By virtue of this high-profile position as New York governor, Smith became a serious presidential aspirant.

By 1924, urban Catholics and Jews, although unable to muster sufficient strength to secure the Democratic nomination for Smith, did manage to block the nomination of rural Protestant hopeful William G. McAdoo. Four years later, as the preeminent national Democrat, Smith was finally awarded the Democratic Party nomination. To some extent, the usually Democratic Protestant South only reluctantly acquiesced in Smith's candidacy. Many Democrats, sensing the electoral appeal of 1920s Republican prosperity, viewed Smith as the Democrats' sacrificial victim offered up to a sure winner—GOP nominee Herbert Hoover.

For a nation that had traditionally elevated a succession of small-town boys to the White House, Smith stood out as an unabashed "city slicker." Moreover, by endorsing a mild position on Prohibition enforcement (then still in effect) and by embracing his Catholic heritage, Smith raised the century's old Protestant fears of Catholic allegiance to the pope. Smith's opponents, political heirs of English Protestants with strong anti-Catholic sentiments stretching back to the sixteenth century, made certain to exploit anti-Catholic fears among the voters.

Finally, by dealing forthrightly with the controversial issue of his Catholicism, Smith opened the way for the later election in 1960 of America's only Catholic president, fellow Irishman John F. Kennedy (served 1961–1963).

Primary Source

Men of Destiny [excerpt]

SYNOPSIS: The premier American syndicated columnist and political observer of the twentieth century,

journalist Walter Lippmann, examined the political and social impact of New York governor Al Smith's presidential candidacy in "The Catholicism of Al Smith," a chapter of his book. Smith, the first Catholic nominee of a major party (the Democrats in 1928), was defeated soundly by Republican Herbert Hoover. But by addressing the religious issue squarely, Smith paved the way for the election of America's first Catholic president, John F. Kennedy, in 1960.

The Catholicism of Al Smith

For more than a century most Americans have believed both that a religion was no test of a man's fitness for public office and that only a Protestant should be elected President of the United States. This paradox has often been noticed, but until about the year 1923 it was a merely theoretical difficulty without practical importance. For until after the second election of Governor Smith there had never been a serious contender for the Presidency who was not a Protestant.

Since the rise of Smith, desperate efforts have been made by Democratic politicians to find some way of avoiding a direct test of the question whether a Catholic is eligible to be President. They have pointed out that he is a wet, that he belongs to Tammany Hall, that he is a cockney. But these objections however sincere and weighty have been regarded by the mass of people as unreal. Protestants and Catholics alike have felt in their bones that any Democrat who can be elected Governor of New York four times would under ordinary circumstances have an irresistible attraction for the politicians. They may cross their hearts and say that they have no objection to Governor Smith's Catholicism, and they may even think they mean it, and yet they will not be believed. Governor Smith is so clearly available by every conventional test, except that of his religion, that the conviction has now become set, among the newer Americans of the cities, and is now, I think, irremovable that his Catholicism alone stands in the way of his nomination. They may misunderstand the deeper sources of the opposition to Smith as an incarnation of the city, but their misunderstanding is nevertheless a fact of dominating importance.

Since the Catholic voters are a predominant part of the Democratic Party outside of the South, the question of Smith's nomination has become one of life and death to the party. He cannot be rejected without alienating an absolutely essential part of the votes on which the only possible chance of a Democratic victory depends. There are now some twenty million Catholics in the United States. They are no longer, as they were a generation ago, largely confined to a class who do the menial work and do not have to be taken into account in the government of the country. They are a substantial and powerful part of the electorate, and few of them are in a mood to acquiesce under a concrete test in the unwritten law that they are second-class citizens who cannot aspire, no matter what their other qualifications, to the highest office in the land. . . .

The argument comes down then to this crucial point: suppose the Church claimed that a question affecting education or marriage or foreign affairs was to be determined by the principles of the Roman Church, and suppose the executive, legislature, and courts of the United States claimed that the question was to be determined by them, which authority, the ecclesiastical or the civil, would Governor Smith or any other good Catholic recognize as final?

Governor Smith's reply, which avowedly was made after consultation with priests of his Church, is as follows:

> . . . In the wildest dreams of your imagination you cannot conjure up a possible conflict between religious principle and political duty in the United States, except on the unthinkable hypothesis that some law were to be passed which violated the common morality of all God-fearing men. If you conjure up such a conflict how would a Protestant resolve it? Obviously by the dictates of his conscience. That is exactly what a Catholic would do. There is no ecclesiastical tribunal which would have the slightest claim upon the obedience of Catholic communicants in the resolution of such a conflict.

Governor Smith's answer to the fundamental question as to which jurisdiction he would recognize as final is that he would follow the dictates of his own conscience in each particular case. This is a very far-reaching declaration. It amounts to saying that there is an authority higher than the utterances of the Church or the law of the land, namely "the common morality of all God-fearing men," and that the conscience of Alfred E. Smith, and of every other individual, is the final interpreter of whether that common morality has been violated. . . .

If any form of words could put an end to so ancient and deep-seated a controversy as that between Protestantism and Catholicism, this avowal would do it. For the deep Protestant fear that Catholics submit their consciences to an alien power with its seat in Rome is here answered by the radical assertion that for American Catholics their consciences are a

higher authority than their Catholicism. I call it a radical assertion, for there is little doubt that Governor Smith in adopting Archbishop Ireland's statement has aligned himself unqualifiedly with that wing of his Church which is furthest removed from the medieval ideal of a truly catholic and wholly authoritative synthesis of all human interests. Governor Smith is the latest, and by no means the least, of a long line of Catholics who have wholly forgotten, indeed may never even have heard of, what the Church conceived itself to be in the days of its greatest worldly splendor and ambitions. Certainly one detects in him no lingering trace of the idea, speculatively at least so magnificent even to those who, like this writer, were not reared in the Catholic tradition—the idea of Catholicism not as a religious sect but as a civilization. The Catholicism of Governor Smith is the typical modern post-reformation nationalistic religious loyalty in which the Church occupies a distinct and closely compartmented section of an otherwise secular life.

Further Resources

BOOKS

Finan, Christopher M. *Alfred E. Smith: The Happy Warrior.* New York: Hill and Wang, 2002.

O'Connor, Richard. *The First Hurrah: A Biography of Alfred E. Smith.* New York: Putnam, 1970.

Steel, Ronald. *Walter Lippmann and the American Century.* Boston: Little, Brown, 1980.

"The Next Revolution"
Journal article

By: Ellsworth Huntington

Date: October 1928

Source: Huntington, Ellsworth. "The Next Revolution." *Eugenics: A Journal of Race Betterment,* October 1928, 6–14.

About the Author: Ellsworth Huntington (1876–1947), a geographer by academic training, was one of the world's leading figures in the controversial eugenics movement. ■

Introduction

Eugenics, the long-forgotten pseudo-science of selective human breeding, was once a major intellectual discipline. It was based on the superficially attractive notion that human reproduction should be carefully channeled, not merely left to random chance, in much the same manner that man has purposefully domesticated plants and animals over the ages.

Concern over birth control arose in some quarters as the upper classes practiced more birth control and the lower classes less, leading some to believe that the more promising members of society were in danger of dying out. © BETTMANN/CORBIS. REPRODUCED BY PERMISSION.

In practice, eugenics contained several facets. It sought to maintain the vigor of the white race through the promotion of strong families and through strengthening the breeding stock. It encouraged those deemed to be especially well fit (that is, possessing desirable physical and mental characteristics) to reproduce, all the while inducing the "unfit" to abstain either through voluntary means or through compulsory (state-mandated) sterilization.

Significance

Aside from the biological and medical aspects, eugenics contained a controversial social dimension, featuring the idea that in America the declining birthrates among peoples of northern and western European ancestry—so-called "old-stock" Americans—should be reversed, with these peoples thus encouraged to breed and others not.

There were some similarities between the basically conservative eugenics movement and the more liberal-oriented birth control movement. The darker side of the birth control campaign did on occasion encourage selective breeding, or selective birth control, partly to liberate women and promote sexual freedom and partly to prevent

the "wrong" sorts of people from having children. Accordingly, many mental defectives or poor women on welfare found themselves involuntarily sterilized, often without their knowledge or consent—an example of the early twentieth-century "social engineering" that has been thoroughly discredited by the excesses of the German Nazi regime that pushed eugenics to its ultimate limits.

Primary Source

"The Next Revolution" [excerpt]

SYNOPSIS: Ellsworth Huntington, a leading eugenicist, outlines the movement's ambitious program in this excerpt from his article "The Next Revolution," which appeared in the magazine *Eugenics: A Journal of Race Betterment*—a title that speaks loudly for the goals of this now-discredited campaign.

The discovery of America, the invention of the steam engine, and the growth of modern invention have revolutionized civilization. . . .

Can so great a revolution ever again occur? I believe that it can. Indeed a far greater revolution already seems to be well under way. . . . The last revolution was mechanical; the next will be biological. The last changed man's environment; the next will change human nature. Already the biological character of modern nations has begun to change with astonishing rapidity. Here is an example. The families of the British nobility which have held an hereditary title for at least three generations may be better or worse than those of the unskilled laborers; but be that as it may, they are nevertheless different. These aristocrats differ from the laborers in physique, in intellect, and in temperament. A century or more ago the two groups differed only a little in the size of their families and in the rate at which they increased through excess of births over deaths. Today they are as far apart in this respect as in others. . . .

A study of the children listed in *Who's Who in America* for 1926–7, which Mr. Leon F. Whitney and myself have published in *The Builders of America*, shows that in practically every group of leading people whether in professions or business, there has been a decline in the birth rate like that among the British nobility. The older lawyers, engineers, ministers, politicians and others, have more children than the younger ones, even when we confine ourselves to persons whose families are complete. This decline is typical of the whole group of people who form what we call the upper classes, that is, the professional people and those engaged in the larger forms of business. . . .

Is there anything to worry about in all this? Are not plenty of people in the lower classes more valuable than such effete and artificial groups as the British nobility or even the professional classes of America? Undoubtedly many competent children are born in the lower classes, but the percentage who become leaders is far lower than in the upper classes, as appears from a dozen different investigations. . . .

Fail to Reproduce

Even when people from the lower social levels do rise to leadership, they do not biologically reenforce the upper class to any great extent. . . .

The net result of all this is that during the last two or three generations an extremely drastic process of natural or social selection has set in. It has arisen because the more thoughtful people in civilized lands have seen the necessity of birth control and have accordingly limited their families, whereas the less thoughtful have not yet realized this need. Its intensity has been greatly increased because during the same period the death rate, especially that of the children, has been greatly reduced among the less competent groups, only a little among the most competent. Thus, to use technical terms, the biological character of our people is today being rapidly changed by a decreasingly intense differential death rate and an increasingly intense differential birth rate, both working in the wrong direction. . . .

If all this is true, it greatly reenforces our previous conclusion that large families are especially desirable among the people of the finest types. But how is it ever going to be possible to get such families? The answer is that already there is a strong tendency in that direction. We have seen it in the relatively large families of the most successful graduates of Yale and Harvard. It is also evident in certain places where birth control has been practiced so long that it is common among all classes and has ceased to be regarded as a fad or a new discovery among the people of greater intelligence. . . .

Low Birth Rate

How far these conditions are due to the wide practice of birth control it is impossible to say. This much however, is clear. A study of the actual conditions in America, England and other countries, leads to the conclusion that one of the crying evils of our day is the low birth rate among the upper classes and the high birth rate among the lower classes. Deeper study however, shows an opposite tendency which manifests itself when people within a single social level are compared. There the highest birth rate is found among the most valuable members of society, while those who are less valuable are dying out. All this suggests that it is imperative that birth control spread widely among the lower classes, but that the upper classes adopt a new ideal and have larger families. Then we turn to the world as a whole and find that in the only city thus far studied where approximately such a condition actually prevails, the status of civilization is extraordinarily high.

Further Resources

BOOKS

Martin, Geoffrey J. *Ellsworth Huntington: His Life and Legend.* Hamden, Conn.: Archon Books, 1973.

Nies, Betsy L. *Eugenic Fantasies: Ideology in the Literature and Popular Culture of the 1920s.* New York: Routledge, 2000.

"The Child Stylites of Baltimore"

Magazine article

By: Frederic Nelson

Date: August 28, 1929

Source: Nelson, Frederic. "The Child Stylites of Baltimore." *The New Republic,* August 28, 1929, 37–38.

About the Publication: *The New Republic* magazine was founded in 1914 by journalists Herbert Croly, Walter Weyl, and Walter Lippmann. Its first issue in November sold 875 copies, but within a year, its monthly sales reached fifteen thousand. While the magazine is and has been regarded as liberal, its editorial positions over the years have not followed a strict ideological line. ■

Introduction

Twentieth-century America has witnessed the sudden appearance of various popular fads. Either because of boredom or the desire for social conformity, crazes have often captured the American public's fancy. Some of these frivolous stunts reflect the lighthearted side of America: college students swallowing goldfish in the 1940s, shoehorning as many people as possible into a telephone booth in the late 1950s, or "streaking" naked in 1974. Even many aspects of the 1960s "Hippie" movement exhibited faddish themes.

The prosperous 1920s boasted one of the century's most famous crazes, "flagpole sitting," an otherwise harmless diversion that featured daredevils nesting atop structures for days, even weeks at a stretch, while a host of bemused spectators were more than willing to waste time reveling in this carnival atmosphere. Meanwhile, the acknowledged champion of flagpole sitters, an otherwise undistinguished gentleman (and former prize fighter) who went by the name Alvin "Shipwreck" Kelly, had become a national celebrity of sorts since 1924 with his flagpole-sitting escapades. By all reckoning, "Shipwreck" spent a grand total of 145 days perched aloft on various flagpoles in calendar year 1929.

These harmless fads may be associated with widespread prosperity on the general proposition that good economic times provide ordinary people the luxury of engaging in such nonsense. Assorted fads such as flagpole sitting clearly highlight the long-standing tension in America between the desire of people to conform and the need for self-expression and self-actualization. A faddist such as "Shipwreck" Kelly serves to bridge the tension between both impulses.

Significance

Social critics often wonder whether these fads serve any higher social or political purpose or are merely entertainment. Regardless, the flagpole-sitting mania of the 1920s reflected the emergence in America of what observers call the "Cult of Celebrity"—the tendency to inflate the importance of athletes or movie stars. The decade's single greatest hero, aviator Charles A. Lindbergh, had basically performed a glorified stunt by becoming the first man to fly solo across the Atlantic Ocean in 1927, for other teams of pilots had already accomplished the transatlantic journey.

The levity that prompted the flagpole sitting craze quickly receded after the stock market crash of October 1929 and the subsequent Great Depression. If flagpole sitting represented the lighthearted, frivolous, and essentially harmless side of American popular culture, then the hard times that followed 1929 revealed a darker, more sinister side of the American psyche. The Depression era featured, for instance, marathon-dance contests ("walkathons," as they were called) that saw punch-drunk couples literally sleepwalking through endless hours of physical torture in hopes of winning a cash prize.

Primary Source

"The Child Stylites of Baltimore"

> **SYNOPSIS:** The amazing flagpole-sitting craze helped define the decade of the 1920s in much the same manner as did the flapper, Al Capone, or Charles Lindbergh. In the following memorable piece, author Frederic Nelson describes the phenomenon and

seeks to find some larger meaning in these flagpole escapades.

An "Obscene Spectacle" in Mr. Mencken's Own Bailiwick, the Free State of Maryland

The scene is almost any of some score of vacant lots and glaring backyards in the meaner sections of Baltimore. Your attention is at first attracted by the inevitable milling throng of small boys who crowd about celebrities and events of importance. This time the center of their concern is a strange coop-like arrangement set on the top of a pole some fifteen or twenty feet high. The pole is kept under control by guy wires from which hang the American flag, electric lights, signs advising you to patronize the pharmacy at the corner or to inform you that Jimmy Jones, twelve, has been "sitting" for eight days.

You then observe that the coop—or it may be a platform covered by an umbrella—is occupied by a small boy (or girl) who ought to be in bed, if you see him by night, or at play, if you see him by day—and you are informed that he (or she) has remained on top of the pole, through the painful Baltimore heat, the fierce summer storms and despite the persecution of mosquitoes, for as much as a week. You are gazing, in other words, upon one of the several contenders for the Juvenile Flagpole Sitting Championship of the World, a contest which is distinguished for a unique fervor on the part of the children, but fully as much for a lamentable imbecility on the part of their parents. Even while you are staring at one of these infant St. Simons, you observe that his "manager" is considerably older. You may perhaps see an officious-looking person gravely inspecting the sitter's equipment, and, if you inspect the autograph album at the foot of the pole, you may be fortunate enough to see, in the position assigned to Abou Ben Adhem, the name of His Honor, William F. Broening, Mayor of Baltimore!

It all started when, a few weeks ago, a curious fellow known as Shipwreck Kelly, who goes about from city to city demonstrating the hardihood of the American posterior by sitting for extended periods on flagpoles, visited the conservative city of Baltimore and "put on a sitting." During his protracted stay aloft, which was long enough to break the world's record for this particular form of virtuosity, Shipwreck attracted large crowds to the park which was the scene of his effort, and the celebration attending his eventual descent was a demonstration of the ease with which almost any form of imbecility becomes important in these States. Inevitably there was a juvenile aspirant to Shipwreck's fame.

Flagpole sitting became a popular spectator attraction during the 1920s, with Shipwreck Kelly being one of the more well-known practitioners. © BETTMANN/CORBIS. REPRODUCED BY PERMISSION.

Boys from time immemorial have wanted to be locomotive engineers, bareback riders, and major generals. Their heroes are, quite naturally, those who cause the most excitement. It was no great surprise, therefore, when one read in the Baltimore newspapers the modest announcement that Avon Foreman, fifteen, had mounted a flagpole and would sit there until he had broken what might be considered the "juvenile record." When he had sat for ten days, ten hours, ten minutes and ten seconds, he decided that the "juvenile record" in this field had been broken, and he came down.

That might have ended the matter had not various people, no longer accounted children, behaved so preposterously. "The older Baltimore" could hardly believe its ears when it learned the details of the hullabaloo following Avon's descent. For days before this amazing event crowds had gathered nightly to see him perched on his platform upon which bright searchlights had been trained by his father, who is an electrician. When Avon decided that his "record" was safe, there was a neighborhood celebration at which Mayor Broening, for whom no occasion lacks its oratorical opportunities, made an address and presented to Avon an autographed testimonial bearing the great seal of Baltimore City. In the course of his remarks the Mayor described Avon's achievement as an exemplification of "the pioneer spirit of early America." It is quite likely His Honor believed it, but it is equally possible that he was merely making a speech. When two or three people are gathered together Mayor Broening makes a speech, and most of his speeches are much the same.

Whatever these occasional remarks meant to the Mayor, they were a Challenge to the Youth of Baltimore. From that moment Baltimore was dotted with boys and girls ranging from eight to thirteen years of age who were determined to upset Avon Foreman's record as a flagpole sitter. Some of them came down as soon as Father got home, but since the ceremonies attending the Avon Foreman descent from a flagpole, there has been an average of some fifteen children roosting in various contrivances atop "flagpoles" ranging from ten to twenty feet high. Two of them have broken legs and one an arm, and one little girl was ill for days from the effects of her experience, but others mount poles to replace the casualties and the sittings go on. Parents, who at first were inclined to forbid their youngsters to enter the lists, lend their aid and provide their offspring with such comforts as are possible on top of a pole. It is difficult to make out a case against a practice which the Mayor of a city of 750,000 people has sanctioned as an exhibition of "grit and stamina so essential to success in the great struggle of life."

Editors in Baltimore and elsewhere promptly suggested a quick mobilization of shingles, hairbrushes, straps and slippers as a means of breaking this children's crusade under the banner of St. Simon Stylites. As a matter of fact, however, the children seem sages in comparison with the imbecility of their elders. When a boy, through the simple expedient of installing himself in a coop at the end of a pole can bring the Mayor to call on him, cause a minister of the Gospel to hold services with sermon at the foot of the pole and be the central occasion for a brass band, scores of popcorn vendors, offers of free dentistry for a year and a "write-up" in the newspapers, parental authority—in the class mainly afflicted with this mania—avails very little. Indeed, the parents of most of these children exhibit a distinct pride in the performance, protected by ignorance and stupidity from appreciating the possible consequences, physical and otherwise, of these idiotic vigils. They rival one another in fitting out the child's flagpole equip-

ment with electric lights and, occasionally, a radio set! The corner druggist pays a dollar or two for the right to advertise his business on the sacred totem and the city officials, perhaps in an effort to restrain the epidemic, add importance to flagpole sitting by solemnly issuing specifications for flagpoles for this use and charging a license fee of one dollar! If stripes could cure this malady, other backs than those of the children might appropriately receive them.

Moralists, in the larger sense, have an opportunity for prolonged and depressing speculation as to the essential significance of the Baltimore phenomenon. They can meditate upon the dullness of lives which find relief in the spectacle of twenty children squatting on top of improvised flagpoles throughout the city; on the low estimate a skillful politician with further ambitions must have made of his fellow citizens before he decided to take up these Stylites in a serious way; on the vacuity of adults who wear collars and own automobiles and permit their children to astound the neighbors in this fashion; on the strange evolution which makes an outbreak of this sort, to be expected in Los Angeles, possible in a conservative city like Baltimore. Consider the smugness installed in the soul of the youngster who mounted his flagpole with a Bible and thus provided the occasion for a religious service! Reflect on the precedent established for sound civil service by a city engineering department announcing without a smile the accepted specifications for a pole to be sat on! Imagine your own child—! Or your own Mayor, which may be less fantastic. Business is still transacted in Baltimore, but, as the flagpole story (with pictures) is bruited about from city, to city, the people who matter become slightly embarrassed. A hell of a thing for the second port on the Atlantic seaboard!

In view of the excitement just south of Baltimore over the various manifestations of Negro ambition, one of the flagpole sitters provides disquieting material for the believers in White supremacy. A Negro boy took up flagpole sitting and contributed his "grit and stamina" to the prevailing "pioneer spirit" now rampant. Be it noted, however, that he, above all the squatters, had the ordinary sense to come down from his perch at night—and for all meals.

Further Resources

BOOKS

Hoffman, Frank W., and William G. Bailey. *Sports and Recreation Fads*. New York: Haworth Press, 1991.

Marum, Andrew, and Frank Parise. *Follies and Foibles: A View of 20th Century Fads*. New York: Facts on File, 1984.

8

THE MEDIA

DAN PROSTERMAN

Entries are arranged in chronological order by date of primary source. For entries with one primary source, the entry title is the same as the primary source title. Entries with more than one primary source have an overall entry title, followed by the titles of the primary sources.

Important Events in the Media, 1920–1929

1920

• AT&T, GE, and RCA enter into a cross-licensing agreement for radio broadcasting.

• *The Freeman* is founded in New York by Francis Neilson and Albert Jay Nock as a mildly radical journal.

• *Screenland* magazine is founded.

• *The Dial* is founded by Scofield Thayer as a journal receptive to avant-garde literature.

• On January 5, Radio Corporation of America (RCA) is officially launched with a capital value of $20 million.

• On November 2, station KDKA in Pittsburgh makes the first radio broadcast for the general public when it announces the Harding-Cox presidential election returns. Although less than a thousand radios are tuned in, the broadcast stimulates the nation's interest in radio.

1921

• *Love Story* magazine (Street & Smith) commences publication; it begins as a quarterly but soon becomes a weekly.

• George T. Delacorte Jr. launches the Dell Publishing Company, which becomes a prolific publisher of pulp, comic, and fan magazines.

• The first regularly scheduled children's radio program, *The Man on the Moon,* commences twice-weekly broadcasting on WJZ Newark.

• On April 11, the first radio sports broadcast is the Johnny Ray-Johnny Dundee bout over KDKA Pittsburgh.

• From October 5 to October 14, in the first World Series radio broadcast (Yankees-Giants) by WJZ Newark, Sandy Hunt telephones play-by-play from the Polo Grounds in Manhattan to announcer Tommy Cowan.

• On November 11, President Warren G. Harding broadcasts the Armistice Day address from the Tomb of the Unknown Soldier, Arlington National Cemetery.

1922

• *Fruit, Garden and Home* begins publication in Des Moines, Iowa; its name is changed to *Better Homes and Gardens* in 1924.

• Haldeman-Julius Publishing Company is founded in Girard, Kansas—publishers of Little Blue Books.

• *True Confessions* is launched by Fawcett Publications.

• *The Fugitive* is founded in Nashville as a magazine of verse.

• Will H. Hays is appointed head of the Motion Picture Producers and Directors of America (the "Hays Office") after the Fatty Arbuckle rape case, the unsolved murder of William Desmond Taylor, and the drug-related death of Wallace Reid.

• President Harding's address to Congress and the first presidential news conference are broadcast.

• *The New York Times Book Review* begins publication as a separate section.

• NANA (North American Newspaper Alliance) is formed by American and Canadian newspapers as a features syndicate.

• On February 5, *The Reader's Digest*, founded by DeWitt and Lila Wallace, begins publication.

• On February 8, President Harding has a radio installed in the White House.

• On August 3, the first radio broadcast of a full-length play, Eugene Walter's *The Wolf,* over WGY Schenectady, is two and one-half hours long.

• On August 28, the first radio commercial is broadcast by WEAF New York; the station "rents" air time at one hundred dollars for ten minutes.

• On October 2, the first broadcast of a football game is Princeton vs. the University of Chicago, over WEAF New York; the broadcast from Chicago uses long-distance telephone lines.

1923

• Warner Bros. movie studio is incorporated in Hollywood, California. The founders—Albert, Harry, Sam, and Jack L. Warner—got their start in the film business in 1903, when they opened a nickelodeon in Newcastle, Pennsylvania.

• The American Society of Composers, Authors, and Publishers (ASCAP), which was formed in 1915, wins a court decision requiring broadcasters to pay for the right to play copyrighted music on the air.

• *Time* magazine begins publication.

• *The Happiness Boys* (Billy Jones and Ernie Hare) radio program begins.

• The *A&P Gypsies,* the *Ipana Troubadours,* and the *Cliquot Club Eskimos* radio programs begin.

• In *Hoover* v. *Intercity Radio Co., Inc.* the U.S. Court of Appeals rules that the secretary of commerce could assign radio wavelengths but not otherwise regulate broadcasting.

• H. V. Kaltenborn becomes the first radio news commentator.

• In December, immigrant inventor Vladimir Zworykin demonstrates his new invention, which he calls an iconoscope, in New York. The Russian-born engineer's crude device is able to send and receive pictures.

1924

• Presidential political conventions are broadcast for the first time.

- The *Herald* and the *Tribune* merge into the *New York Herald Tribune.*
- *The Saturday Review of Literature* begins publication under the editorship of Henry Seidel Canby.
- Two lurid picture tabloids are launched in New York City: William Randolph Hearst's *Daily Mirror* and Bernarr Macfadden's *New York Evening Graphic.*
- *The New York Daily Worker* is launched as the Communist Party newspaper.
- In January, *The American Mercury* begins publication under the editorship of H. L. Mencken and George Jean Nathan.
- In April, Richard L. Simon and M. Lincoln Schuster publish the *Cross Word Puzzle Book* (Plaza Publishing Co.).
- On August 5, Harold Gray's new comic strip *Little Orphan Annie* begins publication in the *New York Daily News.*
- On September 20, Walter Winchell's "Your Broadway and Mine" begins in the *Graphic.*
- On November 30, RCA sends photographs from London to New York by wireless transmission.

1925

- *EWSM Barn Dance* begins broadcasting from Nashville; it is later renamed *Grand Ole Opry.*
- On February 12, *The New Yorker* begins publication. It bills itself as a magazine for "caviar sophisticates" and not for the "old lady in Dubuque."
- *Cosmopolitan* begins publication.
- *Children* begins publication; its title is changed to *Parents' Magazine* in 1929.
- Electrical recordings utilizing microphones and amplifiers replace acoustical recordings. The first electronic phonograph with a loudspeaker was the Brunswick Panatrope.
- *Screen Play* magazine begins publication.

1926

- The movie *Don Juan* (Warner Bros.) has music and sound effects.
- The tabloid market grows. *True Story* sells two million copies by publishing stories such as "The Diamond Bracelet She Thought Her Husband Didn't Know About." The *Evening Graphic* is referred to as the Porno-Graphic in some circles.
- *The New Masses* begins publication as a radical magazine emulating *The Masses,* which had been suppressed by the government in 1917 because of its militant pacifism.
- On January 12, *Sam 'n' Henry* (Freeman Gosden and Charles Correll) begins broadcasting on WGN Chicago.
- In April, the Book-of-the-Month Club is launched. The first selection, *Lolly Willowes* by Sylvia Townsend Warner, is sent to 4,750 members.
- On October 9, GE, Westinghouse, and RCA form the National Broadcasting Company.
- On November 15, Regular network broadcasting is initiated with a variety show originated by WEAF New York and carried by twenty-one NBC-affiliated stations, with remote pickups from Chicago and Kansas City.

1927

- The Literary Guild of America is founded.
- The Jack Dempsey-Gene Tunney heavyweight championship fight is broadcast.
- Paramount News begins.
- Car radios are introduced by the Philadelphia Storage Battery Co. (Philco).
- The Fox Movietone sound newsreels begin.
- After five years of work, the Motion Picture Producers and Distributors of America issues a code for the industry. The regulations prohibit "licentious or suggestive nudity," "indecent or undue exposure," "excessive and lustful kissing," and "ridicule of clergy" on film. However, actual hangings or electrocutions, as well as "brutality" and "gruesomeness," may be shown, "within the careful limits of good taste."
- On January 1, the Rose Bowl football game is the first coast-to-coast broadcast.
- On January 5, *National Geographic* publishes the first underwater photographs.
- On February 23, President Calvin Coolidge signs a bill creating the Federal Radio Commission, the predecessor of the Federal Communications Commission. Sponsored by Secretary of Commerce Herbert Hoover, the FRC is empowered to grant licenses for assigned radio channels.
- On April 7, Hoover speaking in Washington, D.C., is seen by a group of bankers and investors in New York. The demonstration is set up by AT&T to promote interest in an invention called television, which has been developed from the 1923 experiments of Vladmir Zwotykin.

1928

- Clarence Mackay merges his Commercial Cable and Postal Telegraph companies with the International Telephone and Telegraph Corporation, thereby forming the first organization to combine radio, cable, and telegraph services.
- The first commercial television receiver is offered for sale by the Daven Corporation of Newark, New Jersey; the price is seventy-five dollars.
- NBC forms two networks: Red and Blue.
- The *Dictionary of American Biography* commences publication.
- The RKO movie studio is formed by GE, Westinghouse, and RCA.
- *The Lights of New York* (Warner Bros.) is the first all-talking movie.
- The first license for a television station (W2XBS) is issued to RCA.
- On January 4, NBC links all forty-eight states in a broadcast of a special radio program starring Al Jolson and Will Rogers.
- On January 18, Walt Disney releases his first animated movie with synchronized sound, *Steamboat Willie,* starring a cartoon character named Mickey Mouse.

- On May 11, WGY Schenectady offers the first scheduled television service, on Tuesdays, Thursdays, and Fridays between 1:30 and 2:00 P.M.

- On July 30, George Eastman demonstrates color motion pictures in Rochester, New York. Scenes include goldfish, peacocks, butterflies, flowers, and Fifth Avenue fashion models.

- On August 22, WGY airs the first televised news broadcast, the nomination of Al Smith for president.

- On September 11, WGY broadcasts the first televised play, J. Hartley Manners's *The Queen's Messenger.*

- On November 6, the nation's first animated electric sign begins operation around the top of *The New York Times* building in Times Square. It is called the "zipper" because of the way the lighted messages circle the building. The first news posted on it is returns from the presidential election.

1929

- Robert S. Lynd and Helen Merrell Lynd publish *Middletown,* a classic sociological study of a Middle America town (Muncie, Indiana) during the early 1920s.

- *The Fleischmann Hour* starring Rudy Vallee begins.

- *Amos 'n' Andy* is broadcast on the NBC network.

- Hearst Metrotone News begins distribution through M-G-M.

- *Screen Romances* and *Screen Stories* begin publication.

- A broadcasting rating service is introduced by Crossley's Cooperative Analysis of Broadcasting.

- RCA acquires the Victor Talking Machine Company.

- In June, the issue of *Scribner's Magazine* with the second installment of Ernest Hemingway's *A Farewell to Arms* is banned in Boston.

- On August 19, *Amos 'n' Andy* moves to the NBC Blue Network.

"First WEAF Commercial Continuity"

Radio advertisement

By: Queensboro Corporation

Date: August 28, 1922

Source: Queensboro Corporation. "First WEAF Commercial Continuity." August 28, 1922. Reprinted in Archer, Gleason L. *History of Radio to 1926.* New York: American Historical Society, 1938. Available online at http://www.midcoast.com/~lizmcl/advt2.html; website home page: http://www.midcoast.com (accessed May 12, 2003). ■

Introduction

Radio at the start of the 1920s featured sporadic programming at best, with only a very limited number of broadcast stations able to send signals to a tiny population of radio receivers. But the rapid development of nationwide radio networks throughout the decade revolutionized communications in the United States and dramatically influenced the structure of American media. The American Telephone and Telegraph Company (AT&T) was more widely known for its development of telephone communication, but the company also provided crucial broadcasting technology that enabled the emergence of nationwide radio networks in the 1920s. In 1922, AT&T formed radio station WEAF (later to become National Broadcasting Company) to serve as a conduit for other groups to transmit their messages to the people of New York City. Rather than providing its own programming, WEAF sold its airtime to companies wishing to advertise their products and services to the small but growing number of radio listeners.

Networks such as the National Broadcasting Company (1926) and the Columbia Broadcasting Company (1928) connected dozens of stations across the country. Although the separate stations could not send signals strong enough to reach receivers in different regions, these new national networks linked the signals from station to station, providing national signal distribution. At mid-decade, more than five hundred stations operated in the country, with about two and a half million radio sets

owned. By the end of the decade, a full-fledged radio industry had formed, with the total number of radios doubling to five million by 1929.

The rapidly advancing popularity of radio changed life in America and the world. Live event broadcasting evolved during the 1920s and permitted people to listen to descriptions of news, sports, or music events thousands of miles away. The radio created a new form of entertainment and, as the saying goes, offered television-style home entertainment before television existed.

Significance

Although other radio stations had offered promotional announcements in exchange for fees or donations, the following commercial is the first time that a radio station sold a block of time expressly for a commercial advertisement. The Queensboro Corporation reportedly paid $100 for fifteen minutes of airtime, from 5:15 to 5:30 on Monday afternoon, August 28, 1922. The commercial opened with an introduction by a WEAF announcer, who prepared the audience for a message concerning famous author Nathaniel Hawthorne and his supposed ideals of community life.

The ensuing announcement encouraged listeners to pay homage to the literary artist who wrote *The Scarlet Letter* and *The House of Seven Gables* by moving to a new apartment complex in Jackson Heights, Queens. "Hawthorne Court," according to the ad, offered New Yorkers, primarily Manhattanites, the ability to leave their cramped abodes for these spacious dwellings apparently inspired by the nineteenth-century novelist. Employing many of the commercial strategies that would shape broadcast ads for generations, this piece relied upon vivid imagery to spark listeners' imaginations and, more importantly, desires. Radio ads of later years added sound effects and music to entice audiences to buy virtually all of the products that had originally been promoted only in print media. By the end of the 1920s, the increased focus on radio advertising created a $20 million market. During the coming Great Depression and Second World War, radio cemented its stature as print's only competitor, with 95 percent of American families owning radio sets by the end of WWII. The boom in television production during the postwar period again radically altered the media landscape, with TV's expansion mirroring radio's emergence during the Roaring Twenties.

Primary Source

"First WEAF Commercial Continuity"

SYNOPSIS: Modern advertising places the following commercial in sharp relief. "Mr. Blackwell of the Queensboro Corporation" spoke for ten minutes, far more time than current advertisers can afford or find

Nation-wide broadcasting, for audiences of millions, has been made possible by the development of RCA Radiotrons for all uses in both transmitting and receiving instruments. They are the acknowledged standard in vacuum tube design in the radio industry.

Radiotrons are the heart of the receiving set. To maintain fine reception the vacuum tubes in your set should be replaced with new Radiotrons at least once a year. Do not use new tubes with old. Best results are obtained by changing all tubes at one time.

RCA Radiotron
MADE BY THE MAKERS OF THE RADIOLA

RADIO CORPORATION OF AMERICA · NEW YORK · CHICAGO · SAN FRANCISCO

An advertisement for RCA Radiotron vacuum tubes for radios, 1928. THE ADVERTISING ARCHIVE, LTD. REPRODUCED BY PERMISSION.

suitable to attract listeners with decreasing attention spans and multiple station options. Despite these stark differences, the WEAF spot for "Hawthorne Court" gave birth to a new form of advertising—one that would soon prove inescapable for anyone tuning in to their favorite radio station.

Broadcasting Program Hawthorne Court Introduction

Read by Vischer A. Randall, WEAF announcer.

This afternoon the radio audience is to be addressed by Mr. Blackwell of the Queensboro Corporation, who through arrangements made by the Griffin Radio Service, Inc., will say a few words concerning Nathaniel Hawthorne and the desirability of fostering the helpful community spirit and the healthful unconfined home life that were Hawthorne ideals. Ladies and Gentlemen: Mr. Blackwell.

Broadcasting Program Hawthorne Court

Talk delivered by Mr. Blackwell of the Queensboro Corporation

It is fifty-eight years since Nathaniel Hawthorne, the greatest of American fictionists, passed away.

To honor his memory the Queensboro Corporation, creator and operator of the tenant-owned system of apartment homes at Jackson Heights, New York City, has named its latest group of high-grade dwellings "Hawthorne Court."

I wish to thank those within the sound of my voice for the broadcasting opportunity afforded me to urge this vast radio audience to seek the recreation and the daily comfort of the home removed from the congested part of the city, right at the boundaries of God's great outdoors, and within a few minutes by subway from the business section of Manhattan. This sort of residential environment strongly influenced Hawthorne, America's greatest writer of fiction. He analyzed with charming keenness the social spirit of those who had thus happily selected their homes with good-natured relish.

There should be more Hawthorne sermons preached about the utter inadequacy and the general hopelessness of the congested city home. The cry of the heart is for more living room, more chance to unfold, more opportunity to get near to Mother Earth, to play, to romp, to plant and to dig.

Let me enjoin upon you as you value your health and your hopes and your home happiness, get away from the solid masses of brick, where the meagre opening admitting a slant of sunlight is mockingly called a light shaft, and where children grow up starved for a run over a patch of grass and the sight of a tree.

Apartments in congested parts of the city have proven failures. The word neighbor is an expression of peculiar irony—a daily joke.

Thousands of dwellers in the congested district apartments want to remove to healthier and happier sections but they don't know and they can't seem to get into the belief that their living situation and home environment can be improved. Many of them balk at buying a house in the country or the suburbs and becoming a commuter. They have visions of toiling down in a cellar with a sullen furnace, or shovelling snow, or of the blistering palms pushing a clanking lawn mower. They can't seem to overcome the pessimistic inertia that keeps pounding into their brains that their crowded, unhealthy, unhappy living conditions cannot be improved.

The fact is, however, that apartment homes on the tenant-ownership plan can be secured by these city martyrs merely for the deciding to pick them— merely for the devoting of an hour or so to the preliminary verification of the living advantages that are within their grasp. And this too within twenty minutes of New York's business center by subway transit.

Those who balk at building a house or buying one already built need not remain deprived of the blessings of the home within the ideal residential environment, or the home surrounded by social advantages and the community benefits where neighbor means more than a word of eight letters.

In these better days of more opportunities, it is possible under the tenant-ownership plan to posses an apartment-home that is equal in every way to the house-home and superior to it in numberless respects.

In these same better days, the purchaser of an apartment-home can enjoy all the latest conveniences and contrivances demanded by the housewife and yet have all of the outdoor life that the city dweller yearns for but has deludedly supposed could only be obtained thru purchase of a house in the country.

Imagine a congested city apartment lifted bodily to the middle of a large garden within twenty minutes travel of the city's business center. Imagine the interior of a group of such apartments traversed by a garden court stretching a block, with beautiful flower beds and rich sward. so that the present jaded congested section dweller on looking out his windows is not chilled with the brick and mortar vista, but gladdened and enthused by colors and scents that make life worth living once more. Imagine an apartment to live in at a place where you and your neighbor join the same community clubs, organizations, and activities, where you golf with your neighbor, tennis with your neighbor, bowl with your neighbor and join him in a long list of outdoor and indoor pleasure-giving health-giving activities.

And finally, imagine such a tenant-owned apartment, where you own a floor in a house the same as you can own an entire house with a proportionate ownership of the ground, the same as the ground attached to an entire house but where you have great spaces for planting and growing the flowers you love, and raising the vegetables for which you are fond.

Right at your door is such an opportunity. It only requires the will to take advantage of it all. You owe it to yourself and you owe it to your family to leave the hemmed-in, sombre-hued, artificial apartment life of the congested city section and enjoy what nature intended you enjoy.

Dr. Royal S. Copeland, Health Commissioner of New York, recently declared that any person who preached leaving the crowded city for the open country was a public-spirited citizen and a benefactor to the race. Shall we not follow this advice and become the benefactors he praises? Let us resolve to do so. Let me close by urging that you hurry to the apartment home near the green fields and the neighborly atmosphere right on the subway without the expense and the trouble of a commuter, where health and community happiness beckon—the community life and friendly environment that Hawthorne advocated.

Further Resources

BOOKS

Banning, William Peck. *Commercial Broadcast Pioneer: The WEAF Experiment, 1922–1926.* Cambridge, Mass.: Harvard University Press, 1946.

Barnouw, Erik. *A Tower of Babel,* vol. 1. New York: Oxford University Press, 1966.

Douglas, Susan. *Inventing American Broadcasting, 1899–1922.* Baltimore, Md.: Johns Hopkins University Press, 1987.

Smulyan, Susan. *Selling Radio: The Commercialization of American Broadcasting, 1920–1934.* Washington, D.C.: Smithsonian Institution Press, 1994.

"See the Children Safely to School"

Magazine advertisement

By: Chevrolet Motor Co.

Date: March 10, 1923

Source: "See the Children Safely to School." *Colliers,* March 10, 1923, 19. Available online at http://azimuth.harcourtcollege.com/history/ayers/chapter23/23.1.car4.html; website home page: http://www.azimuth.harcourtcollege.com (accessed April 25, 2003).

About the Organization: Born in Switzerland in 1878, Louis Chevrolet began his vehicle manufacturing career as a young boy, managing a bicycle shop with his two brothers after his family moved to France. Louis spent much of his life making, repairing, and racing automobiles. In 1911, heralded as one of the world's best racers, he teamed with a former Buick Company executive to establish the Chevrolet Motor Company. Although his involvement with the company was in name only after 1913, Chevrolet continued to expand its operations and eventually joined the Ford Motor Company and General Motors Corporation as one of the "Big Three" U.S. automobile manufacturers. The company's marketing campaigns excelled through much of the century, symbolized by perhaps the most famous jingle in car broadcast advertising, "See the U.S.A., in your Chevrolet," from the 1950s. ■

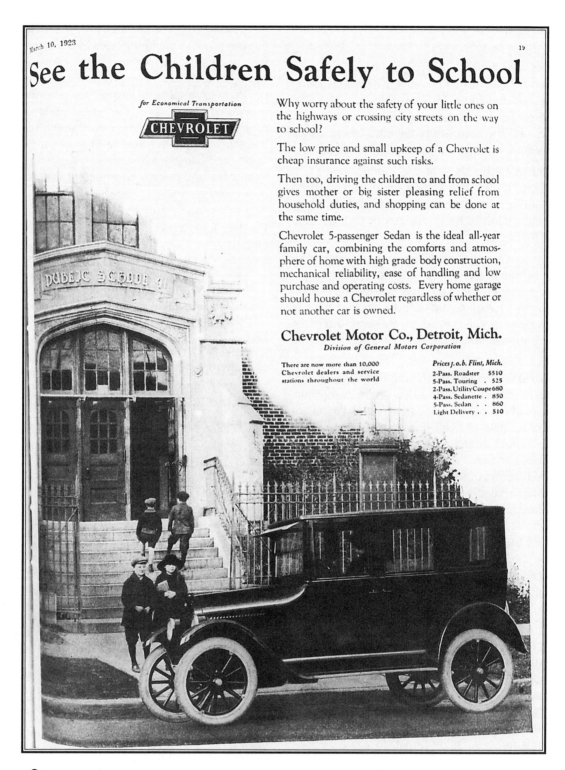

Primary Source

"See the Children Safely to School"

SYNOPSIS: Appearing in 1923, only a few years after the end of the Great War, this Chevrolet ad conveys the shift in advertisers' focus toward family-oriented mass consumption and away from international concerns. Much as the 1950s came to represent an America moving to the comfort of the home following the end of the Second World War, the 1920s saw Americans attempting to experience the pleasures of the modern world without the worries of war abroad and domestic strife. Moreover, the ad depicts the critical role the mass media saw women playing in the postwar period. *COLLIER'S*, MARCH 10, 1923.

Introduction

For nearly a century, automobile advertisements have touted the symbolic qualities of car ownership. The right car may bring style, luxury, and sex appeal. Or, depending upon the market focus, the perfect auto signifies safety, dependability, and durability. The links between cars, charisma, and character began almost as the first Model Ts rolled off the Ford assembly line in Detroit in 1908.

With those cars came advertisers who sought to attract customers for these new-fangled machines with promises of reliability, romance, and class. Just as millions of increasingly affluent Americans sought refuge from the pressures of war and domestic insurrection during the 1910s, manufacturers, ad agencies, and mass media teamed to revolutionize the national marketing of automobiles. By the end of the decade, nearly half of all American families owned automobiles.

Significance

Automobile ads blanketed print media throughout the Roaring Twenties, with magazines offering full-page, often full-color tributes to the burgeoning car industry. Much as car ads do today, the displays focused on particular sectors of the buying population. The major automakers ran various ads during the period that reflected either men's desire to woo with a car or women's growing independence and buying power. These pieces paid particular attention to the perceived needs of women. For example, the Ford Motor Company advertised its De Luxe Sedan with the heading, "An easy car for a woman to drive." In a campaign for the Sport Coupe, Ford focused on enticing men eager to impress. With language suitable for a work of art, the full-page ad began, "Women's eyes are quick to note and appreciate the trim, graceful lines of the new Ford, its exquisite two-tone color harmonies, the rich simplicity and quiet good taste reflected in every least little detail of finish and appointment." The automobile's admirers in the ad included a driver and a maid, and a pair of flappers standing with a gentlemen, all dressed in a manner befitting their respective social standing.

Likewise, advertisers championed the safety and security of certain models in the hopes of attracting female customers depicted in ads either as independent ladies on the town or caring mothers dutifully taking their children to school. The ad for Chevrolet ran in the weekly magazine *Collier's* in 1923. "See the Children Safely to School" touts the Chevrolet "5-passenger Sedan" as "the ideal all-year family car," both economical and durable. As implied by the advertisement, the copywriters viewed possible consumers as not only mothers hoping to drive their children safely to school but also as women striving for a little free time "from household duties."

Further Resources

BOOKS

Banham, Russ Banham. *The Ford Century: Ford Motor Company and the Innovations That Shaped the World.* New York: Artisan, 2002.

Hounshell, David A. *From the American System to Mass Production, 1800–1932: Development of Manufacturing Technology in the United States.* Baltimore, Md.: Johns Hopkins University Press, 1985.

Leinwand, Gerald Leinwand. *1927: High Tide of the 1920s.* New York: Four Walls Eight Windows, 2001.

Rubenstein, James M. *Making and Selling Cars: Innovation and Change in the U.S. Automotive Industry.* Baltimore, Md.: Johns Hopkins University Press, 2001.

PERIODICALS

"An easy car for women to drive." *McCall's Magazine,* July 1930. Available online at http://www.ahooga.com/info/ads /1930mc.jpg; website home page: http://www.ahooga.com (accessed April 25, 2003).

"Greater Even Than Its Beauty is the Reliability of the New Ford." *McCall's Magazine,* September 1928. Available online at http://www.ahooga.com/info/ads/1928mc.jpg; website home page: http://www.ahooga.com (accessed April 25, 2003).

"Louis Chevrolet" (obituary). *The New York Times,* June 7, 1941.

Advertising for Women

"Teachers and Mothers are Allies in Fighting Dirt"; "What the World Expects of Women Today"; "If Only I Could Tell This to Every Business Girl"

Advertisements

By: Lever Brothers; Kotex Company

Date: 1923; 1926; 1929

Source: "Teachers and Mothers are Allies in Fighting Dirt." *Ladies' Home Journal,* 1923; "What the World Expects of Women Today." *Ladies' Home Journal,* 1926; "If Only I Could Tell This to Every Business Girl." *Boston Post,* 1929. Available online at Ad*Access (Ad nos. BH1181, BH0020, BH0244): http://scriptorium.lib.duke.edu/adaccess/ (accessed April 24, 2003).

About the Publication: Started in 1883 as a supplement for women in the publication *Tribune and Farmer,* the *Ladies' Home Journal* quickly increased in readership to become not only the most popular women's publication but also one of the nation's most popular magazines through much of the twentieth century. The *Journal* holds the distinction of being

The
Deputy Mother

The school teacher is the finest expression of American ideals that exists today.

The culture, usefulness, morals and health of twenty-five million future citizens are in her loving charge.

She labors loyally and with trained intelligence without hope of appreciation or special reward.

She is making America.

Teachers and Mothers
are Allies in Fighting Dirt

The Health
Doctor *says*

Habits of personal cleanliness which children learn at home and school are their surest protection through life against the danger of disease germs which lurk on everything touched by many hands.

The wholesome Lifebuoy odor tells you that it is a true health soap. This odor vanishes—but the protection remains

OUTSIDE the safe home haven, your children find at least one protectress as lovingly relentless as any mother in warring against the dangers to health that lurk on all dirty things.

Even though Johnny's finger nails and suspiciously tanned neck should escape detection at home, his alert teacher applies that most effective discipline—public censure—and thereafter Johnny is more reconciled to cleanliness.

Why is Dirt Dangerous?

Why are doctors, mothers, teachers and health authorities waging determined war against personal uncleanliness?

It is because science has proved that almost all sickness is spread by the hands. Thousands of people deposit disease germs on everything they touch—doorknobs, rails, money, car straps, books, papers, telephones. The next hand that touches the object picks up the germs and very likely transfers them to nose or mouth or food.

The sensible protection is to *purify* hands and face frequently with a true health soap. Lifebuoy has become the most widely used toilet soap in the world because mothers know that it combats the dangers of dirt.

Lifebuoy is more than pure soap, although the bland, creamy Lifebuoy lather of the oils of palm fruit and cocoanut is gratefully soothing. It is more than a beauty soap, although women have learned that it keeps the skin texture of face, hands and body soft, fine and sweet.

How Lifebuoy Protects

Lifebuoy is first of all a *skin purifier*. Its lather releases a wonderful, non-irritating antiseptic which is carried deep into every pore, removing all impurities and leaving the skin safe, odorless and stimulated.

Mothers and teachers—"Health Doctors" both of you—let Lifebuoy guard the health of your children. Place a cake at every place where there is running water.

LEVER BROS. CO.
Cambridge,
Mass.

LIFEBUOY HEALTH SOAP

Primary Source

"Teachers and Mothers are Allies in Fighting Dirt"

SYNOPSIS: The marketing designs presented here were ubiquitous during the 1920s. Newspapers and magazines geared toward both female and general readerships addressed the changing roles of women with ads that played upon the concerns of women assuming unprecedented socioeconomic roles in American society. Certain ads appeared almost identical to stories and commentaries written by the publications' editorial staff that appeared elsewhere in the magazines. The text inserted below the primary images often read like an actual news report, with advertisers presenting their assertions as unbiased fact. This ad urges the purchase of Lifebuoy Soap. AD*ACCESS ON-LINE PROJECT - AD #BH1181 JOHN W. HARTMAN CENTER FOR SALES, ADVERTISING & MARKETING HISTORY DUKE UNIVERSITY RARE BOOK, MANUSCRIPT, AND SPECIAL COLLECTIONS LIBRARY HTTP://SCRIPTORIUM.LIB.DUKE.EDU/ADACCESS/

132   *The Ladies* HOME JOURNAL   October, 1926

What the World Expects of Women Today

In society—in business—demands the discarding of makeshift hygienic methods

Easy
Disposal

*and 2 other
important factors*

① No laundry. As easy to dispose of as a piece of tissue—thus ending the trying problem of disposal.

*Eight in every ten women have adopted this NEW way
which solves woman's most important hygienic problem
so amazingly . . . by ending the uncertainty of old
ways . . . and adding the convenience of disposability.*

By ELLEN J. BUCKLAND, *Registered Nurse*

THE lives of women today are different from those of yesterday. More is accomplished, more is *expected*. The modern woman, unlike her predecessors, cannot afford to lose precious days.

Thus makeshift hygienic methods had to go. There is a *new* way. A way that supplants the uncertainty of old-time methods with scientific security.

You meet *all* exactments every day. You wear filmiest frocks and sheerest things without a second's thought. You meet every day in confidence . . . unhandicapped, *at your best*.

These new advantages

This new way is Kotex, the scientific sanitary pad. Nurses in war-time France first discovered it. It is made of the super-absorbent Cellucotton. It absorbs and holds instantly sixteen times its own weight in moisture. It is five times

as absorbent as cotton. Kotex also deodorizes by a new disinfectant. And thus solves another trying problem.

You can get it anywhere, today

If you have not tried Kotex, please do. It will make a great difference in your viewpoint, in your peace of mind *and your health*. Many ills, according to leading medical authorities, are traced to the use of unsafe and unsanitary makeshift methods.

Thus today, on eminent medical advice, millions are turning to this new way.

There is no bother, no expense, of laundry. Simply discard Kotex as you would waste paper—without embarrassment.

Only Kotex is "like" Kotex

In purchasing, take care that you get the genuine Kotex. It is the *only* pad embodying the super-absorbent Cellucotton. It is the *only* napkin made by this company. Only Kotex itself is "like" Kotex.

You can obtain Kotex at better drug and department stores everywhere. Comes in sanitary sealed packages of 12 in two sizes, the Regular and Kotex-Super. Cellucotton Products Co., 166 West Jackson Blvd., Chicago.

② Utter protection—Kotex absorbs 16 times its own weight in moisture; 5 times that of cotton, and it deodorizes, thus assuring double protection.

③ Easy to buy anywhere.* Many stores keep them ready-wrapped in plain paper—simply help yourself, pay the clerk, that is all.

"Ask for them by name"

KOTEX
PROTECTS—DEODORIZES

*Supplied also in personal service cabinets
in rest-rooms by
West Disinfecting Co.

Kotex Regular:
65c per dozen

Kotex-Super:
90c per dozen

*No laundry—discard as
easily as a piece of tissue*

Primary Source

"What the World Expects of Women Today"

An ad for Kotex sanitary napkins, 1926 COURTESY OF KIMBERLY CLARK WORLD WIDE, INC. AD*ACCESS ON-LINE PROJECT - AD #BH0244 JOHN W. HARTMAN CENTER FOR SALES, ADVERTISING & MARKETING HISTORY DUKE UNIVERSITY RARE BOOK, MANUSCRIPT, AND SPECIAL COLLECTIONS LIBRARY HTTP://SCRIPTORIUM.LIB.DUKE.EDU/ADACCESS/

"If only I could tell this to every business girl"

Says an Office Manager

Women in business find that this modern sanitary protection means better health, greater opportunity for accomplishment.

IN offices throughout the country–in offices all over the world–women are realizing the full value of every working day, free from the problems which once retarded their progress. Kotex has not only meant new comfort and better health but it has brought a priceless mental relief.

Doctors and nurses have helped to teach women the importance of this new sanitary protection. They stress its soft, soothing comfort, its correct absorbency.

Fleecy, soft filler

Cellucotton absorbent wadding, which fills Kotex, offers a type of softness that no substitutes can equal. Surgeons in 85% of the company's leading hospitals insist upon Cellucotton absorbent wadding to give patients the greatest possible degree of hygienic comfort.

The new deodorant

To assure the utmost daintiness of person, Kotex now deodorizes by a process discovered and perfected in Kotex laboratories. This process has been patented* and is found in no other sanitary pad.

Corners cut and rounded

The fact that corners of the pad are now rounded and tapered means greater mental as well as physical comfort. This one improvement alone has impressed thousands of women, who write us in appreciation of its advantages.

Layers of filler are adjustable. The gauze, as well as the filler, is softer and gentler than ever. And Kotex is disposed of just like tissue. That fact alone has helped to change the hygienic habits of women all over the world.

SUPER-SIZE KOTEX

Formerly 90c–Now 65c

Some women find Super-size Kotex a special comfort. Exactly the same as the Regular size Kotex, but with added layers of Cellucotton absorbent wadding.

Try the new Kotex. It is 45c for a box of twelve at any drug, dry goods or department store. Also obtained in vending cabinets of rest-rooms. Kotex Company, 180 No. Michigan Ave., Chicago.

KOTEX

The New Sanitary Pad which deodorizes

*Kotex is the only sanitary pad that deodorizes by patented process. (Patent No. 1,670,587.)

Primary Source

"If Only I Could Tell This to Every Business Girl"

An ad for Kotex sanitary napkins, 1929 COURTESY OF KIMBERLY CLARK WORLD WIDE, INC. AD*ACCESS ON-LINE PROJECT - AD #BH0020 JOHN W. HARTMAN CENTER FOR SALES, ADVERTISING & MARKETING HISTORY DUKE UNIVERSITY RARE BOOK, MANUSCRIPT, AND SPECIAL COLLECTIONS LIBRARY HTTP://SCRIPTORIUM.LIB.DUKE.EDU/ADACCESS/

the first magazine to reach a circulation of one million monthly subscribers. ■

Introduction

Women dramatically altered their roles in American society during the 1920s. The flapper image of women during the Jazz Age incorporated an independent sense of style and greater social power. Following the massive increase in female employment outside the home during World War I, women continued to seek wage-earning positions in greater numbers during the next decade. This employment brought greater economic freedom and, therefore, enhanced the position of women in the economy. The ratification of the Nineteenth Amendment meant victory for women's rights activists and brought a steady advancement in the political sphere to match women's economic gains. As a result of these changes, publications devoted to women's issues, such as *McCall's, Good Housekeeping,* and the *Ladies' Home Journal,* soared in popularity. Companies devoted more advertising funds to marketing plans aimed at cultivating female consumers. Female laborers were disproportionately single, as married women continued to find their primary responsibilities in caring for their families.

Significance

Leafing through the pages of *Ladies' Home Journal* over its history gives a glimpse of the changing social expectations for women through the decades. "Teachers and Mothers are Allies in Fighting Dirt," published in 1923, combined the ideals of women as both wage earners and mothers. The duty that linked the two was care for children, a social expectation undeterred by Jazz Age visions of "new women." Despite the millions of women entering the workforce during the decade, the primary concern, according to Lifebuoy Soap, remained maintaining clean homes and children. The two ads for Kotex emphasized the changing status of women in the Roaring Twenties. The drive to gain employment and keep pace with the changes of modern society placed pressures on women that advertisers both manufactured and attempted to solve. To gain "better health, [and] greater opportunity for accomplishment," as well as "priceless mental relief," women apparently needed to purchase these particular items. Advertisers supported their claims by employing stereotypes of menstruation as dirty and unhealthy—something that "once retarded their progress." Noting the massive changes under way in American social relations, the final ad explained, "The lives of women today are different from those of yesterday. More is accomplished, more is *expected*. The modern woman, unlike her predecessors, cannot afford to lose precious days." The implication was that only Kotex

brand hygiene products provided necessary protection against office or social embarrassment.

Further Resources

BOOKS

Fox, Stephen. *The Mirror Makers: A History of American Advertising and Its Creators.* New York: Vintage, 1984.

Kessler-Harris, Alice. *Out to Work: A History of Wage-Earning Women in the United States.* New York: Oxford University Press, 1982.

Marchand, Roland. *Advertising the American Dream: Making Way for Modernity, 1920–1941.* Berkeley, Calif.: University of California Press, 1986.

Sedition or Propaganda?

"Spider Web Chart"
Chart

By: Lucia Maxwell
Date: March 22, 1924
Source: Maxwell, Lucia. "Spider Web Chart: The Socialist-Pacifist Movement in America Is an Absolutely Fundamental and Integral Part of International Socialism." *Dearborn Independent,* March 22, 1924, 11. Available online at http://womhist.binghamton.edu/wilpf/doc3.htm; website home page: http://womhist.binghamton.edu (accessed April 23, 2003).

"Poison Propaganda"
Editorial

By: Carrie Chapman Catt
Date: May 31, 1924
Source: Catt, Carrie Chapman. "Poison Propaganda." *The Woman Citizen,* May 31, 1924, 32–33. Available online at http://womhist.binghamton.edu/wilpf/doc4.htm; website home page: http://womhist.binghamton.edu (accessed April 25, 2003).
About the Author: Carrie Clinton Lane Chapman Catt (1859–1947) was born in Ripon, Wisconsin. After working with the Woman's Christian Temperance Union, Catt became a suffragist and helped found the National American Woman Suffrage Association (NAWSA) in 1890. She served as the organization's president from 1900 to 1904 and from 1915 until 1920. She also founded the International Woman Suffrage Association in 1902. With Catt leading the New York Woman Suffrage Party, the state of New York granted women the vote in 1917. Two years later, the Nineteenth Amendment to the Constitution, which granted women equal voting rights throughout the United States, gained ratification. The NAWSA changed its name to the League of Women Voters and continued to urge social reforms to benefit women throughout the twentieth century. ■

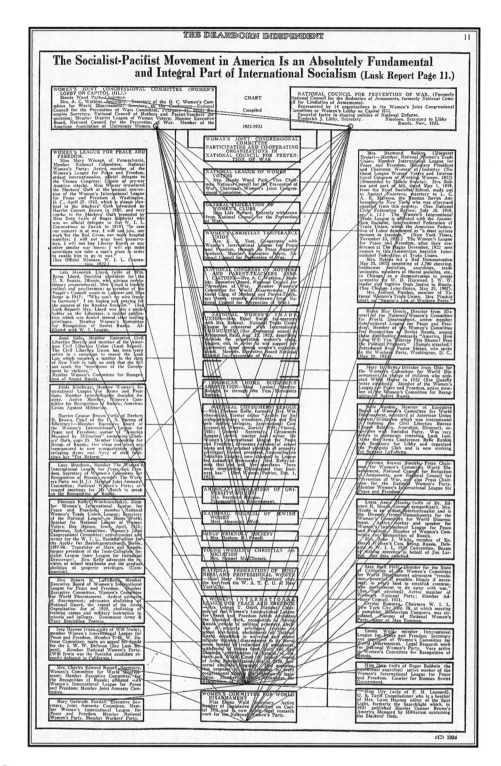

Primary Source

"Spider Web Chart"

SYNOPSIS: The "Spider Web Chart" as it appeared in *The Dearborn Independent,* March 22, 1924. The chart asserts that many American political interest groups, including pacifists and feminists, are linked to international Socialism and Communism. FROM THE COLLECTIONS OF HENRY FORD MUSEUM & GREENFIELD VILLAGE. REPRODUCED BY PERMISSION.

Introduction

In the years preceding the Roaring Twenties, enormous protest and controversy reverberated throughout the United States. The Great Migration, the suffrage movement, and the First World War (1914–1918) engendered great social unrest. The repercussions of these events impacted the early 1920s in vital ways. The Espionage and Sedition Acts, passed during the war, continued to threaten leftist groups who called for radical change in government, business, and social relations. In addition to punishing antiwar protesters, federal officials used these laws to ban feminist and Communist publications, break up labor unions, arrest more than 1,500 agitators, and deport several hundred more in the late 1910s and early 1920s.

Many activists saw reform needed in multiple sectors of American society and therefore often participated in more than one reform organization. Carrie Chapman Catt, for instance, served in both women's rights and pacifist groups. Even as the NAWSA supported the war effort, the Woman's Peace Party formed to oppose American participation in the conflict. Catt, a founding member of the NAWSA, argued that war negatively impacted the struggle for suffrage. The Woman's Peace Party, like the Women's International League for Peace and Freedom (WILPF), faced government scrutiny for its pacifist platform. According to the language of the Sedition Act of 1918, any criticism of U.S. policy during the war threatened the nation's ability to conduct the war and must be prohibited. Pacifism, by its very nature, opposed U.S. involvement in the war and therefore could be construed as sedition. The end of the war did not bring the end of prosecution for violating these repressive laws. Even after the armistice of 1918, advocates of peace faced the charge of treason into the next decade.

Significance

Conservative industrialist Henry Ford owned the *Dearborn Independent* in Michigan and greatly influenced its news coverage. His manufacturing firms received millions of dollars worth of military contracts during and after World War I. Ford, therefore, vehemently opposed the pacifist movement. The *Independent* published Lucia Maxwell's "Spider Web Chart" on March 22, 1924, while Maxwell served as an assistant in the U.S. Chemical Warfare Bureau. Pacifist groups, including many of those listed in the graphic, called for the outlawing of the chemical weapons used during the Great War and thereby threatened the U.S. War Department's chemical weapons program.

The title for the chart came from a New York State Senate Committee investigation of socialist influence in the state and nation. Compiled for the Lusk Committee in 1920, the "Report on Seditious Activities" provided the membership information used in the Spider Web Chart. Ostensibly geared to reveal socialists in prominent political positions, the chart implicated several women's rights organizations as seditious threats to national security.

As a prominent member of several organizations labeled in Maxwell's article, Catt argued vociferously against the chart's assertion that pacifists and feminists threatened national security. Catt labeled the associations depicted in the Spider Web as slanderous, and she counterattacked by linking the U.S. government to conservative groups opposed to both pacifism and women's rights. As depicted by these articles, activists on both sides of the Red Scare debate battled for power in postwar America through the mass media.

Primary Source

"Poison Propaganda" [excerpt]

SYNOPSIS: In her editorial "Poison Propaganda," Carrie Chapman Catt responded to the allegations of the Spider Web Chart.

Some time ago insidious comments upon all educational peace movements and their leaders began to appear in the press. In 1922 there was a widespread circularization of the newspapers with a fanciful declaration that the "Law, not War" day celebrated in many cities was being financed by Moscow, and an especially virulent attack was made upon Mr. Libby, Quaker, of the National Council for the Prevention of War, who was promoting these demonstrations. Many papers reprinted the matter. In 1923 the American Defense Society sent out similar propaganda declaring that Russian communism and American efforts to promote peace were working hand in hand.

From time to time similar attacks have been made upon individuals, any individuals, who have appealed to public opinion on behalf of world peace. The charge has been implied in these stories that various women's organizations, well known and composed of highly honorable memberships, were being financed by Moscow because they were promoting peace sentiment.

On March 15 1924, the *Dearborn Independent* carried an amazing story, continued in the number of March 22, under the starting title "Are Women's Clubs Used by Bolshevists?" These articles asserted that the masses women within the many well-known organizations were being weakly played upon by a few women in "key positions" who were linked to world communism and its aim to overturn all governments. The second instalment [sic] was accompanied by a chart compiled from the Lusk report and connecting the highest and best organizations with socialist-pacifist activities. A definite attack was made upon the Women's Joint Congressional Committee, its seventeen component organizations and many of its members.

This Committee thereupon named a sub-committee, of which Mrs. Maud Wood Park was Chairman, to investigate the source of this attack, although its libelous character would have warranted a suit against Henry Ford, whose paper had published the articles. Quiet and efficient search revealed the astonishing source—the Chemical Warfare Bureau of our own government.

Things sometimes happen in this strange world that are so amazing one's senses are fairly paralyzed by the revelation. This is one of them. Here are women conducting themselves as they always have when they want something which can only be attained by political action, that is, speaking, arranging meetings, petitioning, reading, investigating, thinking, how to abolish war, the world's greatest crime. Yet, in this supposedly most tolerant republic in the world, boasting of its free speech and liberty for all, they suddenly discover that a department of their own government is systematically discrediting them by the distribution of false and libelous charges, which, because of their source, carry abnormal influence. These women, trying to attain their hopes through constructive, educational measures, are accused of being in conspiracy with communists whose aim is the overthrow of governments through revolution. For trying to teach men and women to think, the public is warned to beware of them. They are called Bolshevist—the world's present-day most damning condemnatory epithet—and the bills for distribution of these libels are quite clearly met by their own tax money! Is this America or Russia? Is this the twentieth century or the middle ages? . . .

At this point, although the incident seems incomplete, probably both sides may "rest their case," the Government having apologized and promised withdrawal of the offending material. It is to be regretted that in its own defense the Joint Congressional Committee could only speak for itself and left the other women, charged by the chart with unpatriotic behavior, out in the cold. It now becomes necessary for them to take up cudgels in their own behalf.

Meantime, the scurrilous articles, somewhat shorn of their sharpest libels, have been reprinted from the *Dearborn Independent* in a leaflet by the Associated Industries of Kentucky (Louisville) and widely distributed by them. Just why should these industries publish this attack upon women? Clearly to intimidate them and prevent something they are sponsoring from becoming law. Is it the abolition of child labor, education or peace?

Women of America, don't get frightened; think. Don't be intimidated; act.

Further Resources

BOOKS

Alonso, Harriet Hyman. *Peace as a Women's Issue: A History of the U. S. Movement for World Peace and Women's Rights.* Syracuse, N.Y.: Syracuse University Press, 1993.

Foster, Catherine. *Women for All Seasons: The Story of the Women's International League for Peace and Freedom.* Athens, Ga.: University of Georgia Press, 1989.

Jensen, Joan M. "All Pink Sisters: The War Department and the Feminist Movement in the 1920s." In *Decades of Discontent: The Women's Movement, 1920–1940,* edited by Lois Scharf and Joan M. Jensen. Westport, Conn.: Greenwood, 1983, 199–222.

Murray, Robert K. *Red Scare: A Study in National Hysteria, 1919–1920.* Minneapolis: University of Minnesota Press, 1955.

WEBSITES

"Women and Social Movements in the United States, 1775–2000." Available online at http://womhist.binghamton.edu (accessed April 25, 2003).

Time and *The New Yorker*

"*Time: The Weekly Newsmagazine (A Prospectus)*"

Prospectus

By: Briton Hadden and Henry Luce

Date: 1949

Source: Hadden, Briton and Henry Luce. "Time: The Weekly Newsmagazine (A Prospectus)." In Busch, Noel F. *Briton Hadden: A Biography of the Co-founder of Time.* New York: Farrar, Straus, 1949, 60–64.

About the Authors: Briton Hadden (1898–1929), along with Henry R. Luce, pioneered magazine journalism in the 1920s. In 1923, the pair, five years after graduating together from Yale University, created an entirely new format for news coverage—the newsweekly. *Time* magazine forever changed the way Americans received their news, offering brief reports and vivid pictures in a "timely" fashion.

Henry R. Luce (1898-1967), American magazine editor and publisher, was a powerful journalistic innovator. Luce worked with Hadden on the *Baltimore News.* They left soon after to raise $86,000 in order to launch *Time* magazine. After Hadden's untimely death, Luce continued to grow *Time* and created the business magazine *Fortune* in 1930 and the photography-based *Life* in 1936.

Cover of the First Edition

Magazine cover

By: *The New Yorker*

Date: February 21, 1925

Source: *The New Yorker,* February 21, 1925. The New Yorker Collection, 1991. Rea Irvin from cartoonbank.com. ∎

Introduction

Sandwiched between the turmoil of the 1910s and the Great Depression, the Roaring Twenties symbolized the cultural changes that permeated the decade. Stereotyped as licentious and boisterous, the music, art, literary, and dance styles of the decade enticed and appalled Americans. In journalism, the sensationalist press of the first twenty years of the twentieth century continued, but gave way at times to magazines new in content and format. Entirely different in both respects, the following texts reveal the changes under way during the Jazz Age as the founders of *Time* and *The New Yorker* began innovative publications that would run for the next eighty years and beyond.

Significance

Briton Hadden and Henry Luce, both twenty-four years old and Yale classmates, desired to alter dramatically the structure of news media. The pair completed the following prospectus for what would become the most widely read newsweekly in the United States—*Time.* From the opening sentences of the piece, Hadden and Luce offered a damning review of contemporary news journals. They wrote that, despite the multitude of daily and periodic publications, Americans remained "uninformed BECAUSE NO PUBLIC HAS ADAPTED ITSELF TO THE TIME WHICH BUSY MEN ARE ABLE TO SPEND ON SIMPLY KEEPING INFORMED." Hadden and Luce concluded that the nation needed a new, weekly magazine that would provide a concise summary of major events in an easily digestible format with visual appeal. Although Hadden and Luce declared that *Time* would not have an editorial page, they noted that the magazine may contain "certain prejudices." For much of its history, *Time* has offered a moderate to conservative slant that mirrored Luce's political leanings. The style proposed in this 1922 prospectus continued to govern the press philosophies of *Time* and its primary competitors,

Newsweek and *U.S. News & World Report,* for the rest of the century.

The first edition of *The New Yorker* featured on of the most memorable icons of the Jazz Age on its cover. The upper-class gentleman who graced the front of the February 21, 1925, issue wore Victorian-era clothing, holding up his monocle to examine a butterfly. Interestingly, the publication whose primary audience was New York's cultural elite devoted this opening image to mocking the snobbery of an apparently bygone era. The new publication offered its Roaring Twenties audience a fresh perspective on the music, arts, literature, and politics of the era. While the opening image critiqued previous generations as staid and aloof, the magazine consistently provided probing, humorous examinations of the Roaring Twenties' upper crust.

Primary Source

"Time: The Weekly Newsmagazine (A Prospectus)" [excerpt]

SYNOPSIS: Noel F. Busch, biographer of Britton Hadden, published the following prospectus verbatim in 1949. Busch noted that Hadden and Luce were only twenty-four years old and lived with their respective families when they wrote this plan. Despite their youth and relatively few years in the journalism industry, the biographer portrayed the pair as "fire-hardened, battle-seasoned veterans" prepared to establish themselves with the formation of a revolutionary publication, *Time* magazine.

The Argument

Although daily journalism has been more highly developed in the United States than in any other country of the world—

Although foreigners marvel at the excellence of our periodicals, *World's Work, Century, Literary Digest, Outlook,* and the rest—

People in America are, for the most part, poorly informed.

This is not the fault of the daily newspapers; they print all the news.

It is not the fault of the weekly "reviews"; they adequately develop and comment on the news.

To say with the facile cynic that it is the fault of the people themselves is to beg the question.

People are uninformed BECAUSE NO PUBLICATION HAS ADAPTED ITSELF TO THE TIME WHICH BUSY MEN ARE ABLE TO SPEND ON SIMPLY KEEPING INFORMED.

Primary Source

Cover of the First Edition

SYNOPSIS: The cover of the February 21, 1925 issue—the first edition—of *The New Yorker,* with an image of Eustace Tilley. Every February Mr. Tilley appears on the cover. © THE NEW YORKER COLLECTION 1991 REA IRVIN FROM CARTOONBANK.COM. ALL RIGHTS RESERVED.

TIME is a weekly news-magazine, aimed to serve the modern necessity of keeping people informed, created on a new principle of COMPLETE ORGANIZATION.

TIME is interested—not in how much it includes between its covers—but in HOW MUCH IT GETS OFF ITS PAGES INTO THE MINDS OF ITS READERS.

The Format

TIME will appear on Friday morning and will contain news up to and including the Wednesday immediately preceding.

The size of TIME's pages and the quality of the paper are the same as in *Life.*

The magazine contains 24 pages of reading matter in addition to advertisements and front and back covers.

There are three columns to a page.

The cover is black and white.

The illustrations are chiefly portraits.

The Process

From virtually every magazine and newspaper of note in the world, TIME collects all available information on all subjects of importance and general interest. The essence of all this information is reduced to approximately 100 short articles, none of which are over 400 words in length (seven inches of type). Each of these articles will be found in its logical place in the magazine, according to a FIXED METHOD OF ARRANGEMENT which constitutes a complete ORGANIZATION of all the news.

This fixed method arrangement is composed of six general "departments," which are:

Name of Department. . . . . Pages
NATIONAL PUBLIC AFFAIRS. 5
FOREIGN NEWS 4
THE ARTS. 6
Books
Theatre
Art
Music
Newspapers and Periodicals
The Columnists
THE PROFESSIONS 3
Education
Religion
Law
Medicine
Science and Invention
Business (including Finance)
SPORTS 1
PEOPLE 2
Imaginary Interviews
Crime

How Time Differs

TIME, like all weeklies, differs from the daily papers in what it omits.

It differs from other weeklies in that it deals *briefly* with EVERY HAPPENING OF IMPORTANCE and presents these happenings as NEWS (fact) rather than as "comment." It further differs in that it is from three to fifteen days more up-to-date than they.

TIME is not like *The Literary Digest* and is in no way modelled after it.

The Literary Digest treats at great length with a few subjects selected more or less arbitrarily from week to week. TIME gives *all* the week's news in a *brief, organized* manner.

The Digest makes its statements through its time-honored formula of editorial excerpts. TIME simply states.

The Digest, in giving both sides of a question, gives little or no hint as to which side it considers to be right. TIME gives both sides, but clearly indicates which side it believes to have the stronger position.

Editorial Bias

There will be no editorial page in TIME.

No article will be written to prove any special case.

But the editors recognize that complete neutrality on public questions and important news is probably as undesirable as it is impossible, and are therefore ready to acknowledge certain prejudices which may in varying measure predetermine their opinions on the news.

A catalogue of these prejudices would include such phrases as:

1. A belief that the world is round and an admiration of the statesman's "view of the world."

2. A general distrust of the present tendency toward increasing interference by government.

3. A prejudice against the rising cost of government.

4. Faith in the things which money cannot buy.

5. A respect for the old, particularly in manners.

6. An interest in the new, particularly in ideas.

But this magazine is not founded to promulgate prejudices, liberal or conservative. "To keep men well-informed"—that, first and last, is the only axe this magazine has to grind.

Further Resources

BOOKS

Douglas, George H. *The Smart Magazine: Fifty Years of Literary Revelry and High Jinks at 'Vanity Fair,' 'The New Yorker,' 'Life,' 'Esquire,' and 'The Smart Set.'"* Hamden, Conn.: Archon Press, 1991.

Kobler, John. *Luce: His Time, Life, and Fortune.* Garden City, N.Y.: Doubleday, 1968.

Peterson, Theodore. *Magazines in the Twentieth Century.* Urbana, Ill.: University of Illinois Press, 1964.

Swanberg, W.A. *Luce and His Empire.* New York: Scribners, 1972.

WEBSITES

Baughman, James L. "Hadden, Briton." *American National Biography Online.* Available online at http://www.anb.org/articles/16/16-03268.html; website home page: http://www.anb.org (accessed April 25, 2003).

Herzstein, Robert Edwin. "Luce, Henry Robinson." *American National Biography Online.* Available online at http://www.anb.org/articles/16/16-02454.html; website home page: http://www.anb.org (accessed April 25, 2003).

"Harlem"

Journal article

By: Alain Locke

Date: March 1925

Source: Locke, Alain. "Harlem." *Survey Graphic,* March 1925, 629–630. Available online at http://etext.lib.virginia.edu/harlem/LocHarlF.html; website home page: http://etext.lib.virginia.edu (accessed April 24, 2003).

About the Author: Alain Leroy Locke (1885–1954) graduated from Harvard in 1907 and taught education at Howard University from 1912 to 1917, then philosophy from 1917 until his death. Locke was the first African American Rhodes scholar. His primary research focused on the theory that race existed only as a social construct. During the Harlem Renaissance, the controversial Locke argued for a sort of cultural pluralism following his notion that culture could be molded and enhanced. His most famous work, *The New Negro,* resulted from the March 1925 edition of *Survey Graphic* devoted to the topic. ∎

Introduction

The Great Migration of the 1910s and 1920s saw well over one million African Americans escape the discrimination of the South to the possibilities and tensions of life in the North and West. As the ensuing race riots in several urban centers revealed, this mass movement did not automatically bring joy and simplicity. In fact, life in the North created a whole new set of problems, limitations, and racial stratifications for African Americans. African American–owned newspapers cultivated growing audiences in the new African American communities of urban America. In this context, the Harlem Renaissance expressed the outpouring of artistic creativity enabled by the exciting and difficult changes of the 1920s.

Significance

Alain Locke's "Harlem" detailed the sweeping changes under way in African America during the Jazz Age and, implicitly, the increasingly powerful role of African American journalists in mass media. Focusing on the impact of the hundreds of thousands of African Americans who had moved to Harlem in recent years, the author provided readers of the nationally circulated journal *Survey Graphic* with a colorful commentary on life in Harlem. Locke depicted the neighborhood as a microcosm of the national changes generated by the Great Migration. The scholar's notion of the "New Negro" characterized the vital role of intrarace relations and development in this cultural renaissance. For Locke, new interactions between African Americans of diverse backgrounds in Harlem made the area "the greatest Negro community the world has known." The advancement of the "New Negro" rested not only on economic prosperity but also on innovations in the arts and letters. The influx of African Americans from all corners of the United States and from various socioeconomic backgrounds had created "a new vision of opportunity" that encompassed the full spectrum of human endeavors, free from social prescriptions and expectations. In dance, business, music, politics, literature, poetry, and journalism, the Harlem Renaissance challenged all Americans to recognize the challenges and opportunities created in the aftermath of world war and domestic strife.

Primary Source

"Harlem"

SYNOPSIS: The following commentary by Alain Locke conveyed the energy of Harlem during the 1920s. By 1925, the Harlem Renaissance was in full swing. Locke conveyed the myriad developments in the neighborhood and asserted that Harlem's innovations in fact reflected much broader social forces. Harlem's demographic and historical characteristics certainly made it unique in many respects. But, as Locke emphasized in the article's closing paragraph, this New York neighborhood's vitality arose from changes affecting the entire African American population.

If we were to offer a symbol of what Harlem has come to mean in the short span of twenty years it would be another statue of liberty on the landward side of New York. It stands for a folk-movement which in human significance can be compared only with the pushing back of the western frontier in the first half of the last century, or the waves of immigration which have swept in from overseas in the last half. Numerically far smaller than either of these movements, the volume of migration is such none the less that Harlem has become the greatest Negro community the world has known—without counterpart in the South or in Africa. But beyond this, Harlem represents the Negro's latest thrust towards Democracy.

The special significance that today stamps it as the sign and center of the renaissance of a people lies, however, layers deep under the Harlem that many know but few have begun to understand. Physically Harlem is little more than a note of sharper color in the kaleidoscope of New York. The metropolis pays little heed to the shifting crystallizations of its own heterogeneous millions. Never having experienced permanence, it has watched, without emotion or even curiosity, Irish, Jew, Italian, Negro, a score of other races drift in and out of the same colorless tenements.

So Harlem has come into being and grasped its destiny with little heed from New York. And to the herded thousands who shoot beneath it twice a day on the subway, or the comparatively few whose daily travel takes them within sight of its fringes or down its main arteries, it is a black belt and nothing more. The pattern of delicatessen store and cigar shop and restaurant and undertaker's shop which repeats itself a thousand times on each of New York's long avenues is unbroken through Harlem. Its apartments, churches and storefronts antedated the Negroes and, for all New York knows, may outlast them there. For most of New York, Harlem is merely a rough rectangle of common-place city blocks, lying between and to east and west of Lenox and Seventh Avenues, stretching nearly a mile north and south—and unaccountably full of Negroes.

Another Harlem is savored by the few—a Harlem of racy music and racier dancing, of cabarets famous or notorious according to their kind, of amusement in which abandon and sophistication are cheek by

Author Alain Locke was also the editor of an anthology entitled *The New Negro* that featured the works of African American writers. He is considered a key figure of the Harlem Renaissance. **THE LIBRARY OF CONGRESS.**

jowl—a Harlem which draws the connoisseur in diversion as well as the undiscriminating sightseer. This Harlem is the fertile source of the "shuffling" and "rollin'" and "runnin' wild" revues that establish themselves season after season in "downtown" theaters. It is part of the exotic fringe of the metropolis.

Beneath this lies again the Harlem of the newspapers—a Harlem of monster parades and political flummery, a Harlem swept by revolutionary oratory or draped about the mysterious figures of Negro "millionaires," a Harlem pre-occupied with naive adjustments to a white world—a Harlem, in short, grotesque with the distortions of journalism.

Yet in final analysis, Harlem is neither slum, ghetto, resort or colony, though it is in part all of them. It is—or promises at least to be—a race capital. Europe seething in a dozen centers with emergent nationalities, Palestine full of a renascent Judaism—these are no more alive with the spirit of a racial awakening than Harlem; culturally and spiritually it focuses a people. Negro life is not only founding new centers, but finding a new soul. The tide of Negro migration, northward and city-ward, is not to be fully explained as a blind flood started by the demands of war industry coupled with the shutting off of foreign migration, or by the pressure of poor crops coupled with increased social terrorism in certain sections of the South and Southwest. Neither labor demand, the boll-weevil nor the Ku Klux Klan is a basic factor, however contributory any or all of them may have been. The wash and rush of this human tide on the beach line of the northern city centers is to be explained primarily in terms of a new vision of opportunity, of social and economic freedom of a spirit to seize, even in the face of an extortionate and heavy toll, a chance for the improvement of conditions. With each successive wave of it, the movement of the Negro migrant becomes more and more like that of the European waves at their crests, a mass movement toward the larger and the more democratic chance—in the Negro's case a deliberate flight not only from countryside to city, but from medieaval America to modern.

The secret lies close to what distinguishes Harlem from the ghettos with which it is sometimes compared. The ghetto picture is that of a slowly dissolving mass, bound by ties of custom and culture and association, in the midst of a freer and more varied society. From the racial standpoint, our Harlems are themselves crucibles. Here in Manhattan is not merely the largest Negro community in the world, but the first concentration in history of so many diverse elements of Negro life. It has attracted the African, the West Indian, the Negro American; has brought together the Negro of the North and the Negro of the South; the man from the city and the man from the town and village; the peasant, the student, the business man, the professional man, artist, poet, musician, adventurer and worker, preacher and criminal, exploiter and social outcast. Each group has come with its own separate motives and for its own special ends, but their greatest experience has been the finding of one another. Proscription and prejudice have thrown these dissimilar elements into a common area of contact and interaction. Within this area, race sympathy and unity have determined a further fusing of sentiment and experience. So what began in terms of segregation becomes more anymore, as its elements mix and react, the laboratory of a great race-welding. Hitherto, it must be admitted that American Negroes have been a race more in name than in fact, or to be exact, more in sentiment than in experience. The chief bond between them has been that of a common condition rather than a common consciousness; a problem in common rather than a life in common. In Harlem, Negro life is seizing upon

its first chances for group expression and self-determination. That is why our comparison is taken with those nascent centers of folk-expression and self-determination which are playing a creative part in the world today. Without pretense to their political significance, Harlem has the same role to play for the New Negro as Dublin has had for the New Ireland or Prague for the New Czechoslovakia.

It is true the formidable centers of our race life, educational, industrial, financial, are not in Harlem, yet here, nevertheless, are the forces that make a group known and felt in the world. The reformers, the fighting advocates, the inner spokesmen, the poets, artists and social prophets are here, and pouring in toward them are the fluid ambitious youth and pressing in upon them the migrant masses. The professional observers, and the enveloping communities as well, are conscious of the physics of this stir and movement, of the cruder and more obvious facts of a ferment and a migration. But they are as yet largely unaware of the psychology of it, of the galvanising shocks and reactions, which mark the social awakening and internal reorganization which are making a race out of its own disunited elements.

A railroad ticket and a suitcase, like a Bagdad carpet, transport the Negro peasant from the cotton-field and farm to the heart of the most complex urban civilization. Here in the mass, he must and does survive a jump of two generations in social economy and of a century and more in civilisation. Meanwhile the Negro poet, student, artist, thinker, by the very move that normally would take him off at a tangent from the masses, finds himself in their midst, in a situation concentrating the racial side of his experience and heightening his race-consciousness. These moving, half-awakened newcomers provide an exceptional seed-bed for the germinating contacts of the enlightened minority. And that is why statistics are out of joint with fact in Harlem, and will be for a generation or so.

Harlem, I grant you, isn't typical—but it is significant, it is prophetic. No sane observer, however sympathetic to the new trend, would contend that the great masses are articulate as yet, but they stir, they move, they are more than physically restless. The challenge of the new intellectuals among them is clear enough—the "race radicals" and realists who have broken with the old epoch of philanthropic guidance, sentimental appeal and protest. But are we after all only reading into the stirrings of a sleeping giant the dreams of an agitator? The answer is in the migrating peasant. It is the "man farthest down" who is most active in getting up. One of the most characteristic symptoms of this is the professional man himself migrating to recapture his constituency after a vain effort to maintain in some Southern corner what for years back seemed an established living and clientele. The clergyman following his errant flock, the physician or lawyer trailing his clients, supply the true clues. In a real sense it is the rank and file who are leading, and the leaders who are following. A transformed and transforming psychology permeates the masses.

When the racial leaders of twenty years ago spoke of developing race-pride and stimulating race-consciousness, and of the desirability of race solidarity, they could not in any accurate degree have anticipated the abrupt feeling that has surged up and now pervades the awakened centers. Some of the recognized Negro leaders and a powerful section of white opinion identified with "race work" of the older orderhave indeed attempted to discount this feeling as a "passing phase," an attack of "race nerves," so to speak, an "aftermath of the war," and the like. It has not abated, however, if we are to gage by the present tone and temper of the Negro press, or by the shift in popular support from the officially recognized and orthodox spokesmen to those of the independent, popular, and often radical type who are unmistakable symptoms of a new order. It is a social disservice to blunt the fact that the Negro of the Northern centers has reached a stage where tutelage, even of the most interested and well-intentioned sort, must give place to new relationships, where positive self-direction must be reckoned with in ever increasing measure.

As a service to this new understanding, the contributors to this Harlem number have been asked, not merely to describe Harlem as a city of migrants and as a race center, but to voice these new aspirations of a people, to read the clear message of the new conditions, and to discuss some of the new relationships and contacts they involve. First, we shall look at Harlem, with its kindred centers in the Northern and Mid-Western cities, as the way mark of a momentous folk movement; then as the center of a gripping struggle for an industrial and urban foothold. But more significant than either of these, we shall also view it as the stage of the pageant of contemporary Negro life. In the drama of its new and progressive aspects, we may be witnessing the resurgence of a race; with our eyes focussed on the Harlem scene we may dramatically glimpse the New Negro. A.L.

Further Resources

BOOKS

Harris, Leonard, ed. *The Philosophy of Alain Locke: Harlem Renaissance and Beyond.* Philadelphia: Temple University Press, 1989.

Hutchinson, George. *The Harlem Renaissance in Black and White.* Cambridge, Mass.: Belknap Press of Harvard University Press, 1995.

Lewis, David L. *When Harlem Was in Vogue.* New York: Knopf, 1981.

Locke, Alain Leroy. *The New Negro: An Interpretation.* New York: Arno Press, 1968.

WEBSITES

Alain L. Locke Society. Available online at http://www.alain-locke.com/ (accessed April 24, 2003)

Harris, Leonard. "Locke, Alain Leroy." *American National Biography Online.* Available online at http://www.anb.org/articles/20/20-00599.html; website home page: http://www.anb.org (accessed April 24, 2003).

Reuben, Paul P. "Chapter 9: Harlem Renaissance—Alaine Locke." *PAL: Perspectives in American Literature—a Research and Reference Guide.* Available online at http://www.csustan.edu/english/reuben/pal/chap9/locke.html; website home page: http://www.csustan.edu (accessed April 24, 2003).

"The Scopes Trial: Aftermath"

Editorial

By: H.L. Mencken

Date: September 14, 1925

Source: Mencken, H.L. "Aftermath" *Baltimore Evening Sun,* September 14, 1925. Available online at http://www.positiveatheism.org/hist/menck05.htm#SCOPESD; website home page: http://www.positiveatheism.org (accessed April 24, 2003).

About the Author: Henry Louis Mencken (1880–1956) emerged as one of the nation's most renowned and controversial social commentators. By age twenty-five, Mencken had risen from entry-level reporter to editor of the *Baltimore Herald*. His criticism of American social norms, and his support of Germany throughout the First World War, brought great criticism. During the war, magazines and newspapers that normally printed Mencken's reports censored him and refused to publish his work. Mencken refused to stop writing and began what would become a six-volume critique, often quite harsh, of American society and culture. Following the war, he returned to prominence by cofounding the *American Mercury* in 1923, which he edited until 1933. He continued to write until a series of strokes crippled him in 1948. ■

Journalist H.L. Mencken, famous for his biting commentary on the Scopes "Monkey Trial" and other news events. © BETTMANN/CORBIS. REPRODUCED BY PERMISSION.

Introduction

The government of Tennessee, in official support of Christian fundamentalist principles, passed the Butler Act in 1925. This law prohibited the teaching of evolutionary biology in the state's public schools. Eager to challenge the policy's constitutionality, the American Civil Liberties Union publicly promised to pay for the defense of any instructor willing to be arrested for teaching the banned material. John Scopes, only twenty-four years old, accepted the offer and soon faced trial for covering evolution in a high school biology class. William Jennings Bryan, three-time presidential candidate, former secretary of state, and the greatest orator of his age, was named special prosecutor. Clarence Darrow, the most renowned trial attorney in the country, joined the defense counsel. On July 21, within ten minutes of beginning deliberations, the jury returned with a guilty verdict, and the judge fined Scopes $100.

Significance

The Scopes trial suited Jazz Age journalism perfectly. The press competed wildly for the most salacious, striking, and, of course, sellable story. Even before the trial began on July 10, 1925, the Scopes case had evolved into a media circus. Scores of newspaper and radio reporters from across the country flooded into the small town of Dayton to cover the great showdown between Darrow and Bryan—and between creationism and evolutionism. Increasingly sensational reports, including live broadcasts, made the trial one of the most popularly followed events in American history. In the most famous courtroom exchange, Darrow called the ardently anti-evolutionist Bryan to the stand and humiliated him before a nationwide audience. The Scopes trial became legendary and eventually spawned a Broadway play later turned into a movie, *Inherit the Wind*, featuring Spencer Tracy as Darrow.

One of the most influential journalists of the 1920s, H. L. Mencken covered the Scopes trial for the *Baltimore Evening Sun*. His reports exploded with abrasive wit, sharp criticism, and a litany of diatribes against William Jennings Bryan and his supporters. Mencken labeled the case the "Monkey Trial," a title that pointedly linked the controversy over evolution with the author's ringing critique of the legal proceedings. While hundreds of reporters crammed the hot, humid Tennessee courtroom to provide breathless coverage of the trial, Mencken raised the stakes by focusing his stinging commentaries on the distinctly American cultural forces that created both the trial and the media frenzy that enveloped it.

Primary Source

"The Scopes Trial: Aftermath"

SYNOPSIS: "Aftermath," published two months after the trial, provided Mencken's reflections on the Scopes case and the media coverage it created. His final barrage spared virtually no one. He attacked Bryan, fundamentalist Christians, the South, and the liberal journals who criticized Darrow for being too harsh in his interrogation of Bryan. The fact that Bryan had died five days after the trial's conclusion did not suppress Mencken's wrath.

I

The Liberals, in their continuing discussion of the late trial of the infidel Scopes at Dayton, Tenn., run true to form. That is to say, they show all their habitual lack of humor and all their customary furtive weakness for the delusions of Homo neanderthalensis. I point to two of their most enlightened organs: the eminent New York World and the gifted New Republic. The World is displeased with Mr. Darrow because, in his appalling cross-examination of the mountebank Bryan, he did some violence to the theological superstitions that millions of Americans cherish. The New Republic denounces him because he addressed himself, not to "the people of Tennessee" but to the whole country, and because he should have permitted "local lawyers" to assume "the most conspicuous position in the trial."

Once more, alas, I find myself unable to follow the best Liberal thought. What the World's contention amounts to, at bottom, is simply the doctrine that a man engaged in combat with superstition should be very polite to superstition. This, I fear, is nonsense. The way to deal with superstition is not to be polite to it, but to tackle it with all arms, and so rout it, cripple it, and make it forever infamous and ridiculous. Is it, perchance, cherished by persons who should know better? Then their folly should be brought out into the light of day, and exhibited there in all its hideousness until they flee from it, hiding their heads in shame.

True enough, even a superstitious man has certain inalienable rights. He has a right to harbor and indulge his imbecilities as long as he pleases, provided only he does not try to inflict them upon other men by force. He has a right to argue for them as eloquently as he can, in season and out of season. He has a right to teach them to his children. But certainly he has no right to be protected against the free criticism of those who do not hold them. He has no right to demand that they be treated as sacred. He has no right to preach them without challenge. Did Darrow, in the course of his dreadful bombardment of Bryan, drop a few shells, incidentally, into measurably cleaner camps? Then let the garrisons of those camps look to their defenses. They are free to shoot back. But they can't disarm their enemy.

II

The meaning of religious freedom, I fear, is sometimes greatly misapprehended. It is taken to be a sort of immunity, not merely from governmental control but also from public opinion. A dunderhead gets himself a long-tailed coat, rises behind the sacred desk, and emits such bilge as would gag a Hottentot. Is it to pass unchallenged? If so, then what we have is not religious freedom at all, but the most intolerable and outrageous variety of religious despotism. Any fool, once he is admitted to holy orders, becomes infallible. Any half-wit, by the simple device of ascribing his delusions to revelation, takes on an authority that is denied to all the rest of us.

I do not know how many Americans entertain the ideas defended so ineptly by poor Bryan, but probably the number is very large. They are preached once a week in at least a hundred thousand rural churches, and they are heard too in the meaner quarters of the great cities. Nevertheless, though they are thus held to be sound by millions, these ideas remain mere rubbish. Not only are they not supported by the known facts; they are in direct contravention of the known facts. No man whose information is sound and whose mind functions normally can conceivably credit them. They are the products of ignorance and stupidity, either or both.

What should be a civilized man's attitude toward such superstitions? It seems to me that the only attitude possible to him is one of contempt. If he admits that they have any intellectual dignity whatever, he admits that he himself has none. If he pretends to a respect for those who believe in them, he pretends falsely, and sinks almost to their level. When he is challenged he must answer honestly, regardless of tender feelings. That is what Darrow did at Dayton, and the issue plainly justified the act. Bryan went there in a hero's shining armor, bent deliberately upon a gross crime against sense. He came out a wrecked and preposterous charlatan, his tail between his legs. Few Americans have ever done so much for their country in a whole lifetime as Darrow did in two hours.

III

The caveat of the New Republic is so absurd that it scarcely deserves an answer. It is based upon a complete misunderstanding of the situation that the Scopes trial revealed. What good would it have done to have addressed an appeal to the people of Tennessee? They had already, by their lawful representatives, adopted the anti-evolution statute by an immense majority, and they were plainly determined to uphold it. The newspapers of the State, with one or two exceptions, were violently in favor of the prosecution, and applauded every effort of the rustic judge and district attorney to deprive the defense of its most elemental rights.

True enough, there was a minority of Tennesseeans on the other side—men and women who felt keenly the disgrace of their State, and were eager to put an end to it. But their time had passed; they had missed their chance. They should have stepped forward at the very beginning, long before Darrow got into the case. Instead, they hung back timorously, and so Bryan and the Baptist pastors ran amok. There was a brilliant exception: John R. Neal. There was another: T.R. Elwell. Both lawyers. But the rest of the lawyers of the State, when the issue was joined at last, actually helped the prosecution. Their bar associations kept up a continuous fusillade. They tried their best to prod the backwoods Dogberry, Raulston, into putting Darrow into jail.

There was but one way to meet this situation and Darrow adopted it. He appealed directly to the country and to the world. He had at these recreant Tennesseeans by exhibiting their shame to all men, near and far. He showed them cringing before the rustic theologians, and afraid of Bryan. He turned the State inside out, and showed what civilization can come to under Fundamentalism. The effects of that cruel exposure are now visible. Tennessee is still spluttering—and blushing. The uproar staggered its people. And they are doing some very painful thinking. Will they cling to Fundamentalism or will they restore civilization? I suspect that the quick decision of their neighbor, Georgia, will help them to choose. Darrow did more for them, in two weeks, than all their pastors and politicians had done since the Civil War.

IV

His conduct of the case, in fact, was adept and intelligent from beginning to end. It is hard, in retrospect, to imagine him improving it. He faced immense technical difficulties. In order to get out of the clutches of the village Dogberry and before judges of greater intelligence he had to work deliberately for the conviction of his client. In order to evade the puerile question of that client's guilt or innocence and so bring the underlying issues before the country, he had to set up a sham battle on the side lines. And in order to expose the gross ignorance and superstition of the real prosecutor, Bryan, he had to lure the old imposter upon the stand.

It seems to me that he accomplished all of these things with great skill. Scopes was duly convicted, and the constitutional questions involved in the law will now be heard by competent judges and decided without resort to prayer and moving pictures. The whole world has been made familiar with the issues, and the nature of the menace that Fundamentalism offers to civilization is now familiar to every schoolboy. And Bryan was duly scotched, and, if he had lived, would be standing before the country today as a comic figure, tattered and preposterous.

All this was accomplished, in infernal weather, by a man of sixty-eight, with the scars of battles all over him. He had, to be sure, highly competent help. At his table sat lawyers whose peculiar talents, in combination, were of the highest potency—the brilliant Hays, the eloquent Malone, the daring and patriotic Tennesseean, Neal. But it was Darrow who carried the main burden, and Darrow who shaped the final result. When he confronted Bryan at last, the whole combat came to its climax. On the one side was bigotry, ignorance, hatred, superstition, every sort of blackness that the human mind is capable of. On the other side was sense. And sense achieved a great victory.

Further Resources

BOOKS

Fitzpatrick, Vincent. *H.L. Mencken.* New York: Continuum, 1989.

Hobson, Fred. *Mencken: A Life.* New York: Random House, 1994.

Manchester, William. *Disturber of the Press: The Life of H.L. Mencken.* New York: Harper, 1951.

Mencken, H.L. *The Diary of H.L. Mencken.* New York: Knopf, 1989.

———. *My Life as Author and Editor.* New York: Knopf, 1992.

WEBSITES

Hobson, Fred Hobson. "Mencken, H.L." *American National Biography Online.* Available online at http://www.anb.org/articles/16/16-01120.html; website home page: http://www.anb.org (accessed April 24, 2003).

AUDIO AND VISUAL MEDIA

Inherit the Wind. Directed by Stanley Kramer. MGM. Videocassette. 1960.

"The Four Horsemen"

Newspaper article

By: Grantland Rice

Date: October 19, 1924

Source: Rice, Grantland. "The Four Horsemen." *New York Herald-Tribune,* October 19, 1924. Available online at http://lamb.archives.nd.edu/rockne/rice.html; website home page: http://lamb.archives.nd.edu (accessed April 24, 2003).

About the Author: Henry Grantland Rice (1880–1954), from an early age, exhibited both a love of sport and a gift for language. After graduating from Vanderbilt University, Rice began reporting stints at several metropolitan dailies before gaining a nationally syndicated column at the *New York Tribune* in 1914. As the nation's most influential sports journalist, he selected the All-American football team for *Collier's* magazine from 1925 until shortly before his death. As a radio broadcaster, he covered the World Series and many other sporting events. Prolific in all media, Rice even won two Academy Awards for his sports short films. He continues to be remembered as the author of the famous lines, "When the Great Scorer comes / To mark against your name, / He'll write not 'won' or 'lost' / But how you played the game." ∎

Introduction

The essay "The Four Horsemen" (and its creation of the moniker of the same name to represent four football players) exhibits why Grantland Rice remains in the pantheon of sportswriters, but the story also reveals the extent to which sports had begun to dominate American popular culture by the 1920s. In the midst of a boisterous economy and public displays of youthful exuberance, spectator sports exploded to unforeseen heights during the decade. The Roaring Twenties ushered in a new period of popular culture and mass entertainment, especially regarding the emergence of spectator sports. The news media, which had covered sporting events for decades, greatly expanded its coverage of sports. These developments included the first national radio broadcasts of sporting events, primarily boxing and baseball. The relative economic prosperity of the era meant that more Americans could afford to pay to attend a boxing match, baseball game, or football contest. In addition, with more people working an increasingly common forty-hour work week, weekend sporting events such as college football rose in popularity.

For millions, the Roaring Twenties represented a time to focus attention away from international conflict and the domestic turbulence of World War I (1914–1918). Americans attempted to recover some sense of what President Warren G. Harding (served 1921–1923) described as "normalcy" in their daily lives following the end of the Great War. Writers such as Grantland Rice, though, seemed to have capitalized on the public's remembrance of war, religious consciousness, and desire for drama.

Significance

"The Four Horsemen," similar to much of Rice's writing of the period, provides its audience with a spectacle of apocalyptic proportions. Molding religious and military symbols, Rice portrayed the Notre Dame vs. Army game of 1924 as a life-or-death struggle between good and evil. The story's lead remains perhaps the most famous in sports journalism: "Outlined against a blue-gray October sky, the Four Horsemen rode again." Making no mistake that he intended to convey the ultimate grandeur of the affair, Rice continued: "In dramatic lore they are known as Famine, Pestilence, Destruction and Death. These are only aliases. Their real names are Stuhldreher, Miller, Crowley and Layden." Without a drop of parody, Rice altered the biblical symbols of the end of the world to become the backfield of the Notre Dame University football team.

Rice never lapses in his depiction of the game as an event of immense consequence. "It was in vain that 1,400 gray-clad cadets pleaded for the Army line to hold. The Army line was giving all it had, but when a tank tears in with the speed of a motorcycle, what chance had flesh and blood to hold?" Considering Rice's wartime experience serving at the western front, it is no surprise that this report seems reminiscent of battle coverage from Verdun or the Somme less than a decade before. Rather than turning off his audience, Rice attracted a greater following precisely because his writing provided a sense of importance to leisure activities. Perhaps the fascination with Rice's commentary provides a sense of restlessness within American society—the war was over, but battles, however small, still needed to be fought and won.

Primary Source

"The Four Horsemen" [excerpt]

> **SYNOPSIS:** Grantland Rice treated the Notre Dame football team's 13-7 victory over Army in 1924 not as mere college football but as a contest of epic proportions. The opening and closing sentences cemented Rice's stature as the Bard of American sports journalism. With his emphasis on the human drama of sport, Grantland Rice remains an influential icon.

Polo Grounds, New York, Oct. 19, 1924—Outlined against a blue-gray October sky, the Four Horsemen rode again. In dramatic lore they are known as Famine, Pestilence, Destruction and Death. These are only aliases. Their real names are Stuhldreher, Miller, Crowley and Layden. They formed the crest of the South Bend cyclone before which another fighting Army football team was swept over the precipice at the Polo Grounds yesterday afternoon as 55,000 spectators peered down on the bewildering panorama spread on the green plain below.

A cyclone can't be snared. It may be surrounded, but somewhere it breaks through to keep on going. When the cyclone starts from South Bend, where the candle lights still gleam through the Indiana sycamores, those in the way must take to storm cellars at top speed.

Yesterday the cyclone struck again as Notre Dame beat the Army, 13 to 7, with a set of backfield stars that ripped and crashed through a strong Army defense with more speed and power than the warring cadets could meet.

Notre Dame won its ninth game in twelve Army starts through the driving power of one of the greatest backfields that ever churned up the turf of any gridiron in any football age. Brilliant backfields may come and go, but in Stuhldreher, Miller, Crowley and Layden, covered by a fast and charging line, Notre Dame can take its place in front of the field.

Coach McEwan sent one of his finest teams into action, an aggressive organization that fought to the last play around the first rim of darkness, but when Rockne rushed his Four Horsemen to the track they rode down everything in sight. It was in vain that 1,400 gray-clad cadets pleaded for the Army line to hold. The Army line was giving all it had, but when a tank tears in with the speed of a motorcycle, what chance had flesh and blood to hold? The Army had its share of stars as Garbisch, Farwick, Wilson, Wood, Ellinger, and many others, but they were up against four whirlwind backs who picked up at top speed from the first step as they swept through scant openings to slip on by the secondary defense. The Army had great backs in Wilson and Wood, but the Army had no such quartet, who seemed to carry the mixed blood of the tiger and the antelope.

Rockne's light and tottering line was just about as tottering as the Rock of Gibraltar. It was something more than a match for the Army's great set of forwards, who had earned their fame before. Yet it was not until the second period that the first big thrill of the afternoon set the great crowd into a cheering whirl and brought about the wild flutter of flags that are thrown to the wind in exciting moments. At the game's start Rockne sent in almost entirely a second-string cast. The Army got the jump and began to play most of the football. It was the Army attack that made three first downs before Notre Dame had caught its stride. The South Bend cyclone opened like a zephyr.

And then, in the wake of a sudden cheer, our rushed Stuhldreher, Miller, Crowley and Layden, the four star backs who helped to beat Army a year ago. Things were to be a trifle different now. After a short opening flurry in the second period, Wood, of the Army, kicked out of bounds on Notre Dame's 20 yard line. There was no sign of a tornado starting. But it happened to be at just this spot that Stuhldreher decided to put on his attack and began the long and dusty hike.

On the first play the fleet Crowley peeled off fifteen yards and the cloud from the west was now beginning to show signs of lightning and thunder. The fleet, powerful Layden got six yards more and then Don Miller added ten. A forward pass from Stuhldreher to Crowley added twelve yards, and a moment later Don Miller ran twenty yards around Army's right wing. He was on his way to glory when Wilson, hurtling across the right of way, nailed him on the 10 yard line and threw him out of bounds. Crowley, Miller and Layden—Miller, Layden and Crowley—one or another, ripping and crashing through, as the Army defense threw everything it had in the way to stop this wild charge that had now come seventy yards. Crowley and Layden added five yards more and then, on a split play, Layden when ten yards across the line as if he had just been fired from the black mouth of a howitzer.

In that second period Notre Dame made eight first downs to the Army's none, which shows the unwavering power of the Western attack that hammered relentlessly and remorselessly without easing up for a second's breath. The Western line was going its full share, led by the crippled Walsh with a broken hand.

But there always was Miller or Crowley or Layden, directed through the right spot by the cool and crafty judgment of Stuhldreher, who picked his plays with the finest possible generalship. The South Bend cyclone had now roared eighty-five yards to a touchdown through one of the strongest defensive teams in the game. The cyclone had struck with too much speed and power to be stopped. It was the preponderance of Western speed that swept the Army back.

The next period was much like the second. The trouble began when the alert Layden intercepted an Army pass on the 48 yard line. Stuhldreher was ready for another march.

Once again the cheering cadets began to call for a rallying stand. They are never overwhelmed by any shadow of defeat as long as there is a minute of fighting left. But silence fell over the cadet sector

The Four Horsemen, from left to right: Don Miller, Elmer Layden, Jim Crowley, and Harry Stuhldreher. The group led Notre Dame to the national collegiate football championship in 1924. This photo helped build on the budding legend created by Grantland Rice by showing the Notre Dame backs posed on horseback. AP/WIDE WORLD PHOTOS. REPRODUCED BY PERMISSION.

for just a second as Crowley ran around the Army's right wing for 15 yards, where Wilson hauled him down on the 33 yard line. Walsh, the Western captain, was hurt in the play but soon resumed. Miller got 7 and Layden got 8 and then, with the ball on the Army's 20 yard line, the cadet defense rallied and threw Miller in his tracks. But the halt was only for the moment. On the next play Crowley swung out and around the Army's left wing, cut in and then crashed over the line for Notre Dame's second touchdown.

On two other occasions the Notre Dame attack almost scored. Yeomans saved one touchdown by intercepting a pass on his 5 yard line as he ran back 35 yards before he was nailed by two tacklers. It was a great play in the nick of time. On the next

drive Miller and Layden in two hurricane dashes took the ball 42 yards to the Army's 14 yard line, where the still game Army defense stopped four plunges on the 9 yard line and took the ball.

Up to this point the Army had been outplayed by a crushing margin. Notre Dame had put underway four long marches and two of these had yielded touchdowns. Even the stout and experienced Army line was meeting more than it could hold. Notre Dame's brilliant backs had been provided with the finest possible interference, usually led by Stuhldreher, who cut down tackler after tackler by diving at some rival's flying knees. Against this, each Army attack had been smothered almost before it got underway. Even the great Wilson, the star from Penn State, one of the great backfield runners of his day

Sportswriter Grantland Rice, right, speaks with Bernard Darwin of the *London Times* at a golf match in 1919. **REPRINTED FROM GRANTLAND RICE, *THE TUMULT AND THE SHOUTING*. BARNES AND COMPANY, 1954.**

and time, rarely had a chance to make any headway through a massed wall of tacklers who were blocking every open route.

The sudden change came late in the third quarter, when Wilson, raging like a wild man, suddenly shot through a tackle opening to run 34 yards before he was finally collared and thrown with a jolt. A few minutes later Wood, one of the best of all punters, kicked out of bounds on Notre Dame's 5 yard line. Here was the chance. Layden was forced to kick from behind his own goal. The punt soared up the field as Yeomans called for a free catch on the 35 yard line. As he caught the ball he was nailed and spilled by a Western tackler, and the penalty gave the Army 15 yards, with the ball on Notre Dame's 20-yard line.

At this point Harding was rushed to quarter in place of Yeomans, who had been one of the leading Army stars. On the first three plays the Army reached the 12 yard line, but it was now fourth down, with two yards to go. Harding's next play was the feature of the game.

As the ball was passed, he faked a play to Wood, diving through the line, held the oval for just a half breath, then, tucking the same under his arm, swung out around Notre Dame's right end. The bril-

liant fake worked to perfection. The entire Notre Dame defense had charged forward in a surging mass to check the line attack and Harding, with open territory, sailed on for a touchdown. He traveled those last 12 yards after the manner of food shot from guns. He was over the line before the Westerners knew what had taken place. It was a fine bit of strategy, brilliantly carried over by every member of the cast.

The cadet sector had a chance to rip open the chilly atmosphere at last, and most of the 55,000 present joined in the tribute to football art. But that was Army's last chance to score. From that point on, it was seesaw, up and down, back and forth, with the rivals fighting bitterly for every inch of ground. It was harder now to make a foot than it had been to make ten yards. Even the all-star South Bend cast could no longer continue to romp for any set distances, as Army tacklers, inspired by the touchdown, charged harder and faster than they had charged before.

The Army brought a fine football team into action, but it was beaten by a faster and smoother team. Rockne's supposedly light, green line was about as heavy as Army's, and every whit as aggressive. What is even more important, it was faster on its feet, faster in getting around.

It was Western speed and perfect interference that once more brought the Army doom. The Army line couldn't get through fast enough to break up the attacking plays; and once started, the bewildering speed and power of the Western backs slashed along for 8, 10, and 15 yards on play after play. And always in front of these offensive drivers could be found the whirling form of Stuhldreher, taking the first man out of the play as cleanly as though he had used a hand grenade at close range. This Notre Dame interference was a marvelous thing to look upon.

It formed quickly and came along in unbroken order, always at terrific speed, carried by backs who were as hard to drag down as African buffaloes. On receiving the kick-off, Notre Dame's interference formed something after the manner of the ancient flying wedge, and they drove back up the field with the runner covered from 25 and 30 yards at almost every chance. And when a back such as Harry Wilson finds few chances to get started, you can figure upon the defensive strength that is barricading the road. Wilson is one of the hardest backs in the game to suppress, but he found few chances yesterday to

Notre Dame Football

In the fall of 1910, Knute Rockne, son of Norwegian immigrants who had settled in Chicago, enrolled at the University of Notre Dame as a twenty-two-year-old freshman. He was older than most of his classmates and a Protestant at a Catholic institution, but his work ethic and football skills enabled him to fit well with the university. After graduating in 1914, he stayed at Notre Dame as a chemistry assistant and assistant football coach under his old coach, Jess Harper. When Harper retired in 1918, Rockne became the head coach. From then until his death in 1931, Notre Dame was the best-known football team in the United States. Rockne was a great motivator and speaker, and he crisscrossed the country in the off-season giving inspirational talks and recruiting for Notre Dame. Harper had begun to modify Notre Dame's schedule to include more recognized football powers and fewer regional small schools. Playing Army, Purdue, Nebraska, and Michigan gave Notre Dame's football program more credibility. By 1921, the Irish had a strong schedule and went 10-1, losing only to Iowa in an upset. In 1922 Rockne unveiled a backfield of four talented and swift players: Elmer Layden from Davenport, Iowa; Don Miller of Defiance, Ohio; Jim Crowley of Green Bay, Wisconsin; and Harry Stuhldreher of Massillon, Ohio. The players did not play together all the time in the same backfield until 1924, the year they earned their collective nickname courtesy of Grantland Rice. In that year, they faced Army in a game that had grown to one of the top rivalries in college football. Before weekly ratings polls and television, few games generated as much interest as the Notre Dame–Army contest.

Under Rockne, Notre Dame football developed not only legions of alumni admirers but also so-called subway alumni, that is, people who were devoted Notre Dame rooters but had never set foot on campus or, for that matter, possibly any college campus. Rockne made Notre Dame football the pride of all Catholics, not just Irish Catholics—even though many of the players were Protestant or, in some cases, Jewish. Grantland Rice attended the Army–Notre Dame games regularly, and his accounts of the games were read beyond New York and the *New York Herald Tribune*. By defeating one of the finest Army teams in recent years, Notre Dame established a reputation that only continued to grow. Notre Dame and college football excellence were forever entwined, and the names of Rockne, the Four Horsemen, Johnny Lujack, Frank Leahy, Ara Parseghian, Terry Hanratty, Joe Montana, and many others became part of American football lore. The Four Horsemen led the first of Rockne's and Notre Dame's national championship teams to an undefeated season. The Army game in 1924 was also one of the first to be broadcast on radio. Rockne's teams would go without a loss or tie in five different seasons. Two national championships followed in 1929 and 1930. The success of this team helped raise money for a new stadium completed in 1930. Notre Dame Stadium, with the university library's "Touchdown Jesus" mosaic overlooking the north end zone, is arguably the best-known college stadium in the country. The Four Horsemen and Rockne have become the stuff of legend, and the story by Rice created and solidified their significance in the sports pantheon of the 1920s and beyond.

show his broken-field ability. You can't run through a broken field unless you get there.

One strong feature of the Army play was its headlong battle against heavy odds. Even when Notre Dame had scored two touchdowns and was well on its way to a third, the Army fought on with fine spirit until the touchdown chance came at last. And when the chance came, Coach McEwan had the play ready for the final march across the line. The Army has a better team than it had last year. So has Notre Dame. We doubt that any team in the country could have beaten Rockne's array yesterday afternoon, East or West. It was a great football team brilliantly directed, a team of speed, power and team play. The Army has no cause to gloom over its showing. It played first-class football against more speed than it could match.

Those who have tackled a cyclone can understand.

Further Resources

BOOKS

Camerer, Dave, ed. *The Best of Grantland Rice.* New York: Franklin Watts, 1963.

Fountain, Charles. *Sportswriter: The Life and Times of Grantland Rice.* New York: Oxford University Press, 1993.

Inabinett, Mark. *Grantland Rice and His Heroes: The Sportswriter as Mythmaker in the 1920s.* Westport, Conn.: Praeger, 1995.

Rice, Grantland. *The Tumult and the Shouting: My Life in Sport.* New York: AS Barnes, 1954.

PERIODICALS

"Grantland Rice." Obituary of Grantland Rice. *The New York Times,* July 14, 1954.

WEBSITES

Brattain, Michelle. "Rice, Grantland." *American National Biography Online.* Available online at http://www.anb.org/articles/19/19-00175.html; website home page: http://www.anb.org (accessed April 24, 2003).

Radio Act of 1927
Law

By: U.S. Congress

Date: February 23, 1927

Source: U.S. Congress. *Radio Act of 1927*. Public Law No. 632, 69th Congress, February 23, 1927. Available online at http://www.geocities.com/a_h_kline/1927act.htm; website home page: http://www.geocities.com (accessed April 24, 2003). ∎

Introduction

With the public broadcast of a program at the Metropolitan Opera House in New York City in January 1910, the era of radio began. World War I (1914–1918) stymied the industry's growth, as civilian radio broadcasts were suspended. Only a handful of stations operated in the years immediately after the war. The relative economic prosperity of the 1920s created the first commercial programs and the installation of hundreds of radio stations nationwide. By the end of the decade, the majority of Americans enjoyed hours of radio programming every day. Radio provided the unprecedented ability to hear music programs, news reports, and sporting events as they transpired miles away. The growing popular appeal of radio spawned a multimillion-dollar industry based upon the sending and receiving of broadcast signals, as well as the marketing of commercial time on expanding radio networks.

The first nationwide network, the National Broadcasting Company (NBC), was formed through the connection of twenty-four stations in 1926. The Radio Corporation of America (RCA), which produced "radio receiving sets," announced its establishment with a bold proclamation that signified radio's status and nearly infinite possibility for growth. RCA noted that five million homes already owned radios and twenty-one million possessed the technology (namely electricity) to use radio. By creating NBC, RCA shrewdly maneuvered to control a nationwide network whose programs would increase Americans' desire to purchase radios produced primarily by RCA. The Columbia Broadcasting System (CBS) began operations in 1928 and linked forty-nine stations by the beginning of 1929. NBC, CBS, and ABC (formed by the division of two NBC networks) dominated radio and television broadcasting in the United States for the rest of the century.

Significance

The *Radio Act of 1927* represented the federal government's attempt to take control of the radio industry. The *Radio Act* attempted to streamline radio communications and resolve interference problems that plagued the industry. The law provided the government with the power to grant licenses that granted "individuals, firms, or corporations" the right to transmit radio signals. This meant that only federal authorities controlled the airwaves and thus prohibited any unsanctioned radio transmission. The act established the Federal Radio Commission (FRC) as the agency that would create and police regulatory guidelines for all broadcasting in the United States. The five-member FRC governed radio channels and granted temporary access, initially three-year licenses, to stations as it saw fit.

Two months after the *Radio Act's* passage, the American Telephone & Telegraph Company (AT&T) successfully demonstrated the first long-distance television broadcast. This event foreshadowed a new dimension of communications that the government would struggle to control in the coming decades.

Primary Source

Radio Act of 1927 [excerpt]

SYNOPSIS: Passed on February 23, 1927, the *Radio Act* established the fundamental structure of federal regulations that would govern the radio industry to the present day. In the midst of the unprecedented expansion of radio broadcasting across the country, the U.S. Congress set the following guidelines for radio communications. Perhaps the most important section of the law featured the creation of the Federal Radio Commission (FRC). Congress, like much of the country, was inexperienced in dealing with this new technology and recognized the likelihood of unforeseen changes in the burgeoning industry. Thus, the FRC received somewhat vague guidelines for its operation.

Public Law No. 632, February 23, 1927, 69th Congress. An Act for the regulation of radio communications, and for other purposes.

Be it enacted by the Senate and House of Representatives of the United States of America in Congress assembled,

That this Act is intended to regulate all forms of interstate and foreign radio transmissions and communications within the United States, its Territories and possessions; to maintain the control of the United States over all the channels of interstate and foreign radio transmission; and to provide for the use of such channels, but not the ownership thereof, by individuals, firms, or corporations, for limited periods of time, under licenses granted by Federal authority, and no such license shall be construed to create any right, beyond the terms, conditions, and periods of the license. . . .

SEC. 3. That a commission is hereby created and established to be known as the Federal Radio Commission, hereinafter referred to as the commission, which shall be composed of five commissioners appointed by the President, by and with the advice and consent of the Senate, and one of whom the President shall designate as chairman: *Provided,* That chairmen thereafter elected shall be chosen by the commission itself. . . .

SEC. 4. Except as otherwise provided in this Act, the commission, from time to time, as public convenience, interest, or necessity requires, shall—

(a) Classify radio stations;

(b) Prescribe the nature of the service to be rendered by each class of licensed stations and each station within any class;

(c) Assign bands of frequencies or wave lengths to the various classes of stations, and assign frequencies or wave lengths for each individual station and determine the power which each station shall use and the time during which it may operate;

(d) Determine the location of classes of stations or individual stations;

(e) Regulate the kind of apparatus to be used with respect to its external effects and the purity and sharpness of the emissions from each station and from the apparatus therein;

(f) Make such regulations not inconsistent with law as it may deem necessary to prevent interference between stations and to carry out the provisions of this Act: *Provided, however,* That changes in the wave lengths, authorized power, in the character of emitted signals, or in the times of operation of any station, shall not be made without the consent of the station licensee unless, in the judgment of the commission, such changes will promote public convenience or interest or will serve public necessity or the provisions of this Act will be more fully complied with;

(g) Have authority to establish areas or zones to be served by any station;

(h) Have authority to make special regulations applicable to radio stations engaged in chain broadcasting;

(i) Have authority to make general rules and regulations requiring stations to keep such records of programs, transmissions of energy, communications, or signals as it may deem desirable;

(j) Have authority to exclude from the requirements of any regulations in whole or in part any ra-

From left to right, vice president of radio station WJZ, David Sarnoff; head of the National Broadcasting Company (NBC), M.H. Aylesworth; and chairman of General Electric, Owen Young participate in the first NBC broadcast, November 15, 1926. © **BETTMANN/CORBIS. REPRODUCED BY PERMISSION.**

dio station upon railroad rolling stock, or to modify such regulations in its discretion;

(k) Have authority to hold hearings, summon witnesses, administer oaths, compel the production of books, documents, and papers and to make such investigations as may be necessary in the performance of its duties. The commission may make such expenditures (including expenditures for rent and personal services at the seat of government and elsewhere, for law books, periodicals, and books of reference, and for printing and binding) as may be necessary for the execution of the functions vested in the commission and, as from time to time may be appropriated for by Congress. All expenditures of the commission shall be allowed and paid upon the presentation of itemized vouchers therefor approved by the chairman.

Further Resources

BOOKS

Archer, Gleason L. *History of Radio to 1926.* New York: Arno/New York Times, 1971.

Barnouw, Erik. *A Tower of Babel,* vol. 1. New York: Oxford University Press, 1966.

Emery, Michael, and Edwin Emery. *The Press and America: An Interpretive History of the Mass Media,* 7th ed. Englewood Cliffs, N.J.: Prentice Hall, 1992.

WEBSITES

Federal Radio Commission Archives home page. Available online at http://www.oswego.edu/~messere/FRCpage.html; website home page: http://www.oswego.edu (accessed April 24, 2003).

"United States Early Radio History." Available online at http://earlyradiohistory.us/ (accessed April 24, 2003).

AUDIO AND VISUAL MEDIA

Empire of the Air: The Men Who Made Radio. PBS Video. Videocassette. 1991.

"Far-Off Speakers Seen as Well as Heard Here in Test of Television"

Newspaper article

By: *The New York Times*

Date: April 8, 1927

Source: "Far-Off Speakers Seen as Well as Heard Here in Test of Television." *The New York Times,* April 8, 1927. Available online at http://www.att.com/spotlight/television /nytimes_article.html; website home page: http://www.att.com (accessed April 24, 2003). ∎

Introduction

Although television would not rival radio in nationwide popularity until after World War II (1939–1945), the development of technologies necessary for both broadcasting media overlapped at the turn of the century. The first radio broadcast occurred in San Jose, California, in 1908, and the first public radio broadcasts began in 1920. The ensuing decade witnessed the development of hundreds of radio stations. In the midst of the explosion of

radio broadcasting during the decade, scientists conducted the first successful television transmissions in 1925.

Herbert Eugene Ives (1882–1953) invented and developed the technology used to televise moving images over long distances. Working at Bell Telephone Laboratories (BTL) in the 1920s, Ives experimented with photoelectric cells. He pursued this research to develop cells that could convert light readings into electric current and thereby transmit pictures over telephone lines. The physicist and inventor directed the first long-distance television broadcast, from Washington, D.C., to New York City, in 1927. Two years later, Ives and his colleagues transmitted moving images in color at the same locations. Elected to the National Academy of Sciences in 1933, Ives received more than a hundred patents for his innovations in physics and television technology.

Herbert Hoover's image, if not his voice, already possessed great notoriety by 1927. The future president of the United States (1929–1933) first gained international acclaim as the director of relief operations in Europe during World War I (1914–1918). Following the conflict, both political parties wooed Hoover for the 1920 presidential race. He opted for service as secretary of commerce from 1921 to 1928 in the administrations of Warren G. Harding (served 1921–1923) and Calvin Coolidge (served 1923–1929). Hoover directed the expansion of government regulation of the young broadcasting industries of radio and television. It was in this capacity that he participated in the first long-distance television broadcast on April 7, 1927.

Significance

The following article reported this transmission of moving images with sound the next day. The story's length and tone conveyed the significance of the demonstration. Although the transmission appears rudimentary by modern standards, the ability to transmit both visual and audio information marked a cornerstone in scientific and cultural history. The black-and-white visage of Secretary Hoover appeared on a screen only two inches by three inches in size. As the reporter described, television's nearly instantaneous presentation of moving pictures and sound accompaniment eliminated "time as well as space."

The importance of television in the twentieth century remains impossible to overestimate. The 1927 transmission ushered in a new era in history. In incalculable ways, television broadcasting changed the fundamental nature of human interaction. By the end of the following year, fifteen television stations had received operating licenses. Herbert Hoover became president less than two years after his starring role in the first television broadcast. But the Great Depression that ensued shortly after his tenure began hindered television's advancement. By the end of the 1930s, except for Chicago and New York

Secretary of Commerce Herbert Hoover participates in the first live television broadcast from Washington, to New York City. Behind him are government officials and executives of AT&T and Chesapeake and Potomac Telephone Co., 1927. **HULTON/ARCHIVE. REPRODUCED BY PERMISSION.**

City, virtually all of the United States remained outside the range of television transmissions. Television technology came at a price, with potential buyers unable to afford TVs priced higher than some automobiles. Although the Federal Communications Commission allowed commercial broadcasting in 1941, American entry into World War II again halted television's development. By 1946, only nine TV stations operated nationwide. The post–World War II economic boom aided television's expansion, much as radio benefited from the post–World War I prosperity of the Roaring Twenties.

Primary Source

"Far-Off Speakers Seen as Well as Heard Here in Test of Television"

> **SYNOPSIS:** The article's subtitle, "Like a Photo Come to Life," conveys the fascination of observers with the transmission of Herbert Hoover's image from Washington, D.C., to New York City on April 7, 1927. In fact, the screen used to display the commerce secretary was about half the size of a modern photographic print. The reporter expressed a sense of awe at the visual and audio presentation, and the article conveys a sense of wonder and amazement that millions of people would one day experience.

Herbert Hoover made a speech in Washington yesterday afternoon. An audience in New York heard him and saw him.

More than 200 miles of space intervening between the speaker and his audience was annihilated by the television apparatus developed by the Bell Laboratories of the American Telephone and Telegraph Company and demonstrated publicly for the first time yesterday.

The apparatus shot images of Mr. Hoover by wire from Washington to New York at the rate of eighteen a second. These were thrown on a screen as motion pictures, while the loudspeaker reproduced the speech. As each syllable was heard, the motion of the speaker's lips and his changes of expression were flashed on the screen in the demonstration room of the Bell Telephone Laboratories at 55 Bethune Street.

When the television pictures were thrown on a screen two by three inches, the likeness was excellent. It was as if a photograph had suddenly come to life and begun to talk, smile and nod its head and look this way and that. When the screen was enlarged to two by three feet, the results were not so good.

Phone Hides His Face

At times the face of the Secretary could not be clearly distinguished. He looked down, as he read his speech, and held the telephone receiver up, so that it covered most of the lower part of his countenance. There was too much illumination also in the background of the screen. When he moved his face, his features became clearly distinguishable. Near the close of his talk he turned his head to one side, and in profile his features became clear and full of detail.

On the smaller screen the face and action were reproduced with perfect fidelity.

After Mr. Hoover had spoken, Vice President J.J. Carty of the American Telephone and Telegraph Company and others in the demonstration room at Washington took his place and conversed one at a time with men in New York. The speaker on the New York end looked the Washington man in the eye, as he talked to him. On the small screen before him appeared the living face of the man to whom he was talking.

Time as well as space was eliminated. Secretary Hoover's New York hearers and spectators were something like a thousandth part of a second later than the person at his side in hearing him and in seeing changes of countenance.

The faces and voices were projected from Washington by wire. It was shown a few minutes later, however, that radio does just as well.

Similar Test by Wireless

In the second part of the program, the group in New York saw and heard performances in the Whippany studio of the American Telephone and Telegraph Company by wireless. The first face flashed on the screen from Whippany, N.J., was that of E.L. Nelson, an engineer, who gave a technical description of what was taking place. Mr. Nelson had a good television face. He screened well as he talked.

Next came a vaudeville act by radio from Whippany. A. Dolan, a comedian. The loudspeaker part went over very well. It was the first vaudeville act that ever went on the air as a talking picture and in its possibilities it may be compared with the Fred Ott sneeze of more than thirty years ago, the first piece of comedy ever recorded in motion pictures. For the commercial future of television, if it has one, is thought to be largely in public entertainment—super-news reels flashed before audiences at the moment of occurrence, together with dramatic and musical acts

shot on the ether waves in sound and picture at the instant they are taking place at the studio.

The next number from the studio at Whippany was a regular radio program piece—a short humorous dialect talk by Mrs. H.A. Frederick of Mountain Lakes. Before and between the acts the announcer of the Whippany studio made a motion picture appearance. He was seen as well as heard.

Phone Girl Is Seen, Too

In the Washington part of the demonstration the telephone girl was visible. She appeared on the miniature screen and asked to whom the caller wished to talk. This one was a good-looking girl with fluffy hair, and as cool and efficient as if she had been at the television-telephone switchboard all her life.

A coincidence is that "Metropolis," the German film now showing what purports to be the New York of a century or centuries hence, has a make-believe screen in connection with the telephone—a case of prophecy being fulfilled about as soon as it started.

The demonstration of combined telephone and television, in fact, is one that outruns the imagination of all the wizards of prophecy. It is one of the few things that Leonardo da Vinci, Roger Bacon, Jules Verne and other masters of forecasting failed utterly to anticipate. Even interpreters of the Bible are having trouble in finding a passage which forecast television. H.G. Wells did not rise to it in his earlier crystal-gazing. It is only within the last few years that prophets have been busy in this field. Science has moved ahead so rapidly in this particular line that one of the men, who played a major part in developing the television apparatus shown yesterday, was of the opinion four years ago that research on this subject was hopeless. More than twenty years ago, however, Dr. Alexander Graham Bell, the inventor of the telephone, predicted at a gathering in the tower of the Times Building that the day would come when the man at the telephone would be able to see the distant person to whom he was speaking.

Light Squares Put on Wire

The demonstration began yesterday afternoon at 2:15 with General Carty at the television apparatus in Washington. As he held the transmitter in his hand and talked the light of an arc lamp flickered on his face. Small circles of light were moving across his face, one after another, but they were traveling at such high speed that they seemed to bathe his face in a uniform bluish light. By a complicated process these lights were dividing his face into a telegraph signal from Washington to New York. Here, with inconceivable rapidity, these squares were assembled as a mosaic. Each square differs in its amount of illumination. These differences of illumination traced the countenance in light and shadow and registered the least changes of expression. The squares rushed across the wire from Washington at the rate of 45,000 a second. The face was done over every eighteenth part of a second. About 2,500 squares—or "units," as they are called—make up each picture.

As General Carty talked his face was thus dissected by light in Washington and reconstructed on the small screen in New York. President Walter S. Gifford of the American Telephone and Telegraph Company was on the New York end of the wire.

"How do you do, General? You are looking well," said Mr. Gifford.

The face of General Carty smiled and his voice inquired after the health of the speaker on the New York end.

"I am instructed to make a little conversation," said President Gifford, "while they are getting the loudspeaker ready. They are having a little power trouble."

"We are all ready and waiting here," said General Carty. "Mr. Hoover is here."

"You screen well, General," said Mr. Gifford. "You look more handsome over the wire."

"Does it flatter me much?" General Carty asked.

"It think it is an improvement," was the reply.

Hoover's Voice Heard

Mr. Hoover was than called on to take a seat before the light which divides the sitter into 45,000 squares a second, and he was informed of the slight delay. A few seconds later, the power trouble was conquered, and the voice of Secretary Hoover was heard over the loudspeaker, as his face appeared on the large screen.

The illuminated transparent screen seemed somewhat corrugated. This is due to the fact that the squares which make up the picture are arranged in fifty rows, one on top of the other. In the center of the screen appeared a white glare, surrounded by darker markings. As the eye became accustomed to looking at the screen in the darkened room, the large luminous patch took shape as the forehead of Secretary Hoover. He was leaning forward in such a way that the forehead was taking up too much of the pic-

ture, while his mouth and chin were blotted out behind the telephone transmitter. When he moved, however, the picture became clearer.

The face was easily recognizable, although the features, which had been sharp and distinct on the miniature screen, had become considerably blurred by the enlargement. It was plain that, enlarged to the size of an ordinary motion picture film, the detail would have been completely lost. The invention is admitted to be far from the motion picture house stage.

Secretary Hoover's Speech

The face looked up from the manuscript, the lips began to move and the first television-telephone speech started as follows:

"It is a matter of just pride to have a part in this historic occasion.

"We have long been familiar with the electrical transmission of sound. Today we have, in a sense, the transmission of sight, for the first time in the world's history.

"Human genius has now destroyed the impediment of distance in a new respect, and in a manner hitherto unknown. What its uses may finally be no one can tell, anymore than man could foresee in past years the modern developments of the telegraph or the telephone. All we can say today is that there has been created a marvelous agency for whatever use the future may find, with the full realization that every great and fundamental discovery of the past has been followed by use far beyond the vision of its creator.

"Every school child is aware of the dramatic beginnings of the telegraph, the telephone and the radio, and this evolution in electrical communications has perhaps an importance as vital as any of these.

"This invention again emphasizes a new era in approach to important scientific discovery of which we have already within the last two months seen another great exhibit—the transatlantic telephone. It is the result of organized, planned and definitely directed scientific research, magnificently coordinated in a cumulative group of highly skilled scientists, loyally supported by a great corporation devoted to the advancement of the art. The intricate processes of this invention could never have been developed under any conditions of isolated individual effort.

A Dramatic Achievement

"The world is under obligation to the American Telephone and Telegraph Company for its vision in

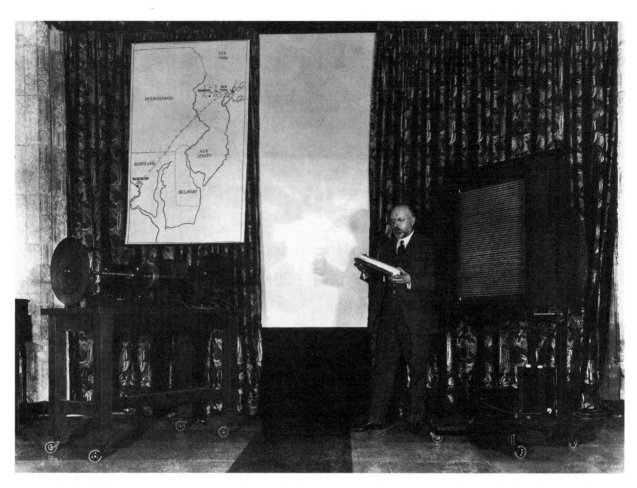

Director of electro-optical research at Bell Telephone Laboratories, Dr. Herbert Ives, with the equipment used in the first intercity television broadcast, April 7, 1927. © HULTON-DEUTSCH COLLECTION/CORBIS. REPRODUCED BY PERMISSION.

the establishment and support of these laboratories, and does tribute to all those who have played their part in this development.

"These laboratories have produced a long list of additions to the telephonic art and a constant contribution to other arts, but no one of them more dramatic or more impressive than this.

"I always find in these occasions a great stimulation of confidence in the future. If we can be assured a flow of new and revolutionary inventions to maintain thought, stimulate spirit, and provide a thousand new opportunities for effort and service, we will have preserved a vital and moving community."

Mrs. Hoover took a seat before the machine which projects living pictures of the sitter and talked to Mr. Gifford.

"What will you invent next?" she said. "I hope you won't invent anything that reads our thoughts."

Half a dozen newspaper men were called to the telephone one after another to talk with men in the demonstration room at Washington. The Times reporter in New York talked to David Lawrence. On the small screen Mr. Lawrence was pictured perfectly. He looked like an excellent daguerreotype which had come to life and started to talk. Even the crinkle of his hair registered perfectly. In these small motion pictures, projected by television, the detail of the face appears in clear-cut black lines against a shining gold background, due to the orange light from neon, which is used in reproducing the pictures.

The pictures were projected only one way yesterday—from Washington to New York. Two-way television-telephone conversations will be held later.

Commercial Use Uncertain

The Bell Laboratories have been directed to concentrate on developing television with all possible speed, although the American Telephone and Telegraph Company has no idea today whether it will ever be commercially valuable. The corporation's attitude is that it wants to know all about the subject, in spite of the fact that its future is vague. Discussing the future possibilities of television yesterday, President Gifford said: "I'll have to leave that to your imagination."

Dr. Frank B. Jewett, Vice President of the American Telephone and Telegraph Company, said yesterday that television was further advanced now than transoceanic telephony was in 1915 when the company held its first successful radio telephone tests from Washington to Paris and Honolulu. Eleven years of development followed that first test in 1915 before transatlantic telephony was placed on a commercial basis.

The television demonstration of yesterday is far in advance of anything that is claimed for any other invention in the same field. John L. Baird, the Scotch inventor, has been considered the leader in television research, but his work is alleged to be crude in comparison with the Bell system. The Alexanderson television project is still in the laboratory, having never been given any public demonstration, and most other television systems are in the talking stage.

Process is Simple in Detail

The process by which yesterday's results were achieved appears infinitely complicated and difficult on first encounter, but becomes fairly simple when traced step by step.

The thing that chiefly staggers the mind is that all that traveled over the wire from Washington to New York or over the ether from Whippany to New York is a series of electrical impulses.

Speed and exactitude are the tremendous achievements in the process. Dots of light are put together at the rate of 45,000 a second to form the motion pictures. Each dot has to be in its exact place. The mosaic of squares would be a jumble—the picture would be completely "pied"—if there was an error of one ninety-thousandth part of a second in the synchronization between the sending apparatus in Washington and the receiving apparatus in New York. Putting aside the terrific speed the problem seemed quite simple, as it was explained yesterday by Dr. Herbert E. Ives, who has been chief of the research work which has resulted in television.

The process begins when the sitter takes his position in front of the television apparatus and the arc light is turned on. Most of this light is shut off from the sitter by a disk. In the disk are a series of holes. As the disk is turned, the light strikes the sitter through the hole nearest the rim. This spot of light travels across the top of his head. The second hole is further from the rim of the disk. The second spot of light travels across the sitter's face, just below the first, the third just below the second, and so on. There are a total of fifty holes and fifty spots of light travel across the sitter or the scene to be photographed, one beneath the other.

If the process could be slowed down infinitely, it would begin with the action of the visible spot of light. In practice, however, the spots move so quickly that the subject seems to be flooded by a steady illumination. There is never more than one spot of light on his face at a time, but the entire fifty spots cross the face or thing to be photographed eighteen times a second.

Spots Vary in Brightness

The lines and contours and colors of the face cause variations in the brightness of the spots they reflect. These variations are turned into variations of electrical current. Facing the sitter are three large photoelectric cells. The moving spots of light are reflected from the face or scene into these cells, where they cause electron showers. The showers are strong or weak, as the light is strong or weak. Electron showers are nothing but electrical current, so that these cells cause a current which constantly varies according to the characteristics of the face or scene to be pictured.

This current is amplified 5,000,000,000,000,000 times before it is strong enough for the work required. Then it is sent, either by wire or radio, to the receiving television station.

This current is a flying picture. Every change in volume is a feature of a scene or portrait. But the question is to make every bit of this flying picture land in the right place.

Arriving at the receiving apparatus, the current is carried to a "brush" or an electrical contact apparatus, which is mounted on a wheel.

As it revolves on this wheel, the "brush" makes and breaks electrical contact approximately 2,500 times. Each contact is made with one of 2,500 wires which are mounted on a circle in which the wheel turns.

Each wire snatches a bit of the electric current or flying picture. To each one of these wires must be delivered eighteen times a second exactly the bit of the picture which is intended for it. The most minute error would scramble the portrait completely.

Neon Gas is Lighted

Each wire carries its bit of current to a square of tin foil behind the television screen. These squares of tin foil are arranged fifty in a row. There are fifty rows. When the bit of current—or fragment of picture—reaches one square of tin foil, it leaps from the tin foil to a wire. It makes the leap through the gas called neon. This is instantaneously illuminated by the passage of electrical current through it. Eighteen times a second there is a flash of neon in front of each of the 2,500 patches of tin foil. The flash is strong or feeble, according to the light or shadow on the particular part of the face or scene. These tiny flashes—occurring at the rate of about 45,000 a second—build up the face on the screen.

The receiving and transmitting of the picture—that is, the taking to pieces of the picture at one place and its reassembling at another—is synchronized by a special system which causes every one of the 2,500 squares or units to fall in its proper place eighteen times a second. This control involves the use of two wires. In the case of radio television, one wavelength is used for sending the picture and two for the synchronization process. Dr. Ives emphasized the difficulty arising here, in view of the congested condition of the "air."

It would take several hundred times as many dots of light a second, under equally perfect control, to make television practical on a large screen for motion picture house purposes. There is one big difficulty here. Television cannot be used on a large screen without using a more powerful light on the person or object sent. The light which is now thrown on the sitter is strong enough to be uncomfortable after a short time. Whether this factor will prove a heavy obstacle is doubtful. A more sensitive photoelectric cell may be developed which would enable television to be extended further without the use of stronger lighting.

How the Eye is Deceived

Dr. Ives called the human eye "a television system." Instead of having only 2,500 wires, the eye has more than a million nerve fibres which carry light impulses to the brain.

As in motion pictures, it is the phenomena of "persistence of vision" which cause the flickering squares of light to fuse together so that the eye sees them as objects in motion. Motion pictures really consists of still pictures shown at the rate of eighteen per second. The eye blends the stills into motion. In television, the eye is even more deceived. Here this is only a series of spots of light flashing on and off, but each spot maintains its effect on the human eye long enough for the brain to comprehend them as an organized picture.

Some of the others who played important parts in the research ending in yesterday's achievement were Dr. Frank Gray, H.M. Stoller, E.R. Morton, R.C. Mathes, J.W. Horton.

Dr. Ives has behind him many years of fruitful research into physical problems. After graduating from the University of Pennsylvania in 1905, he studied three years at Johns Hopkins, receiving the degree of Doctor of Philosophy. During the next ten years as research physicist for a number of organizations he developed, among other things, an "artificial eye" for use in photometry; a method for the description of colors in precise numerical terms; and the first practical lamp for the production of artificial daylight. This lamp is now in general use in retail stores for color comparisons. Another elaborate research was the demonstration of the "mechanical equivalent of light," a fundamental factor in comparing efficiencies of lamps of different kinds. Early in his career, Dr. Ives took up the study of the photoelectric cell, and applied it to a simulation of the eye for experimental work on the human response to light flashes. Conclusions drawn from this study have been applied in the development of the television system.

Dr. Ives's Service in the War

As a captain in the Signal Corps, Dr. Ives during the war had charge of three laboratories for the development of airplane photography. His book on this subject is regarded as the classical work in its field.

Returning to civil life, he entered Bell Telephone Laboratories. When Bell System executives decided that the time was ripe to develop a practical picture-transmission system, Dr. Ives was placed in charge of the work. In addition to general supervisor, Dr. Ives was specifically responsible for the optical aspects of the problem, and for the photoelectric cell. He also continued the study of photoelectric cells and of related problems which have led up to the development of the television system.

Dr. Ives was born in Philadelphia, the son of Frederick E. Ives, scientist and inventor of the halftone process of reproduction.

Further Resources

BOOKS

Leinwand, Gerald. *1927: High Tide of the 1920s.* New York: Four Walls Eight Windows, 2001.

Lyon, Eugene. *David Sarnoff.* New York: Harper & Row, 1966.

Sobel, Robert. *RCA.* New York: Stein and Day, 1986.

WEBSITES

Carey, Charles W., Jr. "Ives, Herbert Eugene." *American National Biography Online.* Available online at http://www .anb.org/articles/13/13-02410.html; website home page: http://www.anb.org (accessed April 24, 2003).

Sacco and Vanzetti Case Political Cartoons

"Is It Freedom?," "Have a Chair!," "An Evening Affair," "The Verdict" and "Death Warrant"

Political cartoon

By: *The Daily Worker*

Date: July 20, July 22, August 9, August 10, and August 22, 1927

Source: Michigan State University, Digital and Multimedia Center. "The Case of Sacco and Vanzetti in Cartoons from the 'Daily Worker.'" Available online at http://digital.lib.msu .edu/onlinecolls/display.cfm?TitleNo=210&FT=gif&I=001; website home page: http://digital.lib.msu.edu (accessed April 24, 2003).

About the Publication: *The Daily Worker* began in 1924 as the official newspaper of the Communist Party of the United States of America (CPUSA). Moving its headquarters from Chicago to New York City in 1927, the paper gradually grew following the 1920s Red Scare. The Great Depression decimated the American economy and provided a wave of support for leftist reform across the country. During this period, circulation increased to over thirty thousand daily subscribers. The paper campaigned for reforming American society rather than for violent revolution. It championed civil rights for African Americans, women's rights, and increased power for labor. As the Communist Party's membership disintegrated during the cold war, the paper's following dissolved as well and it ceased publication in 1957. ∎

Introduction

Police officers arrested Nicola Sacco and Bartolomeo Vanzetti on May 5, 1920, for the murder of a guard and paymaster during a payroll robbery that occurred on April 15, 1920, in South Braintree, Massachusetts. The ensuing trials, convictions, appeals, and the executions of both created one of the more controversial

IS IT FREEDOM?   *July 20, 1927*

Copyright, 1927, by
THE DAILY WORKER PUBLISHING CO.
33 First Street—New York

Primary Source

"Is It Freedom?" (1 OF 5)

SYNOPSIS: *The Daily Worker* published the following political cartoons during the weeks leading to the execution of Nicola Sacco and Bartolomeo Vanzetti on August 23, 1927. Though Sacco and Vanzetti received their sentences for murder in 1921, these drawings reveal the significant attempts made in 1927 to stop the execution. Day by day, the images expressed the hatred and despair of Sacco and Vanzetti's supporters as the cause became more and more bleak. The cartoon above is from July 20, 1927. REFERENCE CENTER FOR MARXIST STUDIES, "DAILY WORKER" PUBLISHER.

episodes in American history. Historians, public officials, and many common citizens continue to debate the innocence or guilt of Sacco and Vanzetti. In the context of the post–World War I Red Scare of 1919–1920, the case inflamed the passions of millions of Americans. Coming on the heals of government repression of antiwar dissent with the wartime Espionage and Sedition Acts, the Federal Bureau of Investigation continued to arrest and deport hundreds of suspected radicals after the war ended in 1918. Fears that Communists, fresh from their victory in the Russian Revolution of 1917, would strike next at the United States, drove the persecution of thousands of leftist activists and their sympathizers. Anarchists, primarily Italian immigrants, responded by bombing the

WITCHES SALEM 1692

LABOR. BOSTON 1927

HAVE A CHAIR!

July 22, 1927

Primary Source

"Have a Chair!" (2 OF 5)

Editorial cartoon comparing the Sacco/Vanzetti trial to the Salem Witch Trials, from the *The Daily Worker,* July 22, 1927.
REFERENCE CENTER FOR MARXIST STUDIES, "DAILY WORKER" PUBLISHER.

AN EVENING AFFAIR   *August 9, 1927*

Primary Source

"An Evening Affair" (3 OF 5)

Editorial cartoon depicting Sacco and Vanzetti's possible fate from the *The Daily Worker,* August 9, 1927. REFERENCE CENTER FOR MARXIST STUDIES, "DAILY WORKER" PUBLISHER.

home of Attorney General A. Mitchell Palmer on June 2, 1919, and Wall Street on September 16, 1920.

Sacco and Vanzetti, Italians who emigrated to the United States in 1908, espoused anarchist philosophies, communicated with the bombers, and are believed to have aided the attacks. The maelstrom that followed their arrest continued decades after the verdict on July 21, 1921, and their execution by the electric chair in 1927. Supporters argued that Sacco and Vanzetti faced murder charges solely because of their Italian descent and radical philosophies. They asserted that the two faced death as punishment for the terrorist attacks of the previous two years. The trials only buttressed these claims, for testimony not only focused on the crimes but revealed the influence of anti-immigrant prejudice on the prosecution and the sitting judge. Defense Attorney Fred Moore stoked the clash when he consistently charged that the trial was directed more at suppressing Italian radicalism than at justice.

Significance

As the CPUSA's press organ, *The Daily Worker* devoted its editorial content to the defense of Sacco and Vanzetti. The paper printed hundreds of articles challenging the evidence presented at the trial. The visceral drawings matched the *Worker*'s strident criticisms of the legal process. The political cartoons shown here exhibit the *Worker*'s core argument that the case represented so much more than the two defendants. In these images, artist Fred Ellis charged that the political, judicial, and economic powers of the American capitalist system conspired to kill an innocent pair of individuals. Ellis's illustrations fused the fate of Sacco and Vanzetti with the destruction of justice and liberty in the United States.

Further Resources

BOOKS

Buhle, Mari Jo, Paul Buhle, and Dan Georgakas, eds. *Encyclopedia of the American Left.* New York: Oxford University

THE VERDICT   *August 10, 1927*

Primary Source

"The Verdict" (4 OF 5)

Editorial cartoon from the *The Daily Worker,* August 10, 1927. REFERENCE CENTER FOR MARXIST STUDIES, "DAILY WORKER" PUBLISHER.

Press, 1998. Entries on *Daily Worker* and Sacco-Vanzetti Case.

Ehrmann, Herbert B. *The Case That Will Not Die: Commonwealth vs. Sacco and Vanzetti.* Boston: Little, Brown, 1969.

Frankfurter, Felix. *The Case of Sacco and Vanzetti: A Critical Analysis for Lawyers and Laymen.* Boston: Little, Brown, 1927.

WEBSITES

Pernicone, Nunzio. "Sacco, Nicola and Bartolomeo Vanzetti." *American National Biography Online.* Available online at http://www.anb.org/articles/15/15-00592.html; website home page: http://www.anb.org (accessed April 24, 2003).

The Sacco-Vanzetti Project. Available online at http://www.saccovanzettiproject.org/pages/home.html; website home page: http://www.saccovanzettiproject.org (accessed April 24, 2003).

August 22, 1927

Primary Source

"Death Warrant" (5 OF 5)

Editorial cartoon from the day before Sacco and Vanzetti are to be executed, from *The Daily Worker,* August 22, 1927. REF-ERENCE CENTER FOR MARXIST STUDIES, "DAILY WORKER" PUBLISHER.

The President's Daughter

Memoir

By: Nan Britton

Date: 1927

Source: Britton, Nan. *The President's Daughter.* New York: Elizabeth Ann Guild, 1927, i–v.

About the Author: Nan Britton (1896–1991) spent her youth in Marion, Ohio, but the known historical details of her life are few. Aside from her autobiography, *The President's Daughter,* little evidence remains from her life and possible relationship with the nation's twenty-ninth president, Warren G. Harding. It was in Marion that Britton became enamored with Harding, who lived much of his adult life in the small town. In 1916, at the age of nineteen, Britton apparently began an affair with the married Senator Harding that continued through his presidency. Britton wrote *The President's Daughter* in 1927, four years after Harding's death. She asserted that Harding had fathered her daughter, Elizabeth Ann Christian, in 1919. ■

Introduction

Historians often rank Warren G. Harding as the worst president in American history. Elected to the White House with more than 60 percent of the vote in 1920, Harding called for a return to "normalcy" after the foreign and domestic turmoil of the war years. Although Harding served for a relatively brief period, from 1921 until his death in 1923, his administration was fraught with unprecedented levels of corruption and scandal. When he died of a cerebral hemorrhage on August 2, 1923, public sympathy staved off congressional investigators and scandal-starved journalists only temporarily.

Several members of the Harding administration, including the attorney general and the head of the Veterans' Bureau, were indicted for fraud. The press flooded readers with stories concerning the eventual indictments, trials, and, in a few cases, convictions. By far, the Teapot Dome scandal ranked as the most flagrant example of wrongdoing in the Harding administration. Senate investigations after Harding's death revealed that his secretary of the interior sold access to naval oil reserves in Teapot Dome, Wyoming, and Elk Hills, California. Secretary Albert B. Fall, who received more than $400,000 in gifts and payments from two oilmen, became the first cabinet member to go to jail for felony crimes committed while serving in a presidential administration. Investigations never connected Harding directly with any of this corruption, but his reputation disintegrated. In 1927, a young, single mother authored an exposé that tarnished Harding's legacy in a manner befitting the Jazz Age media's fascination with sex.

Significance

American presidents from Thomas Jefferson (served 1801–1809) to William Jefferson Clinton (served 1993–2001) have faced media scrutiny for their supposed sexual misconduct. As the first mass-market publication devoted to this topic, *The President's Daughter* pioneered the field of political "sexposés." In a period when the press published countless pages devoted to sexual affairs, Nan Britton took a different tack. She dedicated the book "with understanding and love to all unwedded mothers, and to their innocent children whose fathers are usually not known to the world." Britton framed the text as a call for legal reform to protect illegitimate children and their mothers rather than a sex exposé.

In the autobiography, Britton declares that she had a six-and-a-half-year affair with Senator, then President Warren G. Harding. She writes of losing her virginity with Harding and then bearing his daughter, Elizabeth Ann Christian, in 1919. According to the book, the relationship continued during Harding's tenure in the White House. In fact, Britton describes in tawdry detail making love to the president in a small closet down the hall from the Oval Office. She even recounts an instant when a secret service officer alerted the pair that Harding's wife had arrived unexpectedly. The warning allowed the lovers to dress and sneak away just in time. Little evidence for her claims remains, Britton notes, because she destroyed Harding's letters to her before the book's publication. Rumors of Harding's dalliances with women other than his wife lingered after his death, and the public proved eager to pay for Britton's story. The book became a best-seller and provided its author with hundreds of thousands of dollars.

Primary Source

The President's Daughter [excerpt]

> **SYNOPSIS:** When this book hit the shelves, the public remained engrossed with the presidency of Warren G. Harding. The mass media ran stories of corruption in the Harding administration on an almost daily basis, as official investigations persisted into the late 1920s. Perhaps recognizing that many would criticize her motives, the author prefaced the book with "The Author's Motive." This section provided readers with Britton's justification for writing this autobiography and exposing her "life-long love for Warren Gamaliel Harding. . . ."

The Author's Motive

If love is the only right warrant for bringing children into the world then many children born in wedlock are illegitimate and many born out of wedlock are legitimate.

In the author's opinion wedlock as a word quite defines itself. Often a man and woman are locked at their wedding in a forced fellowship which soon proves to be loveless and during which the passions of the two express themselves in witless and unwanted progeny. And yet we wonder what is wrong with the world!

The story of my life-long love for Warren Gamaliel Harding and his love for me and our love for our child is told in these pages, together with the family, community, and political circumstances under which this relationship continued for the six and one-half years preceding the sudden passing of the President on August 2, 1923.

The author has had but one motive in writing for publication the story of her love-life with Mr. Harding. This motive is grounded in what seems to her to be *the need for legal and social recognition and protection of all children in these United States born out of wedlock.*

To the author, this cause warrants the unusual and conscious frankness with which she has written this book, and the apparent disregard for the so-called conventions, because she feels that *the issue is greater than all the personal sacrifices involved.*

Indeed, even like frankness on the part of thousands of mothers who could divulge similar life-tragedies might well be added to that of the author's if such sacrifice would insure the aggressive agitation of a question involving one of the gravest wrongs existent today, with a view toward a legislative remedy.

Because of the political stature of the man-character involved, this fact-story would no doubt get to the public sooner or later, as news, or as court testimony in trials such as have recently involved men who are or have been national figures. In such case the story so sacred to the author would doubtless be garbled by news writers, or told only partially to serve some legal, personal or party interest. The author feels therefore that through her experiences she has been led to see the need for telling it herself, truly and completely, and in making it the basis for an appeal in behalf of the unfathered children of unwedded mothers, in the sincere hope that this book may result in happier conditions for childhood and motherhood throughout these United States of America.

Much consideration has been given by the author to all probable reactions resulting from the publication of this book. The fact that this narrative is bound up with the life of a man who has held the

Author of *The President's Daughter* Nan Britton holds her daughter Elizabeth Ann. © BETTMANN/CORBIS. REPRODUCED BY PERMISSION.

highest office in this land may mean that temporarily he may be misjudged. But the author, who has shrined him in reverent memory, feels in her heart that these revelations cannot but inspire added love for him after his trials and humanities are perceived and acknowledged.

Moreover, the author is obliged to introduce to a none-too-kindly world the daughter of her love-union with Mr. Harding and thus subject her to curious gaze and speculation. The author regrets this as any mother would, but feels that in no way can she effectively show her understanding love for all children except by baring her own experience, in the hope that the notability of the case itself may influence regard for the welfare of children and help to right an old and current wrong.

Nor, indeed, does the author herself hope to escape criticism unless her real motive is definitely apprehended and conceded. It has required no little heartbreak on her part to relive the story of her love-life, but it had to be relived in memory that the story might be portrayed truthfully. Only by keeping before her the human cause which impelled the writing, and a constant hope that through her own suffering she might be instrumental in preventing the heartaches of thousands of potential mothers, has this been possible.

Knowing the real President Harding as she does, the author feels that if he could be brought back today to witness the futile struggle the mother of his only child has suffered, he himself would proclaim his own fatherhood, and seek to open eyes blinded by convention to a situation which is depriving thousands of innocent children of their natural birthright in denying them legal recognition before the world. In the author's opinion, *there should be no so-called "illegitimates" in these United States.*

It is to be remembered that all children must be precious in the sight of our Father, otherwise he would not be a heavenly father, and that Jesus of Nazareth did *not* say, "Suffer little children born in wedlock to come unto me for of such is the kingdom of heaven." Jesus loved and honored all little children and didn't bother at all about who their parents were or about the manner of their birth. He himself was born in a manger which was most unconventional.

As a result of the author's own personal experiences written in this book, and because of the thousands of prospective mothers who face unknowingly like tragic situations, she feels that an organized effort should be made to secure State and Federal legislation providing the following benefits for unwedded mothers and unfathered children:

> *First:* That on the birth of a child the name of the father be *correctly* registered in the public records, and that failure to do so shall constitute a criminal offense.

> *Second:* That every child born in the United States of America be regarded as legitimate whether born within or without wedlock.

The enactment of these statutes would not, in the author's opinion, detract from the dignity of the marriage-union which automatically legalizes children born therein, but would insure protection for those innocent children born of a love-union in which one or both parents are unmarried.

Readers of this book who agree with the author that this entire situation constitutes a Cause, and who feel with her that members should be gathered into the Elizabeth Ann League to collectively urge the proposed legislation suggested above to provide social equality among children, are invited to write her a personal letter in care of the publishers {see title page}.

The Author

Further Resources
BOOKS
Allen, Frederick L. *Only Yesterday: An Informal History of the 1920s.* New York: Wiley, 1997.

Anthony, Carl Sferrazza. *Florence Harding: The First Lady, the Jazz Age, and the Death of America's Most Scandalous President.* New York: William Morrow, 1998.

Ferrell, Robert H. *The Strange Deaths of President Harding.* Columbia, Mo.: University of Missouri Press, 1996.

Murray, Robert K. *The Harding Era: Warren G. Harding and His Administration.* Minneapolis: University of Minnesota Press, 1969.

Russell, Francis. *The Shadow of Blooming Grove: Warren G. Harding in His Times.* New York: McGraw-Hill, 1968.

WEBSITES
Hawley, Ellis W. "Harding, Warren Gamaliel." *American National Biography Online.* Available online at http://www.anb.org/articles/06/06-00253.html; website home page: http://www.anb.org (accessed April 25, 2003).

"Dead!"
Photograph

By: New York *Daily News*
Date: January 13, 1928
Source: Execution of Woman in Sing Sing Prison. *Daily News,* January 13, 1928, 1. Available online at *Daily News* Pix: The Photo Archive of The New York Daily News, http://www.dailynewspix.com (accessed April 24, 2003).
About the Publication: The New York *Daily News,* started by Joseph Medill Patterson in 1919, was the nation's first tabloid-style paper. By the mid-1920s the *Daily News* reached a circulation of over one million. At the time of Patterson's death in 1946, it stood as the nation's highest-circulation paper, selling well over two million copies every weekday and more than four and a half million copies on Sundays. Patterson had a long family heritage in newspaper publishing. His father, Robert W. Patterson, served as editor of the *Chicago Tribune,* and his mother's father, Joseph Medill, owned it. By the early twentieth century, Joseph was copublishing the *Tribune* with his cousin, Robert R. McCormick, before founding the New York *Daily News.* ∎

Introduction
Joseph Medill Patterson's New York *Daily News* lowered the bar, so to speak, of American journalism during the 1920s. Though the paper did not create sensational coverage, it was the first tabloid paper. *Tabloid* technically referred to the smaller length and width of the newspaper, but the term soon developed its current connotation from the reporting offered by the tabloid papers that emerged during the Jazz Age. The *Daily News* faced stiff competition from several other New York tabloid

RUTH SNYDER'S DEATH PICTURED!—This is perhaps the most remarkable exclusive picture in the history of criminology. It shows the actual scene in the Sing Sing death house as the lethal current surged through Ruth Snyder's body at 11:06 last night. Her helmeted head is stiffened in death, her face masked and an electrode strapped to her bare right leg. The autopsy table on which her body was removed is beside her. Judd Gray, mumbling a prayer, followed her down the narrow corridor at 11:11. "Father, forgive them, for they don't know what they are doing?" were Ruth's last words. The picture is the first Sing Sing execution picture and the first of a woman's electrocution.—Story p. 3; other pics. p. 28 and back page.

Primary Source

"Dead!"

SYNOPSIS: This front page greeted more than one million *Daily News* subscribers on the morning of January 13, 1928. Reporter Tom Howard illegally sneaked a camera into the execution chamber at the Sing Sing maximum-security prison. He apparently raised his pant leg, revealing the camera strapped to his leg just above the ankle, and clicked the shutter at the moment of Ruth Snyder's execution. The full caption is: "Ruth Snyder's Death Pictured! This is perhaps the most remarkable exclusive picture in the history of criminology. It shows the actual scene in the Sing Sing death house as the lethal current surged through Ruth Snyder's body at 11:06 last night. Her helmeted head is stiffened in death, her face masked and an electrode strapped to her bare right leg. The autopsy table on which her body was removed is beside her. Judd Gray, mumbling a prayer, followed her down the narrow corridor at 11:14. 'Father, forgive them, for they don't know what they are doing?' were Ruth's last words. The picture is the first Sing Sing execution picture and the first of a woman's electrocution." **THE NEW YORK DAILY NEWS. REPRODUCED BY PERMISSION.**

Ruth Snyder, on trial for murder and facing capital punishment, sits with her lawyer, 1923. AP/WIDE WORLD PHOTOS. REPRODUCED BY PERMISSION.

papers, including the *Graphic* and William Randolph Hearst's *Daily Mirror,* for the raunchiest, most controversial stories. The reports often featured sex scandals and murder trials.

The murder trial of Ruth Snyder and Judd Gray combined both sex and murder, ultimately climaxing in perhaps the most disturbing news photo ever published. In May 1927, Snyder and Gray, her lover, murdered Snyder's husband. The tabloid press leapt at covering the subsequent police investigation, murder trial, and the eventual executions of both perpetrators. Reflecting press coverage of similar scandals of the period, the press printed every salacious detail of the troubled marriage, love affair, and murder. Hoping to cash in on their new-found infamy, Snyder and Gray each wrote autobiographical exposés for mass publication.

Significance

The nation's highest-circulation daily paper at the time, the New York *Daily News* provided readers with dramatic, and shocking, coverage of the scandal. The grisly photograph of Ruth Snyder's body stiffening as electricity raced through it brings to mind ongoing, present-day debates about the broadcasting of executions. Tom Howard, a reporter for the *Daily News,* secretly taped a mini-camera onto his ankle and began clicking the shutter when the switch was pulled. The result is one of the most disturbing front pages ever printed. This photograph certainly did not begin the practice of sensational news coverage, nor did it precipitate its downfall. Rather, "DEAD!" distills twentieth-century American tabloid journalism into a single image of a masked women clenching at the moment of death.

Further Resources

BOOKS

Bessie, Simon Michael. *Jazz Journalism: The Story of Tabloid Newspapers.* New York: Dutton, 1938.

Leinwand, Gerald. *1927: High Tide of the 1920s.* New York: Four Walls Eight Windows, 2001.

Tebbel, John W. *American Dynasty: The Story of the Mc-Cormicks, Medills, and Pattersons.* Garden City, N.Y.: Doubleday, 1947.

9

MEDICINE AND HEALTH

SCOTT A. MERRIMAN

Entries are arranged in chronological order by date of primary source. For entries with one primary source, the entry title is the same as the primary source title. Entries with more than one primary source have an overall entry title, followed by the titles of the primary sources.

Important Events in Medicine and Health, 1920–1929

1920

- University of Rochester scientist George Whipple cures anemia in dogs by feeding them raw liver. His work on the cause and treatment of anemia would win him the 1934 Nobel Prize in physiology or medicine.

- Phenobarbital (discovered in 1911) is introduced in the treatment of epilepsy.

- Harvey Cushing pioneers new techniques in brain surgery.

1921

- In January, German psychologist Hermann Rorschach introduces the inkblot test for the study of personality.

- In February, James Collip isolates pure insulin.

- In May, British physician Alexander Fleming discovers an antibacterial substance, lysozyme, in saliva, mucus, and tears.

- In May, the first American birth control conference convenes in New York City.

- In July, Franklin Delano Roosevelt contracts polio. Throughout his political career he will hide his ailment from the public, doing nothing to promote public awareness of the disease.

- In July, Albert Calmette and Camille Guerin develop a tuberculosis vaccine.

- In October, Frederick Banting and Charles Best extract insulin from the pancreas and begin experiments using the substance on dogs.

1922

- Joseph Erlanger and Herbert Gasser use an oscilloscope to study electrical impulses in a single nerve fiber.

- In January, Elmer V. McCollum leads a team of scientists at Johns Hopkins University that discovers vitamin D, a substance they found in cod-liver oil that prevents rickets, a skeletal-deformity disease. This discovery leads to vitamin-fortified milk.

- In January, Frederick Hopkins discovers glutathione, a sequence of three amino acids essential for a cell to use oxygen.

- In February, Herbert Evans discovers vitamin E, which he believes to be vital to fertility.

- In April, Elmer McCollum uses vitamin D to treat rickets.

- On June 14, the U.S. Supreme Court affirmed the right of states to compel its citizens to be vaccinated from diseases. The court held that vaccination was in the public interest and that states had a right to act in the public interest.

- In August, Frederick Banting and Charles Best use insulin to treat a diabetic.

1923

- George and Gladys Dick, who discover that streptococcus causes scarlet fever, develop an antitoxin.

- Reuben Kahn makes available a faster and more sensitive test for syphilis.

- In October, the first birth control clinic opens in New York City under the leadership of Margaret Sanger.

1924

- Acetylene is used as an anesthetic.

- Rudolph Matas introduces the use of intravenous saline solution to prevent dehydration.

- In February, Theodor Svedberg invents the ultracentrifuge, which makes it possible to isolate viruses.

- In July, Harry Steenbock finds that ultraviolet light stimulates the body to produce vitamin D.

- In October, Willem Einthoven invents the electrocardiograph.

1925

- James Collip discovers parathormone, a hormone secreted by the parathyroid gland.

- On May 26, Canadian physicians Frederick Grant Banting and John J. Macleod deliver the Nobel Lectures on their work using insulin to treat diabetes. The two shared the 1923 Nobel Prize in physiology or medicine but did not deliver their addresses until 1925.

- In November, George Whipple demonstrates that iron is essential in the formation of red blood cells.

- On December 12, Leiden University professor and physician Willem Einthoven delivers his Nobel Lecture on his development of the electrocardiogram. This work won him the 1924 Nobel Prize in physiology or medicine, though he did not deliver his address until 1925.

1926

- A chemical (later identified as acetylcholine) is shown to be involved in the transmission of nerve impulses.

- Spiroptera carcinoma, a cancer caused by a parasite, is discovered.

- In March, dairy scientist William E. Kraus at the Ohio Agricultural Experiment Station in Wooster, Ohio develops the first vitamin A and D fortified milk.

- In April, George Whipple, George Minot, and William Murphy show that a diet rich in liver can control pernicious anemia, usually a fatal disease.

• In August, Massachusetts biochemist James Sumner crystallizes the enzyme urease.

1927

• Frank A. Hartman isolates cortin from the adrenal glands.

• On July 28, the U.S. Supreme Court in *Buck v. Bell* affirmed the right of states to order surgeons to sterilize those deemed criminals, the insane and idiots.

1928

• Research by Oscar Riddle shows that prolactin, a pituitary hormone, causes the production of milk in the breasts.

• Austrian-born physician George Goldberger, working on a cure for pellagra, finds that a heated yeast extract, later shown to contain the B vitamin niacin, will cure black-tongue, a dog disease analogous to pellagra in humans.

• In January, microbiologist Frederick Griffith demonstrated that an animal exposed to a dead bacterium may manufacture a live strain of that bacterium.

• In February, George Papanicolaou develops the Pap test for diagnosing uterine cancers.

• In March, Alexander Fleming discovers penicillin in a mold. Penicillin, Fleming discovers, kills bacteria and so has the potential to cure humans of bacterial infections.

• In June, Albert Szent-Györgyi isolates hexuronic acid, later proved to be vitamin C.

• In December, Philip Drinker and Louis Shaw at Harvard University invent the "iron lung" as an aid to breathing, especially for polio sufferers.

• On December 10, Charles Jules Henri Nicolle, French physician and director of the Pasteur Institute in Tunis (then part of the French empire in North Africa), received the Nobel Prize in physiology or medicine for his discovery that lice transmit typhus to humans.

1929

• Hans Berger develops the electroencephalograph (EEG).

• Edward Doisy discovers theelin, a female sex hormone, in urine of pregnant women.

• Adolph Butenandt, German biochemist, determines the chemical structure of estrone, a female sex hormone.

• Adenosine triphosphate (ATP) is isolated from muscle.

• Manfred J. Sakel uses insulin shock as a treatment for schizophrenia.

• The first human heart catheterization is performed.

• On December 11, Utrecht University professor Christiaan Eijkman and Cambridge University professor Frederick Hopkins share the Nobel Prize in physiology or medicine for their discovery of vitamins.

The Compulsory Insurance Debate

"Report of the Reference Committee on Hygiene and Public Health"

Report

By: *The Journal of the American Medical Association*

Date: May 8, 1920

Source: "Report of the Reference Committee on Hygiene and Public Health." *Journal of the American Medical Association* 74, no. 19 (May 8, 1920): 1319.

"Report of the Committee on Medical Economics"

Report

By: *The New York State Journal of Medicine*

Date: June 1925

Source: "Report of the Committee on Medical Economics." *The New York State Journal of Medicine* 25, no. 17 (June 1925): 788.

About the Organizations: The American Medical Association (AMA) was founded in 1847 by Nathan Davis. It began publication of the *The Journal of the American Medical Association (JAMA)* in 1883. In the 1890s and into the twentieth century, the publication gained importance under the editorship of Dr. George H. Simmons. *The New York State Journal of Medicine* began publication in 1900 and ceased publication in 1993. In the 1920s it published articles on such topics as diabetes, cardiac disease, botulism, and tuberculosis. ∎

Introduction

Medical insurance is relatively new in American history. In the past, most doctors personally collected their bills, and some even accepted payment in kind, such as eggs or butter. Those who were insured carried insurance through a fraternal order, lodge, or insurance company, but policies were generally for disability rather than payment for medical care. The insurance policies that did provide medical care usually mandated the physician and fee and were opposed by doctors. Not until the early twentieth century did interest in medical insurance grow after many European countries, including Germany and England, passed compulsory insurance laws. The American Association for Labor Legislation (AALL) took up the crusade for government-provided taxpayer-funded insurance and began introducing bills on the state level.

At first doctors favored the idea, as it would guarantee a certain level of income for many. Soon, however, they began to believe that insurance would limit or reduce their incomes. Insurance companies also opposed compulsory insurance, which would make them obsolete. Timing also hurt the idea, for during World War I (1914–1918) some patriots believed that anything German, including compulsory insurance, was "un-American," even renaming hamburgers "liberty sausages" and sauerkraut "liberty cabbage." New York and California both defeated compulsory insurance bills, and many doctors urged the AMA and their local medical societies to take stands against compulsory insurance. The results of their efforts are reproduced here.

Significance

With the defeat of compulsory medical insurance in the late 1910s, perhaps the best chance for state-level insurance expired. Physicians, who disliked the new workmen's compensation insurance, mobilized against the idea and effectively squelched it. Insurance returned to the forefront in the Great Depression, when physicians, like the rest of America, were harmed by the economic collapse. They began to see the economic benefits of voluntary insurance, but they still opposed compulsory care and blocked an effort by President Franklin D. Roosevelt (served 1933–1945) to add health insurance to Social Security.

Voluntary insurance received two boosts in the 1940s: Health insurance became an untaxed workplace benefit, making it attractive to employers and employees during the wage controls of World War II (1939–1945); and the U.S. Supreme Court held that health insurance benefits could be a subject for collective bargaining by organized labor. Later in the decade President Harry S. Truman (served 1945–1953) backed the Wagner-Murray-Dingell bill to provide compulsory insurance at the federal level. The AMA mobilized, raising over $2 million, and public opinion was swayed against compulsory insurance again.

The issue remained dormant until the 1960s, when President John F. Kennedy (served 1961–1963) supported insurance for the elderly. His successor, President Lyndon Johnson (served 1963–1969), brought this idea to fruition, passing Medicare to help the elderly and Medicaid to help the poor. Although the AMA opposed these programs, most doctors benefited financially from them. In 1992, universal health insurance was an important plank in presidential candidate Bill Clinton's platform. More recent calls for a prescription drug benefit for the elderly have also faced opposition, in part because of uncertainty over the role government would play in such a program. Thus, the issues raised in these two articles from the 1920s have returned repeatedly to public attention.

Primary Source

"Report of the Reference Committee on Hygiene and Public Health" [excerpt]

SYNOPSIS: The article from *JAMA* reports a resolution putting the American Medical Association on record as strongly opposed to any compulsory medical insurance, whether from the state or federal government.

Dr. J.W. Schereschewsky, U.S.P.H.S., Chairman, presented the report of the Reference Committee on Hygiene and Public Health, as follows:

Your committee has carefully considered the resolutions on compulsory sickness insurance, and reports it with amendments as follows:

> *Resolved,* That the American Medical Association declares its opposition to the institution of any plan embodying the system of compulsory contributory insurance against illness, or any other plan of compulsory insurance which provides for medical service to be rendered contributors or their dependents, provided, controlled, or regulated by any state or the Federal government.

Primary Source

"Report of the Committee on Medical Economics" [excerpt]

SYNOPSIS: The *New York State Journal of Medicine* article regards the defeat of compulsory medical insurance as a victory and urges the Medical Society of the State of New York to continue its opposition.

3. Health Insurance:

Your Committee is of the opinion that Health Insurance, as such, is a dead issue in the United States. [There] are, however, many indications in the activities of various groups of social workers that Unemployment Insurance of some type is being sought. Care of the unemployed sick has been one phase of the subject which has had considerable attention and which will continue to be an important part of the whole subject. The stand taken against health

insurance by the medical profession in New York State undoubtedly had a far reaching influence and did more to unify the profession than any other one thing in the history of medicine. It is not conceivable that any serious effort will again be made to subsidize medicine as the hand-maiden of the public. But it is essential, if we are to maintain the position which we have won by our unified fight, that we should show ourselves willing to become a deciding and guiding factor in any social efforts which we consider will be of benefit to the public of the State. We recommend, therefore, that if any definite effort is made toward the above ends this Society indicate its desire to be considered willing to participate in general discussions and to act in an advisory capacity where occasion offers.

Further Resources

BOOKS

American Health Security Act of 1994: Report. Washington, D.C.: U.S. Government Printing Office, 1994.

Hoffman, Beatrix Rebecca. *The Wages of Sickness: The Politics of Health Insurance in Progressive America.* Chapel Hill: University of North Carolina Press, 2001.

Moss, David A. *Socializing Security: Progressive-Era Economists and the Origins of American Social Policy.* Cambridge, Mass.: Harvard University Press, 1996.

Muntz, Earl E. *Social Security: An Analysis of the Wagner-Murray Bill.* New York: American Enterprise Association, 1944.

Women in Science

"Wants Women in Science"
Newspaper article

By: *The New York Times*
Date: June 3, 1921
Source: "Wants Women in Science: Dr. Flexner Tells Bryn Mawr Door of Opportunity Is Open." *The New York Times,* June 3, 1921, 32.

"Scientific Careers for Women"
Editorial

By: *The New York Times*
Date: June 4, 1921
Source: "Scientific Careers for Women." *The New York Times,* June 4, 1921, 12.
About the Publication: Founded in 1850 as the *New-York Daily Times, The New York Times* was originally a relatively

With the success of Marie Curie, more women were being urged to pursue a career in the sciences. AP/WIDE WORLD PHOTOS. REPRODUCED BY PERMISSION.

obscure local paper. By the early twentieth century, however, it had grown into a widely known, well-respected news source. Its banner, "All the News That's Fit to Print," is recognized across the United States and throughout the world. ∎

Introduction

Until the twentieth century, women were generally excluded from scientific and medical careers. In the early eighteenth century, women were accepted as midwives and delivered most babies, but by midcentury, opinion was shifting to the belief that male doctors provided better care. By the mid-nineteenth century, a new medical role for women opened up: nursing. But women were still discouraged from pursuing science, because they were considered less rational than men and viewed as "hysterical," particularly when menstruating. Science was viewed as a "man's world," in part because science was based heavily on math, and women were stereotyped as being poor mathematicians. These views had not changed much by the early twentieth century, so most medical schools and graduate science programs remained closed to women. Thus, it came as a shock when Dr. Simon Flexner, director of the Rockefeller Institute for Medical Research, in his commencement address at Bryn Mawr College on June 2, 1921, called for more women to be scientists.

Significance

Even though Flexner could cite such examples of women scientists as Marie Curie, his call met with only a limited response. Throughout the conservative 1920s and the Great Depression of the 1930s, doors remained closed to women scientists. The same was true for women doctors: In 1950, only 5 percent of doctors in the United States were women. Women who wanted to pursue medical or scientific research were discouraged or not allowed to take chemistry or biology, or they were encouraged to be technicians rather than scientists. The editorial reaction to Flexner's call reflects the thinking of the 1920s: that men had more "latent" scientific and mechanical ability than women, were better able than women to view facts "abstractly," and were more adept at weighing facts in the light of accepted theories. Ironically, *The New York Times* itself endorsed the "previously accepted theory" by holding that women were less suited to careers in science.

This attitude has not entirely disappeared. When Mattel Toys introduced its first talking Barbie doll in 1992, she said, among other things, "Math class is tough." This ignited a firestorm of controversy among parents and teachers, who claimed that the doll perpetuated stereotypes about women's aptitude for science and math. By 2003, nearly half of all science graduates in the United States were female, and enrollments in most college science classes were relatively balanced between men and women (though engineering classes generally remained overwhelmingly male). Science careers were also slowly becoming more gender-balanced than they used to be, though only 21 percent of the members of the American Chemical Society were women. Simon Flexner's call represented the beginnings of a slow change in favor of women in the medical community, but *The New York Times*' editorial response represents the sexist attitudes that made it difficult for them to gain respect in these fields.

Primary Source

"Wants Women in Science"

> **SYNOPSIS:** This article from the June 3, 1921, edition of *The New York Times* discusses Dr. Simon Flexner's address to the graduating class of Bryn Mawr College and his call for more women to pursue careers in science.

Philadelphia, June 2.—A plea for young women to take up the pursuit of science was made by Dr. Simon Flexner, Director of the Rockefeller Institute for Medical Research, New York, in an address at the Bryn Mawr College commencement today.

Dr. Flexner paid a tribute to Mme. Curie, and said that now that the doors of opportunity have been thrown open to women one may expect many more will pass its portals and enter upon a career of science. Already they are feeling the lure and perceiving their aptitude, he said.

One hundred students received their degrees at today's exercises. A feature of the day was a gift of 1,000 books from Bryn Mawr to the Sorbonne in Paris, France, which recently established a chair of American literature and civilization.

Primary Source

"Scientific Careers for Women"

SYNOPSIS: This editorial response from *The New York Times* scoffs at Dr. Flexner's idea, suggesting that those few women attracted to science are among those who have cooler heads and more rational minds.

Dr. Simon Flexner, speaking with authority as the Director of the Rockefeller Institute for Medical Research, urged the young women who are graduated at Bryn Mawr this year to undertake work in one or another of the sciences as offering for their sex careers congenial, useful to others, and more than possibly profitable to themselves.

He had no difficulty, of course, in naming many women, beginning with Mme. Curie as the most illustrious modern instance, who have attained eminence in some domain of science, but instinct or something else must have told a good many of his young and properly attentive hearers that such achievement was not for them.

That women can be efficient in laboratories—that some of them are capable of doing there original investigation as well as the routine labor that often is called drudgery—needs no proof at this late day. It is still true, however, that the majority of women are still to develop either the scientific or the mechanical mind.

This is not an essential inferiority to men. Far from all men, indeed, have such minds. But more of men than of women have latent capacities in those directions, and more of them have the power—a necessary qualification for any real achievement in science—of viewing facts abstractly rather than relationally, without overestimating them because they harmonize with previously accepted theories or justify established tastes and proprieties, and with-

out hating and rejecting them because they have the opposite tendencies.

The woman whom science attracts can yield safely to the call, and no more than that can be said to any man. But if Dr. Flexner advised all of the young women graduates to "go into science"—which he probably didn't, though the dispatches gave that impression—he made a mistake and proved that wisdom will not die with him.

Further Resources

BOOKS

Barr, Jean, and Lynda Birke. *Common Science? Women, Science, and Knowledge.* Bloomington, Ind.: Indiana University Press, 1998.

Davis, Cinda-Sue, et al. *The Equity Equation: Fostering the Advancement of Women in the Sciences, Mathematics, and Engineering.* San Francisco: Jossey-Bass, 1996.

Etzkowitz, Henry, et al. *Athena Unbound: The Advancement of Women in Science and Technology.* New York: Cambridge University Press, 2000.

Judson, Horace Freeland. *The Eighth Day of Creation: Makers of the Revolution in Biology.* New York: Simon & Schuster, 1980.

Keller, Evelyn Fox. *A Feeling for the Organism: The Life and Work of Barbara McClintock.* New York: W.H. Freeman, 1983.

Parker, Lesley H., Léonie J. Rennie, and Barry J. Fraser, eds. *Gender, Science, and Mathematics: Shortening the Shadow.* Boston: Kluwer, 1996.

"Police Veto Halts Birth Control Talk; Town Hall in Tumult"

Newspaper article

By: *The New York Times*

Date: November 14, 1921

Source: "Police Veto Halts Birth Control Talk; Town Hall in Tumult." *The New York Times,* November 14, 1921, 1, 7.

About the Publication: Founded in 1850 as the *New-York Daily Times,* The New York Times was originally a relatively obscure local paper. By the early twentieth century, however, it had grown into a widely known, well-respected news source. Its banner, "All the News That's Fit to Print," is recognized across the United States and throughout the world. ■

Introduction

Birth control is by no means solely a modern issue. Eighteenth-century families were forced to use rather ineffective methods such as breast-feeding (which generally halts a woman's menstrual cycle) and coitus interruptus. In the nineteenth century birth control came increasingly to be viewed as "radical," in part because its promoters came from the same camps as those promoting other radical ideas. The federal government stepped in during the nineteenth century by passing the Comstock Act, which banned mailing any obscene materials, including those promoting contraception. The penalty for violating this act was up to ten years in jail and a $5,000 fine. States passed similar acts; for example, Connecticut banned the use of contraceptives. The U.S. Supreme Court upheld the Comstock Act in *Ex Parte Jackson* (1877), assigning to the U.S. government a strong role in enforcing morality.

Margaret Sanger (1883–1966), who coined the term "birth control" in 1914, was a nurse who believed in social reform and thought that the best way to improve people's conditions was to give them control over the number of children they had. She founded the organization that became Planned Parenthood and repeatedly violated the Comstock Act. Imprisoned several times for violating a variety of ordinances, she brought attention to the cause. She also challenged laws that forbade discussing birth control or forbade anyone who was not a physician from discussing it. The federal government indicted Sanger in 1916 for sending birth control information through the mail, although the charges were later dropped. In *People v. Sanger* (1918), the New York Court of Appeals upheld the constitutionality of a law prohibiting the selling of contraceptive devices or the discussion of them. Sanger had to serve thirty days in jail for violating this law. These court cases kept Sanger in the news and slowly swayed public opinion. She continued to hold public meetings, and it was one such meeting that brought the arrest discussed in this newspaper article.

Significance

Sanger drew large audiences and kept the issue of birth control before the public. Planned Parenthood, which she founded, convinced many doctors—previously hostile to her views—that birth control was an acceptable practice. It took time, however, for not until 1937 did the American Medical Association reverse its stand against contraception. Sanger's efforts extended beyond the United States, as she helped to found the International Planned Parenthood Federation, which has over fifty member countries.

One factor hampering Sanger was the lack of effective birth control devices. Intrauterine devices (IUDs), for example, had long been around, but they involved health risks and were not infection-free until the early 1960s. That changed with the development of oral contraceptives, or "the pill," in the 1950s. Then in 1965 the U.S. Supreme Court struck down Connecticut's contra-

ceptive ban in *Griswold v. Connecticut,* holding that there was a "zone of privacy" that surrounded marriage. The whole sexual revolution of the 1960s was the result in large part of changing attitudes toward birth control and the availability of the pill, and Margaret Sanger would have been proud to see freedom of choice in contraceptives realized.

Primary Source

"Police Veto Halts Birth Control Talk; Town Hall In Tumult"

> **SYNOPSIS:** *The New York Times* reported on the arrest by New York City police of Margaret Sanger and several others as they attempted to address a meeting on birth control. The article notes that many of those in attendance were "socially prominent" and urged the speakers to defy the police.

Police Veto Halts Birth Control Talk; Town Hall In Tumult

Mrs. Sanger and Mary Winsor, Leaders in Movement, Arrested at Meeting.

Audience Swarms Stage

Sergeant Seizes Mrs. Sanger as She Starts to Speak—Police Buffeted by Crowd.

Order from Headquarters

No Further Explanation Offered by Raiders— 100 Reserves on Guard in 43d Street.

A mass meeting to discuss "Birth Control: Is It Moral?" was broken up by the police at the Town Hall last night. Hundreds of men and women, many socially prominent, derided the police and urged the speakers to defy the order not to speak.

After an hour of uproar and disorder, during which the police were buffeted about in the crowd that swarmed upon the stage, Mrs. Margaret Sanger and Mary Winsor, both conspicuous figures in the birth control movement, were placed under arrest, charged with disorderly conduct.

The police appeared before the speaking had begun, but while the hall was half filled. The doors were locked and the crowd that was inside had to stay there, while hundreds of others in West Forty-third Street clamored for admittance. Among those locked out were Mrs. Sanger and Harold Cox of England, editor of The Edinburgh Review and a former member of Parliament. When the doors were opened to dismiss the audience, the crowd swept the police aside and carried Mrs. Sanger and Mr. Cox inside. The attempts to speak and the arrests followed.

The leaders of the birth control clinic outside of court, from left to right, Sigrid Brestwell; Mrs. A. L. Field; Dr. Elizabeth Pissiot; Margaret Sanger, leader; Dr. Hanna Stone; Marcella Sideri, 1929. © BETTMANN/CORBIS. REPRODUCED BY PERMISSION.

The meeting was to have been the culmination of the First American Birth Control Conference, which held sessions at the Plaza on Friday and Saturday. The Town Hall had been engaged three weeks ago and $250 had been paid for the use of it. When the doors opened at 7 o'clock hundreds crowded in. By 7:45 the hall was filled except for the reserved seats which had been set aside for persons identified with the movement. There was still a large crowd of ticket holders outside and the street was filled with limousines on their way to the hall when, at about 8 o'clock, Police Captain Thomas Donahue, of the West Forty-seventh Street station went to the hall and ordered the doors closed.

Crowd Sweeps Into Hall

Mrs. Sanger and others who were caught outside appealed in vain for admittance. They were told that the meeting had been ordered stopped by a telephone message from Police Headquarters. Telephonic inquiries to headquarters brought the reply that the orders had been issued by one of the Commissioners, and that none of the Commissioners nor any one who could give any information as to the cause for the order, was at headquarters last night.

One hundred reserves from the West Forty-seventh Street Station were posted in front of the door. The announcement that the meeting had been called off, instead of scattering the crowd, served to increase it. At 8:30 Captain Donahue, who was inside the hall, announced that the doors would be opened to allow those who had entered to leave. As soon as the doors had swung back, the crowd outside, with Mrs. Sanger and Mr. Cox in the van, brushed the police aside and swept into the hall, and Mrs. Sanger was lifted to the stage.

"Defy them! Defy them!" came from all parts of the hall.

Mrs. Sanger motioned for silence, then cried: "One would certainly suppose that this display of liberty and freedom of speech was in Germany, not in America."

"Go on with the meeting," some one shouted, and an outburst of applause followed.

Mrs. Sanger Mounts Stage

Mrs. Sanger stepped to the front of the stage again and began to speak. She was checked by another demonstration, but before she could continue Sergeant August Handwerg and Patrolman Thomas Gaine walked onto the stage and seized her by the arms.

"You can't speak here," the Sergeant said.

"They don't dare arrest you," a woman called out. "Where's the warrant? What is the charge?"

Mrs. Sanger, stepping away from the two policemen, began her address: "The calling of this meeting tonight," she said, "is the greatest compliment you have ever had. I believe you and I are able to discuss the question whether birth control is moral or not—."

Sergeant Handwerg again told Mrs. Sanger she could not speak and advised her not to cause any disorder. When the policeman took her by the arms again scores of persons in the audience jumped upon the stage. "Arrest her—you don't dare arrest her," they cried. Robert M. C. Marsh was among those who went on the stage, and he told Mrs. Sanger that if she desired he would act as her legal adviser. Others who appeared on the stage in Mrs. Sanger's defense were Mrs. Ogden Reid, Mrs. Juliet Barrett Rublee, Mrs. Ernest R. Adee, Dr. Lydia Allen De Vilbis and Lowell Brentano.

The stage was then in a tumult. Several women began to address the audience, and as fast as one was seized by the police another began to speak. Mrs. Sanger was still the storm-centre, and her friends crowded around her and all but swept the policemen off their feet.

"If you would help us," one woman told the audience, "we could remove the police from this platform."

There were cries of "Put out the police!" but wiser counsel prevailed and the audience contented itself with booing the two policemen, who up to that time had made no attempt to clear the stage. The attempts to speak persisted. Mr. Cox, the British editor who had been scheduled to speak, was pushed to the front of the platform and introduced to the audience.

London Editor Cut Short

"I have come across the Atlantic to address you," he began, but further remarks were cut off by the policemen.

Captain Donahue, who up to this time had been watching the scene from the front of the hall, then appeared on the stage and addressed Mrs. Sanger. "Please get off this stage before you cause some disorder," he told her. Mrs. Sanger refused to move.

"If you arrest her you'll have to arrest me too," one woman cried.

"The captain informs me that this meeting has been stopped by an order by telephone," Mrs. Sanger called out to the audience. "I asked him who was at the other end of the wire and he couldn't tell me."

When it became apparent that his orders to leave the hall were not to be obeyed Captain Donahue ordered the arrest of Mrs. Sanger and Miss Winsor, who were taken out of the hall between the two policemen, while the audience sang "My Country, 'Tis of Thee, Sweet Land of Liberty."

Mrs. Sanger, hatless, led the procession across Broadway and up Eighth Avenue to Forty-seventh Street. Nearly all of those in the hall had followed and hundreds joined them on Broadway. Many of those in the hall had gone directly to the police station, some on foot and some in limousines, and the police had to fight their way through a big crowd to get their prisoners inside.

At the police station, Mrs. Sanger described herself as a writer and gave her address as 104 Fifth Avenue, the headquarters of the Birth Control Committee. Miss Winsor, who has been prominent in the suffrage movement, said her home was in Haverford, Pa. Patrolman Gaine told Lieutenant Courtney, in charge at the station, that the arrests had been on the order of Captain Donahue and that the charge was "refusing to leave the stage in the Town Hall when ordered by the Captain and me."

Prisoners Sent to Night Court

The prisoners were ordered to be taken to Night Court at 316 West Fifty-fourth Street. While they were in the police station the congestion in Forty-seventh Street had become so great that reserves were placed at Eighth Avenue, half a block from the station, to keep the throng back. When the prisoners left the station in a patrol wagon, they passed through cheering crowds, which followed on a run to the court.

The two women were again applauded as they entered the court room. Accompanying them were Robert M. C. Marsh and Jonah J. Goldstein as counsel, and as witnesses Mrs. Ogden Mills Reid, Mrs. Ernest R. Adee, Mrs. Juliet Barrett Rublee and Mrs. William A. McGraw of Detroit.

Magistrate Francis X. McQuade released the two prisoners without bail in the custody of their counsel until today, when they will appear for examination in West Side Court. After they left the court room, they went to the home of Mrs. Rublee, at 242 West Forty-ninth Street.

Mrs. Sanger, after leaving Night Court, declared that immediate steps would be taken to get out an injunction to permit the meeting to be held this week. She said that a daughter of a Supreme Court Justice, who was in the audience, called up her father last night and was informed that there was not enough time last night to get the injunction.

"We have reason to believe," Mrs. Sanger declared, "that this meeting was closed by the influence of the Catholic Church."

Mrs. Ann Kennedy, one of the officers of the First American Birth Control Conference, told reporters that she had seen in the hall after the police locked the doors a man who said he was Mgr. Joseph P. Dineen, secretary to Archbishop Patrick J. Hayes. Mgr. Dineen, Mrs. Kennedy said, declared that he had been sent by the Archbishop to the meeting.

In a formal statement which she gave out later, Miss Sanger said:

> My idea of calling the public together tonight was in the belief that this subject could be discussed at the Town Hall with as much dignity and delicacy as it was discussed the last two days at the Hotel Plaza. We were in no way violating the law. I consider my arrest in violation of every principle of liberty that America stands for, and I shall take this case to the highest courts, if necessary, to preclude the possibility of its ever happening again.
>
> My arrest will in no way stop the opening of the Mother's Health Centre at 317 East Tenth Street.

Anne Lifshitz, Mrs. Sanger's secretary, complained after the meeting that she had been roughly handled by the police while attempting to reach Mrs. Sanger after her arrest. She said that she was at the rear of the crowd that followed Mrs. Sanger across Forty-third Street and Broadway. She displayed a torn coat, which, she said, was the result of the rough handling.

Both Mrs. Sanger and Miss Winsor have served jail sentences for participation in militant movements. Mrs. Sanger was indicted in 1916 by the Federal authorities here on the charge of sending improper matter through the mails. This consisted of copies of "The Woman Rebel" containing an article on birth control. Later the charge was dropped.

In the same year Mrs. Sanger opened a birth control clinic at 46 Amboy Street, Brownsville, and as a result of a police raid she and her sister, Mrs. Ethel Byrne, were arrested. She was sentenced to thirty days in the workhouse. Mrs. Byrne started a hunger strike against her imprisonment and was pardoned by Governor Whitman. Mrs. Sanger agreed at the time to be governed by the law as it stood, and Governor Whitman promised her that he would have a commission investigate the subject of birth control.

Miss Winsor was one of the militant suffragists who, after disturbances in Washington in 1919, were sentenced to Occoquan jail, outside of Washington.

Further Resources

BOOKS

Chesler, Ellen. *Woman of Valor: Margaret Sanger and the Birth Control Movement in America.* New York: Simon & Schuster, 1992.

Douglas, Emily Taft. *Margaret Sanger: Pioneer of the Future.* New York: Holt, Rinehart and Winston, 1969.

Gray, Madeline. *Margaret Sanger: A Biography of the Champion of Birth Control.* New York: R. Marek, 1979.

Kennedy, David M. *Birth Control in America: The Career of Margaret Sanger.* New Haven, Conn.: Yale University Press, 1970.

Knowles, Jon, and Marcia Ringel. *All About Birth Control: A Personal Guide.* New York: Three Rivers Press, 1998.

Lader, Lawrence. *The Margaret Sanger Story and the Fight for Birth Control.* Garden City, N.Y.: Doubleday, 1955.

Moore, Gloria, and Ronald Moore. *Margaret Sanger and the Birth Control Movement: A Bibliography, 1911–1984.* Metuchen, N.J.: Scarecrow Press, 1986.

Sanger, Margaret. *Margaret Sanger: An Autobiography.* New York: Dover Publications, 1971.

WEBSITES

"Margaret Sanger: Biographical Sketch." Available online at http://www.nyu.edu/projects/sanger/msbio.htm; website home page: http://www.nyu.edu/projects/sanger/index.html (accessed May 13, 2003).

The Care and Feeding of Children

Guidebook

By: L. Emmett Holt

Date: 1922

Source: Holt, L. Emmett. *The Care and Feeding of Children: A Catechism for the Use of Mothers and Children's Nurses.* New York: D. Appleton and Company, 1922, xii, 186–187, 192–193, 214–215.

About the Author: L. Emmett Holt (1855–1924) was best known for his work in pediatrics. Twice president of the American Pediatric Society, he is credited with broadening preventative pediatrics to include health education, leading to a sharp decrease in infant mortality in New York City between 1916 and 1920. He was president of both the Child Health Organization and the Child Hygiene Association, which he successfully merged into the American Child Health Association. In 1921 he resigned as Carpentier Professor of Diseases of Children at Columbia University, and three years later he set out for Peking to discuss children's health with the Chinese. ■

Introduction

In the early 1900s both the proliferation of college-educated people and the rise of progressivism encouraged a reliance on experts in many fields, including child rearing. These trends led to a devaluing of the mother's role, even as her responsibility for her children increased. At the same time, however, necessary information about basic child care, especially disease prevention, was distributed to households throughout the world. Possibly the best-known early child care expert was L. Emmett Holt, whose book, *The Care and Feeding of Children: A Catechism for the Use of Mothers and Children's Nurses,* went through ten editions. The title suggests the social class to which this book was aimed, as Holt wrote it for children's nurses as well as mothers, and only the well-to-do had nurses. By calling his book a "catechism," a word with religious connotations, Holt put himself in the role of a minister not to be questioned.

Significance

Holt's book offers advice that is markedly different from that given to parents today. The first excerpt deals with the issue of crying. Holt's suggestion that babies should be allowed to cry if nothing is wrong differs from advice found in many later child care books, which suggest picking up the child, although some more recent child care books again suggest allowing children to cry themselves to sleep. Holt also dislikes pacifiers, unlike many current child care experts, who recommend their use until the child reaches an age at which they can harm the development of the teeth.

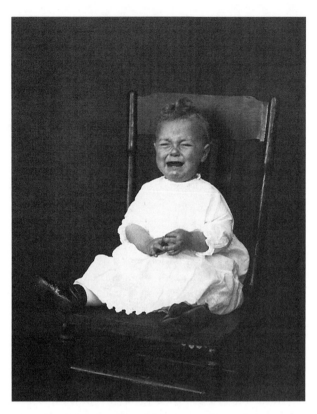

L. Emmett Holt believed that a crying child should be allowed to "cry it out." © BETTMANN/CORBIS. REPRODUCED BY PERMISSION.

The second excerpt deals with playing with children. Holt suggests that those under six months should never be played with, and older children should be played with sparingly. Later child care books suggest just the opposite—that interacting with others is how children learn language and begin to read, and that children need to be intellectually and emotionally stimulated. Holt's last section deals with masturbation, even by children less than a year old. Reflecting the traditional morality of the day, Holt describes this as the worst behavior a child can have and even suggests restraints with infants. More recent child care books and medical studies, in contrast, express a different view, holding that masturbation causes no irreparable harm. Holt's views in general suggest his belief that children should be viewed largely as little adults. While ideas about child rearing have changed substantially from Holt's day, Holt was a pioneer in the field, and works like the one excerpted here led to a thriving field of expert child care advice.

Primary Source

The Care and Feeding of Children [excerpt]

SYNOPSIS: The section on crying suggests that parents should not pick up their children unless there is a need. The section on nervousness suggests that babies should not be played with. Finally, the section on masturbation reflects the beliefs of the time on masturbation, correlates negative behaviors with masturbation, and reveals an inordinate concern with a child's rubbing of himself or herself.

What is the cry of hunger?

It is usually a continuous, fretful cry, rarely strong and lusty.

What is the cry of temper?

It is loud and strong and accompanied by kicking or stiffening of the body, and is usually violent.

What is the cry of illness?

There is usually more of fretfulness and moaning than real crying, although crying is excited by very slight causes.

What is the cry of indulgence or from habit?

This is often heard even in very young infants, who cry to be rocked, to be carried about, sometimes for a light in the room, for a pacifier to suck, or for the continuance of any other bad habit which has been acquired.

How can we be sure that a child is crying to be indulged?

If it stops immediately when it gets what it wants, and cries when this is withdrawn or withheld.

What should be done if a baby cries at night?

One should see that the child is comfortable—the clothing smooth under the body, the hands and feet warm, and the napkin not wet or soiled. If all these matters are properly adjusted and the child simply crying to be taken up, it should not be further interfered with. If the night cry is habitual some other cause should be sought.

How is an infant to be managed that cries from temper, from habit, or to be indulged?

It should simply be allowed to "cry it out." This often requires an hour, and, in extreme cases, two or three hours. A second struggle will seldom last more than ten or fifteen minutes, and a third will rarely be necessary. Such discipline is not to be carried out unless one is sure as to the cause of the habitual crying.

Is it likely that rupture will be caused from crying?

Not in healthy young infants if the abdominal band is properly applied, and seldom after infancy even when no abdominal support. . . .

What are the principal causes of excessive nervousness in infants and young children?

The most important predisposing causes are an inherited nervous constitution, and the delicate

Holt's List of Contagious Diseases

The table of contents of Holt's *The Care and Feeding of Children* directs readers to a section on feared children's contagious diseases that at that time could readily lead to death:

- Measles
- German measles
- Scarlet fever
- Whooping cough
- Chicken pox
- Diphtheria
- Mumps.

Holt emphasized the need for proper hygiene in the prevention and treatment of these diseases. By the close of the twentieth century, most of these diseases could be cured or prevented by vaccines, demonstrating one clear difference in the way experts look at children today versus the 1920s.

SOURCE: Holt, L. Emmett. *The Care and Feeding of Children: A Catechism for the Use of Mothers and Children's Nurses.* New York: D. Appleton and Company, 1922, xii

structure and rapid growth of the brain in early life. It should be remembered that the brain grows as much during the first year as during all the rest of life. Important exciting causes of nervousness are anemia, disturbances of digestion and malnutrition; children who are much below normal weight are especially prone to develop nervous symptoms.

What can be done to prevent or cure this condition of nervousness?

Causes which are discovered should be removed so far as possible. It should be recognized that all infants need quiet peaceful surroundings for the normal growth and development of the brain; those of nervous families, especially. Such infants should see but few people, should be left much alone, should not be romped or played with. They should never be quieted by means of soothing syrups or the "pacifier."

At what age may playing with babies be begun?

Babies under six months old should never be played with; and the less of it at any time the better for the infant.

What harm is done by playing with very young babies?

They are made nervous and irritable, sleep badly, and suffer from indigestion and cease to gain in weight.

When may young children be played with?

If at all, in the morning, or after the mid-day nap; but never just before bedtime. . . .

What is masturbation?

It is the habit of rubbing the genital organs with the hands, with the clothing, against the bed, or rubbing the thighs together. Sometimes a child sits upon the floor, crosses its thighs tightly and rocks backward and forward. Many of these things are passed over lightly and are regarded for months as simply a "queer trick" of the child. It may be seen at any age, even in those not more than a year old. In infancy it is more frequent in girls. It occurs particularly in very nervous children.

To what does masturbation lead?

It increases the nervousness of the child, exaggerates the lack of self-control and when practiced frequently often leads to impairment of the general health, lowered moral sense and sometimes to other sexual propensities.

Does it cause feeble-mindedness?

There is no evidence that this is the case. Feeble-minded children very commonly practice this habit but it is to be regarded as the result rather than the cause of the mental condition.

How should a child with this habit be treated?

Masturbation is the most injurious of all the bad habits, and should be broken up just as early as possible. Children should especially be watched at the time of going to sleep and on first waking. Punishments and mechanical restraint are of little avail except with infants. With older children they usually make matters worse. Rewards are much more efficacious. It is of the utmost importance to watch the child closely, to keep his confidence, and by all possible means to teach self-control.

Some local cause of irritation is often present, which can be removed. Medical advice should at once be sought.

Further Resources
BOOKS

Cable, Mary. *The Little Darlings: A History of Child Rearing in America.* New York: Scribner, 1975.

Cleverley, John, and D. C. Phillips. *Visions of Childhood: Influential Models From Locke to Spock.* New York: Teachers College Press, 1986.

DeMause, Lloyd. *The History of Childhood.* New York: Psychohistory Press, 1974.

Greven, Philip J. *Child-Rearing Concepts, 1628–1861.* Itasca, Ill.: F.E. Peacock, 1973.

Hardyment, Christina. *Dream Babies: Three Centuries of Good Advice on Child Care.* New York: Harper & Row, 1983.

Thompson, Thea, ed. *Edwardian Childhoods.* Boston: Routledge & Kegan Paul, 1981.

Wishy, Bernard W. *The Child and the Republic: The Dawn of Modern American Child Nurture.* Philadelphia: University of Pennsylvania Press, 1972.

"The Kahn Test for Syphilis in the Public Health Laboratory"
Journal article

By: C.C. Young

Date: February 1923

Source: Young, C.C. "The Kahn Test for Syphilis in the Public Health Laboratory." *The American Journal of Public Health* 13, no. 2 (February 1923): 96–99.

About the Scientist: Reuben L. Kahn (1887–1974) is most famous for simplifying the Wassermann test for syphilis in 1923. In the 1950s, however, he also developed the universal serological reaction, and his work in immunology was highly respected. ■

Introduction

An extremely virulent strain of syphilis rampaged across Europe around 1500. Each nation had a different name for it, and most labeled it with the name of their enemy; the French, for instance, called it the Spanish disease. By 1550 the symptoms and progression of syphilis were very similar to today's disease. Treatment, though, was not soon in coming. The only possible cure was mercury, but this treatment ran a high risk of also killing the patient. Another difficulty with syphilis was that there was no reliable test for it. In 1905, though, two German scientists found the cause of syphilis, a microorganism named *Treponema pallidum*. The next year, another German, August von Wassermann, developed a reliable test for the disease, the Wassermann test. This test, however, was complicated, had several sources of error, and had a long incubation period. Thus, a better test was needed, which Kahn provided in 1923. In the meantime, a new drug called arsphenamine, which treated syphilis much more effectively than mercury without the fatal side effects, had been developed in 1910.

Significance

After the development of the Kahn test, diagnosis was relatively quick and certain. The remedies available, including arsphenamine and a similar compound, arsenoxide, treated syphilis with some success. The concern became controlling the disease, but at the time it was not socially acceptable even to mention syphilis, let alone admit having it or seek treatment or testing. In the 1930s the U.S. surgeon general began to discuss sexual diseases more openly, and states began successfully testing prospective marriage partners and pregnant women using the Kahn test. Some states even required every person to be tested for syphilis, and cities opened hospitals for intensive treatment. The real break in the treatment of syphilis was penicillin, which cut the mortality rate nearly 98 percent and infant deaths from congenital syphilis 99 percent. Although penicillin worked wonders in alleviating many of the disease's effects, it did not wipe out the disease. The rate of syphilis nearly quadrupled between 1957 and 1970, as attitudes towards sex liberalized. In the early twenty-first century, syphilis remained a serious concern, even though penicillin generally cures its effects and no state has mandatory tests for it anymore. People cannot be forced to consider whether they have the disease, but one carrier can rapidly spread the disease through a large population.

Primary Source

"The Kahn Test for Syphilis in the Public Health Laboratory" [excerpt]

> **SYNOPSIS:** The journal article reports that the Wassermann test, the best test at the time for syphilis, had many possible "sources of error." It then discusses the Kahn test, noting that it more clearly and simply identifies presence of the disease. The article compares the results of the Kahn test with those of the Wassermann on a large number of samples and suggests that the Kahn test should be used along with the Wassermann.

Few problems give the public health laboratory director greater concern than the laboratory diagnosis of syphilis. On the one side, he deals with a disease which expresses itself in every conceivable clinical form and on the other, with a diagnostic test which possesses many inherent possibilities for error. The Wassermann test is being utilized more and more by many physicians as a routine examination without regard to clinical findings. The laboratory is called upon to pass its opinion on the possibility of syphilitic infection on blood specimens received through the mails without the slightest knowledge of the condition of the patient. It is clear that the laboratory carries a heavy responsibility in furnishing results of the highest accuracy. This applies particularly to the public health laboratory because there

is little opportunity for the laboratory worker and physician to talk over the findings as is true, for example, in the case of the hospital laboratory.

Granting the importance of correct serum diagnosis of syphilis, it must be admitted that the Wassermann test does not entirely supply such a diagnosis. The many variable elements of this test give it numerous sources of error, so many indeed, that it is not uncommon for even dependable workers to vary in their findings on the same specimen of blood.

In order to help overcome many of the variable factors of the Wassermann test, public health laboratory workers have attempted at various times to standardize this test. In Great Britain the Medical Research Committee has done excellent work along this line. In this country also several attempts have been made to standardize the test. The work of the New York City Department of Health, the U.S. Public Health Service, the Massachusetts State Board of Health, and more recently of Kolmer, are conspicuous examples. In Michigan also we have for some time been endeavoring to help standardize this test. While serving as chairman of the Laboratory section of the Michigan Public Health Association at the 1921 meeting, the writer appointed a Wassermann standardization committee, the work of which, however, will be reported in detail in another place.

The standardization of the Wassermann test will bring about greater uniformity in the procedure and will undoubtedly enhance the diagnostic value of the Wassermann test. But it is questionable whether the mere standardization will solve the problem—at least not until we learn more of the laws which underlie the Wassermann test.

When Meinicke, and Sachs and Georgi, published their precipitation tests for syphilis it appeared that at last we might have a simple test to check the Wassermann and in time perhaps replace the older and more complicated test. Although studied to a considerable degree in Germany these two tests have not given promising results in this country. The Sachs and Georgi test has been favorably mentioned by several American workers. Kilduffe more recently subjected 430 serums to parallel Wassermann and Sachs-Georgi tests and concluded that the reaction is neither as delicate nor as trustworthy as the Wassermann test. To our knowledge no laboratory worker in this country has found it worth while to report the results of either the Meinicke or Sachs-Georgi tests to physicians as a check on the Wassermann. Probably the greatest drawback for the laboratory worker is the long incubation period (48 hours) required for these two tests, permitting organisms to develop which interfere with the determination of correct results.

The Kahn Precipitation Test

This leads us to the precipitation test for syphilis which forms the basis of this paper. This test was evolved about a year ago by Kahn in the laboratories of the Michigan Department of Health, and has from the very beginning given promising results. The main features are:

1. The spontaneous reaction in the case of strongly positive serums. About 80 per cent of the serums giving a four plus reaction with the Wassermann test, show spontaneous precipitation after mixing serum with antigen.

2. The clumping of the precipitates after incubation. The four plus and three plus reactions show clumps instead of precipitates. This coagulation of the precipitates makes the stronger reactions unmistakable.

3. The simplicity of the procedure. We have not found it necessary to increase the laboratory personnel in adding this test to our routine procedures because it requires comparatively little time and effort in its manipulation.

We were particularly encouraged by the favorable clinical results obtained with this test by Keim and Wile at the Dermatological Clinic of the University of Michigan. The findings of these workers entirely corroborated our own in connection with examinations made of syphilitic inmates of the Michigan penal institutions where there are 560 cases under treatment. Our findings also showed that the combined results of the Wassermann and Kahn Precipitation tests approached a higher degree of correct diagnosis as well as a better check on treatment than the Wassermann test alone.

On July 1st, 1922, after 15,400 Kahn tests had been carried out in this laboratory in conjunction with the Wassermann test, it was decided to add this test to our routine procedures. Since that date, over 8,000 precipitation tests have been reported parallel with the Wassermann test to physicians, with entirely satisfactory results. . . .

Comparative Results of Wassermann and Kahn Tests

About 93 per cent of serums give the same results with the Wassermann and Kahn tests. Close to six per cent of serums give, what we consider a relative check. These serums give doubtful reactions with the Wassermann test and either negative or positive reactions with the Kahn test, or doubtful reactions with the latter test and negative or positive reactions with the Wassermann test. Close to one per cent of serums do not check, giving a negative reaction with one test and positive with the other or vice versa. . . .

Experience gained with over 23,000 Kahn tests, 8,000 of which have been reported to physicians parallel with the Wassermann test, leads us to the following conclusions:

1. The laboratory diagnosis of syphilis based on the combined results of the Wassermann and Kahn tests possesses a higher degree of accuracy than that of the Wassermann test alone.

2. The clinical application of the Kahn test both in the diagnosis and treatment of syphilis compares favorably with the Wassermann test.

3. The simplicity of the procedure of the Kahn test makes it readily applicable as a routine procedure in a public health laboratory.

4. The employment of the Kahn test as a check on the Wassermann test will help reduce the element of skepticism associated with the older test.

Further Resources

BOOKS

Durkee, Silas. *Gonorrhoea, Syphilis, and other Venereal Diseases: Their Symptoms, Treatment, etc.* Philadelphia: P. Blakiston, Son & Co., 1882.

Goodman, Herman. *Notable Contributors to the Knowledge of Syphilis.* New York: Froben Press, 1943.

Meyer, Oscar Daniel. *That Degenerate Spirochete.* New York: Vantage Press, 1952.

Pusey, William Allen. *The History and Epidemiology of Syphilis.* Springfield, Ill.: C.C. Thomas, 1933.

Syphilis: A Report from the National Institutes of Health. Bethesda, Md.: National Institutes of Health, 1989.

Thomas, Evan W. *Management of Syphilis.* Albany, N.Y.: New York State Department of Health, Bureau of Epidemiology and Communicable Disease Control, 1959.

Ziporyn, Terra. *Disease in the Popular American Press: The Case of Diphtheria, Typhoid Fever, and Syphilis, 1870–1920.* New York: Greenwood Press, 1988.

Insulin

"Insulin Saves Lives at Montefiore Home"

Newspaper article

By: *The New York Times*

Date: April 16, 1923

Source: "Insulin Saves Lives at Montefiore Home." *The New York Times,* April 16, 1923, 19.

"Ex-Secretary Lansing, Ill from Diabetes, Improves Under Treatment with Insulin"

Newspaper article

By: *The New York Times*

Date: June 21, 1923

Source: "Ex-Secretary Lansing, Ill from Diabetes, Improves Under Treatment with Insulin." *The New York Times,* June 28, 1923, 1.

"'Insulin' is Much Easier to Get. No 'Cure' Has Yet Been Found"

Editorial

By: *The New York Times*

Date: June 28, 1923

Source: "'Insulin' is Much Easier to Get. No 'Cure' Has Yet Been Found." *The New York Times,* June 21, 1923, 18.

About the Publication: Founded in 1850 as the *New-York Daily Times, The New York Times* was originally a relatively obscure local paper. By the early twentieth century, however, it had grown into a widely known, well-respected news source. Its banner, "All the News That's Fit to Print," is recognized across the United States and throughout the world. ∎

Introduction

Diabetes was one of the first diseases diagnosed by the ancient Greeks, who noted that diabetics can be identified by the sweet smell of the urine; in fact, the more formal term *diabetes mellitus* literally means "honey-sweet diabetes." Unfortunately, medicine did not move past the diagnosis stage for many centuries. As recently as 1900, there still was no proven treatment for diabetes, although some scientists had made advances in understanding its cause by studying animal pancreases. Two East Coast physicians, Elliot Joslin and Frederick Allen, tried to control diabetes mellitus with diet, but with limited success. Patients lost large amounts of weight, but they generally survived longer. Also, Joslin also tried to understand the disease by studying how diabetics burned calories. Despite the efforts of researchers, many diabetics lapsed into co-

mas and died. The introduction of insulin in 1921, however, was a major step in the treatment of diabetes.

Significance

The three articles show insulin's extraordinary importance at the time. The article on Montefiore Hospital reports a study of insulin and testifies to its effectiveness. It was viewed as a wonder drug, and special resources were devoted to Dr. Ringer so that he could carry out his research. The article also notes that diabetics must inject insulin every day for the rest of their lives and that insulin poses dangers. The article discussing former Secretary of State Robert Lansing serves as the equivalent of today's celebrity endorsement, suggesting that if Lansing trusted it enough to try it, then others should too. The editorial notes the limitations of insulin and praises Dr. Banting of the Toronto General Hospital, who helped to discover it. It also notes the role of John D. Rockefeller Jr., who donated money to increase the supply of insulin and to train doctors.

Since the 1920s, much more research has been done into diabetes and better testing apparatuses are available. Thus, although one can still die from diabetes and its complications, the introduction of insulin made diabetes much more manageable.

Even in the 1920s, some thought that scientists might patent their inventions and deny average patients access to them. Similar concerns exist in the twenty-first century about AIDS drugs and the pharmaceutical companies that have discovered, patented, and profit from them. Had Banting patented his discovery, he would not have been alone, for other scientists in the 1920s did patent their inventions and keep them away from the public and other scientists.

Primary Source

"Insulin Saves Lives at Montefiore Home" [excerpt]

> **SYNOPSIS:** The "Montefiore Home" article discusses how insulin saved lives at one hospital and how those treated with insulin will have to keep taking it for the rest of their lives.

Insulin Saves Lives at Montefiore Home

New Diabetes Serum Used With Complete Success on Patients in Local Hospital

Eighty Cases Treated

"The World Enormously Richer" as a Result of the Discovery, Says Dr. Simon Flexner

The use of insulin in the treatment of diabetes has met with complete success at Montefiore Hospital, where eighty patients, five of whom were in the

Canadian Frederick Banting won the Nobel Prize for his discovery of insulin to combat diabetes. © HULTON-DEUTSCH COLLECTION/CORBIS. REPRODUCED BY PERMISSION.

last stages of the disease, have been treated with the recently discovered serum. This was made known by Dr. A.I. Ringer, attending physician at the hospital, following the annual meeting yesterday in the auditorium.

Dr. Simon Flexner, director of the Rockefeller Institute for Medical Research, who was the chief speaker at the meeting, devoted a part of his address to the new discovery, asserting that "the world is enormously richer that it has ever been before," because of the discovery of the serum by Dr. F.G. Banting of the University of Toronto.

The first reference to the pancreatic serum at yesterday's meeting was made by S.G. Rosenbaum, President of the hospital, who said:

Last August, following the discovery in Toronto of insulin, the active principle of the pancreas, which is a specific in the treatment of diabetes, arrangements were made by the Toronto investigators to distribute some of this preparation to six of the leading institutions in the United States to determine its clinical value. Montefiore Hospital was fortunate in being among these six, and under the direction of Dr. A.I. Ringer active work has been pur-

sued within the last eight months in the treatment of diabetes with this new preparation.

Dr. Ringer in Charge

In order to accomplish this work the metabolic service was reorganized, a special ward was set aside for the patients and extra nurses were employed to assist in the work. Dr. Ringer was given special laboratory facilities and granted a chemist to assist him. In addition to this, Dr. Ringer himself generously contributed the sum of $800 annually for a fellowship in metabolism, which enabled him to have a second assistant.

While the final results of these studies are not yet ready for publication, it can be stated that our results have confirmed the statements of the Toronto investigators that insulin is of the greatest value in the treatment of diabetes, and in severe cases will often save the lives of individuals who in former years succumbed in spite of the best medical care.

Dr. Ringer said that of the eighty patients treated, five had been in coma from which only few heretofore had ever come out. Only a few days ago, said Dr. Ringer, a young man of 22 was brought to the hospital in the last stages of the disease. Three injections of insulin were administered each day, and yesterday the man was seen sitting up in bed, reading a magazine.

Another case, said Dr. Ringer, was that of a man past 50, pronounced incurable. The serum was injected and the man is now on his way to Europe.

Insulin, Dr. Ringer pointed out, must be injected from time to time, permanently. The patients are taught how to administer the serum, so the services of a physician or nurse are unnecessary. For the most severe cases, said Dr. Ringer, the cost per day for insulin is about $1.25.

"From the results we have obtained at Montefiore Hospital," Dr. Ringer said, "I can state unequivocally that no person should die from diabetes. Of course, diabetic patients will die of other diseases, but they ought not to die from diabetes itself. Insulin is undoubtedly the greatest discovery of the age."

Within a week or two Dr. Ringer will give lectures at the hospital on the proper administration of the serum. The danger lies in giving the sufferer too large a dose.

Dr. Flexner on the Discovery

Dr. Flexner made his first reference to insulin after praising the work of Louis Pasteur, the French chemist and biologist, whose hundredth anniversary was recently celebrated.

"As a result of Dr. Banting's discovery, the world is enormously richer today that it ever has been before," he said, "and it seems to me now that the world will never again be in the grip of diabetes as it was before. Toronto, of course, is not the only place that will benefit through the discovery. There is not a city in the globe that will not profit by it. And where the details are worked out and the hazards in the administration are removed so that the average doctor can use it safely there will not be a hamlet in the whole world where that discovery will not be applied."

Dr. Flexner, whose topic was "Discovery in Medicine," referred to vaccination as a cure for smallpox.

"Now," he said, "nobody need have smallpox if they don't want it, and the only ones who do want it, it seems, are the anti-vaccinationists, and they'll get it if they don't watch out. . . ."

Primary Source

"Ex-Secretary Lansing, Ill from Diabetes, Improves Under Treatment With Insulin"

SYNOPSIS: This article relates how former Secretary of State Lansing's life was improved with insulin.

Washington, June 27—Robert Lansing, former Secretary of State, has been seriously ill from diabetes but is said by his physicians to have shown great improvement under the administration of insulin, the new remedy recently developed in Canada.

Unknown to any but his most intimate friends, Mr. Lansing has suffered from diabetes for several years and has confined himself to a severe diet, which resulted in a state of great physical disability. Six weeks ago he entered a hospital and under the care of Dr. Sterling Ruffin of Washington received the insulin treatment. He responded at once, it is said, and after he left the hospital continued the treatment at his residence here.

Not only has he gained greatly in flesh and in strength, but his dietary restrictions have been completely removed, so that now he is permitted to eat as much as he desires of all varieties of food. When he started last week for his Summer home at Watertown, N.Y., he was said to have appeared to be well on the road to complete recovery.

John D. Rockefeller Jr. donated money to train doctors and increase the supply of insulin. **AP/WIDE WORLD PHOTOS. REPRODUCED BY PERMISSION.**

Miss Elizabeth Hughes, daughter of the Secretary of State, has also been taking insulin treatment for diabetes and is said to be practically cured.

Special to the New York Times

Watertown, N.Y., June 27—Mr. and Mrs. Robert Lansing are at their Summer cottage, Henderson Harbor, where Mr. Lansing is enjoying bass fishing daily. They arrived late Friday by motor from Washington, having left the capital Wednesday. It was not known here, even by near relatives, that Mr. Lansing had suffered from diabetes although it was known he was not in best of health.

Primary Source

"'Insulin' is Much Easier to Get. No 'Cure' Has Yet Been Found"

SYNOPSIS: The editorial notes that John D. Rockefeller Jr.'s donation would provide insulin to many more people and that insulin is a treatment, not a cure.

"Insulin" is Much Easier to Get

John D. Rockefeller Jr. has given $10,000 to each of fifteen hospitals scattered through this country and Canada, the money to be used in making more widely available to diabetics the pancreatic extract which is known as "insulin." The gift is another evidence—for Rockefeller gifts never are made except after careful investigation by experts—of the wonderful speed with which the value of this curious substance has won recognition. Unlike most innovations in medical treatment, this one received almost instant recognition as fully justifying all the claims made for it, and if now, though only a year has elapsed since its discovery, there is a single doctor who does not believe in its efficacy he is maintaining a silence as wise as it is cautious.

The Rockefeller fund will be spent partly in increasing the supply of insulin—which as yet, unfortunately, is so scarce, and therefore so expensive, that it can be administered in few except the most desperate cases—and partly in teaching physicians the technique of its administration—in giving them the knowledge required to avoid mistakes and misunderstandings the effect of which might be disastrous both to patients and to the reputation of the drug.

Insulin has been patented, not to make money out of it, but in order that it may be controlled and kept out of the hands of charlatans and those who would exploit its large commercial possibilities.

No "Cure" Has Yet Been Found

In spite of its wonderful powers, insulin is not a cure for all diabetics. What it does for the diabetic is to supply him with the substance which his own pancreas, through some functional failure or physical deterioration, has ceased to give him. By this failure or cessation the balance of metabolism is disturbed, seriously or fatally, just as it is when other glands of the sort called "endocrine" suffer either atrophy or hypertrophy.

It is easy enough to understand why insulin simply overcomes the effects of a pancreatic insufficiency and why its administration must be continued in the case of most patients. This is a characteristic which insulin shares with the extract of the thyroid gland, which saves from idiocy the victims of one form of goitre. In both cases the nature of the help given is not that of a curative substance like quinine—curative as to a special malady by destroying its cause, that is—but like that which a one-legged man gets from a crutch, or one with astigmatism from properly adjusted glasses.

The wise generosity of the younger Rockefeller will bring insulin within the reach of many for whom it now is unavailable, and by it many lives otherwise doomed to more or less speedy extinction will be saved. Discovered by Dr. F. G. Banting of the Toronto General Hospital, it entitles him to honor as one of the world's benefactors, for he has placed it at the world's disposal, making no secret either of its nature or of the method of its administration. It will not make him rich, but it will make him famous.

Further Resources

BOOKS

Bliss, Michael. *The Discovery of Insulin.* Chicago: The University of Chicago Press, 1982.

Insulin-Dependent Diabetes. Bethesda, Md.: National Institutes of Health, 1994.

Krahl, Maurice Edward. *The Action of Insulin on Cells.* New York: Academic Press, 1961.

Macleod, John James Richard. *Insulin: Its Use in the Treatment of Diabetes.* Baltimore: Williams & Wilkins, 1925.

Scott, Aleita Hopping. *Great Scott: Ernest Lyman Scott's Work with Insulin in 1911.* Bogota, N.J.: Scott Publishing Co., 1972.

Wrenshall, Gerald Alfred. *The Story of Insulin: Forty Years of Success Against Diabetes.* London: Bodley Head, 1962.

WEBSITES

"The Discovery of Insulin." Available online at http://www.utoronto.ca/bandb/discovery.html (accessed December 16, 2002). This site lists articles about Dr. F.G. Banting.

AUDIO AND VISUAL MEDIA

Insulin: Basic Clinical Skills. Garden Grove, Calif.: Medcom, 1986.

"Scarlet Fever"

Journal article

By: George F. Dick and Gladys H. Dick

Date: December 1924

Source: Dick, George F., and Gladys H. Dick. "Scarlet Fever." *The American Journal of Public Health* 14 (December 1924): 1022–1028.

About the Authors: George Dick (1881–1967) was born in

Fort Wayne, Indiana, and Gladys Henry (1881–1963) in Pawnee City, Nebraska. They met while working together in etiological research at the University of Chicago and married in 1914. Both worked as physicians at the John McCormick Memorial Institute for Infectious Diseases in Chicago. Their work on scarlet fever generated controversy when they patented their method of preparing and manufacturing diagnostic tests for it. ∎

Introduction

As late as 1900, scarlet fever killed 10 out of 100,000 people, making it one of the leading infectious disease killers, as it had been for many generations. Scarlet fever was related to several other diseases caused by streptococci bacteria, including rheumatic fever and puerperal sepsis, but it was not until the late 1800s that scientists knew enough about bacteriology to understand this. Another complication was that scarlet fever was often confused with measles or diphtheria, making diagnosis difficult. A third complication was that streptococci bacteria were found in the throats of healthy individuals, leading some scientists to suggest that other organisms were responsible for the disease. Without knowing what caused scarlet fever, it was difficult to suggest a mechanism for treating it or to know who was susceptible to it.

Significance

George and Gladys Dick drew several wrong conclusions from their research. For example, they argued that a specific type of streptococcus, hemolytic streptococci, was the source of the disease. They also suggested that only one specific toxin was responsible for all of the disease and most of the damage. These conclusions were soon disproved. The article excerpted here, however, describes a revolutionary skin test, still called the Dick test, that reveals which people are susceptible to scarlet fever and convinced researchers that the streptococcus was responsible for the disease. The Dicks suggested immunization against scarlet fever, but no effective immunization was ever developed.

Besides the Dicks, the work of Alphonse Dochez, Oswald Avery, and Rebecca Lancefield was also important in discovering how the disease worked, as was the support of universities and clinical research facilities. The next significant breakthrough in the battle against scarlet fever came with penicillin, which proved successful in destroying the bacteria and became the accepted therapy—not only for scarlet fever but also for rheumatic fever and puerperal sepsis.

Scarlet fever was greatly feared until the middle of the twentieth century, but modern books on parenting point out that the disease occurs rarely and is treatable. Of course, even now it should be treated quickly, but it poses much less danger since it can be treated with antibiotics. The

Dick test was thus an important step on the road to the containment of scarlet fever, one of many infectious diseases that are no longer as feared in the twenty-first century as they once were.

Primary Source

"Scarlet Fever" [excerpt]

SYNOPSIS: The article notes that when the Dicks put scarlet fever from an infected person onto the throats of others, only some became infected. They also describe how they developed a test to determine if one is susceptible to the disease. The article suggests that a specific type of streptococcus caused scarlet fever and that a specific toxin was the causative agent of the disease's complications.

The intelligent prevention treatment of a disease must depend on a definite knowledge of its cause. Attempts to learn the etiology of scarlet fever have long been hampered by failure to obtain the disease experimentally. Symptoms that might represent scarlet fever in animals had been described by various authors; but these symptoms were indefinite and inconstant, and had followed inoculation with different materials and cultures. No organism had produced in animals a condition that could be accepted as experimental scarlet fever. . . .

Even with human volunteers, we did not expect to obtain experimental scarlet fever readily; for it was known that less than half of the persons exposed to scarlet fever contract the disease.

Healthy young adults who said that they had not had scarlet fever were chosen. In the first series of human inoculations, reported in 1921, volunteers were inoculated with fresh whole blood and fresh blood serum from acute cases of scarlet fever; also with filtered throat mucus from early cases. The results of these inoculations were negative. Then since the hemolytic streptococcus is the organism most constantly associated with scarlet fever, and the one to which immune bodies are most constantly produced, the next volunteers were inoculated with pure cultures of hemolytic streptococci isolated from scarlet fever. In this series, we obtained an occasional sore throat and fever, but no rash. We thought that failure to obtain the rash might be due to a relative insusceptibility on the part of the volunteers, and decided to do some further inoculation experiments using volunteers of an intelligent type who could give their full personal and family history, and to choose them, so far as possible, from those who had never been exposed to scarlet fever.

Health inspectors remove immigrants suspected of being infected with scarlet fever in 1928. Fever suspects were then sent to a quarantine hospital.
© BETTMANN/CORBIS. REPRODUCED BY PERMISSION.

In this series, reported in 1923, we obtained a case of typical scarlet fever by inoculation with a pure culture of a hemolytic streptococcus. This streptococcus had been isolated from a lesion on the finger of a nurse who acquired the disease while caring for a convalescent scarlet fever patient. This was the first case of typical scarlet fever produced experimentally with a pure culture of any organism.

It was still necessary to learn whether the experimental scarlet fever had been produced by the hemolytic streptococcus or by a filterable virus associated with it in the culture. A second group of vol-

unteers were inoculated with a culture of the same organism after it had been passed through a Berkefeld "V" filter. These volunteers remained well. After two weeks had elapsed, and they were still well, they were inoculated with the unfiltered culture. Forty-eight hours later, one of them developed scarlet fever. This experiment furnished evidence that the experimental disease was not caused by a filterable virus but was due to the hemolytic streptococcus itself.

There were still some difficulties. Not all of the hemolytic streptococci associated with scarlet fever are of the same cultural type. Some ferment mannite, while others do not ferment mannite. And it was necessary to show that each type is capable of producing the disease. This was done by inoculating other volunteers with the second cultural type, and obtaining another case of experimental scarlet fever.

The requirement of Koch's laws had now been fully met, and we were justified in concluding that scarlet fever is caused by the hemolytic streptococcus.

Since the hemolytic streptococcus is found in the throat, and is seldom present in the blood, it is evident that the rash of scarlet fever is not produced by the direct action of the streptococcus on the skin. It was still important to learn by what means the streptococcus, growing in the throat, caused the rash.

We found that the scarlet fever streptococci produce a toxin. When this toxin is absorbed into the blood, it produces the rash. The toxin is obtained by inoculating plain broth with the strains of streptococci that produced experimental scarlet fever in human beings. A small amount of blood is usually added to the broth at the time of inoculation. After incubation, the broth cultures are passed through porcelain filters to remove the bacteria. The filtrate is cultured for sterility, and kept in a refrigerator.

When suitable amounts of toxin are injected in susceptible persons, it may cause a reaction characterized by general malaise, nausea, vomiting, fever, and a generalized scarlatinal rash. In other words, the sterile toxin alone is capable of producing the characteristic symptoms of scarlet fever, including the rash. These symptoms appear within a few hours after injection of the toxin, and disappear within forty-eight hours.

The toxin is resistant to heat at temperatures ordinarily employed to kill bacteria, but is destroyed by still higher temperatures.

It is neutralized by convalescent scarlet fever serum due to the presence of an antitoxin in the blood of recovered patients. If persons susceptible to scarlet fever are immunized by injections of small doses of toxin, their blood serum acquires similar antitoxic properties.

These facts indicate that we are dealing with a true soluble toxin specific for scarlet fever.

While minute quantities of the toxin will produce symptoms of scarlet fever in susceptible adults, laboratory animals are comparatively insusceptible to it, so that it is necessary to standardize the toxin on human beings.

The discovery of this toxin offered a scientific basis for:

First, The recognition of scarlet fever streptococci.

Second, The development of a skin test for susceptibility to scarlet fever.

Third, Preventive immunization.

Fourth, The production of an antitoxin.

The two strains of streptococci that caused experimental scarlet fever in man differed culturally, and were not agglutinated by the same immune serum; but they had in common the property of producing the specific toxin of scarlet fever.

Up to the present time, there has been no satisfactory way of identifying scarlet fever streptococci. Since the recognition of the specificity of the agglutination test, and its application to the diagnosis of typhoid fever, many observations have been made on the agglutination of streptococci in relation to scarlet fever. The results of early investigators indicated that most, but not all, of the streptococci associated with scarlet fever are agglutinated by the same immune serum.

But the agglutination test has not furnished a reliable means of identifying scarlet fever streptococci. Certain strains cannot be tested because of spontaneous agglutination. No serum agglutinates specifically streptococci from all cases of scarlet fever. And agglutination of streptococci from other sources is not uncommon.

A study of the toxin production of hemolytic streptococci offers a more hopeful means of identifying those organisms that are capable of causing scarlet fever. . . .

In our first series of skin tests reported in January, 1924, we found positive, or strongly positive, reactions in 41.6 per cent of the persons who gave no history of scarlet fever, and negative, or only slightly positive reactions in all of the convalescent scarlet fever patients tested.

Branch and Edwards reported 40 per cent positive, or strongly positive, reactions in persons with no history of scarlet fever and negative reactions in all convalescent scarlet fever patients tested.

Zingher found a similar relation between immunity to scarlet fever and skin tests with scarlet fever toxin.

Zingher showed that there is a parallelism between immunity to scarlet fever and immunity to diphtheria in various age and social groups. He demonstrated a placental transmission of scarlet fever antitoxin from mother to child. According to his results, most infants show negative reactions during the first months of life, and the skin test becomes positive toward the end of the first year. In this connection it is interesting to note that nearly one hundred years ago, Most, in speaking of the possibility of inoculating against scarlet fever, recommended that such inoculations should not be attempted in children under two years of age because of the insusceptibility of the young child.

Since Jenner's success with smallpox vaccination, many attempts have been made to inoculate human beings with scarlet fever in the hope of preventing more severe attacks. . . .

After demonstration of the specific toxin of scarlet fever and the development of the skin test for susceptibility, we began immunization of susceptible persons by subcutaneous injections of small doses of toxin. We found that by beginning with a small dose, it is possible to avoid severe reactions.

In any large series of skin tests, there will be found a group of clearly negative reactions, another group of definitely positive reactions, and a third group of slightly positive reactions.

Persons who show negative skin tests do not require immunization. We are immunizing all those who show any degree of positive reaction. The immunization consists of three doses of toxin given at five-day intervals.

Following immunization, a skin test should be made to determine the degree of immunity that has been obtained.

A type of skin reaction frequently found after immunization is one that appears quickly, but fades within twenty-four hours, and is, therefore, negative.

If the skin test is still positive after three immunizing doses, the third dose should be repeated, or a larger dose may be given.

Experience has shown that immunization must be carried to the point of a negative skin test.

Prevention of scarlet fever, after exposure, is more complicated. In case of definite exposure, skin tests are made as soon as possible, and at the same time, a culture of the throat is made on blood agar plates. If the skin test is negative, nothing more is done.

In those with positive skin tests, the next step depends on the throat culture. If the plates show no hemolytic streptococci, and further exposure can be avoided, active immunization is carried out with three doses of toxin.

If the throat culture shows hemolytic streptococci, passive immunization is accomplished by injection of convalescent scarlet fever serum, or concentrated scarlet fever antitoxin. We use convalescent serum when it is available to avoid sensitization to horse serum.

The passive immunity is transient. It does not protect for more than a few weeks.

These preventive measures were carried out in a series of 200 persons exposed to scarlet fever. One hundred of this series were nurses in contagious disease hospitals who were tested and immunized before exposure; 100 were children who were not seen until after exposure. Ten of the children with positive skin tests showed hemolytic streptococci in their throat cultures. They received convalescent serum. Five already had sore throat and fever at the time they received the serum. None of these 200 persons exposed to scarlet fever developed the disease.

Controls were afforded by 42 nurses and interns on whom skin tests were not made, and by 2 nurses who were exposed to scarlet fever before their immunization was completed. These 2 nurses and 7 others of this control series contracted scarlet fever.

The toxic element of scarlet fever has long been recognized by clinicians. Variation in degree of toxaemia has served as a basis for the differentiation of clinical types. Thus, Osler, in describing the fulminant toxic type, wrote:

> With all the characteristics of an acute intoxication, the patient is overwhelmed by the intensity of the poison, and may die within twenty-four or thirty-six hours.

And Holt said of the malignant type:

> Death occurs apparently from scarlatinal toxaemia.

When the use of convalescent serum in the treatment of scarlet fever became general, it was learned that it is the severe, toxic type of scarlet fever in which it is the most useful; and that the symptoms most benefited are those commonly attributed to the toxaemia. . . .

Scarlet fever throughout the country has been comparatively mild for several years. The present low death rate from this disease shows that not many lives will be actually saved by any serum.

In 430 cases of scarlet fever admitted to the Durand Hospital in one and a half years, there were only 5 deaths. All of these fatal cases were admitted comparatively late in the disease, and were septic. Three had broncho-pneumonia, empyema, and nephritis; on had suppurating cervical lymph glands and nephritis and the other was a case of puerperal sepsis with sloughed perineal stitches, foul lochia, and persistent vomiting. It is not probable that any serum could have saved the lives of these patients after the complications had developed. . . .

We had found that, if the antitoxin is given early in the disease, a definite fading of the rash is apparent within 24 hours, and there is an improvement in the toxic symptoms. So the antitoxin may be said to remove the toxic element of the disease, including the rash. The subsequent course depends on the local infection in the nose and throat.

The sinuses, glands and ears are frequently involved early in the disease. After enough antitoxin has been given to relieve the patient of the necessity for combating the toxaemia, these local complications should receive careful attention.

Because complications may occur so early in scarlet fever, and the damage done by the disease is to be estimated not so much in the number of deaths as in the after effects, the importance of preventive immunization is apparent.

Further Resources

BOOKS

Bowers, John Z., and Elizabeth F. Purcell. *Advances in American Medicine: Essays at the Bicentennial.* New York: Josiah Macy Jr. Foundation, 1976.

Dick, George F., and Gladys Henry Dick. *Scarlet Fever.* Chicago: Yearbook Publishers, 1938.

Dowling, Harry F. *Fighting Infection: Conquests of the Twentieth Century.* Cambridge, Mass.: Harvard University Press, 1977.

Jürgensen, Theodor von, and Northrup, William P. *Measles, Scarlatina, German Measles.* Translated from the German under the editorial supervision of Alfred Stengel. Philadelphia: W.B. Saunders, 1904.

Ricketts, H.T. *Infection, Immunity and Serum Therapy: In Relation to the Infectious Diseases of Man,* 2d rev. ed. Chicago: American Medical Association Press, 1911.

Shearer, Benjamin F., and Barbara S. Shearer. *Notable Women in the Life Sciences: A Biographical Dictionary.* Westport, Conn.: Greenwood Press, 1996.

"Tularemia"

Journal article

By: Edward Francis

Date: April 25, 1925

Source: Francis, Edward. "Tularemia." *The Journal of the American Medical Association* 84, no. 17 (April 25, 1925): 1243–1250.

About the Author: Ohio native Edward Francis (1872–1957) graduated from the University of Cincinnati and Ohio State University. He was best known for identifying and developing methods to fight tularemia, an infectious disease he contracted five times over the course of his life as a result of his research. For his work, he was awarded a gold medal from the American Medical Association in 1928 and honorary doctorates of science from Ohio State and Miami University in Ohio. ∎

Introduction

Tularemia was officially recognized in 1911, though it had been noted as early as 1907. The disease was wholly American until it was reported in other countries starting in about 1925. It was first noted among people who had been skinning wild rabbits, but it was also observed in those exposed to squirrels, deer flies, and wild fowl. The disease lasts from about seven days to several months, and its severity ranges from a light fever to death. Symptoms generally include a boil at the location of a bite, enlarged lymph nodes, swollen glands, and intestinal difficulties. A person who inhales the bacteria can contract tularemic pneumonia.

Efforts to unravel the mystery of tularemia began in 1902 when the Public Health and Marine Hospital Service and the U.S. Hygienic Laboratory, which provided scientific assistance for the states, were created. Under the auspices of the Hygienic Laboratory, Edward Francis studied tularemia in Utah and noted that the deer fly could transmit the disease. Then in 1912, the Public Health Service's George McCoy and C.W. Chapin discovered the bacterium that causes the disease, naming it *Bacterium tularense,* for Tulare County, California, where they studied the disease.

Although the disease is caused by a bacterium, it is carried by insects, which pick up the disease from animals or contaminated water. In the early twentieth century tularemia was known as "rabbit fever" because rabbits were a prime carrier of the disease. Hunters knew not to shoot a calm rabbit, which might be a carrier, and to fully cook rabbit meat to kill the bacteria.

Significance

After tularemia was identified, a number of unsuccessful treatment methods were tried. Success came in 1944 with the discovery of streptomycin, an antibiotic that generally caused a patient's fever to disappear, even in severe cases. Streptomycin is still widely used, but other antibiotics such as tetracycline and chloramphenicol can be used with equal effectiveness, as can aminoglycosides, macrolides, and fluoroquinolones. A vaccine has been developed for people with a high risk of infection, but it is not recommended for general use.

Tularemia was considered by both the United States and Japan for use as a biological weapon during World War II (1939–1945). After World War II, the United States and the Soviet Union stockpiled the active ingredient in tularemia for this purpose. The United States had destroyed its stocks by 1973, while the Soviets continued to produce them through the 1980s.

In more contemporary times, tularemia has become relatively rare and generally not contagious. Diagnosis and treatment have greatly advanced such that recent mortality rates have been around 2 percent. Left untreated, though, the disease's mortality rate can reach 60 percent.

Tularemia research also led to better methods for preparing and treating rabbit meat between slaughter and sale—an important advance that made rabbit a safer meat to eat.

Primary Source

"Tularemia" [excerpt]

SYNOPSIS: Francis summarizes the disease's behavior, how it is contracted, and where in the United States it is found. He then discusses the disease's progression, how to test for it, methods of transmission, and how immunity may be developed. Francis ends by discussing the treatments available.

Tularemia occurs in nature as a very fatal bacteremia of various rodents (especially rabbits) and is due to *Bacterium tularense;* it is transmissible to man as an accidental infection by the bite of an infected blood-sucking insect or tick, or by the lodgment on his hands of the blood or internal organs of an infected rodent, as in the case of market men, cooks, hunters or laboratory workers.

Among the few diseases of man that have been discovered in the last fifteen years is tularemia. It is the only disease of man that has been elucidated from beginning to end by American investigators alone. These investigators have worked in widely separated states, and in most instances each made his first contribution while in ignorance of the work of the others.

The first observations of each were characterized by the nature of the work for which he was especially trained; thus, a serologist first noted the presence of antitularense amboceptors in his own blood after a febrile attack, and in the blood of his attendant while dissecting infected rodents in his laboratory. A clinician first described the symptoms and course of the disease in a group of six cases occurring in his practice, which he differentiated as due to the bite of a blood-sucking fly found on horses. Finally, a bacteriologist isolated the causative organism from a human case in which the site of infection was the eye.

In consequence of these circumstances, a variety of names or synonyms sprang up, according to the conditions under which the disease was first encountered by each, and we find plaguelike disease of rodents, deer-fly fever, *Bacillus tularense* infection of the eye, rabbit fever and glandular type of tick fever. . . .

Geographic Distribution in Man and Rodents

So far as is now known, tularemia is confined to the United States. It has been authentically reported from thirteen states and the District of Columbia, extending from the Pacific to the Atlantic coast—California, Utah, Wyoming, Idaho, Colorado, Ohio, Indiana, Tennessee, North Carolina, Montana, New Mexico, Virginia, West Virginia and the District of Columbia. . . .

Symptoms and Course of Tularemia

Case histories and notes have been recorded for forty-nine cases, of which fourteen were caused by fly bite in Utah and Idaho, one was caused by tick bite in Montana; ten patients had cut up jack-rabbits for hog feed, chicken feed and fish bait in New Mexico; ten had dressed wild cottontail rabbits for food in Ohio, Washington, D.C., North Carolina, Virginia and West Virginia, and fourteen were laboratory workers who had performed necropsy on infected guinea-pigs or rabbits in laboratories in San Francisco, Washington, D.C., Hamilton, Mont., and London, England.

Two clinical types of symptoms are encountered in analyzing these cases.

Of thirty-five cases in which the patients were flybitten, tick-bitten or had cut up jack-rabbits or dressed cottontail rabbits, thirty-three were of the glandular type, with enlarged glands and an evident local site of infection; in only two of the thirty-five was there a record of absence of enlarged glands or absence of a local site of infection.

Fourteen cases of infection of laboratory workers were free from enlarged glands or local site of infection, and to the clinician they simulated typhoid fever and were therefore of the typhoid type. . . .

Agglutination Tests

The definite diagnosis of tularemia in fourteen laboratory workers rested finally on the agglutination of *Bacterium tularense* by their blood serum in each instance. The fever in each was such as to suggest typhoid, but the only records of positive Widal tests were in two patients who had received three injections of single typhoid vaccine; a slightly positive Widal reaction is recorded in these cases.

The laboratory cases afforded an unusual opportunity to study the early appearance of agglutinins and their long persistence. . . .

Portal of Entry in Laboratory Workers

Two of three laboratory cases occurring in England gave moderate evidence of pain, tenderness and swelling localized in the cervical glands, but otherwise there was an absence of local lesions.

None of the eleven laboratory cases occurring in America showed any evident site of infection or enlarged glands. It is difficult to account for this absence. The portal of entry of the infection in laboratory workers is unknown. All of them had either performed necropsy on infected animals or removed the animals from the dissection boards. Presumably, infected tissue and blood found lodgment on their hands, and then the infection either penetrated the skin or found its way to the mouth and was swallowed. If it penetrated the skin of the hand, one would expect a local lesion or glandular enlargement of the arm, or both; if it found entrance to the mouth, one might expect glandular enlargement of the neck. To support the view that the infection in these cases penetrated the unbroken skin of the hands, we know that guinea-pigs on the normal skin of which infected spleen juice is placed die acutely of typical tularemia, in the absence of any clipping of the hair or rubbing of the skin or of any possibility that the infection might have gained entrance to the animal's mouth. We know that, in culture mediums, cystin is a requirement of growth of the organism, and that the cystin content of the skin is high; hence the possibility must be considered that the cystin of the skin supplies conditions for growth of the organism and subsequent penetration of the skin.

The mechanism of infection of laboratory workers is discussed by Ledingham and Fraser of England, with special reference to one of their three cases. Their third patient, S., dated his infection

Dr. Edward Francis is credited for identifying tularemia and developing methods to fight it. © BETTMANN/CORBIS. REPRODUCED BY PERMISSION.

from one exposure only, while performing a necropsy on a chloroformed guinea-pig and passing the virus to another. He remembered distinctly that the animal had coughed in his presence during anesthesia. Nine days later the illness set in. This was his sole association with tularemia. The view is expressed that a droplet respiratory infection might explain such cases. . . .

Noncontagiousness

No instance has been reported of the spread of the infection from man to man by mere contact or by the bite of insects which previously have bitten a patient. Dr. C.E. Harris, however, reported a case of direct transmission to a mother who, while dressing an ulcer and an opened gland on the neck of her son, pricked her thumb with a safety pin, resulting in a severe infection of the thumb; typical fever and prostration, with rather early suppuration of the epitrochlear and axillary glands, but without red streaks on the arm, followed.

Immunity

The only instance that has been reported of a second attack in man was in a laboratory worker engaged daily in performing necropsies, without gloves, on laboratory animals in the Hygienic Laboratory, Washington, D.C. The second attack developed two years and five months after the first attack; there was a papule engrafted on a crack on the finger from which *Bacterium tularense* was isolated by guinea-pig inoculation. There was also a lymphadenitis involving the epitrochlear and axillary glands of the same arm, but an absence of fever or other notable constitutional symptoms.

The long persistence of agglutinins in the blood of recovered patients may be an indication of their immunity.

Susceptible laboratory animals (guinea-pigs, rabbits and white mice) have exhibited no evidence of immunity in our laboratory; all have died with the single exception of one rabbit, which survived a severe attack. . . .

Treatment

The treatment is symptomatic. Rest in bed is most important. Those who have had most experience with the enlarged glands do not advise excision or even incision until a very evident soft, thin place appears in the skin overlying the glands. No preventive vaccine or curative serum has been perfected.

Further Resources

BOOKS

Jellison, William L. *Tularemia in North America.* Missoula, Mont.: University of Montana, 1974.

Parker, R.R., et al. *Contamination of Natural Waters and Mud with Pasteurella Tularensis and Tularemia in Beavers and Muskrats in the Northwestern United States.* Washington, D.C.: U.S. Government Printing Office, 1951.

The Pathology of Tularemia. Washington, D.C.: U.S. Government Printing Office, 1937.

Pollitzer, Robert. *Review of Russian Papers on Tularemia.* Bethesda, Md.: National Institute of Health, 1958.

Sansberry, Margaret H. "Cellular Immunity in Tularemia." Master's thesis, University of Tennessee, 1960.

Simpson, Walter M. *Tularemia: History, Pathology, Diagnosis and Treatment.* New York: P.B. Hoeber, 1929.

Yeatter, Ralph E., and David H. Thompson. *Tularemia, Weather, and the Rabbit Populations.* Urbana, Ill.: University of Illinois Press, 1952.

WEBSITES

"Tularemia as a Biological Weapon." Available online at http://www.jama.ama-assn.org/issues/v285n21/ffull/jst10001.html (accessed December 16, 2002).

Smallpox

"Mayor Is Vaccinated Against Smallpox to Set a Good Example for the Public"
Newspaper article

By: *The New York Times*
Date: May 15, 1925
Source: "Mayor Is Vaccinated Against Smallpox To Set a Good Example for the Public." *The New York Times,* May 15, 1925, 21.

"City Votes $80,000 to Fight Smallpox"
Newspaper article

By: *The New York Times*
Date: May 16, 1925
Source: "City Votes $80,000 to Fight Smallpox." *The New York Times,* May 16, 1925, 18.

"Public Duty and Self-Interest"
Editorial

By: *The New York Times*
Date: June 4, 1925
Source: "Public Duty and Self-Interest." *The New York Times,* June 4, 1925, 18.

About the Publication: Founded in 1850 as the *New-York Daily Times, The New York Times* was originally a relatively obscure local paper. By the early twentieth century, however, it had grown into a widely known, well-respected news source. Its banner, "All the News That's Fit to Print," is recognized across the United States and throughout the world. ∎

Introduction

By 1900, smallpox was no longer one of the top ten causes of death. Indeed, it had been largely eradicated through vaccination. Before the eighteenth century, though, the only "cure" was to isolate those who had the disease and quarantine ships that had smallpox outbreaks on board, but nearly a quarter of those exposed to smallpox died. By that time, however, one method of dealing with smallpox had been created: an inoculation with material from a pustule on a person who was suffering from smallpox. This procedure, known as variolation, generally produced a light case of smallpox. It did, however, produce a significant number of deaths, especially when done on a wide scale, and those who caught smallpox from this method still posed a threat to others.

In the nineteenth century, Dr. Edward Jenner began inoculation with cowpox, a procedure that quickly replaced variolation. Not everyone was inoculated, however, because the number of antivaccinationists grew and medical opinion on vaccination was split. By the turn of the twentieth century, health officials had begun to emphasize the health benefits of inoculation, a standard and effective method of inoculation was created, and a 1905 Supreme Court case, *Jacobsen v. Massachusetts,* upheld the right of states to require the inoculation of children before they attended school. Outbreaks still occurred, however, such as the one New York City suffered in 1901, when there were over 2,500 confirmed cases and seven hundred deaths. Even in the 1920s, fears of similar outbreaks ran high.

Significance

By 1920 New York City required the immunization of children before they entered school. The disease, however, still posed a risk. In 1925 several cases of smallpox were found, increasing fears of a wide-scale outbreak, and city officials had to determine what steps to take. They decided on a campaign of public persuasion rather than compulsion, for they did not want people to complain that their liberties had been violated. As these articles discuss, Mayor Hylan was vaccinated in front of the press, and extra monies were voted for a citywide vaccination campaign, though vaccination remained voluntary. Buttons were handed out to children in school to congratulate those who had been vaccinated. The effort was successful, as no wave of smallpox arrived, though it did break out in other places that year. Politics, though, reared its ugly head. The health commissioner's opponents suggested that there had never been a threat of smallpox and that the scare had been whipped up only to give the commissioner's friends jobs.

New York City's next smallpox panic was in 1947. A full-scale press alert announced the need for mass vaccination. It was done carefully, however, and no panic resulted. Nearly two hundred vaccination sites were opened to the public, including police precincts, and even President Harry S. Truman (served 1945–1953) was inoculated before he traveled to New York City. Within two weeks, five million people were vaccinated, and by the end of the month, the number had topped six million. A massive number of volunteers were mobilized to handle the volume, and pharmaceutical companies were cajoled into producing more vaccine cheaply. The inoculation worked, as only twelve new cases emerged and only two people died. Thus, in both 1925 and 1947 public education campaigns rather than compulsion succeeded. The success of these methods has strong implications as Americans consider the possibility of smallpox being used as a terrorist weapon in the twenty-first century.

Primary Source

"Mayor Is Vaccinated Against Smallpox to Set a Good Example for the Public"

SYNOPSIS: This article suggests that citizens should follow their mayor's good example and get vaccinated.

Mayor Hylan, at the personal request of Dr. Frank J. Monaghan, Commissioner of the Department of Health, submitted yesterday to vaccination with anti-smallpox virus. As the Mayor and Dr. Monaghan after explained, the former permitted himself to be vaccinated not only as a precaution against the disease but also as a good example to the public.

The Health Commissioner added that it would be wise if every citizen of New York were to follow the Mayor's example. Though there was no cause for alarm, Dr. Monaghan said, yesterday's official reports to the Board of Health listed six cases of smallpox as now under treatment in this city. To avert all possibility of an epidemic, Dr. Monaghan recommended that everybody who had not been vaccinated within a comparatively recent period should fall in line behind Mayor Hylan.

Dr. Monaghan called at the City Hall in person. He was accompanied by Dr. Frank D. Oberwager. They were admitted to the Mayor's office late in the afternoon. Mayor Hylan promptly bared his left arm and Dr. Oberwager applied the lancet and the serum.

New York City of late has been almost entirely free from smallpox, though a considerable number of cases of that disease have been under treatment in Philadelphia, Washington and other cities. It was recalled that President Coolidge and other public men of prominence in the national capital recently had been vaccinated.

Dr. Monaghan said also that yesterday's reports showed under treatment in New York City sixty cases of diphtheria, which is twenty in excess of the number listed on the same date of last year and considerably above normal. The total number of infectious or epidemic diseases now under treatment in his jurisdiction, the Health Commissioner added, aggregated about 400.

In making this statement Dr. Monaghan again emphasized his belief, and requested his hearers to accentuate it, that all this justifies precaution, but not serious alarm, as every case is isolated and is under careful observation and treatment.

Following the discovery of six cases of smallpox in Bayonne since last Saturday, Dr. Bert J. Daly,

Hudson County physician, announced yesterday that all inmates of county institutions had been ordered vaccinated. At the same time Dr. W.W. Brooke, Health Officer of Bayonne, made a public appeal to all citizens of Bayonne to submit to vaccination.

Primary Source

"City Votes $80,000 to Fight Smallpox"

SYNOPSIS: This article discusses the six cases of smallpox already in the city but hints that outside communities may have produced these. It also suggests that the number of travelers coming in and out of New York City make it a prime candidate for a smallpox outbreak.

City Votes $80,000 to Fight Smallpox

Dr. Monaghan Minimizes Actual Peril Here, But Warns of Cases in Suburbs.

Board Heeds His Advice

Health Head Sees No Reason for Compulsory Vaccination Now—Cites Purposes of Fund.

In response to a personal appeal made by Dr. Frank J. Monaghan, Commissioner of the Department of Health, who appeared before them, the Board of Estimate yesterday appropriated a special fund of $80,000 to be expended for vaccine virus and other supplies, for additional emergency personnel, and to meet the cost of a campaign of education to prevent any spread of smallpox in this city.

Dr. Monaghan told the board that, while he did not wish to be regarded as an alarmist, there was no ignoring the fact that there have been outbreaks of smallpox in neighboring cities and a good many cases as near as in Bayonne, N.J. "It is a fact also," he declared, "that the disease has taken on this year a more virulent form than is usual and that every State in the Union has shown an increased number of victims. In some communities the disease has become epidemic.

"The six smallpox cases that now have been reported in this city," the Health Commissioner continued, "were in all probability brought here from outside communities. Our worst afflicted neighbor is Philadelphia, which now has 150 cases. The people are generally negligent and heedless of the importance of vaccination. I am no alarmist, but I should rather be thought an alarmist than to have to hold myself accountable later for an epidemic or for having neglected to take every proper precaution against such a misfortune.

"This city is the gate of entry for a never-ceasing flow of travelers, visitors and residents coming and going, every one of whom becomes a potential source of this disease if he or she has passed through one of the cities where smallpox is prevalent. It is not the increase in the number of cases that causes us so much concern, but it is also the unusual virulence of the disease. Its increased prevalence may be seen from the following figures:

"During last year there have been 4,527 cases and 227 deaths in Michigan, 3,845 cases and 24 deaths in North Carolina, and 3,751 cases and 8 deaths in Indiana. These figures and others show a sufficiently grave situation existing in many parts of the country.

With a sidelong glance at Controller Craig, who has been among those in the past who have criticized the Health Department chief for obtaining special appropriations and augmented personnel under a plea of what the critics have called "fake epidemic scares." Dr. Monaghan went on: "I should rather be criticized for asking for this money to prevent any possible spread of this disease than to have to take the criticism that would be directed against me if smallpox should enter this city and spread on a large scale."

"Go ahead and ask for your appropriation," advised Mayor Hylan, also with a significant look toward the Controller. "Pay no attention to the political fakers and their allies who attack you."

Commissioner Monaghan then made formal application for the $80,000, and the appropriation was voted without a dissenting voice.

"I do not believe in making vaccination compulsory as yet," said Dr. Monaghan after the meeting, "but the disease is a most insidious one, which creeps upon you without warning, and our aim is to prevent its getting a foothold."

Primary Source

"Public Duty and Self-Interest"

SYNOPSIS: This editorial points out that citizens should be vaccinated both for their own protection and to prevent the disease from spreading.

New Yorkers who still have neglected to be vaccinated ought to feel a sense of duty unperformed, as well as a good deal of apprehension, as they read, day after day, of new smallpox cases in or near this city. On Tuesday one victim, not knowing what was the matter with him, and as yet but slightly ill,

With 62 citizens testing positive for smallpox, residents of Middlesboro, Massachusetts, line up for the smallpox inoculation in 1929.
© BETTMANN/CORBIS. REPRODUCED BY PERMISSION.

traveled to the hospital in a crowded subway train. How many he infected may be discovered later, but he would have been entirely harmless as a close neighbor if all of his fellow-travelers had taken the very small amount of trouble needed to insure their own safety.

As vaccination now is performed, it is the most trivial of "operations," so far as giving pain is concerned, and the precautions taken against getting the commoner and irrelevant infections in the minute wound—which alone can give rise to extensive inflammation—are practically sure to be successful.

Further Resources

BOOKS

Dixon, C.W. *Smallpox.* London: J. & A. Churchill, 1962.

Goodman, Brian L. *A History of Epidemic Smallpox in the New World.* Lexington, Ky.: University Press of Kentucky, 1955.

Hopkins, Donald R. *Princes and Peasants: Smallpox in History.* Chicago: University of Chicago Press, 1983.

Shurkin, Joel N. *The Invisible Fire: The Story of Mankind's Victory Over the Ancient Scourge of Smallpox.* New York: Putnam, 1979.

Tucker, Jonathan B. *Scourge: The Once and Future Threat of Smallpox.* New York: Atlantic Monthly Press, 2001.

Wilkinson, Paul Biddulph. *Variations on a Theme by Sydenham: Small Pox.* Bristol, England: J. Wright, 1960.

AUDIO AND VISUAL MEDIA

The History Channel. *Smallpox: Deadly Again?* New York: A&E Television Networks; distributed by New Video Group, 1999.

"Cancer Studies in Massachusetts"

Study

By: Herbert L. Lombard and Carl R. Doering

Date: April 26, 1928

Source: Lombard, Herbert L., and Carl R. Doering. "Cancer Studies in Massachusetts. 2. Habits, Characteristics and Environment of Individuals with and without Cancer." *The New England Journal of Medicine* 198, no. 10 (April 26, 1928): 481–487.

About the Publication: *The New England Journal of Medicine and Surgery and the Collateral Branches of Science* was founded in 1812 by future Massachusetts Medical Society president John Collins Warren, M.D. After a merger and name change, the publication was called *The Boston Medical and Surgical Journal* until, in 1928, it became known as *The*

New England Journal of Medicine. Officially owned by the Massachusetts Medical Society since 1921, the journal is highly respected by both doctors and medical schools. ∎

Introduction

During the colonial period tobacco was the crop that kept Virginia alive, and it quickly became popular in Europe. The tobacco market, though, was unstable, so in the early 1800s many farmers began growing cotton and wheat instead. Tobacco processing, particularly for cigarettes, grew up in the American South in the late nineteenth century. Cigarettes became a mass consumption item in the 1920s as more people could afford them. There was little concern, though, about the health effects of tobacco in the nineteenth and early twentieth centuries, partly because cancer itself was not widely studied. The development of better glass in the nineteenth century led to cellular microscopes, and physicians developed the ability to operate on cancerous tumors. Around the turn of the twentieth century, researchers began to transplant tumors into animals in order to study them, and statisticians started to compile tables of cancer mortality rates.

Significance

Lombard and Doering were among the first researchers to suggest that smoking caused cancer, and this is the most famous article on the subject from the 1920s. They studied the lifestyles of those who had and did not have cancer, and by showing a correlation between smoking and cancer, particularly cancer of the mouth, they were able to suggest causation. Their study demonstrates how the smoking habits of America have changed, as 33 percent of the people they studied were heavy smokers, much higher than in the early twenty-first century, when only about 25 percent even smoke regularly. It took decades for the medical establishment and the government to fully accept the link recognized by Lombard and Doering. Cigarettes got a boost during World War II (1939–1945) as the U.S. Army placed cigarettes, along with chewing gum, in K rations. They were often the only sense of warmth for the infantryman, and nicotine produced relaxation under stressful circumstances. It was not until the 1950s that the medical establishment conclusively determined that smoking causes cancer.

Tobacco companies, then and now, fought this conclusion, even establishing their own research institutes to disprove the link. In the 1950s some U.S. senators suggested that the government place warning labels on cigarettes, but they were opposed by other senators, particularly those from tobacco-growing states. The cigarette companies fought the perception that cigarettes were dangerous through advertisements with figures such as the Marlboro Man and promises that with certain brands, there was not "a cough in a carload."

In 1964, though, public attitudes began to change. Two years earlier, the U.S. surgeon general had established an advisory committee on the issue, and it reported in 1964 that smoking causes cancer. In 1965 Congress passed a law requiring the warning label "Caution: Cigarette smoking may be hazardous to your health." The weak language in the warning indicated the power of the tobacco lobby, but the labels were strengthened over the years. States also began to ban smoking in certain places, and research on the deadly effects of secondhand smoke have challenged the attitude that "it's my body and I'll do what I want with it." Cigarette companies in recent years have lost multimillion-dollar lawsuits, cigarettes are heavily taxed, and certain types of tobacco advertising have been banned.

Primary Source

"Cancer Studies in Massachusetts" [excerpt]

> **SYNOPSIS:** The article begins with a discussion of the methodology of the study, noting how a control group of those without cancer was included. It then surveys a large number of variables and discusses the relationship between cancer and several variables, including smoking, suggesting a connection between smoking and cancer. The article closes by noting the differences between the cancer group and those without cancer.

At the inception of the Massachusetts program for cancer control Dr. Frederick Hoffman was consulted for suggestions. He advised that the Massachusetts study should include a collection of questionnaires similar to those that he was collecting in his San Francisco Survey. As Dr. Hoffman is probably the greatest collector of figures of our time, any advice from him should be most seriously considered. A few of these questionnaires were obtained in the 1925 study but as the number was too small for tabulation they were given to Dr. Hoffman to incorporate with his other records.

During 1927 a somewhat similar study was made by this Department, with the assistance of several of the visiting nurses' organizations throughout the State. Our method of approach was somewhat different from that of Dr. Hoffman. We feel that any study of the habits of individuals with cancer is of little value without a similar study of individuals without cancer. To know that a large percentage of patients with cancer have certain habits is of little value for inference unless we know what percentage of the community at large has the same habits. . . .

The use of tobacco has long been considered a factor in the incidence of cancer of the buccal cav-

Percent of Excessive Smokers by Type of Cancer

	Percent	No. of cases
Cancer of the throat	54	13
Cancer of the intestines	100	5
Cancer of the pancreas	33	3
Cancer of the rectum	88	8
Cancer of the lung	100	5
Cancer of the bladder	60	10
Cancer of the lip	92	12
Cancer of the jaw	100	5
Cancer of the neck	83	6
Cancer of the cheek	100	12
Cancer of the oesophagus	77	13
Cancer of the prostate	100	9
Cancer of tongue	100	7
Cancer of the stomach	82	39
Cancer of the leg	50	2
Sarcoma	73	15
Miscellaneous	60	20

SOURCE: Table 19 from "Cancer Studies in Massachusetts. 2. Habits, Characteristics and Environment of Individuals With and Without Cancer." *New England Journal of Medicine*, vol. 198, no. 10, April 26, 1928, p. 485.

Cancer Sites by Smoking

	Sites supposed to be affected by smoking	Sites not supposed to be affected by smoking	Sarcoma	Total
Heavy smokers	34	100	11	145
Not heavy smokers	1	34	4	39
Total	35	134	15	184
Percent of heavy smokers	97.2	74.6	73.3	78.8

SOURCE: Table 20 from "Cancer Studies in Massachusetts. 2. Habits, Characteristics and Environment of Individuals With and Without Cancer." *New England Journal of Medicine*, vol. 198, no. 10, April 26, 1928, p. 485.

ity. Dr. Hoffman gives the smoking habits of cancer patients by the site of the disease in his San Francisco Survey. We have realigned Dr. Hoffman's figures in preparing table, "Percent of Excessive Smokers by Type of Cancer". . . .

If we postulate that only cancers of certain sites should be affected by heavy smoking, and that those of other sites should not be so affected, and that sarcoma also should not be influenced by tobacco smoking, we can then compare the sites supposed to be affected by smoking with the other two groups which now can be regarded somewhat as controls. These figures, however, give no light upon the relation of smoking to cancer in general. Including under "sites supposed to be affected by smoking" cancers of the lip, jaw, cheek and tongue, and under "sites not supposed to be affected by smoking" all other cancers, we show the results in the table, "Cancer Sites by Smoking".

Of all males who have cancer in the above sample 78.8 per cent. are heavy smokers. Dr. Hoffman found in his larger sample of 834 male patients that 44.1 per cent. were heavy smokers. In our sample, 47.3 per cent. were found to be heavy smokers. What is the true percentage of heavy smokers among males with cancer? Evidently the sample quoted in the table, "Percent of Excessive Smokers by Type of Cancer" is not representative of the cancer population. What is the percentage of heavy smokers in the general population? We do not know. Dublin,

Fiske and Kopf, among 16,662 male policy holders in the Metropolitan Life Insurance Company, found 33.1 per cent. to be heavy smokers. In our control sample we found twenty per cent. heavy smokers and in our total group, including both cancers and controls, we found 33.7 per cent.

The difference between our control group and the cancer group in respect to heavy smoking is twenty-seven per cent. This is highly significant which suggests that heavy smoking has some relation to cancer in general. Of the heavy smoking . . . group, pipe smoking seems to be the most important, as 73.1 per cent. of the heavy smokers in the cancer group are pipe smokers and 72.6 per cent. of the heavy smokers in the control group are pipe smokers.

In the table, "Cancer Sites by Smoking" there is a difference of eighteen per cent. between the heavy smokers who had cancer of the buccal cavity and the total per cent. of heavy smokers. This is statistically significant and indicates that a small part of the buccal cavity cancers may be due to smoking.. . .

Conclusions:

Variations in the habits of cancer patients cannot be studied without the use of good controls, which are most difficult to obtain. We believe our sample to be as nearly satisfactory as is reasonably possible to get on a large scale.

As only large differences between controls and cancers need be considered the size of the sample is adequate.

The collection of data on cancer patients without similar data on controls is valueless in the determination of factors influencing the causation of cancer.

Bad teeth in males are more common among the cancer group than among the controls. This applies to cancer in general and is not limited to buccal cavity cancer.

Heavy smoking is more common in the cancer group than among the controls. In our sample heavy smoking was largely pipe smoking and was particularly more common in those individuals with cancer of the buccal cavity.

The figures gave a suggestion of a hereditary predisposition to cancer but the volume of unknowns made definite conclusions impossible.

The cancer group ate less than the controls but this probably is wholly due to the presence of the disease.

Although we realize that the figures in this study are too small and incomplete for significant conclusions to be drawn, they are presented to show the methods used in order that others may conduct similar studies. We feel that other independent samples collected in a like manner would do much to either prove or disprove our findings.

Further Resources

BOOKS

Adverse Health Effects of Smoking and the Occupational Environment. Cincinnati, Ohio: U.S. Department of Health, Education, and Welfare, Public Health Service, Centers for Disease Control, National Institute for Occupational Safety and Health, 1983.

Cancer Prevention Research Summary: Tobacco. Bethesda, Md.: U.S. Department of Health and Human Services, Public Health Service, National Institutes of Health, National Cancer Institute, 1984.

Petrone, Gerard S. *Tobacco Advertising: The Great Seduction* Atglen, Penn.: Stiffer, 1996.

United States Office of the Surgeon General. "If There's a Baby in the House, Please Don't Smoke." Rockville, Md.: U.S. Department of Health and Human Services, 1986.

U.S. Senate Committee on the Judiciary. *Cigarette Advertising and the First Amendment to the Constitution.* 105th Congress, 2d sess., February 10, 1998. S. Doc. 1530.

"The Wealthiest Nation in the World: Its Mothers and Children"

Journal article

By: Frontier Nursing Service

Date: March 1929

Source: Frontier Nursing Service. "The Wealthiest Nation in the World: Its Mothers and Children." *Quarterly Bulletin* 4, no. 4, March 1929, 1–3.

About the Organization: Mary Breckinridge (1881–1965) created the *Quarterly Bulletin* of the Frontier Nursing Service in 1925 at the behest of the board of directors of the group, then called the Kentucky Committee for Mothers and Babies. As the group's official publication, the *Quarterly Bulletin* carried items of interest to its members and to nurses. ∎

Introduction

Nursing services were generally not available before the middle of the nineteenth century. The American Civil War (1861–1865) and the Crimean War (1853–1856) in Europe, though, changed the concept of medicine to include nurses. But while nurses were generally available to the rich, medical care in rural areas lagged behind that in the cities. Pregnant women, in particular, lacked access to trained medical personnel, since most rural midwives were trained in folklore rather than modern medicine. Childbirth was extremely dangerous in the United States and was the second-leading cause of death for American women well into the twentieth century (trailing only tuberculosis). Childbearing, even before delivery, also had a high mortality rate.

Stepping in to help the situation in rural Kentucky was Mary Breckinridge, who began her career as a nurse. Breckinridge had lost her two children at very early ages and, when helping out in France after World War I (1914–1918), had met many British nurse-midwives. Believing that she could make a difference in the United States, she returned to Kentucky and surveyed Leslie County, in the eastern part of the state. She then traveled to London and was educated at the British Hospital for Mothers and Babies, where she received certification from England's Central Midwives' Board. She then returned to Leslie County, where, in 1925, she founded the Frontier Nursing Service (FNS) to provide health care service in rural eastern Kentucky.

Significance

Because there was no American school of midwifery until it established one, the FNS imported trained English nurses along with some Americans trained in England. These nurse-midwives worked hard to win the confidence of the residents of eastern Kentucky and to improve medical care in the area. A hospital was built in the town of Hyden, and the nurses inoculated people against the many infectious diseases that ravaged the area. They also suggested better ways to build outhouses to deal with sanitation issues. As midwives, of course, they also attended deliveries. People trusted these nurses, and local labor built outposts that were then staffed by them. Fees were reasonable, and the FNS accepted payment in kind.

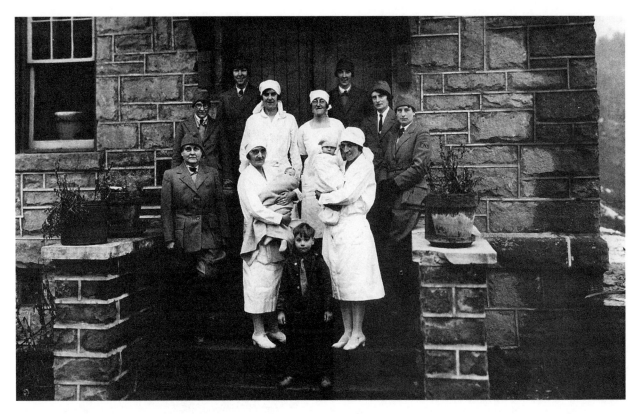

Mary Breckenridge (front row, left) established the Frontier Nursing Service in 1925. The organization has provided quality maternity care for thousands of mothers. AP/WIDE WORLD PHOTOS. REPRODUCED BY PERMISSION.

The FNS had financial difficulties when funds dried up during the Great Depression. The group faced further difficulty in 1939, when the outbreak of World War II (1939–1945) forced many of the nurse-midwives in training to return home. The FNS then established the Frontier Graduate School of Midwifery, the first of its kind in America. Since 1939, the school has trained hundreds of midwives. More recently, the school formed a Community-Based Nurse-Midwifery Education Program, which has used technology to train nearly a thousand midwives throughout the United States. The school also trains nurse-practitioners. In addition to creating the school, the FNS has replaced the original hospital with a larger and more up-to-date facility, where thousands of people have been treated and thousands of babies successfully born.

Primary Source

"The Wealthiest Nation in the World: Its Mothers and Children"

> **SYNOPSIS:** This article from the March 1929 issue of the FNS's *Quarterly Bulletin* opens with accounts of three maternal deaths. It then discusses three other difficult cases FNS nurses and doctors had handled, noting that the FNS saved all three women and suggesting that FNS nurses could have prevented the three deaths.

Perhaps, an accident
Perhaps, an intention.

—*Bridge of San Luis Rey*

In the course of three weeks there have been three maternal deaths in territories not far removed from our nursing stations, for complications which could have been handled by good medical care. One mother, we hear, left a three day old baby. One died following a miscarriage. Of course we haven't the details of these cases, since we didn't see them, but from the information we glean it is apparent that these women died from complications not unlike similar conditions our service has met successfully during almost exactly the same period of time.

Let us illustrate just by telling the story of the last three abnormal cases which we have handled.

No. 1 was a miscarriage, like the one which died on Wolf Creek. Ours was in the Possum Bend territory. The miscarriage was incomplete and the patient shot up a temperature on the third day. We located our consulting surgeon in the distant mining town of Hazard, through a relayed conversation by telephone. He agreed to come in on the evening train the next day. This train passes a flag station after dark. There the surgeon was met by horses and rode on in to the patient's house—a one room log cabin. At nine at night, assisted by two nurses, he did a curettage—the only light from a lantern, an electric flash and the open fire. One nurse gave the anaesthetic, the other waited on him. On another bed in the same room the patient's children lay sleeping. After the surgeon left, one of the nurses remained in the cabin to special the patient, who was given special nursing at night as long as she needed it. Her tenure of life hung by the narrowest thread, but brilliant surgery and good nursing saved the day, and she is now restored to her family.

No 2, a young married woman of seventeen, expecting her first baby, came on a visit to her parents in the Beech Fork territory in order to be near the nurse-midwives for her confinement. They did not know of her arrival, though she had been there two days. She was seven months pregnant. At two in the morning there came a call that she was in convulsions. She had seven terrible convulsions one right after the other. Her young husband rode off for the nearest doctor in an adjoining county, but it was twenty-one and a half hours before he could come. Meanwhile the nurse-midwives proceeded with the routine authorized by our Medical Advisory Committee for cases of eclampsia, and this the doctor continued after his arrival. He stayed the night, leaving directions for the procedures to be carried on after he had gone, because it would be impossible for him to return. His territory covers a thousand square miles. Influenza and pneumonia were raging and the patients in the Beech Fork area were the only ones, except at his own headquarters, getting even nursing care. This patient also had a special nurse every night as long as one was needed. The baby, dead from the profound toxaemia, was born spontaneously a few days later. The girl-mother is alive today, with youth and hope still beckoning her, and health nearly restored.

No. 3. This patient, another young married woman, had such small measurements that it was plain she could not give birth normally to any but a very small baby. This type of case we try to persuade to let us take altogether out of the mountains, on passes furnished by the Louisville & Nashville Railroad, and put under one of our consulting obstetricians in one of the large cities, who give their services. But this patient was timid and could not face the thought of leaving home. We failed in persuading her, but, as we could not abandon her to her fate, we arranged a medical examination with the same doctor from an adjoining county who had handled the eclamptic. He carried the confinement through, and Baby Betty, though tiny, is all the reward any of us need for the weeks of anxiety we have felt on her mother's behalf.

These illustrations are given to show that the Frontier Nursing Service is not only able to take care of normal confinements, but that it can meet the abnormal also, through its medical and surgical consultants. Within a comparatively few miles there have occurred over a short period of time these six abnormal obstetrical cases. The three who had only old neighbors to take care of them are all dead. The three who called in the nurse-midwives of the Frontier Nursing Service, and through them got the skilled medical care they could not have reached alone, are all living. The difference is one between life and death.

Further Resources

BOOKS

Breckinridge, Mary. *Wide Neighborhoods: A Story of the Frontier Nursing Service*. New York: Harper & Brothers, 1952.

Leavitt, Judith Walter. *Brought to Bed: Childbearing in America, 1750–1950*. New York: Oxford University Press, 1986.

———. *Women and Health in America*. Madison, Wis.: University of Wisconsin Press, 1984.

Litoff, J.B. *American Midwives: 1860 to the Present*. Westport, Conn.: Greenwood, 1978.

Stewart, David, and Lee Stewart. *Compulsory Hospitalization: Freedom of Choice in Childbirth?* Marble Hill, Mo.: NAP-SAC, 1979.

Wertz, R.W., and D.C. Wertz. *Lying-In: A History of Childbirth in America*. New York: The Free Press, 1977.

PERIODICALS

Brown, H.E., and G. Isaacs. "The Frontier Nursing Service." *The American Journal of Obstetrics and Gynecology* 124, 1976, 16.

WEBSITES

"History of Frontier Nursing Service." Frontier Nursing Service. Available online at http://www.frontiernursing.org /history_of_fsn.htm; website home page: http://www .frontiernursing.org (accessed December 16, 2002).

"On the Antibacterial Action of Cultures of a Penicillium, with Special Reference to Their Use in the Isolation of B. Influenzæ"

Journal article

By: Alexander Fleming

Date: 1929

Source: Fleming, Alexander. "On the Antibacterial Action of Cultures of a Penicillium, with Special Reference to Their Use in the Isolation of *B. Influenzæ*." *The British Journal of Experimental Pathology* 10, no. 3 (1929): 226–236.

About the Author: Born in Scotland, Alexander Fleming (1881–1955) moved with his brothers to London at the age of thirteen. In 1906 he became a bacteriologist in the Inoculation Department at St. Mary's Hospital, and in 1908 he completed his education at the University of London. He won the Nobel Prize in 1945 for his discovery of penicillin. ∎

Introduction

Research on antibiotics had started over fifty years before Fleming's and has continued ever since. In the 1870s scientists first noted that some materials slowed the growth of organisms. In the 1880s scientists noted that some microorganisms produced antibiotics (although the term was not used at that time). Around the turn of the century, researchers tried to use the antibiotic pyocynase to combat disease, but it proved to be too toxic. It was in this context that Fleming made his discovery.

At this time, there was a serious need for antibiotics, particularly in wartime, when more people died from disease than from wounds. In the Spanish-American War (1898), for example, 460 Americans died in battle or from wounds, but 5,200 perished from malaria, dysentery, and typhoid. In 1900 influenza and pneumonia (combined) were the leading causes of death.

Fleming's discovery of penicillin was accidental. As he notes in the article excerpted here, a number of plates on which he was trying to grow microorganisms did not work because a mold killed off the bacteria. The mold in question was penicillin.

Significance

Fleming was never able to test penicillin on actual patients, and it took years to develop it as an antibiotic. One obstacle was that he had difficulty purifying it. In 1932, though, researchers at the London School of Tropical Medicine and Hygiene found better ways to grow the mold and extract the penicillin. During this time, Howard Florey and his team of researchers developed test methods and ways to create larger amounts of penicillin. When World War II (1939–1945) started, Florey came to the United States, where large amounts of penicillin were being produced. After enough penicillin had been made, it was tested successfully on those who had staphylococcal infections, infected war wounds, and surgical infections. By June 6, 1944, enough penicillin had been produced to treat all British and American troops who became ill or were wounded during the D-Day invasion of Europe.

While these events were occurring, opinion was divided over who should be given credit for discovering penicillin. Some pointed out that Fleming had been the one who initially discovered it. Others noted that Florey was the one who purified penicillin, proved its value, and helped to produce it on a usable scale. In fact, both deserve credit, particularly since neither ever patented his products or made money directly off them. Florey and Fleming, along with Ernst Chain, who chemically extracted penicillin, all were awarded the Nobel Prize.

After penicillin's effectiveness was demonstrated, the question became how to make it as effective as possible, for it was not a "silver bullet." One difficulty was that penicillin was excreted from the body quickly, so ways were developed to keep it in the blood at a steady level. Another was the development of resistant strains, particularly of staphylococci. A third was that some people developed allergic, even fatal, reactions to it. Nonetheless, penicillin produced dramatic results in the treatment of gonorrhea, pneumonia, syphilis, and rheumatic fever. Regardless of who gets the credit for its discovery, penicillin was a major advance in antibiotics.

Primary Source

"On the Antibacterial Action of Cultures of a Penicillium, with Special Reference to Their Use in the Isolation of *B. Influenzæ*" [excerpt]

> **SYNOPSIS:** Fleming first notes the accidental nature of penicillin's discovery. He next discusses how penicillin killed a number of bacteria, including staphylococci. The article notes that penicillin is a good antibacterial agent on a number of substances, including diphtheria bacteria and the bacteria that cause pneumonia.

While working with staphylococcus variants a number of culture-plates were set aside on the laboratory bench and examined from time to time. In the examinations these plates were necessarily exposed to the air and they became contaminated with various micro-organisms. It was noticed that around a large colony of a contaminating mould the staphylococcus colonies became transparent and were obviously undergoing lysis. . . .

Subcultures of this mould were made and experiments conducted with a view to ascertaining something of the properties of the bacteriolytic substance which had evidently been formed in the mould culture and which had diffused into the surrounding medium. It was found that broth in which the mould had been grown at room temperature for one or two weeks had acquired marked inhibitory, bactericidal and bacteriolytic properties to many of the more common pathogenic bacteria. . . .

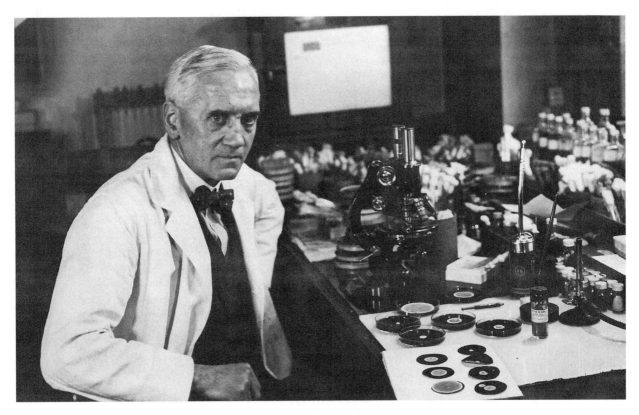

Alexander Fleming is credited with the discovery of penicillin. © BETTMANN/CORBIS. REPRODUCED BY PERMISSION.

Toxicity of Penicillin

The toxicity to animals of powerfully antibacterial mould broth filtrates appears to be very low. Twenty c.c. injected intravenously into a rabbit were not more toxic than the same quantity of broth. Half a c.c. injected intra-peritoneally into a mouse weighing about 20 gm. induced no toxic symptoms. Constant irrigation of large infected surfaces in man was not accompanied by any toxic symptoms, while irrigation of the human conjunctiva every hour for a day had no irritant effect.

In vitro penicillin which completely inhibits the growth of staphylococci in a dilution of 1 in 600 does not interfere with leucocytic function to a greater extent than does ordinary broth. . . .

Discussion

It has been demonstrated that a species of penicillium produces in culture a very powerful antibacterial substance which affects different bacteria in different degrees. Speaking generally it may be said that the least sensitive bacteria are the Gram-negative bacilli, and the most susceptible are the pyogenic cocci. Inhibitory substances have been described in old cultures of many organisms; generally the inhibition is more or less specific to the microbe which has been used for the culture, and the inhibitory substances are seldom strong enough to withstand even slight dilution with fresh nutrient material. Penicillin is not inhibitory to the original penicillium used in its preparation.

Emmerich and other workers have shown that old cultures of *B. pyocyaneus* acquire a marked bacteriolytic power. The bacteriolytic agent, pyocyanase, possesses properties similar to penicillin in that its heat resistance is the same and it exists in the filtrate of a fluid culture. It resembles penicillin also in that it acts only on certain microbes. It differs however in being relatively extremely weak in its action and in acting on quite different types of bacteria. The bacilli of anthrax, diphtheria, cholera and typhoid are those most sensitive to pyocyanase, while the pyogenic cocci are unaffected, but the percentages of pyocyaneus filtrate necessary for the inhibition of these organisms was 40, 33, 40 and 60 respectively (Bocchia, 1909). This degree of inhibition is hardly comparable with 0.2% or less of penicillin which is necessary to completely inhibit the pyogenic cocci or the 1% necessary for *B. diphtheriæ*.

Penicillin, in regard to infections with sensitive microbes, appears to have some advantages over the well-known chemical antiseptics. A good sample will completely inhibit staphylococci, *Streptococcus pyogenes* and pneumococcus in a dilution of 1 in 800. It is therefore a more powerful inhibitory agent than is carbolic acid and it can be applied to an infected surface undiluted as it is non-irritant and non-toxic. If applied, therefore, on a dressing, it will still be effective even when diluted 800 times which is more than can be said of the chemical antiseptics in use. Experiments in connection with its value in the treatment of pyogenic infections are in progress.

In addition to its possible use in the treatment of bacterial infections penicillin is certainly useful to the bacteriologist for its power of inhibiting unwanted microbes in bacterial cultures so that penicillin insensitive bacteria can readily be isolated. A notable instance of this is the very easy isolation of Pfeiffers bacillus of influenza when penicillin is used.

■ ■ ■

In conclusion my thanks are due to my colleagues, Mr. Ridley and Mr. Craddock, for their help in carrying out some of the experiments described in this paper, and to our mycologist, Mr. la Touche, for his suggestions as to the identity of the penicillium.

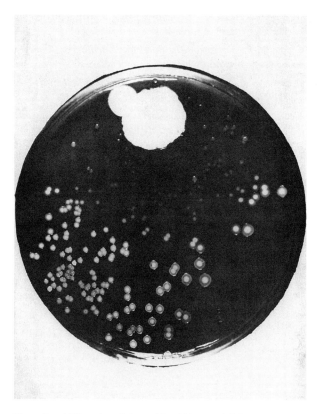

View of penicillin and staphylococci (staph) in a petri dish.
© BETTMANN/CORBIS. REPRODUCED BY PERMISSION.

Summary

1. A certain type of penicillium produces in culture a powerful antibacterial substance. The antibacterial power of the culture reaches its maximum in about 7 days at 20° C. and after 10 days diminishes until it has almost disappeared in 4 weeks.

2. The best medium found for the production of the antibacterial substance has been ordinary nutrient broth.

3. The active agent is readily filterable and the name "penicillin" has been given to filtrates of broth cultures of the mould.

4. Penicillin loses most of its power after 10 to 14 days at room temperature but can be preserved longer by neutralization.

5. The active agent is not destroyed by boiling for a few minutes but in alkaline solution boiling for 1 hour markedly reduces the power. Autoclaving for 20 minutes at 115° C. practically destroys it. It is soluble in alcohol but insoluble in ether or chloroform.

6. The action is very marked on the pyogenic cocci and the diphtheria group of bacilli. Many bacteria are quite insensitive, *e.g.* the coli-typhoid group, the influenza-bacillus group, and the enterococcus.

7. Penicillin is non-toxic to animals in enormous doses and is non-irritant. It [does] not interfere with leucocytic function to a greater degree than does ordinary broth.

8. It is suggested that it may be an efficient antiseptic for application to, or injection into, areas infected with penicillin-sensitive microbes.

9. The use of penicillin on culture plates renders obvious many bacterial inhibitions which are not very evident in ordinary cultures.

10. Its value as an aid to the isolation of *B. influenzæ* has been demonstrated.

Further Resources
BOOKS

Bickel, Lennard. *Rise Up to Life: A Biography of Howard Walter Florey Who Gave Penicillin to the World.* New York: Charles Scribner's Sons, 1972.

Hare, Ronald. *The Birth of Penicillin, and the Disarming of Microbes.* London: Allen and Unwin, 1970.

Fleming, Alexander. *Penicillin, Its Practical Application.* Philadelphia: Blakiston, 1946.

Goldsmith, Margaret L. *The Road to Penicillin: A History of Chemotherapy.* London: L. Drummond, 1946.

Hobby, Gladys L. *Penicillin: Meeting the Challenge.* New Haven, Conn.: Yale University Press, 1985.

Keefer, Chester S., and Donald G. Anderson. *Penicillin and Streptomycin in the Treatment of Infections.* New York: Oxford University Press, 1950.

Macfarlane, Gwyn. *Alexander Fleming, the Man and the Myth.* Cambridge, Mass.: Harvard University Press, 1984.

Smith, Lawrence Weld, and Ann Dolan Walker. *Penicillin Decade, 1941–1951: Sensitizations and Toxicities.* Washington, D.C.: Arundel Press, 1951.

WEBSITES

"Sir Alexander Fleming—Biography." Available online at http://www.nobel.se/medicine/laureates/1945/fleming-bio .html (accessed December 16, 2002).

10

RELIGION

DENNIS A. CASTILLO

Entries are arranged in chronological order by date of primary source. For entries with one primary source, the entry title is the same as the primary source title. Entries with more than one primary source have an overall entry title, followed by the titles of the primary sources.

Important Events in Religion, 1920–1929

1920

- The Hartford Theological Seminary in Hartford, Connecticut, announces that it will no longer require female applicants for admission to declare they do not intend to seek ordination.

1921

- The American Association of Women Preachers begins publication of *Woman's Pulpit.*
- Junior Hadassah is founded as an auxiliary of Hadassah, the Women's Zionist Organization of America.
- The Greek Orthodox Archdiocese of North and South America is created by the Ecumenical Patriarch.
- On May 25, the General Assembly of the Presbyterian Church U.S.A. (Northern) urges federal marriage and divorce laws.
- On November 10, Margaret Sanger founds the American Birth Control League in New York City. It is a combination of the Birth Control League, which she founded in 1914, and the Voluntary Parenthood League, founded by Mary Ware Dennett in 1919. The issue of contraception becomes a major topic in religious circles, with liberals such as Harry Emerson Fosdick and the Universalist Church approving and conservatives such as the Protestant Episcopal House of Bishops and the Roman Catholic Church opposing.

1922

- On May 21, Harry Emerson Fosdick, a Baptist but also an associate pastor of First Presbyterian Church in New York City, preaches his widely circulated sermon "Shall the Fundamentalists Win?" This intensifies the debate between modernist and fundamentalist Protestants.
- On September 12, the House of Bishops of the Protestant Episcopal Church vote 36-27 to remove the word *obey* from the marriage service.
- In November, Bishop Platon is elected Metropolitan of the Orthodox Church of All the Americas and Canada, the former Diocese of the Aleutians and North America of the Russian Orthodox Church.

1923

- Rabbi Benjamin Frankel founds Hillel Foundation at the University of Illinois. This campus religious group is pat-

terned after the Methodist Wesley Foundation. In 1925 B'nai B'rith assumes responsibility for this largest Jewish campus organization.
- On May 18, the all-male General Assembly of the Presbyterian Church U.S.A. (Northern) votes to merge the Women's Board of Home Missions with the Presbyterian Board of Home Missions, ending the female control of this aspect of church work.

1924

- The Methodist Episcopal Church begins to allow ordination of women for local congregations. They are not allowed to belong to the General Conference, however, thus limiting their activities and careers.
- The Presbyterian Church U.S. (Southern) elects women to national service boards for the first time.
- The Woman's Branch of the Union of Orthodox Jewish Congregations of America is founded.
- Aimee Semple McPherson begins broadcasting from her new radio station KFSG (Kall Full Square Gospel) from her Angelus Temple in Los Angeles. This is the first full-time religious radio station in America.
- The editors and critics of *Film Daily* choose Cecil B. De-Mille's *The Ten Commandments* as one of the best movies of 1923.
- Metropolitan Platon declares the Diocese of All America and Canada autonomous from the Russian Patriarch.
- On March 31, the Supreme Court strikes down a law of the state of Oregon that requires all children to attend public schools. The law was intended to end parochial education, particularly Catholic schools.
- On May 27, the General Conference of the Methodist Episcopal Church ends its ban on dancing and theater attendance.
- On June 2, a proposed amendment to the Constitution ending child labor is sent to the states. While twenty-six states ratify the amendment, it falls short of passage. A major force in opposition is the Roman Catholic Church, which fears giving the state excessive control over children.

1925

- The Presbyterian Church U.S.A. (Northern) publishes The Auburn Affirmation, a revision of the points established in the Westminster Confession of Faith. The affirmation permits Presbyterians to have differing interpretations of the principles of their faith.
- Bruce Barton's *The Man Nobody Knows,* a life of Jesus, enters the best-seller list, where it stays for two years. More than 750,000 copies are sold.
- The largest Buddhist temple in the United States is opened in Los Angeles.
- The Jewish Institute of Religion graduates its first class.
- The Protestant Episcopal Church expels Bishop William M. Brown for heresy because he supported communism as a modern form of Christianity.

• On May 13, the state of Florida passes a law requiring daily Bible reading in public schools.

• From July 10 to July 21, the trial of John T. Scopes in Dayton, Tennessee, for teaching evolution in a science class attracts the nation's attention. This is one of the first media events in the nation's history. The radio station WGN of Chicago arranges for remote broadcast of the event. The high point of the trial comes on July 20, when William Jennings Bryan, serving as a lawyer for the prosecution, agrees to take the witness stand. His testimony fails to satisfy his fundamentalist allies. Sophisticates, however, enjoy the humiliating questioning Bryan endures from defense lawyer Clarence Darrow, who focuses on the inconsistencies in the Bible. Scopes is found guilty of teaching evolution, and fined one hundred dollars.

• On October 16, the Texas State Text Book Board prohibits the discussion of the theory of evolution in its school textbooks.

• On November 9, the cornerstone of the nave of St. John the Divine, the largest Episcopal church in the United States, is laid in New York City.

1926

• Henry Sloane Coffin becomes professor of homiletics and president of Union Theological Seminary in New York City, positions he will hold until 1945.

• Bob Jones founds the college with his name in Clearwater, Florida. After a period in Tennessee the school moves to Greenville, South Carolina, in 1946.

• On May 18, Aimee Semple McPherson, founder of the Full Square Gospel Church and pastor of the Angelus Temple in Los Angeles, disappears while swimming in the ocean. She reappears six weeks later in the Arizona desert claiming to have been kidnapped. The sensational charge that she spent part of that time with a man in Carmel, California, makes her a national figure.

• On June 20, the first Eucharistic Congress in the United States opens in Chicago.

• On July 26, the Sanctuary of Our Lady of Victory in Lackawanna, New York, becomes the first Roman Catholic church in the United States to be consecrated as a basilica.

1927

• Mary Katherine Jones Bennett, former president of the Women's Board of Home Missions of the northern Presbyterian Church publishes "Causes of Unrest Among Women of the Church" reflecting a growing feminist current in that denomination. In 1929 she publishes "Status of Women in the Presbyterian Church, U.S.A. with References to Other Denominations."

• Sinclair Lewis's biting satire on a get-ahead Protestant minister, *Elmer Gantry,* immediately goes on the best-seller list.

• On April 17, Gov. Alfred E. Smith of New York, leading contender for the Democratic presidential nomination, responds to a question about potential conflict between his Roman Catholicism and his adherence to the Constitution by stating, "I recognize no power in the institution of my Church to interfere with the operations of the Constitution of the United States or the enforcement of the law of the land."

• On May 8, the Serbian Orthodox Church holds its first American National Church Assembly in Chicago.

• On May 10, the Evangelical Church rules that only celibate women may be ordained.

1928

• Governor Smith of New York becomes the first Roman Catholic to be nominated for the presidency by a major party. Although both candidates try to keep religious prejudice out of the campaign, the issue of Smith's religion becomes both a positive factor, bringing Catholic votes to the Democratic column, and a negative issue, pushing Protestants into the Republican column. Hoover wins in this Republican year and carries five states in the Democratic Solid South.

1929

• The General Assembly of the Presbyterian Church U.S.A. (Northern) reorganizes Princeton Theological Seminary, weakening the conservative dominance both on the board of trustees and in the curriculum. J. Gresham Machen resigns in protest and begins the Westminster Seminary in Philadelphia.

• The Daughters of the American Revolution demand a Senate investigation into communist influences in the Federal Council of Churches of Christ.

"Get on the Water Wagon"

Sermon

By: William Ashley Sunday

Date: 1908

Source: Sunday, William Ashley. "Get on the Water Wagon." Reprinted in *The Best of Billy Sunday: Seventeen Burning Sermons From the Most Spectacular Evangelist the World Has Ever Known.* John R. Rice, ed. Murfreesboro, Tenn.: Sword of the Lord Publishers, 1965, 63–66.

About the Author: William Ashley Sunday (1862–1935) was born in Ames, Iowa. A professional baseball player, he left the sport after his religious conversion and became a well-known evangelist. In his charismatic sermons, Sunday condemned alcohol use and was a strong supporter of Prohibition. He died on November 6, 1935, just short of his seventy-third birthday. ∎

Introduction

William Ashley Sunday's father died in the Civil War (1861–1865) when William was only a month old. The boy lived in the Soldiers' Orphans' Home in Glenwood, Iowa, and then in Davenport, Iowa. He left at the age of fourteen and eventually began playing baseball in a small-town league in Iowa. In 1883, he was discovered by the Chicago White Sox and played professional baseball for eight years. In 1887, while in Chicago, he experienced a profound religious conversion. In 1891, he left baseball to begin religious work.

When Sunday left baseball, he first worked for the Young Men's Christian Association from 1891 to 1895. During that time, he became associated with the Presbyterian itinerant evangelist J. Wilbur Chapman. At first, Sunday worked as Chapman's advance agent, and then he began to do a little preaching himself.

He began his independent career in 1896 by leading a successful revival in Garner, Iowa. Sunday soon became the well-known "Baseball Evangelist." Although he lacked a formal seminary education, he was licensed to preach by the Chicago Presbytery in 1898 and ordained in 1903.

He began with revivals using churches and tents. Soon, Sunday began to draw large crowds to his revivals

with his flamboyant style. Drawing on the same athleticism that led to success on the baseball field, he performed all types of acrobatic feats as he preached his message. Thousands came to see him leap about the stage and put up his fists to fight the Devil. Sunday claimed three hundred thousand converts.

The first social issue that revivalism addressed was temperance in the 1820s, and this continued to be a recurring theme with this form of Christianity. Sunday's sermon "Get on the Water Wagon" is one of the best examples of this issue in the early twentieth century.

Significance

Sunday preached a rough, homespun version of Fundamentalism, one that in particular exhibited contempt for higher education. Regarding modernism, he had no use for what he called the "bastard theory of evolution" or for the "deodorized and disinfected sermons" of "hireling ministers" who abandoned the age-old faith of their fathers to please their liberal parishioners. Sunday also attacked the Social Gospel movement, ridiculing liberal theologians who, he claimed, tried to "make a religion out of social service with Jesus Christ left out."

Sunday believed in preaching what he called a masculine "muscular" Christianity. This equated salvation with decency and manliness ("the man who has real, rich, red blood in his veins instead of pink tea and ice water"). During World War I (1914–1918), this notion of masculine Christianity was combined with patriotism, leading Sunday to claim that "Christianity and patriotism are synonymous terms" just as "hell and traitors are synonymous." In a jab at modernism, he even attributed the supposed atrocities committed by the Germans to the corrosive influence of biblical criticism on the German people.

Unlike Aimee Semple McPherson, Sunday preached divine wrath, rather than divine love. A major target for his fire-and-brimstone preaching was alcohol. Sunday's sermons concentrated on the evils of drinking and the need for prohibition laws. After Prohibition passed, he continued to press this theme, pushing for the enforcement of Prohibition laws and opposing attempts at repeal. "There isn't a man who votes for the saloon who doesn't deserve to have his boy die a drunkard. He deserves to have his girl live out her life with a drunken husband." Sunday attacked drinkers as "dirty, low-down, whiskey-soaked, beer-guzzling, bull-necked, foul-mouthed, hypocrites."

Primary Source

"Get on the Water Wagon" [excerpt]

> **SYNOPSIS:** Sunday was one of the most famous revivalist preachers in the early twentieth century. Dedicated to Prohibition, he focused his preaching on the evils of alcohol. The following excerpt is from

one of Sunday's most popular Prohibition sermons, "Get on the Water Wagon." Also known as his "Booze Sermon," Sunday preached it numerous times in many cities in the 1920s.

I am the sworn, eternal, uncompromising enemy of the liquor traffic. I ask no quarter and I give none. I have drawn the sword in defense of God, home, wife, children and native land, and I will never sheathe it until the undertaker pumps me full of embalming fluid, and if my wife is alive, I think I shall call her to my bedside and say, "Nell, when I am dead, send for the butcher and skin me, and have my hide tanned and made into drum heads and hire men to go up and down the land and beat the drums and say, 'My husband, "Bill" Sunday still lives and gives the whiskey gang a run for its money.'"

After all is said that can be said on the open licensed saloon, its degrading influence upon the individual, upon business, upon public morals, upon the home (for the time is long gone by when there is any ground for argument; even its friends are forced to admit its vile corruption) there is one prime reason why the saloon has not been driven from the land long ago—that is the lying argument that saloons are needed to lighten taxes. I challenge you to show me any community where a saloon license policy has lightened taxes.

Alcohol—Worse than War

Seventy-five per cent of our idiots came from intemperate parents.

Ninety per cent of our adult criminals are drinking men, and committed their crimes while under the influence of booze. The *Chicago Tribune* kept track of the number of murders committed in the saloons over a ten-year period before prohibition and the number was 53,436.

Archbishop Ireland said,

I find social crime and ask what caused it? They say "drink!" I find poverty. What caused it? "Drink!" I find families broken up and ask what caused it; they tell me "drink!" I find men behind prison bars and ask, "What put you here?" They say "drink!" I stand by the scaffold and ask, "What made you a murderer?" They cry "drink!" "drink!"

If God would place in my hand a wand with which to dispel the evils of intemperance, I would strike at the door of every brewery, and every distillery, and every saloon until the accursed traffic was driven from the land.

A famous evangelist with a flamboyant style, Billy Sunday's sermons attracted large audiences. He often preached against the use of alcohol and urged support for Prohibition. © BETTMANN/CORBIS. REPRODUCED BY PERMISSION.

The saloon is the sum of all villainies. It is worse than war, worse than pestilence, worse than famine. It is the crime of crimes. It is the mother of sins. It is the appalling source of misery, pauperism, and crime. It is the source of three-fourths of all the crime; thus it is the source of three-fourths of all the taxation necessary to prosecute the criminals and care for them after they are in prison. To license such an incarnate fiend of Hell is one of the blackest spots on the American government.

The Devil in Solution

"Why anti-saloon?" asks someone. "Why not anti-grocery store, anti-dry goods, anti-furniture, anti-bakery, anti-butcher shop, anti-boot and shoe store, anti-coal yard? Why single out this one business and attack that?"

Who is against the saloon? The church is against it; the school is against it; the home is against it; the scientific world is against it; the military world is against it; the business world is against it; the railroads are against it; and every world-wide interest on earth is against it, except the underworld, the criminal world and the world of crime. All cry, "Away with the saloon. Down with these licensed distributing centers of crime, misery and drunkenness!"

What is this traffic in rum? "The Devil in solution," said Sir Wilfred Lawson, and he was right. "Distilled damnation," said Robert Hall, and he was right. "An artist in human slaughter," said Lord Chesterfield, and he was right. "Prisoners' General driving men to Hell," said Wesley, and he was right. "More destructive than war, pestilence and famine," said Gladstone, and he was right. "A cancer in human society, eating out its vitals and threatening its destruction," said Abraham Lincoln; he was right.

"The most ruinous and degrading of all human pursuits," said William McKinley; he was right. "The most criminal and artistic method of assassination ever invented by the bravos of any age or nation," said Ruskin; he was right. "The most prolific hotbeds of anarchy, vile politics, profane ribaldry and unspeakable sensuality," said Charles Parkhurst; he was right. "A public, permanent agency of degradation," said Cardinal Manning; he was right.

"A business that tends to lawlessness on the part of those who conduct it and criminality on the part of those that patronize it," said Theodore Roosevelt; he was right. "A business that tends to produce idleness, disease, pauperism and crime," said the United States Supreme Court, and it was right. "That damned stuff called alcohol," said Bob Ingersoll; and Bob was right that time sure.

Lord Chief Justice Alverstone, at the International Congress on Alcoholism, said, "After forty years at the bar and ten years as a judge, I have no hesitancy in saying that ninety per cent of the crime is caused by strong drink."

Working Man Pays

Who foots the bills? The landlord who loses his rent; the baker, butcher, grocer, coal man, dry goods merchant, whose goods the drunkard needs for himself and family, but cannot buy; the charitable people, who pity the children of drunkards, and go down in their pockets to keep them from starving; the taxpayers who are taxed to support the jails, penitentiaries, hospitals, alms houses, reformatories, that this cursed business keeps filled.

Who makes the money? The brewers, distillers, saloon-keepers, who are privileged to fill the land with poverty, wretchedness, madness, crime, disease, damnation, and death, authorized by the sovereign right of the people, who vote for this infamous business.

For every $800 spent in producing useful and necessary commodities, the working man receives $143.50 in wages. For every $800 spent in producing booze, the working man receives $9.85 in wages.

The saloon comes as near being a rathole for the working man to dump his wages in as anything I know of.

To know what the Devil will do, find out what the saloon is doing.

The man who votes for the saloon helps the Devil get his boy. The man who doesn't believe in a Hell has never seen a drunkard's home. The Devil and the saloon-keeper are always pulling on the same rope.

Further Resources

BOOKS

Bruns, Roger. *Preacher: Billy Sunday and Big-Time American Evangelism.* New York: Norton, 1992.

Knickerbocker, Wendy. *Sunday at the Ballpark: Billy Sunday's Professional Baseball Career, 1883–1890.* Lanham, Md.: Scarecrow, 2000.

Martin, Robert Francis. *Hero of the Heartland: Billy Sunday and the Transformation of American Society, 1862–1935.* Bloomington: Indiana University Press, 2002.

McLoughlin, William Gerald. *Billy Sunday Was His Real Name.* Chicago: University of Chicago Press, 1955.

WEBSITES

Billy Sunday Online: Life and Ministry of William Ashley Sunday. Available online at http://billysunday.org/ (accessed January 16, 2003).

"Divine Healing"

Sermon

By: Aimee Semple McPherson

Date: September 1920

Source: McPherson, Aimee Semple. "Divine Healing." *Bridal Call,* September 1920. Reprinted at the International Church of the Foursquare Gospel website. Available online at http://www.foursquare.org/files/divine_sermon.pdf; website home page: http://www.foursquare.org (accessed March 25, 2003).

About the Author: Aimee Semple McPherson (1890–1944) was born near Ingersoll, Ontario. A famous revivalist preacher in the 1920s and 1930s, she was one of the first major women religious leaders in the United States. McPherson died on September 27, 1944, twelve days before her fifty-fourth birthday. ■

Introduction

Aimee Semple McPherson was baptized Aimee Elizabeth Kennedy, the only child of James Morgan Kennedy and Minnie Kennedy. Her father was a Methodist and her mother was the foster daughter of a captain in the Salvation Army. Aimee was influenced by her mother's work in the Salvation Army, in particular its unique combination of traditional religion, charitable work, and military organization. She briefly turned from religion, then in 1907 she experienced a religious conversion prompted by the preaching of an itinerant Pentecostal preacher named Robert James Semple. A year later, at the age of seventeen, she married Semple and thus embarked on her ministerial career.

The newly married couple conducted revival meetings together, both in Canada and the United States. In 1910, they went to Asia to do missionary work, but Robert died of typhoid fever just one month before the birth of Roberta Star Semple, their only child.

After Robert's death, Aimee went to live with her mother in New York City. Her mother was working for the Salvation Army at the time, and Aimee became active in revivals. She married Harold Stewart McPherson in 1912 and gave birth to Rolf Kennedy McPherson a year later. Aimee did not settle down, however, but rather felt called to continue doing revival work. Her religious career began to take off in 1916. She traveled up and down the East Coast in what she called her "Gospel Automobile," which featured religious slogans painted on the side. Having already traveled north and south along the East Coast, she headed west across the country in 1918. She ended up in Los Angeles and decided to make it her base of operations. While initially supportive of her missionary activities, her husband began to be resentful of her work, and they divorced in 1921.

Significance

McPherson's ministry flourished. In 1922 in San Francisco, she became the first woman to preach a sermon over the radio. On January 1, 1923, she opened the Angelus Temple in Los Angeles. Also in 1923, McPherson acquired a radio station, becoming the first woman to do so. She used the station to broadcast her services, and KFSG remains the oldest operating radio station in the United States. In 1927, she formally incorporated her movement as the International Church of the Foursquare Gospel. McPherson's theology emphasized Jesus as "Savior, Healer, Baptizer, and Soon-Coming King." The healing aspect became a major focus of her church, with the promise of faith healing drawing thousands to her services at Angelus Temple. McPherson continued to travel, holding revivals across the United States and in England, France, the Holy Land, and Asia. Her unique brand of

Aimee McPherson was one of the first famous women preachers, and the first to have a radio station devoted to evangelism. The focus of her sermons emphasized healing and God's love, which contrasted sharply with many of her contemporaries. **AP/WIDE WORLD PHOTOS. REPRODUCED BY PERMISSION.**

Fundamentalism, emphasizing love and healing, combined with her charismatic personality, led to great growth, which continued after her death in 1944. Today, the denomination she founded includes 1,834 churches in the United States and almost 30,000 worldwide, with a total membership of 3.5 million in 123 countries.

McPherson had many critics. Liberals disliked her religious conservatism, and conservatives thought it was inappropriate for a woman to be a minister. Some writers criticized her preaching as insubstantial, more effective in its delivery than its content. Her own flamboyant character gave further fuel to her detractors. In 1928, Shelton Bissell, a local Los Angeles minister, published an article in *The Outlook* magazine entitled "Vaudeville at Angelus Temple." Having attended an evening service at the temple, he called it "a sensuous debauch served up in the name of religion."

Primary Source

"Divine Healing"

SYNOPSIS: The following document is from a sermon McPherson preached and that the International

The Angelus Temple, Los Angeles. American evangelist Aimee Semple McPherson set up the Angelus Temple as the headquarters for her International Church of the Foursquare Gospel. The church drew thousands who sought the promise of faith healing and services of Sister Aimee. © HULTON-DEUTSCH COLLECTION/CORBIS. REPRODUCED BY PERMISSION.

Church of the Foursquare Gospel continues to make available as representative of its views. It shows her emphasis on healing and God's love, which differed from the fire-and-brimstone preaching of other popular Fundamentalist preachers of the day, such as William Ashley Sunday.

Whether it is easier to say, thy sins be forgiven thee, or take up thy bed and walk.

In the Bible days, when they brought the man sick of the palsy to Jesus, the power of Christ to heal had become a known and an accepted fact. But when He said, "thy sins be forgiven thee," they shook their heads and called it blasphemy. They admitted the power to heal, but doubted the power to save.

Today, the attitude of mankind is reversed—they admit Christ's power to forgive sins, but lift remonstrating, unbelieving hands when it comes to His power to heal.

But the facts of the case are that it is no more difficult for the Savior to do the one than the other. For "whether is it easier to say, thy sins be forgiven thee, or rise, take up thy bed and walk?" That was the poser Jesus gave the doubters so many years ago. The answer is just the same today. Jesus upon Calvary bore not only our sins but our sicknesses in His own body on the tree. He is not only our Savior but our Great Physician. Not only was He wounded for our transgressions, but by His stripes we were healed. Not only does He forgive "our iniquities," but He also "healed all our diseases."

In the plan of Christ and on the pages of the Bible, salvation for the soul and healing for the body went hand in hand. Man through unbelief has sought to divorce them. The mind of God has never changed however, nor His mercy lessened; and what God has joined together, let not man put asunder. In the beginning, sickness came as a result of sin. On Calvary, Jesus bore not only our sins but the results of sin—sickness. "Himself took our infirmities, and bare our sicknesses" (Matthew 8:17). Now if Jesus bore the burden of sickness, why should we continue to struggle beneath the load?

The needs of humanity have never changed—their heartaches, their sorrows, their bodily sufferings—have never changed. He is still a satisfying portion who can meet and supply every need for body and soul. He is still "Jesus the same yesterday, today, and forever."

In coming to Christ for healing, do not ask Him to become your Physician until you have made Him your Savior. There are some sinners who, if healed, would go out to serve the devil so much the harder. Give Jesus Christ your heart first: surrender to Him your life, your love, your all. Then come and ask Him to heal your body, not for your sake and convenience only, but that you may serve Him better, more wholeheartedly and efficiently.

"Is any sick among you? Let him call for the elders of the church; and let them pray over him, anointing him with oil in the name of the Lord: And the prayer of faith shall save the sick and the Lord shall raise him up; and if he has committed sins, they shall be forgiven him. Confess your faults one to another. The effectual fervent prayer of a righteous man availeth much" (James 5:14–16). Here again salvation and healing walk hand in hand.

Jesus waits to save and heal—waits to wash away your every sin, and remove your heavy burden. The secret of receiving both these blessings is a simple, child-like faith.

Believe on the Lord and ye shall be saved. Faith is an absolute necessity in receiving salvation. It is also an absolute necessity in receiving divine healing.

When the two blind men followed Christ in Matthew 9:28, imploring His merciful touch, He turned to them and said, "Believe ye that I am able to do this?" They said unto Him, "Yea, Lord." Then touched He their eyes, and said, "According to your faith be it unto you," and their eyes were opened.

When the woman of Matthew 9:20 pressed through the multitude saying within herself, "If I may but touch His garment, I shall be whole," Jesus turned and said, "Daughter, be of good comfort, thy faith hath made thee whole."

They who rebuke Christ's followers of today for daring to believe and claim His power to heal the sick should bear in mind—that Jesus never rebuked a soul for his faith—but did ever chide their unbelief.

There is not one passage in Scripture to bear out the assertion that the days of miraculously answered prayer were ever to pass away. Here are some of Christ's instructions that have never been recalled:

"As ye go, preach, saying, the kingdom of heaven is at hand. Heal the sick cleanse the lepers, cast out devils; freely ye have received, freely give."—Matthew 10:7–8.

"Go ye into all the world, and preach the Gospel to every creature. He that believeth and is baptized shall be saved; but he that believeth not shall be damned."

"And these signs shall follow them that believe: in my name they shall cast out devils; they shall speak with new tongues; they shall lay hands on the sick and they shall recover" (Mark 16:15). If the signs do not follow, something is wrong with our "believing." The preaching of God's word is still confirmed "with signs following." Amen.

Let us cast off the shackles of unbelief and rise up in faith to believe and claim the mighty promises of God.

Further Resources
BOOKS
Bahr, Robert. *Least of All Saints: The Story of Aimee Semple McPherson.* Englewood Cliffs, N.J.: Prentice-Hall, 1979.

Blumhofer, Edith Waldvogel. *Aimee Semple McPherson: Everybody's Sister.* Grand Rapids, Mich.: Eerdmans, 1993.

Epstein, Daniel Mark. *Sister Aimee: The Life of Aimee Semple McPherson.* San Diego: Harcourt Brace, 1994.

McPherson, Aimee Semple. *In the Service of the King: The Story of My Life.* New York: Boni and Liveright, 1927.

———. *This Is That.* Los Angeles: Bridal Call, 1919.

PERIODICALS

Bissell, Shelton. "Vaudeville at Angelus Temple." *The Outlook* 149, no. 4, May 23, 1928, 126–27, 158.

WEBSITES

Aimee Semple McPherson Resource Center. Available at http://members.aol.com/xbcampbell/asm/indexasm.htm (accessed January 16, 2003).

International Church of the Foursquare Gospel. Available at http://www.foursquare.org (accessed January 16, 2003).

Liberty Harbor Foursquare Church. Available at http://www.libertyharbor.org/aimee.htm; website home page: http://www.libertyharbor.org/ (accessed January 16, 2003).

In His Image

Theological work

By: William Jennings Bryan

Date: 1922

Source: Bryan, William Jennings. *In His Image.* New York: Revell, 1922, 120–123.

About the Author: William Jennings Bryan (1860–1925), a famous orator and politician, unsuccessfully ran as the Democratic presidential candidate in 1896, 1900, and 1908. He helped Woodrow Wilson get elected in 1912 and served as his secretary of state. Bryan later became active in conservative religious causes, such as opposing the teaching of evolution in public schools. He died at the age of sixty-five on July 26, 1925. ■

Introduction

William Jennings Bryan graduated from Illinois College in 1881 and afterwards studied law before he pursued a career in politics. Making unsuccessful bids for the U.S. presidency, he eventually served as Woodrow Wilson's secretary of state from 1913 to 1915.

A pacifist, Bryan opposed the American practice of claiming neutrality while still allowing American ships to transport munitions to belligerents. His differences with Wilson's foreign policy led to his resignation as secretary of state. Despite their differences, Bryan supported Wilson in his reelection in 1916.

Throughout his political life, whether it was fighting for the silver standard in monetary policy or opposing American expansionism, Bryan saw himself as the champion of the common, hardworking masses against the rich and powerful elites of the world. He would bring this devotion to the cause of the ordinary citizen to the field of religion after his political career was over.

Bryan had been a member of the Presbyterian Church since his youth. After his political defeat in 1900, he became more active in church affairs. As his political ca-

reer faded, his involvement in church matters increased. Bryan began to turn his famous oratorical skills to religious subjects and in time became a major force in the fundamentalist opposition to modernism. He had received no formal theological training but relied on the childlike faith of his youth to reject what he saw as the impious undermining of traditional Christian beliefs by liberal theologians. In his book *In His Image* (1922), he showed his distaste for those professors who were undermining the Christian faith of their students. Bryan dedicated the book to his parents, "to whom I am indebted for a Christian environment in youth, during which they instilled into my mind and imprinted upon my heart the religious principles which I have set forth."

Significance

Since Bryan viewed modernism as an assault by elitist university-trained theologians on the simple views of the common people, the conflict reflected his earlier political battles. Just as he energetically opposed the gold standard, he also opposed modernist reinterpretations of the Bible and Christian teaching. In the 1920s Bryan became active in the fundamentalist movement, which attempted to remove theological liberals from positions of authority in the Presbyterian Church, promoted the involvement of the church in the Interchurch World Movement, and fought evolution.

Of all of these issues, Bryan's most strenuous fight was against the teaching of evolution in the public schools. In 1924, he drafted the resolution passed by the Florida state legislature banning the teaching of evolution. Copies of his lecture "Is the Bible True?" were also distributed among Tennessee lawmakers and helped the passage of another such antievolution law. When a teacher in Dayton, Tennessee, was put on trial for violating this law, Bryan was invited to join the prosecuting attorneys. He gladly accepted and threw himself into what became his last fight. While Bryan won the case, Clarence Darrow, the famous attorney for the defense, had put Bryan on the witness stand and ridiculed Bryan's simple religious faith, thus winning in the court of public opinion. The fundamentalist cause suffered greatly from the unflattering depictions of it in the nation's newspapers, and the movement disappeared from public view until the 1980s.

Bryan died five days after the conclusion of the trial. It was ironic that, after so many defeats in his political career, his only victory should be a Pyrrhic one.

Primary Source

In His Image [excerpt]

> **SYNOPSIS:** Bryan, the famous populist, ran unsuccessfully for the U.S. presidency three times. After

William Jennings Bryan, September 20, 1922. Bryan, a famous lawyer, politician, and author, became actively involved in the Fundamentalist movement in the 1920s and fought vehemently against the teaching of Charles Darwin's theory of evolution in public schools. © **BETTMANN/CORBIS.** **REPRODUCED BY PERMISSION.**

his political career was over, Bryan became involved in the controversy between fundamentalism and modernism. His most notable contribution to this conflict was his opposition to the teaching of evolution in the public schools. This opposition, grounded in his Christian faith, can be seen in the following excerpt taken from his book *In His Image.*

The Origin of Man

Is any other proof needed to show the irreligious influence exerted by Darwinism applied to man? At the University of Wisconsin (so a Methodist preacher told me) a teacher told his class that the Bible was a collection of myths. When I brought the matter to the attention of the President of the University, he criticized me but avoided all reference to the professor. At Ann Arbor a professor argued with students against religion and asserted that no thinking man could believe in God or the Bible. At Columbia

(I learned this from a Baptist preacher) a professor began his course in geology by telling his class to throw away all that they had learned in the Sunday school. There is a professor in Yale of whom it is said that no one leaves his class a believer in God. (This came from a young man who told me that his brother was being led away from the Christian faith by this professor.) A father (a Congressman) tells me that a daughter on her return from Wellesley told him that nobody believed in the Bible stories now. Another father (a Congressman) tells me of a son whose faith was undermined by this doctrine in a Divinity School. Three preachers told me of having their interest in the subject aroused by the return of their children from college with their faith shaken. The Northern Baptists have recently, after a spirited contest, secured the adoption of a Confession of Faith; it was opposed by the evolutionists.

In Kentucky the fight is on among the Disciples, and it is becoming more and more acute in the Northern branches of the Methodist and Presbyterian Churches. A young preacher, just out of a theological seminary, who did not believe in the virgin birth of Christ, was recently ordained in Western New York. Last April I met a young man who was made an atheist by two teachers in a Christian college.

These are only a few illustrations that have come under my own observation—nearly all of them within a year. What is to be done? Are the members of the various Christian churches willing to have the power of the pulpit paralyzed by a false, absurd and ridiculous doctrine which is without support in the written Word of God and without support also in nature? Is "thus saith the Lord" to be supplanted by guesses and speculations and assumptions? I submit three propositions for the consideration of the Christians of the nation:

First, the preachers who are to break the bread of life to the lay members should believe that man has in him the breath of the Almighty, as the Bible declares, and not the blood of the brute, as the evolutionists affirm. He should also believe in the virgin birth of the Saviour.

Second, none but Christians in good standing and with a spiritual conception of life should be allowed to teach in Christian schools. Church schools are worse than useless if they bring students under the influence of those who do not believe in the religion upon which the Church and church schools are built. Atheism and Agnosticism are more dangerous when hidden under the cloak of religion than when they are exposed to view.

Third, in schools supported by taxation we should have a real neutrality wherever neutrality in religion is desired. If the Bible cannot be defended in these schools it should not be attacked, either directly or under the guise of philosophy or science. The neutrality which we now have is often but a sham; it carefully excludes the Christian religion but permits the use of the schoolrooms for the destruction of faith and for the teaching of materialistic doctrines.

It is not sufficient to say that *some* believers in Darwinism retain their belief in Christianity; some survive smallpox. As we avoid smallpox because *many* die of it, so we should avoid Darwinism because it *leads many astray.*

If it is contended that an instructor has a right to teach anything he likes, I reply that the parents who pay the salary have a right to decide what shall be taught. To continue the illustration used above, a person can expose himself to the smallpox if he desires to do so, but he has no right to communicate it to others. So a man can believe anything he pleases but he has no right to teach it against the protest of his employers.

Acceptance of Darwin's doctrine tends to destroy one's belief in immortality as taught by the Bible. If there has been no break in the line between man and the beasts—no time when by the act of the Heavenly Father man became "a living Soul," at what period in man's development was he endowed with the hope of a future life? And, if the brute theory leads to the abandonment of belief in a future life with its rewards and punishments, what stimulus to righteous living is offered in its place?

Darwinism leads to a denial of God. Nietzsche carried Darwinism to its logical conclusion and it made him the most extreme of anti-Christians. I had read extracts from his writings—enough to acquaint me with his sweeping denial of God and of the Saviour—but not enough to make me familiar with his philosophy.

Further Resources

BOOKS

Bryan, William Jennings. *The Memoirs of William Jennings Bryan, by Himself and His Wife Mary Baird Bryan.* Port Washington, N.Y.: Kennikat, 1971.

Cherney, Robert W. *A Righteous Cause: The Life of William Jennings Bryan.* Norman: University of Oklahoma Press, 1994.

Levine, Lawrence W. *Defender of the Faith: William Jennings Bryan, the Last Decade, 1915–1925.* Cambridge, Mass.: Harvard University Press, 1987.

The Faith of Modernism
Theological work

By: Shailer Mathews

Date: 1924

Source: Mathews, Shailer. *The Faith of Modernism.* New York: Macmillan, 1924, 37–39.

About the Author: Shailer Mathews (1863–1941), a noted liberal theologian, became a professor at the Divinity School of the new University of Chicago in 1894. He was a strong advocate of employing modern methods for the study of Scripture, which eventually led to conflicts with Fundamentalists. He died on October 23, 1941, at the age of seventy-eight. ■

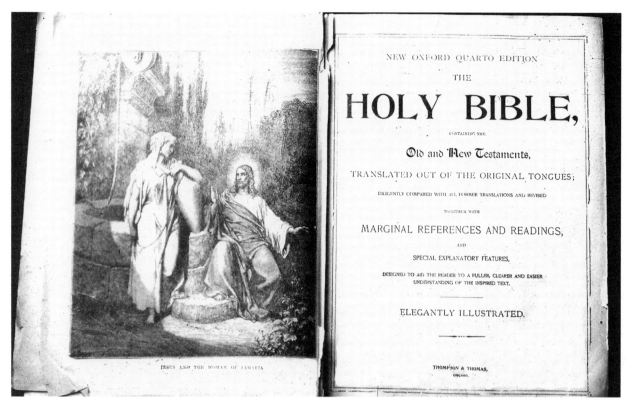

The cornerstone of the Christian religion, the events of the Bible and its writing underwent new scrutiny with the development of scientific methods. Modernists, including Shailer Mathews, supported such study of its history. **FIELD MARK PUBLICATIONS. REPRODUCED BY PERMISSION.**

Introduction

Shailer Mathews graduated from Newton Theological Institution in 1887. Not feeling a call to ministry, he decided to become a teacher. He taught rhetoric at Colby College and then became professor of history and political economy.

The early part of Mathews' career was spent in the fields of history, economics, and sociology. Two years after the University of Chicago was founded (1892), Mathews was recruited to the Divinity School, where he became associate professor of New Testament history and interpretation. Various elements of Mathews' life came together at this point. While he was licensed to preach, he did not pursue a career in the ministry, opting instead for studying new developments in the social sciences. Now he would bring these new historical-critical methods to the study of religion at the Divinity School. In doing so, he became a leading modernist in American religious thought.

In 1908, he became dean of the Divinity School, a position he held for twenty-five years. Under Mathews' leadership, the Divinity School became a center of liberal theology, known at the time as modernism. With the support of William Rainey Harper, the first president of the university, Mathews strove to educate the public in a critical understanding of religion and the Bible. This was done in various ways, including distributing pamphlets through the American Institute of Sacred Literature and offering extension classes. Mathews himself promoted this work through numerous talks and publications, as well as by directing for many summers the religious programs at the famous Chautauqua Institution in western New York.

Chief among his writings advocating modernism was his 1924 work *The Faith of Modernism,* in which he argued that science was not a threat to the Christian faith. In fact, Mathews stated that Christianity would benefit from the application of the scientific method to the study of the Bible.

Significance

Religious conservatives believed that the teachings of scholars like Mathews were leading people astray. Fundamentalism, in fact, originated in reaction to modernism and rejected its more liberal treatment of the Bible. One Fundamentalist stated: "Modernism with its 'Bible' of myth and legend is leading multitudes to everlasting punishment in the lake of fire. They are *lost.* Turn from these false prophets to the Bible which is in fact the infallible Word of the Living God."

For religious liberals like Washington Gladden, Harry Emerson Fosdick, and Mathews, the scientific study of the Bible was done in order to gain deeper insights into these sacred texts and then to apply these truths to the needs of the modern world. In *The Faith of Modernism,* he described what he believed to be the true task of the biblical scholar, that is, "to study the Bible with full respect for its sanctity but with equal respect for the student's intellectual integrity. . . . Only thus can it properly minister to our spiritual needs."

Mathews believed that Christianity was more than its dogmas. In order to get beyond these dogmas to understand the true nature of Christianity, Mathews argued in *The Faith of Modernism* that science was an ally of religion, not its enemy. He advocated the application of the scientific method to the study of religion in general and the Bible in particular. The consequence of this study, Mathews believed, would be a revitalized Christianity that could then be applied to address the social problems of the modern world. As dean of the influential Divinity School of the University of Chicago, Mathews was able to influence a generation of American ministers and religious scholars.

Primary Source

The Faith of Modernism [excerpt]

> **SYNOPSIS:** In *The Faith of Modernism,* Mathews claimed that Christianity had become out of touch with the modern world. The following excerpt highlights Mathews' argument that what was required was the application of the scientific method to the study of the Bible in order to make Christianity relevant again.

Modernism and the Bible

Deep within the Modernist movement is a method of appreciating and using the Bible. This is inevitable. Even the most superficial observer knows that the Bible is the basis upon which much of our religion has been built. But how shall men accustomed to scientific methods of thought use it for religious ends? Need they use it at all? They would be foolish not to. In using it, shall they give up their scientific attitude? That is impossible. Shall they treat the Bible merely as one of the ethnic literatures? That would be of incalculable injury to the religious life.

The true method is followed by the Modernist: to study the Bible with full respect for its sanctity but with equal respect for the student's intellectual integrity. We must begin with the facts concerning it, interpret its actual value and use it for what it is actually worth. Only thus can it properly minister to our spiritual needs.

I.

The Modernist, when he appeals to biblical teachings, wants, first of all, to find the facts concerning the Bible.

For nearly a century the Bible has been studied scientifically. Such study has not started from the assumption of supernatural revelation, but has sought information regarding the origin, time of writing, and the integrity of the biblical material. No one doubts the legitimacy of such attempts. They do not spring from theological bias; they do not deny doctrine; they simply seek to obtain information. They are those used by all students of literature and history and are no more anti-religious than a textbook in chemistry is anti-chemical. But no sooner do men thus study the Bible than facts appear which make belief in its verbal inerrancy untenable. As facts they naturally must be accounted for. In consequence there has grown up a general view of the Bible which is basis of the Modernist position. It was never voted upon or formally adopted by any group of scholars. Like views commonly held in biology or any other science, it is the result of investigators working without collusion, sometimes in rivalry, but without dogmatic assumptions, seeking to find and organize facts by scientific methods. Now that their work in the critical field is largely done, we find general agreement as to how the Bible originated, how it was composed, where it was written, why it was written. Differences as to details exist but the world of undogmatic biblical scholarship is certainly as much at one as to these matters as are the various theologies. How complete is the result of this study can be seen from the fact that there is no serious attempt to refute its conclusions by its own methods. There is plenty of anti-critical literature, plenty of denunciation of higher critics as enemies of the faith, plenty of attempts to enforce conformity in views of doctrines declared to be the teaching of the Bible; but there is little appeal to method and facts. It could not be otherwise. One cannot use the methods of critical scholarship without adopting them. Once adopted they can be trusted to give trustworthy results.

At the present time, although men may differ in their theology, in the extent to which they follow their methods, and in the frankness with which they give utterance to their views, there is no recognized biblical investigator who does not use the methods of criticism when studying the Bible to obtain knowledge of its origin, time of writing and composition, or who does not accept the general theory of the structure of the Pentateuch and synoptic gospels. Even so conservative a theologian as A. H. Strong declares "we may concede the substantial correctness" of the Pentateuchal analysis, and limits inspiration to religious ends.

Further Resources

BOOKS

Lindsey, William D. *Shailer Mathews' Lives of Jesus: The Search for a Theological Foundation for the Social Gospel.* Albany: State University of New York Press, 1997.

Mathews, Shailer. *New Faith for Old: An Autobiography by Shailer Mathews.* New York: Macmillan, 1936.

Pierce v. Society of the Sisters of the Holy Names of Jesus and Mary

Supreme Court decision

By: James Clark McReynolds

Date: June 1, 1925

Source: *Pierce v. Society of the Sisters of the Holy Names of Jesus and Mary.* 268 U.S. 510 (1925). Available online at http://caselaw.lp.findlaw.com/scripts/getcase.pl?navby =case&court=us&vol=268&invol=510; website home page: http://www.findlaw.com (accessed October 21, 2002).

About the Author: James Clark McReynolds (1862–1946) was born in Kentucky. McReynolds served as Woodrow Wilson's attorney general and in 1914 was appointed by him to the U.S. Supreme Court. McReynolds wrote the opinion in the Supreme Court's decision in *Pierce v. Society of the Sisters.* He died on August 24, 1946, at the age of eighty-four. ∎

Introduction

Nativism is the view that the United States should be composed of American-born Protestants of Anglo-Saxon origin. While this attitude resulted in much discrimination against Jews and Lutherans, most of the discrimination took the form of anti-Catholicism. It seems like every generation had its outbreak of this form of anti-Catholic bigotry, with episodes in the 1820s, 1850s, 1880s, 1920s, and 1960s. Catholics often felt targeted for proselytism in the public schools and, like the Lutherans, they responded by establishing their own school system. In 1922, the state of Oregon passed a law that prohibited these parochial schools and compelled all Catholic children to attend public schools.

Walter Pierce of Oregon was a Democrat in a largely Republican state. In 1916, he succeeded in being elected to the Oregon legislature and then ran for the office of governor in 1918 on a progressive platform. He lost the

Justice James Clark McReynolds handed down the decision in *Pierce v. Society of Sisters.* This unanimous decision affirmed the right of parents to choose to send their children to parochial schools. © **CORBIS. REPRODUCED BY PERMISSION.**

gubernatorial election by fifteen thousand votes and two years later lost his seat in the Oregon State Senate by twenty-seven votes.

Undaunted, Pierce ran again for the governorship in 1922. He was aided in his campaign by allying himself with a ballot initiative that would forbid children from attending private schools, the vast majority of these being Catholic parochial schools. Called the Compulsory Education Act, it would require all children ages eight to sixteen to attend public schools.

The bill was supported by the Ku Klux Klan (KKK), which was growing in Oregon. Like other nativist groups, the KKK saw Catholic immigrants and institutions as a threat to American liberty. Thus, because Pierce supported the bill, the KKK rallied behind him.

Ben Olcott, the Republican candidate, denounced the KKK six days prior to his party's primary. This cost him votes and he narrowly won the nomination. Olcott became vulnerable going into the general election.

Significance

On November 7, 1922, Pierce won by thirty-four thousand votes. And even though Catholics (who comprised 8 percent of Oregon's population), other minorities (such as Jews, German Lutherans, Seventh-Day Adventists, and African Americans), and liberal clergy from the Presbyterian, Unitarian, and Congregational churches opposed the act, it passed by nearly twelve thousand votes. The new law was immediately challenged on legal grounds and eventually was taken up by the U.S. Supreme Court. Pierce found that the price he had to pay for the election was having to defend the KKK-sponsored law. The state argued that the greatest danger confronting the American people was class hatred and that the best defense was to require all to "meet in the common schools, which are the great American melting pot, there to become . . . the typical American of the future."

The opposing view was taken by the Society of the Sisters of the Holy Names of Jesus and Mary, a Catholic women's religious order that supported many schools in Oregon and that had been active in the region since 1859. It was also supported in this action by Hill Military Academy. The Court ruled in favor of the Society of the Sisters and unanimously voided the Compulsory Education Act by a vote of 9 to 0.

Justice James Clark McReynolds delivered the written opinion. Not only did he acknowledge that the law would have practically eliminated parochial schools, he also argued for parents having the right to choose how to educate their children, stating, "The child is not the mere creature of the State."

Primary Source

Pierce v. Society of the Sisters of the Holy Names of Jesus and Mary [excerpt]

> **SYNOPSIS:** There were many forms of nativism in the 1920s, from opposition to a Catholic running for president in 1928 to the passage of restrictive immigration laws. One instance of successful opposition to nativism was the U.S. Supreme Court's overturning of the KKK-sponsored Compulsory Education Act, a law that would have prohibited children from attending Catholic schools.

These appeals are from decrees, based upon undenied allegations, which granted preliminary orders restraining [268 U.S. 510, 530] appellants from threatening or attempting to enforce the Compulsory Education Act adopted November 7, 1922 (Laws Or. 1923, p. 9), under the initiative provision of her Constitution by the voters of Oregon. Judicial Code, 266 (Comp. St. 1243). They present the same points of law; there are no controverted questions of fact. Rights said to be guaranteed by the federal Constitution were specially set up, and appropriate prayers asked for their protection.

The challenged act, effective September 1, 1926, requires every parent, guardian, or other person having control or charge or custody of a child between 8 and 16 years to send him "to a public school for the period of time a public school shall be held during the current year" in the district where the child resides; and failure so to do is declared a misdemeanor. . . . The manifest purpose is to compel general attendance at public schools by normal children, between 8 and 16, who have not completed the eight grade. And without doubt enforcement of the statute would seriously impair, perhaps destroy, the profitable features of appellees' business and greatly diminish the value of their property.

Appellee the Society of Sisters is an Oregon corporation, organized in 1880, with power to care for orphans, educate and instruct the youth, establish and maintain academies or schools, and acquire necessary real and personal [268 U.S. 510, 532] property. It has long devoted its property and effort to the secular and religious education and care of children, and has acquired the valuable good will of many parents and guardians. It conducts interdependent primary and high schools and junior colleges, and maintains orphanages for the custody and control of children between 8 and 16. In its primary schools many children between those ages are taught the subjects usually pursued in Oregon public schools during the first eight years. Systematic religious instruction and moral training according to the tenets of the Roman Catholic Church are also regularly provided. All courses of study, both temporal and religious, contemplate continuity of training under appellee's charge; the primary schools are essential to the system and the most profitable. It owns valuable buildings, especially constructed and equipped for school purposes. The business is remunerative—the annual income from primary schools exceeds $30,000—and the successful conduct of this requires long time contracts with teachers and parents. The Compulsory Education Act of 1922 has already caused the withdrawal from its schools of children who would otherwise continue, and their income has steadily declined. The appellants, public officers, have proclaimed their purpose strictly to enforce the statute.

After setting out the above facts, the Society's bill alleges that the enactment conflicts with the right of parents to choose schools where their children will receive appropriate mental and religious training, the right of the child to influence the parents' choice of a school, the right of schools and teachers therein to engage in a useful business or profession, and is accordingly repugnant to the Constitution and void. And, further, that unless enforcement of the measure is enjoined the corporation's business and property will suffer irreparable injury. . . .

No question is raised concerning the power of the state reasonably to regulate all schools, to inspect, supervise and examine them, their teachers and pupils; to require that all children of proper age attend some school, that teachers shall be of good moral character and patriotic disposition, that certain studies plainly essential to good citizenship must be taught, and that nothing be taught which is manifestly inimical to the public welfare.

The inevitable practical result of enforcing the act under consideration would be destruction of appellees' primary schools, and perhaps all other private primary schools for normal children within the state of Oregon. Appellees are engaged in a kind of undertaking not inherently harmful, but long regarded as useful and meritorious. Certainly there is nothing in the present records to indicate that they have failed to discharge their obligations to patrons, students, or the state. And there are no peculiar circumstances or present emergencies which demand extraordinary measures relative to primary education.

Under the doctrine of *Meyer v. Nebraska,* 262 U.S. 390, 43 S. Ct. 625, 29 A. L. R. 1146, we think it entirely plain that the Act of 1922 unreasonably interferes with the liberty of parents and guardians to direct the upbringing and education of children [268 U.S. 510, 535] under their control. As often heretofore pointed out, rights guaranteed by the Constitution may not be abridged by legislation which has no reasonable relation to some purpose within the competency of the state. The fundamental theory of liberty upon which all governments in this Union repose excludes any general power of the state to standardize its children by forcing them to accept instruction from public teachers only. The child is not the mere creature of the state; those who nurture him and direct his destiny have the right, coupled with the high duty, to recognize and prepare him for additional obligations. . . .

The suits were not premature. The injury to appellees was present and very real, not a mere possibility in the remote future. If no relief had been possible prior to the effective date of the act, the injury would have become irreparable. Prevention of impending injury by unlawful action is a well-recognized function of courts of equity.

The decrees below are affirmed.

Further Resources

BOOKS

Ellis, John Tracy. *Documents of American Catholic History.* Milwaukee: Bruce, 1962.

WEBSITES

"Children Not Mere Creatures of the State." Available online at http://www.cascadepolicy.org/edpubs.asp; website home page: http://www.cascadepolicy.org (accessed January 16, 2003).

Pierce v. Society of the Sisters of the Holy Name of Jesus and Mary. Available online at http://religiousfreedom.lib .virginia.edu/court/pier_v_soci.html; website home page: religiousfreedom.lib.virginia.edu (accessed May 9, 2003).

"Walter Marcus Pierce, 1923–27." Available online at http://www.osl.state.or.us/lib/governors/wmp.htm; website home page: http://www.osl.state.or.us/ (accessed January 16, 2003).

"The Hebrew Union College of Yesterday and a Great Desideratum in Its Curriculum Today"
Essay

By: Kaufmann Kohler

Date: 1925

Source: Kohler, Kaufmann. "The Hebrew Union College of Yesterday and a Great Desideratum in Its Curriculum Today." *Hebrew Union College Jubilee Volume (1875–1925).* New York: Ktav, 1968, 74–76.

About the Author: Kaufmann Kohler (1843–1926) was born in Germany. Raised in an orthodox Jewish family, he later became a leader in Reform Judaism. Kohler immigrated to the United States in 1869 and after serving various congregations became president of Hebrew Union College in 1903. He died on January 28, 1926, at the age of eighty-two. ∎

Introduction

Kaufmann Kohler was a major figure in Reform Judaism in the United States. Born in Germany, he studied at universities in Munich and Berlin and received his doctorate from Erlangen in 1867. Influenced by the critical methods he learned in his studies, Kohler believed that Judaism was the product of historical development and that it needed to adapt to modern times. Such views made finding a rabbinical position in Germany difficult, so in 1869 he came to the United States to take a position at Temple Beth-El in Detroit. In 1871, he went on to Sinai Temple in Chicago, and he succeeded his father-in-law as rabbi of Temple Beth-El in New York City in 1879. In all of these positions, Kohler sought to modernize Judaism.

The innovations that Kohler instituted included holding Sunday services, in addition to those held on Saturday in accordance with Jewish tradition. Such a change, along with the addition of sermons, organ music, and the use of vernacular languages, were all aspects of the Reform movement in Judaism. Its goal was to modernize Jewish life and practice. In addition to liturgical changes, the Reform movement also addressed those areas, such as dress and diet, that had served to separate Jews from the rest of society. Particularly in the United States, the Reform movement sought to break down barriers and promote assimilation in American society.

An important step in the development of Reform Judaism in the United States was the founding of Hebrew Union College in Cincinnati. In 1883, the first class graduated. At the graduation dinner celebrating this momentous event, shrimp was served, which violated kosher law. The more conservative attendants, who believed this to be a blatant disregard for Jewish tradition, stormed out of the banquet hall. The new college survived this rocky beginning and continues to this day to train Jewish leaders in the Reform tradition.

Significance

In 1885, Kohler invited a number of Reform rabbis to gather for a conference in Pittsburgh to discuss the principles of their movement. The Pittsburgh conference disagreed with the Orthodox notion of preserving the old traditions. On the contrary, it declared that Judaism was "a progressive religion, ever striving to be in accord with the postulates of reason." More specifically, the fourth principle of the Pittsburgh declaration rejected a strict observance of the kosher laws and other regulations of the past that segregated Jews from the rest of society.

Kohler participated in the preparation of the Union Prayer Book in 1894, which drastically edited prayers and almost completely eliminated those in Hebrew. His major scholarly work was *Jewish Theology Systematically and Historically Considered,* which was published originally in German in 1910 and appeared in English in 1918. His most significant contributions were on the Jewish origins of Christianity and on the origin and development of Jewish liturgy.

Kohler became president of Hebrew Union College on February 19, 1903. Serving in this capacity for eighteen years, he was responsible for raising the school's academic standards. An active scholar, he taught homiletics (the study of the homilies), theology, and Hellenistic (Greek) literature.

In 1925, Hebrew Union College celebrated its fiftieth anniversary. Kohler took this opportunity to comment on the Jews' place in American society. In an article written to commemorate the anniversary, he condemned as fanatics and fools those Jews who argued for segregation from Gentiles. Instead, representing a lifetime of commitment to the ideals of the Reform movement, he called for closer relations with non-Jews. These ideals continue today in Reform Judaism, which strives to foster the distinct identity of its faith community while at the same time maintaining cordial relations and cooperation with those of other faiths.

Primary Source

"The Hebrew Union College of Yesterday and a Great Desideratum in Its Curriculum Today" [excerpt]

SYNOPSIS: The following excerpt is taken from a collection of writings marking the fiftieth anniversary of Hebrew Union College in 1925. It was written by Kohler four years after his retirement from the school and one year before his death. In this piece, Kohler clearly expresses the Reform view that Jews cannot live in seclusion, but rather have to establish contact and dialogue with their non-Jewish neighbors.

. . . To be sure, we American Jews no longer live in seclusion. Our life is interwoven by a thousand threads with that of the surrounding world. Even those who still observe the dietary laws do not want to be alienated, as ex-President Eliot suggests, from the rest of men. Our whole thinking, reading and speaking brings us into closest contact with our non-Jewish fellow citizens, and we are constantly confronted with the question: what is, and should be, our attitude as Jews towards the Christian world. Only blind fanatics and fools speak of the unbridgeable gulf between Jews and Gentiles. Even the Middle Ages, with all their hostility to us, found or sought ways of approach, if not socially, then by means of scientific cooperation and competition. And today when we see a majestic Cathedral rise in our midst, with the motto: "The Fatherhood of God and the Brotherhood of Men" rallying all the creeds in friendship around it, we ought to have a better mutual understanding of each other's idealism and faith than we had hitherto. Yet nowhere is this demand felt so clearly as in our seats of learning, where the students are trained for the leadership of Congregations as ministers. It was well said the other day by Cardinal Hayes: "Tolerance is not enough." What we need today is mutual recognition. Much as we differ from each other in our creeds and doctrines or rites, we have a great deal in common, and we can well afford to learn from each other. If reason is the predominant force of our faith, there are sentiment and mysticism prevalent in the Church. Judaism has made science the sister of our faith; Christianity allied art with its religion. The mighty passion for justice is the characteristic of the Jew throughout the ages, whereas Christianity laid all the stress on love.

We can well understand why the New Testament became a *Noli me tangere* to the Jew, and why the very name of Jesus was shunned by them all these centuries. As soon as the man Jesus was deified, the law forbidding the very mention of the name of other gods (Exodus XXIII, 13) was applied to him, too, and so were the Jews actually called deicides or Christ-killers and laden with curses by the New Testament writers. Nor was there any attempt made by the ruling Church to establish friendlier relations with the maligned race. Only our own great mediae-val authorities took a broader view, and beheld in Christianity, as well as in Mohammedanism, God-appointed agencies for the spreading of the Jewish truth over the world. We to-day have obtained a bet-ter knowledge of the sources and of the accom-plishments of the Christian faith, and it is in our own interest to learn to know more about them. After all, the New Testament, centered on Jesus as the sav-iour, has, notwithstanding all its Jew-hatred and ma-licious charges against the Jews, won the pagan world for Israel's God and for the higher ethics rooted in the belief in Him. Moreover, ever so many phrases of the New Testament have become parts of our ordinary language in Western civilization.

From whatever point then we may look at it, it becomes the imperative duty of the Jewish students in our days to familiarize himself with the New Tes-tament as an off-shoot of Judaism. We proudly claim Jesus as our own, even if we cannot go as far as does Claude Montefiore who wants to raise him to the rank of Israel's great prophets. Likewise should the Jewish teacher be acquainted with the principal facts of Church history as it affected the destinies of the whole Western civilization. This study ought to find a place in the curriculum of the Jewish Col-lege, and accordingly there should be a certain time fixed for a *course on the Relations between Judaism and Christianity in the past and at the present time.*

No Jewish minister today can fail to come in touch with his Christian fellows, whether through the press or in personal conversation, and he owes it to himself, as well as to the sacred cause he rep-resents, to be fully prepared and able to stand up in defense of our faith as its fairminded champion, while maintaining a firm scientific footing in accord with the best results of modern research. Very fre-quently he is called upon to discuss themes per-taining to those relations, and there he finds the opportunity of enlightening his non-Jewish hearers on many points new to them, and this requires a systematic training.

Further Resources

BOOKS

Goldstein, Niles, and Peter S. Knobel. *Duties of the Soul: The Role of the Commandments in Liberal Judaism.* New York: UAHC Press, 1999.

Hirsch, Ammiel, and Yosef Reinman. *One People, Two Worlds: An Orthodox Rabbi and a Reform Rabbi Explore the Issues that Divide Them.* New York: Schocken, 2002.

Kohler, Kaufmann. *The Origins of the Synagogue and the Church.* New York: Macmillan, 1929.

Philipson, David. *Studies in Jewish Literature: Issued in Honor of Professor Kaufmann Kohler.* New York: Arno, 1979.

The Man Nobody Knows
Nonfiction work

By: Bruce Barton

Date: 1925

Source: Barton, Bruce. *The Man Nobody Knows.* Indianapo-lis: Bobbs-Merrill, 1925. Reprint, Bobbs-Merrill, 1983, 11–13.

About the Author: Bruce Barton (1886–1967) was born in Robbins, Tennessee. A man of varied experiences, Barton was an advertising executive, author, and U.S. congressman. He is best known for his 1925 book on Jesus, *The Man No-body Knows.* Barton died a month before his eighty-first birthday on July 5, 1967. ∎

Introduction

Bruce Barton began working at the age of nine sell-ing newspapers and worked his way through college, graduating from Amherst College in 1907. After gradu-ation, he moved to Chicago, where he worked for small newspaper and magazine publishers. In 1912, he moved to New York City, where he became assistant sales man-ager at *Collier's* magazine.

Though his main duties were writing and editing for *Collier's,* he also helped in its advertising department. In his free time, he volunteered for the Salvation Army and discovered a gift for coining catchy slogans, his first be-ing, "A man may be down but he is never out." During World War I (1914–1918), he supervised the publicity for the United War Work fund drive. In the course of this work, Barton met Roy Durstine and Alex Osborn. Together, they formed an advertising agency that, after

Advertising executive and author Bruce Barton in the 1920s. Barton's *The Man Nobody Knows* (1925) was the decade's most popular work on Jesus. It sat atop the best-seller list for two years, selling over a half million copies in hardcover. **THE LIBRARY OF CONGRESS.**

a later merger with another company, became one of the largest agencies in the country: Batten, Barton, Durstine and Osborn (BBDO).

Barton was a great success in advertising. Soon, his agency counted Dunlop Tires, General Electric, General Motors, Lever Brothers, and U.S. Steel among its clients. Barton also created the character Betty Crocker.

Not only was Barton a success in business, but business itself, on the eve of the 1929 stock market crash, was a great success. President Calvin Coolidge had declared that the business of America was business, and this high esteem

for commerce found its way into religion as well. Known as the Gospel of Wealth, this view held that possessing wealth was not only acceptable for Christians, but rather it was their moral obligation to amass riches. Barton made use of his considerable business experience to contribute two procapitalism books to the movement: *The Man Nobody Knows* (1925) and *The Book Nobody Knows* (1926).

Significance

The Gospel of Wealth flourished in the late nineteenth and early twentieth centuries, when the social standing and popularity of businessmen was high. Theologically, wealth was the result not only of hard work, but also of God's blessings. Likewise, the condition of the poor was the result of their moral failings, so it was not the responsibility of society to help them. This view lasted until the stock market crash and the Great Depression.

The Gospel of Wealth and its fascination with business influenced American churches in various ways. Churches adopted modern financial planning and employed advertising and promotional campaigns to increase memberships. A 1921 article in the *Independent* stated, "The sanest religion is business. Any relationship that forces a man to follow the Gold Rule rightfully belongs amid the ceremonials of the church. A great business enterprise includes and presupposes this relationship."

Barton is one of the best representatives of the Gospel of Wealth in the 1920s. Besides living a life that had a natural relationship between religion and business, Barton found the time to combine his advertising experience and religious faith to compose the popular book *The Man Nobody Knows* in 1925. The book pictures Jesus as a master salesman, psychologist, and forceful young executive who forged twelve men from the lower ranks of society into the best management team of all time.

The Man Nobody Knows became the decade's most popular work on Jesus. It sold over five hundred thousand copies and was at the top of the nonfiction best-seller list for two years. At one point in the book, Barton examines the characteristics of Jesus presented in the Bible and contrasts them with the image of Jesus given by scholars and liberal ministers, exclaiming that "[t]his is a man nobody knows!" He followed this book with another that focused on the Bible, entitled *The Book Nobody Knows*.

Primary Source

The Man Nobody Knows [excerpt]

> **SYNOPSIS:** *The Man Nobody Knows* was one of the most popular books associated with the Gospel of Wealth movement. This biography of Jesus, written by Barton, an advertising executive, went through twenty-two printings between 1925 and 1927 alone. Rather than portraying Jesus as a reclusive, passive figure, the book depicts the founder of Christianity

as both a dynamic individual and a model for the modern American businessman.

How It Came to Be Written

The little boy sat bolt upright and still in the rough wooden chair, but his mind was very busy.

This was his weekly hour of revolt.

The kindly lady who could never seem to find her glasses would have been terribly shocked if she had known what was going on inside the little boy's mind.

"You must love Jesus," she said every Sunday, "and God."

The little boy did not say anything. He was afraid to say anything; he was almost afraid that something would happen to him because of the things he thought.

Love God! Who was always picking on people for having a good time and sending little boys to hell because they couldn't do better in a world which He had made so hard! Why didn't God pick on someone His own size?

Love Jesus! The little boy looked up at the picture which hung on the Sunday-school wall. It showed a pale young man with no muscle and a sad expression. The young man had red whiskers.

Then the little boy looked across to the other wall. There was Daniel, good old Daniel, standing off the lions. The little boy liked Daniel. He liked David, too, with the trusty sling that landed a stone square on the forehead of Goliath. And Moses, with his rod and his big brass snake. They were fighters—those three. He wondered if David could whip the champ. Samson could! That would have been a fight!

But Jesus! Jesus was the "Lamb of God." The little boy did not know what that meant, but it sounded like Mary's little lamb, something for girls—sissified. Jesus was also "meek and lowly," a "man of sorrows and acquainted with grief." He went around for three years telling people not to do things.

Sunday was Jesus' day; it was wrong to feel comfortable or laugh on Sunday.

The little boy was glad when the superintendent rang the bell and announced, "We will now sing the closing hymn." One more bad hour was over. For one more week the little boy had left Jesus behind.

Years went by and the boy grew up.

He began to wonder about Jesus.

He said to himself: "Only strong men inspire greatly and build greatly. Yet Jesus has inspired millions; what he founded changed the world. It is extraordinary."

The more sermons the man heard and the more books he read the more mystified he became.

One day he decided to wipe his mind clean of books and sermons.

He said, "I will read what the men who knew Jesus personally said about Him. I will read about Him as though He were a character in history, new to me, about whom I had never heard anything at all."

The man was amazed.

A physical weakling! Where did they get that idea? Jesus pushed a plane and swung an adz; He was a good carpenter. He slept outdoors and spent His days walking around His favorite lake. His muscles were so strong that when He drove the moneychangers out, nobody dared to oppose Him!

A kill-joy! He was the most popular dinner guest in Jerusalem! The criticism which proper people made was that He spent too much time with publicans and sinners (very good fellows, on the whole, the man thought) and enjoyed society too much. They called Him a "wine bibber and a gluttonous man."

A failure! He picked up twelve humble men and created an organization that won the world.

When the man had finished his reading, he exclaimed, "This is a man nobody knows!

"Someday," said he, "someone will write a book about Jesus. He will describe the same discovery I have made about Him, that many other people are waiting to make." For, as the man's little-boy notions and prejudices vanished, he saw the day-to-day life of Him who lived the greatest life and was alive and knowable beyond the mists of tradition.

So the man waited for someone to write the book, but no one did. Instead, more books were published that showed the vital Christ as one who was weak and unhappy, passive and resigned.

The man became impatient. One day he said, "I believe I will try to write that book myself."

And he did.

Further Resources

BOOKS

Barton, Bruce. *The Book Nobody Knows.* Indianapolis: Bobbs-Merrill, 1926.

———. *The Man of Galilee: Twelve Scenes from the Life of Christ.* New York: Cosmopolitan, 1928.

PERIODICALS

"Classic Optimist." *Time* 90, no. 18, July 14, 1967.

"Word Man." *Newsweek* 70, nos. 78–79, July 17, 1967.

"Campaign Address of Governor Alfred E. Smith, Oklahoma City, September 20, 1928"

Speech

By: Alfred E. Smith

Date: September 20, 1928

Source: Smith, Alfred E. "Campaign Address of Governor Alfred E. Smith, Oklahoma City, September 20, 1928." Printed in *Campaign Addresses of Governor Alfred E. Smith.* Washington, D.C.: Democratic National Committee, 1929. Reprinted in John Tracy Ellis, ed. *Documents of American Catholic History.* Milwaukee: Bruce, 1962, 613–617.

About the Author: Alfred E. Smith (1873–1944) was born in New York City. He served as governor of New York State for four terms and was noted for his progressive reforms. Smith became the first Roman Catholic nominated for the U.S. presidency in 1928, losing to Herbert Hoover. He died on October 4, 1944, at the age of seventy. ∎

Introduction

Alfred E. Smith was born in 1873 on New York City's Lower East Side. He attended Catholic school and served as an altar boy at St. James Roman Catholic Church. While an average student, he won a citywide oratory contest at the age of eleven. Smith dropped out of school after the death of his father and went to work. He became involved in the Democratic Party and was elected to his first office in 1903 in the New York State Assembly. A successful reformer, he was elected governor of New York State in 1918.

Smith's record made him a logical choice to be the standard bearer for the Democrats in the 1924 presidential election. The 1924 Democratic convention, however, was divided between the Protestant, pro-Prohibition members from the rural southern and western states, and the Catholic, anti-Prohibition members from the urban northeast. A bitter fight over whether or not to add a platform condemning the Ku Klux Klan (KKK) illustrated the intensity of the religion issue. In the end, after two weeks of stalemate and over a hundred ballots, Smith withdrew himself from consideration.

After the crushing defeat of the Democrats in 1924, losing by an almost two to one margin to the Republicans, it was widely felt that Smith would seek the nomination again. This prospect led Charles C. Marshall, a prominent Protestant layman, to argue in the April 1927 issue of *The Atlantic Monthly* that there was a fundamental conflict between Smith's Catholic faith and the U.S. Constitution. Smith responded in the following issue that he believed in the separation of church and state and that he saw no conflict between being a Catholic and being president. His most eloquent statement on this issue, however, came in his September 20, 1928, Oklahoma City speech.

Significance

In 1928, Smith again ran for the nomination and secured it on the first ballot. He decided to address the religion issue directly in Oklahoma, a state where crosses were burned along the railroad tracks where his campaign trains passed. His speech in Oklahoma City was passionate and touched on the core principles of American democratic values but could not overcome the religious bigotry unleashed against him. Smith lost Oklahoma to Hoover.

The election turnout was very high, 57 percent compared to 49 percent in the previous election, and this included a large number of anti-Catholic votes. Methodist bishop J.M. Cannon urged Protestants to "vote as you pray," and in the South the traditional Democratic vote was reduced. The KKK also lobbied heavily against Smith.

In addition to his Catholicism, another reason many voted against Smith was his opposition to Prohibition, a cause supported by both conservative and liberal Protestants. A publication by the Anti-Saloon League in Ohio stated, "If you believe in Anglo-Saxon Protestant domination, . . . if you believe in prohibition, its observance and enforcement, . . . then whether you are a Republican or a Democrat, you will vote for Hoover rather than Smith." The Prohibition issue undoubtedly silenced those liberal Protestants who might have supported Smith as a reformer or, at the very least, on the principle of religious liberty.

The religion issue did help Smith gain two states (Massachusetts and Rhode Island) with large Catholic populations that had gone Republican in 1924, but it cost him six traditionally Democratic southern states. Even though the Democrats under Smith polled fifteen million votes compared to eight million in 1924, the loss of the southern states resulted in his gaining only eighty-seven electoral votes, the worst showing in the Electoral College for the Democrats since Ulysses S. Grant's victory in 1872.

Primary Source

"Campaign Address of Governor Alfred E. Smith, Oklahoma City, September 20, 1928" [excerpt]

> **SYNOPSIS:** The following is the speech that Smith gave in Oklahoma City in which he clearly addressed the religion issue. While it did not lead to his winning the presidential election, it remains one of the most eloquent attacks on religious bigotry to be delivered by a national figure.

. . . In a presidential campaign there should be but two considerations before the electorate: The platform of the party, and the ability of the candidate to make it effective.

In this campaign an effort has been made to distract the attention of the electorate from these two considerations and to fasten it on malicious and un-American propaganda.

I shall tonight discuss and denounce that wicked attempt. I shall speak openly on the things about which people have been whispering to you. . . .

Twenty-five years ago I began my active public career. I was then elected to the Assembly, representing the neighborhood in New York City where I was born, where my wife was born, where my five children were born and where my father and mother were born. I represented that district continuously for twelve years, until 1915, when I was elected Sheriff of New York county.

Two years later I was elected to the position of President of the Board of Aldermen, which is really that of Vice-Mayor of the City of New York.

In 1918 I was elected by the delegates to the State convention as the candidate of the Democratic Party for Governor and was elected.

Running for re-election in 1920, I was defeated in the Harding landslide. However, while Mr. Harding carried the State of New York by more than 1,100,000 plurality, I was defeated only by some 70,000 votes.

After this defeat I returned to private life, keeping up my interest in public affairs, and accepted appointment to an important State body at the hands of the man who had defeated me.

In 1922 the Democratic Convention, by unanimous vote, renominated me for the third time for Governor. I was elected by the record plurality of 387,000, and this in a State which had been normally Republican.

In 1924, at the earnest solicitation of the Democratic presidential candidate, I accepted nomination. The State of New York was carried by President Coolidge by close to 700,000 plurality, but I was elected Governor. On the morning after election I found myself the only Democrat elected on the State ticket, with both houses of the Legislature overwhelmingly Republican.

Renominated by the unanimous vote of the convention of 1926, I made my fifth State-wide run for

Alfred Emanuel Smith, Ashville, North Carolina, 1928. Smith, a Catholic, spoke out against religious bigotry when his religion was attacked during the 1928 presidential campaign. **AP/WIDE WORLD PHOTOS. REPRODUCED BY PERMISSION.**

the governorship and was again elected the Democratic Governor of a normally Republican State.

Consequently, I am in a position to come before you tonight as the Governor of New York finishing out his fourth term.

The record of accomplishment under my four administrations recommended me to the Democratic Party in the nation, and I was nominated for the presidency at the Houston convention on the first ballot.

To put the picture before you completely, it is necessary for me to refer briefly to this record of accomplishment. . . . [Governor Smith then went into detail concerning the main legislative enactments, appointments, etc., of his administrations.]

One scandal connected with my administration would do more to help out the Republican National Committee in its campaign against me than all the millions of dollars now being spent by them in malicious propaganda. Unfortunately for them, they cannot find it, because the truth is it is not there. I challenge Senator Owen and all his kind to point to one single flaw upon which they can rest their case.

But they won't find it. They won't try to find it, because I know what lies behind all this, and I will tell you before I sit down to-night. . . .

I know what lies behind all this and I shall tell you. I specifically refer to the question of my religion. Ordinarily, that word should never be used in a political campaign. The necessity for using it is forced on me by Senator Owen and his kind, and I feel that at least once in this campaign, I, as the candidate of the Democratic Party, owe it to the people of this country to discuss frankly and openly with them this attempt of Senator Owen and the forces behind him to inject bigotry, hatred, intolerance and un-American sectarian division into a campaign which should be an intelligent debate of the important issues which confront the American people. . . .

A recent newspaper account in the City of New York told the story of a woman who called at the Republican National headquarters in Washington, seeking some literature to distribute. She made the request that it be of a nature other than political. Those in charge of the Republican Publicity Bureau provided the lady with an automobile and she was driven to the office of a publication notorious throughout the country for its senseless, stupid, foolish attacks upon the Catholic Church and upon Catholics generally.

I can think of no greater disaster to this country than to have the voters of it divide upon religious lines. It is contrary to the spirit, not only of the Declaration of Independence, but of the Constitution itself. During all of our national life we have prided ourselves throughout the world on the declaration of the fundamental American truth that all men are created equal.

Our forefathers, in their wisdom, seeing the danger to the country of a division on religious issues, wrote into the Constitution of the United States in no uncertain words the declaration that no religious test shall ever be applied for public office, and it is a sad thing in 1928, in view of the countless billions of dollars that we have poured into the cause of public education, to see some American citizens proclaiming themselves 100 per cent. American, and in the document that makes that proclamation suggesting that I be defeated for the presidency because of my religious belief.

The Grand Dragon of the Realm of Arkansas, writing to a citizen of that State, urges my defeat because I am a Catholic, and in the letter suggests to the man, who happened to be a delegate to the Democratic convention, that by voting against me he was upholding American ideals and institutions as established by our forefathers.

The Grand Dragon that thus advised a delegate to the national convention to vote against me because of my religion is a member of an order known as the Ku Klux Klan, who had the effrontery to refer to themselves as 100 per cent. Americans.

Yet totally ignorant of the history and tradition of this country and its institutions and, in the name of Americanism, they breathe into the hearts and souls of their members hatred of millions of their fellow countrymen because of their religious belief. . . .

I would have no objection to anybody finding fault with my public record circularizing the whole United States, provided he would tell the truth. But no decent, right-minded, upstanding American citizen can for a moment countenance the shower of lying statements, with no basis in fact, that have been reduced to printed matter and sent broadcast through the mails of this country.

One lie widely circulated, particularly through the southern part of the country, is that during my governorship I appointed practically nobody to office but members of my own church.

What are the facts? On investigation I find that in the cabinet of the Governor sit fourteen men. Three of the fourteen are Catholics, ten Protestants, and one of Jewish faith. In various bureaus and divisions of the Cabinet officers, the Governor appointed twenty-six people. Twelve of them are Catholics and fourteen of them are Protestants. Various other State officials, making up boards and commissions, and appointed by the Governor, make a total of 157 appointments, of which thirty-five were Catholics, 106 were Protestants, twelve were Jewish, and four I could not find out about.

I have appointed a large number of judges of all our courts, as well as a large number of county officers, for the purpose of filling vacancies. They total in number 177, of which sixty-four were Catholics, ninety were Protestants, eleven were Jewish, and twelve of the officials I was unable to find anything about so far as their religion was concerned.

This is a complete answer to the false, misleading and, if I may be permitted the use of the harsher word, lying statements that have found their way through a large part of this country in the form of printed matter.

If the American people are willing to sit silently by and see large amounts of money secretly pour into false and misleading propaganda for political purposes, I repeat that I see in this not only a danger to the party, but a danger to the country. . . . [Here other instances of bigotry in the campaign were cited.]

I have been told that politically it might be expedient for me to remain silent upon this subject, but so far as I am concerned no political expediency will keep me from speaking out in an endeavor to destroy these evil attacks.

There is abundant reason for believing that Republicans high in the councils of the party have countenanced a large part of this form of campaign, if they have not actually promoted it. A sin of omission is some times as grievous as a sin of commission. They may, through official spokesmen, disclaim as much as they please responsibility for dragging into a national campaign the question of religion, something that according to our Constitution, our history and our traditions has no part in any campaign for elective public office. . . .

One of the things, if not the meanest thing, in the campaign is a circular pretending to place someone of my faith in the position of seeking votes for me because of my Catholicism. Like everything of this kind, of course it is unsigned, and it would be impossible to trace its authorship. It reached me through a member of the Masonic order who, in turn, received it in the mail. It is false in its every line. It was designed on its very face to injure me with members of churches other than my own.

I here emphatically declare that I do not wish any member of my faith in any part of the United States to vote for me on any religious grounds. I want them to vote for me only when in their hearts and consciences they become convinced that my election will promote the best interests of our country.

By the same token, I cannot refrain from saying that any person who votes against me simply because of my religion is not, to my way of thinking, a good citizen. . . .

The constitutional guaranty that there should be no religious test for public office is not a mere form of words. It represents the most vital principle that ever was given any people.

I attack those who seek to undermine it, not only because I am a good Christian, but because I am a good American and a product of America and of American institutions. Everything I am, and everything I hope to be, I owe to those institutions.

The absolute separation of State and Church is part of the fundamental basis of our Constitution. I believe in that separation, and in all that it implies. That belief must be a part of the fundamental faith of every true American. . . .

Further Resources

BOOKS

Finan, Christopher M. *Alfred E. Smith: The Happy Warrior.* New York: Hill and Wang, 2002.

Handlin, Oscar. *Al Smith and His America.* Boston: Northeastern University Press, 1987.

Moore, Edmund Arthur. *A Catholic Runs for President: The Campaign of 1928.* Gloucester, Mass.: Smith, 1968.

Slayton, Robert A. *Empire Statesman: The Rise and Redemption of Al Smith.* New York: The Free Press, 2001.

The Catholic Spirit in America

Nonfiction work

By: George N. Shuster

Date: 1928

Source: Shuster, George N. *The Catholic Spirit in America.* New York: Dial, 1928. Reprint, New York: Arno, 1978, 278–279.

About the Author: George N. Shuster (1894–1977) was a prominent American Catholic educator and author. He taught at the University of Notre Dame, was editor of *Commonweal* magazine, and was president of Hunter College in New York City. He died on January 25, 1977, at the age of eighty-two. ■

Introduction

George N. Shuster was educated in the Catholic school system and graduated from the University of Notre Dame in 1915. After college, he worked as a journalist in Chicago until World War I (1914–1918). After the war, Shuster remained with the army of occupation in Germany and took advantage of his extended stay in Europe to further his education. The experience opened his eyes to the wide gap between Catholic institutions and culture in the United States and Europe.

Shuster returned to Notre Dame, serving as chair of the English department from 1920 to 1924. During this time, he published his first book, *The Catholic Spirit in Modern English Literature* (1922). Shuster believed that Catholic colleges and universities had an obligation to promote Catholic culture in the United States, and a big part of that, he believed, meant encouraging scholarship from their faculty. Frustrated that the Notre Dame administration regarded scholarship as a luxury rather than a necessity, he resigned in protest in 1924.

Shuster moved to New York and continued to teach English at St. Joseph's College for Women. More significant, however, was his return to journalism. In 1925, he became an editor at *Commonweal*. From this "pulpit," Shuster was able to comment on a variety of issues.

One of these was his complaint that Catholicism was intellectually asleep and exhibited "a terrible contempt for thought." As a Catholic, Shuster was ashamed at the lack of an intellectual tradition in his church. As an American, he also felt that there was much in the way of Catholic political philosophy and social teaching that was not being appreciated, a view that he related in his 1928 book *The Catholic Spirit in America*: "[W]ithout the riches of the Church our conception of nationhood would be poorer and meaner."

Significance

Shuster was also a strong advocate for the right of Catholics to equality in the United States. Despite the tradition of religious liberty, Catholics were often treated as second-class citizens. While not as serious as the discrimination suffered by African Americans, Catholics often suffered in the areas of employment, housing, and political life. The latter is best symbolized by the opposition to Alfred E. Smith because of his Catholic faith in the 1924 and 1928 presidential campaigns. In *The Catholic Spirit in America,* Shuster argued for a spirit of cooperation, not competition, between Protestants and Catholics, as well as for the fact that there was much that Catholicism could contribute to American society.

Shuster was at *Commonweal* for twelve years, until he was forced to resign in 1937. He condemned the oppressive acts of the Nazi government in Germany and had led the editorial staff in calling for an American boycott of the 1936 Olympic Games in Berlin. In 1937, many felt he went too far in condemning Francisco Franco's fascists in Spain. Shuster tried to make the argument that fascism was just as opposed to Catholic ideals as communism, but the prevailing opinion in the Catholic community was that communism was the greater threat. Unable to agree with his colleagues on this point, Shuster resigned.

Shuster went on to become president of New York's Hunter College in 1939 and became involved in a variety of civic activities. In time, other Catholic scholars, in particular the historian John Tracy Ellis, joined his call for Catholic scholarship, resulting in increased intellectual activity. Shuster retired from Hunter in 1960 and made peace with Notre Dame. He worked with that university in various capacities, including serving on the

board of trustees from 1967 to 1971. He died six years after leaving that post, in South Bend, Indiana.

Primary Source

The Catholic Spirit in America [excerpt]

> **SYNOPSIS:** *The Catholic Spirit in America* was published the year of Catholic Alfred E. Smith's failed 1928 presidential bid. In it, Shuster insisted on the compatibility of Catholicism and American culture. He called for a revived Catholic intellectual life that could make its rightful contribution to the future of American culture.

Of course a living faith will avoid identifying tolerance with indifference. No Christian who understands the true origins and norms of his faith can agree to abandon anything essential in that faith, or fail to view as wholly deplorable such outlandish excresences as belief in the imminent return to earth of Mary Baker Eddy. Catholics, therefore, will frankly stand apart from Protestants. But they realize also that the day upon which Protestantism really dies in this country will be ominous, indeed. This death could only add further to the strength of that "enlightenment" which is so contagious all about us. Our danger now lies in the influence for cynicism wielded by a myriad deserters from the ranks of belief—deserters whose romantic haloes cater to the instinct for irreverence, carelessness and denial. If those who feel that much contemporary whacking away at the limitations of Protestantism is doing good are in earnest, let them consider whether they should prefer to place their children in the company of a man who devoutly professes the Christian creed, with whatever narrow anarchies, or in the company of illuminati who have long since tossed the Bible and the Fathers into a handy waste-basket. Nor can one fail to remember that Protestantism is being assaulted in this country because it is still the "official" creed—just as the Catholic Church was besieged in eighteenth-century France because it was the "official" creed.

All these things having been voiced, one could sum up all that has been said in this book by declaring that though there is room for and even need of an intelligent, discerning normative definition of "American," there is absolutely no justification for excluding from that definition anything that is really Catholic. Indeed both past and present, theory and practice, demonstrate that without the riches of the Church our conception of nationhood would be poorer and meaner, in numberless ways. On the other hand, Catholics, grateful for the shelter spread over them by the republic, will continue to believe, with the assembled bishops of 1884, "that our country's heroes were the instruments of the God of Nations in establishing this home of freedom; to both the Almighty and to His instruments in the work, we look with grateful reverence; and to maintain the inheritance which they have left us, should it ever—which God forbid—be imperiled, our Catholic citizens will be found ready to stand forward, as one man, ready to pledge anew 'their lives, their fortunes and their sacred honor.'"

Further Resources

BOOKS

Blantz, Thomas E. *George N. Shuster: On the Side of Truth.* Notre Dame, Ind.: University of Notre Dame Press, 1993.

Lannie, Vincent P., ed. *On the Side of Truth, George N. Shuster: An Evaluation with Readings.* Notre Dame, Ind.: University of Notre Dame Press, 1974.

Shuster, George N. *Catholic Education in a Changing World.* New York: Holt, Rinehart and Winston, 1967.

"Should the Churches Keep Silent?"

Editorial

By: Charles Clayton Morrison

Date: February 7, 1929

Source: Morrison, Charles Clayton. "Should the Churches Keep Silent?" *The Christian Century,* February 7, 1929, 190–192.

About the Author: Charles Clayton Morrison (1874–1966) was a liberal Protestant who edited the influential journal *The Christian Century* for almost forty years. In that time, he became involved in a host of social issues, including temperance, civil rights, and pacifism. Under Morrison, *The Christian Century* was the first national publication to print Martin Luther King Jr.'s "Letter from Birmingham Jail." Morrison died at the age of ninety-one on March 2, 1966. ∎

Introduction

Charles Clayton Morrison, a member of the Disciples of Christ Church, was a leading liberal Protestant in the early twentieth century. Like Harry Emerson Fosdick and Shailer Mathews, he was a follower of the progressive theology that accepted the teaching of evolution. In 1908, with the help of others, Morrison purchased a small magazine named *The Christian Century* and became its editor and publisher. Under his leadership, the magazine became a major voice for liberal Protestantism on the issues of the

day. Its editorials supported such causes as woman suffrage, pacifism, and ecumenism (the promotion of unity throughout the Christian Church). It was also a strong supporter of Prohibition, even though in the minds of many the temperance movement was associated with conservative revivalists such as William Ashley Sunday.

Beginning in 1846 with the famous Maine law, there were repeated efforts on the part of Protestant Christians across the United States to prohibit the sale and consumption of alcohol. The founding of the Women's Christian Temperance Union in 1874 strengthened the movement for Prohibition. This group was joined by the Anti-Saloon League, which was founded in 1895. Between 1905 and 1915, the number of churches supporting Prohibition doubled. The Anti-Saloon League's strength came from combining rural, small-town, middle-class, and progressive Protestants to rescue American civilization from the evils of "demon rum."

Prohibition drew the support of both liberal and conservative Protestants, as well as the support of some liberal Catholics. Many leaders of the Social Gospel movement supported the cause in their speeches and writings. For liberal Protestants, Prohibition was part of the progressive drive to reform American life and to curb the excessive power of big business. *The Christian Century* supported Prohibition in many editorials, such as the one published on February 7, 1929.

Significance

The liquor industry, with its increasing monopolistic tendencies, spent large amounts of money on politicians to gain desired legislation and to block the enforcement of the few regulations that were adopted. It was frequently exposed by the press and political reformers as a principal source of political corruption. Many believed that Prohibition would eliminate in one stroke the primary cause not only of political corruption, vice, and crime, but also of poverty, disease, and marital discord.

While the temperance movement had originally sought to limit the abuse of alcohol, it soon shifted to the goal of total prohibition. Since this movement was able to enlist the support of both liberal and conservative Protestants, it became a great, unified crusade akin to the Abolitionist movement. This united effort paid off with the passage of the Eighteenth Amendment, and Prohibition went into effect January 16, 1920.

Whether or not to repeal Prohibition became a major political issue in the presidential campaigns after the Eighteenth Amendment went into effect. In the February 7, 1929, editorial of *The Christian Century,* Morrison made a strong case for the maintenance and enforcement of the Prohibition laws. He addressed not only the particular issue of Prohibition, but also the need for the

AIN'T IT FUNNY

A Deacon who preached Prohibition
To a bad city went on a mission,
In histea they put rum,he got loaded,ByGum!
And returned in this awful condition.

Postcard from the 1920s that portrays opposition to Christians' organized support of Prohibition. © RYKOFF COLLECTION/CORBIS. REPRODUCED BY PERMISSION.

churches to address the moral and ethical problems of society. He rejected the notion that churches should remain aloof from social issues and that addressing worldly matters was beyond their purely spiritual mission. On the contrary, this engagement in social reform was an important part of liberal Protestantism.

Primary Source

"Should the Churches Keep Silent?"

SYNOPSIS: Prohibition was a major issue for American Protestantism in the nineteenth and early twen-

tieth centuries. With liberals and conservatives disagreeing over virtually everything else, the struggle for Prohibition was the one thing on which modernists and fundamentalists could agree. The following excerpt is an editorial, from the liberal magazine *The Christian Century,* that advocates the enforcement of laws prohibiting alcohol.

The frenzied protest of the world to the church, whenever it has shown signs of dangerous hostility to entrenched evils and institutionalized iniquities, has always been the echo of that cry with which the evil spirit on the Gadarene shore met the church's Master: "What have I to do with thee; I beseech thee torment me not." It is a torment, no less, to have at large in the world a company of people who, however far they may fall short of perfection and however incomplete may be their program for the amelioration of the conditions of men, nevertheless take some things seriously enough to want to do something about it. The church is such a company. Throughout all the centuries it has dissipated much of its energy in taking care of its own interests, accumulating and administering property, protecting its prestige and guarding its privileges; and the more it has done these things the less Christian it has been. But back of all that, there has always been, in varying measure, a solicitude to accomplish something not merely for itself but for men.

It is betraying no secret to say that the church is not satisfied with the world. Even in the dark ages it was not. Civilization has improved, but the Christian conscience has grown sensitive more rapidly than the world has grown virtuous, and it is less satisfied now than it has ever been before. Not all of the divine discontent and the creative idealism is in the church, but much of it is, and in no other organization is it more articulate or more effectively massed for constructive action. If the church ever finds that it has nothing to say in regard to the evils of the world as it now is, it may as well pull down its steeples and put up its shutters.

But how shall the church speak and act— through and to organizations, or through and to individuals, or both? It has a gospel for the individual man; no one denies that. And it would be generally, though not universally, admitted that the individual Christian may sound his note and put his own shoulder under any corner of the world's load to which he can gain access. But the burden which presses upon the lives of men is a burden solidified by institutions, pressed down by consolidated and coordinated forces of self-interest, cemented by every form of social integration, sanctioned by legislation, and bound in place by the structure of government itself. Are Christian men, whose consciences have been awakened to the evils of society, confined to purely individual efforts to remedy these conditions, while every destructive force and every selfish interest is free to organize for the effective pursuit of its objectives? Must Christians engage in a desultory guerilla warfare in the presence of an enemy carrying out a carefully planned campaign? As well send bushwhackers against a phalanx.

The question at issue is not any effort of the church to get something for itself. When it tries that, let it be dealt with no more gently than any other organization which forms a cabal or a lobby to advance its own interests. Nor does it concern the question of mobilizing the members of churches to put over some program which has been delivered to them ready-made by their ecclesiastical superiors—"by ministers as ministers, or by bishops as bishops." It has to do with the right of the church, or of churches, to bring to bear upon government the force of an enlightened Christian opinion democratically formed and held by the people who constitute the churches. We have no sympathy with any conceivable campaign conducted by the church to get special privileges for itself, or with any effort to line up millions of votes to put over some program determined by a handful of hierarchs. These are undemocratic and indefensible tactics. The question that has been raised is wholly unrelated to any such thing.

But in spite of the absence of these objectionable features of clericalism as it has appeared at other times and places, the ancient bogey of church activity in politics is rising again to alarm those who are opposed to the ideas of morality to which the churches, for the most part, stand committed. And, as usual, hostility to some particular program sponsored by the church is generalized into a sweeping denial of the right of the church to sponsor any program and to take the steps which are necessary to make it effective. Perhaps it is just as well that the matter should be discussed as a question of principle and not upon the merits of some particular episode or item.

Most Protestant Christians have arrived at the conclusion that the beverage use of alcohol is personally and socially injurious. Having some knowledge of the futility of various types of regulation that have been practiced at various times and places, and having had experience of the trickeries and subtleties, the bad faith and lawlessness, with which

The Shadow of Danger

If you believe that the traffic in Alcohol does more harm than good- *help stop it!*

A poster that shows support for Prohibition. The "shadow of danger" is cast onto a mother and child by a whiskey bottle depicting the harm alcohol brings to families. © CORBIS. REPRODUCED BY PERMISSION.

the liquor interests have always met all regulative measures, most of them have arrived at the conclusion that the only way to regulate is to prohibit. It has therefore come to be, not an article of faith, but the predominant conviction of the members of the Protestant churches in the United States that the prohibition law should be maintained, obeyed, and enforced. The question of the moment is not whether or not they are right in this belief, but whether, since it is their belief, they have a right to act upon it, and to act through those agencies which they have created to bring the force of public opinion to bear upon those who make and enforce the laws.

The most insolent and bare-faced demand that religion should get off the earth could scarcely go farther than the doctrine, lately announced by the world's wettest newspaper, that "it is not the privilege of citizens [to influence legislative action] when it is to promote ideas derived from religious belief, association, organization and teaching through the efforts of such [church] organizations." According to this interesting theory, any group of citizens may

Protesters rally against prohibition. Many groups organized in either support of or opposition to the Eighteenth Amendment, often for different reasons. However, many argued that Christians should not be allowed to organize since their collective voice in support of the legal ban on alcohol allegedly violated the separation of church and state. © BETTMANN/CORBIS. REPRODUCED BY PERMISSION.

unite to make effective by appropriate legislation any ideas that they may have, either for private gain or for public weal, *unless these ideas have a religious sanction or were derived from a religious source!* Butchers, bakers and candlestick makers, oil producers and steel manufacturers can form their associations, maintain their lobbies at Washington, and bring to bear upon government all the influence that they can command to secure legislation in their several interests, but Christians, as Christians, may not organize to secure legislation which they believe to be for the general welfare. Self-interest may freely utilize the power that comes with concerted action, but those who seek only the common interest must confine themselves to such disjoined and sporadic activities as alone are possible without organization. Citizens may organize to promote by political means whatever ideas they may have derived from the consideration of their own financial advantage, or from their knowledge of business, science, education, or things in general. But organization to influence legislation "is not the privilege of citizens when it is to promote ideas derived from religious belief, association, organization and teaching through the efforts of such organizations." The idea does not

seem reasonable. And it is no more reasonable than it seems.

What then may Christian people do without incurring the displeasure of their critics? They may use moral suasion upon individuals. They may promote temperance, for example, by preaching temperance. This they ought to have done—it may be added parenthetically—but not to have left the other undone. The theory of the church's critics is that an appeal to law is an appeal to force, because behind the law must stand the policeman to enforce it, and that when the church thus "takes the sword" there is little to choose between drawing the sword to enforce acceptance of its creed and drawing it to enforce conformity with its code of conduct.

This too is fallacious. Behind the law stands the policeman, to be sure; but behind the policeman stands the power of public opinion, without which the policeman is impotent and futile. In a democratic country, the law is presumed to be an expression of public opinion. If it represents the will of an organized and effective minority, prevailing over an unorganized majority, it is useless and iniquitous. This is true whether the organized minority is the Anti-saloon league or the brewers' association. The old charge that the dry sentiment of this country is merely that of a militant minority falls to the ground in the presence of such an unblushing claim that everybody else has a right to organize, but not the churches—which, for this purpose, means the drys. Protestantism has no such inherent force of cohesion and no such supreme skill in political manipulation as to be able to make a minority sentiment dominant over a majority. What the critics want is not a fair test of strength—in fact, they have already had that on many a hard-fought field, and they have lost. What they want is a fight in which their enemy's hands will be tied while theirs will be free; a contest in which the opposition to prohibition or any other form of moral legislation will be solidly compacted by organization, while its advocates will be disintegrated and disunited.

The fear that churches which get into the habit of enforcing their codes of conduct by law may go on (or back) to the practice of enforcing acceptance of their creeds by similar means, is pure bunkum. Law deals with conduct; it does not deal with beliefs. If no aspects of conduct are to be controlled by law, then the whole structure of law crumbles. The argument against controlling conduct by law is an argument for anarchy. It is indeed edifying to find a newspaper clamoring so loudly for an increased navy and hooting so scornfully at the idea of maintaining peace among the nations by any means other than armed force, yet laying it so tenderly upon the consciences of Christian men that they should put up the sword, dismiss the policeman, take no interest in any legislation for the common interest, lest they should find themselves defiled by the use of force for a moral purpose.

Slavery was not abolished in this country until it became a moral issue. Perhaps we should repeal the fourteenth amendment as well as the eighteenth, and rely wholly upon moral suasion addressed to individuals to restrain them from holding their fellowmen in involuntary servitude! The truth is that neither emancipation nor prohibition is a matter of private morals, or of forcing conformity to a moral code. But they are matters of public morals, involving the welfare of society as a whole. In such issues, the church has a direct concern, and in such conflicts it will utilize the full force of its influence, so far as its conscience has been enlightened, to secure and enforce such legislation as the common welfare may demand.

Further Resources

BOOKS

Detloff, Linda-Marie. *A Century of the Century*. Grand Rapids, Mich.: Eerdmans, 1987.

Morrison, Charles Clayton. *Can Protestantism Win America?* New York: Harper, 1948.

———. *The Social Gospel and the Christian Cultus*. New York: Harper, 1933.

Schmidt, Jean Miller. *Souls or the Social Order: The Two-Party System in American Protestantism*. Brooklyn, N.Y.: Carlson, 1991.

Leaves From the Notebook of a Tamed Cynic

Diary

By: Reinhold Niebuhr

Date: 1929

Source: Niebuhr, Reinhold. *Leaves From the Notebook of a Tamed Cynic*. 1929. Reprint, San Francisco: Harper and Row, 1980, 78–79.

About the Author: Reinhold Niebuhr (1892–1971) was an Evangelical Synod minister and theologian. Serving as a pastor for thirteen years in Detroit, he then went on to teach social ethics at Union Theological Seminary in New York City. He was the author of numerous books, including *Moral Man and Immoral Society* (1932) and the two-volume *The Nature and Destiny of Man: A Christian Interpretation* (1941–1943). ∎

Introduction

Reinhold Niebuhr was born on June 21, 1892, in Wright City, Missouri. Niebuhr came from a devout family. His father, Gustav, was a minister in the Evangelical Synod, a Lutheran-oriented denomination that had spun off the Prussian Church Union. Reinhold also became a minister of the Evangelical Synod. He graduated from Elmhurst College in 1910 and Eden Theological Seminary in 1913. He then earned a master's degree at Yale Divinity School in 1915 and was ordained. Niebuhr then served as pastor of Bethel Evangelical Church in Detroit from 1915 to 1928.

Niebuhr learned much of human nature from his thirteen years of ministry in Detroit. He took an active interest in a variety of social issues, including war, international relations, industrial relations, and race. These experiences were recorded in his diary and published as *Leaves From the Notebook of a Tamed Cynic* in 1929. In addition to including his commentary on the social issues of the day, Niebuhr also noted in his diary the various challenges, both great and small, of his

Packard Motor Car Co., Detroit, MI, 1920s. A tour of such a factory led Detroit minister and theologian Reinhold Niebuhr to question the social injustices of modern industrial civilization. **AP/WIDE WORLD PHOTOS. REPRODUCED BY PERMISSION.**

ministry as the pastor of a small congregation. While many Christians today may be unaware of his teachings, they would be familiar with his famous Serenity Prayer.

Niebuhr wrote extensively on social issues but rejected liberal views regarding the perfectibility of humanity and human institutions. While an advocate of social reform, he nonetheless believed that the reality of human sin also needed to be taken into consideration. This combination of social progressivism and original sin came to be known as Christian Realism.

Niebuhr's struggles for social justice as a pastor influenced his later writings. His most famous works were *Christianity and Power Politics* (1940), *Faith and History* (1949), *Christian Realism and Political Problems* (1953), and *The Irony of American History* (1955).

Significance

Some of Niebuhr's most severe criticisms of human nature were in the areas of labor and economics. "Look at the industrial enterprise anywhere and you find criminal indifference on the part of the strong to the fate of the weak. The lust for power and the greed for gain are the dominant note in business." One local example of such indifference occurred in 1927 with the Ford Motor Company. Henry Ford was warned by subordinates

that the Model T, of which the company had produced fifteen million, was outdated and needed to be replaced. Ford stubbornly refused until it was too late and then simply stopped production to design a new car. Automobile production dropped 25 percent nationwide and sixty thousand workers in Detroit were laid off for a year with no compensation. Their plight led Niebuhr to write, "I have . . . come to the conclusion that the car cost Ford workers at least fifty million in lost wages during the past year. No one knows how many hundreds lost their homes in the period of unemployment, and how may children were taken out of school to help fill the depleted family exchequer . . . Mr. Ford refuses to concede that he made a mistake in bringing the car out so late . . . No one bothers to ask whether an industry which can maintain a cash reserve of a quarter of a billion ought not make some provision for its unemployed."

Niebuhr's criticisms were ignored, and by the time his diary was published in 1929 he had left Detroit to go on to Union Theological Seminary in New York, where he published numerous books and further developed his system of social ethics. For those who failed to heed Niebuhr's words on the problems with American capitalism, they would get a crash course the year his diary came out—when the Great Depression hit.

Primary Source

Leaves From the Notebook of a Tamed Cynic
[excerpt]

SYNOPSIS: This book is the diary of the thirteen-year pastorate of one of the most important American social theorists in the twentieth century, Reinhold Niebuhr. As a minister, he became involved in a host of social justice issues and was not afraid to criticize noted men of industry, including Henry Ford. In the following excerpt written in 1925, we see his discomfort with industrial society in the United States and his own participation in it.

We went through one of the big automobile factories today. So artificial is life that these factories are like a strange world to me though I have lived close to them for many years. The foundry interested me particularly. The heat was terrific. The men seemed weary. Here manual labor is a drudgery and toil is slavery. The men cannot possibly find any satisfaction in their work. They simply work to make a living. Their sweat and their dull pain are part of the price paid for the fine cars we all run. And most of us run the cars without knowing what price is being paid for them.

Looking at these men the words of Markham's "The Man with the Hoe" came to me. A man with a hoe is a happy creature beside these suffering souls.

The emptiness of ages in his face

· · · · · · ·

Who made him dead to rapture and despair,
A thing that grieves not and that never hopes,
Stolid and stunned, a brother to the ox?

We are all responsible. We all want the things which the factory produces and none of us is sensitive enough to care how much in human values the efficiency of the modern factory costs. Beside the brutal facts of modern industrial life, how futile are all our homiletical spoutings! The church is undoubtedly cultivating graces and preserving spiritual amenities in the more protected areas of society. But it isn't changing the essential facts of modern industrial civilization by a hair's breadth. It isn't even thinking about them.

The morality of the church is anachronistic. Will it ever develop a moral insight and courage sufficient to cope with the real problems of modern society? If it does it will require generations of effort and not a few martyrdoms. We ministers maintain our pride and self-respect and our sense of importance only through a vast and inclusive ignorance. If we knew the world in which we live a little better we would perish in shame or be overcome by a sense of futility.

Further Resources

BOOKS

Brown, Charles C. *Niebuhr and His Age: Reinhold Niebuhr's Prophetic Role and Legacy.* Harrisburg, Penn.: Trinity Press International, 2002.

Clark, Henry B. *Serenity, Courage, and Wisdom: The Enduring Legacy of Reinhold Niebuhr.* Cleveland, Ohio: Pilgrim, 1994.

Dibble, Ernest F. *Young Prophet Niebuhr: Reinhold Niebuhr's Early Search for Social Justice.* Washington, D.C.: University Press of America, 1977.

Harries, Richard, ed. *Reinhold Niebuhr and the Issues of Our Time.* London: Mowbray, 1986.

Kegley, Charles W. *Reinhold Niebuhr: His Religious, Social, and Political Thought.* New York: Pilgrim, 1984.

Landon, Harold R., ed. *Reinhold Niebuhr: A Prophetic Voice in Our Time: Essays in Tribute, by Paul Tillich, John C. Bennett and Hans J. Morgenthau.* Greenwich, Conn.: Seabury, 1992.

Scott, Nathan. *The Legacy of Reinhold Niebuhr.* Chicago: University of Chicago Press, 1975.

The Living of These Days
Autobiography

By: Harry Emerson Fosdick

Date: 1956

Source: Fosdick, Harry Emerson. *The Living of These Days: An Autobiography.* New York: Harper and Row, 1956, 144–147.

About the Author: Harry Emerson Fosdick (1878–1969) was born in Buffalo, New York. A Baptist minister, Fosdick was a famous author and preacher who served prominent churches in New York City. A theological liberal, Fosdick opposed Fundamentalism in the 1920s. He died on October 5, 1969, at the age of ninety-one. ■

Introduction

Harry Emerson Fosdick's parents were devout Baptists, but they encouraged freedom of inquiry and the discussion of unorthodox ideas. An excellent student, Fosdick graduated from Colgate University in Hamilton, New York, in 1900. He decided to enter the ministry and enrolled in Hamilton Theological Seminary, where he studied with the liberal evangelical theologian William Newton Clarke and pro-evolution theologian John Fiske. While these teachers appealed to Fosdick's liberal mindset, in 1901 he transferred to the even more progressive Union Theological Seminary in New York City. He graduated from Union in 1904.

Fosdick was ordained a Baptist minister, and his first congregation was First Baptist Church in Montclair, New

Jersey. He ministered there for eleven years, before leaving in 1915 to return to Union to assume the position of professor of practical theology, which he held until 1946.

Fosdick became nationally famous for his preaching ability and was widely sought after as a speaker and visiting minister. In 1918, while remaining on the Union faculty, he reduced his teaching load so that he could also serve as minister at the prestigious First Presbyterian Church in New York City. Eventually, conservatives, led by William Jennings Bryan, opposed the employment of a Baptist at the church, and Fosdick resigned in 1925 rather than convert.

Prominent Baptists, led by John D. Rockefeller Jr., recruited Fosdick for the Park Avenue Baptist Church in New York in 1926. Because of the thousands who came to hear Fosdick preach, the congregation built the magnificent Riverside Church in the neighborhood of Morningside Heights. This beautiful church was dedicated in 1931, and Fosdick served as a minister there until his retirement in 1946. During these fifteen years at Riverside, Fosdick was arguably the nation's most influential Protestant preacher.

Significance

The effort to remove Fosdick from the pulpit of First Presbyterian was not an isolated case of discrimination but rather was but one episode in the broader struggle between Fundamentalists and modernists in the 1920s. A theological liberal, Fosdick became one of the leaders of the modernist camp. For Fosdick and many like him, orthodoxy was too rigid and stifling; he would have liberal Christianity or no Christianity at all. In his autobiography, he stressed that liberalism was an "absolute necessity to multitudes of us who could not have been Christians at all unless we could thus have escaped the bondage of the then reigning orthodoxy."

Fosdick demonstrated his support for the modernist cause in his 1924 book *The Modern Use of the Bible*. In this work, he tried to summarize the results of modern biblical scholarship in a way that the average Protestant churchgoer could understand and not feel threatened by. Fosdick stressed that the Bible became even more meaningful, not less, when one understood its different periods of development. While these views were welcomed by many, they also brought opposition from Fundamentalists who felt such liberal views undermined the authority of the scripture.

Fosdick gave one of the noted defenses of liberalism two years earlier in his May 22, 1922, sermon "Shall the Fundamentalists Win?" In this sermon, he pleaded for greater tolerance for diverse beliefs—the very kind of tolerance that had allowed a Baptist like himself to be welcomed at a Presbyterian church. Fosdick warned that the

fighting between conservative and liberal parties, both between denominations and within denominations, was further dividing Protestantism. The text of the sermon was distributed to 130,000 ordained Protestants by Fosdick's supporters. Ironically, it was the reaction to this very sermon that galvanized the Fundamentalists to remove Fosdick from First Presbyterian.

Primary Source

The Living of These Days [excerpt]

> **SYNOPSIS:** Fosdick was one of the most famous preachers in the first half of the twentieth century. His liberal views on the Bible and religious tolerance conflicted with those of the Fundamentalists in the 1920s. In the following excerpt, taken from his autobiography that was written over thirty years after the fact, Fosdick reflects on the controversy that spanned three years and led to his being forced to leave First Presbyterian Church in New York City.

The Fundamentalist Controversy

The conflict between liberal and reactionary Christianity had long been moving toward a climax. There were faults on both sides. The modernists were tempted to make a supine surrender to prevalent cultural ideas, accepting them wholesale, and using them as the authoritarian standard by which to judge the truth or falsity of classical Christian affirmations. The reactionaries, sensing the peril in this shift of authority, were tempted to retreat into hidebound obscurantism, denying the discoveries of science, and insisting on the literal acceptance of every Biblical idea, which even Christians of the ancient church had avoided by means of allegorical interpretation. As Reinhold Niebuhr neatly sums it up: "That part of the church which maintained an effective contact with modern culture stood in danger of capitulating to all the characteristic prejudices of a 'scientific' and 'progressive' age; and that part of the church which was concerned with the evangelical heritage chose to protect it in the armor of a rigorous biblicism."

When the storm did break, chance placed me near the center, and I tell the story of the controversy, as I experienced it, not because my share in it was more important than many others', but because I did have an interesting opportunity to see it from the inside.

My sermon, "Shall the Fundamentalists Win?" was a plea for tolerance, for a church inclusive enough to take in both liberals and conservatives without either trying to drive the other out. I stated the honest differences of conviction dividing these two groups on such matters as the virgin birth of Jesus, the inerrancy of the Scriptures and the second coming of Christ, and then made my plea that the desirable solution was not a split that would tear the evangelical churches asunder, but a spirit of conciliation that would work out the problem within an inclusive fellowship.

Since the liberals had no idea of driving the fundamentalists out of the church, while the fundamentalists were certainly trying to drive the liberals out, the impact of this appeal fell on the reactionary group. "Just now," I said, "the fundamentalists are giving us one of the worst exhibitions of bitter intolerance that the churches of this country have ever seen. As one watches them and listens to them, one remembers the remark of General Armstrong of Hampton Institute: 'Cantankerousness is worse than heterodoxy.' There are many opinions in the field of modern controversy concerning which I am not sure whether they are right or wrong, but there is one thing I am sure of: courtesy and kindliness and tolerance and humility and fairness are right. Opinions may be mistaken; love never is."

If ever a sermon failed to achieve its object, mine did. It was a plea for good will, but what came of it was an explosion of ill will, for over two years making headline news of a controversy that went the limit of truculence. The trouble was, of course, that in stating the liberal and fundamentalist positions, I had stood in a Presbyterian pulpit and said frankly what the modernist position on some points was—the virgin birth no longer accepted as historic fact, the literal inerrancy of the Scriptures incredible, the second coming of Christ from the skies an outmoded phrasing of hope.

There might have been no unusual result had it not been for Ivy Lee. Head of one of the nation's foremost publicity organizations, he was a liberal Presbyterian, and the sermon, printed in pamphlet form by the church, caught his attention. He asked the privilege of distributing it to his nation-wide clientele, and I consented. Mr. Lee cut out a few innocuous sentences of the homiletical introduction and conclusion, provided a fresh title, "The New Knowledge and the Christian Faith," broke up the sermon into sections with attractive subcaptions, and distributed it with a commendatory message calling attention to its importance. None of us foresaw the stormy consequence. Mr. Lee and I subsequently became warm friends, and I know that he always took pride in the way he put that sermon over.

The attack that followed was launched by Clarence Edward Macartney, then minister of a Presbyterian church in Philadelphia. He was very decent

Although Harry Emerson Fosdick was a famous Protestant preacher and theologian, the larger conflict between Fundamentalists and Modernists resulted in Fosdick's forced resignation from the prestigious First Presbyterian Church in 1925. © **BETTMAN/CORBIS. REPRODUCED BY PERMISSION.**

and dignified in his attitude. While his theological position was in my judgment incredible, he was personally fair-minded and courteous. Indeed, when the storm was just breaking, he wrote me directly, in order to be sure that he was not misquoting me. After that we had some frank and not unfriendly correspondence, in which he presented his own unbending orthodoxy, shocked at my doctrinal looseness; and I, still hoping that tolerance might win, tried in a conciliatory way to make him see that while I differed from him in my intellectual formulations, I was endeavoring to maintain, just as much as he was, the timeless values and truths of the gospel. It was, however, a vain attempt.

I returned to my preaching after a summer's vacation in 1922 to face a tense situation. The congregation at the church was solidly behind me, but around the horizon storm clouds were gathering. Fundamentalism, especially among Presbyterians and Baptists, was fighting mad, and I was an easily accessible object of attack. One immediate result was that the congregations at the church, which always had filled the auditorium, now overflowed all available auxiliary spaces and took up every foot of standing room. This went on until even the chancel steps were crowded, and when I went into the pulpit someone sat down in the seat I vacated until the sermon was finished.

Among fundamentalist Presbyterians the attack naturally took the form of a determined endeavor to get me out of that pulpit. It was bad enough, they thought, to have heresy preached in a Presbyterian church, but to have a Baptist do it was intolerable. The General Assembly of the Presbyterian Church which met in 1923 had before it overtures from ten presbyteries wanting something done to stop my heretical preaching. William Jennings Bryan, then at the top of his form as a defender of the faith against

evolution, was one of the leading figures of the Assembly, and his oratory helped to achieve a fundamentalist victory. Anyone who ever heard Bryan speak can understand that.

Further Resources

BOOKS

Crocker, Lionel. *Harry Emerson Fosdick's Art of Preaching: An Anthology.* Springfield, Ill.: Thomas, 1971.

Fosdick, Harry Emerson. *A Preaching Ministry: Twenty-one Sermons Preached by Harry Emerson Fosdick at the First Presbyterian Church in the City of New York, 1918–1925.* New York: The Church, 2000.

Miller, Robert Moats. *Harry Emerson Fosdick: Preacher, Pastor, Prophet.* New York: Oxford University Press, 1985.

Scruggs, Julius Richard. *Baptist Preachers with Social Consciousness: A Comparative Study of Martin Luther King, Jr., and Harry Emerson Fosdick.* Philadelphia: Dorrance, 1978.

11

SCIENCE AND TECHNOLOGY

CHRISTOPHER CUMO

Entries are arranged in chronological order by date of primary source. For entries with one primary source, the entry title is the same as the primary source title. Entries with more than one primary source have an overall entry title, followed by the titles of the primary sources.

Important Events in Science and Technology, 1920–1929

1920

- In February, physicist William D. Harkins posits the existence of the neutron, a subatomic particle with a neutral charge and a mass equal to that of a proton. In 1932, British physicist James Chadwick will discover the neutron.

- In March, physicist Otto Stern announces that electrons have a spin expressible in either whole numbers (bosons) or half numbers (fermions).

- In July, American inventor Earl Charles Hanson invents the first hearing aid using vacuum tubes. It is marketed in 1921 as the Vactuphone.

- In November, John Thompson, a retired U.S. Army officer, receives a patent for his machine gun, later nicknamed the "tommy gun."

- On November 2, Station KDKA in Pittsburgh transmits the first regular licensed radio broadcast.

- On December 13, at the Mount Wilson Observatory in California, physicist Albert Michelson uses a stellar interferometer to calculate the diameter of the large star Betelgeuse, the first star—other than the sun—to be measured.

1921

- The American Radio League and Paul Godley in Scotland exchange the first intercontinental communication by shortwave radio.

- In March, John Augustus Larson and Leonarde Keeler, policemen in Berkeley, California invent the lie detector, or polygraph. Proponents claim it can detect lies by measuring changes in pulse rate, blood pressure, respiration, and perspiration.

- In April, petroleum engineer Thomas Midgley Jr. invents an improved gasoline by adding tetraethyl, which increases octane and prevents engine knock. It is marketed as Ethyl gasoline.

- In July, German-born physiologist Otto Loewi announces that nerve impulses are chemical signals. His work implies that human thought is the sum of all chemical activity in the brain.

- On August 3, John H. Houser, an entomologist at the Ohio Agricultural Experiment Station in Wooster, Ohio, supervises the world's first crop dusting.

1922

- Herbert T. Kalmus produces the first full-length technicolor motion picture, *The Toll of the Sea.*

- In January, Elmer V. McCollum, leading a team of scientists at Johns Hopkins University, discovers vitamin D in cod liver oil. The discovery of vitamin D, which prevents the skeletal-deformity disease rickets, leads to the invention of vitamin-fortified milk.

- On February 27, Secretary of Commerce Herbert Hoover convenes a national conference of radio, telephone, and telegraph experts.

- On August 3, Station WGY in Schenectady, New York, uses the first sound effects on radio.

- In October, William Howell discovers heparin, a chemical that prevents blood from clotting during transfusions.

- In November, Herbert Evans and K.J. Scott assert the existence of a vitamin in foods such as wheat germ, alfalfa, and lettuce. Barnett Sure names it vitamin E in 1923, and Evans's team finally isolates it in 1936.

- In December, American mathematician John R. Carson works out the equations for a new form of radio broadcasting: frequency modulation (FM). FM varies the time between wave pulses, whereas amplitude modification (AM) varies the height of radio waves.

1923

- Two U.S. Army pilots perform the first in-flight refueling.

- In February, Edwin H. Armstrong constructs the first FM radio, using the mathematics developed in 1922 by John R. Carson.

- In March, George Eastman produces 16-mm film for use by the general public, beginning the era of home movies. Later that year, Bell and Howell Company market a 16-mm camera, and Victor Animatograph offers a projector.

- In April, American physicist Arthur Holly Compton publishes a paper demonstrating that gamma rays come in tiny packets called quanta, evidence that supports the quantum theory of German physicist Max Planck. This property of gamma rays is called the Compton Effect.

- In June, Russian-born Vladimir Zworykin invents the first television camera, a light-ray-tube scanning device that he calls the iconoscope. In 1924, he patents the kinescope, a television picture tube using a cathode-ray tube.

- In June, at the Mount Wilson Observatory, astronomer Edwin Hubble discovers that nebulae (fuzzy points of light seen in the sky) are actually clusters of stars.

1924

- Transatlantic radio transmission of still photographs begins.

- FM radio is introduced.

- In January, about 2.5 million Americans own a radio, compared with 2,000 in 1920.

- In May, Edwin Hubble proves that the clusters of stars he discovered in 1923 are independent galaxies and so cannot be part of our galaxy, the Milky Way.

- On May 23, American physicist Robert Andrews Millikan delivers his Nobel Lecture. He had received the 1923 Nobel Prize in physics for his discovery of the charge on an electron and for his confirmation of Albert Einstein's photoelectric effect.

- In June, the Harvard Observatory publishes the Henry Draper Catalogue, compiled by astronomer and mathematician Annie J. Cannon, giving the spectra of 225,300 stars.

- In June, American Telephone and Telegraph and General Electric join forces to found Bell Telephone Laboratories.

- In August, British anatomist Raymond Dart discovers the ancient skull of a 6-year-old child in South Africa and christens a new species, *Australopithecus africanus*.

- On November 30, RCA sends photos by wireless from London to New York City.

1925

- G.L. McCarthy patents a microfilm camera for use by banks to make reduced copies of checks.

- In January, George Whipple, a pathologist at the University of Rochester School of Medicine and Dentistry, demonstrates that iron is an essential element in red blood cells.

- On February 24, Congress passes the Purnell Act, doubling federal appropriations to each agricultural experiment station from $30,000 to $60,000 a year. The act reaffirms the federal government's commitment to fund scientific research.

- In March, Vladimir Zworykin applies for a patent for color television. The U.S. Patent Office grants Zworykin a patent in 1928.

- In July, a court in Dayton, Tennessee, finds high school biology teacher John Scopes guilty of violating a state law that forbids the teaching of the theory of evolution in public schools.

- On September 3, a storm over Ava, Ohio, destroys the U.S. Navy dirigible *Shenandoah.*

- On September 12, President Calvin Coolidge appoints a National Aircraft Board with Dwight Morrow as chairman.

- In October, American physicist Clinton J. Davisson, using nickel crystals to diffract X rays, confirms French physicist Louis de Broglie's 1924 theory that particles have wavelike properties.

- In November, American physicist Robert A. Millikan discovers cosmic rays as yet another type of light invisible to humans. In 1911, Austrian physicist Victor Hess had proposed their existence.

1926

- The National Broadcasting Company (NBC) links twenty-four radio stations into a "network."

- James B. Sumner proves that enzymes are proteins and that they catalyze biochemical reactions in the body.

- Vitamin B1 is discovered. Its existence has been presumed since 1896.

- Farmers throughout the south use the mule-drawn cotton stripper, ending the need to pick cotton by hand.

- On February 18, Harcourt, Brace publishes Paul de Kruif's *Microbe Hunters,* a popular book on bacteriology.

- On March 16, in Auburn, Massachusetts, Robert H. Goddard launches first rocket propelled by liquid fuel.

- In April, American inventor Harold Sinclair develops one of the earliest fluid-drive automatic transmissions for automobiles.

- On May 9, explorers Richard E. Byrd and Floyd Bennett fly over the North Pole.

- In June, Italian physicist Enrico Fermi and French scientist Paul Dirac compile the Fermi-Dirac statistics, which calculate the spin of electrons.

- On August 6, Warner Brothers releases the first commercial motion picture with sound, *Don Juan.*

- In October, Bell Labs produces a voiceprint machine, the voice coder, to analyze the frequency (pitch) and energy content of speech.

1927

- J.A. O'Neill invents the first magnetic recording tape. It is first made of paper, which is replaced by plastic in 1932.

- On January 7, the first radiotelephone connection is made between New York and London.

- On February 23, Congress creates the Federal Radio Commission to certify new radio stations and to regulate the operation of all stations.

- On April 7, Walter Gifford, president of AT&T, shows television, the first demonstration of its kind, in the Washington, D.C., office of Secretary of Commerce Herbert Hoover.

- From May 20 to May 21, Charles A. Lindbergh makes the first nonstop, solo flight across the Atlantic Ocean, flying from New York City to Paris in thirty-three and one-half hours.

- In September, University of Texas professor Hermann J. Muller irradiates *Drosophila,* the common fruit fly, to cause genetic mutations. A mutation is a change in the chemistry or location of a gene or group of genes.

- In October, Warner Brothers releases the first feature-length talking picture, *The Jazz Singer.*

1928

- General Electric and New York radio station WRNY make the first effort at television broadcasting.

- Austrian-born physician George Goldberger, working on a cure for pellagra, finds that a heated yeast extract, later shown to contain the B vitamin niacin, will cure blacktongue, a dog disease analogous to pellagra in humans.

- Minnesota Mining and Manufacturing (3M) markets cellophane tape as Scotch Tape.

- Margaret Mead publishes *Coming of Age in Samoa,* which argues that sexual mores among Samoan women are different than those in the U.S. Mead's work corroborates that of her mentor, Franz Boas, who claimed that no absolute standards of conduct exist.

- On March 5, Vannevar Bush and associates at the Massachusetts Institute of Technology invent an analog computer to solve differential equations.

- In June, explorer and aviator Richard E. Byrd establishes a base in Antarctica from which he flies over the South Pole.

- In June, Charles G. King at the University of Pittsburgh discovers Vitamin C. Hungarian scientist Albert Szent-Gyorgyi, working independently from King, makes the same discovery two weeks later.

- On July 30, George Eastman of Kodak introduces color cinema.

- On December 12, delegates from forty countries assemble in Washington, D.C., for a conference on civil aeronautics.

- In December, Philip Drinker and Louis Shaw at Harvard University invent the "iron lung" as an aid to breathing, especially for polio sufferers.

1929

- Further efforts at television broadcasting are made. NBC puts on the air a station with a scanning rate of sixty lines per second.

- Bell Labs produces a color television prototype using a scanning rate of fifty lines per second.

- The Dunlop Rubber Company develops the first foam rubber.

- In March, Edwin Hubble recalculates the distance between Earth and the Andromeda galaxy as 930,000 light years.

- On July 17, Robert Goddard launches the first instrumented rocket, complete with camera, barometer, and thermometer.

- On November 29, Richard E. Byrd flies over the South Pole.

"The Airplane in Catalpa Sphinx Control"

Report

By: John S. Houser

Date: July–August 1922

Source: Houser, John S. "The Airplane in Catalpa Sphinx Control." *Monthly Bulletin [of the] Ohio Agricultural Experiment Station,* July–August 1922, 132–133.

About the Author: John Samuel Houser (1881–1947) was born on a farm near Oxford, Kansas, and received an M.S. in entomology from Cornell University in 1911. He joined the staff of the Ohio Agricultural Experiment Station in Wooster as assistant entomologist in 1903. In 1926, he became head of the department, a position he held until his death in 1947. He was a charter member of the Entomological Society of America, and in 1931 served as president of the American Association of Economic Entomologists. ∎

Introduction

In the eighteenth century, many prominent landowners wanted to infuse farming with science. Thomas Jefferson conducted his own experiments and urged others to do the same. George Washington asked Congress to create a national college to train farmers in the latest science.

During the nineteenth century, chemists began to clarify the details of plant nutrition, and in 1840 the German chemist Justus Liebig identified nitrogen as essential to plant growth. His efforts to popularize agricultural chemistry succeeded in the United States, where journalists and scientists urged Congress to fund agricultural science. Southern Democrats blocked action, but their departure from Congress during the Civil War freed Republicans to act. In 1862 Congress created the U.S. Department of Agriculture (USDA) and a system of agricultural and mechanical colleges to conduct research. But administrative and teaching duties limited the resources the colleges could devote to science, leading scientists to advocate that the individual states create institutions that would devote themselves solely to research. The German states provided the model, having funded agricultural experiment stations since the 1850s. In 1875 Connecticut created the first experiment station in the United States. Other states followed, and in 1887 Congress passed the Hatch Act, giving every state $15,000 annually to create or maintain an agricultural experiment station.

As early as 1881, research focused on the control of insects harmful to crops. That year the USDA created a Division of Entomology, which by 1918 was using insecticides, many of them arsenic compounds, against insects harmful to citrus, apple, and elm trees, and corn, wheat, alfalfa, clover, and sugarcane. The experiment stations and agricultural colleges had similar programs and often coordinated their work with the USDA. The effort of spraying insecticides on plants and trees was laborious, requiring hours to cover a few acres. By 1920 scientists were eager for a quick method of applying insecticides.

The airplane was the obvious solution, for it could cover in seconds ground that would otherwise require hours to traverse. In August 1921, John Houser, an entomologist at the Ohio Agricultural Experiment Station in Wooster, directed an Army pilot to make several passes over an apple orchard near Troy, Ohio, spraying the trees with insecticide. The plane covered the grove with insecticide in less than a minute, an operation that would otherwise have taken most of the day. Crowds cheered as the plane passed overhead, and Houser estimated that the insecticide had killed 99 percent of caterpillars that had infested the orchard.

Significance

The first crop dusting had been a success, and the next year the USDA repeated the feat in Louisiana, where the target was the boll weevil, cotton's nemesis. In 1923 Huff-Deland Dusters Inc., the forerunner of Delta Airlines, made the first commercial dusting and the era of crop dusting had arrived.

The success of crop dusting marked the 1920s as a decade of growth for agricultural science. In 1925 Congress began to fund the study of rural economics and rural sociology at the experiment stations. No less important, the science of plant breeding matured during that decade. As early as 1917, Donald F. Jones, a plant breeder at the Connecticut Agricultural Experiment Station, applied the work of two geneticists in breeding the first varieties of hybrid corn. Hybrid corn had higher yield than traditional varieties and often had better tolerance of drought, insects, and diseases. During the 1920s, the USDA and the experiment stations covered the Midwest and South with hybrid corn, and in 1926 industry joined this work. That year Henry A. Wallace, a plant breeder and son of Agriculture Secretary Henry C. Wallace, founded Pioneer Hi-Bred, a company that develops and sells hybrid seeds. Private industry and public science had united, and by

Figure 11—In the operation of applying the dust the plane flew at an altitude of from 20 to 35 feet in a path parallel to and 53 yards to the windward of the grove. **THE MONTHLY BULLETIN. OHIO AGRICULTURAL EXPERIMENT STATION. VOL. VII, NOS. 7 & 8, JULY–AUGUST, 1922, 134.**

1940 farmers planted hybrids on more than 90 percent of corn acreage in the United States. Agricultural science, using the technology of the airplane and the science of genetics, came of age during the 1920s.

Primary Source

"The Airplane in Catalpa Sphinx Control" [excerpt]

SYNOPSIS: In this excerpt, entomologist John Houser describes the world's first crop dusting. He emphasized that the airplane enabled scientists to cover acreage with insecticide in seconds rather than hours and boasted a kill rate of 99 percent. Houser had not been in the plane but had instead joined the crowd that watched this historic flight.

Details of Applying the Dust

The dusting plane left McCook Field shortly after noon on August 3, 1921, and flew to a previously selected landing field about a mile and a quarter distant from the grove to be treated. There the hopper was filled and the work of applying the dust began.

The meteorological conditions were ideal. The sunlight was excellent for photographing, and a steady wind, estimated at about 11 miles an hour, was blowing in the direction indicated by the arrows in the photographic record of flight. The dusting plane traveled at the rate of 80 miles and hour, and as shown by the photographs, flew along the windward side and parallel to the grove rather than over the trees. Six flights were made past the grove, the plane taking the same path for each passage, which was about 53 yards to the windward. The altitude varied from 20 to 35 feet.

The poison trail was controlled for a few seconds after leaving the plane by the impetus of the "slip stream," but this was soon lost, and the steadily moving wind grasped the poison cloud and carried it, as a wartime barrage, toward the caterpillar-infested grove. When the dust reached the grove, a new influence or force was observed to be at work, for it was noted that air currents were rising from among the trees and the influence of these rising currents, combined with the steady push of the wind was sufficient to carry the poison cloud to all parts of the grove, and even beyond, since some dust settled in a corn field as much as 500 feet to the leeward of the last row of trees.

Figure 12—After the dust was liberated it was floated through the grove by a wind varying from eight to eleven miles per hour. Every leaf was covered by the poison. **THE MONTHLY BULLETIN. OHIO AGRICULTURAL EXPERIMENT STATION. VOL. VII, NOS. 7 & 8, JULY–AUGUST, 1922, 135.**

Each flight past the grove required 9 seconds and, since six flights in all were made, the total time consumed in the act of liberating the dust was 54 seconds. To have done the same amount of work with a liquid sprayer would have required many hours.

The total amount of lead used was 175 pounds. In all probability this was more than was actually necessary.

After the final passage of the plane, a critical examination of the foliage in all parts of the grove was made. Not a catalpa leaf could be found anywhere which did not bear particles of arsenate of lead in sufficient quantity to constitute a killing dose.

The most gratifying phase of the act of applying the dust was the excellent distribution obtained and the remarkable manner in which it could be controlled and thus deposited where intended. By correlating altitude, wind currents, etc., the behavior of the dust can be fairly estimated. After this is done a "trial puff" of the powder can be made and the "range" secured. Using the trial puff as a basis for correction the actual work of dusting can be begun with a fair degree of confidence that the cloud will settle where desired.

The Effect on the Caterpillars

The morning following the application of the dust some dead caterpillars were to be found in the grove and many were ailing. Forty-six hours after the poison was applied evidence of the wholesale slaughter of the insects was apparent on every hand. Every part of the grove was literally polluted by the dead and dying larvae. Their bodies were hanging in every conceivable position on the trunks, branches, and foliage of the trees, fence posts, and weeds; and they were lying in the greatest profusion on the refuse of the forest floor; while still others had sought seclusion beneath fallen leaves, twigs, etc. Not a single step could be taken without crushing numbers of them.

The large as well as the small caterpillars were killed. Previous to the test it was feared that the full grown horn-worms might be able to withstand the treatment, since it is well known that the large horn-worms are rather difficult to kill.

The most careful and painstaking observations indicated that the poison had destroyed at least 99 percent of the caterpillars present at the time of its application.

Further Resources

BOOKS

Baker, Gladys L., et al. *Century of Service: The First 100 Years of the United States Department of Agriculture.* Washington: U.S. Department of Agriculture, 1963.

Bunker, Nancy J., and Tom Dupree. *100 Years: A Century of Growth through Agricultural Research.* Atlanta: University of Georgia Press, 1975.

Busch, Lawrence, ed. *Science and Agricultural Development.* Totowa, N.J.: Allanheld, Osmun, 1981.

Cumo, Christopher M. *Seeds of Change: A History of the Ohio Agricultural Research and Development Center.* Wooster, Ohio: The Wooster Book Company, 2000.

Harding, T. Swann. *Two Blades of Grass: A History of Scientific Development in the USDA.* Norman, Okla.: University of Oklahoma Press, 1947.

Kerr, Norwood Allen. *The Legacy: A Centennial History of Agricultural Experiment Stations, 1887–1987.* Columbia, Mo.: University of Missouri Press, 1988.

Knoblauch, Harold C., Ernest M. Law, and W.P. Meyer. *State Agricultural Experiment Stations: A History of Research Policy and Procedure.* Washington: U.S. Department of Agriculture, 1962.

Perkins, John. *Insects, Experts and the Insecticide Crisis.* New York: Plenum, 1982.

PERIODICALS

Blasé, Melvin G., and Arnold Paulsen. "The Agricultural Experiment Station: An Institutional Development Perspective." *Agricultural Science Review,* 1972, 11–16.

Bonnen, J.T. "The First 100 Years of the Department of Agriculture—Land-Grant College System." *Journal of Farm Economics,* 1962, 1279–1294.

Parks, T.H. "John Samuel Houser, 1881–1947." *Journal of Economic Entomology,* August 1947, 611–613.

WEBSITES

"20th Century Insect Control." ARS Timeline: 138 Years of Agricultural Research. Available online at http://www.ars.usda.gov/is/timeline/insect.htm; website home page: http://www.ars.usda.gov (accessed January 29, 2003).

My Life and Work
Autobiography

By: Henry Ford

Date: 1922

Source: Ford, Henry, and Samuel Crowther. *My Life and Work.* Garden City, N.Y.: Garden City Publishing, 1922, 33–35.

About the Author: Henry Ford (1863–1947) was born on a farm near Dearborn, Michigan. During his late teens he began tinkering with the internal-combustion engine and in 1899 formed the Detroit Automobile Company, which later became the Cadillac Motor Car Company. In 1903 he founded the Ford Motor Company, which he eventually transformed into a multinational conglomerate in thirty-three countries. ■

Introduction

The development of the steam engine in England in the eighteenth century led to the locomotive in the early nineteenth century and the automobile later in the century. Although the steam engine powered the first cars, it was too large and did not generate sufficient power. These shortcomings led inventors to experiment with the electric motor and the gasoline engine. Its power and compactness led the gasoline engine to dominate auto design during the last quarter of the nineteenth century. French and German inventors built gasoline engines as early as the 1860s, and in 1872 Gottlieb Daimler, a German engineer, began manufacturing stationary gasoline engines. In 1885 Daimler mounted a gasoline engine on a bicycle. That year another German engineer, Karl Benz, built his first car, a tricycle. The next year Daimler built a car with four wheels, and in 1887 Benz made his first sale.

As early as the 1870s, New York attorney George Selden had tinkered with the gasoline engine, and by the 1890s American companies were manufacturing cars. That decade Italian firms also joined an industry that was spreading throughout Europe and the United States.

The first automobile companies were small, undercapitalized, and often went bankrupt after only a few years in business. Their concept of the car may have contributed to their failure. The first car manufacturers did not expect to sell cars in volume; they thought of the car as a luxury and priced it beyond the means of all but the wealthy. So long as this view prevailed, the car remained more a curiosity than a technology capable of transforming countryside and city. The car needed someone who could envision its mass appeal.

Henry Ford had this vision. "I will build a motor car for the great multitude," he said upon unveiling the Model T in 1908. Cheap, durable, and capable of traveling on poor roads, the Model T was a departure from the idea of the car as status symbol. Ford cut costs by building all Model Ts from standard parts; even the paint was standard—every car was black. This reconception of the car was a success. By 1927 the Ford Motor Company had sold 15.5 million Model Ts in the United States, 1 million in Canada, and 250,000 in Britain, accounting for half the world's output of cars.

Henry Ford with his first and ten millionth automobile. June 4, 1924. **THE LIBRARY OF CONGRESS.**

Significance

Ford's vision made the 1920s the decade of the car. In 1921 he had captured 55 percent of the U.S. auto market. That year Ford and his competitors churned out 1.5 million cars, and Americans owned 10.5 million cars. By 1929 automobile production leapt to 4.8 million, and Americans owned 26.5 million cars. Nearly half of all American families owned a car in 1929. By 1929 the car accounted for 13 percent of the value of all manufactured goods in the United States. That year Ford employed 375,000 workers, and millions more held jobs dependent on the auto industry, which used 15 percent of all steel manufactured in the United States and 80 percent of all rubber.

During the 1920s, the car and tractor replaced the horse. Its disappearance from the farm left farmers free to plant corn, wheat, and other crops on land that had gone to hay. By giving Americans greater mobility, the car allowed them to live farther from their work, stimulating the growth of the first suburbs and housing developments. During the 1920s Americans began to connect the country in a network of paved roads and highways. Americans took Sunday drives and summer vacations in their cars, spawning tourism. Thanks to the car, modern American emerged during the 1920s.

Primary Source

My Life and Work [excerpt]

> **SYNOPSIS:** In this excerpt from a chapter entitled "What I Learned about Business" from his autobiography, Henry Ford describes the sensation his first car caused in Detroit. By the time he wrote this passage, Ford was among the wealthiest men in the United States and could look back upon his achievements with pride. Characteristic of this pride are the passages in which Ford writes of his foresight in sticking with the gasoline engine when others thought the future lay with the electric motor.

What I Learned About Business

My "gasoline buggy" was the first and for a long time the only automobile in Detroit. It was considered to be something of a nuisance, for it made a racket and it scared horses. Also it blocked traffic. For if I stopped my machine anywhere in town a crowd was around it before I could start up again. If I left it alone even for a minute some inquisitive person always tried to run it. Finally, I had to carry a chain and chain it to a lamp post whenever I left it anywhere. And then there was trouble with the police. I do not know quite why, for my impression is that there were no speed-limit laws in those days.

Anyway, I had to get a special permit from the mayor and thus for a time enjoyed the distinction of being the only licensed chauffeur in America. I ran that machine about one thousand miles through 1895 and 1896 and then sold it to Charles Ainsley of Detroit for two hundred dollars. That was my first sale. I had built the car not to sell but only to experiment with. I wanted to start another car. Ainsley wanted to buy. I could use the money and we had no trouble in agreeing upon a price.

It was not at all my idea to make cars in any such petty fashion. I was looking ahead to production, but before that could come I had to have something to produce. It does not pay to hurry. I started a second car in 1896; it was much like the first but a little lighter. It also had the belt drive which I did not give up until some time later; the belts were all right excepting in hot weather. That is why I later adopted gears. I learned a great deal from that car. Others in this country and abroad were building cars by that time, and in 1895 I heard that a Benz car from Germany was on exhibition in Macy's store in New York. I travelled down to look at it but it had no features that seemed worth while. It also had the belt drive, but it was much heavier than my car. I was working for lightness; the foreign makers have never seemed to appreciate what light weight means. I built three cars in all in my home shop and all of them ran for years in Detroit. I still have the first car; I bought it back a few years later from a man to whom Mr. Ainsley had sold it. I paid one hundred dollars for it.

During all this time I kept my position with the electric company and gradually advanced to chief engineer at a salary of one hundred and twenty-five dollars a month. But my gas-engine experiments were no more popular with the president of the company than my first mechanical leanings were with my father. It was not that my employer objected to experiments—only to experiments with a gas engine. I can still hear him say:

"Electricity, yes, that's the coming thing. But gas—no."

He had ample grounds for his skepticism—to use the mildest terms. Practically no one had the remotest notion of the future of the internal combustion engine, while we were just on the edge of the great electrical development. As with every comparatively new idea, electricity was expected to do much more than we even now have any indication that it can do. I did not see the use of experimenting with electricity for my purposes. A road car could not run on a trolley even if trolley wires had been less expensive; no storage battery was in sight of a weight that was practical. An electrical car had of necessity to be limited in radius and to contain a large amount of motive machinery in proportion to the power exerted. That is not to say that I held or now hold electricity cheaply; we have not yet begun to use electricity. But it has its place, and the internal combustion engine has its place. Neither can substitute for the other—which is exceedingly fortunate.

Further Resources

BOOKS

Gelderman, Carol W. *Henry Ford: The Wayward Capitalist.* New York: Dial Press, 1981.

Lacey, Robert. *Ford: The Men and the Machine.* Boston: Little, Brown, 1986.

Nevins, Allan, and Frank Ernest Hill. *Ford: The Times, the Man and the Company.* New York: Scribner, 1954.

Rae, John B. *The Road and the Car in American Life.* Cambridge: MIT Press, 1971.

Sward, Keith. *The Legend of Henry Ford.* New York: Rinehart, 1948.

PERIODICALS

Lewis, David L. "Man of the Century." *Automotive News,* December 27, 1999, 34–36.

Stewart, Thomas A., et al. "The Businessman of the Century." *Fortune,* November 22, 1999, 108–119.

WEBSITES

"Henry Ford Is Dead at 83 in Dearborn." *The New York Times.* Available onlineat http://www.nytimes.com/learning/general /onthisday/bday/0730.html; website home page: http://www .nytimes.com (accessed January 28, 2003).

"The Life of Henry Ford." OnlineExhibits, Henry Ford Museum & Greenfield Village. Available online at http://www .hfmgv.org/exhibits/hf; website home page: http://www .hfmgv.org (accessed January 28, 2003).

"The Present Status of Eugenical Sterilization in the United States"

Presentation

By: Harry H. Laughlin

Date: 1923

Source: Laughlin, Harry H. "The Present Status of Eugenical Sterilization in the United States." In *Scientific Papers of the Second International Congress of Eugenics. Vol. II: Eugenics in Race and State.* Baltimore: Williams and Wilkins, 1923, 286–291.

About the Author: Harry H. Laughlin (1880–1943) was born in Oskaloosa, Iowa, and received a Ph.D. in biology from Princeton University. He directed the Eugenics Record Office of the Carnegie Institute in Washington, D.C., between 1910 and 1940, using his authority to advance the claim that states had a duty to sterilize "socially inadequate" people. He lobbied Congress to ban immigrants from southern and eastern Europe, people Laughlin believed to be inferior to northern Europeans. He died in 1943 in Kirksville, Missouri. ∎

Introduction

In *The Origin of Species* (1859), Charles Darwin argued that natural selection changes species over time. His cousin Francis Galton believed the pace and direction of that change in human beings could be controlled by ensuring that the "best" people reproduced. He coined the word "eugenics" for the science of selective human breeding. During the nineteenth century, eugenics held wide humanitarian appeal. Journalists and scientists saw it as a way of improving the human condition beyond what was possible through environmental influences such as education and nutrition.

Eugenics took concrete form after 1900. That year, three scientists rediscovered a paper on pea hybridization by the Austrian monk Gregor Mendel. The paper laid the foundation of genetics. Scientists came to understand, as had Mendel, that discrete units called genes determine the traits of an organism. Genes are the blueprint that cells read in assembling an organism, be it a pea plant or a human being.

The alliance between genetics and eugenics was natural. All that was required was the belief that certain genes coded for, or determined, intelligence and character, that the most intelligent and ethical people had these genes in abundance, and that policymakers should encourage them in passing these genes to offspring. A corollary of this position held that the mentally retarded, criminals, the insane, and the indolent and lazy had genes that coded for these deficiencies, genes that policymakers should discourage from being passed to offspring.

By the 1920s, science had become entangled with ideology. Racists and reactionaries bent the claims of eugenics to their own purposes, stamping entire races, ethnic groups, and social classes as "degenerates." Social ills were traced to genes whose deletion from the population became the goal of the most militant eugenicists. They elevated reproduction, the most private of choices, to public policy. Criminals and their ilk would never stop having children on their own, they maintained. Therefore, if humans were to improve their species, the riffraff had to be stopped from procreating. Government must bar them from reproducing—or even make them unable to reproduce by forcing them to undergo surgical sterilization procedures.

Significance

This rationale led more than thirty states to pass sterilization laws between 1907 and 1930. Judges in these states could order physicians to sterilize men and women for a long list of mental and physical defects, even blindness and deafness. The U.S. Supreme Court upheld these laws in 1927. Justice Oliver Wendell Holmes wrote for the majority that "It is better for all the world, if instead of waiting to execute degenerate offspring for crime, or to let them starve for their imbecility, society can prevent those who are manifestly unfit from continuing their kind. The principle that sustains compulsory vaccination is broad enough to cover cutting the Fallopian tubes." Before their repeal, these laws led surgeons to sterilize some 20,000 people in the United States, nearly half in California. These laws prompted Adolf Hitler in 1933 to enact a sterilization law in Germany, under which surgeons sterilized some 375,000 people. The horrors of Nazism sunk their roots in the soil of American eugenics.

Eugenics was an example of American science at its worst and most naive. The premise that all deficiencies are hereditary is simplistic. Education, nutrition, and parents shape people as surely as do genes. In their quest for easy answers to social ills, eugenicists ignored these influences. Eugenics thus cast genetics in its most dogmatic, uncompromising form.

Eugenics also exaggerated the ability of science to engineer society. Eugenicists believed they could identify the talents, and the genes undergirding them, that government should preserve and the deficiencies it should eradicate. But even today people cannot agree on what mix of talents is ideal. From the beginning eugenicists had no real conception of what they meant by "cognate races" or "degenerate stock." But this lack of clarity did not prevent them from making sweeping assertions about human worth.

The 1920s saw science at its most arrogant. Perhaps at no other time in American history has a group of scientists been so sure of its right to control the reproductive destiny of others. Eugenics was considered legitimate science in the United States during 1920s. For example, some two hundred scientists, mostly from the United States and Great Britain, attended the Second International Congress of Eugenics, held in New York in September 1921. Twenty scientific papers were presented, including "The Present Status of Eugenical Sterilization in the United States" by Harry H. Laughlin. Two other such conferences were held.

From the beginnning, organizations that supported minority groups and immigrants fought eugenics for the racism that it was. But it was Hitler's embrace of eugenics that finally discredited the movement in the 1930s. Eugenics quickly lost its base of support, as U.S. scientists lined up against Hitler. The history of eugenics in America reminds us that science is imperfect.

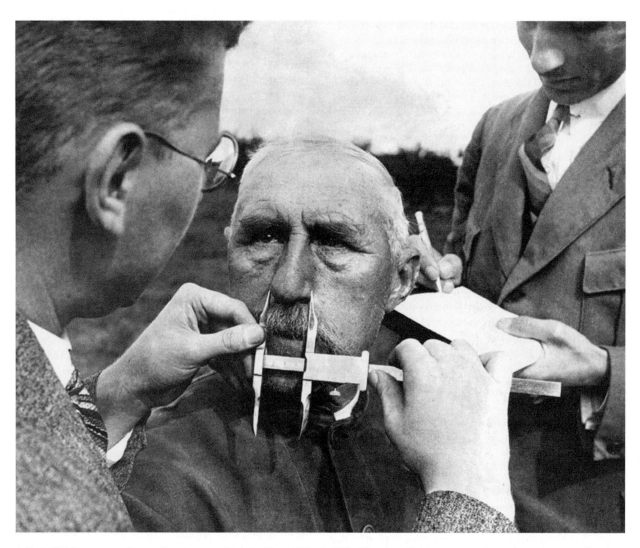

A Nazi official measures a German citizen's nose to determine his racial "purity." The Nuremberg Code's goal was to ban such practices, as well as the types of medical experiments conducted in concentration camps. © HULTON-DEUTSCH COLLECTION/CORBIS. REPRODUCED BY PERMISSION.

Primary Source

"The Present Status of Eugenical Sterilization in the United States" [excerpt]

SYNOPSIS: In this excerpt from a paper presented at the Second International Congress of Eugenics, held in New York in September 1921, Harry H. Laughlin defends the right of states to sterilize "degenerate and worthless" people. Laughlin, like most writers of eugenics tracts, does not define his terms with precision. He is precise only when enumerating the number of people sterilized, statistics he seems to relish. He hints that these sterilizations mark a trend he expects to grow.

At the First International Congress of Eugenics, Mr. Bleecker Van Wagenen reported the progress which legalized eugenical sterilization had made in

the United States prior to the year 1912. Since that time legislation, litigation and administrative advance have extended, and made more secure, the field of activity of this particular means of preventing reproduction by certain members of degenerate human stocks. No one, not even the most ardent advocate of sterilization, proposes to use this remedy as the sole agency for preventing parenthood on the part of human degenerates, but among advanced peoples, it must be rated as one of the four or five most practicable measures for purging the human stock of its more degenerate and worthless strains. . . .

Legislative Notes

. . . It is clear that in order to affect the future population favorably, by improving its hereditary endowments to a considerable degree, the number of eugenical sterilizations must be numbered by thousands instead of by tens.

For the purpose of making the state the arbiter in such matters, a duty which it cannot avoid, fifteen of the American states have enacted statutes governing eugenical sterilization. . . .

Motives of the Statutes

. . . Race betterment is the only motive which eugenical sterilization laws have to justify them. The most successful statutes omit punitive or therapeutic purposes, and set forth only eugenical aims. Their one purpose is to exercise the undoubted right of the state to prevent reproduction by persons of proven degenerate stock, that is persons whose children, because of the inheritance of certain handicapping mental, physical and moral qualities, would probably be unable to develop into self-sustaining and valuable members of society, but which children, on the other hand, would constitute a drag upon the self-supporting portion of the commonwealth. . . .

Persons Subject

It is possible, however, to circumvent such possible attacks by the courts by making all persons of the same natural hereditary degeneracy of the same specific type, whether in institutions or without them, subject to the law. Indeed so long as a person remains in a modern custodial institution, there is no great danger of parenthood. Cacogenic persons in the population at large, and also such persons in custodial institutions who are to be discharged while still potential parents, are the logical individuals to make subject to sterilization for eugenical purposes.

It is clear that if a sterilization statute is to function eugenically, it must provide for the sterilization, early in life, of individuals whose degeneracy is of an hereditary nature, which degeneracy is of such a type as to prevent the making of useful citizens out of the possible offspring. . . .

Statistical Summary

. . . Prior to January 1, 1921, 2233 persons have been legally sterilized in the United States; 1853 were males, 1380 were females. By radicalness of operation, 3061 were the less radical surgically. Of these 1781 consisted in vasectomy of the male, and 1280 in slapingectomy of the female. Of the more radical operations there were 172, of these 72 were castration of the male, and 100 were ovariotomy of the female. By classes, 403 were feebleminded, 2700 insane, and 130 criminalistic. . . .

Institutions Subject

There have been legalized eugenical sterilizations in state institutions for the (1) insane, (2) feebleminded and (3) criminalistic. No operations legalized primarily for eugenical purposes have yet been performed in

a. State Institutions for the (1) inebriate, (2) the diseased, (3) the blind, (4) the deaf, (5) the deformed, (6) the dependent, (7) the epileptic, nor in

b. County, municipal or private institutions for any type of the socially inadequate, nor

c. Among the socially inadequate and cacogenic individuals in the population at large.

Conclusion

The extension of the provisions of the sterilization law to all cacogenic persons of a given legal standard, whether within public or private custodial institutions or in the population at large, is both a legal necessity and a practical requirement for eugenical effectiveness.

Further Resources

BOOKS

Grether, Judith K. *Sterilization and Eugenics: An Examination of Early Twentieth Century Population Control in the United States.* Ann Arbor: University of Michigan Press, 1980.

Haller, Mark. *Eugenics: Hereditarian Attitudes in American Thought.* New Brunswick, N.J.: Rutgers University Press, 1963.

Hassencahl, Frances J. *Harry H. Laughlin, "Expert Eugenics Agent" for the House Committee on Immigration and Naturalization, 1921 to 1931.* Ann Arbor: University of Michigan Press, 1971.

Kevles, Daniel J. *In the Name of Eugenics: Genetics and the Uses of Human Heredity.* New York: Knopf, 1985.

Ludmerer, Kenneth L. *Genetics and American Society: A Historical Appraisal.* Baltimore: Johns Hopkins University Press, 1972.

Robitscher, Jonas, ed. *Eugenic Sterilization.* Springfield, Ill.: Thomas Press, 1973.

PERIODICALS

Gould, Stephen Jay. "The Case of Carrie Buck's Daughter." *Natural History,* July 1984, 14–18.

Vecoli, Rudolph J. "Sterilization: A Progressive Measure." *Wisconsin Magazine of History,* Spring 1960, 190–202.

WEBSITES

"Eugenic Sterilization Laws." Image Archive on the American Eugenics Movement. Available online at http://www.eugenicsarchive.org/html/eugenics/essay8text.html; website home page http://www.eugenicsarchive.org (accessed January 29, 2003).

"Harry H. Laughlin." Harry H. Laughlin Papers, Truman State University, Kirksville, Missouri. Available online at http://library.truman.edu/manuscripts/laughlinbio.htm; website home page http://library.truman.edu (accessed February 7, 2003).

AUDIO AND VISUAL MEDIA

The Lynchburg Story: Eugenic Sterilization in America. Filmakers Library, 1994, VHS.

"The Electron and the Light-Quant from the Experimental Point of View"

Lecture

By: Robert A. Millikan

Date: May 23, 1924

Source: Millikan, Robert A. "The Electron and the Light-Quant from the Experimental Point of View." Nobel Lecture, May 23, 1924. Available online at http://www.nobel.se/physics/laureates/1923/millikan-lecture.html; website home page: http://www.nobel.se (accessed January 28, 2003).

About the Author: Robert Andrews Millikan (1868–1953) was born in in Morrison, Illinois, and received a Ph.D. in physics from Columbia University in 1895. That year he studied at two German universities, returning to the United States the next year to conduct research at the University of Chicago's Ryerson Laboratory. There he performed the oil-drop experiment that eventually would win him the 1923 Nobel Prize in physics. In 1921 he joined the faculty of the California Institute of Technology, where he remained until retirement in 1945. He died in 1953. ■

Introduction

Around 400 B.C.E., the Greek philosopher Democritus proposed that indivisible particles, atoms, compose all matter. Another Greek philosopher, Epicurus, accepted this idea in the fourth century B.C.E., as did the Roman poet Lucretius in the first century B.C.E. With the fragmentation of the Roman Empire in the fifth century C.E., "atomism" fell from favor.

Only in 1802 did British chemist John Dalton revive it. Later in the century, British physicist Michael Faraday inferred that atoms consist of heavy, positively charged nuclei, and light, negatively charged particles, implying that atoms were not indivisible after all. British physicist Joseph John Thomson sought to isolate the negatively charged particles. In 1897 he placed two electrodes in a vacuum tube and passed an electric current between them. The negative electrode emitted Faraday's negatively charged particles, which Thomson called electrons. He measured the mass of an electron, finding it to be less than a trillion trillionth of a gram. Thomson's work made plain that the electron occupied only the tinest fraction of an atom. But Thomson did not know the magnitude of the charge on an electron. This detail was not trivial. The fact that an atom is electrically neutral means that to know the magnitude of the charge on an electron is also to know the magnitude of the charge on the proton, the positively charged particle in an atom's nucleus, for these charges must be equal but opposite. Quantifying electrons and protons in as many ways as possible helped scientists convince the world—and themselves—that they were a physical reality.

Robert Millikan supplied the missing detail with his oil-drop experiment. He sprayed a mist of oil droplets above a chamber with a pinhole at the top. Gravity pulled the droplets down to the chamber, some of which fell through the pinhole. These droplets had received a negative charge from the friction of having passed through the sprayer's nozzle. The chamber had plates at top and bottom such that when Millikan passed an electric current through them, the top plate was positively charged and the bottom negatively charged. By turning on the current Millikan could counteract the force of gravity, for like charges repel and opposites attract. Because this is so, a negatively charged droplet always traveled toward the top of the chamber when Millikan turned on the current.

But the negatively charged droplets did not travel to the top at the same speed. Each electron is one negative charge, and the more electrons a droplet had, the faster it went up, because the intensity of attraction to the top and repulsion from the bottom increased as its negative charge increased. Millikan measured the speed of the droplets as they traveled toward the top of the chamber. The velocity always varied by a multiple of the same tiny amount—a fraction of a billionth of an elecrostatic unit. This fraction, therefore, was the charge on one electron. (A simpler way to think of this is to say, for example, that Droplet #1 traveled at the speed of ten units, Droplet #2 at twenty, Droplet #3 at thirty, and Droplet 4 at forty. All the velocities are multiples of ten. Therefore, in this imaginary case, the charge on one electron would be ten, and Droplet #1 would have one electron, Droplet #2, two electrons, and so on.)

Significance

Millikan's work typified American physics during the 1920s. He had filled in a detail of atomic theory rather than developed a new idea. The flow of ideas had been from Europe to the United States. In the United States, the focus was on precise measurement and careful experimentation. American physics during the 1920s was empirical rather than theoretical, and in his 1924 Nobel address Millikan made much of the fact that the electron was a physical reality, not a theoretical construct. For Millikan and his colleagues in the United States, physics was the study of the concrete.

This preoccupation with the concrete and with empiricism was a hallmark of American science during the 1920s. American physicists fastened on the atom as the concrete building block of matter just as surely as American biologists focused on the gene as the building block of life. Particulars rather than abstractions held the interest of American scientists during the 1920s. In his attention to the concrete, Millikan was the archetypal American scientist.

Primary Source

"The Electron and the Light-Quant from the Experimental Point of View" [excerpt]

SYNOPSIS: Robert Millikan won the 1923 Nobel Prize in physics though he did not deliver his address until May 1924. In this excerpt from his address, Millikan describes the oil-drop experiment that allowed him to measure the charge on an electron. Millikan, in emphasizing that electrons are a reality and not a hypothesis, revealed his commitment to empiricism, a commitment that was a hallmark of American science during the 1920s.

Robert A. Milikan, Nobel Prize–winning physicist and discoverer of the charge on the electron. **AP/WIDE WORLD PHOTOS. REPRODUCED BY PERMISSION.**

The most direct and unambiguous proof of the existence of the electron will probably be generally admitted to be found in an experiment which for convenience I will call the oil-drop experiment. . . .

In order to be able to measure very accurately the force acting upon the charged oil-droplet it was necessary to give it about a centimeter of path in which the speed could be measured. . . .

The observations which gave an unambiguous answer to the questions as to the atomic nature of electricity consisted in putting a charge upon the drop, in general by the frictional process involved in blowing the spray, letting the charged drop drift through a pin-hole in the center of plate C into the space between C and D, and then in changing its charge in a considerable number of different ways; for example, by ionizing the air just beneath it by al-

pha, beta, or gamma rays from radium and letting the field throw these ions into the drop; by illuminating the surface of the drop itself with ultraviolet light; by shooting X-rays both directly at it and beneath it, etc. The results of those changes in charge in a constant field, as is now well-known, . . . were

1. that it was found possible to discharge the droplet completely so that within the limits of observational error—a small fraction of one per cent—*it fell its centimeter undergravity, when the 6,000 volt electrical-field was on, in precisely the same time required to fall the same distance when there was no field;*

2. that it could become endowed with a particular speed in the electrical field (corresponding to 67.7 sec in the particular case shown), which *could be reproduced as often as desired, but which was the smallest speed that the given field ever communicated to it*—nor was this change in speed due to the capture of an electron a small one, difficult to observe and measure. It was often larger than the speed due to gravity itself and represented, as in

this case shown, a reversal in *direction* so that it was striking and unmistakable;

3. that *speeds exactly two times, three times, four times, five times, etc.* (always within the limits of observational error—still less than a percent) *could be communicated to the droplet, but never any fraction of these speeds.*

He who has seen that experiment, and hundreds of investigators have observed it, has literally *seen* the electron.

Further Resources

BOOKS

Kargon, Robert H. *The Rise of Robert Millikan: Portrait of a Life in American Science.* Ithaca, N.Y.: Cornell University Press, 1982.

Kevles, Daniel J. *The Physicists: The History of a Scientific Community in Modern America.* New York: Knopf, 1978.

Motz, Lloyd, and Jefferson Hane Weaver. *The Story of Physics.* New York: Plenum Press, 1989.

Reingold, Nathan. ed. *The Sciences in the American Context.* Washington D.C.: Smithsonian Institution Press, 1979.

PERIODICALS

Dubridge, Lee A., and Paul Epstein. "Robert A. Millikan." *National Academy of Sciences Biographical Memoirs.* 1959, 241–82.

Epstein, Paul. "Robert A. Millikan as Physicist and Teacher." *Review of Modern Physics,* 1948, 10–25.

Kargon, Robert H. "The Conservative Mode: Robert A. Millikan and the Twentieth Century Revolution in Physics." *Isis,* 1977, 590–626.

Kevles, Daniel J. "Millikan: Spokesman for Science in the Twenties." *Engineering and Science,* April 1969, 17–22.

Romer, Alfred. "Robert A. Millikan, Physics Teacher." *Physics Teacher,* February 1978, 78–85.

WEBSITES

"Robert Andrews Millikan, 1868–1953." Selected Papers of Great American Physicists, The Center for History of Physics. Available online at http://www.aip.org/history/gap /Millikan/Millikan.html; website home page http://www .aip.org/history/ (accessed February 7, 2003).

"Mencken Likens Trial to a Religious Orgy, with Defendant a Beelzebub"

Newspaper article

By: H.L. Mencken

Date: July 11, 1925

Source: Mencken, H.L. "Mencken Likens Trial to a Religious Orgy, with Defendant a Beelzebub." *Baltimore Evening Sun,* July 11, 1925. Available online at http://www.etsu.edu /cas/history/docs/menckenorgy.htm; website homepage: http:// www.etsu.edu/cas/history/hist.htm (accessed May 7, 2003).

About the Author: Henry Louis Mencken (1888–1956) was born in Baltimore, Maryland, and joined the *Baltimore Herald* as a reporter in 1899. Seven years later he moved to the *Baltimore Sun,* where he wrote until 1948. Throughout his career Mencken was a polarizing figure. Supporters admired his wit and literary taste. Critics disliked his pro-German bias, his contempt for the poor, and his hatred of Franklin D. Roosevelt. He died in in Baltimore in 1956. ∎

Introduction

As early as 1838, Charles Darwin hit upon the idea of natural selection as the mechanism for evolution, the change in species over time. Yet he did not publish this idea for more than twenty years for fear of controversy. A literal reading of *Genesis* maintained that God had created all species, including humans, in six days and in unalterable form. The theory of evolution by natural selection contradicts this view on three grounds. First, it says that species have evolved from the first primitive life to their current diversity; they were not constant. Second, it maintains that natural selection required millions of years, not six days, to ascend from bacterium to human. Third, it holds that natural selection is a mechanistic process that required neither God's intervention nor His existence.

Reluctant to court controversy, Darwin remained silent until another British naturalist, Alfred Russell Wallace, wrote him in 1858 to say that he, too, had fastened on natural selection as way of explaining evolution. If Darwin wanted to claim the idea of natural selection as his own, he would have to publish his theory. The result, Darwin's *The Origin of Species* appeared the next year and unleashed the torrent of indignation he had foreseen. Religious leaders excoriated Darwin in the month following the book's publication. But by the end of the century they had spent their fury and either made peace with Darwinism or ignored it.

Only in the United States did religious opposition to Dawinsm linger into the twentieth century. In 1921, religious fundamentalists in the South joined former presidential candidate William Jennings Bryan in a movement to ban the teaching of evolution in public schools. Texas governor Miriam Ferguson vowed not "to let that kind of rot go into Texas schoolbooks," and in March 1925 the Tennessee legislature banned the teaching of evolution in its public schools.

The American Civil Liberties Union, founded in 1920 to protect the free expression of ideas, offered to defend any teacher willing to defy the law. In Dayton,

An Anti-Evolution League holds a book sale at the opening of the Scopes "Monkey" Trial in which biology teacher John T. Scopes was being prosecuted for teaching evolution in his class. July 10, 1925. © BETTMANN/CORBIS. REPRODUCED BY PERMISSION.

Tennessee, prominent men saw an opportunity to put the town in the spotlight and convinced high school biology teacher John Scopes to break the law. Scopes' guilt and sure conviction did not deter the ACLU from retaining Clarence Darrow, the era's most celebrated lawyer, to defend the teacher. Bryan countered by offering to assist the prosecution. When the judge refused to hear scientific testimony, Darrow called Bryan to testify as an expert on the Bible. Bryan admitted his belief that a big fish had swallowed Jonah, that Joshua had made the sun stand still, and that God had created the universe and all life in six days, though he hedged on the length of a day, contradicting his insistence that the Bible be interpreted literally. His testimony meant little to the outcome. The jury convicted Scopes and fined him a hundred dollars, though the state supreme court overturned the conviction on a technicality.

The trial received widespread coverage in the press. H.L. Mencken, the most well-known journalist in America at the time, covered it for the *Baltimore Sun,* and other major newspapers sent reporters to the trial.

Significance

In an article published in the *Baltimore Sun* on July 11, 1925, Mencken described the carnival atmosphere that enveloped the Scopes trial and the anti-evolution bias of the jury and townspeople. Mencken considered these people on the fringe of American society and cast them as opponents of scientific progress. His sympathy is with Scopes and Darrow in particular and Darwinism in general. This article was typical of Mencken's style in that he infused it with his convictions, a practice now uncommon in journalism outside of editorials. The views expressed in the article, however, were shared by the majority of Americans at the time.

In the larger context, Bryan's testimony underscored the ferocity of fundamentalist opposition to Darwinism. But this ferocity appealed only to a small sect of Christians. By the 1920s most Americans has accepted Darwin's theories of evolution and natural selection. That decade anthropologists unearthed the oldest prehuman fossils in Africa, evidence that Darwin had been right in assigning humans and apes a common ancestor. By then geneticists understood the mechanism of heredity that had baffled Darwin and that explained how favorable traits passed from one generation to the next. By the 1920s Darwin had been dead forty years, but his ideas had entered the mainstream of science. Opposition to his ideas might be sporadic and intense, as it was in 1925, but by then it was a symbolic gesture rather than

Clarence Darrow during the Scopes "Monkey" Trial in which biology teacher John Scopes was prosecuted for teaching the theory of evolution. Dayton, Tennessee. July 1925. © BETTMANN/CORBIS. REPRODUCED BY PERMISSION.

substantive. The religious opposition that Darwin had feared had dwindled to a shrill minority.

Primary Source

"Mencken Likens Trial to a Religious Orgy, with Defendant a Beelzebub" [excerpt]

SYNOPSIS: In this excerpt, H.L. Mencken describes the Scopes trial in Dayton, Tennessee, in a way that makes his disagreement with the townspeople and their beliefs unmistakable. Such editorializing would be considered improper in a modern newspaper story. The trial was an early example of a "media event," covered by newspapers across the country.

To call a man a doubter in these parts is equal to accusing him of cannibalism. Even the infidel Scopes himself is not charged with any such infamy. What they say of him, at worst, is that he permit-

ted himself to be used as a cat's paw by scoundrels eager to destroy the anti-evolution law for their own dark and hellish ends. There is, it appears, a conspiracy of scientists afoot. Their purpose is to break down religion, propagate immorality, and so reduce mankind to the level of the brutes. They are the sworn and sinister agents of Beelzebub, who yearns to conquer the world, and has his eye especially upon Tennessee. Scopes is thus an agent of Beelzebub once removed, but that is as far as any fair man goes in condemning him. He is young and yet full of folly. When the secular arm has done execution upon him, the pastors will tackle him and he will be saved.

The selection of a jury to try him, which went on all yesterday afternoon in the atmosphere of a blast furnace, showed to what extreme lengths the salvation of the local primates has been pushed. It was obvious after a few rounds that the jury would be unanimously hot for Genesis. The most that Mr. Darrow could hope for was to sneak in a few men bold enough to declare publicly that they would have to hear the evidence against Scopes before condemning him. The slightest sign of anything further brought forth a peremptory challenge from the State. Once a man was challenged without examination for simply admitting that he did not belong formally to any church. Another time a panel man who confessed that he was prejudiced against evolution got a hearty round of applause from the crowd.

The whole process quickly took on an air of strange unreality, at least to a stranger from heathen parts. The desire of the judge to be fair to the defense, and even polite and helpful, was obvious enough—in fact, he more than once stretched the local rules of procedure in order to give Darrow a hand. But it was equally obvious that the whole thing was resolving itself into the trial of a man by his sworn enemies. A local pastor led off with a prayer calling on God to put down heresy; the judge himself charged the grand jury to protect the schools against subversive ideas. And when the candidates for the petit jury came up Darrow had to pass fundamentalist after fundamentalist into the box— some of them glaring at him as if they expected him to go off with a sulphurous bang every time he mopped his bald head.

In brief this is a strictly Christian community, and such is its notion of fairness, justice and due process of law. Try to picture a town made up wholly of Dr. Crabbes and Dr. Kellys, and you will have a reasonably accurate image of it. Its people are simply unable to imagine a man who rejects the literal authority of the Bible. The most they can conjure up, straining until they are red in the face, is a man who is in error about the meaning of this or that text. Thus one accused of heresy among them is like one accused of boiling his grandmother to make soap in Maryland. He must resign himself to being tried by a jury wholly innocent of any suspicion of the crime he is charged with and unanimously convinced that it is infamous. Such a jury, in the legal sense, may be fair. That is, it may be willing to hear the evidence against him before bumping him off. But it would certainly be spitting into the eye of reason to call it impartial.

The trial, indeed, takes on, for all its legal forms, something of the air of a religious orgy. The applause of the crowd I have already mentioned. Judge Raulston rapped it down and threatened to clear the room if it was repeated, but he was quite unable to

still its echoes under his very windows. The courthouse is surrounded by a large lawn, and it is peppered day and night with evangelists. One and all they are fundamentalists and their yells and bawlings fill the air with orthodoxy. I have listened to twenty of them and had private discourse with a dozen, and I have yet to find one who doubted so much as the typographical errors in Holy Writ. They dispute raucously and far into the night, but they begin and end on the common ground of complete faith. One of these holy men wears a sign on his back announcing that he is the Bible champion of the world. He told me today that he had studied the Bible four hours a day for thirty-three years, and that he had devised a plan of salvation that would save the worst sinner ever heard of, even a scientist, a theater actor or a pirate on the high seas, in forty days.

Further Resources

BOOKS

Chittick, Donald E. *The Controversy: The Roots of the Creation-Evolution Conflict.* Portland, Ore.: Multnomah Press, 1984.

De Camp, L. Sprague. *The Great Monkey Trial.* Garden City, N.Y.: Doubleday, 1968.

Gatewood, William B., ed. *Controversy in the Twenties: Fundamentalism, Modernism, and Evolution.* Nashville, Tenn.: Vanderbilt University Press, 1969.

Nelkin, Dorothy. *The Creation Controversy: Science or Scripture in the Schools.* New York: Norton, 1982.

Ruse, Michael. *Darwinism Defended.* Reading, Mass.: Addison-Wesley, 1982.

Szasz, Ferenc Morton. *The Divided Mind of Protestant America, 1880–1930.* University, Ala.: University of Alabama Press, 1982.

PERIODICALS

Callaghan, Catherine A. "Evolution and Creationist Arguments." *American Biology Teacher,* 1980, 422–427.

Grabiner, Judith V., and Peter D. Miller. "Effects of the Scopes Trial." *Science,* 1974, 832–837.

Popper, Karl. "Evolution." *New Scientist,* 1980, 611

WEBSITES

"The Scopes 'Monkey Trial'—July 10, 1925–July 25, 1925." American Studies at the University of Virginia. Available online at http://xroads.virginia.edu/~UG97/inherit/1925home.html; website home page http://xroads.virginia.edu (accessed February 10, 2003).

"Tennessee vs. John Scopes: The 'Monkey Trial.'" Famous Trials. Available online at http://www.law.umkc.edu/faculty/projects/ftrials/scopes/scopes.htm; website home page http://www.law.umkc.edu/faculty/projects/ftrials/ftrials.htm (accessed February 10, 2003).

Chromosomes and Genes

Evolution and Genetics

Nonfiction work

By: Thomas Hunt Morgan

Date: 1925

Source: Morgan, Thomas Hunt. *Evolution and Genetics.* Princeton, N.J.: Princeton University Press, 2d revised ed., 1925, 117–118. (First published as *A Critique of the Theory of Evolution.* Princeton, N.J.: Princeton University Press, 1916. Based on the Louis Clark Vanuxem Foundation lectures, delivered at Princeton University, February 24, March 1, 8, 15, 1916.)

About the Author: Thomas Hunt Morgan (1866–1945) was born in Kentucky and received a Ph.D. in embryology from Johns Hopkins University in 1891. In 1904 he became professor of experimental zoology at Columbia University, where his experiments with fruit flies became a cornerstone of genetics and won him the 1933 Nobel Prize in physiology or medicine. In 1928 he became professor of biology at the California Institute of Technology, where he remained until his death in 1945.

"The Gene as the Basis of Life"

Presentation

By: Hermann J. Muller

Date: 1929

Source: Muller, Hermann J. "The Gene as the Basis of Life." *Proceedings of the International Congress of Plant Sciences,* 1929, 1, 897–921. Reprinted in *Studies in Genetics: The Selected Papers of H.J. Muller.* Bloomington, Ind.: Indiana University Press, 1962, 190–191.

About the Author: Hermann Joseph Muller (1890–1966) was born in New York City. He joined Thomas Hunt Morgan's research team at Columbia University in 1911. In 1920 he became professor of biology at the Unviersity of Texas, where his work in mapping the genome of the fruit fly won him the 1946 Nobel Prize in physiology or medicine. In 1945 he joined the faculty at the University of Indiana, where he remained until retirement in 1964. He died two years later in Indianapolis, Indiana. ∎

Introduction

In 1866 the Austrian monk Gregor Mendel published a paper on pea hybridization that laid the foundation for the science of genetics. Two of his ideas were central to the work of Thomas Hunt Morgan and Hermann J. Muller. First, Mendel inferred from his experiments that pea plants and by extension all organisms are comprised of discrete units, later called genes, that determine traits in the organism. In the pea, genes code for stem length, pea color, smoothness of skin, and other traits. Second, Mendel believed that genes assorted independently. That

is, each gene is an independent unit—they are not linked, just as dimes and pennies are not linked, but can be sorted at random in one's pocket. Unfortunately, only the idea of particulate inheritance (that genes determined traits in an organism) was correct. The idea of independent assortment of genes was wrong and would confuse the study of genetics until Morgan and Muller solved the problem between 1909 and 1927.

In the meantime, biologists were preoccupied with understanding how parents pass their genes to offspring. By 1904, cytologists Walter Sutton and Theodore Boveri had an important clue. They realized that every cell contains a nucleus, and that every nucleus contains chromosomes, which they understood to be strands in each cell that were passed from generation to generation in a recombined and rearranged form. During meosis—cell division that produces gametes or sex cells—each gamete receives half the chromosomes of a somatic or non-sex cell. For example, every cell in the human male except sperm contains forty-six chromosomes, whereas each sperm contains twenty-three chromosomes. The union of sperm and egg, which as a gamete also has twenty-three chromosomes in the human, restores the full complement of forty-six chromosomes. But the relationship between chromosomes and genes was unclear. Were they equivalent? Did chromosomes contain genes, and if so, what was their arrangement on a chromosome?

Morgan and Muller answered these questions. To be fair, other scientists contributed to the solution, though Morgan was the leader of the research team at Columbia University, and Muller, for a time, a member of the group, which published a paper in 1927 that summarized the union between gene and chromosome theories that Morgan and his group had forged. In 1909 Morgan began breeding Drosophila, the fruit fly, and found that genes coding for eye color were on the sex chromosomes. Genes and chromosomes therefore were not equivalent. Chromosomes contained genes, but in what arrangement? Morgan realized that the farther apart two genes were on a chromosome, the more often they would be separated whenever chromosomes exchanged portions of themselves, a rare occurance, when they crossed over during meiosis. This reasoning enabled Morgan to establish that genes are in a line on a chromosome, just as mints are in a line in a roll of Certs, with each mint analogous to a gene and each roll analogous to a chromosome. In 1926 Muller began irradiating fruit flies with X rays to hasten crossing over, a technique that allowed him to map the fruit fly's genome. That is, he determined the linear arrangement of the genes on each of the four chromosomes of the fruit fly. Again, Muller was not alone is this work; other contributed to the mapping of the Drosophila genome.

Significance

By playing a principal role in unifying the gene and chromosome theories, Morgan and Muller helped found the modern science of genetics by 1927. They confirmed Mendel's idea of particulate inheritance and demonstrated that chromosomes, not genes, sort independently, an important correction of Mendel. They demonstrated that the arrangement of genes on a chromosome remains constant unless altered by crossing over. Equally important, their work in confirming particulate inheritance raised the question of the gene's chemistry, opening the way to the discovery of DNA.

In these excerpts, Morgan and Muller summarized the results of more than a decade of breeding experiments with the fruit fly: chromosomes sort independently and genes are in a line on chromosomes. Their language, particularly Muller's, is technical, and the statistics undergirding it and not included here are formidable. Their writing stems from a commitment to empiricism, the belief that reality can be pared down to what one can observe from experiments.

Primary Source

Evolution and Genetics [excerpt]

SYNOPSIS: In this book, Thomas Hunt Morgan unified Charles Darwin's theory of evolution by natural selection with Gregor Mendel's theory of the gene.

Crossing-Over

If the linkage were never broken we should expect to find that groups of characters would be inherited together. There would be as many such groups of characters as there are pairs of chromosomes. To a certain extent this is true, but the study of the inheritance of two or more characters in the same linkage group has revealed a further fact of great interest, namely, that there takes place an interchange at times between the two members of the same linkage group, and, it may be added, only between members of the same linkage group and never between different linkage groups. This interchange gives rise to a new phenomenon in inheritance that is called crossing-over. . . .

From the genetic evidence for crossing-over it is possible to determine the relative location of the genes in the chromosomes. The method can not be given here in detail but the general point of view may be stated. If the genes lie along the length of the chromosomes and if crossing-over is as likely to occur at one level as at another, then, the nearer together two genes lie the less likely is a break between them, or conversely the further apart in the

Thomas Hunt Morgan, Nobel Prize winner and one of the founders of the modern science of genetics. © BETTMANN/CORBIS. REPRODUCED BY PERMISSION.

chromosome they lie the more likely is crossing-over to take place. In other words the percentage of crossovers is an index of the distance apart of the genes. On this basis the location of the genes . . . has been determined. . . . One is enabled to calculate what the inheritance of any gene will be with respect to any other gene in its group provided its relation to two other genes is known.

The theory of crossing-over enables the geneticist to predict the results of a given experiment with the same precision that Mendel's two laws allow prediction for a single pair of characters in the same chromosome pair, or for two or more pairs of characters in different chromosome pairs.

Primary Source

"The Gene as the Basis of Life" [excerpt]

SYNOPSIS: Hermann J. Muller presented this paper at the International Congress of Plant Sciences in 1929. In it he defines a gene as that portion of a chromosome that tells a cell what chemical to manufacture, where to transport it, and what to do with it once it has reached its destination.

The Interrelations of Genes in the Chromosome

Although we may speak of genes as units, either in the sense of Mendelian differentiators or in the sense of independently propagable elements, it must be recognized that they may be only *potential* units, and that in the chromosome they may conceivably exist not as separate particles, or even as chemically disunited substances, but in the form of a linearly continuous structure. True, there is a tendency for a given differential to hold together as a unit when it crosses over against its allelomorph in the heterozygous, but we must also remember that in cases of mutation of an entire region, so-called "deficiency," this region, comprising numerous ordinary separable loci, now holds together as a unit too, when crossing over occurs in the heterozygote. In the case of the unequal crossing over of bar eye, however, we can determine that the bar gene holds together as a unit even in the homozygous condition, for the askew crossing over here occurs just to the right or left of it, but never within it. Furthermore, in cases of chromosome breakage, fusion, or inversion of a region, such as is sometimes found in *Drosophila,* if the genetic material in the chromosome did not have some kind of segmental structure, then the rearrangement of its parts, at the point of breakage or reunion, should always be equivalent, in its effects, to what we now call a "gene mutation"; a number of cases are known in which no such effect has been observed, although in others "mutation" has apparently accompanied the rearrangement. More observations will be necessary on this point. Further important observations of Sturtevant on bar eye do suggest that the spatial relations of the genes with their neighbors are of genetic consequence, as well as their internal arrangements. In finding that two bar genes in contiguity in the same chromosome exert more effect than two lying in homologous chromosomes, he discovered that the local pattern of the genes is a fact which may itself become, in effect, genic in its significance. Nevertheless, this does not make improbable a segmental structure of the gene material.

If we accept the inferences, later to be drawn, that the self-propagable material everywhere is fundamentally alike, and that the smallest independently reproducing portion of it is exceedingly minute, then the chromosome must have some kind of linearly repetitive structure. It also would follow from the "gene-element" interpretation of eversporting genes, presently to be discussed, that the gene material at times at least may be non-linearly repetitive in its formation. Finally, the regularity of the mathe-

matical relations observed in linear linkage, with its corollary, interference, proves that the disunion of parts of the chromatin structure from each other (in crossing over) is determined by geometrical and physical factors and not by chemical bonds or affinities of a sort that would differ from point to point according to the atomic configurations within the gene material. This fact too, then, connotes a chain-like, segmental arrangement of those atomic connections that must exist within the "chromatin" thread, allowing of breaks, between these segments, which are governed by "mechanical" circumstances.

Admitting as yet, however, the provisional nature of our conclusions regarding genic discontinuity, it is still quite legitimate to speak of the number or size of "genes," as suggested in the beginning, in the sense of the number or size of linearly connected regions so taken that in them non-overlapping genetic differences, separable by crossing over, can occur, and these differentiable parts fit our conception of genes in being concerned in the propagation of their own specific structure largely independently of what other kinds of genetic material they may happen to be associated with.

Further Resources

BOOKS

Allen, Garland. *Thomas Hunt Morgan: The Man and His Science.* Princeton, N.J.: Princeton University Press, 1978.

Carlson, Elof Axel. *Genes, Radiation, and Society: The Life and Work of H.J. Muller.* Ithaca, N.Y.: Cornell University Press, 1981.

Mayr, Ernest. *The Growth of Biological Thought: Diversity, Evolution, and Inheritance.* Cambridge, Mass.: Belknap Press of Harvard University Press, 1982.

PERIODICALS

Allen, Garland. "Thomas Hunt Morgan and the Problem of Natural Selection." *Journal of the History of Biology,* 1968, 113–139.

Gilbert, Scott F. "The Embryological Origins of the Gene Theory." *Journal of the History of Biology,* 1978, 307–351.

Mountain, Elizabeth Morgan. "The Place of Thomas Hunt Morgan in American Biology." *American Zoologist,* 1983, 825–876.

Roll-Hansen, Nils. "Drosophila Genetics: A Reductionist Research Program." *Journal of the History of Biology,* 1978, 159–210.

Sturtevant, Alfred H. "The Early Mendelians." *Proceedings of the American Philosophical Society,* 1965, 199–204.

WEBSITES

"Hermann Joseph Muller—Biography." Available online at http://www.nobel.se/medicine/laureates/1946/muller-bio .html; website home page http://www.nobel.se (accessed January 31, 2003).

"Thomas Hunt Morgan—Biography." Available online at http://www.nobel.se/medicine/laureates/1933/morgan-bio .html; website home page http://www.nobel.se (accessed January 31, 2003).

Winged Defense

Nonfiction work

By: William Mitchell

Date: 1925

Source: Mitchell, William. *Winged Defense: The Development and Possibilities of Modern Air Power—Economic and Military.* New York: G.P. Putnam's Sons, 1925, ix–x, 3.

About the Author: William "Billy" Mitchell (1879–1936) served in the U.S. infantry during the Spanish-American War (1898) and in 1909 graduated from the U.S. Army Staff College at Fort Leavenworth, Kansas. During World War I, he served as aviation officer of the American Expeditionary Force, and was promoted to brigadier general. After the war, he was appointed assistant chief of the air service. In 1925 the Army court-martialed him for insubordination because he blamed the Navy's loss of a dirigible on "criminal negligence." Mitchell resigned the next year and died ten years later. ∎

William "Billy" Mitchell, proponent of a strong military and commercial air power. October 6, 1925. **THE LIBRARY OF CONGRESS.**

Introduction

World War I (1914–1918) shaped Billy Mitchell's understanding of the airplane's military potential. When the war began in 1914, the airplane was a technology little more than a decade old, and military observers would have been justified in predicting a minor role for it. Although European armies had used the airplane in small wars in Libya and the Balkans, senior generals had developed their strategies for a possible world war by 1905 and could hardly have foreseen its use at that time. The first offensives of World War I relied on infantry and artillery, not the airplane. Traditionalists saw greater potential in the dirigible, an airship filled with a gas (hydrogen or helium) that is lighter than the Earth's atmosphere. At that time, dirigibles had greater range, speed, and load-carrying capacity than airplanes. By January 1915, the German army was using dirigibles to carry 5,000 pounds of bombs, a larger load than any plane could then carry.

Both the Allies and Central Powers first used the airplane in reconnaissance, by late 1914 equipping it with a camera to photograph the deployment of enemy forces. Within weeks of the opening campaign, observers in two-seated planes had mounted machine guns on the fuselage. But these soon gave way to machine guns mounted on the front of the plane. These guns had an interrupter gear, which synchronized the firing of the gun with the pro-

peller's rotation. Planes could now fire on one another and strafe ground troops. The British army developed a mechanism to release bombs, and by 1918 it had a bomber that could carry more than three thousand pounds of bombs. By then the British had developed a prototype of the aircraft carrier, extending the airplane's role to include naval combat. The airplane had become so important that in 1918, the war's last year, the British manufactured 25,685 military planes, the French 24,652, and the Germans 17,000.

In February 1917, two months before the United States entered the war, the Army dispatched Billy Mitchell to Europe as an observer, and in June General John Pershing appointed him aviation officer of the American Expeditionary Force. Mitchell had little to work with at first. In 1917 the United States had only fifty-five military planes, almost all too obsolete for combat. Mitchell recognized the superiority of European aircraft and relied on the French for planes. Mitchell never had more than 650 planes under his command, though in the Battle of St. Mihiel he combined with the British and French to amass a force of 1,481 planes, not one built in the United States, in the war's largest air battle. The fleet overwhelmed the German force of 283 planes, and Pershing, pleased with the victory, promoted Mitchell to brigadier general.

American Air Force BT-7s on parade at Randolph Field, Texas. **HULTON/ARCHIVE. REPRODUCED BY PERMISSION.**

Significance

World War I elevated Billy Mitchell to the leading authority on airpower in the United States. He understood that the airplane had performed vital roles during the war: strategic bombing, interdiction (the cutting of enemy supply lines), close air support, reconnaissance (information gathering), and air defense. He emerged from the war with boundless enthusiasm for the airplane's potential and during the 1920s attempted to convince military and civilian leaders that the airplane had become the key to victory, replacing the army and navy in importance. So sure was he of the airplane's superiority that he urged Congress to create a separate air force.

Mitchell's views found little support during the 1920s. Generals and admirals resented his claim that airpower had supplanted traditional land and naval forces. Perhaps more important, the combination of isolationism and Republican fiscal conservatism meant that the United States would not spend money on military technology during the 1920s.

It was not until the 1930s that Mitchell's ideas began to win converts. During that decade, the German military created an independent air force, the Luftwaffe, and both the United States and Japan built aircraft carriers, guaranteeing that the airplane would be crucial in any war in the Pacific. Congress stopped short, however, of creating a separate air force, as U.S. commanders insisted that the army and navy maintain their own air wings. Only after World War II (1939–1945) would Congress fulfill Mitchell's goal of creating a separate U.S. Air Force.

Primary Source

Winged Defense [excerpt]

> **SYNOPSIS:** In this excerpt, Billy Mitchell asserts that the airplane has created a new age in commerce and war. As brigadier general, his real interest was in the airplane's military potential. He finds in America's "characteristics and temperament" the makings of a great air power. The strength of this passage does not lie in its innovative strategies but in Mitchell's enthusiasm for the airplane despite his lack of concrete ideas.

Forward

. . . As transportation is the essence of civilization, aviation furnishes the quickest and most expeditious means of communication that the world has ever known. Heretofore, we have been confined to either the earth or the water as the medium of transportation. Now, we can utilize the air which covers both the earth and the water, and the north and south poles, as the medium through which to travel.

With us air people, the future of our nation is indissolubly bound up in the development of air power. Not only will it insure peace and contentment throughout the nation because, in case of national emergency, air power, properly developed, can hold off any hostile air force which may seek to fly over and attack our country, but it can also hold off any hostile shipping which seeks to cross the oceans and menace our shores. At the same time, our national air power can be used in time of peace for some useful purpose. In this it differs very greatly from the old standing armies and navies which, in time of peace, have to be kept up, trained and administered for war only and are therefore a source of expenditure from which little return is forthcoming until an emergency arises.

The time has come when aviation must be developed for aviation's sake and not as an auxiliary to other existing branches. Unless the progressive elements that enter into our makeup are availed of, we will fall behind in the world's development.

Air power has rudely upset the traditions of the older services. It has been with the greatest difficulty that this new and dominating element has gone forward in the way it has. In the future, no nation can call itself great unless its air power is properly organized and provided for, because air power, both from a military and an economic standpoint, will not only dominate the land but the sea as well. Air power in the future will be a determining factor in international competitions, both military and civil. American characteristics and temperament are particularly suitable to its development. . . .

The Aeronautical Era

The world stands on the threshold of the "aeronautical era." During this epoch the destinies of all people will be controlled through the air.

Our ancestors passed through the "continental era" when they consolidated their power on land and developed their means of communication and intercourse over the land or close to it on the seacoast.

Then came the "era of the great navigators," and the competition for the great sea lanes of power, commerce, and communication, which were hitched up and harnessed to the land powers created in the continental era. Now the competition will be for the possession of the unhampered right to traverse and control the most vast, the most important, and the farthest reaching element of the earth, the air, the atmosphere that surrounds us all, that we breathe, live by, and which permeates everything.

Air power has come to stay.

Further Resources

BOOKS

Brown, David, Christopher Shores, and Kenneth Macksey. *The Guinness History of Air Warfare.* Enfield, England: Guinness Superlatives, 1976.

Burlingame, Roger. *General Billy Mitchell, Champion of Air Defense.* Westport, Conn.: Greenwood Press, 1952.

Doughty, Robert A., et al. *Warfare in the Western World: Military Operations Since 1871.* Lexington, Mass.: Heath, 1996.

Hurley, Alfred F. *Billy Mitchell: Crusader for Air Power.* New York: F. Watts, 1964.

Levine, Isaac D. *Mitchell: Pioneer of Air Power.* New York: Arno, 1943.

PERIODICALS

Schwarz, Frederic D. "1925."*American Heritage,* October 2000, 95–98.

WEBSITES

"General Billy Mitchell, Milwaukee Native and Air Force Pioneer." University of Wisconsin—Milwaukee Archives. Available online at http://www.uwm.edu/Dept/Library/arch /mitchell/exhibit.htm; website home page http://www.uwm .edu/Library/arch/index.html (accessed January 30, 2003).

"William 'Billy' Mitchell's Air Power." College of Aerospace Doctrine, Research and Education. Available online at http:// www.cadre.maxwell.af.mil/ar/MITCHELL/Mitchell.htm; website home page http://www.cadre.maxwell.af.mil/ (accessed January 30, 2003).

AUDIO AND VISUAL MEDIA

Billy Mitchell. Coronet Film and Video, 1963.

Journal Entry, May 5, 1926
Personal journal

By: Robert H. Goddard

Date: May 5, 1926

Source: Goddard, Robert H. Journal entry, May 5, 1926. In *The Papers of Robert H. Goddard, Volume II: 1925–1937.* Esther C. Goddard and Edward G. Pendray, eds. New York: McGraw-Hill, 1970, 588–589.

About the Author: Robert Hutchins Goddard (1882–1945) was born in Worcester, Massachusetts, and received a Ph.D. in physics from Clark University in 1911. He returned to Clark University as assistant professor of physics, and in 1919 he was promoted to full professor. He began experimenting with liquid-fuel rockets in the 1910s and during World War I developed a prototype of the bazooka. He launched the first liquid-fuel rocket in 1926. In recognition of his achievements, the Goddard Space Flight Center in Maryland was named in his honor in 1961. ∎

Introduction

The origins of rocketry lay in China. In 1232, Chinese soldiers repelled a Mongol attack by firing at them what some scholars believe were the first rockets. By then the Chinese may have invented gunpowder, which would likely have propelled these rockets. Europeans learned of the rocket from the Mongols, who used it in the Battle of Legnica in Poland in 1241, and Arabs used rockets in Spain in 1249.

By the fourteenth century, Italians were using rockets in their wars. In 1668, a German colonel built what was then the largest rocket in Europe; it was 132 pounds, with a sixteen-pound gunpowder charge. In the eighteenth century, an Indian prince developed a rocket with a range of three-quarters of a mile, and by the end of the century Indian troops were using rockets against British forces. The British in turn used rockets against the French in 1806, and in the War of 1812 both American and British forces enhanced firepower with massive rocket bombardments. By 1815, British experimenter William Congreve built a rocket with a two-mile range. By the middle of the century, British engineer William Hale mounted curved vanes on his rockets, giving them a spin and thus a straight trajectory, just as a football thrown with a spiral follows a straight path. The U.S. Army used rockets in both the Mexican War (1846–1848) and the Civil War (1861–1865).

During World War I (1914–1918), American inventors concentrated on improving the rocket. In 1917, New York inventor Elmer Sperry built a rocket with a gyroscope to give it greater precision. The U.S. Army Signal Corps established a program in 1918 to build rockets modeled after Sperry's invention.

These early rockets relied on solid-fuel propulsion. No one had succeeded in tapping the potential for greater thrust that liquid fuel promised. Robert Goddard was the first to fulfill this promise and the first to understand that thrust and consequent propulsion can take place in a vacuum, needing no air to push against. In 1926 he launched a rocket with a mixture of liquid oxygen and gasoline, the world's first liquid-propelled rocket.

Significance

The test launch of the liquid-propelled rocket on March 16, 1926, which Goddard described in his journal, also launched the modern era of rocketry. In 1931 the German Rocket Society built a liquid-propelled rocket that reached a height of one mile, and a member of the society, physicist Wernher von Braun, developed the V-2 rocket during World War II (1939–1945). Goddard was thus the first to see beyond the military potential of rockets and to glimpse the possibility of space travel. Goddard's rocket made possible supersonic aircraft, intercontinental ballistic missiles, and high-altitude research rockets, and laid a foundation for space travel, the moon landings, and the unmanned probes of our solar system.

Goddard was unique in the 1920s in that he worked without the benefit of a large research team and generous funding. Most other leading scientists of the 1920s headed research laboratories that lived off the largess of government. Although Goddard benefited from occasional grants from the Smithsonian Institution, his resources were so sparse that he had to use his aunt's farm as a launchpad in 1926.

Despite these limitations, Goddard was a pioneer. In 1935 he launched the first rocket that exceeded the speed of sound and was the first to use rockets with stages to gain high altitude. He also developed the first pumps for rocket fuel and the first self-cooling rocket motors. After his death, Congress bought the rights to these and other patents for one million dollars. The space age would have been unimaginable without the work of Robert Goddard.

Primary Source

Journal Entry, May 5, 1926 [excerpt]

SYNOPSIS: In this entry in his personal journal, Robert Goddard describes the first launch of a liquid-fuel rocket in 1926. He was then working on a shoestring budget, and this passage makes clear his concern about the cost of his research. He proposed the possibility of additional launchings but discounted them as a waste of money.

Test of March 16, 1926

Although the problem of satisfactory operation was solved, it was not possible to have a flight unless a larger model were made, or a different principle, permitting greater lightness, were employed. The construction of a larger model was not undertaken because of expense, and another plan of construction was used, which involved back pressure in the supply tanks, and eliminated the pumps, engines, and most of the moving parts, but did not permit such accurate control of the combustion, or the use of the lightest form of supply tanks, as did the previous model. A test of January 20, in the testing frame above mentioned, indicated a pull throughout the test of more than 9 lb, and a similar model, of as light construction as possible, was accordingly made. The lack of control of combustion manifested itself in the frequent burning out of the nozzles.

In a test made March 16, out of doors, with a model of this lighter type, weighting 5 ¾ lb empty and 10 ¼ lb loaded with liquids, the lower part of the nozzle burned through and dropped off, leaving, however, the upper part intact. After about 20 sec the rocket rose without perceptible jar, with no smoke and with no apparent increase in the rather small flame, increased rapidly in speed, and after describing a semicircle, landed 184 ft from the starting point—the curved path being due to the fact that the nozzle had burned through unevenly, and one side was longer than the other. The average speed, from the time of the flight measured by a stopwatch, was 60 miles per hour. This test was very significant, as it was the first time that a rocket operated by liquid propellants traveled under its own power.

Several trials have since been made, using most of the original rocket, with less weight of propelling liquids and with other minor changes, but although it has left the frame and traveled as much as 50 ft away, the handicap of weight has left it in its frame for a half minute or more before lifting has begun.

Remarks

To me, personally, these tests, taken together, prove conclusively the practicality of the liquid-propelled rocket, which means that the multiple-charge idea, or the feeding into a combustion chamber of successive portions of propellant material from extremely light containers or tanks, is realizable.

In case the person or organization which is willing to finance the development of a high-altitude rocket for serious work is not satisfied with the flight of March 16, it will be necessary to make the rocket on a larger scale, in order to increase the lift in proportion to the weight. I believe that such a larger model can be made for $500. Incidentally, however, some of the materials would require from three to five weeks for delivery.

On the other hand, I believe that to make this additional trial flight would be a waste of time and money, for several reasons. First, all the principles involved in the construction of a rocket to beat the

Robert H. Goddard, at the first successful flight of his liquid-propellant rocket. March 16, 1926. **THE LIBRARY OF CONGRESS.**

altitude records have been worked out satisfactorily. Further, the latest model, although useful, no doubt, for some work, and representing the acme of simplicity, makes accurate control of combustion a difficult matter, and does not permit the use of extremely light fuel tanks, which do not have to withstand pressure. Hence I should not consider using the principle of the latest model in a rocket intended for reaching great heights, and I cannot predict beforehand just what can be accomplished by its use.

Further Resources

BOOKS

Dewey, Anne Perkins. *Robert Goddard: Space Pioneer.* Boston: Little, Brown, 1962.

Emme, Eugene Morlock. *Robert Goddard, American Rocket Pioneer.* Greenbelt, Md.: Goddard Space Flight Center, 1968.

Lehman, Milton. *This High Man: The Life of Robert H. Goddard.* New York: Farrar, Straus, 1963.

Streissguth, Thomas. *Rocket Man: The Story of Robert Goddard.* Minneapolis: Carolrhoda Books, 1995.

PERIODICALS

Crouch, Tom D. "Reaching Toward Space." *Smithsonian,* February 2001, 38–41.

Kluger, Jeffrey. "Robert Goddard." *Time,* March 29, 1999, 99–102.

Wicks, Frank. "Trailblazer into Space." *Mechanical Engineering,* October 2000, 70–75.

WEBSITES

"Robert Goddard and His Rockets." NASA. Available online at http://www-istp.gsfc.nasa.gov/stargaze/Sgoddard.htm; website home page http://www.nasa.gov (accessed January 31).

AUDIO AND VISUAL MEDIA

Father of the Space Age. Hearst Metrotone News, 1976, VHS.

The Rocket Man: Robert Goddard and the Adventure of Space Exploration. Goldhil Home Media International, 1994, VHS.

"X-Rays as a Branch of Optics"

Lecture

By: Arthur Holly Compton

Date: December 12, 1927

Source: Compton, Arthur H. "X-Rays as a Branch of Optics." Lecture presented at Nobel Prize for Physics awards ceremony, December 12, 1927. Reproduced in "Arthur H. Compton—Nobel Lecture." Available online at http://www.nobel.se/physics/laureates/1927/compton-lecture.html; website home page: http://www.nobel.se (accessed May 5, 2003).

About the Author: Arthur Holly Compton (1892–1962) was born in Wooster, Ohio, and received his Ph.D. in 1916 from Princeton University. He taught at the University of Minnesota before joining the U.S. Army Signal Corps during World War I (1914–1918). After the war, he taught at Washington University in St. Louis until 1923, when he became professor of physics at the University of Chicago. In 1927, he shared the Nobel Prize in physics for his discovery of the Compton effect. During World War II (1939–1945), he helped develop the atomic bomb. In 1945, he returned to Washington University, where he remained until 1961. He died the next year. ■

Introduction

The classical physics that Isaac Newton founded in the seventeenth century, and that physicists elaborated during the eighteenth and nineteenth centuries, gave way to a revolution during the early twentieth century. In one phase of this revolution, physicists came to understand energy—and, by extension, all radiation—not as a continuum (the nineteenth-century view) but as comprised of discrete units, or quanta.

This conceptual change began in 1900, when German physicist Max Planck heated an object that emitted radiation of all wavelengths. He was able to graph the relationship between temperature and wavelength only by

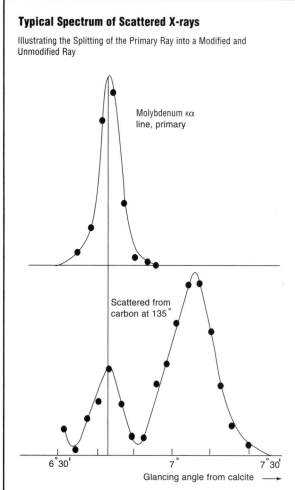

Typical Spectrum of Scattered X-rays

Illustrating the Splitting of the Primary Ray into a Modified and Unmodified Ray

Molybdenum κα line, primary

Scattered from carbon at 135°

6° 30'   7°   7° 30'

Glancing angle from calcite ⟶

SOURCE: Figure 8 from Compton, Arthur H. *X-rays as a branch of optics.* Lecture presented at Nobel Prize for Physics awards ceremony, December 12, 1927. Reproduced in "Arthur H. Compton—Nobel Lecture." Available online at http://www.nobel.se/physics/laureates/1927/compton-lecture.html; Website home page: http://www.nobel.se (accessed May 30, 2002).

supposing that the object had emitted radiation in tiny packets, which he called quanta.

In 1905, Albert Einstein extended Planck's finding to light. In what he called the photoelectric effect, Einstein observed that light always knocked electrons free from a metal with an energy that was some multiple of a quantum. Because the electrons had received that energy from light, it too must be comprised of quanta. At one level, Einstein's conclusion should have surprised no one. What Planck had found true for radiation in general, Einstein had found true for light, that small bandwidth of radiation that humans can see. But at another level the photoelectric effect astonished physicists, for it contradicted the tenet that light was a wave, a cornerstone of physics since the nineteenth century.

Because the quantum undermined the classical understanding of energy, and of light in particular, physicists wanted additional evidence of it.

Significance

Arthur Compton provided this evidence in 1923. By colliding X rays with electrons, Compton was able to measure the energy that a ray transmitted to an electron, just as the cue ball imparts energy to the eight ball upon striking it in a game of pool. He was also able to measure the energy that an electron radiated back to a ray in recoiling from the collision. In both cases, the energy was some multiple of a quantum, evidence that quanta really existed and were not merely a mathematical contrivance. In his Nobel Address of 1927, Compton called these quanta "photons," the name physicists give light quanta.

As important as it was, Compton's work demonstrated that even the best American science of the 1920s was often derivative. Compton had not added a new concept to physics but had confirmed the findings of Planck and Einstein. The flow of ideas had been from Europe to the United States, with an American scientist in the role of verifier rather than originator.

The power of American physics, Compton's work showed, lay in precision of measurement rather than in novelty of idea. Compton, like other American physicists of the 1920s, was an experimenter, not a theoretician. In this sense American physics was subordinate to European physics, but this does not mean it was inferior. Theory is empty without verification. The quantum needed the experimental confirmation of Compton in order for physicists to accept it as more than a heuristic device.

Equally important, Compton's work illustrated the coziness between physics and government. He had served the Army during both world wars and depended on federal grants to fund his laboratory. By the 1920s, American physics had become too costly for someone to pursue without a largess from government. Then, as now, government expected concrete results from its investment, a circumstance that may partly explain why American physicists concentrated more on applied than theoretical work.

Primary Source

"X-Rays as a Branch of Optics" [excerpt]

> **SYNOPSIS:** In this excerpt from his 1927 Nobel Address, Compton outlines the experiments that led him to conclude that X rays are comprised of quanta, which he called photons. Because he was a cautious experimenter, Compton did not extend the implications of his experiments beyond X rays. Consequently, he did not mention either Max Planck or Albert Einstein, though their work is the silent underpinning of his address.

Dr. Arthur H. Compton, Nobel Prize winner and discoverer of the particle nature of radiation, looking at the electric motor he created as an undergraduate. **HULTON/ARCHIVE. REPRODUCED BY PERMISSION.**

A series of experiments performed during the last few years has shown that secondary X-rays are of greater wavelength than the primary rays which produce them. This work is too well-known to require description. On the other hand, careful experiments to find a similar increase in wavelength in light diffusely scattered by a turbid medium have failed to show any effect. An examination of the spectrum of the secondary X-rays shows that the primary beam has been split into two parts, as shown in [illustration, "Typical Spectrum of Scattered X-rays], one of the same wavelength and the other of increased wavelength. When different primary wavelengths are used, we find always the same difference in wavelength between these two components; but the relative intensity of the two components changes. For the longer wavelengths the unmodified ray has the greater energy, while for the shorter wavelengths the modified ray is predominant. In fact when hard γ-rays are employed, it is not possible to find any radiation of the original wavelength.

Thus in the wavelength of secondary radiation we have a gradually increasing departure from the classical electron theory of scattering as we go from the optical region to the region of X-rays and γ-rays.

The question arises, are these secondary X-rays of increased wavelength to be classed as scattered X-rays or as fluorescent? An important fact bearing on this point is the intensity of the secondary rays. From the theories of Thomson, Debye, and others it is possible to calculate the absolute intensity of the scattered rays. It is found that this calculated intensity agrees very nearly with the total intensity of the modified and unmodified rays, but that in many cases the observed intensity of the unmodified ray taken alone is very small compared with the calculated intensity. If the electron theory of the intensity of scattering is even approximately correct, we must thus include the modified with the unmodified rays as scattered rays.

Information regarding the origin of these secondary rays is also given by their state of polarization. We have called attention to the fact that the electron theory demands that the X-rays scattered at 90 degrees should be completely plane polarized. If the rays of increased wavelength are fluorescent, however, we should not expect them to be strongly polarized. You will remember the experiments performed by Barkla some twenty years ago in which he observed strong polarization in X-rays scattered at right angles. It was this experiment which gave us our first strong evidence of the similar character of X-rays and light. But in this work the polarization was far from complete. In fact the intensity of the secondary rays at 90 degrees dropped only to one third its maximum value, where as for complete polarization it should have fallen to zero.

The fact that no such unpolarized rays exist was established by repeating Barkla's experiment with scattering blocks of different sizes. When very small blocks were used, we found that the polarization was nearly complete. The lack of complete polarization in Barkla's experiments was due chiefly to the multiple scattering of the X-rays in the large blocks that he used to scatter the X-rays. It would seem that the only explanation of the complete polarization of the secondary rays is that they consist wholly of scattered rays.

According to the classical theory, an electromagnetic wave is scattered when it sets the electrons which it traverses into forced oscillations, and these oscillating electrons reradiate the energy which they receive. In order to account for the change in wavelength of the scattered rays, however, we have had to adopt a wholly different picture of the scattering process. . . . Here we do not think of the X-rays as waves but as light corpuscles, quanta, or, as we may call them, photons.

Further Resources

BOOKS

Cline, Barbara Lovett. *The Questioners: Physicists and the Quantum Theory.* New York: Crowell, 1965.

Heathcote, Neils H. de V. *Nobel Prize Winners in Physics, 1901–1950.* New York: Shuman, 1953.

Johnson, Marjorie. ed. *The Cosmos of Arthur Holly Compton.* New York: Knopf, 1967.

Kevles, Daniel J. *The Physicists: The History of a Scientific Community in Modern America.* New York: Knopf, 1978.

Mackinnon, Edward M. *Scientific Explanation and Atomic Physics.* Chicago: University of Chicago Press, 1982.

Miller, Arthur I. *Imagery in Scientific Thought: Creating 20th Century Physics.* Cambridge: Birkhauser, 1984.

Stuewer, Roger H. *The Compton Effect: Turning Point in Physics.* New York: Science History, 1975.

PERIODICALS

Agassi, Joseph. "The Structure of the Quantum Revolution." *Philosophy of the Social Sciences,* 1983: 367–381.

Wheaton, Bruce R. "Impulse X-Rays and Radiant Intensity: The Double Edge of Analogy." *Historical Studies in the Physical Sciences,* 1981: 367–390.

WEBSITES

American Institute of Physics. *Arthur Holly Compton, 1892–1962.* Available online at http://www.aip.org/history/gap/Compton/Compton.html; website home page: http://www.aip.org (accessed May 30, 2002).

We

Autobiography

By: Charles A. Lindbergh

Date: 1927

Source: Lindbergh, Charles A. *We.* New York: G.P. Putnam's Sons, 1927, 224–226.

About the Author: Charles Augustus Lindbergh (1902–1974) was born in in Detroit, Michigan. He enrolled in an Army flying school in Texas in 1924, becoming an airmail pilot in 1926. That year he received funding to compete for the $25,000 prize for the first nonstop flight between New York City and Paris. His flight the next year brought him world celebrity. Afterwards, Lindbergh flew across the United States, lecturing and making personal appearance to promote air travel. Thereafter he served as consultant to Ford Motor Company, United Aircraft Corporation, Pan American World Airway, and the U.S. Department of Defense. He died in 1974 in Hawaii. ∎

Crowds gather as Charles Lindbergh arrives in Paris, France, at the Le Bourget Aerodrome. May 31, 1927. © **BETTMANN/CORBIS. REPRODUCED BY PERMISSION.**

Introduction

Flight has intrigued humans since antiquity, but only in the nineteenth century did British experimenter George Cayley derive the scientific principles of flight. In the 1890s Otto Lilienthal, a German engineer, built the first glider.

By then American innovators were committed to surpassing their European rivals. In 1891, Samuel P. Langley, director of the Smithsonian Institution, believed that "Mechanical flight is possible with engines we now possess." As early as 1887 he had experimented with model airplanes weighing thirty pounds. In 1903, he built an airplane, the Aerodrome, with a five-cylinder engine, and twice pilot Charles M. Manley attempted but failed to fly it. Nine days after the second failure, Wilbur and Orville Wright flew their plane at Kitty Hawk, North Carolina.

But flight was far from routine and safe. In 1908 Thomas Selfridge became the first American to die in an air accident when he crashed while flying with Orville Wright. Alexander Graham Bell, who had formed the Aerial Experiment Association in 1907, considered the Wrights' plane dangerous because it required high speed to take off and remain aloft. Crashes made headlines, none more spectacular than the 1925 wreck of the Navy dirigible *Shenandoah,* which killed fourteen of the forty-

three-man crew. Army brigadier general Billy Mitchell, a World War I hero and perhaps the nation's leading advocate for the airplane, blamed the crash on "criminal negligence." If the military was incompetent in aviation, who could the public trust? The uproar following Mitchell's statement led the Army to court-martial him for insubordination and suspend him from duty for five years. Rather than accept the verdict, Mitchell resigned the next year. The airplane had lost its most colorful exponent. Who would recapture the élan of aviation for the American public?

Charles Lindbergh was the answer. The airmail pilot wanted the $25,000 Orteig prize for the first nonstop flight from New York City to Paris. Already five Navy aviators had hopped across the Atlantic, flying from Newfoundland to the Azores to Portugal to England. Lindbergh convinced a group of St. Louis businessmen to fund construction of a $10,000 Curtis-Wright plane with a nine-cylinder, air-cooled engine. It had two ignition systems, a double carburetor, and no radiator. Grateful to his benefactors, Lindbergh named the plane *The Spirit of St. Louis.* He prepared for the flight across the Atlantic by depriving himself of sleep for long periods. Despite the rigors of this training, Lindbergh fell asleep several times during his thirty-three-hour flight, always awakening before crashing into the ocean. His youth and stamina saved

Charles A. Lindbergh, first aviator to fly solo across the Atlantic Ocean. THE LIBRARY OF CONGRESS

him, and he landed in Paris on May 21, 1927, to a jubilant reception.

Significance

As this excerpt from his autobiography attests, Lindbergh's flight captured the imagination of the world and made him an instant celebrity. But the flight was more than a personal achievement. Lindbergh had restored confidence in aviation, erasing the doubts that had lingered after the *Shenandoah* debacle and Mitchell's humiliation. The transatlantic flight convinced Americans in a tangible way, as no amount of rhetoric could have done, that air travel over long distances was safe.

Although the press played up Lindbergh's flight as a solo affair, it was really a corporate venture. He had needed money from prominent businessmen to cross the Atlantic, an illustration of how money had come to dominate science and technology by the 1920s. The era of big science and technology in the form of large research laboratories had arrived, and these labs needed capital financing to conduct their research as much as Lindbergh did to finance his flight. With only the occasional exception, the days of the lone scientist or inventor were over.

Equally important, Lindbergh's flight underscored the power of technology to shrink distance and time. The

car had begun this compression of distance and time. The airplane accelerated it. The oceanliner needed weeks to cross the Atlantic. Lindbergh had accomplished the feat in little more than a day.

Primary Source

We [excerpt]

> **SYNOPSIS:** In this excerpt Charles Lindbergh described the tumultuous reception he received upon landing *The Spirit of St. Louis* in Paris. The detail with which he describes the mania that greeted his landing makes it evident that he enjoyed his new-found celebrity status. Literally overnight, "Lucky Lindy," as the press dubbed him, became a superstar on a par with contemporary entertainers and athletes.

I first saw the lights of Paris a little before ten P.M., or five P.M. New York time, and a few minutes later I was circling the Eiffel Tower at an altitude of about four thousand feet.

The lights of Le Bourget were plainly visible, but appeared to be very close to Paris. I had understood that the field was farther from the city, so continued out to the northeast into the country for four or five miles to make sure that there was not another field farther out which might be Le Bourget. Then I returned and spiralled down closer to the lights. Presently I could make out long lines of hangars, and the roads appeared to be jammed with cars.

I flew low over the field once, then circled around into the wind and landed.

After the plane stopped rolling I turned it around and started to taxi back to the lights. The entire field ahead, however, was covered with thousands of people all running towards my ship. When the first few arrived, I attempted to get them to hold the rest of the crowd back, away from the plane, but apparently no one could understand, or would have been able to conform to my request if he had.

I cut the switch to keep the propeller from killing some one, and attempted to organize an impromptu guard for the plane. The impossibility of any immediate organization became apparent, and when parts of the ship began to crack from the pressure of the multitude I decided to climb out of the cockpit in order to draw the crowd away.

Speaking was impossible; no words could be heard in the uproar and nobody apparently cared to hear any. I started to climb out of the cockpit, but as soon as one foot appeared through the door I was dragged the rest of the way without assistance on my part.

For nearly half an hour I was unable to touch the ground, during which time I was ardently carried around in what seemed to be a very small area, and in every position it is possible to be in. Every one had the best of intentions but no one seemed to know just what they were.

The French military flyers very resourcefully took the situation in hand. A number of them mingled with the crowd; then, at a given signal, they placed my helmet on an American correspondent and cried: "Here is Lindbergh." That helmet on an American was sufficient evidence. The correspondent immediately became the center of attraction, and while he was being taken protestingly to the Reception Committee via a rather devious route, I managed to get inside one of the hangars.

Further Resources

BOOKS

Berg, A. Scott. *Lindbergh.* New York: G.P. Putnam's Sons, 1998.

Davies, Ronald E.G. *Charles Lindbergh: An Airman, His Aircraft, and His Great Flights.* McLean, Va: Paladwr Press, 1997.

Gray, Susan M. *Charles A. Lindbergh and the American Dilemma: The Conflict of Technology and Human Values.* Bowling Green, Ohio: Bowling Green State University Popular Press, 1988.

Hixson, Walter L. *Charles A. Lindbergh, Lone Eagle.* New York: HarperCollins, 1996.

PERIODICALS

Bradley, Perry. "Lindbergh's Legacy." *Business and Commercial Aviation,* February 1999, 9.

Phillips, Edward H. "Barnstormers, Lindbergh Dominate 'Roaring Twenties.'" *Aviation Week and Space Technology,* December 20, 1999, 102–104.

WEBSITES

Charles Lindbergh: An American Aviator. Available online at http://www.CharlesLindbergh.com (accessed January 30, 2003).

"The Flyer: Charles Lindbergh." The *Time* 100. Available online at http://www.time.com/time100/heroes/profile/lindbergh01.html; website home page http://www.time.com/time (accessed January 30, 2003).

AUDIO AND VISUAL MEDIA

Charles A. Lindbergh. Questar Video, 1991, VHS.

Lindbergh. PBS Video, 1990, VHS.

Coming of Age in Samoa
Nonfiction work

By: Margaret Mead

Date: 1928

Source: Mead, Margaret. *Coming of Age in Samoa: A Psychological Study of Primitive Youth for Western Civilization.* New York: Blue Ribbon Books, 1928. Reprint, American Museum of Natural History Special Members Edition. New York: American Museum of Natural History, in agreement with William Morrow and Co., 1973, 2–5.

About the Author: Margaret Mead (1901–1978) was born in Philadelphia, Pennsylvania, and earned a Ph.D. in anthropology from Columbia University in 1929. From 1926 until her death in 1978, she was a curator in the Department of Anthropology at the American Museum of Natural History in New York City. She wrote twenty-three books, coauthored more than twenty others, and wrote articles for *Redbook* magazine. She championed women's rights and opposed the nuclear arms race. At her death she was the world's most famous anthropologist. ∎

Introduction

The early twentieth century, and the 1920s in particular, witnessed a debate between scientists over the role of heredity and the environment in shaping human intelligence, personality, and behavior. Scientists label this debate "nature versus nurture," with "nature" being heredity and "nurture" being the environment.

Scientists who favored the nature side drew support from the new science of genetics. In 1900, three scientists rediscovered a paper on pea hybridization by the Austrian monk Gregor Mendel. In 1866 he had written that discrete units (genes) determined specific traits in pea plants. Scientists came to understand that genes are the blueprints that cells read in assembling a new living thing. Between 1909 and 1927, Columbia University embryologist Thomas Hunt Morgan led a research team in mapping the genes of the fruit fly.

Other scientists, taking their cue from Mendel and Morgan, began matching genes with traits in humans. By the 1920s, hard-line hereditarians believed that humans were solely a product of their genes. Heredity formed a person's intelligence, personality, and behavior, they maintained, and no amount of education, nutrients, or parental affection could compensate for poor heredity. The most militant were eugenicists, scientists who believed humans could improve their species by controlling who reproduced. Eugenicists labeled southern and eastern Europeans as carriers of deficient genes and convinced Congress in 1924 to restrict their immigration to the United States. By 1930 they also persuaded more than thirty states to empower judges to authorize surgeons to sterilize adults with mental, physical, and moral deficiencies in the belief that genes were destiny.

Margaret Mead, noted anthropologist and proponent of the environment as a principal determiner of human development. New Guinea, 1928. **AP/WIDE WORLD PHOTOS. REPRODUCED BY PERMISSION.**

Opposing the hereditarians were environmentalists. In 1925 psychologist John B. Watson published *Behaviorism,* which defined human behavior as a response to stimuli. Because stimuli came from the environment, it, rather than heredity, must shape humans. Environmentalists stressed the role of education, nutrition, and parents in shaping the destiny of human beings. Hereditarians were wrong, environmentalists believed, to the degree they tried to reduce people to a composite of genes. If hereditarians ignored the environment, environmentalists were equally myopic in ignoring genes. The sharp difference in these views exacerbated the bitterness of the nature-nurture debate during the 1920s.

Margaret Mead sided with the environmentalists. During the 1920s she lived with Samoans and found that adolescence is a calm period for female Samoans, whereas it is often a tumultuous time for adolescent girls in the United States. Mead traced this contrast to differences in the cultures—that is, the environments—of Samoa and the United States. She published these conclusions in 1928 in *Coming of Age in Samoa.*

Significance

Coming of Age in Samoa is a landmark of cultural anthropology. Mead did more than buttress the argument

of environmentalists. She treated Samoan culture as a valid alternative to Western culture. In making this case, she popularized the notion of cultural relativism, the idea that all cultural traditions have equal validity, that no culture can claim superiority over another. This idea has since been a core belief of anthropologists. But during the 1920s conservatives rejected it, insisting on the superiority of white Protestant culture, the dominant tradition in the United States. Mead thus challenged the conservative hegemony of the 1920s.

Mead also challenged the notion of who could aspire to a scientific career. In an era when men dominated the natural and social sciences, Mead was conspicuous in being a woman. Her mentor at Columbia had been a man, as had been most of her professors. The leading scientists of the 1920s, from Thomas Hunt Morgan to Robert Millikan, were men. Although women had worked in factories during World War I, during the 1920s they returned home to raise families. Mead was an exception in choosing a career, and a high-profile one, over life as a homemaker.

Mead was also exceptional in reaching beyond an academic audience. In an era when most academics wrote for their own cadre of intellectuals, Mead wrote *Coming of Age in Samoa* for a broad audience. As the first popular work of its kind, it introduced cultural anthropology to the American public and helped establish the writing of scholarship accessible to the public as a legitimate endeavor.

Primary Source

Coming of Age in Samoa [excerpt]

> **SYNOPSIS:** In this excerpt Mead announces the thesis of *Coming of Age in Samoa:* Differences between adolescent females in Samoa and the United States stem from cultural differences. The environment rather than heredity shapes us. Mead avoids scientific jargon, preferring the language of ordinary discourse. Unlike other scholars, who tend to write solely for one another, she decided to write *Coming of Age in Samoa* for a broad audience.

The anthropologist, as he pondered his growing body of material upon the customs of primitive people, grew to realise the tremendous rôle played in an individual's life by the social environment in which each is born and reared. One by one, aspects of behaviour which we had been accustomed to consider invariable complements of our humanity were found to be merely a result of civilisation, present in the inhabitants of one country, absent in another country, and this without a change of race. He learned that neither race nor common humanity can be held responsible for many of the forms which even such basic human emotions as love and fear and anger take under different social conditions.

So the anthropologist, arguing from his observations of the behaviour of adult human beings in other civilisations, reaches many of the same conclusions which the behaviourist reaches in his work upon human babies who have as yet no civilisation to shape their malleable humanity.

With such an attitude towards human nature the anthropologist listened to the current comment upon adolescence. He heard attitudes which seemed to him dependent upon social environment—such as rebellion against authority, philosophical perplexities, the flowering of idealism, conflict and struggle—ascribed to a period of physical development. And on the basis of his knowledge of the determinism of culture, of the plasticity of human beings, he doubted. Were these difficulties due to being adolescent or to being adolescent in America? . . .

What method then is open to us who wish to conduct a human experiment but who lack the power either to construct the experimental conditions or to find controlled examples of those conditions here and there throughout our own civilisation? The only method is that of the anthropologist, to go to a different civilisation and make a study of human beings under different cultural conditions in some other part of the world. For such studies the anthropologist chooses quite simple peoples, primitive peoples, whose society has never attained the complexity of our own. In this choice of primitive peoples like the Eskimo, the Australian, the South Sea islander, or the Pueblo Indian, the anthropologist is guided by the knowledge that the analysis of a simpler civilisation is more possible of attainment.

In complicated civilisations like those of Europe, or the higher civilisations of the East, years of study are necessary before the student can begin to understand the forces at work within them. A study of the French family alone would involve a preliminary study of French history, of French law, of the Catholic and Protestant attitudes towards sex and personal relations. A primitive people without a written language present a much less elaborate problem and a trained student can master the fundamental structure of a primitive society in a few months.

Furthermore, we do not choose a simple peasant community in Europe or an isolated group of mountain whites in the American South, for these people's ways of life, though simple, belong essentially to the historical tradition to which the complex parts of European or American civilisation belong. Instead, we choose primitive groups who have had thousands of years of historical development along completely different lines from our own, whose language does not possess our Indo-European categories, whose religious ideas are of a different nature, whose social organisation is not only simpler but very different from our own. From these contrasts, which are vivid enough to startle and enlighten those accustomed to our own way of life and simple enough to be grasped quickly, it is possible to learn many things about the effect of a civilisation upon the individuals within it.

So, in order to investigate the particular problem, I chose to go not to Germany or to Russia, but to Samoa, a South Sea island about thirteen degrees from the Equator, inhabited by a brown Polynesian people. Because I was a woman and could hope for greater intimacy in working with girls rather than with boys, and because owing to a paucity of women ethnologists our knowledge of primitive girls is far slighter than our knowledge of boys, I chose to concentrate upon the adolescent girl in Samoa.

Further Resources

BOOKS
Cassidy, Robert. *Margaret Mead: A Voice for the Century.* New York: Universe Books, 1983.

Harris, Marvin. *The Rise of Anthropological Theory.* New York: Crowell, 1968.

Howard, Jane. *Margaret Mead: A Life.* New York: Simon & Schuster, 1984.

Leaf, Murray J. *Man, Mind, and Science: A History of Anthropology.* New York: Columbia University Press, 1979.

Rice, Edward. *Margaret Mead: A Portrait.* New York: Harper and Row, 1979.

Silverman, Sydel. *Totems and Teachers: Perspectives on the History of Anthropology.* New York: Columbia University Press, 1981.

PERIODICALS
Ardener, Shirley. "The Social Anthropology of Women and Feminist Anthropology." *Anthropology Today,* 1985, 2–4, 26.

Rensberger, Boyce. "The Nature-Nurture Debate I: Margaret Mead." *Science,* 1983, 28–37.

Sanday, Peggy Reeves. "Margaret Mead's View of Sex Roles in Her Own and Other Societies." *American Anthropologist,* 1980, 340–348.

WEBSITES
"Margaret Mead." American Museum of Natural History. Available online at http://www.amnh.org/exhibitions/expeditions/treasure_fossil/Treasures/Margaret_Mead/mead.html;

website home page: http://www.amnh.org (accessed January 30, 2003).

"Mead's Life and Works." The Margaret Mead Centennial, 2001. Available online at http://www.mead2001.org/biography.html; website home page: http://www.mead2001.org (accessed January 30, 2003).

"The Exploration of Space"
Magazine article

By: Edwin P. Hubble

Date: May 1929

Source: Hubble, Edwin P. "The Exploration of Space." *Harper's Magazine,* May 1929, 732–733.

About the Author: Edwin Powell Hubble (1889–1953) was born in Kentucky. He majored in mathematics and astronomy at the University of Chicago and won a Rhodes Scholarship in 1910 to study law at Oxford University. He opened a law office in Kentucky in 1913, but the law bored Hubble, so he returned to the University of Chicago for a Ph.D. in astrophysics in 1917. Two years later he became an astronomer at Mount Wilson Observatory in California, where he spent most of his career. Hubble provided the first evidence that the universe is expanding, laying the foundation for the Big Bang theory. NASA's Hubble Space Telescope, launched in 1990, was named in his honor. ∎

Introduction

Edwin Hubble's field of study, cosmology, may be the oldest science. The ancient Sumerians, Babylonians, Phoenicians, Egyptians, Chaldeans, Maya, and Aztecs all mapped the heavens. The Greek Aristarchus understood that the earth revolves around the sun, an idea Nicholas Copernicus revived in the sixteenth century.

Yet Copernicus, like the ancients, had no inkling of the universe's vastness. In the seventeenth century, Galileo turned his telescope toward the heavens, finding the universe more immense than the naked eye suggested. During that century Isaac Newton opened the way to classical cosmology by stating that the physical laws that operated on earth also operated in the heavens. Despite the modernity of this idea, Newton held the ancient belief in a static universe, one that was neither expanding nor contracting, and in a universe in which stars were spread evenly and without relation to one another rather than as clusters we now call galaxies. Newton never considered the possibility that our solar system might be merely one of many and the Milky Way, our galaxy, one of innumerable galaxies.

In the eighteenth century, the German philosopher Immanuel Kant proposed that the cosmos might contain many "island universes," or galaxies, and by 1918 the

100-inch reflecting telescope used by Edwin Hubble in his astronomical research. © **MICHAEL MASLAN HISTORIC PHOTOGRAPHS/ CORBIS. REPRODUCED BY PERMISSION.**

American astronomer Harlow Shapley mapped the outline of the Milky Way. The stars within this outline were part of our galaxy, but those beyond it had to be part of other galaxies. The universe had innumerable galaxies, but how far apart were they from one another, and were their distances constant? That is, was the universe static as Newton had thought?

These questions were at the heart of Edwin Hubble's work. Using the telescope at the Mount Wilson Observatory, then the world's most powerful, Hubble calculated that the diameter of the visible universe was some two hundred million light years and inferred that this distance was only a fraction of the universe's size. "We can write the figures but they are utterly beyond our comprehension," Hubble admitted. He found this vast expanse studded with innumerable galaxies, which he classified by shape.

Even more astonishing, Hubble discovered evidence that the universe was expanding. Hubble knew that as early as 1912 Vesto Slipher at Lowell Observatory in Arizona had applied the Doppler Effect to the light from stars in other galaxies. According to the Doppler Effect, the wavelength of visible light should lengthen, that is, shift toward red, if it comes from a star that is moving away from an observer. Slipher observed this "Red Shift" in stars from distant galaxies. Hubble discovered that the farther a galaxy was from the Milky Way, the faster it was receding. This finding, Hubble's Law, so astonished him that as late as 1936 he denied that the universe was expanding. Albert Einstein too at first refused to believe that the universe was expanding. Hubble and Einstein shared a philosophical commitment to Newton's static universe.

Significance

In this excerpt from an article in *Harper's Magazine*, Hubble describes the immensity of the universe, acknowledging that what astronomers can see with the most powerful telescopes is merely a fraction of the universe. The article was published in 1929, when Hubble had already amassed evidence that the universe was expanding. Yet he does not mention this idea, evidence of his discomfort with it.

But others were unwilling to ignore Hubble's findings. An expanding universe implied that if one went back to time's beginning, one would find a universe of no dimensions. All matter must have been concentrated in a dense mass at the beginning of time. The explosion of this mass marked the origin of the universe, and the recession of the galaxies is the aftershock of this initial expansion, proposed the French mathematician Georges Lemaitre in 1927. The Big Bang theory thus stems from the work of Slipher and Hubble.

It is also significant that Hubble was writing for a popular magazine. The universe and its mysteries had caught the public's fancy ever since the famous eclipse of 1919 proved Einstein's General Theory of Relativity. Press coverage of the event in the United States and around the world made Einstein an international celebrity, and astronomy as a whole basked in the glow of Einstein's work.

Primary Source

"The Exploration of Space" [excerpt]

SYNOPSIS: In this excerpt from a May 1929 article in *Harper's Magazine*, Edwin Hubble acknowledges the limits of astronomy as much as its triumphs. With the best telescopes, astronomers can know only a fraction of the vast universe. Astronomy, like science itself, remains a work in progress, with lit-

Edwin Hubble, astronomer responsible for discovering that the universe is expanding and is much larger than previously believed. 1926.
© BETTMANN/CORBIS. REPRODUCED BY PERMISSION.

tle flickers of light here and there to illuminate tiny spheres of knowledge.

The romance of science lies in its explorations. Equipped with his five senses, man explores the universe around him and calls the adventure Science. He is confined to the surface of the planet Earth, hence his explorations of outer space are restricted to the interpretation of light-waves which come flooding in from all directions. In this manner he has found that the sun is merely one of the stars, one of the many millions which, together, make up the stellar system—the system of the Milky Way. From his position in the midst of this system, man looks out through the swarm of stars, past the boundaries, into the universe beyond. For ages he has speculated upon those distant realms, but only to-day have his instruments reached the powers required for the actual exploration.

The last and greatest of these instruments is on Mt. Wilson in southern California. With the 100-inch reflector one could detect a candle at 5,000 miles, one could detect an arc-light on the moon. And with this magic mirror we are now exploring the remoter regions of the universe, far beyond the Milky Way. There is the habitat of the nebulæ—those faint patches of light which have been identified as vast independent stellar systems, comparable with our own system, the system of the Milky Way. There they lie, thinly scattered through the depths of space, out as far as the telescope can reach.

We know something of their actual dimensions, something of their real luminosities, hence their mere appearance in the telescope indicates the general order of their distances. We see a few that appear large and bright: these are the nearer nebulæ. Then we find them smaller and fainter in constantly increasing numbers, and we know that we are reaching out into space farther and ever farther until, with the faintest nebulæ that can be detected with the greatest telescope, we have reached the frontiers of the known universe.

It is distant, this last horizon. Light travels for two hundred million years to make the journey. Yet it defines the observable region of space and restricts our knowledge to a definite portion of the universe. Within the vast sphere are scattered several millions of nebulæ—stellar systems—in various stages of their evolutionary histories. One of the multitude is our own stellar system, the system of the Milky Way. It is, we believe, one of the older and more mature organizations.

The nebulæ are found singly, in groups, and even in great clusters; but when large volumes of space are considered, the tendency to cluster averages out and, to the limits of the telescopes, the distribution is approximately uniform. There is no evidence of a thinning out, no trace of a physical boundary. The universe, we must suppose, stretches out beyond the frontiers, far into the realms of speculation.

Yet it cannot continue indefinitely. An infinite homogeneous universe is not compatible with the laws and the phenomena of nature. The best working hypothesis of the day, the general theory of relativity, postulates a universe which is finite. The dimensions can be calculated, in a tentative way, by assuming the observable region to be typical of space in general. It then appears that we are actually observing an appreciable, though very minute, fraction of the entire universe. Such is the present status of the explorations of space—our adventures in cosmography. A definite region has been sketched in outline, a definite boundary established, at least as a working hypothesis, and astronomers are now proceeding with the task of mapping in the details.

Further Resources

BOOKS

Berendzen, Richard, Richard Hart, and Daniel Seeley. *Man Discovers the Galaxies.* New York: Scientific History, 1976.

DeVorkin, David H. *The History of Modern Astronomy and Astrophysics.* New York: Garland, 1982.

Lang, Kenneth R., and Owen Gingerich, eds. *Source Book in Astronomy and Astrophysics, 1900–1975.* Cambridge, Mass.: Harvard University Press, 1979.

Moltz, Lloyd, and Jefferson Hane Weaver. *The Story of Physics.* New York: Plenum Press, 1989.

Smith, Robert W. *The Expanding Universe.* New York: Cambridge University Press, 1982.

Struve, Otto, and Velta Zebergs. *Astronomy of the 20th Century.* New York: Macmillan, 1962.

PERIODICALS

Hetherington, Norriss S. "Philosophical Values and Observation in Edwin Hubble's Choice of a Model of the Universe." *Historical Studies in the Physical Sciences,* 1983, 41–68.

Mendillo, Michael, David DeVorkin, and Richard Berendzen. "The Universe Unfolds: 1900–1950." *Astronomy,* 1976, 87–95.

Whitrow, G.J. "Edwin Powell Hubble." *Dictionary of Scientific Biography,* 1972, 528–532.

WEBSITES

"Edwin Hubble." *The Journal of the Royal Astronomical Society of Canada.* Available online at http://antwrp.gsfc.nasa.gov/diamond_jubilee/1996/sandage_hubble.html; website home page: http://antwrp.gsfc.nasa.gov (accessed May 8, 2003).

"Edwin Hubble." PBS Online. Available online at http://www.pbs.org/wnet/hawking/cosmostar/html/cstars_hubble.html; website home page: http://www.pbs.org (accessed January 31, 2003).

Dynamo
Play script

By: Eugene O'Neill

Date: 1929

Source: O'Neill, Eugene. *Dynamo.* New York: H. Liveright, 1929. Reprinted in *O'Neill: Complete Plays 1920–1931.* New York: Viking Press, 1988, 873–874.

About the Author: Eugene Gladstone O'Neill (1888–1953) was born in New York City. His father's success as an actor did not at first lead O'Neill to the theater. After a year at Princeton University, he drank and drifted. In 1912 he contracted tuberculosis and vowed that if he recovered he would become a playwright. He wrote more than thirty plays before a degenerative disease undermined his health in the 1940s. Four of his plays were awarded the Pulitzer Prize, and critical acclaim culminated in the Nobel Prize for literature in 1936. He was the first and (as of 2002) remains the only American playwright to have won a Nobel Prize. ■

American Theater Guild production of the Eugene O'Neill play *Dynamo*, 1928–1929. **THE LIBRARY OF CONGRESS.**

Introduction

Salient developments in science and technology influenced American literature during the 1920s. One development was atomic theory, which traced its roots to the ancient Greeks and which British chemist John Dalton revived in 1802. Later that century, British physicist Michael Faraday inferred that atoms are comprised of heavy positively charged nuclei and light negatively charged particles. In 1897 British physicist Joseph John Thomson isolated the negatively charged particle, the electron, and in 1913 he isolated the positively charged particle, the proton. By then, British physicist Ernest Rutherford had derived a model of the atom: a tiny, dense nucleus containing protons surrounded by even smaller electrons. It was clear that atoms, and by extension protons and electrons, comprised all matter.

A second important development came in the science of geology. In the nineteenth century, geologists and naturalists identified the fossils of marine invertebrates as the most ancient life. In *The Origin of Species* (1859), Charles Darwin speculated that life had originated in the primeval ocean, and British and German naturalists searched for fossils of this first life. By the end of the century, the orthodox view held that life had originated in the ocean and evolved into its current aquatic, terrestrial, and avian diversity.

A third significant development was the harnessing of electricity as a source of power. Engineers built the first hydroelectric plant in Wisconsin in 1882. The United States had thirty-eight hydroelectric power plants by the end of 1882, and three thousand by 1899. In 1879, Cleveland and San Francisco installed the first electric streetlights, and the next year Thomas Edison patented the lightbulb. By 1890 Edison was manufacturing more than one million lightbulbs a year. By 1920 hydroelectric plants dotted the nation's rivers. Hydroelectric power heralded an age of plentiful and cheap electricity.

Eugene O'Neill cut to the essence of these developments in his 1929 play, *Dynamo*. The play's main character, Reuben, is preoccupied with the power of electricity to shape human destiny. He likens hydroelectric power plants to temples in the secular America of the 1920s, an America of science and technology rather than Christianity. Reuben's real faith is in scientific and technological progress, and he seems ready to reduce humans to the interaction of protons and electrons, and all life to the first aquatic microorganisms.

Significance

For Eugene O'Neill, science and technology were central pillars of American life. The fact that O'Neill centered *Dynamo* on a hydroelectric plant illustrates the

Eugene G. O'Neill, Nobel Prize and Pulitzer Prize winning playwright.
THE LIBRARY OF CONGRESS.

degree to which science and technology penetrated American literature during the 1920s. Other literary works of 1929 also had scientific and technological themes. Sinclair Lewis's *Dodsworth* is a novel about an auto manufacturer who acts as though his life derives value solely from his relationship to the car. Also in 1929, William Faulkner published *The Sound and the Fury*, in which he abolished absolute time as we reckon it with our clocks, just as Albert Einstein had abolished absolute time, replacing its with the notion of relative time in his Special Theory of Relativity (1905). Faulkner gives readers no real indication of when or in what order the events of the novel take place.

The prevalence of science and technology in *Dynamo* and other American literary works suggests how deeply the two had penetrated American culture by the 1920s. Science and technology were no longer the pursuit of obscure intellectuals in underfunded laboratories. By the 1920s Henry Ford had made technology, in the form of the car, central to American life, and Einstein had become a celebrity when a solar eclipse in 1919 confirmed his General Theory of Relativity. In his popularity and eccentricity, Einstein elevated science to the high status it has enjoyed ever since in the United States. Science and technology had become powerful society forces

by the 1920s, and it was this power that influenced Eugene O'Neill.

Primary Source

Dynamo [excerpt]

SYNOPSIS: In this excerpt, O'Neill sets the scene for Act III of *Dynamo*, a scene suffused by the hum of a hydroelectric plant. It is the plant more than the characters that dominates the scene. The main character, Reuben, venerates the plant as the temple of modern America and is confident of the inevitability of scientific and technological progress.

Act Three

Scene One

Same as Act Two, Scene Three—Exterior of the power house four months later. It is a little after sunset and the equipment on the roof is outlined blackly against a darkening crimson sky.

The door of the dynamo room is shut but the interior is brilliantly lighted and the dynamo can be partly seen through the window. There is a dim light above in the switch galleries as in the previous scene. The overtone of rushing water from the dam sounds louder because of the closed door which muffles the noise of the dynamo to a minor strain.

Reuben enters from the left accompanied by Mrs. Fife. He has grown very thin, his dungarees sag about his angular frame. His face is gaunt and pale. His eyes are deeply sunken. He is talking with unnatural excitement as they come in. Mrs. Fife is unchanged. If anything, her moony dreaminess is more pronounced. She listens to Reuben with a fascinated, far-away look, as if the sound of his voice hypnotized her rather than the meaning of the words.

Reuben: *(insistently)* You understood all I explained to you up on the dam, didn't you?— about how life first came out of the sea?

Mrs. Fife: *(nods dreamily)* Yes, Reuben. It sounds like poetry—"life out of the sea."

Reuben: It is like poetry. Her song in there— Dynamo's—isn't that the greatest poem of all—the poem of eternal life? And listen to the water rushing over the dam! Like music! It's as if that sound was cool water washing over my body!—washing all dirt and sin away! Like some one singing me to sleep—my mother— when I was a kid—calling me back to somewhere far off where I'd been once long ago and known peace! *(He sighs with longing, his body suddenly gone limp and weary.)*

Mrs. Fife: *(dreamily)* That's awful pretty, Reuben. *(She puts her arm around him—sentimentally)* I'll be your mother—yours and Ada's. I've always wanted a boy.

Reuben: *(leans against her gratefully, his head almost on her shoulder, his eyes half closed)* Yes. You're like her—Dynamo—the Great Mother—big and warm—*(with a sudden renewal of his unnatural excitement, breaks away from her)* But I've got to finish telling you all I've come to know about her—how all things end up in her! Did I tell you that our blood plasm is the same right now as the sea was when life came out of it? We've got the sea in our blood still! It's what makes our hearts live! And it's the sea rising up in clouds, falling on the earth in rain, made that river that drives the turbines that drive Dynamo! The sea makes her heart beat, too!—but the sea is only hydrogen and oxygen and minerals, and they're only atoms, and atoms are only protons and electrons—even our blood and the sea are only electricity in the end! And think of the stars! Driving through space, round and round, just like the electrons in the atom! But there must be a center around which all this moves, mustn't there? There is in everything else! And that center must be the Great Mother of Eternal Life, Electricity, and Dynamo is her Divine Image on earth! Her power houses are the new churches!

Further Resources

BOOKS

Alioto, Anthony M. *A History of Western Science.* Englewood Cliffs, N.J.: Prentice Hall, 1987.

Brush, Stephen G. *The History of Modern Science: A Guide to the Second Scientific Revolution, 1800–1950.* Ames, Iowa: Iowa State University Press, 1988.

Floyd, Virginia, ed. *The Plays of Eugene O'Neill: A New Assessment.* New York: F. Ungar, 1985.

Gould, Stephen Jay. *The Panda's Thumb: More Reflections in Natural History.* New York: Norton, 1980.

Moorton, Richard F., ed. *Eugene O'Neill's Century: Centennial Views on America's Foremost Tragic Dramatist.* New York: Greenwood Press, 1991.

PERIODICALS

Webber, Bruce. "All of a Sudden, Eugene O'Neill Is Everywhere." *New York Times,* August 4, 1996, H5.

Wilkins, F.C. "O'Neill at 100." *Americana,* August 1988, 47–53.

WEBSITES

eOneill.com: An Electronic Eugene O'Neill Archive. Available online at http://www.eoneill.com (accessed January 30, 2003).

"Eugene O'Neill—Autobiography." Nobel eMuseum. Available online at http://www.nobel.se/literature/laureates/1936/oneill-autobio.html; website home page: http://www.nobel.se (accessed January 30, 2003).

AUDIO AND VISUAL MEDIA

Eugene O'Neill: A Concise Biography. Academy Media, 1996, VHS.

12

SPORTS

MURRY R. NELSON

Entries are arranged in chronological order by date of primary source. For entries with one primary source, the entry title is the same as the primary source title. Entries with more than one primary source have an overall entry title, followed by the titles of the primary sources.

Important Events in Sports, 1920–1929

1920

- On January 1, in the Rose Bowl Harvard beats the University of Oregon 7-6.

- On January 5, Babe Ruth is sold by the Boston Red Sox to the New York Yankees.

- On February 14, the National Negro Baseball League (NNBL) is founded.

- On May 1, the Brooklyn Dodgers play the Boston Braves to a 1-1 tie in twenty-six innings. Boston's Joe Oeschger and Brooklyn's Leon Cadore pitch the entire game.

- On May 6, Johnny Wilson wins the world middleweight championship in a decision over Mike O'Dowd.

- On May 14, Walter Johnson of the Washington Senators wins his 300th game.

- On June 12, Man o' War runs the mile and 3/8 in 2 minutes 14 1/5 seconds at Belmont.

- On July 1, Walter Johnson of the Washington Senators pitches a no-hitter against the Boston Red Sox.

- On July 3, William Tatem Tilden II becomes the first American to win the men's singles title at Wimbledon by defeating Australian Gerald Patterson 2-6, 6-3, 6-2, 6-4.

- On July 10, Man o' War beats John P. Grier in a match race at Aqueduct. He sets a new world record of 1 minute 49 1/5 seconds for the mile and 1 1/6 distance.

- From July 15 to July 27, the U.S. yacht *Resolute* defeats Great Britain's *Shamrock IV* in the America's Cup race.

- On July 16, Babe Ruth breaks his own record of twenty-nine home runs in a single season against St. Louis. He finished the season with fifty-four homers.

- On August 17, the Cleveland Indians' Ray Chapman dies after being hit in the head by a ball pitched by the Yankees' Carl Mays. This is the only game-related fatality in Major League Baseball history.

- On September 4, Man o' War runs the mile and 5/8 in 2 minutes 40 4/5 seconds at Belmont.

- On September 7, "Big Bill" Tilden beats fellow American "Little Bill" Johnston to claim the men's title at the U.S. Championships 6-1, 1-6, 7-5, 5-7, 6-3.

- On September 15, Exterminator runs two miles in 3 minutes 21 4/5 seconds at Belmont.

- On September 17, the American Professional Football Association (APFA), predecessor of the National Football League, is formed in Canton, Ohio with Jim Thorpe as president; franchises are sold for one hundred dollars.

- On September 19, Norwegian-born Molla Bjurdstedt Mallory defeats American Marion Zinderstein 6-3, 6-1 for the women's title at the U.S. Championships.

- On September 28, eight Chicago White Sox players are indicted by a Chicago grand jury on charges that they conspired to throw the 1919 World Series.

- On October 2, Cincinnati and Pittsburgh schedule a triple-header but are forced to call the third game because of darkness.

- On October 10, William "Wamby" Wambsganss, the Cleveland Indians second baseman, makes an unassisted triple play in the World Series. This is the only triple play in World Series history.

- On October 12, in his last race, Man o' War beats Sir Barton, the 1919 Triple Crown winner, for the Kenilworth Gold Cup.

- On October 10, Jim Bagby of the Cleveland Indians is the first pitcher to hit a home run in the World Series. The Indians defeat the Brooklyn Dodgers 5 games to 2.

- On November 25, WTAW, College Station, Texas, broadcasts the University of Texas-Texas A&M game, which the University of Texas wins 7-3.

- On December 14, Notre Dame's All-American halfback George Gipp dies of pneumonia.

- On December 22, Joe Lynch wins the world bantamweight championship from Pete Herman on a decision.

- From December 30 to January 1, the U.S. Davis Cup tennis team defeats Australasia 5-0 in Auckland, New Zealand.

1921

- The U.S. Figure Skating Association is founded.

- On January 1, the University of California beats Ohio State University 28-0 in the Rose Bowl.

- On January 12, Judge Kenesaw Mountain Landis is appointed commissioner of baseball.

- On April 23, Charles Paddock runs the 100 meters in 10.4 seconds and the 300 meters in 33.2 seconds.

- On June 10, Babe Ruth becomes the all-time home run leader with 120 career homers.

- On June 19, during the first National Collegiate Athletics Association (NCAA) track-and-field championships, Paddock runs 220 yards twice in 20.8 seconds.

- On June 25, Pete Herman regains the world bantamweight championship from Joe Lynch on a decision.

- On June 26, Jock Hutchison wins the British Open championship with a score of 296.

- On July 3, Bill Tilden defeats South Africa's Brian Ivan Cobb "Babe" Norton 4-6, 2-6, 6-1, 6-0, 7-5 in the Wimbledon men's final.

- On July 21, Jack Dempsey defends his world heavyweight crown against Georges Carpentier in the first boxing match to have a "million-dollar gate."

- On August 3, when witnesses disappears, the eight members of the Chicago White Sox accused of fixing the 1919 World Series are found not guilty. Commissioner Landis subsequently bans them for life.

- On August 14, English-born American golfer Jim Barnes wins the U.S. Open with a score of 289.

- On August 19, Ty Cobb of the Detroit Tigers gets his 3,000th base hit.

- On August 21, Molla Bjurdstedt Mallory defeats American Mary K. Browne to take the women's crown at the U.S. Championships 4-6, 6-4, 6-2.

- On September 2, the United States beats Japan in Davis Cup play.

- On September 20, Bill Tilden beats American Wallace Johnson 4-6, 6-4, 6-2 for the men's title at the U.S. Championships.

- On September 23, Johnny Buff wins the world bantamweight championship from Pete Herman on a decision.

- On September 29, Walter Hagen wins his first PGA Championship.

- On October 13, the New York Giants defeat the New York Yankees in the World Series, 5 games to 3.

- On November 25, the American Olympic Association, an organizing board for U.S. teams, is established.

1922

- George Halas renames his Chicago Staleys professional football team; they will now be known as the Chicago Bears.

- Jim Furey assembles the first true professional basketball team, which he calls the "Original Celtics."

- On January 1, the University of California ties with Washington & Jefferson 0-0 in the Rose Bowl.

- On April 22, Ken Williams of the St. Louis Browns is the first American Leaguer to hit three home runs in a single game.

- On April 30, Charles Robertson of the Chicago White Sox pitches a perfect game against the Detroit Tigers.

- On May 7, Jesse Barnes of the New York Giants pitches a no-hitter against the Philadelphia Phillies.

- On June 24, Walter Hagen becomes the first American-born winner of the British Open golf tournament with a score of 300.

- On July 9, Molla Bjurdstedt Mallory reaches the women's final at Wimbledon but loses to France's Suzanne Lenglen 2-6, 0-6.

- On July 10, Joe Lynch regains the world bantamweight championship by knocking out Johnny Buff.

- On July 16, Gene Sarazen wins the U.S. Open golfing championship with a score of 288.

- On June 24, the American Professional Football Association (APFA) changes its name to the National Football League (NFL).

- On August 7, Ken Williams of the St. Louis Browns is the first American Leaguer to hit two home runs in the same inning.

- On August 19, Gene Sarazen wins the PGA title.

- On August 20, Molla Bjurdstedt Mallory beats Helen Wills 6-3, 6-1 to take the U.S. Championships women's title.

- On August 20, Bill Tilden defeats Bill Johnston for the U.S. Championships men's title 4-6, 3-6, 6-2, 6-3, 6-4.

- On August 26, the first Walker Cup golf matches are played at the National Links of America, Southampton, Long Island. The United States defeats Great Britain and Ireland 8-4.

- On September 1, the United States defeats Australasia 4-1 in Davis Cup play.

- On October 1, Glenna Collett wins her first Women's National Championships golfing crown.

- On October 8, the New York Giants defeat the New York Yankees in the World Series, 4 games to none, plus one tie.

- On October 28, WEAF, New York, is the first radio station to broadcast a football game coast to coast: Princeton beats Chicago 21-18.

- On October 29, in the first game they play together, Stuhldreher, Miller, Crowley, and Layden—the Four Horseman of Notre Dame—lead their team to victory over Georgia Tech 13-3.

1923

- The National Negro Baseball League (NNBL) draws more than four hundred thousand spectators and earns two hundred thousand dollars in gate receipts.

- On January 1, the University of Southern California beats Pennsylvania State University 14-3 in the Rose Bowl.

- On March 17, Mike McTigue wins the world light heavyweight championship, outpointing Battling Siki in 20 rounds.

- On April 18, Yankee Stadium opens in New York. Babe Ruth hits a three run homer to beat his former teammates 4-1.

- On June 2, Eugene Criqui wins the world featherweight championship from Johnny Kilbane on a knockout.

- On June 18, Pancho Villa wins the world flyweight championship by knocking out Jimmy Wilde.

- On July 8, Bill Johnston wins the men's title at Wimbledon by defeating fellow American Francis T. Hunter 6-0, 6-3, 6-1.

- On July 16, Bobby Jones wins his first U.S. Open title with a score of 296.

- On July 26, Johnny Dundee wins the world featherweight championship from Eugene Criqui on a decision.

- In August, a new tennis stadium opens at Forest Hills, New York; a permanent concrete structure, it is the first of its kind for the sport. The Wightman Cup matches are the inaugural event for the facility.

- On August 11, in the first Wightman Cup tennis competition the U.S. women defeat the British women 7-0.

- On August 19, Helen Wills wins her first singles title at the U.S. Championships by defeating Molla Bjurdstedt Mallory 6-2, 6-1.

- On August 31, Harry Greb wins the world middleweight championship in a decision over Johnny Wilson.
- From August 31 to September 3, the U.S. Davis Cup team defeats Australia 4-1.
- On September 14, first baseman George Burns of the Boston Red Sox turns an unassisted triple play against Cleveland.
- On September 14, Jack Dempsey defends his world heavyweight crown against Luis Angel Firpo. Dempsey floors Firpo ten times in the bout.
- On September 16, Bill Tilden takes the men's U.S. Championships title by overpowering Bill Johnston 6-4, 6-1, 6-4.
- On September 27, Lou Gehrig clubs his first home run against Boston. Exactly fifteen years later, he hits his last home run (493) against Washington.
- On September 30, Gene Sarazen takes the PGA Championship for the second time in a row.
- On October 6, Boston Braves' shortstop Ernie Padgett completes an unassisted triple play against Philadelphia.
- On October 15, the New York Yankees defeat the New York Giants in the World Series, 4 games to 2.
- On October 25, the American Power Boat Association (APBA), adopting the rules of the Mississippi Valley Power Boat Association, begins to sanction power-boat races.

1924

- The Boston Bruins become the first U.S. team to join the National Hockey League (NHL).
- On January 1, the University of Washington ties Navy 14-14 in the Rose Bowl.
- On March 21, Abe Goldstein wins the world bantamweight championship from Joe Lynch in a decision.
- On June 7, American golfer Cyril Walker wins the U.S. Open Championship with a score of 297.
- From June 18 to June 19, Great Britain defeats the United States in the Wightman Cup 6-1.
- On June 28, Walter Hagen wins his second British Open with a score of 301.
- On July 6, American tennis star Helen Wills plays for the women's singles title at Wimbledon but loses to Great Britain's Kathleen "Kitty" McKane 6-4, 4-6, 4-6.
- On August 16, Helen Wills defeats Molla Bjurdstedt Mallory 6-1, 6-2 to retain her women's title at the U.S. Championships.
- On September 3, Bill Tilden wins the U.S. Championships men's singles title with a 6-1, 9-7, 6-2 victory over Bill Johnston.
- From September 11 to September 13, the United States wins 5-0 over Australia in Davis Cup play.
- On September 20, Grover Alexander of the Chicago Cubs wins his 300th game.
- On September 21, Walter Hagen wins the PGA title.
- On September 24, Paddy Driscoll of the Chicago Cardinals drop-kicks a fifty-yard field goal; he repeats this feat on October 11, 1924.

- Bobby Jones wins his first U.S. Amateur Championship.
- On October 5, Rogers Hornsby of the St. Louis Cardinals finishes the season with a .424 average—the highest in the history of major-league baseball.
- On October 10, the Washington Senators defeat the New York Giants in the World Series, 4 games to 3.
- On October 18, Halfback Harold "Red" Grange of the University of Illinois scores touchdowns on each of his first five carries against the University of Michigan. He also passes for a sixth score. He rushes for a total of 402 yards.
- On December 19, Eddie Martin wins the world bantamweight championship from Abe Goldstein on a decision.

1925

- On January 1, Notre Dame defeats Stanford 27-10 in the Rose Bowl.
- On March 20, Charlie Rosenberg wins the world bantamweight championship from Eddie Martin in a decision.
- On May 3, Paul Berlenbach wins the world light heavyweight championship by outpointing Mike McTigue.
- On May 7, Pittsburgh shortstop Glenn Wright completes an unassisted triple play against St. Louis.
- On May 17, Cleveland Indian Tris Speaker earns his 3,000th hit.
- On June 1, Lou Gehrig begins his record of playing 2,130 consecutive games, over the course of fourteen years, when he pinch-hits for Yankees shortstop Wally Pipp.
- On June 3, Eddie Collins of the Chicago White Sox collects his 3,000th hit.
- On June 6, American Willie MacFarlane defeats Bobby Jones in a play-off to take the U.S. Open with a score of 291.
- On June 27, Jim Barnes wins the British Open with a score of 300.
- From August 14 to August 15, Great Britain beats the United States in the Wightman Cup.
- On August 25, Helen Wills defeats England's Kathleen "Kitty" McKane 3-6, 6-0, 6-2 to win her third straight title at the U.S. Championships.
- From September 10 to September 12, the United States defeats France 5-0 in Davis Cup play.
- On September 20, Bill Tilden defeats Bill Johnston 4-6, 11-9, 6-3, 4-6, 6-3 in the men's U.S. Championships finals.
- On September 27, Walter Hagen takes his second consecutive PGA Championship.
- On October 5, Glenna Collett wins her second Women's National Championships golfing crown.
- On October 15, the Pittsburgh Pirates defeat the Washington Senators in the World Series, 4 games to 3.
- On November 26, Red Grange plays his first professional football game with the Chicago Bears against the Chicago Cardinals. It is the first professional football game to be broadcast nationally.
- On November 24, a new Madison Square Garden designed by architect Thomas W. Lamb opens on Eighth Avenue be-

tween Forty-ninth and Fiftieth Streets. It remains in operation until February 1968.

- On December 7, Rocky Kansas wins the world lightweight boxing championship from Jimmy Goodrich on a decision.

1926

- On January 1, in the most important football game in the history of the South, Alabama beats the University of Washington 20-19 in the Rose Bowl.

- On February 16, at Cannes, Suzanne Lenglen defeats Helen Wills in the tennis "Match of the Century."

- On February 28, in two thirty-six-hole rounds on consecutive Sundays, Walter Hagen beats Bobby Jones.

- On May 20, Pete Latzo wins the world welterweight championship from Mickey Walker on a decision.

- On May 22, Branch Rickey is replaced by Rogers Hornsby as manager of the St. Louis Cardinals.

- On June 17, the United States defeats Great Britain in Wightman Cup competition 4-3.

- On June 26, Bobby Jones wins the British Open with a score of 291.

- On July 3, Sammy Mandell wins the world lightweight championship from Rocky Kansas on a decision.

- On July 3, American Howard Kinsey plays in the Wimbledon men's finals but loses to France's Jacques Boratra 6-8, 1-6, 3-6.

- On July 11, Bobby Jones wins the U.S. Open with a score of 293; he becomes the first American to win the British and U.S. titles in a single year.

- On August 6, Gertrude Ederle becomes the first woman to swim the English Channel; her time is 14 hours 39 minutes.

- On August 11, Tris Speaker of Cleveland collects his 700th career double.

- On August 19, Tiger Flowers retains the world middleweight championship, winning by a decision over Harry Greb.

- On August 24, Molla Bjurdstedt Mallory wins her eighth and final U.S. Championships singles title with a 4-6, 6-4, 9-7 victory over Great Britain's Elizabeth Ryan.

- From September 9 to September 11, the United States defeats France 4-1 in Davis Cup competition.

- On September 23, in Philadelphia, Gene Tunney wins the world heavyweight championship from Jack Dempsey in a ten-round unanimous decision.

- On September 25, the New York Rangers, the Chicago Blackhawks, and the Detroit Cougars join the National Hockey League.

- On September 26, Walter Hagen takes his third consecutive PGA Championship.

- On October 6, Babe Ruth hits three home runs in the fourth game of the World Series against St. Louis.

- On October 10, the St. Louis Cardinals defeat the New York Yankees in the World Series, 4 games to 3.

- On December 3, Mickey Walker wins the world middleweight championship by a controversial decision over Tiger Flowers.

1927

- On January 1, Alabama ties Stanford 7-7 in the Rose Bowl.

- On April 5, Johnny Weissmuller sets two swimming records in the 220-meters and the 100-yard freestyle.

- On May 4, Weissmuller sets swimming records for 200 yards (1 minute 56⅘; seconds), 200 meters (2 minutes 2 seconds), and 220 yards (2 minutes 9 seconds).

- On May 30, Chicago Cub shortstop Jimmy Cooney completes an unassisted triple play against Pittsburgh.

- On May 31, Detroit Tiger first baseman Johnny Neun completes an unassisted triple play against Cleveland.

- On June 3, Joe Dundee wins the world welterweight championship from Pete Latzo by a decision.

- On June 5, the first Ryder Cup golf competition is played at the Worcester, Massachusetts, Country Club. The United States defeats Great Britain 9 1/2 to 2 1/2.

- On July 3, American Helen Wills wins the first of her eight Wimbledon singles titles by defeating Lili de Alvarez of Spain 6-2, 6-4.

- On July 16, Bobby Jones wins his second British Open title with a score of 285.

- On July 18, Ty Cobb of the Detroit Tigers gets his 4,000th hit.

- On August 13, the United States beats Great Britain 5-2 in the Wightman Cup.

- On August 31, Helen Wills defeats England's Betty Nuthall 6-1, 6-4 to take the women's title at the U.S. Championships.

- From September 8 to September 10, France defeats the United States 3-2 in Davis Cup competition; Bill Tilden loses to René Lacoste, and Bill Johnston loses to Lacoste and Henri Cochet.

- On September 12, Benny Bass wins the world featherweight championship by outpointing Red Chapman.

- On September 17, Walter Hagen wins his fourth consecutive PGA title, which is his fifth PGA Championship of the decade.

- On September 18, Bill Tilden loses to René Lacoste 9-11, 3-6, 9-11 in the men's final of the U.S. Championships.

- On September 22, the Gene Tunney-Jack Dempsey world heavyweight championship fight at Soldier Field, Chicago, draws $2.65 million—the first sports gate to top $2 million; Tunney keeps his title because of the legendary "long count" in the tenth round.

- On September 30, Babe Ruth hits his record-breaking 60th home run of the season. The record would last for the next thirty-four years.

- On October 7, Tommy Loughran wins the world light heavyweight championship by a decision over Mike McTigue.

• On October 8, the New York Yankees defeat the Pittsburgh Pirates in the World Series, 4 games to none.

1928

• On January 1, Stanford beats Pittsburgh 7-6 in the Rose Bowl.

• On February 10, Tony Canzoneri wins the world featherweight championship from Benny Bass on a decision.

• On April 15, the New York Rangers are the first American team to win the National Hockey League Stanley Cup. They beat the Montreal Maroons 3 games to 2.

• On May 12, Walter Hagen wins his third British Open title with a score of 292.

• From June 15 to June 16, Great Britain defeats the United States in the Wightman Cup 4-3.

• On June 25, American Johnny Farrell beats Bobby Jones in a play-off to win the U.S. Open with a score of 294.

• On July 8, Helen Wills defends her Wimbledon title by defeating Lili de Alvarez 6-2, 6-3.

• From July 27 to July 29, the United States loses 4-1 in Davis Cup play against France; Bill Tilden gets the only U.S. victory by beating René Lacoste.

• On September 18, Francis Hunter loses to France's Henri Cochet 6-4, 4-6, 6-3, 5-7, 3-6 in the men's final of the U.S. Championships.

• On September 25, Helen Wills defeats American Helen Jacobs 6-2, 6-1 to take the women's singles final of the U.S. Championships.

• On September 28, André Routis wins the world featherweight championship from Tony Canzoneri on a decision.

• On September 30, Glenna Collett wins her third Women's National Championships golfing crown.

• On October 9, the New York Yankees defeat the St. Louis Cardinals in the World Series, 4 games to 0; this is the Yankees's second Series sweep in a row, and for the second time in his career Babe Ruth hits three home runs in a single World Series game.

• On November 6, American Leo Diegel wins the PGA Championship.

• On December 26, Johnny Weissmuller retires from competition after never having lost a freestyle race in eight years. He set sixty-seven world swimming records and at one time held all freestyle world records from 50 to 880 yards.

1929

• On January 1, California linebacker Roy Riegels scoops up a fumble and runs sixty yards the wrong way before being tackled by his teammate on the one-yard line. Georgia blocks the ensuing California punt for a safety and wins 8-7, in the Rose Bowl.

• On May 11, Walter Hagen wins his fourth British Open title with a score of 292.

• On July 1, Bobby Jones beats Al Espinosa to win the U.S. Open with a score of 294.

• On July 6, in the Wimbledon women's singles title match, which features America's two Helens—Wills and Jacobs—Wills defeats Jacobs 6-1, 6-2; Wills will win the title again in 1930, 1932, 1933, 1935, and 1938.

• From August 9 to August 10, the United States beats Great Britain in Wightman Cup play 4-3.

• On August 25, Helen Wills wins the women's title at the U.S. Championships with a victory over Mrs. P. H. Watson 6-4, 6-2; Wills will win again in 1931 for a total of seven U.S. Championships singles titles.

• On September 13, Bill Tilden defeats Francis Hunter 3-6, 6-3, 4-6, 6-2, 6-4 in the men's finals of the U.S. championships; this is Tilden's seventh and last U.S. Championships singles title.

• On October 6, Glenna Collett wins her fourth Women's National Championships golfing crown; she will take her fifth in 1930 and her sixth in 1935.

• On October 14, the Philadelphia Athletics defeat the Chicago Cubs in the World Series, 4 games to 1.

• On October 24, the Carnegie Foundation for the Advancement of Teaching releases *American Collegiate Athletics,* a report documenting abuses in college athletics programs, especially football, and calls for reforms.

• On December 7, Leo Diegel wins his second consecutive PGA Championship.

The Chicago "Black Sox"

Statement of Commissioner Landis

Statement

By: Kenesaw Mountain Landis

Date: August 3, 1921

Source: Landis, Kenesaw Mountain. Statement of Commissioner Landis, August 3, 1921. Available online at http://1919blacksox.com/trial.htm; website home page: http://1919blacksox.com (accessed May 8, 2003).

About the Author: Kenesaw Mountain Landis (1866–1944) was born in 1866. Landis was a federal judge in Chicago, where he was known for frequently making outrageous decisions later overturned on appeal. He was also known as an ardent patriot and great fan of baseball. To provide strong leadership in an effort to bring order out of baseball's near anarchy, Landis accepted the newly created position of commissioner in 1920, while still retaining his federal judgeship. He served as commissioner until his death in 1944.

"Black Sox" Baseball Scandal Inquiry

Photograph

By: Associated Press

Date: 1921

Source: Kenesaw Landis and others at the "Black Sox" baseball scandal inquiry. 1921. AP/Wide World Photos. Available online at http://www.apwideworld.com (accessed May 8, 2003). ∎

Introduction

Baseball has long been known as the national pastime, and through the first half of the twentieth century, it was unquestionably the most popular sport in America. Players were usually poorly educated, second-generation immigrants from small towns and rural areas. In contrast to today, they were not well paid, but most were happy to have a relatively good-paying job playing a game they loved. Most of the money made in baseball was made by the owners, who fought off attempts to begin rival leagues and created a monopoly of sorts in professional baseball.

Just as American as baseball was gambling. From the country's earliest days, Americans had gambled, particularly on such sporting events as horse racing. As sports became more entrenched and organized, betting on games and contests increased. Boxing, baseball, and horse racing were the three most popular professional sports that people bet on. Most of the betting was local and had no bearing on the contests themselves. Once professional gamblers entered the picture, however, the situation changed dramatically. Politicians tried to control or restrict gambling, but evidence suggests that many of those same politicians were not only supporting gambling in some way but also making money from gamblers. By the late 1800s, many newspapers were condemning gambling and the effect it was having on how baseball games were played. Owners knew that they had to cleanse their sport of the taint of gambling or risk losing their fan base. With no outside revenues from modern sources—such as television, commercial enterprises, or endorsements—owners were totally reliant on the revenue from game attendance to make a profit. Profits were not large, and players were not highly paid. A good player could either play on the team that signed him, for a salary set by that club, or not play at all. In the off-season, players held second jobs including everything from laborers and farmers to salesmen and shopkeepers.

The owner of the Chicago White Sox in 1919 was Charles Comiskey, an early baseball player who, over time, had acquired the White Sox and built them into an excellent team. His players, however, were tremendously underpaid. Even worse, Comiskey promised various bonus payments for performance but usually reneged, claiming he did not have the money. In 1919, the White Sox, from the American League, faced the National League's Cincinnati Reds in the World Series. As the Series neared, rumors that such big-time professional gamblers as Arnold Rothstein were seeking to get players to throw the games were widespread. The rumors persisted throughout the Series, which the heavily favored White Sox lost to the Reds, five games to three.

Significance

Without proof of the allegations, the rumors diminished as the 1920 season came and went. In September 1920, though, it was revealed that the 1919 Series had indeed been fixed, despite great efforts by baseball owners to deny or hide the evidence. Eight White Sox players—Eddie Cicotte, Chick Gandil, Oscar Felsch, Joe Jackson, Fred McMullin, Swede Risberg, Buck Weaver, and Claude Williams—admitted accepting payments of $5,000–$10,000 (more than most of their salaries) to throw games. The trial was held in 1921, but all the players retracted their confessions, leaving only the confession of a professional gambler as evidence against them.

Primary Source

"Black Sox" Baseball Scandal Inquiry

SYNOPSIS: Kenesaw Mountain Landis (upper left) with Chas "Swede" Risberg and Arnold "Chick" Gandil (left to right) at an inquiry held in Chicago in 1921. Landis banned the eight players involved in the "Black Sox" scandal from playing professional baseball for life. AP/WIDE WORLD PHOTOS. REPRODUCED BY PERMISSION.

The jury acquitted both the players and the gamblers. Nevertheless, the new commissioner of baseball, Judge Kenesaw Landis, barred all eight players from organized baseball for life.

The so-called Black Sox scandal had both immediate and long-term effects on baseball. Over the next four years, Landis suspended thirty-eight more players and banned seven others for either gambling or simply not reporting a bribe attempt to their teams. Soon, the integrity of baseball was reestablished, and the game became more popular than ever. Coincident with this was an increase in home runs, which thrilled the fans and led to more attendance at games. Other sports, though, remained tainted by the gambling scandal, and the specter of gambling hung over boxing, basketball, and horse racing for decades. Landis's actions greatly affected baseball in the 1920s, and they continue to do so today. Joe Jackson, one of the original eight players banned, remains ineligible for the Baseball Hall of Fame despite his lifetime batting average of .356, third best in baseball history. The spirit of the 1919 scandal was revived in 1989, when Pete Rose, the game's all-time hits leader and then manager of the Cincinnati Reds, was banned from baseball (and the Hall of Fame) for allegedly betting on games, including those in which his own team participated.

Primary Source

Statement of Commissioner Landis

SYNOPSIS: In the following statement, provided on August 3, 1921, baseball commissioner Kenesaw Mountain Landis officially bans for life the eight Chicago White Sox players accused of fixing games in the 1919 World Series. Issued immediately after the court's decision to acquit all eight players, Landis's statement illustrates his absolute power in baseball.

Regardless of the verdict of juries, no player who throws a ballgame, no player that undertakes or promises to throw a ballgame, no player that sits in conference with a bunch of crooked players and gamblers where the ways and means of throwing a game are discussed and does not promptly tell his club about it, will ever play professional baseball.

Further Resources

BOOKS

Asinof, Eliot. *Eight Men Out.* New York: Holt, Rinehart and Winston, 1979.

Pietrusza, David. *Judge and Jury: The Life and Times of Kenesaw Mountain Landis.* South Bend, Ind.: Diamond Communications, 1998.

Spink, J.G. Taylor. *Judge Landis and 25 Years of Baseball.* St. Louis: Sporting News Publishing, 1974.

PERIODICALS

Watson, Bruce. "The Judge Who Ruled Baseball." *Smithsonian,* October 2000.

WEBSITES

"The Black Sox." Chicago Historical Society. Available online at http://www.Chicagohs.org/history/blacksox.html; website home page: http://www.chicagohs.org (accessed December 3, 2002).

"The Black Sox Trial: 1921." *Famous American Trials.* Doug Linder, ed. Available online at http://www.umkc.edu/famoustrials (accessed May 8, 2003).

Linder, Douglas. "The Black Sox Trial: An Account." School of Law, University of Missouri–Kansas City. Available online at http://www.law.umkc.edu/faculty/projects/ftrials/blacksox/blacksox.html; website home page: http://www.law.umkc.edu (accessed December 3, 2002).

"1919 World Series: Black Sox Scandal." History and Political Science home page, Montgomery College. Available online at http://www.mc.cc.md.us/Departments/hpolscrv/blacksox.htm; website home page: http://www.montgomerycollege.edu (accessed December 3, 2002).

AUDIO AND VISUAL MEDIA

Eight Men Out. Directed by John Sayles. Warner Home Video. 1988, VHS.

George Halas and the Birth of the NFL

Halas by Halas

Autobiography

By: George S. Halas

Date: 1979

Source: Halas, George, with Gwen Morgan and Arthur Veysey. *Halas by Halas: The Autobiography of George Halas.* New York: McGraw-Hill, 60–61.

About the Author George S. Halas (1885–1983) was the founder, owner, and coach of the Chicago Bears professional football team from 1920 until his death. He played football at Crane Tech High School in Chicago and under Bob Zuppke at the University of Illinois. As a coach, he won eight National Football League (NFL) titles and is second on the all-time career list with 324 wins. His name was virtually synonymous with the NFL through its first fifty seasons.

Letter to George Halas

Letter

By: A.E. Staley

Date: October 6, 1921

Source: Staley, A.E. Letter from A.E. Staley to George Halas, October 6, 1921. Reprinted in Halas, George, with Gwen Morgan and Arthur Veysey. *Halas by Halas: the Autobiography of George Halas.* New York: McGraw-Hill, 1979, 72. Available online at http://www.webwaymonsters.com/staleys.html; website home page: http://webwaymonsters.com (accessed May 9, 2003).

About the Author Augustus Eugene Staley was a forward-thinking businessman whose first business was begun in 1898 when he began repackaging corn starch that he had bought wholesale into bags bearing his name in his apartment. He quickly convinced investors to back his plan to buy a defunct corn processing plant in Decatur, Illinois, and began producing his own product. Staley looked out for his employees, and his company was highly personal and one of the first to have a company journal, credit union, Fellowship Club (forerunner of a labor union), and football team—which later became the NFL's Chicago Bears. ∎

Introduction

The first football game was an intercollegiate game played in 1869, with Rutgers defeating Princeton. The game, a variant of rugby, continued to evolve over the years, constantly running the risk of abolition because of its excessive roughness. Players played with little or no padding and no helmets. When a number of deaths occurred in games in the early 1900s, President Theodore Roosevelt (served 1901–1909) considered banning the game at colleges, but after a series of reforms, it was allowed to continue in 1905. The first professional football team, from Greensburg, Pennsylvania, began play in 1893, and the first short-lived league was formed in 1902. The game became more of a spectator sport as the rules changed and improved, but few leagues lasted for more than a year or two. Regional rivalries became more important, and that between the teams from Canton and Massillon, Ohio, was one of the most heated. The Canton Bulldogs recruited Jim Thorpe, the famous player from the Carlisle Indian School in Pennsylvania, and Thorpe brought in other great players. By 1919 a number of top teams had emerged in Ohio, and that summer four of them—Canton, Columbus, Dayton, and Akron—plus a team from Rochester, New York, formed the American Professional Football Association (APFA). The next year is credited as the "birth" of the league that became the NFL, with teams from Massillon and Cleveland in Ohio; Decatur, Chicago, and Rock Island in Illinois; Muncie and Hammond in Indiana; and Racine, Wisconsin, combining with the five original clubs to form the APFA. The meeting at which the league was formed was held in Canton, Ohio, on September 17, 1920. All

A.E. Staley Manufacturing Company

CORN PRODUCTS

Decatur, Ill. October 6, 1921.

The Staley Football Team,
Decatur, Illinois.

Gentlemen:

Confirming our verbal agreement with you, we agree to place the names of all your football players (Total number not to exceed nineteen) on our payrolls at a salary of $25.00 per week with the exception of those already being taken care of in that manner on regular jobs.

We also agree to enter into an advertising contract with you whereby we undertake to pay you Three Thousand ($3,000.00) Dollars for such advertising in your score book as you have suggested.

It is our wish and plan that when the football team goes to Chicago on October 15th, it remain there until the end of the season.

In this event while the team is in Chicago we will maintain on the payroll the entire nineteen men on the team at $25.00 per week until this Company shall have paid you in total, including both advertising and salary amounts, the sum of Five Thousand ($5,000.00) Dollars.

In consideration of these various payments, it is agreed that the team is to operate under the name of "The Staley Football Club" That you are to use your best efforts to disseminate information regarding, and to facilitate the business of the A.E.Staley Manufacturing Company; that you are to secure the utmost publicity in the newspapers for the team and the Company; that you are to so conduct the team, its playing and management as to reflect credit upon the A.E.Staley Manufacturing Company; that you will enter into no contracts or obligations in any way binding upon the A.E.Staley Manufacturing Company with this present exception.

It is understood that this arrangement shall terminate at the end of the present football season.

Please indicate your acception of the provisions of this agreement. I remain

Accepted by
Staley Football Club
a
Geo.S.Halas

Yours very truly,
A.E.STALEY MANUFACTURING CO.

President.

Primary Source

Letter to George Halas

SYNOPSIS: This letter of agreement from A.E. Staley, President of A.E. Staley Manufacturing Company, illustrates how pro football was arranged and organized in its formative years in the 1920s. Staley sponsored the football team in order to publicize his company, and the team was called the Staleys. After encouraging the move to Chicago, Staley agreed to provide "seed money" for Halas and his team during its first year in that city. From this modest agreement came the Chicago Bears, still one of the most successful franchises in professional sports. A.E. STALEY MANUFACTURING COMPANY. REPRODUCED BY PERMISSION.

The 1920 Staley football team. George Halas, a Chicago Cubs baseball fan, changed the name of his team to the Bears in 1922. **A.E. STALEY MANUFACTURING COMPANY. REPRODUCED BY PERMISSION.**

paid a one-hundred-dollar fee to join the new league. Jim Thorpe was named the league's first president.

Significance

The American Professional Football Association changed its name in 1925 to the National Football League and has operated continuously since that time. Halas became the dominant owner in the league, and his team, the Chicago Bears (which changed its name from the Staleys in 1922) became the most successful franchise in the league. Halas signed Harold "Red" Grange out of the University of Illinois in 1925, setting off a wave of criticism from colleges and the media but increasing fan interest exponentially. Halas, the last owner to coach in the NFL, led his team to professional championships in 1921, 1932, 1933, 1940, 1941, 1943, 1946, and 1963.

Over the years the National Football League has absorbed various competitor leagues. The All America Football Conference merged with the NFL in the early 1950s, and the American Football League gradually merged with the NFL beginning with the AFL-NFL Super Bowl in 1967. The need for sponsorship is clearly indicated in the Staley letter, and most professional leagues sought such help until they could stand on their own. Since games were not broadcast on television or radio, the president of the Staley Manufacturing Company indicated that newspaper coverage of the team and, thus, the company, would be in the interest of both. It was evident that a professional football league needed to appeal to fans through publicity, since professional teams lacked the natural constituency of college teams (students and alumni). The letter also shows that long-term success could only come by seeking venues with a larger fan base. In other words, the day of the small-town league was passing and the era of big-city franchises was dawning. This remains true in the NFL of the early twenty-first century; the exception is Green Bay, Wisconsin, whose Packers are owned by many members of that community.

Primary Source

Halas by Halas [excerpt]

SYNOPSIS: George Halas's autobiography traces both his personal life and his life in football, which were hard to separate at times. After buying the Decatur Staleys from A.E. Staley, he ran the team as a family enterprise. He also saw the NFL as one of his "children," and his account reflects that. This excerpt focuses on the creation of the American Professional Football Association.

I thought the Staleys had gone beyond this mobile situation. I wrote various teams suggesting games. Replies were indifferent and vague. We needed an organization.

I wrote to Ralph Hay, the manager of the Canton Bulldogs, one of the best run and most prominent teams. I mentioned our need for a league. He had already discussed the idea with Stan Cofall, a former Notre Dame star who was running the Massillon Tigers. They met with Frank Nied and A.F. Ranney of Akron and representatives from Cleveland and Dayton on August 20 in Akron. Hay was appointed temporary chairman. He called a meeting on September 17, 1920, at his automobile showroom in Canton.

Morgan O'Brien, a Staley engineer and a football fan who was being very helpful in administrative matters, and I went to Canton on the train. Twelve teams were represented. They were the Canton Bulldogs; Cleveland Indians; Dayton Triangles; Akron Professionals; Massillon Tigers; Rochester, New York; Rock Island, Illinois; Muncie, Indiana; Staleys of Decatur, Illinois; Chicago Cardinals; Racine, Wisconsin; and Hammond, Indiana. The showroom, big enough for four cars—Hupmobiles and Jordans—occupied the ground floor of the three-story brick Odd Fellows building. Chairs were few. I sat on a runningboard.

We all agreed on the need for a league. In two hours we created the American Professional Football Association.

To give the Association some financial standing, we voted to issue franchises on payment of $100. Twelve teams were awarded franchises on the spot—Akron, Canton, Cleveland, Dayton, Decatur Staleys, Hammond, Massillon, Muncie, Chicago Cardinals, Racine (Wisconsin), Rochester and Rock Island. Massillon withdrew for the 1920 season.

The Association needed someone with a name. Our minds turned to Jim Thorpe, absent but the biggest name in sport. Unanimously, we elected him our president.

When I told other managers about the top players I had lined up, there was great eagerness to meet us on the field.

Further Resources

BOOKS

Carroll, Robert, ed. *Total Football: The Official Encyclopedia of the NFL.* New York: HarperCollins, 1999.

Neft, David. *The Football Encyclopedia.* New York: St. Martin's Press, 1994.

Whittingham, Richard. *The Chicago Bears from George Halas to Super Bowl XX: An Illustrated History.* New York: Simon and Schuster, 1986.

WEBSITES

"Chicago Bears." Pro Football Hall of Fame. Available online at http://www.profootballhof.com/history/teams/bears.cfm; website home page: http://www.profootballhof.com (accessed May 9, 2003).

"Real Men: George Halas." Manlyweb.com. Available online at http://www.manlyweb.com/realmen/GeorgeHalas.html; website home page: http://www.manlyweb.com (accessed May 9, 2003).

Federal Club v. National League

Supreme Court decision

By: Oliver Wendell Holmes Jr.

Date: May 29, 1922

Source: *Federal Baseball Club of Baltimore, Inc. v. National League of Professional Baseball Clubs, et al.* 259 U.S. 200 (1922). Available online at http://caselaw.lp.findlaw.com /scripts/getcase.pl?navby=search&court=US&case=/us/259 /200.html; website home page: http://findlaw.com (accessed December 3, 2002).=US&case=/us/259/200.html; website home page: http://findlaw.com (accessed December 3, 2002).

About the Author: Oliver Wendell Holmes Jr. (1841–1935) was an associate justice of the U.S. Supreme Court from 1902 to 1932, one of the longest tenures in the history of the Court. He began his legal career as a professor of law at Harvard University. Then, in 1883, he was appointed to the Massachusetts Supreme Judicial Court, where he rose to chief justice in 1899, before President Theodore Roosevelt appointed him to the U.S. Supreme Court. Legal scholars consistently rank him among the most brilliant and respected Supreme Court justices of all time. ∎

Introduction

Professional baseball began in the late 1800s. By 1876, the National League of Professional Baseball Clubs had been established as the top professional league. Over the next twenty-five years, other, short-lived rival leagues were formed, including the American Association in 1881, the Players League in 1890, and the American Association in 1891. Another rival league, the Western League, changed its name to the American League in 1900 and battled the National League for top players. In 1903, though, the two leagues signed an agreement that seemed to bring peace to major league baseball.

Just eleven years later, in 1914, yet another league, the Federal League, brought economic crisis to baseball once again. The owners of National and American League clubs agreed to offer various financial inducements to some Federal League owners to drive the league out of business. Not all Federal League owners were included in these financial arrangements, and one club, from Baltimore, brought a lawsuit against the National League under U.S. antitrust laws. These laws prohibit a company or group of companies engaged in interstate commerce—commerce that crosses state lines—from forming a monopoly that allows them to reap unchecked profits by setting prices, restricting services, and eliminating competition. The question facing baseball—and the Supreme Court—in 1922 was this: Was baseball more in the nature of sport, or was it a business? If it was deemed more sport, the courts and the government would have no say in how it ran its affairs, and the antitrust laws would not apply to it. This would have made legal and acceptable such practices as the reserve clause, which forced a player to play only with one club (unless it released him) or not play major league baseball.

Significance

Supreme Court Justice Oliver Wendell Holmes recognized that baseball was a business and that it sold its product (games) in many different cities, suggesting that it was interstate commerce. Nevertheless, he affirmed the finding of the lower court that baseball presented entertainment, which is considered a local matter even though participants may come from other states. For this reason, he saw baseball games as state (not interstate) contests, and therefore not subject to federal antitrust laws. This reasoning greatly affected baseball in the decades that followed. In the late 1950s and early 1960s, for example, an effort was made to start a third major league, the Continental League. Existing major league baseball owners, however, successfully deflected that effort by agreeing to expand their league, essentially buying out potential rivals just as they had earlier in the century. A congressional subcommittee chaired by Emanuel Cellar of New York held hearings that reexamined, and ultimately reaffirmed, baseball's exemption from antitrust laws. Although in the 1970s the reserve clause was found to be an unfair restraint on players—and thus illegal—baseball's exemption from antitrust law continued. In 1997, the Senate Judiciary Committee held hearings on applying antitrust legislation to baseball. Then, in 2002, baseball officials again testified before a congressional subcommittee about the need for continued exemption from antitrust law. Thus, the 1922 decision by the Supreme Court and Justice Holmes continues to be a significant factor in the economics of baseball.

Joe Tinker, a manager for the Chicago Federal League club, in 1914. The owners of National and American League clubs offered financial inducements to some Federal League owners to drive the league out of business. **AP/WIDE WORLD PHOTOS. REPRODUCED BY PERMISSION.**

Primary Source

Federal Club v. National League

> **SYNOPSIS:** *Federal Club v. National League* was filed in U.S. district court. After a decision in favor of the plaintiff (the Baltimore club), the case was appealed, and the decision at the U.S. Court of Appeals was for the defendants (the National League). The case was then appealed to the U.S. Supreme Court. The key question on which the case focuses is whether the business of baseball is interstate commerce. Baseball's continued monopoly depends on whether the court determines baseball to be more a business or a sport. The case was argued on April 19, 1922, and decided on May 29, 1922.

Mr. Justice Holmes delivered the opinion of the Court.

This is a suit for threefold damages brought by the plaintiff in error under the Anti-Trust Acts of July 2, 1890, c. 647, 7, 26 Stat. 209, 210 (Comp. St. 8829), and of October 15, 1914, c. 323, 4, 38 Stat. 730, 731 (Comp. St. 8835d). The defendants are the National League of Professional Base Ball Clubs and the American League of Professional

Base Ball Clubs, unincorporated associations, composed respectively of groups of eight incorporated base ball clubs, joined as defendants; the presidents of the two Leagues and a third person, constituting what is known as the National Commission, having considerable powers in carrying out an agreement between the two Leagues; and three other persons having powers in the Federal League of Professional Base Ball Clubs, the relation of which to this case will be explained. It is alleged that these defendants conspired to monopolize the base ball business, the means adopted being set forth with a detail which, in the view that we take, it is unnecessary to repeat.

The plaintiff is a base ball club incorporated in Maryland, and with seven other corporations was a member of the Federal League of Professional Base Ball Players, a corporation under the laws of Indiana, that attempted to compete with the combined defendants. It alleges that the defendants destroyed the Federal League by buying up some of the constituent clubs and in one way or another inducing all those clubs except the plaintiff to leave their League, and that the three persons connected with the Federal League and named as defendants, one of them being the President of the League, took part in the conspiracy. Great damage to the plaintiff is alleged. The [259 U.S. 200, 208] plaintiff obtained a verdict for $80,000 in the Supreme Court and a judgment for treble the amount was entered, but the Court of Appeals, after an elaborate discussion, held that the defendants were not within the Sherman Act. The appellee, the plaintiff, elected to stand on the record in order to bring the case to this Court at once, and thereupon judgment was ordered for the defendants. *National League of Professional Baseball Clubs v. Federal Baseball Club of Baltimore,* 269 Fed. 681, 688, 50 App. D. C. 165. It is not argued that the plaintiff waived any rights by its course. *Thomsen v. Cayser,* 243 U.S. 66, 37 Sup. Ct. 353, Ann. Cas. 1917D, 322.

The decision of the Court of Appeals went to the root of the case and if correct makes it unnecessary to consider other serious difficulties in the way of the plaintiff's recovery. A summary statement of the nature of the business involved will be enough to present the point. The clubs composing the Leagues are in different cities and for the most part in different States. The end of the elaborate organizations and sub-organizations that are described in the pleadings and evidence is that these clubs shall play against one another in public exhibitions for money, one or the other club crossing a state line in order to make the meeting possible. When as the result of these contests one club has won the pennant of its League and another club has won the pennant of the other League, there is a final competition for the world's championship between these two. Of course the scheme requires constantly repeated travelling on the part of the clubs, which is provided for, controlled and disciplined by the organizations, and this it is said means commerce among the States. But we are of opinion that the Court of Appeals was right.

The business is giving exhibitions of base ball, which are purely state affairs. It is true that in order to attain for these exhibitions the great popularity that they have achieved, competitions must be arranged between clubs from different cities and States. But the fact that in order [259 U.S. 200, 209] to give the exhibitions the Leagues must induce free persons to cross state lines and must arrange and pay for their doing so is not enough to change the character of the business. According to the distinction insisted upon in *Hooper v. California,* 155 U.S. 648, 655, 15 S. Sup. Ct. 207, the transport is a mere incident, not the essential thing. That to which it is incident, the exhibition, although made for money would not be called trade of commerce in the commonly accepted use of those words. As it is put by defendant, personal effort, not related to production, is not a subject of commerce. That which in its consummation is not commerce does not become commerce among the States because the transportation that we have mentioned takes place. To repeat the illustrations given by the Court below, a firm of lawyers sending out a member to argue a case, or the Chautauqua lecture bureau sending out lecturers, does not engage in such commerce because the lawyer or lecturer goes to another State.

If we are right the plaintiff's business is to be described in the same way and the restrictions by contract that prevented the plaintiff from getting players to break their bargains and the other conduct charged against the defendants were not an interference with commerce among the States.

Judgment affirmed.

Further Resources

BOOKS

Abrams, Roger. *Legal Bases: Baseball and the Law.* Philadelphia: Temple University Press, 1998.

Burton, David. *Oliver Wendell Holmes, Jr.* Boston: Twayne, 1980.

Nowick, Sheldon. *Honorable Justice.* Boston: Little, Brown, 1989.

Rader, Benjamin. *Baseball: A History of America's Game.* Urbana, Ill.: University of Illinois Press, 2002.

Voigt, David Q. *Baseball: An Illustrated History.* University Park, Pa.: Penn State University Press, 1994.

White, G. Edward. *Justice Oliver Wendell Holmes—Law and the Inner Self.* New York: Oxford University Press, 1993.

WEBSITES

"The Federal League." Available online at http://www.toyou .com/fl (accessed May 8, 2003).

"Federal League Had Brief Run but Made an Impact on MLB." Historic Baseball. Available online at http://www .historicbaseball.com/federalleague.html; website home page: http://www.historicbaseball.com (accessed December 3, 2002).

"Oliver Wendell Holmes, Jr." Arlington National Cemetery Website. Available online at http://www.arlingtoncemetery .com/owholmes.htm; website home page: http://www .arlingtoncemetery.com (accessed December 3, 2002).

"Why the Finns Are Champion Athletes"

Magazine article

By: *The Literary Digest*

Date: August 2, 1924

Source: "Why the Finns Are Champion Athletes." *The Literary Digest* 82, no. 5, August 2, 1924, 42–44, 46.

About the Publication: *The Literary Digest* began publishing in 1890 and in the first quarter of the twentieth century was one of the most popular magazines in the United States. Its modern-day counterparts are *Time* or *Newsweek* magazines. ■

Introduction

The modern Olympics began in 1896 in Athens, Greece, largely through the efforts of Baron Pierre de Coubertin of France. The Olympics of ancient Greece were primarily track and field events, so these were the featured events in the reconstituted Olympics. By the 1912 Games in Stockholm, Sweden, performers were being hailed internationally for their accomplishments. More than twenty-five countries sent delegations, and teams were now outfitted in national uniforms. At this Olympics, Jim Thorpe won acclaim as the greatest athlete in the world, but the games also presented the world with the first great distance runners from Finland, Hannes Kolehmainen and Albin Stenroos. Kolehmainen and Stenroos won four medals in Stockholm, three of which went to Kolehmainen. In 1916 the games were not held because of the World War I (1914–1918), and the next Olympics, in Antwerp in 1920, came close on the heels of the end of the war. Despite the economic gloom that came with the aftermath of the war, the Games were the first large stage for a new Finnish runner, Paavo Nurmi, who would be called the greatest of the "Flying Finns."

Nurmi was born in Turku, Finland, on June 13, 1897, and first came to international prominence with his performance at the 1920 Games in Antwerp. He won three gold medals: one for the ten thousand-meter run, one for the ten thousand-meter cross-country run, and one as a member of the Finnish ten thousand-meter cross-country team. (The latter two events were dropped from the Olympics after the 1924 Games.) He also finished second in the five thousand-meter run. Nurmi was the most victorious of the Finns at Antwerp, where Kolehmainen won the Olympic marathon. Finns also won the shotput, discus, and javelin, so Nurmi's victories were seen as part of an overall "onslaught" by the Finns. With a more peaceful world and better opportunities for training, it was anticipated that even greater feats were possible at the 1924 Games in Paris. In the intervening years, Nurmi began setting world records at distances ranging from fifteen hundred to ten thousand meters, including the mile, two miles, three miles, two thousand meters, and three thousand meters.

Significance

Paavo Nurmi was arguably the greatest Olympic long-distance runner in history and the greatest track star of the 1920s. His fame was spread both by newspapers and telegraph and through his tours of the United States and Europe after his Olympic victories in 1924 and 1928. In 1924 he won five gold medals in Paris: at fifteen hundred meters, five thousand meters, the ten thousand-meter cross-country run, the team cross-country race, and the three thousand-meter team event. He won at fifteen hundred and five thousand meters on the same day in races run only fifty-five minutes apart—and set an Olympic record in each event. In 1923 he set the record for the mile run and the three-mile run, records which stood until 1931 and 1932 respectively. Then in 1928 he set the ten-mile record and the record distance in the one-hour run, both not broken until 1945. His six-mile run record, set in 1930, lasted seven years. In the 1928 Olympics in Amsterdam, he won the ten thousand-meter race, an event he had chosen not to run in Paris four years earlier. He finished second at five thousand meters to another Finn, Ville Ritola. Both Nurmi's use of systematic stopwatch-based training and the appearance fees he received for running angered amateur track officials, and he was banned from the 1932 Olympics in Los Angeles. Two years later, at the age of thirty-seven,

Paavo Nurmi crosses the finish line at the 1,500 meter Olympic race, July 19, 1924. © BETTMANN/CORBIS. REPRODUCED BY PERMISSION.

he retired from competitive racing after having set twenty-five world records. He died in 1973 in Finland, where he was buried with full national honors.

Primary Source

"Why the Finns Are Champion Athletes" [excerpt]

SYNOPSIS: This article shows the enormous interest in and respect for Paavo Nurmi and his fellow Finnish runners. The article attributes their running success to diet, training, and simply their physical characteristics. The article was written shortly after Nurmi's success in the Paris Olympics and before his first successful American tour. The distance to Finland and its relative isolation made the runners seem more "exotic," and the American fascination with Nurmi endured through the 1920s.

Nurmi proved his greatness not only by winning two distance events in one afternoon, but in each event he smashed the Olympic record with seconds to spare, and then finished as cool, unwearied and serene as if he never had taken a step. His two conquering marches in the 1,500 and 5,000 meter races were epoch-making events, which none among the great crowd ever will forget as excited thousands stood up to pay deserved acclaim to his running greatness.

The fair-haired Finn ran H. B. Stallard, star English miler, into complete unconsciousness over the 1,500-meter route and then, a short while later on, outpaced the stout-hearted Ritola, a son of his native turf, in the most spectacular 5,000-meter race any Olympic game ever has known. In the longer distance Nurmi had to break the Olympic record by more than five seconds and his own world's record by more than four seconds, in order to beat the last desperate drive of Ritola by a stride, but, in spite of the unbelievable double test, he had enough left to finish with a gallant sprint and then to leave the track at a fast jog in the direction of his quarters.

It is no wonder that the largest gathering of the week turned on a vocal cataclysm that must have swept northward to Helsingfors and told the eager thousands throughout all Finland. No runner in track history ever had attempted before any such prodigious fiber-shattering test in one afternoon. To smash two Olympic and one world's record under such conditions stamps Nurmi as the marvel of all track marvels whose like will never again be seen within this generation. Twice within a short interval the blue and white flag of Finland went up because one man stood superior to all his tribe where only a heart of iron could have remained unbroken. Nurmi's first test came in the 1,500-meter race where the durable Finn faced Scharer, star Swiss runner; Stallard and Lowe, of England, and Baker, Hahn and Watson, of the United States. After the well-bunched field had traversed the first 100 yards Nurmi suddenly darted into the lead, and Ray Watson clung to the Finn's heels.

Nurmi swung immediately into a fast, even pace, still using his watch for timing as he finished each lap. Facing the final lap Nurmi had a lead of forty yards, and Watson finally faltered and broke, unable to cling to any such flawless machine in human form. Rounding the far turn Scharer and Stallard came to the front with a rush with a final but vain hope of closing the gap, but Nurmi calmly looked over his shoulder and increased his stride to open a wider gap, winning without the slightest extra effort. He then ran off the track, picked up his sweater and trotted to his quarters. He had broken the Olympic record by three and one-fifth seconds and easily could have broken his own world's record of 3:52^3/$_{10}$ if he had not been faced with the 5,000-meter task.

In the meanwhile Stallard and Scharer in a last heart-breaking sprint came tearing on with the latter in front as Stallard fell unconscious across the finish line. Two physicians were needed to bring the game English miler out of poppyland dreams, where he remained unconscious for thirty minutes. As Nurmi finished a great ovation followed him along the field until he disappeared beneath the big stadium. Fifty minutes later Nurmi returned to start in the 5,000-meter race.

Almost from the crack of the starter's gun Ritola, of Finland, and Wide, of Sweden, hung on to Nurmi's clock-like, effortless spin, as if a ghost were in motion. For five laps Ritola led, but then one look at his watch told Nurmi that it was time he was on his way. Out into the front he glided to the accompaniment of a thundering tumult, and at this point Wide began to drop back. On the final lap Ritola was only two strides away, but still running with valiant courage. Here was a race that was a race, a battle that thousands will hold in memory.

Struggling with all he had Ritola could not close that gap, but near the finish as Nurmi turned to look, his rival countryman came within a stride of his conqueror's heels. This time Nurmi broke the Olympic record by more than five seconds, and again he ran for his sweater on the turf near by, jogging swiftly back to his quarters with a roar of applause following like the thundering of surf in a storm.

Before the race Sparrow Robertson, one of the greatest of all judges, called the turn. "The King of the Track," he said, "has come. They might as well measure him for the crown." . . .

Nurmi is in truth "the iron man of the cinder-path." His like may never be seen again.

You will note that Nurmi invariably finishes his races fresh as a daisy and full of running. Even when prest to the limit by Ritola in the 5,000, Paavo showed no signs of distress. After breasting the tape he picked up his sweater and joy-trotted blithely to his training-quarters.

When men were collapsing right and left in the 10,000-meter cross-country race yesterday Nurmi alone appeared undistrest by the merciless heat. Edwin Wide, a tall, strapping Viking from Sweden, collapsed from sunstroke and had to be carried to the hospital. Frenchmen, Americans, Swedes, Britons and Finns wilted under that grilling heat. But Nurmi romped over hill and dale as tho enjoying a pleasure run. As he entered the vast stadium the little Finn was moving as smoothly and as strongly as tho he

had motored over that six-mile stretch of broken country, steaming under a sun of tropic intensity.

Some one said that the test of a great horse was whether he could run under any track conditions. The same test applies to athletes. Nurmi can run on any sort of footing. He is equally at home on a cinderpath, a plowed field or city pavements. He can run cross-country as well as he can run "on the flat." No excuses are ever needed for the Fantom Finn.

Nurmi is a running freak. He is supreme at any distance, from one mile to ten. We believe that he would be invincible at the half-mile, too. Paavo is not a "spurt runner." He doesn't change his pace as Alfred Shubb did, now hanging back deliberately, now cutting loose a speed burst that left his rivals groggy.

Nurmi "goes out" right from the cut, setting an even, steady pace that no other human can maintain. Moving like an automaton, Nurmi simply glides imperceptibly away from his rivals. It's like running against some grim, inscrutable Robot—some mechanical Frankenstein created to annihilate time.

As Nurmi completes a lap he cocks his blond head to the right to glance at the stop-watch concealed in his clenched fist. This was the characteristic mannerism that Joie Ray, the American mile-runner, a born buffoon, mimicked to the delight of the crowd in the stands.

Nurmi is a post-war product of Finland's public-school system of athletics for all. Each young Finlander is required to take up distance-running as part of the curriculum. It was in this practical school of "involuntary" running that Nurmi developed from a promising novice to the greatest star the cinder-path has known. At Antwerp, still a green kid, Nurmi broke into the victory column twice. Four years have passed since Antwerp held the Olympics and Paris sees Nurmi in the full flush of his athletic manhood.

Further Resources

BOOKS

Uschen, Michael. *Male Olympic Champions*. San Diego, Calif.: Lucent Books, 2000.

WEBSITES

Brady, Joe. "Paavo Nurmi." Virtual Finland. Available online at http://virtual.finland.fi/finfo/english/paavo.html; website home page: http://virtual.finland.fi (accessed May 12, 2003).

"Great Olympian: Biographies." Available online at http://users.skynet.be/hermandw/olymp/bionu.htm#RMP (accessed December 6, 2002).

"Grange Thrills Huge Crowd by Racing to 5 Touchdowns"

Newspaper article

By: James Crusinberry

Date: October 19, 1924

Source: Crusinberry, James. "Grange Thrills Huge Crowd by Racing to 5 Touchdowns." *Chicago Tribune,* October 19, 1924.

About the Publication: The *Chicago Tribune* has been published continuously since it was founded in 1849, making it one of the oldest newspapers in the United States. Under Joseph Medill and, later, Robert McCormick, the *Tribune* was a keen observer of sports, particularly in Illinois. The *Tribune,* which had the largest circulation of any newspaper in Chicago and the Midwest, closely followed and reported on the sporting fortunes of the Big Ten Conference and, specifically, the University of Illinois. ∎

Introduction

College football was revived by rule changes in 1906, and it grew in popularity as the number of alumni from various institutions grew. Strong regional loyalties and powerful teams emerged among schools in the Southeast, in the East with Ivy League and independent teams, and in the Midwest with the Big Ten Conference. Michigan and Illinois were consistently two of the top teams both in the Big Ten and in the country. After winning Big Ten titles in 1918 and 1919, the fortunes of the Fighting Illini plummeted in 1921 and 1922, when they won a total of only three league games. They then went undefeated in 1923 and opened a new stadium, Memorial Field, which seated sixty thousand compared to the fewer than twenty thousand that could fit in the old stadium. Illinois's undefeated season was matched by the University of Michigan, which also went 8–0, but the two teams did not meet that year. The next year, Michigan came to Champaign-Urbana for both teams' Big Ten opener. The contest was also the first to be broadcast on WGN radio of Chicago, the largest station in the Midwest.

Significance

With this game Red Grange established himself as a legendary hero for the rest of his lifetime. His feat of five touchdowns was amazing enough, but the fact that he scored the first four of them over a span of less than twelve minutes was staggering. Though many players had had great performances in a game, Grange's heroics came against one of the strongest teams in the nation. The feat was given wide publicity because of both radio coverage and the extensive press coverage coinciding with the dedication of the new stadium. The excitement and popular-

ity of the game made football a fixture on WGN radio for the next ten years, and many observers believe that Grange's great game contributed to the surge in radio purchases over the next ten years. In 1926, with Grange now a professional, at least one network (NBC) began broadcasting football games.

The media coverage of the game made Grange an instant folk hero; the Wheaton Ice Man—so called because of his summer job delivering ice in his home town of Wheaton, Illinois—became the Galloping Ghost, a nickname that stayed with him throughout his life and is instantly recognizable by even casual fans of football history. As a result of Grange's feats, Eastern papers, particularly *The New York Times,* began regularly covering Illinois football games. The best-known American sportswriter, Grantland Rice, even decided to forgo coverage of some Eastern football games in order to cover Grange, and, beginning in 1925, often highlighted Grange in his *Sportlight News,* a weekly series of sports features shown in motion-picture theaters each week. Grange was signed to a professional contract by the Chicago Bears in November 1925, immediately after the Illinois season ended. His signing was a key to the success of the fledgling National Football League. Grange was elected to the Pro Football Hall of Fame in 1963.

Primary Source

"Grange Thrills Huge Crowd by Racing to 5 Touchdowns" [excerpt]

> **SYNOPSIS:** Led by legendary coaches Fielding Yost of Michigan and Bob Zuppke of Illinois, the game on October 18, 1924, was not just a battle of unbeatens but the dedication day for the new Memorial Stadium. The *Chicago Tribune* featured this account of the game on the front page of the Sunday sports section.

Champaign, Ill., Oct. 18.—[Special.]—Michigan never knew Red Grange, the Illinois wildcat, until today. Now Michigan knows him well.

This great runner of Bob Zuppke's football team ran all over Michigan in the first quarter of their grid battle today at the new Illinois stadium and crushed the Ann Arbor boys before they realized they were in a contest. The final score was 39 to 14 in favor of the boys of Illinois, but was 27 to 0 at the end of the first period when Grange raced down the field four times for touchdowns.

Grange had torn Michigan to pieces before the game had gone more than fifteen seconds because he received the first kickoff from Capt Steger of the Wolverines, and from his own 5 yard line ran and on those four plays and Michigan was a crushed and beaten foe.

The second quarter had hardly begun when Coach Zuppke called his star from the game to save him for other foes to come later in the season, though he was back in the fray for the entire second half, but content to make one touchdown, the final run for it being only 11 yards. He did a lot of plunging and passing in the second half, but never again got loose for a long and thrilling dash.

Further Resources

BOOKS

Carroll, John. *Red Grange and the Rise of Modern Football.* Urbana, Ill.: University of Illinois Press, 1999.

Smith, Ronald A. *Sports and Freedom: The Rise of Big Time College Athletics.* New York: Oxford University Press, 1988.

Young, Linda. *Hail to the Orange and Blue: 100 Years of Illinois Football Tradition.* Champaign, Ill.: Sagamore Publishing, 1990.

WEBSITES

"Harold 'Red' Grange." Pro Football Hall of Fame. Available online at http://www.profootballhof.com/players/enshrinees/hgrange.cfm; website home page: http://www.profootballhof.com (accessed May 12, 2003).

"Robert R. McCormick Museum." Cantigny Park. Available online at http://www.cantignypark.com/rrm_museum_virtual_tour.htm; website home page: http://www.cantignypark.com (accessed May 12, 2003).

University of Michigan Athletics. "Michigan Football History." Available online at http://www.mgoblue.com/section_display.cfm?section_id=419&top=2&level=3; website home page: http://www.mgoblue.com (accessed May 12, 2003).

Red Grange breaks loose for one of his five touchdowns in a 39–14 defeat of the University of Michigan on October 18, 1924.
REPRODUCED COURTESY OF THE UNIVERSITY OF ILLINOIS AT URBANA-CHAMPAIGN ARCHIVES.

dodged and tore his way 95 yards for a touchdown. Right then and there Michigan knew it was up against something it hadn't seen in football before.

Three More Long Runs.

Three more times in that first period Grange got loose for long runs for touchdowns. His second one came after about five minutes of play and was 67 yards in length. The joyful Illini rooters were hardly through cheering that thrilling play before the red headed Wheaton lad got loose again for another, 56 yards in length, and before the quarter was ended he took the ball on the Michigan 44 yard line and dashed through the whole team for a fourth touchdown.

In that first period he made four as sensational open field runs as have been seen in years.

It is doubtful if anything near its equal has been seen in the West since the days of Walter Eckersall. Going into the game, Michigan was figured to have an equal chance to win. The four startling runs in the first quarter by young Grange made Illinois a 130 to 1 shot. He carried the ball for a total of 262 yards

"Original Celtics of New York"
Guidebook

By: Maurice G. Rosenwald

Date: 1924–25

Source: Rosenwald, Maurice G. "Original Celtics of New York." In *Reach Official Basket Ball Guide.* Philadelphia: A.J. Reach Company, 1924–25, 167.

About the Publication: The 1924–1925 *Reach Official Basket Ball Guide* was published by the Reach sporting goods company in Philadelphia. The writer, Maurice G. Rosenwald, worked in public relations, often for the Celtics. The editor of the Reach guide was William Scheffer, who made most of the decisions about the guide and, through the guide, was most responsible for keeping basketball records for the period 1900–1927. ■

The 1923 Celtics basketball team. From left are: Joe Lapchick, Chris Leonard, Dutch Dehnert, Pete Barry, Nat Holman, Johnny Whitty, manager; Johnny Beckman and Eddie Burke. AP/WIDE WORLD PHOTOS. REPRODUCED BY PERMISSION.

Introduction

The Original Celtics were formed initially as an all-Irish team playing around the Celtic Park area of Manhattan. The team was restructured after World War I (1914–1918) and in 1919 added such top players as Johnny Beckman, Joe Trippe, and Ernie Reich. Starting in 1921, the Celtic lineup was set when George Haggerty, Nat Holman, and Chris Leonard joined the team. Except for the addition of Joe Lapchick in 1923 and Davey Banks in 1926, and the loss of Beckman in 1927, the nucleus of the team remained stable throughout the 1920s. The Celtics' stability allowed them to know each other's offensive and defensive moves much better than any other team of the period. That knowledge, combined with their tremendous individual skills, made the Celtics the undisputed top basketball team of the 1920s. They invented modern basketball, perfecting the pivot play, the give-and-go, and the switching man-to-man defense, techniques now a part of every basketball team's repertoire. The Celtics dominated every league in which they competed, and their success drove most of these leagues out

of business because no other squad could compete with them. This lack of competition made fans lose interest in league play, so the Celtics began "barnstorming," that is, playing various top teams on tours throughout the East, Midwest, and South. In a period when most people hardly traveled, the Celtics often played nearly two hundred games per year and journeyed a hundred thousand miles by train and car. In 1926 the Celtics joined the American Basketball League, the first truly national professional basketball league, with teams stretching from Boston to Chicago. The Celtics easily won the league title the next two years, but after that year the team was forced to disband to provide league parity. In the 1930s a Celtics team was resurrected with a number of the old players and toured throughout the Depression era, but the Celtics were no longer the undisputed kings of basketball.

Significance

The Original Celtics created the modern game of basketball and, through their travels, brought the game to outposts throughout America—and not just the game: many people first saw modern athletic shoes and equipment at a touring Celtics game. The owners of the Celtics were the first to sign basketball players to exclusive contracts, allowing the team to stay together for many years. The success of such a system was evident, as the Celtics played before large crowds wherever they went and also provided clinics to introduce the game to newcomers. The Celtics were the first professional team to offer a stable lineup, since most players in the early 1920s contracted with owners for individual games and played on three or more different teams within the same week.

Professional basketball was a very popular sport among working-class citizens, often because the teams were composed of representatives from one ethnic group or sponsored by one craft, such as electricians or shoemakers. Unlike most teams of the era, though, the Celtics were composed of players from various ethnic groups, including Irish Catholics, German Catholics, Jews, and a player of Czech extraction. By not limiting the team to one ethnic group, the team's owners were able to recruit on the basis of skill, and the team's varied ethnic composition provided it with broader fan appeal. Still, the appeal of the Celtics (and of professional basketball generally) was limited in some cities, often by class. *The New York Times,* for instance, gave no coverage to the Celtics until 1926, yet most of the other New York newspapers covered them extensively, reflecting the class split in sport interest and media readership. The Celtics were the best-known team in basketball, and when the Basketball Association of America (a predecessor of the National Basketball Association) began in 1946, the owner of the Boston franchise chose the name Celtics for his team as a tribute to the Original Celtics, and also to demonstrate the high quality of play he envisioned for his team.

Primary Source

"Original Celtics of New York" [excerpt]

SYNOPSIS: *The Reach Guide* was the best—often the only—source of information about professional basketball during the 1920s until it ceased publication in 1928. The guide, which was available nationally, reviewed the previous year's accomplishments of most pro, college, and club teams throughout the United States.

In years to come when the present generation of basketball players have laid aside their shoes for good and the youngsters who are now attending games have youngsters of their own playing the game, the players of that future day will get tin ears listening to, "Well, when the Original Celtics of New York played here in the early part of 1924 they certainly were the greatest aggregation of basketball players ever gotten together. They could do anything that any other basketball quintet could do and then turn around and beat them."

And it will all be true. For the Original Celtics, with Johnnie Beckman and Nat Holman, the two greatest forwards that ever wore the suction shoe; Joe Lopchick, the giant center, and Dutch Dehnert and Chris Leonard, without a doubt the peer of any of the cage game's guards, are the greatest of all.

No team has ever won a series from them. No team has ever had them beaten until the final blast of the whistle. Diggers from the word go, they have played any and all rules and have carried the shamrock jersey to victory in practically every State in the Middle West and Eastern Atlantic sector.

The Original Celtics have probably done more to advance basketball than any other individual or aggregation. Wherever they have gone basketball has taken on a new lease of life. Tremendous audiences have greeted them wherever Jimmie Furey, their manager, has booked them. Dirty playing has never bothered them. They have swung along making the free tries good, and some teams soon learned that the way not to beat the Celtics was to keep on fouling.

Perhaps the greatest record of the Original Celtics was made on their wonderful tour that started January 1st, carrying them up through New York State, through New England, across the Alleghenies, out to Milwaukee, back through Fort Wayne, Cleveland, Detroit, Toledo, Warren, Ohio; Keyser, W. Va.; Washington, D.C.; Richmond, Va.; up to Pennsylvania to Pittsburgh, Oil City, Erie, Reading, Butler, stopping off to play return games in Rochester, Buffalo, Kingston, Catskill and Mt. Vernon, where a previous defeat was wiped out.

The mileage record of the Celtics this season is considerably over 130,000 miles. During that time they have played in nineteen States and in eighty different cities. The Celtics lost but one game out of seventy played during October, November and December, the loss going to the Brooklyn Whirlwinds by a score of 33-32.

Further Resources

BOOKS

Lapchick, Joe. *50 Years of Basketball.* Englewood Cliffs, N.J.: Prentice-Hall, 1968.

Nelson, Murry. *The Originals: The New York Celtics Invent Modern Basketball.* Bowling Green, Ohio: Bowling Green University Popular Press, 1999.

Peterson, Robert. *Cages to Jump Shots.* Lincoln, Neb.: University of Nebraska Press, 2002.

WEBSITES

"Hall of Famers: The Original Celtics." Naismith Memorial Basketball Hall of Fame. Available online at http://www.hoophall.com/halloffamers/Celtics%20Original.htm; website home page: http://www.hoophall.com (accessed May 8, 2003).

"The Original Celtics: The Beginning of Team Basketball." Available online at http://www.tomdawg.de/farbeit/docs/0106.htm (accessed December 6, 2002).

The "Long Count"

"Boxing"

Essay

By: James P. Dawson

Date: 1948

Source: Dawson, James P. "Boxing." In Danzig, Allison, and Peter Brandwein, eds. *Sport's Golden Age: A Close-Up of the Fabulous Twenties.* New York: Harper & Brothers, 1948, 77–78.

About the Author: James P. Dawson (1896–1953) was hired by *The New York Times* as a copy boy in 1908. He became the boxing editor of *The New York Times* and covered boxing and baseball until his death in 1953. The annual award presented to the top rookie in the Yankees' training camp is named in his honor. ■

Gene Tunney Floored by Dempsey

Photograph

Date: September 22, 1927

Source: "Gene Tunney Floored by Dempsey." September 22, 1927. Bettman/Corbis. Image no. U184391ACME. Available online at http://pro.corbis.com (accessed May 8, 2003).

Gene Tunney and Jack Dempsey in Boxing Match

Photograph

Date: September 22, 1927

Source: "Gene Tunney, Jack Dempsey In Boxing Match." September 22, 1927. Bettman/Corbis. Image no. BE053762. Available online at http://pro.corbis.com (accessed May 8, 2003). ■

Introduction

In the latter part of the nineteenth century, boxing was largely dominated by bare-knuckled British fighters. But in 1888 John L. Sullivan, an Irish American from Boston, became the heavyweight champion of the world and began a reign of American fighters who have dominated the weight class ever since. Boxing was popular with many classes of Americans, but its most zealous fans often came from the immigrant groups that produced many early twentieth-century champions, including Irish, Italian, and Jewish fighters. Fights, particularly heavyweight title fights, were staged all over the world, including Cuba, Australia, and England. In 1908 Jack Johnson, an African American, became the heavyweight champion. Johnson's intelligence and arrogance frightened many white people, who hoped for a white fighter to come along to defeat him. In 1915, Jess Willard, a huge (six-foot six-inch) man, defeated Johnson in twenty-six rounds in a fight that Johnson claimed he threw. His claim had some plausibility, for boxing was then plagued by corruption and many fight outcomes were influenced by gamblers and bribes.

Willard was champion for four years until Jack Dempsey, "discovered" by fight promoter Tex Rickard in the mining towns of the West, crushed Willard in three rounds in Toledo, Ohio, in July 1919. The victory of the six-foot one-inch, 190-pound Dempsey made him an instant legend, and people began calling him the greatest heavyweight ever. Dempsey defended his title less than once a year, and some of his opponents were not very challenging, but his contests against Georges Carpentier and Luis Angel Firpo were rousing battles that added to the Dempsey mystique. In 1926 Rickard engineered a fight in Philadelphia between Dempsey and Jack Tunney, a well-spoken former World War I Marine from New York City. In a tremendous upset Tunney defeated Dempsey before more than 120,000 spectators. The next year a rematch was held at Chicago's Soldier Field before 105,000 fans, and the first six rounds resembled the previous fight, with Tunney controlling the action. Then, in the seventh round Dempsey smashed Tunney with a combination of six or seven punches and Tunney went down, one hand clutching the rope. Rather than instantly retreating to a neutral corner, Dempsey lingered near Tunney, then went to the closest corner, the referee all the while signaling him to retreat and *not* counting Tunney out. By the time Dempsey moved to a neutral corner, at least five seconds had elapsed and Tunney was able to recover by nine and rise. He won the next two rounds and successfully defended his title.

Significance

Boxing became more of an attraction to all classes because of Dempsey's success and Tex Rickard's promotional skills. The two Dempsey-Tunney fights each had gate receipts of more than two million dollars, the first fights to produce such revenues at a time when in-

Primary Source

Gene Tunney Floored by Dempsey

SYNOPSIS: Jack Dempsey heads toward the neutral corner as Gene Tunney struggles to get up after being knocked down in the seventh round. Dempsey's failure to immediately head to the neutral corner caused the referee to delay the start of the count. © BETTMANN/CORBIS. REPRODUCED BY PERMISSION.

comes averaged less than two thousand dollars a year. The fights also were aided by radio broadcasting, and the excitement of Graham McNamee's broadcast made the second Dempsey-Tunney fight one that listeners would never forget. Although he lost, Dempsey became a tragic American hero. The "long count" match is probably the most famous fight in boxing history, and Dempsey was able to live comfortably until his death more than fifty years later. His restaurant, Jack Dempsey's Broadway Restaurant, located across from New York City's Madison Square Garden from 1935 to 1974, also kept the memory of Dempsey and the long count alive. People flocked to the restaurant, and Dempsey was a frequent attendee at major sports events in New York City.

Primary Source

"Boxing" [excerpt]

> **SYNOPSIS:** In 1948 Allison Danzig and Paul Brandewein edited a collection of essays about sport in the 1920s entitled *Sport's Golden Age*. This excerpt is from the chapter entitled "Boxing" by James P. Dawson, who covered the fights while working for *The New York Times*. Photos of the fight in 1927 are some of the most famous in sports history.

Everybody, it seemed, wanted to be at this fight. The top price was $40.

The fight itself was a resumption of Philadelphia for six rounds. Dempsey chased Tunney, and Tunney

Primary Source

Gene Tunney and Jack Dempsey in Boxing Match

SYNOPSIS: A view of the tenth round. Although this blow by Gene Tunney failed to connect, the damage to Jack Dempsey had already been done. Tunney successfully defended his title thanks in part to the seventh round "long count." © BETTMANN/CORBIS. REPRODUCED BY PERMISSION.

boxed circles around the ex-champion, thrusting aside Dempsey's savage lunges for the most part with no more effort than would have been necessary in a gymnasium workout. The champion was the epitome of boxing skill, courage, grace, and resourcefulness. Dempsey couldn't hit him with a solid punch to a vital spot—until the seventh round.

Then it happened. Dempsey banged Tunney against the ropes with a long left hook to the head out of his crouch. The champion fell backward into the ropes almost above me, shaken and hurt. Like a tiger, Dempsey was upon his foe, vicious, savage, a man berserk. A volley of wicked left and rights to the head and jaw, and Tunney crumpled, his brain numbed, his consciousness gone, oblivious of the earsplitting din which grew into a crescendo of wild cries echoing ever Soldier Field's excited populace.

Referee Dave Barry stepped to the side of the prostrate Tunney to begin his count. The knockdown timekeeper, Paul Boeler, rose across the ring to tick off the seconds on the watch in his band. Dempsey, his arms spread over the ropes in the corner above me, stood tense, waiting for Tunney to be counted out or come up for further punishment.

Barry's arm swung down in "one," and he motioned Dempsey to leave the corner above Tunney and cross to the opposite neutral corner. Dempsey ignored the motion. I was shouting myself hoarse trying to tell him to heed the referee. Tunney was heaving convulsively there on the floor. The count went to "five" before Dempsey moved. Tunney now was an inert mass struggling to grasp the rope, with the instinctive effort of pulling himself erect. Dempsey finally raced to the corner diagonally across from the fallen Tunney.

Barry resumed his counting—at "one." That was "six" in elapsed time. Tunney was still feebly pawing the air, as thoroughly "out" as any boxer I have ever seen. At "seven" he managed to grasp a rope. That was "twelve" in elapsed time. By superhuman effort he was up at "nine," which should have been "fourteen." Dempsey leaped after him in a furious bid for a knockout that was frustrated only because

Gene Tunney shakes hands with fight promoter Tex Rickard before the September 22, 1927, heavyweight title fight. © UNDERWOOD & UNDERWOOD/CORBIS. REPRODUCED BY PERMISSION.

Tunney had recovered enough of his senses to dodge out of the way of Dempsey's annihilating fists as the ex-champion rushed in. They resumed near the knockdown spot, and then Tunney danced away from harm through the remainder of the round.

In the eighth round Tunney was himself. He came boldly forth with a right to the jaw, under which Dempsey went down to one knee. But, even before Dempsey hit the canvas, Referee Barry was above him, photographic records show, with his arm raised aloft in the count of "one."

Tunney was on the floor for anywhere from 14 to 21 seconds in the seventh, independent watches held on the event showed. I have always maintained Dempsey was the victim of an injustice that night. It has been and always will be my contention that Dempsey knocked out Tunney in Chicago. His popularity since seems to reflect a pretty general support for this view.

Yet, whatever injustice occurred was brought on by Dempsey. Had he obeyed Barry and raced to the farthest neutral corner without delay, Tunney must have been counted out. Or, even surviving a "slow" count, must have been in such helpless condition as to have been finished with the next onslaught. Instead, Dempsey stood there above Tunney, wasting precious seconds in futile insistence to Barry that "you start counting."

There has been no more controversial ring issue in history. Tunney always insisted he knew what was going on at "seven." That was "twelve." If he had heard "five," it was "ten."

Further Resources

BOOKS

Dempsey, Jack, with Barbara Piattelli Dempsey. *Dempsey*. New York: Harper and Row, 1977.

Evensen, Bruce. *When Dempsey Fought Tunney: Heroes, Hokum and Storytelling in the Jazz Age.* Knoxville, Tenn.: University of Tennessee Press, 1996.

Heimer, Mel. *The Long Count.* New York: Atheneum, 1969.

Roberts, Randy. *Jack Dempsey, the Manassa Mauler.* Baton Rouge, La.: Louisiana State University Press, 1979.

Tunney, Gene. *A Man Must Fight.* Boston: Houghton Mifflin, 1932.

PERIODICALS

Nack, William. "The Long Count." *Sports Illustrated,* September 22, 1997, 72–87.

WEBSITES

"Tunney/Dempsey 1927 Fight Announcement." Gene Tunney, 1926–28 Heavyweight Boxing Champion. Available online at http://www.genetunney.org/radio.html; website home page: http://www.genetunney.org (accessed May 8, 2003). *This site contains both a written transcription and audio of the 1927 Tunney-Dempsey match.*

"Jack Dempsey: The Manassa Mauler." CMG Worldwide. Available online at http://www.cmgww.com/sports/dempsey; website home page: http://www.cmgww.com (accessed May 8, 2003).

"Jack Dempsey." International Boxing Hall of Fame. Available online at http://www.ibhof.com/dempsey.htm; website home page: http://www.ibhof.com (accessed May 8, 2003).

Babe Ruth's Sixtieth Home Run

"Ruth Crashes 60th to Set New Record"

Newspaper article

By: *The New York Times*

Date: October 1, 1927

Source: "Ruth Crashes 60th to Set New Record." *New York Times,* October 1, 1927, 12. Reprinted in "History This Month." *Black Tree History Group.* Available online at http://www.blacktreehistory.com/editorial/bte-hismonFeb02 .html; website home page: http://www.blacktreehistory.com (accessed May 8, 2003).

About the Publication: Founded in 1851, *The New York Times* began as one of many daily newspapers in New York City. By the beginning of the twentieth century, however, it had established itself as the city's preeminent paper. A century later, it is one of the world's most successful newspapers, boasting, among other things, a highly respected sports section.

"Babe Ruth at Bat"

Photograph

Date: September 30, 1927

Source: "Babe Ruth at Bat." September 30, 1927. Bettmann/Corbis. Image no. U47535ACME. Available online at http://pro.corbis.com (accessed May 8, 2003). ■

Introduction

The 1920s began with baseball struggling for credibility. In 1921, the Chicago "Black Sox" scandal—in which eight Chicago White Sox players were accused of throwing the 1919 World Series against the Cincinnati Reds—was fully exposed in court. Fortunately for the sport, the emergence of Babe Ruth and his prodigious home-run hitting captured the imagination and interest of fans throughout the United States. Ruth was originally signed as a pitcher by the Boston Red Sox, but his hitting was so outstanding that he began playing the outfield on days he did not pitch. Although he hit twenty-nine home runs in 1919, he was sold to the New York Yankees on December 26, 1919, by financially embattled Red Sox owner Harry Frazee. Ruth soon became the hero of New York and the nation, particularly because of his great appeal to youngsters of all ages. He shattered the home-run record in 1920 by hitting fifty-four, more than any other entire *team* in the league. He broke that record the next year with fifty-nine home runs, and he continued to clobber homers at an amazing rate over the next five years. He began 1927 at a pace that promised to establish a new record. He slowed in midsummer, but in September picked up again, and fans speculated daily on whether he could break his old record by hitting sixty home runs. The Yankees' last games of the year were against the Washington Senators, and on the last day of the season Ruth faced Washington pitcher Tom Zachary. In the eighth inning, in his last at-bat of the game, Ruth homered off Zachary for number sixty.

Significance

Despite a troubled childhood that included a long stay in a Baltimore reformatory, George Herman "Babe" Ruth is often seen as the man who "saved" baseball. After the gambling scandal that tainted the 1919 World Series, as well as earlier incidents and rumors of gambler involvement with the sport, baseball's integrity was in shambles. There was little faith in the honesty of the game, and heroes were few. Ruth and his boisterousness recaptured the interest of the fans, and his home runs were seen as legitimate feats of power and skill.

The aftereffects of Ruth's record-setting sixtieth home run were long lasting. The record stood for thirty-four years, until 1961, when another home run race ensued. This one involved two Yankee players, Roger Maris and Mickey Mantle, and the excitement arose largely because of Ruth's earlier feat. Even when Maris broke Ruth's record, the commissioner of baseball at the time, Ford Frick, determined that Ruth's record would stay in the books along with Maris's because Ruth set his record in fewer games. Twenty-seven years later, the home run race between Mark McGwire and Sammy Sosa rekindled interest in Ruth's record year. Even today, the number *60* is readily associated with his 1927 accomplishment. Ruth remains one of the most recognizable figures not just in baseball but in American history and legend. His image is still used and immediately recognized in advertising. Ruth was also the best-known player on what was the top team of the 1920s: the New York Yankees. Before him, the Yankees had never won a pennant. Ruth's home-run hitting and all-around play led to both increased attendance and improved play by the team. With the acquisition of Ruth, the Yankees began a record run of world titles that continues today. The Yankee uniform (pinstripes), Yankee Stadium (known as the "House That Ruth Built"), and the Yankee mystique (somehow they would win, no matter what) were all shaped by the life and legend of Babe Ruth.

Primary Source

"Ruth Crashes 60th to Set New Record"

> **SYNOPSIS:** The following article is one of the most well-known sports documents of the era. The tension that was released with Ruth's swing is noted in the article's subheadline, "Fans Go Wild."

Ruth Crashes 60th to Set New Record

Babe Makes It A Real Field Day By Accounting For All Runs in 4-2 Victory.

1921 Mark Of 59 Beaten

Fans Go Wild as Ruth Pounds Ball Into Stands With One On, Breaking 2-2 Tie.

Connects Last Time Up

Zachary's Offering Converted Into Epochal Smash, Which Old Fan Catches—Senators Then Subside.

Babe Ruth scaled the hitherto unattained heights yesterday. Home run 60, a terrific smash off the southpaw pitching of Zachary, nestled in the Babe's favorite spot in the right field bleachers, and before the roar had ceased it was found that this drive not only had made home run record history, but also was the winning margin in a 4 to 2 victory over the Senators. This also was the Yanks' 109th

Primary Source

"Babe Ruth at Bat"

SYNOPSIS: Babe Ruth follows through on his 60th home run of the 1927 season. This photograph is also one of the most well-known sports documents of the era, reproduced hundreds, if not thousands, of times. The ball flies swiftly off Ruth's bat into the right-field stands, while Ruth follows through beautifully on his swing. The intensity of his gaze as he follows the flight of the ball is apparent. © BETTMANN/CORBIS. REPRODUCED BY PERMISSION.

triumph of the season. Their last league game of the year will be played today.

When the Babe stepped to the plate in that momentous eighth inning the score was deadlocked. Koenig was on third base, the result of a triple, one man was out and all was tense. It was the Babe's fourth trip to the plate during the afternoon, a base on balls and two singles resulting on his other visits plateward.

The first Zachary offering was a fast one, which sailed over for a called strike. The next was high. The Babe took a vicious swing at the third pitched ball and the bat connected with a crash that was audible in all parts of the stand. It was not necessary to follow the course of the ball. The boys in the bleachers indicated the route of the record homer. It dropped about half way to the top. Boys, No. 60 was some homer, a fitting wallop to top the Babe's record of 59 in 1921.

While the crowd cheered and the Yankee players roared their greetings the Babe made his tri-

umphant, almost regal tour of the paths. He jogged around slowly, touched each bag firmly and carefully, and when he embedded his spikes in the rubber disk to record officially homer 60, hats were tossed into the air, papers were torn up and tossed liberally and the spirit of celebration permeated the place.

The Babe's stroll out to his position was the signal for a handkerchief salute in which all the bleacherites, to the last man, participated. Jovial Babe entered into the carnival spirit and punctuated his Ringly strides with a succession of snappy military salutes.

Ruth 4, Senators 2

Ruth's honor was a fitting climax to a game which will go down as the Babe's personal triumph. The Yanks scored four runs, the Babe personally crossing the plate three times and bringing in Koenig for the fourth. So this is one time where it would be fair, although not original, to record Yankee victory 109 as Ruth 4, Senators 2. There was not much else to the game. The 10,000 persons who came to the Stadium were there for no other purpose than to see the Babe make home run history. After each of the Babe's visits to the plate the expectant crowd would relax and wait for his next effort. They saw him open with a base on balls, follow with two singles then clout the epoch-making circuit smash.

The only unhappy individual within the Stadium was Zachary. He realized he was going down in the records as the historical home run victim, in other words the goat. Zachary was one of the most interested spectators of the home run flight. He tossed his glove to the ground, muttered to himself, turned to his mates for consolation and got everything but that. There is no denying that Zachary was putting everything he had on the ball. No pitcher likes to have recorded after his name the fact that he was Ruth's victim on his sixtieth homer.

The ball that the Babe drove, according to the word of the official sources was a pitch that was fast, low and on the inside. The Babe pulled away from the plate, then stepped into the ball and wham! According to Umpire Bill Dinneen at the plate and Catcher Muddy Ruel the ball traveled on a line and landed a foot inside fair territory about half way to the top of the bleachers. But when the ball reached the bleacher barrier it was about ten feet fair and curving rapidly to the right.

Fan Rushes to Babe With Ball

The ball which became Homer 60 was caught by Joe Forner of 1937 First Avenue, Manhattan. He is about 40 years old and has been following baseball for thirty-five, according to his own admission. He was far from modest and as soon as the game was over rushed to the dressing room to let the Babe know who had the ball.

For three innings both sides were blanked. The Senators broke through in the fourth for two runs.

The Yanks came back with one run in their half of the fourth. Ruth opened with a long single to right and moved to third on Gehrig's single to center. Gehrig took second on the throw to third. Meusel drove deep to Goslin, Ruth scoring and Gehrig taking third after the catch.

With two out in the sixth Ruth singled to right. Gehrig's hit was so fast that it went right through Gillis for a single, Ruth holding second. The Babe tied the score on Meusel's single to center. Lazzeri was an easy third out.

Further Resources

BOOKS

Creamer, Robert. *Babe: The Legend Comes to Life.* New York: Simon & Schuster, 1974.

Mosedale, John. *The Greatest of All: The 1927 New York Yankees.* New York: Dial, 1974.

Robertson, John. *The Babe Chases Sixty: That Fabulous 1927 Season, Home Run by Home Run.* Jefferson, N.C.: McFarland, 1999.

Ruth, Babe, and Robert Considine. *The Babe Ruth Story.* New York: Dutton, 1948.

Ruth, Claire (Merritt), with Bill Slocum. *The Babe and I.* Englewood Cliffs, N.J.: Prentice Hall, 1959.

Smelser, Marshall. *The Life That Ruth Built: A Biography.* New York: Quadrangle/New York Times Books, 1975.

WEBSITES

"Babe Ruth." Baseball-Reference.com. Available online at http://www.baseball-reference.com/r/ruthba01.shtml; website home page: http://www.baseball-reference.com (accessed December 3, 2002).

Babe Ruth.com. Available online at http://www.baberuth.com (accessed December 3, 2002).

"Hall of Famers." National Baseball Hall of Fame. Available online at http://www.baseballhalloffame.org/hofers_and_honorees/index.htm; website home page: http://www.baseballhalloffame.org (accessed December 3, 2002).

The Unofficial 1927 New York Yankees Home Page. Available online at http://www.angelfire.com/pa/1927 (accessed December 3, 2002).

AUDIO AND VISUAL MEDIA

The Babe Ruth Story. Directed by Roy Del Ruth. Twentieth Century Fox Home Entertainment. 1990, VHS.

Down the Fairway

Autobiography

By: Bobby Jones

Date: 1927

Source: Jones, Robert T., Jr., and O.T. Keeler. *Down the Fairway.* New York: Blue Ribbon, 1927, 148–149.

About the Author: Robert Tyre "Bobby" Jones Jr. (1902–1971) was born in Atlanta of well-to-do parents and began playing golf with sawed-off clubs at age three. He received a law degree from Emory University in 1927 and, before his retirement from competitive golf in 1930, he won a remarkable string of major titles. He then returned to his legal career in Atlanta. He also took up other business interests, including the making of instructional golf films and designing courses. ∎

Introduction

Golf was born in Scotland (although similar games were played at the same time in Holland and France) sometime in the thirteenth or fourteenth century, but it was officially recognized in the mid-1400s. It was slow to arrive in the United States; the first American "golf course" was a three-hole version in a cow pasture in Yonkers, New York, laid out in 1888. The first formal golf club was formed in that same town later that year, but the first duly incorporated golf club was Shinnecock Hills in Southampton, New York, in 1891. The game grew slowly among wealthy males in the eastern United States. Then in 1900 and 1913 Harry Vardon, the great English champion, made two extended visits to the United States and popularized golf wherever he made an appearance. One such appearance was in Atlanta, where the eleven-year-old Bobby Jones followed Vardon for an entire round and Vardon became an early idol. In 1913 Francis Ouimet, a gardener's son and former caddy from Brookline, Massachusetts, won the U.S. Open, defeating both Vardon and countryman Ted Ray in a playoff, and this victory was front-page news in many American newspapers. Golf lost some of its "snobbishness" and began to attract more adherents among the less affluent. In 1916 young Jones attracted attention in golf circles when he shot a 74 in the opening round of the National Amateur in Philadelphia and won two matches before losing to the eventual champion. In 1919 he went to the finals of the National Amateur before losing. Jones made the Walker Cup team in 1922 and helped it defeat the British team in matches held in England. Despite playing well, Jones, the biggest name in amateur golf, did not win a major tournament until 1923, when he won the U.S. Open. Following that victory, Jones went on to seven years of tournament victories.

Significance

Bobby Jones is often called the greatest golfer of the 1920s. Indeed, GolfEurope.com noted that considering how much he accomplished in a short career, Jones could easily be the greatest golfer ever. Will Grimsley, a noted golf historian, referred to him in *Golf: Its History, People, and Events* as "the fairway giant of the fabulous Golden Twenties." Paul Gallico credited Jones with the increase in the number of American golfers from a half million in 1915 to five million in 1925. Jones was U.S. Amateur champion in 1924, 1925, 1927, 1929, and 1930, and the fact that he retained his amateur status throughout his career made his feats seem more possible to everyday golfers, who admired him greatly. Jones was also U.S. Open champion four times, British Open champion three times, and British Amateur champion in 1930. At that time these four tournaments constituted the "Grand Slam" in golf, and his legendary accomplishment was revisited in recent years as Tiger Woods sought to win a modern Grand Slam: the Masters, the U.S. Open, the British Open, and the PGA Championship. Jones's ca-

---

Bobby Jones's Golf Record

U.S. Amateur Champion: 1924, 1925, 1927, 1928, 1930. (Runner-up in 1919, 1926.)
U.S. Open Champion: 1923, 1926, 1929, 1930. (Tied for the title in 1925 and 1928 but lost in play-offs.)
British Open Champion: 1926, 1927, 1930.
British Amateur Champion: 1930.
Walker Cup Competition: Won five matches, lost none.

SOURCE: Grimsley, Will. *Golf; Its History, People & Events. With Special Section by Robert Trent Jones.* Englewood Cliffs, New Jersey: Prentice-Hall, 1966, p. 83.

---

reer was even more significant because at the age of twenty-eight he retired while he was still the top golfer in the world.

Primary Source

Down the Fairway [excerpt]

SYNOPSIS: In this excerpt from Jones's autobiography, written in 1927—at age twenty-five while he was still playing golf—Jones looks back on 1926, when he won both the U.S. and British Opens and was runner-up in the U.S. Amateur.

The Biggest Year

Golf is a very queer game. I started the year 1926 with one glorious licking and closed it with another. And it was the biggest golf-year I'll ever have. Walter Hagen gave me the first drubbing, and of all the workmanlike washings-up I have experienced, this was far and away the most complete. He was national professional champion; I was national amateur champion; we liked to play against each other; and a match was arranged for the late winter season in Florida; a 72-hole affair, the first half at the Whitfield Estates Country Club at Sarasota, where I was spending the winter, and the second half a week later at Walter's course at Pasadena. Walter was simply too good for me. My irons were rather seriously out of line, it is true, but no excuses are to be offered when the other fellow, on two really great courses—I regard the Whitfield Estates course as one of the best in America—is never over par on any round, and is four strokes better than par at the finish on the sixty-first green, where the match ended with me sinking a forty-five foot putt for a birdie 3 in the effort to go a little farther, and Walter sinking a forty-footer for a half, to chop my head off. Walter played the most invincible match golf in those two days I have ever seen, let alone confronted. And I

Bobby Jones, left, is presented with the National Open Championship Tournament cup on July 11, 1926. © BETTMANN/CORBIS. REPRODUCED BY PERMISSION.

may add that I can get along very comfortably if I never confront any more like it. He beat me 12-11.

That match did me a lot of good, I think. I had been playing very good golf all winter, and in a series of seven fourball matches, with Tommy Armour as a partner, against pairs of the best professionals in the country, Tommy and I had not lost a match. I fancied I was in for a good season, and then this drubbing came along and showed up glaringly the defect in my iron play which had started troubling me at Skokie, in the open championship of 1922. I set to work on that department, and I think it was Jimmy Donaldson, who was with Armour at Sarasota, who gave me the correct line—too much right hand in the stroke. I worked on the irons whenever I had a chance up to the British invasion. And the irons served me fairly well the rest of the year. . . . Whenever I could get the feel that I was pulling the club down and through the stroke with the left arm—indeed, as if I were hitting the shot with the left hand—it seemed impossible to get much off the line. Curious thing. The older school of professionals always insisted the golf stroke was a left-hand stroke, you know.

Further Resources

BOOKS

Gallico, Paul. *The Golden People.* Garden City, N.Y.: Doubleday, 1965.

Grimsley, Will. *Gold: Its History, People, and Events.* Englewood Cliffs, N.J.: Prentice-Hall, 1966.

Jones, Robert T., Jr. *Golf Is My Game.* New York: Doubleday, 1960.

Miller, Dick. *Triumphant Journey: The Saga of Bobby Jones and the Grand Slam of Golf.* New York: Holt, Rinehart and Winston, 1980.

WEBSITES

Bobby Jones. Available online at http://www.bobbyjones.com (accessed May 8, 2003).

"Bobby Jones (1902–1971)." GolfEurope.com. Available online at http://www.golfeurope.com/almanac/players/jones .htm; website home page: http://www.golfeurope.com (accessed May 8, 2003).

"Robert Tyre (Bobby) Jones." Netstate.com. Available online at http://www.netstate.com/states/peop/people/ga_rtj.htm; website home page: http://netstate.com (accessed May 8, 2003).

Schwartz, Larry. "Bobby Jones Was Golf's Fast Study." ESPN. com Available online at http://www.espn.go.com /sportscentury/features/00014123.html; website home page: http://www.espn.com (accessed May 8, 20032).

Swimming the American Crawl

Autobiography

By: Johnny Weissmuller

Date: 1930

Source: Weissmuller, Johnny, with Clarence A. Bush. *Swimming the American Crawl.* Boston: Houghton Mifflin, 1930, 148–150.

About the Author: Peter John "Johnny" Weissmuller (1904–1984) was an athlete, actor, and author. He was best known as the swimmer and Olympic gold medalist who became the motion-picture star of the popular "Tarzan" movies. A dominating swimmer, Weissmuller won five gold medals at the 1924 and 1928 Olympics, set sixty-seven world records, and won fifty-two swimming championships. His film career began in 1931 when he played the role of Tarzan, created by Edgar Rice Burroughs. He later appeared as "Jungle Jim" on the television series that lasted ten years. His subsequent career in business included ventures in health-food stores and cocktail lounges. ∎

Introduction

Swimming is as old as human contact with bodies of water, but competitive swimming is relatively new.

It is often traced to races in England in the 1830s, although the Japanese had swimming meets as early as the 1600s. Three swimming events—the one hundred meters, the five hundred meters, and the twelve hundred meters (all for men and all freestyle)—were part of the first modern Olympics held in Athens in 1896. The events were largely unnoticed, but in 1900 the swimming events were announced as world championships and attracted more interest. In St. Louis in 1904, the events for the first time were held in still water in an artificial lake, and the times were recorded and recognized. In 1908 the International Federation for Amateur Swimming was founded, and it set rules for recognized distances and strokes.

From 1870 to 1910, racing techniques changed to incorporate the overhand stroke (which replaced the breaststoke for speed) and the scissors kick (which replaced the whip kick used in the breaststroke). Recorded times dropped dramatically for most distances. Americans held most of the records for the most important events at this time because the United States did not enter World War I (1914–1918) until 1917, allowing American swimmers to continue to swim and set records while Europe was at war. In 1920, American dominance at the freestyle swimming events continued at the Antwerp Olympics as Duke Kahanamoku won the one hundred meters, repeating his victory in the 1912 Olympics in Stockholm. Norman Ross of Chicago won both the four hundred- and fifteen hundred-meter freestyle events in Antwerp. In October 1920 Johnny Weissmuller began swimming at the Illinois Athletic Club under coach Bill Bachrach, and the next year he won the National AAU Championship at one hundred yards. He also finished second in the five hundred-yard freestyle to Olympic champion Norman Ross. By 1924 Weissmuller had established world marks at a number of freestyle distances and went on to win the one hundred- and four hundred-meter races at the Olympics in Paris.

Significance

Johnny Weissmuller is credited with perfecting the American crawl, which was first developed by Charles Daniels in about 1906. This version of the crawl was based on the Australian crawl of Australians Frederick Cavill and his sons. Before Weissmuller, the kick was different, but Weissmuller's strength and buoyancy allowed him to fully modify the crawl kick to a straight-legged flutter technique. His success and popularity propelled the stroke to widespread use nationally and internationally. Weissmuller's relative modesty is revealed in his account of his swimming success (and small failure) in 1921. He went on to finish his swimming career not only as an undefeated Olympic champion but also, nearly, as an undefeated racer in any swim meet. He es-

Johnny Weissmuller anticipates the start of a race at Brighton Beach, New York, 1922. © BETTMANN/CORBIS. REPRODUCED BY PERMISSION.

tablished sixty-seven world records while winning five gold medals in two Olympics, fifty-two national championships at distances from fifty yards to five hundred yards in the period from 1923 to 1928, and the national pentathlon in 1922 and 1923 (tied). He was voted the greatest swimmer of the first half of the twentieth century and was inducted into the International Swimming Hall of Fame and the American Olympic Hall of Fame. He later continued to be remembered as a great Olympic hero of the 1924 and 1928 Games by becoming a Hollywood movie star. He was the first "Tarzan" in 1932 and went on to make a dozen of those movies. His Olympic success in the 1920s added athletic credibility to the fantasy role as Tarzan, King of the Jungle.

Primary Source

Swimming the American Crawl [excerpt]

SYNOPSIS: Weissmuller's book, written in 1930 shortly after he retired from competitive swimming, is both an autobiography and an instructional volume. The chapter from which the excerpt is taken, entitled "Early Appearances in Competition," discusses his first competition in swimming in 1921. The foreshadowing of his successes soon after is clear.

During this, my first season outdoors, I also won the two-hundred-and-twenty-yard National championship at Indianapolis, Indiana, defeating Ludy Langer of the Hui Nalu, Hawaii, and my team mate, Ross, in the fast time of two minutes, twenty-eight seconds. I had won the fifty-yard National, and the Central hundred-yard free style, as well as swimming on National and Central championship four-hundred-yard relay teams.

These first performances of mine naturally remain more clearly in my memory than those that have come in the years between then and now, and that is why I am going into them in some detail.

My second free-style world's record was made indoors, in the I.A.C. Pool, which is of the sixty-foot variety. An article in the 'Tri-Color' for December told about it as follows:

> On November 21, Johnny took it upon himself to make a mark in swimming history. The I.A.C. staged an open swimming meet for the benefit of a visiting delegation of A.A.U. officials from all over the country. These officials were here to pass on new records for the year, and also to award various athletic events to clubs bidding for them.
>
> Bachrach had a premonition that something was going to happen. He felt that certain records were threatened, so every precaution was taken to see that any records made would be authentic. The A.A.U. officials measured the tank to the fraction of an inch. The stop-watches used for timing—and there were plenty—were all previously tested for accuracy. All the possibilities for a fluke were eliminated.
>
> Johnny was nervous and made a false start, but when he actually started, good-night! He made the fastest time ever negotiated through water by a human being, covering one hundred yards in fifty-two and three fifths seconds. Think of it—fifty-two and three fifths seconds for one hundred yards!
>
> After the race, spectators were more out of breath than Johnny was. Timers, judges, and watches all agreed that then and there a record was made that will remain a record for some time to come. It is safe to say that those who were so fortunate as to witness that marvelous exhibition of swimming will never forget the thrills it afforded them.

Further Resources

BOOKS

Fury, David. *Johnny Weissmuller: Twice the Hero.* Minneapolis: Artist's Press, 2000.

Weissmuller, Johnny, Jr., with William Reed and W. Craig Reed. *Tarzan, My Father.* Toronto, Ontario: ECW Press, 2002.

WEBSITES

Hillman, Bill. "Johnny Weissmuller: A Career Scrapbook." Available online at http://geocities.com/hillmans12/erbz394 .html (accessed May 9, 2003).

"Johnny Weissmuller Pools: The Legend of Excellence." Available online at http://delairgroup.com/pools/jw/history.html; website home page: http://delairgroup.com (accessed May 9, 2003).

St. Andrews, Geoff. "Biography of Johnny Weissmuller." Available online at http://www.mergetel.com/~geostan/bio .html; website home page: http://www.mergetel.com /~geostan (accessed May 9, 2003).

The Negro in Sports

Reference work

By: Edwin Bancroft Henderson

Date: 1939

Source: Henderson, Edwin Bancroft. *The Negro in Sports.* Washington, D.C.: Associated Publishers, 1939. Revised edition, 1949, 154, 156–157.

About the Author: Edwin Bancroft Henderson (1883–1977), a native of Washington, D.C., headed the Department of Physical Education in Washington's segregated school system from 1925 until 1951. He is often credited with being the "father" both of African American basketball and of African American sports history. In the early 1900s he introduced basketball to the African American youth of Washington, D.C., and was a player, referee, and teacher of the game for many years. He also chronicled the contributions of African Americans to sport in his book, *The Negro in Sports.* ∎

Introduction

Basketball was invented in 1891 in Springfield, Massachusetts. It spread rapidly, largely because it was introduced at YMCAs and Settlement Houses by men trained in the game at YMCA-sponsored classes throughout the Northeast and, later, the rest of the country. Early on the game was introduced in this manner to African Americans, and there were African American teams as well as African Americans playing on prominent white teams as early as 1904. Basketball was also played as an athletic pastime at many social clubs, African American and white. African American basketball champions were declared during these early years, with most of the outstanding teams coming from New York City, but some also had Washington or Pittsburgh as their home. Such pioneers as Edwin Henderson, Will Madden, and Cumberland Posey played and promoted the game, which was extremely popular in African American communities. The game was as much social interaction as sporting event; often men's games were followed by dancing or a women's basketball game. In 1923, a New York messenger and porter named Bob Douglas, who had been man-

THE RENAISSANCE, THE GREATEST COLORED BASKETBALL TEAM OF ALL-TIME
Left to right: Clarence "Fat" Jenkins, Bill Yancey, John Holt, James "Pappy" Ricks, Eyre Saitch, Charles "Tarzan" Cooper and "Wee Willie" Smith. Inset: Owner Robert L. Douglas, who organized club in 1922-23.

The New York Renaissance basketball team, circa late 1920s–early 1930s. The Rens were a dominant team in the late 1920s and probably the best professional team of the 1930s. **BASKETBALL HALL OF FAME, SPRINGFIELD, MA. REPRODUCED BY PERMISSION.**

aging and promoting basketball for fifteen years, formed a new professional all-African American basketball team called the Renaissance. The team was given practice and playing space by the Renaissance Casino in Harlem in return for using its name. The team, usually referred to as the Rens, quickly became a feared team in basketball, African American or white. The team debuted on November 3, 1923, beating a white team, the Collegiate Five, 28–22 before a large crowd at the Renaissance Casino.

Significance

Basketball was a uniquely American sport that, early on, appealed to immigrants and various ethnic groups, including African Americans. The New York Renaissance team was the first great African American basketball team and, indeed, one of the most dominant basketball teams ever. Crowds packed the Renaissance Casino in Harlem to watch the team, which then became a touring team later in the 1920s. It toured all over the East and, in the 1930s and 1940s, in the Midwest. Some bigots had implied that African Americans were not smart enough to be successful at basketball (or other team sports) or that the African American game would wilt against white teams. These criticisms proved to be totally unfounded, for the Rens showed thousands of Americans, African American and white, that African Americans could play exciting and intelligent basketball.

The Rens were a dominant team in the late 1920s and probably the best professional team of the 1930s. They demonstrated skill at all aspects of the game and, most importantly, demonstrated the team concepts that brought their greatest successes. Players like Clarence "Fats" Jenkins, George Fiall, Eyre "Bruiser" Saitch, Hilton "Kid" Slocum, and James "Pappy" Ricks were heroes to African American youth not only in New York but throughout the eastern half of the country. African

American newspapers like the *Chicago Defender,* the *Pittsburgh Courier,* the *New York Age,* and the *New York Amsterdam News* followed their games and made the Rens the best-known African American team in any sport in the 1920s. During each of the last three years of the 1920s, the Rens played over 125 games, winning at least 107 each year. The Rens played the best teams, both African American and white, as well as local teams as they toured the country. Still, they often met discrimination at hotels and dining establishments, but this failed to affect their play or diminish the respect they won among African Americans. The Rens continued their basketball dominance for two more decades, and in 1963 they were one of only four teams ever inducted into the Basketball Hall of Fame.

Primary Source

The Negro in Sports [excerpt]

SYNOPSIS: Henderson's book was the first volume to fully address the issue of African American participation in sports and was the inspiration for later works in the 1970s, 1980s, and 1990s. He wrote the book to provide African American youth with knowledge of great African American athletes as well as to "encourage young people to maintain . . . [their] health and vigor." The revised edition updates the postwar strivings of "colored Americans . . . in all lines of endeavor for full citizenship" (ix). In this sense it is as much a civil rights document as one about sport.

It was in October, 1923, that Bob Douglas organized the Rens. An ardent follower of the game which he had played himself for more than a dozen years, Douglas watched the amateur game sink lower and lower during 1921 and 1922 and conceived the idea that putting out a professional team might prove a worthwhile enterprise. On that first team, Bob had such men as Hilton Slocum, Frank Forbes, Leon Monde, Hy Monte, Zack Anderson, Harold Mayers. Slocum was made captain from the beginning and retained that post until his connection with the team was severed in 1932.

Spartans Become "Rens"

The naming of the team the Renaissance Big Five was purely accidental, or perhaps it would be better to call it a result of circumstances. Douglas himself admits that he did not care for the name at all; he had intended to call the team the Spartans after his old club. In seeking to procure as a home court, the Renaissance Casino, which had just been built, however, Bob offered to use that name for the team and thus gave the place itself additional pub-

licity when the aggregation played elsewhere. The proposition was accepted and the name stuck. Outside of Harlem, though, the team is seldom if ever known by the full name Renaissance. To the countless thousands of fans all over the country who await their visits annually, the crack New Yorkers are known as the "Rens" or the "Rennies." . . .

Professional Basketball

The outstanding professional basketball club was the Renaissance team of New York. This team (1923–1939) was the peer of all teams playing the court game for several seasons. There were very few teams that could beat the "Rens" when this team really got going. So uneven was much of its competition, that few people saw the team perform at its best. The general feeling is that the players were instructed not to run up a large score against weak opponents. Frequently the team gave an exhibition of fancy and trick passing that for machine-like precision beggars description.

There never was a basketball team among white players that excelled, for individual and team contribution, the playing of the old Celtic aggregation consisting of "Nat" Holman, Beckman, Haggerty, Barry, Lapschick and Banks. They were the marvels of the time. However, in 1928, the Renaissance team, made up of Ricks, Fiall, Slocum, Sanders, Mayer and Captain Jenkins easily defeated the Celtics in a crucial seasonal test. Since then the "Rens" beat all the best professional teams. Under the leadership of the owner and manager, "Bob" Douglas, and the captaincy of Jenkins, the Renaissance floor machine made an enviable record for basketball and sportsmanship. . . .

The Rens and Their Record

Over a period of nearly sixteen years the Renaissance players won 1,588 games and lost 239.

Further Resources

BOOKS

Ashe, Arthur. *A Hard Road to Glory: A History of the African American Athlete.* New York: Amistad, 1988.

Peterson, Robert. *Cages to Jump Shots—Pro Basketball's Early Years,* Lincoln, Neb.: University of Nebraska Press, 2002.

Rust, Art, and Edna Rust. *Art Rust's Illustrated History of the Black Athlete.* Garden City, N.Y.: Doubleday, 1985.

Wiggins, David. *Glory Bound: Black Athletes in a White America.* Syracuse, N.Y.: Syracuse University Press, 1997.

PERIODICALS

Henderson, Edwin B. "The Negro in Sport." *Negro History Bulletin* 15, 1951, 42–46.

WEBSITES

"Hall of Famers." Naismith Memorial Basketball Hall of Fame. Available at http://www.hoophall.com/halloffamers/NY%20Renaissance.htm; website home page: http://www.hoophall.com (accessed May 8, 2003).

Frommer, Harvey. "Remembering the New York Renaissance Five." Available online at http://www.travel-watch.com/littleleague.htm; website home page: http://www.travel-watch.com (accessed May 8, 2003).

My Story: A Champion's Memoirs

Autobiography

By: William Tilden

Date: 1948

Source: Tilden, William T., II. *My Story: A Champion's Memoirs.* New York: Hellman, Williams, 1948, 65–66.

About the Author: William Tatem "Bill" Tilden II (1893–1953) was the greatest male tennis player of the 1920s. In 1915, almost totally without roots or direction, Tilden decided to make a study and a career of tennis. He committed himself to the game completely, beginning by coaching at the Germantown Academy without pay. He was first given a national rating as a player in 1915, and a year later entered the U.S. championship matches. He emerged as one of the giants of the game, though later his professional career was cut short when knowledge of his homosexuality finally surfaced. He then moved to Hollywood and had a career in theater. ∎

Introduction

Tennis developed in the late nineteenth century and remained largely an upper-class sport with little mass appeal until around 1912, when the construction of more public courts made the game more accessible to the American public. The game had been largely dominated by players in the Northeast, but by the 1910s a number of Californians became leading players, widening the sport's appeal. The late 1910s and 1920s were a period when great popular tennis heroes appeared. Among the women, Suzanne Lenglen and Helen Wills Moody were preeminent. On the male side, Bill Tilden was challenged for supremacy by René Lacoste and Henri Cochet of France, Manuel Alonso of Spain, Zenzo Shimizu of Japan, and, from the United States, Vincent Richards and William Johnston. Tennis was largely an amateur game, though many of these amateurs got expense money (the amount of which they often inflated) and tennis became popular enough that amateur tennis organizations were suddenly making profits rather than breaking even or covering losses.

Bill Tilden was born in Philadelphia and began playing on the public courts there. In 1912 he began his amateur career, and the next year he and Mary Browne won the U.S. mixed doubles title. Beginning in 1920, he was the dominant player of the decade: From 1920 to 1930 he won Wimbledon three times, the U.S. singles title seven times, and the French Open three times, and he was on the U.S. Davis Cup team every year. Tall and lean, Tilden was able to keep matches close and have fans sitting on the edge of their seats in anticipation.

Significance

Before Tilden's success, tennis held little mass appeal; but his tempestuous conduct and dramatic flair—anticipating such modern-era players as Jimmy Connors and John McEnroe—made him the idol of thousands of new tennis fans. He was seen as a gadfly who played to the fans and their emotions. In addition, he was seen as someone who refused to engage in hypocrisy. At that time many tennis amateurs made a relatively good living through padded expense and appearances fees, which the amateur tennis federations allowed. Tilden refused to do this and, in fact, spoke out against such practices. Those who controlled tennis took umbrage and went out of their way to find fault with him and bring his amateur status into question. He was chastened, for example, for writing a column about tennis for a newspaper syndicate and suspended from Davis Cup play in 1928. France, the United States' opponent for the second round, complained bitterly about the loss of Tilden, the greatest drawing card in tennis. The American ambassador to France intervened and telephoned the chairman of the Davis Cup committee of the United States Lawn Tennis Association (USLTA). The association rescinded the suspension, but then reimposed it when Tilden returned to the United States after the American loss to France.

Tilden was reinstated the next year, but in 1930 he became the first significant amateur to turn professional. He remained a top-flight player for the next ten years. He laid the groundwork for the open era that began in the 1960s, allowing amateurs and professionals to play in the same tournaments, and soon most of the top tennis players turned professional. Later, players as young as fourteen, such as Tracy Austin in 1977, were competing in international tournaments. Tilden was also a stage actor and playwright, making him one of the first sports personalities to combine athletics and the theater. Tilden was also gay and was arrested because of his homosexuality; he even served a short prison term in the late 1940s. Toward the end of his life he was shunned by much of the sports world. He died in 1953, nearly penniless.

Bill Tilden returns a volley in a finals match for the National Singles Title, Forest Hills, N.Y., October 19, 1925. © BETTMANN/CORBIS. REPRODUCED BY PERMISSION.

Primary Source

My Story: A Champion's Memoirs [excerpt]

SYNOPSIS: Tilden's autobiography, *My Story: A Champion's Memoirs,* was one of nine books he wrote (in addition to at least eight published plays). The period he examines here foreshadows his troubles with the officials of United States Lawn Tennis Association over the next ten years.

End of an Era

The opening of 1921 found me champion of the world, champion of England, champion of the United States—and champion battler with the U.S.L.T.A. It seemed incumbent on them to return me to Europe to defend my Wimbledon title, and they were anxious for me to go over some weeks earlier and play for the championship of France. It was this desire, coupled with what I took to be a parsimonious attitude on their part, that led to the first serious dispute between us.

Figuring that I had an income of my own, the Association decided not to take care of my living and traveling expenses completely on this trip. When they extended the invitation to lead an American group abroad, they informed me that I would be graciously allowed one thousand dollars. Out of that enormous sum I was supposed to pay my boat fare over and back, live three weeks in Paris—and then four weeks in London! Anyone who has ever made such a trip has a pretty good idea of how far the amount would go. Besides, I felt it beneath the dignity of the United States to have its champion travel in any way except first class. I so notified the Association, and told them that unless they were willing to pay my complete expenses, both traveling and living, I had no intention of going abroad.

That was where matters stood in early April. Just as the Association and I had reached a complete impasse, the United States Davis Cup team received an invitation from the President of the United States, Warren G. Harding, to take part in exhibitions at the White House.

President Harding received the team officially, and as we were leaving his office he asked me to remain a moment after the others.

"I hear you are not planning to go to Europe to defend at Wimbledon," said Mr. Harding.

"That's true, Mr. President," I replied.

"I have no desire to intrude into your private affairs or to influence you against your will, but we at the head of the Government feel that international sports are more valuable than diplomacy in obtaining friendship and understanding among nations. We hope that any American champions who hold titles abroad will defend them if possible, and will use all their influence to bring our foreign friends to our shores. If you can see your way to reconsidering, I would appreciate it."

That ended that. Naturally I changed my mind on the spot and agreed to go to Europe. After I had told Mr. Harding so, he said, "I suppose I'm prying into your affairs, but I'm curious about your reasons for having previously felt that you would not go. Will you tell me them?"

"With pleasure," I said, and frankly explained the exact situation. Mr. Harding expressed himself to the effect that it was a damned disgrace. I do not know whether Mr. Harding's views reached the Association or not, but I do know that forty-eight hours later I received word that they would pay my complete expenses.

I was far from well when we sailed for France. A long, hard winter of play had left me very much run down. Almost the first thing I did on arriving in France was to pick up an infection which resulted in a series of serious boils. Sanitation and bathing facilities in France in 1921, particularly at the club in St. Cloud where the tournament was to be held, were anything but satisfactory; I'm inclined to think that it was there I picked up the germ which almost cost me both the French and British titles.

Further Resources

BOOKS

Danzig, Allison. "Tennis." In Danzig, Allison and Peter Brandwein, eds. *Sport's Golden Age: A Close-Up of the Fabulous Twenties*. New York: Harper & Brothers, 1948, 208–227.

Deford, Frank. *Big Bill Tilden: The Triumphs and the Tragedy*. New York: Simon and Schuster, 1975.

WEBSITES

"Bill Tilden." Available online at http://www.tennisfame.org /enshrinees/bill_tilden.html; website home page: http://www .tennisfame.org (accessed December 6, 2002).

Borges, Ron. "Tilden Brought Theatrics to Tennis." ESPN.com. Available online at http://espn.go.com/sportscentury/features /00016509.html; website home page: http://espn.com (accessed May 8, 2003).

"Man o' War's Record"
Table

By: George Gipe

Date: 1978

Source: Gipe, George. *The Great American Sports Book: A Casual but Voluminous Look at American Spectator Sports From the Civil War to the Present Time*. Garden City, N.J.: Doubleday, 1978, 252.

About the Author: George Gipe (1933–1986) was an author, television producer, and screenwriter. He began his career as a cameraman at WJZ-TV in Baltimore, Maryland, and later moved to WMAR-TV, where he produced many documentary films. His writings include *The Last Time When, The Great American Sports Book,* and the novel *Coney Island Quickstep*. Gipe was also the author of a number of film novelizations, among them *Melvin and Howard* and *Gremlins,* and a contributor to such popular magazines as *Sports Illustrated* and *Mad*. He was best known for his collaborations on

Man O' War's Record, 1919–1920

1919—2-year old:

Date	Track	Event	Finish
June 6	Belmont	Purse Race	1st
June 9	Belmont	Keene Memorial Stakes	1st
June 21	Jamaica	Youthful Stakes	1st
June 23	Aqueduct	Hudson Stakes	1st
July 5	Aqueduct	Tremont Stakes	1st
Aug. 2	Saratoga	U.S. Hotel Stakes	1st
Aug. 13	Saratoga	Sanford Memorial Stakes	2nd
Aug. 23	Saratoga	Grand Union Hotel Stakes	1st
Aug. 30	Saratoga	Hopeful Stakes	1st
Sept. 13	Belmont	Futurity Stakes	1st

1920—3-year-old:

Date	Track	Event	Finish
May 18	Pimlico	Preakness Stakes	1st
May 29	Belmont	Withers Stakes	1st
June 12	Belmont	Belmont Stakes	1st
June 22	Jamaica	Stuyvesant Handicap	1st
July 10	Aqueduct	Dwyer Stakes	1st
Aug. 7	Saratoga	Miller Stakes	1st
Aug. 21	Saratoga	Travers Stakes	1st
Sept. 4	Belmont	Lawrence Realization Stakes	1st
Sept. 11	Belmont	Jockey Club Stakes	1st
Sept. 18	Havre de Grace	Potomac Handicap	1st
Oct. 12	Kenilworth Park	Kenilworth Park Gold Cup	1st

SOURCE: Gipe, George. *The Great American Sports Book: A Casual But Voluminous Look at American Spectator Sports From the Civil War to the Present Time*. Garden City, New Jersey: Doubleday, 1978, p. 252

Primary Source

"Man o' War's Record"

SYNOPSIS: On paper, Man o' War's racing record forms a document more impressive than that associated with almost any other racehorse. Observers at the time marveled at Man o' War's speed and strength, but today we have to marvel at the written record of his accomplishments.

Man o' War suffers his first and only loss to Upset at the Sanford Stakes in 1919. The controversial loss was alternatively blamed on a poor job of starting the race by starter C.H. Pettingill and a poor ride by jockey Johnny Loftus. AP/WIDE WORLD PHOTOS. REPRODUCED BY PERMISSION.

scripts for the film comedies *Dead Men Don't Wear Plaid* and *The Man With Two Brains.* ∎

Introduction

Horse racing can be traced back to twelfth-century England, though stakes racing (racing for prizes) seems to date to the 1700s. In the United States, Kentucky has been a center of horse breeding and racing for more than two hundred years, and Virginia and New York even longer. The first racetrack in Kentucky was erected in 1797 in Lexington, and a new one built in 1828 operated until 1935. Churchill Downs, site of the Kentucky Derby, was built in 1875 and set off a wave of track building in the eastern United States, particularly near large cities. Famous races were covered in newspapers in the late 1800s, and by the early twentieth century, regular horse-racing newspapers were being published. Racing became even more popular with the growth of legalized betting. In 1913, though, New York outlawed legalized gambling, and by 1919, attendance at racetracks was at a twenty-year low. By 1922, that had all changed because of one horse: Man o' War. To date, no horse had ever captured the public's attention and admiration as had Man o' War, whose racing feats earned him national hero status.

Significance

Man o' War's owner, Samuel D. Riddle, believed that racing one and a quarter miles in May was too taxing for a three-year-old. Thus, Man o' War was not entered in the 1920 Kentucky Derby and had no opportunity to win the legendary Triple Crown: the Derby, the Preakness at Pimlico in Maryland, and the Belmont Stakes in New York. At that time, these three races, taken together, were not considered as noteworthy as they are today. Thus, Man o' War is not listed as a Triple Crown winner anywhere. The horse's performance during the remainder of 1920 season, however, was impressive. He raced eleven times and won all eleven races. He was so dominant that some large-stakes races went off with only two or three horses because no owners thought their horses had a chance against Man o' War. When the season ended, Riddle decided to end his horse's racing career and put him out to stud. Over the rest of his life, more than a half-million visitors came to see him on the farm in Kentucky where he was stabled. Upon his death on November 1, 1947, at the age of thirty, five hundred people attended the funeral, which was broadcast on radio. Even in death, the great horse was honored as the "chief tourist attraction" of Lexington, Kentucky.

Further Resources

BOOKS

Bowen, Edward L. *Man o' War.* Lexington, Ky.: Eclipse, 2000.

Farley, Walter. *Man o' War.* New York: Random House, 1970.

WEBSITES

"Man o' War." About.com. Available online at http://www
.horseracing.about.com/library/weekly/aa110197.htm; web-site home page: http://www.horseracing.about.com (accessed December 3, 2002).

"Man o' War Came Close to Perfection." ESPN. Available online at http://www.espn.go.com/sportscentury/features /00016132.html; website home page: http://www.espn .go.com (accessed December 3, 2002).

GENERAL RESOURCES

General

Allen, Frederick Lewis. *Only Yesterday: An Informal History of the Nineteen-Twenties.* New York: Harper, 1931.

The American Heritage History of the 20's and 30's. New York: American Heritage, 1970.

Baldwin, Douglas. *The 1920s.* Calgary: Weigl, 2000.

Blackman, Cally. *The 20s and 30s.* Milwaukee: Gareth Stevens, 2000.

Blocksma, Mary, and Susan Dennen. *Ticket to the Twenties: A Time Traveler's Guide.* Boston: Little, Brown and Company, 1993.

Cable, Mary. *Top Drawer: American High Society From the Gilded Age to the Roaring Twenties.* New York: Atheneum, 1984.

Cummins, D. Duane, and William Gee White. *Contrasting Decades, the 1920s and 1930s.* Encino, Calif.: Glencoe, 1980.

Farshtey, Greg. *1920s.* San Diego: Kidhaven, 2004.

Hanson, Mary. *The 1920s.* San Diego: Lucent, 1999.

King, David C. *The Roaring Twenties.* Carlisle, Mass.: Discovery Enterprises, 1997.

Lindop, Edmund. *Modern America: The Dazzling Twenties.* New York: F. Watts, 1970.

Severn, Bill. *The End of the Roaring Twenties; Prohibition and Repeal.* New York: J. Messner, 1969.

Sharman, Margaret. *1920s.* Austin: Raintree Steck-Vaughn, 1993.

Stewart, Gail. *1920s.* New York: Crestwood House, 1989.

Tames, Richard. *The 1920s.* New York: F. Watts, 1991.

United States History Society. *1921–1932: Prosperity and Panic.* Skokie, Ill.: United States History Society, 1962–1968.

The Arts

Aaron, Daniel. *Writers on the Left.* New York: Harcourt, Brace & World, 1961.

Albertson, Chris. *Bessie.* New York: Stein & Day, 1972.

Armitage, Shelley. *John Held Jr.: Illustrator of the Jazz Age.* Syracuse, N.Y.: Syracuse University Press, 1987.

Armstrong, Louis. *Satchmo: My Life in New Orleans.* New York: Prentice-Hall, 1954.

Arnason, H.H. *History of Modern Art: Painting · Sculpture · Architecture.* Englewood Cliffs, N.J.: Prentice-Hall / New York: Abrams, 1968.

Baker, Carlos. *Ernest Hemingway: A Life Story.* New York: Scribners, 1969.

Baur, John I. H., ed. *New Art in America: Fifty Painters of the 20th Century.* Greenwich, Conn.: New York Graphic Society, 1957.

Beach, Sylvia. *Shakespeare & Company.* New York: Harcourt, Brace, 1959.

Bell, Bernard. *The Afro-American Novel and Its Tradition.* Amherst: University of Massachusetts Press, 1987.

Bergreen, Laurence. *As Thousands Cheer: The Life of Irving Berlin.* New York: Viking, 1990.

Berkow, Ita G. *Edward Hopper: An American Master.* New York: Smithmark, 1996.

Blair, Walter, and Hamlin Hill. *America's Humor.* New York: Oxford University Press, 1978.

Blum, Daniel. *A New Pictorial History of the Talkies,* revised and enlarged by John Kobal. New York: Putnam, 1982.

Boyer, Paul S. *Purity in Print.* New York: Scribners, 1968.

Brown, Milton W. *American Painting From the Armory Show to the Depression.* Princeton: Princeton University Press, 1955.

Bruccoli, Matthew J. *Some Sort of Epic Grandeur: The Life of F. Scott Fitzgerald,* revised edition. New York: Carroll & Graf, 1993.

———. *F. Scott Fitzgerald: A Life in Letters.* New York: Scribners, 1994.

Chaplin, Charlie. *Charlie Chaplin's Own Story.* Bloomington: Indiana University Press, 1985.

———. *My Autobiography.* New York: Simon & Schuster, 1964.

The Collected Catalogues of Dr. A.S.W. Rosenbach, 1904–1951. New York: Arno/McGraw-Hill, 1967.

Collier, James L. *Louis Armstrong: An American Genius.* New York: Oxford University Press, 1988.

———. *The Making of Jazz: A Comprehensive History.* New York: Dell, 1979.

Cowart, Jack, and Juan Hamilton. *Georgia O'Keefe: Art and Letters.* Washington, D.C.: National Gallery of Art, 1987.

Cowen, Louise. *The Fugitive Group: A Literary History.* Baton Rouge: Louisiana State University Press, 1959.

Cowley, Malcolm. *A Second Flowering: Works and Days of the Lost Generation.* New York: Viking, 1973.

Craven, Wayne. *American Art: History and Culture.* New York: Harry N. Abrams, Inc., 1994.

Elder, Donald. *Ring Lardner: A Biography.* Garden City, N.Y.: Doubleday, 1956.

Ewen, David. *New Complete Book of the American Musical Theater.* New York: Holt Rinehart and Winston, 1970.

Ford, Hugh. *Published in Paris: American and British Writers, Printers, and Publishers in Paris, 1920–1939.* New York: Macmillan, 1975.

Freedland, Michael. *Jolson.* New York: Stein & Day, 1972.

Furia, Philip. *The Poets of Tin Pan Alley: A History of America's Great Lyricists.* New York: Oxford University Press, 1990.

Goldman, Herbert G. *Jolson.* New York: Oxford University Press, 1988.

Goulart, Ron. *The Hardboiled Dicks: An Anthology and Study of Pulp Detective Fiction.* Los Angeles: Sherbourne, 1965.

Gregory, Horace, and Marza Zaturensha. *A History of American Poetry, 1900–1940.* New York: Harcourt, Brace, 1946.

The Harlem Renaissance: An Historical Dictionary of the Era. Westport, Conn.: Greenwood Press, 1984.

Harriman, Margaret Case. *The Vicious Circle: The Story of the Algonquin Round Table.* New York: Rinehart, 1951.

Harris, Trudier, ed. *Afro-American Writers From the Harlem Renaissance to 1940; Dictionary of Literary Biography,* vol. 51. Detroit: Bruccoli Clark/Gale Research, 1986.

Hoffman, Frederic. *The Twenties; American Writing in the Postwar Decade,* rev. ed. New York: Collier, 1962.

Huggins, Nathan Irving. *Harlem Renaissance.* New York: Oxford University Press, 1977.

———. *Voices From the Harlem Renaissance.* New York: Oxford University Press, 1995.

Hughes, Langston. *I Wonder as I Wander: An Autobiographical Journey.* New York: Rinehart, 1956.

Jablonski, Edmund. *The Gershwin Years.* Garden City, N.Y.: Doubleday, 1958.

Kerr, Walter. *The Silent Clowns.* New York: Knopf, 1975.

Kimbel, Bobby Ellen, ed. *American Short-Story Writers, 1910–1945,* series 1 and 2; *Dictionary of Literary Biography,* vols. 86 and 102. Detroit: Bruccoli Clark Layman/Gale Research, 1989, 1991.

Koszarski, Richard. *An Evening's Entertainment: The Age of the Silent Feature Picture 1915–1928.* New York: Scribners, 1990.

Lewis, Felice F. *Literature, Obscenity, and Law.* Carbondale: Southern Illinois University Press, 1976.

MacCann, Richard Dyer. *The Silent Comedians.* Metuchen, N.J.: Scarecrow Press, 1993.

MacNicholas, John, ed. *Twentieth-Century American Dramatists; Dictionary of Literary Biography,* vol. 7. Detroit: Bruccoli Clark/Gale, 1981.

Madden, Ethan. *Better Foot Forward: The History of American Musical Theater.* New York: Grossman, 1976.

Martine, James J. *American Novelists, 1910–1945; Dictionary of Literary Biography,* vol. 9. Detroit: Bruccoli Clark/Gale Research, 1981.

Marx, Samuel. *Mayer and Thalberg: The Make-Believe Saints.* New York: Random House, 1975.

Miller, Marc H., ed. *Louis Armstrong: A Cultural Legacy.* New York Queens Museum of Art / Seattle: University of Washington Press, 1994.

Moley, Raymond. *The Hays Office.* Indianapolis: Bobbs-Merrill, 1945.

The Most of John Held Jr. Introduction by Carl J. Weinhardt. Brattleboro, Vt.: Stephen Green Press, 1972.

Perkins, David. *A History of Modern Poetry From the 1890s to the High Modern Mode.* Cambridge, Mass.: Harvard University Press, 1976.

Quartermain, Peter, ed. *American Poets, 1880–1945,* series 1–3; Dictionary of Literary Biography, vols. 45, 48, and 54. Detroit: Bruccoli Clark/Gale, 1986–1987.

Raeburn, John. *Fame Became of Him: Hemingway as Public Writer.* Bloomington: Indiana University Press, 1984.

Rampersad, Arnold. *The Life of Langston Hughes.* New York: Oxford University Press, 1986.

Rideout, Walter B. *The Radical Novel in the United States 1900–1954.* Cambridge, Mass.: Harvard University Press, 1956.

Robinson, David. *Chaplin: His Life and Art.* New York: McGraw-Hill, 1985.

Robinson, Roxanna. *Georgia O'Keefe: A Life.* New York: Harper & Row Publishers, 1989.

Rood, Karen Lane, ed. *American Writers in Paris, 1920–1939; Dictionary of Literary Biography,* vol. 4. Detroit: Bruccoli Clark/Gale Research, 1980.

Rosenberg, Deena. *Fascinating Rhythm: The Collaboration of George and Ira Gershwin.* New York: Dutton, 1991.

Roth, Leland M. *A Concise History of American Architecture.* New York: Harper & Row, 1979.

Rubin, Louis D., Jr., ed. *The History of Southern Literature.* Baton Rouge: Louisiana State University Press, 1985.

Schuller, Gunther. *Early Jazz: Its Roots and Musical Development.* New York: Oxford University Press, 1968.

Sennett, Mack. *King of Comedy.* Garden City, N.Y.: Doubleday, 1954.

Sheaffer, Louis. *O'Neill: Son and Artist.* Boston: Little, Brown, 1973.

———. *O'Neill: Son and Playwright.* Boston: Little, Brown, 1968.

Smith, Scottie Fitzgerald, et al., eds. *The Romantic Egoists: A Pictorial Autobiography From the Scrapbooks and Albums of Scott and Zelda Fitzgerald.* New York: Scribners, 1974.

Stewart, John L. *The Burden of Time: The Fugitives and Agrarians . . .* Princeton: Princeton University Press, 1965.

Taylor, Deems. *A Pictorial History of the Movies.* New York: Simon & Schuster, 1943.

Terry, Walter. *The Dance in America.* New York: Harper, 1956.

Thomas, Bob. *Thalberg.* Garden City, N.Y.: Doubleday, 1969.

Thrasher, Frederic, ed. *Okay for Sound . . . How the Screen Found Its Voice.* New York: Duell, Sloan & Pearce, 1946.

Ulanov, Barry. *A History of Jazz in America.* New York: Da Capo, 1972.

Wasserman, Herman, ed. *George Gershwin's Song-book,* rev. ed. New York: Simon & Schuster, 1941.

Whitcomb, Ian. *Irving Berlin and Ragtime America.* New York: Limelight, 1988.

Wolfe, Edwin, II, and John F. Fleming. *Rosenbach.* Cleveland & New York: World, 1960.

Business and the Economy

Babson, Steve. *Working Detroit: The Making of a Union Town.* Detroit: Wayne State University Press, 1986.

Baruch, Bernard. *The Public Years.* New York: Holt, Rinehart & Winston, 1960.

Bender, Marilyn, and Seliq Altschul. *The Chosen Instrument: Pan Am, Juan Trippe, the Rise and Fall of an American Entrepreneur.* New York: Simon & Schuster, 1982.

Benson, Susan P. *Counter Cultures: Saleswomen, Managers, and Customers in American Department Stores, 1890–1940.* Urbana: University of Illinois Press, 1988.

Brooks, John. *Once in Golconda.* New York: Norton, 1969.

———. *Telephone: The First Hundred Years.* New York: Harper & Row, 1975.

Bruchey, Stuart. *Enterprise: The Dynamic Economy of a Free People.* Cambridge: Harvard University Press, 1990.

Bryant, Keith L., Jr., and Henry C. Dethloff. *A History of American Business.* 2d ed. Englewood Cliffs, N.J.: Prentice Hall, 1990.

Bryant, Keith L., Jr., ed. *Encyclopedia of American Business History and Biography: Railroads in the Age of Regulation, 1900–1980.* New York and Oxford: Manly/Facts On File, 1988.

Caldwell, Mark. *The Last Crusade: The War on Consumption, 1862–1954.* New York: Antheneum, 1988.

Chandler, Alfred D., Jr. *Giant Enterprise: Ford, General Motors and the Automobile Industry.* New York: Harcourt, Brace & World, 1964.

Chandler, Alfred D., Jr., and Stephen Salsbury. *Pierre S. du Pont and the Making of the Modern Corporation.* New York: Harper & Row, 1971.

Chrysler, Walter P. *Life of an American Workman.* New York: Dodd, Mead, 1927.

Cohen, Lizabeth. *Making a New Deal: Industrial Workers in Chicago, 1919–1939.* New York: Cambridge University Press, 1991.

Cray, Ed. *Chrome Colossus: General Motors and Its Times.* New York: McGraw-Hill, 1980.

Dobson, John M. *A History of American Enterprise.* Englewood Cliffs, N.J.: Prentice Hall, 1988.

Dutton, William S. *Du Pont: One Hundred and Thirty Years.* New York: Scribners, 1942.

Eichengreen, Barry. *Golden Fetters: The Gold Standard and the Great Depression, 1919–1939.* New York: Oxford University, 1995.

Epstein, Ralph. *The Automobile Industry: Its Economic and Commercial Development.* Chicago: University of Chicago Press, 1928.

Fisher, Irving. *The Stock Market Crash—and After.* New York: Macmillan, 1930.

Galbraith, John Kenneth. *The Great Crash.* Boston: Houghton Mifflin, 1961.

———. *The New Industrial State.* Boston: Houghton Mifflin, 1971.

Gelderman, Carol W. *Henry Ford: The Wayward Capitalist.* New York: Dial, 1981.

Gilder, George. *The Spirit of Enterprise.* New York: Simon & Schuster, 1984.

Gilland, Charles E., Jr., ed. *Readings in Business Responsibility.* Braintree, Mass.: Mark, 1969.

Gordon, Thomas, and Morgan Witts. *The Day the Bubble Burst.* Garden City, N.Y.: Doubleday, 1979.

Green, James R. *The World of the Worker: Labor in Twentieth-Century America.* New York: Hill & Wang, 1980.

Gunderson, Gerald. *A New Economic History: America.* New York: McGraw-Hill, 1976.

Gustin, Lawrence. *Billy Durant.* Grand Rapids, Mich.: Eerdmans, 1973.

Hall, Jacquelyn D. *Like a Family: The Making of a Southern Cotton Mill World.* Chapel Hill: University of North Carolina Press, 2000.

Harris, Leon A. *Merchant Princes: An Intimate History of Jewish Families Who Built Great Department Stores.* New York: Harper & Row, 1979.

Harris, S.H. *Twenty Years of Federal Reserve Policy.* Cambridge: Harvard University Press, 1933.

Heilbroner, Robert, and Aaron Singer. *The Economic Transformation of America.* New York: Harcourt Brace Jovanovich, 1977.

Higgs, Robert. *Crisis and Leviathon.* New York: Oxford University Press, 1987.

Holbrook, Stewart. *Age of the Moguls.* Garden City, N.Y.: Doubleday, 1954.

Hughes, Jonathan. *The Governmental Habit.* New York: Basic Books, 1977.

James, F. Cyril. *The Economics of Money, Credit and Banking,* 3rd ed. New York: Ronald Press, 1940.

Keynes, John M. *The General Theory of Employment, Interest and Money.* London: Macmillan, 1936.

Lawrence, Joseph Stagg. *Wall Street and Washington.* Princeton: Princeton University Press, 1929.

Leach, William. *Land of Desire.* New York: Pantheon, 1993.

Leary, William M., ed. *Encyclopedia of American Business History and Biography: The Airline Industry.* New York and Oxford: Manly/Facts On File, 1992.

Lefevre, Edwin. *Reminiscences of a Stock Operator.* Garden City, N.Y.: Doubleday, 1930.

Leuchtenburg, William E. *The Perils of Prosperity, 1914–1932.* Chicago: University of Chicago Press, 1958.

Lewis, David L. *The Public Image of Henry Ford.* Detroit: Wayne State University Press, 1976.

Liebhafsky, H.H. *American Government and Business.* New York: Wiley, 1971.

Lyons, Eugene. *David Sarnoff: A Biography.* New York: Harper & Row, 1966.

May, George S., ed. *Encyclopedia of American Business History and Biography: The Automobile Industry, 1920–1980.* New York and Oxford: Manly/Facts On File, 1990.

McDonald, Forrest. *Insull.* Chicago: University of Chicago Press, 1962.

Nance, John J. *Splash of Color: The Self-Destruction of Braniff International.* New York: Morrow, 1984.

Norton, Hugh S. *Economic Policy: Government and Business.* Columbus, Ohio: Merrill, 1966.

Patterson, James T. *America's Struggle Against Poverty, 1900–1980.* Cambridge: Harvard University Press, 1986.

Pecora, Ferdinand. *Wall Street Under Oath.* New York: Simon & Schuster, 1939.

Peterson, Joyce S. *American Automobile Workers, 1900–1933.* Albany: State University of New York Press, 1987.

Porter, Glenn, ed. *Encyclopedia of American Economic History: Studies of the Principal Movements and Ideas.* 3 vols. New York: Scribners, 1980.

Pusateri, Joseph C. *A History of American Business.* Arlington Heights, Ill.: Davidson, 1984.

Rae, John B. *The American Automobile: A Brief History.* Chicago and London: University of Chicago Press, 1965.

Rich, Doris. *Amelia Earhart: A Biography.* Washington, D.C.: Smithsonian Institute Press, 1989.

Robinson, Graham. *Pictorial History of the Automobile.* New York: Smith, 1987.

Schweikart, Larry, ed. *Encyclopedia of American Business History and Biography: Banking and Finance, 1913–1989.* New York and Oxford: Manly/Facts On File, 1990.

Seely, Bruce E., ed. *Encyclopedia of American Business History and Biography: Iron and Steel in the Twentieth Century.* New York and Oxford: Manly/Facts On File, 1994.

Shannon, David A. *Twentieth Century America.* Chicago: Rand, McNally, 1963.

Sloan, Alfred P., Jr. *Adventures of a White Collar Man.* New York: Doubleday, Doran, 1941.

———. *My Years With General Motors.* Garden City, N.Y.: Doubleday, 1964.

Smith, Henry Ladd. *Airways.* New York: Knopf, 1942.

Soule, George. *Prosperity Decade: From War to Depression, 1917–1929.* New York: Rinehart, 1947.

Stein, Herbert. *The Fiscal Revolution in America.* Washington, D.C.: American Enterprise Institute, 1990.

Traub, Marvin. *Like No Other Store: The Bloomingdales Legend.* New York: Times Books, 1993.

van Metre, Thurman W. *Transportation in the United States.* Chicago: Foundation Press, 1939.

Watson, D.S. *Business and Government.* New York: McGraw-Hill, 1958.

Weisberger, Bernard M. *The Dream Maker.* Boston: Little, Brown, 1979.

Wheelock, David. *The Strategy and Consistency of Federal Reserve Monetary Policy, 1924 to 1932–33.* Cambridge: Cambridge University Press, 1991.

Whitehouse, Arch. *The Sky's the Limit: History of U.S. Airlines.* New York: Macmillan, 1971.

Wylie, Irvin G. *The Self-Made Man in America: The Myth of Rags to Riches.* New Brunswick, N.J.: Rutgers University Press, 1954.

Zieger, Robert. *American Workers, American Unions, 1920–1985.* Baltimore: Johns Hopkins University Press, 1986.

Websites

"1920s Income Tax Cuts Sparked Economic Growth and Raised Federal Revenues." Available online at http://www.cato.org/dailys/03-04-03.html (accessed May 26, 2003).

"1929 Stock Market Crash and the Great Depression." Available online at http://www.jasmts.com/library.php?page=depression (accessed May 26, 2003).

Bittinger, Cyndy. "The Business of America Is Business?" Available online at http://www.calvin-coolidge.org/pages/history/research/ccmf/bitt02.html (accessed May 26, 2003).

"Chronology of Monetary History, 1920–1938." Available online at http://www.ex.ac.uk/RDavies/arian/amser/chrono15.html (accessed May 29, 2003).

"The Crash of 1929." Available online at http://mypage.direct
.ca/r/rsavill/Thecrash.html (accessed May 26, 2003).

"Model A Ford Club of America (MAFCA)." Available online
at http://www.mafca.com (accessed May 26, 2003).

"An Outline of American History (1994): Chapter Nine: The
Booming 1920's." Available online at http://odur.let.rug.nl
/usa/H/1994/ch9_p5.htm (accessed May 26, 2003).

"RCA." Available online at http://www.rca.com (accessed May
26, 2003).

"Regulation and Bank Failures: New Evidence From the Agricultural Collapse of the 1920s." Available online at http://
econpapers.hhs.se/paper/fipfedlwp/91-006.htm (accessed May
26, 2003).

"The Roaring Twenties." Available online at http://econ161
.berkeley.edu/TCEH/Slouch_roaring13.html (accessed May
26, 2003).

Education

Anderson, James D. *The Education of Blacks in the South,
1860–1935.* Chapel Hill: University of North Carolina Press,
1988.

Beale, Howard K. *A History of Freedom of Teaching in American Schools.* Report of the Commission on the Social Studies, American Historical Association, part 16. New York &
Chicago: Scribners, 1941.

Beck, Lynn G., and Joseph Murphy. *Understanding the Prin-
cipalship: Metaphorical Themes, 1920s–1990s.* New York:
Teachers College Press, Columbia University, 1993.

Berube, Maurice R. *American School Reform: Progressive,
Equality, and Excellence Movements, 1883–1993.* Westport,
Conn: Praeger, 1994.

Brubacher, John S., and Willis Rudy. *Higher Education in
Transition.* New York: Harper & Row, 1976.

Butler, Nicholas. *Across the Busy Years: Recollections and Reflections.* 2 vols. New York: Scribners, 1939, 1940.

Button, H. Warren, and Eugene F. Provenzo, Jr. *History of Education and Culture in America.* Englewood Cliffs, N.J.:
Prentice-Hall, 1983.

Church, Robert L., and Michael W. Sedlak. *Education in the
United States: An Interpretive History.* New York: Free
Press, 1976.

Cremin, Lawrence. *American Education, The Metropolitan Experience, 1876–1980.* New York: Harper & Row, 1988.

———. *The Transformation of the School: Progressivism in
American Education, 1876–1957.* New York: Knopf, 1961.

———. *The Wonderful World of Ellwood Patterson Cubberley: An Essay on the Historiography of American Education.* New York: Columbia University Teachers College,
Bureau of Publications, 1965.

Dawson, Howard A., and M.C.S. Noble, Jr. *Handbook on Rural
Education: Factual Data on Rural Education, Its Social and
Economic Backgrounds.* Washington, D.C.: National Edu-
cation Association of the United States, Department of Rural
Education, 1961.

De Camp, L. Sprague. *The Great Monkey Trial.* New York:
Doubleday, 1968.

De Vane, William Clyde. *The American University in the Twentieth Century.* Baton Rouge: Louisiana State University
Press, 1957.

Dulles, Foster R. *America Learns to Play.* Englewood Cliffs,
N.J.: Prentice-Hall, 1940.

Dworkin, Martin. *Dewey on Education.* New York: Columbia
University Teachers College Press, 1959.

Dykhuizen, George. *The Life and Mind of John Dewey.* Carbondale: Southern Illinois University Press, 1973.

Eaton, William Edward. *The American Federation of Teachers, 1916–1961: A History of the Movement.* Carbondale:
Southern Illinois University Press, 1975.

Goodstein, Judith R. *Millikan's School: A History of the California Institute of Technology.* New York: Norton, 1991.

Hofstadter, Richard, and Wilson Smith. *American Higher Education: A Documentary History.* 2 vols. Chicago: University of Chicago Press, 1961.

James, Thomas. *Public versus Nonpublic Education in Histor-
ical Perspective.* Stanford, Calif.: Institute for Research on
Educational Finance and Governance, School of Education,
Stanford University, 1982.

Karier, Clarence J. *Roots of Crisis: American Education in the
Twentieth Century.* Chicago: Rand, McNally, 1973.

———. *Shaping the American Education State, 1900 to the
Present.* New York: Free Press, 1975.

Kliebard, Herbert M. *The Struggle for the American Curriculum, 1893–1958.* 2d ed. New York: Routledge, 1995.

Krug, Edward A. *The Shaping of the American High School.*
vol. 2, *1920–1941.* New York: Harper & Row, 1972.

Lazerson, Marvin, ed. *American Education in the Twentieth
Century: A Documentary History.* New York: Teachers College Press, Columbia University, 1987.

Lowell, Abbott L. *At War With Academic Tradition in America.* Cambridge: Harvard University Press, 1934.

———. *What a College President Has Learned.* New York:
Macmillan, 1938.

Marrin, Albert. *Nicholas Murray Butler.* Boston: G.K. Hall,
1976.

Morgan, Harry. *Historical Perspectives on the Education of
Black Children.* Westport, Conn.: Praeger, 1995.

Morison, Samuel Eliot. *The Development of Harvard University Since the Inauguration of President Eliot, 1869–1929.*
Cambridge: Harvard University Press, 1930.

Murphy, Majorie. *Blackboard Unions: The AFT and the NEA,
1900–1980.* Ithaca, N.Y.: Cornell University Press, 1990.

Nelkin, Dorothy. *The Creation Controversy: Science or Scripture in the Schools.* New York: Norton, 1982.

———. *Science Textbook Controversies and the Politics of
Equal Time.* Cambridge, Mass.: MIT Press, 1977.

Pulliam, John D. *History of Education in America.* 3rd ed.
Columbus, Ohio: Merrill, 1986.

Seller, Maxine Schwartz, ed. *Women Educators in the United
States, 1820–1993: A Bio-Bibliographical Sourcebook.* Westport, Conn.: Greenwood Press, 1994.

Sokal, Michael M. *Psychological Testing and American Society, 1890–1930.* New Brunswick, N.J.: Rutgers University Press, 1987.

Tenenbaum, Samuel. *William Heard Kilpatrick: Trail Blazer in Education.* New York: Harper, 1951.

Thayer, Vivian Trow. *Formative Ideas in American Education, From the Colonial Period to the Present.* New York: Dodd, Mead, 1965.

Vassar, Rena L. *Social History of American Education.* Chicago: Rand, McNally, 1965.

Westbrook, Robert. *John Dewey and American Democracy.* Ithaca, N.Y.: Cornell University Press, 1991.

Yeomans, Henry A. *Abbott Lawrence Lowell, 1856–1943.* Cambridge: Harvard University Press, 1948.

Websites

"1920s EDUCATION." Available online at http://www.gjhistory .org/pix/1920s_education.htm (accessed May 29, 2003).

"Bryn Mawr Summer School for Women Workers in Industry." Available online at http://www.library.pitt.edu/labor _legacy/BRYNMAWR.HTM (accessed May 29, 2003).

"California Institute of Technology." Available online at http:// www.caltech.edu (accessed May 29, 2003).

"Changes in Education during the 1920s." Available online at http://web.bryant.edu/history/h497/prof_wmn/education.htm (accessed May 29, 2003).

"The Duke Endowment." Available online at http://www .dukeendowment.org(accessed May 29, 2003).

"History of Indian Education in the United States." Available online at http://www.aiefprograms.org/history_facts/history.html#1920 (accessed May 29, 2003).

"NEA: Events—American Education Week—History of AEW." Available online at http://www.nea.org/aew/history.html (accessed May 29, 2003).

"OSU [Oregon State University] Chronological History, 1920–1929." Available online at http://osulibrary.oregonstate .edu/archives/chronology/chron_1920.html (accessed May 29, 2003).

"*Pierce v. Society of Sisters,* 268 U.S. 510 (1925)." Available online at http://michaelariens.com/ConLaw/cases/pierce.htm (accessed May 29, 2003).

"The Scopes 'Monkey Trial'—July 10, 1925–July 25, 1925." Available online at http://xroads.virginia.edu/UG97/inherit /1925home.html (accessed May 29, 2003).

Fashion and Design

Armi, C. Edson. *The Art of American Car Design: The Profession and Personalities.* University Park: Pennsylvania State University Press, 1988.

Batterberry, Michael, and Ariane Batterberry. *Mirror, Mirror: A Social History of Fashion.* New York: Holt, Rinehart & Winston, 1977.

Bayer, Herbert, Walter Gropius, and Ise Gropius, eds. *Bauhaus 1919–1928.* New York: Museum of Modern Art, 1938.

Bayer, Patricia. *Art Deco Interiors: Decoration and Design Classics of the 1920s and 1930s.* Boston: Bullfinch Press/ Little, Brown, 1990.

Blackman, Cally. *20th Century Fashion: The 20s & 30s: Flappers and Vamps.* Milwaukee: Gareth Stevens Publishing, 2000.

Brazendale, Kevin, and Enrica Enceti, eds. *Classic Cars: Fifty Years of the World's Finest Automobile Design.* New York: Exeter, 1981.

Brockman, Helen L. *The Theory of Fashion Design.* New York: Wiley, 1965.

Burchard, John, and Albert Bush-Brown. *The Architecture of America: A Social and Cultural History.* Boston: Atlantic Monthly/Little, Brown, 1961.

Calloway, Stephen. *Twentieth-Century Decoration: The Domestic Interior From 1900 to the Present Day.* London: Weidenfeld & Nicolson, 1988.

Calloway, Stephen, and Elizabeth Cromley, eds. *The Elements of Style.* New York: Simon & Schuster, 1991.

Carson, Richard Burns. *The Olympian Cars: The Great American Luxury Automobiles of the Twenties & Thirties.* New York: Knopf, 1976.

Carter, Ernestine. *The Changing World of Fashion.* New York: Putnam, 1977.

The Changing American Woman: Two Hundred Years of American Fashion. New York: Fairchild, 1976.

Chase, Edna Woolman, and Ilka Chase. *Always in Vogue.* Garden City, N.Y.: Doubleday, 1954.

Clark, Clifford Edward, Jr. *The American Family Home, 1800–1960.* Chapel Hill: University of North Carolina Press, 1986.

Contini, Mila. *Fashion: From Ancient Egypt to the Present Day.* New York: Odyssey, 1965.

Curl, Donald W. *Mizner's Florida: American Resort Architecture.* New York: Architectural History Foundation / Cambridge, Mass.: MIT Press, 1984.

de Marly, Diana. *Fashion for Men: An Illustrated History.* New York: Holmes & Meier, 1985.

———. *The History of Haute Couture, 1850–1950.* New York: Holmes & Meier, 1980.

Dolan, Maryanne. *Vintage Clothing, 1880–1960: Identification and Value Guide.* Florence, Ala.: Books Americana, 1984.

Etherington-Smith, Meredith. *Patou.* New York: St. Martin's Press/Marek, 1983.

Ewing, Elizabeth. *History of Twentieth Century Fashion,* rev. and updated ed. London: Batsford, 1992; Lanham, Md.: Barnes & Noble, 1992.

Flink, James J. *The Automobile Age.* Cambridge, Mass. & London: MIT Press, 1988.

Gaines, Jane, and Charlotte Herzog, eds. *Fabrications: Costume and the Female Body.* New York: Routledge, 1990.

Gallico, Paul. *The Golden People.* Garden City, N.Y.: Doubleday, 1965.

Goldberger, Paul. *The Skyscraper.* New York: Knopf, 1981.

Hall, Ben M. *The Best Remaining Seats: The Story of the Golden Age of the Movie Palace.* New York: Clarkson N. Potter, 1961.

Herald, Jacqueline. *Fashions of a Decade: The 1920s.* New York: Facts On File, 1991.

Hildebrand, Grant. *The Architecture of Albert Kahn.* Cambridge, Mass.: MIT Press, 1974.

Jenkins, Alan. *The Twenties.* New York: Universe Books, 1974.

Johnston, Alva. *The Legendary Mizners.* New York: Farrar, Straus & Young, 1953.

Jones, Edgar R. *Those Were the Good Old Days: A Happy Look at American Advertising, 1880–1930.* New York: Simon & Schuster, 1989.

Kilham, Walter H., Jr. *Raymond Hood, Architect: Form Through Function in the American Skyscraper.* New York: Architectural Book Publishing, 1973.

Lençek, Lena, and Gideon Bosker. *Making Waves: Swimsuits and the Undressing of America.* San Francisco: Chronicle, 1989.

Ley, Sandra. *Fashion for Everyone: The Story of Ready-to-Wear, 1870–1970.* New York: Scribners, 1975.

Liebs, Chester H. *Main Street to Miracle Mile: American Roadside Architecture.* Boston: Little, Brown, 1985.

Lloyd, Valerie. *McDowell's Directory of Twentieth Century Fashion.* Englewood Cliffs, N.J.: Prentice-Hall, 1985.

Maddex, Diane, ed. *Master Builders: A Guide to Famous American Architects.* Washington, D.C.: Preservation Press, 1985.

Maxwell, Elsa. *R.S.V.P.: Elsa Maxwell's Own Story.* Boston: Little, Brown, 1954.

McAlester, Virginia, and Lee McAlester. *A Field Guide to American Houses.* New York: Knopf, 1992.

Milbank, Caroline Rennolds. *New York Fashion: The Evolution of American Style.* New York: Abrams, 1989.

Mirken, Alan, ed. *The 1927 Edition of the Sears, Roebuck Catalogue.* New York: Bounty, 1970.

Mulvagh, Jane. *Vogue History of 20th Century Fashion.* Harmondsworth, U.K.: Viking, 1988.

Murray, Maggie Pexton. *Changing Styles in Fashion: Who, What, Why.* New York: Fairchild, 1989.

Nash, Eric Peter. *Frank Lloyd Wright: Force of Nature.* New York: Smithmark Publishers, 1996.

Naylor, David. *Great American Movie Theaters.* Washington, D.C.: Preservation Press, 1987.

Pildas, Ave, and Lucinda Smith. *Movie Palaces.* New York: Clarkson N. Potter, 1980.

Pool, Mary Jane, ed. *20th-Century Decorating, Architecture & Gardens: 80 Years of Ideas & Pleasure From House & Garden.* New York: Holt, Rinehart & Winston, 1980.

Rogers, Meyric R. *American Interior Design: The Traditions and Development of Domestic Design From Colonial Times to the Present.* New York: Norton, 1947.

Roth, Leland M. *A Concise History of American Architecture.* New York: Icon Editions/Harper & Row, 1979.

Ryan, Mary Shaw. *Clothing: A Study in Human Behavior.* New York: Holt, Rinehart & Winston, 1966.

Schoeffler, O.E., and William Gale. *Esquire's Encyclopedia of 20th Century Men's Fashion.* New York: McGraw-Hill, 1973.

Schulze, Franz. *Mies van der Rohe: A Critical Biography.* Chicago: University of Chicago Press, 1985.

Scully, Vincent. *American Architecture and Urbanism.* New York: Praeger, 1969.

Seal, Ethel Davis. *Furnishing the Little House.* New York: Century, 1924.

Sears, Stephen W. *The American Heritage History of the Automobile in America.* New York: American Heritage, 1977.

Sichel, Marion. *History of Men's Costume.* London: Batsford Academic & Educational, 1984.

Steinwedel, Louis William, and J. Herbert Newport. *The Duesenberg: The Story of America's Premier Car.* Philadelphia: Chilton, 1970.

Stern, Robert A. M., with Thomas P. Catalano. *Raymond Hood.* New York: Institute for Architecture and Urban Studies/Rizzoli, 1982.

Stowell, Donald, and Erin Wertenberger. *A Century of Fashion 1865–1965.* Chicago: Encyclopaedia Britannica, 1987.

Trahey, Jane. *The Mode in Costume.* New York: Scribners, 1958.

———. *Harper's Bazaar: One Hundred Years of the American Female.* New York: Random House, 1967.

Tyrrell, Anne V. *Changing Trends in Fashion: Patterns of the Twentieth Century, 1900–1970.* London: Batsford, 1986.

Whiffen, Marcus, and Frederick Koeper. *American Architecture 1607–1976.* Cambridge, Mass.: MIT Press, 1981.

Wood, Barry James. *Show Windows: Seventy-five Years of the Art of Display.* New York: Congdon & Weed, 1982.

Government and Politics

Barry, John M. *Rising Tide: The Great Mississippi Flood of 1927 and How It Changed America.* New York: Simon & Schuster, 1997.

Bernstein, Irving L. *The Lean Years: A History of the American Worker 1920–1933.* Boston: Houghton Mifflin, 1960.

Burner, David. *Herbert Hoover: A Public Life.* New York: Knopf, 1979.

Carter, Dan T. *Scottsboro: A Tragedy of the Modern South.* Baton Rouge: Louisiana University Press, 1969.

Chalmers, David M. *Hooded Americanism: The First Century of the Ku Klux Klan, 1865–1965.* Garden City, N.Y.: Doubleday, 1965.

DeBenedetti, Charles. *Origins of the Modern American Peace Movement, 1915–1929.* Millwood, N.Y.: KTO Press, 1978.

Dorsett, Lyle W. *Billy Sunday and the Redemption of Urban America.* Grand Rapids, Mich.: Eerdmans, 1991.

Fass, Paula. *The Damned and the Beautiful: American Youth in the 1920s.* New York: Oxford University Press, 1977.

Ferrell, Robert H. *The Presidency of Calvin Coolidge.* Lawrence: University of Kansas Press, 1998.

Feuerlicht, Roberta Strauss. *Justice Crucified: The Story of Sacco and Vanzetti.* New York: McGraw-Hill, 1977.

Flink, James K. *The Car Culture.* Cambridge, Mass.: MIT Press, 1975.

Hicks, John Donald. *Republican Ascendancy, 1921–1933.* New York: Harper, 1960.

Kneeshaw, Stephen J. *In Pursuit of Peace: The American Reaction to the Kellogg-Briand Pact, 1928–1929.* New York: Garland, 1991.

Moore, Edmund Arthur. *A Catholic Runs for President; The Campaign of 1928.* New York: Ronald Press, 1956.

Mowry, George E. *The Twenties: Fords, Flappers, and Fanatics.* Englewood Cliffs, N.J.: Prentice-Hall, 1963.

Murray, Robert K. *Red Scare: A Study in National Hysteria, 1919–1920.* Minneapolis: University of Minnesota Press, 1955.

Noggle, Burl. *Teapot Dome: Oil and Politics in the 1920s.* Baton Rouge: Louisiana State University Press, 1962.

Sinclair, Andrew. *The Available Man: The Life Behind the Masks of Warren Gamaliel Harding.* New York: MacMillan, 1965.

———. *Era of Excess: A Social History of the Prohibition Movement.* New York: Harper & Row, 1962.

Trani, Eugene P., and David L. Wilson. *The Presidency of Warren G. Harding.* Lawrence: Regents Press of Kansas, 1977.

Law and Justice

Abraham, Henry J. *Justices, Presidents, and Senators: A History of the U.S. Supreme Court Appointments From Washington to Clinton.* Rowman & Littlefield, 1999.

Avrich, Paul. *Sacco and Vanzetti: The Anarchist Background.* Princeton: Princeton University Press, 1996.

Caudill, Edward. *The Scopes Trial: A Photographic History.* University of Tennessee Press, 2000.

Franklin, John Hope, and Alfred Moss Jr. *From Slavery to Freedom: A History of African Americans.* New York: Knopf, 2000.

Hall, Kermit L., ed. *The Oxford Companion to the Supreme Court.* New York: Oxford University Press, 1992.

Harrison, Maureen, and Steve Gilbert, eds. *Landmark Decisions of the United States Supreme Court II.* Beverly Hills: Excellent Books, 1992.

Kelly, Alfred H., Winfred A. Harbison, and Herman Belz. *The American Constitution: Its Origins and Development—Vol. II.* 7th ed. New York: Norton, 1991.

Kelly, Robert J. *Encyclopedia of Organized Crime in the United States: From Capone's Chicago to the New Urban Underworld.* Westport, Conn.: Greenwood Press, 2000.

Mikula, Mark F., and L. Mpho Mabunda, eds. *Great American Court Cases.* Detroit: Gale Group, 2000.

Palmer, Kris E., ed. *Constitutional Amendments: 1789 to the Present.* Detroit: Gale Group, 2000.

Scopes, John T., and James Presley. *Center of the Storm: Memoirs of John T. Scopes.* New York: Holt, Rinehart & Winston, 1967.

Smith, Page. *Redeeming the Time: A People's History of the 1920s and the New Deal.* New York: Penguin, 1991.

Weinberg, Arthur, ed. *Attorney for the Damned: Clarence Darrow in the Courtroom.* Chicago: University of Chicago Press, 1989.

West's Encyclopedia of American Law, 2d ed. 12 vols. St. Paul, Minn.: West Publishing Co., 1998.

Websites

"The American Experience: The Monkey Trial." Available online at http://www.pbs.org/wgbh/amex/monkeytrial/peopleevents/p_scopes.html; website home page: http://www.pbs.org (accessed April 20, 2003).

Linder, Doug. "Famous Trials." Available online at http://www.umkc.edu/famoustrials (accessed June 18, 2003).

"The Oyez Project of Northwestern University, a U.S. Supreme Court Multimedia Database." Available online at http://www.oyez.com (accessed April 20, 2003).

"The Presidents of the United States." Available online at http://www.whitehouse.gov/history/presidents/; website home page: http://www.whitehouse.gov (accessed April 20, 2003).

"U.S. Supreme Court Opinions." Available online at http://www.findlaw.com/casecode/supreme.html; website home page: http://www.findlaw.com (accessed March 16, 2003).

Lifestyles and Social Trends

Behr, Edward. *Prohibition: Thirteen Years That Changed America.* New York: Arcade, 1996.

Brown, Dorothy M. *Setting a Course: American Women in the Twenties.* Boston: Twayne, 1987.

Carson, Mina J. *Settlement Folk: Social Thought and the American Settlement Movement, 1885–1930.* Chicago: University of Chicago Press, 1990.

Chafe, William. *The American Woman: Her Changing Social, Economic, and Political Roles, 1920–1970.* New York: Oxford University Press, 1972.

Chesler, Ellen. *Women of Valor: Margaret Sanger and the Birth Control Movement in America.* New York: Simon & Schuster, 1992.

Chudacoff, Howard P. *The Age of the Bachelor.* Princeton, N.J.: Princeton University Press, 2000.

Coffey, Frank, and Joseph Layden. *America on Wheels: The First 100 Years: 1896–1996.* Los Angeles: General Pub. Group, 1998.

Cott, Nancy M. *The Grounding of Modern Feminism.* New Haven: Yale University Press, 1987.

Cowan, Ruth Schwartz. *More Work for Mother.* New York: Basic Books, 1983.

Dumenil, Lynn. *The Modern Temper: American Culture and Society in the 1920s.* New York: Hill and Wang, 1995.

Fairclough, Adam. *Better Day Coming: Blacks and Equality, 1890–2000.* New York: Viking, 2001.

Fass, Paula. *The Damned and the Beautiful: American Youth in the 1920s.* New York: Oxford University Press, 1977.

Flink, James. *The Automobile Age.* Cambridge, Mass.: MIT Press, 1990.

———. *Car Culture.* Cambridge, Mass.: MIT Press, 1975.

Franklin, John Hope, and Isidore Starr. *The Negro in Twentieth Century America.* New York: Random House, 1967.

Freedman. Estelle B., and John D'Emilio. *Intimate Matters: A History of Sexuality in America.* New York: Harper & Row, 1988.

Green, Harvey. *The Uncertainty of Everyday Life, 1915–1945.* New York: HarperCollins, 1992.

Hale, Grace E. *Making Whiteness: The Culture of Segregation in the South, 1890–1940.* New York: Vintage Books, 1999.

Hawes, Joseph. *Children Between the Wars: American Childhood, 1920–1940.* New York: Twayne Publishers, 1997.

Horn, Margo. *Before It's Too Late: The Child Guidance Movement in the United States, 1922–1945.* Philadelphia: Temple University Press, 1989.

Jackson, Kenneth T. *The Ku Klux Klan in the City: 1915–1930.* Chicago: Ivan R. Dee, 1992.

Jacobson, Matthew F. *Whiteness of a Different Color: European Immigrants and the Alchemy of Race.* Cambridge, Mass.: Harvard University Press, 1999.

Kallen, Stuart A., ed. *The Roaring Twenties.* San Diego, Calif.: Greenhaven Press, 2002.

Kennedy, David M. *Birth Control in America: The Career of Margaret Sanger.* New Haven, Conn.: Yale University Press, 1991.

Kessler-Harris, Alice. *Out to Work: A History of Wage-Earning Women in the United States.* New York: Oxford University Press, 1982.

Kisseloff, Jeff. *You Must Remember This: An Oral History of Manhattan From the 1890s to World War Two.* Baltimore: John Hopkins University Press, 2000.

Kyvig, David. *Daily Life in the United States, 1920–1939: Decades of Promise and Pain.* Westport, Conn.: Greenwood Press, 2002.

Latham, Angela J. *Posing a Threat: Flappers, Chorus Girls, and Other Brazen Performers of the American 1920s.* Hanover, N.H.: University Press of New England, 2000.

Lemann, Nicholas. *The Promised Land: The Great Black Migration and How It Changed America.* New York: A.A. Knopf, 1991.

Lender, Mark Edward, and James Kirby Martin. *Drinking in America.* New York: Free Press, 1987.

MacLean, Nancy K. *Behind the Mask of Chivalry: The Making of the Second Ku Klux Klan.* New York: Oxford University Press, 1995.

Marks, Carole. *Farewell, We're Good and Gone: The Great Black Migration.* Bloomington: Indiana University Press, 1989.

Marks, Carole, and Diana Edkins. *The Power of Pride: Stylemakers and Rulebreakers of the Harlem Renaissance.* New York: Crown Publishers, 1999.

Martin, Carol. *Dance Marathons: Performing American Culture of the 1920s and 1930s.* Jackson: University Press of Mississippi, 1994.

McCalley, Bruce W. *Model T Ford: The Car That Changed the World.* Iola, Wis.: Krause Publications, 1994.

Mintz, Steven, and Susan Kellogg. *Domestic Revolutions: A Social History of American Family Life.* New York: Free Press, 1988.

Modell, John. *Into One's Own: From Youth to Adulthood in the United States, 1920–1975.* Berkeley: University of California Press, 1989.

Parrish, Michael E. *Anxious Decades: America in Prosperity and Depression, 1920–1941.* New York: W.W. Norton, 1992.

Pegram, Thomas R. *Battling Demon Rum: The Struggle for a Dry America, 1800–1933.* Chicago: Ivan R. Dee, 1998.

Rosenberg, Rosalind. *Divided Lives: American Women in the Twentieth Century.* New York: Hill & Wang, 1992.

Sann, Paul. *Fads, Follies and Delusions of the American People.* New York: Bonanza Books, 1968.

Smith, Page. *Redeeming the Time: A People's History of the 1920's and the New Deal.* New York: McGraw-Hill, 1986.

Solomon, Barbara Miller. *In the Company of Educated Women.* New Haven, Conn.: Yale University Press, 1985.

Stein, Judith. *The World of Marcus Garvey: Race and Class in Modern Society.* Baton Rouge: Louisiana State University Press, 1986.

Strasser, Susan. *Never Done.* New York: Pantheon, 1982.

Watson, Steven. *The Harlem Renaissance: Hub of African-American Culture, 1920–1930.* New York: Pantheon Books, 1995.

Winnewisser, Peter. *The Legendary Model A Ford: The Ultimate History of One of America's Great Automobiles.* Iola, Wis.: Krause Publications, 1999.

Wukovits, John F., ed. *The 1920s.* San Diego, Calif.: Greenhaven Press, 2000.

Zelizer, Viviana. *Pricing the Priceless.* New York: Basic Books, 1985.

Websites

"The 1920s: Primary Sources From American Popular Culture." Available online at http://www.authentichistory.com/1920s.html (accessed April 22, 2003).

"American Prohibition in the 1920s." Available online at http://prohibition.history.ohio-state.edu/proh1920.htm (accessed April 22, 2003).

"A Biography of America: The Twenties." Available online at http://www.learner.org/biographyofamerica/prog20/index.html (accessed April 22, 2003).

"Harlem, 1900–1940: An African American Community." Available online at http://www.si.umich.edu/CHICO/Harlem/index.html (accessed April 22, 2003).

"Harlem Renaissance." Available online at http://www.levity.com/corduroy/harlem.htm (accessed April 22, 2003).

"The Jazz Age Page." Available online at http://www.btinternet.com/dreklind/Jazzhomemac.htm (accessed April 22, 2003).

"The Scopes Monkey Trial." Available online at http://www.courttv.com/archive/greatesttrials/scopes/index.html (accessed April 22, 2003).

The Media

Barfield, Ray. *Listening to Radio, 1920–1950.* Westport, Conn.: Praeger, 1996.

Barnouw, Erik. *A Tower in Babel: A History of Broadcasting in the United States, Volume I, to 1933.* New York: Oxford University Press, 1966.

Berg, A. Scott. *Maxwell Perkins: Editor of Genius.* New York: Dutton, 1978.

The Book of the Month: Sixty Years of Books in American Life. Boston: Little, Brown, 1986.

Boylan, James, ed. *The World and the 20's: The Golden Years of New York's Legendary Newspaper.* New York: Dial Press, 1973.

Cohn, Jan. *Creating America: George Horace Lorimer and The Saturday Evening Post.* Pittsburgh: University of Pittsburgh Press, 1989.

Craig, Douglas. *Fireside Politics: Radio and Political Culture in the United States, 1920–1940.* Baltimore: Johns Hopkins University Press, 2000.

Dardis, Tom. *Firebrand: The Life of Horace Liveright.* New York: Random House, 1995.

Douglas, George H. *The Smart Magazines: 50 Years of Literary Revelry and High Jinks at Vanity Fair, the New Yorker, Life, Esquire, and the Smart Set.* New Haven, Conn.: Archon Books, 1991.

Durstine, Roy S. *This Advertising Business.* New York: Scribners, 1928.

Dzwonkoski, Peter, ed. *American Literary Publishing Houses, 1900–1980: Trade and Paperback; Dictionary of Literary Biography.* Vol. 46. Detroit: Bruccoli Clark/Gale Research, 1986.

Editor to Author: The Letters of Maxwell E. Perkins. Compiled by Maxwell E. Perkins. New York: Scribners, 1950.

Ely, Melvin Patrick. *The Adventures of Amos 'n' Andy: A Social History of an American Phenomenon.* New York: Free Press, 1991.

Emery, Michael, and Edwin Emery. *The Press and America: An Interpretive History of the Mass Media.* Boston: Allyn and Bacon, 1996.

Fielding, Raymond. *The American Newsreel, 1911–1967.* Norman: University of Oklahoma Press, 1972.

Gabler, Neal. *Winchell: Gossip, Power, and the Culture of Celebrity.* New York: Knopf, 1994.

Gelatt, Roland. *The Fabulous Phonograph: From Edison to Stereo.* New York: Appleton-Century, 1966.

Goulart, Ron. *Cheap Thrills: An Informal History of the Pulp Magazines.* New Rochelle, N.Y.: Arlington House, 1972.

Haining, Peter. *The Classic Era of American Pulp Magazines.* Chicago: Chicago Review Press, 2001.

Heidenry, John. *Theirs Was the Kingdom: Lila and DeWitt Wallace and the Story of the Reader's Digest.* New York: Norton, 1993.

Hilmes, Michele. *Radio Voices: American Broadcasting, 1922–1952.* Minneapolis: University of Minnesota Press, 1997.

Hunt, William R. *Body Love: The Amazing Career of Bernard MacFadden.* Bowling Green, Ohio: Bowling Green University Popular Press, 1989.

Kobler, John. *Luce: His Time, Life, and Fortune.* Garden City, N.Y.: Doubleday, 1968.

Kunkel, Thomas. *Genius in Disguise: Harold Ross of the New Yorker.* New York: Random House, 1995.

Lyon, Eugene. *David Sarnoff.* New York: Harper & Row, 1966.

MacDonald, J. Fred. *Don't Touch That Dial: Radio Programming in American Life From 1920 to 1960.* Chicago: G.K. Hall, 1979.

Mencken, H.L. *My Life as Author and Editor.* New York: Knopf, 1992.

Morey, Anne. *Hollywood Outsiders: The Adaptation of the Film Industry, 1913–1934.* Minneapolis: University of Minnesota Press, 2003.

O'Connor, Richard. *Heywood Broun.* New York: Putnam, 1975.

Paley, William S. *As It Happened: A Memoir.* Garden City, N.Y.: Doubleday, 1979.

Ponce De Leon, Charles L. *Self-Exposure: Human-Interest Journalism and the Emergence of Celebrity in America, 1890–1940.* Chapel Hill: University of North Carolina Press, 1992.

Ritchie, Michael. *Stand By: The Prehistory of Television.* Woodstock, N.Y.: Overlook Press, 1994.

Robinson, Jerry. *The Comics: An Illustrated History of Comic Strip Art.* New York: Putnam, 1974.

Schwartz, Evan I. *The Last Lone Inventor: A Tale of Genius, Deceit, and the Birth of Television.* New York: HarperCollins, 2002.

Smith, Sally Bedell. *In All His Glory: The Life and Times of William S. Paley and the Birth of Modern Broadcasting.* New York: Random House, 2002.

Sobel, Robert. *RCA.* New York: Stein & Day, 1986.

Sterling, Christopher H., and John M. Kittross. *Stay Tuned: A Concise History of American Broadcasting, 2nd ed.* Belmont, Calif.: Wadsworth, 1990.

Swanberg, W.A. *Luce and His Empire.* New York: Scribners, 1972.

Tebbel, John. *A History of Book Publishing in the United States.* Vol. 3. New York: Bowker, 1978.

Tebbel, John, and Mary Ellen Zuckerman. *The Magazine in America, 1741–1990.* New York: Oxford University Press, 1991.

Thomas, Dana Lee. *The Media Moguls: From Joseph Pulitzer to William S. Paley, the Wheelings and Dealings of America's News Merchants.* New York: Putnam, 1981.

Vincent, Theodore G., ed. *Voices of a Black Nation: Political Journalism in the Harlem Renaissance.* Palo Alto, Calif.: Ramparts Press, 1973.

Walker, Alexander. *The Shattered Silents: How the Talkies Came to Stay.* London: Elm Tree Books, 1978.

Websites

"Conrad's Garage: Replaying the Earliest Days of Radio." Available online at http://www.npr.org/programs/atc/features

/2001/nov/garage/011130.garage.html; website home page: http://www.npr.org (accessed April 22, 2003).

"Greatest [Radio] Hits of the 1920s and 1930s." Available online at http://www.absintheradio.com (accessed April 22, 2003).

"Harlem: Mecca of the New Negro." Available online at http://etext.lib.virginia.edu/harlem (accessed April 22, 2003).

"United States Early Radio History." Available online at http://EarlyRadioHistory.us (accessed June 17, 2003).

"Voices of the 20th Century: Sounds From the Past." Available online at http://www.ibiscom.com/vofrm.htm (accessed April 22, 2003).

Medicine and Health

Astor, Gerald. *The Disease Detectives: Deadly Medical Mysteries and the People Who Solved Them.* New York: New American Library, 1984.

Bailey, Herbert. *The Vitamin Pioneers.* Emmaus, Pa.: Rodale Books, 1968.

Bates, Barbara. *Bargaining for Life: A Social History of Tuberculosis, 1876–1938.* Philadelphia: University of Pennsylvania Press, 1992.

Bender, Arnold E. *A Dictionary of Food and Nutrition.* New York: Oxford University Press, 1995.

Bliss, Michael. *Banting: A Biography.* Toronto: McClelland & Stewart, 1984.

———. *The Discovery of Insulin.* Toronto: McClelland & Stewart, 1982.

Bochner, Ruth. *Clinical Application of the Rorschach Test.* New York: Grune & Stratton, 1942.

Bordley, James, and A. McGehee Harvey. *Two Centuries of American Medicine, 1776–1976.* Philadelphia: Saunders, 1976.

Brandt, Allan M. *No Magic Bullet: A Social History of Venereal Disease in the United States Since 1880.* New York: Oxford University Press, 1985.

Carmichael, Daniel E. *The Pap Smear: Life of George Papanicolaou.* Springfield, Ill.: Thomas, 1973.

Cassedy, James H. *Medicine in America: A Short History.* Baltimore: Johns Hopkins University Press, 1991.

Drogin, Elash. *Margaret Sanger: Father of Modern Society.* New Hope, Ky.: CUL Publications, 1989.

Duffy, John. *The Healers: The Rise of the Medical Establishment.* New York: McGraw-Hill, 1976; republished as *The Healers: A History of American Medicine.* Urbana: University of Illinois Press, 1979.

Erlichman, Mary. *Electroencephalographic (EEG) Video Monitoring.* Rockville, Md.: United States Department of Health and Human Services, 1990.

Etheridge, Elizabeth. *The Butterfly Caste: A Social History of Pellagra in the South.* Westport, Conn.: Greenwood Press, 1972.

Fulton, John Farquhar. *Harvey Cushing: A Biography.* Springfield, Ill.: Thomas, 1946.

Kiple, Kenneth F., ed. *The Cambridge World History of Human Disease.* New York: Cambridge University Press, 1993.

Magner, Lois A. *A History of Medicine.* New York: Marcel Dekker, 1992.

Marks, Geoffrey, and William K. Beatty. *The Story of Medicine in America.* New York: Scribners, 1973.

Martin, Wayne. *Medical Heroes and Heretics.* Old Greenwich, Conn.: Devon-Adair, 1977.

Mateles, Richard I. *Penicillin: A Paradigm for Biotechnology.* Chicago: Candida, 1998.

McCollum, Elmer V. *From Kansas Farm Boy to Scientist.* Lawrence: University of Kansas Press, 1964.

———. *A History of Nutrition.* Boston: Houghton Mifflin, 1957.

Moss, Ralph W. *Free Radical: Albert Szent-Gyorgyi and the Battle Over Vitamin C.* New York: Paragon House, 1988.

Professional Guide to Diseases. 6th ed. Springhouse, Pa.: Springhouse, 1998.

Puetel, Claude. *History of Syphilis.* Baltimore: Johns Hopkins University Press, 1992.

Rather, L.J. *The Genesis of Cancer: A Study in the History of Ideas.* Baltimore: Johns Hopkins University Press, 1978.

Reilly, Philip. *The Surgical Solution: A History of Involuntary Sterilization in the United States.* Baltimore: Johns Hopkins University Press, 1991.

Scott, Donald F. *Understanding EEG: An Introduction to Electroencephalography.* Philadelphia: Lippincott, 1976.

Sebel, Peter, et al. *Respiration: The Breath of Life.* New York: Torstar, 1985.

Sheehan, John C. *The Enchanted Ring: The Untold Story of Penicillin.* Cambridge, Mass.: MIT Press, 1982.

Smith, Wrynn. *A Profile of Health and Disease in America: Cancer.* New York: Facts On File, 1987.

Taber, Charles W. *Taber's Cyclopedic Medical Dictionary,* 16th ed. Clayton L. Thomas, ed. Philadelphia: F. A. Davis, 1989.

Wasson, Tyler, ed. *Nobel Prize Winners.* New York: Wilson, 1987.

Weisse, Allen B. *Medical Odysseys.* New Brunswick, N.J.: Rutgers University Press, 1991.

Websites

"*Buck v. Bell,* 274 U.S. 200 (1927)." Available online at http://www.law.du.edu/russell/lh/alh/docs/buckvbell.html (accessed June 17, 2003).

Carpenter, Kenneth J., and Ling Zhao. "Forgotten Mysteries in the Early History of Vitamin D." Available online at http://www.nutrition.org/cgi/content/full/129/5/923?maxtoshow=&HITS=10&hits=.

"Historical Development of Inkblot Technique." Available online at http://schatz.sju.edu/introlec/rorschach/history.html.

"The History of Penicillin." Available online at http://oh.essortment.com/historyofpen_pnd.htm.

"History of Vitamin D." Available online at http://vitamind.ucr.edu/history.html.

"Margaret Sanger and the 1920's Birth Control Movement." Available online at http://www.msu.edu/course/mc/112/1920s/Sanger.

"Medicine and Madison Avenue—Timeline." Available online at http://scriptorium.lib.duke.edu/mma/timeline.html.

"Polio History Timeline." Available online at http://www.pbs.org/storyofpolio/polio/timeline/1921.html.

"United States Cancer Mortality From 1900 to 1992." Available online at http://www.healthsentinel.com/Vaccines/DiseaseAndRelatedData_files/she.

"Whipple, George H. Hemoglobin Regeneration as Influenced by Diet and Other Factors." Available online at http://www.nobel.se/medicine/laureates/1934/whipple-lecture.html.

Religion

Ahlstrom, Sydney E. *A Religious History of the American People.* 2 vols. Garden City, N.Y.: Doubleday, 1975.

Albanese, Catherine. *America, Religions and Religion.* Belmont, Calif.: Wadsworth, 1981.

Ammerman, Nancy T. *Bible Believers: Fundamentalists in the Modern World.* New Brunswick, N.J.: Rutgers University Press, 1987.

Balmer, Randall, and John R. Fitsmeier. *The Presbyterians.* Westport, Conn.: Greenwood Press, 1993.

Blumhofer, Edith. *Aimee Semple McPherson: Everybody's Sister.* Grand Rapids, Mich.: Eerdmans, 1993.

Brauer, Jerald C. *Protestantism in America: A Narrative History.* Philadelphia: Westminster, 1953.

Cavert, Samuel McCrea. *The American Churches in the Ecumenical Movement, 1900–1968.* New York: Association Press, 1968.

Cross, Robert D. *The Emergence of Liberal Catholicism in America.* Cambridge, Mass.: Harvard University Press, 1958.

Dolan, Jay P. *The American Catholic Experience: A History From Colonial Times to the Present.* Garden City, N.Y.: Doubleday, 1985.

Dorset, Lyle W. *Billy Sunday and the Redemption of Urban America.* Grand Rapids, Mich.: Eerdmans, 1991.

Epstein, Daniel M. *Sister Aimee: The Life of Aimee Semple McPherson.* New York: Harcourt Brace Jovanovich, 1993.

Hennesey, James J. *American Catholics: A History of the Roman Catholic Community in the United States.* New York: Oxford University Press, 1981.

Hertzberg, Arthur. *The Jews in America: Four Centuries of an Uneasy Encounter—A History.* New York: Simon & Schuster, 1989.

Hudson, Darril. *The Ecumenical Movement in World Affairs.* London: Weidenfeld & Nicolson, 1969.

Hudson, Winthrop S. *Religion in America: An Historical Account of the Development of American Religious Life.* New York: Scribners, 1981.

Marsden, George. *Reforming Fundamentalism: Fuller Seminary and the New Evangelicalism.* Grand Rapids, Mich.: Eerdmans, 1987.

Marty, Martin E. *Pilgrims in Their Own Land: Five Hundred Years of Religion in America.* Boston: Little, Brown, 1984.

McLoughlin, William G. *Billy Sunday Was His Real Name.* Chicago: University of Chicago Press, 1955.

Miller, Robert Moats. *Harry Emerson Fosdick: Preacher, Pastor, Prophet.* New York: Oxford University Press, 1985.

Modern Revivalism: Charles Grandison Finney to Billy Graham. New York: Ronald Press, 1959.

Nelson, John K. *Peace Prophets: American Pacifist Thought, 1919–1945.* Chapel Hill: University of North Carolina Press, 1967.

Norwood, Frederick A. *The Story of American Methodism: A History of the United Methodists and Their Relations.* Nashville, Tenn.: Abingdon, 1974.

Sachar, Howard M. *A History of the Jews in America.* New York: Knopf, 1992.

Stonehouse, Ned B. *J. Gresham Machen: A Biographical Memoir.* Grand Rapids, Mich.: Eerdmans, 1954.

Science and Technology

Aitken, Hugh G. J. *The Continuous Wave: Technology and the American Radio, 1900–1922.* Princeton: Princeton University Press, 1985.

Allen, Garland. *Life Science in the Twentieth Century.* Cambridge: Cambridge University Press, 1978.

Angelucci, Enzo. *Airplanes From the Dawn of Flight to the Present Day.* New York: McGraw-Hill, 1973.

Archer, Gleason. *History of the Radio to 1926.* New York: American Historical Society, 1938.

Asimov, Isaac. *Asimov's New Guide to Science.* New York: Basic Books, 1984.

Baldwin, Neil. *Edison: Inventing the Century.* New York: Hyperion, 1995.

Banister, Robert C. *Social Darwinism: Science and Myth in American Social Thought.* Philadelphia: Temple University Press, 1979.

Billstein, Roger. *Flight in America.* Baltimore: Johns Hopkins University Press, 1985.

Bunch, Bryan, and Alexander Hellemans. *The Timetables of Technology.* New York: Simon & Schuster, 1993.

Burlingame, Roger. *Henry Ford: A Great Life in Brief.* New York: Knopf, 1954.

Carnegie Library of Pittsburgh, Science and Technology Department. *Science and Technology Desk Reference.* Detroit: Gale Research, 1993.

Cochrane, Dorothy, Von Hardesty, and Russell Lee. *The Aviation Careers of Igor Sikorsky.* Los Angeles: Washington University Press for the National Air and Space Museum, 1989.

Corn, Joseph J. *The Winged Gospel: America's Romance With Aviation, 1900–1950.* New York: Oxford University Press, 1983.

———, ed. *Imagining Tomorrow.* Cambridge, Mass.: MIT Press, 1987.

Cravens, Hamilton. *The Triumph of Evolution: American Scientists and the Heredity-Environment Controversy, 1900–1941.* Philadelphia: University of Pennsylvania Press, 1978.

Degler, Carl N. *In Search of Human Nature: The Decline and Revival of Darwinism in American Social Thought.* New York: Oxford University Press, 1991.

Dick, Harold, and Douglas Robinson. *The Golden Age of the Great Passenger Airships.* Washington, D.C.: Smithsonian Institution Press, 1985.

Douglas, George H. *All Aboard! The Railroad in American Life.* New York: Paragon House, 1992.

Farber, Eduard. *Nobel Prize Winners in Chemistry, 1901–1961.* London & New York: Abelard-Schuman, 1963.

Field, George B., Halton Arp, and Jonathan N. Bahcall. *The Redshift Controversy.* Reading, Mass.: Benjamin, 1973.

Freeman, Derek. *Margaret Mead and Samoa: The Making and Unmaking of an Anthropological Myth.* Cambridge, Mass.: Harvard University Press, 1983.

Gillespie, Charles Coulston, ed. *Dictionary of Scientific Biography.* 18 vols. New York: Scribners, 1970–1990.

Gingerich, Owen, ed. *Astrophysics and Twentieth-Century Astronomy to 1950.* New York: Cambridge University Press, 1984.

Goddard, Stephen B. *Getting There: The Epic Struggle Between Road and Rail in the American Century.* New York: Basic Books, 1992.

Halley, James J. *The Role of the Fighter in Air Warfare.* London: Barrie & Jenkins, 1979.

Hallion, Richard P. *Legacy of Flight: The Guggenheim Contribution to American Aviation.* Seattle: University of Washington Press, 1977.

Hanscom, C. Dean, ed. *Dates in American Telephone Technology.* New York: Bell Telephone Laboratories, 1961.

Hartcup, Guy. *The Achievement of the Airship: A History of the Development of Rigid, Semi-Rigid and Non-Rigid Airships.* Newton Abbot, U.K. & North Pomfret, Vt.: David & Charles, 1974.

Heathcote, Niels H. de V. *Nobel Prize Winners in Physics, 1901–1950.* New York: Schuman, 1953.

Hellemans, Alexander, and Bryan Bunch. *The Timetables of Science,* upd. ed. New York: Simon & Schuster, 1991.

Hounshell, David A., and John Kenly Smith Jr. *Science and Corporate Strategy: Du Pont R&D, 1902–1980.* Cambridge. Mass.: Cambridge University Press, 1988.

Kalmus, Herbert T., and Eleanore King Kalmus. *Mr. Technicolor.* Absecon, N.J.: Magic Image Filmbooks, 1990.

Kass-Simon, G., and Patricia Farnes, eds. *Women of Science.* Bloomington: University of Indiana Press, 1990.

Kevles, Daniel J. *In the Name of Eugenics: Genetics and the Uses of Human Heredity.* New York: Knopf, 1985.

———. *The Physicists: The History of a Scientific Community in Modern America.* New York: Knopf, 1978.

King, H.F., comp. *Kitty Hawk to Concorde: Jane's 100 Significant Aircraft.* London: Jane's Yearbooks, 1970.

Lahti, Paul, and Pamela Mittelstaedt. *Foundations of Modern Physics.* Philadelphia: Taylor and Francis, 1986.

Larson, Edward J. *Trial and Error: The American Controversy Over Creation and Evolution.* New York: Oxford University Press, 1985.

Magill, Frank N., ed. *Great Events From History II, Science and Technology Series. Vol 2, 1910–1931.* Pasadena, Calif.: Salem Press, 1991.

Mayr, Ernst. *The Growth of Biological Thought: Diversity, Evolution, and Inheritance.* Cambridge: Harvard University Press, 1982.

Mayr, Ernst, and William B. Provine. *The Evolutionary Synthesis: Perspectives on the Unification of Biology.* Cambridge, Mass.: Harvard University Press, 1980.

McGraw-Hill Encyclopedia of Science and Technology, 4th ed. 14 vols. New York: McGraw-Hill, 1977.

Mount, Ellis, and Barbara List. *Milestones in Science and Technology,* 2d ed. Phoenix: Oryx Press, 1993.

Nye, David. *American Technological Sublime.* Cambridge: MIT Press, 1994.

Oakes, Claudia M., and Kathleen L. Brooks-Pazmany, comps. *Aircraft of the National Air and Space Museum,* 4th ed. Washington, D.C.: Smithsonian Institution Press, 1991.

Oslin, George P. *The Story of Telecommunications.* Macon, Ga.: Mercer University Press, 1992.

Pursell, Carroll W., ed. *Technology in America.* Washington, D.C.: USIA Forum Series, 1979.

Rainger, Ronald, Keith Benson, and Jane Maienschen, eds. *The American Development of Biology.* Philadelphia: University of Pennsylvania Press, 1988.

Robinson, Douglas H., and Charles L. Keller. *"Up Ship!" A History of the U.S. Navy's Rigid Airships, 1919–1935.* Annapolis, Md.: Naval Institute Press, 1982.

Rossiter, Margaret W. *Women Scientists in America: Struggles and Strategies to 1940.* Baltimore: Johns Hopkins University Press, 1982.

Schodek, Daniel L. *Landmarks in American Civil Engineering.* Cambridge, Mass.: MIT Press, 1987.

Schubert, Paul. *The Electric Word: The Rise of Radio.* New York: Macmillan, 1928.

Smith, Robert W. *The Expanding Universe: Astronomy's Great Debate, 1900–1931.* New York: Cambridge University Press, 1982.

Spencer, Frank., ed. *A History of American Physical Anthropology, 1830–1930.* New York: Academic Press, 1982.

Thomas, Lowell, and Lowell Thomas Jr. *Famous First Flights That Changed History.* Garden City, N.Y.: Doubleday, 1969.

Vare, Ethlie Ann, and Greg Ptacek. *Mothers of Invention, From the Bra to the Bomb: Forgotten Women & Their Unforgettable Ideas.* New York: Morrow, 1988.

Wheeler, John A., and Hubert Z. Wojciech, eds. *Quantum Theory and Measurement.* Princeton: Princeton University Press, 1983.

Websites

"20th Century Insect Control." Available online at http://www.ars.usda.gov/is/timeline/insect.htm (accessed June 17, 2003).

"Charles Lindbergh: An American Aviator." Available online at http://www.CharlesLindbergh.com (accessed June 17, 2003).

"Compton, Arthur H. X-Rays as a Branch of Optics." Available online at http://www.nobel.se/physics/laureates/1927/compton-lecture.html (accessed June 17, 2003).

"Edwin Hubble." Available online at http://www.pbs.org/wnet/hawking/cosmostar/html/cstars_hubble.html (accessed June 17, 2003).

"General Billy Mitchell, Milwaukee Native and Air Force Pioneer." Available online at http://www.uwm.edu/Dept/Library/arch/mitchell/exhibit.htm (accessed June 17, 2003).

"Human Ancestors Hall: Taung 1." Available online at http://www.mnh.si.edu/anthro/humanorigins/ha/taung1.html (accessed June 17, 2003).

"The Human Gene Mutation Database." Available online at http://archive.uwcm.ac.uk/uwcm/mg/hgmd0.html (accessed June 17, 2003).

"Margaret Mead." Available online at http://www.amnh.org/exhibitions/expeditions/treasure_fossil/Treasures/Margaret_Mead/mead.html (accessed June 17, 2003).

"Robert Goddard and His Rockets." Available online at http://www-istp.gsfc.nasa.gov/stargaze/Sgoddard.htm (accessed June 17, 2003).

"The Scopes 'Monkey Trial'—July 10, 1925–July 25, 1925." http://xroads.virginia.edu/UG97/inherit/1925home.html (accessed June 17, 2003).

Sports

Adler, David A., and Terry Widener. *America's Champion Swimmer: Gertrude Ederle.* San Diego: Harcourt, 2000.

Aldrich, Nelson W. *Tommy Hitchcock: An American Hero.* Gaithersburg, Md.: Fleet Street, 1984.

Alexander, Charles C. *Rogers Hornsby: A Biography.* New York: H. Holt, 1995.

Anderson, C. W. *Horse of the Century, Man O' War.* New York: Macmillan, 1970.

Asinof, Eliot. *Eight Men Out: The Black Sox and the 1919 Series.* New York: Holt, Rinehart & Winston, 1977.

Bevis, Charley. *Mickey Cochrane: The Life of a Baseball Hall of Fame Catcher.* Jefferson, N.C.: McFarland, 1998.

Bubka, Bob. *The Ryder Cup: Golf's Greatest Event.* New York: Crown, 1999.

Chelland, Patrick. *George Gipp, Knute Rockne and Notre Dame.* Chicago: H. Regnery, 1973.

Clark, Dick, and Laryy Lester, eds. *The Negro Leagues Book.* Cleveland: Society for American Baseball Research, 1994.

Collett, Glenna, and James M. Neville. *Ladies in the Rough.* New York: Knopf, 1929.

Cooper, Michael L. *Playing America's Game: The Story of the Negro League Baseball.* New York: Lodestar, 1993.

Cooper, Page, and Roger L. Treat. *Man O' War.* New York: Messner, 1950.

Cottrell, Robert C. *Blackball, the Black Socks and the Babe: Baseball's Crucial 1920 Season.* Jefferson, N.C.: McFarland, 2002.

Creamer, Robert W. *Babe: The Legend Comes to Life.* New York: Simon & Schuster, 1974.

Deford, Frank. *Big Bill Tilden: The Triumphs and the Tragedy.* New York: Simon & Schuster, 1976.

Engleman, Larry. *The Goddess and the American Girl: The Story of Suzanne Lenglen and Helen Wills.* New York: Oxford University Press, 1988.

Fleischer, Nat. *Gene Tunney: The Enigma of the Ring.* New York: F. Huber, 1931.

———. *Jack Dempsey.* New Rochelle, N.Y.: Arlington House, 1972.

Fleitz, David L. *Shoeless: The Life and Times of Joe Jackson.* Jefferson, N.C.: McFarland, 2001.

Fury, David. *Johnny Weissmuller: "Twice the Hero".* Waterville, Maine: Thorndike Press, 2001.

Graham, Frank. *Lou Gehrig: A Quiet Hero.* New York: Putnam, 1942.

Grange, Red, and Ira Morton. *The Red Grange Story: An Autobiography.* Urbana: University of Illinois Press, 1993.

Guttman, Allen. *A Whole New Ball Game: An Interpretation of American Sports.* Chapel Hill: University of North Carolina Press, 1988.

Hagen, Walter, and Margaret Seaton Heck. *The Walter Hagen Story.* Melbourne: Heinemann, 1957.

Halas, George Stanley, and Gwen Morgan. *Halas.* New York: McGraw-Hill, 1979.

Heimer, Mel. *The Long Count.* New York: Atheneum, 1969.

Hirshberg, Albert. *The Glory Runners.* New York: Putnam, 1968.

Humphrey, Kathryn Long. *Satchel Paige.* New York: Watts, 1988.

Inabinett, Mark. *Grantland Rice and His Heroes: The Sportswriter as Mythmaker in the 1920s.* Knoxville: University of Tennessee Press, 1994.

Kahn, Roger. *A Flame of Pure Fire: Jack Dempsey and the Roaring Twenties.* New York: Harcourt Brace and Company 1999.

Katcher, Leo. *The Big Bankroll: The Life and Times of Arnold Rothstein.* New York: Harper, 1959.

Kavanagh, Jack. *Rogers Hornsby.* New York: Chelsea House, 1991.

Kaye, Ivan N. *Good Clean Violence: A History of College Football.* Philadelphia: Lippincott, 1973.

Keene, Kerry. *The Babe in Red Stockings: An In-depth Chronicle of Babe Ruth With the Boston Red Socks, 1914–1919* Champaign: Sagamore, 1977.

Lipsyte, Robert. *Jim Thorpe: 20th Century Jock.* New York: HarperCollins, 1993.

Macht, Norman L. *Lou Gehrig.* New York: Chelsea House, 1993.

McFarlane, Brian. *Brian McFarlane's Original Six.* Toronto: Stoddart, 1999.

Miller, Dick. *Triumphant Journey: The Saga of Bobby Jones, and the Grand Slam of Golf.* New York: Holt, Reinhart and Winston, 1980.

Murdock, Eugene Converse. *Baseball Players and Their Times: Oral Histories of the Game, 1920–1940.* Westport: Meckler, 1991.

Paddock, Charles W. *The Fastest Human.* New York: T. Nelson & Sons, 1932.

Polner, Murray. *Branch Rickey: A Biography.* New York: Atheneum, 1982.

Reeder, Red. *On the Mound: Three Great Pitchers.* Champaign: Garrard, 1966.

Ribowsky, Mark. *Don't Look Back: Satchel Paige in the Shadows of Baseball.* New York: Simon & Schuster, 1994.

Roberts, Randy. *Jack Dempsey: The Manassa Mauler.* Baton Rouge: Louisiana State University Press, 1979.

Ryan, Bob. *The Boston Celtics: The History, Legends, and Images of America's Most Celebrated Team.* Reading, Mass.: Addison-Wesley, 1989.

Sarazen, Gene. *Thirty Years of Championship Golf; The Life and Times of Gene Sarazen.* New York: Prentice-Hall 1950.

Schoor, Gene. *Red Grange: Football's Greatest Halfback.* New York: J. Messner, 1952.

Shaughnessy, Dan. *The Curse of the Bambino.* New York: Penguin, 1991.

Sowell, Mike. *The Pitch that Killed.* New York: MacMillan, 1989.

Sperber, Murray. *Shake Down the Thunder: The Creation of Notre Dame Football.* New York: Holt, 1993.

Spink, C.G. Taylor. *Judge Landis and Twenty-Five Years of Baseball.* New York.: Thomas Y. Crowell, 1947.

Steele, Michael R. *Knute Rockne: A Bio-Bibliography.* Westport, Conn.: Greenwood Press, 1983.

Stump, Al. *Cobb: A Biography.* Chapel Hill, N.C.: Algonquin Books, 1994.

Treat, Roger L. *Walter Johnson, King of the Pitchers.* New York: J. Messner, 1948.

Twombly, Wells. *Shake Down the Thunder!: The Official Biography of Notre Dame's Frank Leahy.* Radnor, Pa.: Chilton, 1974.

Vincent, Ted. *Mudville's Revenge: The Rise and Fall of American Sport.* New York: Seaview, 1981.

PRIMARY SOURCE TYPE INDEX

Primary source authors appear in parentheses. Page numbers in italics indicate images, and those followed by the letter t *indicate tables.*

Primary source authors appear in parentheses. Page numbers in italics indicate images, and those followed by the letter *t* indicate tables.

Primary source authors appear in parentheses. Page numbers in italics indicate images, and those followed by the letter *t* indicate tables.

Primary source authors appear in parentheses. Page numbers in italics indicate images, and those followed by the letter *t* indicate tables.

GENERAL INDEX

Page numbers in bold indicate primary sources; page numbers in italic indicate images; page numbers in bold italic indicate primary source images; page numbers followed by the letter t indicate tables. Primary sources are indexed under the entry name with the author's name in parentheses. Primary sources are also indexed by title. All primary sources can be identified by bold page locators.

A

Abrams v. U.S. (1919), 321

Academic freedom
language instruction, 156, 157
Lusk Laws, 145

Academics
Edwards, Paul Kenneth, 135
Frankfurter, Felix, 334–335,
335–337
Mathews, Shailer, 528–531
Pound, Roscoe, 335–337, *336*
Pritchett, Henry S., 185–188

Activists
Brestwell, Sigrid, *485*
Dennett, Mary Ware, 398–400
Garvey, Marcus, 277–278,
277–281, *278*
Mosgrove, Alice, *361*
Pissiot, Elizabeth, *485*
Randolph, A. Philip, 108–109
Sanger, Margaret, 269, 270–273,
398, *399*, 484–487, *485*
Sideri, Marcella, *485*
Stone, Hanna, *485*

Actors
Besserer, Eugenie, *45*
Brooks, Louise, 57–60, *58*
Crawford, Joan, *209*
Gilpin, Charles, *8,* 8–10
Jolson, Al, 43–46, *44, 45*
Keaton, Buster, 40–43

Address to Congress (Harding), **392–393**

Advertising
African American consumers,
135–140
Arrow Collars and Shirts, 201–205,
202, 203
Cheney Brothers silks, 231
Chevrolet Sedan, *434*
Chicago Bears, 604
cigarettes, 417–418
Ford Coupe, *218*
Kotex sanitary napkins, *437, 438*
Lifebuoy Soap, *436*
radio, 431–433, *432*
Red Diving Girl, 210–213, *211,
212*
and religion, 535–536
Studebaker Roadster, *217*
women in, 435–439
youth in, 403–405

Advertising for Women, 435–439
"If Only I Could Tell This to Every
Business Girl" (Kotex Co.), **438**
"Teachers and Mothers are Allies
in Fighting Dirt" (Lever Bros.),
436
"What the World Expects of
Women Today" (Kotex Co.),
437

*Advertising Response: A Research Into
Influences That Increase Sales,*
403–405

nonfiction work (Donovan),
404–405

A.E. Staley Manufacturing Company,
604

African Americans
actors, *8,* 8–10, *9*
athletes, 616, 626–629, *627*
businesses, 278
consumers, 135–140
cultural pride, 277–281, 446–449
dancers, 209
and KKK, 384
leaders, 449
musicians, 28–30, *29,* 209
NAACP anti-lynching campaign,
264–269, *265, 266*
newspapers, 627–628
organizations, 112
poets and writers, 21–23, 446–449
portrayal in theater, 8–11
property ownership, 352–355, *353*
Pullman porters, 108–113, *112*
suffrage, 356–357
women, 74–77
workers, 74–77

African nationalism, 278

Agriculture. *See* Farming and farmers

"The Airplane in Catalpa Sphinx Control," 557–560
report (Houser), **558–560**

Airplanes. *See* Aviation

Page numbers in bold indicate primary sources; page numbers in italic indicate images;
page numbers in bold italic indicate primary source images; page numbers followed by the letter *t* indicate tables.

Page numbers in bold indicate primary sources; page numbers in italic indicate images;
page numbers in bold italic indicate primary source images; page numbers followed by the letter *t* indicate tables.

Page numbers in bold indicate primary sources; page numbers in italic indicate images;
page numbers in bold italic indicate primary source images; page numbers followed by the letter *t* indicate tables.

Page numbers in bold indicate primary sources; page numbers in italic indicate images;
page numbers in bold italic indicate primary source images; page numbers followed by the letter *t* indicate tables.

Page numbers in bold indicate primary sources; page numbers in italic indicate images; page numbers in bold italic indicate primary source images; page numbers followed by the letter *t* indicate tables.

Page numbers in bold indicate primary sources; page numbers in italic indicate images;
page numbers in bold italic indicate primary source images; page numbers followed by the letter *t* indicate tables.

Page numbers in bold indicate primary sources; page numbers in italic indicate images; page numbers in bold italic indicate primary source images; page numbers followed by the letter *t* indicate tables.

Page numbers in bold indicate primary sources; page numbers in italic indicate images;
page numbers in bold italic indicate primary source images; page numbers followed by the letter *t* indicate tables.

Page numbers in bold indicate primary sources; page numbers in italic indicate images; page numbers in bold italic indicate primary source images; page numbers followed by the letter *t* indicate tables.

Page numbers in bold indicate primary sources; page numbers in italic indicate images;
page numbers in bold italic indicate primary source images; page numbers followed by the letter *t* indicate tables.

Page numbers in bold indicate primary sources; page numbers in italic indicate images; page numbers in bold italic indicate primary source images; page numbers followed by the letter *t* indicate tables.

Page numbers in bold indicate primary sources; page numbers in italic indicate images;
page numbers in bold italic indicate primary source images; page numbers followed by the letter *t* indicate tables.

Page numbers in bold indicate primary sources; page numbers in italic indicate images; page numbers in bold italic indicate primary source images; page numbers followed by the letter *t* indicate tables.

Page numbers in bold indicate primary sources; page numbers in italic indicate images; page numbers in bold italic indicate primary source images; page numbers followed by the letter *t* indicate tables.

Page numbers in bold indicate primary sources; page numbers in italic indicate images; page numbers in bold italic indicate primary source images; page numbers followed by the letter *t* indicate tables.

Page numbers in bold indicate primary sources; page numbers in italic indicate images;
page numbers in bold italic indicate primary source images; page numbers followed by the letter *t* indicate tables.

Page numbers in bold indicate primary sources; page numbers in italic indicate images; page numbers in bold italic indicate primary source images; page numbers followed by the letter *t* indicate tables.

Page numbers in bold indicate primary sources; page numbers in italic indicate images;
page numbers in bold italic indicate primary source images; page numbers followed by the letter *t* indicate tables.

Page numbers in bold indicate primary sources; page numbers in italic indicate images;
page numbers in bold italic indicate primary source images; page numbers followed by the letter *t* indicate tables.

Page numbers in bold indicate primary sources; page numbers in italic indicate images;
page numbers in bold italic indicate primary source images; page numbers followed by the letter *t* indicate tables.

Page numbers in bold indicate primary sources; page numbers in italic indicate images; page numbers in bold italic indicate primary source images; page numbers followed by the letter *t* indicate tables.

Page numbers in bold indicate primary sources; page numbers in italic indicate images;
page numbers in bold italic indicate primary source images; page numbers followed by the letter *t* indicate tables.

Page numbers in bold indicate primary sources; page numbers in italic indicate images;
page numbers in bold italic indicate primary source images; page numbers followed by the letter *t* indicate tables.

Page numbers in bold indicate primary sources; page numbers in italic indicate images;
page numbers in bold italic indicate primary source images; page numbers followed by the letter *t* indicate tables.

Page numbers in bold indicate primary sources; page numbers in italic indicate images;
page numbers in bold italic indicate primary source images; page numbers followed by the letter *t* indicate tables.